Directory of Public and Private Programs for Emotionally Disturbed Children and Youth

Directory of Public and Private Programs for Emotionally Disturbed Children and Youth

Edited by Ronald E. Fritsch

ORYX PRESS
1985

The rare Arabian Oryx is believed to have inspired the myth of the unicorn. This desert antelope became virtually extinct in the early 1960s. At that time several groups of international conservationists arranged to have 9 animals sent to the Phoenix Zoo to be the nucleus of a captive breeding herd. Today the Oryx population is over 400, and herds have been returned to reserves in Israel, Jordan, and Oman.

Library of Congress Cataloging-in-Publication Data

Fritsch, Ronald E.
    Directory of public and private programs for emotionally disturbed children and youth.

    Includes indexes.
        1. Mental retardation facilities—United States—
States—Directories.   2. Mentally ill children—
Services for—United States—States—Directories.
3. Mentally ill children—Education—United States—
States—Directories.   I. Title.
HV3006.A4F75   1985   362.2'0425'088054   85-15285
ISBN 0-89774-199-4

Contents

Foreword

With the passage and implementation of P.L. 94-142 tremendous pressure has been placed on the public schools of the United States to provide special educational services to seriously emotionally disturbed children and adolescents. However, passage of the law has not proven to be the solution we thought it would be. A number of problems still exist. First, while the public schools have increased programs for the seriously disturbed student, the increase has been rather small. Nationally, less than two percent of the school age population is being served in special education programs even though the research indicates that from five to fifteen percent of the school age population needs these services.

A second problem presented by P.L. 94-142 has to do with the requirement that all seriously emotionally disturbed students must be served. Prior to P.L. 94-142, school systems could be selective in deciding which students they accepted into special education programs. These programs, for the most part, selected emotionally disturbed students who were "manageable." That is, students placed in public school programs were those who could handle the relative open setting of a public school. Students who could not be controlled in public schools or who needed residential placement were often denied public school services. Parents of these students were left to their own devices in the search for services for their children. Now that P.L. 94-142 has been enacted the public schools do not have the "luxury" of denying services to any student who is seriously emotionally disturbed. If the school cannot provide the required program they must purchase services from some other provider, public or private.

A third problem relates to the nature of treatment programs. As the public schools have increased their involvement with seriously disturbed students it has become clear that the needs of these students extend beyond what can be provided in the public schools. It has become clear that the public schools alone cannot deal with all of the needs of these students. Very often these students also need psychotherapy or other services. Parents may also need some type of assistance. Clearly what is called for is the development of cooperative programs between the public schools, private schools, mental health agencies, correctional services, etc. No one agency can meet enough of the needs of these students to maximize success of treatment.

This *Directory of Public and Private Programs for Emotionally Disturbed Children and Youth* will prove to be a most useful guide. It offers a listing of programs and facilities, both public and private, that serve the varying needs of seriously emotionally disturbed children and adolescents. Parents, social workers, psychologists, psychiatrists, juvenile officers, diagnosticians, teachers, and school administrators will find it most useful as they deal with these students. The reader will find the text highly readable and the information presented will allow one to begin the process of selecting appropriate services. As such, it represents the first step in the solution to the identified problems. Those involved in finding the most appropriate placement for students will find it a valuable beginning point in that search. As professionals become aware of the range of services available, both the number of children and adolescents being served and the quality of the programs should increase.

Robert Harth, Ed.D.
Chairman, Department of Special Education
National College of Education

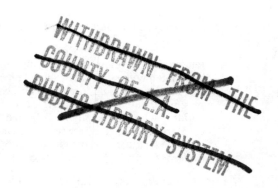
Introduction

Ancient history reveals that children and adolescents deviating significantly from the ''norm'' were banished, forced to conform, and often put to death. In other areas of the world, demonic possession was viewed as a prime contributor to deviant behavior and resulted in trephining, exorcism, witch hunts, and child sacrifices.

During the eighteenth century, Pinel of France, Tuke of England, and Dix and Beers of the United States were prime advocates of moral treatment for the mentally ill. Such support asylums as state hospitals and mental institutions offered young patients with severe mental disorders a variety of innovative interventions from bloodletting, tranquility chairs, chains and cages to drug therapy. In other instances, mentally ill children and youth were committed to prisons, reform schools, and training schools. Treatment in these facilities rotated between solitary confinement and agrarian skill development.

During the Industrial Revolution, with its immigrant waves and passage of compulsory attendance laws, schools were inundated with mild to severely disturbed children. Teachers quickly learned that both immigrant and disturbed students could be placed into self-contained ''steamer'' classrooms away from the other ''normal'' children.

THE RIGHTS OF THE DISABLED

The impetus to change and improve legal-correctional, mental health, and educational opportunities for children and adolescents with severe mental disorders gained support when various constitutional issues arose surrounding questions regarding the eighth and fourteenth amendments. What rights did children and adolescents have who suffered from severe mental disorders? Should such persons be provided the right to fair classification, the right to education and in addition, the

right to treatment? If these rights were withheld, the severely mentally ill person might not be afforded equal treatment under the law, certain due process provisions, and might possibly be subjected to cruel and unusual punishment. These were just a few of the issues arising during the Age of Reform that resulted in extensive litigation culminating in several landmark decisions in the early 1970s. This litigation resulted in the development of specific criteria to ensure that children and adolescents with severe mental disorders had the right to be classified fairly (*Lebanks v. Spears*, 1973), the right to education (*Mills v. Board of Education of the District of Columbia*, 1972), and the right to treatment (*Wyatt v. Stickney*, 1972).

As a result of extensive litigation and lobbying, Congress passed P.L. 94-142 (Education for All Handicapped Children Act) in 1975. This comprehensive law requires in part the identification of children and adolescents with severe mental disorders as seriously emotionally disturbed and outlines specific policies concerning identification, assessment, individualized education programs, placement, confidentiality, and due process. P.L. 94-142 effects educational programming of seriously emotionally disturbed children and adolescents between the ages of three and 21 in least restrictive environments ranging from public schools to institutional settings. The law defines ''seriously emotionally disturbed'' children as follows:

> The term means a condition exhibiting one or more of the following characteristics over a long period of time and to a marked degree, which adversely affects educational performance: (a) an inability to learn which cannot be explained by intellectual, sensory, or health factors; (b) an inability to build or maintain satisfactory interpersonal relationships with peers and teachers; (c) inappropriate types of behavior or feelings under normal circumstances; (d) a general pervasive mood of unhappiness or depression; or (e) a

tendency to develop physical symptoms or fears associated with personal or school problems. The term includes children who are schizophrenic or autistic. The term does not include children who are socially maladjusted, unless it is determined that they are seriously emotionally disturbed. (Education of Handicapped Children, *Federal Register*, Section 121a.5, 1977)

Although general, this definition provides professionals with a common perception of seriously emotionally disturbed children and youth undefined prior to its inception.

SERVING THE NEEDS OF THE EMOTIONALLY DISABLED

With all of the extensive litigation and passage of P.L. 94-142, one could easily assume that since 1975 great advances have been made in serving emotionally disturbed and mentally ill children and youth. The common assumption is that when laws are enacted and their mandates fulfilled problems are resolved. Although many programs and facilities are operating to serve children and adolescents with serious emotional disturbances and severe mental disorders, the incidence of mental health need in the United States has increased dramatically. Grosenick and Huntze (1979) summarize incidence figures from the 1978 *Report to the President from the President's Commission on Mental Health* (U.S. Government Printing Office, 1978):

> For the past few years the most commonly used estimate has been that, at any one time, 10 percent of the population needs some form of mental health service. . . . There is new evidence that this figure may be nearer 15 percent of the population.
>
> Of the estimated two million Americans who have been or would be diagnosed as schizophrenic, approximately 600,000 receive active treatment in any one year. Most current estimates state that about one percent of the population suffers from profound depressive disorders. . . . More than one million Americans have organic psychoses of toxic or neurologic origin or permanently disabling mental conditions of varying causes.
>
> Because diagnostic criteria vary so widely, different surveys of general populations show that the overall prevalence of persistent handicapping mental health problems among children aged three to fifteen ranges from 5 to 15 percent.
>
> As much as 25 percent of the population is estimated to suffer from mild to moderate depression, anxiety, and other indicators of emotional disorder at any given time. (p.8)
>
> By conservative estimates, at least two million American children have learning disabilities

which if neglected, can have profound mental health consequences for the child and the family.

> There are 40 million physically handicapped Americans, many of whom suffer serious emotional consequences because of their disabilities. (p.9)
>
> There has been a dramatic increase in the use and misuse of psychoactive drugs, including alcohol, among young people and nearly a threefold increase in the suicide rate of adolescents. (p.6)

Although great strides have been made to define emotional disturbances important ambiguous questions need consideration. Knoblock (1983) asks, "Who are these children and youth who present the schools, society, and themselves with so many difficulties?"

Although a number of mental health services exist, parents and professionals are continually seeking a comprehensive informational source that will allow them to analyze programs and facilities that will meet their child's individual special needs. *The Directory of Public and Private Programs for Emotionally Disturbed Children and Youth* has been compiled to serve as a basic guide for parents, social workers, psychologists, psychiatrists, juvenile officers, diagnosticians, teachers, and others involved in the process of identifying programs and facilities in a number of least restrictive settings for disturbed children and adolescents. This directory provides in a readable, logical format an overview of programs and facilities available for children and adolescents exhibiting serious emotional disturbances and classified as having severe mental disorders within the United States. In addition to information on student/patient characteristics and pscyhological and educational services, this resource provides demographic data on programs and facilities, describes placement types, provides information on student/patient capacity, tuition and sources of funding available, the types of learning and behavioral problems with a listing of psychopathological conditions treated, and least restrictive educational options offered.

Procedures for compiling the directory consisted of questionnaire development, generation of an address list, and data collection. Questionnaire development and refinement was accomplished by reviewing a variety of survey instruments and extensive interaction with colleagues in the area of emotional disturbance and at The Oryx Press. Programs and facilities were identified from varied sources, namely, Sargents' 1983–84 *The Directory For Exceptional Children,* the 1977 *Directory of U.S. Facilities and Programs for Children with Severe Mental Disorders,* * the National Institute of Mental Health, juvenile courts, and selected advocate

---

*Directory was discontinued as of 1977.

organizations for behaviorally disordered, emotionally disturbed, autistic, and schizophrenic children. Data were collected from both mailings and telephone contacts. Returned questionnaires were then edited and sent to The Oryx Press for encoding and publication.

REFERENCES

Education of Handicapped Children, Federal Register, Section 121A.5, 1977.

Grosenick, J. & Huntze, S., *National needs analysis in behavior disorders: A model for a comprehensive needs analysis in behavior disorders*. Columbia, MO: University of Missouri Press, 1979.

Knoblock, Peter. *Teaching Emotionally Disturbed Children*. Boston: Houghton Mifflin, 1983. p. 4.

Lebanks v. Spears, 60 Federal Rules Decisions 135 (1973).

Mills v. Board of Education of the District of Columbia, 348 Federal Supplement 866 (1972).

National Institute of Mental Health, U.S. Facilities and Programs for Children with Severe Mental Illnesses, 2nd ed. Washington: U.S. Government Printing Office, 1977.

Report to the President from the President's Commission on Mental Health. Washington, DC: U.S. Government Printing Office, 1978. p. 6, 8, 9.

Sargent, K. *The Directory for Exceptional Children* (10th ed. Boston: Porter Sargent Publishers, 1984.)

Wyatt v. Stickney, 344 Federal Supplement 373 (1972).

How to Use This Directory

Entries in this publication are based on a 32 item, 2-page questionnaire which was mailed to programs and facilities providing services to children and adolescents exhibiting serious emotional disturbances and/or classified as having severe mental disorders. The survey was conducted on programs and facilities within the United States. If these programs requested not to be included or did not respond to the questionnaire such entries were omitted from the directory.

The Directory is arranged alphabetically by state with entries listed alphabetically by facility name. Each entry begins with the name of the school district, school, program or facility, the street address, a telephone number for each contact person, the year established, and name of a contact person for more information. Additional information includes type of placement, number of beds in the facility or program for children and adolescents under the age of 21, total number of children served, students'/patients' sex, approximate cost of daily room and board, approximate annual tuition, sources of funding used by the program, availability of summer school, levels of teacher certification, and areas of teacher certification or endorsements. This is followed by information in 2 categories which deal with programs and facilities for children and adolescents with serious emotional disturbances and severe mental disorders; student/patient characteristics; and services provided. Only those questions answered affirmatively are included.

Student/patient characteristics include the approximate ages arranged according to early childhood ages 0–4, early elementary ages 5–8, older elementary ages 9–11, middle school or junior high school ages 12–14, early high school ages 15–17, older high school ages 18–21, and after high school ages over 21. Approximate IQ ranges were included: profoundly low IQs of 0–25, severely low IQs of 26–40, trainable IQs of 41–55, educable IQs of 56–70, borderline/normal IQs of 71–85, normal IQs of 85–130 and high IQs, above 130. Additional items were arranged according to exceptionality categories, learning problems, behavioral problems, and psychopathological conditions treated.

The services category includes affirmative responses regarding psychological and educational offerings: therapeutic services, therapeutic professional types and numbers, educational services within school and outside of school setting and number of rooms arranged in terms of least restrictive environments, educational professional type and numbers, curricula offered, educational intervention approaches used, and the types of degrees/certificates awarded.

The last optional item provided comments highlighting the description of the program or facility.

Following the listing of facilities are two indexes. The first index, the Exceptionalities Index, lists the types of exceptionalities treated at the facilities. The index lists the exceptionalities alphabetically with names of appropriate facilities listed alphabetically with each exceptionality. The second index, The Psychopathological Conditions Treated Index lists the psychopathological conditions treated listed in the facilities section with names of appropriate facilities listed with each condition.

The questionnaire used is reprinted:

Please respond to the items below as completely as possible. Even if you do not wish to be included, please complete items 1-5, return the questionnaire in the enclosed envelope and I will delete your name from my files.

Please duplicate as needed

Programs and Facilities Directory for Children and Adolescents with Serious Emotional Disturbances and Severe Mental Disorders

1. Name of School District, School, Program, or Facility _____

2. Street Address _____

3. City _____ 4. State _____ 5. Zip Code _____

6. Telephone Number ( ) _____ 7. Year Established _____

8. Contact Person _____
   name   title

9. Please indicate the type of placement provided.

    _____ a. Public School   _____ e. Private Day Care
    _____ b. Special School   _____ f. Public Day Care
    _____ c. Public Residential Care _____ g. Special Program
    _____ d. Private Residential Care _____ h. Other (please specify) _____

10. How many beds in your facility are allocated for children and adolescents under the age of 21? _____

11. What is the total number of children and adolescents that can be served in your program or facility? _____

12. Please indicate the sex of students/patients who are served _____ a. Male _____ b. Female _____ c. Both

13. What is the cost of daily room and board? _____

14. What is the annual cost of tuition? _____

15. What sources of funding are used for the program?

    _____ a. State Funds   _____ e. Medicare
    _____ b. HEW   _____ f. P.L. 94-142
    _____ c. Health Insurance _____ g. Other (please specify) _____
    _____ d. Medicaid

16. Is summer school available?   17. For what levels are your teachers certified?

    _____ a. Yes   _____ a. Elementary School
    _____ b. No   _____ b. Jr. High School/Middle School
                            _____ c. High School

18. In what areas do your teachers have endorsements or certification?

    _____ a. ED   _____ e. Reading
    _____ b. LD   _____ f. Math
    _____ c. MR   _____ g. Other (please specify) _____
    _____ d. Career/Vocational Education

Student/Patient Characteristics

19. Please indicate the ages of the students/patients served.

    _____ a. 0-4   _____ e. 15-17
    _____ b. 5-8   _____ f. 18-21
    _____ c. 9-11   _____ g. over 21
    _____ d. 12-14

20. Please indicate the IQ ranges of the students/patients served.

    _____ a. 0-25   _____ e. 71-85
    _____ b. 26-40   _____ f. 85-130
    _____ c. 41-55   _____ g. above 130
    _____ d. 56-70

21. Please indicate which of the following student/patient exceptionalities are served by the program.

    _____ a. Autistic   _____ g. Visually Impaired/Blind
    _____ b. Emotionally Disturbed   _____ h. Physically Handicapped
    _____ c. Learning Disabled   _____ i. Other Health Impaired
    _____ d. Mentally Handicapped   _____ j. Gifted
    _____ e. Communication Disordered _____ k. Other (please specify) _____
    _____ f. Hearing Impaired/Deaf

22. Please indicate the learning problems exhibited by your students/patients.

    _____ a. Memory Disabilities   _____ f. Handwriting Disabilities
    _____ b. Perceptual Disabilities   _____ g. Spelling Disabilities
    _____ c. Thinking Disabilities   _____ h. Arithmetic Disabilities
    _____ d. Oral Language Disabilities _____ i. Written Expression
    _____ e. Reading Disabilities   _____ j. Other (please specify) _____

23. Please indicate the behavioral problems exhibited by your students/patients.

    _____ a. Attention Deficits   _____ g. Physical Aggression
    _____ b. Hyperactivity   _____ h. Indirect Aggression
    _____ c. Hypoactivity   _____ i. Passive Aggression
    _____ d. Impulsivity   _____ j. Withdrawal
    _____ e. Self-Aggression   _____ k. Other (please specify) _____
    _____ f. Verbal Aggression

24. Please indicate the psychopathological conditions treated.

    _____ a. Alcohol Abuse and/or Drug Dependence   _____ k. Depression
    _____ b. Other Substance Abuse or Dependence   _____ l. Suicide
    _____ c. Early Infantile Autism   _____ m. Asthma
    _____ d. Disintegrative Psychoses   _____ n. Anorexia Nervosa
    _____ e. Schizophrenia   _____ o. Ulcerative Colitis
    _____ f. Aphasia   _____ p. Inadequacy/Immaturity
    _____ g. Convulsive Disorders   _____ q. Personality Problems
    _____ h. Phobias   _____ r. Socialized Aggressive Reaction
    _____ i. Obsessions and Compulsions   _____ s. Unsocialized Aggressive Reaction
    _____ j. Hysteria   _____ t. Other (please specify) _____

Services

25. Please indicate which of the following services are offered.

    _____ a. Individual Therapy   _____ i. Drug Therapy
    _____ b. Group Therapy   _____ j. Art Therapy
    _____ c. Parent Involvement   _____ k. Music Therapy
    _____ d. Behavior Therapy   _____ l. Reality Therapy
    _____ e. Cognitive Developmental Therapy _____ m. Play Therapy
    _____ f. Biofeedback   _____ n. Psychodrama
    _____ g. Family Therapy   _____ o. Other (please specify) _____
    _____ h. Filial Therapy

26. Please indicate with a check in the left-hand column which of the following professionals provide services. Please indicate in the right-hand column the number of professionals in each category.

	#professionals			#professionals
_____ a. Psychiatrists	_____	_____ e. Child Care Staff		_____
_____ b. Psychologists	_____	_____ f. Nurses		_____
_____ c. Counselors	_____	_____ g. Other (please specify)		_____
_____ d. Social Workers	_____			

27. Please indicate with a check in the left-hand column which of the following services are offered. Please indicate in the right-hand column the number of rooms that are available for each.

WITHIN School Setting	#rooms	OUTSIDE School Setting	#rooms
_____ a. Consultative (ER1)	_____	_____ g. Special School	_____
_____ b. Itinerants	_____	_____ h. Hospital School	_____
_____ c. Resource Rooms	_____	_____ i. On-Campus Residential School	_____
_____ d. Transition Rooms	_____	_____ j. Homebound Instruction	_____
_____ e. Self-Contained Rooms	_____	_____ k. Other (please specify)	_____
_____ f. Other (please specify)	_____		

28. Please indicate with a check in the left-hand column which of the following educational professionals participate in the program. Please indicate in the right-hand column the number of professionals in each category.

	#professionals			#professionals
_____ a. Regular School Teachers	_____	_____ e. Special Education Counselors		_____
_____ b. Special Education Teachers	_____	_____ f. Paraprofessionals		_____
_____ c. Career/Vocational Teachers	_____	_____ g. Other (please specify)		_____
_____ d. Crisis Teachers	_____			

29. Please indicate which of the following curricula are offered.

    _____ a. Traditional Academic   _____ d. Basic Skills
    _____ b. Career/Vocational Education   _____ e. Prevocational
    _____ c. Individualized   _____ f. Other (please specify) _____

30. Please indicate which of the following educational intervention approaches are used.

    _____ a. Engineered Classroom   _____ e. Behavior Modification
    _____ b. Precision Teaching   _____ f. Applied Behavior Analysis
    _____ c. Progressive Discipline _____ g. Creative Conditioning
    _____ d. Self-Control   _____ h. Other (please specify) _____

31. Please indicate which of the following degrees/certificates are awarded.

    _____ a. Certificate of Attendance _____ c. Graduate Equivalency Diploma
    _____ b. High School Diploma   _____ d. Other (please specify) _____

32. Please use this space to briefly provide (50 words or less) any other information that would highlight the description of your program or facility.

    _____
    _____
    _____
    _____

Name _____

Date _____

By completing, signing, and returning this questionnaire, you are in no way obligated to purchase a copy of the directory.

Please return the questionnaire in the enclosed envelope by November 30, 1984 to Ronald Fritsch, The Oryx Press, P.O. Box 147, Lewisville, Texas 75067-9990

Abbreviations List

The following abbreviations were used throughout this directory:

act-acting
admin-administration, administrative, administrator
assoc-associate
asst-assistant
Ave-Avenue
bldg-building
Blvd-Boulevard
Br-Brother
chair-chairperson
cir-circle
coord-coordinator
corp-corporate, corporation
dept-department, departmental
dir-director
div-division, divisional
Dr-Doctor, Drive
E-East
ed-education, educational
exec-executive

Hwy-Highway
Ln-Lane
med-medical, medicine
mgr-manager
Mt-Mount
N-North
Pkwy-Parkway
Pl-Place
PO Box-Post Office Box
Pres-President
prog-programs
proj-project
Rd-Road
Rt-Route
S-South
St-Saint, Street
serv-services
Sq-Square
Sr-Senior, Sister
supv-supervisor
supt-superintendent
W-West

Alabama

Alabama Youth Services—Chalkville Campus

PO Box 9486, Birmingham, AL 35220-0486 (205) 681-8841
Contact Richard Ray, Supt; Ellen Dossett, Principal
Facility Information *Placement* Public Residential Care. *Number of Beds* 120. *Children/Adolescents Served* 120. *Sexes Served* Both. *Tuition Fees (Approx)* $11,000. *Sources of Funding* State Funds; P.L. 94-142; Dept of Education, Chapter I, II, IV, VI (Federal). Summer school available. *Teacher Certification Level* High School. *Special Certification Level* ED; LD; MR; Career/Vocational Education; Math; Art, English, History.
Student/Patient Characteristics *Age Levels* 12-14; 15-17. *IQ Ranges* 56-70; 71-85; 85-130. *Exceptionalities Served* Emotionally Disturbed; Learning Disabled; Mentally Handicapped. *Learning Problems* Thinking Disabilities; Oral Language Disabilities; Reading Disabilities; Spelling Disabilities; Arithmetic Disabilities; Written Expression. *Behavioral Problems* Attention Deficits; Hyperactivity; Impulsivity; Self-Aggression; Verbal Aggression; Physical Aggression; Passive Aggression; Withdrawal. *Conditions Treated* Alcohol Abuse and/or Drug Abuse; Depression; Suicide; Inadequacy/Immaturity; Socialized Aggressive Reaction; Unsocialized Aggressive Reaction.
Services Provided Individual Therapy; Group Therapy; Behavior Therapy; Family Therapy; Drug Therapy; Art Therapy; Reality Therapy. *Professionals on Staff* Psychiatrists; Psychologists; Counselors 8; Nurses 2. *Service Facilities Available (with number of rooms)* On-Campus Residential School 11. *Educational Professionals* Regular School Teachers 8; Special Education Teachers 5; Career/Vocational Teachers 3. *Curricula* Traditional Academic; Career/Vocational Education; Individualized; Basic Skills; Prevocational; Art; Physical Education; Health; Parenting Skills. *Educational Intervention Approaches* Progressive Discipline; Behavior Modification. *Degrees Awarded* Certificate of Attendance; Graduate Equivalency Diploma.

Birmingham City Board of Education

PO Drawer 10007, Birmingham, AL 35201 (205) 583-4760
Year Established 1884
Contact JoAnne Hamrick, Exceptional Childrens Coord
Facility Information *Placement* Public School; Special School; Public Day Care. *Sexes Served* Both. *Sources of Funding* State Funds; P.L. 94-142; Alabama Act 106. *Teacher Certification Level* Elementary School; Junior High/Middle School; High School. *Special Certification Level* ED; LD; MR.
Student/Patient Characteristics *Age Levels* 5-8; 9-11; 12-14; 15-17; 18-21. *IQ Ranges* 56-70; 71-85; 85-130; Above 130. *Exceptionalities Served* Autistic; Emotionally Disturbed; Learning Disabled; Mentally Handicapped; Communication Disordered; Physically Handicapped; Gifted. *Learning Problems* Memory Disabilities; Perceptual Disabilities; Thinking Disabilities; Oral Language Disabilities; Reading Disabilities; Handwriting Disabilities; Spelling Disabilities; Arithmetic Disabilities; Written Ex-

pression. *Behavioral Problems* Attention Deficits; Hyperactivity; Hypoactivity; Impulsivity; Self-Aggression; Verbal Aggression; Physical Aggression; Indirect Aggression; Passive Aggression; Withdrawal; Social Maladjustments; Sexual Identity Problems. *Conditions Treated* Alcohol Abuse and/or Drug Abuse; Early Infantile Autism; Disintegrative Psychoses; Schizophrenia; Aphasia; Convulsive Disorders; Phobias; Obsessions and Compulsions; Hysteria; Depression; Suicide; Inadequacy/Immaturity; Personality Problems; Socialized Aggressive Reaction; Unsocialized Aggressive Reaction.
Services Provided Behavior Therapy; Cognitive Developmental Therapy. *Professionals on Staff* Psychologists 2; Counselors 11; Nurses 7. *Service Facilities Available (with number of rooms)* Itinerants 1; Self-Contained Rooms 16; Special School 9; On-Campus Residential School 3; Homebound Instruction 1. *Educational Professionals* Special Education Teachers 28; Crisis Teachers 2; Special Education Counselors 11; Paraprofessionals 18; Program Coordinator 1. *Curricula* Traditional Academic; Career/Vocational Education; Individualized; Basic Skills; Prevocational. *Educational Intervention Approaches* Precision Teaching; Self-Control; Behavior Modification; Applied Behavior Analysis. *Degrees Awarded* Certificate of Attendance.

Comments The emotional conflict program is currently in a state of change. Current plans reflect an increase in vocational services, interagency cooperation, and a preventative approach to be offered through mental health curricula.

Brewer-Porch Children's Center

PO Box 2232, University, AL 35486 (205) 348-7236
Year Established 1970
Contact Robert D Lyman, Exec Dir
Facility Information *Placement* Public Residential Care. *Number of Beds* 20. *Children/Adolescents Served* 20. *Sexes Served* Both. *Room and Board Fees (Approx)* $75. *Tuition Fees (Approx)* $27,000. *Sources of Funding* State Funds; Title XX. Summer school available. *Teacher Certification Level* Elementary School; Junior High/Middle School. *Special Certification Level* ED; MR.
Student/Patient Characteristics *Age Levels* 5-8; 9-11; 12-14. *IQ Ranges* 71-85; 85-130; Above 130. *Exceptionalities Served* Emotionally Disturbed; Learning Disabled; Physically Handicapped. *Learning Problems* Perceptual Disabilities; Thinking Disabilities; Oral Language Disabilities; Reading Disabilities; Handwriting Disabilities; Arithmetic Disabilities; Written Expression. *Behavioral Problems* Attention Deficits; Hyperactivity; Hypoactivity; Impulsivity; Self-Aggression; Verbal Aggression; Physical Aggression; Indirect Aggression; Passive Aggression; Withdrawal. *Conditions Treated* Schizophrenia; Aphasia; Convulsive Disorders; Phobias; Obsessions and Compulsions; Hysteria; Depression; Inadequacy/Immaturity; Personality Problems; Socialized Aggressive Reaction; Unsocialized Aggressive Reaction.

Services Provided Individual Therapy; Group Therapy; Parent Involvement; Behavior Therapy; Cognitive Developmental Therapy; Family Therapy; Drug Therapy; Play Therapy. *Professionals on Staff* Psychiatrists .25; Psychologists 3; Counselors 2; Social Workers 2; Child Care Staff 21; Nurses 2. *Service Facilities Available (with number of rooms)* Self-Contained Rooms 3; On-Campus Residential School 3. *Educational Professionals* Special Education Teachers 3; Paraprofessionals 2. *Curricula* Individualized. *Educational Intervention Approaches* Engineered Classroom; Behavior Modification; Applied Behavior Analysis. *Degrees Awarded* Certificate of Attendance.

Child Mental Health Services Inc—Allan Cott School McDonough House

PO Box 7638, Birmingham, AL 35253 (205) 879-1890
Year Established 1974
Contact Betty Milner, Dir

Facility Information *Placement* Special School; Private Residential Care. *Number of Beds* 18. *Children/Adolescents Served* 40. *Sexes Served* Both. *Tuition Fees (Approx)* $30,000-$36,000. *Sources of Funding* State Funds; P.L. 94-142. Summer school available. *Teacher Certification Level* Elementary School; Junior High/Middle School; High School. *Special Certification Level* ED.

Student/Patient Characteristics *Age Levels* 5-8; 9-11; 12-14; 15-17; 18-21. *IQ Ranges* 0-25; 26-40; 41-55; 56-70; 71-85; 85-130; Above 130. *Exceptionalities Served* Autistic. *Learning Problems* Perceptual Disabilities; Thinking Disabilities; Oral Language Disabilities. *Behavioral Problems* Hyperactivity; Self-Aggression; Physical Aggression; Withdrawal. *Conditions Treated* Early Infantile Autism.

Services Provided Parent Involvement; Behavior Therapy. *Professionals on Staff* Psychiatrists 2; Psychologists 1; Social Workers 1; Child Care Staff 12; Nurses 1; Coordinators and Directors 3; Speech Therapists 2. *Service Facilities Available (with number of rooms)* Resource Rooms 1; Self-Contained Rooms 9. *Educational Professionals* Special Education Teachers 8; Career/Vocational Teachers 1; Paraprofessionals 8; Director 1; Parent Advocate 1. *Curricula* Traditional Academic; Individualized; Basic Skills; Prevocational; Special and Language Stimulation. *Educational Intervention Approaches* Behavior Modification.

East Alabama Mental Health Retardation Center

614 2nd Ave, Opelika, AL 36801 (205) 749-3346
Year Established 1967
Contact Carol Skelton, Clinical Dir

Facility Information *Placement* Outpatient Assessment and Treatment Services. *Sexes Served* Both. *Sources of Funding* State Funds; Health Insurance; Medicaid; Medicare; Client Self Pay.

Student/Patient Characteristics *Age Levels* 0-4; 5-8; 9-11; 12-14; 15-17; 18-21; Over 21. *IQ Ranges* 0-25; 26-40; 41-55; 56-70; 71-85; 85-130; Above 130. *Exceptionalities Served* Emotionally Disturbed; Learning Disabled; Mentally Handicapped; Communication Disordered; Hearing Impaired/Deaf; Visually Impaired/Blind; Other Health Impaired; Physically Handicapped; Gifted. *Behavioral Problems* Attention Deficits; Hyperactivity; Hypoactivity; Impulsivity; Self-Aggression; Verbal Aggression; Physical Aggression; Indirect Aggression; Passive Aggression; Withdrawal. *Conditions Treated* Alcohol Abuse and/or Drug Abuse; Other Substance Abuse or Dependence; Early Infantile Autism; Disintegrative Psychoses; Schizophrenia; Aphasia; Convulsive Disorders; Phobias; Obsessions and Compulsions; Hysteria; Depression; Suicide; Asthma; Anorexia Nervosa; Ulcerative Colitis; Inadequacy/Immaturity; Personality Problems; Socialized Aggressive Reaction; Unsocialized Aggressive Reaction.

Services Provided Individual Therapy; Group Therapy; Parent Involvement; Behavior Therapy; Family Therapy; Drug Therapy; Reality Therapy; Play Therapy. *Professionals on Staff* Psychiatrists; Psychologists; Counselors; Social Workers; Child Care Staff; Nurses.

Comments The center provides services to persons residing in Lee, Chambers, Russell, and Tallapoosa counties. Each county has a child/family therapist at least 3/4 time. Services are available to all, regardless of race, creed, sex, religion, nationality, ethnic background, handicap, or disability. Outpatient services, aftercare, transitional services, residential services, and brief inpatient services are available. Fees are on an ability-to-pay basis.

Huntsville City School System

PO Box 1256, Hunstville, AL 35807 (205) 532-4716
Contact Norma Bell, Dir Special Ed

Facility Information *Placement* Public School. *Sexes Served* Both. *Sources of Funding* State Funds; P.L. 94-142. *Teacher Certification Level* Elementary School; Junior High/Middle School; High School. *Special Certification Level* ED; LD; MR.

Student/Patient Characteristics *Age Levels* 5-8; 9-11; 12-14; 15-17; 18-21. *IQ Ranges* 0-25; 26-40; 41-55; 56-70; 71-85; 85-130; Above 130. *Exceptionalities Served* Autistic; Emotionally Disturbed; Learning Disabled; Mentally Handicapped; Communication Disordered; Hearing Impaired/Deaf; Visually Impaired/Blind; Other Health Impaired; Physically Handicapped.

Services Provided Educational. *Professionals on Staff* Psychiatrists; Psychologists; Counselors; Nurses. *Service Facilities Available (with number of rooms)* Itinerants; Resource Rooms; Transition Rooms; Self-Contained Rooms. *Educational Professionals* Regular School Teachers; Special Education Teachers; Career/Vocational Teachers; Crisis Teachers; Paraprofessionals. *Curricula* Traditional Academic; Individualized; Basic Skills. *Educational Intervention Approaches* Engineered Classroom; Precision Teaching; Self-Control; Behavior Modification. *Degrees Awarded* High School Diploma.

Alaska

Alaska State Department of Education—Office of Special Services

Pouch F, Juneau, AK 99811 (907) 465-2970
Contact William Mulnix, Admin
Facility Information *Placement* State Department.

Kenai Peninsula Borough School District

148 N Berkley, Soldotna, AK 99669 (907) 262-5846
Year Established 1964
Contact Kris Rogers, Exec Dir Personnel
Facility Information *Placement* Public School. *Sexes Served* Both.
Sources of Funding State Funds. Summer school available.
Teacher Certification Level Elementary School; Junior High/Middle School; High School. *Special Certification Level* ED; LD; MR.
Student/Patient Characteristics *Age Levels* 0-4; 5-8; 9-11; 12-14; 15-17. *IQ Ranges* 26-40; 41-55; 56-70. *Exceptionalities Served* Autistic; Emotionally Disturbed; Learning Disabled; Mentally Handicapped; Communication Disordered; Hearing Impaired/Deaf; Visually Impaired/Blind; Other Health Impaired; Physically Handicapped; Gifted. *Learning Problems* Memory Disabilities; Perceptual Disabilities; Thinking Disabilities; Oral Language Disabilities; Reading Disabilities; Handwriting Disabilities; Spelling Disabilities; Arithmetic Disabilities; Written Expression. *Behavioral Problems* Attention Deficits; Hyperactivity; Hypoactivity; Impulsivity; Self-Aggression; Verbal Aggression; Physical Aggression; Indirect Aggression; Passive Aggression; Withdrawal. *Conditions Treated* Early Infantile Autism; Schizophrenia; Aphasia; Convulsive Disorders; Phobias; Obsessions and Compulsions; Hysteria; Depression; Suicide; Inadequacy/Immaturity; Personality Problems; Socialized Aggressive Reaction; Unsocialized Aggressive Reaction.

Services Provided Individual Therapy; Group Therapy; Parent Involvement; Behavior Therapy; Family Therapy; Drug Therapy; Reality Therapy; Play Therapy. *Professionals on Staff* Psychiatrists 1; Psychologists 4; Counselors 12. *Service Facilities Available (with number of rooms)* Itinerants 15; Resource Rooms 60; Transition Rooms 4; Self-Contained Rooms 11. *Educational Professionals* Special Education Teachers 75; Paraprofessionals 30. *Curricula* Career/Vocational Education; Individualized; Basic Skills. *Educational Intervention Approaches* Precision Teaching; Behavior Modification; Creative Conditioning. *Degrees Awarded* High School Diploma.

Arizona

Arizona Baptist Children's Services—Little Canyon Campus

Box 27128, Phoenix, AZ 85061 (602) 264-3292
Year Established 1958
Contact C Truett Baker, Exec Dir

Facility Information *Placement* Special School; Private Residential Care. *Number of Beds* 30. *Children/Adolescents Served* 30. *Sexes Served* Both. *Room and Board Fees (Approx)* $73. *Sources of Funding* State Funds; Donations. Summer school available. *Teacher Certification Level* Junior High/Middle School; High School. *Special Certification Level* ED; LD.

Student/Patient Characteristics *Age Levels* 12-14; 15-17. *IQ Ranges* 71-85; 85-130. *Exceptionalities Served* Emotionally Disturbed; Learning Disabled; Physically Handicapped. *Learning Problems* Perceptual Disabilities; Thinking Disabilities; Reading Disabilities. *Behavioral Problems* Attention Deficits; Hyperactivity; Impulsivity; Self-Aggression; Verbal Aggression; Physical Aggression; Indirect Aggression; Passive Aggression; Withdrawal. *Conditions Treated* Convulsive Disorders; Hysteria; Depression; Suicide; Inadequacy/Immaturity; Personality Problems; Socialized Aggressive Reaction; Unsocialized Aggressive Reaction.

Services Provided Individual Therapy; Group Therapy; Parent Involvement; Behavior Therapy; Family Therapy; Drug Therapy; Recreation; Religious Education. *Professionals on Staff* Psychiatrists 1; Psychologists 1; Social Workers 2; Child Care Staff 20; Nurses 1; Recreation Therapist 1. *Service Facilities Available (with number of rooms)* Consultative (ERT) 1; Resource Rooms 1; Self-Contained Rooms 2. *Educational Professionals* Special Education Teachers 2; Special Education Counselors 2. *Curricula* Traditional Academic; Individualized; Basic Skills. *Educational Intervention Approaches* Progressive Discipline; Self-Control; Behavior Modification; Applied Behavior Analysis. *Degrees Awarded* Certificate of Attendance; High School Diploma; Eighth Grade Diploma.

Arizona Boys' Ranch

Boys Ranch, AZ 85224 (602) 892-9550
Year Established 1949
Contact Denice Natt, Treatment Dir

Facility Information *Placement* Public School; Special School; Private Residential Care; Special Program. *Number of Beds* 96. *Children/Adolescents Served* 96. *Sexes Served* Male. *Room and Board Fees (Approx)* $47. *Tuition Fees (Approx)* $3,913. *Sources of Funding* State Funds; P.L. 94-142; Private; Contributions. Summer school available. *Teacher Certification Level* Elementary School; Junior High/Middle School; High School. *Special Certification Level* ED; LD; Career/Vocational Education; Reading.

Student/Patient Characteristics *Age Levels* 9-11; 12-14; 15-17. *IQ Ranges* 71-85; 85-130. *Exceptionalities Served* Emotionally Disturbed; Learning Disabled; Communication Disordered; Gifted. *Learning Problems* Memory Disabilities; Perceptual Disabilities; Thinking Disabilities; Oral Language Disabilities; Reading Disabilities; Handwriting Disabilities; Spelling Disabilities; Arithmetic Disabilities; Written Expression. *Behavioral Problems* Attention Deficits; Hyperactivity; Impulsivity; Self-Aggression; Verbal Aggression; Physical Aggression; Indirect Aggression; Passive Aggression; Withdrawal. *Conditions Treated* Alcohol Abuse and/or Drug Abuse; Other Substance Abuse or Dependence; Convulsive Disorders; Depression; Asthma; Inadequacy/Immaturity; Socialized Aggressive Reaction; Unsocialized Aggressive Reaction.

Services Provided Group Therapy; Parent Involvement; Behavior Therapy; Reality Therapy. *Professionals on Staff* Psychologists 1; Social Workers 5; Child Care Staff 25; Nurses 1. *Service Facilities Available (with number of rooms)* On-Campus Residential School; Departmentalized Academic and Vocational Public School. *Educational Professionals* Special Education Teachers; Career/Vocational Teachers; Paraprofessionals; Certified Vocational Evaluator. *Curricula* Traditional Academic; Career/Vocational Education; Individualized; Basic Skills; Prevocational; Vocational Evaluation. *Educational Intervention Approaches* Contingency Management. *Degrees Awarded* High School Diploma; Graduate Equivalency Diploma; Elementary.

Comments Arizona Boys Ranch is a reality-oriented, goal-directed, activity-centered residential facility that stresses an individualized approach to residents within a structured, disciplined environment.

Arizona Children's Home

2700 S 8th Ave, Tucson, AZ 85713 (602) 622-7611
Year Established 1912
Contact Tim Sikkema, Treatment Dir

Facility Information *Placement* Public School; Special School; Private Residential Care; Special Program. *Number of Beds* 55. *Children/Adolescents Served* 55. *Sexes Served* Both. *Tuition Fees (Approx)* $4,772. *Sources of Funding* State Funds; Health Insurance; P.L. 94-142; CHAMPUS; School Contracts. *Teacher Certification Level* Elementary School; Junior High/Middle School; High School. *Special Certification Level* ED; LD; Cross Categorical.

Student/Patient Characteristics *Age Levels* 5-8; 9-11; 12-14; 15-17. *IQ Ranges* 71-85; 85-130; Above 130. *Exceptionalities Served* Emotionally Disturbed; Learning Disabled; Gifted. *Learning Problems* Memory Disabilities; Perceptual Disabilities; Thinking Disabilities; Oral Language Disabilities; Reading Disabilities; Handwriting Disabilities; Spelling Disabilities; Arithmetic Disabilities; Written Expression. *Behavioral Problems* Attention Deficits; Hyperactivity; Hypoactivity; Impulsivity;

Self-Aggression; Verbal Aggression; Physical Aggression; Indirect Aggression; Passive Aggression; Withdrawal. *Conditions Treated* Convulsive Disorders; Phobias; Obsessions and Compulsions; Hysteria; Depression; Asthma; Anorexia Nervosa; Inadequacy/Immaturity; Personality Problems; Socialized Aggressive Reaction; Unsocialized Aggressive Reaction; Adjustment Reaction to Childhood.

Services Provided Individual Therapy; Group Therapy; Parent Involvement; Behavior Therapy; Cognitive Developmental Therapy; Family Therapy; Filial Therapy; Drug Therapy; Art Therapy; Music Therapy; Reality Therapy; Play Therapy; Psychodrama. *Professionals on Staff* Psychiatrists 1; Psychologists .5; Social Workers 15; Child Care Staff 50; Nurses 1. *Service Facilities Available (with number of rooms)* Resource Rooms 1; Transition Rooms 1; Self-Contained Rooms 4; On-Campus Residential School 6. *Educational Professionals* Special Education Teachers 5; Crisis Teachers 1; Paraprofessionals 4; Counselors 3. *Curricula* Traditional Academic; Individualized; Basic Skills; Prevocational. *Educational Intervention Approaches* Engineered Classroom; Self-Control; Behavior Modification; Creative Conditioning; Diagnostic Teaching. *Degrees Awarded* Eighth Grade Diploma.

Arizona State Hospital

2500 E Van Buren, Phoenix, AZ 85008 (602) 244-1331
Year Established 1887
Contact Bob Marsh, Asst Admin

Facility Information *Placement* State Mental Hospital. *Number of Beds* 25. *Children/Adolescents Served* 25. *Room and Board Fees (Approx)* $150. *Sources of Funding* State Funds. *Teacher Certification Level* High School.

Student/Patient Characteristics *Age Levels* 12-14; 15-17; 18-21; Over 21. *IQ Ranges* 0-25; 26-40; 41-55; 56-70; 71-85; 85-130; Above 130. *Exceptionalities Served* Autistic; Emotionally Disturbed; Learning Disabled; Mentally Handicapped; Communication Disordered; Hearing Impaired/Deaf; Visually Impaired/Blind; Other Health Impaired; Physically Handicapped. *Learning Problems* Memory Disabilities; Perceptual Disabilities; Thinking Disabilities; Oral Language Disabilities; Reading Disabilities; Handwriting Disabilities; Spelling Disabilities; Arithmetic Disabilities; Written Expression. *Behavioral Problems* Attention Deficits; Hyperactivity; Hypoactivity; Impulsivity; Self-Aggression; Verbal Aggression; Physical Aggression; Indirect Aggression; Passive Aggression; Withdrawal. *Conditions Treated* Disintegrative Psychoses; Schizophrenia; Aphasia; Convulsive Disorders; Phobias; Obsessions and Compulsions; Hysteria; Depression; Suicide; Anorexia Nervosa; Inadequacy/Immaturity; Personality Problems; Socialized Aggressive Reaction; Unsocialized Aggressive Reaction.

Services Provided Individual Therapy; Group Therapy; Behavior Therapy; Art Therapy; Music Therapy; Reality Therapy. *Professionals on Staff* Psychiatrists 13; Psychologists 8; Counselors; Social Workers 22; Child Care Staff; Nurses 85. *Educational Professionals* Special Education Teachers 8. *Curricula* Traditional Academic; Basic Skills. *Educational Intervention Approaches* Behavior Modification; Creative Conditioning. *Degrees Awarded* Graduate Equivalency Diploma.

Comments The hospital admits residents of the state of Arizona who, because of mental illness, are dangerous to themselves or others or gravely disabled, for the purpose of diagnosis, evaluation, and treatment. It provides treatment programs that are directed toward the development and enhancement of strengths, abilities, and interests of the patients.

Arizona State Hospital—Nueva Vista School

2500 E Van Buren, Phoenix, AZ 85008 (602) 244-1331
Contact Bernice Powell

Facility Information *Placement* State Hospital. *Number of Beds* 23. *Children/Adolescents Served* 16. *Sexes Served* Both. Summer school available. *Teacher Certification Level* Elementary School; Junior High/Middle School; High School. *Special Certification Level* ED; LD; MR; Elementary Education.

Student/Patient Characteristics *Age Levels* 12-14; 15-17. *IQ Ranges* 56-70; 71-85; 85-130; Above 130. *Exceptionalities Served* Emotionally Disturbed; Mentally Handicapped; Communication Disordered. *Learning Problems* Memory Disabilities; Perceptual Disabilities; Thinking Disabilities; Oral Language Disabilities; Reading Disabilities; Handwriting Disabilities; Spelling Disabilities; Arithmetic Disabilities; Written Expression. *Behavioral Problems* Attention Deficits; Hyperactivity; Hypoactivity; Impulsivity; Self-Aggression; Verbal Aggression; Physical Aggression; Indirect Aggression; Passive Aggression; Withdrawal. *Conditions Treated* Alcohol Abuse and/or Drug Abuse; Other Substance Abuse or Dependence; Disintegrative Psychoses; Schizophrenia; Phobias; Obsessions and Compulsions; Hysteria; Depression; Suicide; Anorexia Nervosa; Personality Problems; Socialized Aggressive Reaction; Unsocialized Aggressive Reaction.

Services Provided Individual Therapy; Group Therapy; Parent Involvement; Behavior Therapy; Family Therapy; Drug Therapy; Recreation Therapy; Occupational Therapy. *Professionals on Staff* Psychiatrists; Psychologists; Counselors; Social Workers; Nurses. *Service Facilities Available (with number of rooms)* Self-Contained Rooms 2; Testing 1; Homebound Instruction 1. *Educational Professionals* Special Education Teachers 4. *Curricula* Individualized; Basic Skills. *Educational Intervention Approaches* Engineered Classroom; Progressive Discipline; Self-Control.

Comments The child and adolescent treatment unit serves severely emotionally disturbed and mentally ill adolescents, ages 12 through 17. The patients receive intensive diagnostic evaluation and treatment carried out by an interdisciplinary team of professionals and paraprofessionals. These activities are closely supervised by the physician and professional nursing personnel.

Brighton School and Diagnostic Center

6503 N 21st Ave, Phoenix, AZ 85015 (602) 242-1870
Year Established 1973
Contact Carolyn Cabanski, Dir

Facility Information *Placement* Special Program. *Children/Adolescents Served* 24. *Sexes Served* Both. *Tuition Fees (Approx)* $7,488. *Sources of Funding* State Funds. *Teacher Certification Level* Elementary School; Junior High/Middle School; High School. *Special Certification Level* ED.

Student/Patient Characteristics *Age Levels* 12-14; 15-17; 18-21; Over 21. *IQ Ranges* 71-85; 85-130. *Exceptionalities Served* Emotionally Disturbed. *Learning Problems* Memory Disabilities; Perceptual Disabilities; Thinking Disabilities; Oral Language Disabilities; Reading Disabilities; Handwriting Disabilities; Spelling Disabilities; Arithmetic Disabilities; Written Expression. *Behavioral Problems* Attention Deficits; Hyperactivity; Hypoactivity; Impulsivity; Self-Aggression; Verbal Aggression; Physical Aggression; Indirect Aggression; Passive Aggression; Withdrawal. *Conditions Treated* Alcohol Abuse and/or Drug Abuse; Other Substance Abuse or Dependence; Disintegrative Psychoses; Schizophrenia; Aphasia; Convulsive Disorders; Phobias; Obsessions and Compulsions; Hysteria; Depression; Suicide; Anorexia Nervosa; Personality Problems; Socialized Aggressive Reaction; Unsocialized Aggressive Reaction.

Services Provided Individual Therapy; Group Therapy; Parent Involvement; Behavior Therapy; Cognitive Developmental Therapy; Family Therapy; Art Therapy; Play Therapy. *Professionals on Staff* Psychologists; Counselors. *Service Facilities Available (with number of rooms)* Self-Contained Rooms 2. *Educational Professionals* Special Education Teachers; Special Education Counselors; Paraprofessionals. *Curricula* Traditional Academic; Career/Vocational Education; Individualized; Basic Skills; Prevocational. *Educational Intervention Approaches* Engineered Classroom; Precision Teaching; Progressive Discipline; Self-Control; Behavior Modification; Applied Behavior Analysis; Creative Conditioning. *Degrees Awarded* High School Diploma; Graduate Equivalency Diploma.

Creative Learning Systems Inc

3926 E Pima, Tucson, AZ 85712 (602) 326-7480
Year Established 1976
Contact Mike Nelson, Exec Dir

Facility Information *Placement* Special School; Public Residential Care; Private Residential Care; Private Day Care; Public Day Care. *Number of Beds* 18. *Children/Adolescents Served* 18 (residential); 20 (day support). *Sexes Served* Both. *Sources of Funding* State Funds; P.L. 94-142; Donations. Summer school available. *Teacher Certification Level* Elementary School; Junior High/Middle School; High School. *Special Certification Level* ED; LD.

Student/Patient Characteristics *Age Levels* 12-14; 15-17. *IQ Ranges* 85-130; Above 130. *Exceptionalities Served* Emotionally Disturbed; Learning Disabled. *Learning Problems* Perceptual Disabilities; Reading Disabilities; Handwriting Disabilities; Spelling Disabilities; Arithmetic Disabilities. *Behavioral Problems* Attention Deficits; Hyperactivity; Hypoactivity; Impulsivity; Self-Aggression; Verbal Aggression; Physical Aggression; Indirect Aggression; Passive Aggression; Withdrawal. *Conditions Treated* Alcohol Abuse and/or Drug Abuse; Other Substance Abuse or Dependence; Obsessions and Compulsions; Depression; Suicide; Asthma; Inadequacy/Immaturity; Personality Problems; Socialized Aggressive Reaction; Unsocialized Aggressive Reaction.

Services Provided Individual Therapy; Group Therapy; Parent Involvement; Behavior Therapy; Family Therapy; Art Therapy; Reality Therapy; Psychodrama. *Professionals on Staff* Psychologists 1; Counselors 6; Child Care Staff 10. *Service Facilities Available (with number of rooms)* Resource Rooms 2; Self-Contained Rooms 1; On-Campus Residential School 4; Homebound Instruction. *Educational Professionals* Regular School Teachers 1; Special Education Teachers 2. *Curricula* Traditional Academic; Individualized; Basic Skills; Prevocational. *Educational Intervention Approaches* Progressive Discipline; Self-Control; Behavior Modification; Creative Conditioning. *Degrees Awarded* High School Diploma; Graduate Equivalency Diploma.

Desert Hills

5245 N Camino De Oeste, Tucson, AZ 85741 (602) 743-7400
Year Established 1973
Contact Guy W Heidinger, Assoc Dir

Facility Information *Placement* Inpatient Psychiatric Facility. *Number of Beds* 62. *Children/Adolescents Served* 78. *Sexes Served* Both. *Room and Board Fees (Approx)* $170. *Sources of Funding* State Funds; Health Insurance; P.L. 94-142. Summer school available. *Teacher Certification Level* Junior High/Middle School; High School. *Special Certification Level* ED; LD; MR; Career/Vocational Education.

Student/Patient Characteristics *Age Levels* 12-14; 15-17. *Exceptionalities Served* Emotionally Disturbed; Learning Disabled. *Learning Problems* Memory Disabilities; Perceptual Disabilities; Thinking Disabilities; Oral Language Disabilities; Reading Disabilities; Handwriting Disabilities; Spelling Disabilities; Arithmetic Disabilities; Written Expression. *Behavioral Problems* Attention Deficits; Impulsivity; Self-Aggression; Verbal Aggression; Physical Aggression; Indirect Aggression; Passive Aggression; Withdrawal. *Conditions Treated* Schizophrenia; Phobias; Obsessions and Compulsions; Hysteria; Depression; Suicide; Asthma; Inadequacy/Immaturity; Personality Problems; Socialized Aggressive Reaction; Unsocialized Aggressive Reaction.

Services Provided Individual Therapy; Group Therapy; Parent Involvement; Behavior Therapy; Family Therapy; Drug Therapy; Art Therapy; Reality Therapy. *Professionals on Staff* Psychiatrists 5; Psychologists 1; Social Workers 6; Child Care Staff 60; Nurses 8. *Service Facilities Available (with number of rooms)* Resource Rooms 2; Self-Contained Rooms 2. *Educational Professionals* Special Education Teachers 6; Career/Vocational Teachers 1; Paraprofessionals 6. *Curricula* Career/Vocational Education; Individualized; Basic Skills; Prevocational. *Degrees Awarded* High School Diploma; Graduate Equivalency Diploma.

The Devereux Center in Arizona

6436 E Sweetwater, Scottsdale, AZ 85254 (602) 998-2920
Year Established 1967
Contact Sean McDevitt, Clinical Dir

Facility Information *Placement* Special School; Private Residential Care. *Number of Beds* 42. *Children/Adolescents Served* 104. *Sexes Served* Both. *Tuition Fees (Approx)* $10,200-$37,200. *Sources of Funding* State Funds; Health Insurance; P.L. 94-142; Private. Summer school available. *Teacher Certification Level* Elementary School; Junior High/Middle School. *Special Certification Level* ED; LD; Reading; Adaptive Physical Education.

Student/Patient Characteristics *Age Levels* 0-4; 5-8; 9-11; 12-14; 15-17. *IQ Ranges* 41-55; 56-70; 71-85; 85-130. *Exceptionalities Served* Autistic; Emotionally Disturbed; Learning Disabled; Communication Disordered. *Learning Problems* Memory Disabilities; Perceptual Disabilities; Thinking Disabilities; Oral Language Disabilities; Reading Disabilities; Handwriting Disabilities; Spelling Disabilities; Arithmetic Disabilities; Written Expression. *Behavioral Problems* Attention Deficits; Hyperactivity; Impulsivity; Verbal Aggression; Physical Aggression; Indirect Aggression; Passive Aggression; Withdrawal. *Conditions Treated* Early Infantile Autism; Schizophrenia; Phobias; Depression; Inadequacy/Immaturity; Personality Problems; Socialized Aggressive Reaction; Unsocialized Aggressive Reaction.

Services Provided Individual Therapy; Group Therapy; Parent Involvement; Behavior Therapy; Cognitive Developmental Therapy; Family Therapy; Play Therapy. *Professionals on Staff* Psychiatrists 1; Psychologists 3; Counselors 3; Social Workers 1; Child Care Staff 32; Nurses 4; Speech and Language Therapists 3; Occupational Therapist 1. *Service Facilities Available (with number of rooms)* Self-Contained Rooms 10; On-Campus Residential School 15. *Educational Professionals* Special Education Teachers 10; Special Education Counselors 3; Paraprofessionals 18. *Curricula* Individualized; Basic Skills; Prevocational. *Educational Intervention Approaches* Progressive Discipline; Self-Control; Behavior Modification. *Degrees Awarded* Certificate of Attendance; High School Diploma.

Comments Devereux provides residential and day programs for special needs children. The programs combine a strong behavioral management approach with intensive clinical services according to identified need. Children with psychiatric disorders and those with specialized educational needs are typically served. Contact the Branch Admissions Officer for details regarding admission criteria and exclusions.

Garfield Girls' School

4820 N 7th Ave, Phoenix, AZ 85013 (602) 274-7318
Year Established 1962
Contact Donna M Leone, Exec Dir

Facility Information *Placement* Private Residential Care. *Number of Beds* 20. *Children/Adolescents Served* 20. *Sexes Served* Female. *Room and Board Fees (Approx)* $55. *Sources of Funding* State Funds; Private Fund Raising. Summer school available. *Teacher Certification Level* Junior High/Middle School; High School. *Special Certification Level* ED; LD; Career/Vocational Education; Reading; Math.

Student/Patient Characteristics *Age Levels* 12-14; 15-17. *IQ Ranges* 71-85; 85-130. *Exceptionalities Served* Emotionally Disturbed; Learning Disabled. *Learning Problems* Thinking Disabilities; Oral Language Disabilities; Reading Disabilities; Spelling Disabilities; Arithmetic Disabilities; Written Expression. *Behavioral Problems* Attention Deficits; Hyperactivity; Impulsivity; Self-Aggression; Verbal Aggression; Physical Aggression; Indirect Aggression; Passive Aggression; Withdrawal. *Conditions Treated* Alcohol Abuse and/or Drug Abuse; Other Substance Abuse or Dependence; Depression; Inadequacy/Immaturity; Personality Problems; Socialized Aggressive Reaction; Unsocialized Aggressive Reaction.

Services Provided Individual Therapy; Group Therapy; Parent Involvement; Family Therapy; Art Therapy; Music Therapy; Reality Therapy. *Professionals on Staff* Counselors 2; Social Workers 2; Child Care Staff 9; Nurses 1. *Service Facilities Available (with number of rooms)* Resource Rooms 1; Self-Contained Rooms 1. *Educational Professionals* Special Education Teachers 2. *Curricula* Traditional Academic; Career/Vocational Education; Individualized; Basic Skills. *Educational Intervention Approaches* Self-Control; Creative Conditioning. *Degrees Awarded* Graduate Equivalency Diploma.

Jane Wayland Center

2613 W Campbell Ave, Phoenix, AZ 85017 (602) 246-4564
Year Established 1929
Contact Richard Geasland, Prog Dir

Facility Information *Placement* Public Residential Care; Private Residential Care; Private Day Care; Public Day Care. *Number of Beds* 23. *Children/Adolescents Served* 23 (residential); 13 (outpatient). *Sexes Served* Both. *Room and Board Fees (Approx)* $81. *Tuition Fees (Approx)* $5,860 (residential students); $7,000 (day only). *Sources of Funding* State Funds; P.L. 94-142; Private. Summer school available. *Teacher Certification Level* Elementary School; Junior High/Middle School; High School. *Special Certification Level* ED; LD; Reading.

Student/Patient Characteristics *Age Levels* 5-8; 9-11; 12-14; 15-17; 18-21; Over 21. *IQ Ranges* 71-85; 85-130; Above 130. *Exceptionalities Served* Autistic; Emotionally Disturbed; Learning Disabled; Communication Disordered. *Learning Problems* Memory Disabilities; Perceptual Disabilities; Thinking Disabilities; Oral Language Disabilities; Reading Disabilities; Handwriting Disabilities; Spelling Disabilities; Arithmetic Disabilities; Written Expression. *Behavioral Problems* Attention Deficits; Hyperactivity; Hypoactivity; Impulsivity; Self-Aggression; Verbal Aggression; Physical Aggression; Indirect Aggression; Passive Aggression; Withdrawal. *Conditions Treated* Disintegrative Psychoses; Schizophrenia; Convulsive Disorders; Phobias; Obsessions and Compulsions; Hysteria; Depression; Suicide; Inadequacy/Immaturity; Personality Problems; Socialized Aggressive Reaction; Unsocialized Aggressive Reaction.

Services Provided Individual Therapy; Group Therapy; Parent Involvement; Behavior Therapy; Cognitive Developmental Therapy; Family Therapy; Drug Therapy; Reality Therapy; Milieu Therapy. *Professionals on Staff* Psychiatrists 1; Psychologists 1; Counselors 1; Social Workers 2; Child Care Staff 23; Nurses 1; Program Director 1. *Service Facilities Available (with number of rooms)* Self-Contained Rooms 3; Special School 3; On-Campus Residential School 3. *Educational Professionals* Special Education Teachers 3; Special Education Counselors 3; Paraprofessionals 3; Special Education Coordinator 1. *Curricula* Traditional Academic; Individualized; Basic Skills; Prevocational. *Educational Intervention Approaches* Engineered Classroom; Progressive Discipline; Behavior Modification; Applied Behavior Analysis; Creative Conditioning. *Degrees Awarded* Graduate Equivalency Diploma.

Comments The center provides the above-stated programs for moderate to severely disturbed children and teenagers. It provides a treatment approach based on a learning model.

Paradise Valley School District No. 69—Therapeutic Educational Activities Milieu

20621 N 32nd St, Phoenix, AZ 85032 (602) 569-1469, 867-5115
Year Established 1983
Contact Bette Eden, Coord; Laura Grothe, Dir of Special Educ

Facility Information *Placement* Public School.
Children/Adolescents Served 40. *Sexes Served* Both. *Sources of Funding* P.L. 94-142. *Teacher Certification Level* Elementary School; Junior High/Middle School; High School. *Special Certification Level* ED; LD.

Student/Patient Characteristics *Age Levels* 12-14; 15-17; 18-21. *IQ Ranges* 85-130. *Exceptionalities Served* Emotionally Disturbed; Learning Disabled. *Learning Problems* Memory Disabilities; Perceptual Disabilities; Thinking Disabilities; Oral Language Disabilities; Reading Disabilities; Handwriting Disabilities; Spelling Disabilities; Arithmetic Disabilities; Written Expression. *Behavioral Problems* Attention Deficits; Hyperactivity; Hypoac-

tivity; Impulsivity; Self-Aggression; Verbal Aggression; Physical Aggression; Indirect Aggression; Passive Aggression; Withdrawal. *Conditions Treated* Disintegrative Psychoses; Schizophrenia; Phobias; Obsessions and Compulsions; Hysteria; Depression; Suicide; Asthma; Personality Problems; Socialized Aggressive Reaction; Unsocialized Aggressive Reaction.

Services Provided Individual Therapy; Group Therapy; Parent Involvement; Behavior Therapy; Family Therapy; Reality Therapy. *Professionals on Staff* Psychologists 1; Social Workers 1; Nurses 1. *Service Facilities Available (with number of rooms)* Self-Contained Rooms. *Educational Professionals* Special Education Teachers 5; Paraprofessionals 6. *Curricula* Individualized. *Educational Intervention Approaches* Behavior Modification. *Degrees Awarded* High School Diploma; Graduate Equivalency Diploma.

Comments This program is a clinical, therapeutic program on a public school campus.

Phoenix Union High School District No. 210

2526 W Osborn Rd, Phoenix, AZ 85017 (602) 251-3932
Contact Karen Smith, Supv of Exceptional Student Prog

Facility Information *Placement* Public School.
Children/Adolescents Served Unlimited. *Sexes Served* Both. *Sources of Funding* State Funds; P.L. 94-142. Summer school available. *Teacher Certification Level* High School. *Special Certification Level* ED; LD; MR; Career/Vocational Education; Reading; Math.

Student/Patient Characteristics *Age Levels* 15-17; 18-21. *IQ Ranges* 0-25; 26-40; 41-55; 56-70; 71-85; 85-130; Above 130. *Exceptionalities Served* Autistic; Emotionally Disturbed; Learning Disabled; Mentally Handicapped; Communication Disordered; Hearing Impaired/Deaf; Visually Impaired/Blind; Other Health Impaired; Physically Handicapped; Gifted. *Learning Problems* Memory Disabilities; Perceptual Disabilities; Thinking Disabilities; Oral Language Disabilities; Reading Disabilities; Handwriting Disabilities; Spelling Disabilities; Arithmetic Disabilities; Written Expression. *Behavioral Problems* Attention Deficits; Hyperactivity; Hypoactivity; Impulsivity; Self-Aggression; Verbal Aggression; Physical Aggression; Indirect Aggression; Passive Aggression; Withdrawal. *Conditions Treated* Aphasia; Phobias; Obsessions and Compulsions; Hysteria; Depression; Suicide; Inadequacy/Immaturity; Personality Problems; Socialized Aggressive Reaction; Unsocialized Aggressive Reaction.

Services Provided Individual Therapy; Group Therapy; Parent Involvement; Behavior Therapy; Cognitive Developmental Therapy; Biofeedback; Family Therapy; Art Therapy; Music Therapy; Reality Therapy; Play Therapy. *Professionals on Staff* Psychologists 10; Counselors 100; Social Workers 8; Nurses 11. *Service Facilities Available (with number of rooms)* Itinerants 8; Resource Rooms; Self-Contained Rooms 8; Homebound Instruction. *Educational Professionals* Regular School Teachers; Special Education Teachers; Career/Vocational Teachers; Special Education Counselors. *Curricula* Traditional Academic; Career/Vocational Education; Individualized; Basic Skills; Prevocational. *Educational Intervention Approaches* Behavior Modification. *Degrees Awarded* Certificate of Attendance; High School Diploma; Certificate of Completion.

Comments This public secondary district provides services to students on 8 comprehensive campuses, a vocational campus, and 5 alternative sites.

Prehab of Arizona Inc—Dorothy Mitchell Residence—Homestead Residence—Helaman House

1134 E University, Mesa, AZ 85203 (602) 969-4024
Year Established 1971
Contact Michael T Hughes, Exec Dir

Facility Information *Placement* Private Residential Care. *Number of Beds* 66. *Children/Adolescents Served* 66. *Sexes Served* Both. *Room and Board Fees (Approx)* $64. *Tuition Fees (Approx)* $4,165. *Sources of Funding* State Funds; P.L. 94-142. Summer school available. *Teacher Certification Level* Elementary School; Junior High/Middle School; High School. *Special Certification Level* ED.

Student/Patient Characteristics *Age Levels* 12-14; 15-17. *IQ Ranges* 71-85; 85-130; Above 130. *Exceptionalities Served* Emotionally Disturbed. *Learning Problems* Memory Disabilities; Oral Language Disabilities; Reading Disabilities; Spelling Disabilities; Arithmetic Disabilities; Written Expression. *Behavioral Problems* Attention Deficits; Hyperactivity; Impulsivity; Self-Aggression; Verbal Aggression; Physical Aggression; Indirect Aggression; Passive Aggression. *Conditions Treated* Alcohol Abuse and/or Drug Abuse; Personality Problems; Socialized Aggressive Reaction; Unsocialized Aggressive Reaction.

Services Provided Individual Therapy; Group Therapy; Parent Involvement; Behavior Therapy; Family Therapy. *Professionals on Staff* Psychologists 1; Counselors 6; Child Care Staff 33. *Service Facilities Available (with number of rooms)* Resource Rooms 2; Self-Contained Rooms 5. *Educational Professionals* Special Education Teachers 5. *Curricula* Individualized; Prevocational. *Educational Intervention Approaches* Behavior Modification. *Degrees Awarded* High School Diploma; Graduate Equivalency Diploma.

Prescott Child Development Center

710 Whipple St, Prescott, AZ 86301 (602) 778-1840
Year Established 1959
Contact Richard A Parry
Facility Information *Placement* Special School; Special Program. *Children/Adolescents Served* 50. *Sexes Served* Both. *Tuition Fees (Approx)* $7,000. *Sources of Funding* State Funds. Summer school available. *Teacher Certification Level* Elementary School; Junior High/Middle School; High School. *Special Certification Level* ED; LD; MR.

Student/Patient Characteristics *Age Levels* 0-4; 5-8; 9-11; 12-14; 15-17. *IQ Ranges* 0-25; 26-40; 41-55; 56-70; 71-85; 85-130; Above 130. *Exceptionalities Served* Autistic; Emotionally Disturbed; Learning Disabled; Mentally Handicapped; Communication Disordered; Hearing Impaired/Deaf; Other Health Impaired; Physically Handicapped. *Learning Problems* Memory Disabilities; Perceptual Disabilities; Thinking Disabilities; Oral Language Disabilities; Reading Disabilities; Handwriting Disabilities; Spelling Disabilities; Arithmetic Disabilities; Written Expression. *Behavioral Problems* Attention Deficits; Hyperactivity; Hypoactivity; Impulsivity; Self-Aggression; Verbal Aggression; Physical Aggression; Indirect Aggression; Passive Aggression; Withdrawal. *Conditions Treated* Alcohol Abuse and/or Drug Abuse; Other Substance Abuse or Dependence; Early Infantile Autism; Disintegrative Psychoses; Schizophrenia; Aphasia; Convulsive Disorders; Phobias; Obsessions and Compulsions; Hysteria; Depression; Suicide; Asthma; Anorexia Nervosa; Ulcerative Colitis; Inadequacy/Immaturity; Personality Problems; Socialized Aggressive Reaction; Unsocialized Aggressive Reaction.

Services Provided Individual Therapy; Group Therapy; Parent Involvement; Behavior Therapy; Family Therapy; Art Therapy; Music Therapy; Reality Therapy; Play Therapy. *Professionals on Staff* Psychiatrists 3; Psychologists 3; Counselors 2; Social Workers 1; Child Care Staff 10. *Service Facilities Available (with number of rooms)* One Room. *Educational Professionals* Special Education Teachers 1; Paraprofessionals 2. *Curricula* Traditional Academic; Individualized; Basic Skills. *Educational Intervention Approaches* Engineered Classroom; Precision Teaching; Progressive Discipline; Behavior Modification; Creative Conditioning.

Rusty's Morningstar Ranch

HC 66, Box 2099, Cornville, AZ 86325 (602) 634-4784
Year Established 1985
Contact Carlene Armstrong, Exec Dir
Facility Information *Placement* Public Residential Care; Private Residential Care; Special Program. *Number of Beds* 12. *Children/Adolescents Served* 12. *Sexes Served* Both. *Room and Board Fees (Approx)* $98. *Tuition Fees (Approx)* $36,000. *Sources of Funding* State Funds; Medicaid; Private.

Student/Patient Characteristics *Age Levels* 18-21; Over 21. *Exceptionalities Served* Autistic; Communication Disordered. *Learning Problems* Perceptual Disabilities; Thinking Disabilities; Oral Language Disabilities; Reading Disabilities; Handwriting Disabilities; Spelling Disabilities; Arithmetic Disabilities; Written Expression. *Behavioral Problems* Attention Deficits; Hyperactivity; Hypoactivity; Impulsivity; Self-Aggression; Verbal Aggression; Physical Aggression; Indirect Aggression; Passive Aggression; Withdrawal. *Conditions Treated* Other Substance Abuse or Dependence.

Services Provided Individual Therapy; Group Therapy; Parent Involvement; Behavior Therapy; Cognitive Developmental Therapy; Art Therapy; Music Therapy; Speech and Language Therapy. *Professionals on Staff* Speech and Language Pathologists 2. *Curricula* Career/Vocational Education; Individualized; Basic Skills; Farm and Ranch Skills; Housekeeping Skills. *Educational Intervention Approaches* Self-Control; Behavior Modification; IMPACT.

Samuel Gompers Memorial Rehabilitation Center Inc

7211 N 7th St, Phoenix, AZ 85020 (602) 943-3484
Year Established 1947
Contact JoAnn Schall-Woodley, Ed Dir
Facility Information *Placement* Special School; Special Program. *Children/Adolescents Served* 60. *Sexes Served* Both. *Tuition Fees (Approx)* $6,100. *Sources of Funding* State Funds; Health Insurance; P.L. 94-142; Department of Economic Security Division. Summer school available. *Teacher Certification Level* Elementary School; Junior High/Middle School; High School. *Special Certification Level* Various Exceptionalities.

Student/Patient Characteristics *Age Levels* 0-4; 5-8; 9-11; 12-14; 15-17; 18-21; Over 21. *IQ Ranges* 0-25; 26-40; 41-55; 56-70; 71-85; 85-130. *Exceptionalities Served* Autistic; Emotionally Disturbed; Mentally Handicapped; Communication Disordered; Hearing Impaired/Deaf; Visually Impaired/Blind; Other Health Impaired; Physically Handicapped. *Learning Problems* Memory Disabilities; Perceptual Disabilities; Thinking Disabilities; Oral Language Disabilities; Reading Disabilities; Handwriting Disabilities; Spelling Disabilities; Arithmetic Disabilities; Written Expression. *Behavioral Problems* Attention Deficits; Hyperactivity; Hypoactivity; Impulsivity; Self-Aggression; Verbal Aggression; Physical Aggression; Indirect Aggression; Passive Aggression; Withdrawal. *Conditions Treated* Early Infantile Autism; Convulsive Disorders.

Services Provided Individual Therapy; Group Therapy; Parent Involvement; Biofeedback; Family Therapy; Music Therapy. *Professionals on Staff* Psychologists; Social Workers; Nurses. *Service Facilities Available (with number of rooms)* Self-Contained Rooms 8. *Educational Professionals* Special Education Teachers; Paraprofessionals. *Curricula* Career/Vocational Education; Individualized; Prevocational; Self Help. *Educational Intervention Approaches* Engineered Classroom; Precision Teaching; Self-Control; Behavior Modification; Creative Conditioning. *Degrees Awarded* Certificate of Attendance.

Comments Gomper's Special Education Programs are structured to respond to a multiplicity of learning needs. Students from 3 to 22 years of age are enrolled in classes designed to meet their individual needs. Grouping is done according to the child's ability and age. Class size ranges from 5 to 9 students with a 1:3 staff-student ratio. The Gompers School program focuses on the abilities of each individual and assists him/her to become as independent as possible.

Scottsdale Public School District

3811 N 44th St, Phoenix, AZ 85018 (602) 952-6181
Contact Betty J Pepper, Dir of Special Educ
Facility Information *Placement* Public School. *Children/Adolescents Served* 2,500. *Sexes Served* Both. *Sources of Funding* State Funds; P.L. 94-142; P.L. 89-313. *Teacher*

Certification Level Elementary School; Junior High/Middle School; High School. *Special Certification Level* ED; LD; MR; Career/Vocational Education; Reading; Math.

Student/Patient Characteristics *Age Levels* 0-4; 5-8; 9-11; 12-14; 15-17; 18-21; Over 21. *IQ Ranges* 0-25; 26-40; 41-55; 56-70; 71-85; 85-130; Above 130. *Exceptionalities Served* Autistic; Emotionally Disturbed; Learning Disabled; Mentally Handicapped; Communication Disordered; Hearing Impaired/Deaf; Visually Impaired/Blind; Other Health Impaired; Physically Handicapped; Gifted. *Learning Problems* Memory Disabilities; Perceptual Disabilities; Thinking Disabilities; Oral Language Disabilities; Reading Disabilities; Handwriting Disabilities; Spelling Disabilities; Arithmetic Disabilities; Written Expression. *Behavioral Problems* Attention Deficits; Hyperactivity; Hypoactivity; Impulsivity; Self-Aggression; Verbal Aggression; Physical Aggression; Indirect Aggression; Passive Aggression; Withdrawal. *Conditions Treated* Phobias; Depression.

Services Provided Parent Involvement; Behavior Therapy. *Professionals on Staff* Psychologists; Counselors; Nurses. *Service Facilities Available (with number of rooms)* Consultative (ERT); Itinerants; Resource Rooms; Self-Contained Rooms; Special School; Homebound Instruction. *Educational Professionals* Special Education Teachers 180; Career/Vocational Teachers 10; Paraprofessionals 89. *Curricula* Traditional Academic; Career/Vocational Education; Individualized; Basic Skills; Prevocational. *Educational Intervention Approaches* Precision Teaching; Behavior Modification. *Degrees Awarded* Certificate of Attendance; High School Diploma.

Washington School District

8610 N 19th Ave, Phoenix, AZ 85021 (602) 864-2643
Contact Joel Davidson, Special Ed Dir
Facility Information *Placement* Public School. *Children/Adolescents Served* 654. *Sexes Served* Both. *Sources of Funding* State Funds; P.L. 94-142. *Teacher Certification Level* Elementary School; Junior High/Middle School. *Special Certification Level* ED; LD.

Student/Patient Characteristics *Age Levels* 5-8; 9-11; 12-14. *IQ Ranges* 71-85; 85-130; Above 130. *Exceptionalities Served* Autistic; Emotionally Disturbed; Learning Disabled. *Learning Problems* Memory Disabilities; Perceptual Disabilities; Thinking Disabilities; Oral Language Disabilities; Reading Disabilities; Handwriting Disabilities; Spelling Disabilities; Arithmetic Disabilities; Written Expression. *Behavioral Problems* Attention Deficits; Hyperactivity; Impulsivity; Verbal Aggression; Physical Aggression; Passive Aggression. *Conditions Treated* Early Infantile Autism; Inadequacy/Immaturity; Personality Problems; Socialized Aggressive Reaction.

Services Provided Individual Therapy; Group Therapy; Parent Involvement; Behavior Therapy. *Professionals on Staff* Psychologists 6; Counselors 3; Nurses 31. *Service Facilities Available (with number of rooms)* Resource Rooms; Self-Contained Rooms. *Educational Professionals* Special Education Teachers 18; Special Education Counselors 3; Paraprofessionals 18. *Curricula* Traditional Academic; Individualized; Basic Skills. *Educational Intervention Approaches* Engineered Classroom; Precision Teaching; Progressive Discipline; Behavior Modification. *Degrees Awarded* Eighth Grade Diploma.

Westbridge

367 N 21st Ave, Phoenix, AZ 85009 (602) 254-0884
Year Established 1983
Contact Helene Boinski-McConnell, Prog Admin
Facility Information *Placement* Inpatient Psychiatric Treatment. *Number of Beds* 20. *Children/Adolescents Served* 20. *Sexes Served* Both. *Room and Board Fees (Approx)* $195-$365. *Sources of Funding* State Funds; Health Insurance; Parents. Summer school available. *Teacher Certification Level* Junior High/Middle School; High School. *Special Certification Level* LD; EMH-Emotionally, Mentally Handicapped.

Student/Patient Characteristics *Age Levels* 12-14; 15-17; 18-21. *IQ Ranges* 71-85; 85-130; Above 130. *Exceptionalities Served* Emotionally Disturbed; Learning Disabled; Communication Disordered; Hearing Impaired/Deaf; Gifted. *Learning Problems* Memory Disabilities; Perceptual Disabilities; Thinking Disabilities; Oral Language Disabilities; Reading Disabilities; Handwriting Disabilities; Spelling Disabilities; Written Expression. *Behavioral Problems* Attention Deficits; Hyperactivity; Impulsivity; Self-Aggression; Verbal Aggression; Physical Aggression; Indirect Aggression; Passive Aggression; Withdrawal. *Conditions Treated* Alcohol Abuse and/or Drug Abuse; Other Substance Abuse or Dependence; Schizophrenia; Convulsive Disorders; Phobias; Obsessions and Compulsions; Hysteria; Depression; Suicide; Anorexia Nervosa; Inadequacy/Immaturity; Personality Problems; Socialized Aggressive Reaction; Unsocialized Aggressive Reaction; Borderline Personality.

Services Provided Individual Therapy; Group Therapy; Parent Involvement; Behavior Therapy; Cognitive Developmental Therapy; Family Therapy; Drug Therapy; Art Therapy; Reality Therapy; Psychodrama; Occupation/Recreational Therapy. *Professionals on Staff* Psychiatrists 7; Psychologists 2; Counselors 1; Social Workers 1; Child Care Staff 10; Nurses 5; Art Therapist 1; Occupational Therapist 1. *Service Facilities Available (with number of rooms)* Consultative (ERT) 1; Resource Rooms 2; Self-Contained Rooms 2. *Educational Professionals* Special Education Teachers 2; Paraprofessionals 2. *Curricula* Traditional Academic; Career/Vocational Education; Individualized; Basic Skills; Prevocational. *Educational Intervention Approaches* Progressive Discipline; Self-Control; Behavior Modification; Applied Behavior Analysis. *Degrees Awarded* Certificate of Attendance; High School Diploma; Graduate Equivalency Diploma.

Youth Evaluation and Treatment Centers (YETC)

801 N 1st Ave, Phoenix, AZ 85003 (602) 258-7282
Year Established 1978
Contact Patricia Miller, Exec Dir
Facility Information *Placement* Special School; Private Residential Care; Crisis Shelter; Day Support. *Number of Beds* 26. *Children/Adolescents Served* 54. *Sexes Served* Both. *Tuition Fees (Approx)* $6,800. *Sources of Funding* State Funds; P.L. 94-142; Private Grants; Donations. *Teacher Certification Level* Elementary School; Junior High/Middle School; High School. *Special Certification Level* ED; Emotionally Handicapped.

Student/Patient Characteristics *Age Levels* 9-11; 12-14; 15-17. *IQ Ranges* 56-70; 71-85; 85-130; Above 130. *Exceptionalities Served* Emotionally Disturbed. *Learning Problems* Memory Disabilities; Perceptual Disabilities; Thinking Disabilities; Oral Language Disabilities; Reading Disabilities; Handwriting Disabilities; Spelling Disabilities; Arithmetic Disabilities; Written Expression. *Behavioral Problems* Attention Deficits; Hyperactivity; Hypoactivity; Impulsivity; Self-Aggression; Verbal Aggression; Physical Aggression; Indirect Aggression; Passive Aggression; Withdrawal. *Conditions Treated* Schizophrenia; Aphasia; Phobias; Obsessions and Compulsions; Hysteria; Depression; Suicide; Inadequacy/Immaturity; Personality Problems; Socialized Aggressive Reaction; Unsocialized Aggressive Reaction.

Services Provided Individual Therapy; Group Therapy; Parent Involvement; Behavior Therapy; Cognitive Developmental Therapy; Family Therapy; Filial Therapy; Art Therapy; Reality Therapy; Play Therapy. *Professionals on Staff* Psychiatrists; Psychologists; Counselors 3; Social Workers 1; Child Care Staff 13; Skills Coordinator 1. *Service Facilities Available (with number of rooms)* On-Campus Residential School 1. *Educational Professionals* Special Education Teachers 1; Career/Vocational Teachers 1; Paraprofessionals 1. *Curricula* Traditional Academic; Career/Vocational Education; Individualized; Basic Skills; Prevocational; GED Preparation. *Educational Intervention Approaches* Precision Teaching; Progressive Discipline; Self-Control; Behavior Modification.

Comments Youth ETC is a multi-program agency (private, nonprofit) which offers a continuum of psychotherapy services to ensure individual needs are met within the least restrictive environment.

Yuma School District One

450 6th St, Yuma, AZ 85364 (602) 782-6581
Contact Wanda Dildine, Special Ed Dir
Facility Information *Placement* Public School.
Children/Adolescents Served 40. *Sexes Served* Both. *Sources of Funding* State Funds; P.L. 94-142. *Teacher Certification Level* Elementary School; Junior High/Middle School. *Special Certification Level* ED; LD; MR.
Student/Patient Characteristics *Age Levels* 5-8; 9-11; 12-14.
Exceptionalities Served Autistic; Emotionally Disturbed; Learning Disabled; Mentally Handicapped; Communication Disordered; Visually Impaired/Blind; Other Health Impaired; Physically Handicapped; Gifted. *Learning Problems* Memory Disabilities; Perceptual Disabilities; Thinking Disabilities; Oral Language Disabilities; Reading Disabilities; Handwriting Disabilities; Spelling Disabilities; Arithmetic Disabilities; Written Expression.
Behavioral Problems Attention Deficits; Hyperactivity; Hypoactivity; Impulsivity; Self-Aggression; Verbal Aggression; Physical Aggression; Indirect Aggression; Passive Aggression; Withdrawal. *Conditions Treated* Inadequacy/Immaturity; Personality Problems.
Services Provided *Professionals on Staff* Psychologists 3; Nurses 1. *Service Facilities Available (with number of rooms)* Resource Rooms 11; Self-Contained Rooms 3. *Educational Professionals* Regular School Teachers 40; Special Education Teachers 32; Paraprofessionals 11. *Curricula* Traditional Academic; Individualized; Basic Skills; Prevocational. *Educational Intervention Approaches* Engineered Classroom; Precision Teaching; Progressive Discipline; Behavior Modification. *Degrees Awarded* Graduate Equivalency Diploma.

Yuma Union High School District

3100 Ave A, Yuma, AZ 85364 (602) 344-3825
Contact M Suzanne Spoden, Spec Ed Prog Advisor

Facility Information *Placement* Public School. *Sexes Served* Both. *Sources of Funding* State Funds; P.L. 94-142. *Teacher Certification Level* High School. *Special Certification Level* ED; LD; MR; Career/Vocational Education; Reading; Math.
Student/Patient Characteristics *Age Levels* 15-17. *IQ Ranges* 0-25; 26-40; 41-55; 56-70; 71-85; 85-130. *Exceptionalities Served* Autistic; Emotionally Disturbed; Learning Disabled; Mentally Handicapped; Communication Disordered; Hearing Impaired/Deaf; Visually Impaired/Blind; Other Health Impaired; Physically Handicapped; Multiply Handicapped. *Learning Problems* Memory Disabilities; Perceptual Disabilities; Thinking Disabilities; Oral Language Disabilities; Reading Disabilities; Handwriting Disabilities; Spelling Disabilities; Arithmetic Disabilities; Written Expression. *Behavioral Problems* Attention Deficits; Hyperactivity; Hypoactivity; Impulsivity; Self-Aggression; Verbal Aggression; Physical Aggression; Indirect Aggression; Passive Aggression; Withdrawal. *Conditions Treated* Alcohol Abuse and/or Drug Abuse; Schizophrenia; Aphasia; Depression; Suicide; Asthma; Inadequacy/Immaturity; Personality Problems; Socialized Aggressive Reaction; Unsocialized Aggressive Reaction.
Services Provided Individual Therapy; Group Therapy; Cognitive Developmental Therapy; Drug Therapy; Reality Therapy. *Professionals on Staff* Psychologists 2; Counselors 10; Nurses 4. *Service Facilities Available (with number of rooms)* Itinerants 2; Resource Rooms 8; Self-Contained Rooms 2. *Educational Professionals* Regular School Teachers 300; Special Education Teachers 11; Career/Vocational Teachers 1; Special Education Counselors. *Curricula* Traditional Academic; Career/Vocational Education; Individualized. *Educational Intervention Approaches* Engineered Classroom; Precision Teaching; Self-Control; Behavior Modification. *Degrees Awarded* High School Diploma; Trainable Mentally Handicapped Awards.

Arkansas

Bridgeway Hospital Youthcare Program

21 Bridgeway Rd, North Little Rock, AR 72118 (501) 771-1500
Year Established 1983
Contact Dusty Maxwell, Prog Coord
Facility Information *Placement* Hospital. *Number of Beds* 24.
Children/Adolescents Served 24. *Sexes Served* Both. *Room and Board Fees (Approx)* $269. *Sources of Funding* Health Insurance.
Teacher Certification Level High School. *Special Certification Level* LD; Secondary Education.
Student/Patient Characteristics *Age Levels* 12-14; 15-17; 18-21.
IQ Ranges 71-85; 85-130; Above 130. *Exceptionalities Served* Emotionally Disturbed; Learning Disabled; Mentally Handicapped; Gifted. *Learning Problems* Memory Disabilities; Perceptual Disabilities; Thinking Disabilities; Oral Language Disabilities; Reading Disabilities; Handwriting Disabilities; Spelling Disabilities; Arithmetic Disabilities; Written Expression.
Behavioral Problems Attention Deficits; Hyperactivity; Hypoactivity; Impulsivity; Self-Aggression; Verbal Aggression; Physical Aggression; Indirect Aggression; Passive Aggression; Withdrawal.
Conditions Treated Alcohol Abuse and/or Drug Abuse; Other Substance Abuse or Dependence; Disintegrative Psychoses; Schizophrenia; Phobias; Obsessions and Compulsions; Hysteria; Depression; Suicide; Anorexia Nervosa; Inadequacy/Immaturity; Personality Problems; Socialized Aggressive Reaction; Unsocialized Aggressive Reaction.
Services Provided Individual Therapy; Group Therapy; Parent Involvement; Behavior Therapy; Family Therapy; Drug Therapy; Art Therapy; Reality Therapy; Play Therapy; Psychodrama.
Professionals on Staff Psychiatrists 4; Psychologists 2; Counselors 6; Social Workers 1; Nurses 18; Physical Therapist; Occupation Therapist 5. *Service Facilities Available (with number of rooms)* Hospital School 2; Homebound Instruction 2. *Educational Professionals* Regular School Teachers 1; Special Education Teachers 1; Special Education Counselors 1; Homebound Teachers 2. *Curricula* Individualized. *Educational Intervention Approaches* Self-Control; Behavior Modification; Applied Behavior Analysis; Creative Conditioning.
Comments Youthcare is a 24 bed private inpatient psychiatric hospital. A variety of treatment modalities are used to work with behavioral and psychopathological conditions. Youthcare utilizes an interdisciplinary approach to treatment.

Harbor View Mercy Hospital

10301 Mayo Rd, Fort Smith, AR 72913 (501) 484-5550
Contact Geraldine Marie Heavrin, Asst Admin
Facility Information *Placement* Special School; Special Program.
Number of Beds 18. *Children/Adolescents Served* 18. *Sexes Served* Both. *Room and Board Fees (Approx)* $255. *Sources of Funding* Health Insurance; Medicaid; Medicare; P.L. 94-142. Summer

school available. *Teacher Certification Level* Elementary School; Junior High/Middle School; High School. *Special Certification Level* ED; MR; Broad Fields K thru 12.
Student/Patient Characteristics *Age Levels* 12-14; 15-17; 18-21; Over 21. *Exceptionalities Served* Autistic; Emotionally Disturbed; Learning Disabled; Mentally Handicapped; Communication Disordered; Hearing Impaired/Deaf; Visually Impaired/Blind; Other Health Impaired; Physically Handicapped; Gifted. *Learning Problems* Memory Disabilities; Perceptual Disabilities; Thinking Disabilities; Oral Language Disabilities; Reading Disabilities; Handwriting Disabilities; Spelling Disabilities; Arithmetic Disabilities; Written Expression. *Behavioral Problems* Attention Deficits; Hyperactivity; Hypoactivity; Impulsivity; Self-Aggression; Verbal Aggression; Physical Aggression; Indirect Aggression; Passive Aggression; Withdrawal; All Psychiatric Diagnoses. *Conditions Treated* Alcohol Abuse and/or Drug Abuse; Other Substance Abuse or Dependence; Early Infantile Autism; Disintegrative Psychoses; Schizophrenia; Aphasia; Convulsive Disorders; Phobias; Obsessions and Compulsions; Hysteria; Depression; Suicide; Asthma; Anorexia Nervosa; Inadequacy/Immaturity; Personality Problems; Socialized Aggressive Reaction; Unsocialized Aggressive Reaction.
Services Provided Individual Therapy; Group Therapy; Parent Involvement; Behavior Therapy; Cognitive Developmental Therapy; Family Therapy; Filial Therapy; Drug Therapy; Art Therapy; Music Therapy; Reality Therapy; Play Therapy; Psychodrama. *Professionals on Staff* Psychiatrists 7; Psychologists; Counselors; Social Workers 2; Nurses; Adjunctive Services Personnel. *Service Facilities Available (with number of rooms)* Consultative (ERT) 3; Resource Rooms 1; Self-Contained Resource Room 1. *Educational Professionals* Regular School Teachers; Special Education Teachers; Career/Vocational Teachers; Crisis Teachers; Special Education Counselors; Paraprofessionals.
Curricula Individualized. *Educational Intervention Approaches* Progressive Discipline; Self-Control; Behavior Modification. *Degrees Awarded* Graduate Equivalency Diploma Prepare for GED.

Little Rock School District

W Markham and Izard, Little Rock, AR 72201 (501) 370-1654
Contact Estelle Matthis, Dir of Special Ed
Facility Information *Placement* Public School. *Sexes Served* Both. *Sources of Funding* State Funds; P.L. 94-142; Local Funds. Summer school available. *Teacher Certification Level* Elementary School; Junior High/Middle School; High School. *Special Certification Level* ED; LD; MR; Speech Impaired; Hearing Impaired; Visually Impaired.
Student/Patient Characteristics *Age Levels* 5-8; 9-11; 12-14; 15-17; 18-21. *IQ Ranges* 26-40; 41-55; 56-70; 71-85; 85-130; Above 130. *Exceptionalities Served* Autistic; Emotionally Disturbed; Learning Disabled; Mentally Handicapped; Communica-

tion Disordered; Hearing Impaired/Deaf; Visually Impaired/ Blind; Other Health Impaired; Physically Handicapped. *Learning Problems* Memory Disabilities; Perceptual Disabilities; Thinking Disabilities; Oral Language Disabilities; Reading Disabilities; Handwriting Disabilities; Spelling Disabilities; Arithmetic Disabilities; Written Expression. *Behavioral Problems* Attention Deficits; Hyperactivity; Hypoactivity; Impulsivity; Self-Aggression; Verbal Aggression; Physical Aggression; Indirect Aggression; Passive Aggression; Withdrawal.

Services Provided Individual Therapy; Group Therapy; Parent Involvement; Behavior Therapy. *Professionals on Staff* Psychiatrists; Psychologists; Counselors; Social Workers; Nurses. *Service Facilities Available (with number of rooms)* Resource Rooms; Self-Contained Rooms; Homebound Instruction; Other Agency Contracts. *Educational Professionals* Regular School Teachers; Special Education Teachers; Career/Vocational Teachers; Special Education Counselors; Paraprofessionals. *Curricula* Traditional Academic; Career/Vocational Education; Individualized; Basic Skills; Prevocational. *Educational Intervention Approaches* Engineered Classroom; Behavior Modification. *Degrees Awarded* High School Diploma.

Ouachita Regional Counseling and Mental Health Center—Children's Specialized Services Unit

PO Box 1106, 700 South Ave, Hot Springs, AR 71902
(501) 624-7111
Year Established 1967
Contact Julius A Adams, Dir Childrens Serv

Facility Information *Placement* Outpatient Mental Health Center. *Sexes Served* Both. *Sources of Funding* Health Insurance; Medicaid; Title XX. Summer school available.

Student/Patient Characteristics *Age Levels* 0-4; 5-8; 9-11; 12-14; 15-17; 18-21; Over 21. *IQ Ranges* 0-25; 26-40; 41-55; 56-70; 71-85; 85-130; Above 130.

Services Provided Individual Therapy; Group Therapy; Parent Involvement; Behavior Therapy; Biofeedback; Family Therapy; Drug Therapy; Art Therapy; Reality Therapy; Play Therapy. *Professionals on Staff* Psychiatrists 1; Psychologists 2; Social Workers 1; Child Care Staff 1; Speech Pathologists 3. *Service Facilities Available (with number of rooms)* Pre-School Classrooms 2.

Comments Children's Specialized Services Unit provides outpatient and evaluation services to children and families in a 5-county area. Services include evaluation and treatment of autistic children, as well as training for parents and professionals.

Pulaski County Special School District

Box 6409, 1500 Dixon Rd, Little Rock, AR 72216
(501) 490-2000
Contact Danny Reed, Dir Special Ed

Facility Information *Placement* Public School. *Sexes Served* Both. *Sources of Funding* State Funds; P.L. 94-142; P.L. 89-313; Local. Summer school available. *Teacher Certification Level* Elementary School; Junior High/Middle School; High School. *Special Certification Level* ED; LD; MR.

Student/Patient Characteristics *Age Levels* 5-8; 9-11; 12-14; 15-17; 18-21. *IQ Ranges* 0-25; 26-40; 41-55; 56-70; 71-85; 85-130; Above 130. *Exceptionalities Served* Autistic; Emotionally Disturbed; Learning Disabled; Mentally Handicapped; Communication Disordered; Hearing Impaired/Deaf; Visually Impaired/ Blind; Other Health Impaired; Physically Handicapped; Gifted.

Learning Problems Memory Disabilities; Perceptual Disabilities; Thinking Disabilities; Oral Language Disabilities; Reading Disabilities; Handwriting Disabilities; Spelling Disabilities; Arithmetic Disabilities; Written Expression. *Behavioral Problems* Attention Deficits; Hyperactivity; Hypoactivity; Impulsivity; Self-Aggression; Verbal Aggression; Physical Aggression; Indirect Aggression; Passive Aggression; Withdrawal.

Services Provided Individual Therapy; Group Therapy; Parent Involvement; Behavior Therapy. *Professionals on Staff* Psychologists 2; Counselors; Social Workers; Physical Therapists 3. *Service Facilities Available (with number of rooms)* Itinerants 25; Resource Rooms; Self-Contained Rooms; Homebound Instruction; Contracted Residential on a Case by Case Basis. *Educational Professionals* Regular School Teachers 1500; Special Education Teachers 150; Career/Vocational Teachers; Speech and Hearing Pathologists 26. *Curricula* Traditional Academic; Career/Vocational Education; Individualized; Basic Skills; Prevocational. *Educational Intervention Approaches* Behavior Modification. *Degrees Awarded* High School Diploma.

Comments The Pulaski County Special School District serves all students aged 5-21 regardless of the nature or severity of their handicap. Every attempt is made to provide or develop educational programs based on individual needs.

University of Arkansas Medical Sciences Division Child Psychiatry—Child Study Center

4301 W Markham, Little Rock, AR 72205 (501) 661-5800
Year Established 1968

Facility Information *Placement* Special School; Outpatient Clinic; Short Term Intensive Psychiatric Inpatient. *Number of Beds* 12. *Children/Adolescents Served* 12 inpatients, unlimited outpatients. *Sexes Served* Both. *Sources of Funding* State Funds; Health Insurance; Medicaid; Medicare. Summer school available. *Teacher Certification Level* Elementary School. *Special Certification Level* ED; LD; Reading.

Student/Patient Characteristics *Age Levels* 0-4; 5-8; 9-11; 12-14. *Exceptionalities Served* Autistic; Emotionally Disturbed; Learning Disabled; Mentally Handicapped; Gifted. *Learning Problems* Memory Disabilities; Perceptual Disabilities; Thinking Disabilities; Oral Language Disabilities; Reading Disabilities; Handwriting Disabilities; Spelling Disabilities; Arithmetic Disabilities; Written Expression. *Behavioral Problems* Attention Deficits; Hyperactivity; Hypoactivity; Impulsivity; Self-Aggression; Verbal Aggression; Physical Aggression; Indirect Aggression; Passive Aggression; Withdrawal. *Conditions Treated* Alcohol Abuse and/or Drug Abuse; Other Substance Abuse or Dependence; Early Infantile Autism; Disintegrative Psychoses; Schizophrenia; Aphasia; Convulsive Disorders; Phobias; Obsessions and Compulsions; Hysteria; Depression; Suicide; Asthma; Anorexia Nervosa; Inadequacy/Immaturity; Personality Problems; Socialized Aggressive Reaction.

Services Provided Individual Therapy; Group Therapy; Parent Involvement; Behavior Therapy; Cognitive Developmental Therapy; Family Therapy; Drug Therapy; Art Therapy; Music Therapy; Play Therapy. *Professionals on Staff* Psychiatrists 5; Psychologists 10; Social Workers 3; Nurses 12. *Service Facilities Available (with number of rooms)* Consultative (ERT); Self-Contained Rooms; Special School; Hospital School; Tutoring. *Educational Professionals* Special Education Teachers 5; Paraprofessionals 5. *Curricula* Traditional Academic; Individualized; Basic Skills. *Educational Intervention Approaches* Behavior Modification.

California

Ahwahnee Hills School

43469 Hwy 49, Ahwahnee, CA 93601 (209) 683-7551
Contact Dan Long, Director

Facility Information *Placement* Private Residential Care. *Number of Beds* 96. *Children/Adolescents Served* 96. *Sexes Served* Male. *Sources of Funding* Medicare. Summer school available. *Teacher Certification Level* Elementary School; Junior High/Middle School; High School.

Student/Patient Characteristics *Age Levels* 12-14; 15-17. *Exceptionalities Served* Emotionally Disturbed; Learning Disabled; Mentally Handicapped; Communication Disordered. *Behavioral Problems* Attention Deficits; Hyperactivity; Impulsivity; Self-Aggression; Verbal Aggression; Physical Aggression; Indirect Aggression; Passive Aggression. *Conditions Treated* Alcohol Abuse and/or Drug Abuse; Depression; Inadequacy/Immaturity; Personality Problems; Socialized Aggressive Reaction; Unsocialized Aggressive Reaction.

Services Provided Individual Therapy; Behavior Therapy; Reality Therapy. *Professionals on Staff* Counselors 2; Social Workers 2; Child Care Staff 8; Houseparents 20. *Service Facilities Available (with number of rooms)* On-Campus Residential School 8. *Educational Professionals* Regular School Teachers 2; Special Education Teachers 8; Special Education Counselors 1; Paraprofessionals 8.

ALA Costa Center for the Developmentally Disabled—After School

1300 Rose St, Berkeley, CA 94702 (415) 527-2550
Contact Lee Turner-Muecke, Dir

Facility Information *Placement* Extended Day-State Funded. *Children/Adolescents Served* 24. *Sexes Served* Both. *Sources of Funding* State Funds; Regional Center Funding. Summer school available. *Teacher Certification Level* Elementary School; High School. *Special Certification Level* ED; MR; Career/Vocational Education.

Student/Patient Characteristics *Age Levels* 5-8; 9-11; 12-14; 15-17; 18-21. *IQ Ranges* 26-40; 56-70. *Exceptionalities Served* Autistic; Learning Disabled; Mentally Handicapped; Communication Disordered; Other Health Impaired. *Learning Problems* Memory Disabilities; Perceptual Disabilities; Thinking Disabilities; Oral Language Disabilities; Reading Disabilities; Handwriting Disabilities; Spelling Disabilities; Arithmetic Disabilities; Written Expression. *Behavioral Problems* Attention Deficits; Hyperactivity; Self-Aggression; Passive Aggression; Withdrawal. *Conditions Treated* Early Infantile Autism.

Services Provided *Professionals on Staff* Counselors; Social Workers; Child Care Staff. *Service Facilities Available (with number of rooms)* Consultative (ERT) 1; Resource Rooms 3; Self-Contained Rooms 3. *Educational Professionals* Special Education Teachers 3; Career/Vocational Teachers 3. *Curricula* Traditional Academic; Career/Vocational Education; Individualized; Basic Skills; Prevocational. *Educational Intervention Approaches* Self-Control; Creative Conditioning.

Almansor Education Center

9 1/2 N Almansor St, Alhambra, CA 91801 (818) 282-6194
Year Established 1974
Contact Nancy Lavelle, Exec Dir

Facility Information *Placement* Special School; Private School. *Children/Adolescents Served* 72. *Sexes Served* Both. *Tuition Fees (Approx)* $9,600. *Sources of Funding* State Funds; Health Insurance; Medicare; P.L. 94-142; Parent Fees. Summer school available. *Teacher Certification Level* Elementary School; Junior High/Middle School; High School. *Special Certification Level* ED; LD; MR; Career/Vocational Education; Reading; Math; Adaptive Physical Education; Speech Therapy; Language Therapy.

Student/Patient Characteristics *Age Levels* 0-4; 5-8; 9-11; 12-14; 15-17; 18-21; Over 21. *IQ Ranges* 41-55; 56-70; 71-85; 85-130; Above 130. *Exceptionalities Served* Emotionally Disturbed; Learning Disabled; Mentally Handicapped; Communication Disordered; Gifted. *Learning Problems* Memory Disabilities; Perceptual Disabilities; Thinking Disabilities; Oral Language Disabilities; Reading Disabilities; Handwriting Disabilities; Spelling Disabilities; Arithmetic Disabilities; Written Expression; Motor Disabilities. *Behavioral Problems* Attention Deficits; Hyperactivity; Hypoactivity; Impulsivity; Self-Aggression; Verbal Aggression; Physical Aggression; Indirect Aggression; Passive Aggression; Withdrawal. *Conditions Treated* Schizophrenia; Aphasia; Convulsive Disorders; Phobias; Obsessions and Compulsions; Hysteria; Depression; Suicide; Asthma; Anorexia Nervosa; Inadequacy/Immaturity; Personality Problems; Socialized Aggressive Reaction; Unsocialized Aggressive Reaction.

Services Provided Individual Therapy; Group Therapy; Parent Involvement; Behavior Therapy; Cognitive Developmental Therapy; Family Therapy; Filial Therapy; Reality Therapy. *Professionals on Staff* Psychologists 1; Social Workers 1; Nurses 1. *Service Facilities Available (with number of rooms)* Resource Rooms 1; Self-Contained Rooms 7. *Educational Professionals* Career/Vocational Teachers 1; Crisis Teachers 3. *Curricula* Traditional Academic; Career/Vocational Education; Individualized; Basic Skills; Prevocational. *Educational Intervention Approaches* Applied Behavior Analysis; Responsibility Training. *Degrees Awarded* Certificate of Attendance; High School Diploma.

Comments The purpose of the center is to enable each student to discover his/her commitment in the form of agreements, goals and objectives; assess each student's unique learning and develop appropriate curriculum and teaching strategies; and to provide a carefully monitered structured environment in which growth in social, language, motor, academic, and vocational areas can take place.

Aseltine School

4027 Normal St, San Diego, CA 92103 (619) 296-2135
Year Established 1968
Contact Marian F Grant, Exec Dir
Facility Information *Placement* Special School.
Children/Adolescents Served 60. *Sexes Served* Both. *Tuition Fees (Approx)* $9,939. *Sources of Funding* P.L. 94-142; Private Tuition. Summer school available. *Teacher Certification Level* Elementary School; Junior High/Middle School; High School. *Special Certification Level* ED; LD; MR; Reading.
Student/Patient Characteristics *Age Levels* 5-8; 9-11; 12-14; 15-17; 18-21. *IQ Ranges* 71-85; 85-130. *Exceptionalities Served* Emotionally Disturbed; Learning Disabled; Visually Impaired/Blind; Gifted. *Learning Problems* Memory Disabilities; Perceptual Disabilities; Thinking Disabilities; Oral Language Disabilities; Reading Disabilities; Handwriting Disabilities; Spelling Disabilities; Arithmetic Disabilities; Written Expression. *Behavioral Problems* Attention Deficits; Hyperactivity; Hypoactivity; Impulsivity; Self-Aggression; Verbal Aggression; Physical Aggression; Indirect Aggression; Passive Aggression. *Conditions Treated* Alcohol Abuse and/or Drug Abuse; Other Substance Abuse or Dependence; Phobias; Obsessions and Compulsions; Depression; Personality Problems; Socialized Aggressive Reaction; Unsocialized Aggressive Reaction.
Services Provided Individual Therapy; Group Therapy; Parent Involvement; Behavior Therapy; Cognitive Developmental Therapy; Family Therapy; Drug Therapy; Music Therapy; Play Therapy; Recreational Therapy. *Professionals on Staff* Psychologists; Counselors 10; Social Workers 1. *Service Facilities Available (with number of rooms)* Consultative (ERT) 3; Resource Rooms 1; Self-Contained Rooms 7. *Educational Professionals* Special Education Teachers 10; Special Education Counselors 10; Paraprofessionals 7. *Curricula* Career/Vocational Education; Individualized; Basic Skills; Prevocational; Remedial Reading. *Educational Intervention Approaches* Progressive Discipline; Self-Control; Behavior Modification; Reality Therapy. *Degrees Awarded* Certificate of Attendance; High School Diploma.
Comments In addition to the basic core curriculum, this school provides career guidance, training in pre-vocational skills, recreation, music, and art. Class size is limited to 8 students. An adult assists the credentialed teacher full time. Activity clubs are offered within the school program. The setting is highly structured and totally individualized with a token economy management system.

Boys' and Girls' Aid Society of San Diego—Cottonwood Center and Community Based Psychiatric Program

2815 Steele Canyon Rd, El Cajon, CA 92020 (619) 442-3363
Year Established 1903
Contact Kathleen Robinson, Dir of Admissions
Facility Information *Placement* Private Residential Care. *Number of Beds* 62. *Children/Adolescents Served* 62. *Sexes Served* Both. *Sources of Funding* Health Insurance; CHAMPUS. Summer school available. *Teacher Certification Level* Junior High/Middle School; High School. *Special Certification Level* ED; LD.
Student/Patient Characteristics *Age Levels* 12-14; 15-17. *IQ Ranges* 85-130; Above 130. *Exceptionalities Served* Emotionally Disturbed; Learning Disabled; Communication Disordered. *Learning Problems* Memory Disabilities; Perceptual Disabilities; Thinking Disabilities; Oral Language Disabilities; Reading Disabilities; Handwriting Disabilities; Spelling Disabilities; Arithmetic Disabilities; Written Expression. *Behavioral Problems* Attention Deficits; Hyperactivity; Hypoactivity; Impulsivity; Self-Aggression; Verbal Aggression; Indirect Aggression; Passive Aggression; Withdrawal. *Conditions Treated* Alcohol Abuse and/or Drug Abuse; Schizophrenia; Depression; Suicide; Inadequacy/Immaturity; Personality Problems; Socialized Aggressive Reaction; Unsocialized Aggressive Reaction.
Services Provided Individual Therapy; Group Therapy; Parent Involvement; Behavior Therapy; Family Therapy; Drug Therapy; Reality Therapy. *Professionals on Staff* Psychiatrists 2; Social Workers 13; Child Care Staff 50; Nurses 6. *Service Facilities Available (with number of rooms)* Self-Contained Rooms 4; On-Campus Residential School 4; Homebound Instruction. *Educational Professionals* Special Education Teachers 4; Paraprofessionals 5. *Curricula* Traditional Academic; Individualized; Basic Skills; Prevocational. *Educational Intervention Approaches* Progressive Discipline; Behavior Modification. *Degrees Awarded* Certificate of Attendance; High School Diploma; Graduate Equivalency Diploma; Junior High Diploma.
Comments The agency provides 24-hour psychiatric treatment in a structured, supportive environment. Cottonwood Center is located in a rural area. The Community Based Program provides a smaller milieu for those adolescents who are able to benefit from a community setting.

Brea Neuropsychiatric Center

875 N Brea, Brea, CA 92621 (714) 529-4963
Year Established 1974
Contact James H Powell, Prog Dir
Facility Information *Placement* Special School; Private Residential Care; Private Day Care. *Number of Beds* 51.
Children/Adolescents Served 51. *Sexes Served* Both. *Room and Board Fees (Approx)* $315. *Sources of Funding* Health Insurance; Medicare. Summer school available. *Teacher Certification Level* Junior High/Middle School; High School. *Special Certification Level* ED; LD; Career/Vocational Education; Reading; Math.
Student/Patient Characteristics *Age Levels* 12-14; 15-17. *IQ Ranges* 71-85; 85-130; Above 130. *Exceptionalities Served* Emotionally Disturbed; Learning Disabled; Communication Disordered. *Learning Problems* Memory Disabilities; Perceptual Disabilities; Thinking Disabilities; Oral Language Disabilities; Reading Disabilities; Handwriting Disabilities; Spelling Disabilities; Arithmetic Disabilities; Written Expression. *Behavioral Problems* Attention Deficits; Hyperactivity; Hypoactivity; Impulsivity; Self-Aggression; Verbal Aggression; Physical Aggression; Indirect Aggression; Passive Aggression; Withdrawal. *Conditions Treated* Alcohol Abuse and/or Drug Abuse; Disintegrative Psychoses; Schizophrenia; Aphasia; Phobias; Obsessions and Compulsions; Hysteria; Depression; Suicide; Anorexia Nervosa; Inadequacy/Immaturity; Personality Problems; Socialized Aggressive Reaction; Unsocialized Aggressive Reaction.
Services Provided Individual Therapy; Group Therapy; Parent Involvement; Behavior Therapy; Biofeedback; Family Therapy; Drug Therapy; Art Therapy; Reality Therapy; Psychodrama. *Professionals on Staff* Psychiatrists 50; Psychologists; Counselors; Social Workers; Child Care Staff 100; Nurses 40. *Service Facilities Available (with number of rooms)* Consultative (ERT) 21; Resource Rooms 3; Self-Contained Rooms 4; Special School 3. *Educational Professionals* Regular School Teachers 4; Special Education Teachers 4; Paraprofessionals 2. *Curricula* Traditional Academic; Career/Vocational Education; Individualized; Basic Skills; Prevocational. *Educational Intervention Approaches* Progressive Discipline; Behavior Modification. *Degrees Awarded* High School Diploma.

Brentwood Center

11828 W Washington Blvd, Los Angeles, CA 90066
(213) 398-4525
Year Established 1973
Contact Barbara Andrews, Principal
Facility Information *Placement* Special School.
Children/Adolescents Served 100. *Sexes Served* Both. *Tuition Fees (Approx)* $15,000 (nonpublic); $7,000-$10,000 (adult programs). *Sources of Funding* P.L. 94-142; Regional Center. Summer school available. *Teacher Certification Level* Elementary School; Junior High/Middle School; High School. *Special Certification Level* ED; LD; MR.
Student/Patient Characteristics *Age Levels* 5-8; 9-11; 12-14; 15-17; 18-21; Over 21. *IQ Ranges* 0-25; 26-40; 41-55; 56-70; 71-85. *Exceptionalities Served* Autistic; Emotionally Disturbed; Mentally Handicapped; Multiply Handicapped. *Learning Problems* Memory Disabilities; Perceptual Disabilities; Thinking

Disabilities; Oral Language Disabilities; Reading Disabilities; Handwriting Disabilities; Spelling Disabilities; Arithmetic Disabilities; Written Expression. *Behavioral Problems* Attention Deficits; Hyperactivity; Hypoactivity; Impulsivity; Self-Aggression; Verbal Aggression; Physical Aggression; Indirect Aggression; Passive Aggression; Withdrawal. *Conditions Treated* Early Infantile Autism; Disintegrative Psychoses; Schizophrenia; Aphasia; Convulsive Disorders; Phobias; Obsessions and Compulsions; Hysteria; Inadequacy/Immaturity; Personality Problems; Unsocialized Aggressive Reaction.

Services Provided Individual Therapy; Group Therapy; Parent Involvement; Behavior Therapy; Family Therapy; Art Therapy; Music Therapy. *Professionals on Staff* Psychiatrists 1; Psychologists 1; Social Workers 1. *Service Facilities Available (with number of rooms)* Self-Contained Rooms 10; Therapy Rooms 4. *Educational Professionals* Special Education Teachers 10; Paraprofessionals 12. *Curricula* Career/Vocational Education; Individualized; Basic Skills; Prevocational. *Educational Intervention Approaches* Applied Behavior Analysis; Individualized Instruction; Developmental Approach. *Degrees Awarded* Certificate of Attendance.

Burt Children's Center

940 Grove St, San Francisco, CA 94121 (415) 922-7700
Year Established 1970
Contact Danielle Lee, Social Serv Dir
Facility Information *Placement* Special School; Private Residential Care. *Number of Beds* 22. *Children/Adolescents Served* 25. *Sexes Served* Both. *Tuition Fees (Approx)* $17,550. *Sources of Funding* State Funds; P.L. 94-142; Regional Centers; County. Summer school available. *Special Certification Level* ED; LD.
Student/Patient Characteristics *Age Levels* 0-4; 5-8; 9-11; 12-14; 15-17; 18-21. *IQ Ranges* 0-25; 26-40. *Exceptionalities Served* Autistic; Emotionally Disturbed. *Learning Problems* Memory Disabilities; Perceptual Disabilities; Thinking Disabilities; Oral Language Disabilities; Reading Disabilities; Handwriting Disabilities; Spelling Disabilities; Arithmetic Disabilities; Written Expression. *Behavioral Problems* Attention Deficits; Hyperactivity; Impulsivity; Self-Aggression; Verbal Aggression; Physical Aggression; Indirect Aggression; Passive Aggression; Withdrawal. *Conditions Treated* Early Infantile Autism; Disintegrative Psychoses; Socialized Aggressive Reaction; Unsocialized Aggressive Reaction.

Services Provided Individual Therapy; Parent Involvement; Cognitive Developmental Therapy; Family Therapy; Art Therapy; Music Therapy; Reality Therapy; Play Therapy; Psychodrama. *Professionals on Staff* Psychiatrists 1; Psychologists 3; Counselors 6; Social Workers 2; Child Care Staff 33. *Service Facilities Available (with number of rooms)* On-Campus Residential School 4. *Educational Professionals* Special Education Teachers 4; Paraprofessionals 8. *Curricula* Traditional Academic; Individualized; Basic Skills. *Educational Intervention Approaches* Progressive Discipline; Self-Control; Creative Conditioning; Psychosocial.

California Center for Educational Therapy

6016 Fallbrook Ave, Ste 201, Woodland Hills, CA 91367
(818) 347-2600
Contact Kenneth Tabachnick, Exec Dir
Facility Information *Placement* Special Program; Evaluation and Remediation of Learning Disorders.
Comments Whether the learning difficulty is labeled neurological dysfunction, perceptual handicap, brain damage, mental retardation or emotional disturbance, the center's emphasis is first on the most careful evaluation of the child's strengths and weaknesses. Following the diagnostic process, the child may either be referred to a more appropriate treatment facility or may be accepted on a one month trial basis at the center. In addition to the remedial work carried on, the center offers both group and individual counseling and psychotherapy for children and parents requiring such help.

California Mental Health Center

134 S Gunston Dr, Los Angeles, CA 90049 (213) 472-6788
Year Established 1946
Contact A B Gottlober, Dir
Facility Information *Placement* Mental Health Center. *Children/Adolescents Served* 10. *Sexes Served* Both. *Sources of Funding* Health Insurance. Summer school available.
Student/Patient Characteristics *Age Levels* 12-14; 15-17; 18-21; Over 21. *IQ Ranges* 85-130; Above 130. *Exceptionalities Served* Emotionally Disturbed; Communication Disordered; Gifted. *Learning Problems* Oral Language Disabilities. *Behavioral Problems* Self-Aggression; Verbal Aggression; Indirect Aggression; Passive Aggression; Withdrawal. *Conditions Treated* Phobias; Obsessions and Compulsions; Hysteria; Depression; Asthma; Anorexia Nervosa; Personality Problems; Socialized Aggressive Reaction.
Services Provided Individual Therapy; Parent Involvement; Behavior Therapy. *Professionals on Staff* Psychiatrists; Psychologists.
Comments The facility is primarily an organization that treats emotionally disturbed adolescents and adults.

Cedu School

PO Box 1176, 3500 Seymour Rd, Running Springs, CA 92382
(714) 867-2722
Year Established 1968
Contact Pat Savage, Dir of Admissions
Facility Information *Placement* Special School. *Number of Beds* 100. *Children/Adolescents Served* 100. *Sexes Served* Both. *Sources of Funding* Health Insurance; P.L. 94-142. Summer school available. *Teacher Certification Level* Junior High/Middle School; High School. *Special Certification Level* ED; LD.
Student/Patient Characteristics *Age Levels* 12-14; 15-17. *IQ Ranges* 85-130; Above 130. *Exceptionalities Served* Emotionally Disturbed. *Behavioral Problems* Impulsivity; Verbal Aggression; Indirect Aggression; Passive Aggression. *Conditions Treated* Alcohol Abuse and/or Drug Abuse; Other Substance Abuse or Dependence; Depression; Inadequacy/Immaturity; Personality Problems; Socialized Aggressive Reaction.
Services Provided Individual Therapy; Group Therapy; Parent Involvement. *Professionals on Staff* Psychologists 1; Counselors 10; Social Workers 1; Primary Care Physicians Assistant 1. *Service Facilities Available (with number of rooms)* On-Campus Residential School 10. *Educational Professionals* Regular School Teachers 6; Special Education Teachers 3. *Curricula* Traditional Academic; Individualized; Basic Skills; Prevocational. *Educational Intervention Approaches* Positive Peer Pressure. *Degrees Awarded* High School Diploma.
Comments Cedu School provides year round residential education for adolescents with special emotional and educational needs. In addition to an individualized academic curriculum, the program includes intensive counseling, vocational education, a wilderness challenge program, and a farm. Average length of stay is 2 to 2-1/2 years.

Children's Health Council

700 Willow Rd, Palo Alto, CA 94304 (415) 326-5530
Year Established 1953
Contact Alan J Rosenthal, Dir
Facility Information *Placement* Special School; Clinic. *Children/Adolescents Served* 50 (in school); 200 (in clinic). *Sexes Served* Both. *Tuition Fees (Approx)* $9,000-$12,000. *Sources of Funding* Health Insurance; P.L. 94-142; Mental Health Funds; Scholarships. Summer school available. *Teacher Certification Level* Elementary School; Junior High/Middle School. *Special Certification Level* ED; LD; MR; Career/Vocational Education; Reading; Math.
Student/Patient Characteristics *Age Levels* 0-4; 5-8; 9-11; 12-14. *IQ Ranges* 56-70; 71-85; 85-130. *Exceptionalities Served* Autistic; Emotionally Disturbed; Learning Disabled; Mentally Handicapped; Communication Disordered; Hearing Impaired/Deaf; Vi-

sually Impaired/Blind; Physically Handicapped. *Learning Problems* Memory Disabilities; Perceptual Disabilities; Thinking Disabilities; Oral Language Disabilities; Reading Disabilities; Handwriting Disabilities; Spelling Disabilities; Arithmetic Disabilities; Written Expression. *Behavioral Problems* Attention Deficits; Hyperactivity; Hypoactivity; Impulsivity; Self-Aggression; Verbal Aggression; Physical Aggression; Indirect Aggression; Passive Aggression; Withdrawal. *Conditions Treated* Early Infantile Autism; Disintegrative Psychoses; Schizophrenia; Aphasia; Phobias; Obsessions and Compulsions; Hysteria; Depression; Anorexia Nervosa; Inadequacy/Immaturity; Personality Problems; Socialized Aggressive Reaction; Unsocialized Aggressive Reaction.

Services Provided Individual Therapy; Group Therapy; Parent Involvement; Behavior Therapy; Cognitive Developmental Therapy; Biofeedback; Family Therapy; Filial Therapy; Drug Therapy; Art Therapy; Play Therapy. *Professionals on Staff* Psychiatrists 5; Psychologists 6; Counselors 3; Social Workers 8; Child Care Staff 6; Teacher/Therapists 12; Speech/Language Therapists 5; Occupational Therapists 3. *Service Facilities Available (with number of rooms)* Consultative (ERT); Resource Rooms; Self-Contained Rooms 6. *Educational Professionals* Special Education Teachers 12; Paraprofessionals 6. *Curricula* Individualized; Basic Skills; Prevocational. *Educational Intervention Approaches* Self-Control; Behavior Modification; Applied Behavior Analysis.

Clearwater Ranch Children's House Inc

PO Box 68, Philo, CA 95466 (707) 895-3120
Year Established 1940
Contact Richard Hall, Ranch Dir
Facility Information *Placement* Special School; Private Non Profit Residential Care. *Number of Beds* 28. *Children/Adolescents Served* 28. *Sexes Served* Both. *Tuition Fees (Approx)* $30,432. *Sources of Funding* State Funds. Summer school available. *Teacher Certification Level* Elementary School; Junior High/Middle School; High School. *Special Certification Level* ED; LD; Reading; Math; Severe Emotionally Disturbed; Sign Language.
Student/Patient Characteristics *Age Levels* 5-8; 9-11; 12-14. *IQ Ranges* 71-85; 85-130; Above 130. *Exceptionalities Served* Emotionally Disturbed; Learning Disabled; Mentally Handicapped; Communication Disordered; Hearing Impaired/Deaf. *Learning Problems* Memory Disabilities; Perceptual Disabilities; Thinking Disabilities; Oral Language Disabilities; Reading Disabilities; Handwriting Disabilities; Spelling Disabilities; Arithmetic Disabilities; Written Expression. *Behavioral Problems* Attention Deficits; Hyperactivity; Hypoactivity; Impulsivity; Self-Aggression; Verbal Aggression; Physical Aggression; Indirect Aggression; Passive Aggression; Withdrawal. *Conditions Treated* Schizophrenia; Aphasia; Phobias; Obsessions and Compulsions; Hysteria; Depression; Suicide; Asthma; Inadequacy/Immaturity; Personality Problems; Socialized Aggressive Reaction; Unsocialized Aggressive Reaction; Borderline Personality.

Services Provided Individual Therapy; Group Therapy; Parent Involvement; Cognitive Developmental Therapy; Family Therapy; Drug Therapy; Art Therapy; Music Therapy; Play Therapy; Psychodrama; Outdoor Recreation Therapy; Relationship Therapy. *Professionals on Staff* Psychiatrists 1; Psychologists 1; Counselors 2; Social Workers 3; Child Care Staff 24; Nurses 1. *Service Facilities Available (with number of rooms)* Consultative (ERT) 2; Resource Rooms 3; On-Campus Residential School 6. *Educational Professionals* Special Education Teachers 3; Paraprofessionals 2; Teacher Aides 3. *Curricula* Traditional Academic; Individualized; Basic Skills. *Educational Intervention Approaches* Precision Teaching; Progressive Discipline; Self-Control; Applied Behavior Analysis; Creative Conditioning.

Comments This program is a clinical treatment program based on relationship therapy and extensive outdoor and wilderness experiences.

College Hospital—College Park School

10802 College Pl, Cerritos, CA 90701 (213) 924-9581
Contact Howard Plass, Ed Dir

Facility Information *Placement* Special School; Private Residential Care; Private Acute Psychiatric Hospital with Private School Program. *Number of Beds* 67. *Children/Adolescents Served* 67. *Sexes Served* Both. *Room and Board Fees (Approx)* $300. *Sources of Funding* Health Insurance. Summer school available. *Teacher Certification Level* Elementary School; Junior High/Middle School; High School. *Special Certification Level* ED; LD; Reading; Math.
Student/Patient Characteristics *Age Levels* 0-4; 5-8; 9-11; 12-14; 15-17; 18-21. *IQ Ranges* 85-130; Above 130. *Exceptionalities Served* Emotionally Disturbed; Learning Disabled; Communication Disordered; Physically Handicapped; Gifted. *Learning Problems* Memory Disabilities; Perceptual Disabilities; Thinking Disabilities; Oral Language Disabilities; Reading Disabilities; Handwriting Disabilities; Spelling Disabilities; Arithmetic Disabilities; Written Expression. *Behavioral Problems* Attention Deficits; Hyperactivity; Hypoactivity; Impulsivity; Self-Aggression; Verbal Aggression; Physical Aggression; Indirect Aggression; Passive Aggression; Withdrawal. *Conditions Treated* Alcohol Abuse and/or Drug Abuse; Other Substance Abuse or Dependence; Aphasia; Phobias; Obsessions and Compulsions; Hysteria; Depression; Suicide; Anorexia Nervosa; Personality Problems; Socialized Aggressive Reaction; Unsocialized Aggressive Reaction.

Services Provided Individual Therapy; Group Therapy; Parent Involvement; Behavior Therapy; Cognitive Developmental Therapy; Biofeedback; Family Therapy; Filial Therapy; Play Therapy; Psychodrama. *Professionals on Staff* Psychiatrists 10; Psychologists 20; Social Workers 4; Child Care Staff 40; Nurses 5. *Service Facilities Available (with number of rooms)* Consultative (ERT); Self-Contained Rooms; Hospital School; On-Campus Residential School. *Educational Professionals* Regular School Teachers 5; Special Education Teachers; Special Education Counselors 2; Paraprofessionals 5. *Curricula* Traditional Academic; Individualized; Basic Skills; Prevocational; Computer Assisted Instruction. *Educational Intervention Approaches* Engineered Classroom; Precision Teaching; Progressive Discipline; Self-Control; Behavior Modification; Applied Behavior Analysis; Creative Conditioning. *Degrees Awarded* High School Diploma; Graduate Equivalency Diploma.

CPC Belmont Hills Hospital

1301 Ralston Ave, Belmont, CA 94002 (415) 593-2143
Year Established 1969
Contact Sharon Sidell-Selick, Marketing Coord
Facility Information *Placement* Special Program. *Number of Beds* 15. *Children/Adolescents Served* 20. *Sexes Served* Both. *Room and Board Fees (Approx)* $395. *Sources of Funding* Health Insurance; Medicaid; Short Doyle (County). Summer school available. *Teacher Certification Level* Elementary School; Junior High/Middle School; High School. *Special Certification Level* ED; LD; MR; Career/Vocational Education; Reading; Math.
Student/Patient Characteristics *Age Levels* 12-14; 15-17. *IQ Ranges* 85-130; Above 130. *Exceptionalities Served* Emotionally Disturbed; Learning Disabled; Mentally Handicapped. *Learning Problems* Memory Disabilities; Perceptual Disabilities; Reading Disabilities; Handwriting Disabilities; Spelling Disabilities; Arithmetic Disabilities. *Behavioral Problems* Attention Deficits; Hyperactivity; Impulsivity; Self-Aggression; Verbal Aggression; Physical Aggression; Indirect Aggression; Passive Aggression; Withdrawal. *Conditions Treated* Alcohol Abuse and/or Drug Abuse; Other Substance Abuse or Dependence; Disintegrative Psychoses; Schizophrenia; Phobias; Obsessions and Compulsions; Hysteria; Depression; Suicide; Anorexia Nervosa; Inadequacy/Immaturity; Personality Problems; Socialized Aggressive Reaction; Unsocialized Aggressive Reaction.

Services Provided Individual Therapy; Group Therapy; Parent Involvement; Behavior Therapy; Cognitive Developmental Therapy; Family Therapy; Drug Therapy; Art Therapy; Play Therapy. *Professionals on Staff* Psychiatrists 8; Psychologists 3; Counselors 4; Social Workers 2; Nurses 4; Occupational Therapy 2; Pharmacist 1; Nutritionist 1. *Service Facilities Available (with number of rooms)* Consultative (ERT) 1; Self-Contained Rooms 2; Hospital School 2. *Educational Professionals* Regular School Teachers 2; Special Education Teachers 1. *Curricula* Traditional Academic; Individualized; Basic Skills; Prevocational. *Educational Intervention Approaches* Behavior Modification.

Developmental Living Center

6518 Lang Ave, Sacramento, CA 95816 (916) 424-9191
Contact K L Pascoe-Stebbins, Dir

Facility Information *Placement* Private Residential Care. *Number of Beds* 12. *Children/Adolescents Served* 12. *Sexes Served* Both. *Sources of Funding* State Funds.

Student/Patient Characteristics *Age Levels* Over 21. *IQ Ranges* 41-55; 56-70. *Exceptionalities Served* Autistic; Communication Disordered. *Learning Problems* Perceptual Disabilities. *Behavioral Problems* Attention Deficits; Hyperactivity; Self-Aggression; Verbal Aggression; Physical Aggression; Withdrawal. *Conditions Treated* Early Infantile Autism.

Services Provided *Educational Intervention Approaches* Behavior Modification; Applied Behavior Analysis.

Comments This facility uses token economics behavior modification and teaches independent living skills as part of an intensive educational residential program in a least restrictive environment.

The Devereux Foundation

PO Box 1079, Santa Barbara, CA 93102 (805) 968-2525
Year Established 1945
Contact Jacob Azain, Dir

Facility Information *Placement* Special School; Private Residential Care; Private Day Care; Public Day Care; Special Program. *Number of Beds* 118. *Children/Adolescents Served* 118. *Sexes Served* Both. *Tuition Fees (Approx)* $24,000-$50,000. *Sources of Funding* State Funds; P.L. 94-142; CA Regional Centers; Mental Health; Department of Social Services; Welfare; Human Services and Probation; OCHAMPUS; Private Insurance. *Teacher Certification Level* Elementary School; Junior High/Middle School; High School. *Special Certification Level* ED; LD; MR; Career/Vocational Education; Reading; Math; Speech and Language; Occupation; Psychomotor; Music; Art; Performing Arts Therapies; Adaptive PE.

Student/Patient Characteristics *Age Levels* 12-14; 15-17; 18-21; Over 21. *IQ Ranges* 41-55; 56-70; 71-85; 85-130. *Exceptionalities Served* Autistic; Emotionally Disturbed; Learning Disabled; Mentally Handicapped; Communication Disordered; Hearing Impaired/Deaf; Other Health Impaired. *Learning Problems* Memory Disabilities; Perceptual Disabilities; Thinking Disabilities; Oral Language Disabilities; Reading Disabilities; Handwriting Disabilities; Spelling Disabilities; Arithmetic Disabilities; Written Expression. *Behavioral Problems* Attention Deficits; Hyperactivity; Hypoactivity; Impulsivity; Self-Aggression; Verbal Aggression; Physical Aggression; Indirect Aggression; Passive Aggression; Withdrawal. *Conditions Treated* Early Infantile Autism; Schizophrenia; Aphasia; Convulsive Disorders; Phobias; Obsessions and Compulsions; Hysteria; Depression; Suicide; Asthma; Anorexia Nervosa; Ulcerative Colitis; Inadequacy/Immaturity; Personality Problems; Socialized Aggressive Reaction; Unsocialized Aggressive Reaction.

Services Provided Individual Therapy; Group Therapy; Parent Involvement; Behavior Therapy; Cognitive Developmental Therapy; Family Therapy; Drug Therapy; Art Therapy; Music Therapy; Reality Therapy; Play Therapy; Psychodrama; Work; Recreational; Occupational; Speech and Language; Psychomotor Therapies. *Professionals on Staff* Psychiatrists 2; Psychologists 8; Counselors 2; Child Care Staff 72; Nurses 4; Physician; Dentist; Psychomotor 4. *Service Facilities Available (with number of rooms)* Self-Contained Rooms 5; On-Campus Residential School 12. *Educational Professionals* Special Education Teachers 21; Career/Vocational Teachers 2; Crisis Teachers; Paraprofessionals 12. *Curricula* Career/Vocational Education; Individualized; Basic Skills; Prevocational. *Educational Intervention Approaches* Progressive Discipline; Self-Control; Behavior Modification; Creative Conditioning. *Degrees Awarded* Certificate of Attendance; High School Diploma; Graduate Equivalency Diploma; Differential Proficiency Standard.

Comments The West Coast branch of The Devereux Foundation primarily provides full residential treatment and special schooling and vocational training for adolescents and young adults presenting multiple educational, emotional, and behavioral disorders.

East Bay Activity Center

2540 Charleston St, Oakland, CA 94602 (415) 531-3666
Year Established 1953
Contact David La Piana, Exec Dir

Facility Information *Placement* Public School; Private Day Treatment and Public Special Education. *Children/Adolescents Served* 20. *Sexes Served* Both. *Tuition Fees (Approx)* $14,874. *Sources of Funding* State Funds; Medicare; P.L. 94-142; Private Donations. Summer school available. *Teacher Certification Level* Elementary School. *Special Certification Level* ED; LD.

Student/Patient Characteristics *Age Levels* 5-8; 9-11. *IQ Ranges* 85-130. *Exceptionalities Served* Emotionally Disturbed; Learning Disabled. *Learning Problems* Memory Disabilities; Perceptual Disabilities; Thinking Disabilities; Oral Language Disabilities; Reading Disabilities; Handwriting Disabilities; Spelling Disabilities; Arithmetic Disabilities; Written Expression. *Behavioral Problems* Attention Deficits; Hyperactivity; Impulsivity; Self-Aggression; Verbal Aggression; Physical Aggression; Indirect Aggression; Withdrawal. *Conditions Treated* Disintegrative Psychoses; Schizophrenia; Depression; Suicide; Personality Problems.

Services Provided Individual Therapy; Group Therapy; Parent Involvement; Family Therapy; Drug Therapy; Art Therapy; Music Therapy; Play Therapy; Occupational Therapy; Speech Therapy. *Professionals on Staff* Psychiatrists 1; Psychologists 1; Counselors 1; Social Workers 2; Child Care Staff 4; Nurses 1. *Service Facilities Available (with number of rooms)* Self-Contained Rooms 3; Play Therapy Room 1. *Educational Professionals* Special Education Teachers 3; School Psychologist 1. *Curricula* Individualized; Basic Skills; Remedial; Tutorial.

Comments The center provides psychiatric day treatment and special education for children, ages 3 to 10, who have severe emotional disorders. The emphasis is on an in-depth assessment and psychodynamic understanding of the nature and genesis of a child's difficulties. The theoretical base is psychoanalytical ego psychology with the modifications and adaptations required by work with severely disturbed children in a day setting.

Eastern Los Angeles Regional Center for the Developmentally Disabled

801 S Garfield Ave No. 305, Alhambra, CA 91801
(818) 570-8620
Year Established 1972
Contact Herman Fogata, Exec Dir

Facility Information *Placement* Special School; Private Residential Care; Private Day Care; Public Day Care; Special Program. *Sexes Served* Both. *Room and Board Fees (Approx)* $17-$32. *Tuition Fees (Approx)* $8,500-$24,000. *Sources of Funding* State Funds. Summer school available.

Student/Patient Characteristics *Age Levels* 0-4; 5-8; 9-11; 12-14; 15-17; 18-21; Over 21. *IQ Ranges* 0-25; 26-40; 41-55; 56-70. *Exceptionalities Served* Autistic; Mentally Handicapped; Physically Handicapped. *Learning Problems* Memory Disabilities; Perceptual Disabilities; Thinking Disabilities; Oral Language Disabilities; Reading Disabilities; Handwriting Disabilities; Spelling Disabilities; Arithmetic Disabilities; Written Expression. *Behavioral Problems* Attention Deficits; Hyperactivity; Impulsivity; Self-Aggression; Indirect Aggression; Withdrawal. *Conditions Treated* Early Infantile Autism.

Services Provided Parent Involvement; Behavior Therapy; Coordination of Services. *Professionals on Staff* Psychologists 1; Social Workers 29; Nurses 1; Physician 1. *Educational Professionals* Special Education Counselors 1. *Educational Intervention Approaches* Behavior Modification.

Comments This center is one of the 21 regional centers in the state of California. The only direct services that this agency provides are diagnosis and evaluation. This agency coordinates the provision and purchasing of a wide range of educational, medical, residential, and other ancillary services.

Edgemont Hospital

4841 Hollywood Blvd, Los Angeles, CA 90027 (213) 666-5252
Year Established 1955
Contact Al Kubat, Clinical Dir Adolescent Serv
Facility Information *Placement* Special School; Private Psychiatric Hospital. *Number of Beds* 24. *Children/Adolescents Served* 24. *Sexes Served* Both. *Room and Board Fees (Approx)* $400. *Sources of Funding* Health Insurance. Summer school available. *Teacher Certification Level* Junior High/Middle School; High School. *Special Certification Level* ED; LD; Reading; Math.
Student/Patient Characteristics *Age Levels* 12-14; 15-17; 18-21. *IQ Ranges* 85-130; Above 130. *Exceptionalities Served* Emotionally Disturbed; Learning Disabled. *Learning Problems* Memory Disabilities; Perceptual Disabilities; Thinking Disabilities; Oral Language Disabilities; Reading Disabilities; Spelling Disabilities; Arithmetic Disabilities; Written Expression. *Behavioral Problems* Attention Deficits; Hyperactivity; Hypoactivity; Impulsivity; Self-Aggression; Verbal Aggression; Physical Aggression; Indirect Aggression; Passive Aggression; Withdrawal. *Conditions Treated* Alcohol Abuse and/or Drug Abuse; Other Substance Abuse or Dependence; Phobias; Obsessions and Compulsions; Hysteria; Depression; Suicide; Asthma; Anorexia Nervosa; Ulcerative Colitis; Inadequacy/Immaturity; Personality Problems; Socialized Aggressive Reaction; Unsocialized Aggressive Reaction.
Services Provided Individual Therapy; Group Therapy; Parent Involvement; Behavior Therapy; Cognitive Developmental Therapy; Family Therapy. *Professionals on Staff* Psychiatrists 4; Psychologists 6; Counselors 1; Child Care Staff 8; Nurses 4. *Service Facilities Available (with number of rooms)* Consultative (ERT) 5; On-Campus Residential School 4. *Educational Professionals* Special Education Teachers 2; Paraprofessionals 4; Educational Psychologists 3. *Curricula* Individualized; Basic Skills. *Educational Intervention Approaches* Behavior Modification; Applied Behavior Analysis. *Degrees Awarded* Certificate of Attendance; High School Diploma; Graduate Equivalency Diploma.

Edgewood Children's Center

1801 Vicente St, San Francisco, CA 94116 (415) 681-3211
Year Established 1851
Contact Barry Feinberg, Dir Residential Treatment
Facility Information *Placement* Private Residential Care. *Number of Beds* 36. *Children/Adolescents Served* 36. *Sexes Served* Both. *Tuition Fees (Approx)* $36,000. *Sources of Funding* State Funds; P.L. 94-142; CHAMPUS. Summer school available. *Teacher Certification Level* Elementary School. *Special Certification Level* ED; LD.
Student/Patient Characteristics *Age Levels* 5-8; 9-11; 12-14. *IQ Ranges* 85-130. *Exceptionalities Served* Emotionally Disturbed; Learning Disabled. *Learning Problems* Perceptual Disabilities; Thinking Disabilities; Oral Language Disabilities; Reading Disabilities; Handwriting Disabilities; Spelling Disabilities; Arithmetic Disabilities; Written Expression. *Behavioral Problems* Attention Deficits; Hyperactivity; Hypoactivity; Impulsivity; Self-Aggression; Verbal Aggression; Physical Aggression; Indirect Aggression; Passive Aggression; Withdrawal. *Conditions Treated* Depression; Suicide; Inadequacy/Immaturity; Personality Problems; Socialized Aggressive Reaction; Unsocialized Aggressive Reaction.
Services Provided Individual Therapy; Group Therapy; Parent Involvement; Behavior Therapy; Cognitive Developmental Therapy; Family Therapy; Drug Therapy; Music Therapy; Play Ther-

apy. *Professionals on Staff* Psychiatrists 1; Social Workers 5; Child Care Staff 33; Nurses 1. *Service Facilities Available (with number of rooms)* Resource Rooms 1; Self-Contained Rooms 4; On-Campus Residential School. *Educational Professionals* Special Education Teachers 4. *Curricula* Traditional Academic; Individualized; Basic Skills.

Edgewood Day Treatment—The Lucinda Weeks Center

2665 28th Ave, San Francisco, CA 94116 (415) 664-7584
Contact David A Reinstein, Dir
Facility Information *Placement* Special School; Private Day Care; Day Treatment. *Children/Adolescents Served* 27. *Sexes Served* Both. *Sources of Funding* P.L. 94-142; Mental Health; Office of Child Development Funds; Private Movies. Summer school available. *Teacher Certification Level* Elementary School. *Special Certification Level* Learning Handicapped; Severely Handicapped.
Student/Patient Characteristics *Age Levels* 5-8; 9-11. *IQ Ranges* 71-85; 85-130. *Exceptionalities Served* Emotionally Disturbed; Learning Disabled; Mentally Handicapped; Communication Disordered; Physically Handicapped. *Learning Problems* Memory Disabilities; Perceptual Disabilities; Thinking Disabilities; Oral Language Disabilities; Reading Disabilities; Handwriting Disabilities; Spelling Disabilities; Arithmetic Disabilities; Written Expression. *Behavioral Problems* Attention Deficits; Hyperactivity; Hypoactivity; Impulsivity; Self-Aggression; Verbal Aggression; Physical Aggression; Indirect Aggression; Passive Aggression; Withdrawal. *Conditions Treated* Schizophrenia; Convulsive Disorders; Phobias; Obsessions and Compulsions; Hysteria; Depression; Inadequacy/Immaturity; Personality Problems; Socialized Aggressive Reaction; Unsocialized Aggressive Reaction.
Services Provided Individual Therapy; Group Therapy; Parent Involvement; Behavior Therapy; Cognitive Developmental Therapy; Family Therapy; Filial Therapy; Drug Therapy; Play Therapy; Psychodrama; Dance Therapy; Milieu Therapy. *Professionals on Staff* Psychiatrists 1; Social Workers 3; Child Care Staff 11; Nurses 1; Creative Arts Therapists 2. *Service Facilities Available (with number of rooms)* Self-Contained Rooms 3. *Educational Professionals* Special Education Teachers 3; Paraprofessionals 11. *Curricula* Traditional Academic; Individualized; Basic Skills. *Educational Intervention Approaches* Engineered Classroom; Precision Teaching; Progressive Discipline; Self-Control; Behavior Modification; Applied Behavior Analysis.
Comments This day treatment program provides individualized special education services, clinical services to both the child and family, and extended day and holiday care.

Escalon Inc

536 E Mendocino St, Altadena, CA 91001 (818) 798-0744
Year Established 1959
Contact Elaine Sleeper, Dir of Ed
Facility Information *Placement* Special School. *Children/Adolescents Served* 125. *Sexes Served* Both. *Tuition Fees (Approx)* $10,325. *Sources of Funding* P.L. 94-142. Summer school available. *Teacher Certification Level* Elementary School; Junior High/Middle School; High School. *Special Certification Level* ED; LD; MR; Severe Emotional Disturbance.
Student/Patient Characteristics *Age Levels* 5-8; 9-11; 12-14; 15-17; 18-21. *IQ Ranges* 41-55; 56-70; 71-85; 85-130; Above 130. *Exceptionalities Served* Autistic; Emotionally Disturbed; Learning Disabled; Mentally Handicapped; Communication Disordered; Physically Handicapped; Gifted. *Learning Problems* Memory Disabilities; Perceptual Disabilities; Thinking Disabilities; Oral Language Disabilities; Reading Disabilities; Handwriting Disabilities; Spelling Disabilities; Arithmetic Disabilities; Written Expression. *Behavioral Problems* Attention Deficits; Hyperactivity; Hypoactivity; Impulsivity; Self-Aggression; Verbal Aggression; Physical Aggression; Indirect Aggression; Passive Aggression; Withdrawal. *Conditions Treated* Early Infantile Autism; Disintegrative Psychoses; Schizophrenia; Aphasia; Convulsive Disorders; Phobias; Obsessions and Compulsions; Depression; Suicide; An-

orexia Nervosa; Inadequacy/Immaturity; Personality Problems; Socialized Aggressive Reaction; Unsocialized Aggressive Reaction.

Services Provided Individual Therapy; Group Therapy; Parent Involvement; Behavior Therapy. *Professionals on Staff* Psychologists 1; Counselors 1. *Service Facilities Available (with number of rooms)* Self-Contained Rooms 3. *Educational Professionals* Special Education Teachers 6; Career/Vocational Teachers 2. *Curricula* Traditional Academic; Career/Vocational Education; Individualized; Basic Skills; Prevocational. *Educational Intervention Approaches* Behavior Modification. *Degrees Awarded* Certificate of Attendance; High School Diploma.

Ettie Lee Homes Inc

5146 N Maine Ave, Baldwin Park, CA 91706 (818) 960-4861
Year Established 1950
Contact John Richardson, Exec Dir
Facility Information *Placement* Private Residential Care. *Number of Beds* 85. *Children/Adolescents Served* 100. *Sexes Served* Male. *Room and Board Fees (Approx)* $57. *Tuition Fees (Approx)* $17,200. *Sources of Funding* State Funds; Medicare; Endowment; Donated Income. Summer school available.

Student/Patient Characteristics *Age Levels* 12-14; 15-17; 18-21. *IQ Ranges* 71-85; 85-130. *Exceptionalities Served* Emotionally Disturbed. *Learning Problems* Memory Disabilities; Perceptual Disabilities; Thinking Disabilities; Oral Language Disabilities; Reading Disabilities; Handwriting Disabilities; Spelling Disabilities; Arithmetic Disabilities; Written Expression. *Behavioral Problems* Attention Deficits; Hyperactivity; Impulsivity; Self-Aggression; Verbal Aggression; Physical Aggression; Indirect Aggression; Passive Aggression; Withdrawal. *Conditions Treated* Alcohol Abuse and/or Drug Abuse; Other Substance Abuse or Dependence; Phobias; Depression; Suicide; Inadequacy/Immaturity; Personality Problems; Socialized Aggressive Reaction; Unsocialized Aggressive Reaction.

Services Provided Individual Therapy; Group Therapy; Parent Involvement; Behavior Therapy; Family Therapy; Drug Therapy; Reality Therapy. *Professionals on Staff* Psychologists 1; Social Workers 9; Child Care Staff 39.

Five Acres Boys' and Girls' Aide Society

760 W Mountain View St, Altadena, CA 91001 (213) 798-6793
Year Established 1888
Contact Jim Carolla, Ed Dir
Facility Information *Placement* Special School; Private Residential Care. *Number of Beds* 50. *Children/Adolescents Served* 68. *Sexes Served* Both. *Room and Board Fees (Approx)* $49. *Tuition Fees (Approx)* $9,840. *Sources of Funding* Medicare; P.L. 94-142; Los Angeles County. Summer school available. *Teacher Certification Level* Elementary School; Junior High/Middle School. *Special Certification Level* LD; Severe Emotional Disturbance.

Student/Patient Characteristics *Age Levels* 0-4; 5-8; 9-11; 12-14. *IQ Ranges* 85-130. *Exceptionalities Served* Emotionally Disturbed; Learning Disabled; Mentally Handicapped; Communication Disordered. *Learning Problems* Memory Disabilities; Perceptual Disabilities; Thinking Disabilities; Oral Language Disabilities; Reading Disabilities; Handwriting Disabilities; Spelling Disabilities; Arithmetic Disabilities; Written Expression. *Behavioral Problems* Attention Deficits; Hyperactivity; Hypoactivity; Impulsivity; Self-Aggression; Verbal Aggression; Physical Aggression; Indirect Aggression; Passive Aggression; Withdrawal. *Conditions Treated* Phobias; Obsessions and Compulsions; Hysteria; Depression; Suicide; Inadequacy/Immaturity; Personality Problems; Socialized Aggressive Reaction; Unsocialized Aggressive Reaction.

Services Provided Individual Therapy; Group Therapy; Parent Involvement; Behavior Therapy; Family Therapy; Drug Therapy; Art Therapy; Play Therapy; Psychodrama. *Professionals on Staff* Psychiatrists 3; Psychologists 1; Counselors 10; Social Workers 5; Child Care Staff 50; Nurses 1. *Service Facilities Available (with number of rooms)* Consultative (ERT) 1; Resource Rooms 2; Transition Rooms 2; Self-Contained Rooms 3; Special School 3; On-Campus Residential School 7. *Educational Professionals* Special Education Teachers 2; Crisis Teachers 2; Special Education Counselors 2; Paraprofessionals 5. *Curricula* Traditional Academic; Career/Vocational Education; Individualized; Basic Skills; Prevocational; Computer Skills. *Educational Intervention Approaches* Progressive Discipline; Self-Control; Behavior Modification.

Comments Five Acres is a residential treatment center, treating moderately to severely emotionally disturbed youngsters who are unable to live at home or in a suitable family setting.

Fred Finch Youth Center

3800 Coolidge Ave, Oakland, CA 94602 (415) 482-2244
Year Established 1891
Contact Jeffrey R Davis, Exec Dir
Facility Information *Placement* Special School; Private Residential Care. *Number of Beds* 50. *Children/Adolescents Served* 50. *Sexes Served* Both. *Room and Board Fees (Approx)* $125. *Tuition Fees (Approx)* $11,000. *Sources of Funding* State Funds; Medicaid; P.L. 94-142; Fees. Summer school available. *Teacher Certification Level* Junior High/Middle School; High School. *Special Certification Level* ED; LD; MR; Reading.

Student/Patient Characteristics *Age Levels* 12-14; 15-17. *IQ Ranges* 71-85; 85-130; Above 130. *Exceptionalities Served* Emotionally Disturbed; Learning Disabled; Mentally Handicapped. *Learning Problems* Memory Disabilities; Perceptual Disabilities; Thinking Disabilities; Oral Language Disabilities; Reading Disabilities; Handwriting Disabilities; Spelling Disabilities; Arithmetic Disabilities; Written Expression. *Behavioral Problems* Attention Deficits; Hyperactivity; Impulsivity; Self-Aggression; Verbal Aggression; Physical Aggression; Withdrawal. *Conditions Treated* Disintegrative Psychoses; Schizophrenia; Depression; Suicide; Inadequacy/Immaturity; Personality Problems; Socialized Aggressive Reaction; Unsocialized Aggressive Reaction.

Services Provided Individual Therapy; Group Therapy; Parent Involvement; Behavior Therapy; Family Therapy; Drug Therapy. *Professionals on Staff* Psychiatrists 2; Psychologists 1; Counselors 5; Social Workers 5; Child Care Staff 45; Nurses 1. *Service Facilities Available (with number of rooms)* Resource Rooms; Self-Contained Rooms; Special School; On-Campus Residential School. *Educational Professionals* Special Education Teachers 4; Paraprofessionals 4. *Curricula* Individualized; Basic Skills; Prevocational. *Educational Intervention Approaches* Self-Control; Behavior Modification. *Degrees Awarded* High School Diploma.

Comments The center provides psychiatric residential services that focus on a treatment milieu augmented by psychotherapy, recreation, health care, psychiatric care, religious counseling and education.

Fremont Unified School District

40775 Fremont Blvd, Fremont, CA 94538 (415) 657-2350
Year Established 1963
Contact John Namkung, Dir Special Ed
Facility Information *Placement* Public School. *Sexes Served* Both. *Sources of Funding* State Funds; P.L. 94-142. Summer school available. *Teacher Certification Level* Elementary School; Junior High/Middle School; High School. *Special Certification Level* ED; LD; MR; Career/Vocational Education.

Student/Patient Characteristics *Age Levels* 5-8; 9-11; 12-14; 15-17; 18-21; Over 21. *IQ Ranges* 26-40; 41-55; 56-70; 71-85; 85-130; Above 130. *Exceptionalities Served* Autistic; Emotionally Disturbed; Learning Disabled; Mentally Handicapped; Communication Disordered; Hearing Impaired/Deaf; Visually Impaired/Blind; Other Health Impaired; Physically Handicapped. *Learning Problems* Memory Disabilities; Perceptual Disabilities; Thinking Disabilities; Oral Language Disabilities; Reading Disabilities; Handwriting Disabilities; Spelling Disabilities; Arithmetic Disabilities; Written Expression. *Behavioral Problems* Attention Deficits; Hyperactivity; Hypoactivity; Impulsivity; Self-Aggression; Verbal Aggression; Physical Aggression; Indirect Aggression; Passive Aggression; Withdrawal. *Conditions Treated* Schizophrenia; Aphasia; Obsessions and Compulsions; Personality Problems.

Services Provided Individual Therapy; Parent Involvement. *Professionals on Staff* Psychologists 15; Counselors 35; Nurses 5; Speech Therapists 17; Adaptive Physical Education Specialists 6. *Service Facilities Available (with number of rooms)* Itinerants 5; Resource Rooms 36; Self-Contained Rooms 56. *Educational Professionals* Special Education Teachers 97; Special Education Counselors 1. *Curricula* Traditional Academic; Career/Vocational Education; Individualized; Basic Skills; Prevocational. *Degrees Awarded* High School Diploma.

Garden Sullivan Learning and Development Program

2750 Geary Blvd, San Francisco, CA 94118 (415) 921-6171
Contact Antje Shadoan, Dir
Facility Information *Placement* Special Program. *Sexes Served* Both. *Sources of Funding* Health Insurance; Private Funds; Grants; Foundations. Summer school available. *Teacher Certification Level* Elementary School; Junior High/Middle School; High School. *Special Certification Level* LD.
Student/Patient Characteristics *Age Levels* 0-4; 5-8; 9-11; 12-14; 15-17; 18-21. *Exceptionalities Served* Autistic; Emotionally Disturbed; Learning Disabled; Mentally Handicapped; Communication Disordered; Other Health Impaired. *Learning Problems* Memory Disabilities; Perceptual Disabilities; Thinking Disabilities; Oral Language Disabilities; Reading Disabilities; Handwriting Disabilities; Spelling Disabilities; Arithmetic Disabilities; Written Expression; Gross and Fine Motor Difficulties. *Behavioral Problems* Attention Deficits; Hyperactivity; Impulsivity; Self-Aggression; Verbal Aggression; Physical Aggression; Indirect Aggression; Passive Aggression; Withdrawal. *Conditions Treated* Aphasia; Convulsive Disorders; Inadequacy/Immaturity.
Services Provided Individual Therapy; Group Therapy; Parent Involvement; Cognitive Developmental Therapy. *Professionals on Staff* Psychologists; Social Workers; Occupational Therapist; Physical Therapist. *Educational Professionals* Special Education Teachers 2. *Curricula* Individualized; Basic Skills. *Educational Intervention Approaches* Behavior Modification.

Gladman Memorial Hospital Adolescent Program

2633 E 27th St, Oakland, CA 94601 (415) 536-8111
Year Established 1967
Contact Ruth J Kaplan, Dir
Facility Information *Placement* Private and Public Inpatient Care. *Number of Beds* 25. *Children/Adolescents Served* 25. *Sexes Served* Both. *Room and Board Fees (Approx)* $365. *Sources of Funding* State Funds; Health Insurance; Short-Doyle Funding. Summer school available. *Teacher Certification Level* Elementary School; Junior High/Middle School; High School. *Special Certification Level* LD; Behavioral Disorders.
Student/Patient Characteristics *Age Levels* 12-14; 15-17. *Exceptionalities Served* Emotionally Disturbed; Learning Disabled; Mentally Handicapped; Gifted; Behaviorally Disordered. *Learning Problems* Memory Disabilities; Perceptual Disabilities; Thinking Disabilities; Reading Disabilities; Handwriting Disabilities; Spelling Disabilities; Arithmetic Disabilities; Written Expression. *Behavioral Problems* Attention Deficits; Hyperactivity; Hypoactivity; Impulsivity; Self-Aggression; Verbal Aggression; Physical Aggression; Indirect Aggression; Passive Aggression; Withdrawal. *Conditions Treated* Alcohol Abuse and/or Drug Abuse; Other Substance Abuse or Dependence; Disintegrative Psychoses; Schizophrenia; Convulsive Disorders; Phobias; Obsessions and Compulsions; Hysteria; Depression; Suicide; Asthma; Anorexia Nervosa; Ulcerative Colitis; Inadequacy/Immaturity; Personality Problems; Socialized Aggressive Reaction; Unsocialized Aggressive Reaction.
Services Provided Individual Therapy; Group Therapy; Parent Involvement; Behavior Therapy; Biofeedback; Family Therapy; Drug Therapy; Art Therapy; Music Therapy; Reality Therapy; Psychodrama. *Professionals on Staff* Psychiatrists 10; Psycholo-

gists 2; Counselors 14; Social Workers 3; Nurses 2. *Service Facilities Available (with number of rooms)* Consultative (ERT) 1; Resource Rooms 1; Self-Contained Rooms 1; Special School 2; Hospital School 2. *Educational Professionals* Special Education Teachers; Paraprofessionals 1. *Curricula* Traditional Academic; Individualized; Basic Skills; Prevocational. *Educational Intervention Approaches* Progressive Discipline; Behavior Modification.

Hathaway School of Hathaway Home for Children

PO Box 3547, Pacoima, CA 91333-3547 (818) 896-2474
Year Established 1919
Contact Milton E Shriner, Admin of Ed
Facility Information *Placement* Public School; Special School; Public Residential Care; Private Residential Care. *Number of Beds* 120. *Children/Adolescents Served* 120 (inpatient); 15 (day school). *Sexes Served* Both. *Room and Board Fees (Approx)* $83. *Tuition Fees (Approx)* $12,750. *Sources of Funding* State Funds; Health Insurance; P.L. 94-142. Summer school available. *Teacher Certification Level* Elementary School; Junior High/Middle School; High School. *Special Certification Level* LD; Career/Vocational Education; Severely Handicapped.
Student/Patient Characteristics *Age Levels* 5-8; 9-11; 12-14; 15-17. *IQ Ranges* 71-85; 85-130; Above 130. *Exceptionalities Served* Emotionally Disturbed; Learning Disabled; Communication Disordered. *Learning Problems* Memory Disabilities; Perceptual Disabilities; Thinking Disabilities; Oral Language Disabilities; Reading Disabilities; Handwriting Disabilities; Spelling Disabilities; Arithmetic Disabilities; Written Expression. *Behavioral Problems* Attention Deficits; Hyperactivity; Hypoactivity; Impulsivity; Self-Aggression; Verbal Aggression; Physical Aggression; Indirect Aggression; Passive Aggression; Withdrawal. *Conditions Treated* Disintegrative Psychoses; Schizophrenia; Phobias; Obsessions and Compulsions; Hysteria; Depression; Suicide; Inadequacy/Immaturity; Personality Problems; Socialized Aggressive Reaction; Unsocialized Aggressive Reaction.
Services Provided Individual Therapy; Group Therapy; Parent Involvement; Behavior Therapy; Cognitive Developmental Therapy; Family Therapy; Drug Therapy; Play Therapy; Psychodrama. *Professionals on Staff* Psychiatrists 4; Psychologists 6; Social Workers 10; Child Care Staff 100; Nurses 4; Speech Pathologist 1. *Service Facilities Available (with number of rooms)* Resource Rooms 3; Self-Contained Rooms 11. *Educational Professionals* Special Education Teachers 11; Career/Vocational Teachers 1; Special Education Counselors 1. *Curricula* Career/Vocational Education; Individualized; Basic Skills; Prevocational. *Educational Intervention Approaches* Progressive Discipline; Self-Control; Behavior Modification. *Degrees Awarded* Certificate of Attendance; High School Diploma; Graduate Equivalency Diploma.
Comments Hathaway Home for Children (and Hathaway School) is a private nonprofit residential treatment facility for severely emotionally disturbed children. Hathaway School is a state certified nonpublic school contracted to Los Angeles Unified School District. Most residential placements are made through Los Angeles County Department of Social Services, Probation, and Department of Adoptions.

Henrietta Weill Memorial Child Guidance Clinic

3628 Stockdale Hwy, Bakersfield, CA 93309 (805) 322-1021
Year Established 1946
Contact Roy Marshall, Exec Dir
Facility Information *Placement* Outpatient Psychiatric Clinic. *Children/Adolescents Served* 350. *Sexes Served* Both. *Sources of Funding* State Funds; Medicaid; United Way; Donations. Summer school available. *Teacher Certification Level* Elementary School. *Special Certification Level* LD.
Student/Patient Characteristics *Age Levels* 9-11. *IQ Ranges* 85-130. *Exceptionalities Served* Emotionally Disturbed; Learning Disabled. *Learning Problems* Memory Disabilities; Perceptual Disabilities; Thinking Disabilities; Oral Language Disabilities; Reading Disabilities. *Behavioral Problems* Attention Deficits; Hy-

peractivity; Hypoactivity; Impulsivity; Self-Aggression; Verbal Aggression; Physical Aggression; Indirect Aggression; Passive Aggression; Withdrawal. *Conditions Treated* Schizophrenia; Phobias; Obsessions and Compulsions; Hysteria; Depression; Suicide; Anorexia Nervosa; Inadequacy/Immaturity; Personality Problems; Socialized Aggressive Reaction; Unsocialized Aggressive Reaction.

Services Provided Individual Therapy; Group Therapy; Parent Involvement; Family Therapy; Play Therapy. *Professionals on Staff* Psychiatrists 1; Psychologists 1; Counselors 10; Social Workers 7; Recreational Therapist 1. *Service Facilities Available (with number of rooms)* Special School 4. *Educational Professionals* Special Education Teachers 2; Classroom Aides 2. *Curricula* Individualized. *Educational Intervention Approaches* Behavior Modification.

Comments The Henrietta Weill Memorial Child Guidance Clinic is an outpatient psychiatric clinic for children (ages 3-18) and their families who are residents of Kern County. The Children's Day Treatment Program is a psychoeducational program that offers a complete academic program within a therapeutic milieu.

Humana Hospital Huntington Beach—Children's Behavioral Center

17772 Beach Blvd, Huntington Beach, CA 92647 (714) 842-1473
Year Established 1974
Contact Robert Wilner, Social Worker
Facility Information *Placement* Inpatient Child Psychiatric Unit. *Number of Beds* 11. *Children/Adolescents Served* 11. *Sexes Served* Both. *Room and Board Fees (Approx)* $255. *Sources of Funding* Health Insurance; Medical. Summer school available. *Teacher Certification Level* Elementary School; Junior High/Middle School. *Special Certification Level* Special Education.
Student/Patient Characteristics *Age Levels* 0-4; 5-8; 9-11; 12-14. *IQ Ranges* 56-70; 71-85; 85-130; Above 130. *Exceptionalities Served* Autistic; Emotionally Disturbed; Learning Disabled; Communication Disordered. *Learning Problems* Memory Disabilities; Perceptual Disabilities; Thinking Disabilities; Oral Language Disabilities; Reading Disabilities; Handwriting Disabilities; Spelling Disabilities; Arithmetic Disabilities; Written Expression. *Behavioral Problems* Attention Deficits; Hyperactivity; Impulsivity; Self-Aggression; Verbal Aggression; Physical Aggression; Passive Aggression; Withdrawal. *Conditions Treated* Schizophrenia; Aphasia; Convulsive Disorders; Phobias; Obsessions and Compulsions; Hysteria; Depression; Suicide; Asthma; Anorexia Nervosa; Inadequacy/Immaturity; Personality Problems; Socialized Aggressive Reaction; Unsocialized Aggressive Reaction.
Services Provided Individual Therapy; Group Therapy; Parent Involvement; Behavior Therapy; Family Therapy; Drug Therapy; Play Therapy. *Professionals on Staff* Psychiatrists 3; Psychologists 1; Social Workers 1; Child Care Staff 5; Nurses 7. *Service Facilities Available (with number of rooms)* Self-Contained Rooms 1. *Educational Professionals* Special Education Teachers 1. *Curricula* Traditional Academic; Individualized. *Educational Intervention Approaches* Behavior Modification.

Ingleside Hospital

7500 E Hellman Ave, Rosemead, CA 91770 (818) 288-1160
Contact Michael Serisawa, Asst Dir of Social Serv
Facility Information *Placement* Private Residential Care. *Number of Beds* 54. *Children/Adolescents Served* 54. *Sexes Served* Both. *Sources of Funding* Health Insurance; Medicare. Summer school available. *Teacher Certification Level* Junior High/Middle School; High School. *Special Certification Level* ED; LD; Career/Vocational Education; Reading; Math.
Student/Patient Characteristics *Age Levels* 9-11; 12-14; 15-17; 18-21; Over 21. *IQ Ranges* 71-85; 85-130; Above 130. *Exceptionalities Served* Emotionally Disturbed; Learning Disabled; Mentally Handicapped. *Learning Problems* Memory Disabilities; Perceptual Disabilities; Thinking Disabilities; Oral Language Disabilities; Reading Disabilities; Handwriting Disabilities; Spelling Disabilities; Arithmetic Disabilities; Written Expression. *Behavioral Problems* Attention Deficits; Hyperactivity; Hypoac-

tivity; Impulsivity; Self-Aggression; Verbal Aggression; Physical Aggression; Indirect Aggression; Passive Aggression; Withdrawal. *Conditions Treated* Alcohol Abuse and/or Drug Abuse; Other Substance Abuse or Dependence; Disintegrative Psychoses; Schizophrenia; Aphasia; Convulsive Disorders; Phobias; Obsessions and Compulsions; Hysteria; Depression; Suicide; Asthma; Anorexia Nervosa; Inadequacy/Immaturity; Personality Problems; Socialized Aggressive Reaction; Unsocialized Aggressive Reaction.
Services Provided Individual Therapy; Group Therapy; Parent Involvement; Behavior Therapy; Cognitive Developmental Therapy; Biofeedback; Family Therapy; Filial Therapy; Drug Therapy; Art Therapy; Music Therapy; Reality Therapy. *Professionals on Staff* Psychiatrists 40; Psychologists 20; Counselors 15; Social Workers 8; Nurses 75. *Service Facilities Available (with number of rooms)* Resource Rooms 2; Self-Contained Rooms 1; Hospital School 7. *Educational Professionals* Regular School Teachers 3; Special Education Teachers 4. *Curricula* Traditional Academic; Career/Vocational Education; Individualized; Basic Skills; Prevocational. *Educational Intervention Approaches* Self-Control; Behavior Modification. *Degrees Awarded* High School Diploma.
Comments Ingleside Hospital is a 146 bed, private, nonprofit psychiatric facility located in the greater Los Angeles area. Ingleside has a 36 bed adolescent program and an 18 bed adolescent chemical dependency program.

John G McGrath School

2100 Napa-Vallejo Hwy, Napa, CA 94559 (707) 253-5565
Year Established 1960
Contact Mark Willoughby, Head Teacher
Facility Information *Placement* State Hospital. *Number of Beds* 200. *Children/Adolescents Served* 200. *Sexes Served* Both. *Room and Board Fees (Approx)* $190. *Sources of Funding* State Funds; HEW. Summer school available. *Teacher Certification Level* Elementary School; Junior High/Middle School; High School. *Special Certification Level* ED; LD; MR; Career/Vocational Education; Reading; Math.
Student/Patient Characteristics *Age Levels* 9-11; 12-14; 15-17; 18-21. *IQ Ranges* 56-70; 71-85; 85-130; Above 130. *Exceptionalities Served* Emotionally Disturbed; Learning Disabled; Mentally Handicapped; Communication Disordered; Hearing Impaired/Deaf; Gifted. *Learning Problems* Memory Disabilities; Perceptual Disabilities; Thinking Disabilities; Oral Language Disabilities; Reading Disabilities; Handwriting Disabilities; Spelling Disabilities; Arithmetic Disabilities; Written Expression. *Behavioral Problems* Attention Deficits; Hyperactivity; Hypoactivity; Impulsivity; Self-Aggression; Verbal Aggression; Physical Aggression; Indirect Aggression; Passive Aggression; Withdrawal. *Conditions Treated* Other Substance Abuse or Dependence; Disintegrative Psychoses; Schizophrenia; Aphasia; Convulsive Disorders; Hysteria; Depression; Suicide; Anorexia Nervosa; Inadequacy/Immaturity; Personality Problems; Socialized Aggressive Reaction; Unsocialized Aggressive Reaction.
Services Provided Individual Therapy; Group Therapy; Parent Involvement; Behavior Therapy; Family Therapy; Drug Therapy; Art Therapy; Music Therapy; Reality Therapy; Play Therapy. *Professionals on Staff* Psychiatrists 5; Psychologists 3; Counselors; Social Workers 7; Child Care Staff; Nurses. *Service Facilities Available (with number of rooms)* Transition Rooms 3; Self-Contained Rooms 8. *Educational Professionals* Special Education Teachers 14; Career/Vocational Teachers 1. *Curricula* Individualized; Basic Skills; Prevocational. *Educational Intervention Approaches* Engineered Classroom; Precision Teaching; Self-Control; Behavior Modification. *Degrees Awarded* Certificate of Attendance; High School Diploma.

Kaplan Foundation

7150 Santa Juanita, Orangevale, CA 95662 (916) 988-0258
Year Established 1980
Contact Karen Kaplan Fitzgerald, Dir

Facility Information *Placement* Special School; Private Residential Care. *Number of Beds* 12. *Children/Adolescents Served* 18. *Sexes Served* Both. *Room and Board Fees (Approx)* $73 (education); $868 (intensive rate). *Sources of Funding* State Funds; Medicare; P.L. 94-142. Summer school available. *Teacher Certification Level* Elementary School; Junior High/Middle School; High School. *Special Certification Level* Severely Handicapped.

Student/Patient Characteristics *Age Levels* 0-4; 5-8; 9-11; 12-14; 15-17; 18-21; Over 21. *IQ Ranges* 0-25; 26-40; 41-55; 56-70; 71-85. *Exceptionalities Served* Autistic. *Learning Problems* Memory Disabilities; Perceptual Disabilities; Thinking Disabilities; Oral Language Disabilities; Reading Disabilities; Handwriting Disabilities; Spelling Disabilities; Arithmetic Disabilities; Written Expression. *Behavioral Problems* Attention Deficits; Hyperactivity; Hypoactivity; Impulsivity; Self-Aggression; Verbal Aggression; Physical Aggression; Indirect Aggression; Passive Aggression; Withdrawal. *Conditions Treated* Early Infantile Autism; Schizophrenia; Aphasia; Convulsive Disorders.

Services Provided Parent Involvement; Behavior Therapy. *Professionals on Staff* Psychiatrists 1; Psychologists 1; Social Workers 3; Speech Pathologist 1. *Service Facilities Available (with number of rooms)* Self-Contained Rooms; On-Campus Residential School. *Educational Professionals* Special Education Teachers 4; Paraprofessionals 50. *Curricula* Traditional Academic; Career/Vocational Education; Individualized; Basic Skills; Prevocational. *Educational Intervention Approaches* Behavior Modification; Applied Behavior Analysis.

La Mel

1801 Bush, San Francisco, CA 94109 (415) 931-1972
Year Established 1970
Contact Josephine LaVonne Lomba

Facility Information *Placement* Public School; Special School; Private Day Care; Public Day Care; Special Program; Vocational. *Children/Adolescents Served* 75. *Sexes Served* Both. *Room and Board Fees (Approx)* $64 (educational); $65 (medical). *Sources of Funding* Health Insurance; P.L. 94-142; Department of Defense; OCHAMPUS. Summer school available. *Teacher Certification Level* Elementary School; Junior High/Middle School; High School. *Special Certification Level* ED; LD; Career/Vocational Education; Reading.

Student/Patient Characteristics *Age Levels* 5-8; 9-11; 12-14; 15-17; 18-21. *IQ Ranges* 71-85; 85-130; Above 130. *Exceptionalities Served* Emotionally Disturbed; Learning Disabled; Communication Disordered; Other Health Impaired; Physically Handicapped; Gifted. *Learning Problems* Memory Disabilities; Perceptual Disabilities; Thinking Disabilities; Oral Language Disabilities; Reading Disabilities; Handwriting Disabilities; Spelling Disabilities; Arithmetic Disabilities; Written Expression. *Behavioral Problems* Attention Deficits; Hyperactivity; Impulsivity; Passive Aggression; Withdrawal. *Conditions Treated* Schizophrenia; Convulsive Disorders; Phobias; Obsessions and Compulsions; Hysteria; Depression; Suicide; Asthma; Anorexia Nervosa; Ulcerative Colitis; Inadequacy/Immaturity; Personality Problems; Socialized Aggressive Reaction; Unsocialized Aggressive Reaction.

Services Provided Individual Therapy; Group Therapy; Parent Involvement; Behavior Therapy; Cognitive Developmental Therapy; Family Therapy; Filial Therapy; Art Therapy; Reality Therapy; Play Therapy; Psychodrama. *Professionals on Staff* Psychiatrists 4; Psychologists 1; Counselors 1; Social Workers 1; Activity Therapists 2; Speech Pathologists 2. *Service Facilities Available (with number of rooms)* Consultative (ERT); Itinerants; Resource Rooms; Transition Rooms; Self-Contained Rooms. *Educational Professionals* Regular School Teachers 12; Special Education Teachers 12; Career/Vocational Teachers 1. *Curricula* Traditional Academic; Career/Vocational Education; Individualized. *Educational Intervention Approaches* Engineered Classroom; Precision Teaching; Progressive Discipline; Self-Control; Behavior Modification; Applied Behavior Analysis; Creative Conditioning. *Degrees Awarded* High School Diploma.

La Puente Valley Community Mental Health Center

160 S 7th Ave, La Puente, CA 91744 (818) 961-8971
Year Established 1979
Contact Geri Curry, Dir

Facility Information *Placement* Referral Agency. *Sexes Served* Both. *Sources of Funding* State Funds; Health Insurance; Medicaid; Medicare; P.L. 94-142.

Student/Patient Characteristics *Age Levels* 0-4; 5-8; 9-11; 12-14; 15-17; 18-21. *IQ Ranges* 41-55; 56-70; 71-85; 85-130; Above 130. *Exceptionalities Served* Autistic; Emotionally Disturbed; Learning Disabled; Mentally Handicapped; Communication Disordered; Gifted. *Learning Problems* Memory Disabilities; Perceptual Disabilities; Thinking Disabilities; Oral Language Disabilities; Reading Disabilities; Handwriting Disabilities; Spelling Disabilities; Arithmetic Disabilities; Written Expression. *Behavioral Problems* Attention Deficits; Hyperactivity; Hypoactivity; Impulsivity; Self-Aggression; Verbal Aggression; Physical Aggression; Indirect Aggression; Passive Aggression; Withdrawal. *Conditions Treated* Other Substance Abuse or Dependence; Disintegrative Psychoses; Schizophrenia; Aphasia; Phobias; Obsessions and Compulsions; Hysteria; Depression; Suicide; Asthma; Anorexia Nervosa; Ulcerative Colitis; Inadequacy/Immaturity; Personality Problems; Socialized Aggressive Reaction; Unsocialized Aggressive Reaction.

Services Provided Individual Therapy; Group Therapy; Parent Involvement; Behavior Therapy; Cognitive Developmental Therapy; Family Therapy; Filial Therapy; Art Therapy; Reality Therapy; Play Therapy; Psychodrama. *Professionals on Staff* Psychiatrists 2; Psychologists 1; Social Workers 2; Nurses 1. *Curricula* Individualized; Basic Skills. *Educational Intervention Approaches* Self-Control; Behavior Modification; Applied Behavior Analysis; Creative Conditioning.

The Los Angeles Child Guidance Clinic

746 W Adams Blvd, Los Angeles, CA 90007 (213) 749-4111
Year Established 1924
Contact Thomas J Ledwith, Pres and Chief Exec Officer

Facility Information *Placement* Special School; Special Program; Adolescent Day Treatment Program; Child Abuse Prevention Program; Outpatient Program. *Children/Adolescents Served* 80. *Sexes Served* Both. *Sources of Funding* State Funds; Health Insurance; Medicare; P.L. 94-142; AB 1733; AB 2994; County; United Way; Private Donations. Summer school available. *Teacher Certification Level* Elementary School; Junior High/Middle School; High School. *Special Certification Level* ED; LD; Career/Vocational Education; Reading; Math; Special Education.

Student/Patient Characteristics *Age Levels* 0-4; 5-8; 9-11; 12-14; 15-17. *IQ Ranges* 56-70; 71-85; 85-130. *Exceptionalities Served* Emotionally Disturbed; Learning Disabled; Communication Disordered. *Learning Problems* Perceptual Disabilities; Thinking Disabilities; Oral Language Disabilities; Reading Disabilities; Handwriting Disabilities; Spelling Disabilities; Arithmetic Disabilities; Written Expression. *Behavioral Problems* Attention Deficits; Hyperactivity; Hypoactivity; Impulsivity; Self-Aggression; Verbal Aggression; Physical Aggression; Indirect Aggression; Passive Aggression; Withdrawal. *Conditions Treated* Alcohol Abuse and/or Drug Abuse; Other Substance Abuse or Dependence; Disintegrative Psychoses; Schizophrenia; Phobias; Obsessions and Compulsions; Depression; Suicide; Personality Problems; Socialized Aggressive Reaction; Unsocialized Aggressive Reaction.

Services Provided Individual Therapy; Group Therapy; Parent Involvement; Behavior Therapy; Cognitive Developmental Therapy; Family Therapy; Filial Therapy. *Professionals on Staff* Psychiatrists 3; Psychologists 3; Social Workers 6; Child Care Staff 2; Nurses 1; Psychology Interns 4. *Service Facilities Available (with number of rooms)* Self-Contained Rooms 5; Special School 6. *Educational Professionals* Special Education Teachers 6; Career/Vocational Teachers 1; Crisis Teachers 1; Paraprofessionals 5; Recreational Therapists 2. *Curricula* Career/Vocational Education; Individualized; Basic Skills; Prevocational.

Educational Intervention Approaches Engineered Classroom; Behavior Modification. *Degrees Awarded* Certificate of Attendance; High School Diploma.

Los Angeles County Office of Education—Division of Special Education

9300 E Imperial Hwy, Downey, CA 90242 (213) 803-8307
Contact Marilyn Armstrong, Dir Special Ed
Facility Information *Placement* Public School. *Sexes Served* Both. *Sources of Funding* State Funds. Summer school available. *Teacher Certification Level* Elementary School; Junior High/Middle School; High School. *Special Certification Level* LD; Severely Handicapped.
Student/Patient Characteristics *Age Levels* 0-4; 5-8; 9-11; 12-14; 15-17; 18-21. *IQ Ranges* 0-25; 26-40; 41-55; 56-70; 71-85; 85-130; Above 130. *Exceptionalities Served* Autistic; Emotionally Disturbed; Learning Disabled; Mentally Handicapped; Communication Disordered; Hearing Impaired/Deaf; Visually Impaired/Blind; Other Health Impaired; Physically Handicapped. *Learning Problems* Memory Disabilities; Perceptual Disabilities; Thinking Disabilities; Oral Language Disabilities; Reading Disabilities; Handwriting Disabilities; Spelling Disabilities; Arithmetic Disabilities; Written Expression. *Behavioral Problems* Attention Deficits; Hyperactivity; Hypoactivity; Impulsivity; Self-Aggression; Verbal Aggression; Physical Aggression; Indirect Aggression; Passive Aggression; Withdrawal.
Services Provided Educational Counseling. *Professionals on Staff* Psychologists 36; Nurses 25. *Service Facilities Available (with number of rooms)* Transition Rooms; Self-Contained Rooms; Special School; Homebound Instruction. *Educational Professionals* Regular School Teachers; Special Education Teachers; Career/Vocational Teachers; Behavior Aides; Psychological School Counselors. *Curricula* Traditional Academic; Career/Vocational Education; Individualized; Basic Skills; Prevocational. *Educational Intervention Approaches* Engineered Classroom; Precision Teaching; Progressive Discipline; Self-Control; Behavior Modification. *Degrees Awarded* Certificate of Attendance; High School Diploma.
Comments County School programs are provided at the request of and in conjunction with school district plans for services to handicapped pupils.

Los Angeles County Office of Education—Mark Twain School

15516 S Doty St, Lawndale, CA 90260 (213) 644-4478
Year Established 1973
Facility Information *Placement* Public School; Special Education. *Children/Adolescents Served* 70. *Sexes Served* Both. *Sources of Funding* State Funds; P.L. 94-142. Summer school available. *Teacher Certification Level* Elementary School; Junior High/Middle School; High School. *Special Certification Level* ED; LD; MR; Career/Vocational Education.
Student/Patient Characteristics *Age Levels* 0-4; 5-8; 9-11; 12-14; 15-17; 18-21. *IQ Ranges* 26-40; 41-55; 56-70. *Exceptionalities Served* Autistic; Emotionally Disturbed; Learning Disabled; Mentally Handicapped; Communication Disordered. *Learning Problems* Memory Disabilities; Perceptual Disabilities; Thinking Disabilities; Oral Language Disabilities; Reading Disabilities; Handwriting Disabilities; Spelling Disabilities; Arithmetic Disabilities; Written Expression. *Behavioral Problems* Attention Deficits; Hyperactivity; Impulsivity; Self-Aggression; Physical Aggression; Indirect Aggression; Passive Aggression. *Conditions Treated* Early Infantile Autism; Disintegrative Psychoses; Schizophrenia; Aphasia; Obsessions and Compulsions; Inadequacy/Immaturity; Unsocialized Aggressive Reaction.
Services Provided *Professionals on Staff* Psychologists 1; Social Workers; Nurses; Teachers. *Service Facilities Available (with number of rooms)* Self-Contained Rooms 15. *Educational Professionals* Special Education Teachers 15; Career/Vocational Teachers 1; Paraprofessionals 3. *Curricula* Traditional Academic; Career/Vocational Education; Individualized; Basic Skills; Prevocational. *Educational Intervention Approaches* Engineered

Classroom; Progressive Discipline; Self-Control; Behavior Modification; Applied Behavior Analysis; Creative Conditioning. *Degrees Awarded* Certificate of Attendance; High School Diploma.

Los Ninos Education Center

6145 Decena Dr, San Diego, CA 92120 (619) 281-5511
Year Established 1970
Contact Martha Morrissey, Admin Asst
Facility Information *Placement* Private Residential Care; Special Program. *Number of Beds* 6. *Children/Adolescents Served* 6 (residential); 100 (educational). *Sexes Served* Both. *Tuition Fees (Approx)* $14,912. *Sources of Funding* P.L. 94-142. Summer school available. *Teacher Certification Level* Elementary School; Junior High/Middle School; High School. *Special Certification Level* ED; LD; MR; Severely Handicapped.
Student/Patient Characteristics *Age Levels* 0-4; 5-8; 9-11; 12-14; 15-17; 18-21; Over 21. *Exceptionalities Served* Autistic; Emotionally Disturbed; Learning Disabled; Mentally Handicapped; Communication Disordered; Hearing Impaired/Deaf; Visually Impaired/Blind. *Learning Problems* Severely Handicapped. *Behavioral Problems* Attention Deficits; Hyperactivity; Hypoactivity; Impulsivity; Self-Aggression; Verbal Aggression; Physical Aggression; Indirect Aggression; Passive Aggression; Withdrawal. *Conditions Treated* Early Infantile Autism; Schizophrenia; Aphasia; Convulsive Disorders; Phobias; Obsessions and Compulsions; Hysteria; Anorexia Nervosa.
Services Provided Individual Therapy; Group Therapy; Parent Involvement; Behavior Therapy; Family Therapy. *Professionals on Staff* Psychiatrists; Psychologists; Child Care Staff. *Educational Professionals* Special Education Teachers. *Curricula* Individualized; Basic Skills; Prevocational. *Educational Intervention Approaches* Self-Control; Behavior Modification.

Mardan Center of Educational Therapy

695 W 19th St, Costa Mesa, CA 92627 (714) 631-6400
Year Established 1962
Contact Richard Schnetzer, Prog Dir
Facility Information *Placement* Special School. *Sexes Served* Both. *Sources of Funding* P.L. 94-142; Scholarships. Summer school available. *Teacher Certification Level* Elementary School; Junior High/Middle School; High School. *Special Certification Level* Learning Handicapped; Severely Handicapped.
Student/Patient Characteristics *Age Levels* 0-4; 5-8; 9-11; 12-14; 15-17; 18-21. *IQ Ranges* 71-85; 85-130; Above 130. *Exceptionalities Served* Emotionally Disturbed; Learning Disabled; Mentally Handicapped; Gifted. *Learning Problems* Memory Disabilities; Perceptual Disabilities; Thinking Disabilities; Oral Language Disabilities; Reading Disabilities; Handwriting Disabilities; Spelling Disabilities; Arithmetic Disabilities; Written Expression. *Behavioral Problems* Attention Deficits; Hyperactivity; Hypoactivity; Impulsivity; Self-Aggression; Verbal Aggression; Physical Aggression; Indirect Aggression; Passive Aggression; Withdrawal.
Services Provided Individual Therapy; Group Therapy; Parent Involvement; Family Therapy; Art Therapy; Play Therapy; Speech and Language Therapy. *Professionals on Staff* Psychologists 1; Counselors 5. *Service Facilities Available (with number of rooms)* Consultative (ERT) 2; Itinerants 6; Resource Rooms 2; Self-Contained Rooms 7. *Educational Professionals* Special Education Teachers 7; Career/Vocational Teachers 1; Paraprofessionals 3. *Curricula* Traditional Academic; Career/Vocational Education; Individualized; Basic Skills; Prevocational. *Educational Intervention Approaches* Engineered Classroom; Progressive Discipline; Self-Control; Behavior Modification; Creative Conditioning. *Degrees Awarded* High School Diploma.
Comments The Mardan Center of Educational Therapy is a private, nonprofit, nonsectarian day school program dedicated to serving the educational, social, and emotional needs of learning disabled and emotionally disturbed children who range in age from 2 to 19 years.

Maryvale

7600 E Graves Ave, Rosemead, CA 91770 (818) 280-6510
Year Established 1856
Contact Michael Giron, Asst Dir

Facility Information *Placement* Private Residential Care; Private Day Care. *Number of Beds* 95. *Children/Adolescents Served* 95 (residential treatment); 84 (day care). *Sexes Served* Both. *Room and Board Fees (Approx)* $87. *Sources of Funding* AFDC; United Way; Contributions. Summer school available. *Teacher Certification Level* Elementary School; Junior High/Middle School; High School. *Special Certification Level* ED; LD.

Student/Patient Characteristics *Age Levels* 0-4; 5-8; 9-11; 12-14; 15-17. *IQ Ranges* 85-130. *Exceptionalities Served* Emotionally Disturbed; Learning Disabled; Abused; Neglected, Dilenquent. *Learning Problems* Memory Disabilities; Perceptual Disabilities; Thinking Disabilities; Oral Language Disabilities; Reading Disabilities; Handwriting Disabilities; Spelling Disabilities; Arithmetic Disabilities; Written Expression. *Behavioral Problems* Attention Deficits; Hyperactivity; Impulsivity; Verbal Aggression; Physical Aggression; Indirect Aggression; Passive Aggression; Withdrawal. *Conditions Treated* Alcohol Abuse and/or Drug Abuse; Phobias; Obsessions and Compulsions; Hysteria; Depression; Asthma; Inadequacy/Immaturity; Personality Problems; Socialized Aggressive Reaction; Unsocialized Aggressive Reaction; Adjustment Reactions.

Services Provided Individual Therapy; Group Therapy; Parent Involvement; Family Therapy; Play Therapy. *Professionals on Staff* Psychiatrists 2; Psychologists 1; Social Workers 7; Child Care Staff 40; Nurses 1. *Service Facilities Available (with number of rooms)* Itinerants; Resource Rooms; Transition Rooms; On-Campus Residential School 6. *Educational Professionals* Special Education Teachers 6; Paraprofessionals 6. *Curricula* Traditional Academic; Individualized; Basic Skills. *Educational Intervention Approaches* Self-Control; Behavior Modification. *Degrees Awarded* High School Diploma.

McKinley Home for Boys

762 W Cypress Ave, San Dimas, CA 91773 (714) 599-1227
Year Established 1900
Contact Jane Van Stedum, Asst Dir

Facility Information *Placement* Private Residential Care. *Number of Beds* 85. *Children/Adolescents Served* 85. *Sexes Served* Male. *Sources of Funding* State Funds. Summer school available. *Teacher Certification Level* Elementary School; Junior High/Middle School; High School. *Special Certification Level* ED.

Student/Patient Characteristics *Age Levels* 5-8; 9-11; 12-14; 15-17. *Exceptionalities Served* Emotionally Disturbed; Learning Disabled. *Learning Problems* Perceptual Disabilities; Oral Language Disabilities; Reading Disabilities; Spelling Disabilities; Arithmetic Disabilities. *Behavioral Problems* Attention Deficits; Hyperactivity; Impulsivity; Verbal Aggression; Physical Aggression. *Conditions Treated* Depression; Inadequacy/Immaturity; Personality Problems.

Services Provided Individual Therapy; Group Therapy; Parent Involvement; Behavior Therapy; Family Therapy; Drug Therapy; Reality Therapy; Play Therapy. *Professionals on Staff* Psychiatrists 1; Psychologists 1; Social Workers 7; Child Care Staff 30; Nurses 1. *Educational Professionals* Special Education Teachers 4; Paraprofessionals 4. *Curricula* Individualized. *Educational Intervention Approaches* Behavior Modification. *Degrees Awarded* High School Diploma.

Comments McKinley is a residential treatment facility for emotionally disturbed boys. Extensive family re-unification efforts are made including multi-family groups, parenting classes, and a full-time family outreach social worker.

Miramonte Mental Health Services Inc

445 Sherman Ave Suite E, Palo Alto, CA 94306 (415) 321-5401
Year Established 1962
Contact Manuel J Costa, Exec Dir

Facility Information *Placement* Private Residential Care; Vocational/Pre-Vocational Day Program. *Children/Adolescents Served* 7. *Sexes Served* Both. *Room and Board Fees (Approx)* $95. *Sources of Funding* State Funds.

Student/Patient Characteristics *Age Levels* 18-21; Over 21. *IQ Ranges* 85-130; Above 130. *Exceptionalities Served* Emotionally Disturbed. *Learning Problems* Memory Disabilities; Perceptual Disabilities; Thinking Disabilities. *Behavioral Problems* Attention Deficits; Hyperactivity; Hypoactivity; Impulsivity; Self-Aggression; Verbal Aggression; Withdrawal. *Conditions Treated* Schizophrenia; Obsessions and Compulsions; Depression; Anorexia Nervosa.

Services Provided Individual Therapy; Group Therapy; Parent Involvement; Family Therapy; Art Therapy. *Professionals on Staff* Psychiatrists 4; Counselors 24. *Educational Professionals* Special Education Teachers 1. *Curricula* Career/Vocational Education; Basic Skills; Prevocational. *Educational Intervention Approaches* Therapeutic Milieu.

Comments Miramonte's programs are directed to voluntary clients, ranging in age from 18 to 65, diagnosed as seriously mentally ill and in need of a therapeutic community in a non-institutional setting. The programs are designed according to the psychosocial rehabilitation model.

Napa State Hospital—Children's Program

2100 Napa Vallejo Hwy, Imola, CA 94558 (707) 253-5571
Year Established 1960
Contact Fred Hollander, Prog Dir

Facility Information *Placement* Public Residential Care. *Number of Beds* 103. *Children/Adolescents Served* 103. *Sexes Served* Both. *Room and Board Fees (Approx)* $200. *Sources of Funding* State Funds; Health Insurance; P.L. 94-142. Summer school available. *Teacher Certification Level* Elementary School; Junior High/Middle School; High School. *Special Certification Level* ED; LD; MR; Career/Vocational Education; Reading; Math.

Student/Patient Characteristics *Age Levels* 5-8; 9-11; 12-14; 15-17. *IQ Ranges* 71-85; 85-130; Above 130. *Exceptionalities Served* Emotionally Disturbed; Learning Disabled; Mentally Handicapped; Communication Disordered; Hearing Impaired/Deaf. *Learning Problems* Memory Disabilities; Perceptual Disabilities; Thinking Disabilities; Oral Language Disabilities; Reading Disabilities; Handwriting Disabilities; Spelling Disabilities; Arithmetic Disabilities; Written Expression. *Behavioral Problems* Attention Deficits; Hyperactivity; Hypoactivity; Impulsivity; Self-Aggression; Verbal Aggression; Physical Aggression; Indirect Aggression; Passive Aggression; Withdrawal. *Conditions Treated* Alcohol Abuse and/or Drug Abuse; Other Substance Abuse or Dependence; Disintegrative Psychoses; Schizophrenia; Aphasia; Convulsive Disorders; Phobias; Obsessions and Compulsions; Hysteria; Depression; Suicide; Asthma; Anorexia Nervosa; Ulcerative Colitis; Inadequacy/Immaturity; Personality Problems; Socialized Aggressive Reaction; Unsocialized Aggressive Reaction.

Services Provided Individual Therapy; Group Therapy; Parent Involvement; Behavior Therapy; Cognitive Developmental Therapy; Family Therapy; Drug Therapy; Art Therapy; Music Therapy; Play Therapy. *Professionals on Staff* Psychiatrists 5; Psychologists 3; Social Workers 7; Child Care Staff 69; Nurses 18; Rehabiltation Therapists 3. *Service Facilities Available (with number of rooms)* Consultative (ERT) 1; Resource Rooms 1; Transition Rooms 1; Self-Contained Rooms 5; Special School 1; On-Campus Residential School 5; Homebound Instruction 1. *Educational Professionals* Special Education Teachers 13.5; Paraprofessionals. *Curricula* Individualized. *Educational Intervention Approaches* Self-Control. *Degrees Awarded* High School Diploma.

National Foundation for the Treatment of the Emotionally Handicapped

15302 Rayen St, Sepulveda, CA 91343 (818) 892-1111
Year Established 1969
Contact Ivelise Markovits, Exec Dir

Facility Information *Placement* Public Residential Care. *Number of Beds* 85. *Children/Adolescents Served* 85. *Sexes Served* Both. *Tuition Fees (Approx)* $18,840. *Sources of Funding* State Funds. Summer school available. *Teacher Certification Level* Junior High/Middle School; High School. *Special Certification Level* ED; LD; Reading; Math.

Student/Patient Characteristics *Age Levels* 12-14; 15-17. *IQ Ranges* 56-70; 71-85; 85-130. *Exceptionalities Served* Emotionally Disturbed; Learning Disabled; Mentally Handicapped. *Learning Problems* Memory Disabilities; Perceptual Disabilities; Thinking Disabilities; Oral Language Disabilities; Reading Disabilities; Handwriting Disabilities; Spelling Disabilities; Arithmetic Disabilities; Written Expression. *Behavioral Problems* Attention Deficits; Hyperactivity; Hypoactivity; Impulsivity; Self-Aggression; Verbal Aggression; Physical Aggression; Indirect Aggression; Passive Aggression; Withdrawal. *Conditions Treated* Obsessions and Compulsions; Hysteria; Depression; Suicide; Inadequacy/Immaturity; Personality Problems; Socialized Aggressive Reaction; Unsocialized Aggressive Reaction.

Services Provided Individual Therapy; Group Therapy; Parent Involvement; Family Therapy; Psychodrama. *Professionals on Staff* Psychiatrists 1; Psychologists 1; Social Workers 7; Child Care Staff 28; Nurses 1. *Service Facilities Available (with number of rooms)* Self-Contained Rooms 5. *Educational Professionals* Regular School Teachers 3; Special Education Teachers 2; Paraprofessionals 4. *Curricula* Traditional Academic; Career/Vocational Education; Individualized; Basic Skills. *Educational Intervention Approaches* Engineered Classroom; Progressive Discipline; Behavior Modification. *Degrees Awarded* Certificate of Attendance; High School Diploma; Graduate Equivalency Diploma.

Office of Riverside County Superintendent of Schools

3939 13th St, Riverside, CA 92502 (714) 788-6635
Contact Steve Eimers, School Psychologist

Facility Information *Placement* Public School; Special Program; Private School. *Children/Adolescents Served* 50. *Sexes Served* Both. *Sources of Funding* State Funds; P.L. 94-142. Summer school available. *Teacher Certification Level* Elementary School; Junior High/Middle School; High School. *Special Certification Level* Severely Handicapped.

Student/Patient Characteristics *Age Levels* 12-14; 15-17; 18-21. *IQ Ranges* 85-130; Above 130. *Exceptionalities Served* Emotionally Disturbed. *Learning Problems* Memory Disabilities; Perceptual Disabilities; Thinking Disabilities; Reading Disabilities; Handwriting Disabilities; Spelling Disabilities; Arithmetic Disabilities; Written Expression. *Behavioral Problems* Attention Deficits; Hyperactivity; Hypoactivity; Impulsivity; Self-Aggression; Verbal Aggression; Physical Aggression; Indirect Aggression; Passive Aggression; Withdrawal. *Conditions Treated* Schizophrenia; Phobias; Obsessions and Compulsions; Hysteria; Depression; Suicide; Inadequacy/Immaturity; Personality Problems; Socialized Aggressive Reaction; Unsocialized Aggressive Reaction.

Services Provided *Professionals on Staff* Psychologists 1; Nurses 1. *Service Facilities Available (with number of rooms)* Consultative (ERT) 5; Self-Contained Rooms 5. *Educational Professionals* Special Education Teachers 5. *Curricula* Traditional Academic; Career/Vocational Education; Individualized; Basic Skills. *Educational Intervention Approaches* Self-Control; Applied Behavior Analysis. *Degrees Awarded* High School Diploma; Graduate Equivalency Diploma.

Pacific Children's Center

303 Van Buren Ave, Oakland, CA 94610 (415) 465-3507
Year Established 1974
Contact Laurie Lambert, Day Treatment Dir

Facility Information *Placement* Special School; Non-Residential Day Treatment Program. *Children/Adolescents Served* 20. *Sexes Served* Both. *Tuition Fees (Approx)* Sliding Scale. *Sources of Funding* State Funds; HEW; Medicare County; Individual Dona-

tions; Grants; Fees. Summer school available. *Teacher Certification Level* Elementary School. *Special Certification Level* ED; LD.

Student/Patient Characteristics *Age Levels* 0-4; 5-8. *Exceptionalities Served* Autistic; Emotionally Disturbed; Learning Disabled; Communication Disordered. *Learning Problems* Thinking Disabilities; Oral Language Disabilities. *Behavioral Problems* Attention Deficits; Hyperactivity; Hypoactivity; Impulsivity; Self-Aggression; Verbal Aggression; Physical Aggression; Indirect Aggression; Passive Aggression; Withdrawal. *Conditions Treated* Early Infantile Autism; Schizophrenia; Obsessions and Compulsions; Depression; Inadequacy/Immaturity; Socialized Aggressive Reaction; Unsocialized Aggressive Reaction.

Services Provided Individual Therapy; Group Therapy; Parent Involvement; Behavior Therapy; Family Therapy; Drug Therapy; Play Therapy. *Professionals on Staff* Psychiatrists 2; Psychologists 3; Counselors 2; Social Workers 2. *Service Facilities Available (with number of rooms)* Transition Rooms 1; Self-Contained Rooms 2; Counseling Center. *Educational Professionals* Regular School Teachers 2; Special Education Teachers 3; Paraprofessionals 4. *Curricula* Emotional and Cognitive Development. *Educational Intervention Approaches* Applied Behavior Analysis; Developmental Interactionalism.

Comments The center serves preschool children with emotional problems ranging from the withdrawn, non-verbal child to the impulsive, acting-out child, including varieties of language delays, behavior problems, and learning disabilities. Simultaneous communication is used with children with language delays. Strong emphasis is placed on parent participation.

Penninsula Children's Center—Children and Youth Services

3860 Middlefield Rd, Palo Alto, CA 94303 (415) 494-1200
Year Established 1960
Contact Gail Switzer, Prog Dir

Facility Information *Placement* Private Non-Profit School. *Children/Adolescents Served* 53. *Sexes Served* Both. *Tuition Fees (Approx)* $15,000. *Sources of Funding* P.L. 94-142; United Way; Short/Doyle Medi-Cal; Private Donation. Summer school available. *Teacher Certification Level* Elementary School; Junior High/Middle School; High School. *Special Certification Level* Severely Handicapped.

Student/Patient Characteristics *Age Levels* 0-4; 5-8; 9-11; 12-14; 15-17; 18-21. *IQ Ranges* 41-55; 56-70; 71-85; 85-130. *Exceptionalities Served* Autistic; Emotionally Disturbed; Learning Disabled; Mentally Handicapped; Communication Disordered; Hearing Impaired/Deaf; Visually Impaired/Blind; Developmentally Disabled; Behaviorally Disabled; Neurologically Disabled. *Learning Problems* Memory Disabilities; Perceptual Disabilities; Thinking Disabilities; Oral Language Disabilities; Reading Disabilities; Handwriting Disabilities; Spelling Disabilities; Arithmetic Disabilities; Written Expression. *Behavioral Problems* Attention Deficits; Hyperactivity; Hypoactivity; Impulsivity; Self-Aggression; Verbal Aggression; Physical Aggression; Indirect Aggression; Passive Aggression; Withdrawal. *Conditions Treated* Early Infantile Autism; Schizophrenia; Aphasia; Phobias; Obsessions and Compulsions; Depression; Suicide; Inadequacy/Immaturity; Personality Problems; Socialized Aggressive Reaction; Unsocialized Aggressive Reaction; Conduct Disorders.

Services Provided Individual Therapy; Group Therapy; Parent Involvement; Behavior Therapy; Cognitive Developmental Therapy; Family Therapy; Filial Therapy; Drug Therapy; Play Therapy; Sign Language; Vocational Training; Speech and Language Therapy; Gross Motor/Sensory Motor Therapy. *Professionals on Staff* Psychiatrists 4; Psychologists 2; Counselors 3; Social Workers 4; Child Care Staff. *Service Facilities Available (with number of rooms)* Home Visits. *Educational Professionals* Special Education Teachers 5; Paraprofessionals 14; Speech and Language Therapists; Recreation Therapists; Occupational Therapist 4. *Curricula* Traditional Academic; Career/Vocational Education; Individualized; Basic Skills; Prevocational. *Educational Intervention Approaches* Progressive Discipline; Self-Control; Behavior Modification.

Comments The center serves children ages 3-22, with a wide range of emotional, behavioral, and developmental problems. Education and mental health specialists use a team approach in planning and implementing the individualized programs for children and their families. The goal is to increase each child's level of functioning so that she/he can be integrated into the public school system and the community.

The Re-Ed West Center for Children Inc

1150 Eastern Ave, Sacramento, CA 95825 (916) 481-8010
Year Established 1966
Contact Nancy Noonan, Exec Dir
Facility Information *Placement* Special School; Private Residential Care. *Number of Beds* 54. *Children/Adolescents Served* 60. *Sexes Served* Both. *Room and Board Fees (Approx)* $51. *Tuition Fees (Approx)* $28,284. *Sources of Funding* State Funds; Health Insurance; Medicare; P.L. 94-142. Summer school available. *Teacher Certification Level* Elementary School. *Special Certification Level* Language Handicapped; Speech Handicapped.
Student/Patient Characteristics *Age Levels* 5-8; 9-11; 12-14. *IQ Ranges* 71-85; 85-130. *Exceptionalities Served* Emotionally Disturbed; Learning Disabled; Mentally Handicapped; Communication Disordered; Gifted. *Learning Problems* Perceptual Disabilities; Thinking Disabilities; Oral Language Disabilities; Reading Disabilities; Handwriting Disabilities; Spelling Disabilities; Arithmetic Disabilities; Written Expression. *Behavioral Problems* Attention Deficits; Hyperactivity; Hypoactivity; Impulsivity; Self-Aggression; Verbal Aggression; Physical Aggression; Indirect Aggression; Passive Aggression; Withdrawal. *Conditions Treated* Alcohol Abuse and/or Drug Abuse; Other Substance Abuse or Dependence; Schizophrenia; Phobias; Obsessions and Compulsions; Depression; Inadequacy/Immaturity; Personality Problems; Socialized Aggressive Reaction; Unsocialized Aggressive Reaction.
Services Provided Individual Therapy; Group Therapy; Parent Involvement; Behavior Therapy; Cognitive Developmental Therapy; Family Therapy; Drug Therapy; Play Therapy. *Professionals on Staff* Psychiatrists 1; Psychologists 1; Counselors 2; Social Workers 5; Child Care Staff 35; Nurses 1. *Service Facilities Available (with number of rooms)* Consultative (ERT) 1; Resource Rooms 1; Special School 4. *Educational Professionals* Special Education Teachers 4; Special Education Counselors 2; Paraprofessionals 8. *Curricula* Traditional Academic; Individualized; Basic Skills; Prevocational. *Educational Intervention Approaches* Engineered Classroom; Progressive Discipline; Behavior Modification. *Degrees Awarded* Graduate Equivalency Diploma.

Sacramento Children's Home—Helen E Cowell Children's Center

2820 14th Ave, Sacramento, CA 95820 (916) 452-4071
Year Established 1867
Contact Barry P Marcus, Asst Dir
Facility Information *Placement* Private Residential Care. *Number of Beds* 20. *Children/Adolescents Served* 20. *Sexes Served* Both. *Tuition Fees (Approx)* $30,024. *Sources of Funding* State Funds; P.L. 94-142. Summer school available. *Special Certification Level* LD.
Student/Patient Characteristics *Age Levels* 5-8; 9-11; 12-14. *IQ Ranges* 71-85; 85-130. *Exceptionalities Served* Emotionally Disturbed; Learning Disabled. *Learning Problems* Memory Disabilities; Perceptual Disabilities; Thinking Disabilities; Oral Language Disabilities; Reading Disabilities; Handwriting Disabilities; Spelling Disabilities; Arithmetic Disabilities; Written Expression. *Behavioral Problems* Attention Deficits; Hyperactivity; Impulsivity; Self-Aggression; Verbal Aggression; Physical Aggression; Indirect Aggression; Passive Aggression; Withdrawal. *Conditions Treated* Depression; Inadequacy/Immaturity; Personality Problems; Socialized Aggressive Reaction.
Services Provided Individual Therapy; Group Therapy; Parent Involvement; Behavior Therapy; Cognitive Developmental Therapy; Family Therapy; Drug Therapy; Art Therapy; Music Therapy; Reality Therapy; Play Therapy. *Professionals on Staff* Psy-

chiatrists; Psychologists; Counselors; Social Workers 2; Child Care Staff 23; Nurses 1. *Service Facilities Available (with number of rooms)* Self-Contained Rooms 1; On-Campus Residential School 4. *Educational Professionals* Special Education Teachers 4. *Curricula* Traditional Academic; Individualized; Basic Skills. *Educational Intervention Approaches* Engineered Classroom; Precision Teaching; Progressive Discipline; Self-Control; Behavior Modification; Applied Behavior Analysis; Creative Conditioning. *Degrees Awarded* Certificate of Attendance.

St George Homes Inc

1727 Euclid Ave, Berkeley, CA 94708 (415) 848-2393
Year Established 1966
Contact Nola Zibaroff, Social Worker
Facility Information *Placement* Special School; Private Residential Care. *Number of Beds* 24. *Children/Adolescents Served* 24. *Sexes Served* Both. *Sources of Funding* State Funds; P.L. 94-142; AFDC. Summer school available. *Teacher Certification Level* High School. *Special Certification Level* Severely Handicapped.
Student/Patient Characteristics *Age Levels* 12-14; 15-17. *IQ Ranges* 71-85; 85-130; Above 130. *Exceptionalities Served* Autistic; Emotionally Disturbed; Learning Disabled; Mentally Handicapped; Communication Disordered. *Learning Problems* Memory Disabilities; Perceptual Disabilities; Thinking Disabilities; Oral Language Disabilities; Reading Disabilities; Handwriting Disabilities; Spelling Disabilities; Arithmetic Disabilities; Written Expression. *Behavioral Problems* Attention Deficits; Hyperactivity; Hypoactivity; Impulsivity; Self-Aggression; Verbal Aggression; Physical Aggression; Indirect Aggression; Passive Aggression; Withdrawal. *Conditions Treated* Disintegrative Psychoses; Schizophrenia; Phobias; Obsessions and Compulsions; Hysteria; Depression; Suicide; Asthma; Inadequacy/Immaturity; Personality Problems; Unsocialized Aggressive Reaction; Psychosis.
Services Provided Individual Therapy; Group Therapy; Parent Involvement; Behavior Therapy; Art Therapy; Music Therapy; Reality Therapy; Play Therapy; Psychodrama; Milieu Therapy. *Professionals on Staff* Psychiatrists; Psychologists; Counselors; Social Workers; Child Care Staff; Nurses. *Service Facilities Available (with number of rooms)* Self-Contained Rooms. *Educational Professionals* Special Education Teachers; Special Education Counselors; Paraprofessionals; Academic Interns. *Curricula* Individualized; Basic Skills; Prevocational. *Educational Intervention Approaches* Creative Conditioning; Analytic Education. *Degrees Awarded* High School Diploma; Graduate Equivalency Diploma.

San Diego County Mental Health Services—Loma Portal Facility

3485 Kenyon St, San Diego, CA 92110 (619) 236-4904
Year Established 1966
Contact Perry B Bach, Child and Adolescent Serv Bureau
Facility Information *Placement* Special Program; Psychiatric Hospital. *Number of Beds* 39. *Children/Adolescents Served* 39. *Sexes Served* Both. *Room and Board Fees (Approx)* $330. *Sources of Funding* State Funds; HEW; Health Insurance; Medicare; P.L. 94-142; CHAMPUS; County Patients. Summer school available. *Teacher Certification Level* Elementary School; Junior High/Middle School; High School. *Special Certification Level* ED; LD; MR; Reading.
Student/Patient Characteristics *Age Levels* 0-4; 5-8; 9-11; 12-14; 15-17. *IQ Ranges* 26-40; 41-55; 56-70; 71-85; 85-130; Above 130. *Exceptionalities Served* Autistic; Emotionally Disturbed; Learning Disabled; Mentally Handicapped; Communication Disordered. *Learning Problems* Memory Disabilities; Perceptual Disabilities; Thinking Disabilities; Oral Language Disabilities; Reading Disabilities; Handwriting Disabilities; Spelling Disabilities; Arithmetic Disabilities; Written Expression. *Behavioral Problems* Attention Deficits; Hyperactivity; Hypoactivity; Impulsivity; Self-Aggression; Verbal Aggression; Physical Aggression; Indirect Aggression; Passive Aggression; Withdrawal. *Conditions Treated* Alcohol Abuse and/or Drug Abuse; Other Substance Abuse or

Dependence; Early Infantile Autism; Disintegrative Psychoses; Schizophrenia; Phobias; Obsessions and Compulsions; Hysteria; Depression; Suicide; Inadequacy/Immaturity; Personality Problems; Socialized Aggressive Reaction; Unsocialized Aggressive Reaction; Affective Disorders; Pervasive Developmental Disabilities.

Services Provided Individual Therapy; Group Therapy; Parent Involvement; Behavior Therapy; Biofeedback; Family Therapy; Drug Therapy; Art Therapy; Music Therapy; Play Therapy; Milieu Therapy. *Professionals on Staff* Psychiatrists 4; Psychologists 3; Counselors 4; Social Workers 2; Nurses 56; Occupational Therapist 2. *Service Facilities Available (with number of rooms)* Consultative (ERT) 4; Transition Rooms 2; Self-Contained Rooms 1; Hospital School. *Educational Professionals* Special Education Teachers 2; Paraprofessionals 5. *Curricula* Traditional Academic; Individualized; Basic Skills; Prevocational. *Educational Intervention Approaches* Engineered Classroom; Precision Teaching; Progressive Discipline; Self-Control; Behavior Modification; Creative Conditioning. *Degrees Awarded* Credits for Attendance.

Comments Programs are licensed acute psychiatric hospitals. One program provides 24-hour diagnostic/treatment services to 19 children and partial day treatment to 4 children. The second program provides 24-hour diagnostic/treatment services to 20 adolescents and partial day treatment to 4 adolescents. Both programs provide on-site classroom instruction.

San Diego Unified School District

4100 Normal St, San Diego, CA 92101 (619) 274-4236
Contact Daniel H Lochtefeld, Dir of Special Ed
Facility Information *Placement* Public School. *Sexes Served* Both. *Sources of Funding* State Funds; P.L. 94-142. Summer school available. *Teacher Certification Level* Elementary School; Junior High/Middle School; High School. *Special Certification Level* ED; LD; MR.

Student/Patient Characteristics *Age Levels* 0-4; 5-8; 9-11; 12-14; 15-17; 18-21; Over 21. *IQ Ranges* 0-25; 26-40; 41-55; 56-70; 71-85; 85-130; Above 130. *Exceptionalities Served* Autistic; Emotionally Disturbed; Learning Disabled; Mentally Handicapped; Communication Disordered; Hearing Impaired/Deaf; Visually Impaired/Blind; Other Health Impaired; Physically Handicapped; Gifted. *Learning Problems* Memory Disabilities; Perceptual Disabilities; Thinking Disabilities; Oral Language Disabilities; Reading Disabilities; Handwriting Disabilities; Spelling Disabilities; Arithmetic Disabilities; Written Expression. *Behavioral Problems* Attention Deficits; Hyperactivity; Hypoactivity; Impulsivity; Self-Aggression; Verbal Aggression; Physical Aggression; Indirect Aggression; Passive Aggression; Withdrawal. *Conditions Treated* Early Infantile Autism; Disintegrative Psychoses; Schizophrenia; Aphasia; Convulsive Disorders; Phobias; Obsessions and Compulsions; Hysteria; Depression; Asthma; Inadequacy/Immaturity; Personality Problems; Socialized Aggressive Reaction; Unsocialized Aggressive Reaction.

Services Provided Parent Involvement; Family Therapy. *Professionals on Staff* Psychologists 41; Social Workers 15; Nurses 12. *Service Facilities Available (with number of rooms)* Consultative (ERT); Itinerants; Resource Rooms; Transition Rooms; Self-Contained Rooms; Special School; Hospital School; Homebound Instruction. *Educational Professionals* Regular School Teachers; Special Education Teachers; Career/Vocational Teachers; Special Education Counselors; Paraprofessionals. *Curricula* Traditional Academic; Career/Vocational Education; Individualized; Basic Skills; Prevocational. *Educational Intervention Approaches* Self-Control; Behavior Modification; Applied Behavior Analysis. *Degrees Awarded* Certificate of Attendance; High School Diploma; Graduate Equivalency Diploma.

San Joaquin County Office of Education—Special Education Programs

3555 Wilmarth Rd, Stockton, CA 95205 (209) 931-4514
Year Established 1955
Contact Jacki Cottingim, Dir

Facility Information *Placement* Public School.
Children/Adolescents Served 400. *Sexes Served* Both. *Sources of Funding* State Funds; P.L. 94-142. Summer school available. *Teacher Certification Level* Elementary School; Junior High/Middle School; High School. *Special Certification Level* ED; LD; MR; Career/Vocational Education; Reading; Math; Severely Handicapped; Communicatively Handicapped.

Student/Patient Characteristics *Age Levels* 0-4; 5-8; 9-11; 12-14; 15-17; 18-21. *IQ Ranges* 0-25; 26-40; 41-55; 56-70; 71-85; 85-130. *Exceptionalities Served* Autistic; Emotionally Disturbed; Learning Disabled; Mentally Handicapped; Communication Disordered; Hearing Impaired/Deaf; Visually Impaired/Blind; Other Health Impaired. *Learning Problems* Memory Disabilities; Perceptual Disabilities; Thinking Disabilities; Oral Language Disabilities; Reading Disabilities; Handwriting Disabilities; Spelling Disabilities; Arithmetic Disabilities; Written Expression. *Behavioral Problems* Attention Deficits; Hyperactivity; Hypoactivity; Impulsivity; Self-Aggression; Verbal Aggression; Physical Aggression; Indirect Aggression; Passive Aggression; Withdrawal. *Conditions Treated* Early Infantile Autism; Aphasia; Phobias; Socialized Aggressive Reaction; Unsocialized Aggressive Reaction.

Services Provided Parent Involvement; Behavior Therapy; Cognitive Developmental Therapy; Music Therapy. *Professionals on Staff* Psychologists 2; Nurses 1. *Service Facilities Available (with number of rooms)* Resource Rooms 10; Self-Contained Rooms 34. *Educational Professionals* Special Education Teachers 34; Career/Vocational Teachers 1; Paraprofessionals 4. *Curricula* Traditional Academic; Career/Vocational Education; Individualized; Basic Skills; Prevocational; Bilingual Instruction; Development Skills. *Educational Intervention Approaches* Precision Teaching; Self-Control; Behavior Modification; Applied Behavior Analysis; Creative Conditioning. *Degrees Awarded* High School Diploma.

San Mateo County Office of Education

333 Main St, Redwood City, CA 94063 (415) 363-5476
Contact H Neufeld, Asst Supt

Facility Information *Placement* Public School; Special School. *Children/Adolescents Served* 40. *Sexes Served* Both. *Sources of Funding* State Funds; P.L. 94-142. Summer school available. *Teacher Certification Level* Elementary School; Junior High/Middle School; High School. *Special Certification Level* Severely Handicapped.

Student/Patient Characteristics *Age Levels* 0-4; 5-8; 9-11; 12-14; 15-17; 18-21. *Exceptionalities Served* Autistic; Emotionally Disturbed; Mentally Handicapped; Communication Disordered; Hearing Impaired/Deaf; Visually Impaired/Blind; Other Health Impaired; Physically Handicapped. *Learning Problems* Memory Disabilities; Perceptual Disabilities; Thinking Disabilities; Oral Language Disabilities; Reading Disabilities; Handwriting Disabilities; Spelling Disabilities; Arithmetic Disabilities; Written Expression. *Behavioral Problems* Attention Deficits; Hyperactivity; Hypoactivity; Impulsivity; Self-Aggression; Verbal Aggression; Physical Aggression; Withdrawal. *Conditions Treated* Early Infantile Autism; Aphasia; Convulsive Disorders; Phobias; Obsessions and Compulsions; Hysteria; Depression; Asthma; Inadequacy/Immaturity; Personality Problems; Socialized Aggressive Reaction; Unsocialized Aggressive Reaction.

Services Provided Individual Therapy; Group Therapy; Parent Involvement; Behavior Therapy; Cognitive Developmental Therapy; Family Therapy; Art Therapy; Music Therapy; Play Therapy; Psychodrama. *Professionals on Staff* Psychologists 5; Social Workers 4; Nurses 5. *Service Facilities Available (with number of rooms)* Itinerants 2; Self-Contained Rooms 106. *Educational Professionals* Special Education Teachers 150; Career/Vocational Teachers 3; Paraprofessionals 110. *Curricula* Career/Vocational Education; Individualized; Basic Skills; Prevocational; Life Skills. *Educational Intervention Approaches* Engineered Classroom; Behavior Modification; Applied Behavior Analysis. *Degrees Awarded* Certificate of Attendance; High School Diploma.

Serendipity Diagnostic and Treatment Center

6441 Matheney Way, Citrus Heights, CA 95621 (916) 726-1955
Year Established 1972
Contact Nancy Lyles, Admissions and Discharge Coord
Facility Information *Placement* Special School; Private Residential Care; Private Day Treatment. *Number of Beds* 24. *Children/Adolescents Served* 36. *Sexes Served* Both. *Room and Board Fees (Approx)* $95. *Tuition Fees (Approx)* $12,360. *Sources of Funding* State Funds; Health Insurance; P.L. 94-142; County. Summer school available. *Teacher Certification Level* Junior High/Middle School; High School. *Special Certification Level* LD; Severely Handicapped.

Student/Patient Characteristics *Age Levels* 12-14; 15-17. *IQ Ranges* 71-85; 85-130; Above 130. *Exceptionalities Served* Emotionally Disturbed. *Learning Problems* Memory Disabilities; Perceptual Disabilities; Thinking Disabilities; Oral Language Disabilities; Reading Disabilities; Handwriting Disabilities; Spelling Disabilities; Arithmetic Disabilities; Written Expression. *Behavioral Problems* Attention Deficits; Hyperactivity; Impulsivity; Self-Aggression; Verbal Aggression; Physical Aggression; Indirect Aggression; Passive Aggression; Withdrawal. *Conditions Treated* Schizophrenia; Convulsive Disorders; Phobias; Obsessions and Compulsions; Hysteria; Depression; Suicide; Anorexia Nervosa; Inadequacy/Immaturity; Personality Problems; Socialized Aggressive Reaction; Unsocialized Aggressive Reaction.

Services Provided Individual Therapy; Group Therapy; Parent Involvement; Behavior Therapy; Family Therapy; Filial Therapy; Drug Therapy; Reality Therapy; Play Therapy; Psychodrama. *Professionals on Staff* Psychiatrists 1; Psychologists 2; Counselors 35; Nurses 1. *Service Facilities Available (with number of rooms)* Therapeutic Classrooms 3. *Educational Professionals* Special Education Teachers 4; Paraprofessionals 4. *Curricula* Individualized; Prevocational; Vocational. *Educational Intervention Approaches* Self-Control; Behavior Modification; Applied Behavior Analysis; Creative Conditioning. *Degrees Awarded* High School Diploma.

Comments Serendipity is a private residential psychiatric treatment program for emotionally disturbed adolescents. It is accredited by the Joint Commission on Accreditation of Hospitals and also provides an on-grounds special education program.

Southwood Psychiatric Residential Treatment Center—Hillcrest

4307 3rd Ave, San Diego, CA 92103 (619) 291-3190
Contact Patti Mellor, Social Serv Dir
Facility Information *Placement* Private Residential Care. *Number of Beds* 48. *Children/Adolescents Served* 48. *Sexes Served* Both. *Room and Board Fees (Approx)* $181. *Sources of Funding* Health Insurance. Summer school available. *Teacher Certification Level* Junior High/Middle School; High School. *Special Certification Level* ED; Reading; Math.

Student/Patient Characteristics *Age Levels* 12-14; 15-17. *IQ Ranges* 71-85; 85-130; Above 130. *Exceptionalities Served* Emotionally Disturbed; Learning Disabled; Gifted. *Learning Problems* Memory Disabilities; Perceptual Disabilities; Thinking Disabilities; Reading Disabilities; Spelling Disabilities; Arithmetic Disabilities; Written Expression. *Behavioral Problems* Attention Deficits; Hyperactivity; Hypoactivity; Impulsivity; Self-Aggression; Verbal Aggression; Indirect Aggression; Passive Aggression; Withdrawal. *Conditions Treated* Alcohol Abuse and/or Drug Abuse; Other Substance Abuse or Dependence; Schizophrenia; Phobias; Obsessions and Compulsions; Hysteria; Depression; Suicide; Inadequacy/Immaturity; Personality Problems; Socialized Aggressive Reaction; Unsocialized Aggressive Reaction.

Services Provided Individual Therapy; Group Therapy; Parent Involvement; Behavior Therapy; Family Therapy; Drug Therapy; Art Therapy; Reality Therapy; Play Therapy; Psychodrama; Occupation Therapy; Recreation Therapy. *Professionals on Staff* Psychiatrists 14; Psychologists 6; Counselors 30; Social Workers 4; Nurses 6; Activity Deptartment 5; Speech Therapist 1. *Service Facilities Available (with number of rooms)* On-Campus Residential School 4. *Educational Professionals* Regular School Teachers 4; Teacher Aides 4. *Curricula* Traditional Academic; Individualized; Basic Skills; Prevocational. *Educational Intervention Approaches* Progressive Discipline; Self-Control; Behavior Modification. *Degrees Awarded* High School Diploma.

Spectrum Center for Educational and Behavioral Development Inc

1916 A Martin Luther King Jr Way, Berkeley, CA 94703 (415) 845-1321
Year Established 1975
Contact Martha Schultz, Prog Coord
Facility Information *Placement* Special School; Private Residential Care; Special Program; Vocational Training Program and Adult Skills Center. *Number of Beds* 18. *Children/Adolescents Served* 18 (residential program); 100 (day school). *Sexes Served* Both. *Sources of Funding* State Funds; P.L. 94-142. Summer school available. *Teacher Certification Level* Elementary School; Junior High/Middle School; High School. *Special Certification Level* ED; LD; MR; Career/Vocational Education; Severely Handicapped.

Student/Patient Characteristics *Age Levels* 5-8; 9-11; 12-14; 15-17; 18-21; Over 21. *IQ Ranges* 0-25; 26-40; 41-55; 56-70; 71-85; 85-130. *Exceptionalities Served* Autistic; Emotionally Disturbed; Learning Disabled; Mentally Handicapped; Communication Disordered; Hearing Impaired/Deaf; Visually Impaired/Blind; Other Health Impaired; Physically Handicapped. *Learning Problems* Memory Disabilities; Perceptual Disabilities; Thinking Disabilities; Oral Language Disabilities; Reading Disabilities; Handwriting Disabilities; Spelling Disabilities; Arithmetic Disabilities; Written Expression. *Behavioral Problems* Attention Deficits; Hyperactivity; Hypoactivity; Impulsivity; Self-Aggression; Verbal Aggression; Physical Aggression; Indirect Aggression; Passive Aggression; Withdrawal. *Conditions Treated* Early Infantile Autism; Disintegrative Psychoses; Schizophrenia; Aphasia; Convulsive Disorders; Inadequacy/Immaturity; Personality Problems; Socialized Aggressive Reaction; Unsocialized Aggressive Reaction.

Services Provided Individual Therapy; Parent Involvement; Behavior Therapy; Cognitive Developmental Therapy; Family Therapy; Drug Therapy. *Professionals on Staff* Psychiatrists 1; Psychologists 3; Counselors 3. *Service Facilities Available (with number of rooms)* Consultative (ERT) 4; Itinerants 4; Self-Contained Rooms 11. *Educational Professionals* Special Education Teachers 13; Career/Vocational Teachers 2; Special Education Counselors 3; Paraprofessionals 18; Speech Therapists; Occupational Therapists. *Curricula* Traditional Academic; Career/Vocational Education; Individualized; Basic Skills; Prevocational. *Educational Intervention Approaches* Engineered Classroom; Precision Teaching; Self-Control; Behavior Modification; Applied Behavior Analysis. *Degrees Awarded* Certificate of Attendance; High School Diploma; Graduate Equivalency Diploma.

Comments The Spectrum Center provides severely handicapped individuals with vocational, communication, and independent living skills.

Sunny Hills Children's Services

300 Sunny Hills Dr, San Anselmo, CA 94960 (415) 487-3200
Year Established 1895
Contact Alice Wilkins, Intake Social Worker
Facility Information *Placement* Private Residential Care. *Number of Beds* 40. *Children/Adolescents Served* 40. *Sexes Served* Both. *Tuition Fees (Approx)* $36,084. *Sources of Funding* State Funds; Health Insurance. Summer school available. *Teacher Certification Level* Junior High/Middle School; High School. *Special Certification Level* Reading; Math; Special Ed.

Student/Patient Characteristics *Age Levels* 12-14; 15-17. *IQ Ranges* 85-130. *Exceptionalities Served* Autistic; Hearing Impaired/Deaf; Visually Impaired/Blind. *Learning Problems* Memory Disabilities; Perceptual Disabilities; Thinking Disabilities; Oral Language Disabilities; Reading Disabilities; Handwriting Disabilities; Spelling Disabilities; Arithmetic Disabilities;

Written Expression. *Behavioral Problems* Attention Deficits; Hyperactivity; Hypoactivity; Impulsivity; Self-Aggression; Verbal Aggression; Physical Aggression; Indirect Aggression; Passive Aggression; Withdrawal.

Switzer Center

1110 Sartori, Torrance, CA 90501 (213) 328-3611
Year Established 1966
Contact Janet Switzer, Exec Dir
Facility Information *Placement* Private Special School. *Children/Adolescents Served* 90. *Sexes Served* Both. *Tuition Fees (Approx)* $9,000 (10 months); $10,350 (extended year). *Sources of Funding* State Funds; Health Insurance; Parent Fees. Summer school available. *Teacher Certification Level* Elementary School; Junior High/Middle School; High School. *Special Certification Level* ED; LD; MR; Reading; Math.
Student/Patient Characteristics *Age Levels* 5-8; 9-11; 12-14; 15-17; 18-21. *IQ Ranges* 71-85; 85-130. *Exceptionalities Served* Emotionally Disturbed; Learning Disabled; Mentally Handicapped; Communication Disordered. *Learning Problems* Memory Disabilities; Perceptual Disabilities; Thinking Disabilities; Oral Language Disabilities; Reading Disabilities; Handwriting Disabilities; Spelling Disabilities; Arithmetic Disabilities; Written Expression; Developmental Dyslexia. *Behavioral Problems* Attention Deficits; Hyperactivity; Hypoactivity; Impulsivity; Self-Aggression; Verbal Aggression; Physical Aggression; Indirect Aggression; Passive Aggression; Withdrawal. *Conditions Treated* Schizophrenia; Aphasia; Convulsive Disorders; Phobias; Obsessions and Compulsions; Depression; Suicide; Inadequacy/Immaturity; Personality Problems; Socialized Aggressive Reaction; Unsocialized Aggressive Reaction.
Services Provided Individual Therapy; Group Therapy; Parent Involvement; Behavior Therapy; Cognitive Developmental Therapy; Family Therapy; Reality Therapy; Play Therapy. *Professionals on Staff* Psychiatrists 1; Psychologists 6; Counselors 2; Social Workers 1; Child Care Staff 26; Sensory Motor 1; Speech Pathologist 1. *Service Facilities Available (with number of rooms)* Special School 8. *Educational Professionals* Regular School Teachers 11; Special Education Teachers 15; Crisis Teachers 2; Special Education Counselors 9; Paraprofessionals 1. *Curricula* Career/Vocational Education; Individualized; Basic Skills; Prevocational. *Educational Intervention Approaches* Precision Teaching; Progressive Discipline; Self-Control; Behavior Modification. *Degrees Awarded* High School Diploma.

Comments Switzer Center provides diagnostic and hourly services in addition to its school. The staff is full-time and assists students in crisis as well as for ongoing counseling. While many therapies are possible, a cognitive-developmental educational approach is used whenever appropriate.

The Sycamores

2933 N El Nido Dr, Altadena, CA 91001 (818) 798-0853
Year Established 1902
Contact Steven E Elson, Exec Dir
Facility Information *Placement* Special School; Private Residential Care. *Number of Beds* 54. *Children/Adolescents Served* 54. *Sexes Served* Male. *Tuition Fees (Approx)* $25,608-$28,800. *Sources of Funding* State Funds; P.L. 94-142 Private Donations. Summer school available. *Teacher Certification Level* Elementary School; Junior High/Middle School; High School. *Special Certification Level* ED; LD; Reading; Math.
Student/Patient Characteristics *Age Levels* 9-11; 12-14. *IQ Ranges* 71-85; 85-130. *Exceptionalities Served* Emotionally Disturbed; Learning Disabled. *Learning Problems* Memory Disabilities; Perceptual Disabilities; Thinking Disabilities; Oral Language Disabilities; Reading Disabilities; Handwriting Disabilities; Spelling Disabilities; Arithmetic Disabilities; Written Expression. *Behavioral Problems* Attention Deficits; Hyperactivity; Impulsivity; Verbal Aggression; Physical Aggression; Indirect Aggression; Passive Aggression; Withdrawal. *Conditions Treated* Phobias; Depression; Personality Problems; Socialized Aggressive Reaction; Unsocialized Aggressive Reaction.

Services Provided Individual Therapy; Group Therapy; Parent Involvement; Behavior Therapy; Family Therapy; Drug Therapy; Art Therapy; Reality Therapy; Play Therapy; Recreational Therapy. *Professionals on Staff* Psychiatrists .5; Psychologists 2; Counselors 2; Social Workers 4; Child Care Staff 30; Nurses 1; Recreational Therapist 1; Art Therapist 1. *Service Facilities Available (with number of rooms)* Consultative (ERT) 2; Resource Rooms 1; Self-Contained Rooms 3. *Educational Professionals* Special Education Teachers 4. *Curricula* Traditional Academic; Individualized; Basic Skills. *Educational Intervention Approaches* Engineered Classroom; Self-Control; Behavior Modification.

Total Living Continuum

391 Loma Dr, Camarillo, CA 90310 (805) 987-9121
Year Established 1979
Contact Barbara Bontrager, Tobias Site Dir
Facility Information *Placement* Private Residential Care. *Number of Beds* 18. *Children/Adolescents Served* 18. *Sexes Served* Both. *Sources of Funding* State Funds; Medicaid; Medicare.
Student/Patient Characteristics *Age Levels* 18-21; Over 21. *IQ Ranges* 26-40; 41-55; 56-70; 71-85. *Exceptionalities Served* Autistic; Emotionally Disturbed; Mentally Handicapped; Hearing Impaired/Deaf. *Learning Problems* Memory Disabilities; Perceptual Disabilities; Thinking Disabilities; Oral Language Disabilities; Reading Disabilities; Handwriting Disabilities; Spelling Disabilities; Arithmetic Disabilities; Written Expression. *Behavioral Problems* Attention Deficits; Hyperactivity; Hypoactivity; Impulsivity; Self-Aggression; Verbal Aggression; Physical Aggression; Indirect Aggression; Passive Aggression; Withdrawal. *Conditions Treated* Early Infantile Autism; Schizophrenia; Convulsive Disorders; Obsessions and Compulsions.
Services Provided Parent Involvement; Behavior Therapy. *Professionals on Staff* Psychiatrists 1; Psychologists 2; Social Workers 1; Behavior Programmers 12. *Educational Professionals* Paraprofessionals 6. *Curricula* Career/Vocational Education; Individualized; Basic Skills. *Educational Intervention Approaches* Self-Control; Behavior Modification; Applied Behavior Analysis.

University of California at Los Angeles—Fernald

405 Hilgard, Los Angeles, CA 90024 (213) 825-3278
Year Established 1921
Contact Linda Taylor, Asst Dir
Facility Information *Placement* Special School. *Children/Adolescents Served* 340. *Sexes Served* Both. *Tuition Fees (Approx)* $4,675. *Sources of Funding* P.L. 94-142; Private Donations. Summer school available. *Teacher Certification Level* Elementary School; Junior High/Middle School; High School. *Special Certification Level* LD; Severely Handicapped.
Student/Patient Characteristics *Age Levels* 5-8; 9-11; 12-14; 15-17; 18-21; Over 21. *IQ Ranges* 85-130; Above 130. *Exceptionalities Served* Emotionally Disturbed; Learning Disabled. *Learning Problems* Memory Disabilities; Perceptual Disabilities; Thinking Disabilities; Oral Language Disabilities; Reading Disabilities; Handwriting Disabilities; Spelling Disabilities; Arithmetic Disabilities; Written Expression. *Behavioral Problems* Attention Deficits; Hyperactivity; Impulsivity; Verbal Aggression; Physical Aggression; Indirect Aggression; Passive Aggression; Withdrawal.
Services Provided Individual Therapy; Group Therapy; Family Therapy; Play Therapy. *Professionals on Staff* Psychologists 13. *Service Facilities Available (with number of rooms)* Homebound Instruction 4; Enrichment Rooms 5. *Educational Professionals* Special Education Teachers 6. *Curricula* Individualized; Basic Skills; Prevocational. *Educational Intervention Approaches* Motivational Program. *Degrees Awarded* High School Diploma.

Ventura County Superintendent of Schools

535 E Main St, Ventura, CA 93009 (805) 652-7321
Contact James Foster, Dir of Special Educ

Facility Information *Placement* Public School; Special Program; Re-ed Day Care with County Mental Health. *Children/Adolescents Served* 26. *Sexes Served* Both. *Sources of Funding* State Funds; P.L. 94-142. Summer school available. *Teacher Certification Level* Elementary School; Junior High/Middle School; High School. *Special Certification Level* ED; LD; MR; Severely Handicapped.

Student/Patient Characteristics *Age Levels* 12-14; 15-17. *IQ Ranges* 71-85; 85-130. *Exceptionalities Served* Emotionally Disturbed; Behavior Disordered. *Learning Problems* Memory Disabilities; Perceptual Disabilities; Thinking Disabilities; Oral Language Disabilities; Reading Disabilities; Handwriting Disabilities; Spelling Disabilities; Arithmetic Disabilities; Written Expression. *Behavioral Problems* Attention Deficits; Hyperactivity; Hypoactivity; Impulsivity; Self-Aggression; Verbal Aggression; Physical Aggression; Indirect Aggression; Passive Aggression; Withdrawal. *Conditions Treated* Disintegrative Psychoses; Schizophrenia; Phobias; Obsessions and Compulsions; Hysteria; Depression; Suicide; Inadequacy/Immaturity; Personality Problems; Socialized Aggressive Reaction; Unsocialized Aggressive Reaction.

Services Provided Individual Therapy; Group Therapy; Parent Involvement; Behavior Therapy; Family Therapy. *Professionals on Staff* Psychiatrists 1; Psychologists 1; Counselors 2; Social Workers 1; Nurses 1; Speech Therapist 1. *Service Facilities Available (with number of rooms)* Self-Contained Rooms 3. *Educational Professionals* Special Education Teachers 2; Paraprofessionals 2; Teacher Counselors 2. *Curricula* Individualized. *Educational Intervention Approaches* Engineered Classroom; Precision Teaching; Behavior Modification.

Comments This program uses a re-ed model. It is a highly structured program utilizing small group process, individual counseling, behavior modification, individualized and group academic instruction and remediation, structured socialization, recreation (including camping) and vocational training.

Villa Esperanza

2116 E Villa St, Pasadena, CA 91107 (818) 449-2919
Year Established 1960
Contact Carol J Zoeller, Educ Admin

Facility Information *Placement* Special School; Private Residential Care; Private Day Care. *Number of Beds* 12. *Children/Adolescents Served* 12 (residential); 60 (day program). *Sexes Served* Both. *Room and Board Fees (Approx)* $50. *Tuition Fees (Approx)* $8,400. *Sources of Funding* State Funds; Medicaid; Medicare; P.L. 94-142; Social Security Insurance. Summer school available. *Teacher Certification Level* Elementary School; Junior High/Middle School; High School. *Special Certification Level* ED; LD; MR.

Student/Patient Characteristics *Age Levels* 0-4; 5-8; 9-11; 12-14; 15-17; 18-21; Over 21. *IQ Ranges* 0-25; 26-40; 41-55; 56-70; 71-85. *Exceptionalities Served* Autistic; Emotionally Disturbed; Learning Disabled; Mentally Handicapped; Communication Disordered. *Learning Problems* Memory Disabilities; Perceptual Disabilities; Thinking Disabilities; Oral Language Disabilities; Reading Disabilities; Handwriting Disabilities; Spelling Disabilities; Arithmetic Disabilities; Written Expression. *Behavioral Problems* Attention Deficits; Hyperactivity; Impulsivity; Self-Aggression; Verbal Aggression; Physical Aggression; Withdrawal. *Conditions Treated* Early Infantile Autism; Obsessions and Compulsions; Inadequacy/Immaturity; Personality Problems.

Services Provided Individual Therapy; Parent Involvement; Music Therapy. *Professionals on Staff* Psychologists 2; Social Workers 1; Child Care Staff 10; Nurses 1. *Service Facilities Available (with number of rooms)* Self-Contained Rooms 8; Hospital School; On-Campus Residential School. *Educational Professionals* Special Education Teachers 4; Career/Vocational Teachers 3; Paraprofessionals 5. *Curricula* Traditional Academic; Career/Vocational Education; Individualized; Basic Skills; Prevocational; Critical Skills Model. *Educational Intervention Approaches* Precision Teaching; Self-Control; Behavior Modification. *Degrees Awarded* High School Diploma.

Vista Del Mar Child Care Service

3200 Motor Ave, Los Angeles, CA 90034 (213) 836-1223
Year Established 1908
Contact Samuel P Berman, Exec Dir

Facility Information *Placement* Public School; Special Program. *Number of Beds* 109. *Sexes Served* Both. *Room and Board Fees (Approx)* Sliding Scale. *Tuition Fees (Approx)* $36,500. *Sources of Funding* State Funds; Private.

Student/Patient Characteristics *Age Levels* 5-8; 9-11; 12-14; 15-17. *IQ Ranges* 85-130. *Exceptionalities Served* Emotionally Disturbed; Learning Disabled; Gifted. *Learning Problems* Memory Disabilities; Perceptual Disabilities; Thinking Disabilities; Oral Language Disabilities; Reading Disabilities; Handwriting Disabilities. *Behavioral Problems* Attention Deficits; Hyperactivity; Hypoactivity; Impulsivity; Self-Aggression; Verbal Aggression; Physical Aggression; Indirect Aggression; Passive Aggression; Withdrawal. *Conditions Treated* Phobias; Obsessions and Compulsions; Depression; Asthma; Anorexia Nervosa; Inadequacy/Immaturity; Personality Problems; Socialized Aggressive Reaction; Unsocialized Aggressive Reaction.

Services Provided Individual Therapy; Group Therapy; Parent Involvement; Behavior Therapy; Family Therapy; Drug Therapy; Art Therapy; Music Therapy; Reality Therapy; Movement Therapy. *Professionals on Staff* Psychiatrists 3; Psychologists 1; Counselors 65; Social Workers 10; Child Care Staff 65; Nurses 3. *Curricula* Traditional Academic; Individualized; Basic Skills; Prevocational. *Educational Intervention Approaches* Behavior Modification. *Degrees Awarded* High School Diploma; Graduate Equivalency Diploma.

Work Training Program Inc

5650 Shoup Ave, Woodland Hills, CA 91367 (818) 999-5080
Year Established 1964
Contact Harriet Rechtman, Proj Mgr

Facility Information *Placement* Special School; Private Residential Care; Special Program. *Number of Beds* 40. *Children/Adolescents Served* 100. *Sexes Served* Both. *Tuition Fees (Approx)* $28,200. *Sources of Funding* Social Security Insurance; CA Regional Centers; Private. Summer school available. *Teacher Certification Level* Elementary School; Junior High/Middle School; High School. *Special Certification Level* ED; LD; MR; Career/Vocational Education.

Student/Patient Characteristics *Age Levels* 18-21; Over 21. *IQ Ranges* 56-70; 71-85; 85-130. *Exceptionalities Served* Autistic; Learning Disabled; Communication Disordered; Visually Impaired/Blind; Other Health Impaired; Physically Handicapped; Developmentally Disabled. *Learning Problems* Memory Disabilities; Perceptual Disabilities; Thinking Disabilities; Oral Language Disabilities; Reading Disabilities; Handwriting Disabilities; Spelling Disabilities; Arithmetic Disabilities; Written Expression. *Behavioral Problems* Attention Deficits; Hyperactivity; Hypoactivity; Impulsivity; Self-Aggression; Verbal Aggression; Physical Aggression; Indirect Aggression; Passive Aggression; Withdrawal. *Conditions Treated* Aphasia; Convulsive Disorders.

Services Provided Individual Therapy; Group Therapy; Parent Involvement; Behavior Therapy; Cognitive Developmental Therapy. *Professionals on Staff* Psychiatrists; Psychologists; Counselors; Behavior Analysts 2. *Educational Professionals* Special Education Teachers 4; Career/Vocational Teachers 10; Paraprofessionals 6. *Curricula* Career/Vocational Education; Individualized; Basic Skills; Prevocational; Consumer Education; Social and Survival Skills. *Educational Intervention Approaches* Behavior Modification; Applied Behavior Analysis. *Degrees Awarded* Certificate of Completion.

Work Training Program Inc

227 N Nopal, Santa Barbara, CA 93103 (805) 963-1685
Year Established 1964
Contact David Farris, Client Services Coord

Facility Information *Placement* Special School; Private Residential Care. *Sexes Served* Both. *Sources of Funding* State Funds; Social Security Insurance; Private. Summer school available. *Special Certification Level* Career/Vocational Education; Adult Basic Education.

Student/Patient Characteristics *Age Levels* 18-21; Over 21. *IQ Ranges* 56-70; 71-85; 85-130. *Exceptionalities Served* Autistic; Emotionally Disturbed; Learning Disabled; Mentally Handicapped. *Learning Problems* Memory Disabilities; Perceptual Disabilities; Thinking Disabilities; Oral Language Disabilities; Reading Disabilities; Handwriting Disabilities; Spelling Disabilities; Arithmetic Disabilities; Written Expression. *Behavioral Problems* Attention Deficits; Hyperactivity; Hypoactivity; Impulsivity; Verbal Aggression; Indirect Aggression; Passive Aggression; Withdrawal. *Conditions Treated* Disintegrative Psychoses; Schizophrenia; Convulsive Disorders; Phobias; Obsessions and Compulsions; Hysteria; Depression; Inadequacy/Immaturity; Personality Problems.

Services Provided Parent Involvement; Behavior Therapy. *Professionals on Staff* Psychiatrists 1; Psychologists 1; Counselors 20; Social Workers 2. *Educational Professionals* Special Education Teachers 3; Career/Vocational Teachers 4; Special Education Counselors 2. *Curricula* Career/Vocational Education; Basic Skills; Prevocational Consumerism; Social Skills; Independent Living Skills. *Educational Intervention Approaches* Behavior Modification; Applied Behavior Analysis. *Degrees Awarded* Certificate of Attendance.

Zonta Children's Center

4300 Bucknall Rd, San Jose, CA 95130 (408) 374-9050
Year Established 1964
Contact Carol Zimbelman, Dir

Facility Information *Placement* Special School; Private Residential Care; Private Day Care. *Number of Beds* 48. *Children/Adolescents Served* 48. *Sexes Served* Both. *Tuition Fees (Approx)* $11,000-$14,000. *Sources of Funding* State Funds; P.L. 94-142; County. Summer school available. *Teacher Certification Level* Elementary School. *Special Certification Level* Severely Handicapped; Learning Handicapped.

Student/Patient Characteristics *Age Levels* 0-4; 5-8; 9-11; 12-14. *IQ Ranges* 0-25; 26-40; 41-55; 56-70; 71-85; 85-130. *Exceptionalities Served* Autistic; Emotionally Disturbed. *Learning Problems* Memory Disabilities; Perceptual Disabilities; Thinking Disabilities; Oral Language Disabilities; Reading Disabilities; Handwriting Disabilities; Spelling Disabilities; Arithmetic Disabilities; Written Expression. *Behavioral Problems* Attention Deficits; Hyperactivity; Hypoactivity; Impulsivity; Self-Aggression; Verbal Aggression; Physical Aggression; Indirect Aggression; Passive Aggression; Withdrawal. *Conditions Treated* Early Infantile Autism; Schizophrenia; Obsessions and Compulsions; Depression; Personality Problems; Socialized Aggressive Reaction; Unsocialized Aggressive Reaction.

Services Provided Group Therapy; Parent Involvement; Behavior Therapy; Family Therapy; Play Therapy. *Professionals on Staff* Social Workers 2; Child Care Staff 4. *Service Facilities Available (with number of rooms)* Self-Contained Rooms 6. *Educational Professionals* Special Education Teachers 4; Paraprofessionals 15. *Curricula* Individualized; Basic Skills; Prevocational. *Educational Intervention Approaches* Self-Control; Behavior Modification.

Colorado

Adams County Adolescent Day Treatment Program

7780 York St, Denver, CO 80229 (303) 288-6638
Year Established 1980
Contact Chris Bonner, Dir

Facility Information *Placement* Mental Health Partial Care Program. *Children/Adolescents Served* 25. *Sexes Served* Both. *Sources of Funding* State Funds; Medicaid; P.L. 94-142. Summer school available. *Teacher Certification Level* Elementary School; Junior High/Middle School; High School. *Special Certification Level* ED; LD.

Student/Patient Characteristics *Age Levels* 12-14; 15-17. *IQ Ranges* 85-130. *Exceptionalities Served* Emotionally Disturbed; Learning Disabled; Physically Handicapped. *Learning Problems* Perceptual Disabilities; Thinking Disabilities; Reading Disabilities; Spelling Disabilities; Arithmetic Disabilities; Written Expression. *Behavioral Problems* Impulsivity; Verbal Aggression; Physical Aggression; Indirect Aggression; Passive Aggression; Withdrawal. *Conditions Treated* Alcohol Abuse and/or Drug Abuse; Convulsive Disorders; Phobias; Obsessions and Compulsions; Depression; Suicide; Asthma; Anorexia Nervosa; Inadequacy/Immaturity; Personality Problems; Socialized Aggressive Reaction; Unsocialized Aggressive Reaction.

Services Provided Individual Therapy; Group Therapy; Parent Involvement; Behavior Therapy; Family Therapy; Filial Therapy; Play Therapy. *Professionals on Staff* Psychiatrists 1; Psychologists 1; Counselors 3; Social Workers 1; Child Care Staff 1. *Educational Professionals* Special Education Teachers 2; Career/Vocational Teachers 1; Paraprofessionals 1. *Curricula* Individualized; Basic Skills; Prevocational. *Educational Intervention Approaches* Precision Teaching; Self-Control; Behavior Modification. *Degrees Awarded* Certificate of Attendance.

Comments This program is an alternative to out-of-home placement for Adams County adolescents. The goals of the program are to return the adolescent to his/her home school district.

Aurora Adolescent Day Resource Center

1646 Elmira, Aurora, CO 80010 (303) 344-9260
Year Established 1980
Contact Maggie Byrnes, Team Leader

Facility Information *Placement* Special School; Private Day Care. *Number of Beds* 16. *Children/Adolescents Served* 16. *Sexes Served* Both. *Tuition Fees (Approx)* $9,600. *Sources of Funding* State Funds; Health Insurance; Medicaid; P.L. 94-142. Summer school available. *Teacher Certification Level* Junior High/Middle School; High School. *Special Certification Level* ED; Reading; Math.

Student/Patient Characteristics *Age Levels* 12-14; 15-17. *IQ Ranges* 85-130; Above 130. *Exceptionalities Served* Emotionally Disturbed; Learning Disabled; Mentally Handicapped. *Learning Problems* Memory Disabilities; Perceptual Disabilities; Thinking Disabilities; Oral Language Disabilities; Reading Disabilities; Handwriting Disabilities; Spelling Disabilities; Arithmetic Disabilities; Written Expression. *Behavioral Problems* Attention Deficits; Hyperactivity; Hypoactivity; Impulsivity; Self-Aggression; Verbal Aggression; Physical Aggression; Indirect Aggression; Passive Aggression; Withdrawal. *Conditions Treated* Alcohol Abuse and/or Drug Abuse; Other Substance Abuse or Dependence; Schizophrenia; Phobias; Obsessions and Compulsions; Hysteria; Depression; Suicide; Asthma; Anorexia Nervosa; Ulcerative Colitis; Inadequacy/Immaturity; Personality Problems; Socialized Aggressive Reaction; Unsocialized Aggressive Reaction.

Services Provided Individual Therapy; Group Therapy; Parent Involvement; Behavior Therapy; Family Therapy; Filial Therapy; Drug Therapy; Art Therapy; Reality Therapy. *Professionals on Staff* Psychiatrists 1; Psychologists 1; Counselors 2; Social Workers 2. *Service Facilities Available (with number of rooms)* Consultative (ERT) 4; Resource Rooms 3. *Educational Professionals* Regular School Teachers 1; Special Education Teachers 2. *Curricula* Traditional Academic; Career/Vocational Education; Individualized; Basic Skills; Prevocational.

Colorado Springs School District No. 11

1115 N El Paso, Colorado Springs, CO 80903 (303) 635-6704
Contact Rod Schofield, Supv

Facility Information *Placement* Public School; Special School; Special Program. *Children/Adolescents Served* 30,000. *Sexes Served* Both. *Tuition Fees (Approx)* $2,600. *Sources of Funding* State Funds; P.L. 94-142. Summer school available. *Teacher Certification Level* Elementary School; Junior High/Middle School; High School. *Special Certification Level* ED; LD; MR; Career/Vocational Education; Reading; Math.

Student/Patient Characteristics *Age Levels* 0-4; 5-8; 9-11; 12-14; 15-17. *IQ Ranges* 26-40; 41-55; 56-70; 71-85; 85-130; Above 130. *Exceptionalities Served* Autistic; Emotionally Disturbed; Learning Disabled; Mentally Handicapped; Communication Disordered; Hearing Impaired/Deaf; Visually Impaired/Blind; Other Health Impaired; Physically Handicapped; Gifted. *Learning Problems* Memory Disabilities; Perceptual Disabilities; Thinking Disabilities; Oral Language Disabilities; Reading Disabilities; Handwriting Disabilities; Spelling Disabilities; Arithmetic Disabilities; Written Expression. *Behavioral Problems* Attention Deficits; Hyperactivity; Hypoactivity; Impulsivity; Self-Aggression; Verbal Aggression; Physical Aggression; Indirect Aggression; Passive Aggression; Withdrawal. *Conditions Treated* Alcohol Abuse and/or Drug Abuse; Other Substance Abuse or Dependence; Phobias; Obsessions and Compulsions; Hysteria; Depression; Suicide; Anorexia Nervosa; Inadequacy/Immaturity; Personality Problems; Socialized Aggressive Reaction; Unsocialized Aggressive Reaction.

Services Provided Individual Therapy; Group Therapy; Parent Involvement; Behavior Therapy; Cognitive Developmental Therapy; Family Therapy; Reality Therapy; Play Therapy. *Professionals on Staff* Psychologists 9; Counselors 30; Social Workers 27; Nurses 9. *Service Facilities Available (with number of rooms)* Consultative (ERT) 10; Itinerants 100; Resource Rooms 55; Transition Rooms 2; Self-Contained Rooms 25; Homebound Instruction. *Educational Professionals* Regular School Teachers 1500; Special Education Teachers 200; Career/Vocational Teachers 10; Paraprofessionals 45. *Curricula* Traditional Academic; Career/Vocational Education; Individualized; Basic Skills. *Educational Intervention Approaches* Precision Teaching; Behavior Modification; Affective Education. *Degrees Awarded* High School Diploma.

Colorado West Regional Mental Health Center

829 Grand Ave, Glenwood Springs, CO 81601 (303) 945-2241
Year Established 1972
Contact Kenneth Stein, Exec Dir

Facility Information *Placement* Mental Health Clinic. *Sexes Served* Both. *Sources of Funding* State Funds; Health Insurance; Medicaid; Medicare; P.L. 94-142; Client Fees.

Student/Patient Characteristics *Age Levels* 0-4; 5-8; 9-11; 12-14; 15-17; 18-21; Over 21. *IQ Ranges* 26-40; 41-55; 56-70; 71-85; 85-130; Above 130. *Exceptionalities Served* Emotionally Disturbed; Learning Disabled; Mentally Handicapped; Communication Disordered; Other Health Impaired; Physically Handicapped. *Learning Problems* Memory Disabilities; Perceptual Disabilities; Thinking Disabilities; Oral Language Disabilities; Reading Disabilities; Handwriting Disabilities; Spelling Disabilities; Arithmetic Disabilities; Written Expression. *Behavioral Problems* Attention Deficits; Hyperactivity; Hypoactivity; Impulsivity; Self-Aggression; Verbal Aggression; Physical Aggression; Indirect Aggression; Passive Aggression; Withdrawal. *Conditions Treated* Alcohol Abuse and/or Drug Abuse; Other Substance Abuse or Dependence; Schizophrenia; Convulsive Disorders; Phobias; Obsessions and Compulsions; Hysteria; Depression; Suicide; Anorexia Nervosa; Ulcerative Colitis; Inadequacy/Immaturity; Personality Problems; Socialized Aggressive Reaction; Unsocialized Aggressive Reaction.

Services Provided Individual Therapy; Group Therapy; Parent Involvement; Behavior Therapy; Family Therapy; Filial Therapy; Drug Therapy; Reality Therapy; Play Therapy. *Professionals on Staff* Psychiatrists 3; Psychologists 8; Counselors; Social Workers 22; Nurses 3.

Excelsior Youth Center

15001 E Oxford Ave, Aurora, CO 80014 (303) 693-1550
Year Established 1973
Contact Terry Hoffman, Admissions Dir

Facility Information *Placement* Special School; Private Residential Care; Special Program. *Number of Beds* 111. *Children/Adolescents Served* 111. *Sexes Served* Female. *Sources of Funding* State Funds; Health Insurance; Medicaid; P.L. 94-142; Private. Summer school available. *Teacher Certification Level* Junior High/Middle School; High School. *Special Certification Level* ED; LD; Career/Vocational Education; Reading; Math; Social Studies; Music/Drama.

Student/Patient Characteristics *Age Levels* 12-14; 15-17; 18-21. *IQ Ranges* 71-85; 85-130; Above 130. *Exceptionalities Served* Emotionally Disturbed; Learning Disabled; Communication Disordered; Hearing Impaired/Deaf; Other Health Impaired; Physically Handicapped; Gifted; Developmental Disabilities. *Learning Problems* Memory Disabilities; Perceptual Disabilities; Thinking Disabilities; Oral Language Disabilities; Reading Disabilities; Spelling Disabilities; Arithmetic Disabilities; Written Expression. *Behavioral Problems* Attention Deficits; Hyperactivity; Impulsivity; Self-Aggression; Verbal Aggression; Physical Aggression; Indirect Aggression; Passive Aggression; Withdrawal. *Conditions Treated* Alcohol Abuse and/or Drug Abuse; Other Substance Abuse or Dependence; Convulsive Disorders; Phobias; Obsessions and Compulsions; Depression; Suicide; Asthma; Anorexia Nervosa; Ulcerative Colitis; Inadequacy/Immaturity; Personality Problems; Socialized Aggressive Reaction; Unsocialized Aggressive Reaction.

Services Provided Individual Therapy; Group Therapy; Parent Involvement; Behavior Therapy; Family Therapy; Filial Therapy; Drug Therapy; Reality Therapy; Play Therapy. *Professionals on Staff* Psychiatrists 2; Psychologists 2; Counselors; Social Workers; Child Care Staff; Nurses 2. *Service Facilities Available (with number of rooms)* Consultative (ERT) 1; Resource Rooms 1; Self-Contained Rooms 7; Library; Gym; Vocational Education 3; Hospital School 1. *Educational Professionals* Regular School Teachers; Special Education Teachers; Career/Vocational Teachers; Crisis Teachers; Special Education Counselors; Paraprofessionals. *Curricula* Traditional Academic; Career/Vocational Education; Individualized; Basic Skills; Prevocational; Remedial. *Educational Intervention Approaches* Progressive Discipline; Self-Control. *Degrees Awarded* High School Diploma; Graduate Equivalency Diploma.

Forest Heights Lodge

PO Box 789, Evergreen, CO 80439 (303) 674-6681
Year Established 1954
Contact Russell H Colburn, Exec Dir

Facility Information *Placement* Private Residential Care. *Number of Beds* 23. *Children/Adolescents Served* 23. *Sexes Served* Male. *Room and Board Fees (Approx)* $87. *Tuition Fees (Approx)* $35,436. *Sources of Funding* Health Insurance; P.L. 94-142. Summer school available. *Teacher Certification Level* Elementary School; Junior High/Middle School; High School. *Special Certification Level* ED; LD.

Student/Patient Characteristics *Age Levels* 5-8; 9-11; 12-14; 15-17. *IQ Ranges* 85-130. *Exceptionalities Served* Autistic; Emotionally Disturbed; Learning Disabled; Communication Disordered. *Learning Problems* Perceptual Disabilities; Thinking Disabilities; Oral Language Disabilities; Reading Disabilities; Handwriting Disabilities; Spelling Disabilities; Arithmetic Disabilities; Written Expression. *Behavioral Problems* Attention Deficits; Hyperactivity; Hypoactivity; Impulsivity; Self-Aggression; Verbal Aggression; Physical Aggression; Indirect Aggression; Passive Aggression; Withdrawal. *Conditions Treated* Early Infantile Autism; Disintegrative Psychoses; Schizophrenia; Aphasia; Phobias; Obsessions and Compulsions; Hysteria; Depression; Suicide; Inadequacy/Immaturity; Personality Problems; Socialized Aggressive Reaction; Unsocialized Aggressive Reaction.

Services Provided Individual Therapy; Group Therapy; Parent Involvement; Cognitive Developmental Therapy; Family Therapy; Filial Therapy; Drug Therapy; Reality Therapy; Play Therapy; Milieu Therapy. *Professionals on Staff* Psychiatrists 2; Psychologists 1; Social Workers 3; Child Care Staff 6; Pediatrician. *Service Facilities Available (with number of rooms)* Resource Rooms 1; Self-Contained Rooms 3. *Educational Professionals* Special Education Teachers 3. *Curricula* Traditional Academic; Individualized; Basic Skills. *Educational Intervention Approaches* Engineered Classroom; Self-Control.

Comments Forest Heights Lodge is a residential treatment center with an on-grounds school. The focus of treatment is on development of trust relationships that allow children to risk relinquishing pathological adjustment. Nurture is emphasized and reality orientation is primary.

Fort Logan Mental Health Center

3520 W Oxford Ave, Denver, CO 80236 (303) 761-0220
Contact Julio Gonzalez, Chief Child-Adolescent Div

Facility Information *Placement* Public Residential Care. *Number of Beds* 74. *Children/Adolescents Served* 74. *Sexes Served* Both. *Room and Board Fees (Approx)* $195. *Sources of Funding* State Funds; P.L. 94-142; Adult Basic Education; ECIA. Summer school available. *Teacher Certification Level* Elementary School; Junior High/Middle School; High School. *Special Certification Level* ED; LD; MR; Career/Vocational Education.

Student/Patient Characteristics *Age Levels* 5-8; 9-11; 12-14; 15-17; 18-21; Over 21. *IQ Ranges* 71-85; 85-130. *Exceptionalities Served* Emotionally Disturbed; Learning Disabled; Mentally Handicapped; Communication Disordered; Hearing Impaired/ Deaf. *Learning Problems* Memory Disabilities; Perceptual Disabilities; Thinking Disabilities; Oral Language Disabilities; Reading Disabilities; Handwriting Disabilities; Spelling Disabilities; Arithmetic Disabilities; Written Expression. *Behavioral Problems* Attention Deficits; Hyperactivity; Hypoactivity; Impulsivity; Self-Aggression; Verbal Aggression; Physical Aggression; Indirect Aggression; Passive Aggression; Withdrawal. *Conditions Treated* Alcohol Abuse and/or Drug Abuse; Other Substance Abuse or Dependence; Schizophrenia; Phobias; Obsessions and Compulsions; Hysteria; Depression; Suicide; Personality Problems; Socialized Aggressive Reaction; Unsocialized Aggressive Reaction.

Services Provided Individual Therapy; Group Therapy; Parent Involvement; Behavior Therapy; Family Therapy; Music Therapy; Play Therapy. *Professionals on Staff* Psychiatrists 4; Psychologists 4; Counselors; Social Workers 6; Nurses 32; Mental Health Workers; Occupational Therapist; Recreation Therapist 40. *Service Facilities Available (with number of rooms)* Resource Rooms 1; Self-Contained Rooms 9. *Educational Professionals* Special Education Teachers 11; Career/Vocational Teachers 2; Paraprofessionals 5; Physical Education 1; Speech Therapist 1. *Curricula* Career/Vocational Education; Individualized; Basic Skills; Prevocational. *Educational Intervention Approaches* Behavior Modification. *Degrees Awarded* Certificate of Attendance; Graduate Equivalency Diploma.

Jefferson County Public Schools

200 Kipling, Lakewood, CO 80226 (303) 237-1379
Year Established 1960
Contact Bob Weiland, Principal
Facility Information *Placement* Public School.
Children/Adolescents Served 170. *Sexes Served* Both. *Sources of Funding* State Funds; P.L. 94-142. Summer school available. *Teacher Certification Level* Elementary School; Junior High/Middle School; High School. *Special Certification Level* ED; LD; MR; Career/Vocational Education.
Student/Patient Characteristics *Age Levels* 5-8; 9-11; 12-14; 15-17; 18-21; Over 21. *IQ Ranges* 26-40; 41-55; 56-70; 71-85. *Exceptionalities Served* Autistic; Emotionally Disturbed; Learning Disabled; Mentally Handicapped; Communication Disordered; Hearing Impaired/Deaf; Visually Impaired/Blind; Other Health Impaired; Physically Handicapped. *Learning Problems* Memory Disabilities; Perceptual Disabilities; Thinking Disabilities; Oral Language Disabilities; Reading Disabilities; Handwriting Disabilities; Spelling Disabilities; Arithmetic Disabilities; Written Expression. *Behavioral Problems* Attention Deficits; Hyperactivity; Hypoactivity; Impulsivity; Self-Aggression; Verbal Aggression; Physical Aggression; Indirect Aggression; Passive Aggression; Withdrawal. *Conditions Treated* Early Infantile Autism; Schizophrenia; Aphasia; Convulsive Disorders; Phobias; Obsessions and Compulsions; Hysteria; Depression; Personality Problems; Socialized Aggressive Reaction; Unsocialized Aggressive Reaction.
Services Provided Individual Therapy; Group Therapy; Parent Involvement; Behavior Therapy; Cognitive Developmental Therapy; Family Therapy; Music Therapy; Reality Therapy; Play Therapy. *Professionals on Staff* Psychologists 1; Counselors 2; Social Workers 2; Child Care Staff 40; Nurses 1. *Service Facilities Available (with number of rooms)* Itinerants 2; Resource Rooms 1; Self-Contained Rooms 10. *Educational Professionals* Regular School Teachers 20; Special Education Teachers 20. *Curricula* Career/Vocational Education; Individualized; Basic Skills; Prevocational. *Educational Intervention Approaches* Behavior Modification; Creative Conditioning. *Degrees Awarded* High School Diploma.

Lookout Mountain School

Golden, CO 80401 (303) 279-7681
Year Established 1881
Contact Ed Greivel, Dir

Facility Information *Placement* Public Residential Care. *Number of Beds* 190. *Children/Adolescents Served* 160. *Sexes Served* Both. *Room and Board Fees (Approx)* $65. *Sources of Funding* State Funds. Summer school available. *Teacher Certification Level* Elementary School; Junior High/Middle School; High School. *Special Certification Level* ED; LD; MR; Career/Vocational Education; Reading; Math.
Student/Patient Characteristics *Age Levels* 12-14; 15-17; 18-21. *IQ Ranges* 56-70; 71-85; 85-130. *Exceptionalities Served* Emotionally Disturbed; Learning Disabled. *Learning Problems* Perceptual Disabilities; Reading Disabilities; Spelling Disabilities; Arithmetic Disabilities; Written Expression. *Behavioral Problems* Attention Deficits; Hyperactivity; Impulsivity; Self-Aggression; Verbal Aggression; Physical Aggression; Withdrawal. *Conditions Treated* Alcohol Abuse and/or Drug Abuse; Other Substance Abuse or Dependence; Obsessions and Compulsions; Depression; Suicide; Asthma; Personality Problems.
Services Provided Individual Therapy; Group Therapy; Parent Involvement; Behavior Therapy; Family Therapy; Drug Therapy; Reality Therapy. *Professionals on Staff* Psychiatrists 1; Psychologists 2; Counselors 28; Child Care Staff 48; Nurses 3. *Service Facilities Available (with number of rooms)* Resource Rooms 2; Self-Contained Rooms; On-Campus Residential School 16. *Educational Professionals* Regular School Teachers; Special Education Teachers; Career/Vocational Teachers. *Curricula* Traditional Academic; Career/Vocational Education; Individualized; Basic Skills; Prevocational. *Educational Intervention Approaches* Engineered Classroom; Precision Teaching; Behavior Modification. *Degrees Awarded* High School Diploma; Graduate Equivalency Diploma.

Mental Health Center of Boulder County—Adolescent Treatment Program

3100 Bucknell Ct, Boulder, CO 80303 (303) 499-1121
Year Established 1983
Contact Carol Tierney, Dir
Facility Information *Placement* Special School; Public Residential Care; Public Day Care; After School Program. *Number of Beds* 7. *Children/Adolescents Served* 12. *Sexes Served* Both. *Sources of Funding* State Funds; Medicaid. Summer school available. *Teacher Certification Level* Junior High/Middle School; High School. *Special Certification Level* ED; LD; Career/Vocational Education; Reading; Math.
Student/Patient Characteristics *Age Levels* 12-14; 15-17. *IQ Ranges* 85-130; Above 130. *Exceptionalities Served* Emotionally Disturbed; Learning Disabled; Other Health Impaired; Gifted. *Learning Problems* Memory Disabilities; Perceptual Disabilities; Thinking Disabilities; Oral Language Disabilities; Reading Disabilities; Handwriting Disabilities; Spelling Disabilities; Arithmetic Disabilities; Written Expression. *Behavioral Problems* Attention Deficits; Hyperactivity; Hypoactivity; Impulsivity; Self-Aggression; Verbal Aggression; Physical Aggression; Indirect Aggression; Passive Aggression; Withdrawal. *Conditions Treated* Alcohol Abuse and/or Drug Abuse; Disintegrative Psychoses; Schizophrenia; Aphasia; Phobias; Obsessions and Compulsions; Hysteria; Depression; Suicide; Anorexia Nervosa; Inadequacy/Immaturity; Personality Problems; Socialized Aggressive Reaction.
Services Provided Individual Therapy; Group Therapy; Parent Involvement; Behavior Therapy; Cognitive Developmental Therapy; Family Therapy; Art Therapy; Reality Therapy. *Professionals on Staff* Psychiatrists 1; Psychologists 3; Counselors 2; Social Workers 1; Child Care Staff 6-8; Nurses 1. *Service Facilities Available (with number of rooms)* Consultative (ERT); Itinerants 2; Transition Rooms 2; Self-Contained Rooms 2; Homebound Instruction. *Educational Professionals* Special Education Teachers 4; Career/Vocational Teachers 1; Itinerants 3. *Curricula* Traditional Academic; Career/Vocational Education; Individualized; Basic Skills; Prevocational; Special Interests. *Educational Intervention Approaches* Precision Teaching; Progressive Discipline; Self-Control; Behavior Modification; Applied Behavior Analysis; Creative Conditioning. *Degrees Awarded* Certificate of Attendance.

Mt Airy Psychiatric Center—Children's Treatment Program—Adolescent Treatment Program

4455 E 12th Ave, Denver, CO 80220 (303) 322-1803
Contact Mary Lou Munroe, Admin Dir
Facility Information *Placement* Acute Psychiatric Hospitalization. *Number of Beds* 48. *Children/Adolescents Served* 48. *Sexes Served* Both. *Room and Board Fees (Approx)* $348 (adolescent program); $426 (childrens program). *Sources of Funding* Health Insurance; P.L. 94-142. Summer school available. *Teacher Certification Level* Elementary School; Junior High/Middle School; High School. *Special Certification Level* ED; LD; Spanish; Speech Therapy.

Student/Patient Characteristics *Age Levels* 9-11; 12-14; 15-17; 18-21. *IQ Ranges* 85-130; Above 130. *Exceptionalities Served* Emotionally Disturbed; Learning Disabled; Mentally Handicapped; Communication Disordered; Hearing Impaired/Deaf; Visually Impaired/Blind; Other Health Impaired; Physically Handicapped. *Learning Problems* Memory Disabilities; Perceptual Disabilities; Thinking Disabilities; Oral Language Disabilities; Reading Disabilities; Handwriting Disabilities; Spelling Disabilities; Arithmetic Disabilities; Written Expression; Behavior Disorders. *Behavioral Problems* Attention Deficits; Hyperactivity; Hypoactivity; Impulsivity; Self-Aggression; Verbal Aggression; Physical Aggression; Indirect Aggression; Passive Aggression; Withdrawal. *Conditions Treated* Alcohol Abuse and/or Drug Abuse; Other Substance Abuse or Dependence; Schizophrenia; Aphasia; Convulsive Disorders; Phobias; Obsessions and Compulsions; Hysteria; Depression; Suicide; Asthma; Anorexia Nervosa; Inadequacy/Immaturity; Personality Problems; Socialized Aggressive Reaction; Unsocialized Aggressive Reaction.

Services Provided Individual Therapy; Group Therapy; Parent Involvement; Family Therapy; Drug Therapy. *Professionals on Staff* Psychiatrists; Psychologists; Counselors 5; Social Workers 5; Child Care Staff 28; Nurses 28; Theraputic Recreation Specialists 3. *Service Facilities Available (with number of rooms)* Self-Contained Rooms 3. *Educational Professionals* Regular School Teachers 2; Special Education Teachers 7; Educational Diagnostician; Director of Education; Speech Therapist. *Curricula* Traditional Academic; Individualized; Basic Skills. *Degrees Awarded* Certificate of Attendance; High School Diploma; Graduate Equivalency Diploma.

Mountain Board of Cooperative Services—Adolescent Day Treatment Program

115 W 10th, Leadville, CO 80461 (303) 486-2603
Year Established 1971
Contact Taylor L Young, Special Ed Dir
Facility Information *Placement* Public School; Public Day Care; Special Program. *Children/Adolescents Served* 15. *Sexes Served* Both. *Sources of Funding* State Funds; HEW; P.L. 94-142; Local Department of Social Services. Summer school available. *Teacher Certification Level* High School. *Special Certification Level* ED; Career/Vocational Education.

Student/Patient Characteristics *Age Levels* 12-14; 15-17. *IQ Ranges* 85-130. *Exceptionalities Served* Emotionally Disturbed; Learning Disabled. *Learning Problems* Memory Disabilities; Perceptual Disabilities; Thinking Disabilities; Oral Language Disabilities; Reading Disabilities; Handwriting Disabilities; Spelling Disabilities; Arithmetic Disabilities; Written Expression. *Behavioral Problems* Attention Deficits; Hyperactivity; Impulsivity; Self-Aggression; Verbal Aggression; Physical Aggression; Indirect Aggression; Passive Aggression; Withdrawal. *Conditions Treated* Alcohol Abuse and/or Drug Abuse; Schizophrenia; Phobias; Obsessions and Compulsions; Depression; Inadequacy/Immaturity; Personality Problems; Socialized Aggressive Reaction; Unsocialized Aggressive Reaction.

Services Provided Individual Therapy; Group Therapy; Parent Involvement; Behavior Therapy; Family Therapy; Art Therapy; Reality Therapy; Play Therapy. *Professionals on Staff* Psychiatrists 1; Psychologists 1; Counselors 1; Social Workers 1. *Service Facilities Available (with number of rooms)* Resource Rooms; Transition Rooms; Special School; Homebound Instruction.

Educational Professionals Special Education Teachers; Career/Vocational Teachers; Special Education Counselors; Paraprofessionals. *Curricula* Traditional Academic; Career/Vocational Education; Individualized; Basic Skills; Prevocational. *Educational Intervention Approaches* Engineered Classroom; Progressive Discipline; Self-Control; Behavior Modification. *Degrees Awarded* High School Diploma.

Northeast Colorado Board of Cooperative Educational Services

PO Box 98, Haxton, CO 80731 (303) 774-6152
Contact Douglas Householder, Special Ed Dir
Facility Information *Placement* BOCES. *Children/Adolescents Served* 8. *Sexes Served* Both. *Tuition Fees (Approx)* $4,500. *Sources of Funding* State Funds; P.L. 94-142; Transfer Tuition. *Teacher Certification Level* Elementary School; Junior High/Middle School. *Special Certification Level* ED; LD; MR; Reading; Math.

Student/Patient Characteristics *Age Levels* 5-8; 9-11; 12-14. *IQ Ranges* 56-70; 71-85; 85-130; Above 130. *Exceptionalities Served* Autistic; Emotionally Disturbed; Learning Disabled; Mentally Handicapped; Other Health Impaired; Gifted. *Learning Problems* Memory Disabilities; Perceptual Disabilities; Thinking Disabilities; Reading Disabilities; Handwriting Disabilities; Spelling Disabilities; Arithmetic Disabilities; Written Expression. *Behavioral Problems* Attention Deficits; Hyperactivity; Hypoactivity; Impulsivity; Self-Aggression; Verbal Aggression; Physical Aggression; Indirect Aggression; Passive Aggression; Withdrawal. *Conditions Treated* Alcohol Abuse and/or Drug Abuse; Other Substance Abuse or Dependence; Early Infantile Autism; Disintegrative Psychoses; Schizophrenia; Aphasia; Convulsive Disorders; Phobias; Obsessions and Compulsions; Hysteria; Depression; Suicide; Anorexia Nervosa; Ulcerative Colitis; Inadequacy/Immaturity; Personality Problems; Socialized Aggressive Reaction; Unsocialized Aggressive Reaction.

Services Provided Individual Therapy; Group Therapy; Parent Involvement; Behavior Therapy; Cognitive Developmental Therapy; Family Therapy; Drug Therapy; Art Therapy; Music Therapy; Reality Therapy; Play Therapy. *Professionals on Staff* Psychologists 3; Counselors 1; Social Workers 2; Child Care Staff 1; Nurses 2; Educational Consultants 2. *Service Facilities Available (with number of rooms)* Itinerants 1; Resource Rooms 1; Transition Rooms 1; Self-Contained Rooms 1. *Educational Professionals* Regular School Teachers 5; Special Education Teachers 2; Career/Vocational Teachers 1; Special Education Counselors 1; Paraprofessionals 2. *Curricula* Traditional Academic; Career/Vocational Education; Individualized; Basic Skills; Prevocational. *Educational Intervention Approaches* Engineered Classroom; Precision Teaching; Progressive Discipline; Self-Control; Behavior Modification; Applied Behavior Analysis. *Degrees Awarded* High School Diploma.

Comments This is a day treatment public school program.

Pikes Peak Board of Cooperative Services

4825 Lorna Pl, Colorado Springs, CO 80915
Contact George Sarter, Dir NEED Prog
Facility Information *Placement* Special School; Special Program. *Children/Adolescents Served* 35. *Sexes Served* Both. *Tuition Fees (Approx)* $8,000. *Sources of Funding* State Funds; P.L. 94-142; Local. Summer school available. *Teacher Certification Level* Junior High/Middle School; High School. *Special Certification Level* ED; Secondary Ed.

Student/Patient Characteristics *Age Levels* 15-17; 18-21. *IQ Ranges* 85-130. *Exceptionalities Served* Emotionally Disturbed; Learning Disabled. *Learning Problems* Perceptual Disabilities; Oral Language Disabilities; Reading Disabilities; Spelling Disabilities; Arithmetic Disabilities; Written Expression. *Behavioral Problems* Attention Deficits; Hyperactivity; Impulsivity; Verbal Aggression; Passive Aggression. *Conditions Treated* Schizophrenia; Obsessions and Compulsions; Depression; Inadequacy/Immaturity; Personality Problems; Socialized Aggressive Reaction; Unsocialized Aggressive Reaction.

Services Provided Individual Therapy; Group Therapy; Parent Involvement; Behavior Therapy; Family Therapy; Drug Therapy. *Professionals on Staff* Psychiatrists 15; Psychologists 2; Social Workers 2. *Service Facilities Available (with number of rooms)* Self-Contained Rooms 4; Special School 4; Homebound Instruction. *Educational Professionals* Special Education Teachers 4; Crisis Teachers 2; Paraprofessionals 3. *Curricula* Individualized; Basic Skills; Prevocational. *Educational Intervention Approaches* Progressive Discipline; Behavior Modification; Applied Behavior Analysis. *Degrees Awarded* High School Diploma.

Comments The day program serves junior and senior high school students who cannot function in the public school due to severe emotional and/or behavioral problems within 16 school districts in 3 counties.

University of Colorado Health Sciences Center—Day Care Center

4200 E 9th Ave, Denver, CO 80262 (303) 394-8244
Year Established 1962
Contact Gordon K Farley, Dir
Facility Information *Placement* Special School; Psychiatric Day Hospital. *Number of Beds* 24. *Children/Adolescents Served* 24. *Sexes Served* Both. *Room and Board Fees (Approx)* $165. *Sources of Funding* State Funds; Health Insurance; Medicaid. Summer school available. *Teacher Certification Level* Elementary School. *Special Certification Level* ED.
Student/Patient Characteristics *Age Levels* 5-8; 9-11. *IQ Ranges* 71-85; 85-130; Above 130. *Exceptionalities Served* Autistic; Emotionally Disturbed; Learning Disabled; Mentally Handicapped; Communication Disordered; Other Health Impaired; Physically Handicapped; Gifted. *Learning Problems* Memory Disabilities; Perceptual Disabilities; Thinking Disabilities; Oral Language Disabilities; Reading Disabilities; Handwriting Disabilities; Spelling Disabilities; Arithmetic Disabilities; Written Expression. *Behavioral Problems* Attention Deficits; Hyperactivity; Impulsivity; Self-Aggression; Verbal Aggression; Physical Aggression; Indirect Aggression; Passive Aggression; Withdrawal. *Conditions Treated* Early Infantile Autism; Schizophrenia; Aphasia; Convulsive Disorders; Phobias; Obsessions and Compulsions; Hysteria; Depression; Suicide; Asthma; Personality Problems; Socialized Aggressive Reaction; Unsocialized Aggressive Reaction.
Services Provided Individual Therapy; Group Therapy; Parent Involvement; Behavior Therapy; Cognitive Developmental Therapy; Family Therapy; Drug Therapy; Art Therapy; Play Therapy. *Professionals on Staff* Psychiatrists 13; Psychologists 3; Social Workers 8. *Service Facilities Available (with number of rooms)* Consultative (ERT) 1; Resource Rooms 1; Self-Contained Rooms 4; Therapy Room 2. *Educational Professionals* Special Education Teachers 5. *Curricula* Traditional Academic; Individualized; Basic Skills. *Educational Intervention Approaches* Engineered Classroom; Precision Teaching; Self-Control; Behavior Modification; Applied Behavior Analysis.

Comments The Day Care Center treats moderately to severely disturbed children using a combined psychodynamic behavior modification, family therapy and biological approach.

University Park Psychological Center

2343 E Evans Ave, Denver, CO 80210 (303) 744-0025
Year Established 1955
Contact Howard Mausner, Consulting Clinical Rehabilitation Psychologist

Facility Information *Placement* Outpatient Psychotherapy and Counseling Center. *Sources of Funding* Health Insurance; Medicaid; Medicare; Private Pay.
Student/Patient Characteristics *Age Levels* 0-4; 5-8; 9-11; 12-14; 15-17; 18-21; Over 21. *IQ Ranges* 71-85; 85-130; Above 130. *Exceptionalities Served* Emotionally Disturbed; Learning Disabled; Mentally Handicapped; Communication Disordered; Hearing Impaired/Deaf; Visually Impaired/Blind; Other Health Impaired; Physically Handicapped; Gifted. *Learning Problems* Memory Disabilities; Perceptual Disabilities; Thinking Disabilities; Oral Language Disabilities; Reading Disabilities; Handwriting Disabilities; Spelling Disabilities; Arithmetic Disabilities; Written Expression. *Behavioral Problems* Attention Deficits; Hyperactivity; Hypoactivity; Impulsivity; Self-Aggression; Verbal Aggression; Physical Aggression; Indirect Aggression; Passive Aggression; Withdrawal. *Conditions Treated* Alcohol Abuse and/or Drug Abuse; Other Substance Abuse or Dependence; Aphasia; Convulsive Disorders; Phobias; Obsessions and Compulsions; Hysteria; Depression; Suicide; Asthma; Anorexia Nervosa; Ulcerative Colitis; Inadequacy/Immaturity; Personality Problems; Socialized Aggressive Reaction; Unsocialized Aggressive Reaction.
Services Provided Individual Therapy; Group Therapy; Parent Involvement; Behavior Therapy; Cognitive Developmental Therapy; Biofeedback; Family Therapy; Filial Therapy; Rational Emotive Therapy. *Professionals on Staff* Psychologists 10; Social Workers 1.

Wallace Village for Children

PO Box 345, Broomfield, CO 80020 (303) 466-7391
Year Established Duane Jones, Clinical Dir
Facility Information *Placement* Private Residential Care; Day Treatment Program. *Children/Adolescents Served* 84 (residential); 35 (day treatment). *Sexes Served* Both. Summer school available. *Teacher Certification Level* Elementary School; Junior High/Middle School; High School. *Special Certification Level* ED; LD; MR; Career/Vocational Education.
Student/Patient Characteristics *Age Levels* 5-8; 9-11; 12-14; 15-17; 18-21. *IQ Ranges* 41-55; 56-70; 71-85; 85-130. *Exceptionalities Served* Emotionally Disturbed. *Learning Problems* Memory Disabilities; Perceptual Disabilities; Thinking Disabilities; Oral Language Disabilities; Reading Disabilities; Handwriting Disabilities; Spelling Disabilities; Arithmetic Disabilities; Written Expression. *Behavioral Problems* Attention Deficits; Hyperactivity; Hypoactivity; Impulsivity; Self-Aggression; Verbal Aggression; Physical Aggression; Indirect Aggression; Passive Aggression; Withdrawal. *Conditions Treated* Schizophrenia; Convulsive Disorders; Depression; Inadequacy/Immaturity; Personality Problems; Socialized Aggressive Reaction; Unsocialized Aggressive Reaction.
Services Provided Individual Therapy; Group Therapy; Parent Involvement; Behavior Therapy; Family Therapy. *Professionals on Staff* Psychiatrists 1; Psychologists 8; Social Workers 3; Child Care Staff 59; Nurses 7. *Service Facilities Available (with number of rooms)* Resource Rooms; Self-Contained Rooms; On-Campus Residential School. *Educational Professionals* Regular School Teachers 4; Special Education Teachers 14; Career/Vocational Teachers 3; Paraprofessionals 6. *Curricula* Traditional Academic; Career/Vocational Education; Individualized; Basic Skills; Prevocational. *Educational Intervention Approaches* Precision Teaching; Self-Control; Behavior Modification. *Degrees Awarded* High School Diploma.

Comments The Village provides a highly structured treatment milieu. It provides a continuum of services for a range of severe to mild emotional and behavioral disorders.

Connecticut

Benhaven

Maple St, East Haven, CT 06512 (203) 469-9819
Year Established 1967
Contact Amy Lettick, Exec Dir

Facility Information *Placement* Special School; Private Residential Care; Private Day Care. *Number of Beds* 28. *Children/Adolescents Served* 45. *Sexes Served* Both. *Tuition Fees (Approx)* $31,344 (residential cost); $54,504 (school and residential cost). *Sources of Funding* State Funds; Medicaid; P.L. 94-142; Local Funding. Summer school available. *Teacher Certification Level* Elementary School; Junior High/Middle School. *Special Certification Level* Special Education.

Student/Patient Characteristics *Age Levels* 0-4; 5-8; 9-11; 12-14; 15-17; 18-21; Over 21. *IQ Ranges* 26-40; 41-55; 56-70; 71-85; 85-130. *Exceptionalities Served* Autistic; Emotionally Disturbed; Mentally Handicapped; Hearing Impaired/Deaf; Visually Impaired/Blind. *Learning Problems* Memory Disabilities; Perceptual Disabilities; Thinking Disabilities; Oral Language Disabilities; Reading Disabilities; Handwriting Disabilities; Spelling Disabilities; Arithmetic Disabilities; Written Expression. *Behavioral Problems* Attention Deficits; Hyperactivity; Hypoactivity; Impulsivity; Self-Aggression; Physical Aggression; Indirect Aggression; Passive Aggression; Withdrawal. *Conditions Treated* Early Infantile Autism; Schizophrenia; Aphasia; Convulsive Disorders.

Services Provided Individual Therapy; Parent Involvement; Behavior Therapy; Drug Therapy; Music Therapy; Play Therapy; Educ Therapy; Speech Therapy; Language Therapy. *Professionals on Staff* Psychiatrists 1; Psychologists 2; Social Workers 1; Child Care Staff 60; Nurses 1; Residential Teachers 14; Coordinators 2. *Service Facilities Available (with number of rooms)* Consultative (ERT); Self-Contained Rooms 9; On-Campus Residential School. *Educational Professionals* Special Education Teachers 8; Career/Vocational Teachers 1; Paraprofessionals 45; Supv Coord 5. *Curricula* Traditional Academic; Career/Vocational Education; Individualized; Basic Skills; Prevocational; Vocational. *Educational Intervention Approaches* Engineered Classroom; Precision Teaching; Behavior Modification; Applied Behavior Analysis.

Comments Benhaven is a residential program for autistic and neurologically impaired individuals. We offer a 12-month 6-day per week school program. The residence never closes. It also serves a day population from local districts. The curriculum and program is individualized and highly structured. Emphasis is on functional education, behavior control, and socialization activities.

Bridgeport Tutoring Center—Counseling Center of Connecticut

893 Clinton Ave, Bridgeport, CT 06604 (203) 333-2611
Year Established 1952
Contact Gerhard H Coler

Facility Information *Placement* Tutoring and Counseling Center. *Sexes Served* Both. *Sources of Funding* Health Insurance; Medicaid; Medicare; Private. Summer school available. *Teacher Certification Level* Elementary School; Junior High/Middle School; High School. *Special Certification Level* ED; Reading; Math.

Student/Patient Characteristics *Age Levels* 0-4; 5-8; 9-11. *Exceptionalities Served* Emotionally Disturbed; Learning Disabled; Communication Disordered; Gifted. *Learning Problems* Memory Disabilities; Perceptual Disabilities; Reading Disabilities; Handwriting Disabilities; Spelling Disabilities; Arithmetic Disabilities; Written Expression. *Behavioral Problems* Attention Deficits; Hyperactivity; Withdrawal. *Conditions Treated* Depression; Personality Problems.

Services Provided Individual Therapy; Parent Involvement; Behavior Therapy; Family Therapy; Reality Therapy. *Professionals on Staff* Counselors 4. *Service Facilities Available (with number of rooms)* Consultative (ERT); Homebound Instruction. *Educational Professionals* Regular School Teachers 30; Special Education Teachers 50; Special Education Counselors 4. *Curricula* Traditional Academic; Individualized; Basic Skills; Prevocational. *Educational Intervention Approaches* Precision Teaching; Self-Control; Behavior Modification; Creative Conditioning. *Degrees Awarded* Certificate of Attendance.

Comments The center is open any time staff is available.

Capitol Region Education Council's Day Treatment Service

212 King Philip Dr, West Hartford, CT 06117 (203) 236-1919
Year Established 1963
Contact Thomas N Parvenski, Dir

Facility Information *Placement* Public School; Public Residential Care. *Number of Beds* 16. *Children/Adolescents Served* 110. *Sexes Served* Both. *Sources of Funding* State Funds; P.L. 94-142; Tuition. Summer school available. *Teacher Certification Level* Elementary School; Junior High/Middle School; High School. *Special Certification Level* ED; LD; MR.

Student/Patient Characteristics *Age Levels* 0-4; 5-8; 9-11; 12-14; 15-17; 18-21. *IQ Ranges* 0-25; 26-40; 41-55; 56-70; 71-85; 85-130. *Exceptionalities Served* Autistic; Emotionally Disturbed; Learning Disabled; Mentally Handicapped; Communication Disordered; Developmentally Disabled. *Learning Problems* Memory Disabilities; Perceptual Disabilities; Thinking Disabilities; Oral Language Disabilities; Reading Disabilities; Handwriting Disabilities; Spelling Disabilities; Arithmetic Disabilities; Written Expression. *Behavioral Problems* Attention Deficits; Hyperactivity; Hypoactivity; Impulsivity; Self-Aggression; Verbal Aggression; Physical Aggression; Indirect Aggression; Passive Aggression; Withdrawal. *Conditions Treated* Early Infantile Autism; Disintegrative Psychoses; Schizophrenia; Phobias; Obsessions and Compulsions; Depression; Inadequacy/Immaturity; Personality Problems; Socialized Aggressive Reaction.

Services Provided Individual Therapy; Group Therapy; Parent Involvement; Behavior Therapy. *Professionals on Staff* Psychologists 1; Social Workers 1; Child Care Staff 55; Nurses 1. *Service Facilities Available (with number of rooms)* Consultative (ERT) 2; Self-Contained Rooms 14. *Educational Professionals* Special Education Teachers 16; Paraprofessionals 39. *Curricula* Traditional Academic; Individualized; Basic Skills; Prevocational. *Educational Intervention Approaches* Behavior Modification; Applied Behavior Analysis. *Degrees Awarded* Certificate of Attendance.

Child Guidance Center of Southern Connecticut

103 W Broad St, Stanford, CT 06902 (203) 326-6127
Year Established 1955
Contact Adrienne Lagin, Chief Psychiatric Social Worker
Facility Information *Placement* Outpatient Child Guidance Clinic. *Children/Adolescents Served* 500. *Sexes Served* Both. *Sources of Funding* State Funds; Health Insurance; United Way. *Special Certification Level* LD.
Student/Patient Characteristics *Age Levels* 0-4; 5-8; 9-11; 12-14; 15-17; 18-21. *IQ Ranges* 71-85; 85-130; Above 130. *Exceptionalities Served* Autistic; Emotionally Disturbed; Learning Disabled. *Learning Problems* Memory Disabilities; Perceptual Disabilities; Oral Language Disabilities; Reading Disabilities; Handwriting Disabilities; Spelling Disabilities; Arithmetic Disabilities; Written Expression. *Behavioral Problems* Attention Deficits; Hyperactivity; Impulsivity; Self-Aggression; Verbal Aggression; Physical Aggression; Indirect Aggression; Passive Aggression; Withdrawal. *Conditions Treated* Early Infantile Autism; Disintegrative Psychoses; Schizophrenia; Phobias; Obsessions and Compulsions; Hysteria; Depression; Suicide; Anorexia Nervosa; Inadequacy/Immaturity; Personality Problems; Socialized Aggressive Reaction; Unsocialized Aggressive Reaction.
Services Provided Individual Therapy; Group Therapy; Parent Involvement; Family Therapy; Drug Therapy; Play Therapy. *Professionals on Staff* Psychiatrists 3; Psychologists 2; Counselors 5; Social Workers 5; Nurses 1. *Educational Professionals* Special Education Counselors 1.

Child Guidance Clinic of Southeastern Connecticut Inc

75 Granite St, New London, CT 06320 (203) 442-0319
Year Established 1954
Contact Walter S Iwanicki, Exec Dir
Facility Information *Placement* Outpatient Psychiatric Clinic. *Children/Adolescents Served* 500. *Sexes Served* Both. *Room and Board Fees (Approx)* $60. *Sources of Funding* State Funds; Health Insurance; Medicaid; P.L. 94-142; United Way.
Student/Patient Characteristics *Age Levels* 0-4; 5-8; 9-11; 12-14; 15-17. *IQ Ranges* 71-85; 85-130; Above 130. *Exceptionalities Served* Autistic; Emotionally Disturbed; Learning Disabled. *Learning Problems* Memory Disabilities; Perceptual Disabilities; Thinking Disabilities; Oral Language Disabilities; Reading Disabilities; Handwriting Disabilities; Spelling Disabilities; Arithmetic Disabilities; Written Expression. *Behavioral Problems* Attention Deficits; Hyperactivity; Hypoactivity; Impulsivity; Self-Aggression; Verbal Aggression; Physical Aggression; Indirect Aggression; Passive Aggression; Withdrawal. *Conditions Treated* Alcohol Abuse and/or Drug Abuse; Other Substance Abuse or Dependence; Early Infantile Autism; Disintegrative Psychoses; Schizophrenia; Phobias; Obsessions and Compulsions; Hysteria; Depression; Suicide; Anorexia Nervosa; Inadequacy/Immaturity; Personality Problems; Socialized Aggressive Reaction; Unsocialized Aggressive Reaction.

Services Provided Individual Therapy; Group Therapy; Parent Involvement; Behavior Therapy; Cognitive Developmental Therapy; Family Therapy; Drug Therapy; Play Therapy. *Professionals on Staff* Psychiatrists 3; Psychologists 4; Social Workers 10.

Children's Center

1400 Whitney Ave, Hamden, CT 06514 (203) 248-2116
Year Established 1833
Contact Vincent Senatore, Dir of Residential Treatment
Facility Information *Placement* Private Residential Care; Private Day Care. *Number of Beds* 60. *Children/Adolescents Served* 80. *Sexes Served* Both. *Room and Board Fees (Approx)* $55. *Tuition Fees (Approx)* $9,500. *Sources of Funding* State Funds. Summer school available. *Teacher Certification Level* Elementary School; Junior High/Middle School. *Special Certification Level* ED; LD; Career/Vocational Education; Reading.
Student/Patient Characteristics *Age Levels* 5-8; 9-11; 12-14; 15-17. *IQ Ranges* 71-85; 85-130. *Exceptionalities Served* Emotionally Disturbed; Learning Disabled. *Learning Problems* Memory Disabilities; Perceptual Disabilities; Thinking Disabilities; Oral Language Disabilities; Reading Disabilities; Handwriting Disabilities; Spelling Disabilities; Arithmetic Disabilities; Written Expression. *Behavioral Problems* Attention Deficits; Hyperactivity; Hypoactivity; Impulsivity; Self-Aggression; Verbal Aggression; Physical Aggression; Indirect Aggression; Passive Aggression; Withdrawal. *Conditions Treated* Alcohol Abuse and/or Drug Abuse; Obsessions and Compulsions; Depression; Inadequacy/Immaturity; Personality Problems; Socialized Aggressive Reaction; Unsocialized Aggressive Reaction.
Services Provided Individual Therapy; Group Therapy; Parent Involvement; Behavior Therapy; Cognitive Developmental Therapy; Family Therapy; Filial Therapy; Drug Therapy; Art Therapy; Reality Therapy; Play Therapy; Psychodrama. *Professionals on Staff* Psychiatrists 1; Psychologists 1; Social Workers 7; Child Care Staff 30; Nurses 2. *Service Facilities Available (with number of rooms)* Transition Rooms 4; Self-Contained Rooms 5. *Educational Professionals* Regular School Teachers 2; Special Education Teachers 8. *Curricula* Traditional Academic; Career/Vocational Education; Individualized; Basic Skills; Prevocational. *Educational Intervention Approaches* Progressive Discipline; Behavior Modification; Creative Conditioning. *Degrees Awarded* Certificate of Attendance.
Comments The Children's Center is a private, nonprofit residential treatment center for emotionally and behaviorally disturbed children.

The Children's School of the Institute of Living

17 Essex St, Hartford, CT 06114 (203) 241-8000
Year Established 1955
Contact Norman Turchi, Special Ed Dir
Facility Information *Placement* Special School; Private School. *Children/Adolescents Served* 50. *Sexes Served* Both. *Tuition Fees (Approx)* $7,000. *Sources of Funding* P.L. 94-142. Summer school available. *Teacher Certification Level* Elementary School; Junior High/Middle School; High School. *Special Certification Level* Special Education.
Student/Patient Characteristics *Age Levels* 0-4; 5-8; 9-11; 12-14. *Exceptionalities Served* Autistic; Emotionally Disturbed; Learning Disabled; Mentally Handicapped; Communication Disordered; Hearing Impaired/Deaf; Other Health Impaired; Neurologically Impaired. *Learning Problems* Memory Disabilities; Perceptual Disabilities; Thinking Disabilities; Oral Language Disabilities; Reading Disabilities; Handwriting Disabilities; Spelling Disabilities; Arithmetic Disabilities; Written Expression. *Behavioral Problems* Attention Deficits; Hyperactivity; Hypoactivity; Impulsivity; Self-Aggression; Verbal Aggression; Physical Aggression; Indirect Aggression; Passive Aggression; Withdrawal. *Conditions Treated* Alcohol Abuse and/or Drug Abuse; Other Substance Abuse or Dependence; Early Infantile Autism; Disintegrative Psychoses; Schizophrenia; Aphasia; Convulsive Disorders; Phobias; Obsessions and Compulsions; Hysteria; Depression; Sui-

cide; Asthma; Anorexia Nervosa; Inadequacy/Immaturity; Personality Problems; Socialized Aggressive Reaction; Unsocialized Aggressive Reaction.

Services Provided Individual Therapy; Group Therapy; Parent Involvement; Behavior Therapy; Family Therapy; Play Therapy. *Professionals on Staff* Psychiatrists 4; Psychologists 4; Social Workers 9. *Service Facilities Available (with number of rooms)* Self-Contained Rooms 7. *Educational Professionals* Special Education Teachers 8; Paraprofessionals 5; Speech Therapist 1. *Curricula* Individualized. *Educational Intervention Approaches* Engineered Classroom; Precision Teaching; Progressive Discipline; Self-Control; Behavior Modification.

Comments The Children's School has a special education program and a continuum of therapeutic services available for both the children and their families.

Community Child Guidance Clinic Preschool

317 Main St, Manchester, CT 06040 (203) 643-2101
Year Established 1974
Contact Susan Schardt, Ed Coord
Facility Information *Placement* Special School.
Children/Adolescents Served 20. *Sexes Served* Both. *Tuition Fees (Approx)* $5,700-$11,000. *Sources of Funding* Tuition. Summer school available. *Teacher Certification Level* Elementary School; Junior High/Middle School; High School. *Special Certification Level* ED; LD; MR.
Student/Patient Characteristics *Age Levels* 0-4; 5-8; 9-11. *IQ Ranges* 0-25; 26-40; 41-55; 56-70; 71-85; 85-130. *Exceptionalities Served* Autistic; Emotionally Disturbed; Learning Disabled. *Learning Problems* Memory Disabilities; Perceptual Disabilities; Thinking Disabilities; Oral Language Disabilities; Reading Disabilities; Handwriting Disabilities; Spelling Disabilities; Arithmetic Disabilities. *Behavioral Problems* Attention Deficits; Hyperactivity; Impulsivity; Verbal Aggression; Passive Aggression; Withdrawal. *Conditions Treated* Early Infantile Autism; Schizophrenia; Inadequacy/Immaturity; Personality Problems.

Services Provided Individual Therapy; Parent Involvement; Family Therapy; Play Therapy. *Professionals on Staff* Psychiatrists 1; Psychologists 1; Social Workers 1. *Service Facilities Available (with number of rooms)* Self-Contained Rooms 5. *Educational Professionals* Special Education Teachers 4; Paraprofessionals 7. *Curricula* Traditional Academic; Basic Skills; Prevocational. *Educational Intervention Approaches* Behavior Modification.

Comments The Community Child Guidance Clinic School is located within a child guidance clinic. The school offers an individualized program designed to meet the student's educational needs with supportive clinical services for both the child and the family within one facility. Two separate educational programs are available. One is for the students with learning disabilities and/or emotional disturbances. The other is for students who have been diagnosed as autistic.

Connecticut College Program for Children with Special Needs

Box 1574, New London, CT 06333
Year Established 1972
Contact Sara Radlinski, Acting Dir
Facility Information *Placement* Preschool Special Needs Program. *Children/Adolescents Served* 35. *Tuition Fees (Approx)* $4,500-$7,500. *Sources of Funding* State Funds; Health Insurance; P.L. 94-142. Summer school available. *Teacher Certification Level* Elementary School. *Special Certification Level* Special Education.
Student/Patient Characteristics *Age Levels* 0-4; 5-8. *Exceptionalities Served* Autistic; Emotionally Disturbed; Learning Disabled; Mentally Handicapped; Communication Disordered; Hearing Impaired/Deaf; Visually Impaired/Blind; Other Health Impaired; Physically Handicapped; Gifted. *Learning Problems* Memory Disabilities; Perceptual Disabilities; Thinking Disabilities; Oral Language Disabilities. *Behavioral Problems* Attention Deficits; Hyperactivity; Hypoactivity; Impulsivity; Verbal Ag-

gression; Physical Aggression; Passive Aggression; Withdrawal. *Conditions Treated* Early Infantile Autism; Schizophrenia; Aphasia; Phobias; Obsessions and Compulsions; Asthma; Personality Problems.

Services Provided Individual Therapy; Parent Involvement; Play Therapy. *Professionals on Staff* Psychiatrists; Psychologists; Social Workers; Child Care Staff; Nurses 1. *Service Facilities Available (with number of rooms)* Self-Contained Rooms 3. *Educational Professionals* Special Education Teachers; Paraprofessionals; Early Children Teachers. *Curricula* Development. *Educational Intervention Approaches* Self-Control; Behavior Modification.

Comments The Connecticut College Program for Children with Special Needs is a preschool (ages birth to 6) program. It is in session from early September to June and for a summer session. The children can attend either small group or individual sessions. The individual sessions may be home or center based. An integral part of the program is the involvement of parents in learning to understand their special child.

Connecticut Junior Republic—Litchfield District

Goshen Rd, Litchfield, CT 06759 (203) 567-9423
Year Established 1909
Contact Bernard Flannery, Intake Coord
Facility Information *Placement* Private Residential Care; Private Day Care. *Number of Beds* 88. *Children/Adolescents Served* 100. *Sexes Served* Male. *Tuition Fees (Approx)* $9,509. Summer school available. *Teacher Certification Level* Elementary School; Junior High/Middle School; High School. *Special Certification Level* ED; LD; Career/Vocational Education; Reading; Math.
Student/Patient Characteristics *Age Levels* 12-14; 15-17. *IQ Ranges* 71-85; 85-130. *Exceptionalities Served* Emotionally Disturbed; Learning Disabled. *Learning Problems* Memory Disabilities; Perceptual Disabilities; Thinking Disabilities; Reading Disabilities; Handwriting Disabilities; Spelling Disabilities; Arithmetic Disabilities; Written Expression. *Behavioral Problems* Attention Deficits; Hyperactivity; Hypoactivity; Impulsivity; Self-Aggression; Verbal Aggression; Physical Aggression; Indirect Aggression; Passive Aggression; Withdrawal. *Conditions Treated* Alcohol Abuse and/or Drug Abuse; Phobias; Hysteria; Depression; Personality Problems; Socialized Aggressive Reaction; Unsocialized Aggressive Reaction.

Services Provided Individual Therapy; Group Therapy; Parent Involvement; Behavior Therapy; Family Therapy; Drug Therapy; Art Therapy; Reality Therapy. *Professionals on Staff* Psychiatrists 2; Psychologists 1; Social Workers 4; Child Care Staff 28; Nurses 2. *Service Facilities Available (with number of rooms)* Self-Contained Rooms. *Educational Professionals* Regular School Teachers 1; Special Education Teachers 10; Career/Vocational Teachers 8. *Curricula* Traditional Academic; Individualized; Prevocational. *Educational Intervention Approaches* Positive Group Interaction. *Degrees Awarded* 8th Grade Diploma.

Comments Connecticut Junior Republic is a residential treatment center for emotionally disturbed boys. Special education, vocational education, intensive group work, and therapeutic use of living situations are components of the program.

Cooperative Educational Services Developmental Learning Center

34 Whipple Rd, Wilton, CT 06897 (203) 762-8526
Year Established 1979
Contact Anthony C Maida, Prog Dir
Facility Information *Placement* Special School; Regional Public School. *Children/Adolescents Served* 60. *Sexes Served* Both. *Tuition Fees (Approx)* $14,030 (pre-vocational); $12,120 (preschool academic); $11,380 (functional academic). *Sources of Funding* Tuitions Paid by Referring School District. Summer school available.
Student/Patient Characteristics *Age Levels* 0-4; 5-8; 9-11; 12-14; 15-17; 18-21. *IQ Ranges* 41-55; 56-70; 71-85. *Exceptionalities Served* Autistic; Emotionally Disturbed; Mentally Handicapped;

Communication Disordered; Hearing Impaired/Deaf. *Learning Problems* Memory Disabilities; Perceptual Disabilities; Thinking Disabilities; Oral Language Disabilities. *Behavioral Problems* Attention Deficits; Hyperactivity; Impulsivity; Self-Aggression; Verbal Aggression; Physical Aggression; Indirect Aggression; Withdrawal. *Conditions Treated* Early Infantile Autism; Schizophrenia; Aphasia; Convulsive Disorders; Asthma; Inadequacy/Immaturity; Socialized Aggressive Reaction; Unsocialized Aggressive Reaction.

Services Provided Behavior Therapy; Cognitive Developmental Therapy. *Professionals on Staff* Psychologists 1; Nurses 1; Physical Therapist 1; Occupational Therapist 1. *Service Facilities Available (with number of rooms)* Resource Rooms 1; Self-Contained Rooms 13. *Educational Professionals* Regular School Teachers 1; Special Education Teachers 20; Career/Vocational Teachers 1; Paraprofessionals 6; Speech Pathologists 3. *Curricula* Traditional Academic; Individualized; Basic Skills; Prevocational; ADL/Functional Academics. *Educational Intervention Approaches* Engineered Classroom; Precision Teaching; Behavior Modification. *Degrees Awarded* Program Diploma.

Comments The Developmental Learning Center (DLC) is a program of Cooperative Educational Services, the public school Regional Educational Service Center for southwestern Connecticut. The program is designed for children 3 to 21 years of age, with severe developmental disability. A full range of special education services are provided.

Elizabeth Ives School

700 Hartford Turnpike, Hamden, CT 06517 (203) 281-3790
Year Established 1963
Contact Betty Sword, Dir
Facility Information *Placement* Special School.
Children/Adolescents Served 34. *Sexes Served* Both. *Tuition Fees (Approx)* $9,285. *Sources of Funding* P.L. 94-142. Summer school available. *Teacher Certification Level* Elementary School. *Special Certification Level* ED; LD; MR; Preschool Handicapped.
Student/Patient Characteristics *Age Levels* 0-4; 5-8; 9-11; 12-14; 15-17. *IQ Ranges* 26-40; 41-55; 56-70; 71-85; 85-130. *Exceptionalities Served* Autistic; Emotionally Disturbed; Learning Disabled; Mentally Handicapped; Communication Disordered. *Learning Problems* Memory Disabilities; Perceptual Disabilities; Thinking Disabilities; Oral Language Disabilities; Reading Disabilities; Handwriting Disabilities; Spelling Disabilities; Arithmetic Disabilities; Written Expression. *Behavioral Problems* Attention Deficits; Hyperactivity; Hypoactivity; Impulsivity; Self-Aggression; Verbal Aggression; Physical Aggression; Indirect Aggression; Passive Aggression; Withdrawal. *Conditions Treated* Early Infantile Autism; Aphasia; Phobias; Obsessions and Compulsions; Inadequacy/Immaturity; Personality Problems.
Services Provided Individual Therapy; Parent Involvement; Behavior Therapy; Cognitive Developmental Therapy; Reality Therapy; Play Therapy. *Professionals on Staff* Social Workers 1; Speech Consultant. *Service Facilities Available (with number of rooms)* Consultative (ERT) 2; Self-Contained Rooms 6. *Educational Professionals* Special Education Teachers 6; Paraprofessionals 5; Mental Health Consultant; Speech Consultant. *Curricula* Traditional Academic; Individualized; Basic Skills; Prevocational. *Educational Intervention Approaches* Precision Teaching; Progressive Discipline; Self-Control; Behavior Modification; Creative Conditioning.

Elmcrest Psychiatric Institute

25 Marlboro St, Portland, CT 06480 (203) 342-0480
Year Established 1970
Contact Elaine Walker, School Principal
Facility Information *Placement* Private Residential Care; Private Day Care. *Number of Beds* 63. *Children/Adolescents Served* 73. *Sexes Served* Both. *Room and Board Fees (Approx)* $270. *Tuition Fees (Approx)* $10,000. *Sources of Funding* Health Insurance. Summer school available. *Teacher Certification Level* Elementary

School; Junior High/Middle School; High School. *Special Certification Level* English; Social Studies; Science; Elementary Education.
Student/Patient Characteristics *Age Levels* 9-11; 12-14; 15-17. *IQ Ranges* 85-130; Above 130. *Exceptionalities Served* Emotionally Disturbed; Learning Disabled; Gifted. *Learning Problems* Memory Disabilities; Perceptual Disabilities; Thinking Disabilities; Oral Language Disabilities; Reading Disabilities; Handwriting Disabilities; Spelling Disabilities; Arithmetic Disabilities; Written Expression. *Behavioral Problems* Attention Deficits; Hyperactivity; Hypoactivity; Impulsivity; Self-Aggression; Verbal Aggression; Physical Aggression; Indirect Aggression; Passive Aggression; Withdrawal. *Conditions Treated* Alcohol Abuse and/or Drug Abuse; Other Substance Abuse or Dependence; Early Infantile Autism; Disintegrative Psychoses; Schizophrenia; Aphasia; Convulsive Disorders; Phobias; Obsessions and Compulsions; Hysteria; Depression; Suicide; Asthma; Anorexia Nervosa; Ulcerative Colitis; Inadequacy/Immaturity; Personality Problems; Socialized Aggressive Reaction; Unsocialized Aggressive Reaction.
Services Provided Individual Therapy; Group Therapy; Parent Involvement; Behavior Therapy; Cognitive Developmental Therapy; Family Therapy; Filial Therapy; Drug Therapy; Art Therapy; Reality Therapy; Play Therapy; Psychodrama. *Professionals on Staff* Psychiatrists 7; Psychologists 5; Social Workers 15; Child Care Staff 100; Nurses 15. *Service Facilities Available (with number of rooms)* Resource Rooms 3; Self-Contained Rooms 8; On-Campus Residential School 11. *Educational Professionals* Regular School Teachers 10; Special Education Teachers 4. *Curricula* Traditional Academic; Career/Vocational Education; Individualized; Basic Skills; Prevocational. *Educational Intervention Approaches* Engineered Classroom; Progressive Discipline; Self-Control; Behavior Modification; Positive Peer Culture. *Degrees Awarded* Certificate of Attendance.

Glenholme School

Sabbaday Ln, Washington, CT 06793 (203) 868-7377
Contact Gary L Fitzherbert, Dir
Facility Information *Placement* Private Residential Care; Special Program. *Number of Beds* 118. *Children/Adolescents Served* 128. *Sexes Served* Both. *Tuition Fees (Approx)* $24,600. *Sources of Funding* State Funds. Summer school available. *Teacher Certification Level* Elementary School; Junior High/Middle School. *Special Certification Level* ED; LD; Career/Vocational Education; Reading.
Student/Patient Characteristics *Age Levels* 5-8; 9-11; 12-14; 15-17. *IQ Ranges* 71-85; 85-130; Above 130. *Exceptionalities Served* Emotionally Disturbed; Learning Disabled; Behavioral Difficulties. *Learning Problems* Memory Disabilities; Perceptual Disabilities; Thinking Disabilities; Reading Disabilities; Handwriting Disabilities; Arithmetic Disabilities. *Behavioral Problems* Attention Deficits; Hyperactivity; Impulsivity; Self-Aggression; Verbal Aggression; Physical Aggression; Indirect Aggression; Passive Aggression. *Conditions Treated* Phobias; Obsessions and Compulsions; Depression; Asthma; Inadequacy/Immaturity; Personality Problems; Socialized Aggressive Reaction.
Services Provided Individual Therapy; Group Therapy; Parent Involvement; Behavior Therapy; Family Therapy. *Professionals on Staff* Psychiatrists 1; Psychologists 2; Counselors 16; Social Workers 6; Child Care Staff 11; Nurses 4. *Service Facilities Available (with number of rooms)* Resource Rooms 3; Self-Contained Rooms 3; On-Campus Residential School 14. *Educational Professionals* Regular School Teachers 5; Special Education Teachers 9; Career/Vocational Teachers 3; Special Education Counselors 2; Paraprofessionals 3. *Curricula* Traditional Academic; Career/Vocational Education; Individualized; Basic Skills; Prevocational. *Educational Intervention Approaches* Behavior Modification; Applied Behavior Analysis; Creative Conditioning. *Degrees Awarded* Certificate of Attendance.

Comments The program serves children with emotional disturbances and/or learning disabilities. The educational program includes: the "Lower School" (self-contained classrooms, K-4); the "Upper School" (classrooms operating on a departmental model, 4-8 grade); the Adaptive Education School (programs concentrating on functional academics and practical life/prevocational skills). Support services include a perceptual/cognitive program, speech therapy, behavior management, physical education, psychological and psychiatric services, and social work services.

Greenshire School

725 Jarvis St, Cheshire, CT 06410 (203) 272-1857
Contact Jeanne Guiliano, Dir
Facility Information *Placement* Special School; Private Residential Care; Special Program. *Number of Beds* 56.
Children/Adolescents Served 56. *Sexes Served* Both. *Room and Board Fees (Approx)* $52. *Tuition Fees (Approx)* $15,900. *Sources of Funding* P.L. 94-142; Local Education Agencies. Summer school available. *Teacher Certification Level* Elementary School; Junior High/Middle School; High School. *Special Certification Level* ED; LD; MR.
Student/Patient Characteristics *Age Levels* 0-4; 5-8; 9-11; 12-14; 15-17. *IQ Ranges* 0-25; 26-40; 41-55; 56-70; 71-85.
Exceptionalities Served Autistic; Emotionally Disturbed; Mentally Handicapped; Communication Disordered; Hearing Impaired/Deaf; Visually Impaired/Blind; Other Health Impaired. *Learning Problems* Memory Disabilities; Perceptual Disabilities; Thinking Disabilities; Oral Language Disabilities; Reading Disabilities; Handwriting Disabilities; Spelling Disabilities; Arithmetic Disabilities; Written Expression. *Behavioral Problems* Attention Deficits; Hyperactivity; Hypoactivity; Impulsivity; Self-Aggression; Verbal Aggression; Physical Aggression; Indirect Aggression; Passive Aggression; Withdrawal. *Conditions Treated* Early Infantile Autism; Disintegrative Psychoses; Schizophrenia; Aphasia; Convulsive Disorders; Phobias; Obsessions and Compulsions; Depression; Asthma; Inadequacy/Immaturity; Personality Problems; Socialized Aggressive Reaction; Unsocialized Aggressive Reaction.
Services Provided Individual Therapy; Group Therapy; Parent Involvement; Behavior Therapy; Family Therapy; Drug Therapy; Reality Therapy; Play Therapy; Psychodrama. *Professionals on Staff* Psychiatrists 1; Psychologists 2; Child Care Staff 40; Nurses 3; Speech Pathologists 2. *Service Facilities Available (with number of rooms)* Consultative (ERT) 2; Self-Contained Rooms 10; On-Campus Residential School 18. *Educational Professionals* Special Education Teachers 9; Career/Vocational Teachers 2; Crisis Teachers 1; Paraprofessionals 22. *Curricula* Career/Vocational Education; Individualized; Basic Skills; Prevocational. *Educational Intervention Approaches* Engineered Classroom; Precision Teaching; Progressive Discipline; Self-Control; Behavior Modification; Applied Behavior Analysis; Creative Conditioning. *Degrees Awarded* Certificate of Attendance.
Comments Greenshire is a small, year round, residential school devoted to the development and adjustment of the autistic, emotionally disturbed, brain damaged or retarded children functioning in the moderate through severe ranges.

Grove School

Box 646, 175 Copse Rd, Madison, CT 06443 (203) 245-2778
Year Established 1934
Contact J Sanford Davis, Exec Dir
Facility Information *Placement* Private Residential Care. *Number of Beds* 80. *Children/Adolescents Served* 80. *Sexes Served* Male. *Tuition Fees (Approx)* $26,000. *Sources of Funding* Health Insurance; Private. Summer school available. *Teacher Certification Level* Elementary School; Junior High/Middle School; High School. *Special Certification Level* ED; LD.
Student/Patient Characteristics *Age Levels* 9-11; 12-14; 15-17; 18-21. *IQ Ranges* 85-130; Above 130. *Exceptionalities Served* Emotionally Disturbed; Learning Disabled. *Behavioral Problems* Attention Deficits; Hyperactivity; Impulsivity; Verbal Aggression; Passive Aggression; Withdrawal. *Conditions Treated* Phobias; Obsessions and Compulsions; Depression; Inadequacy/Immaturity; Personality Problems; Socialized Aggressive Reaction; Unsocialized Aggressive Reaction.

Services Provided Individual Therapy; Group Therapy; Parent Involvement; Family Therapy; Drug Therapy; Art Therapy; Reality Therapy. *Professionals on Staff* Psychiatrists 4; Psychologists 4; Social Workers 1; Child Care Staff 22; Nurses 1. *Service Facilities Available (with number of rooms)* Resource Rooms 1; Self-Contained Rooms 23; On-Campus Residential School. *Educational Professionals* Special Education Teachers 22. *Curricula* Traditional Academic; Individualized. *Educational Intervention Approaches* Engineered Classroom; Precision Teaching; Progressive Discipline; Self-Control; Applied Behavior Analysis. *Degrees Awarded* High School Diploma.
Comments Grove School is designed to meet the needs of boys (10 years of age and older) with average or above average intelligence, who have failed to make a satisfactory adjustment in their homes, schools, or social relationships.

Hall-Brooke Foundation—Hall-Brooke Hospital—Hall-Brooke School

47 Long Lots Rd, Westport, CT 06881 (203) 227-1251
Contact Admissions Officer
Facility Information *Placement* Special School; Private Residential Care; Private Day Care; Special Program. *Number of Beds* 30. *Children/Adolescents Served* 30 (inpatient); 20 (partial hospital); 60 (school). *Sexes Served* Both. *Sources of Funding* Health Insurance; Medicaid; Medicare; P.L. 94-142. Summer school available. *Teacher Certification Level* Elementary School; Junior High/Middle School; High School. *Special Certification Level* LD; Reading; Math; Science; Foreign Language; Art; English; Social Studies.
Student/Patient Characteristics *Age Levels* 5-8; 9-11; 12-14; 15-17; 18-21; Over 21. *IQ Ranges* 56-70; 71-85; 85-130; Above 130. *Exceptionalities Served* Emotionally Disturbed; Learning Disabled. *Learning Problems* Memory Disabilities; Perceptual Disabilities; Thinking Disabilities; Oral Language Disabilities; Reading Disabilities; Handwriting Disabilities; Spelling Disabilities; Arithmetic Disabilities; Written Expression. *Behavioral Problems* Attention Deficits; Hyperactivity; Hypoactivity; Impulsivity; Self-Aggression; Verbal Aggression; Physical Aggression; Indirect Aggression; Passive Aggression; Withdrawal. *Conditions Treated* Alcohol Abuse and/or Drug Abuse; Other Substance Abuse or Dependence; Schizophrenia; Phobias; Obsessions and Compulsions; Hysteria; Depression; Suicide; Anorexia Nervosa; Inadequacy/Immaturity; Personality Problems; Socialized Aggressive Reaction; Unsocialized Aggressive Reaction.
Services Provided Individual Therapy; Group Therapy; Parent Involvement; Family Therapy; Filial Therapy; Drug Therapy; Art Therapy; Music Therapy. *Professionals on Staff* Psychiatrists 10; Psychologists 11; Counselors 2; Social Workers 10; Nurses 30; Specialty Therapists; Administrators; Volunteers 300.

Highland Heights—St Francis Home for Children Inc

PO Box 1224, 651 Prospect St, New Haven, CT 06505 (203) 777-5513
Contact Sr Mary Frances McMahon, Exec Dir
Facility Information *Placement* Special School; Private Residential Care; Private Day Care. *Number of Beds* 48. *Children/Adolescents Served* 48 (residential); 16 (day treatment). *Sexes Served* Both. *Tuition Fees (Approx)* $10,000-$16,333 (school). *Sources of Funding* State Funds; Medicaid; P.L. 94-142. Summer school available. *Teacher Certification Level* Elementary School. *Special Certification Level* ED; LD; Reading; Library; Speech; Early Childhood.
Student/Patient Characteristics *Age Levels* 5-8; 9-11; 12-14; 15-17. *IQ Ranges* 71-85; 85-130. *Exceptionalities Served* Emotionally Disturbed; Learning Disabled. *Learning Problems* Perceptual Disabilities; Oral Language Disabilities; Reading Disabilities; Handwriting Disabilities; Spelling Disabilities; Arithmetic Disabilities; Written Expression. *Behavioral Problems* Attention Deficits; Hyperactivity; Impulsivity; Self-Aggression; Verbal Aggression; Indirect Aggression; Passive Aggression; Withdrawal.

Conditions Treated Other Substance Abuse or Dependence; Phobias; Inadequacy/Immaturity; Personality Problems; Socialized Aggressive Reaction.

Services Provided Individual Therapy; Group Therapy; Parent Involvement; Family Therapy; Play Therapy. *Professionals on Staff* Psychiatrists; Social Workers 8; Child Care Staff 32; Nurses 1. *Service Facilities Available (with number of rooms)* Consultative (ERT) 1; Transition Rooms 4; Self-Contained Rooms 2. *Educational Professionals* Special Education Teachers 6; Special Education Counselors 1; Paraprofessionals 4; Educational Diagnostician; Program Coordinator. *Curricula* Individualized; Basic Skills; Early Childhood. *Educational Intervention Approaches* Engineered Classroom; Self-Control; Learning Center.

Comments Highland Heights is a residential and intensive day treatment center and community based services program for emotionally disturbed children. The program offers comprehensive special education services, intensive psychotherapy for children, family therapy, milieu therapy, therapeutic child care, specialized foster care, and adoption services.

The Institute of Living School

400 Washington St, Hartford, CT 06106 (203) 241-6923
Contact John E Gaisford, Dir

Facility Information *Placement* Hospital School. *Number of Beds* 125. *Children/Adolescents Served* 100. *Sexes Served* Both. *Room and Board Fees (Approx)* $250. *Tuition Fees (Approx)* $9,000-$10,000. *Sources of Funding* State Funds; Health Insurance; Medicaid; P.L. 94-142. *Teacher Certification Level* Elementary School; Junior High/Middle School; High School. *Special Certification Level* ED; LD; Reading; Math; Secondary.

Student/Patient Characteristics *Age Levels* 12-14; 15-17; 18-21. *IQ Ranges* 85-130. *Exceptionalities Served* Emotionally Disturbed; Learning Disabled. *Learning Problems* Perceptual Disabilities; Reading Disabilities; Spelling Disabilities; Arithmetic Disabilities. *Behavioral Problems* Attention Deficits; Hyperactivity; Hypoactivity; Impulsivity; Self-Aggression; Verbal Aggression; Physical Aggression; Indirect Aggression; Passive Aggression; Withdrawal. *Conditions Treated* Alcohol Abuse and/or Drug Abuse; Other Substance Abuse or Dependence; Early Infantile Autism; Disintegrative Psychoses; Schizophrenia; Aphasia; Convulsive Disorders; Phobias; Obsessions and Compulsions; Hysteria; Depression; Suicide; Asthma; Anorexia Nervosa; Ulcerative Colitis; Inadequacy/Immaturity; Personality Problems; Socialized Aggressive Reaction; Unsocialized Aggressive Reaction.

Services Provided Individual Therapy; Group Therapy; Parent Involvement; Biofeedback; Family Therapy; Drug Therapy. *Professionals on Staff* Psychiatrists 58; Psychologists 14; Counselors 25; Nurses 60; Psychological Technician. *Service Facilities Available (with number of rooms)* Self-Contained Rooms 1; Hospital School 14. *Educational Professionals* Regular School Teachers; Special Education Teachers; Special Education Counselors. *Curricula* Traditional Academic; Basic Skills. *Educational Intervention Approaches* Multidisciplinary Teams. *Degrees Awarded* High School Diploma; Graduate Equivalency Diploma.

Comments Entry to the school follows hospital admission.

The Mid Fairfield Child Guidance Center Inc

74 Newtown Ave, Norwalk, CT 06851 (203) 847-3891
Contact Charles T Sansoho, Chief Psychiatric Social Worker

Facility Information *Placement* Outpatient Child Guidance Center. *Sexes Served* Both. *Sources of Funding* State Funds; Health Insurance; United Way; Grants.

Student/Patient Characteristics *Age Levels* 0-4; 5-8; 9-11; 12-14; 15-17. *Exceptionalities Served* Autistic; Emotionally Disturbed; Learning Disabled; Communication Disordered. *Learning Problems* Memory Disabilities; Perceptual Disabilities; Thinking Disabilities; Oral Language Disabilities; Reading Disabilities; Handwriting Disabilities; Spelling Disabilities; Arithmetic Disabilities; Written Expression. *Behavioral Problems* Attention Deficits; Hyperactivity; Hypoactivity; Impulsivity; Self-Aggression; Verbal Aggression; Physical Aggression; Indirect Aggression; Passive Aggression; Withdrawal. *Conditions Treated*

Phobias; Obsessions and Compulsions; Hysteria; Depression; Suicide; Inadequacy/Immaturity; Personality Problems; Socialized Aggressive Reaction; Unsocialized Aggressive Reaction.

Services Provided Individual Therapy; Group Therapy; Parent Involvement; Behavior Therapy; Cognitive Developmental Therapy; Family Therapy; Drug Therapy; Art Therapy; Reality Therapy; Play Therapy. *Professionals on Staff* Psychiatrists 1; Psychologists 3; Counselors 2; Social Workers 8; Parents Aids 4.

Comments The center is a nonprofit agency providing evaluation and treatment services to youngsters ages 2-18 experiencing emotional, developmental, and behavioral problems.

North Central Connecticut Mental Health Systems Inc

1077 Enfield St, Enfield, CT 06082 (203) 745-2438
Year Established 1965
Contact Karen Snyder, Senior Therapist

Comments The North Central Connecticut Mental Health Systems, provides emergency services, psychiatric day treatment for the mentally ill, and outpatient counseling with a specialty in sexual abuse work. It services an 11 town catchment area.

Psychiatric Clinic of the Charlotte Hungerford Hospital

540 Litchfield St, Torrington, CT 06790 (203) 496-6350
Year Established 1962
Contact Alan Marinaccio, Mgr

Facility Information *Placement* Outpatient Psychiatric Clinic. *Sexes Served* Both. *Sources of Funding* State Funds; Health Insurance; Medicaid.

Student/Patient Characteristics *Age Levels* 0-4; 5-8; 9-11; 12-14; 15-17. *IQ Ranges* 0-25; 26-40; 41-55; 56-70; 71-85; 85-130; Above 130. *Exceptionalities Served* Emotionally Disturbed; Mentally Handicapped. *Learning Problems* Memory Disabilities; Perceptual Disabilities; Thinking Disabilities; Oral Language Disabilities; Reading Disabilities; Handwriting Disabilities; Spelling Disabilities; Arithmetic Disabilities; Written Expression. *Behavioral Problems* Attention Deficits; Hyperactivity; Hypoactivity; Impulsivity; Self-Aggression; Verbal Aggression; Physical Aggression; Indirect Aggression; Passive Aggression; Withdrawal. *Conditions Treated* Alcohol Abuse and/or Drug Abuse; Other Substance Abuse or Dependence; Early Infantile Autism; Disintegrative Psychoses; Schizophrenia; Aphasia; Convulsive Disorders; Phobias; Obsessions and Compulsions; Hysteria; Depression; Suicide; Asthma; Anorexia Nervosa; Inadequacy/Immaturity; Personality Problems; Socialized Aggressive Reaction; Unsocialized Aggressive Reaction.

Services Provided Individual Therapy; Group Therapy; Parent Involvement; Behavior Therapy; Cognitive Developmental Therapy; Family Therapy; Filial Therapy; Drug Therapy; Reality Therapy; Play Therapy. *Professionals on Staff* Psychiatrists 5; Psychologists 2; Social Workers 6.

Sheldon Community Guidance Clinic Inc

26 Russell St, New Britain, CT 06107 (203) 223-2778
Year Established 1942
Contact William R Poe, Dir

Facility Information *Placement* Special School; Private Day Care; Outpatient Guidance Clinic. *Children/Adolescents Served* 15 (day program); 840 (outpatient). *Sexes Served* Both. *Room and Board Fees (Approx)* $60. *Sources of Funding* State Funds; Health Insurance; Medicaid. *Teacher Certification Level* High School. *Special Certification Level* ED; LD; Reading; Math.

Student/Patient Characteristics *Age Levels* 15-17. *IQ Ranges* 85-130; Above 130. *Exceptionalities Served* Emotionally Disturbed; Learning Disabled; Communication Disordered. *Learning Problems* Perceptual Disabilities; Thinking Disabilities; Reading Disabilities; Handwriting Disabilities; Spelling Disabilities; Arithmetic Disabilities; Written Expression. *Behavioral Problems* Attention Deficits; Impulsivity; Verbal Aggression; Passive Aggression; Withdrawal. *Conditions Treated* Alcohol Abuse and/or Drug Abuse; Phobias; Depression; Anorexia Nervosa; Inadequacy/Immaturity; Personality Problems.

Services Provided Individual Therapy; Group Therapy; Parent Involvement; Family Therapy; Reality Therapy; Psychodrama. *Professionals on Staff* Psychiatrists 1; Psychologists 3; Social Workers 1. *Service Facilities Available (with number of rooms)* Resource Rooms 1; Special School 6. *Educational Professionals* Special Education Teachers 4; Therapists 4. *Curricula* Individualized. *Educational Intervention Approaches* Self-Control. *Degrees Awarded* High School Diploma.

Southbury Training School

Rt 172, Southbury, CT 06488 (203) 264-8231
Year Established 1940
Contact Francis X Bean, Asst Supt

Facility Information *Placement* Public Residential Care. *Number of Beds* 26. *Children/Adolescents Served* 1100. *Sexes Served* Both. *Room and Board Fees (Approx)* $85. *Tuition Fees (Approx)* $31,096. *Sources of Funding* State Funds. Summer school available. *Special Certification Level* ED; LD; MR.

Student/Patient Characteristics *Age Levels* 12-14; 15-17; 18-21; Over 21. *IQ Ranges* 0-25; 26-40; 41-55; 56-70; 71-85; 85-130. *Exceptionalities Served* Autistic; Emotionally Disturbed; Learning Disabled; Mentally Handicapped; Communication Disordered; Hearing Impaired/Deaf; Visually Impaired/Blind; Other Health Impaired; Physically Handicapped. *Learning Problems* Memory Disabilities; Perceptual Disabilities; Thinking Disabilities; Oral Language Disabilities; Reading Disabilities; Handwriting Disabilities; Spelling Disabilities; Arithmetic Disabilities; Written Expression. *Behavioral Problems* Attention Deficits; Hyperactivity; Hypoactivity; Impulsivity; Self-Aggression; Verbal Aggression; Physical Aggression; Indirect Aggression; Passive Aggression; Withdrawal. *Conditions Treated* Early Infantile Autism; Disintegrative Psychoses; Schizophrenia; Aphasia; Convulsive Disorders; Phobias; Obsessions and Compulsions; Depression; Suicide; Asthma; Inadequacy/Immaturity; Personality Problems; Socialized Aggressive Reaction; Unsocialized Aggressive Reaction.

Services Provided Individual Therapy; Group Therapy; Parent Involvement; Behavior Therapy; Drug Therapy; Art Therapy; Music Therapy. *Professionals on Staff* Psychiatrists 1; Psychologists 16; Social Workers 17; Child Care Staff 700; Nurses 71. *Service Facilities Available (with number of rooms)* Self-Contained Rooms 45; On-Campus Residential School; Homebound Instruction 2. *Educational Professionals* Special Education Teachers 45; Paraprofessionals 6; Vocational Instructors 15. *Curricula* Individualized; Basic Skills; Prevocational; Functional Education. *Educational Intervention Approaches* Behavior Modification; Applied Behavior Analysis.

Comments Southbury is a state institution for mentally retarded. The complications are commonplace: behavior disorders, seizures disorders, physical handicaps, non-ambulatory, sensory deficits.

Sunny Hill Children's Center Inc

977 King St, Greenwich, CT 06830 (203) 531-9706
Year Established 1964
Contact Edith L Bickle, Exec Dir

Facility Information *Placement* Special School; Day Treatment. *Children/Adolescents Served* 10 and their families. *Sexes Served* Both. *Tuition Fees (Approx)* $11,020. *Sources of Funding* P.L. 94-142; Private Gifts; Thrift Shop; Auxilliary. Summer school available. *Teacher Certification Level* Elementary School; Junior High/Middle School. *Special Certification Level* ED; LD; Career/Vocational Education; Reading.

Student/Patient Characteristics *Age Levels* 0-4; 5-8; 9-11; 12-14; 18-21. *IQ Ranges* Above 130. *Exceptionalities Served* Autistic; Emotionally Disturbed; Learning Disabled; Communication Disordered; Multi Handicapped. *Behavioral Problems* Attention Deficits; Hyperactivity; Hypoactivity; Impulsivity; Self-Aggression; Physical Aggression; Indirect Aggression; Passive Aggression; Withdrawal. *Conditions Treated* Early Infantile Autism;

Disintegrative Psychoses; Schizophrenia; Personality Problems; Socialized Aggressive Reaction; Unsocialized Aggressive Reaction.

Services Provided Individual Therapy; Parent Involvement; Family Therapy; Art Therapy; Music Therapy; Reality Therapy; Play Therapy. *Professionals on Staff* Psychiatrists 1; Psychologists 1; Counselors 5; Social Workers 1; Child Care Staff 6. *Service Facilities Available (with number of rooms)* Consultative (ERT) 1; Resource Rooms 1; General Use Rooms; Music Room 2; Special School 3. *Educational Professionals* Regular School Teachers 3; Special Education Teachers 3; Paraprofessionals 1; Crisis Counselors 5. *Curricula* Individualized; Prevocational.

Comments Sunny Hill is a private agency working with seriously disturbed young children and their families. The program focuses on the school phobic child, the autistic child, and the child with severe behavior disorders.

Vitam Center Inc—Vitam School

57 W Rocks Rd, Norwalk, CT 06851 (203) 846-2091
Year Established 1970
Contact Norman M Levy, Med Dir

Facility Information *Placement* Public School; Special School; Private Residential Care; Private Day Care. *Number of Beds* 99. *Children/Adolescents Served* 120. *Sexes Served* Both. *Room and Board Fees (Approx)* $58. *Tuition Fees (Approx)* $8,289. *Sources of Funding* State Funds; Health Insurance; P.L. 94-142; Chapter I; Chapter II. *Teacher Certification Level* Elementary School; Junior High/Middle School; High School. *Special Certification Level* ED; LD; Career/Vocational Education; Reading; Math; Special Education.

Student/Patient Characteristics *Age Levels* 12-14; 15-17. *IQ Ranges* 85-130; Above 130. *Exceptionalities Served* Emotionally Disturbed; Learning Disabled; Gifted. *Learning Problems* Perceptual Disabilities; Thinking Disabilities; Oral Language Disabilities; Reading Disabilities; Handwriting Disabilities; Spelling Disabilities; Arithmetic Disabilities; Written Expression. *Behavioral Problems* Attention Deficits; Hyperactivity; Hypoactivity; Impulsivity; Verbal Aggression; Indirect Aggression; Passive Aggression; Withdrawal. *Conditions Treated* Alcohol Abuse and/or Drug Abuse; Phobias; Obsessions and Compulsions; Depression; Asthma; Anorexia Nervosa; Inadequacy/Immaturity; Personality Problems; Socialized Aggressive Reaction; Unsocialized Aggressive Reaction.

Services Provided Individual Therapy; Group Therapy; Parent Involvement; Behavior Therapy; Cognitive Developmental Therapy; Family Therapy; Drug Therapy; Art Therapy; Music Therapy; Reality Therapy; Play Therapy; Psychodrama. *Professionals on Staff* Psychiatrists 1; Counselors 9; Social Workers 2; Child Care Staff 13; Nurses 6. *Service Facilities Available (with number of rooms)* Special School 7. *Educational Professionals* Special Education Teachers 16. *Curricula* Career/Vocational Education; Individualized; Basic Skills; Prevocational. *Educational Intervention Approaches* Behavior Modification.

Comments The primary objective of the treatment program is to provide rehabilitative services to youth in crisis.

Waterford Country School

78 Hunts Brook Rd, Quaker Hill, CT 06375 (203) 442-9454
Year Established 1922
Contact David B Moorehead, Exec Dir

Facility Information *Placement* Special School; Private Residential Care; Specialized Foster Care. *Number of Beds* 60. *Children/Adolescents Served* 60. *Sexes Served* Both. *Room and Board Fees (Approx)* $45. *Tuition Fees (Approx)* $10,200. *Sources of Funding* State Funds; Health Insurance; P.L. 94-142. Summer school available. *Teacher Certification Level* Junior High/Middle School; High School. *Special Certification Level* ED; LD; MR; Career/Vocational Education; Reading; Math; Speech Therapy.

Student/Patient Characteristics *Age Levels* 9-11; 12-14; 15-17; 18-21. *IQ Ranges* 26-40; 41-55; 56-70; 71-85; 85-130; Above 130. *Exceptionalities Served* Autistic; Emotionally Disturbed; Learning Disabled; Mentally Handicapped; Communication Disordered;

Other Health Impaired; Physically Handicapped. *Learning Problems* Memory Disabilities; Perceptual Disabilities; Thinking Disabilities; Oral Language Disabilities; Reading Disabilities; Handwriting Disabilities; Spelling Disabilities; Arithmetic Disabilities; Written Expression. *Behavioral Problems* Attention Deficits; Hyperactivity; Hypoactivity; Impulsivity; Self-Aggression; Verbal Aggression; Physical Aggression; Indirect Aggression; Passive Aggression; Withdrawal. *Conditions Treated* Convulsive Disorders; Phobias; Obsessions and Compulsions; Hysteria; Depression; Suicide; Asthma; Inadequacy/Immaturity; Personality Problems; Socialized Aggressive Reaction; Unsocialized Aggressive Reaction.

Services Provided Individual Therapy; Group Therapy; Parent Involvement; Behavior Therapy; Cognitive Developmental Therapy; Family Therapy; Filial Therapy; Art Therapy; Music Therapy; Reality Therapy; Play Therapy. *Professionals on Staff* Psychiatrists 1; Psychologists 2; Counselors 2; Social Workers 5; Child Care Staff 30; Nurses 2. *Service Facilities Available (with number of rooms)* On-Campus Residential School 12. *Educational Professionals* Regular School Teachers 2; Special Education Teachers 6; Career/Vocational Teachers 2; Paraprofessionals 2. *Curricula* Career/Vocational Education; Individualized; Basic Skills; Prevocational. *Educational Intervention Approaches* Engineered Classroom; Self-Control; Behavior Modification. *Degrees Awarded* Certificate of Attendance; Progression Into Public School Placement Diploma.

West Hartford Public Schools Off-Campus Program

211 Steele Rd, West Hartford, CT 06117 (203) 236-6081
Year Established 1983
Contact Anne Gauvin, Pupil Serv Coord
Facility Information *Placement* Public School.
Children/Adolescents Served 20. *Sexes Served* Both. *Sources of Funding* P.L. 94-142. Summer school available. *Teacher Certification Level* High School. *Special Certification Level* ED; LD; MR; Career/Vocational Education.
Student/Patient Characteristics *Age Levels* 15-17; 18-21. *IQ Ranges* 85-130. *Exceptionalities Served* Emotionally Disturbed; Learning Disabled; Gifted. *Learning Problems* Memory Disabilities; Perceptual Disabilities; Thinking Disabilities; Reading Disabilities; Handwriting Disabilities; Spelling Disabilities; Arithmetic Disabilities; Written Expression. *Behavioral Problems* Attention Deficits; Hyperactivity; Impulsivity; Self-Aggression; Verbal Aggression; Physical Aggression; Indirect Aggression; Passive Aggression; Withdrawal. *Conditions Treated* Alcohol Abuse and/or Drug Abuse; Other Substance Abuse or Dependence; Disintegrative Psychoses; Schizophrenia; Convulsive Disorders; Phobias; Obsessions and Compulsions; Hysteria; Depression; Suicide; Asthma; Anorexia Nervosa; Inadequacy/Immaturity; Personality Problems; Socialized Aggressive Reaction.
Services Provided Individual Therapy; Group Therapy; Parent Involvement; Family Therapy; Reality Therapy. *Professionals on Staff* Psychiatrists 1; Social Workers 2. *Service Facilities Available (with number of rooms)* Consultative (ERT) 2; Self-Contained Rooms 2. *Educational Professionals* Special Education Teachers 2; Career/Vocational Teachers 1; Paraprofessionals 2. *Curricula* Traditional Academic; Career/Vocational Education;

Individualized; Basic Skills; Prevocational. *Educational Intervention Approaches* Progressive Discipline; Behavior Modification; Applied Behavior Analysis. *Degrees Awarded* High School Diploma.

Wheeler Clinic Inc—Northwest Village School

91 Northwest Dr, Plainville, CT 06062 (203) 747-6801
Year Established 1973
Contact John Mattas, Ed Dir
Facility Information *Placement* Special School; Private Residential Care; Private Day Care; Special Program; Family Services. *Number of Beds* 13. *Sexes Served* Both. *Room and Board Fees (Approx)* $60. *Tuition Fees (Approx)* $16,000. *Sources of Funding* State Funds; Health Insurance; Medicaid; Medicare; P.L. 94-142; Third Party. Summer school available. *Teacher Certification Level* Elementary School; Junior High/Middle School; High School. *Special Certification Level* ED; LD; MR; Reading; Math; Physical Education.
Student/Patient Characteristics *Age Levels* 0-4; 5-8; 9-11; 12-14; 15-17. *IQ Ranges* 26-40; 41-55; 56-70; 71-85; 85-130; Above 130. *Exceptionalities Served* Autistic; Emotionally Disturbed; Learning Disabled; Mentally Handicapped; Communication Disordered; Physically Handicapped. *Learning Problems* Memory Disabilities; Perceptual Disabilities; Thinking Disabilities; Oral Language Disabilities; Reading Disabilities; Handwriting Disabilities; Spelling Disabilities; Arithmetic Disabilities; Written Expression; Gross and Fine Motor Deficits. *Behavioral Problems* Attention Deficits; Hyperactivity; Hypoactivity; Impulsivity; Self-Aggression; Verbal Aggression; Physical Aggression; Indirect Aggression; Passive Aggression; Withdrawal. *Conditions Treated* Alcohol Abuse and/or Drug Abuse; Other Substance Abuse or Dependence; Early Infantile Autism; Disintegrative Psychoses; Schizophrenia; Aphasia; Convulsive Disorders; Phobias; Obsessions and Compulsions; Hysteria; Depression; Suicide; Asthma; Anorexia Nervosa; Inadequacy/Immaturity; Personality Problems; Socialized Aggressive Reaction; Unsocialized Aggressive Reaction.
Services Provided Individual Therapy; Group Therapy; Parent Involvement; Behavior Therapy; Cognitive Developmental Therapy; Biofeedback; Family Therapy; Reality Therapy; Play Therapy; Psychodrama. *Professionals on Staff* Psychiatrists 2; Psychologists 15; Counselors 15; Social Workers 25; Child Care Staff 10; Nurses 1; Occupation Therapy 3; Speech Therapy 3. *Service Facilities Available (with number of rooms)* Consultative (ERT) 20; Itinerants 5; Resource Rooms 5; Transition Rooms 5; Self-Contained Rooms 15; On-Campus Residential School 6. *Educational Professionals* Regular School Teachers 5; Special Education Teachers 15; Crisis Teachers 10; Paraprofessionals 50. *Curricula* Traditional Academic; Career/Vocational Education; Individualized; Basic Skills; Prevocational; Alternative; Wilderness. *Educational Intervention Approaches* Engineered Classroom; Precision Teaching; Progressive Discipline; Self-Control; Behavior Modification; Applied Behavior Analysis. *Degrees Awarded* Certificate of Attendance.

Comments The Wheeler Clinic has served Central Connecticut for 12 years. Services include work with children and their families in a wide range of human services, especially mental health and education.

Delaware

Delaware Guidance Services for Children and Youth Inc

1213 Delaware Ave, Wilmington, DE 19806 (302) 652-3948
Year Established 1952
Contact Allen Oliver, Exec Dir

Facility Information *Placement* Outpatient Psychiatric Clinic. *Sexes Served* Both. *Sources of Funding* Health Insurance; P.L. 94-142; Grants; United Way. *Special Certification Level* ED; LD.

Student/Patient Characteristics *Age Levels* 0-4; 5-8; 9-11; 12-14; 15-17. *IQ Ranges* 56-70; 71-85; 85-130; Above 130. *Exceptionalities Served* Emotionally Disturbed; Learning Disabled; Mentally Handicapped; Hearing Impaired/Deaf; Other Health Impaired; Physically Handicapped. *Learning Problems* Memory Disabilities; Perceptual Disabilities; Thinking Disabilities; Oral Language Disabilities; Reading Disabilities; Handwriting Disabilities; Spelling Disabilities; Arithmetic Disabilities; Written Expression. *Behavioral Problems* Attention Deficits; Hyperactivity; Hypoactivity; Impulsivity; Self-Aggression; Verbal Aggression; Physical Aggression; Indirect Aggression; Passive Aggression; Withdrawal. *Conditions Treated* Schizophrenia; Convulsive Disorders; Phobias; Obsessions and Compulsions; Hysteria; Depression; Suicide; Asthma; Anorexia Nervosa; Ulcerative Colitis; Inadequacy/Immaturity; Personality Problems; Socialized Aggressive Reaction; Unsocialized Aggressive Reaction.

Services Provided Individual Therapy; Group Therapy; Parent Involvement; Behavior Therapy; Cognitive Developmental Therapy; Family Therapy; Drug Therapy; Play Therapy. *Professionals on Staff* Psychiatrists 2; Psychologists 4; Social Workers 8.

Comments This program provides a multi-disciplinary approach to outpatient psychiatric services for children and adolescents and their families.

Department of Public Instruction

PO Box 1402, Townsend Bldg, Dover, DE 19903 (302) 736-4667
Contact Carl M Haltom, Dir Exceptional Children Special Prog Div

Facility Information *Placement* Public School; Special School. *Children/Adolescents Served* 10,000. *Sexes Served* Both. *Sources of Funding* State Funds; P.L. 94-142; P.L. 89-313. Summer school available. *Teacher Certification Level* Elementary School; Junior High/Middle School; High School. *Special Certification Level* ED; LD; MR.

Student/Patient Characteristics *Age Levels* 0-4; 5-8; 9-11; 12-14; 15-17; 18-21. *IQ Ranges* 0-25; 26-40; 41-55; 56-70; 71-85; 85-130; Above 130. *Exceptionalities Served* Autistic; Emotionally Disturbed; Learning Disabled; Mentally Handicapped; Communication Disordered; Hearing Impaired/Deaf; Visually Impaired/Blind; Other Health Impaired; Physically Handicapped; Gifted; Deaf/Blind. *Learning Problems* Memory Disabilities; Perceptual Disabilities; Thinking Disabilities; Oral Language Disabilities; Reading Disabilities; Handwriting Disabilities; Spelling Disabilities; Arithmetic Disabilities; Written Expression. *Behavioral Problems* Attention Deficits; Hyperactivity; Hypoactivity; Impulsivity; Self-Aggression; Verbal Aggression; Physical Aggression; Indirect Aggression; Passive Aggression; Withdrawal. *Conditions Treated* Early Infantile Autism; Schizophrenia; Convulsive Disorders; Obsessions and Compulsions.

Services Provided Individual Therapy; Group Therapy; Parent Involvement; Behavior Therapy; Cognitive Developmental Therapy; Music Therapy; Physical Therapy; Occupational Therapy; Speech Therapy. *Professionals on Staff* Psychologists; Counselors; Nurses; Physical Therapy. *Service Facilities Available (with number of rooms)* Consultative (ERT); Resource Rooms; Transition Rooms; Self-Contained Rooms; Special School; Hospital School; Homebound Instruction. *Educational Professionals* Regular School Teachers; Special Education Teachers; Career/Vocational Teachers; Crisis Teachers; Special Education Counselors; Paraprofessionals. *Curricula* Traditional Academic; Career/Vocational Education; Individualized; Basic Skills; Prevocational. *Educational Intervention Approaches* Engineered Classroom; Precision Teaching; Progressive Discipline; Self-Control; Behavior Modification; Applied Behavior Analysis. *Degrees Awarded* Certificate of Attendance; High School Diploma; Graduate Equivalency Diploma.

Comments The State of Delaware has 19 school districts, of which 17 provide services to handicapped children. There are special schools for the OH, MR, severe LD/SEM, and Hard of Hearing. Complex/Rare children are served in private placement to meet their needs. All districts provide educational services through level 4 of the continuum of services within the home school. Special schools are level 5.

Terry Children's Psychiatric Center

10 Central Ave, New Castle, DE 19720 (215) 421-6661
Year Established 1970
Contact Elizabeth A Waters, Special Ed Assist

Facility Information *Placement* Special School; Public Residential Care. *Number of Beds* 25. *Children/Adolescents Served* 50. *Sexes Served* Both. *Tuition Fees (Approx)* $18,000. *Sources of Funding* State Funds. Summer school available. *Teacher Certification Level* Elementary School. *Special Certification Level* ED; LD; MR.

Student/Patient Characteristics *Age Levels* 0-4; 5-8; 9-11; 12-14. *Exceptionalities Served* Emotionally Disturbed; Learning Disabled; Mentally Handicapped; Communication Disordered. *Learning Problems* Perceptual Disabilities; Oral Language Disabilities; Reading Disabilities; Handwriting Disabilities; Spelling Disabilities; Arithmetic Disabilities; Written Expression. *Behavioral Problems* Attention Deficits; Hyperactivity; Hypoactivity; Impulsivity; Self-Aggression; Verbal Aggression; Physical Aggression; Indirect Aggression; Passive Aggression; Withdrawal.

Conditions Treated Schizophrenia; Phobias; Obsessions and Compulsions; Hysteria; Depression; Suicide; Anorexia Nervosa; Inadequacy/Immaturity; Personality Problems; Socialized Aggressive Reaction; Unsocialized Aggressive Reaction.

Services Provided Individual Therapy; Group Therapy; Parent Involvement; Family Therapy; Drug Therapy; Music Therapy; Play Therapy. *Professionals on Staff* Psychiatrists 5; Psychologists 4; Counselors 10; Social Workers 5; Child Care Staff 28; Nurses 7; Recreational Therapist 3. *Service Facilities Available (with number of rooms)* Resource Rooms 1; Transition Rooms 1; On-Campus Residential School 6. *Educational Professionals* Special Education Teachers 8; Paraprofessionals 1. *Curricula* Traditional Academic; Individualized; Basic Skills. *Educational Intervention Approaches* Engineered Classroom; Behavior Modification.

District of Columbia

District of Columbia Public Schools—Division of Special Education and Pupil Personnel Services

10th and H Sts NW, Washington, DC 20001 (202) 724-4018
Contact Doris A Woodson, Asst Supt

Facility Information *Placement* Public School; Special School; Public Residential Care; Private Residential Care; Private Day Care; Public Day Care. *Children/Adolescents Served* 727. *Sexes Served* Both. *Sources of Funding* State Funds; P.L. 94-142. *Teacher Certification Level* Elementary School; Junior High/Middle School; High School. *Special Certification Level* ED.

Student/Patient Characteristics *Age Levels* 0-4; 5-8; 9-11; 12-14; 15-17; 18-21. *Exceptionalities Served* Emotionally Disturbed; Learning Disabled. *Learning Problems* Memory Disabilities; Perceptual Disabilities; Thinking Disabilities; Oral Language Disabilities; Reading Disabilities; Handwriting Disabilities; Spelling Disabilities; Arithmetic Disabilities; Written Expression. *Behavioral Problems* Attention Deficits; Hyperactivity; Hypoactivity; Impulsivity; Self-Aggression; Verbal Aggression; Physical Aggression; Indirect Aggression; Passive Aggression; Withdrawal.

Services Provided Individual Therapy; Group Therapy; Parent Involvement. *Professionals on Staff* Psychologists; Counselors; Social Workers. *Service Facilities Available (with number of rooms)* Itinerants; Resource Rooms; Self-Contained Rooms; Learning Centers; Special School; Hospital School; On-Campus Residential School. *Educational Professionals* Special Education Teachers; Paraprofessionals. *Curricula* Traditional Academic; Individualized; Competency Based Curriculum Guide; Affective Domain. *Educational Intervention Approaches* Expressive Therapies; Crisis Intervention; Surface Management; Life Space Interviewing; Operant Procedures. *Degrees Awarded* Certificate of Attendance; High School Diploma.

The Episcopal Center for Children

5901 Utah Ave NW, Washington, DC 20015 (202) 363-1333
Year Established 1959
Contact Alan C Korz, Dir

Facility Information *Placement* Private Residential Care; Private Day Care. *Number of Beds* 22. *Children/Adolescents Served* 50. *Sexes Served* Both. *Tuition Fees (Approx)* $17,960 (day program); $24,608 (residential program). *Sources of Funding* P.L. 94-142; United Way; Contributions; Memberships; Endowment. *Teacher Certification Level* Elementary School. *Special Certification Level* ED; LD.

Student/Patient Characteristics *Age Levels* 5-8; 9-11; 12-14. *IQ Ranges* 71-85; 85-130; Above 130. *Exceptionalities Served* Emotionally Disturbed; Learning Disabled. *Learning Problems* Memory Disabilities; Perceptual Disabilities; Oral Language Disabilities; Reading Disabilities; Written Expression. *Behavioral Problems* Attention Deficits; Hyperactivity; Impulsivity; Self-Aggression; Verbal Aggression; Physical Aggression; Indirect Ag-

gression; Passive Aggression; Withdrawal. *Conditions Treated* Schizophrenia; Depression; Socialized Aggressive Reaction; Unsocialized Aggressive Reaction.

Services Provided Individual Therapy; Group Therapy; Parent Involvement; Behavior Therapy; Family Therapy; Drug Therapy; Music Therapy; Psychodrama. *Professionals on Staff* Psychiatrists 2; Psychologists 2; Social Workers 6; Child Care Staff 10; Nurses 2; Art Therapist 1; Speech Therapist 1. *Service Facilities Available (with number of rooms)* Resource Rooms 2; Transition Rooms 1; Self-Contained Rooms 6. *Educational Professionals* Special Education Teachers 7; Adaptive Physical Education 1; Workshop Teacher 1. *Curricula* Traditional Academic; Individualized; Basic Skills. *Educational Intervention Approaches* Engineered Classroom; Progressive Discipline; Self-Control; Behavior Modification.

Comments The Episcopal Center is a residential and day treatment facility (5-day) for emotionally disturbed children and their families from the greater Washington D.C. metropolitan area. The average stay is 3 years and the age at time of intake ranges from 5 to 10-1/2.

St Elizabeth's Hospital—Division of Child and Adolescent Services

2700 Martin Luther King Jr Ave SE, Washington, DC 20032
(202) 574-7100
Year Established 1978
Contact Michael W Mills, Dir; Arthur Strauss, Med Dir

Facility Information *Placement* Psychiatric Hospital. *Number of Beds* 32. *Children/Adolescents Served* 32. *Sexes Served* Both. *Room and Board Fees (Approx)* $224. *Sources of Funding* HEW; Health Insurance; Medicaid. Summer school available. *Teacher Certification Level* Elementary School; Junior High/Middle School; High School. *Special Certification Level* Reading; Math.

Student/Patient Characteristics *Age Levels* 5-8; 9-11; 12-14; 15-17. *Exceptionalities Served* Emotionally Disturbed. *Learning Problems* Memory Disabilities; Perceptual Disabilities; Thinking Disabilities; Oral Language Disabilities; Reading Disabilities; Handwriting Disabilities; Spelling Disabilities; Arithmetic Disabilities; Written Expression. *Behavioral Problems* Attention Deficits; Hyperactivity; Hypoactivity; Impulsivity; Self-Aggression; Verbal Aggression; Physical Aggression; Indirect Aggression; Passive Aggression; Withdrawal. *Conditions Treated* Alcohol Abuse and/or Drug Abuse; Other Substance Abuse or Dependence; Disintegrative Psychoses; Schizophrenia; Phobias; Obsessions and Compulsions; Hysteria; Depression; Suicide; Asthma; Inadequacy/Immaturity; Personality Problems; Socialized Aggressive Reaction; Unsocialized Aggressive Reaction.

Services Provided Individual Therapy; Group Therapy; Parent Involvement; Behavior Therapy; Family Therapy; Drug Therapy; Art Therapy; Music Therapy; Play Therapy; Psychodrama; Recreational Therapy; Occupational Therapy. *Professionals on Staff*

Psychiatrists 4; Psychologists 4; Social Workers 3; Child Care Staff 26; Nurses 14; Pediatrian. *Service Facilities Available (with number of rooms)* Hospital School 3. *Educational Professionals* Special Education Teachers 6. *Curricula* Traditional Academic; Individualized; Basic Skills; Prevocational. *Educational Intervention Approaches* Behavior Modification. *Degrees Awarded* Certificate of Attendance.

Comments The Child and Adolescent Division of Saint Elizabeth's Hospital is a 32 bed inpatient program which offers acute and intermediate inpatient care to children and adolescents aged 6-17 years. Comprehensive diagnostic services are provided. Limited treatment services are offered.

St John's Child Development Center

5005 MacArthur Blvd NW, Washington, DC 20016
(202) 363-7032
Year Established 1868
Contact Thomas Wilds, Dir

Facility Information *Placement* Special School; Private Residential Care; Special Program. *Number of Beds* 15. *Children/Adolescents Served* 100. *Sexes Served* Both. *Tuition Fees (Approx)* $14,000. *Sources of Funding* State Funds; Health Insurance; Medicaid; P.L. 94-142; Private Donations. Summer school available. *Special Certification Level* ED; MR; Career/Vocational Education.

Student/Patient Characteristics *Age Levels* 0-4; 5-8; 9-11; 12-14; 15-17; 18-21; Over 21. *Exceptionalities Served* Autistic. *Learning Problems* Memory Disabilities; Perceptual Disabilities; Thinking Disabilities; Oral Language Disabilities; Reading Disabilities; Handwriting Disabilities; Spelling Disabilities; Arithmetic Disabilities; Written Expression. *Behavioral Problems* Attention Deficits; Hyperactivity; Hypoactivity; Impulsivity; Self-Aggression; Verbal Aggression; Physical Aggression; Indirect Aggression; Passive Aggression; Withdrawal. *Conditions Treated* Early Infantile Autism; Convulsive Disorders; Obsessions and Compulsions; Socialized Aggressive Reaction; Unsocialized Aggressive Reaction.

Services Provided Individual Therapy; Group Therapy; Parent Involvement; Behavior Therapy; Family Therapy; Speech Therapy; Physical Therapy; Adaptive Physical Education; Occupational Therapy; Dance Movement Therapy; Medical Diagnostic. *Professionals on Staff* Psychologists; Social Workers; Nurses. *Service Facilities Available (with number of rooms)* Special School 15. *Educational Professionals* Special Education Teachers 15; Career/Vocational Teachers 2; Special Education Counselors 1; Paraprofessionals 15. *Curricula* Traditional Academic; Career/Vocational Education; Individualized; Basic Skills; Prevocational. *Educational Intervention Approaches* Engineered Classroom; Precision Teaching; Progressive Discipline; Self-Control; Behavior Modification; Applied Behavior Analysis; Creative Conditioning. *Degrees Awarded* Certificate of Completion.

Sibley Hospital—Groome Center—Hayes Hall

5225 Loughboro Rd NW, Washington, DC 20016
(202) 362-7644
Year Established 1969
Contact Helen F Rehwaldt, Dir

Facility Information *Placement* Family Therapy Center. *Children/Adolescents Served* 100. *Sexes Served* Both. *Sources of Funding* Health Insurance; Fees; Contributions.

Student/Patient Characteristics *Age Levels* 5-8; 9-11; 12-14; 15-17; 18-21; Over 21. *IQ Ranges* 85-130; Above 130. *Exceptionalities Served* Emotionally Disturbed; Learning Disabled. *Behavioral Problems* Hyperactivity; Impulsivity; Self-Aggression; Verbal Aggression. *Conditions Treated* Alcohol Abuse and/or Drug Abuse; Schizophrenia; Phobias; Obsessions and Compulsions; Depression; Suicide; Anorexia Nervosa; Ulcerative Colitis; Personality Problems.

Services Provided Individual Therapy; Group Therapy; Family Therapy; Drug Therapy. *Professionals on Staff* Psychiatrists 1; Social Workers 5; Nurses 2.

Comments Groome Center is a nonprofit outpatient mental health facility serving the metropolitan Washington DC area. All treatment is based on Bowen Family Therapy Theory.

Walter Reed Army Medical Center Child and Adolescent Psychiatry Service

Washington, DC 20307 (202) 576-1855
Year Established 1960
Contact Robert O Shearer, Chief of Serv

Facility Information *Placement* Psychiatric Outpatient Services. *Children/Adolescents Served* 400. *Sexes Served* Both. *Sources of Funding* Federal.

Student/Patient Characteristics *Age Levels* 0-4; 5-8; 9-11; 12-14; 15-17; 18-21. *IQ Ranges* 0-25; 26-40; 41-55; 56-70; 71-85; 85-130; Above 130. *Exceptionalities Served* Autistic; Emotionally Disturbed; Learning Disabled; Mentally Handicapped; Communication Disordered; Hearing Impaired/Deaf; Visually Impaired/Blind; Other Health Impaired; Physically Handicapped; Gifted. *Learning Problems* Memory Disabilities; Perceptual Disabilities; Thinking Disabilities; Oral Language Disabilities; Reading Disabilities; Handwriting Disabilities; Spelling Disabilities; Arithmetic Disabilities; Written Expression. *Behavioral Problems* Attention Deficits; Hyperactivity; Hypoactivity; Impulsivity; Self-Aggression; Verbal Aggression; Physical Aggression; Indirect Aggression; Passive Aggression; Withdrawal. *Conditions Treated* Alcohol Abuse and/or Drug Abuse; Other Substance Abuse or Dependence; Early Infantile Autism; Disintegrative Psychoses; Schizophrenia; Aphasia; Convulsive Disorders; Phobias; Obsessions and Compulsions; Hysteria; Depression; Suicide; Asthma; Anorexia Nervosa; Ulcerative Colitis; Inadequacy/Immaturity; Personality Problems; Socialized Aggressive Reaction; Unsocialized Aggressive Reaction.

Services Provided Individual Therapy; Group Therapy; Parent Involvement; Behavior Therapy; Family Therapy; Drug Therapy; Art Therapy; Play Therapy. *Professionals on Staff* Psychiatrists 7; Psychologists 1; Social Workers 5; Art Therapists 3.

Comments Walter Reed is a full service medical center with a full range of specialist and subspecialist services.

Florida

All Children's Hospital

801 6th St S, St Petersburg, FL 33701 (813) 898-7451
Year Established 1978
Contact Joseph Crum, Dir
Facility Information *Placement* Evaluation, Consultation and Hospital Referral. *Sexes Served* Both. *Sources of Funding* State Funds; Health Insurance; Private. .
Student/Patient Characteristics *Age Levels* 0-4; 5-8; 9-11; 12-14; 15-17; 18-21. *IQ Ranges* 0-25; 26-40; 41-55; 56-70; 71-85; 85-130; Above 130. *Exceptionalities Served* Autistic; Emotionally Disturbed; Learning Disabled; Mentally Handicapped; Communication Disordered; Hearing Impaired/Deaf; Visually Impaired/Blind; Other Health Impaired; Physically Handicapped; Gifted. *Learning Problems* Memory Disabilities; Perceptual Disabilities; Thinking Disabilities; Oral Language Disabilities; Reading Disabilities; Handwriting Disabilities; Spelling Disabilities; Arithmetic Disabilities; Written Expression. *Behavioral Problems* Attention Deficits; Hyperactivity; Hypoactivity; Impulsivity; Self-Aggression; Verbal Aggression; Physical Aggression; Indirect Aggression; Passive Aggression; Withdrawal. *Conditions Treated* Early Infantile Autism; Disintegrative Psychoses; Schizophrenia; Aphasia; Convulsive Disorders; Phobias; Obsessions and Compulsions; Hysteria; Depression; Suicide; Asthma; Anorexia Nervosa; Ulcerative Colitis; Inadequacy/Immaturity; Personality Problems; Socialized Aggressive Reaction; Unsocialized Aggressive Reaction.
Services Provided Individual Therapy; Parent Involvement; Behavior Therapy; Cognitive Developmental Therapy; Family Therapy; Play Therapy. *Professionals on Staff* Psychologists 3. *Curricula* Individualized. *Educational Intervention Approaches* Precision Teaching; Behavior Modification.

Bunche Park Elementary School

16001 Bunche Park School Dr, Opa Locka, FL 33054
(305) 621-1469
Contact Betty Angel, Principal
Facility Information *Placement* Public School.
Children/Adolescents Served 200. *Sexes Served* Both. *Sources of Funding* State Funds; HEW; P.L. 94-142. Summer school available. *Teacher Certification Level* Elementary School; Junior High/Middle School. *Special Certification Level* LD; MR.
Student/Patient Characteristics *Age Levels* 5-8; 9-11; 12-14. *IQ Ranges* 0-25. *Exceptionalities Served* Autistic; Emotionally Disturbed; Learning Disabled; Mentally Handicapped; Other Health Impaired; Trainable, Severe and Profound. *Learning Problems* Memory Disabilities; Perceptual Disabilities; Thinking Disabilities; Oral Language Disabilities; Reading Disabilities; Handwriting Disabilities; Spelling Disabilities; Arithmetic Disabilities; Written Expression. *Behavioral Problems* Attention Deficits; Hyperactivity; Impulsivity; Self-Aggression; Verbal Aggression; Physical Aggression; Withdrawal.

Services Provided Individual Therapy; Group Therapy; Parent Involvement; Behavior Therapy; Cognitive Developmental Therapy; Art Therapy; Music Therapy. *Professionals on Staff* Psychologists 1; Counselors 1; Social Workers 10. *Service Facilities Available (with number of rooms)* Consultative (ERT) 1; Itinerants 1; Resource Rooms 1; Self-Contained Rooms 18; Homebound Instruction 1. *Educational Professionals* Regular School Teachers 20; Special Education Teachers 21; Special Education Counselors 1; Paraprofessionals 18. *Curricula* Traditional Academic; Individualized; Basic Skills; Prevocational. *Educational Intervention Approaches* Behavior Modification.

Cantwell Academy Inc

8571 SW 112th St, Miami, FL 33156 (305) 271-4500
Year Established 1979
Contact Ronald J Cantwell, Dir
Facility Information *Placement* Special School.
Children/Adolescents Served 45. *Sexes Served* Both. *Tuition Fees (Approx)* $4,950. *Sources of Funding* Health Insurance; Tuition. Summer school available. *Teacher Certification Level* Elementary School. *Special Certification Level* ED; LD; MR; Reading; Math.
Student/Patient Characteristics *Age Levels* 5-8; 9-11; 12-14; 15-17. *IQ Ranges* 71-85; 85-130; Above 130. *Exceptionalities Served* Emotionally Disturbed; Learning Disabled; Communication Disordered. *Learning Problems* Memory Disabilities; Perceptual Disabilities; Thinking Disabilities; Oral Language Disabilities; Reading Disabilities; Handwriting Disabilities; Spelling Disabilities; Arithmetic Disabilities; Written Expression. *Behavioral Problems* Attention Deficits; Hyperactivity; Hypoactivity; Impulsivity; Verbal Aggression; Physical Aggression; Indirect Aggression; Passive Aggression; Withdrawal. *Conditions Treated* Convulsive Disorders; Obsessions and Compulsions; Hysteria; Depression; Asthma; Anorexia Nervosa; Ulcerative Colitis; Inadequacy/Immaturity; Personality Problems.
Services Provided Individual Therapy; Group Therapy; Parent Involvement; Behavior Therapy; Cognitive Developmental Therapy; Family Therapy; Drug Therapy. *Professionals on Staff* Psychologists 1; Counselors 1; Child Care Staff 1. *Service Facilities Available (with number of rooms)* Self-Contained Rooms 5. *Educational Professionals* Special Education Teachers 3; Medical Administrative 1. *Curricula* Traditional Academic; Individualized; Basic Skills; Prevocational. *Educational Intervention Approaches* Engineered Classroom; Progressive Discipline; Behavior Modification; Applied Behavior Analysis. *Degrees Awarded* Certificate of Attendance.

Comments This is a multi-disciplinary treatment facility for combined management of learning and/or behavioral difficulties.

Child Development Service—Lakeview Center Inc

1200 W Avery, Pensacola, FL 32501 (904) 432-1222
Year Established 1972
Contact John Bilbney, Dir

Facility Information *Placement* Special School; Public Residential Care; Private Residential Care; Community Mental Health Center. *Number of Beds* 36. *Children/Adolescents Served* 106. *Sexes Served* Both. *Room and Board Fees (Approx)* $90. *Tuition Fees (Approx)* $5,000. *Sources of Funding* State Funds; Health Insurance; Medicaid; Fees. Summer school available. *Teacher Certification Level* Elementary School; Junior High/Middle School; High School. *Special Certification Level* ED.

Student/Patient Characteristics *Age Levels* 5-8; 9-11; 12-14; 15-17. *IQ Ranges* 56-70; 71-85; 85-130. *Exceptionalities Served* Autistic; Emotionally Disturbed; Mentally Handicapped. *Behavioral Problems* Attention Deficits; Hyperactivity; Hypoactivity; Impulsivity; Self-Aggression; Verbal Aggression; Physical Aggression; Indirect Aggression; Passive Aggression; Withdrawal. *Conditions Treated* Early Infantile Autism; Schizophrenia; Convulsive Disorders; Phobias; Obsessions and Compulsions; Hysteria; Depression; Suicide; Inadequacy/Immaturity; Personality Problems; Socialized Aggressive Reaction; Unsocialized Aggressive Reaction.

Services Provided Individual Therapy; Group Therapy; Parent Involvement; Behavior Therapy; Family Therapy; Drug Therapy. *Professionals on Staff* Psychiatrists 1; Psychologists 6; Counselors 20; Social Workers 4; Child Care Staff 30; Nurses 25. *Service Facilities Available (with number of rooms)* Consultative (ERT); Self-Contained Rooms; On-Campus Residential School. *Educational Professionals* Special Education Teachers 10; Crisis Teachers 1; Paraprofessionals 20. *Curricula* Career/Vocational Education; Individualized; Basic Skills. *Educational Intervention Approaches* Behavior Modification.

Cousins Respite Care Program of the Parent Resource Center Inc

42 E Jackson St, Orlando, FL 32801 (305) 425-3663
Year Established 1976
Contact Joanne M Clark, Exec Dir

Facility Information *Placement* Short Term Residential Respite Care. *Children/Adolescents Served* 80. *Sexes Served* Both. *Sources of Funding* State Funds.

Student/Patient Characteristics *Age Levels* 0-4; 5-8; 9-11; 12-14; 15-17; 18-21; Over 21. *Exceptionalities Served* Autistic; Mentally Handicapped; Hearing Impaired/Deaf; Visually Impaired/Blind; Other Health Impaired; Physically Handicapped.

Services Provided Short Term Residential Respite Care. *Degrees Awarded* Certificate of Attendance.

Comments The Parent Resource Center, Inc. is a family service agency offering a wide variety of services to the community. One of the services, the Cousins Respite Care Program, offers short-term residential respite care (professional sitter service) to families with handicapped children at home and who are H.R.S.-referred.

CRATER of Broward Inc—Retreat Ranch Facility—24 Hour Residential Treatment Center

11301 SW 49th Pl, Fort Lauderdale, FL 33301 (305) 434-1492
Year Established 1982
Contact Frances Madiwale, Exec Dir

Facility Information *Placement* Public School; Special School; Private Residential Care; Special Program. *Number of Beds* 8. *Children/Adolescents Served* 8. *Sexes Served* Male. *Room and Board Fees (Approx)* $65-$200. *Tuition Fees (Approx)* $73,000. *Sources of Funding* State Funds; Health Insurance. Summer school available. *Teacher Certification Level* Elementary School; Junior High/Middle School; High School. *Special Certification Level* ED; LD; MR; Career/Vocational Education; Reading; Math.

Student/Patient Characteristics *Age Levels* 5-8; 9-11; 12-14. *IQ Ranges* 56-70; 71-85; 85-130. *Exceptionalities Served* Emotionally Disturbed; Learning Disabled; Mentally Handicapped; Communication Disordered; Hearing Impaired/Deaf; Visually Impaired/Blind; Other Health Impaired; Physically Handicapped. *Learning Problems* Thinking Disabilities; Reading Disabilities; Handwriting Disabilities; Spelling Disabilities; Arithmetic Disabilities; Written Expression. *Behavioral Problems* Attention Deficits; Hyperactivity; Hypoactivity; Impulsivity; Self-Aggression; Verbal Aggression; Physical Aggression; Indirect Aggression; Passive Aggression; Withdrawal. *Conditions Treated* Phobias; Obsessions and Compulsions; Depression; Inadequacy/Immaturity; Personality Problems; Socialized Aggressive Reaction; Unsocialized Aggressive Reaction.

Services Provided Individual Therapy; Group Therapy; Parent Involvement; Behavior Therapy; Family Therapy; Drug Therapy; Art Therapy; Music Therapy; Reality Therapy; Play Therapy; Psychodrama. *Professionals on Staff* Psychiatrists 1; Psychologists 1; Counselors 2; Social Workers 1; Child Care Staff 2; Nurses 1. *Service Facilities Available (with number of rooms)* Special School; Hospital School; Homebound Instruction. *Educational Professionals* Regular School Teachers; Special Education Teachers; Special Education Counselors.

Comments CRATER is a 24-hour residential treatment center for emotionally disturbed boys in a home-like setting, with 8 beds and in the process of expanding to 16. The children go off-grounds to school. The boys learn daily basic living skills and receive individual, group, and family therapies.

Daniel Memorial Inc

3725 Belfort Rd, Jacksonville, FL 32216 (904) 737-1677
Year Established 1883
Contact Dan Cook, Exec Dir

Facility Information *Placement* Private Residential Care. *Number of Beds* 45. *Children/Adolescents Served* 75. *Sexes Served* Both. *Room and Board Fees (Approx)* $136. *Sources of Funding* State Funds; Health Insurance; United Way; Trusts; Donations. Summer school available. *Teacher Certification Level* Junior High/Middle School; High School. *Special Certification Level* ED; Reading; Math.

Student/Patient Characteristics *Age Levels* 9-11; 12-14; 15-17. *IQ Ranges* 85-130. *Exceptionalities Served* Emotionally Disturbed. *Learning Problems* Memory Disabilities; Perceptual Disabilities; Thinking Disabilities; Oral Language Disabilities; Reading Disabilities; Handwriting Disabilities; Spelling Disabilities; Arithmetic Disabilities; Written Expression. *Behavioral Problems* Attention Deficits; Hyperactivity; Hypoactivity; Impulsivity; Self-Aggression; Verbal Aggression; Physical Aggression; Indirect Aggression; Passive Aggression; Withdrawal. *Conditions Treated* Schizophrenia; Obsessions and Compulsions; Depression; Suicide; Personality Problems; Socialized Aggressive Reaction; Unsocialized Aggressive Reaction.

Services Provided Individual Therapy; Group Therapy; Parent Involvement; Behavior Therapy; Cognitive Developmental Therapy; Family Therapy; Filial Therapy; Art Therapy; Music Therapy; Play Therapy. *Professionals on Staff* Psychiatrists 2; Psychologists 1; Social Workers 6; Child Care Staff 45; Nurses 3. *Service Facilities Available (with number of rooms)* Resource Rooms 2; Self-Contained Rooms 6; On-Campus Residential School 6. *Educational Professionals* Special Education Teachers 7. *Curricula* Traditional Academic; Individualized; Basic Skills; Prevocational. *Educational Intervention Approaches* Progressive Discipline; Self-Control; Behavior Modification.

Comments Daniel Memorial attempts to help emotionally troubled youngsters and their families toward responsible citizenship. On Daniel Memorial's heavily pine-wooded 10 acre tract in the southeastern section of Jacksonville, youngsters are exposed to a new climate of life offering understanding, recognition, acceptance, and effective help.

The Eckerd Wilderness Educational System Camping System

PO Box 7450, Clearwater, FL 33518 (813) 461-2990
Year Established 1968
Contact Dwight Lord, Dir Agency Relations

Facility Information *Placement* Public Residential Care; Private Residential Care; Educational Services. *Number of Beds* 280. *Children/Adolescents Served* 280. *Sexes Served* Both. *Room and Board Fees (Approx)* $42. *Tuition Fees (Approx)* $15,330. *Sources of Funding* State Funds; Donations. Summer school available. *Teacher Certification Level* Elementary School; Junior High/Middle School; High School. *Special Certification Level* ED; LD; Career/Vocational Education; Reading; Math.

Student/Patient Characteristics *Age Levels* 5-8; 9-11; 12-14; 15-17. *IQ Ranges* 56-70; 71-85; 85-130; Above 130. *Exceptionalities Served* Emotionally Disturbed; Learning Disabled; Adjudicated Delinquent; Socially Maladjusted. *Learning Problems* Perceptual Disabilities; Reading Disabilities; Handwriting Disabilities; Spelling Disabilities; Arithmetic Disabilities; Written Expression. *Behavioral Problems* Attention Deficits; Hyperactivity; Impulsivity; Verbal Aggression; Physical Aggression; Passive Aggression; Withdrawal. *Conditions Treated* Alcohol Abuse and/or Drug Abuse; Obsessions and Compulsions; Depression; Inadequacy/Immaturity; Personality Problems; Socialized Aggressive Reaction; Unsocialized Aggressive Reaction.

Services Provided Group Therapy; Parent Involvement; Behavior Therapy; Reality Therapy. *Professionals on Staff* Counselors 14; Social Workers 3. *Service Facilities Available (with number of rooms)* Resource Rooms 1; On-Campus Residential School. *Educational Professionals* Regular School Teachers 15; Special Education Teachers 1; Special Education Counselors 14; Paraprofessionals 1. *Curricula* Traditional Academic; Career/Vocational Education; Individualized; Basic Skills; Prevocational. *Educational Intervention Approaches* Self-Control. *Degrees Awarded* Certificate of Attendance; Graduate Equivalency Diploma.

Comments This program is a system of 11 wilderness camping programs for emotionally troubled youths. The treatment program is eclectic in nature, utilizing a blend of current interventions found effective with youngsters. The year-round program is designed to serve children between the ages of 7 and 17. It is accredited by the Southern Association of Colleges and Schools as an alternative school and member of the National Association of Homes for Children.

Escambia District Schools

5404 Lillian Hwy, Pensacola, FL 32506 (904) 432-6121
Contact Martha E Stokes, Dir Exceptional Student Ed

Facility Information *Placement* Public School. *Sexes Served* Both. *Sources of Funding* State Funds; P.L. 94-142; P.L. 89-313. Summer school available. *Teacher Certification Level* Elementary School; Junior High/Middle School; High School. *Special Certification Level* ED; LD; MR; Career/Vocational Education.

Student/Patient Characteristics *Age Levels* 5-8; 9-11; 12-14; 15-17; 18-21. *IQ Ranges* 0-25; 26-40; 41-55; 56-70; 71-85; 85-130; Above 130. *Exceptionalities Served* Autistic; Emotionally Disturbed; Learning Disabled; Mentally Handicapped; Communication Disordered; Hearing Impaired/Deaf; Visually Impaired/Blind; Other Health Impaired; Physically Handicapped; Gifted. *Learning Problems* Memory Disabilities; Perceptual Disabilities; Thinking Disabilities; Oral Language Disabilities; Reading Disabilities; Handwriting Disabilities; Spelling Disabilities; Arithmetic Disabilities; Written Expression. *Behavioral Problems* Attention Deficits; Hyperactivity; Hypoactivity; Impulsivity; Self-Aggression; Verbal Aggression; Physical Aggression; Indirect Aggression; Passive Aggression; Withdrawal. *Conditions Treated* Alcohol Abuse and/or Drug Abuse; Other Substance Abuse or Dependence; Early Infantile Autism; Aphasia; Convulsive Disorders; Phobias; Obsessions and Compulsions; Depression; Asthma; Anorexia Nervosa; Personality Problems; Socialized Aggressive Reaction; Unsocialized Aggressive Reaction.

Services Provided Individual Therapy; Group Therapy; Parent Involvement; Behavior Therapy; Family Therapy; Drug Therapy. *Professionals on Staff* Psychiatrists; Psychologists; Counselors. *Service Facilities Available (with number of rooms)* Consultative (ERT); Itinerants; Resource Rooms; Transition Rooms; Self-Contained Rooms; Special School; Hospital School; Homebound Instruction. *Educational Professionals* Special Education Teachers 350. *Curricula* Traditional Academic; Career/Vocational Education; Individualized; Basic Skills; Prevocational. *Educational Intervention Approaches* Engineered Classroom; Precision Teaching; Behavior Modification; Applied Behavior Analysis. *Degrees Awarded* Certificate of Attendance; High School Diploma.

Grant Center Hospital

20601 SW 157th Ave, Miami, FL 33187 (305) 251-0710
Year Established 1976
Contact Judy Ford, Admin

Facility Information *Placement* Special School; Psychiatric Hospital. *Number of Beds* 100. *Children/Adolescents Served* 100. *Sexes Served* Both. *Room and Board Fees (Approx)* $305-$360. *Sources of Funding* State Funds; Health Insurance; P.L. 94-142. Summer school available. *Teacher Certification Level* Elementary School; Junior High/Middle School; High School. *Special Certification Level* ED; LD; Content Areas.

Student/Patient Characteristics *Age Levels* 0-4; 5-8; 9-11; 12-14; 15-17; 18-21. *IQ Ranges* 85-130; Above 130. *Exceptionalities Served* Emotionally Disturbed; Learning Disabled. *Learning Problems* Perceptual Disabilities; Thinking Disabilities. *Behavioral Problems* Attention Deficits; Hyperactivity; Hypoactivity; Impulsivity; Self-Aggression; Verbal Aggression; Physical Aggression; Indirect Aggression; Passive Aggression; Withdrawal. *Conditions Treated* Schizophrenia; Phobias; Obsessions and Compulsions; Depression; Suicide; Anorexia Nervosa; Inadequacy/Immaturity; Personality Problems; Socialized Aggressive Reaction; Unsocialized Aggressive Reaction.

Services Provided Individual Therapy; Group Therapy; Parent Involvement; Behavior Therapy; Cognitive Developmental Therapy; Biofeedback; Family Therapy; Filial Therapy; Drug Therapy; Art Therapy; Music Therapy; Reality Therapy; Play Therapy. *Professionals on Staff* Psychiatrists 6; Psychologists 9; Counselors 24; Social Workers 3; Child Care Staff 167; Nurses 27; Activity Therapists 5; Horticulturists 2. *Service Facilities Available (with number of rooms)* Hospital School 16. *Educational Professionals* Special Education Teachers 18; Speech Therapists 2. *Curricula* Traditional Academic; Individualized; Basic Skills; Prevocational. *Educational Intervention Approaches* Precision Teaching; Behavior Modification. *Degrees Awarded* High School Diploma.

Henderson Mental Health Center

330 SW 27th Ave, Fort Lauderdale, FL 33312 (305) 791-4300
Contact Dale Paulison, Chief of Youth Serv

Facility Information *Placement* Outpatient Mental Health Center. *Children/Adolescents Served* 1,540. *Sexes Served* Both. *Sources of Funding* State Funds; Medicaid; P.L. 94-142; County; United Way.

Student/Patient Characteristics *Age Levels* 0-4; 5-8; 9-11; 12-14; 15-17. *Exceptionalities Served* Emotionally Disturbed; Learning Disabled; Mentally Handicapped. *Behavioral Problems* Attention Deficits; Hyperactivity; Hypoactivity; Impulsivity; Self-Aggression; Verbal Aggression; Physical Aggression; Indirect Aggression; Passive Aggression; Withdrawal. *Conditions Treated* Schizophrenia; Phobias; Obsessions and Compulsions; Hysteria; Depression; Suicide; Asthma; Anorexia Nervosa; Inadequacy/Immaturity; Personality Problems; Socialized Aggressive Reaction; Unsocialized Aggressive Reaction.

Services Provided Individual Therapy; Group Therapy; Parent Involvement; Behavior Therapy; Cognitive Developmental Therapy; Family Therapy; Filial Therapy; Drug Therapy; Play Therapy. *Professionals on Staff* Psychiatrists 4; Psychologists 2; Counselors 3; Social Workers 12.5; Case Manager 1.

Comments In addition to outpatient health services at the center, other services are offered at the Henderson Adolescent Pregnancy Program, and the Individual Family Crisis Program. A North and South branch also exist.

ISIS Programs Inc—Individual Support Through Innovative Services for Autistic Persons

PO Box 5086, 1219 Cypress St, Orlando, FL 32855-5086 (305) 422-8645
Year Established 1979
Contact V Suz Baumann, Exec Dir
Facility Information *Placement* Developmental Training Center. *Children/Adolescents Served* 15. *Sexes Served* Both. *Room and Board Fees (Approx)* $32. *Tuition Fees (Approx)* $8,150. *Sources of Funding* State Funds; P.L. 94-142; County Funds; City Funds; Corporate and Private Donations. Summer school available. *Special Certification Level* MR.
Student/Patient Characteristics *Age Levels* Over 21. *IQ Ranges* 41-55; 56-70; 71-85. *Exceptionalities Served* Autistic; Mentally Handicapped; Hearing Impaired/Deaf. *Learning Problems* Memory Disabilities; Perceptual Disabilities; Thinking Disabilities; Oral Language Disabilities; Reading Disabilities; Handwriting Disabilities; Spelling Disabilities; Arithmetic Disabilities; Written Expression. *Behavioral Problems* Attention Deficits; Hyperactivity; Hypoactivity; Impulsivity; Self-Aggression; Physical Aggression; Indirect Aggression; Withdrawal; Self-stimulation. *Conditions Treated* Early Infantile Autism; Aphasia; Convulsive Disorders; Obsessions and Compulsions; Asthma; Anorexia Nervosa; Inadequacy/Immaturity; Socialized Aggressive Reaction; Unsocialized Aggressive Reaction.
Services Provided Individual Therapy; Group Therapy; Parent Involvement; Behavior Therapy; Cognitive Developmental Therapy; Art Therapy; Music Therapy. *Professionals on Staff* Psychologists 1; Counselors 1; Social Workers 5. *Service Facilities Available (with number of rooms)* Self-Contained Rooms 3; On the job vocational training. *Educational Professionals* Special Education Teachers 1; Curriculum Resource Specialist. *Curricula* Career/Vocational Education; Individualized; Basic Skills; Prevocational. *Educational Intervention Approaches* Precision Teaching; Self-Control; Behavior Modification.

Comments The program focuses on functional skills in a community based setting. Students are out in the community every day. Basic academic skills complement job readiness skills.

La Amistad Foundation

357 Knowles Ave, Winter Park, FL 32789 (305) 645-4620
Year Established 1969
Contact Debra Stallworth, Admissions Coord
Facility Information *Placement* Private Residential Care. *Sexes Served* Both. *Room and Board Fees (Approx)* $135. *Sources of Funding* State Funds; Health Insurance. Summer school available. *Teacher Certification Level* High School. *Special Certification Level* ED.
Student/Patient Characteristics *Age Levels* 15-17; 18-21; Over 21. *IQ Ranges* 85-130. *Exceptionalities Served* Emotionally Disturbed. *Learning Problems* Memory Disabilities; Perceptual Disabilities; Thinking Disabilities; Oral Language Disabilities; Reading Disabilities; Spelling Disabilities; Arithmetic Disabilities; Written Expression. *Conditions Treated* Schizophrenia; Depression; Inadequacy/Immaturity; Personality Problems.
Services Provided Individual Therapy; Group Therapy; Parent Involvement; Behavior Therapy; Biofeedback; Family Therapy; Art Therapy; Music Therapy; Play Therapy. *Professionals on Staff* Psychiatrists 2; Psychologists 3; Counselors 4; Child Care Staff 3; Nurses 5. *Service Facilities Available (with number of rooms)* Special School; Hospital School; On-Campus Residential School 1. *Educational Professionals* Regular School Teachers 1; Special Education Teachers 1; Career/Vocational Teachers 2; Paraprofessionals 3. *Curricula* Traditional Academic; Career/Vocational Education; Individualized; Basic Skills; Prevocational.

Educational Intervention Approaches Behavior Modification. *Degrees Awarded* High School Diploma; Graduate Equivalency Diploma.

LaVoy Exceptional Center

4410 W Main St, Tampa, FL 33607 (813) 876-0862
Contact Paul E Rich
Facility Information *Placement* Public School; Special School. *Children/Adolescents Served* 200. *Sexes Served* Both. *Sources of Funding* State Funds; P.L. 94-142; P.L. 89-313. Summer school available. *Teacher Certification Level* Elementary School; Junior High/Middle School; High School. *Special Certification Level* ED; MR; Career/Vocational Education.
Student/Patient Characteristics *Age Levels* 12-14; 15-17; 18-21; Over 21. *IQ Ranges* 0-25; 26-40; 41-55. *Exceptionalities Served* Autistic; Emotionally Disturbed; Mentally Handicapped. *Learning Problems* Memory Disabilities; Perceptual Disabilities; Thinking Disabilities; Oral Language Disabilities; Reading Disabilities; Handwriting Disabilities; Spelling Disabilities; Arithmetic Disabilities; Written Expression. *Behavioral Problems* Attention Deficits; Hyperactivity; Hypoactivity; Impulsivity; Self-Aggression; Verbal Aggression; Physical Aggression; Indirect Aggression; Passive Aggression; Withdrawal. *Conditions Treated* Early Infantile Autism.
Services Provided Behavior Therapy; Cognitive Developmental Therapy; Music Therapy. *Professionals on Staff* Psychiatrists 1; Psychologists 1; Social Workers 1; Nurses 1. *Service Facilities Available (with number of rooms)* Consultative (ERT) 2; Resource Rooms 1; Self-Contained Rooms 28. *Educational Professionals* Special Education Teachers 27; Career/Vocational Teachers 4. *Curricula* Career/Vocational Education; Individualized; Basic Skills; Prevocational. *Educational Intervention Approaches* Behavior Modification. *Degrees Awarded* Certificate of Attendance.

Mental Health Care Center of the Lower Keys

PO Box 488, Key West, FL 33040 (305) 294-5237
Year Established 1983
Contact Keith R D'Amato, Exec Dir
Facility Information *Placement* Outpatient Treatment Crisis Stabilization. *Children/Adolescents Served* 2. *Sexes Served* Both. *Sources of Funding* State Funds; Health Insurance; Medicaid; Medicare.
Student/Patient Characteristics *Age Levels* 5-8; 9-11; 12-14; 15-17; 18-21; Over 21. *IQ Ranges* 56-70; 71-85; 85-130; Above 130. *Exceptionalities Served* Emotionally Disturbed; Learning Disabled. *Behavioral Problems* Attention Deficits; Hyperactivity; Impulsivity; Self-Aggression; Verbal Aggression; Physical Aggression; Withdrawal. *Conditions Treated* Alcohol Abuse and/or Drug Abuse; Disintegrative Psychoses; Schizophrenia; Convulsive Disorders; Phobias; Depression; Suicide; Anorexia Nervosa; Inadequacy/Immaturity; Personality Problems; Socialized Aggressive Reaction; Unsocialized Aggressive Reaction.
Services Provided Individual Therapy; Group Therapy; Parent Involvement; Behavior Therapy; Cognitive Developmental Therapy; Biofeedback; Family Therapy; Drug Therapy; Reality Therapy; Play Therapy. *Professionals on Staff* Psychiatrists 2; Psychologists 3; Counselors 4; Social Workers 2.

Comments The center is predominately an outpatient treatment facility receiving referrals through the local school system, Department of Health and Rehabilitation and other social agencies, as well as individual self-referral.

Northwest Florida Mental Health Center

624 1/2 N Cove Blvd, Panama City, FL 32401 (904) 769-9481
Year Established 1952
Contact Ann M Tabor, Dir Children's Serv
Facility Information *Placement* Special School. *Children/Adolescents Served* 42. *Sexes Served* Both. *Sources of Funding* State Funds; Medicare; P.L. 94-142. Summer school

available. *Teacher Certification Level* Elementary School; Junior High/Middle School; High School. *Special Certification Level* ED.

Student/Patient Characteristics *Age Levels* 0-4; 5-8; 9-11; 12-14; 15-17; 18-21. *IQ Ranges* 71-85; 85-130; Above 130. *Exceptionalities Served* Autistic; Emotionally Disturbed. *Learning Problems* Memory Disabilities; Perceptual Disabilities; Thinking Disabilities; Oral Language Disabilities; Reading Disabilities; Handwriting Disabilities; Spelling Disabilities; Arithmetic Disabilities; Written Expression. *Behavioral Problems* Attention Deficits; Hyperactivity; Hypoactivity; Impulsivity; Self-Aggression; Verbal Aggression; Physical Aggression; Indirect Aggression; Passive Aggression; Withdrawal. *Conditions Treated* Early Infantile Autism; Disintegrative Psychoses; Schizophrenia; Phobias; Obsessions and Compulsions; Hysteria; Depression; Suicide; Anorexia Nervosa; Inadequacy/Immaturity; Personality Problems; Socialized Aggressive Reaction; Unsocialized Aggressive Reaction.

Services Provided Individual Therapy; Group Therapy; Parent Involvement; Behavior Therapy; Cognitive Developmental Therapy; Family Therapy; Drug Therapy; Play Therapy. *Professionals on Staff* Psychiatrists 2; Psychologists 3; Counselors 5; Child Care Staff 6. *Service Facilities Available (with number of rooms)* Special School 5. *Educational Professionals* Special Education Teachers 4; Career/Vocational Teachers 1; Paraprofessionals 6. *Curricula* Traditional Academic; Career/Vocational Education; Individualized; Basic Skills; Prevocational. *Educational Intervention Approaches* Precision Teaching; Progressive Discipline; Self-Control; Behavior Modification; Applied Behavior Analysis. *Degrees Awarded* Certificate of Attendance; Graduate Equivalency Diploma.

Comments This is a day treatment program for severely disturbed students run jointly by the mental health center and the local school system. Evaluation, consultation and therapy services are offered on an outpatient basis as well.

Orange County Public School System—Gateway School

4000 Silver Star Rd, Orlando, FL 32808 (305) 293-6252
Contact Mary Louise Wicks, Principal

Facility Information *Placement* Public School; Special School. *Children/Adolescents Served* 215. *Sexes Served* Both. *Sources of Funding* State Funds; P.L. 94-142. Summer school available. *Teacher Certification Level* Elementary School. *Special Certification Level* ED; LD; MR.

Student/Patient Characteristics *Age Levels* 0-4; 5-8; 9-11; 12-14. *IQ Ranges* 56-70; 71-85; 85-130; Above 130. *Exceptionalities Served* Emotionally Disturbed; Learning Disabled; Communication Disordered. *Learning Problems* Memory Disabilities; Perceptual Disabilities; Thinking Disabilities; Oral Language Disabilities; Reading Disabilities; Handwriting Disabilities; Spelling Disabilities; Arithmetic Disabilities; Written Expression. *Behavioral Problems* Attention Deficits; Hyperactivity; Impulsivity; Self-Aggression; Verbal Aggression; Physical Aggression; Indirect Aggression; Passive Aggression; Withdrawal. *Conditions Treated* Depression.

Services Provided Individual Therapy; Group Therapy; Parent Involvement; Behavior Therapy; Family Therapy; Art Therapy; Music Therapy; Play Therapy. *Professionals on Staff* Psychologists 1; Social Workers 1; Nurses 1; Therapists 2. *Service Facilities Available (with number of rooms)* Self-Contained Rooms 19; Special School 19. *Educational Professionals* Special Education Teachers 30; Paraprofessionals 23. *Curricula* Traditional Academic; Career/Vocational Education; Individualized; Basic Skills; Prevocational. *Educational Intervention Approaches* Precision Teaching; Behavior Modification.

Orlando Regional Medical Center—Mental Health Department—Children's Services

1500 Orange Ave, Orlando, FL 32806 (305) 841-5171
Year Established 1968
Contact Katherine Wecherle, Outpatient Coord

Facility Information *Placement* Childrens Mental Health Services. *Number of Beds* 5. *Children/Adolescents Served* 300 (outpatient); 5 (inpatient). *Sexes Served* Both. *Sources of Funding* State Funds; Health Insurance; Medicaid; Medicare.

Student/Patient Characteristics *IQ Ranges* 71-85; 85-130; Above 130. *Exceptionalities Served* Emotionally Disturbed; Learning Disabled; Physically Handicapped. *Learning Problems* Memory Disabilities; Perceptual Disabilities; Thinking Disabilities; Oral Language Disabilities; Reading Disabilities. *Behavioral Problems* Attention Deficits; Hyperactivity; Impulsivity; Verbal Aggression; Physical Aggression; Indirect Aggression; Passive Aggression; Withdrawal. *Conditions Treated* Alcohol Abuse and/or Drug Abuse; Other Substance Abuse or Dependence; Early Infantile Autism; Disintegrative Psychoses; Schizophrenia; Convulsive Disorders; Phobias; Obsessions and Compulsions; Hysteria; Depression; Suicide; Asthma; Anorexia Nervosa; Ulcerative Colitis; Inadequacy/Immaturity; Personality Problems; Socialized Aggressive Reaction; Unsocialized Aggressive Reaction.

Services Provided Individual Therapy; Group Therapy; Parent Involvement; Behavior Therapy; Biofeedback; Family Therapy; Drug Therapy; Art Therapy; Reality Therapy; Play Therapy. *Professionals on Staff* Psychiatrists 2; Psychologists 5; Counselors 2; Social Workers 4; Nurses 3.

Peace River Center for Personal Development Inc

1745 Hwy 17 S, Bartow, FL 33830 (813) 533-3141
Contact Barbara O'Brien, Planner Evaluator

Facility Information *Placement* Emotionally Disturbed Residential Facility. *Number of Beds* 8. *Children/Adolescents Served* 8. *Sexes Served* Both. *Room and Board Fees (Approx)* Sliding Scale. *Sources of Funding* State Funds; Health Insurance; Medicaid; Fees.

Student/Patient Characteristics *Age Levels* 5-8; 9-11; 12-14; 15-17. *IQ Ranges* 71-85; 85-130; Above 130. *Exceptionalities Served* Emotionally Disturbed. *Behavioral Problems* Physical Aggression; Indirect Aggression; Passive Aggression; Withdrawal. *Conditions Treated* Disintegrative Psychoses; Schizophrenia; Phobias; Obsessions and Compulsions; Hysteria; Depression; Suicide; Inadequacy/Immaturity; Personality Problems; Socialized Aggressive Reaction; Unsocialized Aggressive Reaction.

Services Provided Individual Therapy; Group Therapy; Parent Involvement; Behavior Therapy; Family Therapy; Play Therapy. *Professionals on Staff* Psychiatrists 1; Psychologists 1; Counselors 2; Social Workers 1.

Seminole County Board of Public Instruction—Programs for Emotionally Handicapped

1211 Mellonville Ave, Sanford, FL 32771 (305) 322-1252
Year Established 1972
Contact Daniel L Scinto, Coord

Facility Information *Placement* Public School; Special School. *Children/Adolescents Served* 480. *Sexes Served* Both. *Sources of Funding* State Funds; P.L. 94-142; Grants. Summer school available. *Teacher Certification Level* Elementary School; Junior High/Middle School; High School. *Special Certification Level* ED.

Student/Patient Characteristics *Age Levels* 5-8; 9-11; 12-14; 15-17; 18-21. *IQ Ranges* 56-70; 71-85; 85-130; Above 130. *Exceptionalities Served* Autistic; Emotionally Disturbed; Severe Emotionally Disturbed. *Learning Problems* Memory Disabilities; Perceptual Disabilities; Thinking Disabilities; Oral Language Disabilities; Reading Disabilities; Handwriting Disabilities; Spelling Disabilities; Arithmetic Disabilities; Written Expression. *Behavioral Problems* Attention Deficits; Hyperactivity; Hypoactivity; Impulsivity; Self-Aggression; Verbal Aggression; Physical Aggression; Indirect Aggression; Passive Aggression; Withdrawal. *Conditions Treated* Early Infantile Autism; Schizophrenia; Convulsive Disorders; Phobias; Obsessions and Compulsions; Hysteria; Depression; Inadequacy/Immaturity; Personality Problems; Socialized Aggressive Reaction; Unsocialized Aggressive Reaction.

Services Provided Parent Involvement; Behavior Therapy; Family Therapy. *Professionals on Staff* Psychiatrists; Psychologists 11; Counselors 1; Social Workers; Nurses. *Service Facilities Available (with number of rooms)* Resource Rooms 20; Self-Contained Rooms 20; Special School 4. *Educational Professionals* Special Education Teachers 45. *Curricula* Traditional Academic; Career/ Vocational Education; Individualized; Basic Skills; Prevocational; Affective. *Educational Intervention Approaches* Engineered Classroom; Precision Teaching; Self-Control; Behavior Modification; Applied Behavior Analysis. *Degrees Awarded* Certificate of Attendance; High School Diploma; Graduate Equivalency Diploma; Special Diploma.

Sunset Learning Center

3775 SW 16th St, Fort Lauderdale, FL 33312 (305) 583-5025
Contact Dr Griffin
Facility Information *Placement* Public School.
Children/Adolescents Served 80. *Sexes Served* Both. *Sources of Funding* State Funds; P.L. 94-142; County; United Way. Summer school available. *Teacher Certification Level* Elementary School; Junior High/Middle School; High School. *Special Certification Level* ED.
Student/Patient Characteristics *Age Levels* 9-11; 12-14; 15-17; 18-21; Over 21. *IQ Ranges* 56-70; 71-85; 85-130; Above 130.
Exceptionalities Served Emotionally Disturbed; Learning Disabled; Other Health Impaired. *Learning Problems* Memory Disabilities; Perceptual Disabilities; Thinking Disabilities; Oral Language Disabilities; Reading Disabilities; Handwriting Disabilities; Spelling Disabilities; Arithmetic Disabilities; Written Expression. *Behavioral Problems* Attention Deficits; Hyperactivity; Impulsivity; Self-Aggression; Verbal Aggression; Physical Aggression; Indirect Aggression; Passive Aggression; Withdrawal. *Conditions Treated* Alcohol Abuse and/or Drug Abuse; Schizophrenia; Convulsive Disorders; Phobias; Depression; Suicide; Personality Problems; Socialized Aggressive Reaction; Unsocialized Aggressive Reaction.
Services Provided Individual Therapy; Group Therapy; Parent Involvement; Behavior Therapy; Cognitive Developmental Therapy; Family Therapy; Reality Therapy; Play Therapy; Psychodrama; Occupational Therapy; Physical Therapy. *Professionals on Staff* Psychiatrists 1; Psychologists 1; Social Workers 5. *Service Facilities Available (with number of rooms)* Resource Rooms 1; Self-Contained Rooms 1. *Educational Professionals* Special Education Teachers 7; Career/Vocational Teachers 3; Special Education Counselors 2; Paraprofessionals 9. *Curricula* Traditional Academic; Career/Vocational Education; Individualized; Basic Skills; Prevocational. *Educational Intervention Approaches* Progressive Discipline; Self-Control; Behavior Modification; Applied Behavior Analysis. *Degrees Awarded* Certificate of Attendance; High School Diploma.
Comments Sunset Day Treatment Program is a mental health service offered and housed on public school grounds.

Threshold Inc

PO Box 1110, Goldenrod, FL 32733 (305) 671-7060
Year Established 1976
Contact Mel Fleck, Dir; Teena Willard, Pres
Facility Information *Placement* Private Residential Care. *Number of Beds* 9. *Children/Adolescents Served* 9. *Sexes Served* Both. *Room and Board Fees (Approx)* $15. *Tuition Fees (Approx)* $31,786. *Sources of Funding* State Funds; Medicaid; Health and Rehabilitative Services. Summer school available. *Teacher Certification Level* High School. *Special Certification Level* MR.
Student/Patient Characteristics *Age Levels* 5-8; 9-11; 12-14; 15-17; 18-21. *IQ Ranges* 0-25; 26-40; 41-55; 56-70.
Exceptionalities Served Autistic; Mentally Handicapped.

Learning Problems Memory Disabilities; Perceptual Disabilities; Thinking Disabilities; Oral Language Disabilities; Reading Disabilities; Handwriting Disabilities; Spelling Disabilities; Arithmetic Disabilities; Written Expression. *Behavioral Problems* Attention Deficits; Hyperactivity; Impulsivity; Self-Aggression; Verbal Aggression; Physical Aggression; Indirect Aggression; Withdrawal. *Conditions Treated* Early Infantile Autism; Schizophrenia; Obsessions and Compulsions.
Services Provided Behavior Therapy. *Professionals on Staff* Psychologists 1; Treatment Workers 16. *Service Facilities Available (with number of rooms)* Special School 8; Residential Treatment 16. *Educational Professionals* Regular School Teachers 1; Paraprofessionals 3. *Curricula* Individualized; Basic Skills; Prevocational. *Educational Intervention Approaches* Behavior Modification; Applied Behavior Analysis. *Degrees Awarded* Certificate of Attendance.

University of South Florida—Florida Mental Health Institute—Department of Child and Family Services

13301 N 30th St, Tampa, FL 33612 (813) 974-4619
Year Established 1973
Contact L Adlai Boyd, Chair
Facility Information *Placement* Public School; Special School; Public Residential Care; Public Day Care; Special Program; University Based Research; Training and Service Mental Health Institute. *Number of Beds* 36. *Children/Adolescents Served* 80. *Sexes Served* Both. *Room and Board Fees (Approx)* $52. *Sources of Funding* State Funds; P.L. 94-142. Summer school available. *Teacher Certification Level* Elementary School; Junior High/Middle School. *Special Certification Level* ED.
Student/Patient Characteristics *Age Levels* 0-4; 5-8; 9-11; 12-14; 15-17. *IQ Ranges* 56-70; 71-85; 85-130; Above 130.
Exceptionalities Served Autistic; Emotionally Disturbed; Learning Disabled; Mentally Handicapped; Communication Disordered; Hearing Impaired/Deaf. *Learning Problems* Memory Disabilities; Perceptual Disabilities; Thinking Disabilities; Oral Language Disabilities; Reading Disabilities; Handwriting Disabilities; Spelling Disabilities; Arithmetic Disabilities; Written Expression. *Behavioral Problems* Attention Deficits; Hyperactivity; Hypoactivity; Impulsivity; Self-Aggression; Verbal Aggression; Physical Aggression; Indirect Aggression; Passive Aggression; Withdrawal. *Conditions Treated* Alcohol Abuse and/or Drug Abuse; Early Infantile Autism; Disintegrative Psychoses; Schizophrenia; Aphasia; Convulsive Disorders; Phobias; Obsessions and Compulsions; Depression; Inadequacy/Immaturity; Personality Problems; Socialized Aggressive Reaction; Unsocialized Aggressive Reaction.
Services Provided Individual Therapy; Group Therapy; Parent Involvement; Behavior Therapy; Cognitive Developmental Therapy; Family Therapy; Filial Therapy; Drug Therapy; Art Therapy; Music Therapy. *Professionals on Staff* Psychiatrists 1; Psychologists 8; Counselors 20; Social Workers 8; Child Care Staff 17; Nurses 4. *Service Facilities Available (with number of rooms)* Consultative (ERT) 11; On-Campus Residential School. *Educational Professionals* Special Education Teachers 12; Special Education Counselors 3; Paraprofessionals 40; Music; Speech. *Curricula* Traditional Academic; Individualized; Basic Skills; Prevocational; Language Conditioning. *Educational Intervention Approaches* Engineered Classroom; Precision Teaching; Behavior Modification; Applied Behavior Analysis. *Degrees Awarded* High School Diploma.
Comments There are 4 distinct research projects within the department: Teaching Family Project (4 group homes for SED kids); Children's Intensive Residential Treatment (group home for 8 using shift model); Adolescent Day Treatment (24): and Early Childhood, Day and Community Project (18 preschoolers and 15 elementary).

Georgia

Albany Area Mental Health and Mental Retardation Center

PO Box 1845, 520 N Jefferson St, Albany, GA 31702
(912) 439-4347

Facility Information *Placement* Outpatient Community Mental Health and Mental Retardation Center. *Sexes Served* Both. *Sources of Funding* State Funds; Health Insurance; Medicaid.

Student/Patient Characteristics *Exceptionalities Served* Emotionally Disturbed; Mentally Handicapped. *Behavioral Problems* Attention Deficits; Hyperactivity; Hypoactivity; Impulsivity; Self-Aggression; Verbal Aggression; Physical Aggression; Indirect Aggression; Passive Aggression; Withdrawal. *Conditions Treated* Alcohol Abuse and/or Drug Abuse; Other Substance Abuse or Dependence; Schizophrenia; Phobias; Obsessions and Compulsions; Depression; Suicide.

Services Provided Individual Therapy; Group Therapy; Parent Involvement; Behavior Therapy; Family Therapy; Drug Therapy; Reality Therapy; Play Therapy. *Professionals on Staff* Psychiatrists 1; Psychologists 2; Counselors 1; Social Workers 4; Nurses 1. *Educational Intervention Approaches* Self-Control; Behavior Modification. *Degrees Awarded* Graduate Equivalency Diploma.

Anneewakee Hospital

4771 Anneewakee Rd, Douglasville, GA 30135 (404) 942-2391
Year Established 1962
Contact Sharon Carter, Admissions Coord

Facility Information *Placement* Private Nonprofit Psychiatric Hospital for Children and Adolescents. *Number of Beds* 455. *Children/Adolescents Served* 455. *Sexes Served* Both. *Room and Board Fees (Approx)* $100. *Sources of Funding* Health Insurance; P.L. 94-142; State Mental Health. Summer school available. *Teacher Certification Level* Elementary School; Junior High/Middle School; High School. *Special Certification Level* ED; LD; MR; Career/Vocational Education; Reading; Math.

Student/Patient Characteristics *Age Levels* 9-11; 12-14; 15-17; 18-21. *IQ Ranges* 85-130; Above 130. *Exceptionalities Served* Emotionally Disturbed; Learning Disabled; Gifted. *Learning Problems* Memory Disabilities; Perceptual Disabilities; Oral Language Disabilities; Reading Disabilities; Handwriting Disabilities; Spelling Disabilities; Arithmetic Disabilities; Written Expression. *Behavioral Problems* Attention Deficits; Hyperactivity; Impulsivity; Verbal Aggression; Passive Aggression; Withdrawal. *Conditions Treated* Alcohol Abuse and/or Drug Abuse; Other Substance Abuse or Dependence; Schizophrenia; Depression; Suicide; Inadequacy/Immaturity; Personality Problems; Socialized Aggressive Reaction; Unsocialized Aggressive Reaction.

Services Provided Individual Therapy; Group Therapy; Parent Involvement; Behavior Therapy; Cognitive Developmental Therapy; Family Therapy; Drug Therapy; Art Therapy; Music Therapy; Play Therapy; Psychodrama; Recreational Therapy.

Professionals on Staff Psychiatrists 8; Psychologists 13; Counselors 16; Social Workers 14; Child Care Staff 80; Nurses 45; Non-psychiatric Medical Specialties 17. *Service Facilities Available (with number of rooms)* Hospital School 45; Resource Rooms, Fine Arts, Vocational Training 12. *Educational Professionals* Regular School Teachers 20; Special Education Teachers 20; Career/Vocational Teachers 6; Special Education Counselors 3; Administrative and Psychoeducational 5. *Curricula* Traditional Academic; Career/Vocational Education; Individualized; Basic Skills; Prevocational. *Educational Intervention Approaches* Progressive Discipline; Applied Behavior Analysis; Creative Conditioning. *Degrees Awarded* High School Diploma; Graduate Equivalency Diploma.

Atlanta Public Schools

2930 Forrest Hill Dr SW, Atlanta, GA 30315 (404) 761-5411
Year Established 1975
Contact Octavia W Milton, Dir; Ann D Newman, B D Coord

Facility Information *Placement* Public School; Public Day Care; Special Program. *Children/Adolescents Served* 130. *Sources of Funding* State Funds; P.L. 94-142. Summer school available. *Teacher Certification Level* Elementary School; Junior High/Middle School; High School. *Special Certification Level* ED; LD; MR; Career/Vocational Education; Reading; Math.

Student/Patient Characteristics *Age Levels* 0-4; 5-8; 9-11; 12-14; 15-17; 18-21. *IQ Ranges* 26-40; 41-55; 56-70; 71-85; 85-130; Above 130. *Exceptionalities Served* Autistic; Emotionally Disturbed; Learning Disabled; Mentally Handicapped; Communication Disordered; Hearing Impaired/Deaf; Visually Impaired/Blind; Other Health Impaired; Physically Handicapped; Gifted. *Learning Problems* Memory Disabilities; Perceptual Disabilities; Thinking Disabilities; Oral Language Disabilities; Reading Disabilities; Handwriting Disabilities; Spelling Disabilities; Arithmetic Disabilities; Written Expression. *Behavioral Problems* Attention Deficits; Hyperactivity; Hypoactivity; Impulsivity; Self-Aggression; Verbal Aggression; Physical Aggression; Indirect Aggression; Passive Aggression; Withdrawal.

Services Provided Individual Therapy; Group Therapy; Parent Involvement; Behavior Therapy; Cognitive Developmental Therapy; Art Therapy; Music Therapy; Reality Therapy; Play Therapy. *Professionals on Staff* Psychiatrists 2; Psychologists 3; Social Workers 6. *Service Facilities Available (with number of rooms)* Itinerants; Resource Rooms; Transition Rooms; Self-Contained Rooms. *Curricula* Traditional Academic; Career/Vocational Education; Individualized; Basic Skills; Prevocational. *Educational Intervention Approaches* Engineered Classroom; Precision Teaching; Behavior Modification. *Degrees Awarded* Certificate of Attendance; High School Diploma.

Burwell Psychoeducational Program

1905 Burwell Rd, Carrollton, GA 30117 (404) 258-7205
Year Established 1972
Contact David Craddock, Dir
Facility Information *Placement* Public School; Special Program.
Children/Adolescents Served 225. *Sexes Served* Both. *Sources of
Funding* State Funds; P.L. 89-313; Title VI-B. Summer school
available. *Teacher Certification Level* Elementary School; Junior
High/Middle School; High School. *Special Certification Level*
ED.
Student/Patient Characteristics *Age Levels* 0-4; 5-8; 9-11; 12-14;
15-17; 18-21. *IQ Ranges* 0-25; 26-40; 41-55; 56-70; 71-85;
85-130; Above 130. *Exceptionalities Served* Autistic; Emotionally
Disturbed. *Behavioral Problems* Attention Deficits; Hyperactivity; Hypoactivity; Impulsivity; Self-Aggression; Verbal Aggression; Physical Aggression; Indirect Aggression; Passive Aggression; Withdrawal.
Services Provided Individual Therapy; Group Therapy; Parent
Involvement; Behavior Therapy; Cognitive Developmental Ther-
apy; Family Therapy; Art Therapy; Music Therapy; Reality Ther-
apy; Play Therapy. *Professionals on Staff* Psychiatrists 1; Psychologists 2; Social Workers 5. *Service Facilities Available (with
number of rooms)* Self-Contained Rooms 2; Special School 10.
Educational Professionals Special Education Teachers 10; Paraprofessionals 11; School Psychologist 1. *Curricula* Traditional
Academic; Career/Vocational Education; Individualized; Basic
Skills; Affective, Social, Behavioral. *Degrees Awarded* Certificate
of Attendance; High School Diploma.

Child and Adolescent Psychoeducational Center

820 N Hamilton St, Dalton, GA 30720 (404) 272-2140
Year Established 1971
Contact George C Andros, Dir
Facility Information *Placement* Special School.
Children/Adolescents Served 250. *Sexes Served* Both. *Sources of
Funding* State Funds; Title VI-B; Title I. Summer school avail-
able. *Teacher Certification Level* Elementary School; Junior
High/Middle School; High School. *Special Certification Level*
ED.
Student/Patient Characteristics *Age Levels* 0-4; 5-8; 9-11; 12-14;
15-17. *IQ Ranges* 56-70; 71-85; 85-130; Above 130.
Exceptionalities Served Autistic; Emotionally Disturbed.
Learning Problems Perceptual Disabilities; Thinking Disabilities;
Oral Language Disabilities; Reading Disabilities; Handwriting
Disabilities; Spelling Disabilities; Arithmetic Disabilities; Written
Expression. *Behavioral Problems* Attention Deficits; Hyperacti-
vity; Hypoactivity; Impulsivity; Self-Aggression; Verbal Aggres-
sion; Physical Aggression; Indirect Aggression; Passive Aggres-
sion; Withdrawal. *Conditions Treated* Early Infantile Autism;
Schizophrenia; Phobias; Depression; Inadequacy/Immaturity;
Personality Problems; Socialized Aggressive Reaction; Un-
socialized Aggressive Reaction.
Services Provided Parent Involvement; Developmental Therapy.
Professionals on Staff Psychiatrists; Psychologists 1.5; Social
Workers 4.5. *Service Facilities Available (with number of rooms)*
Self-Contained Rooms. *Educational Professionals* Special Educa-
tion Teachers 9; Paraprofessionals 10; Administrative 3.
Curricula Basic Skills; Prevocational.
Comments The center provides psychoeducational services to
severely emotionally disturbed and behaviorally disordered chil-
dren and youth. A main center in Dalton and satellite centers in
Canton and Blue Ridge provide services to 6 Northwest Georgia
counties: Whitfield, Murray, Gitner, Fannin, Cherokee and Pic-
kens.

Cobb County—Cobb Douglas Psychoeducation Children's Program

353 Lemon St, Marietta, GA 30060 (404) 425-2712
Contact Pauline Terrell, Prog Coord

Facility Information *Placement* Public School; Special School;
Special Program. *Children/Adolescents Served* 70. *Sexes Served*
Both. *Sources of Funding* State Funds; Psycho Ed Network.
Summer school available. *Teacher Certification Level* Elementary
School; Junior High/Middle School. *Special Certification Level*
LD; Behavior Disorders.
Student/Patient Characteristics *Age Levels* 5-8; 9-11; 12-14. *IQ
Ranges* 71-85; 85-130; Above 130. *Exceptionalities Served* Aut-
istic; Emotionally Disturbed; Learning Disabled; Mentally
Handicapped; Communication Disordered; Visually Impaired/
Blind; Other Health Impaired; Physically Handicapped; Gifted.
Learning Problems Perceptual Disabilities; Thinking Disabilities;
Oral Language Disabilities; Reading Disabilities; Written Expres-
sion. *Behavioral Problems* Attention Deficits; Hyperactivity; Im-
pulsivity; Self-Aggression; Verbal Aggression; Physical Aggres-
sion; Indirect Aggression; Passive Aggression; Withdrawal.
Conditions Treated Early Infantile Autism; Schizophrenia; Pho-
bias; Depression; Suicide; Personality Problems; Socialized Ag-
gressive Reaction; Unsocialized Aggressive Reaction.
Services Provided Individual Therapy; Group Therapy; Parent
Involvement; Behavior Therapy; Family Therapy; Reality Therapy. *Professionals on Staff* Psychiatrists 1; Psychologists 2; Social
Workers 5. *Service Facilities Available (with number of rooms)*
Self-Contained Rooms 8. *Educational Professionals* Special Education Teachers 8; Paraprofessionals 8. *Curricula* Traditional
Academic; Career/Vocational Education; Individualized; Basic
Skills; Prevocational. *Educational Intervention Approaches* Preci-
sion Teaching; Self-Control; Behavior Modification; Applied Behavior Analysis.
Comments This program provides followup service to those stu-
dents that return to their home schools.

Devereux in Georgia

1980 Stanley Rd, Kennesaw, GA 30144 (404) 427-0147
Year Established 1973
Contact Lyn H Crowe, Admissions Dir
Facility Information *Placement* Private Residential Care; Special-
ized Psychiatric Hospital. *Number of Beds* 77. *Sexes Served* Both.
Room and Board Fees (Approx) $109 (open treatment milieu);
$184 (acute care units). *Tuition Fees (Approx)* $39,900 (open
treatment milieu); $67,200 (acute care unit). *Sources of Funding*
State Funds; Health Insurance; P.L. 94-142; CHAMPUS Ap-
proved. Summer school available. *Teacher Certification Level*
Elementary School; Junior High/Middle School; High School.
Special Certification Level LD; MR; Reading; Math; Social Studies; Art; Science.
Student/Patient Characteristics *Age Levels* 12-14; 15-17. *IQ
Ranges* 71-85; 85-130. *Exceptionalities Served* Emotionally Disturbed; Learning Disabled. *Learning Problems* Memory Disabilities; Perceptual Disabilities; Thinking Disabilities; Oral Language Disabilities; Reading Disabilities; Handwriting Disabilities;
Spelling Disabilities; Arithmetic Disabilities; Written Expression.
Behavioral Problems Attention Deficits; Hyperactivity; Hypoactivity; Impulsivity; Self-Aggression; Verbal Aggression; Impulsivity; Indirect Aggression; Passive Aggression; Withdrawal.
Conditions Treated Schizophrenia; Convulsive Disorders; Phobias; Obsessions and Compulsions; Hysteria; Depression; Suicide; Asthma; Anorexia Nervosa; Ulcerative Colitis; Inadequacy/
Immaturity; Personality Problems; Socialized Aggressive Reaction; Unsocialized Aggressive Reaction.
Services Provided Individual Therapy; Group Therapy; Parent
Involvement; Behavior Therapy; Cognitive Developmental Ther-
apy; Family Therapy; Filial Therapy; Drug Therapy; Art Ther-
apy; Reality Therapy; Psychodrama. *Professionals on Staff* Psychiatrists 2; Psychologists 3; Counselors 5; Social Workers 9;
Child Care Staff 65; Nurses 9; Occupational Therapist; Speech
and Language Therapist; Nutritionist. *Service Facilities Available
(with number of rooms)* Resource Rooms 2; Self-Contained
Rooms 1. *Educational Professionals* Regular School Teachers 6;
Special Education Teachers 4; Career/Vocational Teachers 2.
Curricula Traditional Academic; Career/Vocational Education;

Individualized; Prevocational. *Educational Intervention Approaches* Self-Control; Behavior Modification. *Degrees Awarded* Graduate Equivalency Diploma.

Grady Memorial Hospital—Division of Child and Adolescent Psychiatry

80 Butler St, Atlanta, GA 30335 (404) 588-4859
Year Established 1972
Contact J Vernon Magnuson, Dir

Facility Information *Placement* Special School; Outpatient Psychiatry Clinic. *Children/Adolescents Served* 110. *Sexes Served* Both. *Sources of Funding* State Funds; Health Insurance; Medicaid; Medicare; P.L. 94-142; County Funds. Summer school available. *Teacher Certification Level* High School. *Special Certification Level* Career/Vocational Education; Reading; Math; Behavior Disorders.

Student/Patient Characteristics *Age Levels* 0-4; 5-8; 9-11; 12-14; 15-17; 18-21. *IQ Ranges* 41-55; 56-70; 71-85; 85-130; Above 130. *Exceptionalities Served* Autistic; Emotionally Disturbed; Learning Disabled; Mentally Handicapped; Other Health Impaired; Physically Handicapped. *Learning Problems* Perceptual Disabilities; Thinking Disabilities; Reading Disabilities; Spelling Disabilities; Arithmetic Disabilities; Written Expression. *Behavioral Problems* Attention Deficits; Hyperactivity; Impulsivity; Self-Aggression; Verbal Aggression; Physical Aggression; Indirect Aggression; Passive Aggression; Withdrawal. *Conditions Treated* Alcohol Abuse and/or Drug Abuse; Other Substance Abuse or Dependence; Early Infantile Autism; Disintegrative Psychoses; Schizophrenia; Phobias; Obsessions and Compulsions; Hysteria; Depression; Suicide; Asthma; Anorexia Nervosa; Ulcerative Colitis; Inadequacy/Immaturity; Personality Problems; Socialized Aggressive Reaction; Unsocialized Aggressive Reaction.

Services Provided Individual Therapy; Group Therapy; Parent Involvement; Behavior Therapy; Cognitive Developmental Therapy; Family Therapy; Drug Therapy; Play Therapy; Recreation Therapy. *Professionals on Staff* Psychiatrists 3.5; Psychologists 3; Counselors 2; Social Workers 3; Nurses 2; Recreation Therapist 1. *Service Facilities Available (with number of rooms)* Consultative (ERT) 3; Resource Rooms 2; Self-Contained Rooms 2. *Educational Professionals* Special Education Teachers 2; Paraprofessionals 2. *Curricula* Career/Vocational Education; Individualized; Basic Skills; Prevocational. *Educational Intervention Approaches* Progressive Discipline; Self-Control; Applied Behavior Analysis. *Degrees Awarded* Certificate of Attendance; High School Diploma.

Comments The child and adolescent psychiatric program is an outpatient and day treatment program which offers a broad range of services to children and families who use Grady Memorial Hospital and/or live within the catchment area of the Central Fulton County Community Mental Health Center.

Hillside Inc

690 Courtnay Dr NE, Atlanta, GA 30306 (404) 875-4551
Year Established 1888
Contact Lori Hogeman, Social Worker

Facility Information *Placement* Private Residential Care. *Number of Beds* 40. *Children/Adolescents Served* 40. *Sexes Served* Both. *Room and Board Fees (Approx)* Sliding Scale. *Tuition Fees (Approx)* Sliding Scale. *Sources of Funding* State Funds; Health Insurance; P.L. 94-142. Summer school available. *Teacher Certification Level* Elementary School; Junior High/Middle School; High School. *Special Certification Level* ED; LD; Behavioral Disorder; Special Education.

Student/Patient Characteristics *Age Levels* 9-11; 12-14; 15-17. *IQ Ranges* 56-70; 71-85; 85-130; Above 130. *Exceptionalities Served* Emotionally Disturbed; Learning Disabled; Mentally Handicapped. *Learning Problems* Perceptual Disabilities; Thinking Disabilities; Oral Language Disabilities; Reading Disabilities; Spelling Disabilities; Arithmetic Disabilities; Written Expression. *Behavioral Problems* Attention Deficits; Hyperactivity; Hypoactivity; Impulsivity; Self-Aggression; Verbal Aggression; Physical Aggression; Indirect Aggression; Passive Aggression; Withdrawal.

Conditions Treated Schizophrenia; Depression; Suicide; Inadequacy/Immaturity; Personality Problems; Socialized Aggressive Reaction; Unsocialized Aggressive Reaction.

Services Provided Individual Therapy; Group Therapy; Parent Involvement; Behavior Therapy; Family Therapy; Reality Therapy; Recreational Therapy. *Professionals on Staff* Psychiatrists 2; Psychologists 3; Counselors 16; Social Workers 1; Nurses 1. *Service Facilities Available (with number of rooms)* Self-Contained Rooms 4. *Educational Professionals* Regular School Teachers 2; Special Education Teachers 2. *Curricula* Traditional Academic; Career/Vocational Education; Individualized; Basic Skills; Prevocational. *Educational Intervention Approaches* Behavior Modification. *Degrees Awarded* High School Diploma.

Comments Hillside is a residential treatment center for severely emotionally disturbed adolescents between the ages of 10 and 18.

North Metro Psychoeducational Program

846 Huff Rd NW, Atlanta, GA 30318 (404) 352-3720
Year Established 1974
Contact Larry Weiner, Dir

Facility Information *Placement* Special Program. *Children/Adolescents Served* 677-734. *Sexes Served* Both. *Sources of Funding* State Funds; P.L. 94-142. Summer school available. *Teacher Certification Level* Elementary School; Junior High/Middle School; High School. *Special Certification Level* ED.

Student/Patient Characteristics *Age Levels* 0-4; 5-8; 9-11; 12-14; 15-17. *IQ Ranges* 0-25; 26-40; 41-55; 56-70; 71-85; 85-130; Above 130. *Exceptionalities Served* Autistic; Emotionally Disturbed. *Learning Problems* Memory Disabilities; Perceptual Disabilities; Thinking Disabilities; Oral Language Disabilities; Reading Disabilities; Handwriting Disabilities; Spelling Disabilities; Arithmetic Disabilities; Written Expression. *Behavioral Problems* Attention Deficits; Hyperactivity; Hypoactivity; Impulsivity; Self-Aggression; Verbal Aggression; Physical Aggression; Indirect Aggression; Passive Aggression; Withdrawal. *Conditions Treated* Early Infantile Autism; Schizophrenia; Phobias; Obsessions and Compulsions; Depression; Inadequacy/Immaturity; Personality Problems; Socialized Aggressive Reaction; Unsocialized Aggressive Reaction.

Services Provided Individual Therapy; Group Therapy; Parent Involvement; Family Therapy; Art Therapy; Occupational Therapy; Speech Therapy; Physical Therapy. *Professionals on Staff* Psychiatrists 1; Psychologists 4; Social Workers 6. *Service Facilities Available (with number of rooms)* Self-Contained Rooms. *Educational Professionals* Special Education Teachers 21; Paraprofessionals 18. *Curricula* Individualized. *Educational Intervention Approaches* Behavior Modification; Developmental Therapy.

Comments North Metro serves severely emotionally disturbed children and youth, ages 0-18. The program provides diagnostic and treatment services for those who attend school in Atlanta I, II, and III areas, North Fulton Co., Gwinnett Co., and Buford City and is funded by the Georgia State Legislature through the Department of Education.

Northwest Psychoeducational Program

200 Reece St, Rome, GA 30161 (404) 291-2625
Contact Georgia Moore, Dir

Facility Information *Placement* Public School; Special Program. *Children/Adolescents Served* 571. *Sexes Served* Both. *Sources of Funding* State Funds; Federal VI-B; P.L. 89-313. Summer school available. *Teacher Certification Level* Elementary School; Junior High/Middle School; High School. *Special Certification Level* ED; Behavior Disorders.

Student/Patient Characteristics *Age Levels* 0-4; 5-8; 9-11; 12-14; 15-17; 18-21. *IQ Ranges* 71-85; 85-130; Above 130. *Exceptionalities Served* Autistic; Emotionally Disturbed; Developmentally Delayed. *Learning Problems* Memory Disabilities; Perceptual Disabilities; Thinking Disabilities; Oral Language Disabilities; Reading Disabilities; Handwriting Disabilities; Spelling Disabilities; Arithmetic Disabilities; Written Expression. *Behavioral Problems* Attention Deficits; Hyperactivity; Hypoac-

tivity; Impulsivity; Self-Aggression; Verbal Aggression; Physical Aggression; Passive Aggression; Withdrawal. *Conditions Treated* Early Infantile Autism; Schizophrenia; Aphasia; Phobias; Obsessions and Compulsions; Depression; Inadequacy/Immaturity; Socialized Aggressive Reaction; Unsocialized Aggressive Reaction.
Services Provided Individual Therapy; Group Therapy; Parent Involvement; Behavior Therapy; Cognitive Developmental Therapy; Family Therapy; Music Therapy; Play Therapy.
Professionals on Staff Psychiatrists contract; Psychologists 3; Counselors 3; Social Workers 10; Child Care Staff 21; Nurses 1; Infant Therapist 2. *Service Facilities Available (with number of rooms)* Consultative (ERT) 2; Itinerants 3; Self-Contained Rooms 21; Special School; Homebound Instruction 2.
Educational Professionals Special Education Teachers 21; Special Education Counselors 5; Paraprofessionals 21. *Curricula* Individualized; Basic Skills; Prevocational. *Educational Intervention Approaches* Developmental Therapy. *Degrees Awarded* High School Diploma.

Comments The center provides community based services for students who otherwise might be institutionalized. It provides evaluation, diagnosis treatment, and followup for students and their parents. The therapeutic program helps children resolve their emotional conflicts by developing new skills and building on existing skills. Praise, encouragement, and positive experiences help children become more confident. The program takes into account the child's age, developmental abilities, specific problems, and emotional concerns. Each child's program is individualized to meet the goals of the I.E.P.

Oconee Area Psycho Educational Program

1801 N Columbia St, Milledgeville, GA 31061 (912) 452-3514
Contact Joseph Fehlig, Dir
Facility Information *Placement* Special Program.
Children/Adolescents Served 175. *Sexes Served* Both. *Sources of Funding* State Funds; P.L. 94-142; P.L. 89-313. Summer school available. *Teacher Certification Level* Elementary School; Junior High/Middle School; High School. *Special Certification Level* ED; Behavior Disorders.
Student/Patient Characteristics *Age Levels* 0-4; 5-8; 9-11; 12-14; 15-17; 18-21. *IQ Ranges* 41-55; 56-70; 71-85; 85-130.
Exceptionalities Served Autistic; Emotionally Disturbed; Behavior Disorders. *Behavioral Problems* Attention Deficits; Hyperactivity; Hypoactivity; Impulsivity; Self-Aggression; Verbal Aggression; Physical Aggression; Indirect Aggression; Passive Aggression; Withdrawal. *Conditions Treated* Alcohol Abuse and/or Drug Abuse; Early Infantile Autism; Disintegrative Psychoses; Schizophrenia; Phobias; Hysteria; Depression; Suicide; Anorexia Nervosa; Inadequacy/Immaturity; Personality Problems; Socialized Aggressive Reaction; Unsocialized Aggressive Reaction.
Services Provided Individual Therapy; Group Therapy; Parent Involvement; Behavior Therapy; Family Therapy; Drug Therapy. *Professionals on Staff* Psychiatrists 1; Psychologists 1; Counselors 4; Social Workers 2. *Service Facilities Available (with number of rooms)* Consultative (ERT); Itinerants; Self-Contained Rooms; Special School; Homebound Instruction. *Educational Professionals* Special Education Teachers 10; Special Education Counselors 3; Paraprofessionals 8. *Curricula* Individualized. *Educational Intervention Approaches* Behavior Modification; Creative Conditioning.

Parkwood Hospital

1999 Cliff Valley Way, Atlanta, GA 30329 (404) 633-8431
Contact Ron Wallace, Nursing Supv
Facility Information *Placement* Inpatient Hospitalization.
Number of Beds 15. *Children/Adolescents Served* 55. *Sexes Served* Both. *Sources of Funding* Health Insurance; P.L. 94-142. Summer school available. *Teacher Certification Level* Elementary School; Junior High/Middle School. *Special Certification Level* ED.
Student/Patient Characteristics *Age Levels* 0-4; 5-8; 9-11; 12-14; 15-17. *IQ Ranges* 85-130; Above 130. *Exceptionalities Served* Autistic; Emotionally Disturbed; Learning Disabled; Commu-

nication Disordered. *Learning Problems* Memory Disabilities; Perceptual Disabilities; Thinking Disabilities; Oral Language Disabilities; Reading Disabilities; Handwriting Disabilities; Spelling Disabilities; Arithmetic Disabilities; Written Expression. *Behavioral Problems* Attention Deficits; Hyperactivity; Impulsivity; Self-Aggression; Verbal Aggression; Physical Aggression; Indirect Aggression; Passive Aggression; Withdrawal. *Conditions Treated* Alcohol Abuse and/or Drug Abuse; Other Substance Abuse or Dependence; Early Infantile Autism; Disintegrative Psychoses; Schizophrenia; Convulsive Disorders; Phobias; Obsessions and Compulsions; Hysteria; Depression; Suicide; Asthma; Anorexia Nervosa; Inadequacy/Immaturity; Personality Problems; Socialized Aggressive Reaction; Unsocialized Aggressive Reaction.
Services Provided Individual Therapy; Group Therapy; Parent Involvement; Family Therapy; Drug Therapy; Art Therapy; Music Therapy; Play Therapy; Movement Therapy. *Professionals on Staff* Psychiatrists; Counselors 15; Social Workers 4; Nurses 12. *Educational Professionals* Special Education Teachers. *Curricula* . *Educational Intervention Approaches* Precision Teaching; Self-Control; Behavior Modification; Applied Behavior Analysis. *Degrees Awarded* High School Diploma.
Comments Parkwood has 3 units (1 child, 2 adolescent programs) which serve children and adolescents with a variety of emotional disorders. For adolescents, a special chemical dependency program has been established. A limited number of autistic children may be served in the children's program.

Richmond County Board of Education—Sand Hills Psychoeducational Program

2403 Mt Auburn Ave, Augusta, GA 50904 (404) 737-7272
Year Established 1974
Contact Harry Goodwin, Dir
Facility Information *Placement* Special Program.
Children/Adolescents Served 300. *Sexes Served* Both. *Sources of Funding* State Funds; P.L. 94-142; 89-313; 6-B Federal. Summer school available. *Teacher Certification Level* Elementary School; Junior High/Middle School; High School. *Special Certification Level* Behavior Disorders.
Student/Patient Characteristics *Age Levels* 0-4; 5-8; 9-11; 12-14; 15-17. *IQ Ranges* 26-40; 41-55; 56-70; 71-85; 85-130; Above 130. *Exceptionalities Served* Autistic; Emotionally Disturbed. *Learning Problems* Memory Disabilities; Perceptual Disabilities; Thinking Disabilities; Oral Language Disabilities; Reading Disabilities; Handwriting Disabilities; Spelling Disabilities; Arithmetic Disabilities; Written Expression. *Behavioral Problems* Attention Deficits; Hyperactivity; Hypoactivity; Impulsivity; Self-Aggression; Verbal Aggression; Physical Aggression; Indirect Aggression; Passive Aggression; Withdrawal. *Conditions Treated* Early Infantile Autism; Disintegrative Psychoses; Schizophrenia; Phobias; Obsessions and Compulsions; Hysteria; Depression; Suicide; Inadequacy/Immaturity; Personality Problems.
Services Provided Individual Therapy; Group Therapy; Parent Involvement; Behavior Therapy; Cognitive Developmental Therapy; Family Therapy; Art Therapy; Music Therapy; Reality Therapy; Play Therapy; Psychodrama. *Professionals on Staff* Psychiatrists 1; Psychologists 2; Social Workers 8; Speech Therapy; Occupational Therapy. *Service Facilities Available (with number of rooms)* Self-Contained Rooms 5; Special School 12.
Educational Professionals Special Education Teachers 18; Paraprofessionals 20. *Curricula* Traditional Academic; Career/Vocational Education; Individualized; Basic Skills; Prevocational. *Educational Intervention Approaches* Self-Control; Behavior Modification; Developmental Therapy. *Degrees Awarded* Certificate of Attendance; High School Diploma; Graduate Equivalency Diploma.
Comments The Sand Hills Psychoeducational Program provides services to severely emotionally disturbed children and youths between ages 0-18. Counselling, social services and educational programs are also provided to families of children and youth served by the center.

Ridgeview Institute

3995 S Cobb Dr, Smyrna, GA 30080 (404) 434-4567
Year Established 1976
Contact Edward J Osborn, Exec VP of Operations
Facility Information *Placement* Acute Care Psychiatric Hospital. *Number of Beds* 92. *Children/Adolescents Served* 92. *Sexes Served* Both. *Room and Board Fees (Approx)* $250. *Sources of Funding* Health Insurance; Medicare; Self Pay. Summer school available. *Teacher Certification Level* Junior High/Middle School; High School. *Special Certification Level* Math; Science; Social Studies; English.
Student/Patient Characteristics *Age Levels* 12-14; 15-17. *IQ Ranges* 71-85; 85-130; Above 130. *Exceptionalities Served* Emotionally Disturbed; Learning Disabled; Behavior Disordered. *Learning Problems* Memory Disabilities; Thinking Disabilities; Reading Disabilities; Spelling Disabilities; Arithmetic Disabilities; Written Expression. *Behavioral Problems* Attention Deficits; Hyperactivity; Hypoactivity; Impulsivity; Self-Aggression; Verbal Aggression; Physical Aggression; Indirect Aggression; Passive Aggression; Withdrawal. *Conditions Treated* Alcohol Abuse and/or Drug Abuse; Other Substance Abuse or Dependence; Disintegrative Psychoses; Schizophrenia; Convulsive Disorders; Phobias; Obsessions and Compulsions; Hysteria; Depression; Suicide; Anorexia Nervosa; Inadequacy/Immaturity; Personality Problems; Socialized Aggressive Reaction; Unsocialized Aggressive Reaction.
Services Provided Individual Therapy; Group Therapy; Parent Involvement; Behavior Therapy; Biofeedback; Family Therapy; Drug Therapy; Art Therapy; Music Therapy; Reality Therapy; Psychodrama. *Professionals on Staff* Psychiatrists; Psychologists; Counselors; Social Workers; Child Care Staff; Nurses. *Service Facilities Available (with number of rooms)* Consultative (ERT) 10; Self-Contained Rooms 2; Special School 20; Hospital School 20. *Educational Professionals* Regular School Teachers 14; Special Education Counselors 3; School Psychometrist 1. *Curricula* Traditional Academic; Career/Vocational Education; Individualized; Basic Skills; Prevocational; GED Preparation. *Educational Intervention Approaches* Engineered Classroom; Self-Control; Behavior Modification.
Comments Ridgeview Institute is located within a private specialized hospital that serves emotionally disturbed, behavior disordered, and chemically dependent adolescents. The full-time education program is accredited by the Georgia Department of Education.

Rutland Psychoeducational Services

125 Minor St, Athens, GA 30602 (404) 549-3030
Contact Georgann Toop, Coord; Diane Weller, Coord
Facility Information *Placement* Special Program. *Children/Adolescents Served* 180. *Sexes Served* Both. *Sources of Funding* State Funds; P.L. 94-142. Summer school available. *Teacher Certification Level* Elementary School; Junior High/Middle School; High School. *Special Certification Level* ED; Home Economics.
Student/Patient Characteristics *Age Levels* 0-4; 5-8; 9-11; 12-14; 15-17; 18-21; Over 21. *IQ Ranges* 56-70; 71-85; 85-130. *Exceptionalities Served* Emotionally Disturbed. *Learning Problems* Memory Disabilities; Perceptual Disabilities; Thinking Disabilities; Oral Language Disabilities; Reading Disabilities; Handwriting Disabilities; Spelling Disabilities; Arithmetic Disabilities; Written Expression. *Behavioral Problems* Attention Deficits; Hyperactivity; Hypoactivity; Impulsivity; Self-Aggression; Verbal Aggression; Physical Aggression; Indirect Aggression; Passive Aggression; Withdrawal. *Conditions Treated* Early Infantile Autism; Schizophrenia; Phobias; Obsessions and Compulsions; Depression; Suicide; Inadequacy/Immaturity; Personality Problems; Socialized Aggressive Reaction; Unsocialized Aggressive Reaction.
Services Provided Individual Therapy; Group Therapy; Parent Involvement; Behavior Therapy; Family Therapy; Art Therapy; Music Therapy; Reality Therapy; Play Therapy; Rational Emotive Therapy; Developmental Therapy. *Professionals on Staff* Psychiatrists 1; Psychologists 2; Social Workers 5; Coordinators 2; Director 1. *Service Facilities Available (with number of rooms)* Consultative (ERT); Self-Contained Rooms; Crisis Intervention; Homebound Instruction. *Educational Professionals* Special Education Teachers; Crisis Teachers 5; Paraprofessionals; Coordinators 2. *Curricula* Career/Vocational Education; Individualized; Basic Skills; Prevocational; Affective Education. *Educational Intervention Approaches* Self-Control; Behavior Modification. *Degrees Awarded* Certificate of Attendance; High School Diploma; Graduate Equivalency Diploma.

Southwest Georgia Psychoeducational Services—Thomas County Schools

PO Box 110-A, Ochlocknee, GA 31773 (912) 547-5123
Year Established 1971
Contact James M Hall, Prog Dir
Facility Information *Placement* Public School. *Sexes Served* Both. *Sources of Funding* State Funds; HEW. Summer school available. *Teacher Certification Level* Elementary School; High School. *Special Certification Level* Behavior Disorders.
Student/Patient Characteristics *Age Levels* 0-4; 5-8; 9-11; 12-14; 15-17; 18-21; Over 21. *Exceptionalities Served* Autistic; Emotionally Disturbed; Severe Behavior Disordered. *Learning Problems* Memory Disabilities; Thinking Disabilities. *Behavioral Problems* Attention Deficits; Hyperactivity; Hypoactivity; Impulsivity; Self-Aggression; Verbal Aggression; Physical Aggression; Indirect Aggression; Passive Aggression; Withdrawal. *Conditions Treated* Early Infantile Autism; Schizophrenia; Phobias; Obsessions and Compulsions; Hysteria; Depression; Personality Problems; Socialized Aggressive Reaction; Unsocialized Aggressive Reaction.
Services Provided Individual Therapy; Group Therapy; Parent Involvement; Behavior Therapy; Biofeedback; Art Therapy; Reality Therapy; Play Therapy. *Professionals on Staff* Psychiatrists 1; Psychologists 1; Social Workers 7. *Service Facilities Available (with number of rooms)* Resource Rooms; Self-Contained Rooms. *Educational Professionals* Special Education Teachers; Paraprofessionals. *Curricula* Traditional Academic; Career/Vocational Education; Individualized; Basic Skills; Prevocational. *Educational Intervention Approaches* Self-Control; Behavior Modification. *Degrees Awarded* High School Diploma.

Village of St Joseph

PO Box 310120, 2969 Butner Rd SW, Atlanta, GA 30331-0120 (404) 349-2400
Year Established 1967
Contact Mable Stevenson, Intake Social Worker; Sr Mary Frances Bruns, Admin
Facility Information *Placement* Private Residential Care; Private Day School Program. *Number of Beds* 39. *Children/Adolescents Served* 39. *Sexes Served* Both. *Room and Board Fees (Approx)* $40. *Tuition Fees (Approx)* $13,200. *Sources of Funding* Health Insurance; P.L. 94-142; Archdiocesan Subsidy Fees. Summer school available. *Teacher Certification Level* Elementary School; Junior High/Middle School. *Special Certification Level* LD; MR; Reading; Math.
Student/Patient Characteristics *Age Levels* 5-8; 9-11; 12-14; 15-17. *IQ Ranges* 71-85; 85-130. *Exceptionalities Served* Emotionally Disturbed; Learning Disabled. *Learning Problems* Memory Disabilities; Perceptual Disabilities; Thinking Disabilities; Reading Disabilities; Handwriting Disabilities; Spelling Disabilities; Arithmetic Disabilities; Written Expression. *Behavioral Problems* Attention Deficits; Hyperactivity; Impulsivity; Verbal Aggression; Physical Aggression; Passive Aggression; Withdrawal. *Conditions Treated* Convulsive Disorders; Obsessions and Compulsions; Depression; Asthma; Inadequacy/Immaturity; Personality Problems; Socialized Aggressive Reaction.
Services Provided Individual Therapy; Group Therapy; Parent Involvement; Behavior Therapy; Family Therapy; Filial Therapy; Play Therapy. *Professionals on Staff* Psychiatrists 1; Psychologists 1; Counselors 4; Social Workers 2; Child Care Staff 4; Nurses 1; Recreational Supervisors 4. *Service Facilities Available (with*

number of rooms) On-Campus Residential School 6. *Educational Professionals* Regular School Teachers 3; Special Education Teachers 4; Paraprofessionals 2. *Curricula* Individualized; Basic Skills. *Educational Intervention Approaches* Behavior Modification. *Degrees Awarded* Certificate of Attendance.

Comments The Village is a 5-day intermediate residential treatment center. Children are accepted only if parents agree to family therapy.

Hawaii

Children's Day Treatment Center

3627 Kilauea Ave No. 542, Honolulu, HI 96816 (808) 735-5232
Year Established 1945
Contact Hecter Robertin, Dir
Facility Information *Placement* Public Day Care.
Children/Adolescents Served 12. *Sexes Served* Both. *Sources of Funding* State Funds. Summer school available. *Special Certification Level* ED.
Student/Patient Characteristics *Age Levels* 9-11; 12-14. *IQ Ranges* 71-85; 85-130; Above 130. *Exceptionalities Served* Emotionally Disturbed. *Learning Problems* Memory Disabilities; Perceptual Disabilities; Oral Language Disabilities; Reading Disabilities; Handwriting Disabilities; Spelling Disabilities; Written Expression. *Behavioral Problems* Attention Deficits; Hyperactivity; Impulsivity; Self-Aggression; Verbal Aggression; Physical Aggression; Indirect Aggression; Passive Aggression; Withdrawal. *Conditions Treated* Phobias; Obsessions and Compulsions; Hysteria; Depression; Suicide; Inadequacy/Immaturity; Personality Problems; Socialized Aggressive Reaction; Unsocialized Aggressive Reaction.
Services Provided Individual Therapy; Group Therapy; Parent Involvement; Behavior Therapy; Family Therapy; Art Therapy; Reality Therapy; Play Therapy. *Professionals on Staff* Psychiatrists 1; Psychologists 1; Social Workers 1; Nurses 1; Educational Therapist 1; Occupational Therapist 1. *Educational Professionals* Special Education Teachers 1; Educational Tutor 1. *Curricula* Traditional Academic; Individualized; Basic Skills. *Educational Intervention Approaches* Self-Control; Behavior Modification. *Degrees Awarded* Completion Certificate.
Comments The center is a semi-military structured program for SED children 4-12. Day care hours are the same as school hours. The average stay is one semester. Twelve to 15 year olds are seen on an outpatient basis.

Department of Education—Windward Oahu District

45-955 Kamehameha Hwy, Kaneohe, HI 96744 (808) 235-2443
Contact Beth Scott, District Ed Specialist Special Ed
Facility Information *Placement* Public School. *Sexes Served* Both. *Sources of Funding* State Funds; P.L. 94-142. Summer school available. *Teacher Certification Level* Elementary School; Junior High/Middle School; High School. *Special Certification Level* ED; LD; MR; Special Education.
Student/Patient Characteristics *Age Levels* 0-4; 5-8; 9-11; 12-14; 15-17; 18-21. *IQ Ranges* 0-25; 26-40; 41-55; 56-70; 71-85; 85-130; Above 130. *Exceptionalities Served* Emotionally Disturbed; Learning Disabled; Mentally Handicapped; Communication Disordered; Hearing Impaired/Deaf; Visually Impaired/Blind; Other Health Impaired; Physically Handicapped; Gifted. *Learning Problems* Memory Disabilities; Perceptual Disabilities;

Thinking Disabilities; Oral Language Disabilities; Reading Disabilities; Handwriting Disabilities; Spelling Disabilities; Arithmetic Disabilities; Written Expression. *Behavioral Problems* Attention Deficits; Hyperactivity; Hypoactivity; Impulsivity; Self-Aggression; Verbal Aggression; Physical Aggression; Indirect Aggression; Passive Aggression; Withdrawal. *Conditions Treated* Convulsive Disorders; Inadequacy/Immaturity; Socialized Aggressive Reaction; Unsocialized Aggressive Reaction.
Services Provided Individual Therapy; Group Therapy; Parent Involvement; Behavior Therapy; Cognitive Developmental Therapy; Play Therapy. *Professionals on Staff* Psychiatrists; Psychologists; Counselors; Social Workers. *Service Facilities Available (with number of rooms)* Consultative (ERT); Itinerants; Resource Rooms; Self-Contained Rooms; Hospital School; Homebound Instruction. *Educational Professionals* Regular School Teachers; Special Education Teachers; Paraprofessionals. *Curricula* Traditional Academic; Career/Vocational Education; Individualized; Basic Skills; Prevocational. *Educational Intervention Approaches* Precision Teaching; Behavior Modification. *Degrees Awarded* Certificate of Attendance; High School Diploma.
Comments Windward District is a public school program which attempts to service all children with all handicapping conditions within a public school program. When appropriate program and placement are not available, we seek program/placement outside our district.

Hawaii State Department of Education—Special Needs Branch

3430 Leahi Ave, Honolulu, HI 96815 (808) 737-2166
Contact Patrick F McGivern, State Ed Specialist
Facility Information *Placement* Public School. *Sexes Served* Both. *Sources of Funding* State Funds; P.L. 94-142. Summer school available. *Teacher Certification Level* Elementary School; Junior High/Middle School; High School. *Special Certification Level* ED; LD; MR; Career/Vocational Education; Reading; Math.
Student/Patient Characteristics *Age Levels* 0-4; 5-8; 9-11; 12-14; 15-17; 18-21. *IQ Ranges* 0-25; 26-40; 41-55; 56-70; 71-85; 85-130; Above 130. *Exceptionalities Served* Autistic; Emotionally Disturbed; Learning Disabled; Mentally Handicapped; Communication Disordered; Hearing Impaired/Deaf; Visually Impaired/Blind; Other Health Impaired; Physically Handicapped; Gifted. *Learning Problems* Memory Disabilities; Perceptual Disabilities; Thinking Disabilities; Oral Language Disabilities; Reading Disabilities; Handwriting Disabilities; Spelling Disabilities; Arithmetic Disabilities; Written Expression. *Behavioral Problems* Attention Deficits; Hyperactivity; Hypoactivity; Impulsivity; Self-Aggression; Verbal Aggression; Physical Aggression; Indirect Aggression; Passive Aggression; Withdrawal. *Conditions Treated* Alcohol Abuse and/or Drug Abuse; Other Substance Abuse or Dependence; Early Infantile Autism; Disintegrative Psychoses; Schizophrenia; Aphasia; Convulsive Disorders; Phobias; Obses-

sions and Compulsions; Hysteria; Depression; Suicide; Asthma; Anorexia Nervosa; Ulcerative Colitis; Inadequacy/Immaturity; Personality Problems; Socialized Aggressive Reaction; Unsocialized Aggressive Reaction.
Services Provided Individual Therapy; Group Therapy; Parent Involvement; Behavior Therapy; Cognitive Developmental Therapy; Biofeedback; Family Therapy; Filial Therapy; Drug Therapy; Art Therapy; Music Therapy; Play Therapy; Psychodrama. *Professionals on Staff* Psychiatrists; Psychologists; Counselors; Social Workers; Child Care Staff; Nurses; Occupational Therapists; Physical Therapists. *Service Facilities Available (with number of rooms)* Consultative (ERT); Itinerants; Resource Rooms; Transition Rooms; Self-Contained Rooms; Special School; Hospital School; On-Campus Residential School; Homebound Instruction. *Educational Professionals* Regular School Teachers; Special Education Teachers; Career/Vocational Teachers; Crisis Teachers; Special Education Counselors; Paraprofessionals. *Curricula* Traditional Academic; Career/Vocational Education; Individualized; Basic Skills; Prevocational. *Educational Intervention Approaches* Engineered Classroom; Precision Teaching; Progressive Discipline; Self-Control; Behavior Modification; Applied Behavior Analysis; Creative Conditioning. *Degrees Awarded* Certificate of Attendance; High School Diploma; Graduate Equivalency Diploma.

Hawaii State Hospital—Adolescent Unit

45-710 Keaahala Rd, Kaneohe, HI 96744 (808) 247-2191
Contact S P Sears, Dir
Facility Information *Number of Beds* 18. *Children/Adolescents Served* 18. *Sexes Served* Both. *Room and Board Fees (Approx)* Sliding Scale. *Sources of Funding* State Funds; Health Insurance; Medicaid. Summer school available. *Teacher Certification Level* Junior High/Middle School; High School.
Student/Patient Characteristics *Age Levels* 12-14; 15-17. *IQ Ranges* 41-55; 56-70; 71-85; 85-130; Above 130. *Exceptionalities Served* Emotionally Disturbed; Mentally Handicapped; Communication Disordered; Hearing Impaired/Deaf; Visually Impaired/Blind; Other Health Impaired. *Learning Problems* Perceptual Disabilities; Thinking Disabilities; Oral Language Disabilities; Reading Disabilities; Spelling Disabilities; Arithmetic Disabilities; Written Expression. *Behavioral Problems* Attention Deficits; Hyperactivity; Hypoactivity; Impulsivity; Self-Aggression; Verbal Aggression; Physical Aggression; Indirect Aggression; Passive Aggression. *Conditions Treated* Alcohol Abuse and/or Drug Abuse; Other Substance Abuse or Dependence; Disintegrative Psychoses; Schizophrenia; Phobias; Depression; Suicide; Personality Problems; Socialized Aggressive Reaction; Unsocialized Aggressive Reaction.
Services Provided Individual Therapy; Group Therapy; Parent Involvement; Behavior Therapy; Cognitive Developmental Therapy; Family Therapy; Drug Therapy; Art Therapy. *Professionals on Staff* Psychiatrists 1; Psychologists .5; Social Workers 1; Child Care Staff 10; Nurses 5. *Service Facilities Available (with number of rooms)* Special School 3; Hospital School 3; On-Campus Residential School 3. *Educational Professionals* Special Education Teachers 2. *Curricula* Traditional Academic; Individualized; Basic Skills; Prevocational. *Educational Intervention Approaches* Behavior Modification. *Degrees Awarded* Certificate of Attendance; High School Diploma; Graduate Equivalency Diploma.

Honolulu District—Special Education Center of Oahu (SECO)

708 Palekaua St, Honolulu, HI 96816 (808) 734-0233
Year Established 1965
Contact Sr Agnes Jerome Murphy, Dir
Facility Information *Placement* Special School; Special Program. *Children/Adolescents Served* 60. *Sexes Served* Both. *Sources of Funding* State Funds; P.L. 94-142; Aloha United Way. Summer

school available. *Teacher Certification Level* Elementary School; Junior High/Middle School; High School. *Special Certification Level* ED; LD; MR; Private School Teaching Certification.
Student/Patient Characteristics *Age Levels* 0-4; 5-8; 9-11; 12-14; 15-17; 18-21; Over 21. *IQ Ranges* 0-25; 26-40; 41-55; 56-70. *Exceptionalities Served* Autistic; Emotionally Disturbed; Learning Disabled; Mentally Handicapped; Communication Disordered; Hearing Impaired/Deaf; Visually Impaired/Blind; Other Health Impaired; Physically Handicapped. *Learning Problems* Memory Disabilities; Perceptual Disabilities; Thinking Disabilities; Oral Language Disabilities. *Behavioral Problems* Attention Deficits; Hyperactivity; Hypoactivity; Impulsivity; Self-Aggression; Verbal Aggression; Physical Aggression; Indirect Aggression; Passive Aggression; Withdrawal. *Conditions Treated* Early Infantile Autism; Disintegrative Psychoses; Schizophrenia; Aphasia; Convulsive Disorders; Obsessions and Compulsions; Personality Problems; Socialized Aggressive Reaction; Unsocialized Aggressive Reaction.
Services Provided Individual Therapy; Group Therapy; Parent Involvement; Behavior Therapy; Cognitive Developmental Therapy; Art Therapy; Music Therapy; Play Therapy; Recreation Therapy. *Professionals on Staff* Adult Habilitation Trainers. *Service Facilities Available (with number of rooms)* Self-Contained Rooms 10. *Educational Professionals* Special Education Teachers 35. *Curricula* Individualized; Basic Skills; Prevocational. *Educational Intervention Approaches* Behavior Modification. *Degrees Awarded* Graduate Equivalency Diploma.
Comments The center provides special education for children and adolescents who, due to the nature and severity of their handicapping conditions, cannot be accommodated in public schools. Students are placed at SECO by contractual agreement with the Department of Education.

The Salvation Army Residential Treatment Facilities for Children and Youth

845 22nd Ave, Honolulu, HI 96816 (808) 732-2802
Year Established 1971
Contact W R Cozens, Exec Dir
Facility Information *Placement* Private Residential Care. *Number of Beds* 42. *Children/Adolescents Served* 42. *Sexes Served* Both. *Room and Board Fees (Approx)* $16 (room and board); $107 (clinical services). *Tuition Fees (Approx)* $6,730 (academic services). *Sources of Funding* State Funds; Health Insurance; P.L. 94-142; OCHAMPUS. Summer school available. *Teacher Certification Level* Elementary School; Junior High/Middle School; High School. *Special Certification Level* ED.
Student/Patient Characteristics *Age Levels* 9-11; 12-14; 15-17. *Exceptionalities Served* Emotionally Disturbed; Learning Disabled. *Learning Problems* Perceptual Disabilities; Thinking Disabilities; Reading Disabilities; Arithmetic Disabilities. *Behavioral Problems* Attention Deficits; Hyperactivity; Impulsivity; Verbal Aggression; Physical Aggression; Indirect Aggression; Passive Aggression; Withdrawal. *Conditions Treated* Inadequacy/Immaturity; Personality Problems; Socialized Aggressive Reaction; Unsocialized Aggressive Reaction.
Services Provided Individual Therapy; Group Therapy; Parent Involvement; Family Therapy; Drug Therapy; Art Therapy; Play Therapy. *Professionals on Staff* Psychiatrists 3; Psychologists 1; Counselors 6; Social Workers 4; Child Care Staff 18; Nurses 2; Recreational and Activity Therapists 4. *Service Facilities Available (with number of rooms)* On-Campus Residential School 8. *Educational Professionals* Regular School Teachers 1; Special Education Teachers 4; Career/Vocational Teachers 1; Public School Liaison 1. *Curricula* Individualized; Basic Skills; Prevocational. *Educational Intervention Approaches* Engineered Classroom. *Degrees Awarded* High School Diploma.

Idaho

Idaho Youth Ranch Inc

Box 256, Rte 3, Rupert, ID 83350 (208) 532-4117
Year Established 1950
Contact Jim Tallmon, Ranch Dir
Facility Information *Placement* Private Residential Care. *Number of Beds* 38. *Children/Adolescents Served* 66. *Sexes Served* Both. *Room and Board Fees (Approx)* $26-$62. *Tuition Fees (Approx)* $1,620. *Sources of Funding* State Funds; Private Donations; Parents. Summer school available. *Teacher Certification Level* Elementary School; Junior High/Middle School; High School. *Special Certification Level* ED; LD; MR; Career/Vocational Education.

Student/Patient Characteristics *Age Levels* 9-11; 12-14; 15-17; 18-21. *IQ Ranges* 85-130; Above 130. *Exceptionalities Served* Emotionally Disturbed; Learning Disabled; Mentally Handicapped; Communication Disordered; Behavior Disordered. *Learning Problems* Memory Disabilities; Perceptual Disabilities; Thinking Disabilities; Oral Language Disabilities; Reading Disabilities; Handwriting Disabilities; Spelling Disabilities; Arithmetic Disabilities; Written Expression. *Behavioral Problems* Attention Deficits; Hyperactivity; Impulsivity; Self-Aggression; Verbal Aggression; Physical Aggression; Indirect Aggression; Passive Aggression. *Conditions Treated* Alcohol Abuse and/or Drug Abuse; Depression; Inadequacy/Immaturity; Personality Problems; Socialized Aggressive Reaction; Unsocialized Aggressive Reaction.

Services Provided Individual Therapy; Group Therapy; Parent Involvement; Behavior Therapy; Family Therapy; Filial Therapy; Drug Therapy; Reality Therapy; Guided Group Interaction. *Professionals on Staff* Psychiatrists 1; Psychologists 1; Counselors 3; Social Workers 6; Child Care Staff 20; Nurses .5; Recreation Staff 2.5. *Service Facilities Available (with number of rooms)* Consultative (ERT) 1; Resource Rooms 1; Self-Contained Rooms 1; On-Campus Residential School 4; Homebound Instruction 1. *Educational Professionals* Regular School Teachers 1; Special Education Teachers 2; Career/Vocational Teachers 1; Paraprofessionals 2. *Curricula* Career/Vocational Education; Individualized; Basic Skills; Prevocational. *Educational Intervention Approaches* Progressive Discipline; Self-Control; Behavior Modification. *Degrees Awarded* Certificate of Attendance; High School Diploma; Graduate Equivalency Diploma.

Comments Idaho Youth Ranch is a self-contained treatment center having an educational center, chapel, full sized gymnasium, recreation center, central dining facility, and a 4-H barn. A riding arena is being built.

Special Care Program

State Hospital North, Orofino, ID 83544 (208) 476-7934
Year Established 1982
Contact Jody Lubrecht, Dir
Facility Information *Placement* Special School; Private Residential Care. *Number of Beds* 16. *Children/Adolescents Served* 16. *Sexes Served* Both. *Room and Board Fees (Approx)* $114. *Sources of Funding* State Funds; HEW; P.L. 94-142. Summer school available. *Teacher Certification Level* Elementary School; Junior High/Middle School; High School. *Special Certification Level* Special Education; Regular Education; Social Studies.

Student/Patient Characteristics *Age Levels* 5-8; 9-11; 12-14; 15-17. *IQ Ranges* 85-130. *Exceptionalities Served* Autistic; Emotionally Disturbed. *Learning Problems* Memory Disabilities; Perceptual Disabilities; Thinking Disabilities; Oral Language Disabilities; Reading Disabilities; Handwriting Disabilities; Spelling Disabilities; Arithmetic Disabilities; Written Expression. *Behavioral Problems* Attention Deficits; Hyperactivity; Hypoactivity; Impulsivity; Self-Aggression; Verbal Aggression; Physical Aggression; Indirect Aggression; Passive Aggression; Withdrawal. *Conditions Treated* Early Infantile Autism; Disintegrative Psychoses; Schizophrenia; Convulsive Disorders; Obsessions and Compulsions; Depression; Suicide; Asthma; Anorexia Nervosa; Inadequacy/Immaturity; Personality Problems; Socialized Aggressive Reaction; Unsocialized Aggressive Reaction.

Services Provided Individual Therapy; Group Therapy; Parent Involvement; Behavior Therapy; Drug Therapy; Art Therapy; Recreation Therapy; Milieu Therapy. *Professionals on Staff* Psychiatrists 2; Psychologists 2; Social Workers 1; Child Care Staff 15; Nurses 5; Recreation Therapist 1. *Service Facilities Available (with number of rooms)* Self-Contained Rooms 2. *Educational Professionals* Special Education Teachers 1; Paraprofessionals 3. *Curricula* Traditional Academic; Career/Vocational Education; Individualized; Basic Skills; Prevocational. *Educational Intervention Approaches* Precision Teaching; Self-Control; Behavior Modification; Applied Behavior Analysis. *Degrees Awarded* Graduate Equivalency Diploma.

Comments This program offers an intensive treatment of intermediate duration (3-12 months) to severely emotionally disturbed children and adolescents ages 6-18. Two special education classrooms within the locked setting house the accredited education component.

Warm Springs Center

740 Warm Springs Ave, Boise, ID 83702 (208) 343-7797
Year Established 1908
Contact Barry Watts, Exec Dir
Facility Information *Placement* Special Program; Day Treatment Outpatient Mental Health Center. *Children/Adolescents Served* 18 (day treatment); 200 (outpatient). *Sexes Served* Both. *Sources of Funding* Health Insurance; Medicaid; Endowment Fund Grants. Summer school available. *Teacher Certification Level* Elementary School. *Special Certification Level* ED; LD.

Student/Patient Characteristics *Age Levels* 0-4; 5-8; 9-11; 12-14; 15-17; 18-21. *IQ Ranges* 71-85; 85-130; Above 130. *Exceptionalities Served* Emotionally Disturbed; Learning Disabled. *Learning Problems* Memory Disabilities; Thinking Disabilities; Reading Disabilities; Handwriting Disabilities; Spelling Disabilities; Arithmetic Disabilities. *Behavioral Problems* Attention Deficits; Hyperactivity; Hypoactivity; Impulsivity; Self-Aggression; Verbal Aggression; Physical Aggression; Indirect Aggression; Passive Aggression; Withdrawal. *Conditions Treated* Disintegrative Psychoses; Schizophrenia; Phobias; Obsessions and Compulsions; Hysteria; Depression; Suicide; Anorexia Nervosa; Inadequacy/Immaturity; Personality Problems; Socialized Aggressive Reaction; Unsocialized Aggressive Reaction.

Services Provided Individual Therapy; Group Therapy; Parent Involvement; Behavior Therapy; Family Therapy; Drug Therapy; Reality Therapy; Play Therapy; Psychodrama. *Professionals on Staff* Psychiatrists 2; Counselors 3; Social Workers 4. *Educational Professionals* Special Education Teachers 1; Paraprofessionals 2. *Curricula* Individualized; Basic Skills. *Educational Intervention Approaches* Self-Control; Behavior Modification.

Illinois

Allendale School

PO Box 277, Lake Villa, IL 60046 (312) 356-2351
Year Established 1897
Contact Robert Mount, Intake Supv

Facility Information *Placement* Special School; Private Residential Care; Special Program; Outpatient Clinic. *Number of Beds* 67. *Children/Adolescents Served* 67 (residential and group home); 15 (specialized foster care). *Sexes Served* Male. *Room and Board Fees (Approx)* $126. *Tuition Fees (Approx)* $12,845. *Sources of Funding* State Funds; Health Insurance; P.L. 94-142. Summer school available. *Teacher Certification Level* Elementary School; Junior High/Middle School; High School. *Special Certification Level* ED; LD; Career/Vocational Education; Reading; Math.

Student/Patient Characteristics *Age Levels* 9-11; 12-14; 15-17; 18-21. *IQ Ranges* 71-85; 85-130. *Exceptionalities Served* Autistic; Emotionally Disturbed; Learning Disabled; Behavior Disordered. *Learning Problems* Memory Disabilities; Perceptual Disabilities; Thinking Disabilities; Oral Language Disabilities; Reading Disabilities; Handwriting Disabilities; Spelling Disabilities; Arithmetic Disabilities; Written Expression. *Behavioral Problems* Attention Deficits; Hyperactivity; Impulsivity; Self-Aggression; Verbal Aggression; Physical Aggression; Indirect Aggression; Passive Aggression; Withdrawal. *Conditions Treated* Schizophrenia; Phobias; Depression; Inadequacy/Immaturity; Personality Problems; Socialized Aggressive Reaction; Unsocialized Aggressive Reaction.

Services Provided Individual Therapy; Group Therapy; Parent Involvement; Behavior Therapy; Family Therapy; Drug Therapy; Art Therapy; Music Therapy; Reality Therapy; Play Therapy. *Professionals on Staff* Psychiatrists 1; Psychologists 2; Social Workers 6; Child Care Staff 64; Nurses 1. *Service Facilities Available (with number of rooms)* Consultative (ERT) 3; Resource Rooms 1; Self-Contained Rooms 9; Special School 3. *Educational Professionals* Special Education Teachers 12; Career/Vocational Teachers 1; Crisis Teachers 1; Special Education Counselors 3; Music; Art; Home Economics; Industrial Arts; Physical Education 5. *Curricula* Traditional Academic; Career/Vocational Education; Individualized; Basic Skills; Prevocational. *Educational Intervention Approaches* Precision Teaching; Behavior Modification; Applied Behavior Analysis. *Degrees Awarded* Certificate of Attendance; High School Diploma; Eighth Grade Diploma.

Arrise Inc—Arrise Group Home for Autistic Children

336 Lathrop, Forest Park, IL 60310 (312) 771-2945
Year Established 1980
Contact Timothy A Andriano, Exec Dir

Facility Information *Placement* Private Residential Care. *Number of Beds* 6. *Children/Adolescents Served* 6. *Sexes Served* Both. *Sources of Funding* State Funds. Summer school available. *Teacher Certification Level* Elementary School; Junior High/Middle School. *Special Certification Level* Behavior Disorders.

Student/Patient Characteristics *Age Levels* 5-8; 9-11; 12-14; 15-17; 18-21. *IQ Ranges* 26-40; 41-55; 56-70; 71-85. *Exceptionalities Served* Autistic. *Learning Problems* Memory Disabilities; Perceptual Disabilities; Thinking Disabilities; Oral Language Disabilities; Reading Disabilities; Handwriting Disabilities; Spelling Disabilities; Arithmetic Disabilities; Written Expression. *Behavioral Problems* Attention Deficits; Hyperactivity; Self-Aggression; Verbal Aggression; Physical Aggression; Withdrawal. *Conditions Treated* Early Infantile Autism.

Services Provided Behavior Therapy. *Professionals on Staff* Psychologists 1; Child Care Staff 8. *Educational Professionals* Special Education Teachers 3. *Curricula* Individualized; Basic Skills. *Educational Intervention Approaches* Self-Control; Behavior Modification; Applied Behavior Analysis.

Comments All children residing in the group home attend public school special education classes. The group home program operates 365 days. Parents of children must reside within the Chicago metropolitan area.

Chaddock

205 S 24th St, Quincy, IL 62301 (217) 222-0034
Year Established 1853
Contact James Real, Principal

Facility Information *Placement* Special School; Private Residential Care. *Number of Beds* 54. *Children/Adolescents Served* 54. *Sexes Served* Both. *Room and Board Fees (Approx)* $30-$47. *Tuition Fees (Approx)* $10,919. *Sources of Funding* State Funds; P.L. 94-142; Private Donations. Summer school available. *Teacher Certification Level* Junior High/Middle School; High School. *Special Certification Level* LD; Reading; Behavior Disorders.

Student/Patient Characteristics *Age Levels* 9-11; 12-14; 15-17; 18-21. *IQ Ranges* 71-85; 85-130. *Exceptionalities Served* Emotionally Disturbed; Learning Disabled. *Learning Problems* Perceptual Disabilities; Reading Disabilities; Spelling Disabilities; Arithmetic Disabilities; Written Expression. *Behavioral Problems* Attention Deficits; Hyperactivity; Hypoactivity; Impulsivity; Self-Aggression; Verbal Aggression; Physical Aggression; Indirect Aggression; Passive Aggression; Withdrawal. *Conditions Treated* Depression; Inadequacy/Immaturity; Personality Problems.

Services Provided Individual Therapy; Group Therapy; Parent Involvement; Behavior Therapy; Family Therapy. *Professionals on Staff* Psychiatrists 1; Psychologists 1; Counselors 1; Social Workers 5; Child Care Staff 80; Nurses 1. *Service Facilities Available (with number of rooms)* Self-Contained Rooms 5; On-

Campus Residential School 11. *Educational Professionals* Special Education Teachers 10; Career/Vocational Teachers; Paraprofessionals 3; Principal 1; Physical Education; Arts and Crafts. *Curricula* Career/Vocational Education; Individualized; Basic Skills. *Educational Intervention Approaches* Team Primacy. *Degrees Awarded* Graduate Equivalency Diploma.

Comments Teaching youth to value caring for themselves and others is the primary focus of this program.

Child Disability Clinic—Carle Clinic

602 W University, Urbana, IL 61801 (217) 337-3100
Contact Annette Lansford, Dir Child Disability Clinic
Facility Information *Placement* Diagnostic Clinic. *Sources of Funding* Health Insurance; School Funding; State Crippled Children Funding.
Student/Patient Characteristics *Age Levels* 0-4; 5-8; 9-11; 12-14; 15-17; 18-21. *IQ Ranges* 0-25; 26-40; 41-55; 56-70; 71-85; 85-130; Above 130. *Exceptionalities Served* Autistic; Emotionally Disturbed; Learning Disabled; Mentally Handicapped; Communication Disordered; Hearing Impaired/Deaf; Visually Impaired/Blind; Other Health Impaired; Physically Handicapped; Gifted. *Learning Problems* Memory Disabilities; Perceptual Disabilities; Thinking Disabilities; Oral Language Disabilities; Reading Disabilities; Handwriting Disabilities; Spelling Disabilities; Arithmetic Disabilities; Written Expression. *Behavioral Problems* Attention Deficits; Hyperactivity; Hypoactivity; Impulsivity; Self-Aggression; Verbal Aggression; Physical Aggression; Indirect Aggression; Passive Aggression; Withdrawal. *Conditions Treated* Alcohol Abuse and/or Drug Abuse; Other Substance Abuse or Dependence; Early Infantile Autism; Disintegrative Psychoses; Schizophrenia; Aphasia; Convulsive Disorders; Phobias; Obsessions and Compulsions; Hysteria; Depression; Suicide; Asthma; Anorexia Nervosa; Ulcerative Colitis; Inadequacy/Immaturity; Personality Problems; Socialized Aggressive Reaction; Unsocialized Aggressive Reaction.
Services Provided *Educational Professionals* Special Education Teachers.

Children's Center for Behavioral Development

353 N 88th St, East Saint Louis, IL 62203 (618) 398-1152
Year Established 1974
Contact Alan Reeves, Exec Dir
Facility Information *Placement* Special School; Special Program. *Children/Adolescents Served* 80. *Sexes Served* Both. *Tuition Fees (Approx)* $5,422. *Sources of Funding* State Funds; P.L. 94-142. Summer school available. *Teacher Certification Level* Elementary School; Junior High/Middle School; High School. *Special Certification Level* ED; LD; MR; Career/Vocational Education; Reading; Math; Behavior Disorders.
Student/Patient Characteristics *Age Levels* 5-8; 9-11; 12-14; 15-17; 18-21. *IQ Ranges* 56-70; 71-85; 85-130. *Exceptionalities Served* Emotionally Disturbed; Learning Disabled; Mentally Handicapped. *Learning Problems* Memory Disabilities; Perceptual Disabilities; Thinking Disabilities; Oral Language Disabilities; Reading Disabilities; Handwriting Disabilities; Spelling Disabilities; Arithmetic Disabilities; Written Expression. *Behavioral Problems* Attention Deficits; Hyperactivity; Impulsivity; Verbal Aggression; Physical Aggression; Passive Aggression; Withdrawal. *Conditions Treated* Alcohol Abuse and/or Drug Abuse; Schizophrenia; Depression; Inadequacy/Immaturity; Personality Problems; Socialized Aggressive Reaction; Unsocialized Aggressive Reaction.
Services Provided Individual Therapy; Group Therapy; Parent Involvement; Behavior Therapy; Cognitive Developmental Therapy; Family Therapy; Drug Therapy; Art Therapy; Reality Therapy; Play Therapy. *Professionals on Staff* Psychiatrists 1; Psychologists 5; Counselors 1; Social Workers 3; Child Care Staff 6; Nurses 1. *Service Facilities Available (with number of rooms)* Self-Contained Rooms 6. *Educational Professionals* Special Education Teachers 6; Career/Vocational Teachers 1; Crisis Teachers 2; Special Education Counselors 2; Paraprofessionals 6. *Curricula* Traditional Academic; Career/Vocational Education; Individual-

ized; Basic Skills; Prevocational. *Educational Intervention Approaches* Progressive Discipline; Self-Control; Behavior Modification; Applied Behavior Analysis. *Degrees Awarded* High School Diploma.

The Clinical Center of Southern Illinois University

Carbondale, IL 62901 (618) 453-2361
Year Established 1959
Contact Carol McDermott, Coord of Social Work Serv Div
Facility Information *Placement* Special Program. *Sexes Served* Both. *Sources of Funding* State Funds; Client Fees. Summer school available. *Teacher Certification Level* Elementary School; Junior High/Middle School; High School. *Special Certification Level* ED; LD; Reading; Math.
Student/Patient Characteristics *Age Levels* 0-4; 5-8; 9-11; 12-14; 15-17; 18-21; Over 21. *IQ Ranges* 26-40; 41-55; 56-70; 71-85; 85-130; Above 130. *Exceptionalities Served* Autistic; Emotionally Disturbed; Learning Disabled; Mentally Handicapped; Communication Disordered; Hearing Impaired/Deaf; Other Health Impaired; Physically Handicapped; Gifted. *Learning Problems* Memory Disabilities; Perceptual Disabilities; Thinking Disabilities; Oral Language Disabilities; Reading Disabilities; Handwriting Disabilities; Spelling Disabilities; Arithmetic Disabilities; Written Expression. *Behavioral Problems* Attention Deficits; Hyperactivity; Hypoactivity; Impulsivity; Self-Aggression; Verbal Aggression; Physical Aggression; Indirect Aggression; Passive Aggression; Withdrawal. *Conditions Treated* Alcohol Abuse and/or Drug Abuse; Other Substance Abuse or Dependence; Early Infantile Autism; Disintegrative Psychoses; Schizophrenia; Aphasia; Convulsive Disorders; Phobias; Obsessions and Compulsions; Hysteria; Depression; Suicide; Anorexia Nervosa; Ulcerative Colitis; Inadequacy/Immaturity; Personality Problems; Socialized Aggressive Reaction; Unsocialized Aggressive Reaction.
Services Provided Individual Therapy; Parent Involvement; Behavior Therapy; Cognitive Developmental Therapy; Biofeedback; Family Therapy; Filial Therapy; Drug Therapy; Reality Therapy; Play Therapy. *Professionals on Staff* Psychiatrists 2; Psychologists 20; Psychologists; Social Workers 5; Nurses 2; Physical Therapists; Communications Specialists; Reading Specialists.

Comprehensive Mental Health Center of St Clair County Inc

3911 State St, East Saint Louis, IL 62205 (618) 482-7330
Year Established 1957
Contact Delores Ray, Exec Dir
Facility Information *Placement* Outpatient Assessment and Treatment. *Sexes Served* Both. *Sources of Funding* State Funds; Health Insurance; Medicaid.
Student/Patient Characteristics *Age Levels* 0-4; 5-8; 9-11; 12-14; 15-17; 18-21; Over 21. *IQ Ranges* 56-70; 71-85; 85-130. *Exceptionalities Served* Emotionally Disturbed; Learning Disabled. *Learning Problems* Perceptual Disabilities; Thinking Disabilities; Oral Language Disabilities; Reading Disabilities; Spelling Disabilities; Arithmetic Disabilities; Written Expression. *Behavioral Problems* Attention Deficits; Hyperactivity; Impulsivity; Verbal Aggression; Physical Aggression; Passive Aggression; Withdrawal. *Conditions Treated* Schizophrenia; Phobias; Obsessions and Compulsions; Hysteria; Depression; Suicide; Anorexia Nervosa; Inadequacy/Immaturity; Personality Problems; Socialized Aggressive Reaction; Unsocialized Aggressive Reaction.
Services Provided Individual Therapy; Group Therapy; Parent Involvement; Behavior Therapy; Family Therapy; Play Therapy. *Professionals on Staff* Psychiatrists 3; Psychologists 1; Counselors 2; Social Workers 1; Nurses; Aide 1. *Service Facilities Available (with number of rooms)* Consultative (ERT) 1.

Covenant Children's Home and Family Services

502 Elm Pl, Princeton, IL 61356 (815) 875-1129
Year Established 1921
Contact Martin L Pratt, Exec Dir

Facility Information *Placement* Public School; Public Residential Care; Private Residential Care. *Number of Beds* 47. *Children/Adolescents Served* 47. *Sexes Served* Both. *Room and Board Fees (Approx)* $81. *Sources of Funding* State Funds; Medicaid; P.L. 94-142. Summer school available. *Teacher Certification Level* Elementary School; Junior High/Middle School; High School. *Special Certification Level* ED; LD; MR.
Student/Patient Characteristics *Age Levels* 5-8; 9-11; 12-14; 15-17; 18-21. *IQ Ranges* 71-85; 85-130; Above 130. *Exceptionalities Served* Emotionally Disturbed; Learning Disabled; Mentally Handicapped; Hearing Impaired/Deaf; Visually Impaired/Blind; Other Health Impaired; Physically Handicapped. *Learning Problems* Memory Disabilities; Perceptual Disabilities; Thinking Disabilities; Oral Language Disabilities; Reading Disabilities; Spelling Disabilities; Arithmetic Disabilities. *Behavioral Problems* Attention Deficits; Hyperactivity; Hypoactivity; Impulsivity; Self-Aggression; Verbal Aggression; Physical Aggression; Indirect Aggression; Passive Aggression; Withdrawal. *Conditions Treated* Alcohol Abuse and/or Drug Abuse; Other Substance Abuse or Dependence; Schizophrenia; Convulsive Disorders; Phobias; Obsessions and Compulsions; Hysteria; Depression; Suicide; Asthma; Anorexia Nervosa; Ulcerative Colitis; Inadequacy/Immaturity; Personality Problems; Socialized Aggressive Reaction; Unsocialized Aggressive Reaction.

Services Provided Individual Therapy; Group Therapy; Parent Involvement; Behavior Therapy; Family Therapy; Filial Therapy; Reality Therapy; Therapeutic Recreation/Sports Program. *Professionals on Staff* Psychiatrists 1; Psychologists 1; Social Workers 4; Child Care Staff; Nurses 1; Masters Degree Therapist 3. *Service Facilities Available (with number of rooms)* Resource Rooms 2; Self-Contained Rooms 4. *Educational Professionals* Special Education Teachers 4. *Curricula* Traditional Academic; Career/Vocational Education; Individualized; Basic Skills. *Educational Intervention Approaches* Progressive Discipline; Self-Control; Behavior Modification. *Degrees Awarded* High School Diploma; Jr High School Diploma.

Dysfunctioning Child Center—Respite Care Unit

800 E 55th St, Chicago, IL 60615 (312) 241-5155
Year Established 1979
Contact Joseph H Thomas
Facility Information *Placement* Special Program. *Number of Beds* 15. *Children/Adolescents Served* 14. *Sexes Served* Both. *Room and Board Fees (Approx)* $3. *Sources of Funding* State Funds; Department of Mental Health. *Special Certification Level* ED; MR.
Student/Patient Characteristics *Age Levels* 0-4; 5-8; 9-11; 12-14. *IQ Ranges* 0-25; 26-40; 41-55; 56-70. *Exceptionalities Served* Autistic; Mentally Handicapped; Hearing Impaired/Deaf; Visually Impaired/Blind. *Learning Problems* Perceptual Disabilities; Thinking Disabilities; Oral Language Disabilities; Multiply Handicapped. *Behavioral Problems* Attention Deficits; Hyperactivity; Impulsivity; Self-Aggression; Physical Aggression; Passive Aggression; Withdrawal. *Conditions Treated* Early Infantile Autism.
Services Provided Behavior Therapy. *Professionals on Staff* Psychiatrists 1; Psychologists 3; Social Workers 1; Child Care Staff 18; Nurses 7; Speech Therapist; Behavior Analyst; Occupational Therapist 3. *Service Facilities Available (with number of rooms)* Resource Rooms 2; Self-Contained Rooms 3. *Curricula* Individualized; Basic Skills. *Educational Intervention Approaches* Behavior Modification.

Comments The Respite Care Unit offers a comprehensive, coordinated, short-term residential service. It is a residential treatment and evaluation program for developmentally disabled children ages 3-12. RCU offers 24 hour care to children of families in crisis, providing evaluation and treatment.

East St Louis Area Joint Agreement—Department of Special Education

1005 State St, East Saint Louis, IL 62201 (618) 875-8800
Year Established 1947
Contact Tunya P Robinson, Dir
Facility Information *Placement* Public School; Special Program. *Children/Adolescents Served* 1743. *Sexes Served* Both. *Sources of Funding* State Funds; P.L. 94-142; Local. Summer school available. *Teacher Certification Level* Elementary School; Junior High/Middle School; High School. *Special Certification Level* ED; LD; MR; Career/Vocational Education; Special Education.
Student/Patient Characteristics *Age Levels* 5-8; 9-11; 12-14; 15-17; 18-21. *IQ Ranges* 0-25; 26-40; 41-55; 56-70. *Exceptionalities Served* Emotionally Disturbed; Learning Disabled; Mentally Handicapped; Communication Disordered; Hearing Impaired/Deaf; Visually Impaired/Blind; Other Health Impaired; Physically Handicapped; Gifted. *Learning Problems* Memory Disabilities; Perceptual Disabilities; Thinking Disabilities; Oral Language Disabilities; Reading Disabilities; Handwriting Disabilities; Spelling Disabilities; Arithmetic Disabilities; Written Expression. *Behavioral Problems* Attention Deficits; Impulsivity; Self-Aggression; Verbal Aggression; Physical Aggression; Indirect Aggression; Passive Aggression; Withdrawal. *Conditions Treated* Depression; Inadequacy/Immaturity; Personality Problems; Socialized Aggressive Reaction; Unsocialized Aggressive Reaction.

Services Provided Individual Therapy; Group Therapy; Parent Involvement; Behavior Therapy; Cognitive Developmental Therapy. *Professionals on Staff* Psychiatrists 1; Psychologists 9; Counselors 14; Social Workers 10; Nurses 1. *Service Facilities Available (with number of rooms)* Resource Rooms 20; Self-Contained Rooms 35. *Educational Professionals* Regular School Teachers; Special Education Teachers; Career/Vocational Teachers; Crisis Teachers; Special Education Counselors. *Curricula* Career/Vocational Education; Prevocational. *Educational Intervention Approaches* Engineered Classroom; Precision Teaching.

Forest Hospital

555 Wilson Ln, Des Plaines, IL 60016 (312) 635-4100
Year Established 1957
Contact Charles Scharenberg, Admin
Facility Information *Placement* Special School; Private Day Care; Hospital School. *Number of Beds* 115. *Children/Adolescents Served* 135. *Sexes Served* Both. *Room and Board Fees (Approx)* $330. *Sources of Funding* State Funds; Health Insurance; P.L. 94-142; Cash. Summer school available. *Teacher Certification Level* Elementary School; Junior High/Middle School; High School. *Special Certification Level* ED; LD; MR; Career/Vocational Education; Reading; Math; Deaf Education.
Student/Patient Characteristics *Age Levels* 5-8; 9-11; 12-14; 15-17; 18-21; Over 21. *IQ Ranges* 71-85; 85-130; Above 130. *Exceptionalities Served* Emotionally Disturbed; Learning Disabled; Communication Disordered; Hearing Impaired/Deaf; Visually Impaired/Blind; Physically Handicapped; Gifted; Behavior Disordered; Educationally Handicapped; Neurologically Impaired. *Learning Problems* Memory Disabilities; Perceptual Disabilities; Thinking Disabilities; Oral Language Disabilities; Reading Disabilities; Handwriting Disabilities; Spelling Disabilities; Arithmetic Disabilities; Written Expression. *Behavioral Problems* Attention Deficits; Hyperactivity; Hypoactivity; Impulsivity; Self-Aggression; Verbal Aggression; Physical Aggression; Indirect Aggression; Passive Aggression; Withdrawal. *Conditions Treated* Alcohol Abuse and/or Drug Abuse; Other Substance Abuse or Dependence; Disintegrative Psychoses; Schizophrenia; Aphasia; Convulsive Disorders; Phobias; Obsessions and Compulsions; Hysteria; Depression; Suicide; Asthma; Anorexia Nervosa; Ulcerative Colitis; Inadequacy/Immaturity; Personality Problems; Socialized Aggressive Reaction; Unsocialized Aggressive Reaction.

Services Provided Individual Therapy; Group Therapy; Parent Involvement; Behavior Therapy; Cognitive Developmental Therapy; Biofeedback; Family Therapy; Filial Therapy; Drug Ther-

apy; Art Therapy; Music Therapy; Reality Therapy; Play Therapy; Psychodrama; Milieu Therapy; Multiple Family Therapy; Pool Relaxation. *Professionals on Staff* Psychiatrists; Psychologists; Social Workers 5; Child Care Staff 55; Nurses 20; Certified Alcoholism Counselor 1. *Educational Professionals* Regular School Teachers 12; Special Education Teachers 4; Career/Vocational Teachers 1; Paraprofessionals 3; Hearing Impaired Teacher 1. *Curricula* Traditional Academic; Career/Vocational Education; Individualized; Basic Skills; Prevocational; Computer. *Educational Intervention Approaches* Engineered Classroom; Precision Teaching; Progressive Discipline; Self-Control; Behavior Modification; Applied Behavior Analysis; Creative Conditioning.
Comments Forest Hospital is a fully accredited private psychiatric hospital. The primary objective at Forest is to provide intensive, comprehensive care to patients in order that they may be re-established within their families and communities as soon as possible.

The Grove School

40 Ed Old Mill Rd, Lake Forest, IL 60045
Facility Information *Placement* Special School; Private Residential Care. *Number of Beds* 66. *Children/Adolescents Served* 100. *Sexes Served* Both. *Room and Board Fees (Approx)* \$75. *Tuition Fees (Approx)* \$5,600. *Sources of Funding* State Funds; Health Insurance; Medicaid; P.L. 94-142; Private Donations. Summer school available. *Teacher Certification Level* Elementary School; Junior High/Middle School; High School. *Special Certification Level* LD; MR; Career/Vocational Education.
Student/Patient Characteristics *Age Levels* 12-14; 15-17; 18-21; Over 21. *IQ Ranges* 0-25; 26-40; 56-70. *Exceptionalities Served* Autistic; Learning Disabled; Mentally Handicapped; Communication Disordered; Other Health Impaired; Physically Handicapped; Severe and Profoundly Handicapped; Multiply Handicapped. *Learning Problems* Memory Disabilities; Perceptual Disabilities; Thinking Disabilities; Oral Language Disabilities; Reading Disabilities. *Behavioral Problems* Attention Deficits; Hyperactivity; Self-Aggression; Verbal Aggression. *Conditions Treated* Early Infantile Autism; Schizophrenia; Aphasia.

Hartgrove Hospital—Hartgrove Academy

520 N Ridgeway, Chicago, IL 60624 (312) 722-3113
Year Established 1977
Contact Donald Pondelick, Dir
Facility Information *Placement* Public School; Special School; Private Residential Care. *Number of Beds* 82. *Children/Adolescents Served* 82. *Sexes Served* Both. *Room and Board Fees (Approx)* \$370. *Tuition Fees (Approx)* \$4,800. *Sources of Funding* State Funds; Health Insurance; P.L. 94-142. Summer school available. *Teacher Certification Level* Elementary School; Junior High/Middle School; High School. *Special Certification Level* ED; LD; MR; Reading; Math.
Student/Patient Characteristics *Age Levels* 5-8; 9-11; 12-14; 15-17; 18-21; Over 21. *IQ Ranges* 56-70; 71-85; 85-130; Above 130. *Exceptionalities Served* Autistic; Emotionally Disturbed; Learning Disabled; Mentally Handicapped; Communication Disordered; Hearing Impaired/Deaf; Physically Handicapped; Gifted. *Learning Problems* Memory Disabilities; Perceptual Disabilities; Thinking Disabilities; Oral Language Disabilities; Reading Disabilities; Handwriting Disabilities; Spelling Disabilities; Arithmetic Disabilities; Written Expression. *Behavioral Problems* Attention Deficits; Hyperactivity; Hypoactivity; Impulsivity; Self-Aggression; Verbal Aggression; Physical Aggression; Indirect Aggression; Passive Aggression; Withdrawal. *Conditions Treated* Alcohol Abuse and/or Drug Abuse; Other Substance Abuse or Dependence; Early Infantile Autism; Disintegrative Psychoses; Schizophrenia; Aphasia; Convulsive Disorders; Phobias; Obsessions and Compulsions; Hysteria; Depression; Suicide; Asthma; Anorexia Nervosa; Ulcerative Colitis; Inadequacy/Immaturity; Personality Problems; Socialized Aggressive Reaction; Unsocialized Aggressive Reaction.

Services Provided Individual Therapy; Group Therapy; Parent Involvement; Behavior Therapy; Cognitive Developmental Therapy; Biofeedback; Family Therapy; Filial Therapy; Drug Therapy; Art Therapy; Music Therapy; Reality Therapy; Play Therapy; Psychodrama. *Professionals on Staff* Psychiatrists 50; Psychologists 50; Counselors 10; Social Workers 10; Child Care Staff 75; Nurses 30. *Service Facilities Available (with number of rooms)* Consultative (ERT); Resource Rooms; Transition Rooms; Self-Contained Rooms; Hospital School; Homebound Instruction. *Educational Professionals* Regular School Teachers 2; Special Education Teachers 10. *Curricula* Traditional Academic; Individualized; Basic Skills; Prevocational. *Educational Intervention Approaches* Engineered Classroom; Behavior Modification; Creative Conditioning. *Degrees Awarded* Certificate of Attendance.

Henry Horner Children and Adolescent Center

4201 N Oak Park Ave, Chicago, IL 60634 (312) 794-3960
Year Established 1974
Contact Alan J Ward, Dir
Facility Information *Placement* Public Psychiatric Hospital. *Number of Beds* 100. *Children/Adolescents Served* 100. *Sexes Served* Both. *Room and Board Fees (Approx)* \$234. *Sources of Funding* State Funds; Health Insurance; Medicaid. Summer school available. *Teacher Certification Level* Elementary School; Junior High/Middle School; High School. *Special Certification Level* ED; LD.
Student/Patient Characteristics *Age Levels* 0-4; 5-8; 9-11; 12-14; 15-17. *IQ Ranges* 56-70; 71-85; 85-130; Above 130. *Exceptionalities Served* Autistic; Emotionally Disturbed; Learning Disabled. *Learning Problems* Memory Disabilities; Thinking Disabilities; Oral Language Disabilities; Reading Disabilities. *Behavioral Problems* Attention Deficits; Hyperactivity; Impulsivity; Self-Aggression; Verbal Aggression; Physical Aggression; Indirect Aggression; Passive Aggression; Withdrawal. *Conditions Treated* Early Infantile Autism; Disintegrative Psychoses; Schizophrenia; Phobias; Obsessions and Compulsions; Hysteria; Depression; Suicide; Anorexia Nervosa; Inadequacy/Immaturity; Personality Problems; Socialized Aggressive Reaction; Unsocialized Aggressive Reaction.
Services Provided Individual Therapy; Group Therapy; Parent Involvement; Behavior Therapy; Family Therapy; Drug Therapy; Art Therapy; Music Therapy; Reality Therapy; Play Therapy. *Professionals on Staff* Psychiatrists 5; Psychologists 7; Social Workers 6; Child Care Staff 70; Nurses 10. *Service Facilities Available (with number of rooms)* Self-Contained Rooms 13; On-Campus Residential School 13. *Educational Professionals* Special Education Teachers 12; Career/Vocational Teachers 5. *Curricula* Traditional Academic; Career/Vocational Education; Individualized. *Degrees Awarded* High School Diploma.

Illinois Center for Autism

10025 Bunkum Rd, Fairview Heights, IL 62208 (618) 398-7500
Year Established 1978
Contact Carol Madison, Dir
Facility Information *Placement* Private Day Care; Mental Health/Educational Facility for the Autistic. *Children/Adolescents Served* 34. *Sexes Served* Both. *Sources of Funding* State Funds; P.L. 94-142; 708 Mental Health Board Funds; Contributions; United Way. Summer school available. *Teacher Certification Level* Elementary School; Junior High/Middle School; High School. *Special Certification Level* Behavioral Disorder; Trainable Mentally Handicapped.
Student/Patient Characteristics *Age Levels* 0-4; 5-8; 9-11; 12-14; 15-17; 18-21. *Exceptionalities Served* Autistic; Hearing Impaired/Deaf. *Behavioral Problems* Attention Deficits; Hyperactivity; Self-Aggression; Verbal Aggression; Physical Aggression; Indirect Aggression; Withdrawal. *Conditions Treated* Early Infantile Autism; Schizophrenia; Aphasia.
Services Provided Individual Therapy; Group Therapy; Parent Involvement; Behavior Therapy; Cognitive Developmental Therapy; Family Therapy; Art Therapy; Music Therapy; Play Ther-

apy; Simultaneous Sign Language Training. *Professionals on Staff* Psychologists 2; Counselors 1; Speech/Language Therapists; Behavior Modification Therapists 4. *Service Facilities Available (with number of rooms)* Self-Contained Rooms 8; Homebound Instruction 1. *Educational Professionals* Special Education Teachers 8; Paraprofessionals 12. *Curricula* Individualized; Basic Skills; Prevocational. *Educational Intervention Approaches* Behavior Modification.

Irene Josselyn Clinic

405 Central, Northfield, IL 60093 (312) 441-5600
Year Established 1952
Contact Mary Giffin, Dir

Facility Information *Placement* Outpatient Psychiatric Care.

Comments This outpatient psychiatric facility is equipped to diagnose and treat most psychiatric illnesses of children including mixed learning and emotional conditions. No in-patient facilities and no educational programs are provided.

Jeanine Schultz Memorial School

2101 W Oakton St, Park Ridge, IL 60068 (312) 696-3315
Year Established 1965
Contact Joseph C Zummo, Dir

Facility Information *Placement* Private Residential School and Special Education Day School. *Number of Beds* 6.
Children/Adolescents Served 6. *Sexes Served* Both. *Room and Board Fees (Approx)* $56. *Tuition Fees (Approx)* $6,300. *Sources of Funding* State Funds; P.L. 94-142. Summer school available.
Teacher Certification Level Elementary School; Junior High/Middle School; High School. *Special Certification Level* ED; LD; Reading.

Student/Patient Characteristics *Age Levels* 5-8; 9-11; 12-14; 15-17; 18-21; Over 21. *IQ Ranges* 85-130; Above 130.
Exceptionalities Served Autistic; Emotionally Disturbed; Learning Disabled. *Learning Problems* Memory Disabilities; Perceptual Disabilities; Thinking Disabilities; Oral Language Disabilities; Reading Disabilities; Handwriting Disabilities; Spelling Disabilities; Arithmetic Disabilities; Written Expression; Social Interaction. *Behavioral Problems* Attention Deficits; Hyperactivity; Hypoactivity; Impulsivity; Self-Aggression; Verbal Aggression; Physical Aggression; Indirect Aggression; Passive Aggression; Withdrawal. *Conditions Treated* Early Infantile Autism; Disintegrative Psychoses; Schizophrenia; Convulsive Disorders; Phobias; Obsessions and Compulsions; Hysteria; Depression; Suicide; Anorexia Nervosa; Ulcerative Colitis; Inadequacy/Immaturity; Personality Problems; Socialized Aggressive Reaction; Unsocialized Aggressive Reaction.

Services Provided Individual Therapy; Group Therapy; Parent Involvement; Art Therapy; Music Therapy; Play Therapy.
Professionals on Staff Psychiatrists 2; Social Workers 5; Child Care Staff 6. *Service Facilities Available (with number of rooms)* Consultative (ERT); Self-Contained Rooms. *Educational Professionals* Special Education Teachers 8. *Curricula* Individualized; Small Group Instruction. *Educational Intervention Approaches* Dynamic Approach; Highly Structured. *Degrees Awarded* High School Diploma.

Comments This program serves 50 seriously emotionally disturbed children and adolescents who have been excluded from public school placement in our day special education program. Milieu therapy and special education services as well as individual and group psychotherapy are also provided. Social workers work with parents to offer child guidance. A residential component is also provided.

Jewish Children's Bureau of Chicago

1 S Franklin, Chicago, IL 60606 (312) 346-6700
Year Established 1894
Contact Ann A Marakis, Intake Coord

Facility Information *Placement* Special School; Private Residential Care; Private Day Care; Special Program. *Number of Beds* 40. *Children/Adolescents Served* 40 (placement services); unlim-

ited (in-home services). *Sexes Served* Both. *Sources of Funding* State Funds; Client Fees. Summer school available. *Teacher Certification Level* Elementary School; Junior High/Middle School; High School. *Special Certification Level* ED; LD; Career/Vocational Education.

Student/Patient Characteristics *Age Levels* 0-4; 5-8; 9-11; 12-14; 15-17; 18-21; Over 21. *IQ Ranges* 71-85; 85-130; Above 130. *Exceptionalities Served* Emotionally Disturbed; Learning Disabled; Physically Handicapped; Gifted. *Learning Problems* Perceptual Disabilities; Thinking Disabilities; Reading Disabilities; Handwriting Disabilities; Spelling Disabilities; Arithmetic Disabilities; Written Expression. *Behavioral Problems* Attention Deficits; Hyperactivity; Impulsivity; Self-Aggression; Verbal Aggression; Physical Aggression; Indirect Aggression; Passive Aggression; Withdrawal. *Conditions Treated* Alcohol Abuse and/or Drug Abuse; Schizophrenia; Phobias; Obsessions and Compulsions; Hysteria; Depression; Suicide; Asthma; Anorexia Nervosa; Ulcerative Colitis; Inadequacy/Immaturity; Personality Problems; Socialized Aggressive Reaction; Unsocialized Aggressive Reaction.

Services Provided Individual Therapy; Group Therapy; Parent Involvement; Family Therapy; Filial Therapy; Reality Therapy; Play Therapy. *Professionals on Staff* Psychiatrists; Social Workers; Child Care Staff. *Service Facilities Available (with number of rooms)* Special School. *Educational Professionals* Special Education Teachers. *Curricula* Traditional Academic; Career/Vocational Education; Individualized; Basic Skills; Prevocational. *Degrees Awarded* Certificate of Attendance; High School Diploma; Elementary School Diploma.

Little Friends Inc—Group Home for Autistic Children

1 N 111 Bloomingdale Rd, Wheaton, IL 60187 (312) 690-7292
Year Established 1981
Contact Patti Suloway Boheme, Prog Dir

Facility Information *Placement* Private Residential Care; Two Year Residential Program; Weekend Respite Program. *Number of Beds* 6. *Children/Adolescents Served* During week 6; weekends 30. *Sexes Served* Both. *Room and Board Fees (Approx)* $102. *Sources of Funding* State Funds; P.L. 94-142; Social Security Insurance; Department of Mental Health and Developmental Disabilities.

Student/Patient Characteristics *Age Levels* 5-8; 9-11; 12-14. *IQ Ranges* 0-25; 26-40; 41-55. *Exceptionalities Served* Autistic. *Learning Problems* Memory Disabilities; Perceptual Disabilities; Thinking Disabilities; Oral Language Disabilities; Reading Disabilities. *Behavioral Problems* Attention Deficits; Hyperactivity; Hypoactivity; Impulsivity; Self-Aggression; Verbal Aggression; Physical Aggression; Indirect Aggression; Passive Aggression; Withdrawal. *Conditions Treated* Early Infantile Autism; Obsessions and Compulsions.

Services Provided Parent Involvement; Behavior Therapy; Cognitive Developmental Therapy; Family Therapy; Drug Therapy. *Professionals on Staff* Psychiatrists 1; Psychologists 1; Counselors 2; Social Workers 1; Child Care Staff 14. *Curricula* Individualized; Basic Skills. *Educational Intervention Approaches* Behavior Modification; Applied Behavior Analysis.

Comments Little Friends Group Home is a 2 year-treatment program working with autistic children in the areas of socialization, communication, independent living skills, community exposure and behavior control so the child can return home after 2 years. Parent training and involvement is also a major part of the program.

Little Friends Inc—Little Friends Parent Infant Program

140 N Wright, Naperville, IL 60540 (312) 355-6870
Year Established 1974
Contact Maryanne Dzik, Prog Coord

Facility Information *Placement* Early Intervention. *Sexes Served* Both. *Tuition Fees (Approx)* Sliding Scale. *Sources of Funding* State Funds; Private Contributions. Summer school available. *Special Certification Level* LD; MR; Early Childhood.

Student/Patient Characteristics *Age Levels* 0-4. *IQ Ranges* 0-25; 26-40; 41-55; 56-70; 71-85; 85-130; Above 130. *Exceptionalities Served* Autistic; Emotionally Disturbed; Learning Disabled; Mentally Handicapped; Communication Disordered; Visually Impaired/Blind; Other Health Impaired; Physically Handicapped. *Behavioral Problems* Attention Deficits; Hyperactivity; Hypoactivity; Impulsivity; Withdrawal. *Conditions Treated* Early Infantile Autism; Disintegrative Psychoses; Schizophrenia; Aphasia; Convulsive Disorders; Depression; Personality Problems.

Services Provided Group Therapy; Parent Involvement; Cognitive Developmental Therapy; Family Therapy; Play Therapy. *Professionals on Staff* Psychiatrists 1; Psychologists 1; Social Workers 1; Child Care Staff 4; Pediatrician; Occupational Therapy; Speech Therapy. *Educational Professionals* Special Education Teachers 4. *Curricula* Early Intervention.

Comments This program serves children ages 0-3 with developmental delays or who are at high risk for normal development. Parent participation is required.

Little Friends Inc—Little Friends School

619 E Franklin, Naperville, IL 60540 (312) 355-6870
Year Established 1965
Contact Dottee Krejci, Dir

Facility Information *Placement* Special School. *Children/Adolescents Served* 125. *Sexes Served* Both. *Tuition Fees (Approx)* $6,879. *Sources of Funding* State Funds; P.L. 94-142; Department of Mental Health. Summer school available. *Teacher Certification Level* Elementary School; Junior High/Middle School; High School. *Special Certification Level* ED; LD; MR.

Student/Patient Characteristics *Age Levels* 5-8; 9-11; 12-14; 15-17. *IQ Ranges* 26-40; 41-55; 56-70; 71-85; 85-130; Above 130. *Exceptionalities Served* Autistic; Emotionally Disturbed; Learning Disabled; Mentally Handicapped; Communication Disordered; Other Health Impaired. *Learning Problems* Memory Disabilities; Perceptual Disabilities; Thinking Disabilities; Oral Language Disabilities; Reading Disabilities; Handwriting Disabilities; Spelling Disabilities; Arithmetic Disabilities; Written Expression. *Behavioral Problems* Attention Deficits; Hyperactivity; Impulsivity; Self-Aggression; Verbal Aggression; Physical Aggression; Indirect Aggression; Passive Aggression; Withdrawal. *Conditions Treated* Early Infantile Autism; Schizophrenia; Aphasia; Phobias; Obsessions and Compulsions; Hysteria; Depression; Suicide; Inadequacy/Immaturity; Personality Problems; Socialized Aggressive Reaction; Unsocialized Aggressive Reaction.

Services Provided Individual Therapy; Group Therapy; Parent Involvement; Behavior Therapy; Cognitive Developmental Therapy; Family Therapy; Music Therapy; Play Therapy; Intrusion Therapy; Occupational Therapy; Physical Therapy. *Professionals on Staff* Psychiatrists 1; Psychologists 4; Counselors 4; Social Workers 5; Nurses 1. *Service Facilities Available (with number of rooms)* Consultative (ERT) 9; Resource Rooms 2; Self-Contained Rooms 30; Special School. *Educational Professionals* Regular School Teachers 10; Special Education Teachers 12. *Curricula* Individualized; Basic Skills; Prevocational. *Educational Intervention Approaches* Self-Control; Behavior Modification. *Degrees Awarded* High School Diploma.

Comments Students referred to the therapeutic program have some history of emotional problems. Most have an IQ within the normal range. A milieu treatment approach is used in all classrooms.

Little Friends Inc—The Therapeutic Workshop

5157 Thatcher Rd, Downers Grove, IL 60540 (312) 964-1722
Year Established 1983
Contact Jerry Lowell, Prog Coord

Facility Information *Placement* Private Day Care. *Children/Adolescents Served* 22. *Sexes Served* Both. *Tuition Fees (Approx)* $8,793. *Sources of Funding* P.L. 94-142. Summer school available. *Teacher Certification Level* High School. *Special Certification Level* ED; LD; MR.

Student/Patient Characteristics *Age Levels* 15-17; 18-21. *IQ Ranges* 71-85; 85-130. *Exceptionalities Served* Emotionally Disturbed; Learning Disabled; Mentally Handicapped. *Learning Problems* Memory Disabilities; Perceptual Disabilities; Thinking Disabilities; Oral Language Disabilities; Reading Disabilities; Spelling Disabilities; Arithmetic Disabilities; Written Expression. *Behavioral Problems* Attention Deficits; Hypoactivity; Impulsivity; Verbal Aggression; Passive Aggression; Withdrawal. *Conditions Treated* Schizophrenia; Obsessions and Compulsions; Hysteria; Depression; Suicide; Inadequacy/Immaturity; Personality Problems.

Services Provided Individual Therapy; Group Therapy; Parent Involvement; Behavior Therapy; Family Therapy. *Professionals on Staff* Psychologists 1; Counselors 1; Social Workers 1. *Service Facilities Available (with number of rooms)* Consultative (ERT) 1; Itinerants 1; Self-Contained Rooms 2. *Educational Professionals* Special Education Teachers 1; Career/Vocational Teachers 1; Special Education Counselors 1; Job Placement Specialist 1. *Curricula* Career/Vocational Education; Individualized; Basic Skills; Prevocational. *Educational Intervention Approaches* Self-Control; Behavior Modification. *Degrees Awarded* Certificate of Attendance; High School Diploma.

Comments Students in this program are involved in 3 program areas; academic instruction, therapeutic support, and vocational training.

Lovellton Academy

600 Villa, Elgin, IL 60120 (312) 695-0077
Year Established 1984
Contact Patricia Carlson, Dir

Facility Information *Placement* Special School; Private Residential Care; Private Day Care. *Number of Beds* 20. *Children/Adolescents Served* 30. *Sexes Served* Both. *Room and Board Fees (Approx)* $45-$76. *Sources of Funding* State Funds; Health Insurance; P.L. 94-142. Summer school available. *Teacher Certification Level* Elementary School; Junior High/Middle School; High School. *Special Certification Level* ED; LD; MR; Career/Vocational Education; Reading; Math.

Student/Patient Characteristics *Age Levels* 12-14; 15-17; 18-21. *IQ Ranges* 71-85; 85-130; Above 130. *Exceptionalities Served* Emotionally Disturbed; Learning Disabled; Communication Disordered; Physically Handicapped; Gifted. *Learning Problems* Memory Disabilities; Perceptual Disabilities; Thinking Disabilities; Oral Language Disabilities; Reading Disabilities; Handwriting Disabilities; Spelling Disabilities; Arithmetic Disabilities; Written Expression. *Behavioral Problems* Attention Deficits; Hyperactivity; Hypoactivity; Impulsivity; Self-Aggression; Verbal Aggression; Physical Aggression; Indirect Aggression; Passive Aggression; Withdrawal. *Conditions Treated* Alcohol Abuse and/or Drug Abuse; Other Substance Abuse or Dependence; Disintegrative Psychoses; Schizophrenia; Aphasia; Convulsive Disorders; Phobias; Obsessions and Compulsions; Hysteria; Depression; Suicide; Asthma; Anorexia Nervosa; Ulcerative Colitis; Inadequacy/Immaturity; Personality Problems; Socialized Aggressive Reaction; Unsocialized Aggressive Reaction.

Services Provided Individual Therapy; Group Therapy; Parent Involvement; Behavior Therapy; Cognitive Developmental Therapy; Biofeedback; Family Therapy; Filial Therapy; Drug Therapy; Art Therapy; Music Therapy; Reality Therapy; Play Therapy; Psychodrama. *Professionals on Staff* Psychologists 2; Social Workers 1; Child Care Staff 8; Nurses 2. *Educational Professionals* Regular School Teachers 2; Special Education Teachers 2; Career/Vocational Teachers 1; Paraprofessionals 2. *Curricula* Traditional Academic; Career/Vocational Education; Individualized; Basic Skills; Prevocational. *Educational Intervention Approaches* Engineered Classroom; Precision Teaching; Progressive Discipline; Self-Control; Behavior Modification; Applied Behavior Analysis; Creative Conditioning.

Comments This program is psychoeducationally oriented for developmentally or emotionally disturbed, or behaviorally disordered students. School attendance is of prime importance while students and their families are actively involved in the treatment process.

Lutherbrook Children's Center

343 W Lake St, Addison, IL 60101 (312) 543-6900
Year Established 1873
Contact Richard J Hass, Dir
Facility Information *Placement* Private Residential Care. *Number of Beds* 36. *Children/Adolescents Served* 36. *Sexes Served* Both. *Room and Board Fees (Approx)* $100. *Tuition Fees (Approx)* $31,966. *Sources of Funding* State Funds. Summer school available. *Teacher Certification Level* Elementary School. *Special Certification Level* ED.
Student/Patient Characteristics *Age Levels* 5-8; 9-11; 12-14. *IQ Ranges* 71-85; 85-130. *Exceptionalities Served* Emotionally Disturbed. *Learning Problems* Memory Disabilities; Perceptual Disabilities; Thinking Disabilities; Oral Language Disabilities; Reading Disabilities; Handwriting Disabilities; Spelling Disabilities; Arithmetic Disabilities; Written Expression. *Behavioral Problems* Attention Deficits; Hyperactivity; Impulsivity; Self-Aggression; Verbal Aggression; Physical Aggression; Indirect Aggression; Passive Aggression. *Conditions Treated* Depression; Inadequacy/Immaturity; Personality Problems; Unsocialized Aggressive Reaction.
Services Provided Individual Therapy; Group Therapy; Family Therapy; Art Therapy. *Professionals on Staff* Counselors 4; Social Workers 2; Child Care Staff 25; Nurses 1. *Service Facilities Available (with number of rooms)* Resource Rooms 1; Self-Contained Rooms 5; On-Campus Residential School 5. *Educational Professionals* Regular School Teachers 4; Special Education Teachers 3; Paraprofessionals 4. *Curricula* Traditional Academic; Individualized; Basic Skills. *Educational Intervention Approaches* Self-Control; Behavior Modification. *Degrees Awarded* Certificate of Attendance.

Madden Mental Health Center Campus—Institute for Juvenile Research—Inpatient Services

1200 S 1st Ave, Hines, IL 60141 (312) 345-9870
Year Established 1968
Contact Norman J Booth, Dir
Facility Information *Placement* Mental Health Center. *Number of Beds* 45. *Children/Adolescents Served* 45. *Sexes Served* Both. *Sources of Funding* State Funds. Summer school available. *Teacher Certification Level* Elementary School; High School. *Special Certification Level* ED; LD; Reading; Math.
Student/Patient Characteristics *Age Levels* 5-8; 9-11; 12-14; 15-17. *IQ Ranges* 71-85; 85-130; Above 130. *Exceptionalities Served* Emotionally Disturbed; Learning Disabled. *Learning Problems* Memory Disabilities; Perceptual Disabilities; Thinking Disabilities; Oral Language Disabilities; Reading Disabilities; Handwriting Disabilities; Spelling Disabilities; Arithmetic Disabilities; Written Expression. *Behavioral Problems* Attention Deficits; Hyperactivity; Hypoactivity; Impulsivity; Self-Aggression; Verbal Aggression; Physical Aggression; Passive Aggression; Withdrawal. *Conditions Treated* Disintegrative Psychoses; Schizophrenia; Convulsive Disorders; Phobias; Obsessions and Compulsions; Hysteria; Depression; Suicide; Anorexia Nervosa; Personality Problems; Socialized Aggressive Reaction; Unsocialized Aggressive Reaction.
Services Provided Individual Therapy; Group Therapy; Parent Involvement; Behavior Therapy; Family Therapy; Drug Therapy; Activity Therapy; Arts and Crafts Therapy; Milieu Therapy. *Professionals on Staff* Psychiatrists 1; Psychologists; Social Workers 5; Child Care Staff 23; Nurses 13.5; Activity Therapists 2; Hearing and Speech Therapist 1; Clerical and Administrative 3.5. *Service Facilities Available (with number of rooms)* Resource Rooms 2; Self-Contained Rooms 5. *Educational Professionals* Special Education Teachers 7; Career/Vocational Teachers 1. *Curricula* Career/Vocational Education; Individualized.

Educational Intervention Approaches Progressive Discipline; Self-Control; Behavior Modification. *Degrees Awarded* Certificate of Attendance.
Comments The Madden Campus program consists of 2 independent inpatient psychiatric units providing hospital care to children (ages 6-12) and adolescents (ages 13-17). Educational services on a limited basis are provided to young adults (18-21) who are hospitalized in the adult section at the center.

The Mansion

126 N Wright St, Naperville, IL 60540 (312) 357-1226
Year Established 1975
Contact Gary Luckey, Prog Dir
Facility Information *Placement* Special School; Special Program. *Children/Adolescents Served* 40. *Sexes Served* Both. *Room and Board Fees (Approx)* $24. *Tuition Fees (Approx)* $5,005. *Sources of Funding* P.L. 94-142. Summer school available. *Teacher Certification Level* High School. *Special Certification Level* ED; LD.
Student/Patient Characteristics *Age Levels* 12-14; 15-17. *IQ Ranges* 85-130. *Exceptionalities Served* Emotionally Disturbed; Learning Disabled. *Learning Problems* Memory Disabilities; Perceptual Disabilities; Thinking Disabilities. *Behavioral Problems* Attention Deficits; Impulsivity; Verbal Aggression; Passive Aggression; Withdrawal. *Conditions Treated* Alcohol Abuse and/or Drug Abuse; Phobias; Obsessions and Compulsions; Hysteria; Depression; Suicide; Inadequacy/Immaturity; Personality Problems; Socialized Aggressive Reaction.
Services Provided Individual Therapy; Group Therapy; Family Therapy; Reality Therapy. *Professionals on Staff* Psychologists 3; Counselors 4; Social Workers 3. *Service Facilities Available (with number of rooms)* Resource Rooms 1. *Educational Professionals* Special Education Teachers 4. *Curricula* Individualized. *Educational Intervention Approaches* Progressive Discipline; Self-Control. *Degrees Awarded* High School Diploma.
Comments The Mansion is a private special education day treatment program serving emotionally disturbed and behavior disordered adolescents ages 14-18. References currently originate within public school districts.

McKinley Therapeutic Center

7939 S Western, Chicago, IL 60620 (312) 778-4365
Year Established 1978
Contact Thomas M Jemilo, Dir
Facility Information *Placement* Therapeutic Day Program. *Children/Adolescents Served* 75. *Sexes Served* Both. *Sources of Funding* P.L. 94-142; DMH Block Grants. Summer school available. *Teacher Certification Level* Elementary School; Junior High/Middle School; High School. *Special Certification Level* ED; LD; Reading; Behavior Disordered; Educable Mentally Handicapped.
Student/Patient Characteristics *Age Levels* 9-11; 12-14; 15-17; 18-21. *IQ Ranges* 56-70; 71-85; 85-130; Above 130. *Exceptionalities Served* Emotionally Disturbed; Learning Disabled; Mentally Handicapped; Behavior Disordered. *Learning Problems* Perceptual Disabilities; Reading Disabilities; Handwriting Disabilities; Spelling Disabilities; Arithmetic Disabilities; Written Expression. *Behavioral Problems* Attention Deficits; Hyperactivity; Impulsivity; Verbal Aggression; Physical Aggression; Passive Aggression; Withdrawal. *Conditions Treated* Inadequacy/Immaturity; Personality Problems; Socialized Aggressive Reaction; Unsocialized Aggressive Reaction.
Services Provided Individual Therapy; Group Therapy; Parent Involvement; Family Therapy. *Professionals on Staff* Psychiatrists 2; Psychologists 2; Social Workers 3. *Service Facilities Available (with number of rooms)* Consultative (ERT) 3; Self-Contained Rooms 12; Reading; Woodshop 3; Gym-Modified P.E. 2. *Educational Professionals* Special Education Teachers 12; Career/Vocational Teachers 1. *Curricula* Career/Vocational Education; Individualized; Basic Skills. *Educational Intervention Approaches* Behavior Modification. *Degrees Awarded* Certificate of Attendance; High School Diploma; Grammer School Diploma.

Comments Therapeutic Day Program for approximately 75 students ages 10-21 who have been formally excluded from the Chicago Public School System with severe/profound behavior disorders and emotional disturbances.

Mental Health Centers of Central Illinois—Child and Adolescent Day Treatment Program

702 E Miller, Springfield, IL 62702 (217) 523-3213
Year Established 1981
Contact Robert J Burmeister, Admin Coord
Facility Information *Placement* Special Program. *Children/Adolescents Served* 9. *Sexes Served* Both. *Sources of Funding* State Funds.
Student/Patient Characteristics *Age Levels* 12-14; 15-17. *IQ Ranges* 71-85; 85-130. *Exceptionalities Served* Emotionally Disturbed; Mentally Handicapped. *Learning Problems* Thinking Disabilities; Reading Disabilities; Spelling Disabilities; Written Expression. *Behavioral Problems* Attention Deficits; Hyperactivity; Impulsivity; Self-Aggression; Verbal Aggression; Physical Aggression; Indirect Aggression; Passive Aggression; Withdrawal. *Conditions Treated* Schizophrenia; Obsessions and Compulsions; Depression; Suicide; Inadequacy/Immaturity; Personality Problems; Socialized Aggressive Reaction.
Services Provided Individual Therapy; Group Therapy; Parent Involvement; Behavior Therapy; Family Therapy; Play Therapy; Psychodrama. *Professionals on Staff* Psychiatrists 1; Psychologists 3; Counselors 3; Social Workers; Nurses 2. *Service Facilities Available (with number of rooms)* Consultative (ERT) 3. *Educational Professionals* Paraprofessionals 2. *Curricula* Individualized. *Educational Intervention Approaches* Self-Control; Behavior Modification. *Degrees Awarded* Certificate of Attendance.
Comments The center is a structured therapeutic milieu program designed to supplement existing outpatient therapy programs. It is geared to working with adolescents between the ages of 12 and 16 years (and their parents) who experience emotional and behavioral problems resulting from high levels of stress and anxiety, but do not require an inpatient 24 hour restricted environment. The program goals are directed toward behavioral, social and psychological self confidence, and self sufficiency.

Mercy Hospital and Medical Center—Community Guidance Center

Stevenson Expwy at King Dr, Chicago, IL 60616 (312) 567-2291
Year Established 1960
Contact Judith Opat, Coord Children and Adolescent Prog
Facility Information *Placement* Outpatient Mental Health Center. *Children/Adolescents Served* 140. *Sexes Served* Both. *Sources of Funding* State Funds; Health Insurance; Medicaid; Private.
Student/Patient Characteristics *Age Levels* 0-4; 5-8; 9-11; 12-14; 15-17; 18-21; Over 21. *IQ Ranges* 56-70; 71-85; 85-130; Above 130. *Exceptionalities Served* Emotionally Disturbed; Mentally Handicapped; Communication Disordered; Hearing Impaired/Deaf; Other Health Impaired. *Learning Problems* Memory Disabilities; Perceptual Disabilities; Thinking Disabilities; Oral Language Disabilities; Reading Disabilities; Handwriting Disabilities; Spelling Disabilities; Arithmetic Disabilities; Written Expression. *Behavioral Problems* Attention Deficits; Hyperactivity; Hypoactivity; Impulsivity; Self-Aggression; Verbal Aggression; Physical Aggression; Indirect Aggression; Passive Aggression; Withdrawal. *Conditions Treated* Disintegrative Psychoses; Schizophrenia; Convulsive Disorders; Obsessions and Compulsions; Hysteria; Depression; Suicide; Asthma; Ulcerative Colitis; Inadequacy/Immaturity; Personality Problems; Socialized Aggressive Reaction; Unsocialized Aggressive Reaction.
Services Provided Individual Therapy; Group Therapy; Parent Involvement; Behavior Therapy; Family Therapy; Filial Therapy; Drug Therapy; Play Therapy; Theraplay. *Professionals on Staff* Psychiatrists 2; Psychologists 3; Social Workers 5.
Comments Comprehensive outpatient mental health services are provided for children from birth through 18 years of age, and their families. This may include individual therapy, play therapy,

family therapy and group therapy. The center also works closely with the Departments of Pediatrics, Occupational Therapy, Speech Pathology, Physical Therapy, and Neurology to provide services to children and adolescents requiring specialized diagnostic evaluation and treatment.

Michael Reese Hospital and Medical Center—Dysfunctioning Child Center

2915 S Ellis, Chicago, IL 60616 (312) 791-3848
Year Established 1963
Contact William J White, Assoc Dir
Facility Information *Placement* Special School; Public Day Care. *Number of Beds* 13. *Children/Adolescents Served* 3,000. *Sexes Served* Both. *Sources of Funding* State Funds; Health Insurance; Medicaid; Multiple Sources. Summer school available. *Teacher Certification Level* Elementary School. *Special Certification Level* ED; LD; MR; Severe Profound Autism.
Student/Patient Characteristics *Age Levels* 0-4; 5-8; 9-11; 12-14; 15-17; 18-21; Over 21. *IQ Ranges* 0-25; 26-40; 41-55; 56-70; 71-85; 85-130; Above 130. *Exceptionalities Served* Autistic; Emotionally Disturbed; Learning Disabled; Mentally Handicapped; Communication Disordered; Visually Impaired/Blind; Other Health Impaired; Physically Handicapped. *Learning Problems* Memory Disabilities; Perceptual Disabilities; Thinking Disabilities; Oral Language Disabilities; Reading Disabilities; Handwriting Disabilities; Spelling Disabilities; Arithmetic Disabilities; Written Expression. *Behavioral Problems* Attention Deficits; Hyperactivity; Hypoactivity; Impulsivity; Self-Aggression; Verbal Aggression; Physical Aggression; Indirect Aggression; Passive Aggression; Withdrawal. *Conditions Treated* Early Infantile Autism; Aphasia; Convulsive Disorders; Depression; Asthma; Inadequacy/Immaturity; Personality Problems; Socialized Aggressive Reaction; Unsocialized Aggressive Reaction; Pervasive Developmental Disorders.
Services Provided Individual Therapy; Group Therapy; Parent Involvement; Behavior Therapy; Family Therapy; Filial Therapy; Drug Therapy; Art Therapy; Music Therapy; Play Therapy. *Professionals on Staff* Psychiatrists; Psychologists; Counselors; Social Workers; Child Care Staff; Nurses; Speech and Language Therapy; Occupational Therapy. *Service Facilities Available (with number of rooms)* Consultative (ERT); Itinerants; Resource Rooms; Self-Contained Rooms. *Educational Professionals* Special Education Teachers; Special Education Counselors; Paraprofessionals. *Curricula* Career/Vocational Education; Individualized; Basic Skills; Prevocational. *Educational Intervention Approaches* Progressive Discipline; Behavior Modification; Applied Behavior Analysis.

Quincy School for the Handicapped

4409 Maine, Quincy, IL 62301 (217) 223-0413
Year Established 1970
Contact Geneva Gerlach, Dir of DD Serv
Facility Information *Placement* Private Day Care. *Children/Adolescents Served* 25. *Sexes Served* Both. *Sources of Funding* State Funds; Donations. *Special Certification Level* MR.
Student/Patient Characteristics *Age Levels* 0-4; 5-8; 9-11; 12-14; 15-17. *IQ Ranges* 0-25; 26-40. *Exceptionalities Served* Autistic; Learning Disabled; Mentally Handicapped; Communication Disordered; Hearing Impaired/Deaf; Visually Impaired/Blind; Other Health Impaired; Physically Handicapped. *Learning Problems* Severe and Profoundly Handicapped; Multiply Handicapped. *Behavioral Problems* Hyperactivity; Self-Aggression; Physical Aggression; Withdrawal. *Conditions Treated* Aphasia; Convulsive Disorders.
Services Provided Parent Involvement; Behavior Therapy; Family Therapy; Drug Therapy. *Professionals on Staff* Psychiatrists 1; Psychologists 1; Social Workers 1; Child Care Staff 7; Nurses 1.5; Pediatric Nuerologist 1. *Service Facilities Available (with number of rooms)* Consultative (ERT) 1; Resource Rooms 1; Transition Rooms 1; Self-Contained Rooms 5. *Educational Professionals* Special Education Teachers 2; Paraprofessionals 7.

Curricula Individualized. *Educational Intervention Approaches* Behavior Modification; Eclectic. *Degrees Awarded* Certificate of Attendance.

The Rimland School for Autistic Children

6759 N Greenview, Chicago, IL 60626 (312) 973-1536
Year Established 1971
Contact Rosalind C Oppenheim, Exec Dir
Facility Information *Placement* Special Program.
Children/Adolescents Served $15. *Sexes Served* Both. *Sources of Funding* State Funds; P.L. 94-142; Philanthropic; United Way; Foundation Grants; Contributions. Summer school available. *Special Certification Level* ED; LD; MR; Math.
Student/Patient Characteristics *Age Levels* 5-8; 9-11; 12-14; 15-17; 18-21; Over 21. *Exceptionalities Served* Autistic; Emotionally Disturbed; Mentally Handicapped; Communication Disordered; Behavior Disordered. *Learning Problems* Perceptual Disabilities; Oral Language Disabilities; Reading Disabilities; Handwriting Disabilities; Spelling Disabilities; Arithmetic Disabilities; Written Expression. *Behavioral Problems* Attention Deficits; Hyperactivity; Hypoactivity; Impulsivity; Self-Aggression; Verbal Aggression; Physical Aggression; Indirect Aggression; Passive Aggression; Withdrawal. *Conditions Treated* Early Infantile Autism.
Services Provided Parent Involvement; Behavior Therapy. *Professionals on Staff* Psychiatrists 1; Psychologists 1; Social Workers 1; Speech-Language Pathologists 2. *Service Facilities Available (with number of rooms)* Self-Contained Rooms 4; Speech-Language Room 1; Gym; Swim Programs. *Educational Professionals* Special Education Teachers 4; Career/Vocational Teachers 1; Paraprofessionals 3. *Curricula* Traditional Academic; Career/Vocational Education; Individualized; Basic Skills; Prevocational. *Educational Intervention Approaches* Behavior Modification.

Rockford School District No. 205

201 S Madison, Rockford, IL 61108 (815) 966-3000
Contact Micheal N Golden, Supv of Behavior Disorder Prog
Facility Information *Placement* Public School; Public Day Care. *Sexes Served* Both. *Tuition Fees (Approx)* $3,030. *Sources of Funding* State Funds; P.L. 94-142. Summer school available. *Teacher Certification Level* Elementary School; Junior High/Middle School; High School. *Special Certification Level* ED; LD.
Student/Patient Characteristics *Age Levels* 0-4; 5-8; 9-11; 12-14; 15-17; 18-21. *IQ Ranges* 71-85; 85-130; Above 130. *Exceptionalities Served* Autistic; Emotionally Disturbed; Learning Disabled; Mentally Handicapped; Communication Disordered; Hearing Impaired/Deaf; Visually Impaired/Blind; Physically Handicapped; Gifted. *Learning Problems* Memory Disabilities; Perceptual Disabilities; Thinking Disabilities; Oral Language Disabilities; Reading Disabilities; Handwriting Disabilities; Spelling Disabilities; Arithmetic Disabilities; Written Expression. *Behavioral Problems* Attention Deficits; Hyperactivity; Hypoactivity; Impulsivity; Self-Aggression; Verbal Aggression; Physical Aggression; Indirect Aggression; Passive Aggression; Withdrawal. *Conditions Treated* Early Infantile Autism; Schizophrenia; Phobias; Obsessions and Compulsions; Depression; Inadequacy/Immaturity; Socialized Aggressive Reaction; Unsocialized Aggressive Reaction.
Services Provided Individual Therapy; Group Therapy; Parent Involvement; Behavior Therapy; Play Therapy. *Professionals on Staff* Psychiatrists; Psychologists 2; Social Workers 1.5; Nurses. *Service Facilities Available (with number of rooms)* Self-Contained Rooms; Special School 3; Hospital School 2. *Educational Professionals* Special Education Teachers. *Curricula* Traditional Academic; Career/Vocational Education; Individualized; Basic Skills; Prevocational. *Educational Intervention Approaches* Progressive Discipline; Self-Control; Behavior Modification; Applied Behavior Analysis. *Degrees Awarded* High School Diploma.

St Joseph's Carondelet Child Center

739 E 35th St, Chicago, IL 60616 (312) 624-7443
Year Established 1872
Contact James B McLaughlin, Exec Dir
Facility Information *Placement* Special School; Private Residential Care. *Number of Beds* 28. *Children/Adolescents Served* 45. *Sexes Served* Both. *Room and Board Fees (Approx)* $49-$53. *Sources of Funding* State Funds; P.L. 94-142. Summer school available. *Teacher Certification Level* Elementary School; Junior High/Middle School. *Special Certification Level* ED; LD; MR.
Student/Patient Characteristics *Age Levels* 5-8; 9-11; 12-14. *IQ Ranges* 71-85; 85-130; Above 130. *Exceptionalities Served* Autistic; Emotionally Disturbed; Learning Disabled. *Learning Problems* Memory Disabilities; Perceptual Disabilities; Thinking Disabilities; Oral Language Disabilities; Reading Disabilities; Handwriting Disabilities; Spelling Disabilities; Arithmetic Disabilities; Written Expression. *Behavioral Problems* Attention Deficits; Hyperactivity; Hypoactivity; Impulsivity; Self-Aggression; Verbal Aggression; Physical Aggression; Indirect Aggression; Passive Aggression; Withdrawal. *Conditions Treated* Early Infantile Autism; Disintegrative Psychoses; Schizophrenia; Aphasia; Phobias; Obsessions and Compulsions; Hysteria; Depression; Suicide; Asthma; Inadequacy/Immaturity; Personality Problems; Socialized Aggressive Reaction; Unsocialized Aggressive Reaction.
Services Provided Individual Therapy; Group Therapy; Parent Involvement; Behavior Therapy; Cognitive Developmental Therapy; Family Therapy; Art Therapy; Music Therapy; Reality Therapy; Play Therapy. *Professionals on Staff* Psychiatrists 1; Social Workers 3; Child Care Staff 15. *Service Facilities Available (with number of rooms)* Itinerants 1; Transition Rooms 1; Self-Contained Rooms 6. *Educational Professionals* Special Education Teachers 6; Special Education Counselors 1; Principal 1. *Curricula* Traditional Academic; Individualized; Basic Skills. *Educational Intervention Approaches* Engineered Classroom; Progressive Discipline; Self-Control; Behavior Modification. *Degrees Awarded* Elementary Diploma.

Sonia Shankman Orthogenic School of the University of Chicago

1365 E 60th St, Chicago, IL 60637 (312) 962-1203
Contact Jacquelyn Sanders, Dir
Facility Information *Placement* Private Residential Care. *Number of Beds* 40. *Children/Adolescents Served* 40. *Sexes Served* Both. *Room and Board Fees (Approx)* $38. *Tuition Fees (Approx)* $35,000. *Sources of Funding* State Funds; Private. Summer school available. *Teacher Certification Level* Elementary School; Junior High/Middle School; High School. *Special Certification Level* ED.
Student/Patient Characteristics *Age Levels* 9-11; 12-14; 15-17; 18-21. *IQ Ranges* 56-70; 71-85; 85-130; Above 130. *Exceptionalities Served* Autistic; Emotionally Disturbed. *Behavioral Problems* Attention Deficits; Hyperactivity; Hypoactivity; Impulsivity; Self-Aggression; Verbal Aggression; Physical Aggression; Indirect Aggression; Passive Aggression; Withdrawal. *Conditions Treated* Early Infantile Autism; Schizophrenia; Phobias; Obsessions and Compulsions; Hysteria; Depression; Anorexia Nervosa; Inadequacy/Immaturity; Personality Problems; Socialized Aggressive Reaction; Unsocialized Aggressive Reaction.
Services Provided Individual Therapy; Group Therapy; Milieu Therapy. *Professionals on Staff* Psychiatrists 2; Psychologists 2; Counselors 19; Social Workers 3.5; Nurses 1. *Service Facilities Available (with number of rooms)* Consultative (ERT) 2; Resource Rooms 3; Self-Contained Rooms 5; PE; Dining Room; TV 10. *Educational Professionals* Special Education Teachers 7; Special Education Counselors 19. *Curricula* Individualized. *Educational Intervention Approaches* Milieu Therapeutic.

South Metropolitan Association—Interventions Residential School

PO Box 79, 4200 Maple Ave, Matteson, IL 60443
(312) 747-7255
Year Established 1984
Contact David A Wilson, Dir

Facility Information *Placement* Special School; Private Residential Care. *Number of Beds* 20. *Children/Adolescents Served* 20. *Sexes Served* Both. *Room and Board Fees (Approx)* $74. *Tuition Fees (Approx)* $5,200. *Sources of Funding* P.L. 94-142. Summer school available. *Teacher Certification Level* High School. *Special Certification Level* ED; LD.

Student/Patient Characteristics *Age Levels* 12-14; 15-17; 18-21. *IQ Ranges* 71-85; 85-130; Above 130. *Exceptionalities Served* Emotionally Disturbed. *Learning Problems* Perceptual Disabilities; Thinking Disabilities; Oral Language Disabilities; Reading Disabilities. *Behavioral Problems* Attention Deficits; Hyperactivity; Impulsivity; Self-Aggression; Verbal Aggression; Passive Aggression; Withdrawal. *Conditions Treated* Disintegrative Psychoses; Schizophrenia; Aphasia; Convulsive Disorders; Phobias; Obsessions and Compulsions; Hysteria; Depression; Inadequacy/Immaturity; Personality Problems; Socialized Aggressive Reaction.

Services Provided Individual Therapy; Group Therapy; Parent Involvement; Behavior Therapy; Family Therapy; Drug Therapy; Reality Therapy; Recreation Therapy. *Professionals on Staff* Psychiatrists 1; Psychologists 1; Counselors 9; Social Workers 2; Child Care Staff 2; Nurses 1. *Service Facilities Available (with number of rooms)* Itinerants 2; Resource Rooms 1; Transition Rooms 1; Self-Contained Rooms 2; On-Campus Residential School 1. *Educational Professionals* Special Education Teachers 10; Career/Vocational Teachers 1; Crisis Teachers 1; Special Education Counselors 2; Paraprofessionals 5. *Curricula* Traditional Academic; Career/Vocational Education; Individualized; Basic Skills; Prevocational. *Educational Intervention Approaches* Precision Teaching; Behavior Modification. *Degrees Awarded* Certificate of Attendance; High School Diploma.

Comments The Residential School is designed to provide comprehensive programming for the psychological, academic, social, and recreational needs of its students. This is accomplished through a treatment/educational system which promotes a therapeutic community, within which students will hopefully learn to function in a nurturing, family-like environment.

Special Education Association of Adams County

1444 Main, Quincy, IL 62301 (217) 223-8700
Year Established 1967
Contact Joe Bocke, Dir

Facility Information *Placement* Public School. *Children/Adolescents Served* 32. *Sexes Served* Both. *Tuition Fees (Approx)* $2,200. *Sources of Funding* State Funds; P.L. 94-142; Local. *Teacher Certification Level* Elementary School; Junior High/Middle School; High School. *Special Certification Level* ED; LD.

Student/Patient Characteristics *Age Levels* 5-8; 9-11; 12-14; 15-17. *IQ Ranges* 85-130. *Exceptionalities Served* Emotionally Disturbed; Learning Disabled; Mentally Handicapped; Communication Disordered; Hearing Impaired/Deaf; Visually Impaired/Blind; Other Health Impaired; Physically Handicapped. *Learning Problems* Memory Disabilities; Perceptual Disabilities; Thinking Disabilities; Oral Language Disabilities; Reading Disabilities; Handwriting Disabilities; Spelling Disabilities; Arithmetic Disabilities; Written Expression. *Behavioral Problems* Attention Deficits; Hyperactivity; Hypoactivity; Impulsivity; Self-Aggression; Verbal Aggression; Physical Aggression; Indirect Aggression; Passive Aggression; Withdrawal. *Conditions Treated* Alcohol Abuse and/or Drug Abuse; Other Substance Abuse or Dependence; Early Infantile Autism; Disintegrative Psychoses; Schizophrenia; Aphasia; Convulsive Disorders; Phobias; Obsessions and Compulsions; Hysteria; Depression; Suicide; Asthma;

Anorexia Nervosa; Ulcerative Colitis; Inadequacy/Immaturity; Personality Problems; Socialized Aggressive Reaction; Unsocialized Aggressive Reaction.

Services Provided Individual Therapy; Group Therapy; Parent Involvement; Behavior Therapy; Cognitive Developmental Therapy; Biofeedback; Family Therapy; Drug Therapy. *Professionals on Staff* Psychiatrists; Psychologists; Counselors; Social Workers; Child Care Staff; Nurses. *Service Facilities Available (with number of rooms)* Consultative (ERT); Itinerants; Resource Rooms; Transition Rooms; Self-Contained Rooms; Special School; Hospital School; On-Campus Residential School; Homebound Instruction. *Educational Professionals* Regular School Teachers; Special Education Teachers; Career/Vocational Teachers; Crisis Teachers; Special Education Counselors; Paraprofessionals. *Curricula* Traditional Academic; Career/Vocational Education; Individualized; Basic Skills; Prevocational. *Educational Intervention Approaches* Engineered Classroom; Precision Teaching; Self-Control; Behavior Modification.

Springfield Public School District No. 186

1900 W Monroe, Springfield, IL 62704 (217) 525-3018
Contact Mary Loken, Dir Alternative and Special Prog

Facility Information *Placement* Public School. *Sexes Served* Both. *Sources of Funding* State Funds; P.L. 94-142; Local Taxes. *Teacher Certification Level* Elementary School; Junior High/Middle School; High School. *Special Certification Level* ED; LD.

Student/Patient Characteristics *Age Levels* 5-8; 9-11; 12-14; 15-17; 18-21. *IQ Ranges* 71-85; 85-130. *Exceptionalities Served* Emotionally Disturbed; Learning Disabled; Behavior Disordered. *Learning Problems* Memory Disabilities; Perceptual Disabilities; Reading Disabilities. *Behavioral Problems* Attention Deficits; Hyperactivity; Impulsivity; Self-Aggression; Verbal Aggression; Physical Aggression; Indirect Aggression; Passive Aggression; Withdrawal. *Conditions Treated* Inadequacy/Immaturity; Personality Problems.

Services Provided Parent Involvement; Behavior Therapy. *Professionals on Staff* Psychologists 6. *Service Facilities Available (with number of rooms)* Resource Rooms 6; Self-Contained Rooms 6; Homebound Instruction. *Educational Professionals* Special Education Teachers 7. *Curricula* Traditional Academic; Individualized; Basic Skills; Prevocational. *Educational Intervention Approaches* Behavior Modification. *Degrees Awarded* High School Diploma.

The Theraplay Institute

333 N Michigan Ave, Chicago, IL 60601 (312) 332-1260
Year Established 1969
Contact Adrienne Allert, Dir of Training

Comments The institute is an outpatient training facility for mental health professionals. Services offered include theraplay, psychodrama, group therapy and other psychodynamic approaches.

The University of Chicago—Departments of Psychiatry and Pediatrics—Child Psychiatry

5841 S Maryland Ave, Chicago, IL 60637 (312) 962-6826
Year Established 1954
Contact Bennett L Leventhal, Dir

Facility Information *Placement* Hospital/Medical Center. *Number of Beds* 100. *Sexes Served* Both. *Sources of Funding* Health Insurance; Medicaid; P.L. 94-142;.

Student/Patient Characteristics *Age Levels* 0-4; 5-8; 9-11; 12-14; 15-17; 18-21; Over 21. *IQ Ranges* 26-40; 41-55; 56-70; 71-85; 85-130; Above 130. *Exceptionalities Served* Autistic; Emotionally Disturbed; Learning Disabled; Mentally Handicapped; Other Health Impaired; Physically Handicapped; Gifted. *Learning Problems* Memory Disabilities; Perceptual Disabilities; Thinking Disabilities; Oral Language Disabilities; Reading Disabilities; Handwriting Disabilities; Spelling Disabilities; Arithmetic Disabilities; Written Expression. *Behavioral Problems* Attention Deficits; Hyperactivity; Hypoactivity; Impulsivity; Self-

Aggression; Verbal Aggression; Physical Aggression; Indirect Aggression; Passive Aggression; Withdrawal. *Conditions Treated* Alcohol Abuse and/or Drug Abuse; Other Substance Abuse or Dependence; Early Infantile Autism; Disintegrative Psychoses; Schizophrenia; Aphasia; Convulsive Disorders; Phobias; Obsessions and Compulsions; Hysteria; Depression; Suicide; Asthma; Anorexia Nervosa; Ulcerative Colitis; Inadequacy/Immaturity; Personality Problems; Socialized Aggressive Reaction; Unsocialized Aggressive Reaction.

Services Provided Individual Therapy; Group Therapy; Parent Involvement; Cognitive Developmental Therapy; Biofeedback; Family Therapy; Filial Therapy; Drug Therapy. *Professionals on Staff* Psychiatrists 10; Psychologists 10; Social Workers 10; Child Care Staff 10; Nurses. *Service Facilities Available (with number of rooms)* Hospital School 2. *Educational Professionals* Special Education Teachers 3; Paraprofessionals 10.

Comments Child Psychiatry is a medical center based program for the evaluation and treatment of children with the full spectrum of psychiatric and other medical disorders.

University of Illinois Medical Center—Child Psychiatry Clinic

912 S Wood, Chicago, IL 60612 (312) 996-7721
Contact Perry Meyers, Assoc Chief

Facility Information *Placement* Outpatient Mental Health. *Sexes Served* Both. *Sources of Funding* State Funds; University.

Student/Patient Characteristics *Age Levels* 0-4; 5-8; 9-11; 12-14; 15-17. *IQ Ranges* 71-85; 85-130; Above 130. *Exceptionalities Served* Autistic; Emotionally Disturbed; Learning Disabled. *Behavioral Problems* Attention Deficits; Hyperactivity; Hypoactivity; Impulsivity; Self-Aggression; Verbal Aggression; Physical Aggression; Indirect Aggression; Passive Aggression; Withdrawal. *Conditions Treated* Schizophrenia; Convulsive Disorders; Phobias; Obsessions and Compulsions; Hysteria; Depression; Suicide; Anorexia Nervosa; Inadequacy/Immaturity; Personality Problems; Socialized Aggressive Reaction; Unsocialized Aggressive Reaction.

Services Provided Individual Therapy; Parent Involvement; Family Therapy; Play Therapy. *Professionals on Staff* Psychiatrists 4; Psychologists 2; Social Workers 2.

Indiana

Children's Bureau of Indianapolis Inc

615 N Alabama, Rm 426, Indianapolis, IN 46204
(317) 634-6481
Year Established 1851
Contact Janice Klein, Supv

Facility Information *Placement* Private Residential Care. *Number of Beds* 38. *Children/Adolescents Served* 38. *Sexes Served* Both. *Room and Board Fees (Approx)* $48. *Sources of Funding* State Funds.

Student/Patient Characteristics *Age Levels* 9-11; 12-14; 15-17. *IQ Ranges* 71-85; 85-130; Above 130. *Exceptionalities Served* Emotionally Disturbed; Learning Disabled; Communication Disordered; Hearing Impaired/Deaf. *Learning Problems* Memory Disabilities; Perceptual Disabilities; Thinking Disabilities; Oral Language Disabilities; Reading Disabilities; Handwriting Disabilities; Spelling Disabilities; Arithmetic Disabilities; Written Expression. *Behavioral Problems* Attention Deficits; Hyperactivity; Impulsivity; Self-Aggression; Verbal Aggression; Physical Aggression; Indirect Aggression; Passive Aggression; Withdrawal. *Conditions Treated* Convulsive Disorders; Phobias; Obsessions and Compulsions; Depression; Anorexia Nervosa; Inadequacy/Immaturity; Personality Problems; Socialized Aggressive Reaction; Unsocialized Aggressive Reaction.

Services Provided Individual Therapy; Parent Involvement; Behavior Therapy; Family Therapy; Drug Therapy; Reality Therapy; Play Therapy. *Professionals on Staff* Psychiatrists 1; Social Workers 4; Child Care Staff 13.

Christian Haven Homes—Central Indiana Campus

Box 17, Rte 1, Wheatfield, IN 46392 (219) 956-3125
Year Established 1956
Contact Rev Carl Lange, Exec Dir

Facility Information *Placement* Private Residential Care. *Number of Beds* 120. *Children/Adolescents Served* 120. *Sexes Served* Male. *Room and Board Fees (Approx)* $48-$50. *Tuition Fees (Approx)* $1,500. *Sources of Funding* Title XX; County Funds; Gifts. Summer school available. *Teacher Certification Level* Elementary School. *Special Certification Level* ED; LD; MR; Career/Vocational Education; Reading.

Student/Patient Characteristics *Age Levels* 9-11; 12-14; 15-17; 18-21. *IQ Ranges* 56-70; 71-85; 85-130. *Exceptionalities Served* Emotionally Disturbed; Learning Disabled; Mentally Handicapped. *Learning Problems* Perceptual Disabilities; Thinking Disabilities; Reading Disabilities; Handwriting Disabilities; Spelling Disabilities; Arithmetic Disabilities; Written Expression. *Behavioral Problems* Attention Deficits; Hyperactivity; Impulsivity; Verbal Aggression; Indirect Aggression; Passive Aggression; Withdrawal. *Conditions Treated* Alcohol Abuse and/or Drug Abuse; Depression; Personality Problems; Socialized Aggressive Reaction; Unsocialized Aggressive Reaction.

Services Provided Individual Therapy; Group Therapy; Behavior Therapy; Family Therapy; Reality Therapy. *Professionals on Staff* Psychologists 11; Counselors 6; Child Care Staff 32. *Service Facilities Available (with number of rooms)* Resource Rooms 2; Self-Contained Rooms 8; On-Campus Residential School. *Educational Professionals* Special Education Teachers 9; Career/Vocational Teachers 4; Paraprofessionals 4. *Curricula* Career/Vocational Education; Individualized. *Educational Intervention Approaches* Behavior Modification. *Degrees Awarded* Certificate of Attendance; Graduate Equivalency Diploma.

Comments Programs are provided for boys ages 15-20. The programs emphasize vocational training.

Evansville Vanderburgh School Corporation

SE 9th St, Evansville, IN 47708 (812) 426-5066
Contact Lewis R Browning, Supv

Facility Information *Placement* Public School. *Children/Adolescents Served* 140. *Sexes Served* Both. *Sources of Funding* State Funds; P.L. 94-142; Local. *Teacher Certification Level* Elementary School; Junior High/Middle School; High School. *Special Certification Level* ED; LD; MR.

Student/Patient Characteristics *Age Levels* 5-8; 9-11; 12-14; 15-17. *IQ Ranges* 0-25; 26-40; 41-55; 56-70; 71-85; 85-130; Above 130. *Exceptionalities Served* Autistic; Emotionally Disturbed; Learning Disabled; Mentally Handicapped; Communication Disordered; Hearing Impaired/Deaf; Visually Impaired/Blind; Other Health Impaired; Physically Handicapped; Multiply Handicapped. *Learning Problems* Memory Disabilities; Perceptual Disabilities; Thinking Disabilities; Oral Language Disabilities; Reading Disabilities; Handwriting Disabilities; Spelling Disabilities; Arithmetic Disabilities; Written Expression. *Behavioral Problems* Attention Deficits; Hyperactivity; Hypoactivity; Impulsivity; Self-Aggression; Verbal Aggression; Physical Aggression; Indirect Aggression; Passive Aggression; Withdrawal. *Conditions Treated* Early Infantile Autism; Disintegrative Psychoses; Schizophrenia; Aphasia; Convulsive Disorders; Obsessions and Compulsions; Hysteria; Depression; Suicide; Asthma; Anorexia Nervosa; Ulcerative Colitis; Inadequacy/Immaturity; Personality Problems; Socialized Aggressive Reaction; Unsocialized Aggressive Reaction.

Services Provided *Professionals on Staff* Psychologists 10; Counselors 30; Nurses 30; Physical Therapy 1; Occupational Therapy 1; Adaptive Physical Education 1. *Service Facilities Available (with number of rooms)* Itinerants 50; Resource Rooms 10; Self-Contained Rooms 80; Special School 3; Hospital School 8; Homebound Instruction 2. *Educational Professionals* Special Education Teachers 140; Crisis Teachers 2; Special Education Counselors 1; Paraprofessionals 50. *Curricula* Traditional Academic; Career/Vocational Education; Individualized; Basic Skills; Prevocational. *Educational Intervention Approaches* Progressive

Discipline; Self-Control; Behavior Modification. *Degrees Awarded* Certificate of Attendance; High School Diploma; Graduate Equivalency Diploma.

Ft Wayne Children's Home—Crossroad

2525 Lake Ave, Fort Wayne, IN 46805 (219) 484-4153
Year Established 1883
Contact Robert H DePew, Dir of Professional Serv
Facility Information *Placement* Public School; Special School; Private Residential Care; Diagnostic. *Number of Beds* 57. *Children/Adolescents Served* 60. *Sexes Served* Both. *Room and Board Fees (Approx)* $72. *Tuition Fees (Approx)* $26,280. *Sources of Funding* Donations; Title XX. Summer school available. *Teacher Certification Level* Elementary School; Junior High/Middle School; High School. *Special Certification Level* ED; LD; MR; Math Social Studies; Science.
Student/Patient Characteristics *Age Levels* 12-14; 15-17. *IQ Ranges* 85-130; Above 130. *Exceptionalities Served* Emotionally Disturbed; Learning Disabled. *Learning Problems* Perceptual Disabilities; Thinking Disabilities; Oral Language Disabilities; Reading Disabilities; Spelling Disabilities; Arithmetic Disabilities; Written Expression. *Behavioral Problems* Attention Deficits; Hyperactivity; Impulsivity; Self-Aggression; Verbal Aggression; Indirect Aggression; Passive Aggression; Withdrawal. *Conditions Treated* Phobias; Obsessions and Compulsions; Hysteria; Depression; Suicide; Anorexia Nervosa; Inadequacy/Immaturity; Personality Problems; Socialized Aggressive Reaction; Bulemia.
Services Provided Individual Therapy; Group Therapy; Parent Involvement; Behavior Therapy; Family Therapy; Drug Therapy; Art Therapy; Music Therapy; Reality Therapy; Play Therapy; Hypnotherapy. *Professionals on Staff* Psychiatrists 1; Psychologists 4; Counselors 6; Social Workers 2; Child Care Staff 24; Nurses 1; Chaplain 1; Acting Specialist 2; Behavioral Management Specialist 1; Family Development Specialist 1. *Service Facilities Available (with number of rooms)* Consultative (ERT) 1; Special School 4; On-Campus Residential School 4. *Educational Professionals* Special Education Teachers 4; Paraprofessionals 2. *Curricula* Traditional Academic; Individualized; Basic Skills; Prevocational; Personal Daily Living Skills. *Educational Intervention Approaches* Precision Teaching; Progressive Discipline; Self-Control; Behavior Modification; Creative Conditioning. *Degrees Awarded* High School Diploma.

Gibault School For Boys

Box 2316, 5901 Dixie Bee Rd, Terre Haute, IN 47802
(812) 299-1156
Year Established 1921
Contact Daniel P McGinley, Exec Dir
Facility Information *Placement* Private Residential Care. *Number of Beds* 104. *Children/Adolescents Served* 104. *Sexes Served* Male. *Room and Board Fees (Approx)* $66. *Sources of Funding* State Funds; Medicaid. Summer school available. *Teacher Certification Level* Elementary School; Junior High/Middle School; High School. *Special Certification Level* ED; LD; Reading; Math.
Student/Patient Characteristics *Age Levels* 9-11; 12-14; 15-17. *IQ Ranges* 71-85; 85-130; Above 130. *Exceptionalities Served* Emotionally Disturbed; Learning Disabled; Juvenile Delinquents. *Learning Problems* Perceptual Disabilities; Reading Disabilities; Handwriting Disabilities; Spelling Disabilities; Arithmetic Disabilities; Written Expression. *Behavioral Problems* Attention Deficits; Hyperactivity; Impulsivity; Self-Aggression; Verbal Aggression; Physical Aggression; Passive Aggression. *Conditions Treated* Alcohol Abuse and/or Drug Abuse; Personality Problems; Unsocialized Aggressive Reaction.
Services Provided Individual Therapy; Group Therapy; Parent Involvement; Behavior Therapy; Drug Therapy; Reality Therapy. *Professionals on Staff* Psychiatrists 1; Psychologists 1; Counselors 6; Social Workers 3; Child Care Staff 21; Nurses 1; Coaches 12. *Service Facilities Available (with number of rooms)* Consultative (ERT) 1; Resource Rooms 1; Transition Rooms 7; Self-Contained Rooms 3. *Educational Professionals* Regular School

Teachers 8; Special Education Teachers 3; Paraprofessionals 1; Learning Disabilities Consultant 1. *Curricula* Traditional Academic; Individualized; Basic Skills; Prevocational. *Educational Intervention Approaches* Self-Control; Behavior Modification. *Degrees Awarded* Certificate of Attendance; Graduate Equivalency Diploma.
Comments Gibault is a residential facility for delinquent boys with emotional problems.

Indiana Girls' School

2596 Girls' School Rd, Indianapolis, IN 46224 (317) 244-3387
Year Established 1906
Contact Carroll Baker, Asst Supt
Facility Information *Placement* Public Residential Care. *Number of Beds* 150. *Children/Adolescents Served* 150. *Sexes Served* Female. *Sources of Funding* State Funds. Summer school available. *Teacher Certification Level* Junior High/Middle School; High School. *Special Certification Level* Career/Vocational Education; Reading; Math.
Student/Patient Characteristics *Age Levels* 12-14; 15-17. *IQ Ranges* 85-130. *Learning Problems* Memory Disabilities; Perceptual Disabilities; Thinking Disabilities; Oral Language Disabilities; Reading Disabilities; Handwriting Disabilities; Spelling Disabilities; Arithmetic Disabilities; Written Expression. *Behavioral Problems* Attention Deficits; Hyperactivity; Self-Aggression; Verbal Aggression; Physical Aggression; Indirect Aggression; Passive Aggression; Withdrawal. *Conditions Treated* Alcohol Abuse and/or Drug Abuse; Hysteria; Depression; Suicide; Inadequacy/Immaturity; Personality Problems; Socialized Aggressive Reaction; Unsocialized Aggressive Reaction.
Services Provided Individual Therapy; Group Therapy; Parent Involvement; Behavior Therapy; Drug Therapy; Positive Peer Culture. *Professionals on Staff* Psychiatrists 1; Psychologists 1; Counselors 9; Social Workers 1; Child Care Staff 60; Nurses 5. *Service Facilities Available (with number of rooms)* On-Campus Residential School 14. *Educational Professionals* Regular School Teachers 22; Career/Vocational Teachers 5. *Curricula* Traditional Academic; Career/Vocational Education; Individualized; Basic Skills. *Educational Intervention Approaches* Progressive Discipline; Self-Control; Positive Peer Culture. *Degrees Awarded* High School Diploma; Graduate Equivalency Diploma.

Indiana University Developmental Training Center

2312 Montclair Ave, Bloomington, IN 47405 (812) 339-4306
Year Established 1969
Contact H D Schroeder, Dir
Facility Information *Placement* Special Program; University Affiliated Program. *Number of Beds* 8. *Children/Adolescents Served* 8. *Sexes Served* Both. *Tuition Fees (Approx)* $45,000. *Sources of Funding* State Funds. Summer school available. *Teacher Certification Level* Elementary School; Junior High/Middle School; High School. *Special Certification Level* ED; LD; MR.
Student/Patient Characteristics *Age Levels* 15-17; 18-21. *IQ Ranges* 26-40; 41-55. *Exceptionalities Served* Autistic. *Learning Problems* Memory Disabilities; Perceptual Disabilities; Thinking Disabilities; Oral Language Disabilities; Reading Disabilities; Handwriting Disabilities; Social Interaction. *Behavioral Problems* Attention Deficits; Hyperactivity; Impulsivity; Self-Aggression; Verbal Aggression; Physical Aggression; Passive Aggression; Withdrawal. *Conditions Treated* Early Infantile Autism; Obsessions and Compulsions.
Services Provided Parent Involvement; Behavior Therapy; Art Education; Music Education. *Professionals on Staff* Psychologists 1; Social Workers 3; Nurses 1. *Service Facilities Available (with number of rooms)* Self-Contained Rooms 3; On-Campus Residential School. *Educational Professionals* Special Education Teachers 3; Career/Vocational Teachers 1; Paraprofessionals 3; Recreational Therapist; Adapted Physical Education; Speech Clinician. *Curricula* Career/Vocational Education; Individualized; Basic Skills; Social; Speech and Language. *Educational Intervention Approaches* Behavior Modification.

Comments The center is a university affiliated program designed to train university students and professionals as well as conduct research. The programs change to reflect the needs in the state and in cooperation with other agencies.

Indianapolis Public Schools—Special Education Department

120 E Walnut St, Indianapolis, IN 46204 (317) 266-4740
Contact Amy Zent, Supv Spec Ed
Facility Information *Placement* Public School; Special School; Special Program. *Children/Adolescents Served* 6405. *Sexes Served* Both. *Sources of Funding* State Funds; P.L. 94-142; Local Tax Funds. Summer school available. *Teacher Certification Level* Elementary School; Junior High/Middle School; High School. *Special Certification Level* ED; LD; MR; Career/Vocational Education; Visual Impaired; Hearing Impaired; Physical Therapy; Occupational Therapy; Speech and Hearing; Physical Handicapped.
Student/Patient Characteristics *Age Levels* 5-8; 9-11; 12-14; 15-17; 18-21. *IQ Ranges* 0-25; 26-40; 41-55; 56-70; 71-85; 85-130. *Exceptionalities Served* Autistic; Emotionally Disturbed; Learning Disabled; Mentally Handicapped; Communication Disordered; Hearing Impaired/Deaf; Visually Impaired/Blind; Other Health Impaired; Physically Handicapped. *Learning Problems* Memory Disabilities; Perceptual Disabilities; Thinking Disabilities; Oral Language Disabilities; Reading Disabilities; Handwriting Disabilities; Spelling Disabilities; Arithmetic Disabilities; Written Expression; Motor Disabilities. *Behavioral Problems* Attention Deficits; Hyperactivity; Impulsivity; Verbal Aggression; Physical Aggression; Withdrawal. *Conditions Treated* Aphasia; Convulsive Disorders; Phobias; Obsessions and Compulsions; Personality Problems.
Services Provided Parent Involvement; Behavior Therapy; Cognitive Developmental Therapy. *Professionals on Staff* Psychologists 21; Counselors 26; Social Workers 50; Nurses 3. *Service Facilities Available (with number of rooms)* Itinerants 48; Resource Rooms 86; Self-Contained Rooms 338; Special School 35; Hospital School 8; Homebound Instruction. *Educational Professionals* Special Education Teachers 386; Career/Vocational Teachers 8; Crisis Teachers 3; Special Education Counselors 26. *Curricula* Traditional Academic; Career/Vocational Education; Individualized; Basic Skills. *Educational Intervention Approaches* Behavior Modification. *Degrees Awarded* Certificate of Attendance; High School Diploma.

Indianapolis Public Schools—James E Roberts School No. 97

1401 E 10th St, Indianapolis, IN 46201 (317) 266-4297
Contact Olivia Gaither, Principal
Facility Information *Placement* Public School; Special School. *Sexes Served* Both. *Sources of Funding* State Funds; P.L. 94-142; Local Taxes. *Teacher Certification Level* Elementary School. *Special Certification Level* ED; LD; MR; Physically Handicapped; Elementary Education.
Student/Patient Characteristics *Age Levels* 5-8; 9-11. *IQ Ranges* 26-40; 41-55; 56-70; 71-85; 85-130. *Exceptionalities Served* Autistic; Other Health Impaired; Physically Handicapped. *Learning Problems* Memory Disabilities; Perceptual Disabilities; Thinking Disabilities; Oral Language Disabilities; Reading Disabilities; Handwriting Disabilities; Spelling Disabilities; Arithmetic Disabilities; Written Expression. *Behavioral Problems* Attention Deficits; Hyperactivity; Impulsivity; Self-Aggression; Withdrawal. *Conditions Treated* Early Infantile Autism; Convulsive Disorders; Asthma; Personality Problems.
Services Provided Individual Therapy; Parent Involvement; Family Therapy; Drug Therapy. *Professionals on Staff* Psychologists 1; Social Workers 1; Nurses 1; Occupational Therapy 1; Speech Therapy 1; Physical Therapy 1. *Service Facilities Available (with number of rooms)* Itinerants; Self-Contained Rooms 2; Special School; Homebound Instruction. *Educational Professionals* Special Education Teachers 9; Paraprofessionals 5. *Curricula* Traditional Academic; Individualized; Basic Skills. *Educational Intervention Approaches* Self-Control; Behavior Modification.
Comments This is a special public school that serves some physically handicapped and autistic students in the Indianapolis Public Schools. The enrollment is small and each student receives individualized attention.

Learning Center

610 Main St, Lafayette, IN 47901 (317) 423-2638
Year Established 1974
Contact Ron Casey, School Psychologist; Marybeth Jansky, Clinical Social Worker
Facility Information *Placement* 2 Special Education Classrooms within Outpatient Mental Health Hospital. *Children/Adolescents Served* 40. *Sexes Served* Both. *Sources of Funding* State Funds; Health Insurance; Medicaid; Medicare; P.L. 94-142; Title XX. *Teacher Certification Level* Elementary School; Junior High/Middle School; High School. *Special Certification Level* ED; LD.
Student/Patient Characteristics *Age Levels* 5-8; 9-11; 12-14; 15-17. *IQ Ranges* 56-70; 71-85; 85-130; Above 130. *Exceptionalities Served* Emotionally Disturbed. *Learning Problems* Memory Disabilities; Oral Language Disabilities; Reading Disabilities; Spelling Disabilities; Arithmetic Disabilities; Written Expression. *Behavioral Problems* Attention Deficits; Hyperactivity; Hypoactivity; Impulsivity; Self-Aggression; Verbal Aggression; Physical Aggression; Indirect Aggression; Passive Aggression; Withdrawal.
Services Provided Individual Therapy; Group Therapy; Parent Involvement; Behavior Therapy; Cognitive Developmental Therapy; Family Therapy; Art Therapy; Music Therapy; Reality Therapy; Play Therapy. *Professionals on Staff* Psychiatrists 2; Psychologists 2; Social Workers 3. *Service Facilities Available (with number of rooms)* Self-Contained Rooms 2. *Educational Professionals* Special Education Teachers 4; Paraprofessionals 3; School Psychologist. *Curricula* Traditional Academic; Individualized; Basic Skills.
Comments The Learning Center is a short-term, intensive therapy program for children in grades K through 12 with emotional/behavioral difficulties. The program is co-sponsored by the Greater Lafayette Area Special Services of the Lafayette School Corporation, Tippecanoe School Corporation, and the West Lafayette School Corporation with the Child and Adolescent Services of the Wabash Valley Hospital Mental Health Center Inc.

Mears House

8619 Indianapolis Blvd, Highland, IN 46322 (219) 398-7050 ext 270
Year Established 1980
Contact James L Scherrer, Prog Supv
Facility Information *Placement* Private Residential Care. *Number of Beds* 20. *Children/Adolescents Served* 20. *Sexes Served* Female. *Room and Board Fees (Approx)* $77. *Tuition Fees (Approx)* $28,105. *Sources of Funding* State Funds; Health Insurance; Medicaid; County Funds. *Teacher Certification Level* Junior High/Middle School; High School. *Special Certification Level* ED; LD; MR; Career/Vocational Education; Reading; Math.
Student/Patient Characteristics *Age Levels* 12-14; 15-17. *IQ Ranges* 71-85; 85-130. *Exceptionalities Served* Emotionally Disturbed. *Learning Problems* Perceptual Disabilities; Reading Disabilities. *Behavioral Problems* Impulsivity; Verbal Aggression; Indirect Aggression; Passive Aggression; Withdrawal. *Conditions Treated* Depression; Inadequacy/Immaturity; Personality Problems; Socialized Aggressive Reaction; Unsocialized Aggressive Reaction.
Services Provided Individual Therapy; Group Therapy; Parent Involvement; Behavior Therapy; Family Therapy; Reality Therapy. *Professionals on Staff* Psychiatrists 2; Psychologists 1; Counselors 1; Social Workers 1; Child Care Staff 8. *Service Facilities*

Available (with number of rooms) Public High School and Middle School. *Curricula* Traditional Academic. *Educational Intervention Approaches* Self-Control. *Degrees Awarded* High School Diploma.

New Hope of Indiana Inc

8450 N Payne Rd, Indianapolis, IN 46268 (317) 872-4210
Year Established 1978
Contact Audrey Douthit, Dir of Admissions
Facility Information *Placement* Special School; Private Residential Care. *Children/Adolescents Served* 200. *Sexes Served* Both. *Room and Board Fees (Approx)* $73. *Sources of Funding* Medicaid; Private Pay. Summer school available. *Special Certification Level* ED; LD; MR; Career/Vocational Education; Reading; Math; Cognitive Rehabilitation.
Student/Patient Characteristics *Age Levels* 18-21; Over 21. *IQ Ranges* 41-55; 56-70; 71-85; 85-130; Above 130. *Exceptionalities Served* Autistic; Learning Disabled; Mentally Handicapped; Communication Disordered; Hearing Impaired/Deaf; Visually Impaired/Blind; Other Health Impaired; Physically Handicapped; Head-Injured. *Learning Problems* Memory Disabilities; Perceptual Disabilities; Thinking Disabilities; Oral Language Disabilities; Reading Disabilities; Handwriting Disabilities; Spelling Disabilities; Arithmetic Disabilities; Written Expression; Motor Impairments. *Behavioral Problems* Attention Deficits; Hyperactivity; Hypoactivity; Impulsivity; Self-Aggression; Verbal Aggression; Indirect Aggression; Passive Aggression; Withdrawal. *Conditions Treated* Early Infantile Autism; Aphasia; Convulsive Disorders; Depression; Inadequacy/Immaturity; Personality Problems; Dementia; Adjustment Reactions.
Services Provided Individual Therapy; Group Therapy; Parent Involvement; Behavior Therapy; Biofeedback; Family Therapy; Drug Therapy; Art Therapy; Music Therapy; Reality Therapy. *Professionals on Staff* Psychiatrists 1; Psychologists 1; Counselors 12; Social Workers 6; Nurses 36; Occupational Therapy; Physical Therapy; Vocational Rehabilitation 50. *Service Facilities Available (with number of rooms)* On-Campus Residential School 12. *Educational Professionals* Special Education Teachers 3; Career/Vocational Teachers 3. *Curricula* Traditional Academic; Career/Vocational Education; Individualized; Basic Skills; Prevocational; Cognitive Rehabilitation; Independent-Living Training. *Educational Intervention Approaches* Engineered Classroom; Precision Teaching; Behavior Modification; Applied Behavior Analysis.
Comments New Hope is certified as an Intermediate Care Facility for the mentally retarded and developmentally disabled (ICF/MR). The program emphasizes service to physically disabled and traumatically brain injured young adults. Rehabilitation programs are individualized and comprehensive.

Northern Indiana State Hospital and Developmental Disabilities Center

1234 N Notre Dame Ave, South Bend, IN 46634-1995 (219) 287-0651
Year Established 1948
Contact J Cockshott, Supt
Facility Information *Placement* Public Residential Care. *Number of Beds* 83. *Children/Adolescents Served* 83. *Sexes Served* Both. *Room and Board Fees (Approx)* $120. *Sources of Funding* State Funds; Health Insurance; Medicaid; P.L. 94-142; Parents.
Student/Patient Characteristics *Age Levels* 0-4; 5-8; 9-11; 12-14; 15-17. *IQ Ranges* 0-25; 26-40. *Exceptionalities Served* Autistic; Mentally Handicapped; Hearing Impaired/Deaf; Visually Impaired/Blind; Other Health Impaired. *Behavioral Problems* Attention Deficits; Hyperactivity; Hypoactivity; Impulsivity; Self-Aggression; Verbal Aggression; Physical Aggression; Indirect Aggression; Passive Aggression; Withdrawal. *Conditions Treated* Early Infantile Autism; Convulsive Disorders.
Services Provided Behavior Therapy; Recreation Therapy; Occupational Therapy; Physical Therapy; Speech Therapy. *Professionals on Staff* Psychologists 2; Social Workers 3; Nurses 13. *Service Facilities Available (with number of rooms)* Special

School. *Educational Professionals* Special Education Teachers 1. *Curricula* Basic Skills; Prevocational. *Educational Intervention Approaches* Behavior Modification; Applied Behavior Analysis.
Comments This is an 83-bed facility for the developmentally disabled with a module especially designed for autistic youths. The program for this module involves outside school instruction during the day, 1 to 1 and small group instruction with ancillary therapists, and data-based programing in self-help, daily living, and prevocational skill areas.

Northwest Indiana Special Education Cooperative

2150 W 97th Ave, Crown Point, IN 46307 (219) 769-4000
Contact Gwenn Sciakitone, Supv
Facility Information *Placement* Therapeutic Day School. *Children/Adolescents Served* 100. *Sexes Served* Both. *Sources of Funding* State Funds; P.L. 94-142. *Teacher Certification Level* Elementary School; Junior High/Middle School; High School. *Special Certification Level* ED; LD; MR.
Student/Patient Characteristics *Age Levels* 5-8; 9-11; 12-14; 15-17; 18-21. *IQ Ranges* 71-85; 85-130. *Exceptionalities Served* Emotionally Disturbed. *Behavioral Problems* Attention Deficits; Hyperactivity; Impulsivity; Self-Aggression; Physical Aggression; Withdrawal.
Services Provided *Professionals on Staff* Psychologists 10. *Service Facilities Available (with number of rooms)* Consultative (ERT); Itinerants; Resource Rooms; Self-Contained Rooms. *Educational Professionals* Special Education Teachers 9; Paraprofessionals 7. *Curricula* Traditional Academic; Individualized. *Degrees Awarded* High School Diploma.

Otis R Bowen Center

PO Box 497, 850 N Harrison St, Warsaw, IN 46580 (219) 267-7169
Year Established 1960
Contact Barry J Van Dyck, Deputy Exec Dir
Facility Information *Placement* Public School; Special Program; Therapeutic Foster Care. *Children/Adolescents Served* 20 (Foster Care); 30 (School Program); 400 (Outpatients). *Sexes Served* Both. *Sources of Funding* State Funds; Health Insurance; Medicaid; Medicare.
Student/Patient Characteristics *Age Levels* 9-11; 12-14; 15-17. *Exceptionalities Served* Emotionally Disturbed. *Learning Problems* Perceptual Disabilities; Thinking Disabilities. *Behavioral Problems* Attention Deficits; Hyperactivity; Hypoactivity; Impulsivity; Self-Aggression; Verbal Aggression; Physical Aggression; Indirect Aggression; Passive Aggression; Withdrawal. *Conditions Treated* Disintegrative Psychoses; Schizophrenia; Aphasia; Phobias; Obsessions and Compulsions; Hysteria; Depression; Suicide; Anorexia Nervosa; Inadequacy/Immaturity; Personality Problems; Socialized Aggressive Reaction; Unsocialized Aggressive Reaction.
Services Provided Individual Therapy; Group Therapy; Parent Involvement; Behavior Therapy; Cognitive Developmental Therapy; Biofeedback; Family Therapy; Drug Therapy; Art Therapy; Reality Therapy; Play Therapy; Psychodrama. *Professionals on Staff* Psychiatrists 1; Psychologists 2; Counselors 3; Social Workers 4. *Service Facilities Available (with number of rooms)* Consultative (ERT) 2; Resource Rooms 2; Transition Rooms 2; Self-Contained Rooms 4. *Educational Professionals* Regular School Teachers; Special Education Teachers 4; Special Education Counselors 3; Paraprofessionals 3. *Curricula* Traditional Academic; Individualized; Basic Skills. *Educational Intervention Approaches* Eclectic. *Degrees Awarded* Certificate of Attendance; High School Diploma; Graduate Equivalency Diploma.

Porter Starke Services Inc—Vale Park Psychiatric Hospital

701 Wall St, Valparaiso, IN 46383 (219) 464-8541
Year Established 1976
Contact Terry Hanson, Dir Community Serv

Facility Information *Placement* Psychiatric Hospital. *Number of Beds* 8. *Children/Adolescents Served* 8. *Sexes Served* Both. *Room and Board Fees (Approx)* $242. *Sources of Funding* State Funds; Health Insurance.

Student/Patient Characteristics *Age Levels* 12-14; 15-17; 18-21; Over 21. *IQ Ranges* 85-130; Above 130. *Exceptionalities Served* Emotionally Disturbed. *Behavioral Problems* Hyperactivity; Hypoactivity; Impulsivity; Self-Aggression; Verbal Aggression; Physical Aggression; Indirect Aggression; Passive Aggression; Withdrawal. *Conditions Treated* Alcohol Abuse and/or Drug Abuse; Other Substance Abuse or Dependence; Schizophrenia; Phobias; Obsessions and Compulsions; Hysteria; Depression; Suicide; Inadequacy/Immaturity; Personality Problems; Socialized Aggressive Reaction; Unsocialized Aggressive Reaction.

Services Provided Individual Therapy; Group Therapy; Parent Involvement; Behavior Therapy; Cognitive Developmental Therapy; Family Therapy; Drug Therapy; Reality Therapy; Play Therapy. *Professionals on Staff* Psychiatrists 4; Psychologists 9; Social Workers 4; Nurses 10. *Service Facilities Available (with number of rooms)* School Work Coordinated Between Schools.

South Bend Community School Corporation—Adolescent Day Treatment Center

635 S Main, South Bend, IN 46601 (219) 282-4130
Year Established 1983
Contact Elizabeth J Lynch, Dir of Special Ed

Facility Information *Placement* Public School; Special Program. *Children/Adolescents Served* 20. *Sexes Served* Both. *Sources of Funding* State Funds; P.L. 94-142. Summer school available. *Special Certification Level* ED.

Student/Patient Characteristics *Age Levels* 12-14; 15-17. *IQ Ranges* 71-85; 85-130; Above 130. *Exceptionalities Served* Emotionally Disturbed. *Behavioral Problems* Attention Deficits; Hyperactivity; Hypoactivity; Impulsivity; Self-Aggression; Verbal Aggression; Physical Aggression; Indirect Aggression; Passive Aggression; Withdrawal. *Conditions Treated* Alcohol Abuse and/or Drug Abuse; Other Substance Abuse or Dependence; Phobias; Obsessions and Compulsions; Hysteria; Depression; Suicide; Inadequacy/Immaturity; Personality Problems; Socialized Aggressive Reaction; Unsocialized Aggressive Reaction.

Services Provided Individual Therapy; Group Therapy; Parent Involvement; Behavior Therapy; Cognitive Developmental Therapy; Family Therapy; Drug Therapy; Play Therapy; Psychodrama. *Professionals on Staff* Psychiatrists 1; Psychologists 1; Counselors 1; Social Workers 2. *Service Facilities Available (with number of rooms)* Consultative (ERT); Itinerants; Resource Rooms; Transition Rooms; Self-Contained Rooms; Special

School; Homebound Instruction. *Educational Professionals* Regular School Teachers 2; Special Education Teachers 1; Paraprofessionals 2. *Curricula* Traditional Academic; Career/Vocational Education; Individualized; Basic Skills; Prevocational. *Educational Intervention Approaches* Engineered Classroom; Precision Teaching; Progressive Discipline; Self-Control; Behavior Modification; Applied Behavior Analysis. *Degrees Awarded* High School Diploma.

Southlake Center for Mental Health

8555 Taft St, Merriville, IN 46410 (219) 769-4005
Year Established 1977
Contact Cheryl Morgavan, Dir of Outpatient Serv

Facility Information *Placement* Therapeutic Summer Day Camp. *Children/Adolescents Served* 30. *Sexes Served* Both. *Tuition Fees (Approx)* $1,550. *Sources of Funding* State Funds; Health Insurance. Summer school available.

Student/Patient Characteristics *Age Levels* 5-8; 9-11; 12-14. *IQ Ranges* 85-130. *Exceptionalities Served* Emotionally Disturbed. *Behavioral Problems* Attention Deficits; Hyperactivity; Hypoactivity; Impulsivity; Self-Aggression; Verbal Aggression; Physical Aggression; Indirect Aggression; Passive Aggression; Withdrawal. *Conditions Treated* Phobias; Obsessions and Compulsions; Hysteria; Depression; Inadequacy/Immaturity; Personality Problems; Socialized Aggressive Reaction; Unsocialized Aggressive Reaction.

Services Provided Individual Therapy; Group Therapy; Parent Involvement; Behavior Therapy; Biofeedback; Family Therapy; Drug Therapy; Play Therapy. *Professionals on Staff* Psychiatrists 2; Psychologists 10; Psychologists; Social Workers 5; Child Care Staff 6.

Comments Southlake Center for Mental Health is a comprehensive community mental health center which offers a full range of outpatient diagnosis and therapy services to children and adolescents. An additional special program of the center is the therapeutic summer day camp for children ages 6 through 14.

Trade Winds Rehabiltiation Center Inc

PO Box 6038, 5901 W 7th Ave, Gary, IN 46406 (219) 949-4000
Year Established 1968
Contact Jean Calabrese, Community Ed Dir

Facility Information *Placement* Rehabilitation Center.

Comments The center is an outpatient rehabilitation center for children and adults. It is open Monday-Firday, 8:30 a.m.-4:00 p.m. year round.

Iowa

Area Education Agency—Education Center

1755 W 11th St, Waterloo, IA 50701 (319) 235-0058
Year Established 1911
Contact Vilas Morris, Admin; Jon Ford, Treatment Supv
Facility Information *Placement* Public Day Care.
Children/Adolescents Served 30. *Sexes Served* Both. *Tuition Fees (Approx)* $4,400. *Sources of Funding* State Funds. Summer school available. *Teacher Certification Level* Elementary School. *Special Certification Level* ED; LD; MR.
Student/Patient Characteristics *Age Levels* 5-8; 9-11; 12-14. *IQ Ranges* 41-55; 56-70; 71-85; 85-130. *Exceptionalities Served* Autistic; Emotionally Disturbed; Learning Disabled; Mentally Handicapped; Communication Disordered; Hearing Impaired/ Deaf. *Learning Problems* Memory Disabilities; Perceptual Disabilities; Thinking Disabilities; Oral Language Disabilities; Reading Disabilities; Handwriting Disabilities; Spelling Disabilities; Arithmetic Disabilities; Written Expression. *Behavioral Problems* Attention Deficits; Hyperactivity; Hypoactivity; Impulsivity; Self-Aggression; Verbal Aggression; Physical Aggression; Indirect Aggression; Passive Aggression; Withdrawal. *Conditions Treated* Early Infantile Autism; Disintegrative Psychoses; Schizophrenia; Aphasia; Phobias; Obsessions and Compulsions; Depression; Inadequacy/Immaturity; Personality Problems; Socialized Aggressive Reaction; Unsocialized Aggressive Reaction.
Services Provided Individual Therapy; Group Therapy; Parent Involvement; Behavior Therapy; Cognitive Developmental Therapy; Family Therapy; Art Therapy; Music Therapy; Reality Therapy; Play Therapy. *Professionals on Staff* Psychologists 1; Social Workers 1; Child Care Staff 15; Nurses 1; Speech Therapist 3; Itinerant Hearing Therapist; Physical Therapist. *Service Facilities Available (with number of rooms)* Consultative (ERT); Itinerants 3; Self-Contained Rooms 6. *Educational Professionals* Special Education Teachers 6; Paraprofessionals 9. *Curricula* Individualized.

Comments The facility provides an intensive day-school treatment experience for severely emotionally disturbed or learning disabled youngsters.

Area Education Agency 4—River Valley School

1800 19th St, Rock Valley, IA 51247 (712) 476-2743
Year Established 1976
Contact Barry Monson, Principal
Facility Information *Placement* Public School.
Children/Adolescents Served 100. *Sexes Served* Both. *Tuition Fees (Approx)* $9,500. *Sources of Funding* State Funds; P.L. 94-142. Summer school available. *Teacher Certification Level* Elementary School; Junior High/Middle School; High School. *Special Certification Level* ED; LD; MR; Career/Vocational Education; Severe and Profoundly Handicapped.

Student/Patient Characteristics *Age Levels* 0-4; 5-8; 9-11; 12-14; 15-17; 18-21. *IQ Ranges* 26-40; 41-55; 56-70. *Exceptionalities Served* Mentally Handicapped; Other Health Impaired. *Learning Problems* Memory Disabilities; Perceptual Disabilities; Thinking Disabilities; Oral Language Disabilities; Reading Disabilities; Handwriting Disabilities; Spelling Disabilities; Arithmetic Disabilities; Written Expression. *Behavioral Problems* Attention Deficits; Hyperactivity; Hypoactivity; Impulsivity; Self-Aggression; Verbal Aggression; Physical Aggression; Indirect Aggression; Passive Aggression; Withdrawal.
Services Provided *Professionals on Staff* Psychologists 1; Social Workers 1; Nurses 1. *Service Facilities Available (with number of rooms)* Itinerants 3; Self-Contained Rooms 13. *Educational Professionals* Special Education Teachers 15; Career/Vocational Teachers 1; Paraprofessionals 17; Foster Grandparents 50. *Curricula* Individualized. *Educational Intervention Approaches* Behavior Modification. *Degrees Awarded* High School Diploma.

Comments River Valley is a special school operated by Area 4. Approximately 1/2 of the enrollment are residents of the area and 1/2 are from outside the area or state. Those from outside the area live in residential space provided by a private agent.

Children's and Adolescent Unit of Mental Health Institute of Cherokee Iowa

1200 W Cedar St, Cherokee, IA 51012 (512) 225-2594
Year Established 1966
Contact Martha Ehbrecht, Chief of Serv
Facility Information *Placement* Special School; Public Residential Care; Public Day Care. *Number of Beds* 50. *Children/Adolescents Served* 50. *Room and Board Fees (Approx)* $137. *Sources of Funding* State Funds; Health Insurance; Medicaid; P.L. 89-313. Summer school available. *Teacher Certification Level* Elementary School; Junior High/Middle School; High School. *Special Certification Level* ED; LD; Career/Vocational Education; Reading; Math.
Student/Patient Characteristics *Age Levels* 5-8; 9-11; 12-14; 15-17. *IQ Ranges* 71-85; 85-130; Above 130. *Exceptionalities Served* Autistic; Emotionally Disturbed; Learning Disabled; Gifted. *Learning Problems* Memory Disabilities; Perceptual Disabilities; Thinking Disabilities; Reading Disabilities; Spelling Disabilities; Arithmetic Disabilities; Written Expression. *Behavioral Problems* Attention Deficits; Hyperactivity; Hypoactivity; Impulsivity; Self-Aggression; Verbal Aggression; Physical Aggression; Indirect Aggression; Passive Aggression; Withdrawal. *Conditions Treated* Early Infantile Autism; Disintegrative Psychoses; Schizophrenia; Convulsive Disorders; Phobias; Obsessions and Compulsions; Hysteria; Depression; Suicide; Asthma; Anorexia Nervosa; Ulcerative Colitis; Inadequacy/Immaturity; Personality Problems; Socialized Aggressive Reaction; Unsocialized Aggressive Reaction.

Services Provided Individual Therapy; Group Therapy; Parent Involvement; Behavior Therapy; Cognitive Developmental Therapy; Family Therapy; Drug Therapy; Art Therapy; Music Therapy; Reality Therapy; Play Therapy. *Professionals on Staff* Psychiatrists 6; Psychologists 2; Social Workers 3; Child Care Staff 28; Nurses 10. *Service Facilities Available (with number of rooms)* Self-Contained Rooms 8; Hospital School 8. *Educational Professionals* Special Education Teachers 8; Career/Vocational Teachers 1. *Curricula* Traditional Academic; Career/Vocational Education; Individualized; Basic Skills; Prevocational. *Educational Intervention Approaches* Progressive Discipline; Self-Control; Behavior Modification; Creative Conditioning. *Degrees Awarded* Certificate of Attendance; High School Diploma; Graduate Equivalency Diploma.

Comments This is a children's unit in a state mental hospital. It is accredited and provides a residency training program for physicians in general psychiatry.

Children's Home of Cedar Rapids—Cedarwood Group Home

1732 Blake Blvd SE, Cedar Rapids, IA 52403 (319) 365-9164
Year Established 1977
Contact Scott Goslin, Intake Coord

Facility Information *Placement* Private Residential Care. *Number of Beds* 8. *Children/Adolescents Served* 8. *Sexes Served* Male. *Room and Board Fees (Approx)* $80. *Sources of Funding* State Funds; Agency Endowment. Summer school available.

Student/Patient Characteristics *Age Levels* 15-17. *IQ Ranges* 85-130. *Exceptionalities Served* Emotionally Disturbed; Learning Disabled; Communication Disordered. *Learning Problems* Perceptual Disabilities; Reading Disabilities; Spelling Disabilities; Arithmetic Disabilities; Written Expression. *Behavioral Problems* Attention Deficits; Impulsivity; Self-Aggression; Verbal Aggression; Physical Aggression; Indirect Aggression; Passive Aggression; Withdrawal. *Conditions Treated* Depression; Inadequacy/Immaturity; Personality Problems; Socialized Aggressive Reaction; Unsocialized Aggressive Reaction.

Services Provided Individual Therapy; Group Therapy; Parent Involvement; Behavior Therapy; Family Therapy; Reality Therapy; Aftercare; Independent Living. *Professionals on Staff* Psychiatrists 1; Psychologists 1; Social Workers 1; Child Care Staff 8; Nurses 1. *Service Facilities Available (with number of rooms)* Community Schools.

Comments Cedarwood Group Home provides residential treatment for older male adolescents preparing for independent living.

Children's Home of Cedar Rapids—Heartwood Diagnostic Evaluation Unit

2309 C St SW, Cedar Rapids, IA 52404 (319) 365-9164
Contact Scott Goslin, Intake Coord

Facility Information *Placement* Private Residential Diagnostic Care. *Number of Beds* 10. *Children/Adolescents Served* 10. *Sexes Served* Both. *Room and Board Fees (Approx)* $110. *Sources of Funding* State Funds; Agency Endowment. *Teacher Certification Level* Junior High/Middle School; High School.

Student/Patient Characteristics *Age Levels* 12-14; 15-17. *IQ Ranges* 85-130. *Exceptionalities Served* Emotionally Disturbed; Learning Disabled; Mentally Handicapped; Communication Disordered; Behavior Disorders. *Learning Problems* Perceptual Disabilities; Thinking Disabilities; Oral Language Disabilities; Reading Disabilities; Spelling Disabilities; Arithmetic Disabilities; Written Expression. *Behavioral Problems* Attention Deficits; Hyperactivity; Impulsivity; Self-Aggression; Verbal Aggression; Physical Aggression; Indirect Aggression; Passive Aggression; Withdrawal.

Services Provided Diagnostic. *Professionals on Staff* Psychiatrists 1; Psychologists 1; Social Workers 3; Child Care Staff 12; Nurses 1; Active Services Coordinator 1. *Service Facilities Available (with number of rooms)* Diagnostic Classroom 1. *Educational*

Professionals Diagnostic Teacher 1. *Curricula* Basic Skills; Evaluative Testing. *Educational Intervention Approaches* Behavior Modification.

Comments The Diagnostic Evaluation Unit provides residential care for 30 days. Educational, psychiatric, psychological, social, family, and medical evaluation are completed during that time. Final report recommends appropriate placement and includes results of all evaluations.

Children's Home of Cedar Rapids—Heartwood Residential Treatment Center

2309 C St SW, Cedar Rapids, IA 52404 (319) 365-9164
Contact Scott Goslin, Intake Coord

Facility Information *Placement* Private Residential Care. *Number of Beds* 20. *Children/Adolescents Served* 20. *Sexes Served* Both. *Room and Board Fees (Approx)* $80. *Sources of Funding* State Funds; Agency Endowment. Summer school available. *Teacher Certification Level* Junior High/Middle School; High School. *Special Certification Level* ED; LD; Behavior Disorders.

Student/Patient Characteristics *Age Levels* 12-14; 15-17. *IQ Ranges* 85-130. *Exceptionalities Served* Emotionally Disturbed; Learning Disabled; Mentally Handicapped; Behavior Disorders. *Learning Problems* Memory Disabilities; Perceptual Disabilities; Thinking Disabilities; Oral Language Disabilities; Reading Disabilities; Handwriting Disabilities; Spelling Disabilities; Arithmetic Disabilities; Written Expression. *Behavioral Problems* Attention Deficits; Hyperactivity; Hypoactivity; Impulsivity; Self-Aggression; Verbal Aggression; Physical Aggression; Indirect Aggression; Passive Aggression; Withdrawal. *Conditions Treated* Convulsive Disorders; Phobias; Obsessions and Compulsions; Hysteria; Depression; Ulcerative Colitis; Inadequacy/Immaturity; Personality Problems; Socialized Aggressive Reaction; Unsocialized Aggressive Reaction.

Services Provided Individual Therapy; Group Therapy; Parent Involvement; Behavior Therapy; Family Therapy; Art Therapy; Reality Therapy. *Professionals on Staff* Psychiatrists 1; Psychologists 1; Social Workers 3; Child Care Staff 20; Nurses 1; Activity Services Coordinators 2. *Service Facilities Available (with number of rooms)* Self-Contained Rooms 2; Community Junior High Schools. *Educational Professionals* Special Education Teachers 1; Paraprofessionals 1. *Curricula* Individualized; Basic Skills; Social Skills Training. *Educational Intervention Approaches* Progressive Discipline; Behavior Modification.

Comments Heartwood Treatment Center serves children aged 12-15 who are in need of highly structured residential placement. Many attend school in the local school system with some attending the on-campus classroom for the behavior disabled. Course of treatment is generally 10-12 months.

Children's Home of Cedar Rapids—Maplewood Group Home

1950 4th Ave SE, Cedar Rapids, IA 52403 (319) 365-9164
Year Established 1974
Contact Scott Goslin, Intake Coord

Facility Information *Placement* Private Residential Care. *Number of Beds* 8. *Children/Adolescents Served* 8. *Sexes Served* Female. *Room and Board Fees (Approx)* $80. *Sources of Funding* State Funds; Agency Endowment. Summer school available.

Student/Patient Characteristics *Age Levels* 15-17. *IQ Ranges* 85-130. *Exceptionalities Served* Emotionally Disturbed; Learning Disabled; Communication Disordered. *Learning Problems* Thinking Disabilities; Reading Disabilities; Spelling Disabilities; Arithmetic Disabilities; Written Expression. *Behavioral Problems* Attention Deficits; Impulsivity; Self-Aggression; Verbal Aggression; Physical Aggression; Indirect Aggression; Passive Aggression; Withdrawal. *Conditions Treated* Depression; Inadequacy/Immaturity; Personality Problems; Socialized Aggressive Reaction; Unsocialized Aggressive Reaction.

Services Provided Individual Therapy; Group Therapy; Parent Involvement; Behavior Therapy; Family Therapy; Reality Therapy; Aftercare; Independent Living. *Professionals on Staff* Psychiatrists 1; Psychologists 1; Social Workers 1; Child Care Staff 8; Nurses 1. *Service Facilities Available (with number of rooms)* Community Schools.

Comments Maplewood Group Home provides residential treatment for older female adolescents preparing for independent living.

Davenport Community School District

1001 Harrison St, Davenport, IA 52806 (319) 326-5005
Contact Betty M Long, Acting Dir of Special Ed
Facility Information *Placement* Public School; Special School.

Comments The Davenport Community School District provides public schools programs but does not operate a residential facility of any kind. Services are provided for ages 3 through 21. Students identified as behavior disordered (including autism and schizophrenia), hearing impaired, visually impaired, learning disabled, mentally disabled, physically disabled, other health related disorders, speech and language disordered are provided for in a public school setting and/or special school setting. Residential facilities in the community are funded and operated by other agencies.

Des Moines Children's Home—Orchard Place

925 SW Porter, Des Moines, IA 50315 (515) 285-6781
Year Established 1886
Contact Earl Kelly, Exec Dir
Facility Information *Placement* Special School; Private Residential Care. *Number of Beds* 71. *Children/Adolescents Served* 116. *Sexes Served* Both. *Room and Board Fees (Approx)* $63. *Tuition Fees (Approx)* $8,000. *Sources of Funding* State Funds; Health Insurance; Medicaid; P.L. 94-142. Summer school available. *Teacher Certification Level* Elementary School; Junior High/Middle School; High School. *Special Certification Level* ED; LD; Career/Vocational Education; Reading; Math.
Student/Patient Characteristics *Age Levels* 5-8; 9-11; 12-14; 15-17; 18-21. *IQ Ranges* 71-85; 85-130; Above 130. *Exceptionalities Served* Emotionally Disturbed; Learning Disabled. *Learning Problems* Memory Disabilities; Perceptual Disabilities; Thinking Disabilities; Oral Language Disabilities; Reading Disabilities; Handwriting Disabilities; Spelling Disabilities; Arithmetic Disabilities; Written Expression. *Behavioral Problems* Attention Deficits; Hyperactivity; Hypoactivity; Impulsivity; Self-Aggression; Verbal Aggression; Physical Aggression; Indirect Aggression; Passive Aggression; Withdrawal. *Conditions Treated* Schizophrenia; Aphasia; Phobias; Obsessions and Compulsions; Hysteria; Depression; Suicide; Anorexia Nervosa; Personality Problems; Socialized Aggressive Reaction; Unsocialized Aggressive Reaction.
Services Provided Individual Therapy; Group Therapy; Parent Involvement; Behavior Therapy; Family Therapy; Drug Therapy; Art Therapy; Reality Therapy; Play Therapy. *Professionals on Staff* Psychiatrists 1; Psychologists 1; Social Workers 12; Child Care Staff 35; Nurses 1. *Service Facilities Available (with number of rooms)* Consultative (ERT); Itinerants; Resource Rooms; Transition Rooms; Self-Contained Rooms; Special School; Hospital School; On-Campus Residential School; Homebound Instruction. *Educational Professionals* Special Education Teachers 13; Career/Vocational Teachers 1; Paraprofessionals 14. *Curricula* Traditional Academic; Career/Vocational Education; Individualized; Basic Skills; Prevocational. *Educational Intervention Approaches* Progressive Discipline; Self-Control; Behavior Modification. *Degrees Awarded* Certificate of Attendance; High School Diploma; Graduate Equivalency Diploma.

Jasper County Mental Health Center

2009 1st Ave E, Newton, IA 50208 (515) 792-4012
Year Established 1963
Contact B Rowe Winecott, Exec Dir
Facility Information *Placement* Community Mental Health Center. *Sexes Served* Both. *Sources of Funding* State Funds; Health Insurance; Medicaid; Medicare; County Funds; Patient Fees.

Student/Patient Characteristics *Age Levels* 0-4; 5-8; 9-11; 12-14; 15-17; 18-21; Over 21. *IQ Ranges* 71-85; 85-130; Above 130. *Exceptionalities Served* Emotionally Disturbed; Learning Disabled; Mentally Handicapped; Communication Disordered; Hearing Impaired/Deaf; Visually Impaired/Blind; Other Health Impaired; Physically Handicapped; Gifted. *Learning Problems* Memory Disabilities; Perceptual Disabilities; Thinking Disabilities; Oral Language Disabilities. *Behavioral Problems* Attention Deficits; Hyperactivity; Hypoactivity; Impulsivity; Self-Aggression; Verbal Aggression; Physical Aggression; Indirect Aggression; Passive Aggression; Withdrawal. *Conditions Treated* Alcohol Abuse and/or Drug Abuse; Other Substance Abuse or Dependence; Disintegrative Psychoses; Schizophrenia; Phobias; Obsessions and Compulsions; Hysteria; Depression; Suicide; Asthma; Anorexia Nervosa; Ulcerative Colitis; Inadequacy/Immaturity; Personality Problems; Socialized Aggressive Reaction; Unsocialized Aggressive Reaction.
Services Provided Individual Therapy; Group Therapy; Parent Involvement; Behavior Therapy; Family Therapy; Drug Therapy; Reality Therapy; Play Therapy. *Professionals on Staff* Psychiatrists 1; Psychologists 3; Social Workers 2.

Kinsman School—Wittenmeyer Youth Center

2800 Eastern Ave, Davenport, IA 52803 (319) 326-6431
Year Established 1975
Contact Michael P Scannell, Head Teacher
Facility Information *Placement* Special School; Public Residential Care. *Number of Beds* 53. *Children/Adolescents Served* 53. *Sexes Served* Both. *Tuition Fees (Approx)* $6,898. *Sources of Funding* State Funds; Local Funds. Summer school available. *Teacher Certification Level* Junior High/Middle School; High School. *Special Certification Level* Behavior Disorders.
Student/Patient Characteristics *Age Levels* 12-14; 15-17. *IQ Ranges* 56-70; 71-85; 85-130; Above 130. *Exceptionalities Served* Emotionally Disturbed; Behavior Disorders. *Learning Problems* Memory Disabilities; Perceptual Disabilities; Thinking Disabilities; Oral Language Disabilities; Reading Disabilities; Handwriting Disabilities; Spelling Disabilities; Arithmetic Disabilities; Written Expression. *Behavioral Problems* Attention Deficits; Hyperactivity; Hypoactivity; Impulsivity; Self-Aggression; Verbal Aggression; Physical Aggression; Indirect Aggression; Passive Aggression; Withdrawal.
Services Provided Individual Therapy; Group Therapy; Parent Involvement; Behavior Therapy; Cognitive Developmental Therapy; Family Therapy; Reality Therapy. *Professionals on Staff* Psychiatrists 1; Psychologists 2; Counselors 20; Social Workers 4; Child Care Staff; Nurses 3. *Service Facilities Available (with number of rooms)* On-Campus Residential School 6. *Educational Professionals* Special Education Teachers 6; Paraprofessionals 3. *Curricula* Traditional Academic; Individualized; Basic Skills; Prevocational. *Educational Intervention Approaches* Engineered Classroom; Progressive Discipline; Behavior Modification; Rational Emotive Therapist. *Degrees Awarded* Certificate of Attendance.

Comments The children are placed in the residential setting by the courts. If they meet Iowa criteria for behavior disorders they are accepted into the on-campus school.

Mental Health Center of Linn County—Child and Adolescent Division

520 11th St NW, Cedar Rapids, IA 52405 (319) 398-3562
Contact Hunter H Comlymd, Chief of Div
Facility Information *Placement* Outpatient Mental Health Center. *Children/Adolescents Served* 400.

Mental Health Center of Mid-Iowa

1 N 4th Ave, Marshalltown, IA 50158 (515) 752-1585
Year Established 1958
Contact Richard M Grimes, Exec Dir
Facility Information *Placement* Outpatient Mental Health Center.

Student/Patient Characteristics *Age Levels* 5-8; 9-11; 12-14; 15-17; 18-21; Over 21. *IQ Ranges* 56-70; 71-85; 85-130; Above 130. *Exceptionalities Served* Emotionally Disturbed. *Learning Problems* Thinking Disabilities. *Behavioral Problems* Attention Deficits; Hyperactivity; Hypoactivity; Impulsivity; Self-Aggression; Verbal Aggression; Physical Aggression; Indirect Aggression; Passive Aggression; Withdrawal. *Conditions Treated* Disintegrative Psychoses; Schizophrenia; Phobias; Obsessions and Compulsions; Hysteria; Depression; Suicide; Anorexia Nervosa; Inadequacy/Immaturity; Personality Problems; Socialized Aggressive Reaction; Unsocialized Aggressive Reaction.

Services Provided Individual Therapy; Group Therapy; Parent Involvement; Behavior Therapy; Family Therapy; Drug Therapy; Reality Therapy; Play Therapy. *Professionals on Staff* Psychiatrists 3; Psychologists 3; Counselors 1; Social Workers 1.

Quad Cities Center for Autistic Children Inc

1505 W 34th St, Davenport, IA 52806 (319) 386-6359
Year Established 1980
Contact Connie Toland, Teacher Dir
Facility Information *Placement* Special Program.
Student/Patient Characteristics *Exceptionalities Served* Autistic. *Conditions Treated* Early Infantile Autism.

Comments To date, the center offers a Saturday program for autistic, or autistic-like, children and youth.

State Training School

Eldora, IA 50627 (515) 858-5402
Year Established 1868
Contact James W Hoy, Supt
Facility Information *Placement* Institution for Adjudicated Delinquent Youth. *Number of Beds* 200. *Children/Adolescents Served* 200. *Sexes Served* Male. *Room and Board Fees (Approx)* $65. *Sources of Funding* State Funds; P.L. 94-142. Summer school available. *Teacher Certification Level* Elementary School; Junior High/Middle School; High School. *Special Certification Level* ED; LD; MR; Career/Vocational Education; Reading; Math.
Student/Patient Characteristics *Age Levels* 12-14; 15-17. *IQ Ranges* 71-85; 85-130; Above 130. *Exceptionalities Served* Emotionally Disturbed; Learning Disabled; Mentally Handicapped; Communication Disordered; Hearing Impaired/Deaf; Visually Impaired/Blind; Other Health Impaired; Delinquents. *Learning Problems* Memory Disabilities; Thinking Disabilities; Oral Language Disabilities; Reading Disabilities; Arithmetic Disabilities; Written Expression. *Behavioral Problems* Attention Deficits; Hyperactivity; Impulsivity; Self-Aggression; Verbal Aggression; Physical Aggression; Indirect Aggression; Passive Aggression; Withdrawal. *Conditions Treated* Alcohol Abuse and/or Drug Abuse; Other Substance Abuse or Dependence; Depression; Inadequacy/Immaturity; Personality Problems; Socialized Aggressive Reaction; Unsocialized Aggressive Reaction.

Services Provided Individual Therapy; Group Therapy; Parent Involvement; Behavior Therapy; Family Therapy; Drug Therapy; Reality Therapy; Positive Peer Culture. *Professionals on Staff* Psychiatrists 2; Psychologists 2; Counselors 18; Social Workers 2; Child Care Staff 45; Nurses 4. *Service Facilities Available (with number of rooms)* Resource Rooms 1; Transition Rooms 2; Self-Contained Rooms 3; Departmentalized 7. *Educational Professionals* Regular School Teachers 10; Special Education Teachers 5; Career/Vocational Teachers 1; Paraprofessionals 2; School Librarian 1. *Curricula* Traditional Academic; Career/Vocational Education; Individualized; Basic Skills. *Educational Intervention Approaches* Engineered Classroom. *Degrees Awarded* High School Diploma; Graduate Equivalency Diploma; Vocational Competency.

Waterloo Community Schools

1516 Washington St, Waterloo, IA 50701 (319) 233-5281
Contact Charles Vaughn, Assoc Supt
Facility Information *Placement* Public School. *Children/Adolescents Served* 30. *Sexes Served* Both. *Sources of Funding* State Funds; P.L. 94-142. Summer school available. *Teacher Certification Level* Elementary School. *Special Certification Level* ED; LD.
Student/Patient Characteristics *Age Levels* 5-8; 9-11; 12-14. *IQ Ranges* 71-85; 85-130. *Exceptionalities Served* Emotionally Disturbed; Learning Disabled. *Learning Problems* Perceptual Disabilities; Thinking Disabilities; Oral Language Disabilities; Reading Disabilities; Handwriting Disabilities; Spelling Disabilities; Arithmetic Disabilities; Written Expression. *Behavioral Problems* Attention Deficits; Hyperactivity; Hypoactivity; Impulsivity; Self-Aggression; Verbal Aggression; Physical Aggression; Indirect Aggression; Passive Aggression; Withdrawal. *Conditions Treated* Early Infantile Autism; Disintegrative Psychoses; Schizophrenia; Phobias; Obsessions and Compulsions; Depression; Inadequacy/Immaturity; Personality Problems; Socialized Aggressive Reaction; Unsocialized Aggressive Reaction.

Services Provided Individual Therapy; Group Therapy; Parent Involvement; Behavior Therapy; Cognitive Developmental Therapy; Family Therapy; Reality Therapy; Play Therapy. *Professionals on Staff* Psychologists 1; Social Workers 1; Nurses 1; Curriculum Consultant 1. *Service Facilities Available (with number of rooms)* Self-Contained Rooms 6. *Educational Professionals* Special Education Teachers 6; Paraprofessionals 10. *Curricula* Traditional Academic; Individualized; Basic Skills; Prevocational. *Educational Intervention Approaches* Engineered Classroom; Precision Teaching; Progressive Discipline; Self-Control; Behavior Modification; Applied Behavior Analysis.

Comments Severe emotionally disturbed and learning disabled students are served in grades kindergarten through 6. Each student has an individual psychological treatment plan and an individual educational plan.

Kansas

Big Lakes Developmental Center Inc

1500 Hayes Dr, Manhattan, KS 66502 (913) 776-9201
Year Established 1973
Contact James K Shaver, Exec Dir

Facility Information *Placement* Special School; Private Residential Care; Special Program. *Children/Adolescents Served* 55 (children); 93 (adult training center); 35 (residential). *Sexes Served* Both. *Tuition Fees (Approx)* Sliding Scale. *Sources of Funding* State Funds; Health Insurance; Medicaid; P.L. 94-142; County Mill Levy; Title XX; CHAMPUS; Donations. Summer school available. *Special Certification Level* Early Childhood Handicapped.

Student/Patient Characteristics *Age Levels* 0-4; 5-8; 18-21; Over 21. *IQ Ranges* 0-25; 26-40; 41-55; 56-70; 71-85. *Exceptionalities Served* Autistic; Emotionally Disturbed; Learning Disabled; Mentally Handicapped; Communication Disordered; Hearing Impaired/Deaf; Visually Impaired/Blind; Other Health Impaired; Physically Handicapped; Developmentally Delayed. *Learning Problems* Memory Disabilities; Perceptual Disabilities; Thinking Disabilities; Oral Language Disabilities; Reading Disabilities; Handwriting Disabilities; Spelling Disabilities; Arithmetic Disabilities. *Behavioral Problems* Attention Deficits; Hyperactivity; Hypoactivity; Impulsivity; Self-Aggression; Verbal Aggression; Indirect Aggression; Passive Aggression; Withdrawal. *Conditions Treated* Early Infantile Autism; Schizophrenia; Aphasia; Convulsive Disorders; Obsessions and Compulsions; Inadequacy/Immaturity; Personality Problems; Socialized Aggressive Reaction; Unsocialized Aggressive Reaction.

Services Provided Individual Therapy; Group Therapy; Parent Involvement; Behavior Therapy; Cognitive Developmental Therapy; Family Therapy; Play Therapy; Speech Therapy; Occupational Therapy; Horticulture Therapy. *Professionals on Staff* Psychologists 1; Social Workers 1; Child Care Staff 10; Speech Therapist 2; Occupational Therapist 1; Horticulture Therapist 2. *Service Facilities Available (with number of rooms)* Developmental Preschools 3; Adult Training Centers 2; Special School; Homebound Instruction 22. *Educational Professionals* Special Education Teachers 3; Paraprofessionals 18; Early Childhood Handicapped Teachers 5. *Curricula* Traditional Academic; Career/Vocational Education; Individualized; Basic Skills; Prevocational. *Educational Intervention Approaches* Engineered Classroom; Precision Teaching; Progressive Discipline; Self-Control; Behavior Modification; Creative Conditioning.

Capital City Schools

2700 W 6th St, Topeka, KS 66606 (913) 296-4343
Year Established 1959
Contact Abigail B Calkin, Principal

Facility Information *Placement* Special School. *Number of Beds* 162. *Children/Adolescents Served* 300. *Sexes Served* Both. *Tuition Fees (Approx)* $4,000. *Sources of Funding* State Funds; P.L. 94-142; Chapter 1; Chapter 2 Funds. Summer school available. *Teacher Certification Level* Elementary School; Junior High/Middle School; High School. *Special Certification Level* ED; LD; MR; Career/Vocational Education; Reading; Math.

Student/Patient Characteristics *Age Levels* 5-8; 9-11; 12-14; 15-17; 18-21; Over 21. *IQ Ranges* 71-85; 85-130; Above 130. *Exceptionalities Served* Emotionally Disturbed. *Learning Problems* Memory Disabilities; Thinking Disabilities; Reading Disabilities; Handwriting Disabilities; Spelling Disabilities; Arithmetic Disabilities; Written Expression. *Behavioral Problems* Attention Deficits; Hyperactivity; Hypoactivity; Impulsivity; Self-Aggression; Verbal Aggression; Physical Aggression; Indirect Aggression; Passive Aggression; Withdrawal. *Conditions Treated* Alcohol Abuse and/or Drug Abuse; Disintegrative Psychoses; Schizophrenia; Phobias; Depression; Suicide; Anorexia Nervosa; Inadequacy/Immaturity; Personality Problems; Socialized Aggressive Reaction; Unsocialized Aggressive Reaction.

Services Provided Individual Therapy; Group Therapy; Parent Involvement; Family Therapy; Drug Therapy; Art Therapy; Music Therapy. *Professionals on Staff* Psychiatrists 8; Psychologists 4; Counselors 1; Social Workers 10; Child Care Staff 12; Nurses 5; Activity Therapists 8. *Service Facilities Available (with number of rooms)* Consultative (ERT) 6; Resource Rooms; Self-Contained Rooms 5; Departmentalized 38; Public School 20. *Educational Professionals* Special Education Teachers 46; Career/Vocational Teachers 2; Special Education Counselors 6; Paraprofessionals 11; Psychologist 1; Social Worker 2; Counselor 1. *Curricula* Traditional Academic; Career/Vocational Education; Individualized; Basic Skills; Prevocational. *Educational Intervention Approaches* Precision Teaching; Behavior Modification; Assertive Discipline. *Degrees Awarded* Certificate of Attendance; High School Diploma; Graduate Equivalency Diploma; Honor Roll Certificates.

Comments Capital City Schools is an accredited special school for children at Topeka State Hospital and community day students who have personal and social adjustment problems beyond what the regular educational system can deal with. The children are 5-21 years old. The school operates officially under the aegis of USD 501 and Topeka State Hospital by contractual arrangements. Each professional staff member is certified in their subject area and in special education.

Early Childhood Developmental Center Inc

94 Lewis Dr, Hays, KS 67601 (913) 625-3257
Year Established 1966
Contact Sheryl Lorance, Dir

Facility Information *Placement* Special School. *Number of Beds* 45. *Children/Adolescents Served* 45. *Sexes Served* Both. *Sources of Funding* State Funds; Health Insurance. Summer school available. *Teacher Certification Level* Elementary School. *Special Certification Level* Early Childhood Handicapped.

Student/Patient Characteristics *Age Levels* 0-4; 5-8. *IQ Ranges* 0-25; 26-40; 41-55; 56-70; 71-85; 85-130; Above 130. *Exceptionalities Served* Autistic; Emotionally Disturbed; Learning Disabled; Mentally Handicapped; Communication Disordered; Hearing Impaired/Deaf; Visually Impaired/Blind; Other Health Impaired; Physically Handicapped; Gifted. *Learning Problems* Memory Disabilities; Perceptual Disabilities; Thinking Disabilities; Oral Language Disabilities. *Behavioral Problems* Attention Deficits; Hyperactivity; Hypoactivity; Impulsivity; Self-Aggression; Verbal Aggression; Physical Aggression; Indirect Aggression; Passive Aggression; Withdrawal. *Conditions Treated* Early Infantile Autism; Aphasia; Convulsive Disorders; Obsessions and Compulsions; Depression; Personality Problems; Socialized Aggressive Reaction; Unsocialized Aggressive Reaction.

Services Provided Group Therapy; Parent Involvement; Behavior Therapy; Cognitive Developmental Therapy; Family Therapy; Art Therapy; Music Therapy; Play Therapy. *Professionals on Staff* Psychiatrists 2; Psychologists 3; Counselors 2; Child Care Staff 6; Nurses 2. *Educational Professionals* Special Education Teachers 6; Paraprofessionals 7. *Curricula* Traditional Academic; Individualized; Basic Skills. *Educational Intervention Approaches* Precision Teaching; Self-Control; Behavior Modification; Applied Behavior Analysis; Creative Conditioning.

Comments The center is a special purpose preschool serving handicapped and non-handicapped children and their families. It serves all types of exceptionalities.

Elm Acres Youth Home Inc

PO Box 1135, Pittsburg, KS 66762 (316) 231-9840
Year Established 1955
Contact Frank Ross, Exec Dir

Facility Information *Placement* Private Residential Care. *Number of Beds* 40. *Children/Adolescents Served* 20 (boys in Pittsburg program); 20 (girls in Columbus program). *Sexes Served* Both. *Room and Board Fees (Approx)* $47. *Sources of Funding* State Funds; Donations; Grants; Fund Drives; Bequests; United Way.
Student/Patient Characteristics *Age Levels* 12-14; 15-17; 18-21. *IQ Ranges* 56-70; 71-85; 85-130; Above 130. *Exceptionalities Served* Emotionally Disturbed; Learning Disabled. *Learning Problems* Memory Disabilities; Perceptual Disabilities; Thinking Disabilities; Oral Language Disabilities; Reading Disabilities; Handwriting Disabilities; Spelling Disabilities; Arithmetic Disabilities; Written Expression; Behavior Disorders. *Behavioral Problems* Attention Deficits; Hyperactivity; Hypoactivity; Impulsivity; Self-Aggression; Verbal Aggression; Physical Aggression; Indirect Aggression; Passive Aggression; Withdrawal. *Conditions Treated* Alcohol Abuse and/or Drug Abuse; Phobias; Obsessions and Compulsions; Hysteria; Depression; Personality Problems; Socialized Aggressive Reaction; Unsocialized Aggressive Reaction.

Services Provided Individual Therapy; Group Therapy; Parent Involvement; Behavior Therapy; Cognitive Developmental Therapy; Family Therapy; Reality Therapy. *Professionals on Staff* Counselors 5; Social Workers 3; Child Care Staff 16. *Service Facilities Available (with number of rooms)* On-Campus Residential School 1; Homebound Instruction. *Educational Intervention Approaches* Progressive Discipline; Self-Control; Behavior Modification.

High Plains Mental Health Center—Colby Office

135 SW 6th, Colby, KS 67701 (913) 462-6774
Contact Ralph G Tremblay, Office Dir

Facility Information *Placement* Primarily Outpatient Mental Health Center. *Number of Beds* 8. *Sexes Served* Both. *Room and Board Fees (Approx)* Sliding Scale. *Sources of Funding* State Funds; Health Insurance; Medicaid; Medicare; Private Pay; Title 19.
Student/Patient Characteristics *Age Levels* 0-4; 5-8; 9-11; 12-14; 15-17; 18-21; Over 21. *IQ Ranges* 0-25; 26-40; 41-55; 56-70; 71-85; 85-130; Above 130. *Exceptionalities Served* Autistic; Emotionally Disturbed; Learning Disabled; Mentally Handicapped; Communication Disordered; Hearing Impaired/Deaf; Visually Impaired/Blind; Other Health Impaired; Physically Handicapped; Gifted. *Learning Problems* Memory Disabilities; Perceptual Disabilities; Thinking Disabilities; Oral Language Disabilities; Reading Disabilities; Handwriting Disabilities; Spelling Disabilities; Arithmetic Disabilities; Written Expression. *Behavioral Problems* Attention Deficits; Hyperactivity; Hypoactivity; Impulsivity; Self-Aggression; Verbal Aggression; Physical Aggression; Indirect Aggression; Passive Aggression; Withdrawal. *Conditions Treated* Alcohol Abuse and/or Drug Abuse; Other Substance Abuse or Dependence; Early Infantile Autism; Disintegrative Psychoses; Schizophrenia; Aphasia; Convulsive Disorders; Phobias; Obsessions and Compulsions; Hysteria; Depression; Suicide; Asthma; Anorexia Nervosa; Ulcerative Colitis; Inadequacy/Immaturity; Personality Problems; Socialized Aggressive Reaction; Unsocialized Aggressive Reaction.

Services Provided Individual Therapy; Group Therapy; Parent Involvement; Behavior Therapy; Biofeedback; Family Therapy; Filial Therapy; Drug Therapy; Art Therapy; Music Therapy; Play Therapy; Psychodrama; Hypnosis; Analytic Therapy. *Professionals on Staff* Psychiatrists 2; Psychologists 10; Counselors 5; Social Workers 6; Nurses 3. *Service Facilities Available (with number of rooms)* Consultative (ERT).

Institute of Logopedics

2400 Jardine Dr, Wichita, KS 67219 (316) 262-8271
Year Established 1949
Contact Mary E Barton, Principal

Facility Information *Placement* Special Purpose School. *Number of Beds* 71. *Children/Adolescents Served* 200. *Sexes Served* Both. *Room and Board Fees (Approx)* $44. *Tuition Fees (Approx)* $16,800. *Sources of Funding* State Funds; Private Pay; Donations; Grants. Summer school available. *Teacher Certification Level* Elementary School. *Special Certification Level* LD; MR.
Student/Patient Characteristics *Age Levels* 0-4; 5-8; 9-11; 12-14; 15-17; 18-21. *Exceptionalities Served* Learning Disabled; Mentally Handicapped; Communication Disordered; Hearing Impaired/Deaf; Visually Impaired/Blind; Other Health Impaired; Physically Handicapped. *Learning Problems* Memory Disabilities; Perceptual Disabilities; Thinking Disabilities; Oral Language Disabilities; Reading Disabilities; Handwriting Disabilities; Spelling Disabilities; Arithmetic Disabilities; Written Expression. *Behavioral Problems* Attention Deficits; Hyperactivity; Hypoactivity; Self-Aggression; Verbal Aggression; Physical Aggression; Withdrawal.

Services Provided Individual Therapy; Group Therapy; Parent Involvement. *Professionals on Staff* Psychologists 1; Child Care Staff; Nurses 2. *Service Facilities Available (with number of rooms)* Self-Contained Rooms 7; Life Skills 7. *Educational Professionals* Special Education Teachers 14; Career/Vocational Teachers 2; Paraprofessionals 25; Client Service Coordinators 2. *Curricula* Traditional Academic; Career/Vocational Education; Individualized; Basic Skills; Prevocational. *Educational Intervention Approaches* Precision Teaching; Behavior Modification; Applied Behavior Analysis. *Degrees Awarded* Certificate of Attendance.

Comments The Mission of the Institute of Logopedics is to provide services for communicatively handicapped children from birth to age 22 years. Because most severely communicatively handicapped individuals have emotional and behavioral problems, there are components of our program designed to meet these needs.

Kansas State Department of Education—Special Education Administration

120 E 10th, Topeka, KS 66612 (913) 296-3868
Contact Jane Rhys, Ed Prog Specialist

Comments The State Department advises parents and guardians to contact the local school district for services. If problems with services in Kansas occur, parents and guardians are encouraged to contact the State Department (1-800-332-6262).

Larned State Hospital—Child Psychiatric Unit—Adolescent Psychiatric Unit/Westside School

Box 89, Rte 3, Larned, KS 67550 (316) 285-2131
Year Established 1974
Contact G W Getz, Acting Supt

Facility Information *Placement* Private Residential Care; Public Residential School. *Number of Beds* 35. *Children/Adolescents Served* 35. *Sexes Served* Both. *Sources of Funding* State Funds; Health Insurance; Medicaid; P.L. 94-142. Summer school available. *Teacher Certification Level* Elementary School; Junior High/Middle School; High School. *Special Certification Level* ED; LD; MR; Career/Vocational Education; Reading; Math.

Student/Patient Characteristics *Age Levels* 5-8; 9-11; 12-14; 15-17. *IQ Ranges* 71-85; 85-130. *Exceptionalities Served* Emotionally Disturbed; Learning Disabled. *Learning Problems* Memory Disabilities; Perceptual Disabilities; Thinking Disabilities; Oral Language Disabilities; Reading Disabilities; Handwriting Disabilities; Spelling Disabilities; Arithmetic Disabilities; Written Expression. *Behavioral Problems* Attention Deficits; Hyperactivity; Hypoactivity; Impulsivity; Self-Aggression; Verbal Aggression; Physical Aggression; Indirect Aggression; Passive Aggression. *Conditions Treated* Socialized Aggressive Reaction; Unsocialized Aggressive Reaction.

Services Provided Individual Therapy; Group Therapy; Parent Involvement; Behavior Therapy; Drug Therapy; Art Therapy; Music Therapy. *Professionals on Staff* Psychiatrists; Psychologists; Counselors; Social Workers; Nurses. *Service Facilities Available (with number of rooms)* Consultative (ERT) 2; Resource Rooms 2; Transition Rooms 3; Self-Contained Rooms 3; Special School 12; Hospital School 12; Homebound Instruction 2. *Educational Professionals* Special Education Teachers 17; Career/Vocational Teachers 3; Crisis Teachers 2; Special Education Counselors 1; Paraprofessionals 7. *Curricula* Traditional Academic; Career/Vocational Education; Individualized; Basic Skills; Prevocational. *Educational Intervention Approaches* Engineered Classroom; Precision Teaching; Self-Control; Behavior Modification; Applied Behavior Analysis. *Degrees Awarded* High School Diploma; Graduate Equivalency Diploma.

Comments Westside School provides educational opportunities for 6 through 21 year old male and female students who are in residential placement for psychiatric care.

The Menninger Foundation—Pre-School Day Treatment Center

PO Box 829, 325 Frazier, Topeka, KS 66601 (913) 273-7500
Year Established 1969
Contact Lucile M Ware, Dir

Facility Information *Placement* Day Treatment and Partial Hospitalization. *Number of Beds* 30. *Children/Adolescents Served* 30. *Sexes Served* Both. *Tuition Fees (Approx)* $9,240 (treatment); Sliding Fee Scale. *Sources of Funding* Health Insurance; Medicaid; P.L. 89-313; Private Funding; Local, State and National Funding. Summer school available. *Teacher Certification Level* Elementary School. *Special Certification Level* ED; LD; MR.

Student/Patient Characteristics *Age Levels* 0-4; 5-8. *Exceptionalities Served* Autistic; Emotionally Disturbed; Learning Disabled; Multiply Handicapped. *Learning Problems* Memory Disabilities; Perceptual Disabilities; Thinking Disabilities; Oral Language Disabilities; Reading Disabilities; Handwriting Disabilities; Arithmetic Disabilities. *Behavioral Problems* Attention Deficits; Hyperactivity; Hypoactivity; Impulsivity; Self-Aggression; Verbal Aggression; Physical Aggression; Indirect Aggression; Passive Aggression; Withdrawal. *Conditions Treated* Early Infantile Autism; Disintegrative Psychoses; Schizophrenia; Phobias; Obsessions and Compulsions; Hysteria; Depression; Suicide; Inadequacy/Immaturity; Personality Problems; Socialized Aggressive Reaction; Unsocialized Aggressive Reaction; Severe Reactive Disorders; Child Abuse.

Services Provided Individual Therapy; Group Therapy; Parent Involvement; Behavior Therapy; Cognitive Developmental Therapy; Family Therapy; Drug Therapy; Play Therapy; Speech Therapy. *Professionals on Staff* Psychiatrists 6; Psychologists 2; Social Workers 5. *Service Facilities Available (with number of rooms)* Day Treatment Center 6. *Educational Professionals* Special Education Teachers 4; Paraprofessionals 3. *Curricula* Traditional Academic; Individualized; Basic Skills; Remedial. *Educational Intervention Approaches* Precision Teaching; Progressive Discipline; Behavior Modification. *Degrees Awarded* Certificate of Attendance.

Comments The Pre-School Day Treatment Center is a partial hospitalization program for youngsters 2 to 7 years of age offering comprehensive evaluations and treatment to emotionally disturbed or learning disabled young children and their families. Family involvement is required. Fees are based on ability to pay and/or medical insurance.

The Menninger Foundation—The Children's Division

Box 829, Topeka, KS 66601 (913) 273-7500
Contact Leslie J Lehulle, Dir Hospital Admissions

Facility Information *Placement* Private Residential Care. *Number of Beds* 69. *Children/Adolescents Served* 69. *Sexes Served* Both. *Room and Board Fees (Approx)* $475 (admissions unit); $337 (long term). *Tuition Fees (Approx)* $140,000. *Sources of Funding* Private Insurance. *Teacher Certification Level* Elementary School; Junior High/Middle School; High School. *Special Certification Level* ED; LD; Reading; Math.

Student/Patient Characteristics *Age Levels* 0-4; 5-8; 9-11; 12-14; 15-17. *IQ Ranges* 85-130; Above 130. *Exceptionalities Served* Emotionally Disturbed; Learning Disabled. *Learning Problems* Memory Disabilities; Perceptual Disabilities; Thinking Disabilities; Oral Language Disabilities; Reading Disabilities; Handwriting Disabilities; Spelling Disabilities; Arithmetic Disabilities; Written Expression. *Behavioral Problems* Attention Deficits; Hyperactivity; Impulsivity; Self-Aggression; Verbal Aggression; Physical Aggression; Indirect Aggression; Passive Aggression; Withdrawal. *Conditions Treated* Alcohol Abuse and/or Drug Abuse; Disintegrative Psychoses; Schizophrenia; Convulsive Disorders; Phobias; Obsessions and Compulsions; Hysteria; Depression; Suicide; Asthma; Anorexia Nervosa; Ulcerative Colitis; Inadequacy/Immaturity; Personality Problems; Socialized Aggressive Reaction; Unsocialized Aggressive Reaction.

Services Provided Individual Therapy; Group Therapy; Parent Involvement; Biofeedback; Family Therapy; Drug Therapy; Art Therapy; Music Therapy; Play Therapy; Psychodrama. *Professionals on Staff* Psychiatrists 8; Psychologists 7; Social Workers 10; Child Care Staff 70; Nurses 6. *Educational Professionals* Special Education Teachers 15. *Curricula* Traditional Academic; Prevocational. *Degrees Awarded* High School Diploma; Graduate Equivalency Diploma.

Comments The Children's Division of the Menninger Foundation offers diagnostic and long-term treatment for severely disturbed children and adolescents. The treatment orientation is largely psychodynamic with much use of group dynamics and family therapy techniques.

Pawnee Mental Health Services

520 Washington Ave, Concordia, KS 66901 (913) 243-1094
Year Established 1978
Contact Fred Prindaville

Facility Information *Placement* Outpatient Psychotherapy. *Children/Adolescents Served* 50. *Sexes Served* Both. *Sources of Funding* State Funds; HEW; Health Insurance; Medicaid; Medicare; Private Pay.

Student/Patient Characteristics *Age Levels* 0-4; 5-8; 9-11; 12-14; 15-17; 18-21; Over 21. *IQ Ranges* 71-85; 85-130; Above 130. *Exceptionalities Served* Emotionally Disturbed; Learning Disabled; Mentally Handicapped; Communication Disordered; Gifted. *Behavioral Problems* Attention Deficits; Hyperactivity; Impulsivity; Verbal Aggression; Physical Aggression; Indirect Aggression; Passive Aggression; Withdrawal. *Conditions Treated* Alcohol Abuse and/or Drug Abuse; Other Substance Abuse or Dependence; Phobias; Obsessions and Compulsions; Hysteria; Depression; Suicide; Anorexia Nervosa; Inadequacy/Immaturity; Personality Problems; Socialized Aggressive Reaction; Unsocialized Aggressive Reaction.

Services Provided Individual Therapy; Group Therapy; Parent Involvement; Behavior Therapy; Biofeedback; Family Therapy; Filial Therapy; Drug Therapy; Art Therapy; Reality Therapy; Play Therapy. *Professionals on Staff* Psychiatrists 1; Psychologists 5; Counselors 2; Social Workers 2; Nurses 2.

The St Francis Boys' Homes Inc

PO Box 1348, 509 E Elm St, Salina, KS 67401 (913) 825-0541
Year Established 1945
Contact Richard W Burnett, Clinical Coord
Facility Information *Placement* Public School; Private Residential Care. *Number of Beds* 52. *Children/Adolescents Served* 52. *Sexes Served* Male. *Room and Board Fees (Approx)* $107. *Sources of Funding* State Funds; HEW; Health Insurance; OCHAMPUS; VA. *Special Certification Level* ED; Reading; Math.
Student/Patient Characteristics *Age Levels* 12-14; 15-17. *IQ Ranges* 85-130; Above 130. *Exceptionalities Served* Emotionally Disturbed. *Behavioral Problems* Attention Deficits; Hyperactivity; Impulsivity; Self-Aggression; Verbal Aggression; Physical Aggression; Indirect Aggression; Passive Aggression; Withdrawal. *Conditions Treated* Socialized Aggressive Reaction; Unsocialized Aggressive Reaction.
Services Provided Individual Therapy; Group Therapy; Parent Involvement; Family Therapy; Drug Therapy; Reality Therapy. *Professionals on Staff* Psychiatrists 1; Psychologists 2.5; Counselors 14; Social Workers 3; Child Care Staff 10; Nurses 1; Treatment Coordinator 2. *Service Facilities Available (with number of rooms)* Consultative (ERT) 4; Resource Rooms 4. *Educational Professionals* Regular School Teachers 2. *Curricula* Traditional Academic; Career/Vocational Education; Individualized. *Degrees Awarded* High School Diploma.

Shawnee County Youth Center Services

2600 E 23rd, Topeka, KS 66605 (913) 233-6459
Contact Keven Pellant, Deputy Dir
Facility Information *Placement* Public Residential Care; Home Supervision; Detention Service; Residential Treatment. *Number of Beds* 22 (detention); 16 (HARTS). *Sexes Served* Both. *Sources of Funding* State Funds. Summer school available. *Teacher Certification Level* Junior High/Middle School; High School. *Special Certification Level* ED; LD.
Student/Patient Characteristics *Age Levels* 12-14; 15-17. *IQ Ranges* 56-70; 71-85; 85-130; Above 130. *Exceptionalities Served* Emotionally Disturbed; Learning Disabled; Mentally Handicapped; Other Health Impaired; Physically Handicapped. *Learning Problems* Memory Disabilities; Perceptual Disabilities; Thinking Disabilities; Oral Language Disabilities; Reading Disabilities; Handwriting Disabilities; Spelling Disabilities; Arithmetic Disabilities; Written Expression. *Behavioral Problems* Attention Deficits; Hyperactivity; Hypoactivity; Impulsivity; Self-Aggression; Verbal Aggression; Physical Aggression; Indirect Aggression; Passive Aggression; Withdrawal. *Conditions Treated* Alcohol Abuse and/or Drug Abuse; Other Substance Abuse or Dependence; Depression; Inadequacy/Immaturity; Personality Problems; Socialized Aggressive Reaction.
Services Provided Individual Therapy; Group Therapy; Parent Involvement; Behavior Therapy; Family Therapy; Reality Therapy; Play Therapy. *Professionals on Staff* Counselors 3; Social Workers 4; Child Care Staff 31; Nurses 1. *Service Facilities Available (with number of rooms)* Transition Rooms 1; Self-Contained Rooms 1; Inhouse Detention School; Special School; Homebound Instruction. *Educational Professionals* Special Education Teachers 2. *Curricula* Traditional Academic; Career/Voca-

tional Education; Individualized; Basic Skills. *Educational Intervention Approaches* Progressive Discipline; Behavior Modification; Creative Conditioning.

Shawnee Mission Public Schools

7235 Antioch, Shawnee Mission, KS 66203 (913) 831-1900
Contact Larry Cyrier, Coord
Facility Information *Placement* Public School. *Children/Adolescents Served* 350. *Sexes Served* Both. *Sources of Funding* State Funds; P.L. 94-142; Local Funds. Summer school available. *Teacher Certification Level* Elementary School; Junior High/Middle School; High School. *Special Certification Level* ED.
Student/Patient Characteristics *Age Levels* 0-4; 5-8; 9-11; 12-14; 15-17; 18-21. *IQ Ranges* 0-25; 26-40; 41-55; 56-70; 71-85; 85-130. *Exceptionalities Served* Autistic; Emotionally Disturbed; Learning Disabled; Mentally Handicapped; Communication Disordered; Hearing Impaired/Deaf; Visually Impaired/Blind; Other Health Impaired; Physically Handicapped; Gifted. *Learning Problems* Memory Disabilities; Perceptual Disabilities; Thinking Disabilities; Oral Language Disabilities; Reading Disabilities; Handwriting Disabilities; Spelling Disabilities; Arithmetic Disabilities; Written Expression. *Behavioral Problems* Attention Deficits; Hyperactivity; Hypoactivity; Impulsivity; Self-Aggression; Verbal Aggression; Physical Aggression; Indirect Aggression; Passive Aggression; Withdrawal. *Conditions Treated* Early Infantile Autism; Disintegrative Psychoses; Schizophrenia; Convulsive Disorders; Phobias; Obsessions and Compulsions; Hysteria; Depression; Suicide; Inadequacy/Immaturity; Personality Problems; Socialized Aggressive Reaction; Unsocialized Aggressive Reaction.
Services Provided Behavior Therapy. *Professionals on Staff* Psychologists 15; Counselors 30; Social Workers 11. *Service Facilities Available (with number of rooms)* Consultative (ERT); Itinerants 3; Resource Rooms 13; Self-Contained Rooms 8; Alternative School; Hospital School 1; Homebound Instruction. *Educational Professionals* Special Education Teachers 24. *Curricula* Traditional Academic; Career/Vocational Education; Individualized; Basic Skills; Prevocational. *Educational Intervention Approaches* Progressive Discipline; Applied Behavior Analysis. *Degrees Awarded* High School Diploma.

Southeast Kansas Mental Health Center

PO Box 39, 1106 S Ninth, Humboldt, KS 66748 (316) 473-2241
Year Established 1961
Contact Paul R Thomas, Admin
Facility Information *Placement* Outpatient Mental Health Center. *Sexes Served* Both. *Sources of Funding* State Funds; Health Insurance; Medicaid; Medicare; Fees.
Student/Patient Characteristics *Age Levels* 0-4; 5-8; 9-11; 12-14; 15-17; 18-21; Over 21. *IQ Ranges* 56-70; 71-85; 85-130; Above 130. *Exceptionalities Served* Emotionally Disturbed; Learning Disabled. *Behavioral Problems* Attention Deficits; Hyperactivity; Hypoactivity; Impulsivity; Self-Aggression; Verbal Aggression; Physical Aggression; Indirect Aggression; Passive Aggression; Withdrawal. *Conditions Treated* Alcohol Abuse and/or Drug Abuse; Early Infantile Autism; Disintegrative Psychoses; Schizophrenia; Phobias; Obsessions and Compulsions; Hysteria; Depression; Suicide; Anorexia Nervosa; Inadequacy/Immaturity; Personality Problems; Socialized Aggressive Reaction; Unsocialized Aggressive Reaction.
Services Provided Individual Therapy; Parent Involvement; Behavior Therapy; Biofeedback; Family Therapy; Drug Therapy; Play Therapy. *Professionals on Staff* Psychiatrists 2; Psychologists 5; Counselors 3; Social Workers 4.

United Methodist Youthville

PO Box 210, Newton, KS 67114 (316) 283-1950
Year Established 1927
Contact Terry Moore, Intake Social Worker

Facility Information *Placement* Private Residential Care. *Number of Beds* 125. *Children/Adolescents Served* 125. *Sexes Served* Both. *Room and Board Fees (Approx)* $52. *Sources of Funding* State Funds. Summer school available. *Teacher Certification Level* Elementary School; Junior High/Middle School; High School. *Special Certification Level* LD; Reading; Math.
Student/Patient Characteristics *Age Levels* 9-11; 12-14; 15-17. *IQ Ranges* 85-130. *Exceptionalities Served* Emotionally Disturbed. *Learning Problems* Memory Disabilities; Perceptual Disabilities; Oral Language Disabilities; Reading Disabilities; Handwriting Disabilities; Spelling Disabilities; Arithmetic Disabilities; Written Expression. *Behavioral Problems* Attention Deficits; Hyperactivity; Impulsivity; Self-Aggression; Verbal Aggression; Physical Aggression; Indirect Aggression; Passive Aggression; Withdrawal. *Conditions Treated* Depression; Inadequacy/Immaturity; Personality Problems; Socialized Aggressive Reaction; Unsocialized Aggressive Reaction; Adjustment Disorders.
Services Provided Individual Therapy; Parent Involvement; Behavior Therapy; Family Therapy; Milieu Therapy. *Professionals on Staff* Psychiatrists 1; Psychologists 2; Counselors; Social Workers 10; Child Care Staff 40. *Service Facilities Available (with number of rooms)* Resource Rooms; Self-Contained Rooms; On-Campus Residential School; Homebound Instruction. *Educational Professionals* Special Education Teachers; Paraprofessionals. *Curricula* Traditional Academic; Individualized; Basic Skills. *Degrees Awarded* High School Diploma.
Comments United Methodist Youthville is a residential treatment program serving predominately Kansas youths who have emotional and social adjustment problems. UMY has 14 resident living units across the state. UMY is accredited by the Council on Accreditation of Services for Families and Children, the Child Welfare League of America, the Certification Council of the United Methodist Church, and the Kansas Department of Health and Environment.

Wichita Guidance Center

415 Poplar, Wichita, KS 67220 (316) 686-6671
Year Established 1930
Contact B L Atkison, Dir
Facility Information *Placement* Private Outpatient Mental Health Center. *Sexes Served* Both. *Sources of Funding* State Funds; Health Insurance; Medicaid; United Way; Fees.
Student/Patient Characteristics *Age Levels* 0-4; 5-8; 9-11; 12-14; 15-17. *IQ Ranges* 41-55; 56-70; 71-85; 85-130; Above 130. *Exceptionalities Served* Emotionally Disturbed; Learning Disabled; Mentally Handicapped. *Learning Problems* Memory Disabilities; Perceptual Disabilities; Thinking Disabilities; Reading Disabilities. *Behavioral Problems* Attention Deficits; Hyperactivity; Hypoactivity; Impulsivity; Self-Aggression; Verbal Aggression; Physical Aggression; Indirect Aggression; Passive Aggression; Withdrawal. *Conditions Treated* Schizophrenia; Phobias; Obsessions and Compulsions; Hysteria; Depression; Suicide; Anorexia Nervosa; Inadequacy/Immaturity; Personality Problems; Socialized Aggressive Reaction; Unsocialized Aggressive Reaction.
Services Provided Individual Therapy; Group Therapy; Parent Involvement; Behavior Therapy; Cognitive Developmental Therapy; Family Therapy; Play Therapy. *Professionals on Staff* Psychiatrists 3; Psychologists 9; Social Workers 12.
Comments Wichita Guidance Center is primarily an outpatient mental health facility. They do work with both residential and inpatient facilities in our general area.

Wyandotte Mental Health Center

36th at Eaton, Kansas City, KS 66103 (913) 831-9500
Year Established 1952
Contact Cassie Thompson, Children and Adolescent Service Mgr
Facility Information *Placement* Outpatient Mental Health Center. *Sexes Served* Both. *Room and Board Fees (Approx)* Sliding Scale. *Sources of Funding* State Funds; Health Insurance; Medicaid; Medicare.

Student/Patient Characteristics *Age Levels* 0-4; 5-8; 9-11; 12-14; 15-17; 18-21; Over 21. *IQ Ranges* 71-85; 85-130; Above 130. *Exceptionalities Served* Emotionally Disturbed; Learning Disabled; Other Health Impaired. *Learning Problems* Reading Disabilities; Handwriting Disabilities; Spelling Disabilities; Arithmetic Disabilities. *Behavioral Problems* Attention Deficits; Hyperactivity; Impulsivity; Self-Aggression; Verbal Aggression; Physical Aggression; Passive Aggression; Withdrawal. *Conditions Treated* Alcohol Abuse and/or Drug Abuse; Other Substance Abuse or Dependence; Schizophrenia; Phobias; Depression; Anorexia Nervosa; Inadequacy/Immaturity; Personality Problems; Socialized Aggressive Reaction.
Services Provided Individual Therapy; Group Therapy; Parent Involvement; Behavior Therapy; Family Therapy; Drug Therapy; Reality Therapy; Play Therapy. *Professionals on Staff* Psychiatrists 2; Psychologists 3; Social Workers 7; Child Care Staff 9; Nurses 3.
Comments This outpatient comprehensive community mental health center serves the population of Wyandotte County, Kansas. It screens for admission to state psychiatric hospitals and provides outpatient psychiatric services. It does not refuse service to anyone due to their inability to pay. It is a not-for-profit private agency.

Wyandotte Special Education Cooperative

625 Minnesota, Kansas City, KS 66101 (913) 621-3073
Year Established 1971
Contact H Lowell Alexander, Dir
Facility Information *Placement* Public School. *Children/Adolescents Served* 130. *Sources of Funding* State Funds; P.L. 94-142; Local. Summer school available. *Teacher Certification Level* Elementary School; Junior High/Middle School; High School. *Special Certification Level* Emotional Disturbance.
Student/Patient Characteristics *Age Levels* 5-8; 9-11; 12-14; 15-17; 18-21. *IQ Ranges* 71-85; 85-130. *Exceptionalities Served* Autistic; Emotionally Disturbed; Learning Disabled; Mentally Handicapped; Communication Disordered; Hearing Impaired/Deaf; Visually Impaired/Blind; Other Health Impaired; Physically Handicapped; Gifted; Teenage Mother. *Learning Problems* Memory Disabilities; Perceptual Disabilities; Thinking Disabilities; Oral Language Disabilities; Reading Disabilities; Handwriting Disabilities; Spelling Disabilities; Arithmetic Disabilities; Written Expression. *Behavioral Problems* Attention Deficits; Hyperactivity; Hypoactivity; Impulsivity; Self-Aggression; Verbal Aggression; Physical Aggression; Indirect Aggression; Passive Aggression; Withdrawal. *Conditions Treated* Early Infantile Autism; Disintegrative Psychoses; Schizophrenia; Aphasia; Convulsive Disorders; Phobias; Obsessions and Compulsions; Hysteria; Depression; Suicide; Asthma; Anorexia Nervosa; Ulcerative Colitis; Inadequacy/Immaturity; Personality Problems; Socialized Aggressive Reaction; Unsocialized Aggressive Reaction.
Services Provided Group Therapy; Parent Involvement; Behavior Therapy; Cognitive Developmental Therapy; Family Therapy; Reality Therapy; Play Therapy. *Professionals on Staff* Psychiatrists .5; Psychologists 22; Social Workers 22; Nurses 3. *Service Facilities Available (with number of rooms)* Transition Rooms 1; Self-Contained Rooms 14; Special School 1; Hospital School 1; Homebound Instruction 1. *Educational Professionals* Special Education Teachers 14; Career/Vocational Teachers 5. *Curricula* Traditional Academic; Career/Vocational Education; Individualized; Basic Skills; Prevocational. *Educational Intervention Approaches* Engineered Classroom; Progressive Discipline; Self-Control; Behavior Modification. *Degrees Awarded* High School Diploma.

Youth Center at Larned—Westside School

Box 89, Rte 3, Larned, KS 67550 (316) 285-2131
Year Established 1974
Contact Maxine Vaughan, Dir

Facility Information *Placement* Public Residential Care; Public Residential School. *Number of Beds* 60. *Children/Adolescents Served* 60. *Sexes Served* Male. *Sources of Funding* State Funds; Health Insurance; Medicaid; P.L. 94-142. Summer school available. *Teacher Certification Level* Junior High/Middle School; High School. *Special Certification Level* ED; LD; MR; Career/Vocational Education; Reading; Math.

Student/Patient Characteristics *Age Levels* 15-17. *IQ Ranges* 85-130. *Exceptionalities Served* Emotionally Disturbed; Learning Disabled. *Learning Problems* Memory Disabilities; Perceptual Disabilities; Thinking Disabilities; Oral Language Disabilities; Reading Disabilities; Handwriting Disabilities; Spelling Disabilities; Arithmetic Disabilities; Written Expression. *Behavioral Problems* Attention Deficits; Hyperactivity; Hypoactivity; Impulsivity; Self-Aggression; Verbal Aggression; Physical Aggression; Indirect Aggression; Passive Aggression; Withdrawal.

Services Provided Individual Therapy; Group Therapy; Parent Involvement; Behavior Therapy; Drug Therapy; Art Therapy; Music Therapy. *Professionals on Staff* Psychiatrists; Psychologists; Counselors; Social Workers; Nurses. *Service Facilities Available (with number of rooms)* Consultative (ERT) 2; Resource Rooms 2; Transition Rooms 3; Self-Contained Rooms 3; Special School 12; Hospital School 12; Homebound Instruction 2. *Educational Professionals* Special Education Teachers 17; Career/Vocational Teachers 3; Crisis Teachers 2; Special Education Counselors 1; Paraprofessionals 7. *Curricula* Traditional Academic; Career/Vocational Education; Individualized; Basic Skills; Prevocational. *Educational Intervention Approaches* Engineered Classroom; Precision Teaching; Self-Control; Behavior Modification; Applied Behavior Analysis. *Degrees Awarded* High School Diploma; Graduate Equivalency Diploma.

Comments Westside School provides educational opportunities for adjudicated 16 through 18 year old male adolescents who are placed in a residential setting by court action.

Youth Center of Beloit—North Beloit High

1720 N Hersey, Beloit, KS 67420 (913) 738-3571
Year Established 1888
Contact Robert Engel, Ed Dir

Facility Information *Placement* Special School; 24 hr Residential Program. *Number of Beds* 94. *Children/Adolescents Served* 104. *Sexes Served* Both. *Sources of Funding* State Funds; P.L. 94-142. Summer school available. *Teacher Certification Level* High School. *Special Certification Level* ED; LD; Career/Vocational Education; Reading; Math.

Student/Patient Characteristics *Age Levels* 12-14; 15-17; 18-21. *IQ Ranges* 56-70; 71-85; 85-130. *Exceptionalities Served* Emotionally Disturbed; Learning Disabled; Mentally Handicapped; Communication Disordered. *Learning Problems* Memory Disabilities; Perceptual Disabilities; Thinking Disabilities; Oral Language Disabilities; Reading Disabilities; Handwriting Disabilities; Spelling Disabilities; Arithmetic Disabilities; Written Expression. *Behavioral Problems* Attention Deficits; Hyperactivity; Hypoactivity; Impulsivity; Self-Aggression; Verbal Aggression; Physical Aggression; Indirect Aggression; Passive Aggression; Withdrawal. *Conditions Treated* Alcohol Abuse and/or Drug Abuse; Other Substance Abuse or Dependence; Phobias; Obsessions and Compulsions; Depression; Suicide; Personality Problems.

Services Provided Individual Therapy; Group Therapy; Behavior Therapy; Biofeedback; Family Therapy; Drug Therapy; Art Therapy; Music Therapy; Horticultural Therapy. *Professionals on Staff* Psychologists 5; Counselors 2; Social Workers 5; Child Care Staff 50; Nurses 2. *Service Facilities Available (with number of rooms)* Resource Rooms 1; Self-Contained Rooms 1; Departmentalized 10. *Educational Professionals* Special Education Teachers 13; Career/Vocational Teachers 2; Special Education Counselors 2; Paraprofessionals 13. *Curricula* Career/Vocational Education; Individualized; Basic Skills; Prevocational; Life Skills. *Educational Intervention Approaches* Self-Control; Behavior Modification. *Degrees Awarded* High School Diploma; Graduate Equivalency Diploma.

Kentucky

Archdiocese of Louisville—Guidance Clinic

2801 S Preston St, Louisville, KY 40217 (502) 635-7139
Year Established 1954
Contact Judy Brock, Exec Sec
Facility Information *Placement* Public School; Special School. *Children/Adolescents Served* $80-$100 (per month). *Sexes Served* Both. *Sources of Funding* Health Insurance; Individual Charges. Summer school available. *Teacher Certification Level* Elementary School; Junior High/Middle School; High School. *Special Certification Level* ED; LD; MR.
Student/Patient Characteristics *Age Levels* 0-4; 5-8; 9-11; 12-14; 15-17; 18-21; Over 21. *IQ Ranges* 0-25; 26-40; 41-55; 56-70; 71-85; 85-130; Above 130. *Exceptionalities Served* Autistic; Emotionally Disturbed; Learning Disabled; Mentally Handicapped; Gifted. *Learning Problems* Memory Disabilities; Perceptual Disabilities; Oral Language Disabilities; Reading Disabilities. *Behavioral Problems* Attention Deficits; Hyperactivity; Impulsivity; Verbal Aggression; Physical Aggression; Withdrawal. *Conditions Treated* Alcohol Abuse and/or Drug Abuse; Phobias; Hysteria; Obsessions and Compulsions; Depression; Suicide; Asthma; Inadequacy/Immaturity; Personality Problems.
Services Provided Individual Therapy; Group Therapy; Parent Involvement; Family Therapy; Play Therapy. *Professionals on Staff* Psychiatrists 1; Psychologists 1; Counselors 1. *Service Facilities Available (with number of rooms)* Consultative (ERT) 4. *Educational Professionals* Special Education Teachers; Special Education Counselors. *Curricula* Traditional Academic; Career/Vocational Education; Basic Skills; Emotional Adjustment; Personality Development. *Educational Intervention Approaches* Self-Control; Behavior Modification. *Degrees Awarded* High School Diploma; Grade School Diploma.

Cabinet for Human Resources—Children's Treatment Service

Lakeland Rd, Louisville, KY 40223 (502) 245-4121, ext 434
Year Established 1970
Contact Thomas D Schell, Prog Dir
Facility Information *Placement* Public Residential Care. *Number of Beds* 44. *Children/Adolescents Served* 52. *Sexes Served* Both. *Room and Board Fees (Approx)* $210. *Sources of Funding* Health Insurance; Medicaid. Summer school available. *Special Certification Level* ED.
Student/Patient Characteristics *Age Levels* 5-8; 9-11; 12-14; 15-17. *Exceptionalities Served* Emotionally Disturbed. *Learning Problems* Memory Disabilities; Perceptual Disabilities; Thinking Disabilities; Oral Language Disabilities; Reading Disabilities; Handwriting Disabilities; Spelling Disabilities; Arithmetic Disabilities; Written Expression. *Behavioral Problems* Self-Aggression; Verbal Aggression; Physical Aggression; Indirect Ag-

gression; Passive Aggression; Withdrawal. *Conditions Treated* Schizophrenia; Phobias; Obsessions and Compulsions; Hysteria; Depression; Suicide; Anorexia Nervosa.
Services Provided Individual Therapy; Group Therapy; Parent Involvement; Family Therapy; Art Therapy; Music Therapy; Reality Therapy; Play Therapy. *Professionals on Staff* Psychiatrists 3; Psychologists 7; Social Workers 10; Child Care Staff 60; Nurses 12; Activity Therapy; Art Therapy. *Service Facilities Available (with number of rooms)* Special School 8. *Educational Professionals* Special Education Teachers 8; Career/Vocational Teachers 1; Paraprofessionals 8. *Curricula* Traditional Academic; Individualized; Prevocational. *Educational Intervention Approaches* Engineered Classroom. *Degrees Awarded* High School Diploma.
Comments The facility is a licensed and accredited psychiatric hospital.

Christian Church—Children's Campus

PO Box 45, Danville, KY 40422 (606) 236-5507
Year Established 1884
Contact Bill Donovan, Admin
Facility Information *Placement* Private Residential Care. *Number of Beds* 40. *Children/Adolescents Served* 40. *Sexes Served* Both. *Room and Board Fees (Approx)* $52. *Tuition Fees (Approx)* $18,980. *Sources of Funding* State Funds; Church Support. Summer school available. *Teacher Certification Level* Elementary School; Junior High/Middle School. *Special Certification Level* ED.
Student/Patient Characteristics *Age Levels* 5-8; 9-11; 12-14. *IQ Ranges* 71-85; 85-130; Above 130. *Exceptionalities Served* Emotionally Disturbed; Learning Disabled; Communication Disordered. *Learning Problems* Memory Disabilities; Perceptual Disabilities; Thinking Disabilities; Oral Language Disabilities; Reading Disabilities; Handwriting Disabilities; Spelling Disabilities; Arithmetic Disabilities; Written Expression. *Behavioral Problems* Attention Deficits; Hyperactivity; Hypoactivity; Impulsivity; Self-Aggression; Verbal Aggression; Physical Aggression; Indirect Aggression; Passive Aggression; Withdrawal. *Conditions Treated* Convulsive Disorders; Phobias; Obsessions and Compulsions; Depression; Asthma; Inadequacy/Immaturity; Personality Problems; Socialized Aggressive Reaction; Unsocialized Aggressive Reaction.
Services Provided Individual Therapy; Parent Involvement; Behavior Therapy; Family Therapy; Reality Therapy; Play Therapy; Psychodrama. *Professionals on Staff* Social Workers 6; Child Care Staff 16. *Service Facilities Available (with number of rooms)* Self-Contained Rooms 2; On-Campus Residential School 2. *Educational Professionals* Special Education Teachers 2; Paraprofessionals 2. *Curricula* Individualized; Basic Skills. *Educational Intervention Approaches* Behavior Modification; Creative Conditioning.

Comments The Children's Campus is a residential treatment center for emotionally disturbed children. In addition to the treatment program it provides a state approved educational program for children who are unable to function in a public school program.

The Cleveland Home

140 Park St, Versailles, KY 40383 (606) 873-3271
Year Established 1875
Contact Gayle L Crossfield, Exec Dir
Facility Information *Placement* Private Residential Care. *Number of Beds* 16. *Children/Adolescents Served* 16. *Sexes Served* Female. *Sources of Funding* State Funds; Private.
Student/Patient Characteristics *Age Levels* 12-14; 15-17; 18-21. *IQ Ranges* 56-70; 71-85; 85-130. *Exceptionalities Served* Emotionally Disturbed; Learning Disabled; Other Health Impaired. *Learning Problems* Thinking Disabilities; Reading Disabilities; Spelling Disabilities. *Behavioral Problems* Verbal Aggression; Passive Aggression; Withdrawal.
Services Provided Individual Therapy; Group Therapy; Parent Involvement; Behavior Therapy; Family Therapy; Reality Therapy. *Professionals on Staff* Counselors 4; Social Workers 1; Child Care Staff 4. *Service Facilities Available (with number of rooms)* Resource Rooms 1. *Educational Professionals* Tutor 1.

Maryhurst School

1015 Dorsey Ln, Louisville, KY 40223 (502) 245-1576
Year Established 1863
Contact Janet McWilliams, Principal; Charles Donlon, Clinical Dir
Facility Information *Placement* Special School; Private Residential Care. *Number of Beds* 40. *Children/Adolescents Served* 42. *Sexes Served* Female. *Room and Board Fees (Approx)* $64. *Sources of Funding* State Funds; P.L. 94-142. Summer school available. *Teacher Certification Level* Junior High/Middle School; High School. *Special Certification Level* ED; Reading.
Student/Patient Characteristics *Age Levels* 12-14; 15-17; 18-21. *IQ Ranges* 71-85; 85-130; Above 130. *Exceptionalities Served* Emotionally Disturbed; Learning Disabled. *Learning Problems* Memory Disabilities; Perceptual Disabilities; Thinking Disabilities; Oral Language Disabilities; Reading Disabilities; Handwriting Disabilities; Spelling Disabilities; Arithmetic Disabilities; Written Expression. *Behavioral Problems* Attention Deficits; Hyperactivity; Impulsivity; Self-Aggression; Verbal Aggression; Indirect Aggression; Passive Aggression; Withdrawal. *Conditions Treated* Alcohol Abuse and/or Drug Abuse; Other Substance Abuse or Dependence; Schizophrenia; Phobias.
Services Provided Individual Therapy; Group Therapy; Parent Involvement; Behavior Therapy; Cognitive Developmental Therapy; Biofeedback; Family Therapy; Filial Therapy; Drug Therapy; Art Therapy; Music Therapy; Reality Therapy; Psychodrama. *Professionals on Staff* Psychiatrists 1; Psychologists 1; Counselors 2; Social Workers 3; Child Care Staff 21. *Service Facilities Available (with number of rooms)* Consultative (ERT) 2; Resource Rooms 1; Self-Contained Rooms 8; On-Campus Residential School 15. *Educational Professionals* Regular School Teachers 6; Special Education Teachers 2; Career/Vocational Teachers 1; Special Education Counselors 3. *Curricula* Tradi-

tional Academic; Individualized; Basic Skills; Prevocational. *Educational Intervention Approaches* Progressive Discipline; Self-Control; Behavior Modification. *Degrees Awarded* High School Diploma; Graduate Equivalency Diploma.

Comments Maryhurst is a 24 hour residential treatment facility for troubled adolescent girls. The Maryhurst program offers individualized education, therapeutic treatment, and group living for young women between the ages of 13-17 who need a highly structured though loving environment to build a more satisfying and rewarding life. Maryhurst is licensed by the Kentucky Department for Human Resources and accredited by the Kentucky Department of Education.

Norton Psychiatric Clinic—Norton Adolescent Treatment Program and Norton Academy

PO Box 35070, Louisville, KY 40232 (502) 562-8850
Year Established 1974
Contact Helen Atchley, Admissions Coord
Facility Information *Placement* Special Program; Psychiatric Clinic. *Number of Beds* 18. *Children/Adolescents Served* 18. *Sexes Served* Both. *Room and Board Fees (Approx)* $305. *Sources of Funding* Health Insurance. Summer school available. *Teacher Certification Level* Junior High/Middle School; High School. *Special Certification Level* ED; LD; Reading; Math.
Student/Patient Characteristics *Age Levels* 12-14; 15-17. *IQ Ranges* 71-85; 85-130; Above 130. *Exceptionalities Served* Emotionally Disturbed. *Learning Problems* Memory Disabilities; Perceptual Disabilities; Thinking Disabilities; Oral Language Disabilities; Reading Disabilities; Handwriting Disabilities; Spelling Disabilities; Arithmetic Disabilities; Written Expression. *Behavioral Problems* Attention Deficits; Hyperactivity; Hypoactivity; Impulsivity; Self-Aggression; Verbal Aggression; Physical Aggression; Indirect Aggression; Passive Aggression; Withdrawal. *Conditions Treated* Alcohol Abuse and/or Drug Abuse; Other Substance Abuse or Dependence; Disintegrative Psychoses; Schizophrenia; Convulsive Disorders; Phobias; Obsessions and Compulsions; Hysteria; Depression; Suicide; Anorexia Nervosa; Ulcerative Colitis; Inadequacy/Immaturity; Personality Problems; Socialized Aggressive Reaction; Unsocialized Aggressive Reaction.
Services Provided Individual Therapy; Group Therapy; Parent Involvement; Behavior Therapy; Cognitive Developmental Therapy; Family Therapy; Drug Therapy; Art Therapy. *Professionals on Staff* Psychiatrists 4; Social Workers 2; Nurses 5. *Service Facilities Available (with number of rooms)* Resource Rooms; Self-Contained Rooms; Hospital School. *Educational Professionals* Special Education Teachers 5; Paraprofessionals 5. *Curricula* Traditional Academic; Basic Skills. *Educational Intervention Approaches* Behavior Modification; Creative Conditioning. *Degrees Awarded* Certificate of Attendance; High School Diploma.

Comments The adolescent program is a short-term (30-120 days) psychiatric inpatient setting offering evaluation and treatment of psychiatric disorders. Norton Academy offers an in-hospital school for inpatients and follow up for outpatients who are residents of Jefferson County. The school is funded by the Jefferson County School System.

Louisiana

Acadiana Mental Health Center

400 St Julien Ave, Lafayette, LA 70506 (318) 233-7500
Year Established 1948
Contact Michael Berrard, Mgr
Facility Information *Placement* Mental Health Center. *Sexes Served* Both.
Student/Patient Characteristics *Age Levels* 0-4; 5-8; 9-11; 12-14; 15-17; 18-21.
Services Provided Individual Therapy; Group Therapy; Parent Involvement; Behavior Therapy; Cognitive Developmental Therapy; Family Therapy; Drug Therapy; Play Therapy. *Professionals on Staff* Psychiatrists 2; Psychologists 3; Social Workers 4. *Service Facilities Available (with number of rooms)* Consultative (ERT) 2. *Educational Professionals* Special Education Teachers 13.

Comments This is a comprehensive community mental health center serving primarily the indigent who have emotional problems and are classified in the DSM III. It does not offer an in-house educational system. The Lafayette Parish School Board, Special Education Department, offers all educational resources.

DePaul Hospital and Residential Treatment Center

1040 Calhoun St, New Orleans, LA 70118 (504) 899-8282
Year Established 1970
Contact Carol Evans, Prog Dir
Facility Information *Placement* Private Residential Care. *Number of Beds* 166. *Children/Adolescents Served* 166. *Sexes Served* Both. *Room and Board Fees (Approx)* $195-$320. *Sources of Funding* State Funds; Health Insurance; Medicaid. Summer school available. *Special Certification Level* ED; Reading; Math; English; Science; Social Studies.
Student/Patient Characteristics *Age Levels* 5-8; 9-11; 12-14; 15-17; 18-21. *IQ Ranges* 56-70; 71-85; 85-130; Above 130. *Exceptionalities Served* Emotionally Disturbed; Learning Disabled; Mentally Handicapped. *Learning Problems* Memory Disabilities; Perceptual Disabilities; Thinking Disabilities; Oral Language Disabilities; Reading Disabilities; Spelling Disabilities; Arithmetic Disabilities; Written Expression. *Behavioral Problems* Attention Deficits; Hyperactivity; Hypoactivity; Impulsivity; Self-Aggression; Verbal Aggression; Physical Aggression; Indirect Aggression; Passive Aggression; Withdrawal. *Conditions Treated* Alcohol Abuse and/or Drug Abuse; Other Substance Abuse or Dependence; Schizophrenia; Convulsive Disorders; Phobias; Obsessions and Compulsions; Hysteria; Depression; Suicide; Anorexia Nervosa; Inadequacy/Immaturity; Personality Problems; Socialized Aggressive Reaction; Unsocialized Aggressive Reaction.

Services Provided Individual Therapy; Group Therapy; Parent Involvement; Behavior Therapy; Biofeedback; Family Therapy; Drug Therapy; Art Therapy; Music Therapy; Reality Therapy; Play Therapy; Psychodrama. *Professionals on Staff* Psychiatrists; Psychologists 1; Counselors 15; Social Workers 10; Child Care Staff 43; Nurses 15.5; Creative Arts Therapists 4. *Service Facilities Available (with number of rooms)* Self-Contained Rooms 15. *Educational Professionals* Special Education Teachers 15. *Curricula* Traditional Academic; Individualized; Basic Skills; G.E.D. Preparation. *Educational Intervention Approaches* Progressive Discipline; Self-Control; Behavior Modification. *Degrees Awarded* Certificate of Attendance; High School Diploma.

Donaldsonville Mental Health Center

419 Memorial Dr, Donaldsonville, LA 70346 (504) 473-7901
Contact Ann Woodward, Mgr
Facility Information *Placement* Outpatient Mental Health Services. *Sexes Served* Both. *Sources of Funding* State Funds.
Student/Patient Characteristics *Age Levels* 0-4; 5-8; 9-11; 12-14; 15-17; 18-21; Over 21. *IQ Ranges* 0-25; 26-40; 41-55; 56-70; 71-85; 85-130; Above 130. *Exceptionalities Served* Emotionally Disturbed; Learning Disabled; Mentally Handicapped; Gifted. *Learning Problems* Memory Disabilities; Perceptual Disabilities; Thinking Disabilities; Oral Language Disabilities; Reading Disabilities; Handwriting Disabilities; Spelling Disabilities; Arithmetic Disabilities; Written Expression. *Behavioral Problems* Attention Deficits; Hyperactivity; Hypoactivity; Impulsivity; Self-Aggression; Verbal Aggression; Physical Aggression; Indirect Aggression; Passive Aggression; Withdrawal. *Conditions Treated* Disintegrative Psychoses; Schizophrenia; Phobias; Obsessions and Compulsions; Hysteria; Depression; Suicide; Anorexia Nervosa; Inadequacy/Immaturity; Personality Problems; Socialized Aggressive Reaction; Unsocialized Aggressive Reaction.

Services Provided Individual Therapy; Group Therapy; Parent Involvement; Behavior Therapy; Cognitive Developmental Therapy; Family Therapy; Drug Therapy; Reality Therapy; Play Therapy. *Professionals on Staff* Psychiatrists 1; Psychologists 1; Counselors 2; Social Workers 3; Nurses 2.

Comments The clinic provides psychiatric outpatient services to the general population of the area.

The Harmony Center Inc

1245 Laurel St, Baton Rouge, LA 70802 (504) 344-1865
Year Established 1978
Contact Soundra J Temple, Prog Dir
Facility Information *Placement* Private Residential Care. *Number of Beds* 26. *Children/Adolescents Served* 36. *Sexes Served* Male. *Sources of Funding* State Funds; P.L. 94-142. Summer school available. *Teacher Certification Level* High School. *Special Certification Level* ED.

Student/Patient Characteristics *Age Levels* 15-17; 18-21; Over 21. *Exceptionalities Served* Emotionally Disturbed; Learning Disabled; Mentally Handicapped; Other Health Impaired. *Learning Problems* Perceptual Disabilities; Thinking Disabilities; Oral Language Disabilities; Reading Disabilities; Spelling Disabilities; Arithmetic Disabilities; Written Expression. *Behavioral Problems* Attention Deficits; Indirect Aggression; Withdrawal. *Conditions Treated* Personality Problems.

Services Provided Individual Therapy; Group Therapy; Parent Involvement; Reality Therapy. *Professionals on Staff* Psychiatrists 1; Psychologists 1; Counselors 3; Social Workers 2; Nurses 1. *Educational Professionals* Special Education Teachers 1; Paraprofessionals 1. *Curricula* Individualized; Basic Skills; Reading. *Educational Intervention Approaches* Behavior Modification. *Degrees Awarded* Certificate of Participation.

Jefferson Parish School System—Department of Special Education

1450 Jefferson St, Gretna, LA 70053 (504) 363-5300
Year Established 1960
Contact Barbara Turner, Dir of Special Ed
Facility Information *Placement* Public School; Special School. *Children/Adolescents Served* $8,000. *Sexes Served* Both. *Sources of Funding* State Funds; P.L. 94-142; P.L. 89-313 Funds. Summer school available. *Teacher Certification Level* Elementary School; Junior High/Middle School; High School. *Special Certification Level* ED; LD; MR; Career/Vocational Education; Pre-School-Non-Categorical Handicapped; Gifted-Talented; Generic; Severe Language Disorder; Hearing Impaired; Visual Impaired.

Student/Patient Characteristics *Age Levels* 0-4; 5-8; 9-11; 12-14; 15-17; 18-21. *IQ Ranges* 0-25; 26-40; 41-55; 56-70; 71-85; 85-130; Above 130. *Exceptionalities Served* Autistic; Emotionally Disturbed; Learning Disabled; Mentally Handicapped; Communication Disordered; Hearing Impaired/Deaf; Visually Impaired/Blind; Other Health Impaired; Physically Handicapped; Gifted; Pre-School-Non-Categorical. *Learning Problems* Memory Disabilities; Perceptual Disabilities; Thinking Disabilities; Oral Language Disabilities; Reading Disabilities; Handwriting Disabilities; Spelling Disabilities; Arithmetic Disabilities; Written Expression. *Behavioral Problems* Attention Deficits; Hyperactivity; Hypoactivity; Impulsivity; Self-Aggression; Verbal Aggression; Physical Aggression; Indirect Aggression; Passive Aggression; Withdrawal. *Conditions Treated* Alcohol Abuse and/or Drug Abuse; Other Substance Abuse or Dependence; Early Infantile Autism; Schizophrenia; Aphasia; Convulsive Disorders; Phobias; Obsessions and Compulsions; Hysteria; Depression; Suicide; Asthma; Anorexia Nervosa; Inadequacy/Immaturity; Personality Problems; Socialized Aggressive Reaction; Unsocialized Aggressive Reaction.

Services Provided Individual Therapy; Group Therapy; Parent Involvement; Behavior Therapy. *Professionals on Staff* Psychiatrists; Psychologists; Social Workers; Nurses. *Service Facilities Available (with number of rooms)* Consultative (ERT); Itinerants; Resource Rooms; Self-Contained Rooms; Special School; On-Campus Residential School; Private/Parochial Schools. *Educational Professionals* Regular School Teachers; Special Education Teachers; Career/Vocational Teachers; Paraprofessionals. *Curricula* Traditional Academic; Career/Vocational Education; Individualized; Basic Skills; Prevocational. *Educational Intervention Approaches* Engineered Classroom; Precision Teaching; Progressive Discipline; Self-Control; Behavior Modification; Applied Behavior Analysis; Creative Conditioning. *Degrees Awarded* Certificate of Attendance; High School Diploma; Graduate Equivalency Diploma.

Comments Jefferson Parish School System is located adjacent to the City of New Orleans. It services a geographical area on 2 sides of the Mississippi River with a regular school population of 55,000 and a special education population of 8,000.

K-Bar-B Youth Ranch—Richard M Wise School

PO Box 1517, Lacombe, LA 70445 (504) 641-1425
Year Established 1971
Contact Herbert W Smith, Exec Clinical Dir
Facility Information *Placement* Special School; Private Residential Care. *Number of Beds* 40. *Children/Adolescents Served* 40. *Sexes Served* Both. *Tuition Fees (Approx)* $20,900. *Sources of Funding* State Funds. Summer school available. *Teacher Certification Level* Elementary School; Junior High/Middle School; High School. *Special Certification Level* ED; LD.

Student/Patient Characteristics *Age Levels* 5-8; 9-11; 12-14; 15-17; 18-21. *IQ Ranges* 71-85; 85-130. *Exceptionalities Served* Emotionally Disturbed; Learning Disabled. *Learning Problems* Memory Disabilities; Perceptual Disabilities; Thinking Disabilities; Oral Language Disabilities; Reading Disabilities; Handwriting Disabilities; Spelling Disabilities; Arithmetic Disabilities; Written Expression. *Behavioral Problems* Attention Deficits; Hyperactivity; Impulsivity; Verbal Aggression; Physical Aggression; Indirect Aggression; Passive Aggression; Withdrawal. *Conditions Treated* Alcohol Abuse and/or Drug Abuse; Other Substance Abuse or Dependence; Convulsive Disorders; Phobias; Obsessions and Compulsions; Hysteria; Depression; Suicide; Asthma; Inadequacy/Immaturity; Personality Problems; Socialized Aggressive Reaction; Unsocialized Aggressive Reaction.

Services Provided Individual Therapy; Group Therapy; Parent Involvement; Behavior Therapy; Cognitive Developmental Therapy; Family Therapy; Reality Therapy. *Professionals on Staff* Psychiatrists 1; Psychologists 3; Counselors 10; Nurses 1. *Service Facilities Available (with number of rooms)* Self-Contained Rooms 4; On-Campus Residential School 4. *Educational Professionals* Special Education Teachers 4; Paraprofessionals 4. *Curricula* Traditional Academic; Career/Vocational Education; Individualized; Basic Skills; Prevocational. *Degrees Awarded* Certificate of Attendance; Graduate Equivalency Diploma.

Comments This program is a special education school for emotionally disturbed and learning disabled children. It uses the self-contained classroom model and individualized instruction based on a diagnostically prescribed educational program. The school operates via an interagency agreement with the local parish school board and all of its resources.

Louisiana State University Medical Center—School of Allied Health Professions—Human Development Center

1100 Florida Ave, Bldg 138, New Orleans, LA 70119-2799
(504) 568-8397
Year Established 1983
Contact Jeanne A Bonck, Exemplary Serv Coord
Facility Information *Placement* Special School; Special Program. *Children/Adolescents Served* 50. *Sexes Served* Both. *Sources of Funding* State Funds; HEW. Summer school available. *Teacher Certification Level* Elementary School. *Special Certification Level* ED; LD; MR.

Student/Patient Characteristics *Age Levels* 0-4. *IQ Ranges* 41-55; 56-70; 71-85; 85-130. *Exceptionalities Served* Autistic; Emotionally Disturbed; Mentally Handicapped; Communication Disordered; Hearing Impaired/Deaf; Visually Impaired/Blind; Other Health Impaired; Physically Handicapped. *Learning Problems* Memory Disabilities; Perceptual Disabilities; Thinking Disabilities; Oral Language Disabilities. *Behavioral Problems* Attention Deficits; Hyperactivity; Hypoactivity; Impulsivity. *Conditions Treated* Early Infantile Autism; Convulsive Disorders.

Services Provided Individual Therapy; Group Therapy; Parent Involvement; Behavior Therapy; Cognitive Developmental Therapy. *Professionals on Staff* Psychiatrists 1; Psychologists 1; Counselors 1; Social Workers 3; Nurses 1. *Service Facilities Available (with number of rooms)* Special School; Homebound Instruction. *Educational Professionals* Special Education Teachers 6; Paraprofessionals 3. *Curricula* Individualized; Self-Help; Readiness. *Educational Intervention Approaches* Engineered Classroom; Precision Teaching; Behavior Modification; Applied Behavior Analysis.

Comments The University Affiliated Program is an interdisciplinary early intervention program for infants and young children with developmental disabilities. Services are provided through center-based classroom programming and home and center-based parent training.

Towering Pines Center

306 Driftwood Cir, Slidell, LA 70459 (504) 641-7542
Year Established 1960
Contact Soledad Martinez, Dir Treatment Serv
Facility Information *Placement* Special School. *Number of Beds* 35. *Children/Adolescents Served* 35. *Sexes Served* Both. *Sources of Funding* P.L. 94-142; P.L. 89-313. Summer school available. *Teacher Certification Level* Junior High/Middle School; High School. *Special Certification Level* ED; MR; Social Studies.
Student/Patient Characteristics *Age Levels* 9-11; 12-14; 15-17. *Exceptionalities Served* Emotionally Disturbed; Learning Disabled; Mentally Handicapped; Communication Disordered.

Learning Problems Memory Disabilities; Perceptual Disabilities; Thinking Disabilities; Oral Language Disabilities; Reading Disabilities; Handwriting Disabilities; Spelling Disabilities; Arithmetic Disabilities; Written Expression. *Behavioral Problems* Attention Deficits; Hyperactivity; Hypoactivity; Impulsivity; Self-Aggression; Verbal Aggression; Physical Aggression; Indirect Aggression; Passive Aggression; Withdrawal. *Conditions Treated* Schizophrenia; Phobias; Obsessions and Compulsions; Depression; Inadequacy/Immaturity; Personality Problems; Socialized Aggressive Reaction; Unsocialized Aggressive Reaction.

Services Provided Individual Therapy; Group Therapy; Behavior Therapy; Cognitive Developmental Therapy. *Professionals on Staff* Psychiatrists 1; Psychologists 1. *Service Facilities Available (with number of rooms)* Self-Contained Rooms. *Educational Professionals* Special Education Teachers 3; Paraprofessionals 3. *Curricula* Individualized; Basic Skills; Prevocational. *Educational Intervention Approaches* Behavior Modification. *Degrees Awarded* Certificate of Attendance; Graduate Equivalency Diploma.

Maine

Augusta School Department

Box 1080, RFD 2, Pierce Dr, Augusta, ME 04330
(207) 622-3724
Contact Wayne Dorr, Dir Special Ed
Facility Information *Placement* Public School.
Children/Adolescents Served 25. *Sexes Served* Both. *Tuition Fees (Approx)* $7,500. *Sources of Funding* State Funds; P.L. 94-142. *Teacher Certification Level* Elementary School; Junior High/Middle School; High School. *Special Certification Level* ED; LD.
Student/Patient Characteristics *Age Levels* 12-14; 15-17; 18-21. *IQ Ranges* 71-85; 85-130. *Exceptionalities Served* Emotionally Disturbed; Learning Disabled; Mentally Handicapped; Hearing Impaired/Deaf. *Learning Problems* Perceptual Disabilities; Reading Disabilities. *Behavioral Problems* Attention Deficits; Hyperactivity; Impulsivity; Self-Aggression; Physical Aggression; Indirect Aggression; Passive Aggression; Withdrawal. *Conditions Treated* Alcohol Abuse and/or Drug Abuse; Disintegrative Psychoses; Schizophrenia; Phobias; Obsessions and Compulsions; Depression; Suicide; Anorexia Nervosa; Personality Problems; Socialized Aggressive Reaction; Unsocialized Aggressive Reaction.
Services Provided Individual Therapy; Group Therapy; Parent Involvement; Behavior Therapy; Family Therapy; Drug Therapy; Reality Therapy; Play Therapy. *Professionals on Staff* Psychiatrists 1; Psychologists 3; Counselors 4; Nurses 1. *Service Facilities Available (with number of rooms)* Resource Rooms 5; Self-Contained Rooms 2; Special School 1; Hospital School 1; Homebound Instruction. *Educational Professionals* Regular School Teachers; Special Education Teachers; Career/Vocational Teachers 3; Special Education Counselors 2. *Curricula* Traditional Academic; Career/Vocational Education; Individualized; Basic Skills; Prevocational; Job Placement. *Educational Intervention Approaches* Engineered Classroom; Progressive Discipline; Self-Control; Behavior Modification; Applied Behavior Analysis. *Degrees Awarded* High School Diploma.

Homes Unlimited Inc

26 5th St, Bangor, ME 04401 (207) 942-6672
Year Established 1973
Contact Gerry Palmer, Admin
Facility Information *Placement* Public Residential Care. *Number of Beds* 3. *Children/Adolescents Served* 18. *Sexes Served* Both. *Room and Board Fees (Approx)* $31. *Tuition Fees (Approx)* $6,000 (outside independent day program). *Sources of Funding* State Funds; Social Security Insurance.
Student/Patient Characteristics *Age Levels* 18-21; Over 21. *IQ Ranges* 41-55; 56-70. *Exceptionalities Served* Autistic; Emotionally Disturbed; Learning Disabled; Mentally Handicapped; Communication Disordered; Hearing Impaired/Deaf; Other Health Impaired. *Learning Problems* Memory Disabilities; Perceptual Disabilities; Thinking Disabilities; Oral Language Disabilities; Reading Disabilities; Handwriting Disabilities; Spelling Disabilities; Arithmetic Disabilities; Written Expression. *Behavioral Problems* Attention Deficits; Hyperactivity; Hypoactivity; Impulsivity; Self-Aggression; Verbal Aggression; Physical Aggression; Indirect Aggression; Passive Aggression; Withdrawal. *Conditions Treated* Schizophrenia; Aphasia; Convulsive Disorders; Phobias; Depression; Suicide; Inadequacy/Immaturity.
Services Provided Individual Therapy; Group Therapy; Parent Involvement. *Professionals on Staff* Psychologists; Counselors; Social Workers; Nurses. *Educational Professionals* Special Education Teachers; Career/Vocational Teachers; Paraprofessionals. *Curricula* Individualized; Basic Skills; Prevocational. *Educational Intervention Approaches* Self-Control; Behavior Modification.

Maryland

Anne Arundel County Health Department Mental Health Clinic

3 Truman Pkwy, Annapolis, MD 21401 (301) 224-7164
Year Established 1934
Contact Admissions Person
Facility Information *Placement* Outpatient Mental Health Clinic. *Children/Adolescents Served* 20. *Sexes Served* Both. *Sources of Funding* State Funds; HEW; Health Insurance; Medicaid; Medicare; County Funds.
Student/Patient Characteristics *Age Levels* 5-8; 9-11; 12-14; 15-17; 18-21; Over 21. *IQ Ranges* 41-55; 56-70; 71-85; 85-130; Above 130. *Exceptionalities Served* Autistic; Emotionally Disturbed; Gifted. *Learning Problems* Thinking Disabilities. *Behavioral Problems* Attention Deficits; Hyperactivity; Hypoactivity; Impulsivity; Self-Aggression; Verbal Aggression; Physical Aggression; Indirect Aggression; Passive Aggression; Withdrawal. *Conditions Treated* Other Substance Abuse or Dependence; Disintegrative Psychoses; Schizophrenia; Phobias; Obsessions and Compulsions; Hysteria; Depression; Suicide; Asthma; Anorexia Nervosa; Ulcerative Colitis; Inadequacy/Immaturity; Personality Problems; Socialized Aggressive Reaction.
Services Provided Individual Therapy; Group Therapy; Parent Involvement; Family Therapy; Filial Therapy; Drug Therapy; Play Therapy. *Professionals on Staff* Psychiatrists 2; Psychologists 5; Counselors 7; Social Workers 6; Nurses 8. *Service Facilities Available (with number of rooms)* Play Therapy Room. *Educational Professionals* Paraprofessionals 7.

Chestnut Lodge Hospital—Adolescent and Child Division

500 W Montgomery Ave, Rockville, MD 20850 (301) 424-8300
Year Established 1910
Contact Patricia Holland, Admissions Coord
Facility Information *Placement* Special School; Private Residential Care. *Number of Beds* 28. *Children/Adolescents Served* 28. *Sexes Served* Both. *Room and Board Fees (Approx)* $284. *Tuition Fees (Approx)* $12,870. *Sources of Funding* Health Insurance; P.L. 94-142; Patients Private Funds. Summer school available. *Teacher Certification Level* Elementary School; Junior High/Middle School; High School. *Special Certification Level* Special Education.
Student/Patient Characteristics *Age Levels* 9-11; 12-14; 15-17; 18-21. *IQ Ranges* 85-130; Above 130. *Exceptionalities Served* Autistic; Emotionally Disturbed. *Learning Problems* Thinking Disabilities. *Behavioral Problems* Attention Deficits; Hyperactivity; Impulsivity; Self-Aggression; Verbal Aggression; Physical Aggression; Indirect Aggression; Passive Aggression; Withdrawal. *Conditions Treated* Schizophrenia; Obsessions and Compulsions;

Hysteria; Depression; Suicide; Anorexia Nervosa; Inadequacy/Immaturity; Personality Problems; Socialized Aggressive Reaction; Unsocialized Aggressive Reaction.
Services Provided Individual Therapy; Group Therapy; Parent Involvement; Family Therapy; Filial Therapy; Drug Therapy; Art Therapy; Music Therapy; Milieu Treatment. *Professionals on Staff* Psychiatrists 30; Psychologists 2; Social Workers 2; Nurses 6; Houseparents 35. *Service Facilities Available (with number of rooms)* Consultative (ERT); Resource Rooms; Transition Rooms; Self-Contained Rooms; Special School; Hospital School; On-Campus Residential School. *Educational Professionals* Special Education Teachers 8; Special Education Counselors; Teacher Assitants 2; Principal 1. *Curricula* Traditional Academic; Individualized. *Educational Intervention Approaches* Engineered Classroom; Precision Teaching; Progressive Discipline; Self-Control; Behavior Modification; Applied Behavior Analysis. *Degrees Awarded* High School Diploma.

The Children's Guild Inc

5921 Smith Ave, Baltimore, MD 21209 (301) 542-3355
Year Established 1953
Contact Stanley Mopsik, Exec Dir
Facility Information *Placement* Private Special School. *Children/Adolescents Served* 113. *Sexes Served* Both. *Tuition Fees (Approx)* $11,250 (and ability to pay). *Sources of Funding* State Funds; P.L. 94-142; United Way. Summer school available. *Teacher Certification Level* Elementary School. *Special Certification Level* ED; LD.
Student/Patient Characteristics *Age Levels* 0-4; 5-8. *IQ Ranges* 71-85; 85-130. *Exceptionalities Served* Emotionally Disturbed; Learning Disabled. *Learning Problems* Memory Disabilities; Perceptual Disabilities; Thinking Disabilities; Oral Language Disabilities; Reading Disabilities; Handwriting Disabilities; Spelling Disabilities; Arithmetic Disabilities; Written Expression. *Behavioral Problems* Attention Deficits; Hyperactivity; Hypoactivity; Impulsivity; Self-Aggression; Verbal Aggression; Physical Aggression; Indirect Aggression; Passive Aggression; Withdrawal. *Conditions Treated* Schizophrenia; Phobias; Obsessions and Compulsions; Hysteria; Depression; Inadequacy/Immaturity; Personality Problems; Socialized Aggressive Reaction.
Services Provided Individual Therapy; Group Therapy; Parent Involvement; Behavior Therapy; Family Therapy; Drug Therapy; Play Therapy; Movement Therapy. *Professionals on Staff* Psychiatrists 2; Psychologists 1; Social Workers 7; Pediatric Neurologist; Psychiatric Social Worker. *Service Facilities Available (with number of rooms)* Self-Contained Rooms 13. *Educational Professionals* Regular School Teachers; Special Education Teachers 26; Crisis Teachers 1. *Curricula* Individualized. *Educational Intervention Approaches* Self-Control; Behavior Modification.

Comments The Childrens Guild Inc is a therapeutic education program providing intensive special education and therapy for children. Comprehensive counseling and therapy for families is also provided.

Christ Church Child Center

8011 Old Georgetown Rd, Bethesda, MD 20814 (301) 986-1635
Year Established 1961
Contact Shari Gelman, Dir
Facility Information *Placement* Special School; Special Program. *Children/Adolescents Served* 140. *Sexes Served* Both. *Tuition Fees (Approx)* $10,200. *Sources of Funding* P.L. 94-142. *Teacher Certification Level* Elementary School. *Special Certification Level* ED; LD; MR; Reading; Math.
Student/Patient Characteristics *Age Levels* 0-4; 5-8; 9-11; 12-14. *IQ Ranges* 56-70; 71-85; 85-130. *Exceptionalities Served* Autistic; Emotionally Disturbed; Learning Disabled; Mentally Handicapped; Communication Disordered; Hearing Impaired/Deaf. *Learning Problems* Memory Disabilities; Perceptual Disabilities; Thinking Disabilities; Oral Language Disabilities; Reading Disabilities; Handwriting Disabilities; Spelling Disabilities; Arithmetic Disabilities; Written Expression. *Behavioral Problems* Attention Deficits; Hyperactivity; Hypoactivity; Impulsivity; Self-Aggression; Verbal Aggression; Physical Aggression; Indirect Aggression; Passive Aggression; Withdrawal. *Conditions Treated* Early Infantile Autism; Aphasia; Convulsive Disorders; Inadequacy/Immaturity; Personality Problems; Socialized Aggressive Reaction; Unsocialized Aggressive Reaction.
Services Provided Individual Therapy; Group Therapy; Parent Involvement; Behavior Therapy; Cognitive Developmental Therapy; Art Therapy; Music Therapy; Reality Therapy; Play Therapy. *Professionals on Staff* Social Workers 2; Child Care Staff 70; Occupational Therapists 8; Speech Therapists 10; Music Therapist 1; Recreational Therapist 1. *Service Facilities Available (with number of rooms)* Consultative (ERT) 2; Self-Contained Rooms 15. *Educational Professionals* Special Education Teachers 15; Crisis Teachers 2; Paraprofessionals 17. *Curricula* Traditional Academic; Individualized. *Educational Intervention Approaches* Engineered Classroom; Precision Teaching; Progressive Discipline; Self-Control; Behavior Modification.

Community Psychiatric Clinic Inc

2424 Reedie Dr; 4803 Hampden Ln; 9081 Shady Grove Court, Wheaton; Bethesda; Gaithersburg, MD 20902; 20814; 20877 (301) 656-5220; (301) 933-2402; (301) 840-9636
Year Established 1935
Contact Miriam Silver, Admin Officer
Facility Information *Placement* Outpatient Mental Health Services. *Sexes Served* Both.
Student/Patient Characteristics *Age Levels* 0-4; 5-8; 9-11; 12-14; 15-17; 18-21. *IQ Ranges* 41-55; 56-70; 71-85; 85-130; Above 130. *Exceptionalities Served* Emotionally Disturbed; Learning Disabled; Mentally Handicapped. *Learning Problems* Memory Disabilities; Perceptual Disabilities; Thinking Disabilities; Oral Language Disabilities; Reading Disabilities; Handwriting Disabilities; Spelling Disabilities; Arithmetic Disabilities; Written Expression. *Behavioral Problems* Attention Deficits; Hyperactivity; Impulsivity; Self-Aggression; Verbal Aggression; Physical Aggression; Indirect Aggression; Passive Aggression; Withdrawal. *Conditions Treated* Alcohol Abuse and/or Drug Abuse; Schizophrenia; Phobias; Obsessions and Compulsions; Hysteria; Depression; Suicide; Personality Problems; Socialized Aggressive Reaction.
Services Provided Individual Therapy; Group Therapy; Parent Involvement; Behavior Therapy; Family Therapy; Drug Therapy. *Professionals on Staff* Psychiatrists 14; Psychologists 18; Counselors 5; Social Workers 25; Nurses 4.

Edgemeade of Maryland

13400 Edgemeade Rd, Upper Marlboro, MD 20772
(301) 888-1330
Contact L Geraghty, Treatment Prog Dir

Facility Information *Placement* Special School; Private Residential Care. *Number of Beds* 48. *Children/Adolescents Served* 48 (residential); 15 (day students). *Sexes Served* Male. *Room and Board Fees (Approx)* $101. *Tuition Fees (Approx)* $17,703-$37,012. *Sources of Funding* State Funds. Summer school available. *Special Certification Level* ED; LD; Reading; Math.
Student/Patient Characteristics *Age Levels* 12-14; 15-17; 18-21. *IQ Ranges* 71-85; 85-130. *Exceptionalities Served* Emotionally Disturbed; Learning Disabled; Mentally Handicapped; Neurologically Impaired. *Learning Problems* Perceptual Disabilities; Thinking Disabilities; Reading Disabilities; Written Expression. *Behavioral Problems* Attention Deficits; Hyperactivity; Impulsivity; Verbal Aggression; Physical Aggression; Withdrawal. *Conditions Treated* Alcohol Abuse and/or Drug Abuse; Schizophrenia; Depression; Personality Problems; Behavioral Disorders; Thought Disorders.
Services Provided Individual Therapy; Group Therapy; Parent Involvement; Behavior Therapy; Family Therapy; Drug Therapy; Art Therapy; Reality Therapy; Play Therapy. *Professionals on Staff* Psychologists 1; Counselors 20; Social Workers 6; Nurses 4; Drug and Substance Abuse Counselor; Speech Therapist; Medical Doctor; Consulting. *Service Facilities Available (with number of rooms)* Resource Rooms 1; Transition Rooms 1; Self-Contained Rooms 1; Local Public School. *Educational Professionals* Special Education Teachers; Career/Vocational Teachers 1; Paraprofessionals 15. *Curricula* Traditional Academic; Individualized; Basic Skills; Prevocational; Socialization. *Educational Intervention Approaches* Behavior Modification. *Degrees Awarded* High School Diploma.

The Frost School

4915 Aspen Hill Rd, Rockville, MD 20853 (301) 933-3451
Year Established 1975
Contact Richard A Miller, Dir
Facility Information *Placement* Special School; Private Day Care. *Children/Adolescents Served* 36. *Sexes Served* Both. *Tuition Fees (Approx)* $12,000. *Sources of Funding* State Funds; P.L. 94-142; Local Public Schools. Summer school available. *Teacher Certification Level* Junior High/Middle School; High School. *Special Certification Level* ED; LD; Career/Vocational Education; Reading; Math.
Student/Patient Characteristics *Age Levels* 12-14; 15-17; 18-21. *IQ Ranges* 85-130; Above 130. *Exceptionalities Served* Emotionally Disturbed; Learning Disabled. *Learning Problems* Memory Disabilities; Perceptual Disabilities; Thinking Disabilities; Oral Language Disabilities; Reading Disabilities; Handwriting Disabilities; Spelling Disabilities; Arithmetic Disabilities; Written Expression. *Behavioral Problems* Attention Deficits; Hyperactivity; Hypoactivity; Impulsivity; Self-Aggression; Verbal Aggression; Physical Aggression; Indirect Aggression; Passive Aggression; Withdrawal. *Conditions Treated* Alcohol Abuse and/or Drug Abuse; Disintegrative Psychoses; Schizophrenia; Aphasia; Phobias; Obsessions and Compulsions; Hysteria; Depression; Suicide; Anorexia Nervosa; Inadequacy/Immaturity; Personality Problems; Socialized Aggressive Reaction; Unsocialized Aggressive Reaction.
Services Provided Individual Therapy; Group Therapy; Parent Involvement; Family Therapy; Reality Therapy. *Professionals on Staff* Psychiatrists .2; Psychologists 3; Counselors 3; Social Workers 2; Nurses 1. *Educational Professionals* Special Education Teachers 4; Career/Vocational Teachers 1; Special Education Counselors 3. *Curricula* Traditional Academic; Career/Vocational Education; Individualized; Basic Skills; Prevocational. *Educational Intervention Approaches* Progressive Discipline; Self-Control.

Hamilton Children's Center

4112 Hamilton St, Hyattsville, MD 20781 (301) 779-0993
Year Established 1970
Contact Carol Fuechsel, Dir

Facility Information *Placement* Mental Health Facility. *Children/Adolescents Served* 75. *Sexes Served* Both. *Tuition Fees (Approx)* Sliding Scale. *Sources of Funding* State Funds; Health Insurance; Medicaid; Individual Fees.

Student/Patient Characteristics *Age Levels* 0-4; 5-8; 9-11; 12-14; 15-17. *IQ Ranges* 0-25; 26-40; 41-55; 56-70; 71-85; 85-130; Above 130. *Exceptionalities Served* Emotionally Disturbed. *Learning Problems* Memory Disabilities; Perceptual Disabilities; Thinking Disabilities; Oral Language Disabilities; Reading Disabilities; Handwriting Disabilities; Spelling Disabilities; Arithmetic Disabilities; Written Expression. *Behavioral Problems* Attention Deficits; Hyperactivity; Hypoactivity; Impulsivity; Self-Aggression; Verbal Aggression; Physical Aggression; Indirect Aggression; Passive Aggression; Withdrawal. *Conditions Treated* Alcohol Abuse and/or Drug Abuse; Other Substance Abuse or Dependence; Disintegrative Psychoses; Schizophrenia; Aphasia; Convulsive Disorders; Phobias; Obsessions and Compulsions; Hysteria; Depression; Suicide; Asthma; Anorexia Nervosa; Ulcerative Colitis; Inadequacy/Immaturity; Personality Problems; Socialized Aggressive Reaction; Unsocialized Aggressive Reaction.

Services Provided Individual Therapy; Group Therapy; Parent Involvement; Behavior Therapy; Family Therapy; Art Therapy; Play Therapy. *Professionals on Staff* Psychiatrists 1; Psychologists 2; Social Workers 1; Art Therapist 1; Mental Health Associate 1.

The Hannah More Center

PO Box 370, Reisterstown, MD 21136 (301) 526-5000
Year Established 1978
Contact Mark Waldman, Exec Dir

Facility Information *Placement* Special School; Private Day Care. *Children/Adolescents Served* 75. *Sexes Served* Both. *Tuition Fees (Approx)* $17,825. *Sources of Funding* State Funds; P.L. 94-142. *Teacher Certification Level* Junior High/Middle School; High School. *Special Certification Level* ED.

Student/Patient Characteristics *Age Levels* 12-14; 15-17; 18-21. *IQ Ranges* 85-130. *Exceptionalities Served* Emotionally Disturbed; Learning Disabled. *Learning Problems* Memory Disabilities; Perceptual Disabilities; Thinking Disabilities; Oral Language Disabilities; Reading Disabilities; Handwriting Disabilities; Spelling Disabilities; Arithmetic Disabilities; Written Expression. *Behavioral Problems* Attention Deficits; Hyperactivity; Impulsivity; Verbal Aggression; Physical Aggression; Indirect Aggression; Passive Aggression; Withdrawal. *Conditions Treated* Alcohol Abuse and/or Drug Abuse; Schizophrenia; Phobias; Obsessions and Compulsions; Hysteria; Depression; Inadequacy/Immaturity; Personality Problems; Socialized Aggressive Reaction; Unsocialized Aggressive Reaction.

Services Provided Individual Therapy; Group Therapy; Parent Involvement; Behavior Therapy; Cognitive Developmental Therapy; Family Therapy; Drug Therapy; Psychodrama. *Professionals on Staff* Psychiatrists 1; Psychologists 2; Social Workers 2. *Service Facilities Available (with number of rooms)* Resource Rooms 1; Transition Rooms 4; Self-Contained Rooms 4. *Educational Professionals* Special Education Teachers 7; Career/Vocational Teachers 1; Crisis Teachers 3; Paraprofessionals 5. *Curricula* Traditional Academic; Career/Vocational Education; Individualized; Basic Skills; Prevocational. *Educational Intervention Approaches* Engineered Classroom; Behavior Modification. *Degrees Awarded* High School Diploma; Graduate Equivalency Diploma.

Harford County Community Mental Health Center

PO Box 191, Hays St, Bel Air, MD 21014 (301) 838-3373
Contact Gregory E Smith, Coord Psychological Serv

Facility Information *Placement* Outpatient Services. *Children/Adolescents Served* 150. *Sexes Served* Both. *Sources of Funding* Health Insurance; Medicaid; Medicare; Sliding Scale.

Student/Patient Characteristics *Age Levels* 0-4; 5-8; 9-11; 12-14; 15-17; 18-21; Over 21. *IQ Ranges* 0-25; 26-40; 41-55; 56-70; 71-85; 85-130; Above 130. *Exceptionalities Served* Autistic; Emotionally Disturbed; Learning Disabled; Mentally Handicapped; Physically Handicapped; Gifted. *Learning Problems* Memory

Disabilities; Perceptual Disabilities; Thinking Disabilities; Oral Language Disabilities; Reading Disabilities; Handwriting Disabilities; Spelling Disabilities; Arithmetic Disabilities; Written Expression. *Behavioral Problems* Attention Deficits; Hyperactivity; Hypoactivity; Impulsivity; Self-Aggression; Verbal Aggression; Physical Aggression; Indirect Aggression; Passive Aggression; Withdrawal. *Conditions Treated* Schizophrenia; Phobias; Obsessions and Compulsions; Hysteria; Depression; Suicide; Anorexia Nervosa; Inadequacy/Immaturity; Personality Problems; Socialized Aggressive Reaction; Unsocialized Aggressive Reaction.

Services Provided Individual Therapy; Group Therapy; Parent Involvement; Behavior Therapy; Cognitive Developmental Therapy; Biofeedback; Family Therapy; Drug Therapy; Reality Therapy; Play Therapy. *Professionals on Staff* Psychiatrists 2; Psychologists 5; Counselors 2; Social Workers 5. *Educational Intervention Approaches* Self-Control; Behavior Modification.

Institute of Psychiatry and Human Behavior—Department of Psychiatry—Child and Adolescent Inpatient Service

645 W Redwood St, Baltimore, MD 21201 (301) 528-6184
Year Established 1983
Contact Laurence W Ford, Principal

Facility Information *Placement* University Hospital Program. *Number of Beds* 12. *Children/Adolescents Served* 12. *Sexes Served* Both. *Room and Board Fees (Approx)* $400. *Sources of Funding* Health Insurance; Medicaid; Social Services. Summer school available. *Teacher Certification Level* Elementary School; Junior High/Middle School; High School. *Special Certification Level* ED; LD.

Student/Patient Characteristics *Age Levels* 9-11; 12-14; 15-17. *IQ Ranges* 56-70; 71-85; 85-130; Above 130. *Exceptionalities Served* Emotionally Disturbed; Learning Disabled; Mentally Handicapped. *Learning Problems* Memory Disabilities; Perceptual Disabilities; Thinking Disabilities; Oral Language Disabilities; Reading Disabilities; Handwriting Disabilities; Spelling Disabilities; Arithmetic Disabilities; Written Expression. *Behavioral Problems* Attention Deficits; Hyperactivity; Hypoactivity; Impulsivity; Self-Aggression; Verbal Aggression; Physical Aggression; Indirect Aggression; Passive Aggression; Withdrawal. *Conditions Treated* Alcohol Abuse and/or Drug Abuse; Other Substance Abuse or Dependence; Disintegrative Psychoses; Phobias; Obsessions and Compulsions; Depression; Suicide; Asthma; Personality Problems; Socialized Aggressive Reaction; Unsocialized Aggressive Reaction.

Services Provided Individual Therapy; Group Therapy; Parent Involvement; Behavior Therapy; Family Therapy; Filial Therapy; Drug Therapy; Art Therapy; Play Therapy; Altrudt Therapy. *Professionals on Staff* Psychiatrists 4; Psychologists 2; Social Workers; Child Care Staff 15; Nurses 8. *Service Facilities Available (with number of rooms)* Consultative (ERT); Itinerants; Resource Rooms; Self-Contained Rooms; Crisis Room; On-Campus Residential School 6. *Educational Professionals* Special Education Teachers; Crisis Teachers. *Curricula* Individualized; Basic Skills; Perceptual Motor Training; Physical Education. *Educational Intervention Approaches* Engineered Classroom.

The John F Kennedy Institute

707 N Broadway, Baltimore, MD 21205 (301) 522-5455
Year Established 1967
Contact Diane Grohs, Patient Serv Coord

Facility Information *Placement* Pediatric Hospital. *Number of Beds* 40. *Children/Adolescents Served* 40 (inpatients); 5000 (outpatients). *Sexes Served* Both. *Room and Board Fees (Approx)* $507. *Sources of Funding* State Funds; Health Insurance; Medicaid; P.L. 94-142. *Teacher Certification Level* Elementary School. *Special Certification Level* ED; LD; MR; Reading; Math.

Student/Patient Characteristics *Age Levels* 0-4; 5-8; 9-11; 12-14; 15-17; 18-21. *IQ Ranges* 0-25; 26-40; 41-55; 56-70; 71-85; 85-130; Above 130. *Exceptionalities Served* Autistic; Emotionally Disturbed; Learning Disabled; Mentally Handicapped; Communication Disordered; Hearing Impaired/Deaf; Visually Impaired/

Blind; Other Health Impaired; Physically Handicapped; Gifted. *Learning Problems* Memory Disabilities; Perceptual Disabilities; Thinking Disabilities; Oral Language Disabilities; Reading Disabilities; Handwriting Disabilities; Spelling Disabilities; Arithmetic Disabilities; Written Expression. *Behavioral Problems* Attention Deficits; Hyperactivity; Hypoactivity; Impulsivity; Self-Aggression; Verbal Aggression; Physical Aggression; Indirect Aggression; Passive Aggression; Withdrawal. *Conditions Treated* Early Infantile Autism; Convulsive Disorders; Phobias; Inadequacy/Immaturity; Socialized Aggressive Reaction; Unsocialized Aggressive Reaction.

Services Provided Individual Therapy; Parent Involvement; Behavior Therapy; Biofeedback; Drug Therapy. *Professionals on Staff* Psychiatrists 4; Psychologists 24; Social Workers 12; Child Care Staff 40; Nurses 25. *Service Facilities Available (with number of rooms)* Consultative (ERT); Resource Rooms; Self-Contained Rooms. *Educational Professionals* Regular School Teachers; Special Education Teachers. *Curricula* Traditional Academic; Career/Vocational Education; Individualized; Basic Skills; Prevocational. *Educational Intervention Approaches* Behavior Modification; Applied Behavior Analysis.

Linwood Children's Center

3421 Church Rd, Elliott City, MD 21043 (301) 463-1352
Year Established 1955
Contact Social Work Dir

Facility Information *Placement* Special School; Private Residential Care. *Number of Beds* 20. *Children/Adolescents Served* 20. *Sexes Served* Both. *Sources of Funding* State Funds; P.L. 94-142. Summer school available. *Teacher Certification Level* Elementary School; Junior High/Middle School; High School. *Special Certification Level* ED; Autistic.

Student/Patient Characteristics *Age Levels* 5-8; 9-11; 12-14; 15-17; 18-21. *IQ Ranges* 26-40; 41-55; 56-70; 71-85; 85-130. *Exceptionalities Served* Autistic; Emotionally Disturbed. *Learning Problems* Perceptual Disabilities; Thinking Disabilities; Oral Language Disabilities; Reading Disabilities; Handwriting Disabilities; Spelling Disabilities; Arithmetic Disabilities; Written Expression. *Behavioral Problems* Attention Deficits; Hyperactivity; Hypoactivity; Impulsivity; Self-Aggression; Verbal Aggression; Physical Aggression; Indirect Aggression; Passive Aggression; Withdrawal. *Conditions Treated* Early Infantile Autism.

Services Provided Individual Therapy; Group Therapy; Parent Involvement; Behavior Therapy; Family Therapy; Drug Therapy; Music Therapy; Play Therapy; Psychodrama; Movement Therapy. *Professionals on Staff* Psychiatrists 1; Psychologists 1; Counselors; Social Workers 2; Child Care Staff 9; Speech Therapy; Physical Therapy. *Service Facilities Available (with number of rooms)* Self-Contained Rooms 6; On-Campus Residential School. *Educational Professionals* Special Education Teachers 11; Career/Vocational Teachers 1; Paraprofessionals 11. *Curricula* Traditional Academic; Career/Vocational Education; Individualized; Basic Skills; Prevocational. *Educational Intervention Approaches* Precision Teaching; Progressive Discipline; Self-Control; Behavior Modification; Creative Conditioning. *Degrees Awarded* Certificate of Attendance.

Montrose School

13700 Hanover Rd, Reisterstown, MD 21136 (301) 833-1500
Contact Leonard F Gmeiner, Supt

Facility Information *Placement* Juvenile State Training School. *Number of Beds* 300. *Children/Adolescents Served* 300. *Sexes Served* Both. *Tuition Fees (Approx)* $19,594. *Sources of Funding* State Funds. Summer school available. *Teacher Certification Level* Elementary School; Junior High/Middle School; High School. *Special Certification Level* Special Education.

Student/Patient Characteristics *Age Levels* 12-14; 15-17. *IQ Ranges* 71-85; 85-130; Above 130. *Exceptionalities Served* Emotionally Disturbed; Learning Disabled; Mentally Handicapped; Communication Disordered. *Learning Problems* Memory Disabilities; Perceptual Disabilities; Thinking Disabilities; Oral Language Disabilities; Reading Disabilities; Handwriting Disabilities;

Spelling Disabilities; Arithmetic Disabilities; Written Expression. *Behavioral Problems* Hyperactivity; Impulsivity; Self-Aggression; Verbal Aggression; Physical Aggression; Indirect Aggression; Passive Aggression; Withdrawal. *Conditions Treated* Alcohol Abuse and/or Drug Abuse; Other Substance Abuse or Dependence; Schizophrenia; Depression; Suicide; Asthma; Personality Problems; Socialized Aggressive Reaction.

Services Provided Individual Therapy; Group Therapy; Parent Involvement; Behavior Therapy; Drug Therapy. *Professionals on Staff* Psychiatrists 2; Psychologists 4; Social Workers 8; Nurses 6. *Service Facilities Available (with number of rooms)* Consultative (ERT) 1; Resource Rooms 2; Self-Contained Rooms 3; On-Campus Residential School 30. *Educational Professionals* Special Education Teachers 21; Paraprofessionals 3. *Curricula* Individualized; Basic Skills; Prevocational. *Educational Intervention Approaches* Behavior Modification; Positive Peer Pressure. *Degrees Awarded* Graduate Equivalency Diploma.

Queen of Angels School—Villa Maria Treatment Center

2300 Dulaney Valley Rd, Timonium, MD 21093 (301) 252-4700
Contact John M Pumphrey, Ed Dir

Facility Information *Placement* Special School; Private Residential Care. *Number of Beds* 80. *Children/Adolescents Served* 90. *Sexes Served* Both. *Sources of Funding* State Funds; P.L. 94-142. Summer school available. *Teacher Certification Level* Elementary School. *Special Certification Level* ED; LD.

Student/Patient Characteristics *Age Levels* 5-8; 9-11. *IQ Ranges* 71-85; 85-130. *Exceptionalities Served* Emotionally Disturbed; Learning Disabled. *Learning Problems* Perceptual Disabilities; Oral Language Disabilities; Reading Disabilities; Handwriting Disabilities; Spelling Disabilities; Arithmetic Disabilities; Written Expression. *Behavioral Problems* Attention Deficits; Hyperactivity; Impulsivity; Self-Aggression; Verbal Aggression; Physical Aggression; Indirect Aggression; Passive Aggression; Withdrawal. *Conditions Treated* Schizophrenia; Convulsive Disorders; Phobias; Obsessions and Compulsions; Depression; Inadequacy/Immaturity; Personality Problems; Socialized Aggressive Reaction; Unsocialized Aggressive Reaction.

Services Provided Individual Therapy; Group Therapy; Parent Involvement; Behavior Therapy; Family Therapy; Drug Therapy; Art Therapy; Music Therapy; Play Therapy; Psychoeducation. *Professionals on Staff* Psychiatrists 4; Psychologists 2; Social Workers 9; Child Care Staff 56; Nurses 1. *Service Facilities Available (with number of rooms)* Itinerants 2; Resource Rooms 4; Self-Contained Rooms 8; On-Campus Residential School 14. *Educational Professionals* Special Education Teachers 13; Crisis Teachers 2; Paraprofessionals 13. *Curricula* Individualized; Basic Skills. *Educational Intervention Approaches* Self-Control; Behavior Modification; Psychoeducation.

School for Contemporary Education

4906 Roland Ave, Baltimore, MD 21210 (301) 235-9292
Year Established 1970
Contact Artha Johansen, Unit Dir

Facility Information *Placement* Special School. *Children/Adolescents Served* 40. *Sexes Served* Both. *Tuition Fees (Approx)* $11,577 (13 and under); $12,177 (14 and over). *Sources of Funding* State Funds; P.L. 94-142. *Teacher Certification Level* Elementary School; Junior High/Middle School; High School. *Special Certification Level* ED.

Student/Patient Characteristics *Age Levels* 9-11; 12-14; 15-17. *IQ Ranges* 71-85; 85-130; Above 130. *Exceptionalities Served* Emotionally Disturbed; Learning Disabled. *Learning Problems* Memory Disabilities; Perceptual Disabilities; Thinking Disabilities; Oral Language Disabilities; Reading Disabilities; Handwriting Disabilities; Spelling Disabilities; Arithmetic Disabilities; Written Expression. *Behavioral Problems* Attention Deficits; Hyperactivity; Impulsivity; Self-Aggression; Verbal Aggression; Physical Aggression; Indirect Aggression; Passive Aggression; Withdrawal.

Conditions Treated Phobias; Obsessions and Compulsions; Depression; Inadequacy/Immaturity; Personality Problems; Socialized Aggressive Reaction; Unsocialized Aggressive Reaction.

Services Provided Individual Therapy; Group Therapy; Parent Involvement; Behavior Therapy; Cognitive Developmental Therapy. *Professionals on Staff* Psychiatrists 1; Psychologists 2; Counselors 1; Social Workers 1. *Service Facilities Available (with number of rooms)* Resource Rooms 1; Self-Contained Rooms 1; Special School 5. *Educational Professionals* Special Education Teachers 5; Paraprofessionals 6; Reading Specialist 1; Curricula Specialist 1. *Curricula* Traditional Academic; Individualized; Basic Skills; Prevocational. *Educational Intervention Approaches* Engineered Classroom; Precision Teaching; Progressive Discipline; Self-Control; Behavior Modification; Applied Behavior Analysis; Creative Conditioning. *Degrees Awarded* Certificate of Attendance.

Taylor Manor Hospital

PO Box 396, College Ave, Ellicott City, MD 21043
(301) 465-3322
Year Established 1907
Contact Bruce Taylor, Dir of Admissions

Facility Information *Placement* Private Residential Care; Special Program. *Number of Beds* 75. *Children/Adolescents Served* 75. *Sexes Served* Both. *Room and Board Fees (Approx)* $290. *Sources of Funding* Health Insurance; Private Funding; Insurance. Summer school available. *Teacher Certification Level* Junior High/Middle School; High School. *Special Certification Level* ED; Reading; Math; Physical Education; Secondary Education.

Student/Patient Characteristics *Age Levels* 12-14; 15-17; 18-21; Over 21. *IQ Ranges* 71-85; 85-130; Above 130. *Exceptionalities Served* Emotionally Disturbed; Learning Disabled; Other Health Impaired; Physically Handicapped. *Learning Problems* Memory Disabilities; Perceptual Disabilities; Thinking Disabilities; Oral Language Disabilities; Reading Disabilities; Handwriting Disabilities; Spelling Disabilities; Arithmetic Disabilities; Written Expression. *Behavioral Problems* Attention Deficits; Hyperactivity; Hypoactivity; Impulsivity; Self-Aggression; Verbal Aggression; Indirect Aggression; Passive Aggression; Withdrawal. *Conditions Treated* Alcohol Abuse and/or Drug Abuse; Other Substance Abuse or Dependence; Disintegrative Psychoses; Schizophrenia; Convulsive Disorders; Phobias; Obsessions and Compulsions; Hysteria; Depression; Suicide; Asthma; Anorexia Nervosa; Inadequacy/Immaturity; Personality Problems; Socialized Aggressive Reaction; Unsocialized Aggressive Reaction; Most PSM III.

Services Provided Individual Therapy; Group Therapy; Parent Involvement; Behavior Therapy; Cognitive Developmental Therapy; Biofeedback; Family Therapy; Filial Therapy; Drug Therapy; Art Therapy; Music Therapy; Reality Therapy; Psychodrama; Milieu Therapy; Recreation Therapy; Dance Therapy. *Professionals on Staff* Psychiatrists 12; Psychologists 12; Counselors 10; Social Workers 14; Child Care Staff 90; Nurses 20; Activity Therapist 20. *Service Facilities Available (with number of rooms)* Resource Rooms 2; Self-Contained Rooms 6; Hospital School 1. *Educational Professionals* Regular School Teachers 4; Special Education Teachers 2; Career/Vocational Teachers 1; Crisis Teachers 1; Special Education Counselors .5; Paraprofes-

sionals 2. *Curricula* Traditional Academic; Individualized; Basic Skills; Prevocational. *Educational Intervention Approaches* Progressive Discipline; Self-Control; Behavior Modification; Applied Behavior Analysis. *Degrees Awarded* High School Diploma; Graduate Equivalency Diploma.

Comments Taylor Manor Hospital is a 185 bed private psychiatric hospital with long- and short-term specialized programs for adolescents age 12 and older. Other specialized programs are available for young adults and adults with addictions, including alcoholism, drug abuse, and compulsive gambling.

Woodbourne Center

1301 Woodbourne Ave, Baltimore, MD 21239 (301) 433-1000
Year Established 1798
Contact John Hodge-Williams, Exec Dir

Facility Information *Placement* Private Residential Care; Private Day Care. *Number of Beds* 36. *Children/Adolescents Served* 36 (residents); 60 (day students). *Sexes Served* Both. *Room and Board Fees (Approx)* $42 (males); $58 (females). *Tuition Fees (Approx)* $8,500. *Sources of Funding* State Funds; Medicaid; P.L. 94-142; Endowment; United Way. Summer school available. *Teacher Certification Level* Junior High/Middle School; High School. *Special Certification Level* ED; LD; Career/Vocational Education; Reading; Math; Physical Education.

Student/Patient Characteristics *Age Levels* 12-14; 15-17. *IQ Ranges* 71-85; 85-130. *Exceptionalities Served* Emotionally Disturbed; Learning Disabled. *Learning Problems* Memory Disabilities; Perceptual Disabilities; Thinking Disabilities; Oral Language Disabilities; Reading Disabilities; Handwriting Disabilities; Spelling Disabilities; Arithmetic Disabilities; Written Expression. *Behavioral Problems* Attention Deficits; Hyperactivity; Impulsivity; Self-Aggression; Verbal Aggression; Physical Aggression; Indirect Aggression; Passive Aggression; Withdrawal. *Conditions Treated* Phobias; Obsessions and Compulsions; Depression; Suicide; Inadequacy/Immaturity; Personality Problems; Socialized Aggressive Reaction; Unsocialized Aggressive Reaction.

Services Provided Individual Therapy; Group Therapy; Parent Involvement; Behavior Therapy; Cognitive Developmental Therapy; Family Therapy; Art Therapy; Reality Therapy; Psychodrama. *Professionals on Staff* Psychiatrists .5; Psychologists 2; Counselors 2; Social Workers 5; Child Care Staff 18; Nurses 1.5; Diagnostic-Prescriptive Clinician 1; Expressive Art Therapist 1; Occupational Therapist .5; Speech Pathologist .5. *Service Facilities Available (with number of rooms)* Consultative (ERT) 3; Itinerants 2; Resource Rooms 5; Transition Rooms 4; Self-Contained Rooms 6; Shop, Computer Room 2; On-Campus Residential School 8. *Educational Professionals* Special Education Teachers 14; Career/Vocational Teachers 2; Crisis Teachers 1; Special Education Counselors 1; Paraprofessionals 12. *Curricula* Career/Vocational Education; Individualized; Basic Skills; Prevocational. *Educational Intervention Approaches* Engineered Classroom; Behavior Modification. *Degrees Awarded* Certificate of Attendance.

Comments Woodbourne is a licensed private residential treatment center and operates a level 5 residential school and day school for the Baltimore Public School System.

Massachusetts

Arlington School

115 Mill St, Belmont, MA 02146 (617) 855-2124
Year Established 1961
Contact John F Dunn
Facility Information *Placement* Public Residential Care; Private Residential Care; Private Day Care; Special Program. *Number of Beds* 8. *Children/Adolescents Served* 60. *Sexes Served* Both. *Room and Board Fees (Approx)* $90. *Tuition Fees (Approx)* $22,600. *Sources of Funding* State Funds; Health Insurance; P.L. 94-142. Summer school available. *Teacher Certification Level* High School. *Special Certification Level* ED; LD; Reading; Math.
Student/Patient Characteristics *Age Levels* 12-14; 15-17; 18-21. *IQ Ranges* 85-130. *Exceptionalities Served* Emotionally Disturbed; Learning Disabled. *Learning Problems* Memory Disabilities; Perceptual Disabilities; Thinking Disabilities; Reading Disabilities; Handwriting Disabilities; Spelling Disabilities; Arithmetic Disabilities; Written Expression. *Behavioral Problems* Attention Deficits; Hyperactivity; Hypoactivity; Impulsivity; Self-Aggression; Verbal Aggression; Physical Aggression; Indirect Aggression; Passive Aggression; Withdrawal. *Conditions Treated* Alcohol Abuse and/or Drug Abuse; Other Substance Abuse or Dependence; Disintegrative Psychoses; Schizophrenia; Convulsive Disorders; Phobias; Obsessions and Compulsions; Hysteria; Depression; Suicide; Anorexia Nervosa; Inadequacy/Immaturity; Personality Problems; Socialized Aggressive Reaction; Unsocialized Aggressive Reaction.
Services Provided Individual Therapy; Group Therapy; Parent Involvement; Family Therapy; Drug Therapy. *Professionals on Staff* Psychiatrists 50; Psychologists 50; Counselors 5; Social Workers 50; Nurses 50. *Service Facilities Available (with number of rooms)* Consultative (ERT); Resource Rooms. *Educational Professionals* Special Education Teachers 10; Crisis Teachers 4; Special Education Counselors 3. *Curricula* Traditional Academic; Individualized; Basic Skills; Prevocational. *Educational Intervention Approaches* Engineered Classroom; Precision Teaching; Progressive Discipline; Self-Control. *Degrees Awarded* High School Diploma.
Comments Accredited by the New England Association of Schools and Colleges, Arlington School offers both a departmentalized curriculum, specialized small-group instruction, and serial (group) tutoring.

Avalon Center—Avalon Schools

Old Stockbridge Rd, Lenox, MA 01240 (413) 637-1821
Year Established 1980
Contact David B Hastings, Prog Dir
Facility Information *Placement* Private Residential Care. *Number of Beds* 55. *Children/Adolescents Served* 55. *Sexes Served* Both. *Tuition Fees (Approx)* $47,000 - $61,000. *Sources of Funding* State Funds; Agencies of States other than MA. Summer school

available. *Teacher Certification Level* Elementary School; Junior High/Middle School. *Special Certification Level* ED; LD; MR; Special Needs.
Student/Patient Characteristics *Age Levels* 9-11; 12-14; 15-17; 18-21; Over 21. *IQ Ranges* 0-25; 26-40; 41-55; 56-70; 71-85. *Exceptionalities Served* Autistic; Emotionally Disturbed; Mentally Handicapped; Communication Disordered; Visually Impaired/Blind; Other Health Impaired. *Learning Problems* Memory Disabilities; Perceptual Disabilities; Thinking Disabilities; Oral Language Disabilities; Reading Disabilities; Handwriting Disabilities; Spelling Disabilities; Arithmetic Disabilities; Written Expression. *Behavioral Problems* Attention Deficits; Hyperactivity; Impulsivity; Self-Aggression; Verbal Aggression; Physical Aggression; Indirect Aggression; Passive Aggression; Withdrawal. *Conditions Treated* Early Infantile Autism; Disintegrative Psychoses; Schizophrenia; Personality Problems; Socialized Aggressive Reaction; Unsocialized Aggressive Reaction.
Services Provided Individual Therapy; Group Therapy; Parent Involvement; Behavior Therapy; Cognitive Developmental Therapy. *Professionals on Staff* Psychiatrists 1; Psychologists 3; Social Workers 1; Child Care Staff 81; Nurses 7. *Educational Professionals* Special Education Teachers 8. *Curricula* Individualized; Basic Skills; Prevocational. *Educational Intervention Approaches* Milieu Therapy.
Comments The premise at Avalon Center is that children improve in a highly-structured, supportive environment. Child care workers at a high ratio serve as the primary therapists, working within Treatment Teams which formulate and execute individual treatment plans. All students attend school in small groups with certified teachers.

Avalon School at High Point

W Mountain Rd, Lenox, MA 01240 (413) 637-2845
Year Established 1976
Contact Lawrence J Anastasi, Dir of Social Serv
Facility Information *Placement* Private Residential Care. *Number of Beds* 45. *Children/Adolescents Served* 45. *Sexes Served* Male. *Tuition Fees (Approx)* $33,000. *Sources of Funding* State Funds; P.L. 94-142. Summer school available. *Teacher Certification Level* Elementary School. *Special Certification Level* ED; LD; MR; Reading; Math.
Student/Patient Characteristics *Age Levels* 12-14; 15-17; 18-21. *IQ Ranges* 26-40; 41-55; 56-70; 71-85. *Exceptionalities Served* Autistic; Emotionally Disturbed; Learning Disabled; Mentally Handicapped; Communication Disordered; Hearing Impaired/Deaf. *Learning Problems* Memory Disabilities; Perceptual Disabilities; Thinking Disabilities; Oral Language Disabilities; Reading Disabilities; Handwriting Disabilities; Spelling Disabilities; Arithmetic Disabilities; Written Expression. *Behavioral Problems* Attention Deficits; Hyperactivity; Impulsivity; Self-Aggression;

Passive Aggression; Withdrawal. *Conditions Treated* Early Infantile Autism; Schizophrenia; Convulsive Disorders; Obsessions and Compulsions; Depression.

Services Provided Individual Therapy; Parent Involvement; Family Therapy; Drug Therapy. *Professionals on Staff* Psychiatrists 1; Psychologists 1; Social Workers 1; Child Care Staff 16; Nurses 1. *Service Facilities Available (with number of rooms)* Resource Rooms 1; Self-Contained Rooms 1; On-Campus Residential School 7. *Educational Professionals* Special Education Teachers 7; Career/Vocational Teachers 1. *Curricula* Prevocational.

Boston Public Schools—The McKinley Schools

108 Babson St, Mattapau, MA 02126 (617) 298-6972
Year Established 1978
Contact John Brown-Verre, Senior Prog Dir

Facility Information *Placement* Public School; Special School. *Children/Adolescents Served* 350. *Sexes Served* Both. *Tuition Fees (Approx)* $9,000. *Sources of Funding* State Funds; Medicaid; P.L. 94-142; City Funds; P.L.94-482. *Teacher Certification Level* Elementary School; Junior High/Middle School; High School. *Special Certification Level* ED; LD; Career/Vocational Education; Regular Education.

Student/Patient Characteristics *Age Levels* 5-8; 9-11; 12-14; 15-17; 18-21; Over 21. *IQ Ranges* 85-130. *Exceptionalities Served* Emotionally Disturbed; Learning Disabled. *Learning Problems* Memory Disabilities; Perceptual Disabilities; Thinking Disabilities; Oral Language Disabilities; Reading Disabilities; Handwriting Disabilities; Spelling Disabilities; Arithmetic Disabilities; Written Expression. *Behavioral Problems* Attention Deficits; Hyperactivity; Hypoactivity; Impulsivity; Self-Aggression; Verbal Aggression; Physical Aggression; Indirect Aggression; Passive Aggression; Withdrawal. *Conditions Treated* Alcohol Abuse and/or Drug Abuse; Other Substance Abuse or Dependence; Schizophrenia; Hysteria; Depression; Suicide; Inadequacy/Immaturity; Personality Problems; Socialized Aggressive Reaction; Unsocialized Aggressive Reaction.

Services Provided Individual Therapy; Group Therapy; Parent Involvement; Behavior Therapy; Family Therapy; Drug Therapy; Reality Therapy. *Professionals on Staff* Psychiatrists 1; Psychologists 2; Social Workers 15; Nurses 2; Psychotherapists 12. *Service Facilities Available (with number of rooms)* Self-Contained Rooms; Shops. *Educational Professionals* Special Education Teachers; Career/Vocational Teachers; Crisis Teachers; Paraprofessionals. *Curricula* Traditional Academic; Career/Vocational Education; Individualized; Basic Skills; Prevocational. *Educational Intervention Approaches* Progressive Discipline; Self-Control; Behavior Modification; Applied Behavior Analysis. *Degrees Awarded* Certificate of Attendance; High School Diploma.

Central Massachusetts Special Education Collaborative—Quimby School

305 Belmont St, Worcester, MA 01604 (617) 753-5159
Year Established 1972
Contact Robert E Hartnett, Dir

Facility Information *Placement* Public School; Special School. *Children/Adolescents Served* 30. *Sexes Served* Both. *Tuition Fees (Approx)* $8,000. *Sources of Funding* P.L. 94-142; Chapter 766. *Special Certification Level* ED; MR.

Student/Patient Characteristics *Age Levels* 9-11; 12-14; 15-17; 18-21. *IQ Ranges* 41-55; 56-70; 71-85; 85-130. *Exceptionalities Served* Autistic; Emotionally Disturbed; Learning Disabled; Mentally Handicapped; Communication Disordered. *Learning Problems* Memory Disabilities; Perceptual Disabilities; Thinking Disabilities; Oral Language Disabilities; Reading Disabilities; Handwriting Disabilities; Spelling Disabilities; Arithmetic Disabilities; Written Expression. *Behavioral Problems* Attention Deficits; Hyperactivity; Hypoactivity; Impulsivity; Self-Aggression; Verbal Aggression; Physical Aggression; Indirect Aggression; Passive Aggression; Withdrawal. *Conditions Treated* Early Infantile Autism; Schizophrenia; Aphasia; Phobias; Obsessions and Compulsions.

Services Provided Individual Therapy; Parent Involvement; Behavior Therapy. *Professionals on Staff* Psychologists. *Educational Professionals* Special Education Teachers 4; Paraprofessionals 5; Speech Therapist 1. *Curricula* Traditional Academic; Career/Vocational Education; Individualized; Basic Skills; Prevocational. *Educational Intervention Approaches* Progressive Discipline; Self-Control; Behavior Modification; Applied Behavior Analysis.

The Children's Study Home

Springfield, MA 01109 (413) 739-5626
Year Established 1865
Contact John R Jackson, Exec Dir

Facility Information *Placement* Special School; Private Residential Care. *Number of Beds* 23. *Children/Adolescents Served* 60. *Sexes Served* Both. *Tuition Fees (Approx)* $23,663 (residence); $29,134 (school and residence). *Sources of Funding* State Funds; Medicaid; Local School System. Summer school available. *Teacher Certification Level* Elementary School; Junior High/Middle School; High School. *Special Certification Level* ED; Speech and Hearing.

Student/Patient Characteristics *Age Levels* 5-8; 9-11; 12-14; 15-17; 18-21. *IQ Ranges* 56-70; 71-85; 85-130. *Exceptionalities Served* Emotionally Disturbed; Learning Disabled; Hearing Impaired/Deaf; Visually Impaired/Blind. *Learning Problems* Memory Disabilities; Perceptual Disabilities; Thinking Disabilities; Oral Language Disabilities; Reading Disabilities; Handwriting Disabilities; Spelling Disabilities; Arithmetic Disabilities; Written Expression. *Behavioral Problems* Attention Deficits; Hyperactivity; Hypoactivity; Impulsivity; Self-Aggression; Verbal Aggression; Physical Aggression; Indirect Aggression; Passive Aggression; Withdrawal. *Conditions Treated* Schizophrenia; Convulsive Disorders; Phobias; Obsessions and Compulsions; Hysteria; Depression; Suicide; Asthma; Anorexia Nervosa; Inadequacy/Immaturity; Personality Problems; Socialized Aggressive Reaction; Unsocialized Aggressive Reaction.

Services Provided Individual Therapy; Parent Involvement; Behavior Therapy; Family Therapy; Play Therapy. *Professionals on Staff* Psychiatrists 1; Psychologists 1; Social Workers 4; Child Care Staff 17; Nurses 1. *Service Facilities Available (with number of rooms)* Itinerants 4; Transition Rooms 1; Self-Contained Rooms 10; On-Campus Residential School 2. *Educational Professionals* Special Education Teachers 12; Paraprofessionals 4. *Curricula* Traditional Academic; Career/Vocational Education; Individualized; Basic Skills; Prevocational. *Educational Intervention Approaches* Self-Control; Behavior Modification; Applied Behavior Analysis. *Degrees Awarded* High School Diploma; Graduate Equivalency Diploma.

Comments The educational programs are fully accredited by the Massachusetts Department of Education. The agency provides an alternative educational experience for children living in residence plus children who may live at home, but are unable to cope with the stresses of public school. Individual educational plans are developed for each child. Small classrooms are provided to enhance learning.

DeSisto Schools Inc

Rte 183 Interlaken, West Stockbridge, MA 01266 (413) 298-3776
Year Established 1978
Contact Constance L Real, Dir of Admissions

Facility Information *Placement* Private Residential Care. *Number of Beds* 165. *Children/Adolescents Served* 165. *Sexes Served* Both. *Tuition Fees (Approx)* $12,900; $3,000 (summer school). *Sources of Funding* Health Insurance. Summer school available. *Teacher Certification Level* High School. *Special Certification Level* ED; LD; MR.

Student/Patient Characteristics *Age Levels* 12-14; 15-17; 18-21. *IQ Ranges* 85-130. *Exceptionalities Served* Emotionally Disturbed; Learning Disabled; Gifted. *Learning Problems* Memory Disabilities; Perceptual Disabilities; Thinking Disabilities; Oral Language Disabilities; Reading Disabilities; Spelling Disabilities; Arithmetic Disabilities; Written Expression. *Behavioral Problems* Attention Deficits; Hyperactivity; Hypoactivity; Impulsivity;

Self-Aggression; Verbal Aggression; Physical Aggression; Indirect Aggression; Passive Aggression; Withdrawal. *Conditions Treated* Alcohol Abuse and/or Drug Abuse; Other Substance Abuse or Dependence; Disintegrative Psychoses; Schizophrenia; Phobias; Obsessions and Compulsions; Hysteria; Depression; Suicide; Asthma; Anorexia Nervosa; Ulcerative Colitis; Inadequacy/Immaturity; Personality Problems; Socialized Aggressive Reaction; Unsocialized Aggressive Reaction; Bipolar Affective Disorders.

Services Provided Individual Therapy; Group Therapy; Parent Involvement; Behavior Therapy; Cognitive Developmental Therapy; Family Therapy; Filial Therapy; Drug Therapy; Reality Therapy; Psychodrama. *Professionals on Staff* Psychiatrists 1; Psychologists 2; Counselors 2; Social Workers 6. *Service Facilities Available (with number of rooms)* Resource Rooms 2; Self-Contained Rooms 12. *Educational Professionals* Regular School Teachers 15; Special Education Teachers 3; Special Education Counselors 1; Therapists. *Curricula* Traditional Academic; Individualized; Basic Skills. *Educational Intervention Approaches* Progressive Discipline; Self-Control; Behavior Modification; Applied Behavior Analysis. *Degrees Awarded* High School Diploma.

Comments DeSisto offers a high school academic program with a therapy component for children with educational and emotional needs. It offers a highly structured environment in which problems are confronted.

The Devereux Schools at Rutland

2 Miles Rd, Rutland, MA 01543 (617) 886-4746
Year Established 1955
Contact Kenneth M Ayers, Admissions Dir

Facility Information *Placement* Private Residential Care. *Number of Beds* 136. *Children/Adolescents Served* 126. *Sexes Served* Both. *Sources of Funding* State Funds; P.L. 94-142; Private. Summer school available. *Teacher Certification Level* Elementary School; Junior High/Middle School. *Special Certification Level* ED; LD; MR; Career/Vocational Education; Reading; Math.

Student/Patient Characteristics *Age Levels* 5-8; 9-11; 12-14; 15-17; 18-21. *IQ Ranges* 26-40; 41-55; 56-70; 71-85; 85-130; Above 130. *Exceptionalities Served* Autistic; Emotionally Disturbed; Learning Disabled; Mentally Handicapped. *Learning Problems* Memory Disabilities; Perceptual Disabilities; Thinking Disabilities; Oral Language Disabilities; Reading Disabilities; Handwriting Disabilities; Spelling Disabilities; Arithmetic Disabilities; Written Expression. *Behavioral Problems* Attention Deficits; Hyperactivity; Hypoactivity; Impulsivity; Self-Aggression; Verbal Aggression; Physical Aggression; Indirect Aggression; Passive Aggression; Withdrawal. *Conditions Treated* Schizophrenia; Convulsive Disorders; Phobias; Obsessions and Compulsions; Hysteria; Depression; Personality Problems; Socialized Aggressive Reaction; Unsocialized Aggressive Reaction.

Services Provided Individual Therapy; Group Therapy; Parent Involvement; Drug Therapy; Music Therapy; Play Therapy. *Professionals on Staff* Psychiatrists 3; Psychologists 2; Counselors 4; Social Workers 7; Child Care Staff; Nurses. *Educational Professionals* Special Education Teachers; Career/Vocational Teachers; Paraprofessionals. *Curricula* Career/Vocational Education; Individualized; Basic Skills; Prevocational. *Educational Intervention Approaches* Behavior Modification.

Doctor Franklin Perkins School

971 Main St, Lancaster, MA 01523 (617) 365-7376
Contact Andrea J Spencer, Prog Dir

Facility Information *Placement* Residential School. *Number of Beds* 57. *Children/Adolescents Served* 57. *Sexes Served* Both. *Sources of Funding* State Funds; P.L. 94-142; State Agencies; Private. Summer school available. *Special Certification Level* MR; Art; Music; Adaptive Physical Education.

Student/Patient Characteristics *Age Levels* 5-8; 9-11; 12-14; 15-17; 18-21; Over 21. *IQ Ranges* 26-40; 41-55; 56-70; 71-85. *Exceptionalities Served* Emotionally Disturbed; Mentally Handicapped; Communication Disordered. *Learning Problems* Memory Disabilities; Perceptual Disabilities; Thinking Disabilities; Oral Language Disabilities; Reading Disabilities. *Behavioral Problems*

Attention Deficits; Hyperactivity; Hypoactivity; Impulsivity; Self-Aggression; Verbal Aggression; Physical Aggression; Indirect Aggression; Passive Aggression; Withdrawal.

Services Provided Parent Involvement; Behavior Therapy; Music Therapy. *Professionals on Staff* Psychiatrists; Psychologists; Social Workers 3; Child Care Staff 72; Nurses 2; Occupational Therapy; Speech Therapy. *Service Facilities Available (with number of rooms)* Self-Contained Rooms. *Educational Professionals* Special Education Teachers 8; Paraprofessionals 18. *Curricula* Career/Vocational Education; Individualized; Basic Skills; Prevocational. *Educational Intervention Approaches* Precision Teaching; Progressive Discipline; Self-Control; Behavior Modification; Applied Behavior Analysis. *Degrees Awarded* Certificate of Attendance.

Douglas A Thom Clinic Inc

315 Dartmouth St, Boston, MA 02116 (617) 266-1222
Year Established 1921
Contact Jean Lau Chin, Co-Dir

Facility Information *Placement* Outpatient Mental Health Clinic. *Children/Adolescents Served* 300. *Sexes Served* Both. *Sources of Funding* HEW; Health Insurance; Medicaid.

Student/Patient Characteristics *Age Levels* 5-8; 9-11; 12-14; 15-17; 18-21. *IQ Ranges* 85-130. *Exceptionalities Served* Emotionally Disturbed; Learning Disabled. *Learning Problems* Memory Disabilities; Perceptual Disabilities; Thinking Disabilities; Oral Language Disabilities; Reading Disabilities; Handwriting Disabilities; Spelling Disabilities; Arithmetic Disabilities; Written Expression. *Behavioral Problems* Attention Deficits; Hyperactivity; Hypoactivity; Impulsivity; Self-Aggression; Verbal Aggression; Physical Aggression; Indirect Aggression; Passive Aggression; Withdrawal. *Conditions Treated* Phobias; Obsessions and Compulsions; Hysteria; Depression; Inadequacy/Immaturity; Personality Problems; Socialized Aggressive Reaction; Unsocialized Aggressive Reaction.

Services Provided Individual Therapy; Group Therapy; Parent Involvement; Cognitive Developmental Therapy; Family Therapy; Play Therapy. *Professionals on Staff* Psychiatrists 2; Psychologists 6; Social Workers 6.

Comments The clinic is an outpatient association providing psychotherapeutic and psychoeducational services to children and families with learning and emotional problems.

Efficacy Research Institute of Framingham

569 Salem End Rd, Framingham, MA 01701 (617) 620-0020
Year Established 1980
Contact Susan E McSweeney, Asst Dir

Facility Information *Placement* Special School; Private Residential Care; Special Program. *Number of Beds* 35. *Children/Adolescents Served* 52. *Sexes Served* Both. *Tuition Fees (Approx)* $21,837-$28,441. *Sources of Funding* State Funds; P.L. 94-142. *Teacher Certification Level* Elementary School; Junior High/Middle School; High School. *Special Certification Level* ED; LD; MR.

Student/Patient Characteristics *Age Levels* 0-4; 5-8; 9-11; 12-14; 15-17; 18-21; Over 21. *IQ Ranges* 0-25; 26-40; 41-55. *Exceptionalities Served* Autistic; Mentally Handicapped; Communication Disordered. *Learning Problems* Memory Disabilities; Perceptual Disabilities; Thinking Disabilities; Oral Language Disabilities; Reading Disabilities; Handwriting Disabilities; Spelling Disabilities; Arithmetic Disabilities; Written Expression. *Behavioral Problems* Attention Deficits; Self-Aggression; Physical Aggression; Withdrawal. *Conditions Treated* Early Infantile Autism.

Services Provided Parent Involvement; Behavior Therapy; Family Therapy. *Professionals on Staff* Psychologists 1; Counselors 9; Nurses 3. *Service Facilities Available (with number of rooms)* On-Campus Residential School. *Educational Professionals* Special Education Teachers 23; Career/Vocational Teachers 1; Special Education Counselors 31. *Curricula* Individualized; Basic Skills; Prevocational. *Educational Intervention Approaches* Behavior Modification; Applied Behavior Analysis.

Efficacy Research Institute of Taunton Inc

Box 2072, 60 Hodges Ave Ext, Taunton, MA 02780
(617) 822-9628
Year Established 1974
Contact Katherine E Foster, Exec Dir
Facility Information *Placement* Private Residential Care. *Number of Beds* 20. *Children/Adolescents Served* 20. *Sexes Served* Both. *Tuition Fees (Approx)* $38,227. *Sources of Funding* State Funds; P.L. 94-142; Division of Mental Health. *Special Certification Level* ED; LD; MR; Severe Special Needs.
Student/Patient Characteristics *Age Levels* 9-11; 12-14; 15-17; 18-21; Over 21. *IQ Ranges* 26-40; 41-55; 56-70. *Exceptionalities Served* Autistic; Emotionally Disturbed; Learning Disabled; Mentally Handicapped; Communication Disordered. *Learning Problems* Memory Disabilities; Perceptual Disabilities; Oral Language Disabilities; Reading Disabilities; Handwriting Disabilities; Spelling Disabilities; Arithmetic Disabilities; Written Expression. *Conditions Treated* Early Infantile Autism.
Services Provided Parent Involvement; Behavior Therapy; Cognitive Developmental Therapy; Family Therapy. *Professionals on Staff* Psychologists 1; Social Workers 1; Nurses 1. *Service Facilities Available (with number of rooms)* Self-Contained Rooms 7; Pre-Vocational 1. *Educational Professionals* Special Education Teachers 20; Adapted Physical Education Instructor 1. *Curricula* Individualized; Basic Skills; Prevocational. *Educational Intervention Approaches* Precision Teaching; Behavior Modification; Applied Behavior Analysis.
Comments The institute is a private, nonprofit, residential facility for students with special education and emotional needs. It serves a co-ed population of 20 students that range in age from 8-21. These students typically have language delays, poor social interactions, and behavior problems including non-compliance, self-stimulatory behavior, moderate aggression, and self-injurious behavior. Individualized behavioral and educational programming is provided in the areas of self-care, language development, behavior problem reduction, social skills development, reading, math, writing, activities of daily living, prevocational skills, and gross motor skills.

Everett House

232 Centre St, Dorchester, MA 02124 (617) 282-0350
Year Established 1854
Contact Judith McCarthy, Prog Dir
Facility Information *Placement* Private Residential Care. *Number of Beds* 8. *Children/Adolescents Served* 8. *Sexes Served* Female. *Room and Board Fees (Approx)* $68. *Tuition Fees (Approx)* $24,950.
Student/Patient Characteristics *Age Levels* 15-17. *IQ Ranges* 71-85. *Exceptionalities Served* Emotionally Disturbed. *Behavioral Problems* Verbal Aggression; Passive Aggression; Withdrawal.
Services Provided Individual Therapy; Group Therapy; Parent Involvement; Behavior Therapy; Family Therapy. *Professionals on Staff* Social Workers 1; Child Care Staff 9.

Gould Farm

Gould Rd, Monterey, MA 01245 (413) 528-0703
Year Established 1913
Contact Kent D Smith, Exec Dir
Facility Information *Placement* Private Residential Care; Psychiatric Rehabilitation. *Children/Adolescents Served* 40. *Sexes Served* Both. *Room and Board Fees (Approx)* $70-$80. *Sources of Funding* Health Insurance; Private Payments; Contributions. Summer school available.
Student/Patient Characteristics *Age Levels* 15-17; 18-21; Over 21. *IQ Ranges* 71-85; 85-130; Above 130. *Exceptionalities Served* Emotionally Disturbed. *Learning Problems* Thinking Disabilities. *Behavioral Problems* Attention Deficits; Impulsivity; Self-Aggression; Verbal Aggression; Indirect Aggression; Passive Aggression; Withdrawal. *Conditions Treated* Other Substance Abuse or Dependence; Disintegrative Psychoses; Schizophrenia; Pho-

bias; Obsessions and Compulsions; Hysteria; Depression; Suicide; Inadequacy/Immaturity; Personality Problems; Socialized Aggressive Reaction.
Services Provided Individual Therapy; Group Therapy; Parent Involvement; Family Therapy; Drug Therapy; Art Therapy; Work Adjustment. *Professionals on Staff* Psychiatrists 1; Counselors 3; Social Workers 1; Nurses 1; Program Coordinators 20. *Curricula* Career/Vocational Education; Individualized; Basic Skills; Prevocational.

Greater Fall River Association for Mental Health Inc Clinic

101 Rock St, Fall River, MA 02720 (617) 676-8187
Contact Arthur F Cassidy, Exec Dir
Facility Information *Placement* Mental Health Clinic. *Children/Adolescents Served* 400. *Sexes Served* Both. *Sources of Funding* State Funds; Health Insurance; Medicaid; Medicare.
Comments The purpose of the clinic is to provide diagnostic treatment and consultation outpatient services to agencies and to children and adults of Greater Fall River who are in need of mental health services. There is sometimes a waiting list for services. About 250 interviews a month are provided.

Hall-Mercer Children's Center of the McLean Hospital

115 Mill St, Belmont, MA 02178 (617) 855-2804
Year Established 1973
Contact Joan M Cottler, Social Work Dir
Facility Information *Placement* Private Residential Care; Private Day Care. *Number of Beds* 43. *Children/Adolescents Served* 43 (inpatients); 130 (outpatients). *Sexes Served* Both. *Room and Board Fees (Approx)* $527. *Sources of Funding* State Funds; Health Insurance; Self-Pay. Summer school available. *Teacher Certification Level* Elementary School; Junior High/Middle School. *Special Certification Level* ED; LD; MR.
Student/Patient Characteristics *Age Levels* 0-4; 5-8; 9-11; 12-14; 15-17. *IQ Ranges* 56-70; 71-85; 85-130; Above 130. *Exceptionalities Served* Autistic; Emotionally Disturbed; Learning Disabled; Mentally Handicapped. *Learning Problems* Memory Disabilities; Perceptual Disabilities; Thinking Disabilities; Oral Language Disabilities; Reading Disabilities; Handwriting Disabilities; Spelling Disabilities; Arithmetic Disabilities; Written Expression; Cognitive Disabilities. *Behavioral Problems* Attention Deficits; Hyperactivity; Hypoactivity; Impulsivity; Self-Aggression; Verbal Aggression; Physical Aggression; Indirect Aggression; Passive Aggression; Withdrawal. *Conditions Treated* Early Infantile Autism; Disintegrative Psychoses; Schizophrenia; Convulsive Disorders; Phobias; Obsessions and Compulsions; Hysteria; Depression; Suicide; Asthma; Anorexia Nervosa; Inadequacy/Immaturity; Personality Problems; Socialized Aggressive Reaction; Unsocialized Aggressive Reaction.
Services Provided Individual Therapy; Group Therapy; Parent Involvement; Behavior Therapy; Cognitive Developmental Therapy; Family Therapy; Filial Therapy; Drug Therapy; Art Therapy; Music Therapy; Reality Therapy; Play Therapy; Psychodrama; Psychopharmacotherapy; Cognitive Control Therapy; Occupational and Recreational Therapy; Milieu Therapy. *Professionals on Staff* Psychiatrists 11.3; Psychologists 8.85; Social Workers 7; Child Care Staff 42; Nurses 31.6; Occupational Therapists; Pediatricians 2. *Service Facilities Available (with number of rooms)* Consultative (ERT) 2; Resource Rooms 1; Transition Rooms 1; Self-Contained Rooms 6; Hospital-Based Psychoeducation Program. *Educational Professionals* Special Education Teachers 12. *Curricula* Traditional Academic; Career/Vocational Education; Individualized; Basic Skills; Prevocational; Cognitive Training. *Educational Intervention Approaches* Precision Teaching; Progressive Discipline; Self-Control; Behavior Modification; Applied Behavior Analysis; Cognitive Restructuring; Cognitive Therapy.

Comments The Hall-Mercer Children's Center of the McLean Hospital offers comprehensive diagnostic and treatment services for children from infancy through adolescence with psychiatric illness. Multidisciplinary teams work with each child and family to assess their biological, developmental, emotional, social, educational, and cognitive difficulties and strengths. Services are integrated with the services of the child's community for continuity of care.

Harbor Schools Inc

11 Market Sq, Newburyport, MA 01950 (617) 462-3151
Year Established 1972
Contact Arthur C DiMauro, Exec Dir

Facility Information *Placement* Private Residential Care. *Number of Beds* 76. *Children/Adolescents Served* 76. *Sexes Served* Both. *Room and Board Fees (Approx)* $83. *Sources of Funding* State Funds; Municipalities; Private. Summer school available. *Teacher Certification Level* Elementary School; Junior High/Middle School; High School. *Special Certification Level* ED.

Student/Patient Characteristics *Age Levels* 9-11; 12-14; 15-17; 18-21. *Exceptionalities Served* Emotionally Disturbed; Behavior Disorders. *Learning Problems* Memory Disabilities; Perceptual Disabilities; Thinking Disabilities; Oral Language Disabilities; Reading Disabilities; Handwriting Disabilities; Spelling Disabilities; Arithmetic Disabilities; Written Expression. *Behavioral Problems* Attention Deficits; Hyperactivity; Impulsivity; Self-Aggression; Verbal Aggression; Physical Aggression; Indirect Aggression; Passive Aggression; Withdrawal. *Conditions Treated* Schizophrenia; Phobias; Obsessions and Compulsions; Hysteria; Depression; Suicide; Inadequacy/Immaturity; Personality Problems; Socialized Aggressive Reaction; Unsocialized Aggressive Reaction.

Services Provided Individual Therapy; Group Therapy; Parent Involvement; Behavior Therapy; Cognitive Developmental Therapy; Family Therapy; Reality Therapy; Play Therapy. *Professionals on Staff* Psychiatrists 2; Psychologists 4; Social Workers 6; Child Care Staff 35; Nurses 1. *Service Facilities Available (with number of rooms)* Self-Contained Rooms 16; On-Campus Residential School 16. *Educational Professionals* Special Education Teachers 8; Career/Vocational Teachers 4. *Curricula* Career/Vocational Education; Individualized; Basic Skills; Prevocational. *Educational Intervention Approaches* Engineered Classroom; Progressive Discipline; Self-Control; Behavior Modification; Applied Behavior Analysis; Creative Conditioning.

Independence House of Avalon Inc

PO Box 90, S Main St, Sheffield, MA 01257 (413) 229-2319
Year Established 1982
Contact Paula J McPeek, Dir

Facility Information *Placement* Private Residential Care. *Number of Beds* 12. *Children/Adolescents Served* 12. *Sexes Served* Male. *Tuition Fees (Approx)* $35,000. *Sources of Funding* State Funds. Summer school available. *Special Certification Level* ED; LD; MR; Special Needs.

Student/Patient Characteristics *Age Levels* 15-17; 18-21. *Exceptionalities Served* Autistic; Emotionally Disturbed; Learning Disabled; Mentally Handicapped; Communication Disordered; Hearing Impaired/Deaf; Other Health Impaired; Physically Handicapped. *Learning Problems* Memory Disabilities; Perceptual Disabilities; Thinking Disabilities; Oral Language Disabilities; Reading Disabilities; Handwriting Disabilities; Spelling Disabilities; Arithmetic Disabilities; Written Expression. *Behavioral Problems* Attention Deficits; Hyperactivity; Hypoactivity; Impulsivity; Self-Aggression; Verbal Aggression; Physical Aggression; Indirect Aggression; Passive Aggression; Withdrawal. *Conditions Treated* Early Infantile Autism; Schizophrenia; Aphasia; Convulsive Disorders; Phobias; Obsessions and Compulsions; Depression; Inadequacy/Immaturity; Unsocialized Aggressive Reaction.

Services Provided Individual Therapy; Parent Involvement; Behavior Therapy; Cognitive Developmental Therapy; Drug Therapy; Art Therapy; Music Therapy; Reality Therapy; Play Therapy. *Professionals on Staff* Psychiatrists 1; Psychologists 1; Counselors 1; Social Workers 1; Child Care Staff 12; Nurses 1. *Service Facilities Available (with number of rooms)* Consultative (ERT) 1; Itinerants 6; Self-Contained Rooms 2; On-Campus Residential School 2. *Educational Professionals* Special Education Teachers 2; Paraprofessionals 8. *Curricula* Individualized. *Educational Intervention Approaches* Precision Teaching; Progressive Discipline; Self-Control; Behavior Modification; Applied Behavior Analysis; Creative Conditioning.

The Institute Day School

475 Varnum Ave, Lowell, MA 01854 (617) 454-4234
Year Established 1978
Contact Lori Fowler, Ed Dir

Facility Information *Placement* Special School. *Children/Adolescents Served* 45. *Sexes Served* Both. *Sources of Funding* State Funds. *Teacher Certification Level* Elementary School; Junior High/Middle School; High School. *Special Certification Level* ED; LD; MR; Career/Vocational Education.

Student/Patient Characteristics *Age Levels* 5-8; 9-11; 12-14; 15-17; 18-21. *IQ Ranges* 71-85; 85-130. *Exceptionalities Served* Emotionally Disturbed; Learning Disabled. *Learning Problems* Perceptual Disabilities; Handwriting Disabilities; Spelling Disabilities; Written Expression. *Behavioral Problems* Attention Deficits; Hyperactivity; Hypoactivity; Impulsivity; Self-Aggression; Verbal Aggression; Physical Aggression; Indirect Aggression; Passive Aggression; Withdrawal. *Conditions Treated* Depression; Suicide; Inadequacy/Immaturity; Personality Problems; Socialized Aggressive Reaction; Unsocialized Aggressive Reaction.

Services Provided Individual Therapy; Group Therapy; Parent Involvement; Behavior Therapy. *Professionals on Staff* Counselors 6; Social Workers 1; Nurses 1. *Service Facilities Available (with number of rooms)* Consultative (ERT) 2; Transition Rooms 1; Self-Contained Rooms 5. *Educational Professionals* Special Education Teachers 5; Career/Vocational Teachers 1; Crisis Teachers 1; Special Education Counselors 4. *Curricula* Traditional Academic; Career/Vocational Education; Individualized; Basic Skills; Prevocational. *Educational Intervention Approaches* Precision Teaching; Self-Control; Creative Conditioning. *Degrees Awarded* Certificate of Attendance; High School Diploma.

Comments The Institute Day School is a private, therapeutic day placement for individuals experiencing social-emotional problems. Treatment is provided mainly through therapeutic peer groups by trained professionals serving ages 8-18.

Institute for Developmental Disabilities—Crystal Springs School

38 Narrows Rd, Assonet, MA 02702 (617) 644-2214
Year Established 1954
Contact Charles B Young, Exec Dir

Facility Information *Placement* Special School; Private Residential Care. *Number of Beds* 95. *Children/Adolescents Served* 105. *Sexes Served* Both. *Tuition Fees (Approx)* $32,398 (regular residential); $40,376 (behavior development unit). *Sources of Funding* State Funds; Health Insurance; Medicaid; P.L. 94-142; Private Payment. Summer school available. *Teacher Certification Level* Elementary School. *Special Certification Level* MR.

Student/Patient Characteristics *Age Levels* 0-4; 5-8; 9-11; 12-14; 15-17; 18-21; Over 21. *IQ Ranges* 0-25; 26-40; 41-55; 56-70. *Exceptionalities Served* Emotionally Disturbed; Mentally Handicapped; Communication Disordered; Hearing Impaired/Deaf; Visually Impaired/Blind; Other Health Impaired; Physically Handicapped. *Learning Problems* Handwriting Disabilities; Spelling Disabilities; Arithmetic Disabilities; Written Expression. *Behavioral Problems* Attention Deficits; Hyperactivity; Hypoactivity; Impulsivity; Self-Aggression; Physical Aggression; Withdrawal. *Conditions Treated* Convulsive Disorders; Unsocialized Aggressive Reaction.

Services Provided Parent Involvement; Behavior Therapy. *Professionals on Staff* Psychiatrists; Psychologists 2; Social Workers 1; Child Care Staff 65; Nurses 11; Physical Therapist 1; Occupational Therapist 1; Adaptive Physical Education 1; Speech and Hearing 2. *Service Facilities Available (with number of rooms)* Self-Contained Rooms; On-Campus Residential School. *Educational Professionals* Special Education Teachers 10; Career/ Vocational Teachers 1; Paraprofessionals 10. *Curricula* Individualized. *Educational Intervention Approaches* Behavior Modification.

Institute for Family and Life Learning Residential School

78 Liberty St, Danvers, MA 01923 (617) 777-4480
Year Established 1976
Contact Shelby Liner, Exec Asst
Facility Information *Placement* Private Residential Care. *Number of Beds* 39. *Children/Adolescents Served* 39. *Sexes Served* Both. *Room and Board Fees (Approx)* $74. *Tuition Fees (Approx)* $27,013. *Sources of Funding* State Funds; P.L. 94-142; Chapter 766. Summer school available. *Teacher Certification Level* High School. *Special Certification Level* ED; LD; Reading.
Student/Patient Characteristics *Age Levels* 15-17; 18-21. *IQ Ranges* 71-85; 85-130; Above 130. *Exceptionalities Served* Emotionally Disturbed; Learning Disabled. *Learning Problems* Memory Disabilities; Perceptual Disabilities; Thinking Disabilities; Oral Language Disabilities; Reading Disabilities; Handwriting Disabilities; Spelling Disabilities; Arithmetic Disabilities; Written Expression. *Behavioral Problems* Attention Deficits; Hyperactivity; Hypoactivity; Impulsivity; Self-Aggression; Verbal Aggression; Physical Aggression; Indirect Aggression; Passive Aggression; Withdrawal. *Conditions Treated* Alcohol Abuse and/or Drug Abuse; Other Substance Abuse or Dependence; Depression; Suicide; Inadequacy/Immaturity; Personality Problems; Socialized Aggressive Reaction; Unsocialized Aggressive Reaction.
Services Provided Individual Therapy; Group Therapy; Parent Involvement; Behavior Therapy; Family Therapy; Reality Therapy. *Professionals on Staff* Psychiatrists 1; Counselors 4; Child Care Staff 10. *Service Facilities Available (with number of rooms)* Self-Contained Rooms 8. *Educational Professionals* Regular School Teachers; Special Education Teachers 6; Career/Vocational Teachers 1; Paraprofessionals 10. *Curricula* Individualized. *Degrees Awarded* High School Diploma.

Italian Home for Children

1125 Centre St, Jamaica Plain, MA 02130 (617) 524-3116
Year Established 1917
Contact Christopher F Small, Exec Dir
Facility Information *Placement* Special School; Private Residential Care. *Number of Beds* 44. *Children/Adolescents Served* 44. *Sexes Served* Both. *Room and Board Fees (Approx)* $57. *Tuition Fees (Approx)* $20,870. *Sources of Funding* State Funds; Donations. Summer school available. *Teacher Certification Level* Elementary School. *Special Certification Level* ED.
Student/Patient Characteristics *Age Levels* 5-8; 9-11; 12-14. *IQ Ranges* 71-85; 85-130; Above 130. *Exceptionalities Served* Emotionally Disturbed; Learning Disabled. *Learning Problems* Memory Disabilities; Perceptual Disabilities; Thinking Disabilities; Oral Language Disabilities; Reading Disabilities; Handwriting Disabilities; Spelling Disabilities; Arithmetic Disabilities; Written Expression. *Behavioral Problems* Attention Deficits; Hyperactivity; Impulsivity; Self-Aggression; Verbal Aggression; Physical Aggression; Passive Aggression. *Conditions Treated* Phobias; Obsessions and Compulsions; Hysteria; Depression; Asthma; Inadequacy/Immaturity; Personality Problems; Unsocialized Aggressive Reaction.
Services Provided Individual Therapy; Group Therapy; Parent Involvement; Behavior Therapy; Family Therapy; Play Therapy; Milieu Therapy. *Professionals on Staff* Psychologists 1; Social Workers 8; Child Care Staff 24. *Service Facilities Available (with number of rooms)* Resource Rooms 1; Self-Contained Rooms 2. *Educational Professionals* Special Education Teachers 2; Occupa-

tional Therapist 1; Speech and Language Therapist 1. *Curricula* Individualized; Basic Skills; Prevocational. *Educational Intervention Approaches* Self-Control; Behavior Modification.
Comments The Italian Home for Children is a residential treatment program for 44 emotionally disturbed, latency-aged children. Residents are integrated into the public schools and participate in community based activities.

John C Corrigan Mental Health Center

49 Hillside St, Fall River, MA 02720 (617) 678-2901
Year Established 1972
Contact Ann Castro, Dir of Children's Serv
Facility Information *Placement* Special Program. *Number of Beds* 2. *Children/Adolescents Served* 200. *Sexes Served* Both. *Sources of Funding* State Funds.
Student/Patient Characteristics *Age Levels* 5-8; 9-11; 12-14; 15-17; 18-21; Over 21. *IQ Ranges* 71-85; 85-130; Above 130. *Exceptionalities Served* Emotionally Disturbed; Learning Disabled; Mentally Handicapped; Communication Disordered. *Learning Problems* Thinking Disabilities; Reading Disabilities. *Behavioral Problems* Attention Deficits; Hyperactivity; Impulsivity; Self-Aggression; Verbal Aggression; Physical Aggression; Indirect Aggression; Passive Aggression; Withdrawal. *Conditions Treated* Disintegrative Psychoses; Schizophrenia; Aphasia; Convulsive Disorders; Phobias; Obsessions and Compulsions; Hysteria; Depression; Suicide; Anorexia Nervosa; Inadequacy/Immaturity; Personality Problems; Socialized Aggressive Reaction.
Services Provided Individual Therapy; Group Therapy; Parent Involvement; Behavior Therapy; Cognitive Developmental Therapy; Biofeedback; Family Therapy; Play Therapy. *Professionals on Staff* Psychiatrists 1; Psychologists 1; Counselors 8; Social Workers 3; Nurses 1. *Service Facilities Available (with number of rooms)* Consultative (ERT).

Judge Baker Guidance Center

295 Longwood Ave, Boston, MA 02115 (617) 232-8390
Contact Mary Phinney, Intake Coord
Facility Information *Placement* Special School; Guidance Center. *Number of Beds* 27. *Sexes Served* Both. *Room and Board Fees (Approx)* Sliding Scale. *Tuition Fees (Approx)* $17,081; Sliding Scale. *Sources of Funding* Health Insurance; Medicaid; P.L. 94-142; Grants; Fundraising; Private Pay. Summer school available. *Teacher Certification Level* Elementary School; Junior High/Middle School.
Student/Patient Characteristics *Age Levels* 0-4; 5-8; 9-11; 12-14; 15-17; 18-21. *Exceptionalities Served* Autistic; Emotionally Disturbed; Learning Disabled; Mentally Handicapped; Other Health Impaired; Physically Handicapped. *Learning Problems* Memory Disabilities; Perceptual Disabilities; Thinking Disabilities; Oral Language Disabilities; Reading Disabilities; Handwriting Disabilities; Spelling Disabilities; Arithmetic Disabilities; Written Expression. *Behavioral Problems* Attention Deficits; Hyperactivity; Hypoactivity; Impulsivity; Self-Aggression; Verbal Aggression; Physical Aggression; Indirect Aggression; Passive Aggression; Withdrawal.
Services Provided Individual Therapy; Parent Involvement; Behavior Therapy; Cognitive Developmental Therapy; Biofeedback; Family Therapy; Drug Therapy; Art Therapy; Play Therapy; Expressive Arts Therapy. *Professionals on Staff* Psychiatrists 18; Psychologists 45; Social Workers 34; Child Care Staff 10; Nurses 20. *Educational Professionals* Special Education Teachers 12; Special Education Counselors 10; Paraprofessionals 20. *Curricula* Individualized; Basic Skills; Prevocational. *Educational Intervention Approaches* Precision Teaching; Progressive Discipline; Self-Control; Behavior Modification. *Degrees Awarded* Certificate of Attendance; 8th Grade Diploma.
Comments JBGC is a multiservice child mental health facility affiliated with a major teaching hospital. It provides services to a predominantly inner city population in a variety of settings and modalities.

League School of Boston Inc

225 Nevada St, Newtonville, MA 02160 (617) 964-3260
Year Established 1966
Contact Barbara T Schaechter, Exec Dir
Facility Information *Placement* Private Day School. *Number of Beds* 7. *Children/Adolescents Served* 65. *Sexes Served* Both. *Tuition Fees (Approx)* $15,085 (day school); $44,084 (group home). *Sources of Funding* State Funds; P.L. 94-142. Summer school available. *Teacher Certification Level* Elementary School; Junior High/Middle School; High School.
Student/Patient Characteristics *Age Levels* 0-4; 5-8; 9-11; 12-14; 15-17; 18-21; Over 21. *IQ Ranges* 26-40; 41-55; 56-70; 71-85; 85-130. *Exceptionalities Served* Autistic; Emotionally Disturbed; Learning Disabled; Mentally Handicapped; Communication Disordered. *Learning Problems* Memory Disabilities; Perceptual Disabilities; Thinking Disabilities; Oral Language Disabilities; Reading Disabilities; Handwriting Disabilities; Spelling Disabilities; Arithmetic Disabilities; Written Expression. *Behavioral Problems* Attention Deficits; Hyperactivity; Hypoactivity; Impulsivity; Self-Aggression; Verbal Aggression; Physical Aggression; Withdrawal. *Conditions Treated* Early Infantile Autism; Disintegrative Psychoses; Schizophrenia; Aphasia; Convulsive Disorders; Phobias.
Services Provided Individual Therapy; Group Therapy; Parent Involvement; Behavior Therapy; Family Therapy; Drug Therapy. *Professionals on Staff* Psychiatrists 1; Social Workers 5.5; Child Care Staff 7; Nurses 1; Occupational Therapist 1; Speech and Language Pathologist 1. *Service Facilities Available (with number of rooms)* Special School 40. *Educational Professionals* Special Education Teachers 28; Career/Vocational Teachers 2. *Curricula* Individualized; Basic Skills; Prevocational; Work Training. *Educational Intervention Approaches* Behavior Modification.

Lighthouse School

180 Old Westford Rd, Chelmsford, MA 01863 (617) 256-9300
Year Established 1968
Contact Timothy Fitzpatrick, Prog Coord
Facility Information *Placement* Private Day Care. *Children/Adolescents Served* 100. *Sexes Served* Both. *Tuition Fees (Approx)* $9,000. *Sources of Funding* State Funds; P.L. 94-142. *Special Certification Level* ED; LD; MR; Career/Vocational Education; Reading; Math; Physical Education; Art; Speech; Occupational Therapy.
Student/Patient Characteristics *Age Levels* 5-8; 9-11; 12-14; 15-17; 18-21. *IQ Ranges* 26-40; 41-55; 56-70; 71-85; 85-130. *Exceptionalities Served* Autistic; Emotionally Disturbed; Learning Disabled; Mentally Handicapped; Communication Disordered; Hearing Impaired/Deaf; Visually Impaired/Blind; Other Health Impaired; Physically Handicapped. *Learning Problems* Memory Disabilities; Perceptual Disabilities; Thinking Disabilities; Oral Language Disabilities; Reading Disabilities; Handwriting Disabilities; Spelling Disabilities; Arithmetic Disabilities; Written Expression. *Behavioral Problems* Attention Deficits; Hyperactivity; Hypoactivity; Impulsivity; Self-Aggression; Verbal Aggression; Physical Aggression; Indirect Aggression; Passive Aggression; Withdrawal. *Conditions Treated* Early Infantile Autism; Schizophrenia; Aphasia; Phobias; Obsessions and Compulsions; Depression; Inadequacy/Immaturity; Personality Problems; Socialized Aggressive Reaction; Unsocialized Aggressive Reaction.
Services Provided Individual Therapy; Group Therapy; Parent Involvement; Behavior Therapy; Biofeedback; Family Therapy; Art Therapy; Music Therapy; Play Therapy. *Professionals on Staff* Psychiatrists 1; Psychologists 1; Counselors 5; Social Workers 3; Child Care Staff 19; Nurses 3; Behavior Specialist 1. *Educational Professionals* Special Education Teachers 6; Career/Vocational Teachers 5; Paraprofessionals 19. *Curricula* Traditional Academic; Career/Vocational Education; Individualized; Basic Skills; Prevocational; Community and Domestic Skills. *Educational Intervention Approaches* Precision Teaching; Progressive Discipline; Behavior Modification.

Main Street Human Resources

60 Cottage St, Great Barington, MA 01230 (413) 528-9155
Year Established 1975
Contact Jeff Liebowitz, Clinic Dir
Facility Information *Placement* Outpatient Mental Health Facility. *Children/Adolescents Served* $150. *Sexes Served* Both. *Sources of Funding* State Funds; Health Insurance; Medicaid; Medicare; Sliding Scale.
Student/Patient Characteristics *Age Levels* 0-4; 5-8; 9-11; 12-14; 15-17; 18-21; Over 21. *IQ Ranges* 41-55; 56-70; 71-85; 85-130; Above 130. *Exceptionalities Served* Emotionally Disturbed; Mentally Handicapped; Communication Disordered. *Learning Problems* Memory Disabilities; Perceptual Disabilities; Thinking Disabilities; Reading Disabilities. *Behavioral Problems* Attention Deficits; Hyperactivity; Hypoactivity; Impulsivity; Self-Aggression; Verbal Aggression; Physical Aggression; Indirect Aggression; Passive Aggression; Withdrawal. *Conditions Treated* Alcohol Abuse and/or Drug Abuse; Other Substance Abuse or Dependence; Disintegrative Psychoses; Schizophrenia; Phobias; Obsessions and Compulsions; Hysteria; Depression; Suicide; Anorexia Nervosa; Ulcerative Colitis; Inadequacy/Immaturity; Personality Problems; Socialized Aggressive Reaction; Unsocialized Aggressive Reaction.
Services Provided Individual Therapy; Group Therapy; Parent Involvement; Family Therapy; Drug Therapy; Art Therapy; Play Therapy; Hypnotherapy. *Professionals on Staff* Psychiatrists 1; Counselors 1; Social Workers 3; Nurses 3.

McAuley Nazareth Home for Boys

77 Mulberry St, Leicester, MA 01524 (617) 892-4886
Year Established 1901
Contact Sr Mary Theresa Barry, Admin
Facility Information *Placement* Private Residential Care. *Number of Beds* 16. *Children/Adolescents Served* 16. *Sexes Served* Male. *Room and Board Fees (Approx)* $55. *Tuition Fees (Approx)* $20,220. *Sources of Funding* State Funds; P.L. 94-142. Summer school available. *Teacher Certification Level* Elementary School. *Special Certification Level* ED.
Student/Patient Characteristics *Age Levels* 5-8; 9-11; 12-14. *IQ Ranges* 71-85; 85-130. *Exceptionalities Served* Emotionally Disturbed. *Learning Problems* Thinking Disabilities; Oral Language Disabilities; Reading Disabilities; Handwriting Disabilities; Spelling Disabilities; Arithmetic Disabilities; Written Expression. *Behavioral Problems* Attention Deficits; Hyperactivity; Hypoactivity; Impulsivity; Self-Aggression; Verbal Aggression; Physical Aggression; Indirect Aggression; Passive Aggression; Withdrawal. *Conditions Treated* Depression; Suicide; Asthma; Personality Problems; Socialized Aggressive Reaction; Unsocialized Aggressive Reaction.
Services Provided Individual Therapy; Parent Involvement; Behavior Therapy; Family Therapy; Reality Therapy; Play Therapy. *Professionals on Staff* Psychiatrists 1; Social Workers 2; Child Care Staff 9. *Service Facilities Available (with number of rooms)* Consultative (ERT) 1; Self-Contained Rooms 2; On-Campus Residential School 3. *Educational Professionals* Special Education Teachers 3; Tutor. *Curricula* Traditional Academic; Individualized; Basic Skills. *Educational Intervention Approaches* Progressive Discipline; Self-Control. *Degrees Awarded* Certificate of Attendance.

Milford Assistance Program Day School

89 Congress St, Milford, MA 01757 (617) 473-3332
Year Established 1974
Contact Daniel R Crawford
Facility Information *Placement* Special School. *Sexes Served* Both. *Tuition Fees (Approx)* $9,027. *Sources of Funding* State Funds; Health Insurance; Medicaid; Medicare; P.L. 94-142; P.L. 89-313. Summer school available. *Teacher Certification Level* Junior High/Middle School; High School. *Special Certification Level* ED; Special Education.

Student/Patient Characteristics *Age Levels* 12-14; 15-17; 18-21; Over 21. *IQ Ranges* 85-130; Above 130. *Exceptionalities Served* Emotionally Disturbed; Learning Disabled. *Learning Problems* Memory Disabilities; Perceptual Disabilities; Thinking Disabilities; Oral Language Disabilities; Reading Disabilities; Handwriting Disabilities; Spelling Disabilities; Arithmetic Disabilities; Written Expression. *Behavioral Problems* Attention Deficits; Hyperactivity; Impulsivity; Self-Aggression; Verbal Aggression; Physical Aggression; Indirect Aggression; Passive Aggression; Withdrawal. *Conditions Treated* Alcohol Abuse and/or Drug Abuse; Other Substance Abuse or Dependence; Disintegrative Psychoses; Schizophrenia; Phobias; Depression; Suicide; Anorexia Nervosa; Inadequacy/Immaturity; Personality Problems; Socialized Aggressive Reaction; Unsocialized Aggressive Reaction.

Services Provided Individual Therapy; Group Therapy; Parent Involvement; Behavior Therapy; Family Therapy; Filial Therapy; Drug Therapy; Reality Therapy; Milieu Therapy. *Professionals on Staff* Psychiatrists; Psychologists; Counselors; Social Workers. *Service Facilities Available (with number of rooms)* Transition Rooms; Self-Contained Rooms; Special School 6. *Educational Professionals* Special Education Teachers; Special Education Counselors; Paraprofessionals. *Curricula* Career/Vocational Education; Individualized; Basic Skills; Prevocational. *Educational Intervention Approaches* Precision Teaching; Self-Control; Behavior Modification; Applied Behavior Analysis; Creative Conditioning. *Degrees Awarded* High School Diploma; Graduate Equivalency Diploma.

Multidisciplinary Institute for Neuropsychological Development Inc—MIND

48 Garden St, Cambridge, MA 02138 (617) 547-9845
Year Established 1970
Contact E Christine Kris, Dir

Facility Information *Placement* Institute for Neuropsychological Development. *Children/Adolescents Served* 150. *Sexes Served* Both. *Sources of Funding* State Funds; HEW; Health Insurance; Medicaid; Medicare; P.L. 94-142; Private Sources. Summer school available.

Student/Patient Characteristics *Age Levels* 0-4; 5-8; 9-11; 12-14; 15-17; 18-21; Over 21. *IQ Ranges* 26-40; 41-55; 56-70; 71-85; 85-130; Above 130. *Exceptionalities Served* Autistic; Emotionally Disturbed; Learning Disabled; Mentally Handicapped; Communication Disordered; Hearing Impaired/Deaf; Visually Impaired/Blind; Other Health Impaired; Gifted. *Learning Problems* Memory Disabilities; Perceptual Disabilities; Thinking Disabilities; Oral Language Disabilities; Reading Disabilities; Handwriting Disabilities; Spelling Disabilities; Arithmetic Disabilities; Written Expression. *Behavioral Problems* Attention Deficits; Hyperactivity; Hypoactivity; Impulsivity; Self-Aggression; Verbal Aggression; Physical Aggression; Indirect Aggression; Passive Aggression; Withdrawal. *Conditions Treated* Early Infantile Autism; Aphasia; Convulsive Disorders; Obsessions and Compulsions; Hysteria; Depression; Suicide; Inadequacy/Immaturity; Personality Problems; Socialized Aggressive Reaction.

Services Provided Individual Therapy; Parent Involvement; Behavior Therapy; Cognitive Developmental Therapy; Biofeedback; Family Therapy; Filial Therapy; Drug Therapy; Art Therapy; Play Therapy; Motor Integration Training. *Professionals on Staff* Psychiatrists; Psychologists 4; Counselors 4; Child Care Staff; Occupational Therapist; Physical Therapist; Speech and Language Therapist; Play Therapist. *Service Facilities Available (with number of rooms)* Consultative (ERT) 2; Tutorial Rooms 2; Homebound Instruction 1. *Educational Professionals* Regular School Teachers; Special Education Teachers; Career/Vocational Teachers; Crisis Teachers; Special Education Counselors; Paraprofessionals; Computer Instruction Tutors. *Curricula* Traditional Academic; Career/Vocational Education; Individualized; Basic Skills; Prevocational; ESL. *Educational Intervention Approaches* Precision Teaching; Progressive Discipline; Self-Control; Applied Behavior Analysis.

Mystic Valley Mental Health Center

186 Bedford St, Lexington, MA 02173 (617) 861-0890
Year Established 1957
Contact Richard Weiss, Exec Dir

Facility Information *Placement* Private Residential Care; Private Day Care; Special Program; Outpatient Counseling and Therapy Center. *Number of Beds* 12. *Children/Adolescents Served* 12 (residential); 56 (day treatment); 175 (outpatient). *Sexes Served* Both. *Room and Board Fees (Approx)* $64. *Sources of Funding* State Funds; Health Insurance; Medicaid; P.L. 94-142; Patient Fees.

Student/Patient Characteristics *Age Levels* 0-4; 5-8; 9-11; 12-14; 15-17; 18-21. *IQ Ranges* 0-25; 26-40; 41-55; 56-70; 71-85; 85-130; Above 130. *Exceptionalities Served* Autistic; Emotionally Disturbed; Learning Disabled; Mentally Handicapped. *Learning Problems* Memory Disabilities; Perceptual Disabilities; Oral Language Disabilities; Reading Disabilities. *Behavioral Problems* Attention Deficits; Hyperactivity; Impulsivity; Self-Aggression; Verbal Aggression; Physical Aggression; Indirect Aggression; Passive Aggression; Withdrawal. *Conditions Treated* Early Infantile Autism; Disintegrative Psychoses; Schizophrenia; Aphasia; Phobias; Obsessions and Compulsions; Hysteria; Depression; Suicide; Anorexia Nervosa; Inadequacy/Immaturity; Personality Problems; Socialized Aggressive Reaction.

Services Provided Individual Therapy; Group Therapy; Parent Involvement; Behavior Therapy; Cognitive Developmental Therapy; Family Therapy; Filial Therapy; Drug Therapy; Art Therapy; Play Therapy; Physical Therapy; Occupational Therapy; Rehabilitation Counseling. *Professionals on Staff* Psychiatrists 5; Psychologists 7; Counselors 4; Social Workers 10; Child Care Staff 8; Nurses 5. *Service Facilities Available (with number of rooms)* Self-Contained Rooms; Local Schools. *Educational Professionals* Regular School Teachers; Special Education Teachers; Crisis Teachers; Special Education Counselors. *Curricula* Traditional Academic; Career/Vocational Education; Individualized. *Degrees Awarded* High School Diploma; Graduate Equivalency Diploma.

Comments Mystic Valley is a comprehensive community-based mental health and mental retardation organization.

New England Home for Little Wanderers—Longview Farm

PO Box 166, 399 Lincoln Rd, Walpole, MA 02081
(617) 668-7703
Year Established 1940
Contact Patrick J Nugent, Dir

Facility Information *Placement* Private Residential Care; Private 766 Approved School. *Number of Beds* 21. *Children/Adolescents Served* 21. *Sexes Served* Male. *Room and Board Fees (Approx)* $72. *Tuition Fees (Approx)* $26,423. *Sources of Funding* State Funds; P.L. 94-142; Chapter 766. *Teacher Certification Level* Elementary School; Junior High/Middle School. *Special Certification Level* ED.

Student/Patient Characteristics *Age Levels* 12-14; 15-17. *IQ Ranges* 71-85; 85-130. *Exceptionalities Served* Emotionally Disturbed; Learning Disabled. *Learning Problems* Memory Disabilities; Perceptual Disabilities; Thinking Disabilities; Oral Language Disabilities; Reading Disabilities; Handwriting Disabilities; Spelling Disabilities; Arithmetic Disabilities; Written Expression. *Behavioral Problems* Attention Deficits; Hyperactivity; Impulsivity; Verbal Aggression.

Services Provided Individual Therapy; Group Therapy; Parent Involvement; Behavior Therapy; Family Therapy. *Professionals on Staff* Counselors 1; Social Workers 2; Child Care Staff 14. *Service Facilities Available (with number of rooms)* Resource Rooms 1; Self-Contained Rooms 2; Pre Vocational Shops 3. *Educational Professionals* Regular School Teachers 1; Special Education Teachers 4; Career/Vocational Teachers 1. *Curricula* Traditional Academic; Career/Vocational Education; Individualized; Basic Skills; Prevocational; Outdoor Education. *Educational Intervention Approaches* Behavior Modification. *Degrees Awarded* High School Diploma.

Comments Longview Farm is a residential educational facility in a rural setting, comprising a residence with 2 distinct living groups and a group home. Each resident is assigned a social worker and a mentor who provide on-going treatment through individual, group, and family work. The structured academic, pre-vocation program allows for a positive learning experience. A summer outdoor education program is provided.

New England Home for Little Wanderers—Orchard Home

917 Belmont St, Watertown, MA 02172 (617) 489-1760
Year Established 1955
Contact Brenda English, Dir
Facility Information *Placement* Special School; Private Residential Care. *Number of Beds* 10. *Children/Adolescents Served* 10. *Sexes Served* Female. *Room and Board Fees (Approx)* $74. *Tuition Fees (Approx)* $27,305. *Sources of Funding* State Funds; Private Contributions. Summer school available. *Teacher Certification Level* Elementary School; Junior High/Middle School. *Special Certification Level* ED; LD; Art.
Student/Patient Characteristics *Age Levels* 9-11; 12-14. *IQ Ranges* 71-85; 85-130. *Exceptionalities Served* Emotionally Disturbed; Learning Disabled; Communication Disordered; Physically Handicapped. *Learning Problems* Memory Disabilities; Perceptual Disabilities; Thinking Disabilities; Oral Language Disabilities; Reading Disabilities; Handwriting Disabilities; Spelling Disabilities; Arithmetic Disabilities; Written Expression. *Behavioral Problems* Attention Deficits; Hyperactivity; Hypoactivity; Impulsivity; Self-Aggression; Verbal Aggression; Physical Aggression; Indirect Aggression; Passive Aggression; Withdrawal. *Conditions Treated* Schizophrenia; Phobias; Obsessions and Compulsions; Hysteria; Depression; Suicide; Asthma; Anorexia Nervosa; Ulcerative Colitis; Inadequacy/Immaturity; Personality Problems; Socialized Aggressive Reaction.
Services Provided Individual Therapy; Group Therapy; Parent Involvement; Behavior Therapy; Family Therapy; Filial Therapy; Drug Therapy; Reality Therapy; Play Therapy. *Professionals on Staff* Psychiatrists 1; Psychologists 1; Social Workers 1; Child Care Staff 10; Nurses 1; Administrators. *Service Facilities Available (with number of rooms)* Resource Rooms 1; Self-Contained Rooms 1. *Educational Professionals* Special Education Teachers 2; Crisis Teachers 1. *Curricula* Traditional Academic; Individualized; Basic Skills. *Educational Intervention Approaches* Self-Control; Behavior Modification.

New England Home for Little Wanderers—Knight Children's Center

161 S Huntington Ave, Boston, MA 02130 (617) 232-8600
Year Established 1950
Contact Daniel Sweeney, Principal
Facility Information *Placement* Special School; Private Residential Care; Private Day Care. *Number of Beds* 24. *Children/Adolescents Served* 42. *Sexes Served* Both. *Room and Board Fees (Approx)* $74. *Tuition Fees (Approx)* $27,046; $13,816 (day rate). *Sources of Funding* State Funds; P.L. 94-142; Chapter 766. Summer school available. *Teacher Certification Level* Elementary School; Junior High/Middle School. *Special Certification Level* ED; LD.
Student/Patient Characteristics *Age Levels* 5-8; 9-11; 12-14. *IQ Ranges* 71-85; 85-130. *Exceptionalities Served* Emotionally Disturbed; Learning Disabled. *Learning Problems* Memory Disabilities; Perceptual Disabilities; Thinking Disabilities; Oral Language Disabilities; Reading Disabilities; Handwriting Disabilities; Spelling Disabilities; Arithmetic Disabilities; Written Expression. *Behavioral Problems* Attention Deficits; Hyperactivity; Impulsivity; Self-Aggression; Verbal Aggression; Physical Aggression; Passive Aggression; Withdrawal. *Conditions Treated* Obsessions and Compulsions; Depression; Inadequacy/Immaturity; Personality Problems; Socialized Aggressive Reaction; Unsocialized Aggressive Reaction.

Services Provided Individual Therapy; Group Therapy; Parent Involvement; Family Therapy; Art Therapy; Music Therapy; Play Therapy. *Professionals on Staff* Psychiatrists 1; Psychologists 1; Social Workers 6; Child Care Staff 17; Nurses 1. *Service Facilities Available (with number of rooms)* Consultative (ERT) 2; Resource Rooms 2; Transition Rooms 1; Self-Contained Rooms 7. *Educational Professionals* Special Education Teachers 10. *Curricula* Traditional Academic; Individualized; Basic Skills; Adaptive Physical Education. *Educational Intervention Approaches* Engineered Classroom; Precision Teaching; Self-Control; Behavior Modification.

New England Medical Center—Bay Cove Day Center for Children Day Hospital

Box 395, 171 Harrison Ave, Boston, MA 02111 (617) 956-5739
Year Established 1979
Contact Margaret B Reber, Div Admin
Facility Information *Placement* Special School; Pediatric Psychiatric Day Hospital. *Children/Adolescents Served* 24. *Sexes Served* Both. *Tuition Fees (Approx)* $11,824 (Educational Component). *Sources of Funding* State Funds; Medicaid; P.L. 94-142; Chapter 766. Summer school available. *Teacher Certification Level* Elementary School. *Special Certification Level* LD; Reading; Math.
Student/Patient Characteristics *Age Levels* 5-8; 9-11; 12-14. *IQ Ranges* 85-130. *Exceptionalities Served* Autistic; Emotionally Disturbed; Learning Disabled. *Learning Problems* Perceptual Disabilities; Thinking Disabilities; Oral Language Disabilities; Reading Disabilities; Handwriting Disabilities; Spelling Disabilities; Arithmetic Disabilities; Written Expression. *Behavioral Problems* Attention Deficits; Hyperactivity; Hypoactivity; Impulsivity; Self-Aggression; Verbal Aggression; Physical Aggression; Indirect Aggression; Passive Aggression; Withdrawal. *Conditions Treated* Early Infantile Autism; Schizophrenia; Phobias; Obsessions and Compulsions; Hysteria; Depression; Suicide; Asthma; Inadequacy/Immaturity; Personality Problems; Socialized Aggressive Reaction; Unsocialized Aggressive Reaction.
Services Provided Individual Therapy; Group Therapy; Parent Involvement; Behavior Therapy; Cognitive Developmental Therapy; Family Therapy; Drug Therapy; Art Therapy; Play Therapy; Psychodrama. *Professionals on Staff* Psychiatrists 1; Psychologists 1; Counselors 4; Social Workers 2; Child Care Staff 4; Nurses 1; Psychiatric Resident. *Service Facilities Available (with number of rooms)* Consultative (ERT) 1; Resource Rooms 2; Transition Rooms 1; Classrooms 3; Gym 1; Hospital School; Arts and Crafts 1; Library 1. *Educational Professionals* Special Education Teachers. *Curricula* Individualized. *Degrees Awarded* Certificate of Attendance.

New England Medical Center—Division of Child Psychiatry

Box 395, 171 Harrison Ave, Boston, MA 02111 (617) 956-5732
Contact Margaret B Reber, Div Admin
Facility Information *Placement* Inpatient and Outpatient Child Psychiatric Services. *Number of Beds* 7. *Children/Adolescents Served* 7 (inpatients); 100 (outpatients). *Sexes Served* Both. *Room and Board Fees (Approx)* $373. *Sources of Funding* Health Insurance; Medicaid.
Student/Patient Characteristics *Age Levels* 0-4; 5-8; 9-11; 12-14; 15-17; 18-21. *IQ Ranges* 85-130. *Exceptionalities Served* Autistic; Emotionally Disturbed; Learning Disabled; Hearing Impaired/Deaf. *Learning Problems* Perceptual Disabilities; Thinking Disabilities; Oral Language Disabilities; Reading Disabilities; Handwriting Disabilities; Spelling Disabilities; Arithmetic Disabilities; Written Expression. *Behavioral Problems* Attention Deficits; Hyperactivity; Hypoactivity; Impulsivity; Self-Aggression; Verbal Aggression; Physical Aggression; Indirect Aggression; Passive Aggression; Withdrawal. *Conditions Treated* Early Infantile Autism; Schizophrenia; Phobias; Obsessions and Compulsions; Hysteria; Depression; Suicide; Asthma; Inadequacy/Immaturity; Personality Problems; Socialized Aggressive Reaction; Unsocialized Aggressive Reaction.

Services Provided Individual Therapy; Group Therapy; Parent Involvement; Family Therapy; Drug Therapy. *Professionals on Staff* Psychiatrists 12; Psychologists 10; Counselors 12; Social Workers 8; Nurses 5. *Service Facilities Available (with number of rooms)* Hospital 20.

Our Lady of Providence Children's Center

2112 Riverdale St, West Springfield, MA 01089-1099
(413) 788-7366
Year Established 1881
Contact Gerard L Malouin, Pres

Facility Information *Placement* Adoption, Foster Care, Diagnostic, Group Home. *Number of Beds* 60. *Children/Adolescents Served* 60 in residence and school, unlimited in outpatient clinic. *Sexes Served* Both. *Room and Board Fees (Approx)* $82 (residential); $98 (intensive residential or diagnostic); $42 (group home); $50 (day treatment). *Sources of Funding* State Funds. Summer school available. *Teacher Certification Level* Elementary School; Junior High/Middle School; High School. *Special Certification Level* ED; Reading.

Student/Patient Characteristics *Age Levels* 5-8; 9-11; 12-14; 15-17. *IQ Ranges* 71-85; 85-130; Above 130. *Exceptionalities Served* Autistic; Emotionally Disturbed; Learning Disabled; Mentally Handicapped; Gifted. *Learning Problems* Memory Disabilities; Perceptual Disabilities; Thinking Disabilities; Oral Language Disabilities; Reading Disabilities; Handwriting Disabilities; Spelling Disabilities; Arithmetic Disabilities; Written Expression. *Behavioral Problems* Attention Deficits; Hyperactivity; Hypoactivity; Impulsivity; Self-Aggression; Verbal Aggression; Physical Aggression; Indirect Aggression; Passive Aggression; Withdrawal. *Conditions Treated* Early Infantile Autism; Disintegrative Psychoses; Schizophrenia; Convulsive Disorders; Phobias; Obsessions and Compulsions; Hysteria; Depression; Suicide; Inadequacy/Immaturity; Personality Problems; Socialized Aggressive Reaction; Unsocialized Aggressive Reaction.

Services Provided Individual Therapy; Group Therapy; Parent Involvement; Behavior Therapy; Family Therapy; Reality Therapy; Play Therapy. *Professionals on Staff* Psychiatrists 1; Psychologists 3; Social Workers 21; Child Care Staff 60; Nurses 3. *Service Facilities Available (with number of rooms)* Transition Rooms 1; Self-Contained Rooms 5; On-Campus Residential School 6. *Educational Professionals* Special Education Teachers 5; Crisis Teachers 1; Paraprofessionals 6. *Curricula* Traditional Academic; Individualized; Basic Skills. *Educational Intervention Approaches* Progressive Discipline; Self-Control; Behavior Modification. *Degrees Awarded* Certificate of Attendance.

Comments Programs are designed along a flexible continuum from prevention-oriented programs to more restrictive treatment programs. This service continuum facilitates and maximizes the child and family's progress by providing all of the necessary services at one agency. The core programs are: Diagnostic Unit, Residential, Group Home, Day Treatment, Foster Care, Adoption, Pregnant and Parenting Services, and Community Education and Advocacy.

Pace School

348 Pond St, Braintree, MA 02184 (617) 848-6894
Contact Barry Rosenwasser, Prog Dir

Facility Information *Placement* Special School. *Children/Adolescents Served* 18. *Sexes Served* Both. *Tuition Fees (Approx)* $16,900. *Sources of Funding* Chapter 766. Summer school available. *Teacher Certification Level* Junior High/Middle School; High School. *Special Certification Level* ED; LD; MR; Career/Vocational Education; Autistic.

Student/Patient Characteristics *Age Levels* 12-14; 15-17; 18-21; Over 21. *IQ Ranges* 0-25; 26-40; 41-55. *Exceptionalities Served* Autistic; Emotionally Disturbed; Mentally Handicapped; Communication Disordered; Behaviorally Disordered. *Learning Problems* Memory Disabilities; Perceptual Disabilities; Thinking Disabilities; Oral Language Disabilities; Reading Disabilities; Handwriting Disabilities; Spelling Disabilities; Arithmetic Disabilities; Written Expression. *Behavioral Problems* Attention

Deficits; Hyperactivity; Hypoactivity; Impulsivity; Self-Aggression; Verbal Aggression; Physical Aggression; Indirect Aggression; Passive Aggression; Withdrawal; Self Stimulation. *Conditions Treated* Early Infantile Autism; Convulsive Disorders; Socialized Aggressive Reaction; Unsocialized Aggressive Reaction.

Services Provided Parent Involvement; Behavior Therapy; Art Therapy; Music Therapy; Speech and Language Therapy. *Professionals on Staff* Child Care Staff 9. *Service Facilities Available (with number of rooms)* Self-Contained Rooms 3. *Educational Professionals* Special Education Teachers 3; Paraprofessionals 6. *Curricula* Career/Vocational Education; Individualized; Basic Skills; Prevocational; Community Skills Training. *Educational Intervention Approaches* Self-Control; Behavior Modification; Applied Behavior Analysis.

Comments Pace provides services for developmentally delayed adolescents with severe behavior and communication deficits The overall goal is to prepare adolescents to function successfully in normative community homes, work, and leisure environments as adults. Pace is open 6 days a week, 52 weeks a year.

Protestant Youth Center

PO Box 23, 19 Hospital Rd, Baldwinville, MA 01436-0023
(617) 939-2101
Year Established 1962
Contact Jerilyn C Niemela

Facility Information *Placement* Private Residential Care. *Number of Beds* 32. *Children/Adolescents Served* 28. *Sexes Served* Female. *Tuition Fees (Approx)* $30,055. *Sources of Funding* Tuition. Summer school available. *Special Certification Level* ED; LD; MR.

Student/Patient Characteristics *Age Levels* 9-11; 12-14; 15-17; 18-21. *IQ Ranges* 71-85; 85-130. *Exceptionalities Served* Emotionally Disturbed; Learning Disabled; Mentally Handicapped; Communication Disordered. *Learning Problems* Memory Disabilities; Perceptual Disabilities; Thinking Disabilities; Oral Language Disabilities; Reading Disabilities; Handwriting Disabilities; Spelling Disabilities; Arithmetic Disabilities; Written Expression. *Behavioral Problems* Attention Deficits; Hyperactivity; Hypoactivity; Impulsivity; Self-Aggression; Verbal Aggression; Physical Aggression; Indirect Aggression; Passive Aggression; Withdrawal. *Conditions Treated* Convulsive Disorders; Phobias; Obsessions and Compulsions; Hysteria; Depression; Inadequacy/Immaturity; Personality Problems; Socialized Aggressive Reaction; Unsocialized Aggressive Reaction.

Services Provided Individual Therapy; Group Therapy; Parent Involvement; Behavior Therapy; Family Therapy; Art Therapy; Music Therapy. *Professionals on Staff* Psychiatrists 1; Psychologists 1; Counselors; Child Care Staff 18; Nurses 1. *Service Facilities Available (with number of rooms)* On-Campus Residential School 9. *Educational Professionals* Special Education Teachers 5; Career/Vocational Teachers 1. *Curricula* Traditional Academic; Career/Vocational Education; Individualized; Basic Skills; Prevocational. *Educational Intervention Approaches* Self-Control; Behavior Modification. *Degrees Awarded* High School Diploma; Graduate Equivalency Diploma.

Psychiatric Services Inc

215 Summer St, Haverhill, MA 01830 (617) 374-0401
Year Established 1972
Contact Michael H Malamud, Dir

Facility Information *Placement* Mental Health Clinic. *Sexes Served* Both. *Sources of Funding* Health Insurance; Medicaid; Medicare; Private Insurance.

Student/Patient Characteristics *Age Levels* 0-4; 5-8; 9-11; 12-14; 15-17; 18-21; Over 21. *IQ Ranges* 41-55; 56-70; 71-85; 85-130; Above 130. *Exceptionalities Served* Emotionally Disturbed; Learning Disabled; Mentally Handicapped; Communication Disordered; Hearing Impaired/Deaf; Visually Impaired/Blind; Other Health Impaired; Physically Handicapped; Gifted. *Learning Problems* Memory Disabilities; Perceptual Disabilities; Thinking Disabilities; Oral Language Disabilities; Reading Disabilities. *Behavioral Problems* Attention Deficits; Hyperactivity; Hypoactivity; Impulsivity; Self-Aggression; Verbal Aggression; Physical Aggression; Indirect Aggression; Passive Aggression; Withdrawal. *Conditions Treated* Alcohol Abuse and/or Drug Abuse; Other Substance Abuse or Dependence; Early Infantile Autism; Disintegrative Psychoses; Schizophrenia; Aphasia; Convulsive Disorders; Phobias; Obsessions and Compulsions; Hysteria; Depression; Suicide; Asthma; Anorexia Nervosa; Ulcerative Colitis; Inadequacy/Immaturity; Personality Problems; Socialized Aggressive Reaction; Unsocialized Aggressive Reaction.

Services Provided Individual Therapy; Group Therapy; Parent Involvement; Cognitive Developmental Therapy; Family Therapy; Filial Therapy; Drug Therapy; Play Therapy. *Professionals on Staff* Psychiatrists 1; Psychologists 2; Social Workers 6. *Service Facilities Available (with number of rooms)* Consultative (ERT).

River Street School

1137 River St, Hyde Park, MA 02136 (617) 364-4213
Year Established 1972
Contact Maryclaire Knight, Exec Dir
Facility Information *Placement* Special School.
Children/Adolescents Served 35. *Sexes Served* Both. *Tuition Fees (Approx)* $13,289. *Sources of Funding* State Funds; RL 89-313. *Teacher Certification Level* Junior High/Middle School; High School. *Special Certification Level* Reading; Math; Moderate Special Needs.

Student/Patient Characteristics *Age Levels* 12-14; 15-17; 18-21. *IQ Ranges* 85-130. *Exceptionalities Served* Emotionally Disturbed; Learning Disabled. *Learning Problems* Oral Language Disabilities; Reading Disabilities; Handwriting Disabilities; Spelling Disabilities; Arithmetic Disabilities; Written Expression. *Behavioral Problems* Attention Deficits; Hyperactivity; Impulsivity; Verbal Aggression; Physical Aggression; Passive Aggression; Withdrawal. *Conditions Treated* Alcohol Abuse and/or Drug Abuse; Disintegrative Psychoses; Obsessions and Compulsions; Depression; Suicide; Asthma; Anorexia Nervosa; Inadequacy/Immaturity; Personality Problems; Socialized Aggressive Reaction.

Services Provided Individual Therapy; Group Therapy; Parent Involvement; Behavior Therapy; Family Therapy; Drug Therapy; Art Therapy; Reality Therapy. *Professionals on Staff* Psychologists 2; Counselors 1; Social Workers 4; Child Care Staff 1; Nurses 1. *Educational Professionals* Regular School Teachers 3; Special Education Teachers 3; Career/Vocational Teachers 3; Paraprofessionals 2; Therapists 4. *Curricula* Traditional Academic; Career/Vocational Education; Individualized; Basic Skills; Prevocational; Computers. *Educational Intervention Approaches* Progressive Discipline; Self-Control; Applied Behavior Analysis. *Degrees Awarded* High School Diploma.

St Ann's Home Inc—Day Treatment and Special Education Program

100A Haverhill St, Methuen, MA 01844 (617) 682-5276
Year Established 1925
Contact Patrick T Villani, Exec Dir
Facility Information *Placement* Special School.
Children/Adolescents Served 35. *Sexes Served* Both. *Tuition Fees (Approx)* $11,559. *Sources of Funding* State Funds; Health Insurance; Medicaid; P.L. 94-142. *Teacher Certification Level* Elementary School; Junior High/Middle School; High School. *Special Certification Level* ED; LD; Reading; Math.

Student/Patient Characteristics *Age Levels* 5-8; 9-11; 12-14; 15-17. *IQ Ranges* 71-85; 85-130; Above 130. *Exceptionalities Served* Emotionally Disturbed; Learning Disabled. *Learning Problems* Memory Disabilities; Perceptual Disabilities; Thinking Disabilities; Oral Language Disabilities; Reading Disabilities; Handwriting Disabilities; Spelling Disabilities; Arithmetic Disabilities; Written Expression. *Behavioral Problems* Attention Deficits; Hyperactivity; Impulsivity; Self-Aggression; Verbal Aggression; Physical Aggression; Indirect Aggression; Passive Aggression; Withdrawal. *Conditions Treated* Phobias; Obsessions

and Compulsions; Hysteria; Depression; Inadequacy/Immaturity; Personality Problems; Socialized Aggressive Reaction; Unsocialized Aggressive Reaction.

Services Provided Individual Therapy; Group Therapy; Parent Involvement; Behavior Therapy; Cognitive Developmental Therapy; Family Therapy; Drug Therapy; Reality Therapy; Play Therapy. *Professionals on Staff* Psychiatrists 2; Psychologists 3; Social Workers 3; Child Care Staff 5; Nurses 2. *Service Facilities Available (with number of rooms)* Consultative (ERT) 3; Resource Rooms 4; Self-Contained Rooms 12. *Educational Professionals* Special Education Teachers 12; Crisis Teachers 4; Paraprofessionals 15. *Curricula* Individualized; Basic Skills. *Educational Intervention Approaches* Progressive Discipline; Behavior Modification; Applied Behavior Analysis. *Degrees Awarded* Certificate of Attendance; High School Diploma.

St Ann's Home Inc—Residential Treatment and Special Education Program

100A Haverhill St, Methuen, MA 01844 (617) 682-5276
Year Established 1925
Contact Patrick T Villani, Exec Dir
Facility Information *Placement* Private Residential Care. *Number of Beds* 80. *Children/Adolescents Served* 80. *Sexes Served* Both. *Tuition Fees (Approx)* $11,559-$20,865. *Sources of Funding* State Funds; Health Insurance; Medicaid; P.L. 94-142. Summer school available. *Teacher Certification Level* Elementary School; Junior High/Middle School; High School. *Special Certification Level* ED; LD; Reading; Math.

Student/Patient Characteristics *Age Levels* 5-8; 9-11; 12-14; 15-17. *IQ Ranges* 71-85; 85-130; Above 130. *Exceptionalities Served* Emotionally Disturbed; Learning Disabled. *Learning Problems* Memory Disabilities; Perceptual Disabilities; Thinking Disabilities; Oral Language Disabilities; Reading Disabilities; Handwriting Disabilities; Spelling Disabilities; Arithmetic Disabilities; Written Expression. *Behavioral Problems* Attention Deficits; Hyperactivity; Impulsivity; Self-Aggression; Verbal Aggression; Physical Aggression; Indirect Aggression; Passive Aggression; Withdrawal. *Conditions Treated* Phobias; Obsessions and Compulsions; Hysteria; Depression; Inadequacy/Immaturity; Personality Problems; Socialized Aggressive Reaction; Unsocialized Aggressive Reaction.

Services Provided Individual Therapy; Group Therapy; Parent Involvement; Behavior Therapy; Cognitive Developmental Therapy; Family Therapy; Drug Therapy; Reality Therapy; Play Therapy. *Professionals on Staff* Psychiatrists 2; Psychologists 3; Social Workers 6; Child Care Staff 70; Nurses 2. *Service Facilities Available (with number of rooms)* Consultative (ERT) 6; Resource Rooms 4; Self-Contained Rooms 12. *Educational Professionals* Special Education Teachers 12; Crisis Teachers 4; Paraprofessionals 15. *Curricula* Individualized; Basic Skills. *Educational Intervention Approaches* Progressive Discipline; Behavior Modification; Applied Behavior Analysis. *Degrees Awarded* Certificate of Attendance; High School Diploma.

Solomon Mental Health Center

391 Varnum Ave, Lowell, MA 01854 (617) 454-8851
Year Established 1967
Contact Fernando A Duran, Supt Area Dir
Facility Information *Placement* Community Mental Health Center. *Sexes Served* Both. *Room and Board Fees (Approx)* $188. *Sources of Funding* State Funds; Health Insurance; Medicaid; Medicare; Self Pay. *Special Certification Level* ED; MR; Special Education.

Student/Patient Characteristics *Age Levels* 5-8; 9-11; 12-14; 15-17; 18-21; Over 21. *IQ Ranges* 0-25; 26-40; 41-55; 56-70; 71-85; 85-130; Above 130. *Exceptionalities Served* Autistic; Emotionally Disturbed; Mentally Handicapped. *Behavioral Problems* Attention Deficits; Hyperactivity; Hypoactivity; Impulsivity; Self-Aggression; Verbal Aggression; Physical Aggression; Indirect Aggression; Passive Aggression; Withdrawal. *Conditions Treated* Disintegrative Psychoses; Schizophrenia; Phobias; Obsessions and Compulsions; Hysteria; Depression; Suicide; Inadequacy/Immaturity; Personality Problems; Socialized Aggressive Reaction; Unsocialized Aggressive Reaction.

Services Provided Individual Therapy; Group Therapy; Parent Involvement; Family Therapy; Drug Therapy; Play Therapy. *Professionals on Staff* Psychiatrists 6; Psychologists 10; Social Workers 16; Nurses 23. *Service Facilities Available (with number of rooms)* Resource Rooms 1. *Educational Professionals* Special Education Teachers 2. *Curricula* Individualized.

Stetson School Inc

PO Box 309, South St, Barre, MA 01005 (617) 355-4541
Year Established 1899
Contact Richard J Robinson, Exec Dir

Facility Information *Placement* Special School; Private Residential Care. *Number of Beds* 34. *Children/Adolescents Served* 34. *Sexes Served* Male. *Room and Board Fees (Approx)* $79. *Tuition Fees (Approx)* $28,883. *Sources of Funding* State Funds; Medicaid; P.L. 89-313; Donations. Summer school available. *Teacher Certification Level* Elementary School; Junior High/Middle School; High School. *Special Certification Level* ED; LD; Career/Vocational Education; Reading; Math.

Student/Patient Characteristics *Age Levels* 9-11; 12-14; 15-17. *IQ Ranges* 71-85; 85-130. *Exceptionalities Served* Emotionally Disturbed; Learning Disabled; Behavior Disordered. *Learning Problems* Memory Disabilities; Perceptual Disabilities; Thinking Disabilities; Reading Disabilities; Handwriting Disabilities; Spelling Disabilities; Arithmetic Disabilities; Written Expression. *Behavioral Problems* Attention Deficits; Hyperactivity; Hypoactivity; Impulsivity; Self-Aggression; Verbal Aggression; Physical Aggression; Indirect Aggression; Passive Aggression; Withdrawal. *Conditions Treated* Phobias; Obsessions and Compulsions; Hysteria; Depression; Inadequacy/Immaturity; Personality Problems; Socialized Aggressive Reaction; Unsocialized Aggressive Reaction.

Services Provided Individual Therapy; Group Therapy; Parent Involvement; Behavior Therapy; Reality Therapy; Play Therapy. *Professionals on Staff* Psychiatrists 1; Psychologists 3; Counselors 1; Child Care Staff 10; Nurses 1; Supervisors 3. *Service Facilities Available (with number of rooms)* Resource Rooms 2; Self-Contained Rooms 3; Vocational Shops 2; On-Campus Residential School 7. *Curricula* Traditional Academic; Individualized; Basic Skills; Prevocational. *Educational Intervention Approaches* Precision Teaching; Progressive Discipline; Self-Control; Behavior Modification; Applied Behavior Analysis; Creative Conditioning. *Degrees Awarded* Certificate of Attendance; High School Diploma; Graduate Equivalency Diploma.

Tri City Community Mental Health and Retardation Center

140A Ferry St, Malden, MA 02148 (617) 324-7300
Contact Pamela M Senesac, Clinical Dir

Facility Information *Placement* Outpatient Mental Health. *Children/Adolescents Served* 100. *Sexes Served* Both. *Sources of Funding* State Funds; Health Insurance; Medicaid.

Student/Patient Characteristics *Age Levels* 5-8; 9-11; 12-14; 15-17. *IQ Ranges* 56-70; 71-85; 85-130. *Exceptionalities Served* Emotionally Disturbed; Learning Disabled; Mentally Handicapped. *Behavioral Problems* Hyperactivity; Impulsivity; Indirect Aggression; Passive Aggression; Withdrawal. *Conditions Treated* Schizophrenia; Phobias; Obsessions and Compulsions; Hysteria; Depression; Suicide; Anorexia Nervosa; Inadequacy/Immaturity; Personality Problems; Socialized Aggressive Reaction.

Services Provided Individual Therapy; Group Therapy; Parent Involvement; Family Therapy; Drug Therapy; Play Therapy. *Professionals on Staff* Psychiatrists 1; Psychologists .5; Social Workers 2.5.

Comments This agency provides community based outpatient mental health services to children and families. It provides limited psychological testing.

Valley View School

Oakham Rd, North Brookfield, MA 01535 (617) 867-6505
Year Established 1970
Contact Philip G Spiva, Dir

Facility Information *Placement* Private Residential Care. *Number of Beds* 34. *Children/Adolescents Served* 34. *Sexes Served* Male. *Tuition Fees (Approx)* $23,250. *Sources of Funding* Private; Chapter 766. *Teacher Certification Level* Junior High/Middle School; High School. *Special Certification Level* ED; Math; Science; Language Arts; Social Studies; Physical Education.

Student/Patient Characteristics *Age Levels* 12-14; 15-17. *IQ Ranges* 85-130; Above 130. *Exceptionalities Served* Emotionally Disturbed; Learning Disabled; Gifted. *Learning Problems* Memory Disabilities; Perceptual Disabilities; Thinking Disabilities; Reading Disabilities; Handwriting Disabilities; Spelling Disabilities; Arithmetic Disabilities; Written Expression. *Behavioral Problems* Attention Deficits; Hyperactivity; Hypoactivity; Impulsivity; Verbal Aggression; Indirect Aggression; Passive Aggression. *Conditions Treated* Inadequacy/Immaturity; Personality Problems; Socialized Aggressive Reaction.

Services Provided Individual Therapy; Group Therapy; Parent Involvement; Cognitive Developmental Therapy; Reality Therapy. *Professionals on Staff* Psychologists 2; Social Workers 2; Child Care Staff 10; Nurses 1. *Service Facilities Available (with number of rooms)* Resource Rooms 2; Special School 8; On-Campus Residential School 8. *Educational Professionals* Regular School Teachers 7; Special Education Teachers 2. *Curricula* Traditional Academic; Individualized; Prevocational. *Educational Intervention Approaches* Progressive Discipline; Self-Control. *Degrees Awarded* Certificate of Attendance; High School Diploma.

Valleyhead Inc

PO Box 714, Reservoir Rd, Lenox, MA 01240 (413) 637-3635
Year Established 1969
Contact Gary Shaw, Admissions

Facility Information *Placement* Special School; Private Residential Care; Special Program. *Number of Beds* 78. *Sexes Served* Female. *Room and Board Fees (Approx)* $69-$80. *Tuition Fees (Approx)* $25,000-$29,000. *Sources of Funding* State Funds; Health Insurance; Private. Summer school available. *Teacher Certification Level* Elementary School; Junior High/Middle School; High School. *Special Certification Level* ED; LD; MR; Career/Vocational Education; Math; Science; Social Studies.

Student/Patient Characteristics *Age Levels* 9-11; 12-14; 15-17; 18-21; Over 21. *IQ Ranges* 41-55; 56-70; 71-85; 85-130; Above 130. *Exceptionalities Served* Emotionally Disturbed; Learning Disabled; Mentally Handicapped; Communication Disordered; Hearing Impaired/Deaf; Visually Impaired/Blind. *Learning Problems* Memory Disabilities; Perceptual Disabilities; Thinking Disabilities; Oral Language Disabilities; Reading Disabilities; Handwriting Disabilities; Spelling Disabilities; Arithmetic Disabilities; Written Expression. *Behavioral Problems* Attention Deficits; Hyperactivity; Impulsivity; Self-Aggression; Verbal Aggression; Physical Aggression; Indirect Aggression; Passive Aggression; Withdrawal. *Conditions Treated* Alcohol Abuse and/or Drug Abuse; Other Substance Abuse or Dependence; Schizophrenia; Convulsive Disorders; Depression; Suicide; Anorexia Nervosa; Inadequacy/Immaturity; Personality Problems; Socialized Aggressive Reaction; Unsocialized Aggressive Reaction.

Services Provided Individual Therapy; Group Therapy; Parent Involvement; Behavior Therapy; Family Therapy; Reality Therapy. *Professionals on Staff* Psychiatrists 1; Psychologists 2; Counselors 2; Social Workers 3; Child Care Staff 25; Nurses 1. *Service Facilities Available (with number of rooms)* Consultative (ERT) 6; Resource Rooms 2; Transition Rooms 2; Self-Contained Rooms 2. *Educational Professionals* Special Education Teachers 12; Career/Vocational Teachers 2; Paraprofessionals 2. *Curricula* Career/Vocational Education; Individualized; Basic Skills; Prevocational. *Educational Intervention Approaches* Precision Teaching; Progressive Discipline; Self-Control; Behavior Modification. *Degrees Awarded* Certificate of Attendance; High School Diploma; Graduate Equivalency Diploma.

Walker Home and School

1968 Central Ave, Needham, MA 02192 (617) 449-4500
Contact Floyd Alwon, Exec Dir

Facility Information *Placement* Special School; Private Residential Care; Private Day Care. *Number of Beds* 34.
Children/Adolescents Served 52. *Sexes Served* Male. *Tuition Fees (Approx)* $35,043 (residential costs); $20,267 (day treatment).
Sources of Funding State Funds; P.L. 94-142; School Districts.
Summer school available. *Teacher Certification Level* Elementary School; Junior High/Middle School. *Special Certification Level* ED; LD; Reading; Math; Speech and Language; Creative Expression.

Student/Patient Characteristics *Age Levels* 5-8; 9-11; 12-14. *IQ Ranges* 85-130; Above 130. *Exceptionalities Served* Emotionally Disturbed; Learning Disabled; Mentally Handicapped; Communication Disordered; Physically Handicapped. *Learning Problems* Memory Disabilities; Perceptual Disabilities; Thinking Disabilities; Oral Language Disabilities; Reading Disabilities; Handwriting Disabilities; Spelling Disabilities; Arithmetic Disabilities; Written Expression. *Behavioral Problems* Attention Deficits; Hyperactivity; Impulsivity; Self-Aggression; Verbal Aggression; Physical Aggression; Indirect Aggression; Passive Aggression; Withdrawal. *Conditions Treated* Phobias; Obsessions and Compulsions; Hysteria; Depression; Suicide; Inadequacy/Immaturity; Personality Problems; Socialized Aggressive Reaction; Unsocialized Aggressive Reaction.

Services Provided Individual Therapy; Group Therapy; Parent Involvement; Behavior Therapy; Family Therapy; Art Therapy; Reality Therapy; Play Therapy. *Professionals on Staff* Psychiatrists 1; Psychologists 1; Social Workers 6; Child Care Staff 17; Nurses 1. *Curricula* Traditional Academic; Individualized; Basic Skills; Prevocational. *Educational Intervention Approaches* Engineered Classroom; Precision Teaching; Progressive Discipline; Self-Control; Behavior Modification; Applied Behavior Analysis; Creative Conditioning. *Degrees Awarded* Certificate of Attendance.

West-Ros-Park Mental Health Center

780 American Legion Hwy, Roslindale, MA 02131
(617) 325-6700
Year Established 1970
Contact Harold Goldberg, Clinical Dir

Facility Information *Placement* Outpatient Treatment. *Sexes Served* Both. *Sources of Funding* State Funds; Health Insurance; Medicaid.

Student/Patient Characteristics *Age Levels* 0-4; 5-8; 9-11; 12-14; 15-17. *IQ Ranges* 85-130. *Exceptionalities Served* Emotionally Disturbed; Learning Disabled; Mentally Handicapped; Communication Disordered. *Learning Problems* Memory Disabilities; Perceptual Disabilities; Thinking Disabilities; Oral Language Disabilities; Reading Disabilities; Handwriting Disabilities; Spelling Disabilities; Arithmetic Disabilities; Written Expression. *Behavioral Problems* Attention Deficits; Hyperactivity; Hypoactivity; Impulsivity; Self-Aggression; Verbal Aggression; Physical Aggression; Indirect Aggression; Passive Aggression; Withdrawal. *Conditions Treated* Alcohol Abuse and/or Drug Abuse; Other Substance Abuse or Dependence; Early Infantile Autism; Disintegrative Psychoses; Schizophrenia; Convulsive Disorders; Phobias; Obsessions and Compulsions; Hysteria; Depression; Suicide; Asthma; Anorexia Nervosa; Ulcerative Colitis; Inadequacy/Immaturity; Personality Problems; Socialized Aggressive Reaction; Unsocialized Aggressive Reaction.

Services Provided Individual Therapy; Group Therapy; Parent Involvement; Behavior Therapy; Cognitive Developmental Therapy; Family Therapy; Filial Therapy; Drug Therapy; Play Therapy. *Professionals on Staff* Psychiatrists 3; Psychologists 7; Social Workers 5; Nurses 3.

Michigan

Arnell Engstrom Children's Center

Box C, Traverse City, MI 49684 (616) 922-5400
Year Established 1971
Contact Paul Surratt, Dir
Facility Information *Placement* Psychiatric Hospital. *Number of Beds* 40. *Children/Adolescents Served* 40. *Sexes Served* Both. *Room and Board Fees (Approx)* $284. *Sources of Funding* State Funds; Health Insurance; Medicaid; First Party. Summer school available. *Teacher Certification Level* Elementary School; Junior High/Middle School; High School. *Special Certification Level* Emotionally Impaired.
Student/Patient Characteristics *Age Levels* 5-8; 9-11; 12-14; 15-17; 18-21. *Exceptionalities Served* Emotionally Disturbed. *Learning Problems* Memory Disabilities; Perceptual Disabilities; Thinking Disabilities; Oral Language Disabilities; Reading Disabilities; Handwriting Disabilities; Spelling Disabilities; Arithmetic Disabilities; Written Expression. *Behavioral Problems* Attention Deficits; Hyperactivity; Hypoactivity; Impulsivity; Self-Aggression; Verbal Aggression; Physical Aggression; Indirect Aggression; Passive Aggression; Withdrawal. *Conditions Treated* Disintegrative Psychoses; Schizophrenia; Aphasia; Convulsive Disorders; Phobias; Obsessions and Compulsions; Hysteria; Depression; Suicide; Anorexia Nervosa; Inadequacy/Immaturity; Personality Problems; Socialized Aggressive Reaction; Unsocialized Aggressive Reaction.
Services Provided Individual Therapy; Group Therapy; Parent Involvement; Behavior Therapy; Drug Therapy. *Professionals on Staff* Psychiatrists 2; Psychologists 2; Counselors; Social Workers 4; Child Care Staff 50; Nurses 10; Occupation Therapist; Recreation Therapist. *Service Facilities Available (with number of rooms)* Self-Contained Rooms 6. *Educational Professionals* Special Education Teachers 7. *Curricula* Traditional Academic; Career/Vocational Education; Individualized; Basic Skills; Prevocational. *Educational Intervention Approaches* Precision Teaching; Behavior Modification. *Degrees Awarded* Certificate of Attendance; High School Diploma.
Comments The center is a psychiatric hospital for children and adolescents.

Barat Human Services—Barat House

5250 John Rd, Detroit, MI 48202 (313) 833-1525
Year Established 1925
Contact Dianne Bostic Robinson, Exec Dir
Facility Information *Placement* Private Residential Care. *Number of Beds* 22. *Children/Adolescents Served* 22. *Sexes Served* Male. *Room and Board Fees (Approx)* $84. *Sources of Funding* State Funds; United Foundation. Summer school available. *Teacher Certification Level* Elementary School; Junior High/Middle School; High School. *Special Certification Level* ED; LD; MR.

Student/Patient Characteristics *Age Levels* 12-14; 15-17. *IQ Ranges* 71-85; 85-130; Above 130. *Exceptionalities Served* Emotionally Disturbed; Learning Disabled; Mentally Handicapped. *Learning Problems* Memory Disabilities; Perceptual Disabilities; Thinking Disabilities; Reading Disabilities; Handwriting Disabilities; Spelling Disabilities; Arithmetic Disabilities; Written Expression. *Behavioral Problems* Attention Deficits; Hyperactivity; Impulsivity; Self-Aggression; Verbal Aggression; Physical Aggression; Indirect Aggression; Passive Aggression; Withdrawal. *Conditions Treated* Depression; Suicide; Asthma; Inadequacy/Immaturity; Personality Problems; Socialized Aggressive Reaction; Unsocialized Aggressive Reaction.
Services Provided Individual Therapy; Group Therapy; Parent Involvement; Behavior Therapy; Family Therapy; Art Therapy; Reality Therapy. *Professionals on Staff* Psychiatrists 1; Social Workers 3; Child Care Staff 5; Nurses 3; Art Therapist. *Educational Professionals* Special Education Teachers 1; Paraprofessionals 3. *Curricula* Traditional Academic; Individualized; Basic Skills. *Educational Intervention Approaches* Progressive Discipline; Behavior Modification; Creative Conditioning.
Comments Barat House is a community based residential treatment program with the majority of the residents attending community schools. In-house individualized educational and tutorial programs are provided for those students who exhibit school phobia and who are out of school.

Battle Creek Child Guidance Center

155 Garfield Ave, Battle Creek, MI 59017 (616) 968-9287
Year Established 1952
Contact Irma M Bradley, Exec Dir
Facility Information *Placement* Outpatient Child Guidance Center. *Children/Adolescents Served* 500. *Sexes Served* Both. *Tuition Fees (Approx)* Sliding Scale. *Sources of Funding* State Funds; Health Insurance; Medicaid; 10% Local Match.
Student/Patient Characteristics *Age Levels* 0-4; 5-8; 9-11; 12-14; 15-17. *IQ Ranges* 56-70; 71-85; 85-130; Above 130. *Exceptionalities Served* Autistic; Emotionally Disturbed; Learning Disabled; Mentally Handicapped; Gifted. *Learning Problems* Memory Disabilities; Perceptual Disabilities; Thinking Disabilities. *Behavioral Problems* Attention Deficits; Hyperactivity; Hypoactivity; Impulsivity; Self-Aggression; Verbal Aggression; Physical Aggression; Indirect Aggression; Passive Aggression; Withdrawal. *Conditions Treated* Alcohol Abuse and/or Drug Abuse; Other Substance Abuse or Dependence; Early Infantile Autism; Disintegrative Psychoses; Schizophrenia; Aphasia; Convulsive Disorders; Phobias; Obsessions and Compulsions; Hysteria; Depression; Suicide; Asthma; Anorexia Nervosa; Inadequacy/Immaturity; Personality Problems; Socialized Aggressive Reaction; Unsocialized Aggressive Reaction.

Services Provided Individual Therapy; Group Therapy; Parent Involvement; Behavior Therapy; Cognitive Developmental Therapy; Biofeedback; Family Therapy; Filial Therapy; Drug Therapy; Art Therapy; Reality Therapy; Play Therapy. *Professionals on Staff* Psychiatrists 3; Psychologists 1; Social Workers 5. *Service Facilities Available (with number of rooms)* Consultative (ERT); Resource Rooms; Transition Rooms; Self-Contained Rooms. *Educational Professionals* Regular School Teachers; Special Education Teachers; Special Education Counselors. *Curricula* Traditional Academic; Career/Vocational Education; Individualized; Basic Skills; Prevocational. *Educational Intervention Approaches* Behavior Modification. *Degrees Awarded* High School Diploma; Graduate Equivalency Diploma.

Comments The Battle Creek Child Guidance Center is an outpatient diagnostic and treatment facility serving all of Calhoun County. It utilizes a team approach (social worker, psychologist and psychiatrist).

Beacon Day Treatment Program

11401 Olive St, Romulus, MI 48174 (313) 941-2770
Year Established 1979
Contact Tom Dolan, Dir
Facility Information *Placement* Day Treatment Program. *Children/Adolescents Served* 200. *Sexes Served* Both. *Sources of Funding* State Funds; Health Insurance; Medicaid. *Teacher Certification Level* Elementary School; Junior High/Middle School; High School. *Special Certification Level* ED.
Student/Patient Characteristics *Age Levels* 5-8; 9-11; 12-14; 15-17; 18-21. *IQ Ranges* 71-85; 85-130; Above 130. *Exceptionalities Served* Emotionally Disturbed. *Learning Problems* Memory Disabilities; Perceptual Disabilities; Thinking Disabilities; Reading Disabilities; Handwriting Disabilities; Spelling Disabilities; Arithmetic Disabilities; Written Expression. *Behavioral Problems* Attention Deficits; Hyperactivity; Impulsivity; Self-Aggression; Verbal Aggression; Physical Aggression; Passive Aggression; Withdrawal. *Conditions Treated* Alcohol Abuse and/or Drug Abuse; Phobias; Obsessions and Compulsions; Hysteria; Depression; Suicide; Anorexia Nervosa; Inadequacy/Immaturity; Personality Problems; Socialized Aggressive Reaction; Unsocialized Aggressive Reaction.
Services Provided Individual Therapy; Group Therapy; Parent Involvement; Behavior Therapy; Cognitive Developmental Therapy; Family Therapy; Filial Therapy; Drug Therapy; Reality Therapy; Play Therapy. *Professionals on Staff* Psychiatrists 1; Psychologists 2; Social Workers 14. *Service Facilities Available (with number of rooms)* Consultative (ERT) 2; Transition Rooms 2; Self-Contained Rooms 20. *Educational Professionals* Special Education Teachers 22; Career/Vocational Teachers 1; Paraprofessionals 24. *Curricula* Traditional Academic; Career/Vocational Education; Individualized; Basic Skills; Prevocational. *Educational Intervention Approaches* Engineered Classroom; Behavior Modification. *Degrees Awarded* High School Diploma.

Berrien County Intermediate School District

711 St Joseph Ave, Berrien Springs, MI 49085 (616) 471-7725
Contact Jerry Reimann, Special Ed
Facility Information *Placement* Public School. *Children/Adolescents Served* 90. *Sexes Served* Both. *Sources of Funding* State Funds; P.L. 94-142. *Teacher Certification Level* Elementary School; Junior High/Middle School; High School. *Special Certification Level* ED; LD; MR.
Student/Patient Characteristics *Age Levels* 0-4; 5-8; 9-11; 12-14; 15-17; 18-21; Over 21. *IQ Ranges* 0-25; 26-40; 41-55; 56-70; 71-85; 85-130. *Exceptionalities Served* Autistic; Emotionally Disturbed.
Comments This program is a public school program, a part of mandatory special education. It serves its area's residents.

Birmingham Autistic Program

1300 Derby, Birmingham, MI 48008 (313) 646-1636
Year Established 1973
Contact Angelynn Martin, Prog Dir
Facility Information *Placement* Public School. *Sexes Served* Both. *Sources of Funding* State Funds; P.L. 94-142. Summer school available. *Teacher Certification Level* Elementary School; Junior High/Middle School; High School. *Special Certification Level* Autistically Impaired.
Student/Patient Characteristics *Age Levels* 0-4; 5-8; 9-11; 12-14. *IQ Ranges* 0-25; 26-40; 41-55; 56-70; 71-85. *Exceptionalities Served* Autistic. *Learning Problems* Perceptual Disabilities; Oral Language Disabilities. *Behavioral Problems* Attention Deficits; Hyperactivity; Hypoactivity; Impulsivity; Self-Aggression; Withdrawal. *Conditions Treated* Early Infantile Autism.
Services Provided Day School Program. *Professionals on Staff* Psychologists 2; Social Workers 1; Speech and Language Pathologists 2; Special Education Teachers 6; Occupational Therapists 1; Physical Therapists 1. *Service Facilities Available (with number of rooms)* Self-Contained Rooms 6. *Educational Professionals* Special Education Teachers 6; Paraprofessionals 8. *Curricula* Individualized. *Educational Intervention Approaches* Precision Teaching; Behavior Modification; Creative Conditioning. *Degrees Awarded* Report Cards; Elementary and Middle School.
Comments The Birmingham Autistic Programs are housed in an elementary and middle school. The autistic students have the same opportunities within the school day as the general education students: art, gym, music, library, home economics. The classrooms are self-contained and students are mainstreamed where appropriate. The students' educational program is individualized.

Boysville of Michigan

8744 Clinton Macon Rd, Clinton, MI 49236
Facility Information *Placement* Public School; Special School; Private Residential Care. *Number of Beds* 200. *Children/Adolescents Served* 200. *Sexes Served* Male. *Room and Board Fees (Approx)* $99. *Sources of Funding* State Funds; Medicaid. Summer school available. *Teacher Certification Level* Junior High/Middle School; High School. *Special Certification Level* ED; LD; Career/Vocational Education; Reading; Math.
Student/Patient Characteristics *Age Levels* 12-14; 15-17. *Exceptionalities Served* Emotionally Disturbed; Learning Disabled. *Learning Problems* Perceptual Disabilities; Thinking Disabilities; Oral Language Disabilities; Reading Disabilities. *Behavioral Problems* Verbal Aggression; Physical Aggression; Indirect Aggression; Passive Aggression.
Services Provided Individual Therapy; Group Therapy; Parent Involvement; Behavior Therapy; Cognitive Developmental Therapy; Family Therapy; Reality Therapy. *Professionals on Staff* Psychologists 3; Counselors 20; Social Workers 25; Child Care Staff 60; Nurses 2. *Educational Professionals* Regular School Teachers; Special Education Teachers; Crisis Teachers. *Curricula* Individualized; Basic Skills; Prevocational. *Degrees Awarded* High School Diploma; Graduate Equivalency Diploma.

Brant Services Corporation—Brant Ryan House

1313 Henry Ruff, Inkster, MI 48141 (313) 721-2700
Contact Adrienne Brant James, Exec Dir
Facility Information *Placement* Public Residential Care. *Children/Adolescents Served* 6. *Sexes Served* Male. *Room and Board Fees (Approx)* $65. *Sources of Funding* State Funds; HEW; Medicaid.
Student/Patient Characteristics *Age Levels* 18-21; Over 21. *IQ Ranges* 26-40; 56-70. *Exceptionalities Served* Autistic; Emotionally Disturbed. *Learning Problems* Memory Disabilities; Perceptual Disabilities; Thinking Disabilities; Oral Language Disabilities; Reading Disabilities; Handwriting Disabilities; Spelling Disabilities; Arithmetic Disabilities; Written Expression. *Behavioral Problems* Attention Deficits; Hyperactivity; Hypoactivity; Impulsivity; Self-Aggression; Physical Aggression; With-

drawal. *Conditions Treated* Early Infantile Autism; Obsessions and Compulsions; Inadequacy/Immaturity; Personality Problems; Socialized Aggressive Reaction; Unsocialized Aggressive Reaction.

Services Provided Individual Therapy; Group Therapy; Parent Involvement; Behavior Therapy; Drug Therapy. *Professionals on Staff* Social Workers 1; Child Care Staff 7; Nurses 1.

Comments Brant House is a state licensed group home for developmentally disabled adults and is currently a home for 6 autistic men 18 years of age and older.

Calhoun Intermediate School District

17111 G Dr N, Marshall, MI 49068 (616) 781-5141
Contact Alfred B Worde, Dir Special Ed
Facility Information *Placement* Public School.

Cheboygan-Otsego-Presque Isle Intermediate School District—Alpine Educational Facility

Box 979, Gaylord, MI 45735 (517) 732-4676
Year Established 1980
Contact Earl A Kilonder, Special Ed Supv
Facility Information *Placement* Special School.
Children/Adolescents Served 65. *Sexes Served* Both. *Sources of Funding* State Funds; P.L. 94-142. Summer school available.
Teacher Certification Level Elementary School; Junior High/Middle School. *Special Certification Level* ED; MR.
Student/Patient Characteristics *Age Levels* 0-4; 5-8; 9-11; 12-14; 15-17; 18-21; Over 21. *IQ Ranges* 0-25; 26-40; 41-55.
Exceptionalities Served Autistic; Mentally Handicapped; Communication Disordered; Hearing Impaired/Deaf; Visually Impaired/Blind; Other Health Impaired; Physically Handicapped. *Learning Problems* Memory Disabilities; Perceptual Disabilities; Thinking Disabilities; Oral Language Disabilities; Reading Disabilities; Handwriting Disabilities; Spelling Disabilities; Arithmetic Disabilities; Written Expression. *Behavioral Problems* Attention Deficits; Hyperactivity; Hypoactivity; Impulsivity; Self-Aggression; Verbal Aggression; Physical Aggression; Withdrawal. *Conditions Treated* Early Infantile Autism.

Services Provided *Professionals on Staff* Psychologists 1; Social Workers 1. *Service Facilities Available (with number of rooms)* Self-Contained Rooms 5. *Educational Professionals* Special Education Teachers 5; Paraprofessionals 10. *Curricula* Individualized; Basic Skills; Prevocational. *Educational Intervention Approaches* Precision Teaching; Progressive Discipline; Self-Control; Behavior Modification.

Cheboygan-Otsego-Presque Isle Intermediate School District—Hawks Programs

Box 101, Hawks, MI 49743 (517) 734-3947
Year Established 1970
Contact Earl A Kilonder, Special Ed Supv
Facility Information *Placement* Special School.
Children/Adolescents Served 30. *Sexes Served* Both. *Sources of Funding* State Funds. Summer school available. *Teacher Certification Level* Elementary School; Junior High/Middle School. *Special Certification Level* ED; LD; MR.
Student/Patient Characteristics *Age Levels* 0-4; 5-8; 9-11; 12-14; 15-17; 18-21; Over 21. *IQ Ranges* 0-25; 26-40; 41-55.
Exceptionalities Served Autistic; Mentally Handicapped; Communication Disordered; Hearing Impaired/Deaf; Visually Impaired/Blind; Other Health Impaired; Physically Handicapped. *Learning Problems* Memory Disabilities; Perceptual Disabilities; Thinking Disabilities; Oral Language Disabilities; Reading Disabilities; Handwriting Disabilities; Spelling Disabilities; Arithmetic Disabilities; Written Expression. *Behavioral Problems* Attention Deficits; Hyperactivity; Hypoactivity; Impulsivity; Self-Aggression; Verbal Aggression; Physical Aggression; Indirect Aggression. *Conditions Treated* Early Infantile Autism.

Services Provided *Professionals on Staff* Psychologists 1; Social Workers 1. *Service Facilities Available (with number of rooms)* Self-Contained Rooms 2. *Educational Professionals* Special Education Teachers 2; Paraprofessionals 5. *Curricula* Individualized; Basic Skills; Prevocational. *Educational Intervention Approaches* Precision Teaching; Progressive Discipline; Self-Control; Behavior Modification.

Cheboygen-Otsego-Presque Isle Intermediate School District—Inverness Elementary

Box 100, Cheboygen, MI 49721 (616) 627-2804
Year Established 1970
Contact Earl A Kilonder, Special Ed Supv
Facility Information *Placement* Public School.
Children/Adolescents Served 15. *Sexes Served* Both. *Sources of Funding* State Funds; P.L. 94-142. Summer school available.
Teacher Certification Level Elementary School; Junior High/Middle School. *Special Certification Level* MR.
Student/Patient Characteristics *Age Levels* 0-4; 5-8; 9-11; 12-14; 15-17; 18-21; Over 21. *IQ Ranges* 0-25; 26-40. *Exceptionalities Served* Autistic; Mentally Handicapped; Communication Disordered; Hearing Impaired/Deaf; Visually Impaired/Blind; Other Health Impaired; Physically Handicapped. *Learning Problems* Memory Disabilities; Perceptual Disabilities; Thinking Disabilities; Oral Language Disabilities; Reading Disabilities; Handwriting Disabilities; Spelling Disabilities; Arithmetic Disabilities; Written Expression. *Behavioral Problems* Attention Deficits; Hyperactivity; Hypoactivity; Impulsivity; Self-Aggression; Verbal Aggression; Physical Aggression. *Conditions Treated* Early Infantile Autism.

Services Provided *Professionals on Staff* Psychologists 1; Social Workers 1. *Service Facilities Available (with number of rooms)* Self-Contained Rooms 1. *Educational Professionals* Special Education Teachers 1; Paraprofessionals 2. *Curricula* Individualized. *Educational Intervention Approaches* Precision Teaching; Progressive Discipline; Self-Control; Behavior Modification.

Child Psychiatry Service—Department of Psychiatry—University Hospitals

1402 Catherine Pl, Ann Arbor, MI 48109-0010 (313) 764-0250
Facility Information *Placement* Child Psychiatry Service. *Number of Beds* 51. *Sexes Served* Both. *Room and Board Fees (Approx)* $415. *Sources of Funding* Health Insurance; Medicaid. Summer school available. *Teacher Certification Level* Elementary School; Junior High/Middle School; High School. *Special Certification Level* ED; LD; MR; Career/Vocational Education; Reading; Math; Science; Social Studies; Language Arts; Deaf Education; Art Education; Music Education.
Student/Patient Characteristics *Age Levels* 0-4; 5-8; 9-11; 12-14; 15-17. *IQ Ranges* 71-85; 85-130; Above 130. *Exceptionalities Served* Emotionally Disturbed; Learning Disabled; Mentally Handicapped. *Learning Problems* Memory Disabilities; Perceptual Disabilities; Thinking Disabilities; Oral Language Disabilities; Reading Disabilities; Handwriting Disabilities; Spelling Disabilities; Arithmetic Disabilities; Written Expression. *Behavioral Problems* Attention Deficits; Hyperactivity; Hypoactivity; Impulsivity; Self-Aggression; Verbal Aggression; Physical Aggression; Indirect Aggression; Passive Aggression; Withdrawal. *Conditions Treated* Schizophrenia; Phobias; Obsessions and Compulsions; Hysteria; Depression; Suicide; Asthma; Anorexia Nervosa; Ulcerative Colitis; Inadequacy/Immaturity; Personality Problems; Socialized Aggressive Reaction; Unsocialized Aggressive Reaction.

Services Provided Individual Therapy; Parent Involvement; Family Therapy; Drug Therapy; Art Therapy; Music Therapy; Play Therapy. *Professionals on Staff* Psychiatrists; Psychologists; Social Workers; Child Care Staff; Nurses; Activity Therapists.
Service Facilities Available (with number of rooms) Consultative (ERT); Itinerants; Resource Rooms; Transition Rooms; Self-Contained Rooms; Special School; Hospital School; On-Campus Residential School; Homebound Instruction. *Educational*

Professionals Special Education Teachers 18; Paraprofessionals 4. *Curricula* Traditional Academic; Career/Vocational Education; Individualized; Basic Skills.

Family Guidance Service—Ingham Community Mental Health Center

407 W Greenlawn, Lansing, MI 48910 (517) 374-8000
Year Established 1967
Contact Steven R Shelton, Prog Supv
Facility Information *Placement* Public Residential Care; Public Day Care; Special Program. *Sexes Served* Both. *Sources of Funding* State Funds; Health Insurance; Medicaid. Summer school available.
Student/Patient Characteristics *Age Levels* 5-8; 9-11; 12-14; 15-17. *IQ Ranges* 56-70; 71-85; 85-130; Above 130. *Exceptionalities Served* Emotionally Disturbed; Learning Disabled. *Learning Problems* Memory Disabilities; Perceptual Disabilities; Thinking Disabilities; Reading Disabilities. *Behavioral Problems* Attention Deficits; Hyperactivity; Impulsivity; Self-Aggression; Verbal Aggression; Physical Aggression; Indirect Aggression; Passive Aggression; Withdrawal. *Conditions Treated* Disintegrative Psychoses; Schizophrenia; Phobias; Obsessions and Compulsions; Hysteria; Depression; Suicide; Anorexia Nervosa; Inadequacy/Immaturity; Personality Problems; Socialized Aggressive Reaction; Unsocialized Aggressive Reaction.
Services Provided Individual Therapy; Group Therapy; Parent Involvement; Cognitive Developmental Therapy; Family Therapy; Filial Therapy; Drug Therapy; Art Therapy; Reality Therapy; Play Therapy. *Professionals on Staff* Psychiatrists 2; Psychologists 2; Social Workers 4; Occupational Therapist 1; Recreational Therapist 1.

Flint Community Schools

923 E Kearsley St, Flint, MI 48502 (313) 762-1915
Contact Sherry A Goodwin, Special Ed Dir
Facility Information *Placement* Public School.
Children/Adolescents Served 50. *Sexes Served* Both. *Sources of Funding* State Funds; P.L. 94-142. *Teacher Certification Level* Elementary School; Junior High/Middle School; High School. *Special Certification Level* ED; LD; MR.
Student/Patient Characteristics *Age Levels* 0-4; 5-8; 9-11; 12-14; 15-17; 18-21. *IQ Ranges* 71-85. *Exceptionalities Served* Autistic; Emotionally Disturbed. *Learning Problems* Perceptual Disabilities; Oral Language Disabilities; Reading Disabilities; Handwriting Disabilities; Spelling Disabilities; Arithmetic Disabilities. *Behavioral Problems* Attention Deficits; Hyperactivity; Hypoactivity; Impulsivity; Self-Aggression; Verbal Aggression; Physical Aggression; Indirect Aggression; Passive Aggression; Withdrawal. *Conditions Treated* Early Infantile Autism; Disintegrative Psychoses; Schizophrenia; Phobias; Depression; Personality Problems; Socialized Aggressive Reaction; Unsocialized Aggressive Reaction.
Services Provided Individual Therapy; Group Therapy; Parent Involvement; Behavior Therapy; Family Therapy; Play Therapy. *Professionals on Staff* Psychiatrists 2.5; Psychologists 11; Social Workers 21; Child Care Staff 4; Mental Health Therapists 4; Child Care Workers 4. *Service Facilities Available (with number of rooms)* Itinerants 1; Transition Rooms 4. *Educational Professionals* Special Education Teachers 4; Special Education Counselors 1; Paraprofessionals 4. *Curricula* Traditional Academic; Career/Vocational Education; Individualized; Basic Skills; Prevocational. *Educational Intervention Approaches* Engineered Classroom; Progressive Discipline; Self-Control; Behavior Modification. *Degrees Awarded* High School Diploma.

Genesee Intermediate School District Center for Autism

2413 W Maple Ave, Flint, MI 48507 (313) 767-4310
Year Established 1976
Contact James D Hilley, Dir Special Serv

Facility Information *Placement* Public School; Special School; Public Day Care. *Children/Adolescents Served* 60. *Sexes Served* Both. *Sources of Funding* State Funds; HEW; P.L. 94-142; Title I; Chapter I. Summer school available. *Teacher Certification Level* Elementary School; Junior High/Middle School; High School. *Special Certification Level* ED; Autism.
Student/Patient Characteristics *Age Levels* 0-4; 5-8; 9-11; 12-14; 15-17; 18-21; Over 21. *IQ Ranges* 0-25; 26-40; 41-55; 56-70; 71-85; 85-130; Above 130. *Exceptionalities Served* Autistic. *Learning Problems* Memory Disabilities; Perceptual Disabilities; Thinking Disabilities; Oral Language Disabilities; Reading Disabilities; Handwriting Disabilities; Spelling Disabilities; Arithmetic Disabilities; Written Expression. *Behavioral Problems* Attention Deficits; Hyperactivity; Hypoactivity; Impulsivity; Self-Aggression; Verbal Aggression; Physical Aggression; Indirect Aggression; Withdrawal. *Conditions Treated* Early Infantile Autism; Schizophrenia; Aphasia; Convulsive Disorders; Depression; Suicide.
Services Provided Individual Therapy; Group Therapy; Parent Involvement; Behavior Therapy; Cognitive Developmental Therapy; Family Therapy; Drug Therapy; Art Therapy; Music Therapy; Play Therapy; Psychodrama Case Work Treatment. *Professionals on Staff* Psychiatrists 10; Psychologists 1; Social Workers 1; Child Care Staff 10; Nurses 1; Physical Education Teacher; Speech Therapist 1. *Service Facilities Available (with number of rooms)* Self-Contained Rooms 10; Special School. *Educational Professionals* Special Education Teachers 10; Paraprofessionals 10. *Curricula* Individualized; Prevocational. *Educational Intervention Approaches* Behavior Modification.

Hawthorn Center

18471 Haggerty Rd, Northville, MI 48167 (313) 349-3000
Year Established 1956
Contact Beverley M Baskins, Admin Mgr
Facility Information *Placement* State Hospital. *Number of Beds* 136. *Children/Adolescents Served* 136. *Sexes Served* Both. *Room and Board Fees (Approx)* $215. *Sources of Funding* State Funds. Summer school available. *Teacher Certification Level* Elementary School; Junior High/Middle School; High School. *Special Certification Level* Special Education.
Student/Patient Characteristics *Age Levels* 5-8; 9-11; 12-14; 15-17. *Exceptionalities Served* Autistic; Emotionally Disturbed; Learning Disabled; Communication Disordered; Hearing Impaired/Deaf. *Learning Problems* Memory Disabilities; Perceptual Disabilities; Thinking Disabilities; Oral Language Disabilities; Reading Disabilities; Handwriting Disabilities; Spelling Disabilities; Arithmetic Disabilities; Written Expression. *Behavioral Problems* Attention Deficits; Hyperactivity; Hypoactivity; Impulsivity; Self-Aggression; Verbal Aggression; Physical Aggression; Indirect Aggression; Passive Aggression; Withdrawal. *Conditions Treated* Alcohol Abuse and/or Drug Abuse; Other Substance Abuse or Dependence; Early Infantile Autism; Disintegrative Psychoses; Schizophrenia; Aphasia; Convulsive Disorders; Phobias; Obsessions and Compulsions; Hysteria; Depression; Suicide; Asthma; Anorexia Nervosa; Ulcerative Colitis; Inadequacy/Immaturity; Personality Problems; Socialized Aggressive Reaction; Unsocialized Aggressive Reaction.
Services Provided Individual Therapy; Group Therapy; Family Therapy. *Professionals on Staff* Psychiatrists 11; Psychologists 11.5; Social Workers 17.5; Child Care Staff 106.5; Nurses 29; Pediatrician .5. *Educational Professionals* Special Education Teachers 41. *Curricula* Traditional Academic; Individualized; Basic Skills. *Degrees Awarded* High School Diploma.
Comments Services are limited to Michigan residents.

Ingham Developmental Center

625 Hagadorn Rd, Mason, MI 48854 (517) 676-3778
Contact David Fuller, Principal

Facility Information *Placement* Day School Program; Special Education. *Children/Adolescents Served* 160. *Sexes Served* Both. *Sources of Funding* State Funds; P.L. 94-142. Summer school available. *Teacher Certification Level* Elementary School. *Special Certification Level* Special Education.

Student/Patient Characteristics *Age Levels* 0-4; 5-8; 9-11; 12-14; 15-17; 18-21; Over 21. *Exceptionalities Served* Autistic; Mentally Handicapped; Communication Disordered; Hearing Impaired/Deaf; Visually Impaired/Blind; Other Health Impaired. *Behavioral Problems* Attention Deficits; Hyperactivity; Hypoactivity; Impulsivity; Self-Aggression; Verbal Aggression; Physical Aggression; Withdrawal. *Conditions Treated* Early Infantile Autism.

Services Provided Individual Therapy; Parent Involvement. *Professionals on Staff* Psychiatrists 1; Psychologists 2; Social Workers 2; Nurses 1. *Educational Professionals* Special Education Teachers 18; Crisis Teachers 1; Paraprofessionals 27; Support Staff 8. *Curricula* Individualized; Prevocational. *Educational Intervention Approaches* Progressive Discipline; Self-Control; Behavior Modification; Applied Behavior Analysis.

Ingham Intermediate School District

2630 W Howell Rd, Mason, MI 48854 (517) 676-5968
Contact Kenneth J Woodring, Dir of Prog and Serv
Facility Information *Placement* Public School. *Children/Adolescents Served* 50. *Sexes Served* Both. *Sources of Funding* State Funds; P.L. 94-142; Local. *Teacher Certification Level* Elementary School; Junior High/Middle School; High School. *Special Certification Level* ED; LD.

Student/Patient Characteristics *Age Levels* 15-17; 18-21; Over 21. *IQ Ranges* 71-85; 85-130; Above 130. *Exceptionalities Served* Emotionally Disturbed; Learning Disabled. *Learning Problems* Memory Disabilities; Perceptual Disabilities; Thinking Disabilities; Oral Language Disabilities; Reading Disabilities; Handwriting Disabilities; Spelling Disabilities; Arithmetic Disabilities; Written Expression. *Behavioral Problems* Attention Deficits; Hyperactivity; Impulsivity; Self-Aggression; Verbal Aggression; Physical Aggression; Indirect Aggression; Passive Aggression; Withdrawal.

Services Provided Parent Involvement; Behavior Therapy. *Professionals on Staff* Psychiatrists; Psychologists .2; Social Workers 1. *Service Facilities Available (with number of rooms)* Itinerants 2; Resource Rooms 1; Self-Contained Rooms 5. *Educational Professionals* Special Education Teachers 6. *Curricula* Traditional Academic; Career/Vocational Education; Individualized; Basic Skills; Prevocational; Personal Adjustments. *Educational Intervention Approaches* Precision Teaching; Progressive Discipline; Self-Control; Behavior Modification. *Degrees Awarded* High School Diploma.

Comments This program serves high school students with learning and adjustment problems. The program is situated in a vocational educational center and is available to students from 11 local school districts. Students may attend for up to a full day.

Jackson County Intermediate School District

6700 Browns Lake Rd, Jackson, MI 49203 (517) 787-2800
Year Established 1970
Contact Dianne Taulbee, Supv
Facility Information *Placement* Public School. *Number of Beds* 60. *Children/Adolescents Served* 75. *Sexes Served* Both. *Sources of Funding* State Funds; P.L. 94-142. *Teacher Certification Level* Elementary School; Junior High/Middle School; High School. *Special Certification Level* ED.

Student/Patient Characteristics *Age Levels* 0-4; 5-8; 9-11; 12-14; 15-17; 18-21; Over 21. *IQ Ranges* 85-130. *Exceptionalities Served* Autistic; Emotionally Disturbed. *Learning Problems* Memory Disabilities; Perceptual Disabilities; Thinking Disabilities; Reading Disabilities; Handwriting Disabilities; Spelling Disabilities; Arithmetic Disabilities. *Behavioral Problems* Attention Deficits; Hyperactivity; Hypoactivity; Impulsivity; Self-Aggression; Verbal Aggression; Physical Aggression; Indirect Aggression; Passive Aggression; Withdrawal. *Conditions Treated* Alcohol Abuse and/or Drug Abuse; Inadequacy/Immaturity; Personality Problems.

Services Provided Individual Therapy; Group Therapy; Parent Involvement; Behavior Therapy; Cognitive Developmental Therapy; Drug Therapy; Play Therapy. *Professionals on Staff* Psychiatrists; Psychologists; Social Workers. *Service Facilities Available (with number of rooms)* Consultative (ERT); Itinerants; Resource Rooms; Transition Rooms; Self-Contained Rooms; Special School; Hospital School; Homebound Instruction. *Educational Professionals* Regular School Teachers; Special Education Teachers; Special Education Counselors; Paraprofessionals. *Curricula* Traditional Academic; Developmental; Affective. *Educational Intervention Approaches* Engineered Classroom; Precision Teaching; Progressive Discipline; Self-Control; Behavior Modification; Applied Behavior Analysis; Creative Conditioning. *Degrees Awarded* Certificate of Attendance; High School Diploma.

Comments This program provides services only to students within Jackson County, who are certified to receive special education services.

Kalamazoo Child Guidance Clinic

2615 Stadium Dr, Kalamazoo, MI 49008 (616) 343-1651
Year Established 1942
Contact Richard E Becker, Exec Dir
Facility Information *Placement* Private Nonprofit Outpatient Clinic. *Children/Adolescents Served* 1200 (outpatient). *Sexes Served* Both. *Sources of Funding* State Funds; Medicaid; Fees.

Student/Patient Characteristics *Age Levels* 0-4; 5-8; 9-11; 12-14; 15-17. *IQ Ranges* 56-70; 71-85; 85-130; Above 130. *Exceptionalities Served* Autistic; Emotionally Disturbed; Learning Disabled. *Learning Problems* Memory Disabilities; Perceptual Disabilities; Thinking Disabilities. *Behavioral Problems* Attention Deficits; Hyperactivity; Hypoactivity; Impulsivity; Self-Aggression; Verbal Aggression; Physical Aggression; Indirect Aggression; Passive Aggression; Withdrawal. *Conditions Treated* Alcohol Abuse and/or Drug Abuse; Other Substance Abuse or Dependence; Early Infantile Autism; Disintegrative Psychoses; Schizophrenia; Phobias; Obsessions and Compulsions; Hysteria; Depression; Suicide; Asthma; Anorexia Nervosa; Inadequacy/Immaturity; Personality Problems; Socialized Aggressive Reaction; Unsocialized Aggressive Reaction.

Services Provided Individual Therapy; Group Therapy; Parent Involvement; Behavior Therapy; Family Therapy; Drug Therapy; Play Therapy. *Professionals on Staff* Psychiatrists 2; Psychologists 6; Counselors 2; Social Workers 6; Nurses 1; Child Development Specialists 2.

Comments The Kalamazoo Child Guidance Clinic is a private nonprofit outpatient psychiatric program. It serves all school-age children as well as infants and preschoolers. It provides diagnostic and treatment services for emotionally disturbed children and their families. It also has a special outreach program serving abused children, the neglected, and emotionally upset adolescents.

Kalamazoo Valley Intermediate School District

1819 E Milham Rd, Kalamazoo, MI 49002 (616) 381-4620
Contact Annlee Decent, Asst Supt

Lafayette Clinic

951 E Lafayette, Detroit, MI 48207 (313) 256-9350
Year Established 1955
Contact Linda Hryhorczuk, Dir Child Adolescent Serv
Facility Information *Placement* Public Residential Care. *Number of Beds* 40. *Children/Adolescents Served* 40. *Sexes Served* Both. *Sources of Funding* State Funds. Summer school available. *Teacher Certification Level* Elementary School; Junior High/Middle School; High School. *Special Certification Level* ED; LD.

Student/Patient Characteristics *Age Levels* 5-8; 9-11; 12-14; 15-17. *IQ Ranges* 56-70; 71-85; 85-130; Above 130. *Exceptionalities Served* Autistic; Emotionally Disturbed; Learning

Disabled; Communication Disordered. *Learning Problems* Memory Disabilities; Perceptual Disabilities; Thinking Disabilities; Oral Language Disabilities; Reading Disabilities; Handwriting Disabilities; Spelling Disabilities; Arithmetic Disabilities; Written Expression. *Behavioral Problems* Attention Deficits; Hyperactivity; Hypoactivity; Impulsivity; Self-Aggression; Verbal Aggression; Physical Aggression; Indirect Aggression; Passive Aggression; Withdrawal. *Conditions Treated* Early Infantile Autism; Disintegrative Psychoses; Schizophrenia; Aphasia; Convulsive Disorders; Phobias; Obsessions and Compulsions; Hysteria; Depression; Suicide; Anorexia Nervosa; Inadequacy/Immaturity; Personality Problems; Socialized Aggressive Reaction; Unsocialized Aggressive Reaction.

Services Provided Individual Therapy; Group Therapy; Parent Involvement; Behavior Therapy; Family Therapy; Drug Therapy; Play Therapy. *Professionals on Staff* Psychiatrists 8; Psychologists 4; Social Workers 5; Child Care Staff 12; Nurses 6; Occupational Therapy; Recreational Therapy 4. *Service Facilities Available (with number of rooms)* Hospital School 6. *Educational Professionals* Special Education Teachers 8. *Curricula* Traditional Academic; Individualized; Basic Skills; Prevocational. *Degrees Awarded* Certificate of Attendance.

Lansing School District

519 W Kalamazoo St, Lansing, MI 48933 (517) 374-4300
Contact Pamela Turner, Prog Consultant

Facility Information *Placement* Public School.
Children/Adolescents Served 80. *Sexes Served* Both. *Sources of Funding* State Funds; P.L. 94-142. *Teacher Certification Level* Elementary School; Junior High/Middle School. *Special Certification Level* ED; LD; MR; Reading; Math.
Student/Patient Characteristics *Age Levels* 5-8; 9-11; 12-14; 15-17. *IQ Ranges* 56-70; 71-85; 85-130. *Exceptionalities Served* Autistic; Emotionally Disturbed; Learning Disabled; Mentally Handicapped. *Learning Problems* Memory Disabilities; Perceptual Disabilities; Thinking Disabilities; Oral Language Disabilities; Reading Disabilities; Handwriting Disabilities; Spelling Disabilities; Arithmetic Disabilities; Written Expression. *Behavioral Problems* Attention Deficits; Hyperactivity; Hypoactivity; Impulsivity; Self-Aggression; Verbal Aggression; Physical Aggression; Indirect Aggression; Passive Aggression; Withdrawal. *Conditions Treated* Obsessions and Compulsions; Depression; Inadequacy/Immaturity; Socialized Aggressive Reaction; Unsocialized Aggressive Reaction.

Services Provided Parent Involvement; Behavior Therapy; Cognitive Developmental Therapy; Reality Therapy. *Professionals on Staff* Social Workers 3. *Service Facilities Available (with number of rooms)* Consultative (ERT) 1; Self-Contained Rooms 8. *Educational Professionals* Special Education Teachers; Special Education Counselors; Paraprofessionals. *Curricula* Traditional Academic; Individualized; Basic Skills; Prevocational. *Educational Intervention Approaches* Progressive Discipline; Self-Control; Behavior Modification; Applied Behavior Analysis; Creative Conditioning.

Monroe County Intermediate School District—Programs for Emotionally Impaired

1101 S Raisinville, Monroe, MI 48101 (313) 242-5454
Year Established 1975
Contact Donald A Spencer, Special Ed Supv

Facility Information *Placement* Public School; Special School.
Children/Adolescents Served 120. *Sexes Served* Both. *Sources of Funding* State Funds; P.L. 94-142. *Teacher Certification Level* Elementary School; Junior High/Middle School; High School. *Special Certification Level* ED; LD; MR; Reading.
Student/Patient Characteristics *Age Levels* 5-8; 9-11; 12-14; 15-17; 18-21; Over 21. *IQ Ranges* 71-85; 85-130; Above 130. *Exceptionalities Served* Autistic; Emotionally Disturbed; Learning Disabled. *Learning Problems* Memory Disabilities; Perceptual Disabilities; Thinking Disabilities; Oral Language Disabilities; Reading Disabilities; Handwriting Disabilities; Spelling Disabilities; Arithmetic Disabilities; Written Expression. *Behavioral*

Problems Attention Deficits; Hyperactivity; Hypoactivity; Impulsivity; Self-Aggression; Verbal Aggression; Physical Aggression; Indirect Aggression; Passive Aggression; Withdrawal. *Conditions Treated* Alcohol Abuse and/or Drug Abuse; Other Substance Abuse or Dependence; Early Infantile Autism; Disintegrative Psychoses; Schizophrenia; Phobias; Obsessions and Compulsions; Depression; Inadequacy/Immaturity; Personality Problems; Socialized Aggressive Reaction; Unsocialized Aggressive Reaction.

Services Provided Individual Therapy; Group Therapy; Parent Involvement; Behavior Therapy; Family Therapy. *Professionals on Staff* Psychiatrists 1; Psychologists 1; Social Workers 4. *Service Facilities Available (with number of rooms)* Consultative (ERT) 1; Transition Rooms 9; Self-Contained Rooms 2; Special School 2; Homebound Instruction. *Educational Professionals* Special Education Teachers 11; Special Education Counselors 1; Paraprofessionals 12. *Curricula* Career/Vocational Education; Individualized; Prevocational. *Educational Intervention Approaches* Progressive Discipline; Self-Control; Behavior Modification. *Degrees Awarded* High School Diploma.

Comments This is a county service program. Students are referred from local districts. Resource rooms and teacher consultants are available at the local level.

Normon Westlund Child Guidance Clinic

3253 Congress St, Saginaw, MI 48602 (517) 793-4790
Year Established 1942
Contact David L Blecke, Admin Dir

Facility Information *Placement* Outpatient; Psychiatric Clinic.
Student/Patient Characteristics *Conditions Treated* Alcohol Abuse and/or Drug Abuse; Disintegrative Psychoses; Aphasia; Phobias; Obsessions and Compulsions; Hysteria; Depression; Suicide; Anorexia Nervosa; Ulcerative Colitis; Inadequacy/Immaturity; Personality Problems.

Services Provided Individual Therapy; Group Therapy; Parent Involvement; Biofeedback; Family Therapy; Filial Therapy; Reality Therapy; Play Therapy. *Professionals on Staff* Psychiatrists 2; Psychologists 3; Social Workers 9; Graduate Students; Medical Residents 14.

Northeast Guidance Center

17000 E Warren, Detroit, MI 48224 (313) 824-8000
Contact Jonathan L York, Exec Dir

Facility Information *Placement* Outpatient Psychiatric Clinic.
Sexes Served Both. *Sources of Funding* Health Insurance; Fees.
Student/Patient Characteristics *Age Levels* 0-4; 5-8; 9-11; 12-14; 15-17; 18-21; Over 21.

Services Provided Individual Therapy; Group Therapy; Family Therapy; Marital Therapy; Psychological Testing and Evaluation; Social and Vocational Rehabilitation; Psychiatric Consultation; Crisis Services. *Professionals on Staff* Psychiatrists; Psychologists; Social Workers; Nurses.

Comments Northeast Guidance Center has 4 locations serving northeast Detroit, the Grosse Pointes, and Harper Woods. It offers outpatient services, older adult services, a program for professionals, a community support program, a community education program, an alcohol and chemical dependency treatment program, and professional evaluation and testing services.

Southgate Regional Center for Developmental Disabilities

16700 Pennsylvania, Southgate, MI 48295 (313) 283-9200
Year Established 1977
Contact Laura Pollaccia, Intake Admission and Discharge Coord
Facility Information *Placement* Public Residential Care. *Number of Beds* 29. *Children/Adolescents Served* 30. *Sexes Served* Both. *Sources of Funding* State Funds; Medicaid.
Student/Patient Characteristics *Age Levels* 9-11; 12-14; 15-17; 18-21; Over 21. *IQ Ranges* 0-25; 26-40; 41-55; 56-70; 71-85. *Exceptionalities Served* Autistic; Mentally Handicapped; Communication Disordered; Hearing Impaired/Deaf; Visually Impaired/

Blind; Other Health Impaired. *Learning Problems* Memory Disabilities; Perceptual Disabilities; Thinking Disabilities.
Behavioral Problems Attention Deficits; Hyperactivity; Self-Aggression; Verbal Aggression; Physical Aggression. *Conditions Treated* Early Infantile Autism; Convulsive Disorders; Unsocialized Aggressive Reaction.

Services Provided Individual Therapy; Group Therapy; Parent Involvement; Behavior Therapy. *Professionals on Staff* Psychiatrists 1; Psychologists 3; Social Workers 4; Child Care Staff 232; Nurses 20. *Service Facilities Available (with number of rooms)* Homebound Instruction 1. *Educational Professionals* Special Education Teachers 1. *Curricula* Prevocational. *Educational Intervention Approaches* Behavior Modification.

Comments Southgate Regional Center for Developmental Disabilities serves primarily the severely and profoundly mentally retarded. Residents are admitted who can no longer reside at home or in a community setting. Residents under age 26 attend special education school programs within the community. Residents over age 26 attend pre-vocational programs on the grounds or in the community.

The Starr Commonwealth Schools

13725 26 Mile Rd (Starr Commonwealth Rd), Albion, MI 49224
(517) 629-5591
Year Established 1913
Contact Olga Kolodica, Intake Coord
Facility Information *Placement* Private Residential Care. *Number of Beds* 170. *Children/Adolescents Served* 170. *Sexes Served* Male. *Room and Board Fees (Approx)* $76. *Tuition Fees (Approx)* $27,875. *Sources of Funding* State Funds; Donations. Summer school available. *Teacher Certification Level* Elementary School; Junior High/Middle School; High School. *Special Certification Level* ED; LD; Career/Vocational Education; Reading; Math; Emotionally Impaired.
Student/Patient Characteristics *Age Levels* 9-11; 12-14; 15-17. *Exceptionalities Served* Emotionally Disturbed; Learning Disabled. *Learning Problems* Perceptual Disabilities; Oral Language Disabilities; Reading Disabilities; Spelling Disabilities; Arithmetic Disabilities. *Behavioral Problems* Verbal Aggression; Physical Aggression; Passive Aggression; Withdrawal. *Conditions Treated* Inadequacy/Immaturity; Personality Problems; Unsocialized Aggressive Reaction.
Services Provided Individual Therapy; Group Therapy; Parent Involvement; Behavior Therapy; Family Therapy; Art Therapy; Music Therapy; Reality Therapy; Play Therapy. *Professionals on Staff* Counselors; Social Workers; Child Care Staff; Nurses. *Service Facilities Available (with number of rooms)* Consultative (ERT); Resource Rooms; On-Campus Residential School. *Educational Professionals* Special Education Teachers. *Curricula* Traditional Academic; Career/Vocational Education; Individualized; Basic Skills; Prevocational; Art; Drama. *Educational Intervention Approaches* Self-Control; Behavior Modification.

Comments Students receive service learning, creative arts, music, recreational therapy, and outdoor education.

Vista Maria

20651 W Warren, Dearborn Heights, MI 48127 (313) 271-3050
Year Established 1941
Contact Mary Beth Sinko, Exec Dir
Facility Information *Placement* Private Residential Care. *Number of Beds* 128. *Children/Adolescents Served* 128. *Sexes Served* Female. *Sources of Funding* State Funds; HEW; Medicaid; Court; County; ACDF Funds. *Teacher Certification Level* Elementary School; Junior High/Middle School; High School. *Special Certification Level* ED; LD.
Student/Patient Characteristics *Age Levels* 12-14; 15-17; 18-21. *IQ Ranges* 41-55; 56-70; 71-85. *Exceptionalities Served* Emotionally Disturbed; Learning Disabled. *Learning Problems* Memory Disabilities; Perceptual Disabilities; Thinking Disabilities; Oral Language Disabilities; Reading Disabilities; Handwriting Disabilities; Spelling Disabilities; Arithmetic Disabilities; Written Expression. *Behavioral Problems* Attention Deficits; Hyperactivity;

Hypoactivity; Impulsivity; Self-Aggression; Verbal Aggression; Physical Aggression; Indirect Aggression; Passive Aggression; Withdrawal. *Conditions Treated* Alcohol Abuse and/or Drug Abuse; Other Substance Abuse or Dependence; Phobias; Obsessions and Compulsions; Depression; Suicide; Anorexia Nervosa; Inadequacy/Immaturity; Personality Problems; Socialized Aggressive Reaction; Unsocialized Aggressive Reaction.

Services Provided Individual Therapy; Group Therapy; Parent Involvement; Behavior Therapy; Cognitive Developmental Therapy; Family Therapy; Filial Therapy; Drug Therapy; Art Therapy; Music Therapy; Reality Therapy; Play Therapy; Psychodrama. *Professionals on Staff* Psychiatrists 1; Psychologists 1; Social Workers; Child Care Staff; Nurses 1. *Service Facilities Available (with number of rooms)* Resource Rooms 3; On-Campus Residential School 9. *Educational Professionals* Special Education Teachers 20; Special Education Counselors 20. *Curricula* Traditional Academic; Individualized; Basic Skills; Prevocational. *Educational Intervention Approaches* Progressive Discipline; Self-Control; Behavior Modification; Applied Behavior Analysis. *Degrees Awarded* Certificate of Attendance; High School Diploma.

Wellerwood Autism Program

800 Wellerwood NE, Grand Rapids, MI 49505 (616) 364-6763
Year Established 1974
Contact Lucy Hough Waite, Prog Dir
Facility Information *Placement* Public School. *Sexes Served* Both. *Sources of Funding* State Funds; P.L. 94-142; Community Mental Health. Summer school available. *Teacher Certification Level* Elementary School; Junior High/Middle School; High School. *Special Certification Level* ED; MR; Autistic Impaired.
Student/Patient Characteristics *Age Levels* 0-4; 5-8; 9-11; 12-14; 15-17; 18-21; Over 21. *IQ Ranges* 0-25; 26-40; 41-55; 56-70; 71-85; 85-130. *Exceptionalities Served* Autistic. *Learning Problems* Memory Disabilities; Perceptual Disabilities; Thinking Disabilities; Oral Language Disabilities; Reading Disabilities; Handwriting Disabilities; Spelling Disabilities; Arithmetic Disabilities; Written Expression. *Behavioral Problems* Attention Deficits; Hyperactivity; Hypoactivity; Impulsivity; Self-Aggression; Physical Aggression; Withdrawal. *Conditions Treated* Early Infantile Autism; Aphasia.
Services Provided Parent Involvement; Behavior Therapy; Speech and Language Therapy; Parent Support Group. *Professionals on Staff* Psychiatrists; Psychologists 1; Social Workers 1; Child Care Staff 12. *Service Facilities Available (with number of rooms)* Resource Rooms 1; Self-Contained Rooms 7; Special School 7. *Educational Professionals* Special Education Teachers 8; Paraprofessionals 12. *Curricula* Traditional Academic; Career/Vocational Education; Individualized; Basic Skills; Prevocational. *Educational Intervention Approaches* Behavior Modification; Psycholinguistic Language Training.

York Woods Center

PO Box B, Ypsilanti, MI 48197 (313) 434-3666
Year Established 1965
Contact Robert St John, Facility Dir
Facility Information *Placement* Public Residential Care. *Number of Beds* 60. *Children/Adolescents Served* 60. *Sexes Served* Both. *Room and Board Fees (Approx)* $319. *Sources of Funding* State Funds; Health Insurance; Medicaid. Summer school available. *Teacher Certification Level* Elementary School; Junior High/Middle School; High School. *Special Certification Level* ED; LD; MR; Career/Vocational Education; Reading; Math.
Student/Patient Characteristics *Age Levels* 5-8; 9-11; 12-14; 15-17. *IQ Ranges* 71-85; 85-130. *Exceptionalities Served* Emotionally Disturbed; Learning Disabled; Mentally Handicapped. *Learning Problems* Memory Disabilities; Perceptual Disabilities; Thinking Disabilities; Oral Language Disabilities; Reading Disabilities; Handwriting Disabilities; Spelling Disabilities; Arithmetic Disabilities; Written Expression. *Behavioral Problems* Attention Deficits; Hyperactivity; Hypoactivity; Impulsivity; Self-Aggression; Verbal Aggression; Physical Aggression; Indirect

Aggression; Passive Aggression; Withdrawal. *Conditions Treated* Alcohol Abuse and/or Drug Abuse; Other Substance Abuse or Dependence; Early Infantile Autism; Schizophrenia; Convulsive Disorders; Phobias; Obsessions and Compulsions; Hysteria; Depression; Suicide; Asthma; Anorexia Nervosa; Inadequacy/Immaturity; Personality Problems; Socialized Aggressive Reaction; Unsocialized Aggressive Reaction.

Services Provided Individual Therapy; Group Therapy; Parent Involvement; Behavior Therapy; Family Therapy; Drug Therapy; Art Therapy; Music Therapy; Play Therapy. *Professionals on Staff* Psychiatrists 4; Psychologists 5; Social Workers 12; Child Care Staff 49; Nurses 17. *Educational Professionals* Special Education Teachers 14. *Curricula* Traditional Academic; Career/Vocational Education; Individualized; Basic Skills; Prevocational. *Educational Intervention Approaches* Engineered Classroom; Precision Teaching; Progressive Discipline; Self-Control; Behavior Modification; Applied Behavior Analysis; Creative Conditioning. *Degrees Awarded* Certificate of Attendance.

Minnesota

Bar-None Residential Treatment Services for Children

22426 St Francis Blvd, Anoka, MN 55303 (612) 753-2554
Contact Verlyn Wenndt, Dir
Facility Information *Placement* Public Residential Care. *Number of Beds* 63. *Children/Adolescents Served* 63. *Sexes Served* Both. *Room and Board Fees (Approx)* $78-$112. *Sources of Funding* State Funds; Health Insurance; P.L. 94-142; County or State Contracts. Summer school available. *Teacher Certification Level* Elementary School; Junior High/Middle School; High School. *Special Certification Level* ED; LD; MR.
Student/Patient Characteristics *Age Levels* 0-4; 5-8; 9-11; 12-14; 15-17; 18-21. *IQ Ranges* 0-25; 26-40; 41-55; 56-70; 71-85; 85-130; Above 130. *Exceptionalities Served* Autistic; Emotionally Disturbed; Learning Disabled; Mentally Handicapped; Communication Disordered; Hearing Impaired/Deaf; Visually Impaired/Blind; Physically Handicapped; Gifted. *Learning Problems* Memory Disabilities; Perceptual Disabilities; Thinking Disabilities; Oral Language Disabilities; Reading Disabilities; Handwriting Disabilities; Spelling Disabilities; Arithmetic Disabilities; Written Expression. *Behavioral Problems* Attention Deficits; Hyperactivity; Hypoactivity; Impulsivity; Self-Aggression; Verbal Aggression; Physical Aggression; Indirect Aggression; Passive Aggression; Withdrawal. *Conditions Treated* Early Infantile Autism; Disintegrative Psychoses; Schizophrenia; Aphasia; Convulsive Disorders; Phobias; Obsessions and Compulsions; Hysteria; Depression; Suicide; Asthma; Inadequacy/Immaturity; Personality Problems; Socialized Aggressive Reaction; Unsocialized Aggressive Reaction.
Services Provided Individual Therapy; Group Therapy; Parent Involvement; Behavior Therapy; Family Therapy; Drug Therapy; Reality Therapy; Play Therapy. *Professionals on Staff* Psychiatrists 1; Psychologists 1; Social Workers 8; Child Care Staff 50; Nurses 2; Pediatric Neurologist 1. *Service Facilities Available (with number of rooms)* Resource Rooms 1; Transition Rooms 1; Self-Contained Rooms 4; On-Campus Residential School 9. *Educational Professionals* Special Education Teachers 12; Career/Vocational Teachers 1; Crisis Teachers 1; Paraprofessionals 15. *Curricula* Traditional Academic; Career/Vocational Education. *Educational Intervention Approaches* Engineered Classroom; Precision Teaching; Progressive Discipline; Self-Control; Behavior Modification; Applied Behavior Analysis.
Comments Bar-None has 3 residential treatment programs: 1) Bar-None Residential Treatment Center for emotionally disturbed/handicapped boys, population of 42; 2) Bar-None Intensive Residential Treatment Center for 17 boys and girls, handicapped by autism, autistic-like characteristics and/or developmentally disabled; 3) Bar-None's Forestrian Annex for 7 boys and girls handicapped by autism, autistic-line characteristics and/or developmentally disabled.

Gerard of Minnesota Inc

Box 715, Austin, MN 55912 (507) 433-1843
Year Established 1969
Contact Peter S Brower
Facility Information *Placement* Private Residential Care. *Number of Beds* 46. *Children/Adolescents Served* 46. *Sexes Served* Both. *Room and Board Fees (Approx)* $121. *Sources of Funding* State Funds; Health Insurance; P.L. 94-142. Summer school available. *Teacher Certification Level* Elementary School; Junior High/Middle School; High School. *Special Certification Level* ED; LD; Reading; Math; Behavior Disorders.
Student/Patient Characteristics *Age Levels* 5-8; 9-11; 12-14; 15-17. *IQ Ranges* 85-130; Above 130. *Exceptionalities Served* Emotionally Disturbed; Learning Disabled; Physically Handicapped. *Learning Problems* Memory Disabilities; Perceptual Disabilities; Thinking Disabilities; Oral Language Disabilities; Reading Disabilities; Handwriting Disabilities; Spelling Disabilities; Arithmetic Disabilities; Written Expression. *Behavioral Problems* Attention Deficits; Hyperactivity; Hypoactivity; Impulsivity; Self-Aggression; Verbal Aggression; Physical Aggression; Indirect Aggression; Passive Aggression; Withdrawal. *Conditions Treated* Disintegrative Psychoses; Schizophrenia; Convulsive Disorders; Phobias; Obsessions and Compulsions; Hysteria; Depression; Suicide; Anorexia Nervosa; Inadequacy/Immaturity; Personality Problems; Socialized Aggressive Reaction; Unsocialized Aggressive Reaction.
Services Provided Individual Therapy; Group Therapy; Parent Involvement; Behavior Therapy; Family Therapy; Filial Therapy; Art Therapy; Music Therapy; Reality Therapy; Play Therapy; Recreation Therapy; Dance and Movement Therapy; Medication; Adjunctive Therapy. *Professionals on Staff* Psychiatrists 3; Psychologists 3; Counselors 1; Social Workers 6; Child Care Staff 39; Nurses 6. *Service Facilities Available (with number of rooms)* Self-Contained Rooms 6; On-Campus Residential School 6; Homebound Instruction. *Educational Professionals* Special Education Teachers 6; Paraprofessionals 1. *Curricula* Traditional Academic; Individualized. *Educational Intervention Approaches* Precision Teaching; Progressive Discipline; Self-Control; Behavior Modification.

Gilfillan Center

Box 744, Bemidji, MN 56601 (218) 751-6553
Year Established 1965
Contact Cyril Murphy, Dir
Facility Information *Placement* Special School; Private Residential Care. *Number of Beds* 51. *Children/Adolescents Served* 51. *Sexes Served* Both. *Room and Board Fees (Approx)* $75. *Tuition Fees (Approx)* $27,641. *Sources of Funding* State Funds; Health Insurance; County; Private. Summer school available. *Teacher Certification Level* Elementary School; Junior High/Middle School; High School. *Special Certification Level* ED; LD.

Student/Patient Characteristics *Age Levels* 9-11; 12-14; 15-17. *IQ Ranges* 85-130. *Exceptionalities Served* Emotionally Disturbed; Learning Disabled; Mentally Handicapped; Communication Disordered; Other Health Impaired. *Learning Problems* Memory Disabilities; Perceptual Disabilities; Thinking Disabilities; Oral Language Disabilities; Reading Disabilities; Handwriting Disabilities; Spelling Disabilities; Arithmetic Disabilities; Written Expression. *Behavioral Problems* Attention Deficits; Hyperactivity; Impulsivity; Self-Aggression; Verbal Aggression; Physical Aggression; Indirect Aggression; Passive Aggression. *Conditions Treated* Other Substance Abuse or Dependence; Phobias; Obsessions and Compulsions; Hysteria; Depression; Suicide; Inadequacy/Immaturity; Personality Problems; Socialized Aggressive Reaction; Unsocialized Aggressive Reaction.

Services Provided Individual Therapy; Group Therapy; Parent Involvement; Behavior Therapy; Family Therapy; Drug Therapy; Art Therapy; Reality Therapy. *Professionals on Staff* Psychiatrists 1; Psychologists 1; Counselors 22; Social Workers 4; Nurses 1. *Service Facilities Available (with number of rooms)* Consultative (ERT) 3; Resource Rooms 2; Transition Rooms 2; Self-Contained Rooms 9; On-Campus Residential School; Homebound Instruction 4. *Educational Professionals* Regular School Teachers 2; Special Education Teachers 10. *Curricula* Traditional Academic; Career/Vocational Education; Individualized; Basic Skills; Prevocational. *Educational Intervention Approaches* Engineered Classroom; Precision Teaching; Behavior Modification; Creative Conditioning. *Degrees Awarded* Certificate of Attendance; High School Diploma; Graduate Equivalency Diploma.

Minneapolis Children's Medical Center—Program for Autistic and Other Exceptional Children

2525 Chicago Ave, Minneapolis, MN 55404 (612) 874-6139
Contact Sheila Merzer and Lyle Chaston, Co Dir
Facility Information *Placement* Special School. *Children/Adolescents Served* 30 (direct treatment); 200 (evaluation). *Sexes Served* Both. *Room and Board Fees (Approx)* $30 (day treatment). *Tuition Fees (Approx)* $5,400. *Sources of Funding* Health Insurance; Medicaid; Medicare; P.L. 94-142. Summer school available. *Teacher Certification Level* Elementary School. *Special Certification Level* ED; LD; MR; Early Childhood Education; Special Education.

Student/Patient Characteristics *Age Levels* 0-4; 5-8; 9-11. *IQ Ranges* 0-25; 26-40; 41-55; 56-70; 71-85; 85-130; Above 130. *Exceptionalities Served* Autistic; Emotionally Disturbed; Learning Disabled; Mentally Handicapped; Communication Disordered. *Learning Problems* Perceptual Disabilities; Thinking Disabilities; Oral Language Disabilities. *Behavioral Problems* Attention Deficits; Hyperactivity; Hypoactivity; Impulsivity; Self-Aggression; Verbal Aggression; Physical Aggression; Withdrawal. *Conditions Treated* Early Infantile Autism; Disintegrative Psychoses; Convulsive Disorders; Developmental; Disorders.

Services Provided Individual Therapy; Group Therapy; Parent Involvement; Play Therapy; Occupational Treatment. *Professionals on Staff* Psychiatrists 1; Psychologists 3. *Service Facilities Available (with number of rooms)* Special School 3. *Educational Professionals* Regular School Teachers; Special Education Teachers 40; Paraprofessionals. *Curricula* Individualized.

Minnesota Learning Center

E Oak St, Brainerd, MN 56401 (218) 828-2317
Year Established 1970
Contact Al Mahling, Acting Dir
Facility Information *Placement* Public Residential Care. *Number of Beds* 48. *Children/Adolescents Served* 48. *Sexes Served* Both. *Room and Board Fees (Approx)* $136. *Sources of Funding* State Funds; HEW; Health Insurance; Medicaid; P.L. 94-142; Private Payers. . *Teacher Certification Level* Junior High/Middle School; High School. *Special Certification Level* LD; MR; Career/Vocational Education; Reading; Math; Adult Education.

Student/Patient Characteristics *Age Levels* 5-8; 9-11; 12-14; 15-17; 18-21. *IQ Ranges* 41-55; 56-70; 71-85; 85-130. *Exceptionalities Served* Emotionally Disturbed; Learning Disabled; Mentally Handicapped; Other Health Impaired; Physically Handicapped. *Learning Problems* Memory Disabilities; Perceptual Disabilities; Thinking Disabilities; Oral Language Disabilities; Reading Disabilities; Handwriting Disabilities; Spelling Disabilities; Arithmetic Disabilities; Written Expression. *Behavioral Problems* Attention Deficits; Hyperactivity; Hypoactivity; Impulsivity; Self-Aggression; Verbal Aggression; Physical Aggression; Indirect Aggression; Passive Aggression; Withdrawal. *Conditions Treated* Schizophrenia; Convulsive Disorders; Phobias; Obsessions and Compulsions; Depression; Suicide; Inadequacy/Immaturity; Socialized Aggressive Reaction; Unsocialized Aggressive Reaction.

Services Provided Individual Therapy; Group Therapy; Parent Involvement; Behavior Therapy; Cognitive Developmental Therapy. *Professionals on Staff* Psychiatrists 1; Psychologists 6; Counselors 13; Social Workers 1; Child Care Staff 15; Nurses 2; Parent Trainers; Recreational Therapists; Staff Trainer 14. *Service Facilities Available (with number of rooms)* Self-Contained Rooms 3; Public School. *Educational Professionals* Special Education Teachers 3; Paraprofessionals 27. *Curricula* Traditional Academic; Individualized; Basic Skills; Social Skills Training. *Educational Intervention Approaches* Engineered Classroom; Precision Teaching; Progressive Discipline; Self-Control; Behavior Modification; Applied Behavior Analysis.

Comments The Minnesota Learning Center is a short-term residential program serving youths whose behavior problems prevent them from being served in their home communities. Since 1970, MLC has served 900 youths and their families.

Northwood Children's Home

714 College St, Duluth, MN 55811 (218) 724-8815
Year Established 1883
Contact James Yoeger, Exec Dir
Facility Information *Placement* Private Residential Care. *Number of Beds* 52. *Children/Adolescents Served* 52 (residential); 8 (day treatment). *Sexes Served* Both. *Room and Board Fees (Approx)* $85. *Sources of Funding* State Funds; Health Insurance; Medicaid; P.L. 94-142. Summer school available. *Teacher Certification Level* Elementary School; Junior High/Middle School. *Special Certification Level* ED; LD; MR.

Student/Patient Characteristics *Age Levels* 5-8; 9-11; 12-14; 15-17. *IQ Ranges* 56-70; 71-85; 85-130; Above 130. *Exceptionalities Served* Autistic; Emotionally Disturbed; Learning Disabled; Mentally Handicapped; Communication Disordered; Gifted. *Learning Problems* Memory Disabilities; Perceptual Disabilities; Thinking Disabilities; Oral Language Disabilities; Reading Disabilities; Handwriting Disabilities; Spelling Disabilities; Arithmetic Disabilities; Written Expression. *Behavioral Problems* Attention Deficits; Hyperactivity; Hypoactivity; Impulsivity; Self-Aggression; Verbal Aggression; Physical Aggression; Indirect Aggression; Passive Aggression; Withdrawal. *Conditions Treated* Early Infantile Autism; Schizophrenia; Convulsive Disorders; Phobias; Obsessions and Compulsions; Depression; Suicide; Inadequacy/Immaturity; Personality Problems; Socialized Aggressive Reaction; Unsocialized Aggressive Reaction.

Services Provided Individual Therapy; Group Therapy; Parent Involvement; Behavior Therapy; Family Therapy; Drug Therapy; Art Therapy; Music Therapy; Reality Therapy; Play Therapy; Speech Therapy; Occupational Therapy. *Professionals on Staff* Psychiatrists 1; Psychologists 2; Social Workers 4; Child Care Staff 45; Nurses 1. *Service Facilities Available (with number of rooms)* Consultative (ERT) 2; Resource Rooms 3; Self-Contained Rooms 6. *Educational Professionals* Special Education Teachers 7; Paraprofessionals 8. *Curricula* Traditional Academic; Career/Vocational Education; Individualized; Basic Skills; Prevocational. *Educational Intervention Approaches* Precision Teaching; Progressive Discipline; Self-Control; Behavior Modification. *Degrees Awarded* Graduate Equivalency Diploma.

Range Mental Health Center

Box 1188, Virginia, MN 55792 (218) 749-2881
Contact Craig Stevens

Facility Information *Placement* Outpatient Mental Health Center. *Sources of Funding* State Funds; Health Insurance; Medicaid; Medicare.

Student/Patient Characteristics *Age Levels* 0-4; 5-8; 9-11; 12-14; 15-17; 18-21; Over 21. *IQ Ranges* 0-25; 26-40; 41-55; 56-70; 71-85; 85-130; Above 130. *Exceptionalities Served* Autistic; Emotionally Disturbed; Learning Disabled; Mentally Handicapped; Communication Disordered; Hearing Impaired/Deaf; Visually Impaired/Blind; Other Health Impaired; Physically Handicapped; Gifted. *Learning Problems* Memory Disabilities; Perceptual Disabilities; Thinking Disabilities; Oral Language Disabilities; Reading Disabilities; Handwriting Disabilities; Spelling Disabilities; Arithmetic Disabilities; Written Expression. *Behavioral Problems* Attention Deficits; Hyperactivity; Hypoactivity; Impulsivity; Self-Aggression; Verbal Aggression; Physical Aggression; Indirect Aggression; Passive Aggression; Withdrawal. *Conditions Treated* Alcohol Abuse and/or Drug Abuse; Other Substance Abuse or Dependence; Early Infantile Autism; Disintegrative Psychoses; Schizophrenia; Aphasia; Convulsive Disorders; Phobias; Obsessions and Compulsions; Hysteria; Depression; Suicide; Asthma; Anorexia Nervosa; Ulcerative Colitis; Inadequacy/Immaturity; Personality Problems; Socialized Aggressive Reaction; Unsocialized Aggressive Reaction.

Services Provided Individual Therapy; Group Therapy; Parent Involvement; Behavior Therapy; Cognitive Developmental Therapy; Biofeedback; Family Therapy; Filial Therapy; Drug Therapy; Play Therapy. *Professionals on Staff* Psychiatrists; Psychologists; Counselors; Social Workers; Child Care Staff; Nurses. *Service Facilities Available (with number of rooms)* Consultative (ERT).

St Cloud Children's Home

1726 S 7th Ave, Saint Cloud, MN 56301 (612) 251-8811
Year Established 1924
Contact John L Doman, Dir

Facility Information *Placement* Private Residential Care. *Number of Beds* 72. *Children/Adolescents Served* 72. *Sexes Served* Both. *Room and Board Fees (Approx)* $75. *Sources of Funding* State Funds; HEW; Health Insurance; Medicaid; P.L. 94-142. Summer school available. *Teacher Certification Level* Elementary School; Junior High/Middle School; High School. *Special Certification Level* ED; LD; MR; Reading; Math; Science; Business Education; English; Social Studies; Home Economics; Industrial Arts.

Student/Patient Characteristics *Age Levels* 9-11; 12-14; 15-17. *IQ Ranges* 85-130; Above 130. *Exceptionalities Served* Emotionally Disturbed; Learning Disabled; Mentally Handicapped; Communication Disordered. *Learning Problems* Memory Disabilities; Perceptual Disabilities; Thinking Disabilities; Oral Language Disabilities; Reading Disabilities; Handwriting Disabilities; Spelling Disabilities; Arithmetic Disabilities; Written Expression. *Behavioral Problems* Attention Deficits; Hyperactivity; Impulsivity; Self-Aggression; Verbal Aggression; Physical Aggression; Passive Aggression; Withdrawal. *Conditions Treated* Schizophrenia; Convulsive Disorders; Phobias; Obsessions and Compulsions; Hysteria; Depression; Suicide; Inadequacy/Immaturity; Personality Problems; Socialized Aggressive Reaction; Unsocialized Aggressive Reaction.

Services Provided Individual Therapy; Group Therapy; Parent Involvement; Behavior Therapy; Family Therapy; Drug Therapy; Art Therapy; Music Therapy; Reality Therapy; Play Therapy; Psychodrama. *Professionals on Staff* Psychiatrists 1; Psychologists 3; Child Care Staff 44; Nurses 2; Therapists 6. *Service Facilities Available (with number of rooms)* Consultative (ERT) 1; Resource Rooms 2; Transition Rooms 6; Hospital School 1; Local Community School. *Educational Professionals* Special Education Teachers 12; Special Education Counselors 1; Paraprofessionals; Special Education Coordinator 1. *Curricula* Traditional Academic; Career/Vocational Education; Individualized; Basic Skills.

Educational Intervention Approaches Engineered Classroom; Precision Teaching; Behavior Modification. *Degrees Awarded* Certificate of Attendance; High School Diploma.

Stevencroft Inc

1436 Ashland Ave, Saint Paul, MN 55104 (612) 644-2514
Year Established 1979
Contact Sandra Bump, Dir

Facility Information *Placement* Private Residential Care. *Number of Beds* 6. *Children/Adolescents Served* 6. *Sexes Served* Both. *Room and Board Fees (Approx)* $79. *Sources of Funding* Minnesota Medical Assistance. *Special Certification Level* ED; LD; MR.

Student/Patient Characteristics *Age Levels* 15-17; 18-21. *IQ Ranges* 41-55; 56-70; 71-85. *Exceptionalities Served* Autistic. *Learning Problems* Memory Disabilities; Perceptual Disabilities; Thinking Disabilities; Oral Language Disabilities; Reading Disabilities; Handwriting Disabilities; Spelling Disabilities; Arithmetic Disabilities; Written Expression. *Behavioral Problems* Attention Deficits; Hyperactivity; Hypoactivity; Impulsivity; Self-Aggression; Verbal Aggression; Physical Aggression; Indirect Aggression; Passive Aggression; Withdrawal. *Conditions Treated* Early Infantile Autism.

Services Provided Individual Therapy; Behavior Therapy; Cognitive Developmental Therapy. *Professionals on Staff* Psychiatrists 1; Psychologists 1; Counselors 10. *Educational Professionals* Special Education Teachers 1; Paraprofessionals 9. *Curricula* Individualized; Basic Skills. *Educational Intervention Approaches* Precision Teaching; Behavior Modification; Applied Behavior Analysis; Creative Conditioning.

Comments This residential facility serves adolescents diagnosed as autistic with a program of behavior management, communication training, and instruction in social, self-care, and practical living skills.

Tri-County Cooperative Center No. 946

Box 657, Grand Rapids, MN 55744 (218) 326-0521
Year Established 972
Contact Ronald J Rubado, Dir

Facility Information *Placement* Public School. *Children/Adolescents Served* 16. *Sexes Served* Both. *Tuition Fees (Approx)* $2,000. *Sources of Funding* State Funds; P.L. 94-142. *Teacher Certification Level* Elementary School; Junior High/Middle School; High School. *Special Certification Level* ED; LD; Early Education; Secondary Education.

Student/Patient Characteristics *Age Levels* 5-8; 9-11; 12-14. *IQ Ranges* 85-130. *Exceptionalities Served* Emotionally Disturbed; Learning Disabled; Other Health Impaired. *Learning Problems* Memory Disabilities; Perceptual Disabilities; Thinking Disabilities; Reading Disabilities; Spelling Disabilities; Arithmetic Disabilities; Written Expression. *Behavioral Problems* Attention Deficits; Impulsivity; Verbal Aggression; Passive Aggression. *Conditions Treated* Obsessions and Compulsions; Personality Problems.

Services Provided *Professionals on Staff* Psychologists 2; Social Workers 2; Child Care Staff 2. *Service Facilities Available (with number of rooms)* Self-Contained Rooms 2. *Educational Professionals* Regular School Teachers 7; Special Education Teachers 2; Paraprofessionals 2; School Psychologists 2. *Curricula* Traditional Academic; Individualized; Basic Skills; Prevocational. *Educational Intervention Approaches* Precision Teaching; Self-Control; Behavior Modification. *Degrees Awarded* High School Diploma.

University of Minnesota Hospitals—Child and Adolescent Psychiatry

420 Delaware St SE, Minneapolis, MN 55079 (612) 373-8871
Year Established 1958
Contact Barry D Garfinkel, Dir

Facility Information *Placement* Psychiatric Inpatient Hospitalization. *Number of Beds* 10. *Children/Adolescents Served* 10. *Sexes Served* Both. *Room and Board Fees (Approx)* $380. *Sources of Funding* Health Insurance; Medicaid; Medicare. Summer school available. *Teacher Certification Level* Elementary School; Junior High/Middle School; High School. *Special Certification Level* ED; LD; MR; Reading; Math.

Student/Patient Characteristics *Age Levels* 0-4; 5-8; 9-11; 12-14. *IQ Ranges* 0-25; 26-40; 41-55; 56-70; 71-85; 85-130; Above 130. *Exceptionalities Served* Autistic; Emotionally Disturbed; Learning Disabled; Mentally Handicapped; Communication Disordered; Hearing Impaired/Deaf; Other Health Impaired; Physically Handicapped; Gifted. *Learning Problems* Memory Disabilities; Perceptual Disabilities; Thinking Disabilities; Oral Language Disabilities; Reading Disabilities; Handwriting Disabilities; Spelling Disabilities; Arithmetic Disabilities; Written Expression. *Behavioral Problems* Attention Deficits; Hyperactivity; Hypoactivity; Impulsivity; Self-Aggression; Verbal Aggression; Physical Aggression; Indirect Aggression; Passive Aggression; Withdrawal. *Conditions Treated* Alcohol Abuse and/or Drug Abuse; Other Substance Abuse or Dependence; Early Infantile Autism; Disintegrative Psychoses; Schizophrenia; Aphasia; Convulsive Disorders; Phobias; Obsessions and Compulsions; Hysteria; Depression; Suicide; Asthma; Anorexia Nervosa; Ulcerative Colitis; Inadequacy/Immaturity; Personality Problems; Socialized Aggressive Reaction; Unsocialized Aggressive Reaction.

Services Provided Individual Therapy; Group Therapy; Parent Involvement; Behavior Therapy; Cognitive Developmental Therapy; Family Therapy; Drug Therapy; Art Therapy; Play Therapy; Psychodrama. *Professionals on Staff* Psychiatrists 4; Psychologists 2; Counselors 1; Social Workers 1; Child Care Staff 4; Nurses 4. *Service Facilities Available (with number of rooms)* Consultative (ERT) 1; Resource Rooms 1; Self-Contained Rooms 1. *Educational Professionals* Regular School Teachers 1; Special Education Teachers 1. *Curricula* Traditional Academic; Individualized; Basic Skills. *Educational Intervention Approaches* Precision Teaching; Progressive Discipline; Behavior Modification.

West Central Community Services Center Inc

Box 787, 1125 SE 6th St, Willmar, MN 56288 (612) 235-4613
Year Established 1958
Contact P V Mehmel

Facility Information *Placement* Mental Health Services. *Children/Adolescents Served* 9 (temporary residence). *Sexes Served* Both. *Room and Board Fees (Approx)* $90. *Sources of Funding* State Funds; Health Insurance; Medicaid; Private Pay.

Student/Patient Characteristics *Age Levels* 0-4; 5-8; 9-11; 12-14; 15-17; 18-21; Over 21. *IQ Ranges* 56-70; 71-85; 85-130; Above 130. *Exceptionalities Served* Emotionally Disturbed; Mentally Handicapped; Hearing Impaired/Deaf. *Learning Problems* Perceptual Disabilities; Thinking Disabilities; Oral Language Disabilities. *Behavioral Problems* Attention Deficits; Hyperactivity; Hypoactivity; Impulsivity; Self-Aggression; Verbal Aggression; Physical Aggression; Indirect Aggression; Passive Aggression; Withdrawal. *Conditions Treated* Alcohol Abuse and/or Drug Abuse; Schizophrenia; Phobias; Obsessions and Compulsions; Hysteria; Depression; Suicide; Anorexia Nervosa; Inadequacy/Immaturity; Personality Problems.

Services Provided Individual Therapy; Group Therapy; Parent Involvement; Biofeedback; Family Therapy; Drug Therapy; Reality Therapy; Play Therapy. *Professionals on Staff* Psychiatrists 3; Psychologists 5; Counselors 3; Social Workers 5; Nurses 5.

Comments The West Central Community Services Center is a comprehensive community mental health program whose primary purpose is to maintain people in community life, while assisting them in coping with the stresses of living.

Wilder Children's Placement

919 Lafond Ave, Saint Paul, MN 55104 (612) 642-4008
Year Established 1865
Contact Gary L Larson, Treatment Coord

Facility Information *Placement* Private Residential Care; Foster Care. *Number of Beds* 84. *Children/Adolescents Served* 90. *Sexes Served* Both. *Room and Board Fees (Approx)* $63-$77. *Sources of Funding* State Funds; Health Insurance. Summer school available. *Teacher Certification Level* Elementary School; Junior High/Middle School. *Special Certification Level* ED; LD; Reading; Math.

Student/Patient Characteristics *Age Levels* 5-8; 9-11; 12-14; 15-17; 18-21. *IQ Ranges* 85-130; Above 130. *Exceptionalities Served* Autistic; Emotionally Disturbed; Learning Disabled; Hearing Impaired/Deaf; Other Health Impaired. *Learning Problems* Memory Disabilities; Perceptual Disabilities; Thinking Disabilities; Oral Language Disabilities; Reading Disabilities; Handwriting Disabilities; Spelling Disabilities; Arithmetic Disabilities; Written Expression. *Behavioral Problems* Attention Deficits; Hyperactivity; Hypoactivity; Impulsivity; Self-Aggression; Verbal Aggression; Physical Aggression; Indirect Aggression; Passive Aggression; Withdrawal. *Conditions Treated* Disintegrative Psychoses; Schizophrenia; Convulsive Disorders; Phobias; Obsessions and Compulsions; Hysteria; Depression; Suicide; Asthma; Anorexia Nervosa; Ulcerative Colitis; Inadequacy/Immaturity; Personality Problems; Socialized Aggressive Reaction; Unsocialized Aggressive Reaction.

Services Provided Individual Therapy; Group Therapy; Parent Involvement; Behavior Therapy; Family Therapy; Drug Therapy; Art Therapy; Play Therapy; Psychodrama; Multi-Family Therapy; Sexuality Therapy. *Professionals on Staff* Psychiatrists 2; Social Workers 12; Child Care Staff 60. *Service Facilities Available (with number of rooms)* Consultative (ERT) 2; Resource Rooms 2; Transition Rooms 2; Self-Contained Rooms 6; Special School; Public Schools. *Educational Professionals* Special Education Teachers 6; Special Education Counselors 7; Sensory Motor; Speech and Language; Physical Education; Art. *Curricula* Traditional Academic; Individualized; Basic Skills; Sex Education. *Educational Intervention Approaches* Progressive Discipline; Self-Control; Behavior Modification. *Degrees Awarded* Certificate of Attendance.

Comments Residential treatment is a service for children and parents. It is a therapeutic setting in which behaviors and relationships can improve to enable the child to function in his/her own school, home, and community. Treatment strives for reunification with the family when possible.

Mississippi

Early Education Center

PO Box 10356, Westland Station, 2307 S Lynch, Jackson, MS 39209 (601) 353-1664
Contact Martha Coppinger, Dir
Facility Information *Placement* Special School.
Children/Adolescents Served 55. *Sexes Served* Both. *Tuition Fees (Approx)* $7,308. *Sources of Funding* State Funds. Summer school available. *Teacher Certification Level* Elementary School. *Special Certification Level* ED; LD; MR; Physically Handicapped.
Student/Patient Characteristics *Age Levels* 0-4; 5-8. *IQ Ranges* 0-25; 26-40; 41-55; 56-70; 71-85; 85-130. *Exceptionalities Served* Autistic; Learning Disabled; Mentally Handicapped; Communication Disordered; Hearing Impaired/Deaf; Visually Impaired/Blind; Other Health Impaired; Physically Handicapped. *Learning Problems* Perceptual Disabilities; Oral Language Disabilities; Reading Disabilities. *Behavioral Problems* Attention Deficits; Hyperactivity; Self-Aggression; Physical Aggression; Withdrawal.
Services Provided Parent Involvement; Behavior Therapy; Cognitive Developmental Therapy. *Professionals on Staff* Psychologists; Social Workers 1; Child Care Staff 15. *Service Facilities Available (with number of rooms)* Self-Contained Rooms 6; Special School 2. *Educational Professionals* Special Education Teachers 7; Paraprofessionals 10. *Curricula* Individualized.
Educational Intervention Approaches Precision Teaching; Behavior Modification; Creative Conditioning.
Comments The Early Education Center, located at two sites in Jackson, serves preschool children who have various handicapping conditions. The center utilizes an interdisciplinary approach, and offers a developmental and individualized educational program for each child.

Harrison County Training Center for Exceptional Children

PO Drawer J, 94 29th St, Gulfport, MS 39501 (601) 863-0583
Year Established 1970
Contact Wilda P Switzer, Dir
Facility Information *Placement* Public School.
Children/Adolescents Served 180. *Sexes Served* Both. *Sources of Funding* State Funds; P.L. 94-142. *Special Certification Level* ED; LD; MR; Career/Vocational Education; Hearing Impaired; Visually Impaired.
Student/Patient Characteristics *Age Levels* 0-4; 5-8; 9-11; 12-14; 15-17; 18-21. *IQ Ranges* 0-25; 26-40; 41-55; 56-70; 71-85; 85-130. *Exceptionalities Served* Autistic; Emotionally Disturbed; Mentally Handicapped; Communication Disordered; Hearing Impaired/Deaf; Visually Impaired/Blind; Other Health Impaired. *Learning Problems* Perceptual Disabilities; Oral Language Disabilities. *Behavioral Problems* Attention Deficits; Hyperactivity.

Services Provided Individual Therapy; Parent Involvement; Art Therapy; Music Therapy. *Professionals on Staff* Psychologists 1; Social Workers 1; Nurses 1; Audiologists 2; Music Therapist 1; Speech Pathologists 2; Occupational Therapist 1; Recreational Therapist 1. *Service Facilities Available (with number of rooms)* Resource Rooms 2; Self-Contained Rooms 16. *Educational Professionals* Special Education Teachers 15; Career/Vocational Teachers 3. *Curricula* Career/Vocational Education; Individualized; Basic Skills; Prevocational. *Educational Intervention Approaches* Behavior Modification. *Degrees Awarded* Certificate of Attendance.

Jackson Municipal Separate School District

1020 Hunter St, Jackson, MS 39204 (601) 355-4818
Contact Yvonne B Brooks, Asst Supt Exception Ed Serv
Facility Information *Placement* Public School. *Sexes Served* Both. *Sources of Funding* State Funds; P.L. 94-142; Local Funds. Summer school available. *Teacher Certification Level* Elementary School; Junior High/Middle School; High School. *Special Certification Level* ED; LD; MR.
Student/Patient Characteristics *Age Levels* 0-4; 5-8; 9-11; 12-14; 15-17; 18-21; Over 21. *IQ Ranges* 0-25; 26-40; 41-55; 56-70; 71-85; 85-130; Above 130. *Exceptionalities Served* Autistic; Emotionally Disturbed; Learning Disabled; Mentally Handicapped; Communication Disordered; Hearing Impaired/Deaf; Visually Impaired/Blind; Other Health Impaired; Physically Handicapped; Gifted. *Conditions Treated* Early Infantile Autism; Inadequacy/Immaturity; Personality Problems; Socialized Aggressive Reaction; Unsocialized Aggressive Reaction.
Services Provided Individual Therapy; Group Therapy; Parent Involvement; Behavior Therapy. *Professionals on Staff* Psychologists 1; Social Workers 1; Nurses 2. *Service Facilities Available (with number of rooms)* Self-Contained Rooms 3; Homebound Instruction. *Educational Professionals* Regular School Teachers; Special Education Teachers 3; Special Education Counselors 1; Paraprofessionals 3. *Curricula* Individualized. *Educational Intervention Approaches* Engineered Classroom; Progressive Discipline; Behavior Modification. *Degrees Awarded* Certificate of Attendance; High School Diploma.

Millcreek Schools Inc

900 1st Ave NW, Magee, MS 39111 (601) 849-4221
Year Established 1976
Contact L T Terrell, Admin
Facility Information *Placement* Special School; Private Residential Care. *Number of Beds* 125. *Children/Adolescents Served* 125. *Sexes Served* Both. *Sources of Funding* State Funds; Medicaid. *Special Certification Level* ED; LD; MR.

Student/Patient Characteristics *Age Levels* 5-8; 9-11; 12-14; 15-17; 18-21. *IQ Ranges* 41-55; 56-70; 71-85; 85-130. *Exceptionalities Served* Autistic; Emotionally Disturbed; Learning Disabled; Mentally Handicapped; Communication Disordered; Visually Impaired/Blind; Other Health Impaired; Physically Handicapped; Gifted. *Learning Problems* Memory Disabilities; Perceptual Disabilities; Thinking Disabilities; Oral Language Disabilities; Reading Disabilities; Handwriting Disabilities; Spelling Disabilities; Arithmetic Disabilities; Written Expression. *Behavioral Problems* Attention Deficits; Hyperactivity; Hypoactivity; Impulsivity; Self-Aggression; Verbal Aggression; Physical Aggression; Indirect Aggression; Passive Aggression; Withdrawal. *Conditions Treated* Early Infantile Autism; Schizophrenia; Convulsive Disorders; Phobias; Obsessions and Compulsions; Depression; Personality Problems; Socialized Aggressive Reaction; Unsocialized Aggressive Reaction.

Services Provided Individual Therapy; Group Therapy; Behavior Therapy; Art Therapy; Music Therapy; Reality Therapy; Play Therapy. *Professionals on Staff* Psychiatrists 1; Psychologists 2; Counselors 4; Social Workers 2; Child Care Staff 6; Nurses 7; Nutritionist 1. *Service Facilities Available (with number of rooms)* Self-Contained Rooms 10. *Educational Professionals* Special Education Teachers; Paraprofessionals. *Curricula* Traditional Academic; Career/Vocational Education; Individualized; Basic Skills; Prevocational. *Educational Intervention Approaches* Progressive Discipline; Self-Control; Behavior Modification. *Degrees Awarded* Graduate Equivalency Diploma.

North Mississippi Retardation Center

PO Box 967, Oxford, MS 38655 (601) 234-1476
Year Established 1973
Contact A R Hendrix, Dir

Facility Information *Placement* Special School; Public Residential Care; Special Program. *Number of Beds* 113. *Children/Adolescents Served* 134. *Sexes Served* Both. *Room and Board Fees (Approx)* $39 (SNF); $49 (ICF). *Tuition Fees (Approx)* $14,136 (SNF); $18,049 (ICF). *Sources of Funding* State Funds; Medicaid; P.L. 89-313. Summer school available. *Teacher Certification Level* Elementary School; Junior High/Middle School; High School. *Special Certification Level* MR.

Student/Patient Characteristics *Age Levels* 0-4; 5-8; 9-11; 12-14; 15-17; 18-21; Over 21. *IQ Ranges* 0-25; 26-40; 41-55; 56-70. *Exceptionalities Served* Autistic; Emotionally Disturbed; Mentally Handicapped; Communication Disordered; Hearing Impaired/Deaf; Visually Impaired/Blind; Other Health Impaired. *Learning Problems* Memory Disabilities; Perceptual Disabilities; Thinking Disabilities; Oral Language Disabilities; Reading Disabilities; Handwriting Disabilities; Spelling Disabilities; Arithmetic Disabilities; Written Expression. *Behavioral Problems* Attention Deficits; Hyperactivity; Hypoactivity; Impulsivity; Self-Aggression; Verbal Aggression; Physical Aggression; Indirect Aggression; Passive Aggression; Withdrawal. *Conditions Treated* Early Infantile Autism; Convulsive Disorders.

Services Provided Individual Therapy; Group Therapy; Parent Involvement; Behavior Therapy; Family Therapy; Music Therapy. *Professionals on Staff* Psychologists 8; Counselors 2; Social Workers 8; Child Care Staff 169; Nurses 22. *Service Facilities Available (with number of rooms)* Self-Contained Rooms 9; Special School 7. *Educational Professionals* Regular School Teachers 2; Special Education Teachers 23; Special Education Counselors 2; Paraprofessionals 2; Speech and Hearing 5. *Curricula* Traditional Academic; Individualized; Basic Skills; Prevocational. *Educational Intervention Approaches* Behavior Modification. *Degrees Awarded* Certificate of Attendance.

Comments The center is a public residential facility for the mentally retarded ages 5 and over. It provides an accredited education program as well as a day program for multiply handicapped infants and young children, ages 0-5, who live in the community.

Sunshine Mountain

Box 37, Chatawa, MS 39632 (601) 783-3426
Year Established 1976
Contact Ralph Hays, Dir

Facility Information *Placement* Private Residential Care. *Number of Beds* 16. *Children/Adolescents Served* 36. *Sexes Served* Both. *Room and Board Fees (Approx)* $10 (sliding scale). *Sources of Funding* Medicare; Donations.

Services Provided Individual Therapy; Group Therapy; Behavior Therapy; Drug Therapy; Music Therapy. *Professionals on Staff* Nurses.

Comments It is a family unit home with male and female dorms. It cares for 6 older persons with body damage.

Tupelo Municipal Public Schools

605 Easton Blvd, Tupelo, MS 38801 (601) 842-9217
Year Established 1878
Contact Drue H Sutherland, Dir

Facility Information *Placement* Special School. *Children/Adolescents Served* 65. *Sexes Served* Both. *Sources of Funding* State Funds; P.L. 94-142; Preschool Incentive Grant; Local Tax Funds. Summer school available. *Teacher Certification Level* Elementary School. *Special Certification Level* ED; LD; MR; Visually Impaired; Physically Handicapped; Multiply Handicapped; Speech and Language.

Student/Patient Characteristics *Age Levels* 0-4; 5-8; 9-11; 12-14. *IQ Ranges* 0-25; 26-40; 41-55; 56-70; 71-85. *Exceptionalities Served* Autistic; Emotionally Disturbed; Learning Disabled; Mentally Handicapped; Communication Disordered; Visually Impaired/Blind; Other Health Impaired. *Learning Problems* Memory Disabilities; Perceptual Disabilities; Thinking Disabilities; Oral Language Disabilities; Reading Disabilities; Handwriting Disabilities; Spelling Disabilities; Arithmetic Disabilities; Written Expression; Self-Help; Functional Social Skills; Functional Living Skills; Pre-Vocational Skills. *Behavioral Problems* Attention Deficits; Hyperactivity; Impulsivity; Self-Aggression; Verbal Aggression; Physical Aggression; Indirect Aggression; Withdrawal. *Conditions Treated* Early Infantile Autism; Schizophrenia.

Services Provided Individual Therapy; Group Therapy; Parent Involvement; Behavior Therapy; Cognitive Developmental Therapy; Biofeedback; Family Therapy; Play Therapy. *Professionals on Staff* Psychiatrists 1; Psychologists 2; Counselors 3; Social Workers 2; Child Care Staff 9; Nurses 1; Aides 11. *Service Facilities Available (with number of rooms)* Consultative (ERT) 3; Self-Contained Rooms 9. *Educational Professionals* Special Education Teachers 9; Paraprofessionals 11. *Curricula* Individualized; Basic Skills; Prevocational. *Educational Intervention Approaches* Progressive Discipline; Self-Control; Behavior Modification; Applied Behavior Analysis. *Degrees Awarded* Certificate of Attendance.

Comments The McDougal program is a day program for a seven county area of Mississippi. The counties are Chickasaw, Pontotoc, Benton, Union, Lee, Itawamba, and Monroe. All handicapping conditions are served by the center.

Missouri

Boys' Town of Missouri Inc

PO Box 189, Saint James, MO 65559 (314) 265-3251
Year Established 1948
Contact Richard C Dunn, Exec Dir

Facility Information *Placement* Private Residential Care. *Number of Beds* 116. *Children/Adolescents Served* 116. *Sexes Served* Male. *Room and Board Fees (Approx)* $55. *Sources of Funding* State Funds; P.L. 94-142. Summer school available. *Teacher Certification Level* Elementary School; Junior High/Middle School. *Special Certification Level* ED; LD.

Student/Patient Characteristics *Age Levels* 9-11; 12-14; 15-17. *IQ Ranges* 85-130. *Exceptionalities Served* Emotionally Disturbed; Learning Disabled; Gifted. *Learning Problems* Perceptual Disabilities; Thinking Disabilities; Reading Disabilities; Handwriting Disabilities; Spelling Disabilities; Arithmetic Disabilities; Written Expression. *Behavioral Problems* Attention Deficits; Hyperactivity; Hypoactivity; Impulsivity; Self-Aggression; Verbal Aggression; Physical Aggression; Indirect Aggression; Passive Aggression; Withdrawal. *Conditions Treated* Other Substance Abuse or Dependence; Schizophrenia; Convulsive Disorders; Depression; Suicide; Inadequacy/Immaturity; Personality Problems; Socialized Aggressive Reaction; Unsocialized Aggressive Reaction.

Services Provided Individual Therapy; Group Therapy; Parent Involvement; Behavior Therapy; Cognitive Developmental Therapy; Family Therapy; Drug Therapy; Music Therapy; Reality Therapy. *Professionals on Staff* Psychiatrists 1; Psychologists 1; Social Workers 8; Child Care Staff 26; Nurses 2. *Service Facilities Available (with number of rooms)* Consultative (ERT); Resource Rooms; Transition Rooms; Self-Contained Rooms; On-Campus Residential School 10. *Educational Professionals* Special Education Teachers 10. *Curricula* Traditional Academic; Individualized; Basic Skills; Prevocational. *Educational Intervention Approaches* Engineered Classroom; Progressive Discipline; Self-Control; Behavior Modification; Creative Conditioning. *Degrees Awarded* Certificate of Attendance; 8th and 9th Grade Diploma.

Center for Urban Living

3827 Enright St, Saint Louis, MO 63108 (314) 535-2600
Year Established 1978
Contact Beverly Mack Martin, Exec Dir

Facility Information *Placement* Special Program. *Children/Adolescents Served* 60. *Sexes Served* Both. *Sources of Funding* State Funds; HEW; P.L. 94-142; Corporate. Summer school available. *Teacher Certification Level* High School. *Special Certification Level* ED; LD; Occupational Therapy; Behavioral Disorders; Speech Therapy.

Student/Patient Characteristics *Age Levels* 0-4; 5-8; 15-17; 18-21. *IQ Ranges* 56-70; 71-85. *Exceptionalities Served* Emotionally Disturbed; Learning Disabled; Mentally Handicapped; Communication Disordered. *Learning Problems* Perceptual Disabilities; Thinking Disabilities; Oral Language Disabilities; Reading Dis-

abilities; Handwriting Disabilities; Spelling Disabilities; Arithmetic Disabilities; Sensory Motor Integration. *Behavioral Problems* Attention Deficits; Hyperactivity; Impulsivity; Self-Aggression; Verbal Aggression; Physical Aggression; Indirect Aggression; Withdrawal. *Conditions Treated* Phobias; Inadequacy/Immaturity; Socialized Aggressive Reaction; Unsocialized Aggressive Reaction.

Services Provided Individual Therapy; Group Therapy; Parent Involvement; Behavior Therapy; Cognitive Developmental Therapy; Art Therapy; Music Therapy; Play Therapy. *Professionals on Staff* Counselors 1; Social Workers 1; Child Care Staff 1. *Service Facilities Available (with number of rooms)* Resource Rooms 5. *Educational Professionals* Special Education Teachers 2; Paraprofessionals 1; Speech Pathologist 1; Occupational Therapist 1. *Curricula* Individualized; Basic Skills; Special Pre-School. *Educational Intervention Approaches* Progressive Discipline; Self-Control; Behavior Modification; Creative Conditioning. *Degrees Awarded* Certificate of Attendance.

Comments This agency has 3 program components; a therapeutic pre-school, a GED Program, and a special Parenting Skills Education Program for parents of LD, BD, and DD children.

Childhaven

369 N Taylor, Saint Louis, MO 63108 (314) 361-4565
Year Established 1977
Contact Estelle McDaniel, Exec Dir

Facility Information *Placement* Special Program; Nonprofit United Way Agency. *Children/Adolescents Served* 35. *Sexes Served* Both. *Sources of Funding* State Funds; Health Insurance; P.L. 94-142; Private; Parent Fee. Summer school available. *Teacher Certification Level* Elementary School. *Special Certification Level* ED; LD; MR; Preschool Special Education.

Student/Patient Characteristics *Age Levels* 0-4; 5-8; 9-11. *IQ Ranges* 41-55; 56-70; 71-85; 85-130. *Exceptionalities Served* Autistic; Emotionally Disturbed; Learning Disabled; Mentally Handicapped; Communication Disordered; Physically Handicapped; Behavior Disordered. *Learning Problems* Memory Disabilities; Perceptual Disabilities; Thinking Disabilities; Oral Language Disabilities; Reading Disabilities; Handwriting Disabilities; Spelling Disabilities; Arithmetic Disabilities; Written Expression. *Behavioral Problems* Attention Deficits; Hyperactivity; Hypoactivity; Impulsivity; Self-Aggression; Verbal Aggression; Physical Aggression; Withdrawal. *Conditions Treated* Early Infantile Autism; Schizophrenia; Aphasia; Convulsive Disorders; Socialized Aggressive Reaction; Unsocialized Aggressive Reaction.

Services Provided Individual Therapy; Group Therapy; Parent Involvement; Behavior Therapy; Cognitive Developmental Therapy; Family Therapy; Occupational Therapy; Communication Therapy. *Professionals on Staff* Counselors 1. *Service Facilities Available (with number of rooms)* Consultative (ERT) 3; Self-

Contained Rooms 6. *Educational Professionals* Special Education Teachers 8; Special Education Counselors 1; Paraprofessionals 2; Occupational Therapists; Communication Therapists 4. *Curricula* Individualized. *Educational Intervention Approaches* Behavior Modification; Creative Conditioning.

Children's Hospital at Washington University Medical Center—Psychiatric Unit

400 S Kingshighway Blvd, Saint Louis, MO 63178
(314) 454-6000
Year Established 1984
Contact Zila Welner
Facility Information *Placement* Childrens Hospital. *Number of Beds* 12-16. *Children/Adolescents Served* 12-16. *Sexes Served* Both. *Room and Board Fees (Approx)* $400. *Sources of Funding* Health Insurance; Medicaid. *Teacher Certification Level* Elementary School; Junior High/Middle School; High School. *Special Certification Level* ED; Career/Vocational Education.
Student/Patient Characteristics *Age Levels* 0-4; 5-8; 9-11; 12-14; 15-17; 18-21. *IQ Ranges* 0-25; 26-40; 41-55; 56-70; 71-85; 85-130; Above 130. *Exceptionalities Served* Autistic; Emotionally Disturbed; Learning Disabled; Mentally Handicapped; Communication Disordered; Other Health Impaired; Physically Handicapped; Gifted. *Learning Problems* Memory Disabilities; Perceptual Disabilities; Thinking Disabilities; Oral Language Disabilities; Reading Disabilities; Handwriting Disabilities; Spelling Disabilities; Arithmetic Disabilities; Written Expression. *Behavioral Problems* Attention Deficits; Hyperactivity; Hypoactivity; Impulsivity; Self-Aggression; Verbal Aggression; Indirect Aggression; Passive Aggression; Withdrawal. *Conditions Treated* Early Infantile Autism; Disintegrative Psychoses; Schizophrenia; Aphasia; Convulsive Disorders; Phobias; Obsessions and Compulsions; Hysteria; Depression; Suicide; Asthma; Anorexia Nervosa; Ulcerative Colitis; Inadequacy/Immaturity; Personality Problems; Socialized Aggressive Reaction; Unsocialized Aggressive Reaction.
Services Provided Individual Therapy; Group Therapy; Parent Involvement; Behavior Therapy; Cognitive Developmental Therapy; Biofeedback; Family Therapy; Drug Therapy; Art Therapy. *Professionals on Staff* Psychiatrists 5; Psychologists 2; Social Workers 1; Nurses 15. *Service Facilities Available (with number of rooms)* Self-Contained Rooms 1; Hospital School 1. *Educational Professionals* Regular School Teachers 1. *Curricula* Traditional Academic; Individualized; Basic Skills. *Educational Intervention Approaches* Behavior Modification. *Degrees Awarded* Graduate Equivalency Diploma.
Comments This program provides comprehensive diagnostic psychiatric evaluations and short-term, intensive treatment for children and their families. The psychiatric program is located on an open unit within Children's Hospital and utilizes the resources of the professional pediatric staff.

The Children's Mercy Hospital—Section of Psychiatry

24th and Gillham, Kansas City, MO 64108 (816) 234-3201
Year Established 1952
Contact Stephen Churchill, Section Chief
Facility Information *Placement* Outpatient Psychiatric Services. *Children/Adolescents Served* $50. *Sexes Served* Both. *Sources of Funding* State Funds; Health Insurance; Medicaid.
Student/Patient Characteristics *Age Levels* 0-4; 5-8; 9-11; 12-14; 15-17; 18-21. *IQ Ranges* 26-40; 41-55; 56-70; 71-85; 85-130; Above 130. *Exceptionalities Served* Autistic; Emotionally Disturbed; Learning Disabled; Mentally Handicapped; Communication Disordered; Hearing Impaired/Deaf; Visually Impaired/Blind; Other Health Impaired; Physically Handicapped; Gifted. *Learning Problems* Memory Disabilities; Perceptual Disabilities; Thinking Disabilities; Oral Language Disabilities; Reading Disabilities; Handwriting Disabilities; Spelling Disabilities; Arithmetic Disabilities; Written Expression. *Behavioral Problems* Attention Deficits; Hyperactivity; Hypoactivity; Impulsivity; Self-Aggression; Verbal Aggression; Physical Aggression; Indirect Aggression; Passive Aggression; Withdrawal. *Conditions Treated* Alcohol Abuse and/or Drug Abuse; Other Substance Abuse or Dependence; Early Infantile Autism; Disintegrative Psychoses; Schizophrenia; Aphasia; Convulsive Disorders; Phobias; Obsessions and Compulsions; Hysteria; Depression; Suicide; Asthma; Anorexia Nervosa; Ulcerative Colitis; Inadequacy/Immaturity; Personality Problems; Socialized Aggressive Reaction; Unsocialized Aggressive Reaction.
Services Provided Individual Therapy; Parent Involvement; Behavior Therapy; Family Therapy; Filial Therapy; Drug Therapy; Play Therapy. *Professionals on Staff* Psychiatrists 1; Psychologists 1; Social Workers 1.
Comments This is an outpatient psychiatric clinic of a private pediatric hospital.

Community Mental Health Center South

769 Tudor Rd, Lee's Summit, MO 64063 (816) 524-7300
Year Established 1975
Contact Sandy Gray, Facility Mgr
Facility Information *Placement* Outpatient Mental Health Services. *Children/Adolescents Served* 12. *Sexes Served* Both. *Room and Board Fees (Approx)* Sliding Scale. *Tuition Fees (Approx)* Sliding Scale. *Sources of Funding* State Funds; Health Insurance; Private Donations.
Student/Patient Characteristics *Age Levels* 15-17. *IQ Ranges* 85-130. *Exceptionalities Served* Emotionally Disturbed; Learning Disabled. *Learning Problems* Thinking Disabilities; Reading Disabilities; Handwriting Disabilities; Spelling Disabilities; Arithmetic Disabilities; Written Expression. *Behavioral Problems* Attention Deficits; Hyperactivity; Impulsivity; Self-Aggression; Verbal Aggression; Physical Aggression; Indirect Aggression; Passive Aggression; Withdrawal. *Conditions Treated* Alcohol Abuse and/or Drug Abuse; Depression; Suicide; Anorexia Nervosa; Personality Problems; Socialized Aggressive Reaction; Unsocialized Aggressive Reaction.
Services Provided Individual Therapy; Group Therapy; Parent Involvement; Behavior Therapy; Family Therapy; Drug Therapy; Art Therapy; Music Therapy. *Professionals on Staff* Psychiatrists 1; Psychologists 2; Social Workers 1.
Comments The Evening Center program is designed to keep the child with serious home and school problems in their own home and school working on the problems. They attend the program 3 days per week from after school until 8:00 p.m. Transportation can usually be provided from the school to the center. Family therapy is required.

Edgewood Children's Center

330 N Gore Ave, Saint Louis, MO 63119 (314) 968-2060
Year Established 1834
Contact Ralph S Lehman, Exec Dir
Facility Information *Placement* Special School; Private Residential Care; Private Day Care. *Number of Beds* 40 (residential). *Children/Adolescents Served* 70. *Sexes Served* Both. *Room and Board Fees (Approx)* $78 (residential); $33 (day). *Sources of Funding* State Funds; United Way; Endowment Income; Contributions. Summer school available. *Teacher Certification Level* Elementary School; Junior High/Middle School. *Special Certification Level* ED; LD; MR; Reading.
Student/Patient Characteristics *Age Levels* 5-8; 9-11; 12-14; 15-17. *IQ Ranges* 85-130. *Exceptionalities Served* Emotionally Disturbed; Learning Disabled; Mentally Handicapped. *Learning Problems* Memory Disabilities; Perceptual Disabilities; Thinking Disabilities; Oral Language Disabilities; Reading Disabilities; Handwriting Disabilities; Spelling Disabilities; Arithmetic Disabilities; Written Expression. *Behavioral Problems* Attention Deficits; Hyperactivity; Hypoactivity; Impulsivity; Self-Aggression; Verbal Aggression; Physical Aggression; Indirect Aggression; Passive Aggression; Withdrawal. *Conditions Treated* Phobias; Obsessions and Compulsions; Hysteria; Depression; Suicide; Inadequacy/Immaturity; Personality Problems; Socialized Aggressive Reaction; Unsocialized Aggressive Reaction.

Services Provided Individual Therapy; Group Therapy; Parent Involvement; Behavior Therapy; Family Therapy; Reality Therapy; Music Therapy; Occupational Therapy; Speech and Language Therapy; Movement Therapy. *Professionals on Staff* Psychiatrists 1; Psychologists 1; Counselors 4; Social Workers 9; Child Care Staff 20; Nurses 1; Recreational Therapists 3. *Service Facilities Available (with number of rooms)* Resource Rooms 5; Self-Contained Rooms 7. *Educational Professionals* Special Education Teachers 7; Paraprofessionals 3; Adjunctive Therapists 5. *Curricula* Traditional Academic; Individualized; Basic Skills; Prevocational. *Educational Intervention Approaches* Behavior Modification; Applied Behavior Analysis; Creative Conditioning. *Degrees Awarded* Certificate of Attendance.

Comments Edgewood is a residential and day treatment center for children with severe emotional disturbances and learning disabilities. Special education in the on-campus school is a component of treatment. A wide range of adjunctive therapies and life skills training opportunities are provided.

Harry S Truman Children's Neurological Center

15600 Woods Chapel Rd, Kansas City, MO 64139
Year Established 1969
Contact Mary Cox, Asst Admin

Facility Information *Placement* Private Residential Care. *Number of Beds* 25. *Children/Adolescents Served* 25. *Sexes Served* Both. *Room and Board Fees (Approx)* $52. *Sources of Funding* State Funds; Private Donations.

Student/Patient Characteristics *Exceptionalities Served* Visually Impaired/Blind; Other Health Impaired; Physically Handicapped.

Services Provided *Professionals on Staff* Psychologists 1; Child Care Staff 30; Nurses 4; Physical Therapy; Speech.

Comments This program is a residential facility for developmentally delayed children and young adults.

Hawthorne Children's Psychiatric Hospital

5247 Fyler, Saint Louis, MO 63139 (314) 644-8000
Contact Ira Eaton, Dir of Therapeutic Serv

Facility Information *Placement* Psychiatric Hospital. *Number of Beds* 50. *Children/Adolescents Served* 74. *Sexes Served* Both. *Room and Board Fees (Approx)* $230. *Sources of Funding* State Funds; Health Insurance; Medicaid. Summer school available. *Teacher Certification Level* Elementary School; Junior High/Middle School; High School. *Special Certification Level* ED; Career/Vocational Education.

Student/Patient Characteristics *Age Levels* 5-8; 9-11; 12-14; 15-17. *IQ Ranges* 71-85; 85-130. *Exceptionalities Served* Emotionally Disturbed; Learning Disabled. *Learning Problems* Memory Disabilities; Perceptual Disabilities; Thinking Disabilities; Oral Language Disabilities; Reading Disabilities; Handwriting Disabilities; Spelling Disabilities; Arithmetic Disabilities; Written Expression. *Behavioral Problems* Attention Deficits; Hyperactivity; Hypoactivity; Impulsivity; Self-Aggression; Verbal Aggression; Physical Aggression; Indirect Aggression; Passive Aggression; Withdrawal. *Conditions Treated* Other Substance Abuse or Dependence; Disintegrative Psychoses; Schizophrenia; Aphasia; Convulsive Disorders; Phobias; Obsessions and Compulsions; Hysteria; Depression; Suicide; Inadequacy/Immaturity; Personality Problems; Socialized Aggressive Reaction; Unsocialized Aggressive Reaction; Abuse.

Services Provided Individual Therapy; Group Therapy; Parent Involvement; Behavior Therapy; Family Therapy; Art Therapy; Chemotherapy. *Professionals on Staff* Psychiatrists 5; Psychologists 10; Social Workers 7; Child Care Staff 80; Nurses 13. *Service Facilities Available (with number of rooms)* Self-Contained Rooms 11; Homebound Instruction 1. *Educational Professionals* Special Education Teachers 9; Career/Vocational Teachers 3; Paraprofessionals 8; Foster Grandparents 4. *Curricula* Traditional Academic; Career/Vocational Education; Individualized; Basic Skills; Prevocational; Art; Outdoor Educa-

tion. *Educational Intervention Approaches* Engineered Classroom; Behavior Modification; Applied Behavior Analysis; Creative Conditioning. *Degrees Awarded* Certificate of Attendance.

Judevine Center for Autistic Children

9455 Rott Rd, Saint Louis, MO 63127 (314) 849-4440
Year Established 1971
Contact Lois J Blackwell, Dir

Facility Information *Placement* Special School; Parent Training. *Children/Adolescents Served* 40. *Sexes Served* Both. *Tuition Fees (Approx)* $13,500. *Sources of Funding* State Funds; Health Insurance; Private Pay. Summer school available. *Teacher Certification Level* Elementary School. *Special Certification Level* ED; LD; MR; Speech.

Student/Patient Characteristics *Age Levels* 0-4; 5-8; 9-11; 12-14; 15-17; 18-21; Over 21. *IQ Ranges* 26-40; 41-55; 56-70; 71-85; 85-130. *Exceptionalities Served* Autistic; Learning Disabled; Mentally Handicapped; Communication Disordered. *Learning Problems* Memory Disabilities; Perceptual Disabilities; Oral Language Disabilities; Reading Disabilities; Handwriting Disabilities; Spelling Disabilities; Arithmetic Disabilities; Written Expression. *Behavioral Problems* Attention Deficits; Hyperactivity; Hypoactivity; Impulsivity; Self-Aggression; Verbal Aggression; Physical Aggression; Withdrawal. *Conditions Treated* Early Infantile Autism.

Services Provided Individual Therapy; Group Therapy; Parent Involvement; Behavior Therapy; Music Therapy. *Professionals on Staff* Language Therapists 3; Occupational Therapist 1. *Service Facilities Available (with number of rooms)* Consultative (ERT) 1; Self-Contained Rooms 6. *Educational Professionals* Special Education Teachers 6; Crisis Teachers 1; Paraprofessionals 4; Language Therapists 3. *Curricula* Traditional Academic; Individualized; Basic Skills; Prevocational; Language Therapy; Occupational Therapy; Social Skill Training; Music Therapy. *Educational Intervention Approaches* Engineered Classroom; Self-Control; Applied Behavior Analysis; Creative Conditioning.

Comments Judevine provides day programing and clinical services to the autistic, communication disordered and behaviorally disordered in the St. Louis area. In addition, Judevine provides intense 3 week training programs for parents and professionals from across the country.

Lakeside Center for Boys

13044 Marine, Saint Louis, MO 63146 (314) 434-4535
Year Established 1961
Contact David McMullan, Exec Dir

Facility Information *Placement* Special School; Public Residential Care. *Number of Beds* 48. *Children/Adolescents Served* 48. *Sexes Served* Male. *Room and Board Fees (Approx)* $55. *Sources of Funding* State Funds; P.L. 94-142; County Funds. Summer school available. *Teacher Certification Level* Elementary School; Junior High/Middle School; High School. *Special Certification Level* ED; LD; MR; Math Social Studies; English; Science; Industrial Arts; Speech Therapy; Physical Education.

Student/Patient Characteristics *Age Levels* 12-14; 15-17. *IQ Ranges* 85-130. *Exceptionalities Served* Emotionally Disturbed; Learning Disabled; Communication Disordered. *Learning Problems* Memory Disabilities; Perceptual Disabilities; Thinking Disabilities; Oral Language Disabilities; Reading Disabilities; Handwriting Disabilities; Spelling Disabilities; Arithmetic Disabilities; Written Expression. *Behavioral Problems* Attention Deficits; Hyperactivity; Hypoactivity; Impulsivity; Self-Aggression; Verbal Aggression; Physical Aggression; Indirect Aggression; Passive Aggression; Withdrawal. *Conditions Treated* Disintegrative Psychoses; Convulsive Disorders; Phobias; Depression; Suicide; Asthma; Inadequacy/Immaturity; Personality Problems; Socialized Aggressive Reaction; Unsocialized Aggressive Reaction.

Services Provided Individual Therapy; Group Therapy; Parent Involvement; Behavior Therapy; Family Therapy; Art Therapy; Reality Therapy. *Professionals on Staff* Psychiatrists 1; Counselors 1; Social Workers 8; Child Care Staff 21. *Service Facilities*

Available (with number of rooms) Self-Contained Rooms 6; On-Campus Residential School 6; Public Junior High and High School. *Educational Professionals* Regular School Teachers; Special Education Teachers 7.5; Paraprofessionals 3. *Curricula* Traditional Academic; Career/Vocational Education; Individualized; Basic Skills; Industrial Arts. *Educational Intervention Approaches* Progressive Discipline; Self-Control; Behavior Modification.

Lutheran Medical Center—Psychiatric Division

2639 Miami St, Saint Louis, MO 63118 (314) 772-1456
Contact Robert Eisenstein, Mental Health Prog Dir
Facility Information *Placement* Psychiatric Inpatient Medical Center. *Number of Beds* 13. *Children/Adolescents Served* 13. *Sexes Served* Both. *Room and Board Fees (Approx)* $275. *Sources of Funding* Health Insurance; Medicaid; Medicare.
Student/Patient Characteristics *Age Levels* 12-14; 15-17; 18-21; Over 21. *Behavioral Problems* Hyperactivity; Impulsivity; Self-Aggression; Verbal Aggression; Physical Aggression; Indirect Aggression; Passive Aggression; Withdrawal. *Conditions Treated* Disintegrative Psychoses; Schizophrenia; Convulsive Disorders; Phobias; Obsessions and Compulsions; Hysteria; Depression; Suicide; Anorexia Nervosa; Personality Problems; Socialized Aggressive Reaction; Unsocialized Aggressive Reaction.
Services Provided Individual Therapy; Group Therapy; Parent Involvement; Family Therapy; Drug Therapy; Art Therapy; Music Therapy. *Professionals on Staff* Psychiatrists; Psychologists; Social Workers; Nurses. *Curricula* Basic Skills.

Lutheran Special Classes

3558 S Jefferson, Saint Louis, MO 63118 (314) 776-0500
Year Established 1956
Contact Lloyd W Haertling, Exec Dir
Facility Information *Placement* Special Program. *Children/Adolescents Served* 84. *Sexes Served* Both. *Tuition Fees (Approx)* $2,150. *Sources of Funding* Tuition; Lutheran Charities. *Teacher Certification Level* Elementary School. *Special Certification Level* LD; MR.
Student/Patient Characteristics *Age Levels* 5-8; 9-11; 12-14. *IQ Ranges* 41-55; 56-70; 71-85; 85-130. *Exceptionalities Served* Emotionally Disturbed; Learning Disabled; Mentally Handicapped; Gifted. *Learning Problems* Memory Disabilities; Perceptual Disabilities; Thinking Disabilities; Reading Disabilities; Handwriting Disabilities; Spelling Disabilities; Arithmetic Disabilities; Written Expression. *Behavioral Problems* Attention Deficits; Impulsivity; Withdrawal. *Conditions Treated* Inadequacy/Immaturity.
Services Provided *Professionals on Staff* Counselors 1. *Service Facilities Available (with number of rooms)* Consultative (ERT) 3; Resource Rooms 7. *Educational Professionals* Regular School Teachers 70; Special Education Teachers 10. *Curricula* Individualized; Basic Skills. *Educational Intervention Approaches* Self-Control; Behavior Modification. *Degrees Awarded* 8th Grade Diploma.

Menorah Medical Center—Hearing and Speech Department

4949 Rockhill Rd, Kansas City, MO 64110 (816) 276-8225
Year Established 1961
Contact Linda Z Solomon, Dir
Facility Information *Placement* Evaluation and Treatment Center. *Number of Beds* 16. *Sexes Served* Both. *Sources of Funding* Health Insurance; Medicaid. *Special Certification Level* LD; Reading; Speech and Language Pathology; Audiology.
Student/Patient Characteristics *Age Levels* 0-4; 5-8; 9-11; 12-14; 15-17; 18-21. *IQ Ranges* 56-70; 71-85; 85-130; Above 130. *Exceptionalities Served* Autistic; Emotionally Disturbed; Learning Disabled; Mentally Handicapped; Communication Disordered; Hearing Impaired/Deaf; Other Health Impaired. *Learning Problems* Memory Disabilities; Perceptual Disabilities; Thinking Disabilities; Oral Language Disabilities; Reading Disabilities; Handwriting Disabilities; Spelling Disabilities; Arithmetic Dis-

abilities; Written Expression. *Behavioral Problems* Attention Deficits; Hyperactivity; Hypoactivity; Impulsivity; Self-Aggression; Verbal Aggression; Physical Aggression; Indirect Aggression; Passive Aggression; Withdrawal. *Conditions Treated* Alcohol Abuse and/or Drug Abuse; Early Infantile Autism; Disintegrative Psychoses; Schizophrenia; Aphasia; Convulsive Disorders; Depression; Suicide; Ulcerative Colitis; Inadequacy/Immaturity; Personality Problems; Socialized Aggressive Reaction; Unsocialized Aggressive Reaction.
Services Provided Cognitive Developmental Therapy; Dyslexia Therapy; Speech and Language Therapy; Educational Therapy; Auditory Perceptual Therapy. *Professionals on Staff* Speech and Language Therapists; Learning Disability Specialists; Audiologist 5. *Service Facilities Available (with number of rooms)* Hospital School 1. *Educational Professionals* Special Education Teachers 2. *Curricula* Individualized.
Comments The center provides comprehensive services for evaluation and treatment of learning disabilities and communicative disorders including auditory perceptual problems. Services are provided to outpatients, from various referral sources. It also participates in evaluation/treatment teams for pediatric/adolescent psychiatric inpatients.

St Louis County Child Mental Health Services

701 S Brentwood Blvd, Saint Louis, MO 63105 (314) 854-6760
Year Established 1950
Contact Larry K Burke, Dir
Facility Information *Placement* Outpatient Mental Health Services. *Children/Adolescents Served* $1,000. *Sexes Served* Both. *Sources of Funding* State Funds; Health Insurance; Medicaid; P.L. 94-142; County.
Student/Patient Characteristics *Age Levels* 0-4; 5-8; 9-11; 12-14; 15-17. *IQ Ranges* 71-85; 85-130; Above 130. *Exceptionalities Served* Emotionally Disturbed; Learning Disabled; Mentally Handicapped; Gifted. *Learning Problems* Memory Disabilities; Perceptual Disabilities; Thinking Disabilities; Oral Language Disabilities; Reading Disabilities; Handwriting Disabilities; Spelling Disabilities; Arithmetic Disabilities; Written Expression. *Behavioral Problems* Attention Deficits; Hyperactivity; Hypoactivity; Impulsivity; Self-Aggression; Verbal Aggression; Physical Aggression; Indirect Aggression; Passive Aggression; Withdrawal. *Conditions Treated* Alcohol Abuse and/or Drug Abuse; Other Substance Abuse or Dependence; Schizophrenia; Phobias; Obsessions and Compulsions; Hysteria; Depression; Suicide; Anorexia Nervosa; Inadequacy/Immaturity; Personality Problems; Socialized Aggressive Reaction; Unsocialized Aggressive Reaction.
Services Provided Individual Therapy; Group Therapy; Parent Involvement; Behavior Therapy; Cognitive Developmental Therapy; Family Therapy; Drug Therapy. *Professionals on Staff* Psychiatrists 4; Psychologists 5; Social Workers 17.

Sherwood Center for The Exceptional Child

7938 Chestnut, Kansas City, MO 64132 (816) 363-4606
Year Established 1974
Contact Elaine Adams, Placement Coord
Facility Information *Placement* Private Day Treatment School. *Children/Adolescents Served* 65. *Sexes Served* Both. *Tuition Fees (Approx)* $15,805. *Sources of Funding* State Funds; P.L. 94-142; School District; Department of Mental Health. Summer school available. *Teacher Certification Level* Elementary School; Junior High/Middle School; High School. *Special Certification Level* ED; MR; Speech Pathology; Physical Education.
Student/Patient Characteristics *Age Levels* 0-4; 5-8; 9-11; 12-14; 15-17; 18-21. *IQ Ranges* 0-25; 26-40; 41-55; 56-70; 71-85. *Exceptionalities Served* Autistic; Emotionally Disturbed; Learning Disabled; Mentally Handicapped; Communication Disordered; Hearing Impaired/Deaf; Developmentally Disabled. *Learning Problems* Memory Disabilities; Perceptual Disabilities; Thinking Disabilities; Oral Language Disabilities; Reading Disabilities; Handwriting Disabilities; Spelling Disabilities; Arithmetic Disabilities; Written Expression. *Behavioral Problems* Attention Deficits; Hyperactivity; Hypoactivity; Impulsivity; Self-

Aggression; Verbal Aggression; Physical Aggression; Indirect Aggression; Passive Aggression; Withdrawal; Self-Stimulation. *Conditions Treated* Early Infantile Autism; Schizophrenia; Obsessions and Compulsions; Personality Problems.

Services Provided Parent Involvement; Behavior Therapy; Speech Therapy. *Professionals on Staff* Psychologists 2; Speech Therapist 1; Physical Education Teacher 1. *Service Facilities Available (with number of rooms)* Resource Rooms 3; Transition Rooms 1; Self-Contained Rooms 6. *Educational Professionals* Special Education Teachers 6; Career/Vocational Teachers 1; Crisis Teachers 1; Paraprofessionals 7; Speech Pathologist; Physical Education 1. *Curricula* Career/Vocational Education; Individualized; Basic Skills; Prevocational. *Educational Intervention Approaches* Precision Teaching; Behavior Modification; Applied Behavior Analysis. *Degrees Awarded* High School Diploma.

Comments Approximately half of Sherwood's students are autistic. All students have severe communication deficits, and/or severe behavioral problems.

The Spofford Home

9700 Grandview Rd, Kansas City, MO 64050 (816) 765-4060
Year Established 1916
Contact Dorothy Wilson-Simpson, Exec Dir

Facility Information *Placement* Public School; Public Residential Care; Private Residential Care; Day Care Students. *Number of Beds* 49. *Children/Adolescents Served* 49. *Sexes Served* Both. *Room and Board Fees (Approx)* $83. *Tuition Fees (Approx)* $30,295. *Sources of Funding* State Funds; Private Funds; Mental Health Levy. Summer school available. *Teacher Certification Level* Elementary School. *Special Certification Level* ED; LD; MR; Reading; Math; Speech; Music; Art; Physical Education.
Student/Patient Characteristics *Age Levels* 5-8; 9-11. *IQ Ranges* 56-70; 71-85; 85-130; Above 130. *Exceptionalities Served* Autistic; Emotionally Disturbed; Learning Disabled; Other Health Impaired. *Learning Problems* Memory Disabilities; Perceptual Disabilities; Thinking Disabilities; Oral Language Disabilities; Reading Disabilities; Handwriting Disabilities; Spelling Disabilities; Arithmetic Disabilities; Written Expression. *Behavioral Problems* Attention Deficits; Hyperactivity; Hypoactivity; Impulsivity; Self-Aggression; Verbal Aggression; Physical Aggression; Indirect Aggression; Passive Aggression; Withdrawal. *Conditions Treated* Schizophrenia; Aphasia; Convulsive Disorders; Phobias; Obsessions and Compulsions; Hysteria; Depression; Suicide; Inadequacy/Immaturity; Personality Problems; Socialized Aggressive Reaction; Unsocialized Aggressive Reaction.

Services Provided Individual Therapy; Group Therapy; Parent Involvement; Behavior Therapy; Family Therapy; Filial Therapy; Art Therapy; Play Therapy. *Professionals on Staff* Psychiatrists 1; Social Workers 4; Child Care Staff 20; Nurses 2; Art Therapist 1. *Service Facilities Available (with number of rooms)* Itinerants 4; Resource Rooms 1; Self-Contained Rooms 5. *Educational Professionals* Special Education Teachers 5. *Curricula* Traditional Academic; Individualized; Basic Skills. *Educational Intervention Approaches* Progressive Discipline; Self-Control; Behavior Modification.

Comments Spofford Home is a psychiatric residential treatment center for the emotionally disturbed child.

Springfield Park Central Hospital—Park Central School

440 S Market, Springfield, MO 65806 (417) 865-5581
Year Established 1984
Contact Roy Grando, Prog Dir; Sherry C Jacobs, Principal

Facility Information *Placement* Private Day Care. *Number of Beds* 49. *Children/Adolescents Served* 49. *Sexes Served* Both. *Room and Board Fees (Approx)* $275-$300. *Sources of Funding* State Funds; Health Insurance; Medicaid; Medicare. Summer school available. *Teacher Certification Level* Elementary School; Junior High/Middle School; High School. *Special Certification Level* LD; MR; Behavior Disorders.
Student/Patient Characteristics *Age Levels* 5-8; 9-11; 12-14; 15-17. *IQ Ranges* 85-130; Above 130. *Exceptionalities Served* Emotionally Disturbed; Learning Disabled; Mentally Handicapped; Gifted. *Learning Problems* Memory Disabilities; Perceptual Disabilities; Thinking Disabilities; Oral Language Disabilities; Reading Disabilities; Handwriting Disabilities; Spelling Disabilities; Arithmetic Disabilities; Written Expression. *Behavioral Problems* Attention Deficits; Hyperactivity; Impulsivity; Self-Aggression; Verbal Aggression; Physical Aggression; Indirect Aggression; Passive Aggression; Withdrawal. *Conditions Treated* Alcohol Abuse and/or Drug Abuse; Other Substance Abuse or Dependence; Schizophrenia; Phobias; Obsessions and Compulsions; Hysteria; Depression; Suicide; Inadequacy/Immaturity; Personality Problems; Socialized Aggressive Reaction; Unsocialized Aggressive Reaction.

Services Provided Individual Therapy; Group Therapy; Parent Involvement; Behavior Therapy; Family Therapy; Activities Therapy. *Professionals on Staff* Psychiatrists 2; Psychologists 3; Counselors 2; Social Workers 4; Nurses 7; Activity Therapists 3; Psychiatric Technicians 20. *Service Facilities Available (with number of rooms)* Hospital School 5; Homebound Instruction 5. *Educational Professionals* Special Education Teachers 4; Paraprofessionals 2. *Curricula* Traditional Academic; Individualized; Basic Skills; Prevocational. *Educational Intervention Approaches* Behavior Modification.

Tri-County Community Mental Health Center

2900 Hospital Dr, Kansas City, MO 64116 (816) 474-5747
Year Established 1972
Contact Kim Martin, Intake Worker

Facility Information *Placement* Psychiatric Hospital. *Number of Beds* 5. *Sexes Served* Both. *Sources of Funding* Health Insurance; County Funds.
Student/Patient Characteristics *Age Levels* 15-17; 18-21; Over 21. *IQ Ranges* 85-130; Above 130. *Conditions Treated* Alcohol Abuse and/or Drug Abuse; Other Substance Abuse or Dependence; Early Infantile Autism; Disintegrative Psychoses; Schizophrenia; Aphasia; Convulsive Disorders; Phobias; Obsessions and Compulsions; Hysteria; Depression; Suicide; Asthma; Anorexia Nervosa; Ulcerative Colitis; Inadequacy/Immaturity; Personality Problems; Socialized Aggressive Reaction; Unsocialized Aggressive Reaction.

Services Provided Individual Therapy; Group Therapy; Parent Involvement; Behavior Therapy; Cognitive Developmental Therapy; Biofeedback; Family Therapy; Filial Therapy; Drug Therapy; Play Therapy. *Professionals on Staff* Psychiatrists; Psychologists; Social Workers. *Service Facilities Available (with number of rooms)* Consultative (ERT). *Curricula* Individualized.

Montana

Yellowstone Boys' and Girls' Ranch

Box 212, Rte 1, Billings, MT 59106 (406) 656-3001
Year Established 1957
Contact Loren Soft, Exec Dir

Facility Information *Placement* Public School; Special School; Private Residential Care; Community Based Group Homes and Diagnostic Assessment. *Number of Beds* 92 (treatment) 8 (assessment) 24 (group homes). *Children/Adolescents Served* 124. *Sexes Served* Both. *Room and Board Fees (Approx)* $92. *Tuition Fees (Approx)* $6,600 (educational tuition). *Sources of Funding* State Funds; Health Insurance; Medicaid; P.L. 94-142; Private Contributions. Summer school available. *Teacher Certification Level* Elementary School; Junior High/Middle School. *Special Certification Level* ED; LD; MR; Reading; Math.

Student/Patient Characteristics *Age Levels* 5-8; 9-11; 12-14; 15-17. *IQ Ranges* 71-85; 85-130. *Exceptionalities Served* Emotionally Disturbed; Learning Disabled; Communication Disordered. *Learning Problems* Memory Disabilities; Perceptual Disabilities; Thinking Disabilities; Oral Language Disabilities; Reading Disabilities; Handwriting Disabilities; Spelling Disabilities; Arithmetic Disabilities; Written Expression. *Behavioral Problems* Attention Deficits; Hyperactivity; Impulsivity; Self-Aggression; Verbal Aggression; Physical Aggression; Indirect Aggression; Passive Aggression; Withdrawal. *Conditions Treated* Alcohol Abuse and/or Drug Abuse; Other Substance Abuse or Dependence; Schizophrenia; Obsessions and Compulsions; Depression; Suicide; Anorexia Nervosa; Inadequacy/Immaturity; Personality Problems; Socialized Aggressive Reaction; Unsocialized Aggressive Reaction.

Services Provided Individual Therapy; Group Therapy; Parent Involvement; Behavior Therapy; Family Therapy; Drug Therapy; Art Therapy; Music Therapy; Reality Therapy; Play Therapy; Recreational Therapy; Work Therapy. *Professionals on Staff* Psychiatrists 2; Psychologists 1; Counselors 6; Social Workers 1; Child Care Staff 82; Nurses 1. *Service Facilities Available (with number of rooms)* Resource Rooms 1; Ungraded Classes 12; On-Campus Residential School 12. *Educational Professionals* Special Education Teachers 12; Career/Vocational Teachers 2; Special Education Counselors 1; Paraprofessionals 18. *Curricula* Career/Vocational Education; Individualized; Basic Skills; Prevocational. *Educational Intervention Approaches* Engineered Classroom; Precision Teaching; Progressive Discipline; Self-Control; Behavior Modification. *Degrees Awarded* High School Diploma; Graduate Equivalency Diploma; Elementary Diploma.

Comments Yellowstone Boys' and Girls' Ranch provides treatment and care for emotionally disturbed children and youth. The treatment program is a comprehensive, holistic treatment program designed to benefit the child spiritually, physically, intellectually, emotionally, and socially.

Nebraska

Educational Service Unit 3—Department of Special Education—Exceptional Children Resource Center

4224 S 133rd St, Omaha, NE 68137 (402) 330-2770
Year Established 1967
Contact Kay Gordon, Special Ed Dir

Facility Information *Placement* Public School. *Sexes Served* Both. *Tuition Fees (Approx)* $4,400 (center based); $2,250 (home based). *Sources of Funding* P.L. 94-142. Summer school available. *Special Certification Level* MR; Severe and Profound; Speech Pathology.

Student/Patient Characteristics *Age Levels* 0-4; 5-8. *IQ Ranges* 26-40; 41-55; 71-85; 85-130. *Exceptionalities Served* Autistic; Emotionally Disturbed; Learning Disabled; Mentally Handicapped; Communication Disordered; Hearing Impaired/Deaf; Visually Impaired/Blind; Other Health Impaired; Physically Handicapped. *Learning Problems* Memory Disabilities; Perceptual Disabilities; Thinking Disabilities; Oral Language Disabilities. *Behavioral Problems* Attention Deficits; Hyperactivity; Impulsivity; Self-Aggression; Verbal Aggression; Physical Aggression; Indirect Aggression. *Conditions Treated* Convulsive Disorders; Inadequacy/Immaturity.

Services Provided Individual Therapy; Group Therapy; Parent Involvement; Behavior Therapy; Play Therapy. *Professionals on Staff* Psychologists 1; Speech Pathology 1; Physical Therapist 2; Occupational Therapist 1. *Service Facilities Available (with number of rooms)* Consultative (ERT); Itinerants; Self-Contained Rooms 2; Homebound Instruction. *Educational Professionals* Special Education Teachers 5; Paraprofessionals 5. *Curricula* Individualized; Basic Skills. *Educational Intervention Approaches* Self-Control; Behavior Modification.

Encor—Family and Medical Support Services—Home Based Services

885 S 72nd St, Omaha, NE 68114 (402) 444-6576
Contact Nancy Cahill, Dir

Facility Information *Placement* In-Home Training. *Children/Adolescents Served* 20. *Sexes Served* Both. *Room and Board Fees (Approx)* $8; Sliding Fee. *Sources of Funding* State Funds; P.L. 94-142; County; Title XX.

Student/Patient Characteristics *Age Levels* 0-4; 5-8; 9-11; 12-14; 15-17; 18-21; Over 21. *IQ Ranges* 0-25; 26-40; 41-55; 56-70. *Exceptionalities Served* Autistic; Emotionally Disturbed; Learning Disabled; Mentally Handicapped; Communication Disordered; Hearing Impaired/Deaf; Visually Impaired/Blind; Other Health Impaired; Physically Handicapped. *Learning Problems* Memory Disabilities; Perceptual Disabilities; Thinking Disabilities; Oral Language Disabilities; Reading Disabilities; Handwriting Disabilities; Spelling Disabilities; Arithmetic Disabilities; Written Expression. *Behavioral Problems* Attention Deficits; Hyperactivity; Hypoactivity; Impulsivity; Self-Aggression; Verbal Aggression; Physical Aggression; Indirect Aggression; Passive Aggression; Withdrawal.

Services Provided Parent Involvement; Behavior Therapy; Parent Training. *Professionals on Staff* Social Workers 7; Child Care Staff 9; Nurses 2; Behavior Specialists 3. *Service Facilities Available (with number of rooms)* Homebound Instruction. *Educational Professionals* Paraprofessionals 9. *Curricula* Individualized; Basic Skills; Prevocational; Parent Training. *Educational Intervention Approaches* Precision Teaching; Behavior Modification; Applied Behavior Analysis.

Encor—Family and Medical Support Services—Respite Services

885 S 72 St, Omaha, NE 68114 (402) 444-6576
Contact Nancy Cahill, Dir

Facility Information *Placement* Respite Care. *Children/Adolescents Served* 100. *Sexes Served* Both. *Room and Board Fees (Approx)* $8 days; Sliding Fee. *Sources of Funding* State Funds; Title XX; County Funding.

Student/Patient Characteristics *Age Levels* 0-4; 5-8; 9-11; 12-14; 15-17; 18-21; Over 21. *IQ Ranges* 0-25; 26-40; 41-55; 56-70. *Exceptionalities Served* Autistic; Emotionally Disturbed; Learning Disabled; Mentally Handicapped; Communication Disordered; Hearing Impaired/Deaf; Visually Impaired/Blind; Other Health Impaired. *Learning Problems* Memory Disabilities; Perceptual Disabilities; Thinking Disabilities; Oral Language Disabilities; Reading Disabilities; Handwriting Disabilities; Spelling Disabilities; Arithmetic Disabilities; Written Expression. *Behavioral Problems* Attention Deficits; Hyperactivity; Hypoactivity; Impulsivity; Self-Aggression; Verbal Aggression; Physical Aggression; Indirect Aggression; Passive Aggression; Withdrawal. *Conditions Treated* Early Infantile Autism; Convulsive Disorders.

Services Provided Respite Care. *Professionals on Staff* Social Workers 7; Child Care Staff 4; Nurses 2; Behavior Specialists 3.

Epworth Village Inc

PO Box 503, 2119 Division Ave, York, NE 68467
(402) 362-3353
Year Established 1890
Contact Ted C Sheely, Ed Coord

Facility Information *Placement* Special School; Private Residential Care. *Number of Beds* 34. *Children/Adolescents Served* 40. *Sexes Served* Both. *Room and Board Fees (Approx)* $26. *Tuition Fees (Approx)* $13,500. *Sources of Funding* State Funds; P.L. 94-142; Private Donations. Summer school available. *Teacher Certification Level* Elementary School; Junior High/Middle School; High School. *Special Certification Level* ED; MR; Reading; Math; Music; Home Economics.

Student/Patient Characteristics *Age Levels* 9-11; 12-14; 15-17; 18-21. *IQ Ranges* 85-130. *Exceptionalities Served* Emotionally Disturbed; Learning Disabled. *Learning Problems* Perceptual Disabilities; Thinking Disabilities; Reading Disabilities; Spelling Disabilities; Arithmetic Disabilities; Written Expression. *Behavioral Problems* Attention Deficits; Hyperactivity; Hypoactivity; Impulsivity; Self-Aggression; Verbal Aggression; Physical Aggression; Indirect Aggression; Passive Aggression; Withdrawal. *Conditions Treated* Alcohol Abuse and/or Drug Abuse; Depression; Suicide; Inadequacy/Immaturity; Personality Problems; Socialized Aggressive Reaction; Unsocialized Aggressive Reaction.

Services Provided Individual Therapy; Group Therapy; Parent Involvement; Behavior Therapy; Family Therapy; Music Therapy; Reality Therapy. *Professionals on Staff* Psychiatrists 1; Psychologists 1; Counselors; Social Workers; Child Care Staff 14; Nurses 1. *Service Facilities Available (with number of rooms)* Consultative (ERT) 2; Resource Rooms 2; Transition Rooms 2; Self-Contained Rooms 1; On-Campus Residential School 5. *Educational Professionals* Regular School Teachers 3; Special Education Teachers 2; Paraprofessionals 1; Regular Education Counselor; Administrator 1. *Curricula* Traditional Academic; Individualized; Basic Skills; Prevocational. *Educational Intervention Approaches* Engineered Classroom; Precision Teaching; Progressive Discipline; Self-Control; Behavior Modification. *Degrees Awarded* Certificate of Attendance.

Comments Epworth Village is a long-term, non-lock-up, residential care center with a special school for behaviorally impaired and specific learning disabled students.

St Joseph Center for Mental Health

819 Dorcas, Omaha, NE 68108 (402) 449-4653
Year Established 1932
Contact Johanna Anderson, Exec Dir

Facility Information *Placement* Special School; Private Residential Care; Private Day Care. *Number of Beds* 56. *Children/Adolescents Served* 56. *Sexes Served* Both. *Room and Board Fees (Approx)* $233. *Teacher Certification Level* Elementary School; Junior High/Middle School; High School. *Special Certification Level* ED; LD; MR; Reading; Math.

Student/Patient Characteristics *Age Levels* 0-4; 5-8; 9-11; 12-14; 15-17; 18-21; Over 21. *IQ Ranges* 56-70; 71-85; 85-130; Above 130. *Exceptionalities Served* Autistic; Emotionally Disturbed; Learning Disabled; Mentally Handicapped; Gifted. *Learning Problems* Memory Disabilities; Perceptual Disabilities; Thinking Disabilities; Oral Language Disabilities; Reading Disabilities; Handwriting Disabilities; Spelling Disabilities; Arithmetic Disabilities; Written Expression. *Behavioral Problems* Attention Deficits; Hyperactivity; Hypoactivity; Impulsivity; Self-Aggression; Verbal Aggression; Physical Aggression; Indirect Aggression; Passive Aggression; Withdrawal. *Conditions Treated* Alcohol Abuse and/or Drug Abuse; Other Substance Abuse or Dependence; Early Infantile Autism; Disintegrative Psychoses; Schizophrenia; Aphasia; Convulsive Disorders; Phobias; Obses-

sions and Compulsions; Hysteria; Depression; Suicide; Asthma; Anorexia Nervosa; Ulcerative Colitis; Inadequacy/Immaturity; Personality Problems; Socialized Aggressive Reaction; Unsocialized Aggressive Reaction.

Services Provided Individual Therapy; Group Therapy; Parent Involvement; Behavior Therapy; Cognitive Developmental Therapy; Biofeedback; Family Therapy; Drug Therapy; Art Therapy; Music Therapy; Reality Therapy. *Professionals on Staff* Psychiatrists 11; Psychologists 3; Social Workers 5; Nurses 50; Educational Therapists 5. *Service Facilities Available (with number of rooms)* Resource Rooms 4; Transition Rooms 4; Self-Contained Rooms 4; Special School 4; Hospital School 4. *Educational Professionals* Regular School Teachers 5; Special Education Teachers 5; Crisis Teachers 5. *Curricula* Traditional Academic; Individualized; Basic Skills. *Educational Intervention Approaches* Engineered Classroom; Precision Teaching; Progressive Discipline; Self-Control; Behavior Modification; Applied Behavior Analysis; Creative Conditioning.

Youth and Family Services

2555 Leavenworth St, Omaha, NE 68105 (402) 444-6326
Year Established 1971
Contact William E Reay, Dir Youth and Family Serv

Facility Information *Placement* Special School; Special Program; Residential Treatment. *Number of Beds* 23. *Children/Adolescents Served* 93. *Sexes Served* Both. *Room and Board Fees (Approx)* $80 (school). *Tuition Fees (Approx)* $16,740-$29,000. *Sources of Funding* State Funds; Health Insurance; Medicaid. Summer school available. *Teacher Certification Level* High School. *Special Certification Level* ED; LD; MR; BI.

Student/Patient Characteristics *Age Levels* 0-4; 5-8; 9-11; 12-14; 15-17; 18-21. *IQ Ranges* 85-130; Above 130. *Exceptionalities Served* Emotionally Disturbed; Learning Disabled. *Learning Problems* Memory Disabilities; Thinking Disabilities; Reading Disabilities. *Behavioral Problems* Attention Deficits; Hyperactivity; Impulsivity; Self-Aggression; Verbal Aggression; Physical Aggression; Indirect Aggression; Passive Aggression; Withdrawal. *Conditions Treated* Alcohol Abuse and/or Drug Abuse; Disintegrative Psychoses; Schizophrenia; Phobias; Obsessions and Compulsions; Depression; Suicide; Personality Problems; Socialized Aggressive Reaction; Unsocialized Aggressive Reaction.

Services Provided Individual Therapy; Group Therapy; Parent Involvement; Behavior Therapy; Cognitive Developmental Therapy; Family Therapy; Reality Therapy; Play Therapy. *Professionals on Staff* Psychiatrists 1; Psychologists 2; Counselors 30; Social Workers 13; Child Care Staff 4. *Educational Professionals* Special Education Teachers 15; Career/Vocational Teachers 2; Crisis Teachers 3; Special Education Counselors 1; Paraprofessionals 2. *Curricula* Traditional Academic; Career/Vocational Education; Individualized; Basic Skills; Prevocational. *Educational Intervention Approaches* Engineered Classroom; Precision Teaching; Progressive Discipline; Self-Control; Behavior Modification; Applied Behavior Analysis; Creative Conditioning.

Nevada

Community Counseling Center—Rural Clinics

Box 187, Ely, NV 89301 (702) 289-4871
Year Established 1978
Contact David Harley, Office Mgr

Facility Information *Placement* Community Counseling Center. *Sexes Served* Both. *Sources of Funding* State Funds; Block Grant. **Student/Patient Characteristics** *Age Levels* 0-4; 5-8; 9-11; 12-14; 15-17; 18-21; Over 21. *IQ Ranges* 71-85; 85-130; Above 130. *Exceptionalities Served* Emotionally Disturbed; Learning Disabled; Mentally Handicapped. *Learning Problems* Memory Disabilities; Perceptual Disabilities; Thinking Disabilities; Oral Language Disabilities; Reading Disabilities; Handwriting Disabilities; Spelling Disabilities; Arithmetic Disabilities; Written Expression. *Behavioral Problems* Attention Deficits; Hyperactivity; Impulsivity; Self-Aggression; Verbal Aggression; Physical Aggression; Indirect Aggression; Passive Aggression; Withdrawal. *Conditions Treated* Alcohol Abuse and/or Drug Abuse; Other Substance Abuse or Dependence; Early Infantile Autism; Disintegrative Psychoses; Schizophrenia; Aphasia; Convulsive Disorders; Phobias; Obsessions and Compulsions; Hysteria; Depression; Suicide; Asthma; Anorexia Nervosa; Ulcerative Colitis; Inadequacy/Immaturity; Personality Problems; Socialized Aggressive Reaction; Unsocialized Aggressive Reaction.

Services Provided Individual Therapy; Group Therapy; Parent Involvement; Behavior Therapy; Cognitive Developmental Therapy; Biofeedback; Family Therapy; Drug Therapy; Reality Therapy; Play Therapy; Relaxation Training. *Professionals on Staff* Psychiatrists 3; Psychologists 2; Social Workers 3; Outreach 1.

New Hampshire

Center for Life Management

44 Stiles Rd, Salem, NH 03079 (603) 893-3548
Contact Ron Michaud, Dir of Family Serv

Facility Information *Placement* Outpatient Mental Health Facilities. *Sexes Served* Both. *Sources of Funding* State Funds; Health Insurance; Medicaid; Medicare; Town Grants.

Student/Patient Characteristics *Age Levels* 0-4; 5-8; 9-11; 12-14; 15-17; 18-21. *IQ Ranges* 71-85; 85-130. *Exceptionalities Served* Emotionally Disturbed; Learning Disabled; Mentally Handicapped. *Learning Problems* Thinking Disabilities. *Behavioral Problems* Impulsivity; Self-Aggression; Verbal Aggression; Physical Aggression; Indirect Aggression; Passive Aggression; Withdrawal. *Conditions Treated* Alcohol Abuse and/or Drug Abuse; Other Substance Abuse or Dependence; Phobias; Obsessions and Compulsions; Depression; Suicide; Asthma; Anorexia Nervosa; Inadequacy/Immaturity; Personality Problems; Socialized Aggressive Reaction; Unsocialized Aggressive Reaction.

Services Provided Individual Therapy; Group Therapy; Parent Involvement; Behavior Therapy; Cognitive Developmental Therapy; Biofeedback; Family Therapy; Drug Therapy; Reality Therapy; Play Therapy. *Professionals on Staff* Psychiatrists 2; Psychologists 5; Counselors 7; Social Workers 2. *Service Facilities Available (with number of rooms)* Consultative (ERT).

Comments The Center for Life Management Children's Program exists to help children and their families solve problems and fulfill their human potential.

Central New Hampshire Community Mental Health Services Inc—Early Intervention Services

Box 2032, 17 Fruit St, Concord, NH 03301 (603) 228-1551
Year Established 1969
Contact F Kristin Hoeveler, Dir

Facility Information *Placement* Early Intervention Mental Health Services. *Children/Adolescents Served* 70. *Sexes Served* Both. *Sources of Funding* State Funds; Health Insurance; Medicaid; United Way. *Special Certification Level* ED; LD; MR.

Student/Patient Characteristics *Age Levels* 0-4. *Exceptionalities Served* Autistic; Learning Disabled; Mentally Handicapped; Communication Disordered; Hearing Impaired/Deaf; Visually Impaired/Blind; Other Health Impaired; Physically Handicapped. *Learning Problems* Perceptual Disabilities; Oral Language Disabilities. *Behavioral Problems* Attention Deficits; Hyperactivity; Impulsivity; Withdrawal. *Conditions Treated* Convulsive Disorders.

Services Provided Individual Therapy; Parent Involvement; Behavior Therapy; Cognitive Developmental Therapy; Physical Therapy; Occupational Therapy; Speech and Language Therapy. *Professionals on Staff* Psychologists 1; Counselors 1; Physical Therapists 2; Occupational Therapist 1; Speech and Language

Therapist 1. *Service Facilities Available (with number of rooms)* Homebound Instruction. *Educational Professionals* Special Education Teachers 1. *Curricula* Early Intervention.

New England Salem Children's Trust

PO Box 56, Stinson Lake Rd, Rumney, NH 03266
(603) 786-9427
Contact Cynthia Collen, Prog Dir

Facility Information *Placement* Private Residential Care. *Number of Beds* 12. *Children/Adolescents Served* 12. *Sexes Served* Both. *Sources of Funding* State Funds; Medicaid; Private; Corporate Donation. Summer school available.

Student/Patient Characteristics *Age Levels* 9-11; 12-14; 15-17; 18-21. *Exceptionalities Served* Emotionally Disturbed; Learning Disabled; Communication Disordered. *Learning Problems* Memory Disabilities; Perceptual Disabilities; Thinking Disabilities; Oral Language Disabilities; Reading Disabilities; Handwriting Disabilities; Spelling Disabilities; Arithmetic Disabilities; Written Expression. *Behavioral Problems* Attention Deficits; Hyperactivity; Impulsivity; Self-Aggression; Verbal Aggression; Physical Aggression; Passive Aggression; Withdrawal. *Conditions Treated* Phobias; Obsessions and Compulsions; Depression; Suicide; Inadequacy/Immaturity; Personality Problems; Socialized Aggressive Reaction; Unsocialized Aggressive Reaction.

Services Provided Individual Therapy; Group Therapy; Parent Involvement; Behavior Therapy; Cognitive Developmental Therapy; Family Therapy; Art Therapy; Music Therapy; Reality Therapy; Play Therapy. *Professionals on Staff* Psychologists; Counselors; Social Workers; Child Care Staff. *Service Facilities Available (with number of rooms)* Consultative (ERT); Resource Rooms; Transition Rooms; Self-Contained Rooms; Homebound Instruction. *Educational Professionals* Regular School Teachers; Special Education Teachers; Paraprofessionals. *Curricula* Traditional Academic; Career/Vocational Education; Individualized; Basic Skills; Prevocational. *Educational Intervention Approaches* Engineered Classroom; Precision Teaching; Progressive Discipline; Self-Control; Behavior Modification; Applied Behavior Analysis. *Degrees Awarded* Certificate of Attendance; High School Diploma; Graduate Equivalency Diploma.

Philbrook Center—Special Education Program

121 S Fruit St, Concord, NH 03301 (603) 224-6531
Contact Ronald P Mills, Chief of Ed Prog

Facility Information *Placement* Special School. *Number of Beds* 20. *Children/Adolescents Served* 40. *Sexes Served* Both. *Room and Board Fees (Approx)* $69 (day treatment); $87 (residential). *Tuition Fees (Approx)* $12,420 (day treatment); $16,020 (residential). *Sources of Funding* State Funds; P.L. 94-142. Summer school available. *Teacher Certification Level* Elementary School; Junior High/Middle School; High School. *Special Certification Level* ED; LD.

Student/Patient Characteristics *Age Levels* 9-11; 12-14; 15-17. *IQ Ranges* 56-70; 71-85; 85-130. *Exceptionalities Served* Emotionally Disturbed; Learning Disabled. *Conditions Treated* Personality Problems; Socialized Aggressive Reaction; Unsocialized Aggressive Reaction.

Services Provided Group Therapy; Parent Involvement; Behavior Therapy; Art Therapy; Reality Therapy. *Professionals on Staff* Psychologists 1; Counselors 4; Social Workers 4; Child Care Staff 6; Nurses 1. *Service Facilities Available (with number of rooms)* Resource Rooms 1; Self-Contained Rooms 2. *Educational Professionals* Regular School Teachers 5; Special Education Teachers 7; Special Education Counselors 3; Paraprofessionals 6. *Curricula* Traditional Academic; Career/Vocational Education; Individualized; Basic Skills; Prevocational. *Educational Intervention Approaches* Progressive Discipline; Self-Control; Behavior Modification. *Degrees Awarded* Certificate of Attendance; Graduate Equivalency Diploma.

Comments The Philbrook Center Special Education Program is designed to meet the educational needs of emotionally handicapped boys and girls, grades K-12, ages 6-21 years, and is approved as a special education school by the NH State Department of Education.

Pine Haven Boys' Center

PO Box 162, River Rd, Suncook, NH 03275 (603) 485-7141
Year Established 1963
Contact Jackie Picard, Social Worker
Facility Information *Placement* Special School; Private Residential Care. *Number of Beds* 24. *Children/Adolescents Served* 24. *Sexes Served* Male. *Room and Board Fees (Approx)* $65. *Tuition Fees (Approx)* $23,800. *Sources of Funding* State Funds; HEW; P.L. 94-142. Summer school available. *Teacher Certification Level* Elementary School; Junior High/Middle School. *Special Certification Level* LD; Career/Vocational Education.

Student/Patient Characteristics *Age Levels* 9-11; 12-14; 15-17. *IQ Ranges* 71-85; 85-130. *Exceptionalities Served* Emotionally Disturbed; Learning Disabled; Mentally Handicapped. *Learning Problems* Memory Disabilities; Thinking Disabilities; Oral Language Disabilities; Reading Disabilities; Handwriting Disabilities; Spelling Disabilities; Arithmetic Disabilities; Written Expression. *Behavioral Problems* Attention Deficits; Hyperactivity; Hypoactivity; Impulsivity; Verbal Aggression. *Conditions Treated* Depression; Inadequacy/Immaturity; Personality Problems; Socialized Aggressive Reaction; Unsocialized Aggressive Reaction; Socialization Skills.

Services Provided Individual Therapy; Group Therapy; Parent Involvement; Behavior Therapy; Family Therapy; Drug Therapy; Art Therapy; Music Therapy. *Professionals on Staff* Psychiatrists 1; Psychologists 1; Counselors 2; Social Workers 2; Child Care Staff 5; Nurses 1. *Service Facilities Available (with number of rooms)* Resource Rooms 1; Self-Contained Rooms 4. *Educational Professionals* Regular School Teachers 3; Special Education Teachers 3; Career/Vocational Teachers 1. *Curricula* Traditional Academic; Career/Vocational Education; Individualized; Prevocational. *Educational Intervention Approaches* Behavior Modification. *Degrees Awarded* Certificate of Attendance; Elementary School Diploma.

Project Second Start's Alternative High School Program

450 N State St, Concord, NH 03301 (603) 225-3318
Year Established 1978
Contact Karl T Bergeron, Prog Coord
Facility Information *Placement* Special School; Special Program; Work Experience and Training Program. *Children/Adolescents Served* 60. *Sexes Served* Both. *Tuition Fees (Approx)* $3,900 (special ed students); $2,200 (non special ed students). *Sources of Funding* P.L. 94-142; Tuition. Summer school available. *Teacher*

Certification Level Junior High/Middle School; High School. *Special Certification Level* ED; LD; Career/Vocational Education; Reading; Math; General Special Education.

Student/Patient Characteristics *Age Levels* 12-14; 15-17; 18-21. *IQ Ranges* 71-85; 85-130; Above 130. *Exceptionalities Served* Emotionally Disturbed; Learning Disabled; Communication Disordered. *Learning Problems* Memory Disabilities; Perceptual Disabilities; Thinking Disabilities; Oral Language Disabilities; Reading Disabilities; Handwriting Disabilities; Spelling Disabilities; Arithmetic Disabilities; Written Expression. *Behavioral Problems* Attention Deficits; Hyperactivity; Hypoactivity; Impulsivity; Self-Aggression; Verbal Aggression; Physical Aggression; Indirect Aggression; Passive Aggression; Withdrawal. *Conditions Treated* Alcohol Abuse and/or Drug Abuse; Other Substance Abuse or Dependence; Convulsive Disorders; Obsessions and Compulsions; Depression; Personality Problems.

Services Provided Group Therapy; Cognitive Developmental Therapy; Drug Therapy. *Professionals on Staff* Psychologists 2; Counselors 1; Social Workers 1. *Service Facilities Available (with number of rooms)* Special School. *Educational Professionals* Special Education Teachers 6; Career/Vocational Teachers 1; Special Education Counselors 2. *Curricula* Traditional Academic; Career/Vocational Education; Individualized; Basic Skills; Prevocational. *Educational Intervention Approaches* Team Approach. *Degrees Awarded* Certificate of Attendance; High School Diploma; Graduate Equivalency Diploma.

Comments The program is designed for students who are coded learning disabled or emotionally handicapped and for adolescents who are not coded but who have been unable to succeed in a traditional school setting. The program is based on the belief that some students need a small, structured, and highly individualized academic program.

Spaulding Youth Center—Autistic Program

PO Box 189, Tilton, NH 03276 (603) 286-8901
Year Established 1972
Contact Lyn Carlson, Admin Coord
Facility Information *Placement* Special School; Private Residential Care; Special Program; Residential and Day Treatment. *Number of Beds* 13. *Children/Adolescents Served* 23. *Sexes Served* Both. *Room and Board Fees (Approx)* Varies. *Tuition Fees (Approx)* Varies. *Sources of Funding* State Funds; P.L. 94-142; Court Ordered. Summer school available. *Teacher Certification Level* Elementary School. *Special Certification Level* ED; MR; Career/Vocational Education; Elementary Education; Special Education; Psychology.

Student/Patient Characteristics *Age Levels* 0-4; 5-8; 9-11; 12-14; 15-17; 18-21. *IQ Ranges* 41-55; 56-70; 71-85; 85-130; Above 130. *Exceptionalities Served* Autistic; Emotionally Disturbed; Mentally Handicapped; Communication Disordered; Hearing Impaired/Deaf; Visually Impaired/Blind; Other Health Impaired; Physically Handicapped. *Learning Problems* Memory Disabilities; Perceptual Disabilities; Thinking Disabilities; Oral Language Disabilities; Handwriting Disabilities; Spelling Disabilities; Arithmetic Disabilities; Written Expression. *Behavioral Problems* Attention Deficits; Hyperactivity; Hypoactivity; Impulsivity; Self-Aggression; Physical Aggression; Indirect Aggression; Passive Aggression; Withdrawal. *Conditions Treated* Early Infantile Autism; Convulsive Disorders; Phobias; Obsessions and Compulsions; Depression; Unsocialized Aggressive Reaction.

Services Provided Group Therapy; Parent Involvement; Behavior Therapy; Cognitive Developmental Therapy. *Professionals on Staff* Psychologists; Counselors; Social Workers; Child Care Staff 4; Nurses 2. *Service Facilities Available (with number of rooms)* Consultative (ERT) 2; Resource Rooms 3; Self-Contained Rooms 3; On-Campus Residential School 3. *Educational Professionals* Special Education Teachers 4; Career/Vocational Teachers 1; Special Education Counselors 4; Paraprofessionals 6. *Curricula* Career/Vocational Education; Individualized; Basic Skills; Prevocational; Adaptive Daily Living. *Educational Intervention Approaches* Precision Teaching; Behavior Modification; Applied Behavior Analysis.

Comments Programs are designed individually to meet the wide and varied needs of our students. Individual Education Plans cover 24 hours a day and are carefully monitored.

Spaulding Youth Center—Emotional Handicap Program

PO Box 189, Tilton, NH 03276 (603) 286-8901
Year Established 1958
Contact Mary Lou Mion, Admin Coord
Facility Information *Placement* Special School; Private Residential Care; Special Program; Residential and Day Treatment. *Number of Beds* 30. *Children/Adolescents Served* 36. *Sexes Served* Male. *Room and Board Fees (Approx)* Varies. *Tuition Fees (Approx)* Varies. *Sources of Funding* State Funds; P.L. 94-142; Court Ordered. Summer school available. *Teacher Certification Level* Elementary School; Junior High/Middle School. *Special Certification Level* ED; LD; MR; Elementary Education; Special Education; Psychology.
Student/Patient Characteristics *Age Levels* 5-8; 9-11; 12-14; 15-17. *IQ Ranges* 56-70; 71-85; 85-130; Above 130. *Exceptionalities Served* Emotionally Disturbed; Learning Disabled; Communication Disordered; Hearing Impaired/Deaf; Visually Impaired/Blind; Other Health Impaired. *Learning Problems* Memory Disabilities; Perceptual Disabilities; Thinking Disabilities; Oral Language Disabilities; Reading Disabilities; Handwriting Disabilities; Spelling Disabilities; Arithmetic Disabilities; Written Expression. *Behavioral Problems* Attention Deficits; Hyperactivity; Hypoactivity; Impulsivity; Self-Aggression; Verbal Aggression; Physical Aggression; Indirect Aggression; Passive Aggression; Withdrawal. *Conditions Treated* Alcohol Abuse and/or Drug Abuse; Other Substance Abuse or Dependence; Aphasia; Convulsive Disorders; Phobias; Obsessions and Compulsions; Depression; Suicide; Inadequacy/Immaturity; Personality Problems; Socialized Aggressive Reaction; Unsocialized Aggressive Reaction.
Services Provided Individual Therapy; Group Therapy; Parent Involvement; Behavior Therapy; Cognitive Developmental Therapy; Reality Therapy; Play Therapy. *Professionals on Staff* Psychiatrists 1; Psychologists 2; Counselors 1; Social Workers 1; Child Care Staff 12; Nurses 2. *Service Facilities Available (with number of rooms)* Consultative (ERT) 2; Resource Rooms 4; Transition Rooms 1; Self-Contained Rooms 2; On-Campus Residential School. *Educational Professionals* Special Education Teachers 6; Career/Vocational Teachers 1; Special Education Counselors 12; Paraprofessionals 4. *Curricula* Traditional Academic; Career/Vocational Education; Individualized; Basic Skills; Prevocational; Experiential and Outdoor Education. *Educational Intervention Approaches* Precision Teaching; Behavior Modification; Applied Behavior Analysis; Creative Conditioning.
Comments Programs are designed individually to meet the wide and varied needs of our students. Individual Education Plans cover 24 hours a day and are carefully monitored.

Strafford Guidance Center Inc

90 Washington St, Dover, NH 03820 (603) 749-4040
Contact Thomas J Maynard, Exec Dir
Facility Information *Placement* Special Program. *Sexes Served* Both. *Sources of Funding* State Funds; Health Insurance; Medicaid; Court Ordered Payment.

Student/Patient Characteristics *Age Levels* 5-8; 18-21. *IQ Ranges* 71-85; 85-130; Above 130. *Exceptionalities Served* Emotionally Disturbed. *Behavioral Problems* Attention Deficits; Hyperactivity; Hypoactivity; Impulsivity; Self-Aggression; Verbal Aggression; Physical Aggression; Indirect Aggression; Passive Aggression; Withdrawal. *Conditions Treated* Disintegrative Psychoses; Schizophrenia; Aphasia; Phobias; Obsessions and Compulsions; Hysteria; Depression; Suicide; Anorexia Nervosa; Ulcerative Colitis; Inadequacy/Immaturity; Personality Problems; Socialized Aggressive Reaction; Unsocialized Aggressive Reaction.
Services Provided Individual Therapy; Group Therapy; Parent Involvement; Behavior Therapy; Family Therapy; Drug Therapy; Play Therapy. *Professionals on Staff* Psychiatrists 1; Psychologists 1; Counselors 2; Social Workers 4.

Strafford Guidance Center—Youth and Family Services

6 Atkinson St, Dover, NH 03820 (603) 742-0730
Comments The center is a community mental health agency. It is not a placement facility. It provides outpatient therapy to children and families.

War Bonnet—Wilderness Pathways

Box 29, RFD No. 1, Canaan, NH 03741 (603) 523-4276
Year Established 1956
Contact Richard E Vandall, Exec Dir
Facility Information *Placement* Private Residential Care; Summer Camp Program. *Number of Beds* 18. *Children/Adolescents Served* 18 (winter); 75 (summer). *Sexes Served* Male. *Room and Board Fees (Approx)* $68 (winter); $63 (summer). *Tuition Fees (Approx)* $19,000 (winter). *Sources of Funding* State Funds; Health Insurance; Medicare; Private Funds. Summer school available. *Teacher Certification Level* Junior High/Middle School; High School. *Special Certification Level* ED; LD; Reading; Math; Outdoor Education.
Student/Patient Characteristics *Age Levels* 12-14; 15-17; 18-21. *IQ Ranges* 85-130; Above 130. *Exceptionalities Served* Autistic; Emotionally Disturbed; Learning Disabled; Communication Disordered; Gifted. *Learning Problems* Memory Disabilities; Perceptual Disabilities; Thinking Disabilities; Oral Language Disabilities; Reading Disabilities; Handwriting Disabilities; Spelling Disabilities; Arithmetic Disabilities; Written Expression. *Behavioral Problems* Attention Deficits; Hyperactivity; Impulsivity; Verbal Aggression; Indirect Aggression; Passive Aggression; Withdrawal. *Conditions Treated* Other Substance Abuse or Dependence; Schizophrenia; Phobias; Obsessions and Compulsions; Depression; Inadequacy/Immaturity; Personality Problems; Socialized Aggressive Reaction; Unsocialized Aggressive Reaction.
Services Provided Individual Therapy; Group Therapy; Parent Involvement; Behavior Therapy; Family Therapy; Reality Therapy. *Professionals on Staff* Psychiatrists 1; Psychologists 3; Counselors 3; Social Workers 1; Child Care Staff 4. *Service Facilities Available (with number of rooms)* Transition Rooms 1; Public School. *Educational Professionals* Regular School Teachers 2; Special Education Teachers 1; Career/Vocational Teachers 1; Special Education Counselors 1; Paraprofessionals 8. *Curricula* Traditional Academic; Individualized. *Educational Intervention Approaches* Behavior Modification. *Degrees Awarded* Certificate of Attendance; High School Diploma; Graduate Equivalency Diploma.

New Jersey

American Institute—The Training School at Vineland

1667 E Landis Ave, Vineland, NJ 08360 (609) 691-0021
Contact Barbara Nyce, Registrar

Facility Information *Placement* Special School; Private Residential Care; Vocational and Senior Enrichment Programming. *Number of Beds* 60. *Children/Adolescents Served* 60. *Sexes Served* Both. *Tuition Fees (Approx)* $30,389. *Sources of Funding* State Funds; Private Tuition. Summer school available. *Teacher Certification Level* Elementary School; Junior High/Middle School; High School. *Special Certification Level* ED; MR.

Student/Patient Characteristics *Age Levels* 9-11; 12-14; 15-17; 18-21; Over 21. *IQ Ranges* 0-25; 26-40; 41-55; 56-70; 71-85. *Exceptionalities Served* Autistic; Emotionally Disturbed; Learning Disabled; Mentally Handicapped; Communication Disordered; Hearing Impaired/Deaf; Visually Impaired/Blind; Other Health Impaired; Multiply Handicapped. *Learning Problems* Memory Disabilities; Perceptual Disabilities; Thinking Disabilities; Oral Language Disabilities; Reading Disabilities; Handwriting Disabilities; Spelling Disabilities; Arithmetic Disabilities; Written Expression. *Behavioral Problems* Attention Deficits; Hyperactivity; Hypoactivity; Impulsivity; Self-Aggression; Verbal Aggression; Physical Aggression; Indirect Aggression; Passive Aggression; Withdrawal.

Services Provided Individual Therapy; Group Therapy; Behavior Therapy; Art Therapy; Music Therapy. *Professionals on Staff* Psychiatrists 2; Psychologists 5; Counselors 6; Social Workers 5; Child Care Staff 114; Nurses 10; Vocational Instructors 30. *Service Facilities Available (with number of rooms)* Resource Rooms; Transition Rooms; Self-Contained Rooms; Special School; Hospital School; On-Campus Residential School; Homebound Instruction. *Educational Professionals* Special Education Teachers 10; Crisis Teachers 1; Paraprofessionals 5; Ancillary 5. *Curricula* Career/Vocational Education; Individualized; Basic Skills; Prevocational. *Educational Intervention Approaches* Self-Control; Behavior Modification.

Comments The American Institute — The Training School at Vineland is a comprehensive resource facility for developmentally disabled persons offering residential, day, and community-based programs. The 200 acre campus offers a Vocational Opportunity Center, a school, a senior center, a small farm and greenhouse complex, and 14 family-like cottages for residents.

Arthur Brisbane Child Treatment Center

Box 625, Allaire Rd, Farmingdale, NJ 07727 (201) 938-5061
Year Established 1946
Contact Mildred Breyer, Chief Exec Officer

Facility Information *Placement* Public Residential Care. *Number of Beds* 70. *Children/Adolescents Served* 70. *Sexes Served* Both. *Room and Board Fees (Approx)* $175. *Sources of Funding* State Funds. Summer school available. *Teacher Certification Level* Elementary School. *Special Certification Level* LD.

Student/Patient Characteristics *Age Levels* 5-8; 9-11; 12-14. *IQ Ranges* 26-40; 41-55; 56-70; 71-85; 85-130; Above 130. *Exceptionalities Served* Autistic; Emotionally Disturbed; Learning Disabled; Mentally Handicapped; Communication Disordered; Hearing Impaired/Deaf; Visually Impaired/Blind; Other Health Impaired; Physically Handicapped; Gifted. *Learning Problems* Memory Disabilities; Perceptual Disabilities; Thinking Disabilities; Oral Language Disabilities; Reading Disabilities; Handwriting Disabilities; Spelling Disabilities; Arithmetic Disabilities; Written Expression. *Behavioral Problems* Attention Deficits; Hyperactivity; Hypoactivity; Impulsivity; Self-Aggression; Verbal Aggression; Physical Aggression; Indirect Aggression; Passive Aggression; Withdrawal.

Services Provided Individual Therapy; Group Therapy; Parent Involvement; Behavior Therapy; Cognitive Developmental Therapy; Drug Therapy; Art Therapy; Music Therapy; Play Therapy. *Professionals on Staff* Psychiatrists 3; Counselors 5; Social Workers 5; Child Care Staff 35; Nurses 14. *Service Facilities Available (with number of rooms)* Self-Contained Rooms; Hospital School. *Educational Professionals* Special Education Teachers 11; Career/Vocational Teachers 1; Paraprofessionals 2. *Curricula* Traditional Academic; Individualized; Basic Skills; Prevocational. *Educational Intervention Approaches* Engineered Classroom; Behavior Modification.

Atlantic Mental Health Center Inc

2002 Black Horse Pike, McKee City, NJ 08232 (609) 645-7600
Year Established 1953
Contact John W Halpin, Exec Dir

Facility Information *Placement* Outpatient Mental Health Services. *Sexes Served* Both. *Room and Board Fees (Approx)* Sliding Scale. *Sources of Funding* State Funds; Medicaid; Private Fees.

Student/Patient Characteristics *Age Levels* 0-4; 5-8; 9-11; 12-14; 15-17; 18-21; Over 21. *IQ Ranges* 56-70; 71-85; 85-130; Above 130. *Exceptionalities Served* Emotionally Disturbed; Learning Disabled; Mentally Handicapped; Other Health Impaired; Physically Handicapped; Gifted. *Behavioral Problems* Attention Deficits; Hyperactivity; Hypoactivity; Impulsivity; Self-Aggression; Verbal Aggression; Physical Aggression; Indirect Aggression; Passive Aggression; Withdrawal. *Conditions Treated* Alcohol Abuse and/or Drug Abuse; Other Substance Abuse or Dependence; Disintegrative Psychoses; Schizophrenia; Phobias; Obsessions and Compulsions; Hysteria; Depression; Suicide; Anorexia Nervosa; Inadequacy/Immaturity; Personality Problems; Socialized Aggressive Reaction; Unsocialized Aggressive Reaction.

Services Provided Individual Therapy; Group Therapy; Parent Involvement; Behavior Therapy; Family Therapy; Drug Therapy; Play Therapy. *Professionals on Staff* Psychiatrists 3; Psychologists 8; Counselors 4; Social Workers 7; Nurses 1.

Comments The Atlantic Mental Health Center provides individual, group, family counseling, and medication management on an outpatient basis for children, adolescents, and adults. The center also offers a day hospital program for individuals over the age of 18.

The Bancroft School

Hopkins Ln, Haddonfield, NJ 08033 (609) 429-0010
Year Established 1883
Contact Claire B Griese, Special Serv Dir

Facility Information *Placement* Special School; Private Residential Care; Outpatient Evaluation and Treatment Center. *Number of Beds* 125. *Children/Adolescents Served* 125. *Sexes Served* Both. *Room and Board Fees (Approx)* $62. *Tuition Fees (Approx)* $12,300-$22,800. *Sources of Funding* State Funds; Medicaid; P.L. 94-142; Private Families; CHAMPUS. Summer school available. *Teacher Certification Level* Elementary School; Junior High/Middle School; High School. *Special Certification Level* ED; LD; MR; Reading; Communications Handicapped.

Student/Patient Characteristics *Age Levels* 0-4; 5-8; 9-11; 12-14; 15-17; 18-21; Over 21. *IQ Ranges* 26-40; 41-55; 56-70; 71-85; 85-130. *Exceptionalities Served* Autistic; Emotionally Disturbed; Learning Disabled; Mentally Handicapped; Communication Disordered; Hearing Impaired/Deaf; Visually Impaired/Blind; Other Health Impaired; Physically Handicapped. *Learning Problems* Memory Disabilities; Perceptual Disabilities; Thinking Disabilities; Oral Language Disabilities; Reading Disabilities; Handwriting Disabilities; Spelling Disabilities; Arithmetic Disabilities; Written Expression. *Behavioral Problems* Attention Deficits; Hyperactivity; Hypoactivity; Impulsivity; Self-Aggression; Verbal Aggression; Physical Aggression; Indirect Aggression; Passive Aggression; Withdrawal. *Conditions Treated* Schizophrenia; Convulsive Disorders; Obsessions and Compulsions; Ulcerative Colitis; Inadequacy/Immaturity; Personality Problems; Socialized Aggressive Reaction.

Services Provided Individual Therapy; Group Therapy; Parent Involvement; Behavior Therapy; Cognitive Developmental Therapy; Art Therapy; Music Therapy. *Professionals on Staff* Psychiatrists 3; Psychologists 4; Social Workers 3; Child Care Staff 120; Nurses 8. *Service Facilities Available (with number of rooms)* Special School 24. *Educational Professionals* Special Education Teachers 20; Career/Vocational Teachers 4; Paraprofessionals 26. *Curricula* Career/Vocational Education; Individualized; Basic Skills; Prevocational. *Educational Intervention Approaches* Progressive Discipline; Behavior Modification; Creative Conditioning. *Degrees Awarded* Certificate of Attendance; High School Diploma.

Bergen Center for Child Development

140 Park St, Haworth, NJ 07641 (201) 385-4857
Year Established 1968
Contact Adrienne Lafebure, Dir

Facility Information *Placement* Special School.
Children/Adolescents Served 75. *Sexes Served* Both. *Sources of Funding* State Funds. *Teacher Certification Level* Elementary School; Junior High/Middle School; High School. *Special Certification Level* ED; LD; MR.

Student/Patient Characteristics *Age Levels* 5-8; 9-11; 12-14; 15-17; 18-21. *IQ Ranges* 26-40; 41-55; 56-70; 71-85; 85-130; Above 130. *Exceptionalities Served* Autistic; Emotionally Disturbed; Learning Disabled; Communication Disordered; Hearing Impaired/Deaf; Visually Impaired/Blind. *Learning Problems* Memory Disabilities; Perceptual Disabilities; Thinking Disabilities; Oral Language Disabilities; Reading Disabilities; Handwriting Disabilities; Spelling Disabilities; Arithmetic Disabilities; Written Expression. *Behavioral Problems* Physical Aggression; Indirect Aggression; Passive Aggression; Withdrawal. *Conditions Treated* Disintegrative Psychoses; Schizophrenia; Aphasia; Con-

vulsive Disorders; Phobias; Obsessions and Compulsions; Depression; Asthma; Inadequacy/Immaturity; Personality Problems; Socialized Aggressive Reaction; Unsocialized Aggressive Reaction.

Services Provided Individual Therapy; Parent Involvement; Behavior Therapy; Cognitive Developmental Therapy; Family Therapy; Art Therapy; Music Therapy. *Professionals on Staff* Psychologists 2. *Service Facilities Available (with number of rooms)* Self-Contained Rooms 8. *Educational Professionals* Special Education Teachers 10; Career/Vocational Teachers 1; Paraprofessionals 10. *Curricula* Traditional Academic; Career/Vocational Education; Individualized; Basic Skills; Prevocational. *Educational Intervention Approaches* Precision Teaching; Behavior Modification; Applied Behavior Analysis. *Degrees Awarded* Certificate of Attendance; Certificate of Completion.

Bergen County Special Services School District—Washington School Autistic Program

327 E Ridgewood Ave, Paramus, NJ 07652 (201) 265-6300
Year Established 1976
Contact James B Lederer, Asst Supt

Facility Information *Placement* Public School.
Children/Adolescents Served 60. *Sexes Served* Both. *Tuition Fees (Approx)* $8,000. *Sources of Funding* State Funds; P.L. 94-142; County; Local. *Teacher Certification Level* Elementary School; Junior High/Middle School; High School. *Special Certification Level* N.J. Teacher of the Handicapped K-12.

Student/Patient Characteristics *Age Levels* 5-8; 9-11; 12-14; 15-17; 18-21. *IQ Ranges* 26-40; 41-55; 56-70; 71-85. *Exceptionalities Served* Autistic. *Learning Problems* Memory Disabilities; Perceptual Disabilities; Thinking Disabilities; Oral Language Disabilities; Reading Disabilities; Handwriting Disabilities; Spelling Disabilities; Arithmetic Disabilities; Written Expression; Behavioral Disorders. *Behavioral Problems* Attention Deficits; Hyperactivity; Impulsivity; Self-Aggression; Physical Aggression. *Conditions Treated* Early Infantile Autism; Schizophrenia.

Services Provided Speech. *Professionals on Staff* Psychiatrists 1; Psychologists 1; Social Workers 1; Nurses 1. *Service Facilities Available (with number of rooms)* Self-Contained Rooms 11; Workshop 1. *Educational Professionals* Special Education Teachers 10; Paraprofessionals 12; Speech 2; Art 1; Music 1; Physical Education 1. *Curricula* Traditional Academic; Individualized; Basic Skills; Prevocational. *Educational Intervention Approaches* Behavior Modification. *Degrees Awarded* High School Diploma.

Bergen Pines Hospital—Children's Psychiatric Unit

E Ridgewood Ave, Paramus, NJ 07652 (201) 967-4000
Year Established 1971
Contact Gerald Meyerhoff, Chief Child Psychiatry

Facility Information *Placement* Public Residential Care. *Number of Beds* 24. *Children/Adolescents Served* 24. *Sexes Served* Both. *Room and Board Fees (Approx)* $200. *Tuition Fees (Approx)* $5,000-$7,000. *Sources of Funding* Health Insurance; Medicaid; Social Security Insurance. Summer school available. *Teacher Certification Level* Elementary School; Junior High/Middle School. *Special Certification Level* ED; LD; MR; Reading; Math.

Student/Patient Characteristics *Age Levels* 5-8; 9-11; 12-14. *IQ Ranges* 56-70; 71-85; 85-130; Above 130. *Exceptionalities Served* Autistic; Emotionally Disturbed; Learning Disabled; Communication Disordered; Physically Handicapped. *Learning Problems* Memory Disabilities; Perceptual Disabilities; Thinking Disabilities; Oral Language Disabilities; Reading Disabilities; Handwriting Disabilities; Spelling Disabilities; Arithmetic Disabilities; Written Expression. *Behavioral Problems* Attention Deficits; Hyperactivity; Hypoactivity; Impulsivity; Self-Aggression; Verbal Aggression; Physical Aggression; Indirect Aggression; Passive Aggression; Withdrawal. *Conditions Treated* Alcohol Abuse and/or Drug Abuse; Other Substance Abuse or Dependence; Early Infantile Autism; Disintegrative Psychoses; Schizophrenia; Aphasia; Convulsive Disorders; Phobias; Obsessions and Compulsions;

Hysteria; Depression; Suicide; Asthma; Anorexia Nervosa; Ulcerative Colitis; Inadequacy/Immaturity; Personality Problems; Socialized Aggressive Reaction; Unsocialized Aggressive Reaction.

Services Provided Individual Therapy; Group Therapy; Parent Involvement; Behavior Therapy; Family Therapy; Filial Therapy; Drug Therapy; Art Therapy; Music Therapy. *Professionals on Staff* Psychiatrists 2; Psychologists 2; Social Workers 1; Child Care Staff 11; Nurses 13. *Educational Professionals* Special Education Teachers 4. *Curricula* Traditional Academic; Individualized; Basic Skills. *Educational Intervention Approaches* Behavior Modification.

Comments This is a short and intermediate stay residential treatment facility for mentally ill and/or seriously behaviorally disturbed children ages 6-12, some with concurrent physical impairment, utilizing an eclectic approach and featuring behavior therapy.

Chancellor Academy

93 W End Ave, Pompton Plains, NJ 07006 (201) 835-4989
Year Established 1981
Contact Richard A Sheridan, Dir

Facility Information *Placement* Private Day Care.
Children/Adolescents Served 64. *Sexes Served* Both. *Tuition Fees (Approx)* $9,300. *Sources of Funding* P.L. 94-142. *Teacher Certification Level* Elementary School; Junior High/Middle School; High School. *Special Certification Level* Special Education.

Student/Patient Characteristics *Exceptionalities Served* Emotionally Disturbed. *Learning Problems* Memory Disabilities; Perceptual Disabilities; Thinking Disabilities; Oral Language Disabilities; Reading Disabilities; Handwriting Disabilities; Spelling Disabilities; Arithmetic Disabilities; Written Expression. *Behavioral Problems* Attention Deficits; Hyperactivity; Hypoactivity; Impulsivity; Self-Aggression; Verbal Aggression; Physical Aggression; Indirect Aggression; Passive Aggression; Withdrawal. *Conditions Treated* Alcohol Abuse and/or Drug Abuse; Obsessions and Compulsions; Hysteria; Depression; Suicide; Asthma; Anorexia Nervosa; Inadequacy/Immaturity; Personality Problems; Socialized Aggressive Reaction; Unsocialized Aggressive Reaction.

Services Provided Individual Therapy; Group Therapy; Parent Involvement; Behavior Therapy; Family Therapy; Art Therapy; Music Therapy. *Professionals on Staff* Psychologists 1; Counselors 3; Social Workers 2. *Educational Professionals* Special Education Teachers 8; Career/Vocational Teachers 1; Crisis Teachers 2; Special Education Counselors 2; Paraprofessionals 3. *Curricula* Traditional Academic; Career/Vocational Education; Individualized; Basic Skills; Prevocational. *Educational Intervention Approaches* Self-Control; Behavior Modification. *Degrees Awarded* High School Diploma.

The Children's Day School

946 Edgewood Ave, Trenton, NJ 08618 (609) 695-8769
Contact Aloysius J Ballisty, Dir

Facility Information *Placement* Special School.
Children/Adolescents Served 50. *Sexes Served* Both. *Sources of Funding* State Funds; Medicaid. Summer school available. *Teacher Certification Level* Elementary School; Junior High/Middle School; High School. *Special Certification Level* ED.

Student/Patient Characteristics *Age Levels* 5-8; 9-11; 12-14; 15-17. *Exceptionalities Served* Autistic; Emotionally Disturbed; Learning Disabled; Communication Disordered. *Learning Problems* Memory Disabilities; Perceptual Disabilities; Thinking Disabilities; Oral Language Disabilities; Reading Disabilities; Handwriting Disabilities; Spelling Disabilities; Arithmetic Disabilities; Written Expression. *Behavioral Problems* Attention Deficits; Hyperactivity; Hypoactivity; Impulsivity; Self-Aggression; Verbal Aggression; Physical Aggression; Indirect Aggression; Passive Aggression; Withdrawal. *Conditions Treated* Disintegrative Psychoses; Schizophrenia; Phobias; Obsessions

and Compulsions; Hysteria; Depression; Suicide; Inadequacy/Immaturity; Personality Problems; Socialized Aggressive Reaction; Unsocialized Aggressive Reaction.

Services Provided Individual Therapy; Group Therapy; Parent Involvement; Behavior Therapy; Cognitive Developmental Therapy; Drug Therapy; Art Therapy; Reality Therapy; Play Therapy. *Professionals on Staff* Psychiatrists 1; Social Workers 2; Nurses 1. *Service Facilities Available (with number of rooms)* Self-Contained Rooms 6. *Educational Professionals* Special Education Teachers 7. *Curricula* Traditional Academic; Individualized; Basic Skills; Prevocational. *Educational Intervention Approaches* Behavior Modification. *Degrees Awarded* Certificate of Attendance; High School Diploma.

The Children's Institute

342 S Ridgewood Rd, South Orange, NJ 07079 (201) 762-0302
Year Established 1963
Contact Bruce Ettinger, Exec Dir

Facility Information *Placement* Special School.
Children/Adolescents Served 50. *Sexes Served* Both. *Tuition Fees (Approx)* $9,300. *Special Certification Level* Special Education.

Student/Patient Characteristics *Age Levels* 5-8; 9-11; 12-14. *IQ Ranges* 85-130. *Exceptionalities Served* Autistic; Emotionally Disturbed; Learning Disabled; Communication Disordered. *Learning Problems* Memory Disabilities; Perceptual Disabilities; Thinking Disabilities; Oral Language Disabilities; Reading Disabilities; Handwriting Disabilities; Spelling Disabilities; Arithmetic Disabilities; Written Expression. *Behavioral Problems* Attention Deficits; Hyperactivity; Impulsivity; Self-Aggression; Verbal Aggression; Physical Aggression; Passive Aggression; Withdrawal. *Conditions Treated* Schizophrenia; Aphasia; Phobias; Obsessions and Compulsions; Hysteria; Depression; Suicide; Personality Problems; Socialized Aggressive Reaction; Unsocialized Aggressive Reaction.

Services Provided Individual Therapy; Group Therapy; Parent Involvement; Behavior Therapy; Art Therapy; Music Therapy; Reality Therapy; Play Therapy; Psychodrama. *Professionals on Staff* Psychiatrists 1; Social Workers 2; Pediatrician 1; Speech Therapist 1. *Service Facilities Available (with number of rooms)* Consultative (ERT) 4; Transition Rooms 1; Self-Contained Rooms 9. *Educational Professionals* Regular School Teachers 3; Special Education Teachers 9; Crisis Teachers 1. *Curricula* Traditional Academic; Individualized; Basic Skills; Prevocational. *Educational Intervention Approaches* Behavior Modification; Psychotherapy.

Comments The Children's Institute is a private, nonprofit school for emotionally disturbed children ages 5-14 who are unable to function within their own school districts. The program includes academics, individual group and family psychotherapy, learning disabilities remediation, gym, art and music. Additionally, it utilizes behavior modification. Every effort is made to provide the same curriculum and requirements as the child's sending district in as normal and least restrictive environment as possible and to accelerate the successful mainstreaming of each child.

The Community School of the Family Service and Child Guidance Center of the Oranges Maplewood and Millburn

395 S Center St, Orange, NJ 07050 (201) 675-3817
Year Established 1972
Contact L Jane Smith, Dir

Facility Information *Placement* Private Day Care.
Children/Adolescents Served 24. *Sexes Served* Both. *Tuition Fees (Approx)* $9,200. *Sources of Funding* P.L. 94-142. Summer school available. *Teacher Certification Level* Elementary School; Junior High/Middle School. *Special Certification Level* ED; Career/Vocational Education.

Student/Patient Characteristics *Age Levels* 5-8; 9-11. *IQ Ranges* 85-130; Above 130. *Exceptionalities Served* Autistic; Emotionally Disturbed. *Learning Problems* Memory Disabilities; Perceptual Disabilities; Thinking Disabilities; Oral Language Disabilities; Reading Disabilities; Handwriting Disabilities; Spelling Disabilities; Arithmetic Disabilities; Written Expression. *Behavioral Problems* Attention Deficits; Hyperactivity; Hypoactivity; Impulsivity; Self-Aggression; Verbal Aggression; Physical Aggression; Indirect Aggression; Passive Aggression; Withdrawal. *Conditions Treated* Early Infantile Autism; Disintegrative Psychoses; Schizophrenia; Aphasia; Phobias; Obsessions and Compulsions; Hysteria; Depression; Suicide; Ulcerative Colitis; Inadequacy/Immaturity; Personality Problems; Socialized Aggressive Reaction; Unsocialized Aggressive Reaction.

Services Provided Individual Therapy; Group Therapy; Parent Involvement; Behavior Therapy; Cognitive Developmental Therapy; Family Therapy; Play Therapy; Dance Therapy. *Professionals on Staff* Psychiatrists 1; Psychologists 1; Social Workers 1; Movement Therapist 1; Speech Therapist 1. *Service Facilities Available (with number of rooms)* Consultative (ERT) 4; Self-Contained Rooms 4. *Educational Professionals* Special Education Teachers 4; Paraprofessionals 1. *Curricula* Traditional Academic; Individualized; Basic Skills. *Educational Intervention Approaches* Self-Control; Behavior Modification; Applied Behavior Analysis.

Cumberland County Guidance Center Inc

PO Box 808, Carmel Rd RD No. 1, Millville, NJ 08332 (609) 825-6810
Year Established 1961
Contact Susan O Crossley, Coord

Facility Information *Placement* Therapeutic Day Treatment Program. *Children/Adolescents Served* 26. *Sexes Served* Both. *Tuition Fees (Approx)* Sliding Scale. *Sources of Funding* State Funds; Health Insurance; Medicaid. Summer school available.
Student/Patient Characteristics *Age Levels* 5-8; 9-11; 12-14; 15-17. *IQ Ranges* 71-85; 85-130. *Exceptionalities Served* Emotionally Disturbed. *Behavioral Problems* Attention Deficits; Hyperactivity; Hypoactivity; Impulsivity; Self-Aggression; Verbal Aggression; Physical Aggression; Indirect Aggression; Passive Aggression; Withdrawal. *Conditions Treated* Disintegrative Psychoses; Schizophrenia; Phobias; Obsessions and Compulsions; Hysteria; Depression; Suicide; Inadequacy/Immaturity; Personality Problems; Socialized Aggressive Reaction; Unsocialized Aggressive Reaction.
Services Provided Individual Therapy; Group Therapy; Parent Involvement; Family Therapy; Art Therapy; Music Therapy; Reality Therapy; Play Therapy; Psychodrama. *Professionals on Staff* Psychiatrists 1; Psychologists 2; Social Workers 2; Child Care Staff 2.

Comments This mental health facility consults with the schools, courts, Division of Youth and Family Services, and private practitioners for an intensive treatment program.

The Devereux Foundation—Deerhaven

PO Box 654, Pottersville Rd, Chester, NJ 07930 (201) 879-4500
Year Established 1982
Contact L Michelle Borden, Dir

Facility Information *Placement* Private Residential Care. *Number of Beds* 42. *Children/Adolescents Served* 42. *Sexes Served* Female. *Room and Board Fees (Approx)* $69. *Tuition Fees (Approx)* $9,300. *Sources of Funding* State Funds; P.L. 94-142. *Teacher Certification Level* Elementary School; Junior High/Middle School; High School. *Special Certification Level* ED; Physical Education; Health.
Student/Patient Characteristics *Age Levels* 9-11; 12-14; 15-17. *IQ Ranges* 85-130. *Exceptionalities Served* Emotionally Disturbed; Learning Disabled. *Learning Problems* Perceptual Disabilities; Oral Language Disabilities; Reading Disabilities; Handwriting Disabilities; Spelling Disabilities; Arithmetic Disabilities; Written Expression. *Behavioral Problems* Attention Deficits; Hyperactivity; Impulsivity; Self-Aggression; Verbal Aggression; Physical Aggression; Passive Aggression; Withdrawal. *Conditions Treated* Obsessions and Compulsions; Hysteria; Depression; Suicide; Inadequacy/Immaturity; Personality Problems; Socialized Aggressive Reaction; Unsocialized Aggressive Reaction.

Services Provided Individual Therapy; Group Therapy; Parent Involvement; Behavior Therapy; Family Therapy; Drug Therapy; Reality Therapy. *Professionals on Staff* Psychiatrists 1; Social Workers 4; Child Care Staff 20; Nurses 3; Pediatrician 1. *Service Facilities Available (with number of rooms)* Self-Contained Rooms 5. *Educational Professionals* Special Education Teachers 5; Crisis Teachers 1; Paraprofessionals 3; Physical Education 1; Health Teacher 1. *Curricula* Individualized; Basic Skills; Prevocational. *Educational Intervention Approaches* Behavior Modification; Applied Behavior Analysis. *Degrees Awarded* Certificate of Attendance; High School Diploma.

Comments Devereux Deerhaven provides treatment to emotionally disturbed girls in a 24-hour residential milieu with the goal of providing emotional, social, and educational treatment based on their individual needs. Return to a community setting is a primary goal.

Douglass College—Gibbons Campus—Douglass Developmental Disabilities Center

New Brunswick, NJ 08903 (201) 932-9137
Year Established 1972
Contact Jan Handleman, Ed Dir

Facility Information *Placement* Special School.
Children/Adolescents Served 30. *Sexes Served* Both. *Sources of Funding* P.L. 94-142; School District Tuition. Summer school available. *Teacher Certification Level* Elementary School; Junior High/Middle School; High School. *Special Certification Level* Teacher of the Handicapped.
Student/Patient Characteristics *Age Levels* 0-4; 5-8; 9-11; 12-14; 15-17. *IQ Ranges* 0-25; 26-40; 41-55; 56-70; 71-85. *Exceptionalities Served* Autistic. *Learning Problems* Oral Language Disabilities. *Behavioral Problems* Attention Deficits; Hyperactivity; Hypoactivity; Impulsivity; Self-Aggression; Physical Aggression; Withdrawal. *Conditions Treated* Early Infantile Autism.
Services Provided Parent Involvement; Behavior Therapy. *Professionals on Staff* Psychologists 1. *Service Facilities Available (with number of rooms)* Self-Contained Rooms 6. *Educational Professionals* Special Education Teachers 4; Paraprofessionals 8. *Curricula* Individualized; Prevocational. *Educational Intervention Approaches* Behavior Modification. *Degrees Awarded* Certificate of Attendance.

Eden Family of Programs

1 Logan Dr, Princeton, NJ 08540 (609) 987-0099
Year Established 1975
Contact David L Holmes, Dir

Facility Information *Placement* Special School; Private Residential Care; Adult Services. *Number of Beds* 6. *Children/Adolescents Served* 50. *Sexes Served* Both. *Tuition Fees (Approx)* $12,000-$25,000. *Sources of Funding* State Funds; P.L. 94-142; Private. Summer school available. *Teacher Certification Level* Elementary School; Junior High/Middle School; High School. *Special Certification Level* ED.
Student/Patient Characteristics *Age Levels* 0-4; 5-8; 9-11; 12-14; 15-17; 18-21; Over 21. *IQ Ranges* 0-25; 26-40; 41-55; 56-70; 71-85. *Exceptionalities Served* Autistic. *Learning Problems* Memory Disabilities; Perceptual Disabilities; Thinking Disabilities; Oral Language Disabilities; Reading Disabilities; Handwriting Disabilities; Spelling Disabilities; Arithmetic Disabilities; Written Expression. *Behavioral Problems* Attention Deficits; Hyperactivity; Hypoactivity; Impulsivity; Self-Aggression; Verbal Aggression; Physical Aggression; Indirect Aggression; Passive Aggression; Withdrawal. *Conditions Treated* Early Infantile Autism.

Services Provided Individual Therapy; Group Therapy; Parent Involvement; Behavior Therapy; Cognitive Developmental Therapy; Family Therapy; Filial Therapy; Occupational Therapy; Speech Therapy. *Professionals on Staff* Psychiatrists 1; Psychologists 3; Child Care Staff 16. *Service Facilities Available (with number of rooms)* Self-Contained Rooms 15. *Educational Professionals* Special Education Teachers 20; Paraprofessionals

40. *Curricula* Individualized; Basic Skills; Prevocational; Survival Skills. *Educational Intervention Approaches* Behavior Modification; Applied Behavior Analysis. *Degrees Awarded* High School Diploma.

The Forum School

107 Wyckoff Ave, Waldwick, NJ 07463 (201) 444-5882
Year Established 1954
Contact Steven Krapes, Dir
Facility Information *Placement* Special School.
Children/Adolescents Served 85. *Sexes Served* Both. *Tuition Fees (Approx)* $10,000. *Sources of Funding* State Funds; P.L. 94-142; Local Sending District. Summer school available. *Teacher Certification Level* Elementary School; Junior High/Middle School. *Special Certification Level* ED; LD; MR; Reading; Math; Special Education.
Student/Patient Characteristics *Age Levels* 0-4; 5-8; 9-11; 12-14; 15-17. *IQ Ranges* 26-40; 41-55; 56-70; 71-85; 85-130; Above 130. *Exceptionalities Served* Autistic; Emotionally Disturbed. *Learning Problems* Memory Disabilities; Perceptual Disabilities; Thinking Disabilities; Oral Language Disabilities; Reading Disabilities; Handwriting Disabilities; Spelling Disabilities; Arithmetic Disabilities; Written Expression. *Behavioral Problems* Attention Deficits; Hyperactivity; Hypoactivity; Impulsivity; Self-Aggression; Verbal Aggression; Physical Aggression; Indirect Aggression; Passive Aggression; Withdrawal. *Conditions Treated* Early Infantile Autism; Schizophrenia; Aphasia; Convulsive Disorders; Socialized Aggressive Reaction; Unsocialized Aggressive Reaction.
Services Provided Parent Involvement; Behavior Therapy; Cognitive Developmental Therapy; Family Therapy; Drug Therapy; Art Therapy; Music Therapy. *Professionals on Staff* Psychiatrists 1; Psychologists 1; Social Workers 1; Nurses 2; Speach 16. *Educational Professionals* Special Education Teachers 16; Paraprofessionals 16; Physical Education Teachers. *Curricula* Basic Skills; Prevocational; Regular Classroom Instruction.

The Gramon School

346 E Mt Pleasant Ave, Livingston, NJ 07039 (201) 533-1313
Year Established 1939
Contact David F Weeks, Dir
Facility Information *Placement* Special School.
Children/Adolescents Served 95. *Sexes Served* Both. *Tuition Fees (Approx)* $10,000. *Sources of Funding* State Funds; P.L. 94-142; Private Tuition. Summer school available. *Teacher Certification Level* Elementary School; Junior High/Middle School; High School. *Special Certification Level* ED; LD; MR; Reading; Math; Elementary, Secondary, Physical Education.
Student/Patient Characteristics *Age Levels* 5-8; 9-11; 12-14; 15-17; 18-21. *IQ Ranges* 56-70; 71-85; 85-130. *Exceptionalities Served* Emotionally Disturbed; Learning Disabled; Mentally Handicapped; Communication Disordered; Other Health Impaired; Gifted. *Learning Problems* Memory Disabilities; Perceptual Disabilities; Thinking Disabilities; Oral Language Disabilities; Reading Disabilities; Handwriting Disabilities; Spelling Disabilities; Arithmetic Disabilities; Written Expression. *Behavioral Problems* Attention Deficits; Hyperactivity; Hypoactivity; Impulsivity; Self-Aggression; Verbal Aggression; Physical Aggression; Passive Aggression; Withdrawal. *Conditions Treated* Schizophrenia; Convulsive Disorders; Phobias; Obsessions and Compulsions; Depression; Anorexia Nervosa; Inadequacy/Immaturity; Personality Problems; Socialized Aggressive Reaction.
Services Provided Individual Therapy; Group Therapy; Parent Involvement; Behavior Therapy; Art Therapy; Reality Therapy. *Professionals on Staff* Psychiatrists 1; Psychologists 1; Counselors 2; Social Workers 2; Nurses 1; Physicians; Speech Therapists; Art Therapists 3. *Service Facilities Available (with number of rooms)* Resource Rooms 1; Self-Contained Rooms 11. *Educational Professionals* Regular School Teachers 3; Special Education Teachers 11; Crisis Teachers 5; Special Education Counselors 4; Paraprofessionals 4. *Curricula* Traditional Academic; Individual-

ized; Basic Skills; Prevocational. *Educational Intervention Approaches* Behavior Modification. *Degrees Awarded* Certificate of Attendance; High School Diploma.

High Point Adolescent School—Children's Psychiatric Center

PO Box 188, Morganville, NJ 07751 (201) 591-1750
Year Established 1969
Contact Wilma Pfeffer, Principal
Facility Information *Placement* Special School; Private Residential Care. *Number of Beds* 26. *Children/Adolescents Served* 76. *Sexes Served* Both. *Tuition Fees (Approx)* $9,000. *Sources of Funding* State Funds; P.L. 94-142. Summer school available. *Teacher Certification Level* High School. *Special Certification Level* ED; Special Education.
Student/Patient Characteristics *Age Levels* 12-14; 15-17; 18-21. *IQ Ranges* 26-40; 41-55; 56-70; 71-85; 85-130. *Exceptionalities Served* Emotionally Disturbed; Learning Disabled; Communication Disordered. *Learning Problems* Memory Disabilities; Perceptual Disabilities; Thinking Disabilities; Oral Language Disabilities; Reading Disabilities; Handwriting Disabilities; Spelling Disabilities; Arithmetic Disabilities; Written Expression. *Behavioral Problems* Attention Deficits; Hyperactivity; Impulsivity; Self-Aggression; Verbal Aggression; Physical Aggression; Indirect Aggression; Passive Aggression; Withdrawal. *Conditions Treated* Disintegrative Psychoses; Schizophrenia; Aphasia; Depression; Suicide; Inadequacy/Immaturity; Personality Problems; Socialized Aggressive Reaction; Unsocialized Aggressive Reaction.
Services Provided Individual Therapy; Group Therapy; Parent Involvement; Behavior Therapy; Family Therapy; Drug Therapy; Play Therapy; Movement Therapy. *Professionals on Staff* Psychiatrists 1; Social Workers 4; Nurses 1. *Service Facilities Available (with number of rooms)* Consultative (ERT) 4; Itinerants 1; Self-Contained Rooms 8; Speech 3. *Educational Professionals* Special Education Teachers 9; Paraprofessionals 20; Speech Therapists 3. *Curricula* Career/Vocational Education; Individualized; Basic Skills; Prevocational. *Educational Intervention Approaches* Progressive Discipline; Self-Control; Behavior Modification; Applied Behavior Analysis. *Degrees Awarded* High School Diploma.

Hunterdon Learning Center

Box 503, RD 2, Hoffman Crossing Rd, Califon, NJ 07830
(201) 832-7200
Year Established 1976
Contact Stephen R Jason, Ed Dir
Facility Information *Placement* Special Program.
Children/Adolescents Served 75. *Sexes Served* Both. *Tuition Fees (Approx)* $9,300. *Sources of Funding* P.L. 94-142. *Teacher Certification Level* Elementary School; Junior High/Middle School; High School. *Special Certification Level* ED; Industrial Arts; Art and Fine Arts; Social Studies.
Student/Patient Characteristics *Age Levels* 12-14; 15-17; 18-21. *IQ Ranges* 85-130. *Exceptionalities Served* Emotionally Disturbed. *Learning Problems* Perceptual Disabilities; Thinking Disabilities; Reading Disabilities; Spelling Disabilities; Arithmetic Disabilities; Written Expression. *Behavioral Problems* Attention Deficits; Impulsivity; Self-Aggression; Verbal Aggression; Physical Aggression; Indirect Aggression; Passive Aggression; Withdrawal. *Conditions Treated* Depression; Inadequacy/Immaturity; Personality Problems; Socialized Aggressive Reaction; Unsocialized Aggressive Reaction.
Services Provided Individual Therapy; Group Therapy; Parent Involvement; Behavior Therapy; Reality Therapy; Psychodrama. *Professionals on Staff* Psychiatrists 1; Psychologists 1; Counselors 2; Social Workers 1; Administrators 2. *Service Facilities Available (with number of rooms)* Fine Arts Building. *Educational Professionals* Regular School Teachers 1; Special Education Teachers 12; Career/Vocational Teachers 1. *Curricula* Traditional Academic; Career/Vocational Education; Individualized; Basic Skills; Prevocational. *Educational Intervention Approaches* En-

gineered Classroom; Precision Teaching; Progressive Discipline; Self-Control; Behavior Modification; Therapeutic Community Concepts.

Jersey Shore Medical Center—Child Evaluation Center

1945 Corlies Ave, Neptune, NJ 07753 (201) 775-5500, ext 784
Contact Janice Grebler, Clinical Supv
Facility Information *Placement* Diagnostic Services. *Sexes Served* Both. *Sources of Funding* State Funds.
Student/Patient Characteristics *Age Levels* 0-4; 5-8; 9-11; 12-14. *IQ Ranges* 0-25; 26-40; 41-55; 56-70; 71-85; 85-130; Above 130. *Exceptionalities Served* Autistic; Emotionally Disturbed; Learning Disabled; Mentally Handicapped; Communication Disordered; Hearing Impaired/Deaf; Visually Impaired/Blind; Other Health Impaired; Physically Handicapped; Gifted. *Learning Problems* Perceptual Disabilities; Reading Disabilities; Spelling Disabilities; Arithmetic Disabilities. *Behavioral Problems* Attention Deficits; Hyperactivity; Impulsivity; Physical Aggression; Passive Aggression; Withdrawal. *Conditions Treated* Early Infantile Autism; Schizophrenia; Aphasia; Convulsive Disorders; Depression; Unsocialized Aggressive Reaction.
Services Provided Diagnostic. *Professionals on Staff* Psychiatrists 1; Psychologists 1; Social Workers 1; Neurologist; Pediatrican; Learning Specialists.

Lord Stirling School

PO Box 369, Lord Stirling Rd, Basking Ridge, NJ 07920
(201) 766-1786
Year Established 1964
Contact Joseph E Gorga, Dir
Facility Information *Placement* Private Day Care.
Children/Adolescents Served 56. *Sexes Served* Both. *Tuition Fees (Approx)* $9,100. *Sources of Funding* State Funds; P.L. 94-142. *Teacher Certification Level* Elementary School; Junior High/Middle School; High School. *Special Certification Level* Career/Vocational Education; Teacher of the Handicapped.
Student/Patient Characteristics *Age Levels* 12-14; 15-17; 18-21. *IQ Ranges* 71-85; 85-130; Above 130. *Exceptionalities Served* Emotionally Disturbed; Learning Disabled. *Learning Problems* Memory Disabilities; Perceptual Disabilities; Thinking Disabilities; Reading Disabilities; Handwriting Disabilities; Spelling Disabilities; Arithmetic Disabilities; Written Expression. *Behavioral Problems* Attention Deficits; Hyperactivity; Impulsivity; Verbal Aggression; Physical Aggression; Indirect Aggression; Passive Aggression; Withdrawal. *Conditions Treated* Inadequacy/Immaturity; Personality Problems; Socialized Aggressive Reaction.
Services Provided Individual Therapy; Group Therapy; Parent Involvement; Art Therapy. *Professionals on Staff* Psychiatrists 1; Psychologists 2; Social Workers 1. *Service Facilities Available (with number of rooms)* Self-Contained Rooms 6. *Educational Professionals* Special Education Teachers 7; Career/Vocational Teachers 2; Crisis Teachers 1. *Curricula* Traditional Academic; Career/Vocational Education; Individualized; Basic Skills; Prevocational. *Educational Intervention Approaches* Self-Control. *Degrees Awarded* Certificate of Attendance; High School Diploma.

The Midland School

PO Box 5026, Readington Rd, North Branch, NJ 08876
(201) 722-8222
Year Established 1960
Facility Information *Placement* Special School.
Children/Adolescents Served 185. *Sexes Served* Both. *Sources of Funding* State Funds; P.L. 94-142. Summer school available. *Teacher Certification Level* Elementary School; Junior High/Middle School; High School. *Special Certification Level* Teacher of the Handicapped.

Student/Patient Characteristics *Age Levels* 5-8; 9-11; 12-14; 15-17; 18-21. *IQ Ranges* 56-70; 71-85. *Exceptionalities Served* Emotionally Disturbed; Learning Disabled; Communication Disordered. *Learning Problems* Memory Disabilities; Perceptual Disabilities; Thinking Disabilities; Oral Language Disabilities; Reading Disabilities; Handwriting Disabilities; Spelling Disabilities; Arithmetic Disabilities; Written Expression. *Behavioral Problems* Attention Deficits; Hyperactivity; Impulsivity; Verbal Aggression.
Services Provided *Professionals on Staff* Psychologists 1; Social Workers 1; Nurses 3; Learning Consultant 1; Speech Therapists 4. *Service Facilities Available (with number of rooms)* Self-Contained Rooms 26. *Educational Professionals* Special Education Teachers 31. *Curricula* Traditional Academic; Career/Vocational Education; Individualized; Basic Skills; Prevocational. *Educational Intervention Approaches* Behavior Modification.
Comments The Midland School is a private rehabilitation center serving the special education needs of children with learning disabilities, communication disorders, or maladaptive behavior.

Mt Scott Institute

PO Box 129, Washington, NJ 07882 (201) 453-2486
Year Established 1971
Contact Rona Silver, Dir
Facility Information *Placement* Private Residential Care. *Number of Beds* 24. *Children/Adolescents Served* 24. *Sexes Served* Male. *Room and Board Fees (Approx)* $60. *Tuition Fees (Approx)* $10,000 (education). *Sources of Funding* State Funds; P.L. 94-142. Summer school available. *Special Certification Level* ED.
Student/Patient Characteristics *Age Levels* 9-11; 12-14; 15-17; 18-21. *IQ Ranges* 71-85; 85-130. *Exceptionalities Served* Emotionally Disturbed; Learning Disabled. *Learning Problems* Memory Disabilities; Perceptual Disabilities; Thinking Disabilities; Oral Language Disabilities; Reading Disabilities; Handwriting Disabilities; Spelling Disabilities; Arithmetic Disabilities; Written Expression. *Behavioral Problems* Attention Deficits; Hyperactivity; Impulsivity; Self-Aggression; Verbal Aggression; Physical Aggression; Indirect Aggression; Passive Aggression; Withdrawal. *Conditions Treated* Schizophrenia; Convulsive Disorders; Phobias; Obsessions and Compulsions; Depression; Asthma; Inadequacy/Immaturity; Personality Problems; Socialized Aggressive Reaction; Unsocialized Aggressive Reaction.
Services Provided Individual Therapy; Group Therapy; Parent Involvement; Behavior Therapy; Cognitive Developmental Therapy; Family Therapy; Filial Therapy; Drug Therapy; Reality Therapy. *Professionals on Staff* Psychiatrists 1; Psychologists 1; Counselors 9; Social Workers 3. *Service Facilities Available (with number of rooms)* On-Campus Residential School 5. *Educational Professionals* Special Education Teachers 5. *Curricula* Traditional Academic; Career/Vocational Education; Individualized; Basic Skills; Prevocational. *Educational Intervention Approaches* Engineered Classroom; Precision Teaching; Progressive Discipline; Self-Control; Behavior Modification; Applied Behavior Analysis; Creative Conditioning. *Degrees Awarded* High School Diploma.

New Jersey Training School for Boys

PO Box 500, State Home Rd, Jamesburg, NJ 08831
(201) 521-0030
Year Established 1866
Contact Willie T Helm, Supt
Facility Information *Placement* Public Residential Care. *Number of Beds* 350. *Children/Adolescents Served* 350. *Sexes Served* Male. *Sources of Funding* State Funds. Summer school available.
Student/Patient Characteristics *Age Levels* 15-17; 18-21. *IQ Ranges* 85-130. *Exceptionalities Served* Juvenile Delinquents. *Behavioral Problems* Impulsivity; Verbal Aggression; Physical Aggression; Indirect Aggression; Passive Aggression. *Conditions Treated* Other Substance Abuse or Dependence; Inadequacy/Immaturity; Personality Problems; Socialized Aggressive Reaction; Unsocialized Aggressive Reaction.

Services Provided Individual Therapy; Group Therapy; Behavior Therapy; Family Therapy; Drug Therapy; Reality Therapy. *Professionals on Staff* Psychiatrists 1; Psychologists 4; Counselors 3; Social Workers 12. *Curricula* Traditional Academic; Career/ Vocational Education; Prevocational. *Educational Intervention Approaches* Behavior Modification. *Degrees Awarded* High School Diploma.

Ocean Institute—Adolescent Day School—Mental Health Clinic of Ocean County

122 Lien St, Toms River, NJ 08753 (609) 597-6494
Year Established 1980
Contact Harry S Cook, Dir

Facility Information *Placement* Special School; Special Program. *Number of Beds* 16. *Children/Adolescents Served* 16. *Sexes Served* Both. *Tuition Fees (Approx)* $9,300. *Sources of Funding* State Funds; Health Insurance; Medicaid; P.L. 94-142. Summer school available. *Teacher Certification Level* Elementary School; Junior High/Middle School; High School. *Special Certification Level* ED; Special Education.

Student/Patient Characteristics *Age Levels* 12-14; 15-17. *IQ Ranges* 85-130; Above 130. *Exceptionalities Served* Emotionally Disturbed; Learning Disabled. *Learning Problems* Memory Disabilities; Perceptual Disabilities; Thinking Disabilities; Reading Disabilities; Handwriting Disabilities; Spelling Disabilities; Arithmetic Disabilities; Written Expression. *Behavioral Problems* Attention Deficits; Hyperactivity; Hypoactivity; Impulsivity; Verbal Aggression; Indirect Aggression; Passive Aggression; Withdrawal. *Conditions Treated* Disintegrative Psychoses; Schizophrenia; Phobias; Obsessions and Compulsions; Hysteria; Depression; Suicide; Inadequacy/Immaturity; Personality Problems.

Services Provided Individual Therapy; Group Therapy; Parent Involvement; Behavior Therapy; Family Therapy; Drug Therapy; Art Therapy; Reality Therapy; Activity Therapy. *Professionals on Staff* Psychiatrists 1; Counselors 3; Social Workers 2; Nurses 1. *Service Facilities Available (with number of rooms)* Self-Contained Rooms 2. *Educational Professionals* Special Education Teachers 2; Paraprofessionals 2; Principal 1. *Curricula* Traditional Academic; Individualized; Basic Skills; Prevocational. *Educational Intervention Approaches* Engineered Classroom; Behavior Modification.

Princeton Child Development Institute

PO Box 2013, Princeton, NJ 08540 (609) 924-6280
Year Established 1971
Contact Lynn E McClannahan, Dir

Facility Information *Placement* Special School; Private Residential Care. *Number of Beds* 10. *Children/Adolescents Served* 23. *Sexes Served* Both. *Room and Board Fees (Approx)* $80. *Tuition Fees (Approx)* $9,300. *Sources of Funding* State Funds; P.L. 94-142; NJ Division of Youth and Family Services; Contributions. Summer school available. *Teacher Certification Level* Elementary School; Junior High/Middle School; High School. *Special Certification Level* LD; Special Education; Preschool.

Student/Patient Characteristics *Age Levels* 0-4; 5-8; 9-11; 12-14; 15-17; 18-21. *IQ Ranges* 0-25; 26-40; 41-55; 56-70; 71-85. *Exceptionalities Served* Autistic. *Learning Problems* Memory Disabilities; Perceptual Disabilities; Thinking Disabilities; Oral Language Disabilities; Reading Disabilities; Handwriting Disabilities; Spelling Disabilities; Arithmetic Disabilities; Written Expression. *Behavioral Problems* Attention Deficits; Hyperactivity; Hypoactivity; Impulsivity; Self-Aggression; Verbal Aggression; Physical Aggression; Withdrawal. *Conditions Treated* Early Infantile Autism.

Services Provided Parent Involvement. *Professionals on Staff* Psychologists; Child Care Staff. *Educational Professionals* Special Education Teachers. *Curricula* Traditional Academic; Career/Vocational Education; Individualized; Basic Skills; Prevocational. *Educational Intervention Approaches* Applied Behavior Analysis.

Ranch Hope Strang School

Box 325, Sawmill Rd, Alleway, NJ 08001 (609) 935-1555
Year Established 1973
Contact Colleen G Cary, School Admin

Facility Information *Placement* Private Residential Care. *Number of Beds* 49. *Children/Adolescents Served* 49. *Sexes Served* Male. *Room and Board Fees (Approx)* $44. *Tuition Fees (Approx)* $9,055 (education); $15,896 (residential). *Sources of Funding* State Funds; Medicaid; P.L. 94-142. Summer school available. *Teacher Certification Level* Junior High/Middle School; High School. *Special Certification Level* Career/Vocational Education; Reading; Math; Special Education.

Student/Patient Characteristics *Age Levels* 12-14; 15-17. *IQ Ranges* 71-85; 85-130. *Exceptionalities Served* Emotionally Disturbed; Learning Disabled. *Learning Problems* Perceptual Disabilities; Reading Disabilities; Handwriting Disabilities; Spelling Disabilities; Arithmetic Disabilities; Written Expression. *Behavioral Problems* Attention Deficits; Hyperactivity; Hypoactivity; Impulsivity; Self-Aggression; Verbal Aggression; Physical Aggression; Indirect Aggression; Passive Aggression; Withdrawal. *Conditions Treated* Schizophrenia; Phobias; Obsessions and Compulsions; Hysteria; Depression; Asthma; Inadequacy/Immaturity; Personality Problems; Socialized Aggressive Reaction; Unsocialized Aggressive Reaction.

Services Provided Individual Therapy; Group Therapy; Parent Involvement; Behavior Therapy; Cognitive Developmental Therapy; Family Therapy; Drug Therapy; Music Therapy; Reality Therapy. *Professionals on Staff* Psychiatrists 1; Psychologists 1; Counselors 5; Social Workers 4; Child Care Staff 15; Nurses 1. *Service Facilities Available (with number of rooms)* Consultative (ERT) 3; Resource Rooms 2; Transition Rooms 7; Departmentalized. *Educational Professionals* Special Education Teachers 6; Career/Vocational Teachers 1; Paraprofessionals 3; Tutors 2. *Curricula* Traditional Academic; Individualized; Basic Skills; Prevocational. *Educational Intervention Approaches* Self-Control; Behavior Modification. *Degrees Awarded* Certificate of Attendance; Certificate of Completion.

Raritan Bay Mental Health Center

570 Lee St, Perth Amboy, NJ 08861 (201) 442-1666
Year Established 1970
Contact Barbara Larsen Jay, Dir of Children's Serv

Facility Information *Sexes Served* Both. *Sources of Funding* State Funds; Health Insurance; Medicaid; County Funds; Individual Fees. *Special Certification Level* ED; Early Childhood Education.

Student/Patient Characteristics *Age Levels* 0-4; 5-8; 9-11; 12-14; 15-17. *IQ Ranges* 85-130. *Exceptionalities Served* Autistic; Emotionally Disturbed; Learning Disabled. *Learning Problems* Perceptual Disabilities; Thinking Disabilities; Oral Language Disabilities; Reading Disabilities. *Behavioral Problems* Attention Deficits; Hyperactivity; Hypoactivity; Impulsivity; Self-Aggression; Verbal Aggression; Physical Aggression; Indirect Aggression; Passive Aggression; Withdrawal. *Conditions Treated* Alcohol Abuse and/or Drug Abuse; Disintegrative Psychoses; Schizophrenia; Phobias; Obsessions and Compulsions; Hysteria; Depression; Suicide; Anorexia Nervosa; Inadequacy/Immaturity; Personality Problems; Socialized Aggressive Reaction; Unsocialized Aggressive Reaction.

Services Provided Individual Therapy; Group Therapy; Parent Involvement; Behavior Therapy; Biofeedback; Family Therapy; Filial Therapy; Drug Therapy; Art Therapy; Reality Therapy; Play Therapy. *Professionals on Staff* Psychiatrists 5; Psychologists 16; Counselors 2; Social Workers 29; Nurses 3; Vocational Rehabilitation 3. *Educational Professionals* Special Education Counselors 2; Paraprofessionals 2. *Educational Intervention Approaches* Self-Control; Behavior Modification. *Degrees Awarded* Pre-school Diploma.

Comments Parents and family participation and use of community resources are integral parts of the outpatient therapeutic program at this center.

St Clare's Hospital—Adult, Child and Family Services

50 Morris Ave, Denville, NJ 07834 (201) 625-7009
Contact Robert B Jones, Dir
Facility Information *Placement* Outpatient Mental Health Services. *Sexes Served* Both. *Sources of Funding* State Funds; Health Insurance; Medicaid.
Student/Patient Characteristics *Age Levels* 0-4; 5-8; 9-11; 12-14; 15-17; 18-21; Over 21. *Exceptionalities Served* Emotionally Disturbed; Mentally Handicapped. *Behavioral Problems* Attention Deficits; Hyperactivity; Hypoactivity; Impulsivity; Self-Aggression; Verbal Aggression; Physical Aggression; Indirect Aggression; Passive Aggression; Withdrawal. *Conditions Treated* Disintegrative Psychoses; Schizophrenia; Convulsive Disorders; Phobias; Obsessions and Compulsions; Hysteria; Depression; Suicide; Anorexia Nervosa; Inadequacy/Immaturity; Personality Problems; Socialized Aggressive Reaction; Unsocialized Aggressive Reaction.
Services Provided Individual Therapy; Group Therapy; Parent Involvement; Behavior Therapy; Cognitive Developmental Therapy; Family Therapy; Drug Therapy; Outreach Services.
Professionals on Staff Psychiatrists 3; Psychologists 7; Social Workers 12; Psychiatric Nurse Clinician 1.
Comments This hospital is a full service mental health facility providing aftercare to a children's inpatient unit as well as a full range of other mental health services to children and families in the community.

SEARCH Day Program Inc

73 Wickapecko Dr, Ocean, NJ 07712 (201) 531-0454
Year Established 1971
Contact Kenneth F Appenzeller, Exec Dir
Facility Information *Placement* Private, Non-Profit, State-Approved, Day School. *Children/Adolescents Served* 50. *Sexes Served* Both. *Sources of Funding* P.L. 94-142. Summer school available. *Teacher Certification Level* Elementary School; Junior High/Middle School; High School. *Special Certification Level* Math Certified Teacher of the Handicapped.
Student/Patient Characteristics *Age Levels* 0-4; 5-8; 9-11; 12-14; 15-17; 18-21. *IQ Ranges* 0-25; 26-40; 41-55; 56-70; 71-85; 85-130; Above 130. *Exceptionalities Served* Autistic; Emotionally Disturbed; Learning Disabled; Mentally Handicapped; Communication Disordered; Hearing Impaired/Deaf. *Learning Problems* Memory Disabilities; Perceptual Disabilities; Thinking Disabilities; Oral Language Disabilities; Reading Disabilities; Handwriting Disabilities; Spelling Disabilities; Arithmetic Disabilities; Written Expression. *Behavioral Problems* Attention Deficits; Hyperactivity; Self-Aggression; Verbal Aggression; Physical Aggression; Withdrawal. *Conditions Treated* Early Infantile Autism; Schizophrenia; Aphasia.
Services Provided Individual Therapy; Parent Involvement; Behavior Therapy; Cognitive Developmental Therapy; Family Therapy; Drug Therapy; Art Therapy; Music Therapy.
Professionals on Staff Psychiatrists 1; Psychologists 1; Social Workers 2; Nurses 1; Teachers 8. *Service Facilities Available (with number of rooms)* Self-Contained Rooms 8; Adapted Physical Education Room 1. *Educational Professionals* Special Education Teachers 8; Paraprofessionals 12; Speech Pathologist 1; Speech Therapist 1; Social Work Specialist 1; Adapted Physical Education Specialist 1; Occupational Therapist 1. *Curricula* Individualized; Basic Skills; Prevocational. *Educational Intervention Approaches* Behavior Modification.

Special Service School District of Bergen County

327 E Ridgewood Ave, Paramus, NJ 07652 (201) 265-6300
Year Established 1972
Contact Irma Leeds, Asst to Supt
Facility Information *Placement* Special School.
Children/Adolescents Served $1,000. *Sexes Served* Both. *Sources of Funding* State Funds; P.L. 94-142; County Fund; Local Funds.

Teacher Certification Level Elementary School; Junior High/Middle School; High School. *Special Certification Level* Teacher of Handicapped, Deaf, and Hard of Hearing.
Student/Patient Characteristics *Age Levels* 0-4; 5-8; 9-11; 12-14; 15-17; 18-21. *IQ Ranges* 26-40; 41-55; 56-70; 71-85; 85-130. *Exceptionalities Served* Autistic; Emotionally Disturbed; Learning Disabled; Mentally Handicapped; Communication Disordered; Hearing Impaired/Deaf; Visually Impaired/Blind; Other Health Impaired. *Learning Problems* Memory Disabilities; Perceptual Disabilities; Thinking Disabilities; Oral Language Disabilities; Reading Disabilities; Handwriting Disabilities; Spelling Disabilities; Arithmetic Disabilities; Written Expression. *Behavioral Problems* Attention Deficits; Hyperactivity; Hypoactivity; Impulsivity; Self-Aggression; Verbal Aggression; Physical Aggression; Indirect Aggression; Passive Aggression; Withdrawal. *Conditions Treated* Alcohol Abuse and/or Drug Abuse; Other Substance Abuse or Dependence; Early Infantile Autism; Disintegrative Psychoses; Schizophrenia; Aphasia; Convulsive Disorders; Phobias; Obsessions and Compulsions; Hysteria; Depression; Suicide; Asthma; Anorexia Nervosa; Ulcerative Colitis; Inadequacy/Immaturity; Personality Problems; Socialized Aggressive Reaction; Unsocialized Aggressive Reaction.
Services Provided Individual Therapy; Group Therapy; Parent Involvement; Behavior Therapy; Cognitive Developmental Therapy; Biofeedback; Family Therapy; Drug Therapy; Art Therapy; Music Therapy; Reality Therapy; Play Therapy. *Professionals on Staff* Psychiatrists 1; Psychologists 3; Counselors; Social Workers 3. *Service Facilities Available (with number of rooms)* Resource Rooms; Self-Contained Rooms. *Educational Professionals* Special Education Teachers 192; Paraprofessionals 78. *Curricula* Traditional Academic; Career/Vocational Education; Individualized; Basic Skills; Prevocational. *Educational Intervention Approaches* Behavior Modification. *Degrees Awarded* Certificate of Attendance.
Comments This is a public school facility educating the most severely affected.

Therapeutic School and Preschool Community Mental Health Services

570 Belleville Ave, Belleville, NJ 07109 (201) 450-3123
Year Established 1971
Contact Elizabeth Callahan, Dir
Facility Information *Placement* Special School.
Children/Adolescents Served 25. *Sexes Served* Both. *Tuition Fees (Approx)* $9,000-$10,000. *Sources of Funding* P.L. 94-142. *Special Certification Level* Teacher of the Handicapped.
Student/Patient Characteristics *Age Levels* 0-4; 5-8; 9-11. *Exceptionalities Served* Autistic; Emotionally Disturbed; Learning Disabled; Communication Disordered. *Learning Problems* Memory Disabilities; Perceptual Disabilities; Thinking Disabilities; Oral Language Disabilities; Reading Disabilities; Handwriting Disabilities; Spelling Disabilities; Arithmetic Disabilities; Written Expression. *Behavioral Problems* Attention Deficits; Hyperactivity; Impulsivity; Self-Aggression; Verbal Aggression; Physical Aggression; Indirect Aggression; Passive Aggression; Withdrawal. *Conditions Treated* Early Infantile Autism; Schizophrenia; Aphasia; Convulsive Disorders; Socialized Aggressive Reaction.
Services Provided Individual Therapy; Group Therapy; Parent Involvement; Behavior Therapy; Family Therapy; Drug Therapy; Music Therapy; Play Therapy. *Professionals on Staff* Psychiatrists; Social Workers; Physical Therapist; Occupational Therapist; Speech Therapist. *Service Facilities Available (with number of rooms)* Self-Contained Rooms. *Educational Professionals* Special Education Teachers; Paraprofessionals. *Curricula* Individualized; Basic Skills. *Educational Intervention Approaches* Self-Control; Applied Behavior Analysis; Psychotherapeutic Teaching.
Comments The Therapeutic School and Preschool provides a therapeutic structured environment for children with emotional and developmental delays. A total treatment approach provides a setting designed to foster emotional, social, cognitive, and language development.

New Mexico

Albuquerque Child Guidance Center

117 Montclaire SE, Albuquerque, NM 87108 (505) 265-8774
Year Established 1952
Contact Britton K Ruebush, Exec Dir

Facility Information *Placement* Outpatient Mental Health Center. *Children/Adolescents Served* 167. *Sexes Served* Both. *Sources of Funding* Health Insurance; Medicaid; United Way.

Student/Patient Characteristics *Behavioral Problems* Attention Deficits; Hyperactivity; Hypoactivity; Impulsivity; Self-Aggression; Verbal Aggression; Physical Aggression; Indirect Aggression; Passive Aggression; Withdrawal. *Conditions Treated* Phobias; Obsessions and Compulsions; Depression; Suicide; Anorexia Nervosa; Personality Problems; Socialized Aggressive Reaction; Unsocialized Aggressive Reaction.

Services Provided Individual Therapy; Group Therapy; Parent Involvement; Behavior Therapy; Cognitive Developmental Therapy; Biofeedback; Family Therapy; Play Therapy. *Professionals on Staff* Psychiatrists 1; Psychologists 8; Social Workers 3.

Albuquerque Special Preschool

3501 Campus NE, Albuquerque, NM 87106 (505) 266-8811
Year Established 1968
Contact Gail C Beam, Dir

Facility Information *Placement* Special School. *Children/Adolescents Served* 66. *Sexes Served* Both. *Tuition Fees (Approx)* $310-$900. *Sources of Funding* State Funds; United Way. *Teacher Certification Level* Elementary School. *Special Certification Level* LD; MR.

Student/Patient Characteristics *Age Levels* 0-4; 5-8. *IQ Ranges* 41-55; 56-70; 71-85; 85-130. *Exceptionalities Served* Autistic; Learning Disabled; Mentally Handicapped; Communication Disordered; Other Health Impaired. *Learning Problems* Memory Disabilities; Perceptual Disabilities; Oral Language Disabilities; Motor Disabilities. *Behavioral Problems* Attention Deficits; Hyperactivity; Impulsivity. *Conditions Treated* Early Infantile Autism; Aphasia; Convulsive Disorders; Asthma.

Services Provided Individual Therapy; Group Therapy; Parent Involvement; Cognitive Developmental Therapy; Family Therapy; Physical Therapy; Occupational Therapy; Speech Therapy. *Professionals on Staff* Counselors 1; Child Care Staff 5; Therapists 2. *Service Facilities Available (with number of rooms)* Self-Contained Rooms 4; Regular Preschools 4. *Educational Professionals* Special Education Teachers 6; Special Education Counselors 1; Paraprofessionals 6; Early Childhood Teachers 2. *Curricula* Individualized; Developmentally Based; Cognitive Curriculum. *Educational Intervention Approaches* Diagnostic Prescriptive.

Los Lunas Hospital and Training School—Behavioral Services Unit

PO Box 1269, Los Lunas, NM 87130 (505) 865-9611
Year Established 1983
Contact Joseph F Mateju, Hospital Admin

Facility Information *Placement* Public Residential Care. *Sexes Served* Both. *Room and Board Fees (Approx)* $91. *Sources of Funding* State Funds; Medicaid; Medicare. Summer school available. *Special Certification Level* ED; MR.

Student/Patient Characteristics *Age Levels* 0-4; 5-8; 9-11; 12-14; 15-17; 18-21; Over 21. *IQ Ranges* 0-25; 26-40; 41-55. *Exceptionalities Served* Autistic; Emotionally Disturbed; Mentally Handicapped; Visually Impaired/Blind; Other Health Impaired. *Behavioral Problems* Attention Deficits; Hyperactivity; Impulsivity; Self-Aggression; Verbal Aggression; Physical Aggression; Indirect Aggression; Passive Aggression; Withdrawal. *Conditions Treated* Early Infantile Autism; Schizophrenia; Convulsive Disorders; Obsessions and Compulsions; Depression; Personality Problems; Socialized Aggressive Reaction.

Services Provided Individual Therapy; Parent Involvement; Behavior Therapy; Drug Therapy; Art Therapy; Music Therapy. *Professionals on Staff* Psychiatrists 1; Psychologists 2; Social Workers 1; Child Care Staff 34; Nurses 5; Physician 1. *Educational Professionals* Special Education Teachers 1; Career/Vocational Teachers 4. *Curricula* Individualized; Prevocational. *Educational Intervention Approaches* Behavior Modification; Applied Behavior Analysis.

Comments The Behavioral Services Unit is a 20 bed psychiatric facility for the mentally retarded. The unit is one of 3 units at Los Lunas Hospital and Training School. The BSU focuses mainly on very difficult psychiatric/behavioral problems both on an acute care and chronic care basis.

New Mexico Boys' School

PO Box 38, Springer, NM 87747 (505) 483-2475
Year Established 1909
Contact Robert Portillos, Supt

Facility Information *Placement* Correctional Facility. *Number of Beds* 200. *Children/Adolescents Served* 250. *Sexes Served* Male. *Sources of Funding* State Funds. Summer school available. *Teacher Certification Level* Elementary School; Junior High/Middle School; High School. *Special Certification Level* ED; LD; MR; Career/Vocational Education; Reading; Math.

Student/Patient Characteristics *Age Levels* 12-14; 15-17; 18-21; Over 21. *IQ Ranges* 56-70; 71-85; 85-130; Above 130. *Exceptionalities Served* Adjudicated Delinquents. *Learning Problems* Memory Disabilities; Perceptual Disabilities; Thinking Disabilities; Oral Language Disabilities; Reading Disabilities; Handwriting Disabilities; Spelling Disabilities; Arithmetic Disabilities; Written Expression. *Behavioral Problems* Attention

Deficits; Hyperactivity; Hypoactivity; Impulsivity; Self-Aggression; Verbal Aggression; Physical Aggression; Indirect Aggression; Passive Aggression; Withdrawal. *Conditions Treated* Alcohol Abuse and/or Drug Abuse; Other Substance Abuse or Dependence; Disintegrative Psychoses; Schizophrenia; Obsessions and Compulsions; Depression; Suicide; Inadequacy/Immaturity; Personality Problems; Socialized Aggressive Reaction; Unsocialized Aggressive Reaction.

Services Provided Individual Therapy; Group Therapy; Parent Involvement; Behavior Therapy; Drug Therapy. *Professionals on Staff* Psychiatrists 1; Psychologists 4; Counselors 8; Social Workers 3; Nurses 1; Dental Hygienist 1. *Educational Professionals* Regular School Teachers 22; Special Education Teachers 4; Career/Vocational Teachers 5; Paraprofessionals 5. *Curricula* Career/Vocational Education; Individualized; Basic Skills; Prevocational. *Educational Intervention Approaches* Progressive Discipline; Self-Control; Behavior Modification; Applied Behavior Analysis. *Degrees Awarded* Graduate Equivalency Diploma.

Comments New Mexico Boys' School is a correctional facility. It receives students from the courts of New Mexico. It does not accept volunteer commitments.

Peanut Butter and Jelly Therapeutic Pre-School

1101 Lopez SW, Albuquerque, NM 87105 (505) 877-7060
Year Established 1972
Contact Angie Vachio, Exec Dir

Facility Information *Placement* Special Program. *Children/Adolescents Served* 100. *Sexes Served* Both. *Sources of Funding* State Funds; Donations. Summer school available. *Teacher Certification Level* Elementary School. *Special Certification Level* ED; LD; MR.

Student/Patient Characteristics *Age Levels* 0-4. *IQ Ranges* 56-70; 71-85; 85-130. *Exceptionalities Served* Autistic; Emotionally Disturbed; Learning Disabled; Mentally Handicapped; Communication Disordered; Physically Handicapped; Gifted. *Learning Problems* Memory Disabilities; Perceptual Disabilities; Thinking Disabilities; Oral Language Disabilities. *Behavioral Problems* Attention Deficits; Hyperactivity; Hypoactivity; Impulsivity; Self-Aggression; Verbal Aggression; Physical Aggression; Indirect Aggression; Passive Aggression; Withdrawal. *Conditions Treated* Early Infantile Autism; Convulsive Disorders; Depression; Personality Problems; Socialized Aggressive Reaction; Unsocialized Aggressive Reaction.

Services Provided Individual Therapy; Group Therapy; Parent Involvement; Family Therapy; Music Therapy; Play Therapy. *Professionals on Staff* Counselors 2; Social Workers 8. *Service Facilities Available (with number of rooms)* Consultative (ERT) 2; Self-Contained Rooms 6. *Educational Professionals* Regular School Teachers 4; Special Education Teachers 4; Crisis Teachers 1; Special Education Counselors 2. *Curricula* Individualized; Basic Skills; Infant Stimulation. *Educational Intervention Approaches* Gentle Teaching. *Degrees Awarded* Preschool Certificate.

University of New Mexico Children's Psychiatric Hospital—Mimbres School

1001 Yale Blvd NE, Albuquerque, NM 87131 (505) 843-2878
Year Established 1979
Contact Virginia A Cavalluzzo, Ed Dir

Facility Information *Placement* Special School; Public Residential Care. *Number of Beds* 53. *Children/Adolescents Served* 53. *Sexes Served* Both. *Room and Board Fees (Approx)* $180. *Sources of Funding* State Funds; Health Insurance; Medicaid; P.L. 89-313. Summer school available. *Teacher Certification Level* Elementary School; Junior High/Middle School. *Special Certification Level* ED.

Student/Patient Characteristics *Age Levels* 0-4; 5-8; 9-11; 12-14. *IQ Ranges* 71-85; 85-130; Above 130. *Exceptionalities Served* Autistic; Emotionally Disturbed; Learning Disabled. *Learning*

Problems Memory Disabilities; Perceptual Disabilities; Thinking Disabilities; Oral Language Disabilities; Reading Disabilities; Handwriting Disabilities; Spelling Disabilities; Arithmetic Disabilities; Written Expression. *Behavioral Problems* Attention Deficits; Hyperactivity; Hypoactivity; Impulsivity; Self-Aggression; Verbal Aggression; Physical Aggression; Indirect Aggression; Passive Aggression; Withdrawal. *Conditions Treated* Early Infantile Autism; Schizophrenia; Phobias; Depression; Suicide; Anorexia Nervosa; Personality Problems; Socialized Aggressive Reaction; Unsocialized Aggressive Reaction.

Services Provided Individual Therapy; Group Therapy; Parent Involvement; Behavior Therapy; Cognitive Developmental Therapy; Family Therapy; Drug Therapy; Art Therapy; Music Therapy; Reality Therapy; Play Therapy. *Professionals on Staff* Psychiatrists 4; Psychologists 6; Social Workers 4; Child Care Staff 76; Nurses 12; Allied Therapists 8. *Service Facilities Available (with number of rooms)* Hospital School 6. *Educational Professionals* Special Education Teachers 6. *Curricula* Traditional Academic; Individualized; Prevocational; Physical Education; Expressive Arts. *Educational Intervention Approaches* Precision Teaching; Behavior Modification; Applied Behavior Analysis.

Comments The school is a fully accredited public school. It functions within the parameters of the hospital, serving only those children who are patients at the hospital. The school is in session year round; the age range is generally 5-14 years.

University of New Mexico—Children's Psychiatric Hospital

1001 Yale Blvd NE, Albuquerque, NM 87131 (505) 843-2945
Year Established 1978
Contact Paul G Rossman, Medical Dir; Patti Ross, Intake Worker

Facility Information *Placement* Psychiatric Hospital. *Number of Beds* 53. *Children/Adolescents Served* 53. *Sexes Served* Both. *Sources of Funding* State Funds; Health Insurance; Medicaid; Medicare; P.L. 94-142. *Teacher Certification Level* Elementary School; Junior High/Middle School; High School. *Special Certification Level* ED; LD; MR; Reading; Math.

Student/Patient Characteristics *Age Levels* 5-8; 9-11; 12-14. *IQ Ranges* 71-85; 85-130; Above 130. *Exceptionalities Served* Autistic; Emotionally Disturbed; Learning Disabled; Communication Disordered; Physically Handicapped; Gifted. *Learning Problems* Memory Disabilities; Perceptual Disabilities; Thinking Disabilities; Oral Language Disabilities; Reading Disabilities; Handwriting Disabilities; Spelling Disabilities; Arithmetic Disabilities; Written Expression. *Behavioral Problems* Attention Deficits; Hyperactivity; Hypoactivity; Impulsivity; Self-Aggression; Verbal Aggression; Physical Aggression; Indirect Aggression; Passive Aggression; Withdrawal. *Conditions Treated* Early Infantile Autism; Disintegrative Psychoses; Schizophrenia; Convulsive Disorders; Phobias; Obsessions and Compulsions; Hysteria; Depression; Suicide; Anorexia Nervosa; Ulcerative Colitis; Inadequacy/Immaturity; Personality Problems; Socialized Aggressive Reaction; Unsocialized Aggressive Reaction.

Services Provided Individual Therapy; Group Therapy; Parent Involvement; Behavior Therapy; Cognitive Developmental Therapy; Family Therapy; Filial Therapy; Drug Therapy; Art Therapy; Music Therapy; Play Therapy. *Professionals on Staff* Psychiatrists; Psychologists; Counselors; Social Workers; Child Care Staff; Nurses. *Service Facilities Available (with number of rooms)* On-Campus Residential School. *Educational Professionals* Special Education Teachers 6; Paraprofessionals 12; Diagnosticians 2. *Curricula* Traditional Academic; Individualized; Basic Skills. *Educational Intervention Approaches* Precision Teaching; Progressive Discipline; Self-Control; Behavior Modification; Applied Behavior Analysis. *Degrees Awarded* Certificate of Attendance; High School Diploma.

Comments This is a psychiatric hospital for the most seriously disturbed children in the state, ages 3-14.

New York

Andrus Children's Home

1156 N Broadway, Yonkers, NY 10701 (914) 965-3700
Year Established 1928
Contact Barbara Smith, Admissions Dir; Gary O Carman, Exec Dir

Facility Information *Placement* Special School; Private Residential Care. *Number of Beds* 57. *Children/Adolescents Served* 57. *Sexes Served* Both. *Room and Board Fees (Approx)* Sliding Scale. *Sources of Funding* Private Foundation. Summer school available. *Teacher Certification Level* Elementary School; Junior High/Middle School. *Special Certification Level* Special Education.

Student/Patient Characteristics *Age Levels* 9-11; 12-14; 15-17. *IQ Ranges* 85-130; Above 130. *Exceptionalities Served* Emotionally Disturbed; Learning Disabled; Gifted. *Learning Problems* Memory Disabilities; Perceptual Disabilities; Thinking Disabilities; Oral Language Disabilities; Reading Disabilities; Handwriting Disabilities; Spelling Disabilities; Arithmetic Disabilities; Written Expression. *Behavioral Problems* Attention Deficits; Hyperactivity; Impulsivity; Verbal Aggression; Passive Aggression; Withdrawal. *Conditions Treated* Depression; Asthma; Inadequacy/Immaturity; Personality Problems; Socialized Aggressive Reaction; Unsocialized Aggressive Reaction; Identity Disorder.

Services Provided Individual Therapy; Group Therapy; Parent Involvement; Family Therapy; Music Therapy; Play Therapy. *Professionals on Staff* Psychiatrists 1; Psychologists 2; Social Workers 5; Child Care Staff 20; Nurses 3; Recreation Director 1. *Service Facilities Available (with number of rooms)* On-Campus Residential School 10; Self-contained Class for Grades 2-4; Departmentalized Program Grades 5-9. *Educational Professionals* Special Education Teachers 10; Career/Vocational Teachers 1; Crisis Teachers 2; Paraprofessionals 1. *Curricula* Traditional Academic; Career/Vocational Education; Individualized; Basic Skills; Prevocational. *Educational Intervention Approaches* Engineered Classroom; Precision Teaching; Progressive Discipline; Self-Control; Behavior Modification; Applied Behavior Analysis; Creative Conditioning.

Comments Andrus is a residential center for youngsters who have mild to moderate emotional problems. It offers a structured setting with individual, group, and family therapy and a special education program. The cottage for older adolescent boys (ages 14-18) is a group residence, with more of a community focus.

The Astor Home for Children—Day Treatment Program

400 Church St, Poughkeepsie, NY 12601 (914) 452-1630
Year Established 1973
Contact John B Mordock, Asst Exec Dir

Facility Information *Placement* Day Treatment. *Children/Adolescents Served* 40. *Sexes Served* Both. *Tuition Fees (Approx)* $10,172. *Sources of Funding* State Funds; Medicaid; P.L. 89-313. Summer school available. *Teacher Certification Level* Elementary School; Junior High/Middle School. *Special Certification Level* Special Education.

Student/Patient Characteristics *Age Levels* 0-4; 5-8; 9-11; 12-14. *IQ Ranges* 71-85; 85-130; Above 130. *Exceptionalities Served* Emotionally Disturbed. *Learning Problems* Memory Disabilities; Perceptual Disabilities; Thinking Disabilities; Oral Language Disabilities; Reading Disabilities; Handwriting Disabilities; Spelling Disabilities; Arithmetic Disabilities; Written Expression. *Behavioral Problems* Attention Deficits; Hyperactivity; Hypoactivity; Impulsivity; Self-Aggression; Verbal Aggression; Physical Aggression; Indirect Aggression; Passive Aggression; Withdrawal. *Conditions Treated* Early Infantile Autism; Disintegrative Psychoses; Schizophrenia; Phobias; Depression; Personality Problems; Socialized Aggressive Reaction; Unsocialized Aggressive Reaction.

Services Provided Individual Therapy; Group Therapy; Parent Involvement; Behavior Therapy; Cognitive Developmental Therapy; Family Therapy; Play Therapy. *Professionals on Staff* Psychiatrists 1; Psychologists 1; Social Workers 2; Nurses 1. *Service Facilities Available (with number of rooms)* Self-Contained Rooms 5. *Educational Professionals* Special Education Teachers 5; Physical Education Teacher 1. *Curricula* Individualized. *Educational Intervention Approaches* Behavior Modification; Learning Centers.

The Astor Home for Children—Day Treatment Program

750 Tilden St, Bronx, NY 10467 (212) 231-3400
Year Established 1974
Contact Theodore H Wasserman, Prog Dir

Facility Information *Placement* Day Treatment. *Children/Adolescents Served* 110. *Sexes Served* Both. *Tuition Fees (Approx)* $900. *Sources of Funding* State Funds; Medicaid. Summer school available. *Teacher Certification Level* Elementary School; Junior High/Middle School. *Special Certification Level* ED; LD; Reading; Math.

Student/Patient Characteristics *Age Levels* 0-4; 5-8; 9-11; 12-14. *IQ Ranges* 71-85; 85-130; Above 130. *Exceptionalities Served* Emotionally Disturbed; Learning Disabled; Mentally Handicapped. *Learning Problems* Memory Disabilities; Perceptual Disabilities; Thinking Disabilities; Oral Language Disabilities; Reading Disabilities; Handwriting Disabilities; Spelling Disabilities; Arithmetic Disabilities; Written Expression. *Behavioral Problems* Attention Deficits; Hyperactivity; Impulsivity; Self-Aggression; Verbal Aggression; Physical Aggression; Indirect Aggression; Passive Aggression; Withdrawal. *Conditions Treated* Disintegrative Psychoses; Schizophrenia; Aphasia; Convulsive Disorders; Phobias; Obsessions and Compulsions; Hysteria; Depression; Suicide; Asthma; Inadequacy/Immaturity; Personality Problems; Socialized Aggressive Reaction; Unsocialized Aggressive Reaction.

Services Provided Individual Therapy; Group Therapy; Parent Involvement; Behavior Therapy; Cognitive Developmental Therapy; Biofeedback; Family Therapy; Filial Therapy; Drug Therapy. *Professionals on Staff* Psychiatrists 1; Psychologists 5; Social Workers 2. *Service Facilities Available (with number of rooms)* Resource Rooms 1; Transition Rooms 1; Self-Contained Rooms 11. *Educational Professionals* Special Education Teachers 25; Crisis Teachers 1; Paraprofessionals 5; Reading Specialist; Learning Disabilities Teacher 2. *Curricula* Traditional Academic; Career/Vocational Education; Individualized; Basic Skills; Prevocational. *Educational Intervention Approaches* Engineered Classroom; Progressive Discipline; Self-Control; Behavior Modification; Applied Behavior Analysis; Creative Conditioning.

Comments The Home is a licensed day hospital program operating in conjunction with the New York City Board of Education. A full range of therapeutic services are available-educational specialties are represented.

The Astor Home for Children—Group Home Program

1967 Turnbull Ave, Bronx, NY 10473 (212) 829-8900
Year Established 1964
Contact John R Levin, Prog Dir

Facility Information *Placement* Private Residential Care. *Number of Beds* 52. *Children/Adolescents Served* 52. *Sexes Served* Both. *Room and Board Fees (Approx)* $80. *Sources of Funding* HEW; Medicaid.

Student/Patient Characteristics *Age Levels* 5-8; 9-11; 12-14; 15-17; 18-21. *IQ Ranges* 71-85; 85-130. *Exceptionalities Served* Emotionally Disturbed; Learning Disabled. *Learning Problems* Perceptual Disabilities; Thinking Disabilities; Oral Language Disabilities; Reading Disabilities; Spelling Disabilities. *Behavioral Problems* Attention Deficits; Hyperactivity; Impulsivity; Self-Aggression; Verbal Aggression; Physical Aggression; Passive Aggression; Withdrawal. *Conditions Treated* Alcohol Abuse and/or Drug Abuse; Other Substance Abuse or Dependence; Depression; Suicide; Personality Problems; Socialized Aggressive Reaction; Unsocialized Aggressive Reaction.

Services Provided Individual Therapy; Group Therapy; Parent Involvement; Behavior Therapy; Cognitive Developmental Therapy; Family Therapy; Reality Therapy; Play Therapy. *Professionals on Staff* Psychiatrists 1; Psychologists 2; Social Workers 4; Child Care Staff 37; Nurses 1.

Comments This program is an open setting group home program located in the Bronx. It is designed to serve severely emotionally disturbed children. All children are in a public school setting.

The Astor Home for Children—Residential Treatment Center—Residential Treatment Facility—Learning Center

36 Mill St, Rhinebeck, NY 12572 (914) 876-4081
Contact Walter J Joseph, Asst Exec Dir

Facility Information *Placement* Special School; Private Residential Care. *Number of Beds* 75. *Children/Adolescents Served* 75. *Sexes Served* Both. *Room and Board Fees (Approx)* $77 (Residential Treatment Center); $117 (Residential Treatment Facility). *Tuition Fees (Approx)* $9,844. *Sources of Funding* State Funds; Medicaid; P.L. 94-142; Article 853 State Education; Chapter I, 89-313. Summer school available. *Teacher Certification Level* Elementary School; Junior High/Middle School; High School. *Special Certification Level* ED; LD; MR; Special Education.

Student/Patient Characteristics *Age Levels* 5-8; 9-11; 12-14. *IQ Ranges* 56-70; 71-85; 85-130. *Exceptionalities Served* Emotionally Disturbed; Learning Disabled; Mentally Handicapped; Communication Disordered. *Learning Problems* Memory Disabilities; Perceptual Disabilities; Thinking Disabilities; Oral Language Disabilities; Reading Disabilities; Handwriting Disabilities; Spelling

Disabilities; Arithmetic Disabilities; Written Expression. *Behavioral Problems* Attention Deficits; Hyperactivity; Impulsivity; Self-Aggression; Verbal Aggression; Physical Aggression; Passive Aggression; Withdrawal. *Conditions Treated* Schizophrenia; Depression; Inadequacy/Immaturity; Personality Problems; Socialized Aggressive Reaction; Unsocialized Aggressive Reaction.

Services Provided Individual Therapy; Group Therapy; Parent Involvement; Behavior Therapy; Drug Therapy; Play Therapy. *Professionals on Staff* Psychiatrists 2; Psychologists 4; Social Workers 6; Child Care Staff 52; Nurses 4. *Service Facilities Available (with number of rooms)* Self-Contained Rooms 9; On-Campus Residential School 9; Reading Lab 1. *Educational Professionals* Special Education Teachers 12; Certified Teaching Assistants 10. *Curricula* Traditional Academic; Individualized; Basic Skills. *Educational Intervention Approaches* Behavior Modification.

Baker Hall Inc

150 Martin Rd, Lackawanna, NY 14218 (716) 827-9671
Contact James J Casion, Exec Dir

Facility Information *Placement* Private Residential Care. *Number of Beds* 95. *Children/Adolescents Served* 95 (residential); 150 (outpatient); 90 (educational). *Sexes Served* Male. *Room and Board Fees (Approx)* $60-$130. *Tuition Fees (Approx)* $12,000. *Sources of Funding* State Funds; Medicaid; P.L. 94-142; County. Summer school available. *Teacher Certification Level* Junior High/Middle School. *Special Certification Level* Reading; Math; Special Education; Physical Education; Industrial Arts.

Student/Patient Characteristics *Age Levels* 12-14; 15-17; 18-21. *IQ Ranges* 56-70; 71-85. *Exceptionalities Served* Emotionally Disturbed; Learning Disabled; Mentally Handicapped. *Learning Problems* Perceptual Disabilities; Thinking Disabilities; Oral Language Disabilities; Reading Disabilities; Handwriting Disabilities; Spelling Disabilities; Arithmetic Disabilities; Written Expression. *Behavioral Problems* Attention Deficits; Hyperactivity; Impulsivity; Self-Aggression; Verbal Aggression; Physical Aggression; Passive Aggression; Withdrawal. *Conditions Treated* Alcohol Abuse and/or Drug Abuse; Other Substance Abuse or Dependence; Disintegrative Psychoses; Schizophrenia; Convulsive Disorders; Depression; Suicide; Inadequacy/Immaturity; Personality Problems; Socialized Aggressive Reaction; Unsocialized Aggressive Reaction.

Services Provided Individual Therapy; Group Therapy; Parent Involvement; Behavior Therapy; Family Therapy; Filial Therapy; Drug Therapy; Reality Therapy; Play Therapy. *Professionals on Staff* Psychiatrists 1; Psychologists 2; Counselors 20; Social Workers 4; Child Care Staff 115; Nurses 4; Child Care Supervisor 7. *Service Facilities Available (with number of rooms)* Resource Rooms; Transition Rooms; Self-Contained Rooms; Crisis Complex; On-Campus Residential School. *Educational Professionals* Special Education Teachers 19; Career/Vocational Teachers 1; Crisis Teachers 8. *Curricula* Traditional Academic; Career/Vocational Education; Individualized; Basic Skills; Prevocational. *Educational Intervention Approaches* Progressive Discipline; Self-Control; Behavior Modification; Applied Behavior Analysis; Creative Conditioning. *Degrees Awarded* Certificate of Attendance; Graduate Equivalency Diploma.

Comments Baker Hall is a comprehensive center for the care of clients who range in age from birth to 21 years of age. The services include: Special Services, Residential Treatment Facility, Residential Services, Group Home Services, Foster Family Boarding Home, Preventive Services and After Care Services. Baker Hall operates a fully approved Special Education Program offering both academic and work/study tracts.

Berkshire Farm Center and Services for Youth

Rte 22, Canaan, NY 12029 (518) 781-4567
Year Established 1886
Contact Harold Novick, Exec Dir

Facility Information *Placement* Special School; Private Residential Care. *Number of Beds* 232. *Children/Adolescents Served* 232. *Sexes Served* Female. *Room and Board Fees (Approx)* $66-$73. *Tuition Fees (Approx)* $8,573. *Sources of Funding* State Funds; Medicaid; County Social Service Districts. Summer school available. *Teacher Certification Level* Junior High/Middle School.

Student/Patient Characteristics *Age Levels* 12-14; 15-17. *Exceptionalities Served* Emotionally Disturbed; Learning Disabled. *Learning Problems* Perceptual Disabilities; Thinking Disabilities; Reading Disabilities; Spelling Disabilities; Arithmetic Disabilities; Written Expression. *Behavioral Problems* Attention Deficits; Hyperactivity; Hypoactivity; Impulsivity; Self-Aggression; Verbal Aggression; Physical Aggression; Indirect Aggression; Passive Aggression; Withdrawal. *Conditions Treated* Alcohol Abuse and/or Drug Abuse; Other Substance Abuse or Dependence; Phobias; Obsessions and Compulsions; Depression; Suicide; Asthma; Inadequacy/Immaturity; Personality Problems; Socialized Aggressive Reaction; Unsocialized Aggressive Reaction.

Services Provided Individual Therapy; Group Therapy; Parent Involvement; Behavior Therapy; Cognitive Developmental Therapy; Family Therapy; Drug Therapy. *Professionals on Staff* Psychiatrists 2; Psychologists 3; Counselors; Child Care Staff; Nurses. *Degrees Awarded* Graduate Equivalency Diploma.

Comments Berkshire Farm Center and Services for Youth is a voluntary, multifunction child caring agency serving adolescents who are experiencing difficulties at home and/or in their communities. The programs offered by Berkshire Farm Center are designed to meet the various levels of need of the youngsters, their families, and the communities in which they live.

Board of Cooperative Educational Services II—Special Education Division Instructional Support Center

8-43, Centereach, NY 11720 (516) 467-3510
Year Established 1948
Contact James V Fogartey Jr, Special Ed Dir

Facility Information *Placement* Public School; Special School; Intermediate School District. *Children/Adolescents Served* 1600. *Sexes Served* Both. *Sources of Funding* State Funds; P.L. 94-142; 89-313 Funds. Summer school available. *Teacher Certification Level* Elementary School; Junior High/Middle School; High School. *Special Certification Level* ED; LD; MR; Career/Vocational Education; Reading; Math; Special Education.

Student/Patient Characteristics *Age Levels* 0-4; 5-8; 9-11; 12-14; 15-17; 18-21. *IQ Ranges* 0-25; 26-40; 41-55; 56-70; 71-85; 85-130; Above 130. *Exceptionalities Served* Autistic; Emotionally Disturbed; Learning Disabled; Mentally Handicapped; Communication Disordered; Hearing Impaired/Deaf; Visually Impaired/Blind; Other Health Impaired; Physically Handicapped; Gifted. *Learning Problems* Memory Disabilities; Perceptual Disabilities; Thinking Disabilities; Oral Language Disabilities; Reading Disabilities; Handwriting Disabilities; Spelling Disabilities; Arithmetic Disabilities; Written Expression. *Behavioral Problems* Attention Deficits; Hyperactivity; Hypoactivity; Impulsivity; Self-Aggression; Verbal Aggression; Physical Aggression; Indirect Aggression; Passive Aggression; Withdrawal. *Conditions Treated* Early Infantile Autism; Disintegrative Psychoses; Schizophrenia; Aphasia; Convulsive Disorders; Phobias; Asthma; Inadequacy/Immaturity; Personality Problems; Socialized Aggressive Reaction; Unsocialized Aggressive Reaction.

Services Provided Individual Therapy; Group Therapy; Parent Involvement; Behavior Therapy; Cognitive Developmental Therapy; Family Therapy. *Professionals on Staff* Psychiatrists 1; Psychologists 5; Social Workers 10; Nurses 4. *Service Facilities Available (with number of rooms)* Itinerants 10; Transition Rooms 5; Self-Contained Rooms 40. *Educational Professionals* Special Education Teachers 40; Career/Vocational Teachers 20; Crisis Teachers 5; Special Education Counselors 10; Paraprofessionals 25; Art Therapist; Music Therapist; Occupational Therapist; Speech Therapist; Physical Therapist 10. *Curricula* Traditional Academic; Career/Vocational Education; Individualized;

Basic Skills; Prevocational. *Educational Intervention Approaches* Engineered Classroom; Precision Teaching; Progressive Discipline; Behavior Modification. *Degrees Awarded* Certificate of Attendance; High School Diploma.

BOCES Nassau

Valentines Rd and Plain Rd, Westbury, NY 11590
(516) 997-8700
Year Established 1967
Contact E McManus, Supv

Facility Information *Placement* Public School; Special School. *Children/Adolescents Served* 3,000. *Sexes Served* Both. *Tuition Fees (Approx)* $11,995-$20,995. *Sources of Funding* State Funds; P.L. 94-142. Summer school available. *Teacher Certification Level* Elementary School; Junior High/Middle School; High School. *Special Certification Level* ED; LD; MR; Career/Vocational Education; Reading; Math.

Student/Patient Characteristics *Age Levels* 0-4; 5-8; 9-11; 12-14; 15-17; 18-21. *IQ Ranges* 0-25; 26-40; 41-55; 56-70; 71-85; 85-130; Above 130. *Exceptionalities Served* Autistic; Emotionally Disturbed; Learning Disabled; Mentally Handicapped; Communication Disordered; Hearing Impaired/Deaf; Visually Impaired/Blind; Other Health Impaired; Physically Handicapped. *Learning Problems* Memory Disabilities; Perceptual Disabilities; Thinking Disabilities; Oral Language Disabilities; Reading Disabilities; Handwriting Disabilities; Spelling Disabilities; Arithmetic Disabilities; Written Expression. *Behavioral Problems* Attention Deficits; Hyperactivity; Hypoactivity; Impulsivity; Self-Aggression; Verbal Aggression; Physical Aggression; Indirect Aggression; Passive Aggression; Withdrawal. *Conditions Treated* Early Infantile Autism; Disintegrative Psychoses; Schizophrenia; Aphasia; Convulsive Disorders; Phobias; Obsessions and Compulsions; Depression; Inadequacy/Immaturity; Personality Problems; Socialized Aggressive Reaction; Unsocialized Aggressive Reaction.

Services Provided Individual Therapy; Group Therapy; Parent Involvement; Behavior Therapy; Cognitive Developmental Therapy; Family Therapy; Filial Therapy; Music Therapy; Play Therapy; Psychodrama. *Professionals on Staff* Psychologists 21; Counselors 4; Social Workers 6; Nurses 19. *Service Facilities Available (with number of rooms)* Consultative (ERT); Itinerants; Transition Rooms; Self-Contained Rooms; Special School. *Educational Professionals* Special Education Teachers; Career/Vocational Teachers; Crisis Teachers; Special Education Counselors; Paraprofessionals. *Curricula* Traditional Academic; Career/Vocational Education; Individualized; Basic Skills; Prevocational. *Educational Intervention Approaches* Engineered Classroom; Precision Teaching; Progressive Discipline; Self-Control; Behavior Modification; Applied Behavior Analysis. *Degrees Awarded* Certificate of Attendance; High School Diploma; Graduate Equivalency Diploma.

BOCES Onondaga Madison

303 Roby Ave, East Syracuse, NY 13057 (315) 433-2641
Contact Susanne Fitzgerald, Prog Supv

Facility Information *Placement* Public School. *Children/Adolescents Served* 42. *Sexes Served* Both. *Sources of Funding* School District Tuition. Summer school available. *Special Certification Level* ED; LD; MR.

Student/Patient Characteristics *Age Levels* 5-8; 9-11; 12-14; 15-17; 18-21. *IQ Ranges* 71-85; 85-130; Above 130. *Exceptionalities Served* Emotionally Disturbed; Learning Disabled; Communication Disordered; Gifted. *Learning Problems* Perceptual Disabilities; Thinking Disabilities; Oral Language Disabilities; Reading Disabilities; Handwriting Disabilities; Spelling Disabilities; Arithmetic Disabilities; Written Expression. *Behavioral Problems* Attention Deficits; Hyperactivity; Hypoactivity; Impulsivity; Self-Aggression; Verbal Aggression; Physical Aggression; Indirect Aggression; Passive Aggression; Withdrawal. *Conditions Treated* Depression; Inadequacy/Immaturity; Personality Problems; Socialized Aggressive Reaction; Unsocialized Aggressive Reaction.

Services Provided Individual Therapy; Parent Involvement; Behavior Therapy. *Professionals on Staff* Psychologists 1; Nurses 1. *Service Facilities Available (with number of rooms)* Self-Contained Rooms 7; Homebound Instruction; Occupational Education Center. *Educational Professionals* Special Education Teachers 7; Paraprofessionals 11; Occupational Education Teachers. *Curricula* Individualized; Basic Skills; Prevocational. *Educational Intervention Approaches* Behavior Modification.

Comments Onondaga Madison BOCES is an intermediate education unit providing cooperative educational services for seventeen (17) school districts. Students are placed there by school district referral. It is a behavior management program for students who have been labeled severely emotionally disturbed. The program offers intensive, individualized programing.

BOCES Southern Westchester—Rye Lake Campus

666 Old Orchard St, White Plains, NY 10604 (914) 761-5055
Contact John McKay, Principal
Facility Information *Placement* Public School.
Children/Adolescents Served 150. *Sexes Served* Both. *Tuition Fees (Approx)* $17,181 (multiply handicapped); $21,974 (autism); $8,103 (therapeutic support). *Sources of Funding* State Funds; P.L. 94-142. Summer school available.
Student/Patient Characteristics *Age Levels* 0-4; 5-8; 9-11; 12-14; 15-17; 18-21. *IQ Ranges* 0-25; 26-40; 41-55; 56-70. *Exceptionalities Served* Autistic; Emotionally Disturbed; Mentally Handicapped; Severely Multiply Handicapped. *Learning Problems* Memory Disabilities; Perceptual Disabilities; Thinking Disabilities; Oral Language Disabilities; Reading Disabilities; Handwriting Disabilities; Spelling Disabilities; Arithmetic Disabilities; Written Expression. *Behavioral Problems* Attention Deficits; Hyperactivity; Hypoactivity; Impulsivity; Self-Aggression; Verbal Aggression; Physical Aggression; Indirect Aggression; Passive Aggression; Withdrawal. *Conditions Treated* Early Infantile Autism; Personality Problems; Unsocialized Aggressive Reaction.
Services Provided Individual Therapy; Group Therapy; Parent Involvement; Behavior Therapy; Play Therapy. *Service Facilities Available (with number of rooms)* Consultative (ERT); Itinerants; Special School. *Curricula* Individualized; Basic Skills; Prevocational; Essential Links. *Educational Intervention Approaches* Behavior Modification; Applied Behavior Analysis; Effective Teaching. *Degrees Awarded* BOCES Diploma.

Comments BOCES Rye Lake Campus provides individualized educational programing to meet the needs of students, ages 4-21, requiring therapeutic support.

Bronx Developmental Center—Respite Service

1200 Waters Pl, Bronx, NY 10461 (212) 430-0755
Year Established 1973
Contact Kenneth Killian, Prog Coord
Facility Information *Placement* Respite Care.
Children/Adolescents Served 60. *Sexes Served* Both. *Sources of Funding* State Funds.
Student/Patient Characteristics *Age Levels* 0-4; 5-8; 9-11; 12-14; 15-17. *IQ Ranges* 0-25; 26-40; 41-55; 56-70; 71-85. *Exceptionalities Served* Autistic; Learning Disabled; Mentally Handicapped. *Learning Problems* Memory Disabilities; Perceptual Disabilities; Thinking Disabilities; Oral Language Disabilities; Reading Disabilities; Handwriting Disabilities; Spelling Disabilities; Arithmetic Disabilities; Written Expression. *Behavioral Problems* Attention Deficits; Hyperactivity; Hypoactivity; Impulsivity; Self-Aggression; Physical Aggression; Indirect Aggression; Passive Aggression; Withdrawal.
Services Provided Recreation. *Professionals on Staff* Child Care Staff 5; Recreation Therapist.

Comments The Respite Service provides day care (after school; Saturdays) for families caring for autistic or mentally retarded children at home. The service is provided at a local state developmental center. The child participates in structured recreational activities while in the program. The program is coordinated by a senior recreation therapist who supervises the direct-care paraprofessional staff.

Brooklyn Community Counseling Center

1683 Flatbush Ave, Brooklyn, NY 11210
Year Established 1957
Contact Milton Russell; Gerald S Weider, Co-Dir
Facility Information *Placement* Outpatient Psychiatric Clinic.
Student/Patient Characteristics *Exceptionalities Served* Emotionally Disturbed; Learning Disabled; Mentally Handicapped; Communication Disordered; Gifted. *Learning Problems* Memory Disabilities; Perceptual Disabilities; Thinking Disabilities; Reading Disabilities. *Behavioral Problems* Attention Deficits; Hyperactivity; Hypoactivity; Impulsivity; Self-Aggression; Verbal Aggression; Physical Aggression; Indirect Aggression; Passive Aggression; Withdrawal. *Conditions Treated* Schizophrenia; Phobias; Obsessions and Compulsions; Hysteria; Depression; Suicide; Asthma; Anorexia Nervosa; Ulcerative Colitis; Inadequacy/Immaturity; Personality Problems; Socialized Aggressive Reaction; Unsocialized Aggressive Reaction.
Services Provided Individual Therapy; Group Therapy; Parent Involvement; Behavior Therapy; Family Therapy; Play Therapy. *Professionals on Staff* Psychiatrists 4; Psychologists 15; Social Workers 20.

Comments It is a state licensed, psychiatric clinic offering the usual range of psychiatric and psychological services on an outpatient basis. Fees are arranged on a sliding scale.

Broom-Tioga Board of Cooperative Educational Services

421 Upper Glenwood Rd, Binghamton, NY 13905
(607) 729-9301
Contact Lyle Green, Spec Ed Dir
Facility Information *Placement* Public School; Special Program.
Children/Adolescents Served 50. *Sexes Served* Both. *Tuition Fees (Approx)* $10,100. *Sources of Funding* P.L. 94-142. *Teacher Certification Level* Elementary School; Junior High/Middle School; High School. *Special Certification Level* Special Education.
Student/Patient Characteristics *Age Levels* 9-11; 12-14; 15-17; 18-21. *IQ Ranges* 85-130. *Exceptionalities Served* Emotionally Disturbed. *Learning Problems* Thinking Disabilities; Reading Disabilities; Arithmetic Disabilities; Written Expression. *Behavioral Problems* Attention Deficits; Impulsivity; Verbal Aggression; Physical Aggression. *Conditions Treated* Obsessions and Compulsions; Inadequacy/Immaturity; Unsocialized Aggressive Reaction.
Services Provided Individual Therapy; Group Therapy; Behavior Therapy; Drug Therapy; Reality Therapy. *Professionals on Staff* Counselors 1; Social Workers 1; Nurses. *Service Facilities Available (with number of rooms)* Special School 12. *Educational Professionals* Special Education Teachers 6; Paraprofessionals 7; Physical Education 1. *Curricula* Individualized. *Educational Intervention Approaches* Behavior Modification. *Degrees Awarded* Certificate of Attendance.

Cantalician Center for Learning

3233 Main St, Buffalo, NY 14214 (716) 833-5353
Year Established 1955
Contact Mary Haberl, Prog Dir
Facility Information *Placement* Special School.
Children/Adolescents Served 350. *Sexes Served* Both. *Sources of Funding* State Funds. Summer school available. *Special Certification Level* ED; LD; MR.
Student/Patient Characteristics *Age Levels* 0-4; 5-8; 9-11; 12-14; 15-17; 18-21. *IQ Ranges* 0-25; 26-40; 41-55; 56-70; 71-85. *Exceptionalities Served* Autistic; Mentally Handicapped; Communication Disordered; Visually Impaired/Blind; Multiply Handicapped. *Behavioral Problems* Attention Deficits; Hyperactivity;

Self-Aggression; Verbal Aggression; Passive Aggression; Withdrawal. *Conditions Treated* Early Infantile Autism; Convulsive Disorders.

Services Provided Parent Involvement; Behavior Therapy; Art Therapy; Music Therapy; Play Therapy. *Professionals on Staff* Psychologists 2; Counselors 2; Social Workers 1; Behavior Specialist 2. *Service Facilities Available (with number of rooms)* Self-Contained Rooms 43. *Educational Professionals* Special Education Teachers 60; Special Education Counselors 2. *Curricula* Career/Vocational Education; Individualized; Basic Skills; Prevocational. *Educational Intervention Approaches* Precision Teaching; Behavior Modification.

Cayuga Home for Children

PO Box 945, 85 Hamilton Ave, Auburn, NY 13021
(315) 253-5383
Year Established 1852
Contact E J Ferrara, Exec Dir

Facility Information *Placement* Private Residential Care. *Number of Beds* 36. *Children/Adolescents Served* 36. *Sexes Served* Both. *Room and Board Fees (Approx)* $62. *Sources of Funding* State Funds; Medicaid; Contributions. Summer school available.

Student/Patient Characteristics *Age Levels* 12-14; 15-17. *IQ Ranges* 71-85; 85-130. *Exceptionalities Served* Emotionally Disturbed; Learning Disabled. *Learning Problems* Reading Disabilities. *Behavioral Problems* Attention Deficits; Impulsivity; Verbal Aggression; Physical Aggression; Passive Aggression; Withdrawal. *Conditions Treated* Depression; Personality Problems; Socialized Aggressive Reaction; Unsocialized Aggressive Reaction.

Services Provided Individual Therapy; Group Therapy; Parent Involvement; Behavior Therapy; Family Therapy; Drug Therapy; Reality Therapy. *Professionals on Staff* Psychiatrists 1; Psychologists 1; Social Workers 4; Child Care Staff 20. *Service Facilities Available (with number of rooms)* Transition Rooms 8; Self-Contained Rooms 2; On-Campus Residential School 2; Homebound Instruction 1. *Educational Professionals* Special Education Teachers 2; Paraprofessionals 2. *Curricula* Traditional Academic; Career/Vocational Education; Individualized; Basic Skills; Prevocational. *Educational Intervention Approaches* Progressive Discipline; Self-Control; Behavior Modification; Creative Conditioning. *Degrees Awarded* High School Diploma; Graduate Equivalency Diploma.

Comments Cayuga is a growth oriented program with daily social and behavior modification programs and evaluations. Group care is also provided.

The Charlton School

PO Box 47, Burnt Hills, NY 12027 (518) 399-8182
Year Established 1895
Contact Thomas P Oles, Dir of Treatment Serv

Facility Information *Placement* Special School; Private Residential Care. *Number of Beds* 35. *Children/Adolescents Served* 35. *Sexes Served* Female. *Room and Board Fees (Approx)* $60. *Tuition Fees (Approx)* $8,640. *Teacher Certification Level* Junior High/Middle School; High School. *Special Certification Level* Math; Special Education; Theatre; English; Home Economics; Physical Education; Science; Social Studies.

Student/Patient Characteristics *Age Levels* 12-14; 15-17; 18-21. *IQ Ranges* 71-85; 85-130; Above 130. *Exceptionalities Served* Emotionally Disturbed; Learning Disabled. *Learning Problems* Memory Disabilities; Perceptual Disabilities; Thinking Disabilities; Reading Disabilities; Arithmetic Disabilities; Written Expression. *Behavioral Problems* Attention Deficits; Hyperactivity; Hypoactivity; Impulsivity; Self-Aggression; Verbal Aggression; Physical Aggression; Indirect Aggression; Passive Aggression; Withdrawal. *Conditions Treated* Phobias; Depression; Suicide; Anorexia Nervosa; Inadequacy/Immaturity; Personality Problems; Socialized Aggressive Reaction; Unsocialized Aggressive Reaction.

Services Provided Individual Therapy; Group Therapy; Parent Involvement; Behavior Therapy; Family Therapy; Drug Therapy; Reality Therapy. *Professionals on Staff* Psychiatrists 1; Psycholo-

gists 1; Social Workers 5; Child Care Staff 17; Nurses 1. *Service Facilities Available (with number of rooms)* On-Campus Residential School 5. *Educational Professionals* Regular School Teachers 4; Special Education Teachers 2; Paraprofessionals 2. *Curricula* Traditional Academic; Individualized; Basic Skills. *Educational Intervention Approaches* Behavior Modification; Applied Behavior Analysis; Creative Conditioning. *Degrees Awarded* High School Diploma.

Child and Adolescent Psychiatric Clinic Inc

3350 Main St, Buffalo, NY 14214 (716) 835-4011
Year Established 1937
Contact Shepard Goldberg, Exec Dir

Facility Information *Placement* Outpatient Mental Health Clinic. *Children/Adolescents Served* 2,000. *Sources of Funding* State Funds; Health Insurance; Medicaid; United Way.

Student/Patient Characteristics *Age Levels* 0-4; 5-8; 9-11; 12-14; 15-17. *IQ Ranges* 71-85; 85-130; Above 130. *Exceptionalities Served* Emotionally Disturbed. *Behavioral Problems* Attention Deficits; Hyperactivity; Impulsivity; Self-Aggression; Verbal Aggression; Physical Aggression; Indirect Aggression; Passive Aggression. *Conditions Treated* Alcohol Abuse and/or Drug Abuse; Other Substance Abuse or Dependence; Phobias; Obsessions and Compulsions; Hysteria; Depression; Suicide; Anorexia Nervosa; Inadequacy/Immaturity; Personality Problems; Socialized Aggressive Reaction; Unsocialized Aggressive Reaction.

Services Provided Individual Therapy; Group Therapy; Parent Involvement; Family Therapy; Play Therapy. *Professionals on Staff* Psychiatrists; Psychologists; Social Workers.

Child Development Center

120 W 57th St, New York, NY 10019 (212) 582-9100
Year Established 1946
Contact Intake Supv

Facility Information *Placement* Private Day Care. *Children/Adolescents Served* 33. *Sexes Served* Both. *Tuition Fees (Approx)* $11,000. *Sources of Funding* State Funds; Health Insurance; Medicaid; P.L. 94-142; Tuition. Summer school available. *Special Certification Level* ED.

Student/Patient Characteristics *Age Levels* 0-4; 5-8. *IQ Ranges* 85-130; Above 130. *Exceptionalities Served* Emotionally Disturbed; Learning Disabled; Communication Disordered. *Learning Problems* Perceptual Disabilities; Thinking Disabilities; Oral Language Disabilities. *Behavioral Problems* Attention Deficits; Hyperactivity; Impulsivity; Verbal Aggression; Physical Aggression; Passive Aggression; Withdrawal. *Conditions Treated* Convulsive Disorders; Depression; Asthma; Inadequacy/Immaturity; Personality Problems.

Services Provided Individual Therapy; Group Therapy; Parent Involvement; Family Therapy; Music Therapy; Play Therapy; Speech and Language Therapy. *Professionals on Staff* Psychiatrists; Psychologists; Social Workers. *Educational Professionals* Special Education Teachers 4; Trainees; Speech and Language Personnel 2. *Curricula* Nursery School.

Child Research and Study Center

1400 Washington Ave, Albany, NY 12203 (518) 455-6267
Contact Linda Zenner, Social Worker

Facility Information *Placement* Clinic. *Sources of Funding* Health Insurance; Fee.

Services Provided Individual Therapy; Parent Involvement; Family Therapy; Assessment. *Professionals on Staff* Psychologists 5; Social Workers 1; Reading Consultant.

Comments This is a university based clinic offering student training, research and assessment services to the community. Children with learning and other developmental disabilities are served by a staff of psychologists, educational specialists, and social workers. Consultation and training to schools and community agencies is available by arrangement with the clinic director.

Children's Day Hospital—New York Hospital—Cornell Medical Center—Westchester Division

Bloomingdale Rd, White Plains, NY 10605 (914) 997-2474
Year Established 1970
Contact Carol Ann Leal, Chief

Facility Information *Placement* Psychiatric Day Treatment and Special Education. *Children/Adolescents Served* 25. *Sexes Served* Both. *Sources of Funding* Health Insurance; Medicaid; P.L. 94-142; Family Fees. Summer school available. *Teacher Certification Level* Elementary School. *Special Certification Level* ED; LD; Career/Vocational Education; Reading; Math; Special Education.

Student/Patient Characteristics *Age Levels* 5-8; 9-11. *IQ Ranges* 56-70; 71-85; 85-130; Above 130. *Exceptionalities Served* Autistic; Emotionally Disturbed; Learning Disabled; Mentally Handicapped; Communication Disordered; Gifted. *Learning Problems* Perceptual Disabilities; Thinking Disabilities; Oral Language Disabilities; Reading Disabilities; Handwriting Disabilities; Spelling Disabilities; Arithmetic Disabilities; Written Expression. *Behavioral Problems* Attention Deficits; Hyperactivity; Hypoactivity; Impulsivity; Self-Aggression; Verbal Aggression; Physical Aggression; Indirect Aggression; Passive Aggression; Withdrawal. *Conditions Treated* Early Infantile Autism; Disintegrative Psychoses; Schizophrenia; Aphasia; Convulsive Disorders; Phobias; Obsessions and Compulsions; Hysteria; Depression; Asthma; Inadequacy/Immaturity; Personality Problems; Socialized Aggressive Reaction; Unsocialized Aggressive Reaction; Dysthmic Disorders.

Services Provided Individual Therapy; Group Therapy; Parent Involvement; Behavior Therapy; Family Therapy; Drug Therapy; Play Therapy; Milieu Therapy. *Professionals on Staff* Psychiatrists 2; Psychologists 3; Counselors 4; Social Workers 2; Nurses 2; Occupational Therapist 1. *Educational Professionals* Special Education Teachers 3; Career/Vocational Teachers 1; Paraprofessionals 3. *Curricula* Individualized; Basic Skills. *Educational Intervention Approaches* Progressive Discipline; Self-Control; Behavior Modification.

Comments The Children's Day Hospital is a clinically based, self-contained integrated system of comprehensive psychiatric and special education long-term treatment programs which operates for 5 days per week from 8:30 A.M. to 2:30 P.M. all year. On educational holidays and during summer and vacation recess the children receive a 5 days per week Psychiatric Day Camp Milieu System of services, including psychotherapy.

Children's Home of Kingston

26 Grove St, Kingston, NY 12401 (914) 331-1448
Year Established 1874
Contact Connie Whitehurst, Exec Dir

Facility Information *Placement* Special School; Private Residential Care. *Number of Beds* 53. *Children/Adolescents Served* 53 (residence); 15 (foster care); 10 (day treatment). *Sexes Served* Male. *Room and Board Fees (Approx)* $66. *Sources of Funding* Medicaid; P.L. 94-142; County Department of Social Services. Summer school available. *Teacher Certification Level* Elementary School; Junior High/Middle School. *Special Certification Level* ED; LD; Reading; Music Therapy; Art; Physical Education.

Student/Patient Characteristics *Age Levels* 9-11; 12-14; 15-17. *IQ Ranges* 85-130. *Exceptionalities Served* Emotionally Disturbed; Learning Disabled; Communication Disordered. *Learning Problems* Memory Disabilities; Perceptual Disabilities; Thinking Disabilities; Oral Language Disabilities; Reading Disabilities; Handwriting Disabilities; Spelling Disabilities; Arithmetic Disabilities; Written Expression. *Behavioral Problems* Attention Deficits; Hyperactivity; Impulsivity; Self-Aggression; Verbal Aggression; Physical Aggression; Indirect Aggression; Passive Aggression; Withdrawal. *Conditions Treated* Alcohol Abuse and/or Drug Abuse; Aphasia; Convulsive Disorders; Phobias; Obsessions and Compulsions; Hysteria; Depression; Asthma; Inadequacy/Immaturity; Personality Problems; Socialized Aggressive Reaction; Unsocialized Aggressive Reaction.

Services Provided Individual Therapy; Group Therapy; Parent Involvement; Behavior Therapy; Family Therapy; Art Therapy; Music Therapy; Reality Therapy; Play Therapy. *Professionals on Staff* Psychiatrists 1; Psychologists 2; Social Workers 5; Child Care Staff 38; Nurses 1. *Service Facilities Available (with number of rooms)* Transition Rooms 1; Self-Contained Rooms 5; On-Campus Residential School 10. *Educational Professionals* Special Education Teachers 6; Paraprofessionals 6. *Curricula* Individualized; Basic Skills. *Educational Intervention Approaches* Progressive Discipline; Behavior Modification. *Degrees Awarded* Certificate of Attendance.

Comments This program provides a residential treatment for emotionally disturbed boys, with an on-campus school and clinical services.

The Children's Village

Echo and Hills, Dobbs Ferry, NY 10522 (914) 693-0600
Year Established 1851
Contact Nan Dale, Exec Dir

Facility Information *Placement* Special School; Public Residential Care. *Number of Beds* 300. *Children/Adolescents Served* 300 (residential); 24 (day students). *Sexes Served* Male. *Room and Board Fees (Approx)* $63. *Sources of Funding* State Funds; Medicaid; Contract. Summer school available. *Teacher Certification Level* Elementary School; Junior High/Middle School. *Special Certification Level* ED; Reading; Math; Special Education.

Student/Patient Characteristics *Age Levels* 0-4; 5-8; 9-11; 12-14. *IQ Ranges* 56-70; 71-85; 85-130; Above 130. *Exceptionalities Served* Emotionally Disturbed; Learning Disabled; Mentally Handicapped. *Learning Problems* Memory Disabilities; Perceptual Disabilities; Thinking Disabilities; Oral Language Disabilities; Reading Disabilities; Handwriting Disabilities; Spelling Disabilities; Arithmetic Disabilities; Written Expression. *Behavioral Problems* Attention Deficits; Hyperactivity; Impulsivity; Self-Aggression; Verbal Aggression; Physical Aggression; Indirect Aggression; Passive Aggression; Withdrawal. *Conditions Treated* Schizophrenia; Convulsive Disorders; Depression; Suicide; Asthma; Personality Problems; Socialized Aggressive Reaction; Unsocialized Aggressive Reaction.

Services Provided Individual Therapy; Group Therapy; Parent Involvement; Behavior Therapy; Family Therapy; Art Therapy; Music Therapy; Play Therapy. *Professionals on Staff* Psychiatrists 5; Psychologists 5; Social Workers 21; Child Care Staff 229; Nurses 10; Psychology Interns and Externs 10; Case Aides 4. *Service Facilities Available (with number of rooms)* Resource Rooms; Self-Contained Rooms; Special School 33. *Educational Professionals* Special Education Teachers 33; Special Education Counselors 2; Paraprofessionals 40; Physical Education; Industrial Arts; Music; Art; Library 6. *Curricula* Individualized; Basic Skills. *Educational Intervention Approaches* Self-Control; Behavior Modification; Applied Behavior Analysis; Counseling.

Clear View School

River Rd and Rte 9, Scarborough, NY 10510 (914) 941-9513
Year Established 1967
Contact Marilyn Lieberman, Dir of Admissions

Facility Information *Placement* Private Day Care. *Children/Adolescents Served* 90. *Sexes Served* Both. *Tuition Fees (Approx)* $14,399. *Sources of Funding* State Funds; P.L. 94-142; School District. Summer school available. *Teacher Certification Level* Elementary School; Junior High/Middle School; High School. *Special Certification Level* ED; MR.

Student/Patient Characteristics *Age Levels* 0-4; 5-8; 9-11; 12-14; 15-17; 18-21. *IQ Ranges* 26-40; 41-55; 56-70; 71-85; 85-130; Above 130. *Exceptionalities Served* Autistic; Emotionally Disturbed; Mentally Handicapped; Communication Disordered. *Learning Problems* Memory Disabilities; Perceptual Disabilities; Thinking Disabilities; Oral Language Disabilities; Reading Disabilities; Handwriting Disabilities; Spelling Disabilities; Arithmetic Disabilities; Written Expression. *Behavioral Problems* Attention Deficits; Hyperactivity; Hypoactivity; Impulsivity;

Self-Aggression; Verbal Aggression; Physical Aggression; Indirect Aggression; Passive Aggression; Withdrawal. *Conditions Treated* Alcohol Abuse and/or Drug Abuse; Other Substance Abuse or Dependence; Early Infantile Autism; Disintegrative Psychoses; Schizophrenia; Depression; Suicide; Personality Problems; Socialized Aggressive Reaction; Unsocialized Aggressive Reaction.

Services Provided Individual Therapy; Group Therapy; Parent Involvement; Behavior Therapy; Cognitive Developmental Therapy; Family Therapy; Filial Therapy; Art Therapy. *Professionals on Staff* Psychiatrists 1; Psychologists 1.5; Counselors 6; Social Workers 7; Nurses 1. *Educational Professionals* Special Education Teachers 30. *Curricula* Traditional Academic; Career/Vocational Education; Individualized; Basic Skills; Prevocational. *Educational Intervention Approaches* Engineered Classroom; Progressive Discipline; Self-Control; Creative Conditioning. *Degrees Awarded* Certificate of Attendance.

Convalescent Hospital for Children

2075 Scottsville Rd, Rochester, NY 14623 (716) 436-4442
Year Established 1885
Contact Sydney Koret, Pres

Facility Information *Placement* Special School; Private Residential Care; Private Day Care. *Number of Beds* 35. *Children/Adolescents Served* 1,500 (outpatient); 119 (day). *Sexes Served* Both. *Room and Board Fees (Approx)* $156. *Tuition Fees (Approx)* $10,000. *Sources of Funding* State Funds; Health Insurance; Medicaid; P.L. 94-142. Summer school available. *Teacher Certification Level* Elementary School; Junior High/Middle School; High School. *Special Certification Level* ED; LD; Reading.

Student/Patient Characteristics *Age Levels* 0-4; 5-8; 9-11; 12-14; 15-17. *IQ Ranges* 85-130; Above 130. *Exceptionalities Served* Autistic; Emotionally Disturbed; Learning Disabled. *Learning Problems* Perceptual Disabilities; Thinking Disabilities; Oral Language Disabilities; Reading Disabilities; Handwriting Disabilities; Arithmetic Disabilities; Written Expression. *Behavioral Problems* Attention Deficits; Hyperactivity; Hypoactivity; Impulsivity; Self-Aggression; Verbal Aggression; Physical Aggression; Indirect Aggression; Passive Aggression; Withdrawal. *Conditions Treated* Early Infantile Autism; Schizophrenia; Phobias; Obsessions and Compulsions; Hysteria; Depression; Inadequacy/Immaturity; Personality Problems; Socialized Aggressive Reaction; Unsocialized Aggressive Reaction.

Services Provided Individual Therapy; Group Therapy; Parent Involvement; Behavior Therapy; Family Therapy; Filial Therapy; Drug Therapy; Art Therapy; Music Therapy; Play Therapy. *Professionals on Staff* Psychiatrists 3; Psychologists 11; Social Workers 26; Child Care Staff 58; Nurses 1; Art Therapist; Audio-Visual; Dance. *Service Facilities Available (with number of rooms)* Resource Rooms 3; Self-Contained Rooms 12; On-Campus Residential School 29. *Educational Professionals* Special Education Teachers 29; Crisis Teachers 3; Paraprofessionals 26. *Curricula* Traditional Academic; Individualized; Basic Skills; Prevocational. *Educational Intervention Approaches* Engineered Classroom; Precision Teaching; Behavior Modification.

Creative Arts Rehabilitation Center Inc

251 W 51st St, New York, NY 11215 (212) 246-3113
Year Established 1958
Contact Leslie Zeigler, Dir of Social Serv

Facility Information *Placement* Rehabilitation Center. *Sexes Served* Both. *Sources of Funding* Private.

Student/Patient Characteristics *Age Levels* 0-4; 5-8; 9-11; 12-14; 15-17; 18-21; Over 21. *IQ Ranges* 85-130. *Exceptionalities Served* Autistic; Emotionally Disturbed; Mentally Handicapped; Gifted. *Learning Problems* Thinking Disabilities. *Behavioral Problems* Attention Deficits; Hyperactivity; Hypoactivity; Impulsivity; Self-Aggression; Verbal Aggression; Physical Aggression; Indirect Aggression; Passive Aggression; Withdrawal. *Conditions Treated* Schizophrenia; Phobias; Obsessions and Compulsions; Hysteria; Depression; Suicide; Asthma; Anorexia Nervosa; Inadequacy/Immaturity; Personality Problems; Socialized Aggressive Reaction.

Services Provided Individual Therapy; Group Therapy; Art Therapy; Music Therapy. *Educational Intervention Approaches* Creative Conditioning.

Education Assistance Center—Developmental Learning Program

382 Main St, Port Washington, NY 11050 (516) 883-3006
Year Established 1971
Contact Nadine Heyman, Dir Developmental Learning Prog

Facility Information *Placement* Special School. *Children/Adolescents Served* 30. *Sexes Served* Both. *Sources of Funding* P.L. 94-142. Summer school available. *Teacher Certification Level* Elementary School; Junior High/Middle School; High School. *Special Certification Level* ED; LD; MR; Reading; Math.

Student/Patient Characteristics *Age Levels* 12-14; 15-17; 18-21. *IQ Ranges* 85-130. *Exceptionalities Served* Emotionally Disturbed; Learning Disabled. *Learning Problems* Memory Disabilities; Perceptual Disabilities; Reading Disabilities; Handwriting Disabilities; Spelling Disabilities; Arithmetic Disabilities; Written Expression.

Services Provided Individual Therapy; Parent Involvement; Educational. *Professionals on Staff* Psychologists 1; Counselors 1. *Service Facilities Available (with number of rooms)* Self-Contained Rooms. *Educational Professionals* Regular School Teachers 10; Special Education Teachers 8. *Curricula* Traditional Academic; Individualized; Basic Skills. *Degrees Awarded* High School Diploma.

Educational Alliance—Camp Cummings

197 E Broadway, New York, NY 10002 (212) 475-6061
Year Established 1960
Contact Jan Morrison, Camp Dir

Facility Information *Placement* Residential Summer Camp. *Number of Beds* 250. *Children/Adolescents Served* 250. *Sexes Served* Both. *Sources of Funding* Family. *Special Certification Level* MR; Career/Vocational Education.

Student/Patient Characteristics *Age Levels* 9-11; 12-14; 15-17; 18-21; Over 21. *IQ Ranges* 41-55; 56-70; 71-85. *Exceptionalities Served* Autistic; Mentally Handicapped. *Learning Problems* Memory Disabilities; Thinking Disabilities; Oral Language Disabilities; Written Expression. *Behavioral Problems* Attention Deficits; Hyperactivity; Impulsivity; Self-Aggression; Verbal Aggression; Physical Aggression; Passive Aggression; Withdrawal. *Conditions Treated* Personality Problems; Socialized Aggressive Reaction.

Services Provided Art Therapy; Music Therapy; Play Therapy; Social Rehabilitation. *Professionals on Staff* Social Workers 2; Child Care Staff 80; Nurses 5. *Educational Professionals* Special Education Teachers 3; Career/Vocational Teachers 2; Paraprofessionals 50. *Curricula* Prevocational; Life Skills. *Educational Intervention Approaches* Behavior Modification; Creative Conditioning.

Elmcrest Children's Center

960 Salt Springs Rd, Syracuse, NY 13224 (315) 446-6250
Year Established 1845
Contact Cynthia Sullivan, Intake Social Worker

Facility Information *Placement* Private Residential Care. *Number of Beds* 75. *Children/Adolescents Served* 75. *Sexes Served* Both. *Room and Board Fees (Approx)* Varies. *Tuition Fees (Approx)* Varies. *Sources of Funding* State Funds; Medicaid; P.L. 89-313. *Teacher Certification Level* Junior High/Middle School. *Special Certification Level* ED.

Student/Patient Characteristics *Age Levels* 9-11; 12-14; 15-17. *IQ Ranges* 85-130. *Exceptionalities Served* Emotionally Disturbed; Learning Disabled. *Behavioral Problems* Attention Deficits; Hyperactivity; Impulsivity; Self-Aggression; Verbal Aggression; Physical Aggression; Indirect Aggression; Passive Aggression; Withdrawal. *Conditions Treated* Alcohol Abuse and/or Drug

Abuse; Depression; Inadequacy/Immaturity; Personality Problems; Socialized Aggressive Reaction; Unsocialized Aggressive Reaction.

Services Provided Individual Therapy; Group Therapy; Parent Involvement; Behavior Therapy; Family Therapy. *Professionals on Staff* Psychiatrists 1; Psychologists 2; Social Workers 12; Child Care Staff 80; Nurses 2; Recreation 3; Pediatrician 1. *Service Facilities Available (with number of rooms)* Self-Contained Rooms 1; On-Campus Residential School 1; Homebound Instruction 2. *Educational Professionals* Special Education Teachers 2. *Curricula* Traditional Academic; Individualized; Basic Skills. *Educational Intervention Approaches* Self-Control; Behavior Modification.

Comments Elmcrest provides residential child care including: short-term diagnostic evaluation units, long-term group homes, boarding homes, and foster care. Family and court referred residents may include delinquents, status offenders, surrendered, abused, neglected, and emotionally disturbed children. The majority attend public school settings.

Fairmount Children's Center

Box 69, Belle Isle Rd, Syracuse, NY 13209 (315) 487-8431
Year Established 1967
Contact Ann E Badger, Dir

Facility Information *Placement* Childrens Day Treatment and Outpatient Center. *Children/Adolescents Served* 50 (day treatment); 400 (outpatient). *Sexes Served* Both. *Sources of Funding* State Funds; Health Insurance; Medicaid; Local Funds. Summer school available. *Teacher Certification Level* Elementary School. *Special Certification Level* ED.

Student/Patient Characteristics *Age Levels* 0-4; 5-8; 9-11; 12-14; 15-17; 18-21. *IQ Ranges* 0-25; 26-40; 41-55; 56-70; 71-85; 85-130; Above 130. *Exceptionalities Served* Emotionally Disturbed. *Learning Problems* Memory Disabilities; Perceptual Disabilities; Thinking Disabilities; Oral Language Disabilities; Reading Disabilities; Handwriting Disabilities; Spelling Disabilities; Arithmetic Disabilities; Written Expression. *Behavioral Problems* Attention Deficits; Hyperactivity; Hypoactivity; Impulsivity; Self-Aggression; Verbal Aggression; Physical Aggression; Indirect Aggression; Passive Aggression; Withdrawal. *Conditions Treated* Schizophrenia; Convulsive Disorders; Phobias; Obsessions and Compulsions; Hysteria; Depression; Suicide; Inadequacy/Immaturity; Personality Problems; Socialized Aggressive Reaction; Unsocialized Aggressive Reaction.

Services Provided Individual Therapy; Group Therapy; Parent Involvement; Behavior Therapy; Cognitive Developmental Therapy; Family Therapy; Drug Therapy; Play Therapy. *Professionals on Staff* Psychiatrists 1; Psychologists 2.5; Social Workers 14; Child Care Staff 24; Nurses 2; Speech Pathologist 1. *Service Facilities Available (with number of rooms)* Resource Rooms 1; Self-Contained Rooms 9; Special School 7; Public School Class 1. *Educational Professionals* Special Education Teachers 8; Paraprofessionals 25. *Curricula* Traditional Academic; Individualized; Basic Skills. *Educational Intervention Approaches* Precision Teaching; Progressive Discipline; Self-Control; Behavior Modification; Psychoeducational Milieu Therapy.

Four Winds Hospital—Adolescent Services

800 Cross River Rd, Katonah, NY 10536 (914) 763-8151
Year Established 1979
Contact Martin A Buccolo, Dir of Adolescent Serv
Facility Information *Placement* Private Hospital. *Number of Beds* 27. *Children/Adolescents Served* 45. *Sexes Served* Both. *Room and Board Fees (Approx)* $530. *Sources of Funding* Health Insurance; Medicaid. Summer school available. *Teacher Certification Level* Junior High/Middle School; High School. *Special Certification Level* LD.
Student/Patient Characteristics *Age Levels* 12-14; 15-17; 18-21. *Exceptionalities Served* Emotionally Disturbed. *Behavioral Problems* Attention Deficits; Hyperactivity; Hypoactivity; Impulsivity; Self-Aggression; Verbal Aggression; Physical Aggression; Indirect Aggression; Passive Aggression; Withdrawal. *Conditions*

Treated Alcohol Abuse and/or Drug Abuse; Other Substance Abuse or Dependence; Depression; Suicide; Anorexia Nervosa; Personality Problems; Socialized Aggressive Reaction.

Services Provided Individual Therapy; Group Therapy; Parent Involvement; Behavior Therapy; Family Therapy; Filial Therapy; Drug Therapy; Art Therapy; Psychodrama. *Professionals on Staff* Psychiatrists 2; Psychologists 3; Social Workers 2; Child Care Staff 25; Nurses 15; Art Therapist; Recreational Therapist; Alcohol and Drug Counselor; Psychodramatist. *Service Facilities Available (with number of rooms)* Hospital School 8. *Educational Professionals* Special Education Teachers 8. *Curricula* Traditional Academic; Individualized; Basic Skills; GED Preparation. *Educational Intervention Approaches* Self-Control; Behavior Modification; Applied Behavior Analysis.

Comments Four Winds is a private psychiatric hospital in a rural setting, with two adolescent units housed in separate "cottages." Treatment emphasizes milieu therapy and positive peer pressure. Due to the open treatment setting, pre-admission interviews are necessary to assess the patient and family willingness to work and change.

Gateway United Methodist Youth Center and Family Services

6350 Main St, Williamsville, NY 14221 (716) 633-7266
Year Established 1890
Contact Howard Weisz, Pres

Facility Information *Placement* Private Residential Care. *Number of Beds* 58. *Children/Adolescents Served* 58 (residential); 60 (special education school). *Sexes Served* Both. *Room and Board Fees (Approx)* $66. *Sources of Funding* State Funds; Medicare; P.L. 94-142; County Contracts. *Special Certification Level* ED; LD; Reading.

Student/Patient Characteristics *Age Levels* 9-11; 12-14; 15-17. *IQ Ranges* 71-85; 85-130. *Exceptionalities Served* Emotionally Disturbed; Learning Disabled. *Learning Problems* Memory Disabilities; Perceptual Disabilities; Oral Language Disabilities; Reading Disabilities; Arithmetic Disabilities; Written Expression. *Behavioral Problems* Attention Deficits; Hyperactivity; Impulsivity; Self-Aggression; Verbal Aggression; Physical Aggression; Passive Aggression. *Conditions Treated* Phobias; Depression; Inadequacy/Immaturity; Personality Problems; Unsocialized Aggressive Reaction.

Services Provided Individual Therapy; Group Therapy; Parent Involvement; Behavior Therapy; Family Therapy; Art Therapy; Reality Therapy; Dance Therapy. *Professionals on Staff* Psychiatrists 1; Psychologists 1; Social Workers 9; Child Care Staff 38; Nurses 1; Foster Care Specialist 1. *Service Facilities Available (with number of rooms)* Resource Rooms 1; Self-Contained Rooms 7; On-Campus Residential School 10. *Educational Professionals* Special Education Teachers 8; Crisis Teachers 3. *Curricula* Career/Vocational Education; Individualized; Basic Skills; Prevocational. *Educational Intervention Approaches* Progressive Discipline; Self-Control; Behavior Modification.

The George Junior Republic Association Inc

Freeville, NY 13068 (607) 844-8613
Year Established 1895
Contact Frank Speno, Exec Dir

Facility Information *Placement* Public School; Special School; Private Residential Care. *Number of Beds* 170. *Children/Adolescents Served* 115 (boys); 55 (girls). *Sexes Served* Both. *Sources of Funding* P.L. 94-142; Private Donations; Fund Raising; Public; Social; Parents. Summer school available. *Teacher Certification Level* Junior High/Middle School; High School. *Special Certification Level* ED; LD; Career/Vocational Education; Reading; Math; Social Studies.

Student/Patient Characteristics *Age Levels* 12-14; 15-17. *IQ Ranges* 71-85; 85-130; Above 130. *Exceptionalities Served* Emotionally Disturbed; Learning Disabled; Gifted; Juvenile Offenders. *Learning Problems* Memory Disabilities; Perceptual Disabilities; Thinking Disabilities; Oral Language Disabilities; Reading Disabilities; Handwriting Disabilities; Spelling Disabilities;

Arithmetic Disabilities; Written Expression. *Behavioral Problems* Attention Deficits; Hyperactivity; Impulsivity; Verbal Aggression; Indirect Aggression; Passive Aggression; Withdrawal. *Conditions Treated* Aphasia; Convulsive Disorders; Obsessions and Compulsions; Depression; Inadequacy/Immaturity; Personality Problems; Unsocialized Aggressive Reaction; Without Mental Illness.

Services Provided Individual Therapy; Group Therapy; Family Therapy. *Professionals on Staff* Psychiatrists 1; Psychologists 1; Counselors; Social Workers 15; Child Care Staff 155; Nurses; Physician; Dentist; Dental Hygienist. *Service Facilities Available (with number of rooms)* Self-Contained Rooms 17; Job. *Educational Professionals* Regular School Teachers; Special Education Teachers; Career/Vocational Teachers; Speech and Language Pathologist. *Curricula* Traditional Academic; Career/Vocational Education; Individualized; Basic Skills; Prevocational. *Educational Intervention Approaches* Self-Control; Practical Living. *Degrees Awarded* High School Diploma; Graduate Equivalency Diploma; Earn High School Credits.

Glens Falls Hospital—Child and Family Services—Community Mental Health Center

80 Park St, Glens Falls, NY 12801 (518) 761-5321
Contact Patrick Cavanagh, Dir Child and Family Serv

Facility Information *Placement* Outpatient Treatment. *Sexes Served* Both. *Sources of Funding* State Funds; Health Insurance; Medicaid.

Student/Patient Characteristics *Age Levels* 0-4; 5-8; 9-11; 12-14; 15-17. *IQ Ranges* 85-130; Above 130. *Exceptionalities Served* Emotionally Disturbed. *Learning Problems* Memory Disabilities; Perceptual Disabilities; Thinking Disabilities. *Behavioral Problems* Attention Deficits; Hyperactivity; Hypoactivity; Impulsivity; Self-Aggression; Verbal Aggression; Physical Aggression; Indirect Aggression; Passive Aggression; Withdrawal. *Conditions Treated* Disintegrative Psychoses; Schizophrenia; Aphasia; Phobias; Obsessions and Compulsions; Hysteria; Depression; Suicide; Asthma; Anorexia Nervosa; Inadequacy/Immaturity; Personality Problems; Socialized Aggressive Reaction; Unsocialized Aggressive Reaction.

Services Provided Individual Therapy; Group Therapy; Parent Involvement; Behavior Therapy; Cognitive Developmental Therapy; Family Therapy; Filial Therapy; Drug Therapy; Reality Therapy; Play Therapy. *Professionals on Staff* Psychiatrists .5; Psychologists 1; Social Workers 2. *Service Facilities Available (with number of rooms)* Play Room 1.

Green Chimneys Children's Services Inc

Putnam Lake Rd, Brewster, NY 10509 (914) 279-2995
Year Established 1947
Contact Myra M Ross, Clinical Coord and Dir of Admissions

Facility Information *Placement* Private Residential Care. *Number of Beds* 139. *Children/Adolescents Served* 139. *Sexes Served* Both. *Room and Board Fees (Approx)* $66. *Tuition Fees (Approx)* $8,241 (10 months); $1,962 (2 summer months). *Sources of Funding* State Funds; Medicaid; P.L. 94-142; Donations. Summer school available. *Teacher Certification Level* Elementary School; Junior High/Middle School. *Special Certification Level* ED; LD; Career/Vocational Education; Reading; Math.

Student/Patient Characteristics *Age Levels* 5-8; 9-11; 12-14; 15-17; 18-21. *IQ Ranges* 56-70; 71-85; 85-130. *Exceptionalities Served* Emotionally Disturbed; Learning Disabled; Mentally Handicapped; Communication Disordered; Neurologically Impaired. *Learning Problems* Memory Disabilities; Perceptual Disabilities; Thinking Disabilities; Oral Language Disabilities; Reading Disabilities; Handwriting Disabilities; Spelling Disabilities; Arithmetic Disabilities; Written Expression; Motor Disabilities. *Behavioral Problems* Attention Deficits; Hyperactivity; Hypoactivity; Impulsivity; Self-Aggression; Verbal Aggression; Physical Aggression; Indirect Aggression; Passive Aggression; Withdrawal. *Conditions Treated* Schizophrenia; Convulsive Disorders; Phobias; Obsessions and Compulsions; Hysteria; Depression; Sui-

cide; Inadequacy/Immaturity; Personality Problems; Socialized Aggressive Reaction; Unsocialized Aggressive Reaction; Organic Brain Syndrome.

Services Provided Individual Therapy; Group Therapy; Parent Involvement; Behavior Therapy; Family Therapy; Filial Therapy; Drug Therapy; Art Therapy; Music Therapy; Reality Therapy; Play Therapy; Psychodrama; Pet Facilitated Therapy. *Professionals on Staff* Psychiatrists 4; Psychologists 2; Social Workers 14; Child Care Staff 70; Nurses 10; Consultative. *Service Facilities Available (with number of rooms)* Consultative (ERT); Resource Rooms; Transition Rooms; Self-Contained Rooms; On-Campus Residential School; Working; Instructional Farm. *Educational Professionals* Special Education Teachers; Career/Vocational Teachers; Crisis Teachers; Special Education Counselors; Paraprofessionals. *Curricula* Career/Vocational Education; Individualized; Basic Skills; Prevocational. *Educational Intervention Approaches* Self-Control; Behavior Modification; Experiential. *Degrees Awarded* Graduate Equivalency Diploma.

Comments Green Chimneys is a voluntary, non-sectarian, multi-service agency dedicated to the development of basic education and daily living skills in each individual. The goal is to strengthen and restore the emotional health and well-being of children and families.

Hawthorne Cedar Knolls School

226 Linda Ave, Hawthorne, NY 10532 (914) 769-2790
Contact Norman E Friedman, Dir

Facility Information *Placement* Private Residential Care. *Number of Beds* 175. *Children/Adolescents Served* 175. *Sexes Served* Both. *Room and Board Fees (Approx)* $82. *Tuition Fees (Approx)* $12,087. *Sources of Funding* State Funds; Medicaid. Summer school available. *Teacher Certification Level* Junior High/Middle School; High School. *Special Certification Level* ED; LD; Career/Vocational Education; Reading; Math; Cosmetology; Business Education; Remedial Education; Special Education.

Student/Patient Characteristics *Age Levels* 9-11; 12-14; 15-17; 18-21. *IQ Ranges* 56-70; 71-85; 85-130; Above 130. *Exceptionalities Served* Emotionally Disturbed; Learning Disabled; Mentally Handicapped. *Learning Problems* Perceptual Disabilities; Thinking Disabilities; Reading Disabilities; Spelling Disabilities; Arithmetic Disabilities. *Behavioral Problems* Attention Deficits; Hyperactivity; Impulsivity; Self-Aggression; Verbal Aggression; Physical Aggression; Indirect Aggression; Passive Aggression; Withdrawal. *Conditions Treated* Depression; Asthma; Inadequacy/Immaturity; Personality Problems; Socialized Aggressive Reaction; Unsocialized Aggressive Reaction.

Services Provided Individual Therapy; Group Therapy; Parent Involvement; Family Therapy; Drug Therapy; Art Therapy; Play Therapy. *Professionals on Staff* Psychiatrists; Psychologists; Social Workers; Child Care Staff; Nurses. *Service Facilities Available (with number of rooms)* Self-Contained Rooms; On-Campus Residential School. *Educational Professionals* Regular School Teachers; Special Education Teachers 46; Career/Vocational Teachers; Crisis Teachers 7; Special Education Counselors; Paraprofessionals 10. *Curricula* Traditional Academic; Career/Vocational Education; Individualized; Basic Skills; Prevocational. *Educational Intervention Approaches* Behavior Modification; Applied Behavior Analysis; Creative Conditioning.

Hillside Children's Center

1183 Monroe Ave, Rochester, NY 14620 (716) 473-5150
Year Established 1837
Contact Barbara Conradt, Intake Dir

Facility Information *Placement* Special School; Private Residential Care; Community Based Group Home. *Number of Beds* 148. *Children/Adolescents Served* 507. *Sexes Served* Both. *Room and Board Fees (Approx)* $63. *Tuition Fees (Approx)* $5,500. *Sources of Funding* State Funds; HEW; Medicaid. Summer school available. *Teacher Certification Level* Elementary School; Junior High/Middle School; High School. *Special Certification Level* ED; LD; Reading; Math.

Student/Patient Characteristics *Age Levels* 5-8; 9-11; 12-14; 15-17. *IQ Ranges* 56-70; 71-85; 85-130; Above 130. *Exceptionalities Served* Emotionally Disturbed; Learning Disabled; Mentally Handicapped; Communication Disordered; Hearing Impaired/Deaf. *Learning Problems* Perceptual Disabilities; Thinking Disabilities; Oral Language Disabilities; Reading Disabilities; Handwriting Disabilities; Spelling Disabilities; Arithmetic Disabilities; Written Expression. *Behavioral Problems* Attention Deficits; Hyperactivity; Impulsivity; Self-Aggression; Verbal Aggression; Physical Aggression; Indirect Aggression; Passive Aggression; Withdrawal. *Conditions Treated* Alcohol Abuse and/or Drug Abuse; Schizophrenia; Convulsive Disorders; Phobias; Obsessions and Compulsions; Hysteria; Depression; Suicide; Asthma; Anorexia Nervosa; Personality Problems; Socialized Aggressive Reaction; Unsocialized Aggressive Reaction.

Services Provided Individual Therapy; Group Therapy; Parent Involvement; Behavior Therapy; Family Therapy; Art Therapy; Music Therapy; Play Therapy; Psychodrama; Dance Therapy. *Professionals on Staff* Psychiatrists 2; Psychologists 3; Social Workers 55; Child Care Staff 130; Nurses 4; Art Therapist 1; Dance Therapist 1. *Service Facilities Available (with number of rooms)* Resource Rooms 5; On-Campus Residential School 12. *Educational Professionals* Special Education Teachers 12; Crisis Teachers 2; Paraprofessionals 12. *Curricula* Traditional Academic; Basic Skills; Prevocational. *Educational Intervention Approaches* Precision Teaching; Progressive Discipline; Self-Control; Behavior Modification; Applied Behavior Analysis.

Comments Hillside is a multi-service agency providing in-home and out-of-home services to emotionally and behaviorally disturbed children and their families.

Ittleson Center for Child Research

5050 Iselin Ave, New York, NY 10471 (212) 549-6700
Contact Marilyn Tamarin, Asst Dir

Facility Information *Placement* Day Treatment; Residential Care. *Number of Beds* 28. *Children/Adolescents Served* 28 (residence); 26 (day treatment). *Sexes Served* Both. *Room and Board Fees (Approx)* $141. *Sources of Funding* Medicaid; Day Treatment; Private Fees. *Teacher Certification Level* Elementary School. *Special Certification Level* ED.

Student/Patient Characteristics *Age Levels* 5-8; 9-11. *IQ Ranges* 56-70; 71-85; 85-130; Above 130. *Exceptionalities Served* Emotionally Disturbed; Learning Disabled; Communication Disordered. *Learning Problems* Perceptual Disabilities. *Behavioral Problems* Attention Deficits; Hyperactivity; Impulsivity; Self-Aggression; Verbal Aggression; Physical Aggression; Indirect Aggression; Passive Aggression; Withdrawal. *Conditions Treated* Early Infantile Autism; Schizophrenia; Phobias; Obsessions and Compulsions; Hysteria; Depression; Personality Problems; Unsocialized Aggressive Reaction; Pervasive Developmental Disorders.

Services Provided Individual Therapy; Group Therapy; Parent Involvement; Family Therapy; Drug Therapy; Art Therapy; Music Therapy. *Professionals on Staff* Psychiatrists 3; Psychologists 2; Counselors 23; Social Workers 5; Child Care Staff 23; Nurses 2. *Service Facilities Available (with number of rooms)* Consultative (ERT) 8; On-Campus Residential School 8. *Educational Professionals* Special Education Teachers 40; Paraprofessionals 6. *Curricula* Traditional Academic; Individualized; Basic Skills; Prevocational. *Educational Intervention Approaches* Self-Control; Behavior Modification.

Jennie Clarkson Child Care Services Inc—St Christopher's

71 Broadway, Dobbs Ferry, NY 10522 (914) 693-3030
Year Established 1881
Contact William H Bennington, Exec Dir

Facility Information *Placement* Private Residential Care. *Number of Beds* 150. *Sexes Served* Both. *Tuition Fees (Approx)* $30,000. *Sources of Funding* Medicaid. Summer school available. *Teacher Certification Level* Elementary School. *Special Certification Level* ED; LD; Reading; Math.

Student/Patient Characteristics *Age Levels* 12-14; 15-17. *IQ Ranges* 71-85. *Exceptionalities Served* Emotionally Disturbed; Learning Disabled; Mentally Handicapped. *Learning Problems* Memory Disabilities; Perceptual Disabilities; Thinking Disabilities; Oral Language Disabilities; Reading Disabilities; Handwriting Disabilities; Spelling Disabilities; Arithmetic Disabilities; Written Expression. *Behavioral Problems* Attention Deficits; Hyperactivity; Hypoactivity; Impulsivity; Self-Aggression; Verbal Aggression; Physical Aggression; Indirect Aggression; Passive Aggression; Withdrawal. *Conditions Treated* Disintegrative Psychoses; Depression; Inadequacy/Immaturity; Personality Problems; Socialized Aggressive Reaction; Unsocialized Aggressive Reaction.

Services Provided Individual Therapy; Group Therapy; Parent Involvement; Behavior Therapy; Family Therapy. *Service Facilities Available (with number of rooms)* Special School 15. *Educational Professionals* Special Education Teachers; Career/Vocational Teachers; Crisis Teachers; Special Education Counselors; Paraprofessionals. *Curricula* Career/Vocational Education; Individualized; Basic Skills; Prevocational. *Educational Intervention Approaches* Behavior Modification. *Degrees Awarded* Certificate of Attendance; High School Diploma.

Jewish Board of Family and Children Services—Linden Hill School

500 Linda Ave, Hawthorne, NY 10532 (914) 769-3206
Year Established 1950
Contact Maureen DeBiccari, Clinical Admin

Facility Information *Placement* Private Residential Care. *Number of Beds* 55. *Children/Adolescents Served* 65. *Sexes Served* Both. *Tuition Fees (Approx)* $52,000. *Sources of Funding* Health Insurance; Medicaid. Summer school available. *Teacher Certification Level* Junior High/Middle School; High School. *Special Certification Level* ED; LD; Reading; Math.

Student/Patient Characteristics *Age Levels* 12-14; 15-17; 18-21. *IQ Ranges* 71-85; 85-130; Above 130. *Exceptionalities Served* Emotionally Disturbed; Learning Disabled. *Learning Problems* Perceptual Disabilities; Thinking Disabilities; Reading Disabilities; Handwriting Disabilities; Spelling Disabilities; Arithmetic Disabilities; Written Expression. *Behavioral Problems* Attention Deficits; Hyperactivity; Impulsivity; Self-Aggression; Verbal Aggression; Passive Aggression; Withdrawal. *Conditions Treated* Schizophrenia; Depression; Suicide; Inadequacy/Immaturity; Personality Problems.

Services Provided Individual Therapy; Group Therapy; Parent Involvement; Family Therapy. *Professionals on Staff* Psychiatrists 3; Psychologists 2; Social Workers 8; Child Care Staff 26; Nurses 2. *Service Facilities Available (with number of rooms)* Resource Rooms; Self-Contained Rooms; Special School; On-Campus Residential School. *Educational Professionals* Regular School Teachers; Special Education Teachers; Special Education Counselors; Paraprofessionals. *Curricula* Traditional Academic; Career/Vocational Education; Individualized; Basic Skills; Prevocational. *Degrees Awarded* High School Diploma; Graduate Equivalency Diploma.

Jewish Child Care Association—Pleasantville Cottage School

PO Box 237, Pleasantville, NY 10570 (914) 769-0164
Year Established 1912
Contact Alex Cohen, Dir Special Prog

Facility Information *Placement* Private Residential Care. *Number of Beds* 182. *Children/Adolescents Served* 182. *Sexes Served* Both. *Room and Board Fees (Approx)* $73. *Tuition Fees (Approx)* $13,000. *Sources of Funding* State Funds; Medicaid. Summer school available. *Teacher Certification Level* Elementary School; Junior High/Middle School; High School. *Special Certification Level* ED; LD; Reading; Math.

Student/Patient Characteristics *Age Levels* 5-8; 9-11; 12-14; 15-17. *IQ Ranges* 71-85; 85-130. *Exceptionalities Served* Emotionally Disturbed; Learning Disabled. *Learning Problems* Memory Disabilities; Perceptual Disabilities; Thinking Disabilities;

Oral Language Disabilities; Reading Disabilities; Handwriting Disabilities; Spelling Disabilities; Arithmetic Disabilities; Written Expression. *Behavioral Problems* Attention Deficits; Hyperactivity; Impulsivity; Self-Aggression; Verbal Aggression; Physical Aggression; Indirect Aggression; Passive Aggression; Withdrawal. *Conditions Treated* Schizophrenia; Phobias; Obsessions and Compulsions; Hysteria; Depression; Suicide; Anorexia Nervosa; Inadequacy/Immaturity; Personality Problems; Socialized Aggressive Reaction; Unsocialized Aggressive Reaction.

Services Provided Individual Therapy; Group Therapy; Parent Involvement; Behavior Therapy; Family Therapy; Art Therapy; Music Therapy; Reality Therapy; Play Therapy. *Professionals on Staff* Psychiatrists 5; Psychologists 5; Social Workers 16; Child Care Staff 63; Nurses 6. *Service Facilities Available (with number of rooms)* Consultative (ERT) 2; Resource Rooms 2; Self-Contained Rooms 1. *Educational Professionals* Special Education Teachers 40; Crisis Teachers 2; Paraprofessionals 20. *Curricula* Traditional Academic; Career/Vocational Education; Individualized; Basic Skills; Prevocational. *Educational Intervention Approaches* Engineered Classroom; Precision Teaching; Progressive Discipline; Self-Control; Behavior Modification. *Degrees Awarded* Certificate of Attendance; Graduate Equivalency Diploma.

Jewish Child Care Association—Youth Residence Center

217 E 87th St, New York, NY 10128 (212) 427-6655
Contact Kenneth Miller, Dir

Facility Information *Placement* Private Residential Care. *Number of Beds* 40. *Children/Adolescents Served* 40. *Sexes Served* Both. *Tuition Fees (Approx)* $25,000. *Sources of Funding* State Funds.

Student/Patient Characteristics *Age Levels* 15-17; 18-21. *IQ Ranges* 71-85; 85-130. *Exceptionalities Served* Emotionally Disturbed. *Learning Problems* Thinking Disabilities; Reading Disabilities. *Behavioral Problems* Attention Deficits; Impulsivity; Self-Aggression; Passive Aggression; Withdrawal. *Conditions Treated* Schizophrenia; Obsessions and Compulsions; Depression; Anorexia Nervosa; Ulcerative Colitis; Personality Problems; Socialized Aggressive Reaction.

Services Provided Individual Therapy; Group Therapy; Parent Involvement. *Professionals on Staff* Psychiatrists 1; Social Workers 3; Child Care Staff 12; Social Workers 2.

Comments The major focus is to provide adolescents with skills to live independently in the community while involved in treatment.

Jowonio School

215 Bassett St, Syracuse, NY 13210 (315) 479-7744
Year Established 1969
Contact Ellen B Barnes, Dir

Facility Information *Placement* Nonpublic Mainstreamed Day Program. *Children/Adolescents Served* 28 (special needs); 44 (typical). *Sexes Served* Both. *Tuition Fees (Approx)* $9,714 (special needs). *Sources of Funding* State Funds; HEW; County; Parent Tuition. Summer school available. *Teacher Certification Level* Elementary School. *Special Certification Level* Generic Special Education.

Student/Patient Characteristics *Age Levels* 0-4; 5-8. *Exceptionalities Served* Autistic; Emotionally Disturbed; Mentally Handicapped; Communication Disordered; Other Health Impaired; Multiply Handicapped. *Learning Problems* Memory Disabilities; Perceptual Disabilities; Thinking Disabilities; Oral Language Disabilities; Reading Disabilities; Fine and Gross Motor Disabilities. *Behavioral Problems* Attention Deficits; Hyperactivity; Hypoactivity; Impulsivity; Self-Aggression; Physical Aggression; Withdrawal. *Conditions Treated* Early Infantile Autism; Aphasia; Convulsive Disorders.

Services Provided Parent Involvement; Cognitive Developmental Therapy. *Professionals on Staff* Psychologists 2. *Service Facilities Available (with number of rooms)* Resource Rooms 1; Mainstream Classrooms 5. *Educational Professionals* Special Educa-

tion Teachers 8; Paraprofessionals 2; Speech Therapists 2; Occupational Therapist 1; Physical Therapist 1. *Curricula* Individualized. *Educational Intervention Approaches* Developmental Therapy. *Degrees Awarded* Certificate of Attendance.

Comments It provides a mainstreamed educational program for young autistic and emotionally handicapped students. The perspective is a developmental one. Children are transitioned into appropriate school programs.

Kings County Hospital—Downstate Medical Center—Division of Child and Adolescent Psychiatry

451 Clarkson Ave J Bldg, Brooklyn, NY 11203 (718) 735-2481
Year Established 1940
Contact Adolph E Christ, MD

Facility Information *Placement* Acute Inpatient Hospital. *Number of Beds* 50. *Children/Adolescents Served* 50. *Sexes Served* Both. *Room and Board Fees (Approx)* $450. *Sources of Funding* Health Insurance; Medicaid. . *Teacher Certification Level* Elementary School; Junior High/Middle School. *Special Certification Level* ED; LD; Reading.

Student/Patient Characteristics *Age Levels* 5-8; 9-11; 12-14; 15-17. *IQ Ranges* 56-70; 71-85; 85-130. *Exceptionalities Served* Autistic; Emotionally Disturbed; Learning Disabled; Mentally Handicapped. *Learning Problems* Perceptual Disabilities; Thinking Disabilities; Oral Language Disabilities; Reading Disabilities; Arithmetic Disabilities; Written Expression. *Behavioral Problems* Attention Deficits; Hyperactivity; Hypoactivity; Impulsivity; Self-Aggression; Physical Aggression; Indirect Aggression; Passive Aggression; Withdrawal. *Conditions Treated* Schizophrenia; Convulsive Disorders; Phobias; Obsessions and Compulsions; Hysteria; Depression; Suicide; Asthma; Anorexia Nervosa; Ulcerative Colitis; Inadequacy/Immaturity; Personality Problems; Socialized Aggressive Reaction; Unsocialized Aggressive Reaction.

Services Provided Individual Therapy; Group Therapy; Parent Involvement; Behavior Therapy; Cognitive Developmental Therapy; Family Therapy; Filial Therapy; Drug Therapy; Art Therapy; Music Therapy; Reality Therapy; Play Therapy. *Professionals on Staff* Psychiatrists 10; Psychologists 15; Counselors 10; Social Workers 30; Child Care Staff 15; Nurses 50. *Service Facilities Available (with number of rooms)* Consultative (ERT); Self-Contained Rooms; Hospital School. *Educational Professionals* Regular School Teachers 10; Special Education Teachers 5; Career/Vocational Teachers 1; Special Education Counselors 1; Paraprofessionals 10. *Curricula* Traditional Academic; Basic Skills; Prevocational. *Educational Intervention Approaches* Engineered Classroom; Precision Teaching; Progressive Discipline; Behavior Modification; Applied Behavior Analysis. *Degrees Awarded* Certificate of Attendance.

Comments KCH/DMC provides an inpatient hospital program and outpatient programs for children and adolescents who are emotionally disturbed, developmentally disabled, and physically or sexually abused.

Lake Grove School

PO Box L, Moriches Rd, Lake Grove, NY 11755 (516) 585-8776
Year Established 1941
Contact Albert A Brayson II, Exec Dir

Facility Information *Placement* Special School; Private Residential Care. *Number of Beds* 60. *Children/Adolescents Served* 60. *Sexes Served* Both. *Sources of Funding* State Funds; Medicaid; P.L. 94-142. Summer school available. *Teacher Certification Level* High School. *Special Certification Level* ED; LD; MR; Career/Vocational Education; Reading Deaf Education.

Student/Patient Characteristics *Age Levels* 12-14; 15-17; 18-21; Over 21. *IQ Ranges* 0-25; 26-40; 41-55; 56-70; 71-85; 85-130. *Exceptionalities Served* Autistic; Emotionally Disturbed; Learning Disabled; Hearing Impaired/Deaf. *Learning Problems* Memory Disabilities; Perceptual Disabilities; Thinking Disabilities; Oral Language Disabilities; Reading Disabilities; Handwriting Disabilities; Spelling Disabilities; Arithmetic Disabilities; Written Expression. *Behavioral Problems* Attention Deficits; Hyperactivity;

Impulsivity; Self-Aggression; Verbal Aggression; Physical Aggression; Indirect Aggression; Passive Aggression; Withdrawal. *Conditions Treated* Early Infantile Autism; Schizophrenia; Convulsive Disorders; Obsessions and Compulsions; Depression; Suicide; Asthma; Inadequacy/Immaturity; Personality Problems; Socialized Aggressive Reaction; Unsocialized Aggressive Reaction.

Services Provided Individual Therapy; Group Therapy; Parent Involvement; Behavior Therapy; Family Therapy; Drug Therapy; Reality Therapy. *Professionals on Staff* Psychiatrists 1; Psychologists 2; Social Workers 3; Child Care Staff 30; Nurses 1. *Service Facilities Available (with number of rooms)* Resource Rooms 1; Self-Contained Rooms 8. *Educational Professionals* Special Education Teachers 12; Career/Vocational Teachers 2; Crisis Teachers 2; Paraprofessionals 15. *Curricula* Traditional Academic; Career/Vocational Education; Individualized; Basic Skills; Prevocational; Library; Computer. *Educational Intervention Approaches* Precision Teaching; Progressive Discipline; Self-Control; Behavior Modification. *Degrees Awarded* Certificate of Attendance; High School Diploma.

Comments Lake Grove School is a mixed program with both hearing and deaf emotionally disturbed students. Development of communication skills is emphasized.

LaSalle School

391 Western Ave, Albany, NY 12203 (518) 489-4731
Contact Br Casimir, Educ Dir
Facility Information *Placement* Private Residential Care. *Number of Beds* 108. *Children/Adolescents Served* 165. *Sexes Served* Male. *Room and Board Fees (Approx)* $66. *Tuition Fees (Approx)* $8,165. *Sources of Funding* State Funds; Medicaid; P.L. 94-142. Summer school available. *Teacher Certification Level* Junior High/Middle School; High School. *Special Certification Level* ED; LD; Reading; Math; Social Studies; Science; Industrial Arts; Fine Arts.

Student/Patient Characteristics *Age Levels* 12-14; 15-17; 18-21. *IQ Ranges* 85-130. *Exceptionalities Served* Emotionally Disturbed. *Learning Problems* Memory Disabilities; Perceptual Disabilities; Thinking Disabilities; Oral Language Disabilities; Reading Disabilities; Handwriting Disabilities; Spelling Disabilities; Arithmetic Disabilities; Written Expression. *Behavioral Problems* Attention Deficits; Hyperactivity; Hypoactivity; Impulsivity; Self-Aggression; Verbal Aggression; Physical Aggression; Indirect Aggression; Passive Aggression; Withdrawal. *Conditions Treated* Alcohol Abuse and/or Drug Abuse; Other Substance Abuse or Dependence; Depression; Suicide; Asthma; Inadequacy/Immaturity; Personality Problems; Socialized Aggressive Reaction; Unsocialized Aggressive Reaction.

Services Provided Individual Therapy; Group Therapy; Parent Involvement; Behavior Therapy; Cognitive Developmental Therapy; Family Therapy; Drug Therapy; Art Therapy; Music Therapy; Reality Therapy. *Professionals on Staff* Psychiatrists 2; Psychologists 3; Counselors 4; Social Workers 18; Child Care Staff 34; Nurses 3. *Service Facilities Available (with number of rooms)* Resource Rooms 2; On-Campus Residential School 30. *Educational Professionals* Special Education Teachers 34. *Curricula* Traditional Academic; Career/Vocational Education; Individualized; Basic Skills; Prevocational. *Educational Intervention Approaches* Behavior Modification. *Degrees Awarded* High School Diploma.

Comments La Salle serves the needs of young men who are experiencing difficulties at home, in school, or in the community. The goal is to develop within each student the skills necessary for self-reliance and responsible participation in his home and community.

The League School

567 Kingston Ave, Brooklyn, NY 11203 (718) 498-2500
Year Established 1953
Contact Elaine K Thompson, Dir
Facility Information *Placement* Special School.
Children/Adolescents Served 120. *Sexes Served* Both. *Sources of Funding* State Funds; HEW; Medicaid; P.L. 94-142. Summer

school available. *Teacher Certification Level* Elementary School; Junior High/Middle School; High School. *Special Certification Level* ED; MR; Career/Vocational Education.
Student/Patient Characteristics *Age Levels* 0-4; 5-8; 9-11; 12-14; 15-17; 18-21. *IQ Ranges* 26-40; 41-55; 56-70; 71-85; 85-130. *Exceptionalities Served* Autistic; Emotionally Disturbed; Mentally Handicapped; Communication Disordered. *Learning Problems* Memory Disabilities; Thinking Disabilities; Oral Language Disabilities; Reading Disabilities; Handwriting Disabilities; Spelling Disabilities; Arithmetic Disabilities; Written Expression. *Behavioral Problems* Attention Deficits; Hyperactivity; Hypoactivity; Impulsivity; Self-Aggression; Verbal Aggression; Physical Aggression; Indirect Aggression; Passive Aggression; Withdrawal.

Lifeline Center for Child Development Inc

80-09 Winchester Blvd, Queens Village, NY 11427
(718) 740-4300
Year Established 1959
Contact Ethel S Wyner, Exec Dir
Facility Information *Placement* Day Treatment Center.
Children/Adolescents Served 130. *Sexes Served* Both. Summer school available. *Special Certification Level* Special Education.
Student/Patient Characteristics *Age Levels* 0-4; 5-8; 9-11; 12-14; 15-17. *Exceptionalities Served* Emotionally Disturbed.

Services Provided Individual Therapy; Group Therapy; Parent Involvement; Family Therapy; Drug Therapy; Art Therapy; Music Therapy; Reality Therapy; Play Therapy. *Professionals on Staff* Psychiatrists; Psychologists; Social Workers. *Educational Professionals* Special Education Teachers; Paraprofessionals. *Curricula* Individualized; Prevocational.

The Little Village School

Bayberry Ave, Garden City, NY 11530 (516) 746-5575
Year Established 1970
Contact Barbara Feingold, Admin Dir
Facility Information *Placement* Special School.
Children/Adolescents Served 138. *Sexes Served* Both. *Tuition Fees (Approx)* $7,380-$10,695. *Sources of Funding* State Funds; P.L. 94-142; Nassau County; Private Donations. Summer school available. *Teacher Certification Level* Elementary School. *Special Certification Level* ED; MR; Multiply Handicapped; Speech and Language.
Student/Patient Characteristics *Age Levels* 0-4; 5-8; 9-11. *IQ Ranges* 0-25; 26-40; 41-55; 56-70; 71-85; 85-130. *Exceptionalities Served* Autistic; Emotionally Disturbed; Learning Disabled; Mentally Handicapped; Communication Disordered; Hearing Impaired/Deaf; Visually Impaired/Blind; Other Health Impaired; Physically Handicapped. *Learning Problems* Memory Disabilities; Perceptual Disabilities; Thinking Disabilities; Oral Language Disabilities; Reading Disabilities; Handwriting Disabilities; Spelling Disabilities; Arithmetic Disabilities; Written Expression; Social Skills. *Behavioral Problems* Attention Deficits; Hyperactivity; Impulsivity; Self-Aggression; Verbal Aggression; Physical Aggression; Passive Aggression; Withdrawal; Self-Mutilization. *Conditions Treated* Early Infantile Autism.

Services Provided Individual Therapy; Group Therapy; Parent Involvement; Behavior Therapy; Family Therapy; Play Therapy; Dance Therapy; Physical Therapy; Occupational Therapy; Speech Therapy. *Professionals on Staff* Psychologists 2; Social Workers 3; Nurses 1. *Service Facilities Available (with number of rooms)* Itinerants 2; Self-Contained Rooms 12. *Educational Professionals* Special Education Teachers 14; Paraprofessionals 28. *Curricula* Individualized. *Educational Intervention Approaches* Progressive Discipline; Self-Control; Behavior Modification.

Comments This is a year-round comprehensive educational and therapeutic program for developmentally disabled children. The developmental curriculum includes individual speech therapy, physical and occupational therapy, special physical education program, dance/movement therapy, auditory screening and parent workshops.

Madeline Burg Counseling Services—Jewish Board of Family and Children Services

990 Pelham Pkwy, Bronx, NY 10461 (212) 931-2600
Contact Patricia Nitzburg, Dir
Facility Information *Placement* Outpatient Psychiatric Clinics. *Sexes Served* Both. *Room and Board Fees (Approx)* Sliding Scale. *Sources of Funding* Health Insurance; Medicaid; Private Fees.
Student/Patient Characteristics *Age Levels* 0-4; 5-8; 9-11; 12-14; 15-17; 18-21; Over 21. *IQ Ranges* 71-85; 85-130; Above 130. *Exceptionalities Served* Emotionally Disturbed; Learning Disabled; Mentally Handicapped; Communication Disordered; Gifted. *Learning Problems* Memory Disabilities; Perceptual Disabilities; Thinking Disabilities; Oral Language Disabilities; Reading Disabilities; Handwriting Disabilities; Spelling Disabilities; Arithmetic Disabilities; Written Expression. *Behavioral Problems* Attention Deficits; Hyperactivity; Hypoactivity; Impulsivity; Self-Aggression; Verbal Aggression; Physical Aggression; Indirect Aggression; Passive Aggression; Withdrawal. *Conditions Treated* Schizophrenia; Phobias; Obsessions and Compulsions; Phobias; Depression; Anorexia Nervosa; Inadequacy/Immaturity; Personality Problems; Socialized Aggressive Reaction; Unsocialized Aggressive Reaction.
Services Provided Individual Therapy; Group Therapy; Parent Involvement; Family Therapy; Filial Therapy; Drug Therapy; Play Therapy. *Professionals on Staff* Psychiatrists; Psychologists; Social Workers.

Manhattan Children's Psychiatric Center

Ward's Island, New York, NY 10035 (212) 369-0500
Year Established 1972
Contact June Price, Assoc Dir
Facility Information *Placement* Psychiatric Hospital. *Number of Beds* 85. *Children/Adolescents Served* 150. *Sexes Served* Both. *Sources of Funding* State Funds; Medicaid; P.L. 94-142. Summer school available. *Teacher Certification Level* Elementary School; Junior High/Middle School; High School. *Special Certification Level* ED; LD; Career/Vocational Education; Reading; Art; Music; Physical Education; Home Economics.
Student/Patient Characteristics *Age Levels* 5-8; 9-11; 12-14; 15-17; 18-21. *IQ Ranges* 41-55; 56-70; 71-85; 85-130; Above 130. *Exceptionalities Served* Emotionally Disturbed; Learning Disabled; Communication Disordered; Hearing Impaired/Deaf; Visually Impaired/Blind. *Learning Problems* Memory Disabilities; Perceptual Disabilities; Thinking Disabilities; Oral Language Disabilities; Reading Disabilities; Handwriting Disabilities; Spelling Disabilities; Arithmetic Disabilities; Written Expression. *Behavioral Problems* Attention Deficits; Hyperactivity; Impulsivity; Self-Aggression; Verbal Aggression; Physical Aggression; Withdrawal. *Conditions Treated* Disintegrative Psychoses; Schizophrenia; Convulsive Disorders; Phobias; Obsessions and Compulsions; Hysteria; Depression; Suicide; Asthma; Inadequacy/Immaturity; Personality Problems; Socialized Aggressive Reaction; Unsocialized Aggressive Reaction.
Services Provided Individual Therapy; Group Therapy; Parent Involvement; Behavior Therapy; Family Therapy; Drug Therapy; Art Therapy; Music Therapy; Play Therapy. *Service Facilities Available (with number of rooms)* Consultative (ERT) 2; Resource Rooms 2; Self-Contained Rooms 29. *Educational Professionals* Regular School Teachers 4; Special Education Teachers 22; Career/Vocational Teachers 4; Vocational Rehabilitation Counselor 2; School Psychologist 1; Speech Pathologist 1. *Curricula* Traditional Academic; Career/Vocational Education; Individualized; Basic Skills; Prevocational; Art; Music; Home Economics; Physical Education. *Educational Intervention Approaches* Engineered Classroom; Precision Teaching; Progressive Discipline; Behavior Modification. *Degrees Awarded* Graduate Equivalency Diploma.

The Martha H Beeman Foundation Child Guidance Clinic

650 4th St, Niagara Falls, NY 14301 (716) 282-2319
Year Established 1929
Contact Jac Giacovelli, Exec Dir
Facility Information *Placement* Psychiatric Outpatient Clinic. *Children/Adolescents Served* 500. *Sexes Served* Both. *Tuition Fees (Approx)* Sliding Scale. *Sources of Funding* State Funds; Health Insurance; Medicaid; County; Beeman; Fees.
Student/Patient Characteristics *Age Levels* 0-4; 5-8; 9-11; 12-14; 15-17. *IQ Ranges* 0-25; 26-40; 41-55; 56-70; 71-85; 85-130; Above 130. *Exceptionalities Served* Emotionally Disturbed. *Behavioral Problems* Attention Deficits; Hyperactivity; Hypoactivity; Impulsivity; Self-Aggression; Verbal Aggression; Physical Aggression; Indirect Aggression; Passive Aggression; Withdrawal.
Services Provided Individual Therapy; Group Therapy; Parent Involvement; Behavior Therapy; Family Therapy; Filial Therapy; Drug Therapy; Art Therapy; Play Therapy. *Professionals on Staff* Psychiatrists 2; Psychologists 1; Counselors 1; Social Workers 4; Nurses 1.

Nannahagur School Day Treatment Program—(JCCA)

PO Box 237, Pleasantville Cottage School, Pleasantville, NY 10570 (914) 769-0164
Year Established 1970
Contact Lorraine Siegel, Dir
Facility Information *Placement* Day Treatment Program. *Children/Adolescents Served* 45. *Sexes Served* Both. *Sources of Funding* State Funds; Medicaid; OMH; Private Endowment. Summer school available. *Teacher Certification Level* Elementary School; Junior High/Middle School. *Special Certification Level* ED; Reading.
Student/Patient Characteristics *Age Levels* 5-8; 9-11; 12-14. *IQ Ranges* 71-85; 85-130; Above 130. *Exceptionalities Served* Emotionally Disturbed; Learning Disabled; Mentally Handicapped. *Learning Problems* Memory Disabilities; Perceptual Disabilities; Thinking Disabilities; Oral Language Disabilities; Reading Disabilities; Handwriting Disabilities; Spelling Disabilities; Arithmetic Disabilities; Written Expression. *Behavioral Problems* Attention Deficits; Hyperactivity; Impulsivity; Self-Aggression; Verbal Aggression; Physical Aggression; Indirect Aggression; Passive Aggression; Withdrawal. *Conditions Treated* Schizophrenia; Convulsive Disorders; Hysteria; Depression; Inadequacy/Immaturity; Personality Problems; Socialized Aggressive Reaction; Unsocialized Aggressive Reaction.
Services Provided Individual Therapy; Group Therapy; Parent Involvement; Behavior Therapy; Family Therapy; Drug Therapy; Art Therapy; Play Therapy. *Professionals on Staff* Psychiatrists 1; Psychologists 1; Social Workers 4. *Service Facilities Available (with number of rooms)* Resource Rooms 2; Self-Contained Rooms 7. *Educational Professionals* Regular School Teachers; Special Education Teachers 6; Paraprofessionals 7; Specialists 6. *Curricula* Traditional Academic; Individualized; Basic Skills. *Educational Intervention Approaches* Behavior Modification. *Degrees Awarded* Certificate of Attendance.
Comments This is a highly integrated educational clinical program.

The Nassau Center for the Developmentally Disabled Inc

72 S Woods Rd, Woodbury, NY 11797 (516) 921-7650
Year Established 1958
Contact A Nora Walden, Dir Family Serv
Facility Information *Placement* Special School; Public Residential Care; Private Residential Care. *Number of Beds* 29. *Children/Adolescents Served* 29 (residential); 110 (day program). *Sexes Served* Both. *Room and Board Fees (Approx)* $118. *Tuition Fees (Approx)* $16,143. *Sources of Funding* State Funds. Summer school available. *Special Certification Level* ED; LD; MR; Reading; Math.

Student/Patient Characteristics *Age Levels* 0-4; 5-8; 9-11; 12-14; 15-17; 18-21. *IQ Ranges* 71-85. *Exceptionalities Served* Autistic; Emotionally Disturbed; Mentally Handicapped; Communication Disordered; Hearing Impaired/Deaf. *Learning Problems* Memory Disabilities; Perceptual Disabilities; Thinking Disabilities; Oral Language Disabilities; Reading Disabilities; Handwriting Disabilities; Spelling Disabilities; Arithmetic Disabilities; Written Expression. *Behavioral Problems* Attention Deficits; Hyperactivity; Hypoactivity; Impulsivity; Self-Aggression; Verbal Aggression; Physical Aggression; Indirect Aggression; Passive Aggression; Withdrawal. *Conditions Treated* Early Infantile Autism.

Services Provided Individual Therapy; Group Therapy; Parent Involvement; Behavior Therapy; Cognitive Developmental Therapy; Art Therapy; Music Therapy. *Professionals on Staff* Psychiatrists 1; Psychologists 3; Counselors; Social Workers 3; Child Care Staff 60; Nurses 10. *Service Facilities Available (with number of rooms)* Self-Contained Rooms 18; On-Campus Residential School 14. *Educational Professionals* Special Education Teachers 18; Paraprofessionals 36. *Curricula* Individualized; Basic Skills. *Educational Intervention Approaches* Behavior Modification.

New Hope Guild

1777 E 21st St, Brooklyn, NY 11229 (212) 252-4200
Year Established 1953
Contact Jane Nurenberg, Admin Dir

Facility Information *Placement* Outpatient Psychiatric Clinic. *Children/Adolescents Served* 150. *Sexes Served* Both. *Sources of Funding* Health Insurance; Medicaid; Fees. *Special Certification Level* LD.

Student/Patient Characteristics *Age Levels* 5-8; 9-11; 12-14; 15-17; 18-21; Over 21. *IQ Ranges* 71-85; 85-130; Above 130. *Exceptionalities Served* Emotionally Disturbed; Learning Disabled. *Learning Problems* Memory Disabilities; Perceptual Disabilities; Thinking Disabilities; Oral Language Disabilities; Reading Disabilities; Handwriting Disabilities; Spelling Disabilities; Arithmetic Disabilities; Written Expression. *Behavioral Problems* Attention Deficits; Hyperactivity; Hypoactivity; Impulsivity; Self-Aggression; Verbal Aggression; Physical Aggression; Indirect Aggression; Passive Aggression; Withdrawal. *Conditions Treated* Alcohol Abuse and/or Drug Abuse; Other Substance Abuse or Dependence; Disintegrative Psychoses; Schizophrenia; Phobias; Obsessions and Compulsions; Hysteria; Depression; Suicide; Anorexia Nervosa; Inadequacy/Immaturity; Personality Problems; Socialized Aggressive Reaction; Unsocialized Aggressive Reaction.

Services Provided Individual Therapy; Group Therapy; Parent Involvement; Family Therapy; Filial Therapy; Drug Therapy; Art Therapy; Reality Therapy; Play Therapy. *Professionals on Staff* Psychiatrists 5; Psychologists 20; Social Workers 50. *Educational Professionals* Special Education Teachers 5. *Curricula* Individualized.

O D Heck Developmental Center Autism Program

Balltown Rd, Schenectady, NY 12304 (518) 370-7505
Year Established 1978
Contact Douglas Wheeler, Psychologist

Facility Information *Placement* Public School; Public Residential Care. *Number of Beds* 40. *Children/Adolescents Served* 48. *Sexes Served* Both. *Sources of Funding* State Funds. Summer school available. *Teacher Certification Level* Elementary School. *Special Certification Level* MR.

Student/Patient Characteristics *Age Levels* 12-14; 15-17; 18-21; Over 21. *IQ Ranges* 26-40; 41-55. *Exceptionalities Served* Autistic. *Learning Problems* Memory Disabilities; Perceptual Disabilities; Thinking Disabilities; Oral Language Disabilities. *Behavioral Problems* Attention Deficits; Hyperactivity; Impulsivity; Self-Aggression; Physical Aggression; Withdrawal. *Conditions Treated* Early Infantile Autism.

Services Provided Parent Involvement; Behavior Therapy; Cognitive Developmental Therapy; Drug Therapy; Music Therapy. *Professionals on Staff* Psychiatrists 1; Psychologists 5; Social

Workers 2; Child Care Staff 45; Nurses 6; Speech Therapists 2. *Service Facilities Available (with number of rooms)* Self-Contained Rooms 8. *Educational Professionals* Special Education Teachers 8; Paraprofessionals 70. *Curricula* Individualized; Basic Skills; Prevocational. *Educational Intervention Approaches* Behavior Modification; Applied Behavior Analysis; Creative Conditioning.

Ohel Children's Home and Family Services

4423 16th Ave, Brooklyn, NY 11204 (718) 851-6300
Year Established 1969
Contact Neal D Levy, Clinical Dir

Facility Information *Placement* Private Residential Care; Foster Boarding Home Service. *Number of Beds* 37. *Children/Adolescents Served* 37. *Sexes Served* Both. *Sources of Funding* State Funds; Private Donations.

Student/Patient Characteristics *Age Levels* 0-4; 5-8; 9-11; 12-14; 15-17. *Exceptionalities Served* Autistic; Emotionally Disturbed; Learning Disabled; Mentally Handicapped; Communication Disordered; Physically Handicapped; Developmental Disabilities. *Learning Problems* Memory Disabilities; Perceptual Disabilities; Thinking Disabilities; Oral Language Disabilities; Reading Disabilities; Handwriting Disabilities; Spelling Disabilities; Arithmetic Disabilities; Written Expression. *Behavioral Problems* Attention Deficits; Hyperactivity; Hypoactivity; Impulsivity; Self-Aggression; Verbal Aggression; Physical Aggression; Indirect Aggression; Passive Aggression; Withdrawal. *Conditions Treated* Early Infantile Autism; Schizophrenia; Aphasia; Phobias; Obsessions and Compulsions; Hysteria; Depression; Suicide; Asthma; Anorexia Nervosa; Ulcerative Colitis; Inadequacy/Immaturity; Personality Problems; Socialized Aggressive Reaction.

Services Provided Individual Therapy; Group Therapy; Parent Involvement; Behavior Therapy; Family Therapy; Filial Therapy; Drug Therapy; Art Therapy; Music Therapy; Reality Therapy; Play Therapy; Art Therapy; Movement Therapy; Recreation Therapy; Speech Therapy. *Professionals on Staff* Psychiatrists 2; Psychologists 3; Counselors; Social Workers 4; Child Care Staff 15-20; Nurses 3. *Service Facilities Available (with number of rooms)* Tutoring; Community Schools. *Educational Professionals* Regular School Teachers 1; Special Education Counselors 1; Paraprofessionals 1. *Curricula* Traditional Academic; Career/Vocational Education; Individualized; Basic Skills; Prevocational. *Educational Intervention Approaches* Self-Control; Behavior Modification. *Degrees Awarded* High School Diploma.

Parsons Child and Family Center

845 Central Ave, Albany, NY 12206 (518) 438-4571
Year Established 1829
Contact H James Hudson, Dir Human Resources

Facility Information *Placement* Special School; Private Residential Care; Outpatient Psychiatric Center. *Number of Beds* 80. *Children/Adolescents Served* 700. *Sexes Served* Both. *Room and Board Fees (Approx)* $60. *Tuition Fees (Approx)* $21,900. *Sources of Funding* State Funds; Health Insurance; Medicaid. Summer school available. *Teacher Certification Level* Elementary School; Junior High/Middle School; High School. *Special Certification Level* ED; LD; MR; Career/Vocational Education; Reading; Special Education.

Student/Patient Characteristics *Age Levels* 9-11; 12-14; 15-17; 18-21. *IQ Ranges* 56-70; 71-85; 85-130. *Exceptionalities Served* Autistic; Emotionally Disturbed; Learning Disabled. *Learning Problems* Memory Disabilities; Perceptual Disabilities; Thinking Disabilities; Oral Language Disabilities; Reading Disabilities; Handwriting Disabilities; Spelling Disabilities; Arithmetic Disabilities; Written Expression. *Behavioral Problems* Attention Deficits; Hyperactivity; Hypoactivity; Impulsivity; Self-Aggression; Verbal Aggression; Physical Aggression; Indirect Aggression; Passive Aggression; Withdrawal. *Conditions Treated* Early Infantile Autism; Disintegrative Psychoses; Schizophrenia; Convulsive Disorders; Phobias; Obsessions and Compulsions; Depression; Suicide; Personality Problems; Socialized Aggressive Reaction; Unsocialized Aggressive Reaction.

Services Provided Individual Therapy; Group Therapy; Parent Involvement; Behavior Therapy; Family Therapy; Drug Therapy; Art Therapy; Music Therapy; Play Therapy; Psychodrama. *Professionals on Staff* Psychiatrists 4; Psychologists 3; Social Workers 45; Child Care Staff 80; Nurses 6. *Service Facilities Available (with number of rooms)* Resource Rooms 20; Transition Rooms 1; Self-Contained Rooms 4. *Educational Professionals* Regular School Teachers 20; Special Education Teachers 20; Career/Vocational Teachers 2; Crisis Teachers 3; Paraprofessionals 5. *Curricula* Traditional Academic; Career/Vocational Education; Individualized; Basic Skills; Prevocational. *Educational Intervention Approaches* Progressive Discipline; Self-Control; Behavior Modification; Applied Behavior Analysis. *Degrees Awarded* High School Diploma.

Parsons Child and Family Center—Neil Hellman School

60 Academy Rd, Albany, NY 12208 (518) 447-5211
Year Established 1829
Contact Mark Borlawsky, Coord Student Serv
Facility Information *Placement* Special School; Private Residential Care; Private Day Treatment. *Number of Beds* 75. *Children/Adolescents Served* 150. *Sexes Served* Both. *Room and Board Fees (Approx)* $75-$125. *Tuition Fees (Approx)* $15,000. *Sources of Funding* State Funds; Medicaid; Medicare; P.L. 94-142. Summer school available. *Teacher Certification Level* Elementary School; Junior High/Middle School; High School. *Special Certification Level* ED; LD; MR; Career/Vocational Education; Reading; Math; Speech/Language; Adaptive Physical Education.
Student/Patient Characteristics *Age Levels* 5-8; 9-11; 12-14; 15-17; 18-21. *IQ Ranges* 0-25; 26-40; 41-55; 56-70; 71-85; 85-130; Above 130. *Exceptionalities Served* Autistic; Emotionally Disturbed; Learning Disabled; Mentally Handicapped; Communication Disordered; Hearing Impaired/Deaf; Multiply Handicapped. *Learning Problems* Memory Disabilities; Perceptual Disabilities; Thinking Disabilities; Oral Language Disabilities; Reading Disabilities; Handwriting Disabilities; Spelling Disabilities; Arithmetic Disabilities; Written Expression. *Behavioral Problems* Attention Deficits; Hyperactivity; Hypoactivity; Impulsivity; Self-Aggression; Verbal Aggression; Physical Aggression; Indirect Aggression; Passive Aggression; Withdrawal. *Conditions Treated* Early Infantile Autism; Schizophrenia; Aphasia; Phobias; Obsessions and Compulsions; Depression; Inadequacy/Immaturity; Personality Problems; Socialized Aggressive Reaction; Unsocialized Aggressive Reaction.
Services Provided Individual Therapy; Group Therapy; Parent Involvement; Behavior Therapy; Cognitive Developmental Therapy; Family Therapy; Art Therapy; Music Therapy; Play Therapy. *Professionals on Staff* Psychiatrists 6; Psychologists 3; Psychologists; Social Workers 20; Child Care Staff 65; Nurses 5. *Service Facilities Available (with number of rooms)* Transition Rooms 2; Self-Contained Rooms 18; Special School; On-Campus Residential School. *Educational Professionals* Special Education Teachers 35; Career/Vocational Teachers 1; Crisis Teachers 6; Special Education Counselors; Paraprofessionals 2. *Curricula* Traditional Academic; Individualized; Basic Skills; Prevocational. *Educational Intervention Approaches* Behavior Modification. *Degrees Awarded* Certificate of Attendance; High School Diploma.

Pomona Mental Health Center—Child Development Center

Sanitorium Rd, Pomona, NY 10970
Facility Information *Placement* Day Treatment and Mental Health Center. *Children/Adolescents Served* 60. *Sexes Served* Both. *Tuition Fees (Approx)* Sliding Scale. *Sources of Funding* Health Insurance; Medicaid. Summer school available. *Special Certification Level* ED.
Student/Patient Characteristics *Age Levels* 0-4; 5-8. *Exceptionalities Served* Emotionally Disturbed. *Behavioral Problems* Attention Deficits; Hyperactivity; Impulsivity; Self-

Aggression; Verbal Aggression; Physical Aggression; Indirect Aggression; Passive Aggression; Withdrawal. *Conditions Treated* Early Infantile Autism; Schizophrenia; Phobias; Depression; Personality Problems; Socialized Aggressive Reaction; Unsocialized Aggressive Reaction.
Services Provided Individual Therapy; Group Therapy; Parent Involvement; Family Therapy; Drug Therapy. *Professionals on Staff* Psychiatrists 1; Psychologists 2; Social Workers 3; Nurses 1; Pediatrician 1; Speech and Language Therapist 1. *Educational Professionals* Special Education Teachers 4; Paraprofessionals 5.

Post Script Consulting Service

5 E Market St, Corning, NY 14830 (607) 936-8092
Year Established 1979
Contact Alice Rahill, Dir
Facility Information *Placement* Educational Evaluation; Consulting Service. *Sexes Served* Both. *Sources of Funding* Health Insurance; Private Payments. Summer school available. *Special Certification Level* Career/Vocational Education.
Student/Patient Characteristics *Age Levels* 5-8; 9-11; 12-14; 15-17; 18-21; Over 21. *IQ Ranges* 85-130; Above 130. *Exceptionalities Served* Emotionally Disturbed; Learning Disabled; Gifted. *Learning Problems* Memory Disabilities; Perceptual Disabilities; Thinking Disabilities; Oral Language Disabilities; Reading Disabilities; Handwriting Disabilities; Spelling Disabilities; Arithmetic Disabilities; Written Expression. *Behavioral Problems* Attention Deficits; Hyperactivity; Self-Aggression; Verbal Aggression; Passive Aggression. *Conditions Treated* Personality Problems.
Services Provided Individual Therapy; Parent Involvement. *Professionals on Staff* Psychologists 1; Counselors 1. *Service Facilities Available (with number of rooms)* Evaluation and Consultation 2.

Public School No. 176

850 Baychester Ave, Bronx, NY 10475 (212) 671-2911
Year Established 1979
Contact Grace Cavanagh, Principal
Facility Information *Placement* Public School; Special School. *Children/Adolescents Served* 130. *Sexes Served* Both. *Sources of Funding* State Funds; P.L. 94-142; P.L. 89-313. Summer school available. *Teacher Certification Level* Elementary School; Junior High/Middle School. *Special Certification Level* ED; MR; Special Education.
Student/Patient Characteristics *Age Levels* 5-8; 9-11; 12-14; 15-17; 18-21; Over 21. *IQ Ranges* 26-40; 41-55; 56-70; 71-85. *Exceptionalities Served* Autistic. *Learning Problems* Perceptual Disabilities; Thinking Disabilities; Oral Language Disabilities. *Behavioral Problems* Self-Aggression; Physical Aggression; Withdrawal. *Conditions Treated* Early Infantile Autism; Convulsive Disorders.
Services Provided Parent Involvement; Behavior Therapy; Music Therapy; Play Therapy; Speech Therapy. *Professionals on Staff* Psychologists 1; Counselors 1; Social Workers 1. *Service Facilities Available (with number of rooms)* Itinerants 7; Self-Contained Rooms 30. *Educational Professionals* Regular School Teachers 1; Special Education Teachers 35; Crisis Teachers 3; Paraprofessionals 32. *Curricula* Traditional Academic; Career/Vocational Education; Individualized; Basic Skills; Prevocational. *Educational Intervention Approaches* Engineered Classroom; Behavior Modification. *Degrees Awarded* Certificate of Attendance.
Comments PS 176 provides a comprehensive program for autistic students ranging in age from 5-21 yrs.

Queens Hospital Center Department of Psychiatry Child and Adolescent Clinic

82-68 164th St, Jamaica, NY 11432 (718) 990-3571
Contact David Kaminsky, Physician-in-Charge
Facility Information *Placement* Outpatient Clinic Services. *Sexes Served* Both.

Student/Patient Characteristics *Age Levels* 0-4; 5-8; 9-11; 12-14; 15-17. *IQ Ranges* 56-70; 71-85; 85-130; Above 130. *Exceptionalities Served* Autistic; Emotionally Disturbed; Learning Disabled; Other Health Impaired; Gifted. *Learning Problems* Perceptual Disabilities; Thinking Disabilities; Reading Disabilities; Handwriting Disabilities; Spelling Disabilities; Arithmetic Disabilities; Written Expression. *Behavioral Problems* Attention Deficits; Hyperactivity; Hypoactivity; Impulsivity; Self-Aggression; Verbal Aggression; Physical Aggression; Passive Aggression; Withdrawal. *Conditions Treated* Schizophrenia; Phobias; Obsessions and Compulsions; Hysteria; Depression; Suicide; Anorexia Nervosa; Inadequacy/Immaturity; Personality Problems; Socialized Aggressive Reaction; Unsocialized Aggressive Reaction.

Services Provided Individual Therapy; Group Therapy; Parent Involvement; Family Therapy; Drug Therapy. *Professionals on Staff* Psychiatrists 3; Psychologists 3; Social Workers 6.

Rensselaer County Mental Health Department—Unified Services for Children and Adolescents

County Office Building, Troy, NY 12180 (518) 270-2800
Year Established 1975
Contact Ara Baligian, Commissioner of Mental Health
Facility Information *Placement* Referral Services.
Children/Adolescents Served 600. *Sexes Served* Both. *Sources of Funding* State Funds; Health Insurance; Medicaid; Medicare; County Funds. *Special Certification Level* Special Education.
Student/Patient Characteristics *Age Levels* 0-4; 5-8; 9-11; 12-14; 15-17; 18-21. *IQ Ranges* 0-25; 26-40; 41-55; 56-70; 71-85; 85-130; Above 130. *Exceptionalities Served* Autistic; Emotionally Disturbed; Learning Disabled; Mentally Handicapped; Communication Disordered; Hearing Impaired/Deaf; Visually Impaired/Blind; Other Health Impaired; Physically Handicapped; Gifted. *Learning Problems* Memory Disabilities; Perceptual Disabilities; Thinking Disabilities; Oral Language Disabilities; Reading Disabilities; Handwriting Disabilities; Spelling Disabilities; Arithmetic Disabilities; Written Expression. *Behavioral Problems* Attention Deficits; Hyperactivity; Hypoactivity; Impulsivity; Self-Aggression; Verbal Aggression; Physical Aggression; Indirect Aggression; Passive Aggression; Withdrawal. *Conditions Treated* Alcohol Abuse and/or Drug Abuse; Other Substance Abuse or Dependence; Early Infantile Autism; Disintegrative Psychoses; Schizophrenia; Aphasia; Convulsive Disorders; Phobias; Obsessions and Compulsions; Hysteria; Depression; Suicide; Asthma; Anorexia Nervosa; Ulcerative Colitis; Inadequacy/Immaturity; Personality Problems; Socialized Aggressive Reaction; Unsocialized Aggressive Reaction.

Services Provided Individual Therapy; Group Therapy; Parent Involvement; Behavior Therapy; Cognitive Developmental Therapy; Family Therapy; Drug Therapy; Reality Therapy; Play Therapy. *Professionals on Staff* Psychiatrists 3; Psychologists 4; Counselors 2; Social Workers 7; Vocational Rehabilitation Counselor 1. *Educational Professionals* Special Education Teachers. *Curricula* Vocational Rehabilitation Consultation.

Comments This is a mental hygiene clinic providing comprehensive diagnostic treatment and rehabilitative services to youngsters aged 0-21 who are physically handicapped, who exhibit emotional or behavioral difficulties, or who are developmentally delayed.

Rise East School

Bldg J Sanatorium Rd, Pomona, NY 10970 (914) 354-0200
Year Established 1974
Contact Peggy Ingham, Acting Dir
Facility Information *Placement* Special School.
Children/Adolescents Served 35. *Sexes Served* Both. *Tuition Fees (Approx)* $17,531. *Sources of Funding* State Funds; P.L. 94-142. Summer school available. *Teacher Certification Level* Elementary School; Junior High/Middle School; High School. *Special Certification Level* MR; Special Education.

Student/Patient Characteristics *Age Levels* 5-8; 9-11; 12-14; 15-17; 18-21. *IQ Ranges* 0-25; 26-40; 41-55. *Exceptionalities Served* Autistic; Emotionally Disturbed; Mentally Handicapped; Communication Disordered; Hearing Impaired/Deaf; Visually Impaired/Blind; Other Health Impaired; Physically Handicapped; Multiply Handicapped. *Learning Problems* Memory Disabilities; Perceptual Disabilities; Thinking Disabilities; Oral Language Disabilities; Reading Disabilities; Handwriting Disabilities; Spelling Disabilities; Arithmetic Disabilities; Written Expression. *Behavioral Problems* Attention Deficits; Hyperactivity; Hypoactivity; Impulsivity; Self-Aggression; Physical Aggression; Passive Aggression; Withdrawal. *Conditions Treated* Early Infantile Autism; Schizophrenia; Aphasia; Convulsive Disorders.

Services Provided Individual Therapy; Group Therapy; Parent Involvement; Behavior Therapy; Drug Therapy. *Professionals on Staff* Psychiatrists 1; Psychologists 1; Nurses 1. *Service Facilities Available (with number of rooms)* Self-Contained Rooms 5; Therapy Rooms 5. *Educational Professionals* Special Education Teachers 5; Paraprofessionals 10; Speech Therapists 2; Occupational Therapist 1; Physical Therapist 1; Adapted Physical Education Teacher 1. *Curricula* Individualized; Basic Skills; Prevocational. *Educational Intervention Approaches* Precision Teaching; Behavior Modification; Applied Behavior Analysis. *Degrees Awarded* Certificate of Attendance.

Comments Rise provides a coordinated program of very small special education classes, along with speech, physical, occupational, and behavior therapies. Many students have chronic medical involvements as well as physical and mental handicaps.

Rochester Mental Health Center Inc—Day Treatment Unit Services—Children and Youth Division

1425 Portland Ave, Rochester, NY 14621 (716) 544-5220
Year Established 1967
Contact Joseph Gold, Dir Day Treatment Unit Serv
Facility Information *Placement* Special School.
Children/Adolescents Served 70. *Sexes Served* Both. *Tuition Fees (Approx)* $9,005-$9,800. *Sources of Funding* State Funds; Medicaid; P.L. 94-142. Summer school available. *Teacher Certification Level* Elementary School; Junior High/Middle School; High School. *Special Certification Level* ED.
Student/Patient Characteristics *Age Levels* 5-8; 9-11; 12-14; 15-17. *IQ Ranges* 56-70; 71-85; 85-130. *Exceptionalities Served* Autistic; Emotionally Disturbed; Communication Disordered. *Learning Problems* Memory Disabilities; Thinking Disabilities; Oral Language Disabilities. *Behavioral Problems* Attention Deficits; Hyperactivity; Impulsivity; Physical Aggression; Indirect Aggression. *Conditions Treated* Early Infantile Autism; Phobias; Depression; Inadequacy/Immaturity; Personality Problems; Socialized Aggressive Reaction; Unsocialized Aggressive Reaction.

Services Provided Individual Therapy; Group Therapy; Parent Involvement; Behavior Therapy; Family Therapy; Drug Therapy; Play Therapy. *Professionals on Staff* Psychiatrists 3; Psychologists 4; Social Workers 6. *Service Facilities Available (with number of rooms)* Self-Contained Rooms; Hospital School. *Educational Professionals* Special Education Teachers 16; Crisis Teachers 1. *Curricula* Career/Vocational Education; Individualized; Basic Skills. *Educational Intervention Approaches* Engineered Classroom; Precision Teaching; Self-Control; Behavior Modification. *Degrees Awarded* Certificate of Attendance; High School Diploma.

Rockland Children's Psychiatric Center

Convent Road, Orangeburg, NY 10583 (914) 359-7400
Contact S Ahluwalia, Acting Exec Dir
Facility Information *Placement* Childrens Pshyciatric Inpatient Hospital. *Number of Beds* 80. *Children/Adolescents Served* 80. *Sexes Served* Both. *Sources of Funding* Health Insurance; Medicaid. Summer school available. *Teacher Certification Level* Elementary School; Junior High/Middle School; High School. *Special Certification Level* ED; LD; Reading; Math.

Student/Patient Characteristics *Age Levels* 15-17. *IQ Ranges* 41-55; 56-70; 71-85; 85-130. *Exceptionalities Served* Emotionally Disturbed. *Learning Problems* Memory Disabilities; Perceptual Disabilities; Thinking Disabilities; Oral Language Disabilities; Reading Disabilities; Handwriting Disabilities; Spelling Disabilities; Arithmetic Disabilities; Written Expression. *Behavioral Problems* Attention Deficits; Hyperactivity; Hypoactivity; Impulsivity; Self-Aggression; Verbal Aggression; Physical Aggression; Indirect Aggression; Passive Aggression; Withdrawal. *Conditions Treated* Disintegrative Psychoses; Schizophrenia; Phobias; Obsessions and Compulsions; Hysteria; Depression; Suicide; Anorexia Nervosa; Inadequacy/Immaturity; Personality Problems; Socialized Aggressive Reaction; Unsocialized Aggressive Reaction.

Services Provided Individual Therapy; Group Therapy; Parent Involvement; Behavior Therapy; Cognitive Developmental Therapy; Family Therapy; Drug Therapy; Art Therapy; Reality Therapy; Play Therapy. *Professionals on Staff* Psychiatrists 7; Psychologists 2; Counselors; Social Workers 5; Child Care Staff 65; Nurses 15.5. *Service Facilities Available (with number of rooms)* Hospital School. *Educational Professionals* Special Education Teachers 17; Occupational Therapists 8; Recreation Therapists 11. *Curricula* Traditional Academic; Career/Vocational Education; Individualized; Basic Skills; Prevocational. *Educational Intervention Approaches* Engineered Classroom; Precision Teaching; Progressive Discipline; Self-Control; Behavior Modification. *Degrees Awarded* High School Diploma.

Rockland Psychological and Educational Center

21 Alturas Rd, Spring Valley, NY 10977 (914) 356-7250
Year Established 1972
Contact Max Frankel, Dir

Facility Information *Placement* Special Program. *Children/Adolescents Served* 100. *Sexes Served* Both. *Sources of Funding* Health Insurance; Medicaid; Medicare; P.L. 94-142. Summer school available. *Teacher Certification Level* Elementary School; Junior High/Middle School; High School. *Special Certification Level* ED; LD; MR; Career/Vocational Education; Reading; Math.

Student/Patient Characteristics *Age Levels* 0-4; 5-8; 9-11; 12-14; 15-17; 18-21; Over 21. *IQ Ranges* 0-25; 26-40; 41-55; 56-70; 71-85; 85-130; Above 130. *Exceptionalities Served* Emotionally Disturbed; Learning Disabled; Mentally Handicapped; Communication Disordered; Other Health Impaired; Gifted. *Learning Problems* Memory Disabilities; Perceptual Disabilities; Thinking Disabilities; Oral Language Disabilities; Reading Disabilities; Handwriting Disabilities; Spelling Disabilities; Arithmetic Disabilities; Written Expression. *Behavioral Problems* Attention Deficits; Hyperactivity; Hypoactivity; Impulsivity; Self-Aggression; Verbal Aggression; Physical Aggression; Indirect Aggression; Passive Aggression; Withdrawal. *Conditions Treated* Alcohol Abuse and/or Drug Abuse; Other Substance Abuse or Dependence; Aphasia; Phobias; Obsessions and Compulsions; Hysteria; Depression; Suicide; Asthma; Anorexia Nervosa; Ulcerative Colitis; Inadequacy/Immaturity; Personality Problems; Socialized Aggressive Reaction; Unsocialized Aggressive Reaction.

Services Provided Individual Therapy; Group Therapy; Parent Involvement; Behavior Therapy; Cognitive Developmental Therapy; Biofeedback; Family Therapy; Filial Therapy; Reality Therapy; Play Therapy; Physical Therapy; Occupational Therapy; Speech Therapy. *Professionals on Staff* Psychiatrists 1; Psychologists 10; Counselors 11; Social Workers 2; Nurses 1. *Service Facilities Available (with number of rooms)* Consultative (ERT). *Educational Professionals* Special Education Teachers 10; Career/Vocational Teachers 2; Special Education Counselors 4. *Educational Intervention Approaches* Progressive Discipline; Self-Control; Behavior Modification. *Degrees Awarded* Graduate Equivalency Diploma.

St Cabrini Home Inc

Rte 9W, West Park, NY 12493 (914) 384-6500
Year Established 1890
Contact James J Lavelle, Exec Dir

Facility Information *Placement* Private Residential Care. *Number of Beds* 80. *Children/Adolescents Served* 80. *Sexes Served* Both. *Sources of Funding* State Funds; Medicaid; County DSS Funds. Summer school available. *Teacher Certification Level* Junior High/Middle School. *Special Certification Level* Special Education.

Student/Patient Characteristics *Age Levels* 12-14; 15-17. *IQ Ranges* 71-85; 85-130. *Exceptionalities Served* Emotionally Disturbed. *Learning Problems* Perceptual Disabilities; Oral Language Disabilities; Reading Disabilities; Handwriting Disabilities; Spelling Disabilities; Arithmetic Disabilities; Written Expression. *Behavioral Problems* Hyperactivity; Impulsivity; Self-Aggression; Verbal Aggression; Physical Aggression; Indirect Aggression; Passive Aggression; Withdrawal. *Conditions Treated* Other Substance Abuse or Dependence; Hysteria; Depression; Personality Problems; Socialized Aggressive Reaction; Unsocialized Aggressive Reaction.

Services Provided Individual Therapy; Group Therapy; Parent Involvement; Behavior Therapy; Family Therapy. *Professionals on Staff* Psychiatrists 2; Psychologists 2; Social Workers 5; Child Care Staff 40; Nurses 11. *Service Facilities Available (with number of rooms)* Resource Rooms; Self-Contained Rooms 8. *Educational Professionals* Special Education Teachers 8; Special Education Counselors 1; Paraprofessionals 12. *Curricula* Individualized; Basic Skills; Prevocational. *Educational Intervention Approaches* Behavior Modification.

Comments This is a residential child care agency for 80 adolescents referred by family court or the department of social services. All counseling and educational services are provided at the facility.

St Francis Boys' Home—Camelot

50 Riverside Dr, Lake Placid, NY 12946 (518) 523-3605
Year Established 1969
Contact Donald A Fava, Treatment Coord

Facility Information *Placement* Private Residential Care. *Number of Beds* 26. *Children/Adolescents Served* 26. *Sexes Served* Male. *Room and Board Fees (Approx)* $113. *Tuition Fees (Approx)* $41,183. *Sources of Funding* State Funds; Health Insurance; Medicaid; Scholarship. Summer school available. *Teacher Certification Level* Junior High/Middle School; High School. *Special Certification Level* ED; LD; Career/Vocational Education; Reading; Math.

Student/Patient Characteristics *Age Levels* 12-14; 15-17. *IQ Ranges* 85-130; Above 130. *Exceptionalities Served* Emotionally Disturbed; Learning Disabled. *Learning Problems* Memory Disabilities; Perceptual Disabilities; Thinking Disabilities; Reading Disabilities; Handwriting Disabilities; Spelling Disabilities; Arithmetic Disabilities. *Behavioral Problems* Attention Deficits; Hyperactivity; Hypoactivity; Impulsivity; Self-Aggression; Verbal Aggression; Indirect Aggression; Passive Aggression; Withdrawal. *Conditions Treated* Phobias; Depression; Inadequacy/Immaturity; Personality Problems; Socialized Aggressive Reaction; Unsocialized Aggressive Reaction.

Services Provided Individual Therapy; Group Therapy; Parent Involvement; Behavior Therapy; Cognitive Developmental Therapy; Family Therapy; Drug Therapy. *Professionals on Staff* Psychiatrists 1; Psychologists 1; Counselors 7; Social Workers 2; Child Care Staff 2; Nurses 1; Recreation Therapist 1. *Service Facilities Available (with number of rooms)* Resource Rooms; Self-Contained Rooms 3; Public School. *Educational Professionals* Regular School Teachers 1; Special Education Teachers 1; Crisis Teachers 1. *Curricula* Traditional Academic; Individualized; Basic Skills. *Educational Intervention Approaches* Progressive Discipline; Self-Control; Behavior Modification; Creative Conditioning. *Degrees Awarded* High School Diploma.

St Vincent's Hospital and Medical Center of New York—Child and Adolescent Psychiatry Service

203 W 12th St, New York, NY 10011 (212) 790-8211
Year Established 1960
Contact Nicholas M Colombo, Social Work Supv

Facility Information *Placement* Clinic. *Sexes Served* Both. *Room and Board Fees (Approx)* $10-$65 Sliding Scale. *Sources of Funding* State Funds; HEW; Health Insurance; Medicaid; P.L. 94-142.

Student/Patient Characteristics *Age Levels* 0-4; 5-8; 9-11; 12-14; 15-17. *IQ Ranges* 56-70; 71-85; 85-130; Above 130. *Exceptionalities Served* Emotionally Disturbed; Learning Disabled; Mentally Handicapped; Communication Disordered; Physically Handicapped; Gifted. *Learning Problems* Memory Disabilities; Perceptual Disabilities; Thinking Disabilities; Oral Language Disabilities; Reading Disabilities; Handwriting Disabilities; Spelling Disabilities; Arithmetic Disabilities; Written Expression. *Behavioral Problems* Attention Deficits; Hyperactivity; Hypoactivity; Impulsivity; Self-Aggression; Verbal Aggression; Physical Aggression; Indirect Aggression; Passive Aggression; Withdrawal. *Conditions Treated* Disintegrative Psychoses; Schizophrenia; Aphasia; Convulsive Disorders; Phobias; Obsessions and Compulsions; Hysteria; Depression; Suicide; Asthma; Anorexia Nervosa; Ulcerative Colitis; Inadequacy/Immaturity; Personality Problems; Socialized Aggressive Reaction; Unsocialized Aggressive Reaction.

Services Provided Individual Therapy; Group Therapy; Parent Involvement; Behavior Therapy; Cognitive Developmental Therapy; Family Therapy; Filial Therapy; Drug Therapy; Reality Therapy; Play Therapy. *Professionals on Staff* Psychiatrists 3; Psychologists .5; Social Workers 2.5; Nurses 1.

Comments This is a comprehensive outpatient service for children, adolescents, and their families. It evaluates and treats children through age 17 and their families with a variety of therapeutic techniques. It has liaisons with all local schools and agencies and has an outreach program in two local schools.

South Oaks Hospital

400 Sunrise Hwy, Amityville, NY 11701 (516) 264-4000
Year Established 1882
Contact Walter Donhesier; Anthony Van Jones

Facility Information *Placement* Private Psychiatric Hospital. *Number of Beds* 80. *Children/Adolescents Served* 80. *Sexes Served* Both. *Sources of Funding* Health Insurance; Medicare. Summer school available. *Teacher Certification Level* Junior High/Middle School; High School. *Special Certification Level* ED; LD; Reading; Math; Special Education.

Student/Patient Characteristics *Age Levels* 12-14; 15-17. *IQ Ranges* 71-85; 85-130; Above 130. *Exceptionalities Served* Emotionally Disturbed; Learning Disabled; Communication Disordered. *Learning Problems* Memory Disabilities; Thinking Disabilities; Oral Language Disabilities; Reading Disabilities; Handwriting Disabilities; Spelling Disabilities; Arithmetic Disabilities; Written Expression. *Behavioral Problems* Attention Deficits; Hyperactivity; Hypoactivity; Impulsivity; Self-Aggression; Verbal Aggression; Physical Aggression; Indirect Aggression; Passive Aggression; Withdrawal. *Conditions Treated* Alcohol Abuse and/or Drug Abuse; Other Substance Abuse or Dependence; Schizophrenia; Aphasia; Convulsive Disorders; Phobias; Obsessions and Compulsions; Hysteria; Depression; Suicide; Anorexia Nervosa; Inadequacy/Immaturity; Personality Problems; Socialized Aggressive Reaction; Unsocialized Aggressive Reaction.

Services Provided Individual Therapy; Group Therapy; Parent Involvement; Behavior Therapy; Family Therapy; Drug Therapy. *Professionals on Staff* Psychiatrists 18; Psychologists 4; Counselors; Social Workers 4; Nurses. *Service Facilities Available (with number of rooms)* Resource Rooms 3; Self-Contained Rooms 3; Hospital School 8; On-Campus Residential School 8. *Educational Professionals* Regular School Teachers 4; Special Education Teachers 4; Special Education Counselors. *Curricula* Individualized. *Educational Intervention Approaches* Behavior Modification. *Degrees Awarded* High School Diploma; Graduate Equivalency Diploma.

South Shore Child Guidance Center

17 W Merrick Rd, Freeport, NY 11572 (516) 868-3030
Year Established 1959
Contact Murray Felson, Exec Dir

Facility Information *Placement* Child Guidance Center. *Children/Adolescents Served* 450. *Sexes Served* Both. *Sources of Funding* State Funds; Health Insurance; Medicaid; County Funds; Private Fees.

Student/Patient Characteristics *Age Levels* 0-4; 5-8; 9-11; 12-14; 15-17; 18-21. *IQ Ranges* 56-70; 71-85; 85-130; Above 130. *Exceptionalities Served* Emotionally Disturbed; Learning Disabled; Mentally Handicapped. *Learning Problems* Memory Disabilities; Perceptual Disabilities; Thinking Disabilities; Oral Language Disabilities; Reading Disabilities; Handwriting Disabilities; Spelling Disabilities; Arithmetic Disabilities; Written Expression. *Behavioral Problems* Attention Deficits; Hyperactivity; Hypoactivity; Impulsivity; Self-Aggression; Verbal Aggression; Physical Aggression; Indirect Aggression; Passive Aggression; Withdrawal. *Conditions Treated* Alcohol Abuse and/or Drug Abuse; Other Substance Abuse or Dependence; Schizophrenia; Phobias; Obsessions and Compulsions; Hysteria; Depression; Anorexia Nervosa; Ulcerative Colitis; Inadequacy/Immaturity; Personality Problems; Socialized Aggressive Reaction; Unsocialized Aggressive Reaction.

Services Provided Individual Therapy; Group Therapy; Parent Involvement; Behavior Therapy; Family Therapy; Filial Therapy; Drug Therapy; Art Therapy; Play Therapy. *Professionals on Staff* Psychiatrists 2; Psychologists 2.5; Social Workers 6; Art Therapist 1.

Spence Chapin Services to Families and Children—The Children's House

3 E 94th St, New York, NY 10128-0697 (212) 427-7500
Year Established 1976
Contact Andronike C Tsamas, Dir

Facility Information *Placement* Special Program; Day Treatment. *Children/Adolescents Served* 28. *Sexes Served* Both. *Tuition Fees (Approx)* $15,000. *Sources of Funding* State Funds; Medicaid; New York City Department of Mental Health; Third Party Payment. Summer school available. *Special Certification Level* ED; LD; Special Education; Preschool.

Student/Patient Characteristics *Age Levels* 0-4. *Exceptionalities Served* Autistic; Emotionally Disturbed; Learning Disabled; Communication Disordered; Hearing Impaired/Deaf; Physically Handicapped. *Learning Problems* Memory Disabilities; Perceptual Disabilities; Thinking Disabilities; Oral Language Disabilities; Handwriting Disabilities. *Behavioral Problems* Attention Deficits; Hyperactivity; Impulsivity; Self-Aggression; Verbal Aggression; Physical Aggression; Withdrawal. *Conditions Treated* Early Infantile Autism; Schizophrenia; Phobias; Obsessions and Compulsions; Depression; Inadequacy/Immaturity; Personality Problems; Unsocialized Aggressive Reaction.

Services Provided Individual Therapy; Group Therapy; Parent Involvement; Cognitive Developmental Therapy; Family Therapy; Drug Therapy; Music Therapy; Play Therapy. *Professionals on Staff* Psychiatrists 1; Psychologists 1; Social Workers 6. *Service Facilities Available (with number of rooms)* Consultative (ERT) 6; Self-Contained Rooms 3. *Educational Professionals* Special Education Teachers 7. *Curricula* Individualized; Basic Skills. *Educational Intervention Approaches* Self-Control; Psychoeducational Treatment.

State Agriculture and Industrial School

Industry, NY 14474 (716) 533-1700
Year Established 1849
Contact Carl W Juztin, Dir

Facility Information *Placement* Public Residential Care. *Number of Beds* 100. *Children/Adolescents Served* 100. *Sexes Served* Male. *Sources of Funding* State Funds. Summer school available.

Teacher Certification Level Elementary School; Junior High/Middle School. *Special Certification Level* ED; LD; Career/Vocational Education; Reading; Math.

Student/Patient Characteristics *Age Levels* 12-14; 15-17. *IQ Ranges* 41-55; 56-70; 71-85; 85-130; Above 130. *Exceptionalities Served* Emotionally Disturbed; Learning Disabled; Hearing Impaired/Deaf; Other Health Impaired. *Learning Problems* Perceptual Disabilities; Thinking Disabilities; Reading Disabilities; Arithmetic Disabilities. *Behavioral Problems* Attention Deficits; Hyperactivity; Impulsivity; Verbal Aggression; Physical Aggression; Passive Aggression; Withdrawal. *Conditions Treated* Other Substance Abuse or Dependence; Convulsive Disorders; Inadequacy/Immaturity; Personality Problems; Socialized Aggressive Reaction; Unsocialized Aggressive Reaction.

Services Provided Individual Therapy; Group Therapy; Parent Involvement; Behavior Therapy. *Professionals on Staff* Psychiatrists 1; Psychologists 2; Counselors 6; Social Workers 8; Child Care Staff 80; Nurses 3. *Service Facilities Available (with number of rooms)* Resource Rooms; On-Campus Residential School 20. *Educational Professionals* Regular School Teachers 12; Special Education Teachers 3; Career/Vocational Teachers 5; Special Education Counselors 1. *Curricula* Traditional Academic; Career/Vocational Education; Individualized; Basic Skills; Prevocational. *Educational Intervention Approaches* Behavior Modification. *Degrees Awarded* Certificate of Attendance; Graduate Equivalency Diploma.

State University of New York at Albany—SUNY Pre-Kindergarten

1400 Washington Ave, Albany, NY 12222 (518) 457-4654
Year Established 1978
Contact Edward Welch, Dir

Facility Information *Placement* Special School; University Campus Program. *Children/Adolescents Served* 60. *Sexes Served* Both. *Tuition Fees (Approx)* $11,000. *Sources of Funding* State Funds; HEW; County Funds. Summer school available. *Special Certification Level* Special Education.

Student/Patient Characteristics *Age Levels* 0-4. *IQ Ranges* 0-25; 26-40; 41-55; 56-70; 71-85; 85-130; Above 130. *Exceptionalities Served* Autistic; Emotionally Disturbed; Learning Disabled; Mentally Handicapped; Communication Disordered; Hearing Impaired/Deaf; Visually Impaired/Blind; Other Health Impaired; Physically Handicapped; Multiply Handicapped. *Learning Problems* Memory Disabilities; Perceptual Disabilities; Thinking Disabilities; Oral Language Disabilities; Handwriting Disabilities. *Behavioral Problems* Attention Deficits; Hyperactivity; Hypoactivity; Impulsivity; Verbal Aggression; Physical Aggression; Indirect Aggression; Passive Aggression; Withdrawal. *Conditions Treated* Early Infantile Autism; Aphasia; Convulsive Disorders; Phobias; Obsessions and Compulsions; Personality Problems; Socialized Aggressive Reaction.

Services Provided Individual Therapy; Group Therapy; Parent Involvement; Behavior Therapy; Cognitive Developmental Therapy; Music Therapy; Play Therapy. *Professionals on Staff* Psychologists 1; Child Care Staff 17; Nurses 1; Occupational Therapist 1; Physical Therapist 1.5; Speech and Language Therapist 3. *Service Facilities Available (with number of rooms)* Resource Rooms 6; Self-Contained Rooms 6. *Educational Professionals* Special Education Teachers 7; Paraprofessionals 10. *Curricula* Individualized. *Educational Intervention Approaches* Engineered Classroom; Precision Teaching; Behavior Modification; Applied Behavior Analysis.

Stuyvesant Residence Club

74 St Marks Pl, New York City, NY 10003 (212) 477-1565
Contact Sheridan Jackson, Asst Dir

Facility Information *Placement* Public Residential Care. *Number of Beds* 26. *Children/Adolescents Served* 26. *Sexes Served* Male. *Sources of Funding* State Funds; Medicaid.

Student/Patient Characteristics *Age Levels* 15-17; 18-21. *IQ Ranges* 85-130; Above 130. *Exceptionalities Served* Emotionally Disturbed. *Learning Problems* Memory Disabilities; Perceptual

Disabilities; Thinking Disabilities; Oral Language Disabilities; Reading Disabilities; Handwriting Disabilities; Spelling Disabilities; Arithmetic Disabilities; Written Expression. *Behavioral Problems* Attention Deficits; Hyperactivity; Impulsivity; Self-Aggression; Verbal Aggression; Indirect Aggression; Passive Aggression; Withdrawal. *Conditions Treated* Alcohol Abuse and/or Drug Abuse; Schizophrenia; Phobias; Obsessions and Compulsions; Depression; Inadequacy/Immaturity; Personality Problems; Socialized Aggressive Reaction; Unsocialized Aggressive Reaction.

Services Provided Individual Therapy; Group Therapy; Parent Involvement; Family Therapy. *Professionals on Staff* Psychiatrists; Psychologists; Counselors; Social Workers; Nurses. *Service Facilities Available (with number of rooms)* Consultative (ERT). *Curricula* Career/Vocational Education.

Suffolk Child Development Center

Hollywood Dr, Smithtown, NY 11787 (516) 724-1717
Contact Dominic Romeo, Ed Dir

Facility Information *Placement* Private Day Care. *Sexes Served* Both. *Tuition Fees (Approx)* $13,500-$19,500. *Sources of Funding* State Funds; P.L. 94-142; Suffolk County. Summer school available. *Special Certification Level* Special Education.

Student/Patient Characteristics *Age Levels* 0-4; 5-8; 9-11; 12-14; 15-17; 18-21; Over 21. *Exceptionalities Served* Autistic; Emotionally Disturbed; Learning Disabled; Mentally Handicapped; Communication Disordered; Physically Handicapped. *Learning Problems* Memory Disabilities; Perceptual Disabilities; Thinking Disabilities; Oral Language Disabilities. *Behavioral Problems* Attention Deficits; Hyperactivity; Hypoactivity; Impulsivity; Self-Aggression; Physical Aggression; Indirect Aggression; Passive Aggression; Withdrawal. *Conditions Treated* Early Infantile Autism; Aphasia; Convulsive Disorders.

Services Provided Parent Involvement; Family Therapy. *Professionals on Staff* Psychiatrists 2; Psychologists 2; Social Workers 4; Nurses 3. *Service Facilities Available (with number of rooms)* Itinerants 1; Self-Contained Rooms 31; Infant Home Program. *Educational Professionals* Special Education Teachers 31; Paraprofessionals 35. *Curricula* Individualized; Prevocational. *Educational Intervention Approaches* Behavior Modification; Applied Behavior Analysis.

Summit Children's Residence Center

339 N Broadway, Upper Nyack, NY 10960 (914) 358-7772
Year Established 1974
Contact Thomas Schaeffer, Dir of Admissions

Facility Information *Placement* Special School; Private Residential Care. *Number of Beds* 85. *Children/Adolescents Served* 100. *Sexes Served* Both. *Room and Board Fees (Approx)* $72. *Tuition Fees (Approx)* $10,318. *Sources of Funding* State Funds; P.L. 94-142. Summer school available. *Teacher Certification Level* Elementary School; Junior High/Middle School; High School. *Special Certification Level* ED; LD; Career/Vocational Education; Reading; Math.

Student/Patient Characteristics *Age Levels* 9-11; 12-14; 15-17; 18-21; Over 21. *IQ Ranges* 71-85; 85-130; Above 130. *Exceptionalities Served* Emotionally Disturbed; Learning Disabled. *Learning Problems* Memory Disabilities; Perceptual Disabilities; Thinking Disabilities; Oral Language Disabilities; Reading Disabilities; Handwriting Disabilities; Spelling Disabilities; Arithmetic Disabilities; Written Expression. *Behavioral Problems* Attention Deficits; Hyperactivity; Hypoactivity; Impulsivity; Self-Aggression; Verbal Aggression; Indirect Aggression; Passive Aggression; Withdrawal. *Conditions Treated* Disintegrative Psychoses; Schizophrenia; Convulsive Disorders; Phobias; Obsessions and Compulsions; Hysteria; Depression; Suicide; Asthma; Anorexia Nervosa; Ulcerative Colitis; Inadequacy/Immaturity; Personality Problems; Socialized Aggressive Reaction; Unsocialized Aggressive Reaction.

Services Provided Individual Therapy; Group Therapy; Parent Involvement; Behavior Therapy; Cognitive Developmental Therapy; Family Therapy; Filial Therapy; Drug Therapy; Art Therapy; Music Therapy; Reality Therapy; Play Therapy; Psychodrama. *Professionals on Staff* Psychiatrists 1; Psychologists 1; Social Workers 7; Child Care Staff 31; Nurses 2; Speech Pathologist. *Educational Professionals* Special Education Teachers 10; Career/Vocational Teachers 1; Crisis Teachers 2; Paraprofessionals 10. *Curricula* Traditional Academic; Career/Vocational Education; Individualized; Basic Skills; Prevocational. *Degrees Awarded* Certificate of Attendance; High School Diploma.

University of Rochester Medical School—Child and Adolescent Psychiatry Clinic

300 Crittenden Blvd, Rochester, NY 14642 (716) 275-3522
Year Established 1948
Contact Christopher Hodgman, Dir of Div of Child and Adolescent Psychiatry

Facility Information *Placement* Outpatient Psychiatry Clinic. *Sexes Served* Both. *Sources of Funding* Health Insurance; Medicaid; Self-Pay.

Student/Patient Characteristics *Age Levels* 0-4; 5-8; 9-11; 12-14; 15-17. *IQ Ranges* 56-70; 71-85; 85-130; Above 130. *Exceptionalities Served* Emotionally Disturbed; Learning Disabled. *Learning Problems* Memory Disabilities; Perceptual Disabilities; Thinking Disabilities; Oral Language Disabilities; Reading Disabilities; Handwriting Disabilities; Spelling Disabilities; Arithmetic Disabilities; Written Expression. *Behavioral Problems* Attention Deficits; Hyperactivity; Hypoactivity; Impulsivity; Self-Aggression; Verbal Aggression; Physical Aggression; Indirect Aggression; Passive Aggression; Withdrawal. *Conditions Treated* Alcohol Abuse and/or Drug Abuse; Other Substance Abuse or Dependence; Early Infantile Autism; Disintegrative Psychoses; Schizophrenia; Convulsive Disorders; Phobias; Obsessions and Compulsions; Hysteria; Depression; Suicide; Asthma; Anorexia Nervosa; Ulcerative Colitis; Inadequacy/Immaturity; Personality Problems; Socialized Aggressive Reaction; Unsocialized Aggressive Reaction.

Services Provided Individual Therapy; Group Therapy; Parent Involvement; Family Therapy; Play Therapy; Diagnostic Evaluations; Psychological Testing; Psychiatric Evaluation.

Comments The Clinic constitutes the clinical and community consultation arm of the division of child and adolescent psychiatry, Department of Psychiatry. It is an outpatient clinic providing diagnostic and treatment services for the families of children and adolescents who reside in upper New York State.

Variety Preschooler's Workshop

47 Humphrey Dr, Syosset, NY 11791 (516) 921-7171
Year Established 1966
Contact Judith Bloch, Dir

Facility Information *Placement* Special School; Special Services to Families. *Children/Adolescents Served* 150. *Sexes Served* Both. *Tuition Fees (Approx)* $12,000 (nursery); $15,000 (kindergarten). *Sources of Funding* State Funds; P.L. 94-142; Family Court. Summer school available. *Teacher Certification Level* Elementary School. *Special Certification Level* ED; LD; MR.

Student/Patient Characteristics *Age Levels* 0-4; 5-8. *IQ Ranges* 0-25; 26-40; 41-55; 56-70; 71-85; 85-130. *Exceptionalities Served* Autistic; Emotionally Disturbed; Learning Disabled; Mentally Handicapped; Communication Disordered. *Learning Problems* Memory Disabilities; Perceptual Disabilities; Thinking Disabilities; Oral Language Disabilities; Reading Disabilities; Handwriting Disabilities. *Behavioral Problems* Attention Deficits; Hyperactivity; Hypoactivity; Impulsivity; Self-Aggression; Verbal Aggression; Physical Aggression; Indirect Aggression; Passive Aggression; Withdrawal. *Conditions Treated* Early Infantile Autism; Disintegrative Psychoses; Schizophrenia; Aphasia; Phobias; Obsessions and Compulsions; Hysteria; Depression; Inadequacy/Immaturity; Personality Problems; Socialized Aggressive Reaction; Unsocialized Aggressive Reaction.

Services Provided Parent Involvement; Behavior Therapy; Family Therapy; Filial Therapy; Art Therapy; Music Therapy; Play Therapy. *Professionals on Staff* Psychologists 2; Social Workers 5; Nurses 1; Physical Therapist; Occupational Therapist; Adaptive

Physical Ed. 4. *Service Facilities Available (with number of rooms)* Self-Contained Rooms 18. *Educational Professionals* Special Education Teachers 18; Crisis Teachers 1; Special Education Counselors 2; Paraprofessionals 32. *Curricula* Individualized; Basic Skills. *Educational Intervention Approaches* Engineered Classroom; Precision Teaching; Self-Control; Behavior Modification; Applied Behavior Analysis; Creative Conditioning Individual Curriculum.

West Nassau Mental Health Center

365 Franklin Ave, Franklin Square, NY 11010 (516) 437-6050
Year Established 1958
Contact Barbara Judge, Asst to Dir

Facility Information *Placement* Special Program; Outpatient Mental Health Center. *Sexes Served* Both. *Sources of Funding* State Funds; Health Insurance; Medicaid; Medicare; County Funds; Patients Fees; Fundraising.

Student/Patient Characteristics *Age Levels* 0-4; 5-8; 9-11; 15-17; 18-21; Over 21. *Behavioral Problems* Attention Deficits; Hyperactivity; Hypoactivity; Impulsivity; Self-Aggression; Verbal Aggression; Physical Aggression; Indirect Aggression; Passive Aggression; Withdrawal. *Conditions Treated* Disintegrative Psychoses; Schizophrenia; Aphasia; Phobias; Obsessions and Compulsions; Hysteria; Depression; Suicide; Anorexia Nervosa; Inadequacy/Immaturity; Personality Problems; Socialized Aggressive Reaction; Unsocialized Aggressive Reaction.

Services Provided Individual Therapy; Group Therapy; Parent Involvement; Behavior Therapy; Family Therapy; Drug Therapy; Play Therapy. *Professionals on Staff* Psychiatrists 4; Psychologists 3; Social Workers 18.

Westchester Day Treatment Program

226 Linda Ave, Hawthorne, NY 10532 (914) 769-2790
Year Established 1964
Contact Joel Simon, Dir

Facility Information *Placement* Public School. *Children/Adolescents Served* 26. *Sexes Served* Both. *Tuition Fees (Approx)* $12,500. *Sources of Funding* State Funds; Health Insurance; Medicaid; Home District COH. Summer school available. *Teacher Certification Level* Elementary School; Junior High/Middle School; High School. *Special Certification Level* ED; LD; Career/Vocational Education; Reading; Math.

Student/Patient Characteristics *Age Levels* 12-14; 15-17; 18-21. *IQ Ranges* 71-85; 85-130. *Exceptionalities Served* Emotionally Disturbed; Learning Disabled. *Learning Problems* Memory Disabilities; Perceptual Disabilities; Thinking Disabilities; Oral Language Disabilities; Reading Disabilities; Handwriting Disabilities; Spelling Disabilities; Arithmetic Disabilities; Written Expression. *Behavioral Problems* Attention Deficits; Hyperactivity; Impulsivity; Self-Aggression; Verbal Aggression; Physical Aggression; Indirect Aggression; Passive Aggression; Withdrawal. *Conditions Treated* Disintegrative Psychoses; Schizophrenia; Phobias; Obsessions and Compulsions; Hysteria; Depression; Suicide; Anorexia Nervosa; Inadequacy/Immaturity; Personality Problems; Socialized Aggressive Reaction.

Services Provided Individual Therapy; Group Therapy; Parent Involvement; Family Therapy; Filial Therapy; Drug Therapy; Play Therapy. *Professionals on Staff* Psychiatrists 1; Social Workers 2; Child Care Staff 2. *Service Facilities Available (with number of rooms)* Consultative (ERT) 1; Resource Rooms 4; Self-Contained Rooms 3. *Educational Professionals* Regular School Teachers; Special Education Teachers; Career/Vocational Teachers; Special Education Counselors; Paraprofessionals. *Curricula* Traditional Academic; Career/Vocational Education; Individualized; Basic Skills; Prevocational. *Educational Intervention Approaches* Behavior Modification. *Degrees Awarded* Certificate of Attendance; Graduate Equivalency Diploma.

Comments The center provides an integrative clinical/educational milieu for adolescents residing in Westchester County and who have been referred by their sending school districts. A residential program is also available serving youngsters within the New York metropolitan area.

Western New York Children's Psychiatric Center

1010 East and West Rd, West Seneca, NY 14224 (716) 674-9730
Year Established 1979
Contact C A Davis, Exec Dir

Facility Information *Placement* Acute Psychiatric Center. *Number of Beds* 58. *Sexes Served* Both. *Room and Board Fees (Approx)* $299. *Sources of Funding* State Funds; Health Insurance; Medicaid. Summer school available. *Teacher Certification Level* Elementary School; Junior High/Middle School; High School. *Special Certification Level* Special Education.

Student/Patient Characteristics *Age Levels* 5-8; 9-11; 12-14; 15-17. *IQ Ranges* 71-85; 85-130; Above 130. *Exceptionalities Served* Emotionally Disturbed; Learning Disabled; Mentally Handicapped; Communication Disordered; Hearing Impaired/ Deaf. *Learning Problems* Memory Disabilities; Perceptual Disabilities; Thinking Disabilities; Oral Language Disabilities; Reading Disabilities; Handwriting Disabilities; Spelling Disabilities; Arithmetic Disabilities; Written Expression. *Behavioral Problems* Attention Deficits; Hyperactivity; Hypoactivity; Impulsivity; Self-Aggression; Verbal Aggression; Physical Aggression; Indirect Aggression; Passive Aggression; Withdrawal. *Conditions Treated* Disintegrative Psychoses; Schizophrenia; Phobias; Obsessions and Compulsions; Hysteria; Depression; Suicide; Anorexia Nervosa; Inadequacy/Immaturity; Personality Problems; Socialized Aggressive Reaction; Unsocialized Aggressive Reaction.

Services Provided Individual Therapy; Group Therapy; Parent Involvement; Behavior Therapy; Cognitive Developmental Therapy; Family Therapy; Drug Therapy; Reality Therapy; Play Therapy. *Professionals on Staff* Psychiatrists 7; Psychologists 10; Counselors 1; Social Workers 12; Child Care Staff 70. *Educational Professionals* Special Education Teachers 10; Paraprofessionals 3.

Woodward Mental Health Center

201 W Merrick Rd, Freeport, NY 11520 (516) 379-0900
Year Established 1957
Contact Nina L Sloan, Exec Dir

Facility Information *Placement* Day Treatment Center. *Children/Adolescents Served* 85. *Sexes Served* Both. *Sources of Funding* State Funds; Court; Fund-Raising. Summer school available. *Teacher Certification Level* Elementary School; Junior High/Middle School; High School. *Special Certification Level* ED; LD; Career/Vocational Education.

Student/Patient Characteristics *Age Levels* 0-4; 5-8; 9-11; 12-14; 15-17; 18-21. *Exceptionalities Served* Emotionally Disturbed. *Learning Problems* Memory Disabilities; Perceptual Disabilities; Thinking Disabilities; Oral Language Disabilities; Reading Disabilities; Handwriting Disabilities; Spelling Disabilities; Arithmetic Disabilities; Written Expression. *Behavioral Problems* Attention Deficits; Hyperactivity; Impulsivity; Self-Aggression; Verbal Aggression; Physical Aggression; Indirect Aggression; Passive Aggression; Withdrawal. *Conditions Treated* Alcohol Abuse and/or Drug Abuse; Other Substance Abuse or Dependence; Schizophrenia; Phobias; Obsessions and Compulsions; Hysteria; Depression; Suicide; Anorexia Nervosa; Inadequacy/Immaturity; Personality Problems; Socialized Aggressive Reaction; Unsocialized Aggressive Reaction.

Services Provided Individual Therapy; Group Therapy; Parent Involvement; Behavior Therapy; Cognitive Developmental Therapy; Family Therapy; Drug Therapy; Art Therapy; Reality Therapy; Play Therapy. *Professionals on Staff* Psychiatrists 2; Psychologists 2; Counselors 1; Social Workers 4; Nurses 1. *Service Facilities Available (with number of rooms)* Consultative (ERT) 12; Resource Rooms 1; Self-Contained Rooms 5. *Educational Professionals* Special Education Teachers 30. *Curricula* Traditional Academic; Career/Vocational Education; Individualized; Basic Skills; Prevocational. *Educational Intervention Approaches* Engineered Classroom; Precision Teaching; Progressive Discipline; Self-Control; Behavior Modification; Applied Behavior Analysis; Creative Conditioning. *Degrees Awarded* High School Diploma.

Comments Woodward is a psychiatric day treatment program for children and adolescents. The program services are clinically-based and treat the emotional disturbance of the youngster. The individual needs of each youngster are met including special education. There is no charge to the family or child.

North Carolina

Alexander Children's Center

PO Box 220632, 6220 Thermal Rd, Charlotte, NC 28222
(704) 366-8712
Year Established 1888
Contact Glenn B Robinson, Exec Dir

Facility Information *Placement* Private Residential Care; Private Day Care. *Number of Beds* 36. *Children/Adolescents Served* 46. *Sexes Served* Both. *Tuition Fees (Approx)* $36,000. *Sources of Funding* State Funds; Health Insurance; P.L. 94-142. Summer school available. *Teacher Certification Level* Elementary School. *Special Certification Level* ED; LD; MR.

Student/Patient Characteristics *Age Levels* 5-8; 9-11; 12-14. *IQ Ranges* 71-85; 85-130. *Exceptionalities Served* Emotionally Disturbed; Learning Disabled. *Learning Problems* Memory Disabilities; Perceptual Disabilities; Thinking Disabilities; Oral Language Disabilities. *Behavioral Problems* Attention Deficits; Hyperactivity; Impulsivity; Self-Aggression; Verbal Aggression; Physical Aggression; Indirect Aggression; Passive Aggression; Withdrawal. *Conditions Treated* Schizophrenia; Obsessions and Compulsions; Hysteria; Depression; Inadequacy/Immaturity; Personality Problems; Socialized Aggressive Reaction; Unsocialized Aggressive Reaction.

Services Provided Individual Therapy; Group Therapy; Parent Involvement; Behavior Therapy; Cognitive Developmental Therapy; Family Therapy; Filial Therapy; Drug Therapy; Reality Therapy; Play Therapy; Psychodrama. *Professionals on Staff* Psychiatrists 1; Psychologists 2; Social Workers 4; Child Care Staff 15; Nurses 1. *Service Facilities Available (with number of rooms)* Resource Rooms; Self-Contained Rooms 2; On-Campus Residential School 6. *Educational Professionals* Special Education Teachers 5; Crisis Teachers 1; Paraprofessionals 2. *Curricula* Individualized; Basic Skills. *Educational Intervention Approaches* Progressive Discipline; Self-Control; Behavior Modification; Creative Conditioning.

Bowman Gray School of Medicine Developmental Evaluation Clinic—Amos Cottage Rehabilitation Hospital

3325 Silas Creek Pkwy, Winston-Salem, NC 27103
(919) 765-9916
Year Established 1961
Contact Alanson Hinman, Med Dir

Facility Information *Placement* Rehabilitation Hospital; Developmental Evaluation Clinic. *Number of Beds* 41. *Children/Adolescents Served* 41 inpatients; 600 new outpatient evaluations. *Sexes Served* Both. *Sources of Funding* State Funds; Health Insurance; Medicaid; P.L. 94-142; Donations; Private Funds. Summer school available.

Student/Patient Characteristics *Age Levels* 0-4; 5-8; 9-11; 12-14; 15-17; 18-21; Over 21. *IQ Ranges* 26-40; 41-55; 56-70; 71-85; 85-130. *Exceptionalities Served* Autistic; Emotionally Disturbed; Learning Disabled; Mentally Handicapped; Communication Disordered; Hearing Impaired/Deaf; Visually Impaired/Blind; Other Health Impaired. *Learning Problems* Memory Disabilities; Perceptual Disabilities; Thinking Disabilities; Oral Language Disabilities; Reading Disabilities; Handwriting Disabilities; Spelling Disabilities; Arithmetic Disabilities; Written Expression. *Behavioral Problems* Attention Deficits; Hyperactivity; Hypoactivity; Impulsivity; Self-Aggression; Verbal Aggression; Physical Aggression; Indirect Aggression; Passive Aggression; Withdrawal. *Conditions Treated* Early Infantile Autism; Aphasia; Convulsive Disorders; Phobias; Obsessions and Compulsions; Hysteria; Depression; Inadequacy/Immaturity; Personality Problems; Socialized Aggressive Reaction; Unsocialized Aggressive Reaction.

Services Provided Individual Therapy; Group Therapy; Parent Involvement; Behavior Therapy; Cognitive Developmental Therapy; Family Therapy; Filial Therapy; Drug Therapy; Art Therapy; Music Therapy; Play Therapy. *Educational Intervention Approaches* Progressive Discipline; Self-Control; Behavior Modification.

Comments Amos Cottage Rehabilitation Hospital/Developmental Evaluation Clinic is a subacute rehabilitation hospital for children with integral outpatient evaluation, treatment planning, and treatment programs. Developmental disabilities are the primary diagnostic and therapeutic entities served.

Child Guidance Clinic—Day Treatment Program

1200 Glade St, Winston-Salem, NC 27101 (919) 723-3571
Year Established 1957
Contact Clyde Benedict, Exec Dir

Facility Information *Placement* Special School; Special Program. *Children/Adolescents Served* 24. *Sexes Served* Both. *Sources of Funding* State Funds; Title XX; United Way; Third Party Pay; Patient Pay. Summer school available. *Teacher Certification Level* Elementary School; Junior High/Middle School. *Special Certification Level* ED.

Student/Patient Characteristics *Age Levels* 0-4; 5-8. *IQ Ranges* 85-130. *Exceptionalities Served* Emotionally Disturbed. *Learning Problems* Perceptual Disabilities; Thinking Disabilities. *Behavioral Problems* Attention Deficits; Hyperactivity; Impulsivity; Self-Aggression; Verbal Aggression; Physical Aggression; Passive Aggression; Withdrawal. *Conditions Treated* Phobias; Obsessions and Compulsions; Depression; Personality Problems; Socialized Aggressive Reaction; Unsocialized Aggressive Reaction.

Services Provided Individual Therapy; Group Therapy; Parent Involvement; Family Therapy; Play Therapy. *Professionals on Staff* Psychiatrists 2; Psychologists 3; Social Workers 1; Child Care Staff 2. *Service Facilities Available (with number of rooms)*

Consultative (ERT) 1; Resource Rooms 1; Self-Contained Rooms 2. *Educational Professionals* Special Education Teachers 2; Paraprofessionals 1. *Curricula* Individualized; Basic Skills. *Educational Intervention Approaches* Psychoeducational Techniques.

Cleveland County Area Mental Health Program—Division of Child and Youth Services

222 Crawford St, Shelby, NC 28150 (704) 482-8941
Contact William Varley, Dir Childrens Serv
Facility Information *Placement* Public Residential Care; Special Program; Mental Health Program. *Number of Beds* 1. *Children/Adolescents Served* 10 (adolescent day treatment); 10 (therapeutic preschool); 15 (severe developmental delays); 100 (outpatients). *Sexes Served* Both. *Room and Board Fees (Approx)* $100. *Sources of Funding* State Funds; Health Insurance; Medicaid; Private Fees. Summer school available. *Teacher Certification Level* Elementary School; Junior High/Middle School; High School. *Special Certification Level* ED; LD; MR.
Student/Patient Characteristics *Age Levels* 0-4; 5-8; 9-11; 12-14; 15-17. *IQ Ranges* 0-25; 26-40; 41-55; 56-70; 71-85; 85-130; Above 130. *Exceptionalities Served* Autistic; Emotionally Disturbed; Learning Disabled; Mentally Handicapped; Communication Disordered; Hearing Impaired/Deaf; Visually Impaired/Blind; Other Health Impaired; Physically Handicapped; Gifted. *Learning Problems* Memory Disabilities; Perceptual Disabilities; Thinking Disabilities; Oral Language Disabilities; Reading Disabilities; Handwriting Disabilities; Spelling Disabilities; Arithmetic Disabilities; Written Expression. *Behavioral Problems* Attention Deficits; Hyperactivity; Hypoactivity; Impulsivity; Self-Aggression; Verbal Aggression; Physical Aggression; Indirect Aggression; Passive Aggression; Withdrawal. *Conditions Treated* Alcohol Abuse and/or Drug Abuse; Other Substance Abuse or Dependence; Early Infantile Autism; Disintegrative Psychoses; Schizophrenia; Aphasia; Convulsive Disorders; Phobias; Obsessions and Compulsions; Hysteria; Depression; Suicide; Anorexia Nervosa; Inadequacy/Immaturity; Personality Problems; Socialized Aggressive Reaction; Unsocialized Aggressive Reaction.
Services Provided Individual Therapy; Group Therapy; Parent Involvement; Behavior Therapy; Cognitive Developmental Therapy; Family Therapy; Drug Therapy; Reality Therapy; Play Therapy. *Professionals on Staff* Psychiatrists 1; Psychologists 4; Social Workers 3; Child Care Staff 6; Nurses 1. *Service Facilities Available (with number of rooms)* Consultative (ERT); Special School. *Educational Professionals* Special Education Teachers 4. *Curricula* Traditional Academic; Individualized; Basic Skills. *Educational Intervention Approaches* Engineered Classroom; Precision Teaching; Behavior Modification; Applied Behavior Analysis. *Degrees Awarded* Certificate of Attendance.
Comments The child and adolescent services program involves outpatient clinical services which include psychotherapy for children and parents, day treatment services for developmentally impaired and delayed, and day treatment services for emotionally handicapped children ages 3-7, 12-18. All services are supported by case management services and psychiatric consultation.

Development Evaluation Center

3403 Melrose Rd, Fayetteville, NC 28304 (919) 485-3696
Year Established 1967
Contact Leo M Croghan, Dir
Facility Information *Children/Adolescents Served* 600. *Sexes Served* Both. *Sources of Funding* State Funds; Health Insurance; Medicaid.
Student/Patient Characteristics *Age Levels* 0-4; 5-8; 9-11; 12-14; 15-17; 18-21. *IQ Ranges* 0-25; 26-40; 41-55; 56-70; 71-85; 85-130; Above 130. *Exceptionalities Served* Autistic; Emotionally Disturbed; Learning Disabled; Mentally Handicapped; Communication Disordered; Hearing Impaired/Deaf; Visually Impaired/Blind; Other Health Impaired; Physically Handicapped; Gifted. *Learning Problems* Memory Disabilities; Perceptual Disabilities; Thinking Disabilities; Oral Language Disabilities; Reading Dis-

abilities; Handwriting Disabilities; Spelling Disabilities; Arithmetic Disabilities; Written Expression; Spelling Disabilities; Arithmetic Disabilities; Written Expression. *Behavioral Problems* Attention Deficits; Hyperactivity; Hypoactivity; Impulsivity; Self-Aggression; Verbal Aggression; Physical Aggression; Indirect Aggression; Passive Aggression; Withdrawal.

Durham County Group Home for Autistic Adults Inc

2010 Holloway St, Durham, NC 27703 (919) 682-2005
Year Established 1979
Contact Kathryn Hill, Dir
Facility Information *Placement* Public Residential Care. *Sexes Served* Male. *Tuition Fees (Approx)* $6,780. *Sources of Funding* State Funds; Social Security Insurance; Special Assistance for Adults.
Student/Patient Characteristics *Age Levels* 18-21; Over 21. *IQ Ranges* 0-25; 26-40. *Exceptionalities Served* Autistic; Communication Disordered. *Learning Problems* Memory Disabilities; Perceptual Disabilities; Thinking Disabilities; Oral Language Disabilities. *Behavioral Problems* Impulsivity; Self-Aggression; Physical Aggression; Withdrawal. *Conditions Treated* Early Infantile Autism; Obsessions and Compulsions.
Services Provided Individual Therapy; Parent Involvement; Behavior Therapy; Cognitive Developmental Therapy; Art Therapy. *Professionals on Staff* Psychiatrists 1; Psychologists 1; Counselors 1; Social Workers 1. *Service Facilities Available (with number of rooms)* Homebound Instruction. *Educational Professionals* Home Teachers 4. *Curricula* Individualized; Basic Skills; Prevocational. *Educational Intervention Approaches* Behavior Modification.
Comments This is a group home for 5 autistic adults. The home-teachers and director are responsible for teaching self help, leisure, and communication skills along with behavioral programing. The residents go to a workshop Monday-Friday where they improve their vocational skills and earn their own spending money.

Eastern Area Residential Treatment Home (EARTH)

3200 S Memorial Dr, Greenville, NC 27834 (919) 756-4432
Year Established 1974
Contact Margaret B Pritchard, Dir
Facility Information *Placement* Public Residential Care. *Number of Beds* 5. *Children/Adolescents Served* 5. *Sexes Served* Both. *Sources of Funding* State Funds. Summer school available. *Teacher Certification Level* Elementary School. *Special Certification Level* ED; MR.
Student/Patient Characteristics *Age Levels* 5-8; 9-11; 12-14. *IQ Ranges* 56-70; 71-85; 85-130. *Exceptionalities Served* Autistic; Emotionally Disturbed; Communication Disordered. *Learning Problems* Memory Disabilities; Perceptual Disabilities; Thinking Disabilities; Oral Language Disabilities; Reading Disabilities; Handwriting Disabilities; Spelling Disabilities; Arithmetic Disabilities; Written Expression. *Behavioral Problems* Attention Deficits; Hyperactivity; Impulsivity; Self-Aggression; Physical Aggression; Indirect Aggression; Passive Aggression; Withdrawal. *Conditions Treated* Early Infantile Autism; Schizophrenia; Personality Problems; Socialized Aggressive Reaction; Unsocialized Aggressive Reaction.
Services Provided Individual Therapy; Parent Involvement; Behavior Therapy; Cognitive Developmental Therapy; Drug Therapy; Music Therapy. *Professionals on Staff* Psychiatrists 1; Psychologists 1; Child Care Staff 3. *Educational Professionals* Special Education Teachers 2. *Curricula* Traditional Academic; Individualized; Basic Skills. *Educational Intervention Approaches* Engineered Classroom; Behavior Modification.
Comments EARTH is a residential treatment facility serving 5 autistic or emotionally disturbed children in a home-like atmosphere with in-house education.

The Group Home for the Autistic Inc

Box 450, Rte 4, Albemarle, NC 28001 (704) 982-9600
Year Established 1979
Contact Dawn Harwood, Dir
Facility Information *Placement* Private Residential Care. *Number of Beds* 5. *Children/Adolescents Served* 5. *Sexes Served* Both. *Sources of Funding* State Funds; Social Security Income.
Student/Patient Characteristics *Age Levels* 5-8; 9-11. *IQ Ranges* 0-25; 26-40. *Exceptionalities Served* Autistic; Communication Disordered. *Learning Problems* Perceptual Disabilities; Oral Language Disabilities; Reading Disabilities. *Behavioral Problems* Attention Deficits; Hyperactivity; Impulsivity; Self-Aggression; Verbal Aggression; Physical Aggression; Indirect Aggression; Withdrawal; Running Away. *Conditions Treated* Early Infantile Autism.
Services Provided Parent Involvement; Behavior Therapy. *Educational Professionals* Special Education Teachers 3. *Curricula* Basic Skills; Prevocational; Behavior Shaping. *Educational Intervention Approaches* Behavior Modification.
Comments This program is a short-term residential facility for austistic, autistic like, or communication handicapped children between the ages of 5-12. The children are contracted for behavior problems. The Group Home trains the child through behavior modification and the parents on how to work with their child. The child is discharged to home when the goals have been met.

Homewood School—Highland Hospital

19 Zillicoa St, Asheville, NC 28801 (704) 254-3201
Contact Joyce Bracewell, Dir of Admissions
Facility Information *Placement* Private Residential Care; Private Day Care. *Number of Beds* 35. *Children/Adolescents Served* 30. *Sexes Served* Both. *Room and Board Fees (Approx)* $284-$320 (day). *Tuition Fees (Approx)* $7,000 (school year). *Sources of Funding* Health Insurance. Summer school available. *Teacher Certification Level* Junior High/Middle School; High School. *Special Certification Level* ED; LD; MR; Academically Gifted.
Student/Patient Characteristics *Age Levels* 12-14; 15-17; 18-21. *IQ Ranges* 71-85; 85-130; Above 130. *Exceptionalities Served* Emotionally Disturbed; Learning Disabled; Mentally Handicapped; Physically Handicapped; Gifted. *Learning Problems* Memory Disabilities; Perceptual Disabilities; Thinking Disabilities; Oral Language Disabilities; Reading Disabilities; Handwriting Disabilities; Spelling Disabilities; Arithmetic Disabilities; Written Expression. *Behavioral Problems* Attention Deficits; Hyperactivity; Hypoactivity; Impulsivity; Self-Aggression; Verbal Aggression; Passive Aggression; Withdrawal. *Conditions Treated* Alcohol Abuse and/or Drug Abuse; Other Substance Abuse or Dependence; Schizophrenia; Phobias; Obsessions and Compulsions; Hysteria; Depression; Suicide; Asthma; Anorexia Nervosa; Inadequacy/Immaturity; Personality Problems; Socialized Aggressive Reaction; Unsocialized Aggressive Reaction.
Services Provided Individual Therapy; Group Therapy; Parent Involvement; Behavior Therapy; Biofeedback; Family Therapy; Drug Therapy; Art Therapy; Music Therapy. *Professionals on Staff* Psychiatrists 8; Psychologists 3; Social Workers 6; Child Care Staff 42; Nurses 36; Activity Therapists 6. *Service Facilities Available (with number of rooms)* Resource Rooms 4; Transition Rooms 3; Self-Contained Rooms 5; Study Rooms 10; On-Campus Residential School. *Educational Professionals* Special Education Teachers 6; Paraprofessionals 2. *Curricula* Traditional Academic; Individualized; Basic Skills; Prevocational. *Educational Intervention Approaches* Progressive Discipline; Self-Control; Behavior Modification; Applied Behavior Analysis; Creative Conditioning.

John Umstead Hospital—Children's Psychiatric Institute

H and 9th Sts, Butner, NC 27509 (919) 575-7621
Year Established 1967
Contact Mary G Holton, Social Work Dir

Facility Information *Placement* Public Residential Care; Outpatient Clinic. *Number of Beds* 64. *Children/Adolescents Served* 64 (patients); 50 (outpatients). *Sexes Served* Both. *Room and Board Fees (Approx)* $184. *Sources of Funding* State Funds; Health Insurance; Medicaid; P.L. 94-142. Summer school available. *Teacher Certification Level* Elementary School; Junior High/Middle School; High School. *Special Certification Level* ED; LD; Reading; Math.
Student/Patient Characteristics *Age Levels* 0-4; 5-8; 9-11; 12-14; 15-17. *IQ Ranges* 56-70; 71-85; 85-130; Above 130. *Exceptionalities Served* Emotionally Disturbed; Learning Disabled; Communication Disordered; Hearing Impaired/Deaf; Visually Impaired/Blind; Other Health Impaired; Physically Handicapped; Gifted. *Learning Problems* Memory Disabilities; Perceptual Disabilities; Thinking Disabilities; Oral Language Disabilities; Reading Disabilities; Handwriting Disabilities; Spelling Disabilities; Arithmetic Disabilities; Written Expression. *Behavioral Problems* Attention Deficits; Hyperactivity; Hypoactivity; Impulsivity; Self-Aggression; Verbal Aggression; Physical Aggression; Indirect Aggression; Passive Aggression; Withdrawal. *Conditions Treated* Disintegrative Psychoses; Schizophrenia; Aphasia; Convulsive Disorders; Phobias; Obsessions and Compulsions; Hysteria; Depression; Suicide; Asthma; Anorexia Nervosa; Ulcerative Colitis; Inadequacy/Immaturity; Personality Problems; Socialized Aggressive Reaction; Unsocialized Aggressive Reaction.
Services Provided Individual Therapy; Group Therapy; Parent Involvement; Behavior Therapy; Cognitive Developmental Therapy; Family Therapy; Drug Therapy; Play Therapy. *Professionals on Staff* Psychiatrists 12; Psychologists 6; Social Workers 12; Child Care Staff 40; Nurses 16; Recreators 10. *Service Facilities Available (with number of rooms)* Hospital School. *Educational Professionals* Special Education Teachers 22; Paraprofessionals 10. *Curricula* Traditional Academic; Career/Vocational Education; Individualized; Basic Skills; Prevocational. *Educational Intervention Approaches* Engineered Classroom; Precision Teaching; Progressive Discipline; Self-Control; Behavior Modification; Applied Behavior Analysis. *Degrees Awarded* High School Diploma.
Comments The Institute is made up of 4 programs including an outpatient psychiatric clinic, a short-term adolescent inpatient program, and 2 long-term residential psychiatric inpatient programs (latency and adolescent). The latency program serves the entire state while the adolescent program serves the north central portion of the state only.

Samarkand Manor

Eagle Springs, NC 27242 (919) 673-3756
Year Established 1917
Contact Carl A Hampton, Facility Dir
Facility Information *Placement* Training School. *Number of Beds* 130. *Children/Adolescents Served* 160. *Sexes Served* Both. *Sources of Funding* State Funds; P.L. 94-142; Chapter I. Summer school available. *Teacher Certification Level* Elementary School; Junior High/Middle School; High School. *Special Certification Level* ED; LD; MR; Career/Vocational Education; Reading; Math.
Student/Patient Characteristics *Age Levels* 12-14; 15-17. *IQ Ranges* 41-55; 56-70; 71-85; 85-130; Above 130. *Exceptionalities Served* Emotionally Disturbed; Learning Disabled; Mentally Handicapped; Communication Disordered; Hearing Impaired/Deaf; Gifted. *Learning Problems* Memory Disabilities; Perceptual Disabilities; Thinking Disabilities; Oral Language Disabilities; Reading Disabilities; Handwriting Disabilities; Spelling Disabilities; Arithmetic Disabilities; Written Expression. *Behavioral Problems* Attention Deficits; Hyperactivity; Impulsivity; Self-Aggression; Verbal Aggression; Physical Aggression; Indirect Aggression; Passive Aggression; Withdrawal. *Conditions Treated* Alcohol Abuse and/or Drug Abuse; Other Substance Abuse or Dependence; Schizophrenia; Obsessions and Compulsions; Depression; Suicide; Inadequacy/Immaturity; Personality Problems; Socialized Aggressive Reaction; Unsocialized Aggressive Reaction.

Services Provided Individual Therapy; Group Therapy; Parent Involvement; Behavior Therapy; Family Therapy; Drug Therapy; Reality Therapy. *Professionals on Staff* Psychiatrists 1; Psychologists 1; Counselors; Social Workers 6; Child Care Staff 93; Nurses 4. *Service Facilities Available (with number of rooms)* Resource Rooms 1; Transition Rooms 20; On-Campus Residential School 1. *Educational Professionals* Regular School Teachers 10; Special Education Teachers 25; Career/Vocational Teachers 7; Paraprofessionals 2; Vocational Counselor 1. *Curricula* Traditional Academic; Career/Vocational Education; Individualized; Basic Skills; Prevocational. *Educational Intervention Approaches* Progressive Discipline; Self-Control; Behavior Modification; Applied Behavior Analysis.

University of North Carolina School of Medicine—Department of Psychiatry—Division TEACCH

310 Medical School Wing E 222H, Chapel Hill, NC 27514
(919) 966-2173
Year Established 1972
Contact Eric Schopler, Dir

Facility Information *Placement* Public School; Community Program. *Sexes Served* Both. *Sources of Funding* State Funds; Health Insurance; Federal Research Funds. *Teacher Certification Level* Elementary School; Junior High/Middle School; High School. *Special Certification Level* ED; LD; MR; Autism.

Student/Patient Characteristics *Age Levels* 0-4; 5-8; 9-11; 12-14; 15-17; 18-21; Over 21. *IQ Ranges* 26-40; 41-55; 56-70; 71-85; 85-130. *Exceptionalities Served* Autistic; Learning Disabled; Communication Disordered. *Learning Problems* Memory Disabilities; Perceptual Disabilities; Thinking Disabilities; Oral Language Disabilities; Reading Disabilities; Handwriting Disabilities; Spelling Disabilities; Arithmetic Disabilities; Written Expression. *Behavioral Problems* Attention Deficits; Hyperactivity; Hypoactivity; Impulsivity; Self-Aggression; Verbal Aggression; Physical Aggression; Indirect Aggression; Passive Aggression; Withdrawal. *Conditions Treated* Early Infantile Autism; Developmental Disorders.

Services Provided Individual Therapy; Group Therapy; Parent Involvement; Behavior Therapy; Family Therapy. *Professionals on Staff* Psychiatrists .5; Psychologists 8; Psychoeducational Specialists 30; Pediatricians 1. *Service Facilities Available (with number of rooms)* Self-Contained Rooms 43. *Educational Professionals* Special Education Teachers 43. *Curricula* Individualized. *Educational Intervention Approaches* Engineered Classroom; Behavior Modification; Communication; Social Skills.

Comments TEACCH is a comprehensive community based program designed to serve autistic and communication handicapped children at home, at school, and in the community. Parent involvement at all three levels is emphasized. Research and training are major program components.

North Dakota

Cass County Social Services—Children's Social Service Center

702 Main Ave, Fargo, ND 58108 (701) 241-5750
Year Established 1955
Contact Roger L Flynn, Supv

Facility Information *Placement* Clinical, Child/Family Guidance Center, Outpatient Only. *Children/Adolescents Served* $150 (per month). *Sexes Served* Both. *Sources of Funding* State Funds; HEW; County Funds and Client Fees. Summer school available.

Student/Patient Characteristics *Age Levels* 0-4; 5-8; 9-11; 12-14; 15-17. *IQ Ranges* 41-55; 56-70; 71-85; 85-130; Above 130.
Exceptionalities Served Autistic; Emotionally Disturbed; Learning Disabled; Mentally Handicapped; Communication Disordered; Hearing Impaired/Deaf; Visually Impaired/Blind; Other Health Impaired; Physically Handicapped; Gifted; Socially and Behaviorally Disturbed. *Learning Problems* Memory Disabilities; Perceptual Disabilities; Thinking Disabilities; Oral Language Disabilities; Reading Disabilities; Handwriting Disabilities; Spelling Disabilities; Arithmetic Disabilities; Written Expression.
Behavioral Problems Attention Deficits; Hyperactivity; Hypoactivity; Impulsivity; Self-Aggression; Verbal Aggression; Physical Aggression; Indirect Aggression; Passive Aggression; Withdrawal. *Conditions Treated* Schizophrenia; Aphasia; Convulsive Disorders; Phobias; Obsessions and Compulsions; Hysteria; Depression; Suicide; Anorexia Nervosa; Inadequacy/Immaturity; Personality Problems; Socialized Aggressive Reaction; Unsocialized Aggressive Reaction.

Services Provided Individual Therapy; Group Therapy; Parent Involvement; Behavior Therapy; Family Therapy; Drug Therapy; Reality Therapy; Play Therapy. *Professionals on Staff* Psychiatrists 1; Psychologists 2; Counselors 3; Social Workers 3.

Dakota Boys' Ranch

Box 396, Minot, ND 58107 (701) 852-3628
Year Established 1953
Contact Charles Fontaine, Dir of Child Care

Facility Information *Placement* Private Residential Care. *Number of Beds* 56. *Children/Adolescents Served* 56. *Sexes Served* Male. *Room and Board Fees (Approx)* $34. *Sources of Funding* State Funds; Medicaid; P.L. 94-142. Summer school available. *Teacher Certification Level* Elementary School; Junior High/Middle School; High School. *Special Certification Level* ED; LD; Career/Vocational Education; Reading.

Student/Patient Characteristics *Age Levels* 12-14; 15-17; 18-21. *IQ Ranges* 85-130. *Exceptionalities Served* Emotionally Disturbed; Learning Disabled. *Learning Problems* Memory Disabilities; Perceptual Disabilities; Thinking Disabilities; Oral Language Disabilities; Reading Disabilities; Handwriting Disabilities; Spelling Disabilities; Arithmetic Disabilities; Written Expression. *Behavioral Problems* Attention Deficits; Hyperactivity; Impul-

sivity; Self-Aggression; Verbal Aggression; Physical Aggression; Indirect Aggression; Passive Aggression; Withdrawal. *Conditions Treated* Inadequacy/Immaturity; Unsocialized Aggressive Reaction.

Services Provided Individual Therapy; Group Therapy; Parent Involvement; Behavior Therapy; Cognitive Developmental Therapy; Family Therapy; Art Therapy; Reality Therapy. *Professionals on Staff* Counselors; Social Workers; Child Care Staff. *Service Facilities Available (with number of rooms)* On-Campus Residential School 10. *Educational Professionals* Regular School Teachers; Special Education Teachers 2; Career/Vocational Teachers 3; Educational Counselor. *Curricula* Traditional Academic; Individualized; Basic Skills; Prevocational. *Educational Intervention Approaches* Self-Control; Behavior Modification; Applied Behavior Analysis. *Degrees Awarded* Certificate of Attendance; Graduate Equivalency Diploma.

Medical Care Rehabilitation Hospital's Child Evaluation and Treatment Program

University of North Dakota University Station, Grand Forks, ND 58202 (701) 780-2477
Year Established 1966
Contact Douglas Knowlton, Dir

Facility Information *Placement* Inpatient and Outpatient Evaluation. *Number of Beds* 8. *Children/Adolescents Served* 350 (outpatient), 8 (inpatient). *Sexes Served* Both. *Sources of Funding* State Funds; Health Insurance; Medicaid; Hill Burton. *Special Certification Level* ED; LD; MR.

Student/Patient Characteristics *Age Levels* 0-4; 5-8; 9-11; 12-14; 15-17; 18-21. *IQ Ranges* 0-25; 26-40; 41-55; 56-70; 71-85; 85-130; Above 130. *Exceptionalities Served* Autistic; Emotionally Disturbed; Learning Disabled; Mentally Handicapped; Communication Disordered; Hearing Impaired/Deaf; Visually Impaired/Blind; Other Health Impaired; Physically Handicapped; Multiply Handicapped. *Learning Problems* Memory Disabilities; Perceptual Disabilities; Thinking Disabilities; Oral Language Disabilities; Reading Disabilities; Handwriting Disabilities; Spelling Disabilities; Arithmetic Disabilities; Written Expression.
Behavioral Problems Attention Deficits; Hyperactivity; Hypoactivity; Impulsivity; Self-Aggression; Verbal Aggression; Physical Aggression; Indirect Aggression; Passive Aggression; Withdrawal. *Conditions Treated* Early Infantile Autism; Aphasia; Convulsive Disorders; Phobias; Obsessions and Compulsions; Hysteria; Depression; Socialized Aggressive Reaction; Unsocialized Aggressive Reaction.

Services Provided Individual Therapy; Parent Involvement; Behavior Therapy; Family Therapy; Play Therapy. *Professionals on Staff* Psychiatrists 1; Psychologists 3; Social Workers 1; Nurses 2; Occupational Therapists 3; Physical Therapists 4; Speech Pathologists 3. *Educational Professionals* Special Education Teachers 2. *Educational Intervention Approaches* Precision Teaching; Progressive Discipline; Self-Control; Behavior Modification.

North Dakota State Mental Hospital—Child and Adolescent Unit

PO Box 476, Jamestown, ND 58401 (701) 252-7733 ext 2772 or 2791
Year Established 1967
Contact Harley H Trefz, Educ Dir

Facility Information *Placement* Public Psychiatric Mental Hospital. *Number of Beds* 48. *Children/Adolescents Served* 64. *Sexes Served* Both. *Room and Board Fees (Approx)* $116. *Tuition Fees (Approx)* $10,702. *Sources of Funding* State Funds; Health Insurance; Medicaid; Medicare; P.L. 94-142. *Teacher Certification Level* Elementary School; Junior High/Middle School; High School. *Special Certification Level* ED; LD; Secondary Education.

Student/Patient Characteristics *Age Levels* 5-8; 9-11; 12-14; 15-17; 18-21. *IQ Ranges* 41-55; 56-70; 71-85; 85-130.
Exceptionalities Served Autistic; Emotionally Disturbed; Learning Disabled; Mentally Handicapped; Communication Disordered; Visually Impaired/Blind; Physically Handicapped; Gifted.
Learning Problems Memory Disabilities; Perceptual Disabilities; Thinking Disabilities; Oral Language Disabilities; Reading Disabilities; Handwriting Disabilities; Spelling Disabilities; Arithmetic Disabilities; Written Expression. *Behavioral Problems* Attention Deficits; Hyperactivity; Hypoactivity; Impulsivity; Self-Aggression; Verbal Aggression; Physical Aggression; Indirect Aggression; Passive Aggression; Withdrawal. *Conditions Treated* Alcohol Abuse and/or Drug Abuse; Other Substance Abuse or Dependence; Early Infantile Autism; Disintegrative Psychoses; Schizophrenia; Aphasia; Convulsive Disorders; Phobias; Obsessions and Compulsions; Hysteria; Depression; Suicide; Asthma; Anorexia Nervosa; Inadequacy/Immaturity; Personality Problems; Socialized Aggressive Reaction; Unsocialized Aggressive Reaction.

Services Provided Individual Therapy; Group Therapy; Parent Involvement; Behavior Therapy; Cognitive Developmental Therapy; Family Therapy; Drug Therapy; Reality Therapy; Play Therapy. *Professionals on Staff* Psychiatrists 1; Psychologists 2; Social Workers 2; Child Care Staff 36; Nurses 5; Recreation Therapists 2. *Service Facilities Available (with number of rooms)* Self-Contained Rooms 10. *Educational Professionals* Special Education Teachers 14; Paraprofessionals 4. *Curricula* Traditional Academic; Individualized; Basic Skills. *Educational Intervention Approaches* Engineered Classroom; Precision Teaching; Progressive Discipline; Self-Control; Behavior Modification; Applied Behavior Analysis; Creative Conditioning. *Degrees Awarded* High School Diploma.

Comments The education program in the Child and Adolescent Center is a public special school and is an adjunctive and integral component of the treatment evaluation process. It works in conjunction with the home school.

Ohio

Berea Children's Home

202 E Bagley Rd, Berea, OH 44017 (216) 234-2006
Year Established 1864
Contact Christopher Cassidy, Admin Asst

Facility Information *Placement* Special School; Private Residential Care; Private Day Care; Childrens Home. *Number of Beds* 53. *Children/Adolescents Served* 80. *Sexes Served* Male. *Room and Board Fees (Approx)* $85. *Sources of Funding* State Funds; P.L. 94-142; County Funds Placements. Summer school available. *Teacher Certification Level* Elementary School. *Special Certification Level* LD; Severely Behaviorally Handicapped.

Student/Patient Characteristics *Age Levels* 5-8; 9-11; 12-14; 15-17; 18-21. *IQ Ranges* 71-85; 85-130. *Exceptionalities Served* Autistic; Emotionally Disturbed; Learning Disabled; Hearing Impaired/Deaf. *Learning Problems* Memory Disabilities; Perceptual Disabilities; Thinking Disabilities; Oral Language Disabilities; Reading Disabilities; Handwriting Disabilities; Spelling Disabilities; Arithmetic Disabilities; Written Expression. *Behavioral Problems* Attention Deficits; Hyperactivity; Hypoactivity; Impulsivity; Self-Aggression; Verbal Aggression; Physical Aggression; Indirect Aggression; Passive Aggression; Withdrawal. *Conditions Treated* Schizophrenia; Obsessions and Compulsions; Depression; Personality Problems; Socialized Aggressive Reaction; Unsocialized Aggressive Reaction.

Services Provided Individual Therapy; Group Therapy; Parent Involvement; Behavior Therapy; Family Therapy; Drug Therapy; Art Therapy; Music Therapy; Eclectic Therapy. *Professionals on Staff* Psychiatrists 1; Psychologists 1; Counselors 3; Social Workers 6; Child Care Staff 30; Nurses 1. *Service Facilities Available (with number of rooms)* Consultative (ERT) 2; Self-Contained Rooms 4; On-Campus Residential School. *Educational Professionals* Special Education Teachers 4; Reading 1. *Curricula* Traditional Academic; Career/Vocational Education. *Educational Intervention Approaches* Behavior Modification.

Comments This program is a multi-service nonprofit agency offering residential day treatment group homes, foster homes, outpatient counseling, and day care services. The school program is supervised by the city school district. Children with emotional/behavioral problems are referred by county children services board and a per diem fee is charged.

Bittersweet Farms

12660 Archbold-Whitehouse Rd, Whitehouse, OH 43571
(419) 875-6986
Year Established 1983
Contact Bettye Ruth Kay, Dir

Facility Information *Placement* Private Residential Care; Private Day Care; Farmstead Skills Training. *Number of Beds* 15. *Children/Adolescents Served* 15. *Sexes Served* Both. *Room and Board Fees (Approx)* $73. *Sources of Funding* Medicaid. Summer school available. *Teacher Certification Level* High School. *Special Certification Level* LD; Agriculture; Adult Education.

Student/Patient Characteristics *Age Levels* 18-21; Over 21. *IQ Ranges* 26-40; 41-55; 56-70; 71-85; 85-130. *Exceptionalities Served* Autistic. *Learning Problems* Memory Disabilities; Perceptual Disabilities; Thinking Disabilities; Oral Language Disabilities; Reading Disabilities; Handwriting Disabilities; Written Expression. *Behavioral Problems* Attention Deficits; Hyperactivity; Hypoactivity; Impulsivity; Self-Aggression; Physical Aggression; Indirect Aggression; Withdrawal. *Conditions Treated* Early Infantile Autism; Inadequacy/Immaturity.

Services Provided Individual Therapy; Behavior Therapy; Drug Therapy; Art Therapy; Music Therapy; Work and Leisure Therapy. *Professionals on Staff* Psychiatrists 1; Psychologists 1; Social Workers 1; Nurses; Occupational Therapist 1. *Service Facilities Available (with number of rooms)* Adult Education Programs 6. *Educational Professionals* Special Education Teachers 2; Career/Vocational Teachers 1; Paraprofessionals 26. *Curricula* Career/Vocational Education; Individualized; Prevocational. *Educational Intervention Approaches* Self-Control; Behavior Modification.

Comments Bittersweet Farms utilizes a variety of therapeutic approaches and is involved in training self-skills, leisure, work, cognitive development, and socialization in a farmstead setting.

Blick Clinic for Developmental Disabilities

640 W Market St, Akron, OH 44303 (216) 762-5425
Year Established 1969
Contact Gregory L LaForme, Exec Dir

Facility Information *Placement* Interdisciplinary Outpatient Services. *Children/Adolescents Served* 300-500. *Sexes Served* Both. *Sources of Funding* State Funds; Health Insurance; Medicaid; Medicare; Fee.

Student/Patient Characteristics *Age Levels* 0-4; 5-8; 9-11; 12-14; 15-17; 18-21; Over 21. *IQ Ranges* 0-25; 26-40; 41-55; 56-70; 71-85. *Exceptionalities Served* Autistic; Emotionally Disturbed; Learning Disabled; Mentally Handicapped; Communication Disordered; Hearing Impaired/Deaf; Visually Impaired/Blind; Other Health Impaired; Physically Handicapped. *Learning Problems* Memory Disabilities; Perceptual Disabilities; Thinking Disabilities; Oral Language Disabilities; Reading Disabilities; Handwriting Disabilities; Spelling Disabilities; Arithmetic Disabilities; Written Expression. *Behavioral Problems* Attention Deficits; Hyperactivity; Hypoactivity; Impulsivity; Self-Aggression; Verbal Aggression; Physical Aggression; Indirect Aggression; Passive Aggression; Withdrawal. *Conditions Treated* Alcohol Abuse and/or Drug Abuse; Other Substance Abuse or Dependence; Early Infantile Autism; Schizophrenia; Aphasia; Convulsive Disorders; Phobias; Obsessions and Compulsions; Hysteria; Depression; Inadequacy/Immaturity; Personality Problems; Socialized Aggressive Reaction; Unsocialized Aggressive Reaction.

Services Provided Individual Therapy; Group Therapy; Parent Involvement; Behavior Therapy; Cognitive Developmental Therapy; Family Therapy; Filial Therapy; Drug Therapy. *Professionals on Staff* Psychiatrists 2; Psychologists 6; Social Workers 5; Child Care Staff 6; Nurses 1; Occupational Therapist; Physical Therapist; Speech; Medical Doctor. *Service Facilities Available (with number of rooms)* Consultative (ERT). *Curricula* Individualized. *Educational Intervention Approaches* Precision Teaching; Progressive Discipline; Self-Control; Behavior Modification; Applied Behavior Analysis.

Boys' Village Inc—Boys' Village School

Box 518, Smithville, OH 44677 (216) 264-3232
Year Established 1946
Contact David Yonas, Clinical Dir
Facility Information *Placement* Public School; Special School; Private Residential Care. *Number of Beds* 68.
Children/Adolescents Served 68. *Sexes Served* Male. *Room and Board Fees (Approx)* $55. Summer school available. *Teacher Certification Level* Elementary School; Junior High/Middle School; High School. *Special Certification Level* LD; Reading; Math.
Student/Patient Characteristics *Age Levels* 12-14; 15-17. *IQ Ranges* 85-130; Above 130. *Exceptionalities Served* Emotionally Disturbed; Learning Disabled. *Learning Problems* Memory Disabilities; Perceptual Disabilities; Thinking Disabilities; Reading Disabilities; Handwriting Disabilities; Spelling Disabilities; Arithmetic Disabilities; Written Expression. *Behavioral Problems* Attention Deficits; Hyperactivity; Impulsivity; Self-Aggression; Verbal Aggression; Physical Aggression; Indirect Aggression; Passive Aggression; Withdrawal. *Conditions Treated* Other Substance Abuse or Dependence; Phobias; Obsessions and Compulsions; Hysteria; Depression; Inadequacy/Immaturity; Personality Problems; Socialized Aggressive Reaction; Unsocialized Aggressive Reaction.
Services Provided Individual Therapy; Group Therapy; Parent Involvement; Behavior Therapy; Cognitive Developmental Therapy; Family Therapy; Art Therapy; Music Therapy. *Professionals on Staff* Psychiatrists 1; Psychologists 1; Social Workers 6; Child Care Staff. *Educational Professionals* Special Education Counselors 9. *Curricula* Traditional Academic; Individualized; Basic Skills; Prevocational.

Buckeye Boys' Ranch Inc

5665 Hoover Rd, Grove City, OH 43123 (614) 875-2371
Year Established 1961
Contact Leslie A Bostic, Exec Dir
Facility Information *Placement* Private Residential Care; Private Day Care; Group Home. *Number of Beds* 60.
Children/Adolescents Served Residential 50; Group Home 10; Day Treatment 15. *Sexes Served* Male. *Room and Board Fees (Approx)* Residential $67; Group Home $53; Day Treatment $19. *Tuition Fees (Approx)* Residential $24,776; Group Home $19,429; Day Treatment $3,487. *Sources of Funding* State Funds; Medicaid; Tuition; United Way; Private Donations. *Teacher Certification Level* Elementary School; Junior High/Middle School. *Special Certification Level* LD; Career/Vocational Education; Behavior Disabled.
Student/Patient Characteristics *Age Levels* 9-11; 12-14; 15-17; 18-21. *IQ Ranges* 71-85; 85-130; Above 130. *Exceptionalities Served* Emotionally Disturbed; Learning Disabled; Severe Behaviorally Handicapped. *Learning Problems* Memory Disabilities; Perceptual Disabilities; Thinking Disabilities; Oral Language Disabilities; Reading Disabilities; Handwriting Disabilities; Spelling Disabilities; Arithmetic Disabilities; Written Expression. *Behavioral Problems* Attention Deficits; Hyperactivity; Hypoactivity; Impulsivity; Self-Aggression; Verbal Aggression; Physical Aggression; Indirect Aggression; Passive Aggression; Withdrawal. *Conditions Treated* Phobias; Obsessions and Compulsions; Hysteria; Depression; Suicide; Inadequacy/Immaturity; Personality Problems; Socialized Aggressive Reaction; Unsocialized Aggressive Reaction.

Services Provided Individual Therapy; Group Therapy; Parent Involvement; Behavior Therapy; Family Therapy; Drug Therapy; Reality Therapy. *Professionals on Staff* Psychiatrists 1; Counselors 4; Social Workers 2; Child Care Staff 40; Nurses 1. *Service Facilities Available (with number of rooms)* Consultative (ERT) 2; Transition Rooms 6; Self-Contained Rooms 6. *Educational Professionals* Special Education Teachers 10; Career/Vocational Teachers 1; Paraprofessionals 2; Administrator 1; Secretary 1. *Curricula* Individualized; Basic Skills; Prevocational. *Educational Intervention Approaches* Precision Teaching; Behavior Modification. *Degrees Awarded* High School Diploma.
Comments The group home program is designed for students 14 to 18. The Day Treatment Program is designed for students primarily in Franklin County. Aftercare services are also available for graduates remaining in-county.

Butler County Mental Health Center Inc

111 Buckeye St, Hamilton, OH 45011 (513) 896-7887
Year Established 1946
Contact Marion S Parish, Center Dir
Facility Information *Placement* Outpatient Mental Health Facility. *Children/Adolescents Served* 150. *Sexes Served* Both. *Sources of Funding* State Funds; Health Insurance; Medicaid; Self-Pay.
Student/Patient Characteristics *Age Levels* 0-4; 5-8; 9-11; 12-14; 15-17; 18-21; Over 21. *IQ Ranges* 56-70; 71-85; 85-130; Above 130. *Exceptionalities Served* Emotionally Disturbed; Mentally Handicapped. *Learning Problems* Memory Disabilities; Perceptual Disabilities; Thinking Disabilities. *Behavioral Problems* Attention Deficits; Hyperactivity; Hypoactivity; Impulsivity; Self-Aggression; Verbal Aggression; Physical Aggression; Indirect Aggression; Passive Aggression; Withdrawal. *Conditions Treated* Alcohol Abuse and/or Drug Abuse; Other Substance Abuse or Dependence; Schizophrenia; Phobias; Obsessions and Compulsions; Hysteria; Depression; Suicide; Anorexia Nervosa; Inadequacy/Immaturity; Personality Problems; Socialized Aggressive Reaction; Unsocialized Aggressive Reaction.
Services Provided Individual Therapy; Group Therapy; Parent Involvement; Family Therapy; Play Therapy. *Professionals on Staff* Psychiatrists 2; Psychologists 3; Counselors 14; Social Workers 8.

Child Adolescent Service Center

1226 Market Ave N, Canton, OH 44714 (216) 454-7917
Year Established 1976
Contact Jon V Thomas, Clinical Dir; Sandra Dragomire, Day Treatment Coord
Facility Information *Placement* Special School; Special Program. *Children/Adolescents Served* 40. *Sexes Served* Both. *Room and Board Fees (Approx)* $65. *Tuition Fees (Approx)* Sliding Scale. *Sources of Funding* State Funds; Health Insurance; Medicaid; United Way. Summer school available. *Teacher Certification Level* Elementary School; Junior High/Middle School. *Special Certification Level* LD; Child Development.
Student/Patient Characteristics *Age Levels* 0-4; 5-8; 9-11; 12-14. *IQ Ranges* 56-70; 71-85; 85-130; Above 130. *Exceptionalities Served* Autistic; Emotionally Disturbed; Learning Disabled; Mentally Handicapped; Communication Disordered; Other Health Impaired; Physically Handicapped. *Learning Problems* Memory Disabilities; Perceptual Disabilities; Thinking Disabilities; Oral Language Disabilities; Reading Disabilities. *Behavioral Problems* Attention Deficits; Hyperactivity; Impulsivity; Self-Aggression; Verbal Aggression; Physical Aggression; Indirect Aggression; Passive Aggression; Withdrawal. *Conditions Treated* Early Infantile Autism; Schizophrenia; Convulsive Disorders; Obsessions and Compulsions; Depression; Inadequacy/Immaturity; Personality Problems; Socialized Aggressive Reaction; Unsocialized Aggressive Reaction.
Services Provided Individual Therapy; Group Therapy; Parent Involvement; Behavior Therapy; Family Therapy; Drug Therapy; Play Therapy. *Professionals on Staff* Psychiatrists 1; Psychologists 1; Social Workers 1; Child Care Staff 6. *Service Facilities*

Available (with number of rooms) Self-Contained Rooms 5.
Educational Professionals Special Education Teachers 2; Para-professionals 2. *Curricula* Traditional Academic; Individualized; Basic Skills. *Educational Intervention Approaches* Behavior Modification; Applied Behavior Analysis; Positive Education Program.

Comments This program is a psychoeducational model which incorporates a variety of therapies with education. The school age program is jointly operated between this agency and the local school district.

Children's Aid Society

10427 Detroit Ave, Cleveland, OH 44102 (216) 521-6511
Contact Catharine D Berwald, Dir of Clinical Serv

Facility Information *Placement* Private Residential Care. *Number of Beds* 36. *Children/Adolescents Served* 36. *Sexes Served* Both. *Sources of Funding* Health Insurance. *Teacher Certification Level* Elementary School; Junior High/Middle School. *Special Certification Level* LD.

Student/Patient Characteristics *Age Levels* 5-8; 9-11; 12-14. *IQ Ranges* 85-130; Above 130. *Exceptionalities Served* Emotionally Disturbed; Learning Disabled; Other Health Impaired. *Learning Problems* Memory Disabilities; Perceptual Disabilities; Thinking Disabilities; Oral Language Disabilities; Reading Disabilities; Handwriting Disabilities; Spelling Disabilities; Arithmetic Disabilities; Written Expression. *Behavioral Problems* Attention Deficits; Impulsivity; Self-Aggression; Verbal Aggression; Physical Aggression; Indirect Aggression; Passive Aggression; Withdrawal. *Conditions Treated* Convulsive Disorders; Phobias; Obsessions and Compulsions; Depression; Socialized Aggressive Reaction; Unsocialized Aggressive Reaction.

Services Provided Individual Therapy; Group Therapy; Parent Involvement; Behavior Therapy; Family Therapy; Art Therapy; Music Therapy. *Professionals on Staff* Psychiatrists; Psychologists; Counselors; Social Workers; Child Care Staff; Nurses. *Service Facilities Available (with number of rooms)* Resource Rooms 1; Self-Contained Rooms 6. *Educational Professionals* Special Education Teachers; Paraprofessionals. *Curricula* Traditional Academic; Individualized; Basic Skills. *Educational Intervention Approaches* Engineered Classroom; Precision Teaching; Progressive Discipline; Self-Control; Behavior Modification; Applied Behavior Analysis. *Degrees Awarded* Certificate of Attendance.

The Children's Home of Cincinnati

5051 Duck Creek Rd, Cincinnati, OH 45227 (513) 272-2800
Year Established 1864
Contact Joseph T Chambers, Exec Dir

Facility Information *Placement* Public School; Special School; Private Residential Care; Private Day Care. *Number of Beds* 36. *Children/Adolescents Served* 36 (residential treatment); 10 (day treatment). *Sexes Served* Both. *Room and Board Fees (Approx)* $107. *Tuition Fees (Approx)* $145,200. *Sources of Funding* State Funds; P.L. 94-142. Summer school available. *Teacher Certification Level* Elementary School; Junior High/Middle School; High School. *Special Certification Level* ED; LD.

Student/Patient Characteristics *Age Levels* 9-11; 12-14; 15-17; 18-21. *IQ Ranges* 71-85; 85-130; Above 130. *Exceptionalities Served* Emotionally Disturbed; Learning Disabled. *Learning Problems* Memory Disabilities; Perceptual Disabilities; Thinking Disabilities; Oral Language Disabilities; Reading Disabilities; Handwriting Disabilities; Spelling Disabilities; Arithmetic Disabilities; Written Expression. *Behavioral Problems* Attention Deficits; Hyperactivity; Hypoactivity; Impulsivity; Self-Aggression; Verbal Aggression; Physical Aggression; Indirect Aggression; Passive Aggression; Withdrawal. *Conditions Treated* Phobias; Obsessions and Compulsions; Depression; Suicide; Anorexia Nervosa; Inadequacy/Immaturity; Personality Problems; Socialized Aggressive Reaction; Unsocialized Aggressive Reaction.

Services Provided Individual Therapy; Group Therapy; Parent Involvement; Behavior Therapy; Family Therapy; Drug Therapy; Art Therapy. *Professionals on Staff* Psychiatrists 1; Psychologists

1; Social Workers 6; Child Care Staff 20; Nurses 2; Director of Professional Services 1. *Service Facilities Available (with number of rooms)* Self-Contained Rooms 1; Departmental Classrooms 5; On-Campus Residential School 6; Public and Parochial Schools. *Educational Professionals* Special Education Teachers 6; Paraprofessionals 1; Director of Education 1. *Curricula* Traditional Academic; Career/Vocational Education; Individualized; Basic Skills. *Educational Intervention Approaches* Engineered Classroom; Self-Control; Behavior Modification; Creative Conditioning. *Degrees Awarded* High School Diploma.

Children's Mental Health Center Inc

721 Raymond St, Columbus, OH 43205 (614) 221-2615
Year Established 1949
Contact Judd F Holder, Exec Dir

Facility Information *Placement* Outpatient Mental Health Center. *Sexes Served* Both. *Sources of Funding* State Funds; Health Insurance; Medicaid; County Levy; Grants. *Special Certification Level* ED; Reading; Math.

Student/Patient Characteristics *Age Levels* 0-4; 5-8; 9-11; 12-14; 15-17. *IQ Ranges* 85-130. *Exceptionalities Served* Emotionally Disturbed. *Learning Problems* Perceptual Disabilities; Reading Disabilities; Spelling Disabilities; Arithmetic Disabilities. *Behavioral Problems* Attention Deficits; Hyperactivity; Hypoactivity; Impulsivity; Self-Aggression; Verbal Aggression; Physical Aggression; Indirect Aggression; Passive Aggression; Withdrawal. *Conditions Treated* Alcohol Abuse and/or Drug Abuse; Phobias; Obsessions and Compulsions; Depression; Suicide; Anorexia Nervosa; Inadequacy/Immaturity; Personality Problems; Socialized Aggressive Reaction; Unsocialized Aggressive Reaction.

Services Provided Individual Therapy; Group Therapy; Parent Involvement; Behavior Therapy; Family Therapy; Play Therapy. *Professionals on Staff* Psychiatrists 4; Psychologists 6; Social Workers 42. *Service Facilities Available (with number of rooms)* Therapy Offices; Group Rooms 50. *Educational Professionals* Special Education Teachers 4. *Educational Intervention Approaches* Self-Control; Behavior Modification.

Comments The Center provides a full range of professional outpatient guidance and counseling mental health services to children through age 18 and their families. Services include the diagnosis and treatment of emotional and behavioral disorders, family and marital counseling, testing and evaluation, alcohol and drug abuse, crisis support, suicide prevention, children and adolescents in trouble on the streets, in the courts, and in the schools, and the Families in Transition Program, which provides the support for families experiencing divorce, separation, death, or illness or who are victims of crime.

Children's Psychiatric Center of the Jewish Hospital

3140 Harvey Ave, Cincinnati, OH 45229 (513) 281-6070
Year Established 1920
Contact Sharon Sorg, Admin Dir

Facility Information *Placement* Psychiatric Center. *Children/Adolescents Served* 756 (outpatients); 79 (day treatment patients). *Sexes Served* Both. *Room and Board Fees (Approx)* $116. *Tuition Fees (Approx)* $20,800. *Sources of Funding* HEW; Health Insurance; Medicaid; P.L. 94-142; Community Chest; Hamilton County Community Mental Health Board. Summer school available. *Teacher Certification Level* Elementary School. *Special Certification Level* Severe Behavioral Handicaps.

Student/Patient Characteristics *Age Levels* 0-4; 5-8; 9-11; 12-14. *Exceptionalities Served* Autistic; Emotionally Disturbed. *Learning Problems* Memory Disabilities; Perceptual Disabilities; Thinking Disabilities; Oral Language Disabilities; Reading Disabilities; Handwriting Disabilities; Spelling Disabilities; Arithmetic Disabilities; Written Expression. *Behavioral Problems* Attention Deficits; Hyperactivity; Impulsivity; Self-Aggression; Verbal Aggression; Physical Aggression; Indirect Aggression; Passive Aggression; Withdrawal. *Conditions Treated* Disintegrative

Psychoses; Phobias; Obsessions and Compulsions; Depression; Suicide; Inadequacy/Immaturity; Personality Problems; Socialized Aggressive Reaction; Unsocialized Aggressive Reaction.

Services Provided Individual Therapy; Group Therapy; Parent Involvement; Behavior Therapy; Cognitive Developmental Therapy; Family Therapy; Drug Therapy; Play Therapy. *Professionals on Staff* Psychiatrists 5; Psychologists 8; Social Workers 3; Child Care Staff 11; Nurses 1. *Service Facilities Available (with number of rooms)* Consultative (ERT) 5; Itinerants 8; Transition Rooms 3; Self-Contained Rooms 11. *Educational Professionals* Special Education Teachers 3; Paraprofessionals 1. *Curricula* Traditional Academic; Individualized; Basic Skills. *Educational Intervention Approaches* Behavior Modification.

Comments This program provides outpatient services to children with emotional, behavior, and learning problems. Parent training on child rearing and in understanding normal and unusual developmental problems is provided. Day treatment services for children with emotional and learning problems needing daily special education and comprehensive treatment with parental counseling is emphasized. The Elementary Program serves children 6 to 12 years of age and the Preschool Program children 3 to 6 years of age. Community Consultation and Education Services are provided to schools, social agencies, health facilities, day care centers, physicians, and parent groups.

Cleveland Christian Home for Children Inc

11401 Lorain Ave, Cleveland, OH 44111 (216) 671-0977
Year Established 1903
Contact James B Daley, Prog Dir
Facility Information *Placement* Private Residential Care. *Number of Beds* 36. *Children/Adolescents Served* 36. *Sexes Served* Both. *Room and Board Fees (Approx)* $88. *Sources of Funding* State Funds; County Funds. *Teacher Certification Level* Elementary School. *Special Certification Level* ED; LD.

Student/Patient Characteristics *IQ Ranges* 56-70; 71-85; 85-130. *Exceptionalities Served* Emotionally Disturbed; Learning Disabled. *Learning Problems* Memory Disabilities; Perceptual Disabilities; Thinking Disabilities; Oral Language Disabilities; Reading Disabilities; Spelling Disabilities; Arithmetic Disabilities; Written Expression. *Behavioral Problems* Attention Deficits; Hyperactivity; Impulsivity; Self-Aggression; Verbal Aggression; Physical Aggression; Indirect Aggression; Passive Aggression; Withdrawal. *Conditions Treated* Obsessions and Compulsions; Depression; Inadequacy/Immaturity; Personality Problems; Socialized Aggressive Reaction; Unsocialized Aggressive Reaction.

Services Provided Individual Therapy; Parent Involvement; Behavior Therapy; Family Therapy; Drug Therapy; Play Therapy. *Professionals on Staff* Psychiatrists 1; Psychologists 1; Social Workers 3; Child Care Staff 37. *Service Facilities Available (with number of rooms)* Self-Contained Rooms 4; On-Campus Residential School 4. *Educational Professionals* Special Education Teachers 3. *Curricula* Individualized; Basic Skills. *Educational Intervention Approaches* Behavior Modification.

Comments The educational component of the Cleveland Christian Home treatment program is provided by the Cleveland City Schools. Teachers are hired jointly by the home and the Cleveland Public Schools. Teachers are compensated by the Cleveland Public School System. Regular public school classes are utilized when appropriate.

Cleveland Clinic Foundation

9500 Euclid Ave, Cleveland, OH 44106 (216) 444-5822
Year Established 1925
Contact Meir Gross, Head of Child and Adolescent Psychiatry
Facility Information *Placement* Hospital Clinic and Day Hospital. *Number of Beds* 20. *Sexes Served* Both. *Room and Board Fees (Approx)* $290. *Sources of Funding* Health Insurance; Medicaid; Medicare; Direct Payment. Summer school available. *Teacher Certification Level* Elementary School; Junior High/Middle School; High School. *Special Certification Level* ED; LD; MR; Reading; Math.

Student/Patient Characteristics *Age Levels* 9-11; 12-14; 15-17; 18-21. *IQ Ranges* 71-85; 85-130; Above 130. *Exceptionalities Served* Emotionally Disturbed; Learning Disabled; Mentally Handicapped; Communication Disordered; Hearing Impaired/Deaf; Other Health Impaired. *Learning Problems* Memory Disabilities; Perceptual Disabilities; Thinking Disabilities; Oral Language Disabilities; Reading Disabilities; Handwriting Disabilities; Spelling Disabilities; Arithmetic Disabilities; Written Expression. *Behavioral Problems* Attention Deficits; Hyperactivity; Hypoactivity; Impulsivity; Self-Aggression; Verbal Aggression; Physical Aggression; Indirect Aggression; Passive Aggression; Withdrawal. *Conditions Treated* Alcohol Abuse and/or Drug Abuse; Other Substance Abuse or Dependence; Early Infantile Autism; Disintegrative Psychoses; Schizophrenia; Aphasia; Convulsive Disorders; Phobias; Obsessions and Compulsions; Hysteria; Depression; Suicide; Asthma; Anorexia Nervosa; Ulcerative Colitis; Inadequacy/Immaturity; Personality Problems; Socialized Aggressive Reaction; Unsocialized Aggressive Reaction.

Services Provided Individual Therapy; Group Therapy; Parent Involvement; Behavior Therapy; Cognitive Developmental Therapy; Biofeedback; Family Therapy; Filial Therapy; Drug Therapy; Art Therapy; Music Therapy; Reality Therapy; Play Therapy; Psychodrama. *Professionals on Staff* Psychiatrists 3; Psychologists 5; Social Workers 4; Nurses 15. *Service Facilities Available (with number of rooms)* Consultative (ERT) 1; Resource Rooms 1; Special School 1; Hospital School 1; On-Campus Residential School 1. *Educational Professionals* Special Education Teachers 3. *Curricula* Traditional Academic; Individualized; Basic Skills; Prevocational. *Educational Intervention Approaches* Progressive Discipline; Self-Control; Behavior Modification; Applied Behavior Analysis; Creative Conditioning. *Degrees Awarded* High School Diploma; Graduate Equivalency Diploma.

The Educational Clinic Inc

867 S James Rd, Columbus, OH 43227-1099 (614) 236-1604
Year Established 1962
Contact Gerald J Pruzan, Dir
Facility Information *Placement* Outpatient Mental Health Clinic. *Sexes Served* Both. *Sources of Funding* Health Insurance; Medicaid; Medicare; P.L. 94-142 Fee. Summer school available. *Teacher Certification Level* Elementary School; Junior High/Middle School; High School. *Special Certification Level* ED; LD; MR; Reading; Speech Pathology.

Student/Patient Characteristics *Age Levels* 5-8; 9-11; 12-14; 15-17; 18-21; Over 21. *IQ Ranges* 71-85; 85-130; Above 130. *Exceptionalities Served* Emotionally Disturbed; Learning Disabled; Mentally Handicapped; Communication Disordered; Hearing Impaired/Deaf; Visually Impaired/Blind; Other Health Impaired; Gifted. *Learning Problems* Memory Disabilities; Perceptual Disabilities; Thinking Disabilities; Oral Language Disabilities; Reading Disabilities; Handwriting Disabilities; Spelling Disabilities; Arithmetic Disabilities; Written Expression. *Behavioral Problems* Attention Deficits; Hyperactivity; Hypoactivity; Impulsivity; Self-Aggression; Verbal Aggression; Physical Aggression; Indirect Aggression; Passive Aggression; Withdrawal. *Conditions Treated* Alcohol Abuse and/or Drug Abuse; Other Substance Abuse or Dependence; Disintegrative Psychoses; Schizophrenia; Aphasia; Convulsive Disorders; Phobias; Obsessions and Compulsions; Hysteria; Depression; Suicide; Anorexia Nervosa; Ulcerative Colitis; Inadequacy/Immaturity; Personality Problems; Socialized Aggressive Reaction; Unsocialized Aggressive Reaction.

Services Provided Individual Therapy; Group Therapy; Parent Involvement; Behavior Therapy; Cognitive Developmental Therapy; Biofeedback; Family Therapy; Reality Therapy; Play Therapy. *Professionals on Staff* Psychologists 2; Counselors 2; Remedial Therapists and Speech Pathologists 5. *Educational Professionals* Regular School Teachers 1; Special Education Teachers 4; Special Education Counselors 2; Paraprofessionals 1. *Curricula* Individualized; Basic Skills. *Educational Intervention Approaches* Self-Control; Behavior Modification. *Degrees Awarded* Certificate of Attendance.

Emerson North

5642 Hamilton Ave, Cincinati, OH 45224 (513) 541-0135
Contact Bruce Weil, Dir Adolescent Prog

Facility Information *Placement* Private Residential Care; Inpatient Psychiatric Hospital. *Number of Beds* 39.
Children/Adolescents Served 39. *Sexes Served* Both. *Room and Board Fees (Approx)* $320. *Sources of Funding* Health Insurance. Summer school available. *Teacher Certification Level* Junior High/Middle School; High School. *Special Certification Level* ED; LD.

Student/Patient Characteristics *Age Levels* 12-14; 15-17; 18-21. *IQ Ranges* 71-85; 85-130; Above 130. *Exceptionalities Served* Emotionally Disturbed; Learning Disabled. *Learning Problems* Perceptual Disabilities; Thinking Disabilities; Reading Disabilities; Spelling Disabilities; Arithmetic Disabilities; Written Expression. *Behavioral Problems* Attention Deficits; Hyperactivity; Hypoactivity; Impulsivity; Self-Aggression; Verbal Aggression; Physical Aggression; Indirect Aggression; Passive Aggression; Withdrawal. *Conditions Treated* Alcohol Abuse and/or Drug Abuse; Other Substance Abuse or Dependence; Disintegrative Psychoses; Schizophrenia; Phobias; Obsessions and Compulsions; Hysteria; Depression; Suicide; Anorexia Nervosa; Personality Problems; Socialized Aggressive Reaction; Unsocialized Aggressive Reaction.

Services Provided Individual Therapy; Group Therapy; Parent Involvement; Behavior Therapy; Cognitive Developmental Therapy; Family Therapy; Drug Therapy; Art Therapy; Music Therapy; Reality Therapy; Play Therapy; Psychodrama; Loss Group; Adoption Issues Group; Recreational Therapy. *Professionals on Staff* Psychiatrists 7; Psychologists 3; Counselors 1; Social Workers 4; Child Care Staff 16; Nurses 20. *Service Facilities Available (with number of rooms)* Traditional Classrooms. *Educational Professionals* Special Education Teachers 4. *Curricula* Traditional Academic; Individualized; Basic Skills. *Educational Intervention Approaches* Self-Control.

Kimwood—Home for Autistic Opportunities Inc

1001 Rice St, Springfield, OH 45505 (513) 322-6460
Year Established 1979

Facility Information *Placement* Family Home. *Number of Beds* 4.
Children/Adolescents Served 4. *Room and Board Fees (Approx)* $51. *Sources of Funding* State Funds.

Student/Patient Characteristics *Age Levels* 12-14. *IQ Ranges* 41-55; 56-70. *Exceptionalities Served* Autistic. *Learning Problems* Memory Disabilities; Perceptual Disabilities; Thinking Disabilities; Oral Language Disabilities; Reading Disabilities; Handwriting Disabilities; Spelling Disabilities; Arithmetic Disabilities; Written Expression. *Behavioral Problems* Impulsivity; Self-Aggression. *Conditions Treated* Early Infantile Autism; Convulsive Disorders; Personality Problems.

Services Provided Parent Involvement. *Service Facilities Available (with number of rooms)* Self-Contained Rooms 1; Special School; Public School 1. *Educational Professionals* Special Education Teachers. *Curricula* Prevocational. *Educational Intervention Approaches* Self-Control; Behavior Modification.

Lake County Mental Health Center—Department of Children's Services

8445 Munson Rd, Mentor, OH 44060 (216) 255-6701
Contact Lillian N Schlachter, Dir Children's Serv

Facility Information *Placement* Mental Health Center.
Children/Adolescents Served 100. *Sexes Served* Both. *Sources of Funding* State Funds; Health Insurance; Medicaid; 648 Bd; Local Mental Health Sources.

Student/Patient Characteristics *Age Levels* 0-4; 5-8; 9-11; 12-14; 15-17. *IQ Ranges* 41-55; 56-70; 71-85; 85-130; Above 130. *Exceptionalities Served* Autistic; Emotionally Disturbed; Learning Disabled; Mentally Handicapped; Other Health Impaired; Physically Handicapped; Gifted. *Learning Problems* Memory Disabilities; Perceptual Disabilities; Thinking Disabilities; Oral Language Disabilities; Reading Disabilities; Handwriting Disabilities; Spelling Disabilities; Arithmetic Disabilities; Written Expression. *Behavioral Problems* Attention Deficits; Hyperactivity; Hypoactivity; Impulsivity; Self-Aggression; Verbal Aggression; Physical Aggression; Indirect Aggression; Passive Aggression; Withdrawal. *Conditions Treated* Alcohol Abuse and/or Drug Abuse; Other Substance Abuse or Dependence; Schizophrenia; Convulsive Disorders; Phobias; Obsessions and Compulsions; Hysteria; Depression; Suicide; Asthma; Anorexia Nervosa; Ulcerative Colitis; Inadequacy/Immaturity; Personality Problems; Socialized Aggressive Reaction; Unsocialized Aggressive Reaction.

Services Provided Individual Therapy; Group Therapy; Parent Involvement; Behavior Therapy; Cognitive Developmental Therapy; Family Therapy; Play Therapy. *Professionals on Staff* Psychiatrists 1; Psychologists 1; Social Workers 5; Child Care Staff 1.

Marymount Hospital Mental Health Center

12300 McCracken Rd, Garfield Heights, OH 44125
(216) 581-0500
Year Established 1972
Contact Mark S Susin, Child-Therapist

Facility Information *Placement* Outpatient Evaluation/Therapy. *Sexes Served* Both. *Sources of Funding* State Funds; Health Insurance; Medicaid; Medicare.

Student/Patient Characteristics *Age Levels* 0-4; 5-8; 9-11; 12-14; 15-17; 18-21; Over 21. *IQ Ranges* 56-70; 71-85; 85-130. *Exceptionalities Served* Emotionally Disturbed; Learning Disabled; Gifted. *Learning Problems* Perceptual Disabilities; Reading Disabilities. *Behavioral Problems* Attention Deficits; Hyperactivity; Impulsivity; Self-Aggression; Verbal Aggression; Indirect Aggression; Passive Aggression; Withdrawal. *Conditions Treated* Depression; Anorexia Nervosa; Inadequacy/Immaturity; Personality Problems; Socialized Aggressive Reaction.

Services Provided Individual Therapy; Group Therapy; Parent Involvement; Behavior Therapy; Cognitive Developmental Therapy; Family Therapy; Art Therapy; Music Therapy; Reality Therapy; Play Therapy; Psychodrama. *Professionals on Staff* Psychiatrists 3; Psychologists 3; Counselors 2; Social Workers 3; Nurses 6.

Marymount Hospital Mental Health Center

12300 McCracken Rd, Garfield Heights, OH 44125
(216) 581-0500
Year Established 1972
Contact John J Moigritt, Medical Dir

Facility Information *Placement* Mental Health Center. *Sexes Served* Both. *Room and Board Fees (Approx)* $330 (inpatient). *Sources of Funding* State Funds; Health Insurance; Medicaid; Medicare; Self Pay.

Student/Patient Characteristics *Age Levels* 9-11; 12-14; 15-17; 18-21; Over 21. *Exceptionalities Served* Autistic; Emotionally Disturbed; Learning Disabled; Mentally Handicapped; Communication Disordered; Hearing Impaired/Deaf; Visually Impaired/Blind; Other Health Impaired; Physically Handicapped. *Learning Problems* Memory Disabilities; Perceptual Disabilities; Thinking Disabilities; Oral Language Disabilities; Reading Disabilities; Handwriting Disabilities; Spelling Disabilities; Arithmetic Disabilities; Written Expression. *Behavioral Problems* Attention Deficits; Hyperactivity; Hypoactivity; Impulsivity; Self-Aggression; Verbal Aggression; Physical Aggression; Indirect Aggression; Passive Aggression; Withdrawal. *Conditions Treated* Alcohol Abuse and/or Drug Abuse; Other Substance Abuse or Dependence; Disintegrative Psychoses; Schizophrenia; Aphasia; Convulsive Disorders; Phobias; Obsessions and Compulsions; Hysteria; Depression; Suicide; Anorexia Nervosa; Ulcerative Colitis; Inadequacy/Immaturity; Personality Problems; Socialized Aggressive Reaction; Unsocialized Aggressive Reaction.

Services Provided Individual Therapy; Group Therapy; Parent Involvement; Behavior Therapy; Cognitive Developmental Therapy; Family Therapy; Filial Therapy; Drug Therapy; Art Therapy; Music Therapy; Reality Therapy; Play Therapy; Psychodrama. *Professionals on Staff* Psychiatrists 8; Psychologists 3; Counselors 7; Social Workers 3; Nurses 14.

Mental Health Services of North Central Hamilton Co Inc

7710 Reading Rd, Cincinnati, OH 45237 (513) 761-6222
Year Established 1974
Contact Maurice Ripley, Asst Exec Dir
Facility Information *Placement* Outpatient Mental Health Services. *Children/Adolescents Served* 200. *Sexes Served* Both. *Sources of Funding* State Funds; Health Insurance; Medicaid; County Funds; Client Fees.
Student/Patient Characteristics *Age Levels* 5-8; 9-11; 12-14; 15-17. *IQ Ranges* 71-85; 85-130; Above 130. *Exceptionalities Served* Emotionally Disturbed. *Learning Problems* Memory Disabilities; Thinking Disabilities. *Behavioral Problems* Attention Deficits; Hyperactivity; Impulsivity; Self-Aggression; Verbal Aggression; Physical Aggression; Indirect Aggression; Passive Aggression; Withdrawal. *Conditions Treated* Disintegrative Psychoses; Schizophrenia; Phobias; Obsessions and Compulsions; Hysteria; Depression; Suicide; Anorexia Nervosa; Personality Problems; Socialized Aggressive Reaction; Unsocialized Aggressive Reaction.
Services Provided Individual Therapy; Group Therapy; Parent Involvement; Behavior Therapy; Family Therapy; Filial Therapy; Drug Therapy; Play Therapy; Psychodrama. *Professionals on Staff* Psychiatrists 2; Psychologists 3; Counselors 2; Social Workers.

The Millcreek Psychiatric Center for Children

66th St and Paddock Rd, Cincinnati, OH 45216 (513) 948-3800
Year Established 1978
Contact Peter B Steele, Supt
Facility Information *Placement* Children's Psychiatric Hospital. *Number of Beds* 64. *Children/Adolescents Served* 64. *Sexes Served* Both. *Room and Board Fees (Approx)* Sliding Scale. *Tuition Fees (Approx)* Sliding Scale. *Sources of Funding* State Funds. Summer school available. *Teacher Certification Level* Elementary School. *Special Certification Level* Behavior Disordered; Learning Impaired.
Student/Patient Characteristics *Age Levels* 5-8; 9-11; 12-14; 15-17. *IQ Ranges* 56-70; Above 130. *Learning Problems* Memory Disabilities; Perceptual Disabilities; Thinking Disabilities; Oral Language Disabilities; Reading Disabilities; Handwriting Disabilities; Spelling Disabilities; Arithmetic Disabilities; Written Expression. *Behavioral Problems* Attention Deficits; Hyperactivity; Hypoactivity; Impulsivity; Self-Aggression; Verbal Aggression; Physical Aggression; Indirect Aggression; Passive Aggression; Withdrawal. *Conditions Treated* Disintegrative Psychoses; Schizophrenia; Convulsive Disorders; Phobias; Obsessions and Compulsions; Hysteria; Depression; Suicide; Anorexia Nervosa; Ulcerative Colitis; Inadequacy/Immaturity; Personality Problems; Socialized Aggressive Reaction.
Services Provided Individual Therapy; Group Therapy; Parent Involvement; Behavior Therapy; Cognitive Developmental Therapy; Family Therapy; Filial Therapy; Drug Therapy; Art Therapy; Music Therapy; Reality Therapy; Play Therapy. *Professionals on Staff* Psychiatrists; Psychologists; Social Workers; Child Care Staff; Nurses. *Service Facilities Available (with number of rooms)* Hospital School. *Educational Professionals* Special Education Teachers; Career/Vocational Teachers; Paraprofessionals. *Curricula* Traditional Academic; Individualized; Basic Skills; Prevocational. *Educational Intervention Approaches* Progressive Discipline; Self-Control; Behavior Modification.

Osterlen Services for Youth

1918 Mechanicsburg Rd, Springfield, OH 45503 (513) 399-6101
Year Established 1903
Contact Walter R Brooker, Exec Dir

Facility Information *Placement* Special School; Private Residential Care; Community Group Homes. *Number of Beds* 48. *Children/Adolescents Served* 61. *Sexes Served* Both. *Room and Board Fees (Approx)* $65. *Sources of Funding* State Funds; Referring Families; Lutheran Church. *Teacher Certification Level* Junior High/Middle School; High School. *Special Certification Level* Severe Behavioral Handicap.
Student/Patient Characteristics *Age Levels* 12-14; 15-17. *IQ Ranges* 71-85; 85-130; Above 130. *Exceptionalities Served* Emotionally Disturbed; Learning Disabled; Mentally Handicapped. *Learning Problems* Memory Disabilities; Perceptual Disabilities; Thinking Disabilities; Oral Language Disabilities; Reading Disabilities; Handwriting Disabilities; Spelling Disabilities; Arithmetic Disabilities; Written Expression. *Behavioral Problems* Attention Deficits; Hyperactivity; Impulsivity; Self-Aggression; Verbal Aggression; Physical Aggression; Indirect Aggression; Passive Aggression; Withdrawal. *Conditions Treated* Depression; Suicide; Asthma; Personality Problems; Socialized Aggressive Reaction; Unsocialized Aggressive Reaction.
Services Provided Individual Therapy; Group Therapy; Parent Involvement; Behavior Therapy; Family Therapy; Drug Therapy; Art Therapy; Reality Therapy; Psychodrama. *Professionals on Staff* Psychiatrists 1; Psychologists 1; Social Workers 4; Child Care Staff 30; Nurses 1; Activity Therapists 3. *Service Facilities Available (with number of rooms)* Resource Rooms 1; Transition Rooms 6; Self-Contained Rooms 1; On-Campus Residential School 9. *Educational Professionals* Special Education Teachers 5; Career/Vocational Teachers 1; Paraprofessionals 1. *Curricula* Individualized; Basic Skills; Prevocational. *Educational Intervention Approaches* Self-Control; Behavior Modification; Reality Approach. *Degrees Awarded* High School Diploma.

Parkview Counseling Center Inc

1001 Covington St, Youngstown, OH 44510 (216) 747-2601
Year Established 1970
Contact Chuck Boris, Prog Dir
Facility Information *Placement* Public School; Private Day Care. *Children/Adolescents Served* 60. *Sexes Served* Both. *Sources of Funding* State Funds; Health Insurance; Medicaid; Medicare. Summer school available. *Teacher Certification Level* Elementary School; Junior High/Middle School; High School.
Student/Patient Characteristics *Age Levels* 0-4; 15-17; 18-21. *IQ Ranges* 56-70; 71-85; 85-130; Above 130. *Exceptionalities Served* Autistic; Emotionally Disturbed; Learning Disabled; Mentally Handicapped; Communication Disordered. *Learning Problems* Memory Disabilities; Perceptual Disabilities; Thinking Disabilities; Oral Language Disabilities; Reading Disabilities; Handwriting Disabilities; Spelling Disabilities; Arithmetic Disabilities; Written Expression. *Behavioral Problems* Attention Deficits; Hyperactivity; Hypoactivity; Impulsivity; Self-Aggression; Verbal Aggression; Indirect Aggression; Passive Aggression; Withdrawal. *Conditions Treated* Early Infantile Autism; Schizophrenia; Aphasia; Phobias; Obsessions and Compulsions; Depression; Suicide; Anorexia Nervosa; Ulcerative Colitis; Inadequacy/Immaturity; Personality Problems; Socialized Aggressive Reaction; Unsocialized Aggressive Reaction.
Services Provided Individual Therapy; Group Therapy; Parent Involvement; Family Therapy; Play Therapy. *Professionals on Staff* Psychiatrists; Psychologists; Counselors; Social Workers; Child Care Staff; Nurses. *Service Facilities Available (with number of rooms)* Consultative (ERT); Special School. *Educational Professionals* Special Education Teachers 6; Paraprofessionals 5. *Curricula* Traditional Academic; Individualized; Basic Skills. *Degrees Awarded* High School Diploma.

Parmadale—The Youth Services Village

6753 State Rd, Parma, OH 44134-4596 (216) 845-7700
Year Established 1925
Contact Anne Mengerink, Intake Dir
Facility Information *Placement* Special School; Private Residential Care; Private Day Care. *Number of Beds* 240. *Children/Adolescents Served* 240. *Sexes Served* Both. *Room and*

Board Fees (Approx) $59. *Sources of Funding* County; Foundations Monies; United Way; Catholic Charities. Summer school available. *Teacher Certification Level* Elementary School; Junior High/Middle School; High School. *Special Certification Level* LD; MR; Career/Vocational Education; Reading; Math.

Student/Patient Characteristics *Age Levels* 12-14; 15-17; 18-21. *IQ Ranges* 56-70; 71-85; 85-130; Above 130. *Exceptionalities Served* Emotionally Disturbed; Learning Disabled; Mentally Handicapped. *Learning Problems* Memory Disabilities; Perceptual Disabilities; Thinking Disabilities; Oral Language Disabilities; Reading Disabilities; Handwriting Disabilities; Spelling Disabilities; Arithmetic Disabilities; Written Expression. *Behavioral Problems* Attention Deficits; Hyperactivity; Hypoactivity; Impulsivity; Self-Aggression; Verbal Aggression; Physical Aggression; Indirect Aggression; Passive Aggression; Withdrawal. *Conditions Treated* Alcohol Abuse and/or Drug Abuse; Other Substance Abuse or Dependence; Depression; Socialized Aggressive Reaction; Unsocialized Aggressive Reaction.

Services Provided Individual Therapy; Group Therapy; Parent Involvement; Behavior Therapy; Family Therapy. *Professionals on Staff* Psychiatrists 1; Psychologists 5; Counselors 10; Social Workers 7; Child Care Staff 75; Nurses 1. *Service Facilities Available (with number of rooms)* Itinerants 3; Resource Rooms 2; Self-Contained Rooms 7; Special School 1; On-Campus Residential School 5. *Educational Professionals* Regular School Teachers 23; Special Education Teachers 5; Paraprofessionals 14. *Curricula* Traditional Academic; Career/Vocational Education; Individualized; Basic Skills; Prevocational. *Educational Intervention Approaches* Self-Control; Behavior Modification; Applied Behavior Analysis. *Degrees Awarded* Certificate of Attendance; High School Diploma; Graduate Equivalency Diploma.

Sagamore Hills Children's Psychiatric Hospital

11910 Dunham Rd, Northfield, OH 44067 (216) 467-7955
Year Established 1961
Contact Patricia McGarry, Intake Coord

Facility Information *Placement* Special School; Public Residential Care. *Number of Beds* 64. *Children/Adolescents Served* 64. *Sexes Served* Both. *Room and Board Fees (Approx)* Sliding Scale. *Sources of Funding* State Funds; Health Insurance; Medicaid; P.L. 94-142. Summer school available. *Teacher Certification Level* Elementary School; Junior High/Middle School; High School. *Special Certification Level* ED; LD; MR; Career/Vocational Education; Reading; Math.

Student/Patient Characteristics *Age Levels* 5-8. *IQ Ranges* 56-70; 71-85; 85-130; Above 130. *Exceptionalities Served* Emotionally Disturbed; Learning Disabled. *Learning Problems* Memory Disabilities; Perceptual Disabilities; Thinking Disabilities; Oral Language Disabilities; Reading Disabilities; Handwriting Disabilities; Spelling Disabilities; Arithmetic Disabilities; Written Expression. *Behavioral Problems* Attention Deficits; Hyperactivity; Hypoactivity; Impulsivity; Self-Aggression; Verbal Aggression; Physical Aggression; Indirect Aggression; Passive Aggression; Withdrawal. *Conditions Treated* Disintegrative Psychoses; Schizophrenia; Convulsive Disorders; Phobias; Obsessions and Compulsions; Hysteria; Depression; Suicide; Anorexia Nervosa; Inadequacy/Immaturity; Personality Problems; Socialized Aggressive Reaction; Unsocialized Aggressive Reaction.

Services Provided Individual Therapy; Group Therapy; Parent Involvement; Behavior Therapy; Drug Therapy; Art Therapy. *Professionals on Staff* Psychiatrists 5; Psychologists 4; Social Workers 5; Child Care Staff 48; Nurses 14. *Service Facilities Available (with number of rooms)* Hospital School 14. *Educational Professionals* Special Education Teachers 11; Career/Vocational Teachers 2; Special Education Counselors 1. *Curricula* Traditional Academic; Career/Vocational Education; Individualized; Basic Skills; Prevocational. *Educational Intervention Approaches* Engineered Classroom; Behavior Modification; Creative Conditioning. *Degrees Awarded* High School Diploma.

Comments This is a state sponsored hospital that provides residential treatment for emotionally disturbed children and adolescents ages 6-17. It offers milieu therapy, individual and group therapy psychotherapy, occupational therapy, art therapy, and chemotherapy.

St Joseph Residential Treatment and Child Care Center

650 St Paul Ave, Dayton, OH 45410 (513) 254-3562
Year Established 1849
Contact Richard P Clair, Exec Dir

Facility Information *Placement* Special School; Private Residential Care; Private Day Care; Boys Group Home; Treatment Foster Care. *Number of Beds* 48. *Children/Adolescents Served* 48. *Sexes Served* Both. *Room and Board Fees (Approx)* $77. *Sources of Funding* Per Diem. Summer school available. *Teacher Certification Level* Elementary School; Junior High/Middle School. *Special Certification Level* LD; Reading; Math Severe Behavioral Handicap.

Student/Patient Characteristics *Age Levels* 5-8; 9-11; 12-14; 15-17. *IQ Ranges* 71-85; 85-130. *Exceptionalities Served* Emotionally Disturbed; Learning Disabled. *Learning Problems* Memory Disabilities; Perceptual Disabilities; Thinking Disabilities; Oral Language Disabilities; Reading Disabilities; Handwriting Disabilities; Spelling Disabilities; Arithmetic Disabilities; Written Expression. *Behavioral Problems* Attention Deficits; Hyperactivity; Hypoactivity; Impulsivity; Self-Aggression; Verbal Aggression; Physical Aggression; Indirect Aggression; Passive Aggression; Withdrawal. *Conditions Treated* Hysteria; Depression; Inadequacy/Immaturity; Personality Problems; Socialized Aggressive Reaction; Unsocialized Aggressive Reaction.

Services Provided Individual Therapy; Group Therapy; Parent Involvement; Behavior Therapy; Cognitive Developmental Therapy; Family Therapy; Filial Therapy; Art Therapy; Music Therapy; Reality Therapy; Play Therapy; Art Therapist. *Professionals on Staff* Psychiatrists 1; Counselors 5; Social Workers 2; Child Care Staff; Nurses. *Service Facilities Available (with number of rooms)* Resource Rooms 1; Transition Rooms 1; Self-Contained Rooms; On-Campus Residential School. *Educational Professionals* Special Education Teachers; Paraprofessionals. *Curricula* Individualized; Basic Skills; Prevocational. *Educational Intervention Approaches* Self-Control; Behavior Modification; Applied Behavior Analysis. *Degrees Awarded* Certificate of Attendance.

Comments St Joseph is a residential center treating emotionally and behaviorally disturbed boys and girls, in a highly structured setting using a behavioral approach and therapy.

St Vincent Children's Center

1490 E Main St, Columbus, OH 43205 (614) 237-0323
Year Established 1875
Contact Sal Piazza, Clinical Dir

Facility Information *Placement* Private Residential Care; Private Day Care. *Number of Beds* 20. *Children/Adolescents Served* 60. *Sexes Served* Both. *Room and Board Fees (Approx)* Sliding Scale. *Sources of Funding* State Funds; Health Insurance; Medicaid; P.L. 94-142. Summer school available. *Teacher Certification Level* Elementary School. *Special Certification Level* ED; Behavior Disorders.

Student/Patient Characteristics *Age Levels* 5-8; 9-11. *IQ Ranges* 56-70; 71-85; 85-130; Above 130. *Exceptionalities Served* Autistic; Emotionally Disturbed; Learning Disabled; Communication Disordered; Hearing Impaired/Deaf. *Learning Problems* Memory Disabilities; Perceptual Disabilities; Thinking Disabilities; Oral Language Disabilities; Reading Disabilities; Handwriting Disabilities; Spelling Disabilities; Arithmetic Disabilities; Written Expression. *Behavioral Problems* Attention Deficits; Hyperactivity; Hypoactivity; Impulsivity; Self-Aggression; Verbal Aggression; Physical Aggression; Indirect Aggression; Passive Aggression; Withdrawal. *Conditions Treated* Schizophrenia; Aphasia; Convulsive Disorders; Obsessions and Compulsions; Hysteria; Depression; Inadequacy/Immaturity; Personality Problems; Socialized Aggressive Reaction; Unsocialized Aggressive Reaction.

Services Provided Individual Therapy; Group Therapy; Parent Involvement; Behavior Therapy; Cognitive Developmental Therapy; Family Therapy; Filial Therapy; Reality Therapy; Play Therapy. *Professionals on Staff* Psychiatrists 1; Psychologists 2; Social Workers 5; Child Care Staff 20; Nurses 1. *Service Facilities Available (with number of rooms)* Resource Rooms 1; Self-Contained Rooms 9. *Educational Professionals* Special Education Teachers 9; Crisis Teachers 2. *Curricula* Individualized; Basic Skills. *Educational Intervention Approaches* Behavior Modification. *Degrees Awarded* Certificate of Attendance.

Starr Commonwealth Schools—Hannah Neil Center for Children

301 Obetz Rd, Columbus, OH 43207 (614) 491-5784
Year Established 1858
Contact JoAnne F Milburn, Dir

Facility Information *Placement* Special School; Private Residential Care; Private Day Care; Outpatient Counseling Program; Treatment Foster Home Program. *Number of Beds* 48. *Children/Adolescents Served* 48 (residential); 20 (day treatment). *Sexes Served* Both. *Room and Board Fees (Approx)* $40 (day treatment); $72 (residential). *Sources of Funding* Health Insurance; Medicaid; Placing Agencies. Summer school available. *Teacher Certification Level* Elementary School. *Special Certification Level* ED; LD.

Student/Patient Characteristics *Age Levels* 5-8; 9-11; 12-14. *IQ Ranges* 71-85; 85-130; Above 130. *Exceptionalities Served* Emotionally Disturbed. *Learning Problems* Memory Disabilities; Perceptual Disabilities; Thinking Disabilities; Oral Language Disabilities; Reading Disabilities; Handwriting Disabilities; Spelling Disabilities; Arithmetic Disabilities; Written Expression. *Behavioral Problems* Attention Deficits; Hyperactivity; Hypoactivity; Impulsivity; Self-Aggression; Verbal Aggression; Physical Aggression; Indirect Aggression; Passive Aggression; Withdrawal. *Conditions Treated* Depression; Suicide; Inadequacy/Immaturity; Personality Problems; Socialized Aggressive Reaction; Unsocialized Aggressive Reaction.

Services Provided Individual Therapy; Group Therapy; Parent Involvement; Family Therapy; Play Therapy. *Professionals on Staff* Psychiatrists 1; Psychologists 2; Counselors 22; Social Workers 8; Child Care Staff 8; Nurses 1; Occupational Therapist 1. *Service Facilities Available (with number of rooms)* On-Campus Residential School 7. *Educational Professionals* Special Education Teachers 7; Crisis Teachers 3; Paraprofessionals 3; Speech Therapist 1. *Curricula* Individualized; Basic Skills. *Educational Intervention Approaches* Peer Tutoring. *Degrees Awarded* Certificate of Attendance.

Training Center for Youth

2280 W Broad St, Columbus, OH 43223 (614) 275-0810
Year Established 1972
Contact Ann Swillinger, Asst Supt

Facility Information *Placement* Public Residential Care. *Number of Beds* 150. *Children/Adolescents Served* 150. *Sexes Served* Male. *Room and Board Fees (Approx)* $68. *Sources of Funding* State Funds; P.L. 94-142; NSLA. Summer school available. *Teacher Certification Level* Elementary School; Junior High/Middle School; High School. *Special Certification Level* ED; LD; MR; Reading; Math.

Student/Patient Characteristics *Age Levels* 12-14; 15-17; 18-21. *IQ Ranges* 56-70; 71-85; 85-130; Above 130. *Exceptionalities Served* Emotionally Disturbed; Learning Disabled; Mentally Handicapped; Communication Disordered; Hearing Impaired/ Deaf; Visually Impaired/Blind; Other Health Impaired; Physically Handicapped; Gifted; Juvenile Delinquents. *Learning Problems* Memory Disabilities; Perceptual Disabilities; Thinking Disabilities; Oral Language Disabilities; Reading Disabilities; Handwriting Disabilities; Spelling Disabilities; Arithmetic Disabilities; Written Expression. *Behavioral Problems* Attention

Deficits; Hyperactivity; Hypoactivity; Impulsivity; Self-Aggression; Verbal Aggression; Physical Aggression; Indirect Aggression; Passive Aggression; Withdrawal. *Conditions Treated* Alcohol Abuse and/or Drug Abuse; Other Substance Abuse or Dependence; Convulsive Disorders; Phobias; Obsessions and Compulsions; Hysteria; Depression; Suicide; Asthma; Inadequacy/Immaturity; Personality Problems; Socialized Aggressive Reaction; Unsocialized Aggressive Reaction.

Services Provided Individual Therapy; Group Therapy; Parent Involvement; Behavior Therapy; Cognitive Developmental Therapy; Family Therapy; Drug Therapy; Art Therapy; Reality Therapy. *Professionals on Staff* Psychiatrists 1; Psychologists 2; Counselors 2; Social Workers 6; Child Care Staff 70; Nurses 6; Physician 1; Speech Therapist 1; Certified Alcoholism Counselor 1. *Service Facilities Available (with number of rooms)* Resource Rooms 6; Transition Rooms 22; Self-Contained Rooms 7. *Educational Professionals* Regular School Teachers 28; Special Education Teachers 7; Special Education Counselors 1; Foster Grandparents 7. *Curricula* Traditional Academic; Individualized; Basic Skills; Prevocational. *Educational Intervention Approaches* Progressive Discipline; Self-Control; Behavior Modification. *Degrees Awarded* High School Diploma.

Comments The training center serves youth adjudicated delinquent by Ohio's 88 county juvenile courts, assigned because of emotional disturbance/severe behavioral problems.

Trumbull County Board of Education

2577 Schenley Ave NE, Warren, OH 44483 (216) 372-2200
Contact Elizabeth A Graban, Asst Supt of Special Serv
Facility Information *Placement* Public School. *Sexes Served* Both. *Sources of Funding* State Funds; P.L. 94-142. *Teacher Certification Level* Elementary School; Junior High/Middle School; High School. *Special Certification Level* ED; LD; MR; Career/Vocational Education; Reading; Math.

Student/Patient Characteristics *Age Levels* 5-8; 9-11; 12-14; 15-17; 18-21; Over 21. *IQ Ranges* 0-25; 26-40; 41-55; 56-70; 71-85; 85-130; Above 130. *Exceptionalities Served* Autistic; Learning Disabled; Mentally Handicapped; Communication Disordered; Hearing Impaired/Deaf; Visually Impaired/Blind; Other Health Impaired; Physically Handicapped; Gifted; Severe Behaviorally Handicapped. *Learning Problems* Memory Disabilities; Perceptual Disabilities; Thinking Disabilities; Oral Language Disabilities; Reading Disabilities; Handwriting Disabilities; Spelling Disabilities; Arithmetic Disabilities; Written Expression. *Behavioral Problems* Attention Deficits; Hyperactivity; Hypoactivity; Impulsivity; Self-Aggression;. Verbal Aggression; Physical Aggression; Indirect Aggression; Passive Aggression; Withdrawal. *Conditions Treated* Aphasia; Convulsive Disorders; Asthma; Socialized Aggressive Reaction; Unsocialized Aggressive Reaction.

Services Provided *Professionals on Staff* Psychologists 11; Counselors. *Educational Professionals* Regular School Teachers; Special Education Teachers; Career/Vocational Teachers; Crisis Teachers; Paraprofessionals. *Curricula* Traditional Academic; Career/Vocational Education; Individualized; Basic Skills; Prevocational. *Degrees Awarded* High School Diploma.

University Hospitals of Cleveland—Hanna Pavilion Child Psychiatric Unit

2040 Abington Rd, Cleveland, OH 44106 (216) 844-1720
Year Established 1966
Contact Thomas Brugger

Facility Information *Placement* Child Psychiatric Hospital Ward. *Number of Beds* 12. *Children/Adolescents Served* 12. *Sexes Served* Both. *Room and Board Fees (Approx)* $498. *Sources of Funding* Medicaid. Summer school available. *Special Certification Level* ED; LD; MR.

Student/Patient Characteristics *Age Levels* 5-8; 9-11; 12-14. *IQ Ranges* 26-40; 41-55; 56-70; 71-85; 85-130; Above 130. *Exceptionalities Served* Autistic; Emotionally Disturbed; Learning Disabled; Mentally Handicapped; Communication Disordered; Hearing Impaired/Deaf; Visually Impaired/Blind; Other Health Impaired; Physically Handicapped. *Learning Problems* Memory

Disabilities; Perceptual Disabilities; Thinking Disabilities; Oral Language Disabilities; Reading Disabilities; Handwriting Disabilities; Spelling Disabilities; Arithmetic Disabilities; Written Expression. *Behavioral Problems* Attention Deficits; Hyperactivity; Hypoactivity; Impulsivity; Self-Aggression; Verbal Aggression; Physical Aggression; Indirect Aggression; Passive Aggression; Withdrawal. *Conditions Treated* Alcohol Abuse and/or Drug Abuse; Other Substance Abuse or Dependence; Early Infantile Autism; Disintegrative Psychoses; Schizophrenia; Aphasia; Convulsive Disorders; Phobias; Obsessions and Compulsions; Hysteria; Depression; Suicide; Asthma; Anorexia Nervosa; Ulcerative Colitis; Inadequacy/Immaturity; Personality Problems; Socialized Aggressive Reaction; Unsocialized Aggressive Reaction.

Services Provided Individual Therapy; Group Therapy; Parent Involvement; Behavior Therapy; Family Therapy; Drug Therapy; Art Therapy; Play Therapy; Milieu Therapy. *Professionals on Staff* Psychiatrists 4; Psychologists 2; Social Workers 2; Child Care Staff 8; Nurses 16; Psychoeducation; Occupational Therapy 4. *Service Facilities Available (with number of rooms)* Hospital School 3. *Educational Professionals* Regular School Teachers; Special Education Teachers 3; Paraprofessionals 3. *Curricula* Traditional Academic; Career/Vocational Education; Individualized; Basic Skills; Prevocational. *Educational Intervention Approaches* Engineered Classroom; Progressive Discipline; Self-Control; Behavior Modification; Applied Behavior Analysis; Creative Conditioning. *Degrees Awarded* Certificate of Attendance.

Oklahoma

Children's Medical Center

5300 E Skelly Dr, Tulsa, OK 74135 (918) 664-6600
Year Established 1926
Contact James D Stansbarger, Admin
Facility Information *Placement* Private, Nonprofit; Psychiatric Medical Hospital. *Number of Beds* 101. *Sexes Served* Both. *Room and Board Fees (Approx)* $140. *Sources of Funding* State Funds; Health Insurance; Medicaid; P.L. 94-142; Private Philanthropy. Summer school available. *Teacher Certification Level* Elementary School; Junior High/Middle School; High School. *Special Certification Level* ED; LD; MR; Career/Vocational Education; Reading; Math; Administration; Psychometrist; Music; Speech; Elementary Education.
Student/Patient Characteristics *Age Levels* 0-4; 5-8; 9-11; 12-14; 15-17. *IQ Ranges* 0-25; 26-40; 41-55; 56-70; 71-85; 85-130; Above 130. *Exceptionalities Served* Autistic; Emotionally Disturbed; Learning Disabled; Mentally Handicapped; Communication Disordered; Hearing Impaired/Deaf; Visually Impaired/Blind; Other Health Impaired; Physically Handicapped. *Learning Problems* Memory Disabilities; Perceptual Disabilities; Thinking Disabilities; Oral Language Disabilities; Reading Disabilities; Handwriting Disabilities; Spelling Disabilities; Arithmetic Disabilities; Written Expression. *Behavioral Problems* Attention Deficits; Hyperactivity; Hypoactivity; Impulsivity; Self-Aggression; Verbal Aggression; Physical Aggression; Indirect Aggression; Passive Aggression; Withdrawal. *Conditions Treated* Early Infantile Autism; Disintegrative Psychoses; Schizophrenia; Aphasia; Convulsive Disorders; Phobias; Obsessions and Compulsions; Hysteria; Depression; Suicide; Asthma; Anorexia Nervosa; Ulcerative Colitis; Inadequacy/Immaturity; Personality Problems; Socialized Aggressive Reaction; Unsocialized Aggressive Reaction.
Services Provided Individual Therapy; Group Therapy; Parent Involvement; Behavior Therapy; Cognitive Developmental Therapy; Biofeedback; Family Therapy; Filial Therapy; Art Therapy; Reality Therapy; Play Therapy; Psychodrama. *Professionals on Staff* Psychiatrists 3; Psychologists 9; Counselors; Social Workers 7; Child Care Staff 89; Nurses 49; Pediatricians 5; Therapists 8; Audiologist 2; Research Physicians 2; Research Technicians 9; Research Doctoral 3. *Service Facilities Available (with number of rooms)* Self-Contained Rooms 6. *Educational Professionals* Regular School Teachers; Special Education Teachers 6; Career/Vocational Teachers; Special Education Counselors; Paraprofessionals; Vocational Training Counselors. *Curricula* Traditional Academic; Career/Vocational Education; Individualized; Basic Skills; Prevocational. *Educational Intervention Approaches* Behavior Modification; Team Recommendations.
Comments Children's Medical Center is a 101 bed hospital accredited by the Joint Commission on the Accreditation of Hospitals. It is comprised of 2 major units, psychiatry and pediatrics. Each has its own medical director and nursing staff.

In addition to the many therapies available for patient's treatments, a full-time recreation department plans activities both on and off the Center's grounds.

Comanche County Guidance Clinic

1010 S Sheridan Rd, Lawton, OK 73502 (405) 248-5890 ext 62
Contact Soren Barrett, Clinic Dir/Psychologist
Facility Information *Placement* County Guidance Clinic; Outpatient Treatment and Evaluation. *Children/Adolescents Served* 160. *Sexes Served* Both. *Sources of Funding* State Funds; Local.
Services Provided Individual Therapy; Group Therapy; Parent Involvement; Behavior Therapy; Cognitive Developmental Therapy; Family Therapy; Play Therapy. *Professionals on Staff* Psychologists 2; Counselors 2; Social Workers 1; Speech Pathologists; Child Development Specialists; Audiologist 4.
Comments The clinic is an outpatient, short-term treatment facility connected to the local health department. Fees are based upon a sliding scale. Families and children (0-18 years) are served by a multiple disciplinary team.

Phil Smalley Children's Center

PO Box 1008, 312 12th Ave NE, Norman, OK 73070
(405) 364-9004
Year Established 1971
Contact Ray Gray, Principal
Facility Information *Placement* Public Residential Care. *Number of Beds* 40. *Children/Adolescents Served* 40. *Sexes Served* Both. *Room and Board Fees (Approx)* $350. *Sources of Funding* State Funds; Health Insurance; Medicaid; P.L. 94-142. *Teacher Certification Level* Elementary School; Junior High/Middle School; High School. *Special Certification Level* ED.
Student/Patient Characteristics *Age Levels* 5-8; 9-11; 12-14. *IQ Ranges* 85-130. *Exceptionalities Served* Emotionally Disturbed. *Learning Problems* Perceptual Disabilities; Thinking Disabilities. *Behavioral Problems* Attention Deficits; Hyperactivity; Impulsivity; Self-Aggression; Verbal Aggression; Physical Aggression; Indirect Aggression; Passive Aggression; Withdrawal.
Services Provided Individual Therapy; Group Therapy; Parent Involvement; Family Therapy; Play Therapy; Occupational Therapy; Recreational Therapy. *Professionals on Staff* Psychiatrists 1; Psychologists 5; Social Workers 4; Child Care Staff 53; Nurses 11. *Service Facilities Available (with number of rooms)* Self-Contained Rooms 9; Placement in Norman Public School. *Educational Professionals* Special Education Teachers 9; Paraprofessionals 9; School Psychologist; Psychometrist 1. *Curricula* Traditional Academic; Individualized; Basic Skills. *Educational Intervention Approaches* Self-Control.

Red Rock Comprehensive Mental Health Center

214 E Madison, Oklahoma City, OK 73105 (405) 524-7711
Year Established 1974
Contact Pat Damron, Dir Community Serv

Facility Information *Placement* Mental Health Center. *Sexes Served* Both. *Sources of Funding* State Funds; HEW; Medicaid; Medicare.

Student/Patient Characteristics *Age Levels* 0-4; 5-8; 9-11; 12-14; 15-17; 18-21; Over 21. *IQ Ranges* 56-70; 71-85; 85-130; Above 130. *Exceptionalities Served* Autistic; Emotionally Disturbed; Learning Disabled; Mentally Handicapped. *Behavioral Problems* Attention Deficits; Hyperactivity; Hypoactivity; Impulsivity; Self-Aggression; Verbal Aggression; Physical Aggression; Indirect Aggression; Passive Aggression; Withdrawal. *Conditions Treated* Alcohol Abuse and/or Drug Abuse; Other Substance Abuse or Dependence; Early Infantile Autism; Disintegrative Psychoses; Schizophrenia; Phobias; Obsessions and Compulsions; Hysteria; Depression; Suicide; Anorexia Nervosa; Inadequacy/Immaturity; Personality Problems; Socialized Aggressive Reaction; Unsocialized Aggressive Reaction.

Services Provided Individual Therapy; Group Therapy; Parent Involvement; Behavior Therapy; Family Therapy; Drug Therapy; Art Therapy; Reality Therapy; Play Therapy. *Professionals on Staff* Psychiatrists 6; Psychologists 25; Social Workers 23.

Shadow Mountain Institute

6262 S Sheridan, Tulsa, OK 74133 (918) 492-8200
Year Established 1978
Contact D Edward, Admin

Facility Information *Placement* Public School; Private Residential Care; Psychiatric Hospital. *Number of Beds* 130. *Children/Adolescents Served* 130. *Sexes Served* Both. *Room and Board Fees (Approx)* $127. *Sources of Funding* State Funds; P.L. 94-142. Summer school available. *Teacher Certification Level* Elementary School; Junior High/Middle School. *Special Certification Level* ED.

Student/Patient Characteristics *Age Levels* 5-8; 9-11; 12-14; 15-17. *IQ Ranges* 85-130. *Exceptionalities Served* Emotionally Disturbed; Learning Disabled; Mentally Handicapped; Physically Handicapped; Gifted. *Learning Problems* Memory Disabilities; Perceptual Disabilities; Thinking Disabilities; Reading Disabilities; Handwriting Disabilities; Spelling Disabilities; Arithmetic Disabilities; Written Expression. *Behavioral Problems* Attention Deficits; Hyperactivity; Hypoactivity; Impulsivity; Self-Aggression; Verbal Aggression; Physical Aggression; Indirect Aggression; Passive Aggression; Withdrawal. *Conditions Treated* Alcohol Abuse and/or Drug Abuse; Other Substance Abuse or Dependence; Disintegrative Psychoses; Schizophrenia; Phobias; Obsessions and Compulsions; Hysteria; Depression; Suicide; Anorexia Nervosa; Inadequacy/Immaturity; Personality Problems; Socialized Aggressive Reaction; Unsocialized Aggressive Reaction.

Services Provided Individual Therapy; Group Therapy; Parent Involvement; Behavior Therapy; Cognitive Developmental Therapy; Family Therapy; Drug Therapy; Art Therapy; Reality Therapy; Play Therapy; Psychodrama. *Professionals on Staff* Psychiatrists; Psychologists; Counselors; Social Workers; Child Care Staff; Nurses. *Educational Professionals* Special Education Teachers; Paraprofessionals. *Curricula* Individualized; Basic Skills. *Educational Intervention Approaches* Precision Teaching; Progressive Discipline; Self-Control; Behavior Modification; Creative Conditioning. *Degrees Awarded* High School Diploma; Graduate Equivalency Diploma.

Timberridge Institute for Children and Adolescents Inc

6001 N Classen Blvd, Oklahoma City, OK 73118 (405) 848-3518
Year Established 1970
Contact Donna Rowlan, Ed Coord

Facility Information *Placement* Special School. *Children/Adolescents Served* 75. *Sexes Served* Both. *Tuition Fees (Approx)* $4,725. *Sources of Funding* Private Tuition. Summer school available. *Teacher Certification Level* Elementary School; Junior High/Middle School; High School. *Special Certification Level* ED; LD.

Student/Patient Characteristics *Age Levels* 5-8; 9-11; 12-14; 15-17. *IQ Ranges* 56-70; 71-85; 85-130; Above 130. *Exceptionalities Served* Autistic; Emotionally Disturbed; Learning Disabled; Mentally Handicapped; Communication Disordered; Visually Impaired/Blind; Other Health Impaired; Physically Handicapped; Gifted. *Learning Problems* Memory Disabilities; Perceptual Disabilities; Thinking Disabilities; Oral Language Disabilities; Reading Disabilities; Handwriting Disabilities; Spelling Disabilities; Arithmetic Disabilities; Written Expression. *Behavioral Problems* Attention Deficits; Hyperactivity; Impulsivity; Self-Aggression; Verbal Aggression; Physical Aggression; Indirect Aggression; Passive Aggression; Withdrawal. *Conditions Treated* Early Infantile Autism; Convulsive Disorders; Phobias; Obsessions and Compulsions; Depression; Personality Problems; Socialized Aggressive Reaction; Unsocialized Aggressive Reaction.

Services Provided Individual Therapy; Group Therapy; Parent Involvement; Behavior Therapy; Cognitive Developmental Therapy; Family Therapy; Music Therapy; Play Therapy. *Professionals on Staff* Psychologists 8. *Service Facilities Available (with number of rooms)* Resource Rooms 1; Transition Rooms 1; Self-Contained Rooms 6. *Educational Professionals* Special Education Teachers 3. *Curricula* Traditional Academic; Individualized; Basic Skills. *Educational Intervention Approaches* Self-Control; Behavior Modification. *Degrees Awarded* Certificate of Attendance; High School Diploma.

Oregon

Christie School

Marylhurst, OR 97036 (503) 635-3416
Year Established 1859
Contact Joanne Baum Falk, Intake Coord

Facility Information *Placement* Private Residential Care; Clinical Program. *Number of Beds* 37. *Children/Adolescents Served* 37. *Sexes Served* Both. *Room and Board Fees (Approx)* $95-$136. *Sources of Funding* State Funds. Summer school available. *Teacher Certification Level* Elementary School; Junior High/Middle School. *Special Certification Level* Handicapped Learner.

Student/Patient Characteristics *Age Levels* 9-11; 12-14; 15-17. *IQ Ranges* 71-85; 85-130; Above 130. *Exceptionalities Served* Emotionally Disturbed; Learning Disabled. *Learning Problems* Memory Disabilities; Perceptual Disabilities; Thinking Disabilities; Oral Language Disabilities; Reading Disabilities; Handwriting Disabilities; Spelling Disabilities; Arithmetic Disabilities; Written Expression. *Behavioral Problems* Attention Deficits; Hyperactivity; Impulsivity; Self-Aggression; Verbal Aggression; Physical Aggression; Indirect Aggression; Passive Aggression; Withdrawal. *Conditions Treated* Alcohol Abuse and/or Drug Abuse; Phobias; Depression; Suicide; Inadequacy/Immaturity; Personality Problems; Socialized Aggressive Reaction; Unsocialized Aggressive Reaction.

Services Provided Individual Therapy; Group Therapy; Parent Involvement; Behavior Therapy; Family Therapy; Play Therapy. *Professionals on Staff* Psychiatrists 1; Psychologists 1; Counselors 3; Social Workers 6; Child Care Staff 50; Nurses 2; Occupational Therapy 1. *Service Facilities Available (with number of rooms)* On-Campus Residential School. *Educational Professionals* Special Education Teachers 5; Paraprofessionals 3. *Curricula* Career/Vocational Education; Individualized; Basic Skills; Prevocational. *Educational Intervention Approaches* Behavior Modification. *Degrees Awarded* Certificate of Attendance.

Edgefield Children's Center

2408 SW Halsey, Troutdale, OR 97060 (503) 665-0157
Year Established 1965
Contact Buell E Goocher, Dir

Facility Information *Placement* Public School; Special School; Private Residential Care; Private Day Care. *Number of Beds* 22. *Children/Adolescents Served* 50. *Sexes Served* Both. *Sources of Funding* State Funds; Health Insurance; Medicaid; Private Sources. Summer school available. *Teacher Certification Level* Elementary School. *Special Certification Level* ED; LD; Reading; Math.

Student/Patient Characteristics *Age Levels* 5-8; 9-11; 12-14. *IQ Ranges* 71-85; 85-130; Above 130. *Exceptionalities Served* Emotionally Disturbed; Learning Disabled; Mentally Handicapped; Communication Disordered; Gifted. *Learning Problems* Memory Disabilities; Perceptual Disabilities; Thinking Disabilities; Oral Language Disabilities; Reading Disabilities; Handwriting Disabil-ities; Spelling Disabilities; Arithmetic Disabilities; Written Expression. *Behavioral Problems* Attention Deficits; Hyperactivity; Impulsivity; Self-Aggression; Verbal Aggression; Physical Aggression; Indirect Aggression; Passive Aggression; Withdrawal. *Conditions Treated* Alcohol Abuse and/or Drug Abuse; Obsessions and Compulsions; Depression; Inadequacy/Immaturity; Personality Problems; Socialized Aggressive Reaction; Unsocialized Aggressive Reaction.

Services Provided Individual Therapy; Group Therapy; Parent Involvement; Behavior Therapy; Family Therapy; Filial Therapy. *Professionals on Staff* Psychiatrists 1; Psychologists 5; Social Workers 7; Child Care Staff 20. *Service Facilities Available (with number of rooms)* Self-Contained Rooms 5. *Educational Professionals* Special Education Teachers 5; Child Care Workers 10. *Curricula* Traditional Academic; Individualized; Basic Skills. *Educational Intervention Approaches* Self-Control; Behavior Modification; Applied Behavior Analysis.

Josephine County Mental Health Program—Children's Resource Team

714 NW A St, Grants Pass, OR 97526 (503) 474-5365
Year Established 1972
Contact Bob Gans Morse, Unit Representative

Facility Information *Placement* Special Program. *Children/Adolescents Served* 300. *Sexes Served* Both. *Sources of Funding* State Funds; Medicaid; P.L. 94-142; Headstart; County Funds.

Student/Patient Characteristics *Age Levels* 0-4; 5-8; 9-11; 12-14; 15-17. *IQ Ranges* 56-70; 71-85; 85-130; Above 130. *Exceptionalities Served* Emotionally Disturbed; Learning Disabled; Mentally Handicapped; Communication Disordered; Hearing Impaired/Deaf; Visually Impaired/Blind; Other Health Impaired; Physically Handicapped; Gifted. *Learning Problems* Memory Disabilities; Perceptual Disabilities; Thinking Disabilities; Oral Language Disabilities; Reading Disabilities; Handwriting Disabilities; Spelling Disabilities; Arithmetic Disabilities; Written Expression. *Behavioral Problems* Attention Deficits; Hyperactivity; Hypoactivity; Impulsivity; Self-Aggression; Verbal Aggression; Physical Aggression; Indirect Aggression; Passive Aggression; Withdrawal. *Conditions Treated* Depression; Suicide; Inadequacy/Immaturity; Personality Problems; Socialized Aggressive Reaction; Unsocialized Aggressive Reaction.

Services Provided Individual Therapy; Group Therapy; Parent Involvement; Behavior Therapy; Cognitive Developmental Therapy; Family Therapy. *Professionals on Staff* Psychologists 1; Social Workers 2. *Educational Intervention Approaches* Self-Control; Behavior Modification; Applied Behavior Analysis.

Klamath County Mental Health Center—Mentally Retarded/Developmentally Disabled Program

3314 Vandenberg Rd, Klamath Falls, OR 97603 (503) 882-7291
Contact Jane Pickett, MR/DD Case Manager
Facility Information *Placement* Public School; Public Day Care; Special Program. *Children/Adolescents Served* 45. *Sexes Served* Both. *Sources of Funding* State Funds; P.L. 94-142. *Teacher Certification Level* Elementary School; Junior High/Middle School; High School. *Special Certification Level* MR; Developmental Disabilities.
Student/Patient Characteristics *Age Levels* 0-4; 5-8; 9-11; 12-14; 15-17; 18-21; Over 21. *IQ Ranges* 0-25; 26-40; 41-55; 56-70. *Exceptionalities Served* Autistic; Mentally Handicapped; Communication Disordered; Hearing Impaired/Deaf; Visually Impaired/Blind. *Learning Problems* Memory Disabilities; Perceptual Disabilities; Thinking Disabilities; Oral Language Disabilities; Reading Disabilities; Handwriting Disabilities; Spelling Disabilities; Arithmetic Disabilities; Written Expression. *Behavioral Problems* Attention Deficits; Hyperactivity; Hypoactivity; Impulsivity; Self-Aggression; Verbal Aggression; Physical Aggression; Indirect Aggression. *Conditions Treated* Early Infantile Autism; Convulsive Disorders.
Services Provided Day Activity Work Program; Residential Program. *Professionals on Staff* Counselors 1. *Service Facilities Available (with number of rooms)* Self-Contained Rooms 6. *Educational Professionals* Special Education Teachers 6; Paraprofessionals 6. *Curricula* Traditional Academic; Career/Vocational Education. *Educational Intervention Approaches* Behavior Modification; Creative Conditioning. *Degrees Awarded* Certificate of Attendance.

Klamath County Mental Health Center—Natural Family Preservation Project

3314 Vandenberg Rd, Klamath Falls, OR 97603 (503) 882-7291
Contact Harold Bailey, NFPP Prog Coord
Facility Information *Placement* Special Program; Juvenile Diversion. *Children/Adolescents Served* 60. *Sexes Served* Both. *Sources of Funding* State Funds; Medicaid.
Student/Patient Characteristics *Age Levels* 9-11; 12-14; 15-17; 18-21. *IQ Ranges* 71-85; 85-130; Above 130. *Exceptionalities Served* Emotionally Disturbed. *Behavioral Problems* Attention Deficits; Hyperactivity; Impulsivity; Verbal Aggression; Physical Aggression; Indirect Aggression; Passive Aggression; Withdrawal. *Conditions Treated* Alcohol Abuse and/or Drug Abuse; Other Substance Abuse or Dependence; Inadequacy/Immaturity; Personality Problems; Socialized Aggressive Reaction; Unsocialized Aggressive Reaction.
Services Provided Individual Therapy; Group Therapy; Parent Involvement; Behavior Therapy; Cognitive Developmental Therapy; Biofeedback; Family Therapy; Drug Therapy; Reality Therapy; Recreation Therapy; Work Activities. *Professionals on Staff* Psychiatrists 1; Psychologists 1; Counselors 1; Social Workers 1; Activities Coordinator 1.
Comments This is a community-based diversion program for youth at high risk of being placed outside the home due to their behavior.

Lane School Programs—Lane Education Service District

Box 2680, 1200 Hwy 99 N, Eugene, OR 97405 (503) 689-6500
Year Established 1984
Contact C Sue McCullough, Supv
Facility Information *Placement* Public School; Special School. *Children/Adolescents Served* 24 (day treatment); 30 (outreach). *Sexes Served* Both. *Sources of Funding* State Funds; P.L. 94-142; County School Funds. *Teacher Certification Level* Elementary School; Junior High/Middle School; High School. *Special Certification Level* LD; Handicapped Learner.
Student/Patient Characteristics *Age Levels* 5-8; 9-11; 12-14; 15-17. *IQ Ranges* 71-85; 85-130. *Exceptionalities Served* Emotionally Disturbed; Learning Disabled. *Learning Problems* Mem-

ory Disabilities; Perceptual Disabilities; Thinking Disabilities; Oral Language Disabilities; Reading Disabilities; Handwriting Disabilities; Spelling Disabilities; Arithmetic Disabilities; Written Expression. *Behavioral Problems* Attention Deficits; Hyperactivity; Impulsivity; Self-Aggression; Verbal Aggression; Physical Aggression; Indirect Aggression; Passive Aggression; Withdrawal. *Conditions Treated* Alcohol Abuse and/or Drug Abuse; Disintegrative Psychoses; Schizophrenia; Convulsive Disorders; Obsessions and Compulsions; Depression; Suicide; Asthma; Anorexia Nervosa; Inadequacy/Immaturity; Personality Problems; Socialized Aggressive Reaction; Unsocialized Aggressive Reaction.
Services Provided Individual Therapy; Group Therapy; Parent Involvement; Behavior Therapy; Cognitive Developmental Therapy; Family Therapy. *Professionals on Staff* Psychologists 1; Counselors 2; Social Workers 2. *Service Facilities Available (with number of rooms)* Consultative (ERT) 3; Itinerants; Resource Rooms 3; Transition Rooms 1; Outreach Consultants. *Educational Professionals* Special Education Teachers 5; Paraprofessionals 4. *Curricula* Traditional Academic; Career/Vocational Education; Individualized; Basic Skills; Prevocational; Outdoor School. *Educational Intervention Approaches* Self-Control; Behavior Modification; Applied Behavior Analysis.

Parry Center for Children

3415 SE Powell Blvd, Portland, OR 97202 (503) 234-9591
Year Established 1867
Contact Shirley J Steele, Social Serv Dir
Facility Information *Placement* Private Residential Care. *Number of Beds* 49. *Children/Adolescents Served* 49. *Sexes Served* Both. *Room and Board Fees (Approx)* $100. *Sources of Funding* State Funds; United Way; Fund Raising; Endowment. Summer school available. *Teacher Certification Level* Elementary School. *Special Certification Level* ED; LD; Reading; Math.
Student/Patient Characteristics *Age Levels* 5-8; 9-11; 12-14; 15-17. *IQ Ranges* 71-85; 85-130. *Exceptionalities Served* Autistic; Emotionally Disturbed; Learning Disabled; Communication Disordered. *Learning Problems* Memory Disabilities; Perceptual Disabilities; Thinking Disabilities; Oral Language Disabilities; Reading Disabilities; Handwriting Disabilities; Spelling Disabilities; Arithmetic Disabilities; Written Expression. *Behavioral Problems* Attention Deficits; Hyperactivity; Hypoactivity; Impulsivity; Self-Aggression; Verbal Aggression; Physical Aggression; Indirect Aggression; Passive Aggression; Withdrawal. *Conditions Treated* Early Infantile Autism; Schizophrenia; Aphasia; Phobias; Obsessions and Compulsions; Depression; Personality Problems; Socialized Aggressive Reaction; Unsocialized Aggressive Reaction.
Services Provided Individual Therapy; Group Therapy; Parent Involvement; Behavior Therapy; Family Therapy; Drug Therapy; Art Therapy; Music Therapy; Play Therapy; Occupational Therapy. *Professionals on Staff* Psychiatrists 1; Psychologists 1; Social Workers; Child Care Staff 45; Nurses 1. *Service Facilities Available (with number of rooms)* Transition Rooms 1; On-Campus Residential School 3. *Educational Professionals* Special Education Teachers 4; Paraprofessionals 2; Speech Therapist 1; Adaptive Physical Education 1. *Curricula* Traditional Academic; Individualized; Basic Skills. *Educational Intervention Approaches* Self-Control; Behavior Modification; Applied Behavior Analysis.

St Mary's Home for Boys

16535 SW TV Hwy, Beaverton, OR 97006 (503) 649-5651
Year Established 1889
Contact Emma L Grosz-Dennis, Asst Dir
Facility Information *Placement* Private Residential Care. *Number of Beds* 48. *Children/Adolescents Served* 48. *Sexes Served* Male. *Room and Board Fees (Approx)* $39-$75. *Tuition Fees (Approx)* $27,375. *Sources of Funding* State Funds; P.L. 94-142. Summer school available. *Teacher Certification Level* Elementary School; Junior High/Middle School; High School. *Special Certification Level* ED; LD; MR; Reading; Math.

Student/Patient Characteristics *Age Levels* 9-11; 12-14; 15-17. *IQ Ranges* 71-85; 85-130; Above 130. *Exceptionalities Served* Emotionally Disturbed; Learning Disabled; Mentally Handicapped; Communication Disordered; Physically Handicapped. *Learning Problems* Memory Disabilities; Perceptual Disabilities; Thinking Disabilities; Oral Language Disabilities; Reading Disabilities; Handwriting Disabilities; Spelling Disabilities; Arithmetic Disabilities; Written Expression. *Behavioral Problems* Attention Deficits; Hyperactivity; Hypoactivity; Impulsivity; Self-Aggression; Verbal Aggression; Physical Aggression; Indirect Aggression; Passive Aggression; Withdrawal. *Conditions Treated* Convulsive Disorders; Phobias; Obsessions and Compulsions; Depression; Asthma; Ulcerative Colitis; Inadequacy/Immaturity; Personality Problems; Socialized Aggressive Reaction; Unsocialized Aggressive Reaction.

Services Provided Individual Therapy; Group Therapy; Parent Involvement; Behavior Therapy; Cognitive Developmental Therapy; Family Therapy; Reality Therapy. *Professionals on Staff* Psychologists 2; Counselors 1; Social Workers 4; Child Care Staff 30; Nurses 1; Physician 1. *Service Facilities Available (with number of rooms)* Resource Rooms 1; Self-Contained Rooms 6; Special School. *Educational Professionals* Special Education Teachers 7; Crisis Teachers .5; Special Education Counselors .5; Paraprofessionals 4. *Curricula* Individualized; Basic Skills; Prevocational. *Educational Intervention Approaches* Precision Teaching; Self-Control; Behavior Modification; Applied Behavior Analysis. *Degrees Awarded* High School Diploma; Graduate Equivalency Diploma.

Waverly Children's Home

3550 SE Woodward St, Portland, OR 97202 (503) 234-7532
Year Established 1888
Contact Cynthia Thompson, Exec Dir

Facility Information *Placement* Public Residential Care; Private Residential Care; Shelter Care; Day Treatment. *Number of Beds* 45. *Children/Adolescents Served* 55. *Sexes Served* Both. *Sources of Funding* State Funds; United Way; Private Donations. Summer school available. *Teacher Certification Level* Elementary School; Junior High/Middle School. *Special Certification Level* ED; LD; MR.

Student/Patient Characteristics *Age Levels* 0-4; 5-8; 9-11; 12-14. *IQ Ranges* 71-85; 85-130. *Exceptionalities Served* Emotionally Disturbed; Learning Disabled; Mentally Handicapped. *Learning Problems* Memory Disabilities; Perceptual Disabilities; Thinking Disabilities; Oral Language Disabilities; Reading Disabilities; Handwriting Disabilities; Spelling Disabilities; Arithmetic Disabilities; Written Expression. *Behavioral Problems* Attention Deficits; Hyperactivity; Impulsivity; Self-Aggression; Verbal Aggression; Physical Aggression; Indirect Aggression. *Conditions Treated* Inadequacy/Immaturity; Personality Problems.

Services Provided Group Therapy; Parent Involvement; Behavior Therapy; Family Therapy. *Professionals on Staff* Psychiatrists; Social Workers 4; Child Care Staff; Nurses 1; Instructional Aides 5; Community Agent; Speech and Language Pathologist 1. *Service Facilities Available (with number of rooms)* Transition Rooms 2; Special School 1; On-Campus Residential School 3. *Educational Professionals* Special Education Teachers 7; Paraprofessionals 7; Speech and Language Pathologist. *Curricula* Traditional Academic; Career/Vocational Education; Individualized; Basic Skills. *Educational Intervention Approaches* Behavior Modification.

Pennsylvania

Berks County Intermediate Unit

PO Box 4097, 2900 St Lawrence Ave, Reading, PA 19606
(215) 779-7111 ext 204
Year Established 1971
Contact Thomas F Schmoyer, Asst Dir of Special Ed
Facility Information *Placement* Public School; Special School.
Sexes Served Both. *Tuition Fees (Approx)* $10,000. *Sources of Funding* State Funds; P.L. 94-142; P.L. 89-313. Summer school available. *Teacher Certification Level* Elementary School; Junior High/Middle School; High School. *Special Certification Level* ED; LD; MR.
Student/Patient Characteristics *Age Levels* 0-4; 5-8; 9-11; 12-14; 15-17; 18-21. *IQ Ranges* 0-25; 26-40; 41-55; 56-70; 71-85; 85-130; Above 130. *Exceptionalities Served* Autistic; Emotionally Disturbed; Learning Disabled; Mentally Handicapped; Communication Disordered; Hearing Impaired/Deaf; Visually Impaired/Blind; Other Health Impaired; Physically Handicapped; Gifted. *Learning Problems* Memory Disabilities; Perceptual Disabilities; Thinking Disabilities; Oral Language Disabilities; Reading Disabilities; Handwriting Disabilities; Spelling Disabilities; Arithmetic Disabilities; Written Expression. *Behavioral Problems* Attention Deficits; Hyperactivity; Impulsivity; Self-Aggression; Verbal Aggression; Physical Aggression; Indirect Aggression; Passive Aggression; Withdrawal. *Conditions Treated* Alcohol Abuse and/or Drug Abuse; Other Substance Abuse or Dependence; Early Infantile Autism; Schizophrenia; Aphasia; Convulsive Disorders; Phobias; Obsessions and Compulsions; Hysteria; Depression; Suicide; Asthma; Anorexia Nervosa; Ulcerative Colitis; Inadequacy/Immaturity; Personality Problems; Socialized Aggressive Reaction; Unsocialized Aggressive Reaction.
Services Provided *Professionals on Staff* Psychiatrists 2; Psychologists 15; Social Workers 3; Nurses 2. *Service Facilities Available (with number of rooms)* Itinerants; Resource Rooms; Transition Rooms; Self-Contained Rooms; Special School; Day Treatment Center. *Educational Professionals* Regular School Teachers; Special Education Teachers; Career/Vocational Teachers. *Curricula* Traditional Academic; Career/Vocational Education; Individualized; Basic Skills; Prevocational. *Educational Intervention Approaches* Precision Teaching; Behavior Modification; Applied Behavior Analysis.
Comments This program provides special education services for 18 school districts.

Bucks County Intermediate Unit—Looking Glass School

Cross Keys Bldg, Doylestown, PA 18901 (215) 348-2940
Year Established 1976
Contact Richard W Dolton, Supv

Facility Information *Placement* Public School; Special School.
Children/Adolescents Served 40. *Sexes Served* Both. *Sources of Funding* State Funds; P.L. 94-142. *Teacher Certification Level* Junior High/Middle School; High School. *Special Certification Level* ED.
Student/Patient Characteristics *Age Levels* 12-14; 15-17. *IQ Ranges* 85-130. *Exceptionalities Served* Emotionally Disturbed. *Learning Problems* Thinking Disabilities; Reading Disabilities; Handwriting Disabilities; Spelling Disabilities; Arithmetic Disabilities; Written Expression. *Behavioral Problems* Attention Deficits; Impulsivity; Self-Aggression; Verbal Aggression; Physical Aggression; Indirect Aggression; Passive Aggression; Withdrawal. *Conditions Treated* Depression; Inadequacy/Immaturity; Personality Problems; Socialized Aggressive Reaction.
Services Provided Individual Therapy; Group Therapy; Parent Involvement; Art Therapy; Music Therapy; Reality Therapy. *Professionals on Staff* Psychiatrists 1; Psychologists 1; Counselors 2; Social Workers 1. *Service Facilities Available (with number of rooms)* Consultative (ERT) 1; Itinerants 1; Self-Contained Rooms 9. *Educational Professionals* Special Education Teachers 4; Crisis Teachers 1; Special Education Counselors 2; Paraprofessionals 3. *Curricula* Traditional Academic; Basic Skills. *Educational Intervention Approaches* Progressive Discipline; Self-Control. *Degrees Awarded* High School Diploma.
Comments This program is designed for students who have not been successful in traditional self-contained classes for emotional development in a public school setting.

Camphill Special Schools Inc

RD 1, Glenmoore, PA 19343 (215) 469-9236
Year Established 1963
Contact Cornelius M Peitzner, Admin
Facility Information *Placement* Private Residential Care; Private Day Care. *Number of Beds* 73. *Children/Adolescents Served* 73. *Sexes Served* Both. *Tuition Fees (Approx)* $8,500-$14,200. *Sources of Funding* State Funds; Private. *Teacher Certification Level* Elementary School. *Special Certification Level* ED; MR; Career/Vocational Education.
Student/Patient Characteristics *Age Levels* 5-8; 9-11; 12-14; 15-17; 18-21. *IQ Ranges* 26-40; 41-55; 56-70; 71-85. *Exceptionalities Served* Autistic; Learning Disabled; Mentally Handicapped. *Learning Problems* Memory Disabilities; Perceptual Disabilities; Thinking Disabilities; Oral Language Disabilities; Reading Disabilities; Handwriting Disabilities; Spelling Disabilities; Arithmetic Disabilities; Written Expression. *Behavioral Problems* Attention Deficits; Hyperactivity; Withdrawal.
Services Provided Individual Therapy; Group Therapy; Parent Involvement; Art Therapy; Music Therapy; Play Therapy; Color and Light Therapy. *Professionals on Staff* Nurses; Physician.

Service Facilities Available (with number of rooms) Special
School. *Educational Professionals* Special Education Teachers.
Curricula Individualized; Basic Skills; Prevocational. *Educational
Intervention Approaches* Creative Conditioning.

Center for Autistic Children

3965 Conshohocken Ave, Philadelphia, PA 19131
(215) 878-3400
Contact Bertram A Ruttenberg, Dir

Facility Information *Placement* Special School; Outpatient Psy-
chiatric. *Children/Adolescents Served* 35. *Sexes Served* Both.
Sources of Funding State Funds; Medicare; P.L. 94-142. Summer
school available. *Teacher Certification Level* Elementary School;
Junior High/Middle School. *Special Certification Level* ED.
Student/Patient Characteristics *Age Levels* 0-4; 5-8; 9-11; 12-14.
Exceptionalities Served Autistic; Emotionally Disturbed; Mentally
Handicapped. *Learning Problems* Memory Disabilities; Percep-
tual Disabilities; Thinking Disabilities; Oral Language Disabil-
ities; Reading Disabilities; Handwriting Disabilities; Spelling
Disabilities; Arithmetic Disabilities; Written Expression.
Behavioral Problems Attention Deficits; Hyperactivity; Hypoactiv-
ity; Impulsivity; Self-Aggression; Verbal Aggression; Physical
Aggression; Indirect Aggression; Passive Aggression; Withdrawal.
Conditions Treated Early Infantile Autism; Disintegrative
Psychoses; Schizophrenia; Phobias; Obsessions and Compulsions.

Services Provided Individual Therapy; Group Therapy; Parent
Involvement; Behavior Therapy; Art Therapy; Music Therapy;
Play Therapy; Recreational Therapy; Movement Therapy; Lan-
guage Therapy. *Professionals on Staff* Psychiatrists 1; Social
Workers 1; Child Care Staff 6; Therapists 4.5. *Service Facilities
Available (with number of rooms)* Self-Contained Rooms 4.
Educational Professionals Special Education Teachers 4.

Centerville Clinics Inc—Partial Hospital Program

RD 1, Fredericktown, PA 15333 (412) 757-6801
Year Established 1975
Contact Ann D Goydos, Dir

Facility Information *Placement* Partial Hospital Programs; Day
Programs. *Sexes Served* Both. *Sources of Funding* Health Insurance. Summer school available. *Teacher Certification Level* Elementary School; Junior High/Middle School; High School.
Special Certification Level LD; MR.
Student/Patient Characteristics *Age Levels* 12-14; 15-17; Over 21.
IQ Ranges 71-85; 85-130; Above 130. *Exceptionalities Served*
Emotionally Disturbed; Learning Disabled; Mentally Handicapped; Communication Disordered; Hearing Impaired/Deaf; Visually Impaired/Blind; Other Health Impaired; Physically Handicapped; Gifted.

Services Provided *Professionals on Staff* Psychiatrists 2; Psychologists 1; Counselors 15; Social Workers. *Service Facilities
Available (with number of rooms)* Consultative (ERT) 1; Transition Rooms 1; Self-Contained Rooms 2. *Educational
Professionals* Regular School Teachers 5; Special Education
Teachers 5. *Curricula* Traditional Academic. *Educational
Intervention Approaches* Progressive Discipline; Self-Control; Behavior Modification; Applied Behavior Analysis; Creative Conditioning. *Degrees Awarded* High School Diploma.

Community Mental Health and Counseling Center

406 N Buhl Farm Dr, Hermitage, PA 16148 (412) 981-7141
Year Established 1960
Contact Elliott T Shinn, Med Dir

Facility Information *Placement* Health and Counseling Center.
Services Provided Individual Therapy; Group Therapy; Parent
Involvement; Behavior Therapy; Family Therapy; Filial Therapy;
Drug Therapy; Art Therapy; Reality Therapy; Play Therapy.
Professionals on Staff Psychiatrists; Psychologists; Counselors;
Social Workers.

Craig House—Technoma

751 N Negley Ave, Pittsburgh, PA 15206 (412) 361-2801
Year Established 1955
Contact Richard L Kerchner, Admin

Facility Information *Placement* Special School; Special Program
Partial Psychiatric Hospital. *Children/Adolescents Served* 200.
Sexes Served Both. *Sources of Funding* State Funds; Health
Insurance; P.L. 94-142. Summer school available. *Teacher
Certification Level* Elementary School; Junior High/Middle
School; High School. *Special Certification Level* LD; Career/
Vocational Education; Reading; Math.
Student/Patient Characteristics *Exceptionalities Served* Autistic;
Emotionally Disturbed; Learning Disabled; Communication Dis-
ordered. *Learning Problems* Memory Disabilities; Perceptual
Disabilities; Thinking Disabilities; Oral Language Disabilities;
Reading Disabilities; Handwriting Disabilities; Spelling Disabil-
ities; Arithmetic Disabilities; Written Expression. *Behavioral
Problems* Attention Deficits; Hyperactivity; Hypoactivity; Impul-
sivity; Self-Aggression; Verbal Aggression; Physical Aggression;
Indirect Aggression; Passive Aggression; Withdrawal. *Conditions
Treated* Alcohol Abuse and/or Drug Abuse; Other Substance
Abuse or Dependence; Early Infantile Autism; Disintegrative
Psychoses; Schizophrenia; Convulsive Disorders; Phobias; Obses-
sions and Compulsions; Hysteria; Depression; Suicide; Asthma;
Anorexia Nervosa; Ulcerative Colitis; Inadequacy/Immaturity;
Personality Problems; Socialized Aggressive Reaction; Un-
socialized Aggressive Reaction.

Services Provided Individual Therapy; Group Therapy; Parent
Involvement; Behavior Therapy; Cognitive Developmental Ther-
apy; Family Therapy; Filial Therapy; Drug Therapy; Art Ther-
apy; Reality Therapy. *Professionals on Staff* Psychiatrists 3; Psy-
chologists 2; Counselors 30; Social Workers 10; Child Care Staff
40; Nurses 2; Pediatrician; Speech Therapist. *Service Facilities
Available (with number of rooms)* Self-Contained Rooms 20.
Educational Professionals Special Education Teachers 25; Career/
Vocational Teachers 5. *Curricula* Traditional Academic; Career/
Vocational Education; Individualized; Basic Skills; Prevocational.
Educational Intervention Approaches Engineered Classroom; Self-
Control; Behavior Modification; Applied Behavior Analysis; Cre-
ative Conditioning. *Degrees Awarded* Certificate of Attendance;
High School Diploma.

The Delacato and Doman Autistic Unit

32 S Morton Ave, Morton, PA 19070 (215) 544-6610
Year Established 1974
Contact James F McGonagle, Clinical Dir

Facility Information *Placement* In-Home Rehabilitation Programs. *Sexes Served* Both. *Tuition Fees (Approx)* $1,000. *Sources
of Funding* Health Insurance. *Special Certification Level* ED.
Student/Patient Characteristics *Age Levels* 0-4; 5-8; 9-11; 12-14;
15-17; 18-21; Over 21. *IQ Ranges* 0-25; 26-40; 41-55; 56-70;
71-85; 85-130; Above 130. *Exceptionalities Served* Autistic;
Learning Disabled; Mentally Handicapped; Communication Dis-
ordered; Hearing Impaired/Deaf; Visually Impaired/Blind.
Learning Problems Memory Disabilities; Perceptual Disabilities;
Thinking Disabilities; Oral Language Disabilities; Reading Dis-
abilities; Handwriting Disabilities; Spelling Disabilities;
Arithmetic Disabilities; Written Expression. *Behavioral Problems*
Attention Deficits; Hyperactivity; Impulsivity; Self-Aggression;
Verbal Aggression; Physical Aggression; Withdrawal. *Conditions
Treated* Early Infantile Autism; Aphasia; Convulsive Disorders;
Obsessions and Compulsions; Inadequacy/Immaturity; Personal-
ity Problems; Socialized Aggressive Reaction; Unsocialized Ag-
gressive Reaction.

Services Provided Individual Therapy; Parent Involvement; Behavior Therapy; Sensory Based. *Educational Professionals* Regular School Teachers 1; Special Education Teachers 1. *Educational
Intervention Approaches* Sensory Integration.

The Delacato and Doman Autistic Unit

Plymouth Plaza, Ste 107, Plymouth Meeting, PA 19462
(215) 828-4881
Year Established 1975
Contact Janice Delacato, Admin
Facility Information *Placement* Outpatient Facility. *Sexes Served* Both. *Sources of Funding* Health Insurance; Parent Pay. *Teacher Certification Level* Elementary School; Junior High/Middle School; High School.
Student/Patient Characteristics *Age Levels* 0-4; 5-8; 9-11; 12-14; 15-17; 18-21; Over 21. *Exceptionalities Served* Autistic; Learning Disabled; Communication Disordered; Hearing Impaired/Deaf. *Learning Problems* Memory Disabilities; Perceptual Disabilities; Thinking Disabilities; Oral Language Disabilities; Reading Disabilities; Handwriting Disabilities; Spelling Disabilities; Arithmetic Disabilities; Written Expression. *Behavioral Problems* Attention Deficits; Hyperactivity; Hypoactivity; Impulsivity; Self-Aggression; Verbal Aggression; Physical Aggression; Indirect Aggression; Passive Aggression; Withdrawal. *Conditions Treated* Early Infantile Autism.
Services Provided Neurological Home Rehabilitative Therapy. *Service Facilities Available (with number of rooms)* Home Program by Family Members. *Educational Intervention Approaches* Sensory System Normalization.

Delta School

3515 Woodhaven Rd, Philadelphia, PA 19154 (215) 632-5904
Year Established 1958
Contact Robert W Long, Ed Dir
Facility Information *Placement* Special School.
Children/Adolescents Served 200. *Sexes Served* Both. *Sources of Funding* State Funds; P.L. 94-142. *Special Certification Level* Reading; Physically Handicapped; Mentally Handicapped.
Student/Patient Characteristics *Age Levels* 5-8; 9-11; 12-14; 15-17; 18-21. *IQ Ranges* 56-70; 71-85; 85-130. *Exceptionalities Served* Emotionally Disturbed; Learning Disabled; Mentally Handicapped. *Learning Problems* Memory Disabilities; Perceptual Disabilities; Thinking Disabilities; Oral Language Disabilities; Reading Disabilities; Handwriting Disabilities; Spelling Disabilities; Arithmetic Disabilities; Written Expression. *Behavioral Problems* Attention Deficits; Hyperactivity; Hypoactivity; Impulsivity; Self-Aggression; Verbal Aggression; Physical Aggression; Indirect Aggression; Passive Aggression; Withdrawal.
Services Provided Individual Therapy; Group Therapy; Behavior Therapy; Cognitive Developmental Therapy; Art Therapy; Music Therapy; Reality Therapy; Play Therapy. *Professionals on Staff* Psychiatrists 1; Psychologists 1; Nurses 1. *Service Facilities Available (with number of rooms)* Resource Rooms 1. *Educational Professionals* Special Education Teachers 20; Career/Vocational Teachers 1; Crisis Teachers 4; Special Education Counselors 1; Paraprofessionals 4. *Curricula* Career/Vocational Education; Basic Skills; Prevocational. *Educational Intervention Approaches* Progressive Discipline; Behavior Modification. *Degrees Awarded* Graduate Equivalency Diploma; Certificate of Completion.

The Devereux Foundation

PO Box 400, 19 S Waterloo Rd, Devon, PA 19333
(215) 964-3100
Year Established 1912
Contact Ellwood M Smith, Admissions Dir
Facility Information *Placement* Private Residential Care; Private Day Care. *Children/Adolescents Served* 950 (residential beds); 150 (day students). *Sexes Served* Both. *Tuition Fees (Approx)* $2,200-$6,900. *Sources of Funding* State Funds; Health Insurance; P.L. 94-142; CHAMPUS. Summer school available. *Teacher Certification Level* Elementary School; Junior High/Middle School; High School.
Student/Patient Characteristics *Age Levels* 9-11; 12-14; 15-17; 18-21; Over 21. *IQ Ranges* 26-40; 41-55; 56-70; 71-85; 85-130. *Exceptionalities Served* Autistic; Emotionally Disturbed; Learning Disabled; Mentally Handicapped; Communication Disordered; Hearing Impaired/Deaf. *Learning Problems* Thinking Disabilities; Arithmetic Disabilities. *Behavioral Problems* Impulsivity; Passive Aggression. *Conditions Treated* Alcohol Abuse and/or Drug Abuse; Other Substance Abuse or Dependence; Early Infantile Autism; Disintegrative Psychoses; Schizophrenia; Aphasia; Convulsive Disorders; Phobias; Obsessions and Compulsions; Hysteria; Depression; Suicide; Asthma; Anorexia Nervosa; Personality Problems; Socialized Aggressive Reaction; Unsocialized Aggressive Reaction.
Services Provided Individual Therapy; Group Therapy; Behavior Therapy; Cognitive Developmental Therapy; Drug Therapy; Art Therapy; Music Therapy; Play Therapy. *Professionals on Staff* Psychiatrists; Psychologists; Counselors; Social Workers; Child Care Staff; Nurses. *Educational Professionals* Special Education Teachers; Career/Vocational Teachers; Crisis Teachers; Special Education Counselors; Paraprofessionals. *Curricula* Career/Vocational Education; Individualized; Basic Skills; Prevocational. *Educational Intervention Approaches* Behavior Modification; Applied Behavior Analysis. *Degrees Awarded* High School Diploma; Graduate Equivalency Diploma.

Educational Department of Institute of Pennsylvania Hospital—Mill Creek School

111 N 49th St, Philadelphia, PA 19139 (215) 471-2169
Year Established 1971
Contact Stanley C Diamond, Dir
Facility Information *Placement* Special School; Hospital. *Number of Beds* 40. *Children/Adolescents Served* 58. *Sexes Served* Both. *Room and Board Fees (Approx)* $400. *Tuition Fees (Approx)* $11,880. *Sources of Funding* State Funds; Health Insurance; Medicaid; Private Funds. Summer school available. *Teacher Certification Level* High School. *Special Certification Level* ED; Math.
Student/Patient Characteristics *Age Levels* 12-14; 15-17; 18-21. *IQ Ranges* 85-130; Above 130. *Exceptionalities Served* Emotionally Disturbed. *Learning Problems* Perceptual Disabilities; Thinking Disabilities; Reading Disabilities; Spelling Disabilities; Arithmetic Disabilities; Written Expression. *Behavioral Problems* Attention Deficits; Hyperactivity; Impulsivity; Self-Aggression; Verbal Aggression; Physical Aggression; Passive Aggression. *Conditions Treated* Alcohol Abuse and/or Drug Abuse; Other Substance Abuse or Dependence; Schizophrenia; Phobias; Obsessions and Compulsions; Depression; Suicide; Anorexia Nervosa; Inadequacy/Immaturity; Personality Problems; Socialized Aggressive Reaction; Unsocialized Aggressive Reaction.
Services Provided Individual Therapy; Group Therapy; Parent Involvement; Behavior Therapy; Biofeedback; Drug Therapy; Art Therapy; Music Therapy. *Professionals on Staff* Psychiatrists; Counselors 1; Social Workers 10. *Service Facilities Available (with number of rooms)* Self-Contained Rooms 1. *Educational Professionals* Regular School Teachers 1; Special Education Teachers 6; Counselor 2. *Curricula* Traditional Academic; Career/Vocational Education; Individualized; Basic Skills; Prevocational. *Educational Intervention Approaches* Behavior Modification Psychoanalytic; Confrontation. *Degrees Awarded* High School Diploma; Graduate Equivalency Diploma.

Elwyn Institutes

111 Elwyn Rd, Elwyn, PA 19063 (215) 358-6520
Year Established 1852
Contact Earl E Leight, Registrar
Facility Information *Placement* Special School; Private Residential Care; Vocational Training. *Number of Beds* 300. *Children/Adolescents Served* (residential); 500 (day care). *Sexes Served* . *Tuition Fees (Approx)* $8,245 (educational tuition). *Sources of Funding* State Funds. Summer school available. *Special Certification Level* ED; MR; Reading; Speech; Hearing Impaired; Visual Impaired; Physical Education; Home Ecomonics; Music.

Student/Patient Characteristics *Age Levels* 5-8; 9-11; 12-14; 15-17; 18-21; Over 21. *IQ Ranges* 26-40; 41-55; 56-70; 71-85. *Exceptionalities Served* Autistic; Emotionally Disturbed; Learning Disabled; Mentally Handicapped; Communication Disordered; Hearing Impaired/Deaf; Visually Impaired/Blind; Other Health Impaired; Physically Handicapped. *Learning Problems* Memory Disabilities; Perceptual Disabilities; Thinking Disabilities; Oral Language Disabilities; Reading Disabilities; Handwriting Disabilities; Spelling Disabilities; Arithmetic Disabilities; Written Expression. *Behavioral Problems* Attention Deficits; Hyperactivity; Impulsivity; Self-Aggression; Verbal Aggression; Physical Aggression; Indirect Aggression; Passive Aggression; Withdrawal. *Conditions Treated* Early Infantile Autism; Aphasia; Convulsive Disorders; Obsessions and Compulsions; Inadequacy/Immaturity; Personality Problems; Socialized Aggressive Reaction.

Services Provided Individual Therapy; Group Therapy; Parent Involvement; Behavior Therapy; Play Therapy; Occupational Therapy; Physical Therapy; Audiology. *Service Facilities Available (with number of rooms)* Resource Rooms 4; Self-Contained Rooms 20. *Educational Professionals* Special Education Teachers 100; Ancillary Staff 50. *Curricula* Traditional Academic; Career/Vocational Education; Individualized; Basic Skills; Prevocational. *Educational Intervention Approaches* Behavior Modification. *Degrees Awarded* Certificate of Attendance; High School Diploma.

Comments Elwyn is a private nonprofit facility which provides a wide range of special education and rehabilitation services for handicapped children and adults on both a residential and day basis.

Family Guidance Center

101 N 5th St, Reading, PA 19601 (215) 378-1641
Year Established 1967
Contact John N Berger, Exec Dir

Facility Information *Placement* Outpatient Psychiatric. *Sexes Served* Both. *Sources of Funding* State Funds; Health Insurance; Medicaid; Medicare; United Fund.

Student/Patient Characteristics *Age Levels* 0-4; 5-8; 9-11; 12-14; 15-17; 18-21; Over 21. *IQ Ranges* 0-25; 26-40; 41-55; 56-70; 71-85; 85-130; Above 130. *Exceptionalities Served* Autistic; Emotionally Disturbed; Mentally Handicapped. *Behavioral Problems* Attention Deficits; Hyperactivity; Hypoactivity; Impulsivity; Self-Aggression; Verbal Aggression; Physical Aggression; Indirect Aggression; Passive Aggression; Withdrawal. *Conditions Treated* Early Infantile Autism; Disintegrative Psychoses; Schizophrenia; Phobias; Obsessions and Compulsions; Hysteria; Depression; Suicide; Asthma; Anorexia Nervosa; Ulcerative Colitis; Inadequacy/Immaturity; Personality Problems; Socialized Aggressive Reaction; Unsocialized Aggressive Reaction.

Services Provided Individual Therapy; Parent Involvement; Behavior Therapy; Biofeedback; Family Therapy; Drug Therapy; Play Therapy. *Professionals on Staff* Psychiatrists 3; Psychologists 6; Counselors 3; Social Workers 6; Nurses 1. *Educational Intervention Approaches* Behavior Modification.

Comments It is a base service unit for the community MH/MR program and provides diagnosis, treatment, case-management and outpatient psychiatric care to persons with a mental disability.

Green Tree School

143 W Walnut Ln, Philadelphia, PA 19144 (215) 843-4528
Year Established 1957
Contact Albert Silverman, Dir

Facility Information *Placement* Special School. *Children/Adolescents Served* 225. *Sexes Served* Both. *Sources of Funding* State Funds; Medicaid; City; Head Start. *Teacher Certification Level* Elementary School. *Special Certification Level* ED; MR; Career/Vocational Education; Reading.

Student/Patient Characteristics *Age Levels* 0-4; 5-8; 9-11; 12-14; 15-17; 18-21. *Exceptionalities Served* Emotionally Disturbed; Physically Handicapped. *Learning Problems* Perceptual Disabil-

ities; Thinking Disabilities; Oral Language Disabilities; Reading Disabilities; Handwriting Disabilities; Spelling Disabilities; Arithmetic Disabilities; Written Expression. *Behavioral Problems* Attention Deficits; Hyperactivity; Impulsivity; Self-Aggression; Verbal Aggression; Physical Aggression; Indirect Aggression; Passive Aggression; Withdrawal. *Conditions Treated* Inadequacy/Immaturity; Personality Problems; Socialized Aggressive Reaction; Unsocialized Aggressive Reaction.

Services Provided Individual Therapy; Group Therapy; Parent Involvement; Art Therapy; Play Therapy; Movement Therapy. *Professionals on Staff* Psychiatrists 2; Counselors 3; Social Workers 3; Nurses 1. *Service Facilities Available (with number of rooms)* Self-Contained Rooms 15. *Educational Professionals* Special Education Teachers 20; Career/Vocational Teachers 2; Crisis Teachers 2; Special Education Counselors 6; Paraprofessionals 15. *Curricula* Individualized; Prevocational. *Degrees Awarded* Certificate of Attendance.

Highland Youth Services—The Highland School

5250 Caste Dr, Pittsburgh, PA 15236 (412) 885-7017
Year Established 1966
Contact Millicent McCathren, School Dir; John Niedzwicki, Prog Dir

Facility Information *Placement* Special School. *Children/Adolescents Served* 136. *Sexes Served* Both. *Room and Board Fees (Approx)* $39. *Sources of Funding* State Funds; Health Insurance. *Teacher Certification Level* Elementary School; Junior High/Middle School; High School. *Special Certification Level* ED; LD; MR; Reading; Math; Special Education Speech; Language Arts; Music; Shop.

Student/Patient Characteristics *Age Levels* 5-8; 9-11; 12-14; 15-17; 18-21; Over 21. *IQ Ranges* 71-85; 85-130; Above 130. *Exceptionalities Served* Emotionally Disturbed; Learning Disabled; Gifted. *Learning Problems* Memory Disabilities; Perceptual Disabilities; Thinking Disabilities; Oral Language Disabilities; Reading Disabilities; Handwriting Disabilities; Spelling Disabilities; Arithmetic Disabilities; Written Expression. *Behavioral Problems* Attention Deficits; Hyperactivity; Hypoactivity; Impulsivity; Self-Aggression; Verbal Aggression; Physical Aggression; Indirect Aggression; Passive Aggression; Withdrawal. *Conditions Treated* Schizophrenia; Phobias; Obsessions and Compulsions; Depression; Inadequacy/Immaturity; Personality Problems; Socialized Aggressive Reaction; Unsocialized Aggressive Reaction.

Services Provided Individual Therapy; Group Therapy; Parent Involvement; Behavior Therapy; Family Therapy; Filial Therapy; Drug Therapy; Reality Therapy; Play Therapy; Psychodrama. *Professionals on Staff* Psychiatrists 2; Social Workers 10; Nurses 2. *Service Facilities Available (with number of rooms)* Self-Contained Rooms 6; Therapy Rooms 3. *Educational Professionals* Regular School Teachers 3; Special Education Teachers 20; Special Education Teachers; Paraprofessionals 1. *Curricula* Traditional Academic; Individualized; Basic Skills; Prevocational. *Educational Intervention Approaches* Progressive Discipline; Self-Control. *Degrees Awarded* High School Diploma.

Comments Highland School—Highland Youth Services is an integrated educational mental health program serving children within commuting distance to a day program. Primary diagnosis must be Emotionally Disturbed and I.Q. within normal ranges.

Institute for Learning

5501 Greene St, Philadelphia, PA 19144 (215) 848-4074
Year Established 1965
Contact Sally Gever

Facility Information *Placement* Outpatient Mental Health Clinic. *Children/Adolescents Served* 200. *Sexes Served* Both. *Sources of Funding* Health Insurance; Medicaid. *Teacher Certification Level* Elementary School; Junior High/Middle School; High School. *Special Certification Level* ED; LD; MR; Reading; Math.

Student/Patient Characteristics *Age Levels* 0-4; 5-8; 9-11; 12-14; 15-17; 18-21; Over 21. *IQ Ranges* 71-85; 85-130. *Exceptionalities Served* Emotionally Disturbed; Learning Disabled. *Learning*

Problems Perceptual Disabilities; Oral Language Disabilities; Reading Disabilities; Handwriting Disabilities; Spelling Disabilities; Arithmetic Disabilities. *Behavioral Problems* Attention Deficits; Hyperactivity; Impulsivity; Verbal Aggression; Indirect Aggression; Passive Aggression; Withdrawal. *Conditions Treated* Phobias; Obsessions and Compulsions; Hysteria; Depression; Personality Problems; Socialized Aggressive Reaction.

Services Provided Individual Therapy; Group Therapy; Parent Involvement; Family Therapy. *Professionals on Staff* Psychiatrists 2; Psychologists 5; Social Workers 3; Learning Therapists 25. *Curricula* Individualized.

The Learning Center

444 E College Ave Ste 500, State College, PA 16801
(814) 234-3450
Year Established 1978
Contact Cynthia Minter, Dir

Facility Information *Placement* Clinical; Tutoring School. *Children/Adolescents Served* 100. *Sexes Served* Both. *Sources of Funding* Private Tuition. Summer school available. *Teacher Certification Level* Elementary School; Junior High/Middle School; High School. *Special Certification Level* ED; LD; MR; Reading; Math; Science.

Student/Patient Characteristics *Age Levels* 9-11; 12-14; 15-17; 18-21; Over 21. *IQ Ranges* 85-130; Above 130. *Exceptionalities Served* Emotionally Disturbed; Learning Disabled; Communication Disordered; Gifted. *Learning Problems* Memory Disabilities; Perceptual Disabilities; Thinking Disabilities; Reading Disabilities; Handwriting Disabilities; Spelling Disabilities; Arithmetic Disabilities; Written Expression. *Behavioral Problems* Attention Deficits; Hyperactivity.

Services Provided Individual Therapy; Parent Involvement; Cognitive Developmental Therapy. *Professionals on Staff* Parenting Specialist. *Educational Professionals* Special Education Teachers 100. *Curricula* Individualized; Basic Skills; Study Skills; Problem Solving. *Educational Intervention Approaches* Precision Teaching; Self-Control.

Lourdesmont—Good Shepherd Youth and Family Services

537 Venard Rd, Clarks Summit, PA 18411 (717) 587-4741
Year Established 1889
Contact Alice Caulson, Admissions Dir

Facility Information *Placement* Private Residential Care; Day Treatment Partial Hospitalization. *Number of Beds* 25. *Children/Adolescents Served* 100. *Sexes Served* Both. *Room and Board Fees (Approx)* $57. *Sources of Funding* State Funds; County Child Welfare Agencies. Summer school available. *Teacher Certification Level* High School. *Special Certification Level* ED; Reading; Math; Secondary Subject Areas.

Student/Patient Characteristics *Age Levels* 12-14; 15-17. *IQ Ranges* 85-130. *Exceptionalities Served* Emotionally Disturbed. *Learning Problems* Perceptual Disabilities; Reading Disabilities; Spelling Disabilities; Arithmetic Disabilities; Written Expression. *Behavioral Problems* Attention Deficits; Hyperactivity; Hypoactivity; Impulsivity; Self-Aggression; Verbal Aggression; Physical Aggression; Indirect Aggression; Passive Aggression; Withdrawal. *Conditions Treated* Phobias; Obsessions and Compulsions; Hysteria; Inadequacy/Immaturity; Personality Problems; Socialized Aggressive Reaction; Unsocialized Aggressive Reaction.

Services Provided Individual Therapy; Group Therapy; Parent Involvement; Behavior Therapy; Family Therapy; Drug Therapy; Art Therapy; Music Therapy; Reality Therapy. *Professionals on Staff* Psychiatrists 1; Psychologists 2; Counselors 4; Social Workers 2; Child Care Staff 12; Nurses 2; Activities Staff 1; Community Workers 2. *Service Facilities Available (with number of rooms)* Resource Rooms 1; On-Campus Residential School 14. *Educational Professionals* Special Education Teachers 11; Career/Vocational Teachers 2; Special Education Counselors 3. *Curricula* Traditional Academic; Individualized; Basic Skills;

Prevocational. *Educational Intervention Approaches* Self-Control; Behavior Modification; Applied Behavior Analysis. *Degrees Awarded* High School Diploma.

Comments The Lourdesmont focus is psycho-social-educational intervention for adolescents who present emotional/social/behavioral maladjustment.

The Mary and Alexander Laughlin Children's Center

Broad and Frederick Sts, Sewickley, PA 15143 (215) 741-4087
Year Established 1956
Contact Mary Beth Duffy, Exec Dir

Facility Information *Placement* Special School. *Sexes Served* Both. *Sources of Funding* Privately Supported; Nonprofit. Summer school available. *Special Certification Level* ED; LD; Reading; Math.

Student/Patient Characteristics *Age Levels* 0-4; 5-8; 9-11; 12-14; 15-17; 18-21; Over 21. *Exceptionalities Served* Emotionally Disturbed; Learning Disabled; Communication Disordered; Hearing Impaired/Deaf; Gifted. *Learning Problems* Memory Disabilities; Perceptual Disabilities; Thinking Disabilities; Oral Language Disabilities; Reading Disabilities; Handwriting Disabilities; Spelling Disabilities; Arithmetic Disabilities; Written Expression. *Behavioral Problems* Attention Deficits; Hyperactivity; Hypoactivity; Impulsivity; Self-Aggression; Verbal Aggression; Physical Aggression; Indirect Aggression; Passive Aggression; Withdrawal. *Conditions Treated* Aphasia; Depression; Inadequacy/Immaturity; Personality Problems; Socialized Aggressive Reaction.

Services Provided Individual Therapy; Parent Involvement; Behavior Therapy; Cognitive Developmental Therapy; Family Therapy; Play Therapy; Psychodrama. *Professionals on Staff* Psychologists 2; Counselors 2. *Educational Professionals* Special Education Teachers 23.

The Mental Health Institute for Children at Allentown State Hospital

1600 Hanover Ave, Allentown, PA 18103 (215) 821-6401
Year Established 1930
Contact John L Wachter, Dir

Facility Information *Placement* Psychiatric Hospital. *Number of Beds* 39. *Children/Adolescents Served* 39. *Sexes Served* Both. *Room and Board Fees (Approx)* $155. *Sources of Funding* State Funds; Medicaid; Medical Assistance. *Teacher Certification Level* Elementary School. *Special Certification Level* Special Education.

Student/Patient Characteristics *Age Levels* 5-8; 9-11; 12-14. *IQ Ranges* 71-85; 85-130; Above 130. *Exceptionalities Served* Emotionally Disturbed. *Learning Problems* Memory Disabilities; Perceptual Disabilities; Thinking Disabilities; Oral Language Disabilities; Reading Disabilities; Handwriting Disabilities; Spelling Disabilities; Arithmetic Disabilities; Written Expression. *Behavioral Problems* Attention Deficits; Hyperactivity; Impulsivity; Self-Aggression; Verbal Aggression; Physical Aggression; Indirect Aggression; Passive Aggression; Withdrawal. *Conditions Treated* Alcohol Abuse and/or Drug Abuse; Other Substance Abuse or Dependence; Disintegrative Psychoses; Schizophrenia; Convulsive Disorders; Depression; Suicide; Personality Problems; Socialized Aggressive Reaction; Unsocialized Aggressive Reaction.

Services Provided Individual Therapy; Group Therapy; Parent Involvement; Behavior Therapy; Cognitive Developmental Therapy; Family Therapy; Filial Therapy; Drug Therapy; Art Therapy; Music Therapy; Play Therapy; Occupational Therapy. *Professionals on Staff* Psychiatrists 2; Psychologists 1; Social Workers 4; Child Care Staff 15; Nurses 6; Recreation Therapy; Art Therapy; Music Therapy 7. *Service Facilities Available (with number of rooms)* Hospital School 6. *Educational Professionals* Special Education Teachers 5. *Curricula* Individualized. *Educational Intervention Approaches* Self-Control; Behavior Modification; Collateral Counseling.

Comments The Mental Health Institute is a psychiatric hospital for emotionally disturbed children serving northeast PA. A total individualized program is offered to each child admitted. This includes psychotherapy special education, activity therapy, and family therapy.

Pace School

200 S Beatty St, Pittsburgh, PA 15206 (412) 441-1111
Year Established 1967
Contact Barbara Bazron, Exec Dir
Facility Information *Placement* Special School. *Children/Adolescents Served* 175. *Sexes Served* Both. *Sources of Funding* P.L. 94-142; Private Contributions. *Teacher Certification Level* Elementary School. *Special Certification Level* ED; LD.
Student/Patient Characteristics *Age Levels* 5-8; 9-11; 12-14; 15-17. *IQ Ranges* 71-85; 85-130. *Exceptionalities Served* Emotionally Disturbed; Learning Disabled; Brain Injured. *Learning Problems* Memory Disabilities; Perceptual Disabilities; Thinking Disabilities; Oral Language Disabilities; Reading Disabilities; Handwriting Disabilities; Spelling Disabilities; Arithmetic Disabilities; Written Expression. *Behavioral Problems* Attention Deficits; Hyperactivity; Hypoactivity; Impulsivity; Self-Aggression; Verbal Aggression; Physical Aggression; Indirect Aggression; Passive Aggression; Withdrawal. *Conditions Treated* Inadequacy/Immaturity; Personality Problems; Socialized Aggressive Reaction; Unsocialized Aggressive Reaction.
Services Provided Individual Therapy; Group Therapy; Parent Involvement; Behavior Therapy; Art Therapy; Play Therapy; Speech and Language Therapy. *Professionals on Staff* Psychiatrists 1; Psychologists 1; Counselors 3; Social Workers 2; Nurses 1. *Service Facilities Available (with number of rooms)* Consultative (ERT) 12; Itinerants 1; Resource Rooms 2; Transition Rooms 4; Self-Contained Rooms 16. *Educational Professionals* Special Education Teachers 18; Career/Vocational Teachers 1; Crisis Teachers 1; Special Education Counselors 5; Paraprofessionals 16; Speech Therapists; Counseling; Adaptive Physical Education 2. *Curricula* Traditional Academic; Career/Vocational Education; Individualized; Basic Skills; Prevocational; Social Skills; Expressive Arts. *Educational Intervention Approaches* Self-Control; Behavior Modification; Eclectic Approach.

Comments Pace is a private, nonprofit day school serving socially-emotionally disturbed/brain injured children aged 6-15. Pace serves children throughout southwestern PA. Pace students are of average or above intelligence, but as a result of their disabilities, cannot be educated adequately in a regular school situation. Pace is licensed by the PA Department of Education.

Partial Hospitalization Program Children's Service Center

335 S Franklin St, Wilkes Barre, PA 18702 (717) 825-6425
Contact Joseph DeVizia, Exec Dir
Facility Information *Placement* Partial Hospitalization. *Children/Adolescents Served* 75. *Sexes Served* Both. *Sources of Funding* State Funds. Summer school available. *Teacher Certification Level* Elementary School; Junior High/Middle School; High School. *Special Certification Level* Special Education.
Student/Patient Characteristics *Age Levels* 0-4; 5-8; 9-11; 12-14; 15-17. *IQ Ranges* 71-85; 85-130. *Exceptionalities Served* Emotionally Disturbed. *Behavioral Problems* Attention Deficits; Hyperactivity; Hypoactivity; Impulsivity; Self-Aggression; Verbal Aggression; Physical Aggression; Indirect Aggression; Passive Aggression; Withdrawal. *Conditions Treated* Early Infantile Autism; Schizophrenia; Phobias; Obsessions and Compulsions; Hysteria; Depression; Suicide; Asthma; Anorexia Nervosa; Inadequacy/Immaturity; Personality Problems; Socialized Aggressive Reaction; Unsocialized Aggressive Reaction.
Services Provided Individual Therapy; Group Therapy; Parent Involvement; Behavior Therapy; Family Therapy; Play Therapy. *Professionals on Staff* Psychiatrists; Psychologists; Social Work-

ers; Child Care Staff; Nurses. *Educational Professionals* Special Education Teachers. *Curricula* Individualized. *Educational Intervention Approaches* Progressive Discipline; Self-Control; Behavior Modification. *Degrees Awarded* High School Diploma.

Penn Foundation for Mental Health

807 Lawn Ave, Sellersville, PA 18960 (215) 257-6551
Year Established 1958
Contact Donald E Kraybill, Dir Child and Family Serv
Facility Information *Placement* Adolescent Partial Hospitalization. *Children/Adolescents Served* 10. *Sexes Served* Both. *Sources of Funding* State Funds; Health Insurance; Medicaid.
Student/Patient Characteristics *Age Levels* 12-14; 15-17. *IQ Ranges* 85-130. *Exceptionalities Served* Emotionally Disturbed. *Behavioral Problems* Attention Deficits; Hyperactivity; Impulsivity; Self-Aggression; Verbal Aggression; Physical Aggression; Indirect Aggression; Withdrawal. *Conditions Treated* Alcohol Abuse and/or Drug Abuse; Other Substance Abuse or Dependence; Schizophrenia; Depression; Suicide; Anorexia Nervosa; Inadequacy/Immaturity; Personality Problems; Socialized Aggressive Reaction.
Services Provided Individual Therapy; Group Therapy; Parent Involvement; Behavior Therapy; Cognitive Developmental Therapy; Biofeedback; Family Therapy; Drug Therapy; Art Therapy; Music Therapy; Reality Therapy; Play Therapy; Psychodrama. *Professionals on Staff* Psychiatrists 1; Psychologists 2; Counselors 1; Nurses 1; Activity Therapists 2. *Service Facilities Available (with number of rooms)* Consultative (ERT); Self-Contained Rooms; Homebound Instruction. *Educational Professionals* Special Education Counselors 1; Paraprofessionals 2. *Curricula* Individualized. *Educational Intervention Approaches* Self-Control; Behavior Modification. *Degrees Awarded* Certificate of Attendance.

Philadelphia Child Guidance Clinic

34th and Civic Center Blvd, Philadelphia, PA 19104
(215) 243-2740
Contact Ida W Philips, Outpatient Dir
Facility Information *Placement* Outpatient Clinic and Hospital. *Number of Beds* 38. *Sexes Served* Both. *Sources of Funding* State Funds; Health Insurance; Medicaid.
Student/Patient Characteristics *Age Levels* 0-4; 5-8; 9-11; 12-14; 15-17; 18-21. *IQ Ranges* 71-85; 85-130; Above 130. *Exceptionalities Served* Emotionally Disturbed; Mentally Handicapped; Communication Disordered; Hearing Impaired/Deaf. *Learning Problems* Memory Disabilities; Perceptual Disabilities; Thinking Disabilities; Oral Language Disabilities; Reading Disabilities; Handwriting Disabilities; Spelling Disabilities; Arithmetic Disabilities; Written Expression. *Behavioral Problems* Attention Deficits; Hyperactivity; Hypoactivity; Impulsivity; Self-Aggression; Verbal Aggression; Physical Aggression; Indirect Aggression; Passive Aggression; Withdrawal. *Conditions Treated* Schizophrenia; Phobias; Obsessions and Compulsions; Hysteria; Depression; Anorexia Nervosa; Inadequacy/Immaturity; Personality Problems; Socialized Aggressive Reaction; Unsocialized Aggressive Reaction.
Services Provided Individual Therapy; Group Therapy; Parent Involvement; Biofeedback; Family Therapy. *Professionals on Staff* Psychiatrists 4; Psychologists 7; Counselors 4; Social Workers 5.

Comments The Philadelphia Child Guidance Clinic Outpatient Department provides the following types of services: individual and family therapy, psychological testing and evaluation, psychological consultation, clinical case management, and school liaison.

Philadelphia Child Guidance Clinic—Child and Family Inpatient Service

34th St and Civic Center Blvd, Philadelphia, PA 19104
(215) 243-2660
Year Established 1925
Contact Connell P O'Brien, Dir Inpatient Serv

Facility Information *Placement* Psychiatric Inpatient Guidance Clinic. *Number of Beds* 38. *Children/Adolescents Served* 38. *Sexes Served* Both. *Sources of Funding* Health Insurance; Medicaid. Summer school available. *Teacher Certification Level* Elementary School; Junior High/Middle School; High School. *Special Certification Level* ED; LD; MR.

Student/Patient Characteristics *Age Levels* 0-4; 5-8; 9-11; 12-14; 15-17; 18-21; Over 21. *IQ Ranges* 71-85; 85-130; Above 130. *Exceptionalities Served* Emotionally Disturbed; Learning Disabled; Mentally Handicapped; Communication Disordered; Hearing Impaired/Deaf; Visually Impaired/Blind; Other Health Impaired; Gifted. *Learning Problems* Memory Disabilities; Perceptual Disabilities; Thinking Disabilities; Oral Language Disabilities; Reading Disabilities; Handwriting Disabilities; Spelling Disabilities; Arithmetic Disabilities; Written Expression. *Behavioral Problems* Attention Deficits; Hyperactivity; Hypoactivity; Impulsivity; Self-Aggression; Verbal Aggression; Physical Aggression; Indirect Aggression; Passive Aggression; Withdrawal. *Conditions Treated* Disintegrative Psychoses; Schizophrenia; Aphasia; Convulsive Disorders; Phobias; Obsessions and Compulsions; Hysteria; Depression; Suicide; Asthma; Anorexia Nervosa; Ulcerative Colitis; Inadequacy/Immaturity; Personality Problems; Socialized Aggressive Reaction; Unsocialized Aggressive Reaction.

Services Provided Individual Therapy; Group Therapy; Parent Involvement; Behavior Therapy; Cognitive Developmental Therapy; Biofeedback; Family Therapy; Drug Therapy; Art Therapy; Recreation Therapy. *Professionals on Staff* Psychiatrists 11; Psychologists 8; Counselors 2; Social Workers 7; Child Care Staff 60; Nurses 14; Psychoeducation Specialist; Adjunctive Specialist 3. *Service Facilities Available (with number of rooms)* Self-Contained Rooms 4; Special School 7; Hospital School 7. *Educational Professionals* Special Education Teachers 4; Crisis Teachers 1; Paraprofessionals 15; Program Coordinators 3. *Curricula* Psychoeducational. *Educational Intervention Approaches* Engineered Classroom; Progressive Discipline; Self-Control; Applied Behavior Analysis; Creative Conditioning; Psychoeducational.

Comments The Inpatient Service of the clinic provides an intense and innovative acute hospitalization program with a 30 day average length of stay. Using a structural (family therapy) and ecological treatment approach each of 5 treatment teams provide services to a broad diagnostic range of children, adolescents, and young adults.

Pressley Ridge School—Day School

530 Marshall Ave, Pittsburgh, PA 15214 (412) 321-3900
Year Established 1969
Contact Andrew Reitz, Prog Dir

Facility Information *Placement* Private Day Care. *Number of Beds* 130. *Children/Adolescents Served* 120. *Sexes Served* Both. *Tuition Fees (Approx)* $12,000. *Sources of Funding* State Funds; Health Insurance; Medicaid; Mental Health. *Teacher Certification Level* Elementary School; Junior High/Middle School; High School. *Special Certification Level* ED.

Student/Patient Characteristics *Age Levels* 9-11; 12-14; 15-17. *IQ Ranges* 71-85; 85-130. *Exceptionalities Served* Emotionally Disturbed. *Learning Problems* Memory Disabilities; Perceptual Disabilities; Thinking Disabilities; Oral Language Disabilities; Reading Disabilities; Handwriting Disabilities; Spelling Disabilities; Arithmetic Disabilities; Written Expression. *Behavioral Problems* Attention Deficits; Hyperactivity; Hypoactivity; Impulsivity; Self-Aggression; Verbal Aggression; Physical Aggression; Indirect Aggression; Passive Aggression; Withdrawal. *Conditions Treated* Alcohol Abuse and/or Drug Abuse; Other Substance Abuse or Dependence; Schizophrenia; Phobias; Obsessions and Compul-

sions; Hysteria; Depression; Suicide; Inadequacy/Immaturity; Personality Problems; Socialized Aggressive Reaction; Unsocialized Aggressive Reaction.

Services Provided Individual Therapy; Group Therapy; Behavior Therapy; Family Therapy. *Professionals on Staff* Psychiatrists 2; Psychologists 6; Counselors 5. *Service Facilities Available (with number of rooms)* Consultative (ERT); Resource Rooms; Self-Contained Rooms. *Educational Professionals* Special Education Teachers 20; Career/Vocational Teachers 1; Special Education Counselors 7. *Curricula* Career/Vocational Education; Individualized; Basic Skills; Prevocational. *Educational Intervention Approaches* Engineered Classroom; Self-Control; Behavior Modification; Applied Behavior Analysis. *Degrees Awarded* Graduate Equivalency Diploma.

Pressley Ridge School—Pryde—Family Based Treatment

530 Marshall Ave, Pittsburgh, PA 15214 (412) 321-6995
Year Established 1982
Contact Pam Meadowcroft, Prog Dir

Facility Information *Placement* Public Residential Care; Family Based Treatment. *Number of Beds* 75. *Children/Adolescents Served* 75. *Sexes Served* Both. *Room and Board Fees (Approx)* $49. *Sources of Funding* State Funds; County Contracts. Summer school available.

Student/Patient Characteristics *Age Levels* 5-8; 9-11; 12-14; 15-17. *IQ Ranges* 71-85; 85-130. *Exceptionalities Served* Emotionally Disturbed; Deliquent. *Learning Problems* Memory Disabilities; Perceptual Disabilities; Thinking Disabilities; Oral Language Disabilities; Reading Disabilities; Handwriting Disabilities; Spelling Disabilities; Arithmetic Disabilities; Written Expression. *Behavioral Problems* Attention Deficits; Hyperactivity; Hypoactivity; Impulsivity; Self-Aggression; Verbal Aggression; Physical Aggression; Indirect Aggression; Passive Aggression; Withdrawal. *Conditions Treated* Alcohol Abuse and/or Drug Abuse; Other Substance Abuse or Dependence; Schizophrenia; Convulsive Disorders; Phobias; Obsessions and Compulsions; Hysteria; Depression; Suicide; Inadequacy/Immaturity; Personality Problems; Socialized Aggressive Reaction; Unsocialized Aggressive Reaction.

Services Provided Individual Therapy; Group Therapy; Parent Involvement; Behavior Therapy; Family Therapy. *Professionals on Staff* Psychiatrists 2; Psychologists 3; Social Workers 11. *Service Facilities Available (with number of rooms)* Consultative (ERT); Self-Contained Rooms; Special School. *Educational Professionals* Regular School Teachers; Special Education Teachers; Special Education Counselors. *Curricula* Traditional Academic; Individualized. *Educational Intervention Approaches* Behavior Modification; Applied Behavior Analysis.

Pressley Ridge School—Wilderness School

Box 25, RD 1, Ohiopyle, PA 15470 (412) 321-6995
Year Established 1975
Contact Peter Salvik, Prog Dir

Facility Information *Placement* Public Residential Care. *Number of Beds* 50. *Children/Adolescents Served* 50. *Sexes Served* Male. *Room and Board Fees (Approx)* $66. *Tuition Fees (Approx)* $24,090. *Sources of Funding* State Funds; County Contracts. Summer school available. *Teacher Certification Level* Elementary School; Junior High/Middle School; High School. *Special Certification Level* ED.

Student/Patient Characteristics *Age Levels* 9-11; 12-14; 15-17. *IQ Ranges* 71-85; 85-130. *Exceptionalities Served* Emotionally Disturbed; Delinquent. *Learning Problems* Memory Disabilities; Perceptual Disabilities; Thinking Disabilities; Oral Language Disabilities; Reading Disabilities; Handwriting Disabilities; Spelling Disabilities; Arithmetic Disabilities; Written Expression. *Behavioral Problems* Attention Deficits; Hyperactivity; Hypoactivity; Impulsivity; Self-Aggression; Verbal Aggression; Physical Aggression; Passive Aggression; Withdrawal. *Conditions Treated* Alcohol Abuse and/or Drug Abuse; Other Substance Abuse or Dependence; Phobias; Obsessions and Compulsions; Hysteria;

Depression; Suicide; Inadequacy/Immaturity; Personality Problems; Socialized Aggressive Reaction; Unsocialized Aggressive Reaction.

Services Provided Group Therapy; Parent Involvement; Family Therapy; Reality Therapy. *Professionals on Staff* Psychiatrists 2; Psychologists 6; Counselors 15; Social Workers 3; Child Care Staff. *Service Facilities Available (with number of rooms)* Consultative (ERT); Self-Contained Rooms 5. *Educational Professionals* Regular School Teachers; Special Education Teachers. *Curricula* Traditional Academic; Career/Vocational Education; Individualized; Basic Skills; Prevocational. *Educational Intervention Approaches* Self-Control; Behavior Modification; Group Process. *Degrees Awarded* Certificate of Attendance; High School Diploma; Graduate Equivalency Diploma.

The Rehabilitation Institute of Pittsburgh

6301 Northumberland St, Pittsburgh, PA 15217 (412) 521-9000
Year Established 1902
Contact Bea Maier, Prog Coord

Facility Information *Placement* Comprehensive Medical Rehab Facility. *Number of Beds* 92. *Children/Adolescents Served* 92 (inpatients); 160 (day patients); unlimited (outpatients). *Sexes Served* Both. *Room and Board Fees (Approx)* $465. *Tuition Fees (Approx)* $12,276. *Sources of Funding* State Funds; Health Insurance. Summer school available. *Teacher Certification Level* Elementary School; Junior High/Middle School; High School. *Special Certification Level* ED; LD; MR; Special Education.

Student/Patient Characteristics *Age Levels* 0-4; 5-8; 9-11; 12-14; 15-17; 18-21; Over 21. *Exceptionalities Served* Emotionally Disturbed; Learning Disabled; Mentally Handicapped; Communication Disordered; Hearing Impaired/Deaf; Visually Impaired/Blind; Other Health Impaired; Physically Handicapped. *Learning Problems* Memory Disabilities; Perceptual Disabilities; Thinking Disabilities; Oral Language Disabilities; Reading Disabilities; Handwriting Disabilities; Spelling Disabilities; Arithmetic Disabilities; Written Expression. *Behavioral Problems* Attention Deficits; Hyperactivity; Hypoactivity; Impulsivity; Self-Aggression; Verbal Aggression; Physical Aggression; Indirect Aggression; Passive Aggression; Withdrawal. *Conditions Treated* Schizophrenia; Convulsive Disorders; Asthma; Anorexia Nervosa; Inadequacy/Immaturity; Personality Problems; Socialized Aggressive Reaction; Unsocialized Aggressive Reaction.

Services Provided Individual Therapy; Group Therapy; Parent Involvement; Behavior Therapy; Cognitive Developmental Therapy; Biofeedback; Family Therapy. *Professionals on Staff* Psychiatrists 1.5; Psychologists 6; Social Workers 4; Child Care Staff 54; Nurses 33; Occupational Therapists 16; Speech-Language Therapists 15; Physical Therapists 11. *Service Facilities Available (with number of rooms)* Resource Rooms 5; Self-Contained Rooms 1; Hospital School 8. *Educational Professionals* Special Education Teachers 25; Rehab Counselors 7. *Curricula* Individualized; Basic Skills; Prevocational. *Educational Intervention Approaches* Behavior Modification.

Comments The Day School Program at the Rehabilitation Institute is licensed by the PA Department of Education, Division of Private Academic Schools to provide special education on the preschool, elementary, and secondary levels for students who are mentally retarded, physically handicapped, brain damaged, or socially/emotionally disturbed.

St Christopher's Hospital Child Psychiatry Center

2603 N 5th St, Philadelphia, PA 19133 (215) 427-5528
Year Established 1952
Contact Joan F Sharp, Asst Admin

Facility Information *Placement* Child Psychiatry Center.

Comments Child Psychiatry Center provides out and day treatment for children and adolescents.

St Gabriel's Hall

Box 13 Audubon, Phoenixville, PA 19407 (215) 666-7970
Year Established 1896
Contact Ralph Stinson, Treatment Dir

Facility Information *Placement* Private Residential Care; Program for Court Committee Deliquents. *Number of Beds* 200. *Children/Adolescents Served* 210. *Sexes Served* Male. *Room and Board Fees (Approx)* $65. *Sources of Funding* State Funds. Summer school available.

Student/Patient Characteristics *Age Levels* 12-14; 15-17; 18-21. *IQ Ranges* 71-85; 85-130; Above 130. *Exceptionalities Served* Emotionally Disturbed; Learning Disabled. *Learning Problems* Perceptual Disabilities; Thinking Disabilities; Oral Language Disabilities; Reading Disabilities. *Behavioral Problems* Attention Deficits; Hyperactivity; Impulsivity; Self-Aggression; Verbal Aggression; Physical Aggression; Indirect Aggression; Passive Aggression; Withdrawal. *Conditions Treated* Alcohol Abuse and/or Drug Abuse; Other Substance Abuse or Dependence; Depression; Suicide; Inadequacy/Immaturity; Personality Problems; Socialized Aggressive Reaction; Unsocialized Aggressive Reaction.

Services Provided Individual Therapy; Group Therapy; Parent Involvement; Behavior Therapy; Cognitive Developmental Therapy; Biofeedback; Family Therapy; Drug Therapy; Reality Therapy. *Professionals on Staff* Psychiatrists 1; Psychologists 7; Counselors 3; Social Workers 10; Child Care Staff 36; Nurses 5. *Service Facilities Available (with number of rooms)* Consultative (ERT) 4; Resource Rooms 1; Self-Contained Rooms 20. *Educational Professionals* Regular School Teachers 25; Special Education Teachers 10. *Curricula* Traditional Academic; Individualized; Basic Skills. *Educational Intervention Approaches* Progressive Discipline; Self-Control; Behavior Modification. *Degrees Awarded* High School Diploma; Graduate Equivalency Diploma.

School District of Philadelphia—Special Education—Stevens Administrative Center

13th and Spring Garden St, Philadelphia, PA 19123
(215) 351-7221
Contact Vivian D Ray, Dir Clinical Serv

Facility Information *Placement* Public School; Special School. *Children/Adolescents Served* 24,000. *Sexes Served* Both. *Sources of Funding* State Funds; P.L. 94-142. Summer school available. *Teacher Certification Level* Elementary School; Junior High/Middle School; High School. *Special Certification Level* ED; LD; MR.

Student/Patient Characteristics *Age Levels* 5-8; 9-11; 12-14; 15-17; 18-21. *IQ Ranges* 0-25; 26-40; 41-55; 56-70; 71-85; 85-130; Above 130. *Exceptionalities Served* Emotionally Disturbed; Learning Disabled; Mentally Handicapped; Communication Disordered; Hearing Impaired/Deaf; Visually Impaired/Blind; Other Health Impaired; Physically Handicapped; Gifted. *Learning Problems* Memory Disabilities; Perceptual Disabilities; Thinking Disabilities; Oral Language Disabilities; Reading Disabilities; Spelling Disabilities; Arithmetic Disabilities; Written Expression. *Behavioral Problems* Attention Deficits; Hyperactivity; Hypoactivity; Impulsivity; Self-Aggression; Verbal Aggression; Physical Aggression; Indirect Aggression; Passive Aggression; Withdrawal.

Services Provided Parent Involvement. *Professionals on Staff* Psychiatrists; Psychologists; Counselors; Social Workers. *Service Facilities Available (with number of rooms)* Consultative (ERT); Itinerants; Resource Rooms; Self-Contained Rooms. *Educational Professionals* Regular School Teachers; Special Education Teachers; Special Education Counselors; Paraprofessionals. *Curricula* Traditional Academic; Career/Vocational Education; Individualized; Basic Skills; Prevocational. *Educational Intervention Approaches* Engineered Classroom; Precision Teaching; Behavior Modification. *Degrees Awarded* Certificate of Attendance; High School Diploma.

Comments The School District of Philadelphia provides comprehensive services for exceptional children.

Scranton Counseling Center—The Louis J Vitale Children and Youth Service

326 Adams Ave, Scranton, PA 18503 (717) 348-6100
Year Established 1974
Contact Frayda Froozan, Community Relations Specialist
Facility Information *Placement* Comprehensive Mental Health; Mental Retardation Center. *Sexes Served* Both. *Sources of Funding* Health Insurance; Sliding Scale; Third Party Insurance.
Student/Patient Characteristics *Exceptionalities Served* Emotionally Disturbed; Hearing Impaired/Deaf; Other Health Impaired; Developmentally Disabled.
Services Provided Individual Therapy; Group Therapy; Family Therapy; Play Therapy. *Professionals on Staff* Psychiatrists; Psychologists; Social Workers; Nurses; Mental Health Workers; Support Staff.

Comments The Children and Youth Service provides diagnostic and treatment services for children and adolescents who have adjustment or emotional problems. Evaluations include family assessment, psychological testing, and psychiatric examination. Treatment services include but are not limited to individual and family therapy, play therapy, and group therapy. Emphasis is placed on prevention of more serious problems.

The Timothy School

625 Montgomery Ave, Bryn Mawr, PA 19010 (215) 525-7101
Year Established 1966
Contact Sr Angela McGinniss, Dir
Facility Information *Placement* Special School.
Children/Adolescents Served 40. *Sexes Served* Both. *Sources of Funding* P.L. 94-142; Donations. Summer school available.
Teacher Certification Level Elementary School. *Special Certification Level* ED.
Student/Patient Characteristics *Age Levels* 5-8; 9-11; 12-14.
Exceptionalities Served Autistic; Emotionally Disturbed.
Learning Problems Memory Disabilities; Perceptual Disabilities; Thinking Disabilities; Oral Language Disabilities; Reading Disabilities; Handwriting Disabilities. *Behavioral Problems* Attention Deficits; Hyperactivity; Impulsivity; Self-Aggression; Physical Aggression; Passive Aggression; Withdrawal. *Conditions Treated* Early Infantile Autism; Aphasia.
Services Provided Parent Involvement; Behavior Therapy. *Professionals on Staff* Psychiatrists; Psychologists. *Service Facilities Available (with number of rooms)* Self-Contained Rooms. *Educational Professionals* Special Education Teachers 8; Paraprofessionals 14. *Curricula* Individualized. *Educational Intervention Approaches* Behavior Modification.

Rhode Island

Behavior Research Institute

240 Laban St, Providence, RI 02909 (401) 944-1186
Year Established 1971
Contact Susan McCrary, Admin Asst
Facility Information *Placement* Private Residential Care. *Children/Adolescents Served* 65. *Sexes Served* Both. *Tuition Fees (Approx)* $69,445-$80,984. *Sources of Funding* P.L. 94-142. Summer school available. *Special Certification Level* Severe and Profoundly Handicapped.
Student/Patient Characteristics *Age Levels* 0-4; 5-8; 9-11; 12-14; 15-17; 18-21; Over 21. *Exceptionalities Served* Autistic; Learning Disabled; Mentally Handicapped; Communication Disordered; Hearing Impaired/Deaf; Visually Impaired/Blind. *Learning Problems* Memory Disabilities; Perceptual Disabilities; Thinking Disabilities; Oral Language Disabilities; Reading Disabilities; Handwriting Disabilities; Spelling Disabilities; Arithmetic Disabilities; Written Expression. *Behavioral Problems* Attention Deficits; Hyperactivity; Hypoactivity; Impulsivity; Self-Aggression; Verbal Aggression; Physical Aggression; Indirect Aggression; Passive Aggression; Withdrawal. *Conditions Treated* Early Infantile Autism; Schizophrenia; Socialized Aggressive Reaction; Unsocialized Aggressive Reaction.
Services Provided Parent Involvement; Behavior Therapy. *Professionals on Staff* Psychiatrists 1.5; Psychologists 1.5; Social Workers .5; Child Care Staff 90; Nurses 3. *Service Facilities Available (with number of rooms)* Self-Contained Rooms 10. *Educational Professionals* Special Education Teachers 20; Behavior Therapist 90. *Curricula* Career/Vocational Education; Individualized; Basic Skills; Prevocational. *Educational Intervention Approaches* Precision Teaching; Behavior Modification.

Behavioral Development Center Inc

86 Mount Hope Ave, Providence, RI 02906 (401) 274-6310
Year Established 1976
Contact Susan E Stevenson, Special Ed Supv
Facility Information *Placement* Private Residential Care; Special Program. *Number of Beds* 10. *Children/Adolescents Served* 75 (day program); 10 (residential). *Sexes Served* Both. *Tuition Fees (Approx)* $9,260-$26,210. *Sources of Funding* State Funds; P.L. 94-142; Local Education Agencies. Summer school available. *Teacher Certification Level* Elementary School; Junior High/Middle School; High School.
Student/Patient Characteristics *Age Levels* 0-4; 5-8; 9-11; 12-14; 15-17; 18-21; Over 21. *IQ Ranges* 0-25; 26-40; 41-55; 56-70; 71-85. *Exceptionalities Served* Autistic; Emotionally Disturbed; Communication Disordered. *Learning Problems* Memory Disabilities; Perceptual Disabilities; Thinking Disabilities; Oral Language Disabilities; Reading Disabilities; Handwriting Disabilities; Spelling Disabilities; Arithmetic Disabilities; Written Expression. *Behavioral Problems* Attention Deficits; Hyperactivity; Hypoactivity; Impulsivity; Self-Aggression; Verbal Aggression; Physical Aggression; Indirect Aggression; Passive Aggression; Withdrawal. *Conditions Treated* Early Infantile Autism; Aphasia; Unsocialized Aggressive Reaction.
Services Provided Individual Therapy; Parent Involvement; Behavior Therapy; Cognitive Developmental Therapy; Biofeedback; Family Therapy; Filial Therapy; Music Therapy; Relaxation Therapy. *Professionals on Staff* Psychiatrists 1; Psychologists 5; Social Workers 1; Child Care Staff 10; Pediatrician 1. *Service Facilities Available (with number of rooms)* Consultative (ERT) 2; Transition Rooms 2; Self-Contained Rooms 10; Vocational Workshop 1; Gym 1. *Educational Professionals* Special Education Teachers 18; Career/Vocational Teachers 2; Teacher Therapist; Art; Speech and Language; Physical Education 37. *Curricula* Traditional Academic; Career/Vocational Education; Individualized; Basic Skills; Prevocational; Socialization. *Educational Intervention Approaches* Precision Teaching; Self-Control; Applied Behavior Analysis; Relaxation; Covert Conditioning. *Degrees Awarded* Certificate of Attendance.

Comments The center is a treatment and educational center for autistic and behaviorally disordered children. The center provides a continuum of services including day programming with clinical and special education services, group residences, early intervention, Saturday therapeutic recreation, transition and integration programs, family intervention, community vocational training, and respite services.

Bradley Hospital

1011 Veterans Memorial Pkwy, East Providence, RI 02915 (401) 434-3400
Contact Kevin P Meyers, Ed Dir
Facility Information *Placement* Hospital. *Number of Beds* 56. *Children/Adolescents Served* 125. *Sexes Served* Both. *Room and Board Fees (Approx)* $306-$479 (inpatient); $101 (day hospital); $92 (preschool). *Sources of Funding* State Funds; Health Insurance; P.L. 94-142; Private Insurance. Summer school available. *Teacher Certification Level* Elementary School; Junior High/Middle School; High School. *Special Certification Level* ED; LD; MR.
Student/Patient Characteristics *Age Levels* 0-4; 5-8; 9-11; 12-14; 15-17. *IQ Ranges* 56-70; 71-85; 85-130; Above 130. *Exceptionalities Served* Autistic; Emotionally Disturbed. *Learning Problems* Memory Disabilities; Perceptual Disabilities; Thinking Disabilities; Oral Language Disabilities; Reading Disabilities; Handwriting Disabilities; Spelling Disabilities; Arithmetic Disabilities; Written Expression. *Behavioral Problems* Attention Deficits; Hyperactivity; Hypoactivity; Impulsivity; Self-Aggression; Verbal Aggression; Physical Aggression; Indirect Aggression; Passive Aggression; Withdrawal. *Conditions Treated* Alcohol Abuse and/or Drug Abuse; Other Substance Abuse or Dependence; Early Infantile Autism; Disintegrative Psychoses; Schizophrenia; Aphasia; Convulsive Disorders; Phobias; Obses-

sions and Compulsions; Hysteria; Depression; Suicide; Asthma; Anorexia Nervosa; Ulcerative Colitis; Inadequacy/Immaturity; Personality Problems; Socialized Aggressive Reaction; Unsocialized Aggressive Reaction.

Services Provided Individual Therapy; Group Therapy; Parent Involvement; Behavior Therapy; Cognitive Developmental Therapy; Biofeedback; Family Therapy; Filial Therapy; Drug Therapy; Play Therapy. *Professionals on Staff* Psychiatrists 10; Psychologists 15; Social Workers 25; Child Care Staff 45; Nurses 20; Teachers 25. *Service Facilities Available (with number of rooms)* Hospital School 82. *Educational Professionals* Special Education Teachers 24; Career/Vocational Teachers 1. *Curricula* Traditional Academic; Career/Vocational Education; Individualized; Basic Skills; Prevocational. *Educational Intervention Approaches* Engineered Classroom; Precision Teaching; Behavior Modification; Applied Behavior Analysis.

Comments The educational program at Bradley Hospital is so designed as to be an integral part of an overall treatment program. The length of stay may range from 30-70 days for inpatients to 60-200 days for day hospital patients.

Emma Pendleton Bradley Hospital Developmental Disabilities Program

1011 Veterans Memorial Pkwy, East Providence, RI 02915 (401) 434-3400
Year Established 1931
Contact Kathy Erickson, Admissions Dir

Facility Information *Placement* Special Program; 90-120 Day Psychiatric-Behavioral Inpatient Program; 9-18 Month Day Hospital. *Number of Beds* 12. *Children/Adolescents Served* 24. *Sexes Served* Both. *Room and Board Fees (Approx)* $92-$306. *Sources of Funding* State Funds; HEW; Health Insurance; P.L. 94-142. Summer school available. *Teacher Certification Level* Elementary School; Junior High/Middle School. *Special Certification Level* ED; LD; MR.

Student/Patient Characteristics *Age Levels* 0-4; 5-8; 9-11; 12-14; 15-17. *IQ Ranges* 0-25; 26-40; 41-55; 56-70; 71-85.
Exceptionalities Served Autistic; Emotionally Disturbed; Mentally Handicapped; Communication Disordered; Hearing Impaired/Deaf; Visually Impaired/Blind. *Learning Problems* Memory Disabilities; Perceptual Disabilities; Thinking Disabilities; Oral Language Disabilities. *Behavioral Problems* Attention Deficits; Hyperactivity; Hypoactivity; Impulsivity; Self-Aggression; Verbal Aggression; Physical Aggression; Indirect Aggression; Passive Ag-

gression; Withdrawal. *Conditions Treated* Early Infantile Autism; Schizophrenia; Convulsive Disorders; Depression; Unsocialized Aggressive Reaction.

Services Provided Individual Therapy; Parent Involvement; Behavior Therapy; Cognitive Developmental Therapy; Family Therapy; Drug Therapy; Art Therapy; Music Therapy; Play Therapy. *Professionals on Staff* Psychiatrists 2; Psychologists 3; Social Workers 2; Child Care Staff 16; Nurses 5; Physical Therapist 1; Speech Therapist 1. *Service Facilities Available (with number of rooms)* Self-Contained Rooms 5; Hospital School 5. *Educational Professionals* Special Education Teachers 3; Paraprofessionals 6. *Curricula* Individualized; Basic Skills. *Educational Intervention Approaches* Behavior Modification; Applied Behavior Analysis. *Degrees Awarded* Certificate of Attendance.

Harmony Hill School Inc

Absalona Hill Rd, Chedachet, RI 02814 (401) 949-0690
Year Established 1976
Contact Terrence J Leary, Exec Dir

Facility Information *Placement* Private Residential Care; Private Day Care. *Number of Beds* 40. *Children/Adolescents Served* 55. *Sexes Served* Male. *Sources of Funding* State Funds; P.L. 94-142. Summer school available. *Teacher Certification Level* Elementary School; Junior High/Middle School. *Special Certification Level* ED.

Student/Patient Characteristics *Age Levels* 9-11; 12-14; 15-17; 18-21. *IQ Ranges* 85-130; Above 130. *Exceptionalities Served* Emotionally Disturbed; Learning Disabled. *Learning Problems* Perceptual Disabilities; Oral Language Disabilities; Reading Disabilities. *Behavioral Problems* Attention Deficits; Hyperactivity; Impulsivity; Verbal Aggression; Physical Aggression; Passive Aggression. *Conditions Treated* Inadequacy/Immaturity; Personality Problems.

Services Provided Individual Therapy; Group Therapy; Parent Involvement; Behavior Therapy; Family Therapy; Reality Therapy; Play Therapy. *Professionals on Staff* Psychiatrists 1; Psychologists 2; Counselors 16; Social Workers 7; Child Care Staff 25; Nurses 2. *Service Facilities Available (with number of rooms)* Itinerants 1; Self-Contained Rooms 7. *Educational Professionals* Special Education Teachers 11; Paraprofessionals 7; Music; Art; Physical Education. *Curricula* Traditional Academic; Career/Vocational Education; Individualized; Basic Skills; Prevocational. *Educational Intervention Approaches* Progressive Discipline; Behavior Modification. *Degrees Awarded* Graduate Equivalency Diploma.

South Carolina

Charles Lea Center—Program for Children, Adolescents, and Young Adults with Autism

195 Burdette St, Spartanburg, SC 29302 (803) 585-0322
Year Established 1973
Contact William K Chidester, Prog Dir

Facility Information *Placement* Public School; Special School; Special Program. *Children/Adolescents Served* 30. *Sexes Served* Both. *Sources of Funding* State Funds; P.L. 94-142; SC Department of Mental Health. Summer school available. *Teacher Certification Level* Elementary School; Junior High/Middle School; High School. *Special Certification Level* ED; Career/ Vocational Education.

Student/Patient Characteristics *Age Levels* 0-4; 5-8; 9-11; 12-14; 15-17; 18-21; Over 21. *IQ Ranges* 0-25; 26-40; 41-55; 56-70; 71-85; 85-130. *Exceptionalities Served* Autistic. *Learning Problems* Memory Disabilities; Perceptual Disabilities; Thinking Disabilities; Oral Language Disabilities; Reading Disabilities; Handwriting Disabilities; Spelling Disabilities; Arithmetic Disabilities; Written Expression. *Behavioral Problems* Attention Deficits; Hyperactivity; Hypoactivity; Impulsivity; Self-Aggression; Verbal Aggression; Physical Aggression; Indirect Aggression; Passive Aggression; Withdrawal. *Conditions Treated* Early Infantile Autism; Schizophrenia.

Services Provided Individual Therapy; Group Therapy; Parent Involvement; Behavior Therapy; Cognitive Developmental Therapy; Family Therapy; Drug Therapy. *Professionals on Staff* Psychiatrists 1; Psychologists 7; Nurses 1; Physical Therapist 1. *Service Facilities Available (with number of rooms)* Consultative (ERT) 2; Transition Rooms 2; Self-Contained Rooms 3; Special School 3; Community Training Sites 5. *Educational Professionals* Special Education Teachers 3; Career/Vocational Teachers 1; Paraprofessionals 5; Speech Pathologist 1. *Curricula* Career/Vocational Education; Individualized; Basic Skills; Prevocational. *Educational Intervention Approaches* Self-Control; Behavior Modification; Applied Behavior Analysis; Creative Conditioning.

Charleston County School District—Charleston Program for the Behaviorally Handicapped

1170 Marquis St, North Charleston, SC 29405 (803) 747-5423
Year Established 1972
Contact Diane Sabiston, Prog Dir

Facility Information *Placement* Public School. *Children/Adolescents Served* 45. *Sexes Served* Both. *Sources of Funding* State Funds; P.L. 94-142. Summer school available. *Teacher Certification Level* Elementary School. *Special Certification Level* ED; MR; Career/Vocational Education; Elementary Education.

Student/Patient Characteristics *Age Levels* 0-4; 5-8; 9-11; 12-14; 15-17; 18-21. *IQ Ranges* 0-25; 26-40; 41-55; 56-70. *Exceptionalities Served* Autistic; Behaviorally Handicapped.

Behavioral Problems Attention Deficits; Hyperactivity; Impulsivity; Self-Aggression; Physical Aggression; Withdrawal. *Conditions Treated* Early Infantile Autism.

Services Provided Parent Involvement; Behavior Therapy; Cognitive Developmental Therapy. *Professionals on Staff* Psychologists 1; Nurses 1. *Service Facilities Available (with number of rooms)* Self-Contained Rooms 8. *Educational Professionals* Special Education Teachers 10; Paraprofessionals 7; Speech Therapists 2. *Curricula* Traditional Academic; Career/Vocational Education; Individualized; Basic Skills; Community Based Training. *Educational Intervention Approaches* Engineered Classroom; Behavior Modification.

Comments This day program is in a public school setting offering classes in functional curriculum, vocational training, community-based training, and opportunities to interact with non-handicapped peers.

The Episcopal Church Home for Children—York Place

234 Kings Mountain St, York, SC 29745 (803) 684-4011
Year Established 1969
Contact Brian L Phelps, Dir of Treatment Serv

Facility Information *Placement* Private Residential Care; Public Day Care. *Number of Beds* 35. *Children/Adolescents Served* 35. *Sexes Served* Both. *Room and Board Fees (Approx)* $91. *Tuition Fees (Approx)* $33,184. *Sources of Funding* State Funds; P.L. 94-142 Private. Summer school available. *Teacher Certification Level* Elementary School. *Special Certification Level* ED; LD.

Student/Patient Characteristics *Age Levels* 5-8; 9-11; 12-14. *IQ Ranges* 85-130. *Exceptionalities Served* Emotionally Disturbed; Learning Disabled. *Learning Problems* Perceptual Disabilities; Thinking Disabilities; Oral Language Disabilities. *Behavioral Problems* Attention Deficits; Hyperactivity; Impulsivity; Self-Aggression; Verbal Aggression; Physical Aggression; Withdrawal. *Conditions Treated* Schizophrenia; Aphasia; Convulsive Disorders; Obsessions and Compulsions; Depression; Asthma; Inadequacy/Immaturity; Personality Problems; Socialized Aggressive Reaction; Unsocialized Aggressive Reaction.

Services Provided Individual Therapy; Group Therapy; Parent Involvement; Behavior Therapy; Cognitive Developmental Therapy; Biofeedback. *Professionals on Staff* Psychiatrists 2; Psychologists 3; Counselors 2; Social Workers 2; Child Care Staff 20; Nurses 1. *Service Facilities Available (with number of rooms)* On-Campus Residential School 3. *Educational Professionals* Special Education Teachers 3; Paraprofessionals 3. *Curricula* Individualized; Basic Skills. *Educational Intervention Approaches* Engineered Classroom; Behavior Modification.

Florence Program for Autistic Children and Adolescents—Lester Elementary School

3500 E Palmetto St, Florence, SC 29501 (803) 665-7608
Contact Christine Foltz, Dir
Facility Information *Placement* Special Program.
Children/Adolescents Served 15. *Sexes Served* Both. *Sources of Funding* State Funds; HEW; P.L. 94-142. Summer school available. *Teacher Certification Level* Elementary School; Junior High/Middle School. *Special Certification Level* ED.
Student/Patient Characteristics *Age Levels* 5-8; 9-11; 12-14; 15-17; 18-21. *IQ Ranges* 0-25; 26-40. *Exceptionalities Served* Autistic. *Learning Problems* Memory Disabilities; Perceptual Disabilities; Thinking Disabilities; Oral Language Disabilities; Reading Disabilities; Handwriting Disabilities; Spelling Disabilities; Arithmetic Disabilities; Written Expression. *Behavioral Problems* Attention Deficits; Hyperactivity; Impulsivity; Physical Aggression; Indirect Aggression; Withdrawal. *Conditions Treated* Early Infantile Autism; Obsessions and Compulsions; Inadequacy/Immaturity.
Services Provided Parent Involvement; Behavior Therapy. *Professionals on Staff* Psychologists 2; Child Care Staff 4; Nurses 2. *Service Facilities Available (with number of rooms)* Resource Rooms 1; Self-Contained Rooms 2. *Educational Professionals* Regular School Teachers 10; Special Education Teachers 3; Paraprofessionals 3. *Curricula* Traditional Academic; Career/Vocational Education; Individualized; Basic Skills; Prevocational. *Educational Intervention Approaches* Engineered Classroom; Precision Teaching; Behavior Modification; Alternatives to Punishment. *Degrees Awarded* Certificate of Attendance.

Medical University of South Carolina—Department of Psychiatry—Youth Division

171 Ashley Ave, Charleston, SC 29425 (803) 792-3051
Contact Donald J Carek, Chief of Youth Div
Facility Information *Placement* Psychiatric Hospital Unit. *Number of Beds* 18. *Children/Adolescents Served* 18. *Sexes Served* Both. *Room and Board Fees (Approx)* $250. *Sources of Funding* Health Insurance; Medicaid. *Teacher Certification Level* Elementary School; Junior High/Middle School; High School. *Special Certification Level* ED.
Student/Patient Characteristics *Age Levels* 0-4; 5-8; 9-11; 12-14; 15-17. *IQ Ranges* 41-55; 56-70; 71-85; 85-130; Above 130. *Exceptionalities Served* Autistic; Emotionally Disturbed; Learning Disabled; Mentally Handicapped; Communication Disordered; Other Health Impaired; Physically Handicapped; Gifted. *Learning Problems* Memory Disabilities; Perceptual Disabilities; Thinking Disabilities; Oral Language Disabilities; Reading Disabilities; Handwriting Disabilities; Spelling Disabilities; Arithmetic Disabilities; Written Expression. *Behavioral Problems* Attention Deficits; Hyperactivity; Hypoactivity; Impulsivity; Self-Aggression; Verbal Aggression; Physical Aggression; Indirect Aggression; Passive Aggression; Withdrawal. *Conditions Treated* Alcohol Abuse and/or Drug Abuse; Early Infantile Autism; Disintegrative Psychoses; Schizophrenia; Aphasia; Convulsive Disorders; Phobias; Obsessions and Compulsions; Hysteria; Depression; Suicide; Asthma; Anorexia Nervosa; Ulcerative Colitis; Inadequacy/Immaturity; Personality Problems; Socialized Aggressive Reaction.
Services Provided Individual Therapy; Group Therapy; Parent Involvement; Behavior Therapy; Cognitive Developmental Therapy; Family Therapy; Drug Therapy; Play Therapy. *Professionals on Staff* Psychiatrists 5; Psychologists 3; Social Workers 3; Child Care Staff 14; Nurses 12. *Service Facilities Available (with number of rooms)* Hospital School 3. *Educational Professionals* Special Education Teachers 4. *Curricula* Individualized. *Degrees Awarded* High School Diploma.
Comments The Youth Division serves children and adolescents ordinarily hospitalized for up to 90 days for evaluation and treatment.

Pine Grove School

PO Box 468, Chestnut Rd, Elgin, SC 29045 (803) 438-3011
Year Established 1969
Contact Carl E Herring, Exec Dir
Facility Information *Placement* Private Residential Care. *Number of Beds* 40. *Children/Adolescents Served* 40. *Sexes Served* Both. *Tuition Fees (Approx)* $26,400. *Sources of Funding* State Funds; P.L. 94-142; Private. Summer school available. *Special Certification Level* ED; MR.
Student/Patient Characteristics *Age Levels* 5-8; 9-11; 12-14; 15-17; 18-21; Over 21. *Exceptionalities Served* Autistic; Emotionally Disturbed; Mentally Handicapped. *Behavioral Problems* Attention Deficits; Hyperactivity; Impulsivity; Self-Aggression; Indirect Aggression. *Conditions Treated* Early Infantile Autism.
Services Provided Individual Therapy; Parent Involvement; Behavior Therapy; Art Therapy; Music Therapy; Play Therapy. *Professionals on Staff* Psychologists 2; Counselors 10; Social Workers 1; Child Care Staff 30; Nurses 2. *Service Facilities Available (with number of rooms)* Resource Rooms 4; Self-Contained Rooms 9; On-Campus Residential School 12. *Educational Professionals* Special Education Teachers 9; Paraprofessionals 10. *Curricula* Individualized; Basic Skills; Prevocational. *Educational Intervention Approaches* Behavior Modification.

South Carolina State College—Autistic Nursery, Speech, Language, and Hearing Clinic

South Carolina State College, Orangeburg, SC 29117
(803) 536-8074
Year Established 1980
Contact Willa A Wilson, Nursery Coord
Facility Information *Placement* Special Program. *Children/Adolescents Served* 10. *Sexes Served* Both. *Sources of Funding* State Funds; Medicaid; P.L. 94-142. Summer school available. *Teacher Certification Level* Elementary School. *Special Certification Level* ED; MR.
Student/Patient Characteristics *Age Levels* 15-17. *IQ Ranges* 0-25. *Exceptionalities Served* Autistic; Communication Disordered. *Learning Problems* Perceptual Disabilities; Oral Language Disabilities. *Behavioral Problems* Attention Deficits; Hyperactivity; Impulsivity; Physical Aggression; Withdrawal. *Conditions Treated* Early Infantile Autism.
Services Provided Individual Therapy; Group Therapy; Parent Involvement. *Professionals on Staff* Child Care Staff 2; Speech Pathologist. *Service Facilities Available (with number of rooms)* Resource Rooms 1; Self-Contained Rooms 1. *Educational Professionals* Special Education Teachers 2; Paraprofessionals 2; Speech Pathologist 1. *Curricula* Individualized. *Educational Intervention Approaches* Behavior Modification.
Comments The program is designed to help preschool autistic children develop behavioral control. The Judevine approach is used.

South Carolina State Hospital—Child and Adolescent Unit—Blanding House

PO Box 119, Columbia, SC 29210 (803) 758-7767
Contact Beth Troy Maris, Dir
Facility Information *Placement* Public Psychiatric Hospital. *Number of Beds* 43. *Children/Adolescents Served* 43. *Sexes Served* Both. *Room and Board Fees (Approx)* $35. *Sources of Funding* State Funds; Health Insurance; Medicaid; P.L. 94-142. Summer school available. *Teacher Certification Level* Elementary School; Junior High/Middle School; High School. *Special Certification Level* ED; LD; MR; Career/Vocational Education; Reading; Math.
Student/Patient Characteristics *Age Levels* 5-8; 9-11; 12-14; 15-17. *IQ Ranges* 56-70; 71-85; 85-130. *Exceptionalities Served* Emotionally Disturbed; Learning Disabled; Mentally Handicapped. *Learning Problems* Memory Disabilities; Perceptual Disabilities; Thinking Disabilities; Oral Language Disabilities; Reading Disabilities; Handwriting Disabilities; Spelling Disabilities;

Arithmetic Disabilities; Written Expression. *Behavioral Problems* Attention Deficits; Hyperactivity; Impulsivity; Self-Aggression; Verbal Aggression; Physical Aggression; Indirect Aggression; Passive Aggression; Withdrawal. *Conditions Treated* Schizophrenia; Convulsive Disorders; Phobias; Obsessions and Compulsions; Hysteria; Depression; Suicide; Anorexia Nervosa; Personality Problems; Socialized Aggressive Reaction; Unsocialized Aggressive Reaction.

Services Provided Individual Therapy; Group Therapy; Parent Involvement; Behavior Therapy; Cognitive Developmental Therapy; Family Therapy; Filial Therapy; Art Therapy; Music Therapy; Reality Therapy; Play Therapy; Psychodrama. *Professionals on Staff* Psychiatrists 1; Psychologists 5; Social Workers 5; Child Care Staff 90; Nurses; Activity Therapists 5. *Service Facilities Available (with number of rooms)* Self-Contained Rooms 4; Hospital School 2; Homebound Instruction 2. *Educational Professionals* Special Education Teachers 5; Career/Vocational Teachers 2; Paraprofessionals 1. *Curricula* Traditional Academic; Individualized; Basic Skills; Prevocational. *Educational Intervention Approaches* Behavior Modification; Applied Behavior Analysis; Creative Conditioning. *Degrees Awarded* Certificate of Attendance.

United Affiliated Facilities Program at Winthrop College

Oakland Ave, Rock Hill, SC 29733 (803) 323-2244
Year Established 1976
Contact Cecilia Strickland, Consultant Trainee

Facility Information *Placement* Extended Diagnostics. *Children/Adolescents Served* 10. *Sexes Served* Both. *Sources of Funding* Department of Mental Health. Summer school available. *Teacher Certification Level* Elementary School. *Special Certification Level* ED; MR; Elementary Education; Early Childhood Education.

Student/Patient Characteristics *Age Levels* 0-4; 5-8. *IQ Ranges* 41-55; 71-85. *Exceptionalities Served* Autistic. *Learning Problems* Perceptual Disabilities; Thinking Disabilities; Oral Language Disabilities. *Behavioral Problems* Attention Deficits; Hyperactivity; Impulsivity; Physical Aggression; Withdrawal. *Conditions Treated* Early Infantile Autism.

Services Provided Parent Involvement; Behavior Therapy; Parent Training Consultation. *Service Facilities Available (with number of rooms)* Special School 1. *Educational Professionals* Special Education Teachers 1. *Curricula* Individualized; Preschool. *Educational Intervention Approaches* Behavior Modification.

South Dakota

Children's Home Society of South Dakota

3209 S Prairie Ave, Sioux Falls, SD 57105 (605) 334-6004
Year Established 1893
Contact David H Wright, Exec Dir
Facility Information *Placement* Special School; Private Residential Care; Day Treatment. *Number of Beds* 61.
Children/Adolescents Served 61. *Sexes Served* Both. *Room and Board Fees (Approx)* $69. *Tuition Fees (Approx)* $8,840 (residential); $10,140 (day students). *Sources of Funding* State Funds; P.L. 94-142; Private; BIA; Title XX. Summer school available. *Teacher Certification Level* Elementary School; Junior High/Middle School. *Special Certification Level* ED; LD; Reading; Math.
Student/Patient Characteristics *Age Levels* 5-8; 9-11; 12-14; 15-17. *IQ Ranges* 26-40; 41-55; 56-70; 71-85; 85-130; Above 130. *Exceptionalities Served* Autistic; Emotionally Disturbed; Learning Disabled; Communication Disordered. *Learning Problems* Memory Disabilities; Perceptual Disabilities; Thinking Disabilities; Oral Language Disabilities; Reading Disabilities; Handwriting Disabilities; Spelling Disabilities; Arithmetic Disabilities; Written Expression. *Behavioral Problems* Attention Deficits; Hyperactivity; Hypoactivity; Impulsivity; Self-Aggression; Verbal Aggression; Physical Aggression; Indirect Aggression; Passive Aggression; Withdrawal. *Conditions Treated* Other Substance Abuse or Dependence; Early Infantile Autism; Disintegrative Psychoses; Schizophrenia; Aphasia; Convulsive Disorders; Phobias; Obsessions and Compulsions; Hysteria; Depression; Suicide; Asthma; Anorexia Nervosa; Ulcerative Colitis; Inadequacy/Immaturity; Personality Problems; Socialized Aggressive Reaction; Unsocialized Aggressive Reaction.
Services Provided Individual Therapy; Group Therapy; Parent Involvement; Behavior Therapy; Cognitive Developmental Therapy; Family Therapy; Drug Therapy; Music Therapy; Reality Therapy; Play Therapy. *Professionals on Staff* Psychiatrists 2; Psychologists 1; Counselors 4; Social Workers 7; Child Care Staff 24; Nurses 1. *Service Facilities Available (with number of rooms)* Self-Contained Rooms 15; On-Campus Residential School. *Educational Professionals* Special Education Teachers 15; Special Education Counselors 3; Paraprofessionals 5. *Curricula* Individualized; Basic Skills. *Educational Intervention Approaches* Precision Teaching; Behavior Modification. *Degrees Awarded* Certificate of Attendance.
Comments The Children's Home provides a residential treatment program for emotionally and behaviorally disordered children with treatment to families during placement. Day treatment is provided within the same setting.

Dakota House

PO Box 550, 1408 S Main, Aberdeen, SD 57401 (605) 225-1010
Year Established 1978
Contact Charles Saylor, Exec Dir

Facility Information *Placement* Public School; Public Residential Care; Private Residential Care; Private Day Care; Public Day Care. *Number of Beds* 16. *Children/Adolescents Served* 16. *Sexes Served* Both. *Room and Board Fees (Approx)* $31-$59. *Sources of Funding* Health Insurance; Medicaid; P.L. 94-142. Summer school available. *Teacher Certification Level* Elementary School; Junior High/Middle School; High School. *Special Certification Level* ED; LD; Reading; Math.
Student/Patient Characteristics *Age Levels* 5-8; 9-11; 12-14; 15-17. *IQ Ranges* 71-85; 85-130; Above 130. *Exceptionalities Served* Emotionally Disturbed. *Learning Problems* Perceptual Disabilities; Thinking Disabilities. *Behavioral Problems* Attention Deficits; Hyperactivity; Hypoactivity; Impulsivity; Self-Aggression; Verbal Aggression; Physical Aggression; Indirect Aggression; Passive Aggression; Withdrawal. *Conditions Treated* Schizophrenia; Aphasia; Convulsive Disorders; Phobias; Obsessions and Compulsions; Hysteria; Depression; Suicide; Anorexia Nervosa; Personality Problems; Socialized Aggressive Reaction; Unsocialized Aggressive Reaction.
Services Provided Individual Therapy; Group Therapy; Parent Involvement; Behavior Therapy; Cognitive Developmental Therapy; Biofeedback; Family Therapy; Drug Therapy; Art Therapy; Reality Therapy; Play Therapy. *Professionals on Staff* Psychiatrists 2; Psychologists 3; Counselors 6; Social Workers 5; Nurses 1. *Service Facilities Available (with number of rooms)* Special School 2; On-Campus Residential School 1. *Educational Professionals* Special Education Teachers 2; Paraprofessionals 2. *Curricula* Traditional Academic; Individualized; Basic Skills. *Educational Intervention Approaches* Self-Control; Behavior Modification. *Degrees Awarded* Certificate of Attendance.

South Dakota Human Services Center

PO Box 76, N Hwy 81, Yankton, SD 57078 (605) 668-3100
Year Established 1879
Contact Jon L Gapa, Asst Admin Medical Support Serv
Facility Information *Placement* Public Residential Care; Special Program. *Number of Beds* 20. *Children/Adolescents Served* 20. *Sexes Served* Both. *Sources of Funding* State Funds; P.L. 94-142. Summer school available. *Special Certification Level* ED; LD.
Student/Patient Characteristics *Age Levels* 12-14; 15-17. *IQ Ranges* 71-85; 85-130; Above 130. *Exceptionalities Served* Emotionally Disturbed; Learning Disabled; Communication Disordered; Physically Handicapped; Gifted. *Learning Problems* Memory Disabilities; Perceptual Disabilities; Thinking Disabilities; Oral Language Disabilities; Reading Disabilities; Handwriting Disabilities; Spelling Disabilities; Arithmetic Disabilities; Written Expression. *Behavioral Problems* Attention Deficits; Hyperactivity; Hypoactivity; Self-Aggression; Verbal Aggression; Physical Aggression; Indirect Aggression; Passive Aggression; Withdrawal. *Conditions Treated* Alcohol Abuse and/or Drug Abuse; Other Substance Abuse or Dependence; Schizophrenia; Convulsive Dis-

orders; Obsessions and Compulsions; Depression; Suicide; Anorexia Nervosa; Inadequacy/Immaturity; Personality Problems; Socialized Aggressive Reaction; Unsocialized Aggressive Reaction.

Services Provided Individual Therapy; Group Therapy; Parent Involvement; Behavior Therapy; Cognitive Developmental Therapy; Family Therapy; Drug Therapy; Art Therapy; Music Therapy; Reality Therapy. *Professionals on Staff* Psychiatrists 1; Psychologists 1; Counselors 3; Social Workers 1; Nurses 6; Pediatricians 1; Support Staff 27. *Service Facilities Available (with number of rooms)* Self-Contained Rooms 4. *Educational Professionals* Special Education Teachers 3.5. *Curricula* Traditional Academic; Career/Vocational Education; Individualized; Basic Skills. *Educational Intervention Approaches* Progressive Discipline; Behavior Modification. *Degrees Awarded* Certificate of Attendance; High School Diploma; Graduate Equivalency Diploma.

Comments The South Dakota Human Services Center, Adolescent Treatment Program is a 24-hour adolescent treatment program serving South Dakota. The Human Services Center is part of the University of South Dakota School of Medicine, Department of Psychiatry. The average length of stay is approximately 90-120 days.

Southeastern Children's Center

2000 S Summit, Sioux Falls, SD 57105 (605) 336-0510
Year Established 1969
Contact Marlys Waller, Dir Children's Serv
Facility Information *Placement* Special School; Private Residential Care. *Number of Beds* 16. *Children/Adolescents Served* 16. *Sexes Served* Both. *Tuition Fees (Approx)* $11,410-$26,172. *Sources of Funding* Medicaid; P.L. 94-142; Social Security Insurance. Summer school available. *Teacher Certification Level* Elementary School. *Special Certification Level* MR.
Student/Patient Characteristics *Age Levels* 0-4; 5-8; 9-11; 12-14; 15-17; 18-21. *IQ Ranges* 0-25; 26-40; 41-55; 56-70. *Exceptionalities Served* Autistic; Emotionally Disturbed; Mentally Handicapped; Communication Disordered; Hearing Impaired/Deaf; Visually Impaired/Blind; Physically Handicapped. *Learning Problems* Memory Disabilities; Perceptual Disabilities; Thinking Disabilities; Oral Language Disabilities; Reading Disabilities; Handwriting Disabilities; Spelling Disabilities; Arithmetic Disabilities; Written Expression. *Behavioral Problems* Attention Deficits; Hyperactivity; Impulsivity; Self-Aggression; Verbal Aggression; Physical Aggression; Indirect Aggression; Withdrawal. *Conditions Treated* Early Infantile Autism; Convulsive Disorders.
Services Provided Parent Involvement; Behavior Therapy; Family Therapy. *Professionals on Staff* Psychiatrists 1; Counselors 6; Child Care Staff 19. *Service Facilities Available (with number of rooms)* Self-Contained Rooms 3. *Educational Professionals* Special Education Teachers 4; Special Education Counselors 1; Paraprofessionals 1. *Curricula* Individualized; Basic Skills; Prevocational. *Educational Intervention Approaches* Behavior Modification; Applied Behavior Analysis.

Comments The program provides services for individuals who are unable to receive special education services in their home school districts due to developmental disabilities and significant behavior problems. Intensive services are provided to enable clients to gain the skills/behaviors necessary to re-enter a less restrictive setting.

West River Children's Center of the Children's Home Society of South Dakota

Box 7801, Keystone Rte, Rapid City, SD 57701 (605) 343-5422
Year Established 1971
Contact F G Tully, Prog Dir
Facility Information *Placement* Special School; Private Residential Care. *Number of Beds* 17. *Children/Adolescents Served* 17. *Sexes Served* Both. *Room and Board Fees (Approx)* $69. *Tuition Fees (Approx)* $8,840 (residential); $10,140 (day students). *Sources of Funding* State Funds; P.L. 94-142; Private Foundation Monies. Summer school available. *Teacher Certification Level* Elementary School Special Education. *Special Certification Level* ED; LD; Special Education.
Student/Patient Characteristics *Age Levels* 5-8; 9-11; 12-14. *IQ Ranges* 71-85; 85-130. *Exceptionalities Served* Autistic; Emotionally Disturbed; Learning Disabled. *Learning Problems* Memory Disabilities; Perceptual Disabilities; Thinking Disabilities; Oral Language Disabilities; Reading Disabilities; Handwriting Disabilities; Spelling Disabilities; Arithmetic Disabilities; Written Expression. *Behavioral Problems* Attention Deficits; Hyperactivity; Hypoactivity; Impulsivity; Self-Aggression; Verbal Aggression; Physical Aggression; Indirect Aggression; Passive Aggression. *Conditions Treated* Early Infantile Autism; Disintegrative Psychoses; Schizophrenia; Aphasia; Convulsive Disorders; Phobias; Obsessions and Compulsions; Hysteria; Depression; Suicide; Anorexia Nervosa; Inadequacy/Immaturity; Personality Problems; Socialized Aggressive Reaction; Unsocialized Aggressive Reaction.

Services Provided Individual Therapy; Group Therapy; Parent Involvement; Cognitive Developmental Therapy; Family Therapy. *Professionals on Staff* Psychiatrists 1; Psychologists 1; Counselors 3; Social Workers 1; Child Care Staff 10. *Service Facilities Available (with number of rooms)* Consultative (ERT); Self-Contained Rooms 7. *Educational Professionals* Special Education Teachers 8; Paraprofessionals 2. *Curricula* Individualized; Basic Skills. *Educational Intervention Approaches* Precision Teaching; Progressive Discipline; Behavior Modification; Applied Behavior Analysis.

Tennessee

Avon Lenox Special Education

310 N Avon Rd, Memphis, TN 38117 (901) 683-5561
Year Established 1977
Contact Angela C Aste, Principal
Facility Information *Placement* Public School; Special School; Special Program. *Children/Adolescents Served* 175. *Sexes Served* Both. *Sources of Funding* Funded through resources of Board of Education-state and local. *Special Certification Level* MR.
Student/Patient Characteristics *Age Levels* 0-4; 5-8; 9-11; 12-14; 15-17; 18-21; Over 21. *IQ Ranges* 0-25; 26-40; 41-55.
Exceptionalities Served Autistic; Mentally Handicapped; Communication Disordered; Other Health Impaired. *Learning Problems* Memory Disabilities; Perceptual Disabilities; Thinking Disabilities; Oral Language Disabilities; Reading Disabilities; Handwriting Disabilities; Spelling Disabilities; Arithmetic Disabilities; Written Expression. *Behavioral Problems* Attention Deficits; Hyperactivity; Hypoactivity; Impulsivity; Self-Aggression; Verbal Aggression; Physical Aggression; Indirect Aggression; Passive Aggression; Withdrawal. *Conditions Treated* Convulsive Disorders; Obsessions and Compulsions; Asthma.
Services Provided Parent Involvement; Behavior Therapy; Cognitive Developmental Therapy. *Professionals on Staff* Psychiatrists; Psychologists; Counselors; Social Workers. *Service Facilities Available (with number of rooms)* Itinerants; Self-Contained Rooms; Workshops. *Educational Professionals* Special Education Teachers 14; Paraprofessionals 26; Speech Therapist 1; Occupational Therapist 1; Physical Therapist; Librarian. *Curricula* Individualized. *Educational Intervention Approaches* Behavior Modification; Applied Behavior Analysis. *Degrees Awarded* Certificate of Attendance.
Comments Avon Lenox is a self-contained public school for trainable and profoundly handicapped students from 4 through 21 years of age. In addition to mental handicaps, the students have additional handicaps such as physical disabilities, behavior disorders and health conditions.

Chattanooga Psychiatric Clinic—Children and Youth Program

1028 E 3rd St, Chattanooga, TN 37403 (615) 266-6751
Contact Theo E Lemaire, Prog Dir
Facility Information *Placement* Outpatient Mental Health Services. *Sources of Funding* State Funds; Health Insurance; Medicaid; Fees.
Services Provided *Professionals on Staff* Psychiatrists; Psychologists.

Child and Family Services

114 Dameron Ave 1, Knoxville, TN 37917 (615) 524-7483
Year Established 1930
Contact Larry R Feezel, Coord Residential Serv
Facility Information *Placement* Private Residential Care. *Number of Beds* 21. *Children/Adolescents Served* 39. *Sexes Served* Both. *Sources of Funding* State Funds; HEW; Donations; Local; United Way.
Student/Patient Characteristics *Age Levels* 12-14; 15-17. *IQ Ranges* 71-85; 85-130; Above 130. *Exceptionalities Served* Emotionally Disturbed; Mentally Handicapped. *Learning Problems* Reading Disabilities; Spelling Disabilities; Arithmetic Disabilities; Written Expression. *Behavioral Problems* Attention Deficits; Hyperactivity; Impulsivity; Self-Aggression; Verbal Aggression; Physical Aggression; Indirect Aggression; Passive Aggression; Withdrawal. *Conditions Treated* Phobias; Obsessions and Compulsions; Hysteria; Depression; Suicide; Inadequacy/Immaturity; Personality Problems; Socialized Aggressive Reaction; Unsocialized Aggressive Reaction.
Services Provided Individual Therapy; Group Therapy; Parent Involvement; Behavior Therapy; Family Therapy; Reality Therapy. *Professionals on Staff* Social Workers 4; Child Care Staff 16. *Service Facilities Available (with number of rooms)* Public. *Degrees Awarded* High School Diploma.

De Neuville Heights School for Girls

3060 Baskin St, Memphis, TN 38127 (901) 357-7316
Year Established 1884
Contact Sr Mary Euphrasia, Social Serv Dir
Facility Information *Placement* Private Residential Care. *Number of Beds* 52. *Children/Adolescents Served* 52. *Sexes Served* Female. *Room and Board Fees (Approx)* $28. *Tuition Fees (Approx)* $9,600. *Sources of Funding* P.L. 94-142; United Way; Title I; Child Care Fee. Summer school available. *Teacher Certification Level* Junior High/Middle School; High School. *Special Certification Level* ED; Reading; Math.
Student/Patient Characteristics *Age Levels* 12-14; 15-17. *IQ Ranges* 71-85; 85-130. *Exceptionalities Served* Emotionally Disturbed; Learning Disabled; Communication Disordered; Hearing Impaired/Deaf; Physically Handicapped; Gifted. *Learning Problems* Memory Disabilities; Perceptual Disabilities; Thinking Disabilities; Oral Language Disabilities; Reading Disabilities; Handwriting Disabilities; Spelling Disabilities; Arithmetic Disabilities; Written Expression. *Behavioral Problems* Attention Deficits; Hyperactivity; Hypoactivity; Impulsivity; Self-Aggression; Verbal Aggression; Physical Aggression; Indirect Aggression; Passive Aggression; Withdrawal. *Conditions Treated* Alcohol Abuse and/or Drug Abuse; Other Substance Abuse or Dependence; Aphasia; Convulsive Disorders; Phobias; Obsessions and Compulsions; Hysteria; Depression; Suicide; Asthma;

Anorexia Nervosa; Ulcerative Colitis; Inadequacy/Immaturity; Personality Problems; Socialized Aggressive Reaction; Unsocialized Aggressive Reaction.

Services Provided Individual Therapy; Group Therapy; Parent Involvement; Behavior Therapy; Family Therapy; Drug Therapy; Art Therapy; Music Therapy; Reality Therapy; Play Therapy; Psychodrama. *Professionals on Staff* Psychiatrists 3; Psychologists 7; Counselors 2; Social Workers 3; Child Care Staff 7; Nurses 2. *Service Facilities Available (with number of rooms)* On-Campus Residential School 10. *Educational Professionals* Regular School Teachers 10; Special Education Teachers 2; Special Education Counselors 2; Paraprofessionals 3. *Curricula* Traditional Academic; Individualized; Basic Skills; Prevocational. *Educational Intervention Approaches* Progressive Discipline; Self-Control; Behavior Modification; Applied Behavior Analysis; Creative Conditioning. *Degrees Awarded* Certificate of Attendance; High School Diploma.

Lakeshore Mental Health Institute—Riverbend School—Children and Youth Services

5908 Lyons View Dr, Knoxville, TN 37919 (615) 584-1561 ext 7390
Year Established 1970
Contact Joe Pritchard, Coord

Facility Information *Placement* State-Funded Residential Care. *Number of Beds* 89. *Children/Adolescents Served* 89. *Sexes Served* Both. *Room and Board Fees (Approx)* $160. *Sources of Funding* Medicaid. Summer school available. *Teacher Certification Level* Elementary School; Junior High/Middle School; High School. *Special Certification Level* ED; LD; Reading; Math.

Student/Patient Characteristics *Age Levels* 0-4; 5-8; 9-11; 12-14; 15-17. *IQ Ranges* 71-85; 85-130; Above 130. *Exceptionalities Served* Autistic; Emotionally Disturbed; Learning Disabled; Communication Disordered. *Learning Problems* Memory Disabilities; Perceptual Disabilities; Thinking Disabilities; Oral Language Disabilities; Reading Disabilities; Handwriting Disabilities; Spelling Disabilities; Arithmetic Disabilities; Written Expression. *Behavioral Problems* Attention Deficits; Hyperactivity; Hypoactivity; Impulsivity; Self-Aggression; Verbal Aggression; Physical Aggression; Indirect Aggression; Passive Aggression; Withdrawal; Depression; Suicidal Tendencies and Gestures. *Conditions Treated* Alcohol Abuse and/or Drug Abuse; Other Substance Abuse or Dependence; Early Infantile Autism; Disintegrative Psychoses; Schizophrenia; Aphasia; Convulsive Disorders; Phobias; Obsessions and Compulsions; Hysteria; Depression; Suicide; Anorexia Nervosa; Inadequacy/Immaturity; Personality Problems; Socialized Aggressive Reaction; Unsocialized Aggressive Reaction.

Services Provided Individual Therapy; Group Therapy; Parent Involvement; Behavior Therapy; Cognitive Developmental Therapy; Family Therapy; Drug Therapy; Art Therapy; Reality Therapy; Play Therapy. *Professionals on Staff* Psychiatrists 2; Psychologists 2; Counselors 20; Social Workers 10; Child Care Staff 30; Nurses 10. *Service Facilities Available (with number of rooms)* Consultative (ERT) 2; Itinerants 2; Resource Rooms 10; Transition Rooms 5; Self-Contained Rooms 5; Special School 10; On-Campus Residential School 10. *Educational Professionals* Regular School Teachers 5; Special Education Teachers 5; Crisis Teachers 10; Special Education Counselors 10; Paraprofessionals 20. *Curricula* Traditional Academic; Career/Vocational Education; Individualized; Basic Skills; Prevocational. *Educational Intervention Approaches* Precision Teaching; Self-Control; Behavior Modification. *Degrees Awarded* High School Diploma; Graduate Equivalency Diploma.

Meharry Community Mental Health Center

1005 D B Todd Blvd, Nashville, TN 37208 (615) 327-6255
Year Established 1973
Contact Hershell A Warren, Exec Dir

Facility Information *Placement* Special School; Public Residential Care; Public Day Care. *Number of Beds* 15. *Children/Adolescents Served* 40. *Sexes Served* Both. *Room and Board Fees (Approx)*

Sliding Scale. *Tuition Fees (Approx)* Sliding Scale. *Sources of Funding* State Funds; Health Insurance; Medicaid; P.L. 94-142. Summer school available. *Teacher Certification Level* Junior High/Middle School; High School. *Special Certification Level* ED; LD; MR.

Student/Patient Characteristics *Age Levels* 12-14; 15-17; 18-21. *IQ Ranges* 56-70; 71-85; 85-130; Above 130. *Exceptionalities Served* Emotionally Disturbed; Learning Disabled; Mentally Handicapped. *Learning Problems* Memory Disabilities; Perceptual Disabilities; Thinking Disabilities; Oral Language Disabilities; Reading Disabilities; Handwriting Disabilities; Spelling Disabilities; Arithmetic Disabilities; Written Expression. *Behavioral Problems* Attention Deficits; Hyperactivity; Hypoactivity; Impulsivity; Self-Aggression; Verbal Aggression; Physical Aggression; Indirect Aggression; Passive Aggression; Withdrawal. *Conditions Treated* Alcohol Abuse and/or Drug Abuse; Schizophrenia; Depression; Suicide; Inadequacy/Immaturity; Personality Problems; Socialized Aggressive Reaction; Unsocialized Aggressive Reaction.

Services Provided Individual Therapy; Group Therapy; Parent Involvement; Behavior Therapy; Family Therapy; Drug Therapy. *Professionals on Staff* Psychiatrists 3; Psychologists 2; Counselors 6; Social Workers 1; Child Care Staff 10; Nurses 5. *Service Facilities Available (with number of rooms)* On-Campus Residential School 3. *Educational Professionals* Regular School Teachers 3; Special Education Teachers 3; Paraprofessionals 1. *Curricula* Traditional Academic; Individualized; Basic Skills; Prevocational. *Educational Intervention Approaches* Behavior Modification. *Degrees Awarded* Certificate of Attendance; High School Diploma.

Comments Two programs are provided; a day treatment program and an alternative school program for emotionally disturbed and behaviorally disordered adolescents. A residential treatment program with an academic component for chemically dependent adolescents is also provided.

Moccasin Bend Mental Health Center—Smallwood Center

Moccasin Bend Rd, Chattanooga, TN 37411 (615) 265-2271
Year Established 1968
Contact Catherine Sumberg, Day Supv

Facility Information *Placement* Public Residential Care. *Number of Beds* 57. *Children/Adolescents Served* 57. *Sexes Served* Both. *Sources of Funding* State Funds; Health Insurance; Medicaid. Summer school available. *Teacher Certification Level* Elementary School. *Special Certification Level* ED.

Student/Patient Characteristics *Age Levels* 5-8; 9-11; 12-14. *IQ Ranges* 56-70; 71-85; 85-130; Above 130. *Exceptionalities Served* Emotionally Disturbed. *Learning Problems* Perceptual Disabilities; Reading Disabilities; Handwriting Disabilities; Spelling Disabilities; Arithmetic Disabilities. *Behavioral Problems* Attention Deficits; Hyperactivity; Impulsivity; Verbal Aggression; Physical Aggression; Passive Aggression; Withdrawal.

Overlook Mental Health Center—Blount County Adolescent Partial Hospitalization Program

219 Court St, Maryville, TN 37801 (615) 984-0625
Year Established 1984
Contact Mark B Potts, Prog Mgr

Facility Information *Placement* Special School; Special Program; Mental Health Center. *Children/Adolescents Served* 12 (day treatment). *Sexes Served* Both. *Sources of Funding* State Funds; Health Insurance; Medicaid; Self-Pay. Summer school available. *Teacher Certification Level* Junior High/Middle School; High School. *Special Certification Level* ED; LD.

Student/Patient Characteristics *Age Levels* 5-8; 9-11; 12-14; 15-17; 18-21; Over 21. *IQ Ranges* 56-70; 71-85; 85-130. *Exceptionalities Served* Emotionally Disturbed; Learning Disabled; Communication Disordered. *Learning Problems* Perceptual Disabilities; Thinking Disabilities. *Behavioral Problems* Attention Deficits; Hyperactivity; Impulsivity; Verbal Aggression; Physical Aggression; Indirect Aggression; Passive Aggression;

Withdrawal. *Conditions Treated* Alcohol Abuse and/or Drug Abuse; Other Substance Abuse or Dependence; Depression; Personality Problems; Socialized Aggressive Reaction; Unsocialized Aggressive Reaction.

Services Provided Individual Therapy; Group Therapy; Parent Involvement; Behavior Therapy; Cognitive Developmental Therapy; Family Therapy; Art Therapy; Reality Therapy; Play Therapy. *Professionals on Staff* Psychiatrists 1; Psychologists 1; Counselors 1; Social Workers 2. *Educational Professionals* Special Education Teachers 1. *Curricula* Individualized; Basic Skills. *Educational Intervention Approaches* Engineered Classroom; Behavior Modification; Applied Behavior Analysis. *Degrees Awarded* Certificate of Completion.

Raineswood Residential Center

3232 E Raines Rd, Memphis, TN 38118 (901) 362-0085
Year Established 1978
Contact Carol McKinney, Prog Mgr

Facility Information *Placement* Public School; Public Residential Care. *Number of Beds* 28. *Children/Adolescents Served* 28. *Sexes Served* Both. *Sources of Funding* Local Funding; Contracts. Summer school available. *Teacher Certification Level* Elementary School; Junior High/Middle School; High School. *Special Certification Level* Generic Special Education.

Student/Patient Characteristics *Age Levels* 5-8; 9-11; 12-14; 15-17; 18-21. *IQ Ranges* 0-25; 26-40; 41-55; 56-70; 71-85. *Exceptionalities Served* Autistic; Mentally Handicapped; Communication Disordered; Hearing Impaired/Deaf. *Learning Problems* Perceptual Disabilities; Thinking Disabilities; Oral Language Disabilities. *Behavioral Problems* Attention Deficits; Hyperactivity; Hypoactivity; Impulsivity; Self-Aggression; Verbal Aggression; Physical Aggression; Indirect Aggression; Passive Aggression; Withdrawal. *Conditions Treated* Early Infantile Autism; Convulsive Disorders; Socialized Aggressive Reaction; Unsocialized Aggressive Reaction.

Services Provided Parent Involvement; Behavior Therapy. *Professionals on Staff* Psychologists 1; Liaison 1. *Service Facilities Available (with number of rooms)* Self-Contained Rooms 6. *Educational Professionals* Special Education Teachers 6; Paraprofessionals 25; Program Manager 1; Liaison 1. *Curricula* Career/Vocational Education; Individualized; Prevocational; Leisure Skill Training. *Educational Intervention Approaches* Behavior Modification.

Comments Raineswood Residential Center provides individualized training in a structured environment 24 hours a day, 12 months per year for autistic-like children. A maximum of 28 children can be served. It is available to Memphis residents free of charge and to non-residents on a tuition basis.

Regional Intervention Program

2400 White Ave, Nashville, TN 37204 (615) 383-7986
Year Established 1969
Contact Matthew A Timm, Dir

Facility Information *Placement* Special Program. *Children/Adolescents Served* 130. *Sexes Served* Both. *Sources of Funding* State Funds; Junior League of Nashville. Summer school available. *Special Certification Level* ED; LD; MR.

Student/Patient Characteristics *Age Levels* 0-4. *IQ Ranges* 0-25; 26-40; 41-55; 56-70; 71-85; 85-130; Above 130. *Exceptionalities Served* Autistic; Emotionally Disturbed; Mentally Handicapped; Communication Disordered; Hearing Impaired/Deaf; Visually Impaired/Blind; Other Health Impaired. *Learning Problems* Memory Disabilities; Perceptual Disabilities; Thinking Disabilities; Oral Language Disabilities. *Behavioral Problems* Attention Deficits; Hyperactivity; Hypoactivity; Impulsivity; Self-Aggression; Verbal Aggression; Physical Aggression; Withdrawal. *Conditions Treated* Early Infantile Autism; Aphasia.

Services Provided Parent Involvement; Behavior Therapy; Cognitive Developmental Therapy; Family Therapy. *Professionals on Staff* Psychiatrists 1; Psychologists 1; Counselors 6; Pediatrics 1; Physical Therapy 1; Speech and Language 1. *Educational Professionals* Special Education Counselors 6; Paraprofessionals

7. *Curricula* Parent Training. *Educational Intervention Approaches* Engineered Classroom; Behavior Modification; Applied Behavior Analysis.

Comments The project is a parent-implemented treatment program for families with behaviorally disordered and/or developmentally delayed preschool children.

Ridgeview Psychiatric Hospital and Center

240 W Tyrone Rd, Oak Ridge, TN 37830 (615) 482-1076
Contact Howard Friedman, Coord Adolescent Treatmemt Prog

Facility Information *Placement* Private Residential Care. *Number of Beds* 16. *Children/Adolescents Served* 16. *Sexes Served* Both. *Sources of Funding* Health Insurance; Medicaid. Summer school available. *Teacher Certification Level* Elementary School; Junior High/Middle School; High School. *Special Certification Level* ED; LD; MR; Math; Elementary Education.

Student/Patient Characteristics *Age Levels* 12-14; 15-17. *IQ Ranges* 71-85; 85-130; Above 130. *Exceptionalities Served* Emotionally Disturbed; Learning Disabled; Mentally Handicapped; Other Health Impaired; Physically Handicapped; Gifted. *Learning Problems* Memory Disabilities; Perceptual Disabilities; Thinking Disabilities; Oral Language Disabilities; Reading Disabilities; Handwriting Disabilities; Spelling Disabilities; Arithmetic Disabilities; Written Expression. *Behavioral Problems* Attention Deficits; Hyperactivity; Impulsivity; Self-Aggression; Verbal Aggression; Physical Aggression; Passive Aggression; Withdrawal. *Conditions Treated* Disintegrative Psychoses; Schizophrenia; Depression; Suicide; Anorexia Nervosa; Inadequacy/Immaturity; Personality Problems; Socialized Aggressive Reaction; Unsocialized Aggressive Reaction; Anxiety Reactions.

Services Provided Individual Therapy; Group Therapy; Parent Involvement; Family Therapy; Art Therapy; Music Therapy; Play Therapy; Psychodrama; Hypnotherapy. *Professionals on Staff* Psychiatrists 3; Psychologists 10; Social Workers 1; Nurses 11; Occupational Therapist 1; Recreational Therapist 1. *Service Facilities Available (with number of rooms)* Resource Rooms 1; Transition Rooms; Self-Contained Rooms 1; Hospital School 1. *Educational Professionals* Special Education Teachers 1; Paraprofessionals 4; Social Worker 1. *Curricula* Traditional Academic; Career/Vocational Education; Individualized; Basic Skills; Prevocational; GED Preparation; College Education. *Educational Intervention Approaches* Progressive Discipline; Self-Control.

Comments Ridgeview's treatment program, while primarily psychotherapeutic, is set up in a way which first establishes consistent controls over behavior. Extensive work with family members is an essential part of the treatment program. Educational needs are met by Ridgeview's own staff.

Southeast Mental Health Center—Child Development Institute

3810 Winchester Rd, Memphis, TN 38181 (901) 369-1400
Contact Vance Stewart, Dir

Facility Information *Placement* Outpatient Mental Health Center. *Sexes Served* Both. *Sources of Funding* State Funds; Health Insurance; Medicaid; Self Pay.

Student/Patient Characteristics *Exceptionalities Served* Autistic; Emotionally Disturbed; Learning Disabled; Mentally Handicapped; Gifted. *Learning Problems* Memory Disabilities; Perceptual Disabilities; Thinking Disabilities; Oral Language Disabilities; Reading Disabilities; Handwriting Disabilities; Spelling Disabilities; Arithmetic Disabilities; Written Expression. *Behavioral Problems* Attention Deficits; Hyperactivity; Hypoactivity; Impulsivity; Self-Aggression; Verbal Aggression; Physical Aggression; Indirect Aggression; Passive Aggression; Withdrawal. *Conditions Treated* Phobias; Obsessions and Compulsions; Hysteria; Depression; Suicide; Asthma; Anorexia Nervosa; Inadequacy/Immaturity; Personality Problems; Socialized Aggressive Reaction; Unsocialized Aggressive Reaction.

Services Provided Individual Therapy; Group Therapy; Parent Involvement; Behavior Therapy; Cognitive Developmental Therapy; Biofeedback; Family Therapy; Filial Therapy; Art Therapy; Reality Therapy; Play Therapy; Diagnosis and Evaluation; Consultation; Aftercare. *Professionals on Staff* Psychologists 1; Social Workers 1; Intern 1. *Service Facilities Available (with number of rooms)* Consultative (ERT). *Educational Intervention Approaches* Behavior Modification; Applied Behavior Analysis; Creative Conditioning; Ecologically Engineered.

Comments This is an outpatient clinic within a mental health center.

University of Tennessee—Child Development Center School

711 Jefferson Ave, Memphis, TN 38105 (901) 767-0957
Year Established 1957
Contact Carolyn P McKellar, Chief Special Ed

Facility Information *Placement* Public School; Special School. *Children/Adolescents Served* 60. *Sexes Served* Both. *Sources of Funding* State Funds; HEW. Summer school available. *Teacher Certification Level* Elementary School. *Special Certification Level* ED; LD; MR; Reading; Deaf; Blind; Multiply Handicapped.

Student/Patient Characteristics *Age Levels* 9-11. *IQ Ranges* 56-70; 71-85. *Exceptionalities Served* Emotionally Disturbed; Learning Disabled; Mentally Handicapped; Hearing Impaired/Deaf; Visually Impaired/Blind. *Learning Problems* Perceptual Disabilities; Oral Language Disabilities; Reading Disabilities; Arithmetic Disabilities; Written Expression. *Behavioral Problems* Attention Deficits; Hyperactivity; Impulsivity; Self-Aggression; Verbal Aggression; Physical Aggression; Withdrawal. *Conditions Treated* Aphasia; Personality Problems; Socialized Aggressive Reaction.

Services Provided Individual Therapy; Group Therapy; Parent Involvement; Behavior Therapy; Family Therapy; Filial Therapy; Drug Therapy; Play Therapy. *Professionals on Staff* Psychiatrists 2; Psychologists 2; Social Workers 2; Child Care Staff 16; Nurses 3. *Service Facilities Available (with number of rooms)* Consultative (ERT); Self-Contained Rooms; Special School; Homebound Instruction. *Educational Professionals* Special Education Teachers 6; Special Education Counselors 5; Paraprofessionals 5. *Curricula* Individualized. *Educational Intervention Approaches* Precision Teaching; Self-Control; Behavior Modification.

Vanderbilt Medical Center—Division of Child and Adolescent Psychiatry

2100 Pierce Ave, Nashville, TN 37212 (615) 322-7588
Year Established 1961
Contact Betty Gumm Willis, Prog Coord

Facility Information *Placement* Medical Center. *Number of Beds* 16. *Children/Adolescents Served* 22. *Sexes Served* Both. *Room and Board Fees (Approx)* $191. *Sources of Funding* State Funds; Health Insurance; Medicaid; P.L. 94-142. Summer school available. *Teacher Certification Level* Elementary School; Junior High/Middle School; High School. *Special Certification Level* ED; LD; MR; Elementary Education.

Student/Patient Characteristics *Age Levels* 0-4; 5-8; 9-11; 12-14. *IQ Ranges* 56-70; 71-85; 85-130; Above 130. *Exceptionalities Served* Autistic; Emotionally Disturbed; Learning Disabled; Mentally Handicapped; Communication Disordered; Hearing Impaired/Deaf; Visually Impaired/Blind; Other Health Impaired; Physically Handicapped; Gifted. *Learning Problems* Memory Disabilities; Perceptual Disabilities; Thinking Disabilities; Oral Language Disabilities; Reading Disabilities; Handwriting Disabilities; Spelling Disabilities; Arithmetic Disabilities; Written Expression. *Behavioral Problems* Attention Deficits; Hyperactivity; Hypoactivity; Impulsivity; Self-Aggression; Verbal Aggression; Physical Aggression; Indirect Aggression; Passive Aggression; Withdrawal. *Conditions Treated* Early Infantile Autism; Disintegrative Psychoses; Schizophrenia; Aphasia; Convulsive Disorders; Phobias; Obsessions and Compulsions; Hysteria; Depression; Suicide; Asthma; Anorexia Nervosa; Ulcerative Colitis; Inadequacy/Immaturity; Personality Problems; Socialized Aggressive Reaction; Unsocialized Aggressive Reaction.

Services Provided Individual Therapy; Parent Involvement; Behavior Therapy; Family Therapy; Drug Therapy; Milieu Therapy; Occupational Therapy; Recreational Therapy. *Professionals on Staff* Psychiatrists 6; Psychologists 2; Social Workers 3; Child Care Staff 8; Nurses 11; Occupational Therapist; Recreational Therapist 1. *Service Facilities Available (with number of rooms)* Self-Contained Rooms 3; Hospital School 3. *Educational Professionals* Special Education Teachers 3; Paraprofessionals 2; Diagnostician. *Curricula* Traditional Academic; Individualized; Basic Skills. *Educational Intervention Approaches* Precision Teaching; Self-Control; Behavior Modification.

Texas

Austin State Hospital

4110 Guadalupe, Austin, TX 78751 (512) 452-0381
Year Established 1857
Facility Information *Placement* Public Psychiatric Hospital.
Number of Beds 103. *Children/Adolescents Served* 103. *Sexes Served* Both. *Room and Board Fees (Approx)* Sliding Scale.
Tuition Fees (Approx) Sliding Scale. *Sources of Funding* State Funds. Summer school available. *Teacher Certification Level* Elementary School; Junior High/Middle School; High School.
Special Certification Level ED; LD; MR; Career/Vocational Education; Reading; Math; Speech.
Student/Patient Characteristics *Age Levels* 0-4; 5-8; 9-11; 12-14; 15-17. *IQ Ranges* 26-40; 41-55; 56-70; 71-85; 85-130; Above 130.
Exceptionalities Served Autistic; Emotionally Disturbed; Learning Disabled; Mentally Handicapped; Communication Disordered; Hearing Impaired/Deaf; Visually Impaired/Blind; Other Health Impaired; Physically Handicapped; Gifted. *Learning Problems* Memory Disabilities; Perceptual Disabilities; Thinking Disabilities; Oral Language Disabilities; Reading Disabilities; Handwriting Disabilities; Spelling Disabilities; Arithmetic Disabilities; Written Expression. *Behavioral Problems* Attention Deficits; Hyperactivity; Impulsivity; Self-Aggression; Verbal Aggression; Physical Aggression; Withdrawal. *Conditions Treated* Early Infantile Autism; Disintegrative Psychoses; Schizophrenia; Aphasia; Convulsive Disorders; Phobias; Obsessions and Compulsions; Hysteria; Depression; Suicide; Asthma; Anorexia Nervosa; Ulcerative Colitis; Inadequacy/Immaturity; Personality Problems; Socialized Aggressive Reaction; Unsocialized Aggressive Reaction.
Services Provided Individual Therapy; Group Therapy; Parent Involvement; Behavior Therapy; Cognitive Developmental Therapy; Family Therapy; Drug Therapy; Art Therapy; Music Therapy; Reality Therapy; Play Therapy. *Professionals on Staff* Psychiatrists; Psychologists; Social Workers; Child Care Staff; Nurses. *Service Facilities Available (with number of rooms)* Self-Contained Rooms; Hospital School. *Educational Professionals* Special Education Teachers; Career/Vocational Teachers; Paraprofessionals. *Curricula* Traditional Academic; Career/Vocational Education; Individualized; Basic Skills; Prevocational.
Educational Intervention Approaches Engineered Classroom; Self-Control; Behavior Modification. *Degrees Awarded* Certificate of Attendance; High School Diploma; Graduate Equivalency Diploma.

Autistic Treatment Center—Richardson

Box 529, Richardson, TX 75080 (214) 644-2076
Year Established 1977
Contact Anna Hundley, Exec Dir

Facility Information *Placement* Private Residential Care. *Number of Beds* 24. *Sexes Served* Both. *Tuition Fees (Approx)*
$20,000-$50,000. *Sources of Funding* State Funds; P.L. 94-142.
Summer school available. *Special Certification Level* ED; LD; MR.
Student/Patient Characteristics *Age Levels* 0-4; 5-8; 9-11; 12-14; 15-17; 18-21; Over 21. *IQ Ranges* 0-25; 26-40; 41-55; 56-70; 71-85. *Exceptionalities Served* Autistic; Hearing Impaired/Deaf.
Learning Problems Perceptual Disabilities; Reading Disabilities.
Behavioral Problems Attention Deficits; Hyperactivity; Hypoactivity; Impulsivity; Self-Aggression; Verbal Aggression; Physical Aggression. *Conditions Treated* Early Infantile Autism.
Services Provided Parent Involvement; Behavior Therapy.
Professionals on Staff Psychiatrists 1; Psychologists 1; Counselors 1; Child Care Staff 12. *Service Facilities Available (with number of rooms)* Special School. *Educational Professionals* Special Education Teachers; Paraprofessionals. *Curricula* Individualized.
Educational Intervention Approaches Behavior Modification.

Autistic Treatment Center—San Antonio

518 Pike, San Antonio, TX 78209 (512) 824-5616
Year Established 1979
Contact Monte Parker, Dir
Facility Information *Placement* Special School; Private Residential Care. *Number of Beds* 12. *Children/Adolescents Served* 14.
Sexes Served Both. *Tuition Fees (Approx)* $10,000-$35,000.
Sources of Funding P.L. 94-142; MH/MR Grant; Endowments.
Summer school available. *Teacher Certification Level* Elementary School. *Special Certification Level* ED; MR; Speech Therapy.
Student/Patient Characteristics *Age Levels* 0-4; 5-8; 9-11; 12-14; 15-17. *IQ Ranges* 0-25; 26-40; 41-55; 56-70. *Exceptionalities Served* Autistic; Emotionally Disturbed; Mentally Handicapped.
Learning Problems Perceptual Disabilities; Thinking Disabilities; Oral Language Disabilities; Reading Disabilities. *Behavioral Problems* Attention Deficits; Hyperactivity; Hypoactivity; Impulsivity; Self-Aggression; Verbal Aggression; Physical Aggression; Indirect Aggression; Passive Aggression; Withdrawal. *Conditions Treated* Early Infantile Autism.
Services Provided Individual Therapy; Group Therapy; Parent Involvement; Behavior Therapy. *Professionals on Staff* Psychologists 1; Child Care Staff 4; Nurses 1; Pediatrician 5. *Service Facilities Available (with number of rooms)* Consultative (ERT); Self-Contained Rooms. *Educational Professionals* Special Education Teachers 4; Special Education Counselors 1; Speech Therapist 1. *Curricula* Individualized; Basic Skills; Prevocational.
Educational Intervention Approaches Precision Teaching; Behavior Modification.

Avondale House

3611 Cummins, Houston, TX 77027 (713) 993-9544
Year Established 1976
Contact Patrick Cox, Exec Dir
Facility Information *Placement* Special School; Private Residential Care; Special Program. *Number of Beds* 10.
Children/Adolescents Served 35. *Sexes Served* Both. *Room and Board Fees (Approx)* Sliding Scale. *Tuition Fees (Approx)* Sliding Scale. *Sources of Funding* State Funds; P.L. 94-142; Private; County. Summer school available. *Teacher Certification Level* Elementary School; Junior High/Middle School; High School. *Special Certification Level* ED; LD; MR; Career/Vocational Education.
Student/Patient Characteristics *Age Levels* 5-8; 9-11; 12-14; 15-17; Over 21. *IQ Ranges* 0-25; 26-40; 41-55; 56-70; 71-85; 85-130. *Exceptionalities Served* Autistic; Emotionally Disturbed; Mentally Handicapped; Communication Disordered. *Learning Problems* Memory Disabilities; Perceptual Disabilities; Oral Language Disabilities. *Behavioral Problems* Attention Deficits; Hyperactivity; Hypoactivity; Impulsivity; Self-Aggression; Verbal Aggression; Physical Aggression; Indirect Aggression; Passive Aggression; Withdrawal. *Conditions Treated* Early Infantile Autism; Aphasia; Convulsive Disorders; Phobias; Obsessions and Compulsions; Socialized Aggressive Reaction; Unsocialized Aggressive Reaction.
Services Provided Individual Therapy; Group Therapy; Parent Involvement; Behavior Therapy; Family Therapy. *Professionals on Staff* Psychologists 2; Counselors 1; Social Workers 1; Child Care Staff 8. *Service Facilities Available (with number of rooms)* Consultative (ERT) 1; Self-Contained Rooms 4. *Educational Professionals* Special Education Teachers 5; Paraprofessionals 4. *Curricula* Traditional Academic; Career/Vocational Education; Individualized; Basic Skills; Prevocational. *Educational Intervention Approaches* Progressive Discipline; Self-Control; Behavior Modification; Creative Conditioning.

The Battin Clinic

3931 Essey Ln, Houston, TX 77027-5199 (713) 621-3072
Year Established 1959
Contact R Ray Battin
Facility Information *Placement* Outpatient Clinic.
Children/Adolescents Served 150. *Sexes Served* Both. *Sources of Funding* State Funds; Health Insurance; Medicare; Foundation Monies. *Special Certification Level* ED; LD; Career/Vocational Education; Reading; Math.
Student/Patient Characteristics *Age Levels* 0-4; 5-8; 9-11; 12-14; 15-17; 18-21; Over 21. *IQ Ranges* 71-85; 85-130; Above 130. *Exceptionalities Served* Emotionally Disturbed; Learning Disabled; Communication Disordered; Hearing Impaired/Deaf; Visually Impaired/Blind; Gifted. *Learning Problems* Memory Disabilities; Perceptual Disabilities; Thinking Disabilities; Oral Language Disabilities; Reading Disabilities; Handwriting Disabilities; Spelling Disabilities; Arithmetic Disabilities; Written Expression. *Behavioral Problems* Attention Deficits; Hyperactivity; Hypoactivity; Impulsivity; Self-Aggression; Verbal Aggression; Physical Aggression; Indirect Aggression; Passive Aggression; Withdrawal; Runaways. *Conditions Treated* Alcohol Abuse and/or Drug Abuse; Other Substance Abuse or Dependence; Aphasia; Phobias; Obsessions and Compulsions; Depression; Suicide; Inadequacy/Immaturity; Socialized Aggressive Reaction; Unsocialized Aggressive Reaction; Stress Syndrome.
Services Provided Individual Therapy; Group Therapy; Parent Involvement; Behavior Therapy; Cognitive Developmental Therapy; Biofeedback; Family Therapy; Reality Therapy; Play Therapy. *Professionals on Staff* Psychologists 3; Counselors 2; Social Workers 1; Speech Pathologist 4; Audiologist 2; Reading Specialist 1. *Educational Professionals* Reading 1. *Curricula* Individualized. *Educational Intervention Approaches* Behavior Modification; Applied Behavior Analysis; Creative Conditioning; Developmental.

Comments This multidiscipline rehabilitation agency does diagnostic neuropsychological, audiological, educational and psychological evaluation, and develops individualized treatment program. It also provides therapy and consultation services to schools, families, and individuals.

Big Spring State Hospital

Box 231, Big Spring, TX 79720 (915) 267-8216
Year Established 1934
Contact John Peptis, Unit Admin
Facility Information *Placement* Public Residential Care. *Number of Beds* 22. *Children/Adolescents Served* 22. *Sexes Served* Both. *Room and Board Fees (Approx)* $104. *Sources of Funding* State Funds; Health Insurance.
Student/Patient Characteristics *Age Levels* 12-14; 15-17. *IQ Ranges* 71-85; 85-130. *Exceptionalities Served* Emotionally Disturbed; Mentally Handicapped. *Learning Problems* Memory Disabilities; Thinking Disabilities. *Behavioral Problems* Attention Deficits; Hyperactivity; Hypoactivity; Impulsivity; Self-Aggression; Verbal Aggression; Physical Aggression; Indirect Aggression; Passive Aggression; Withdrawal. *Conditions Treated* Disintegrative Psychoses; Schizophrenia; Convulsive Disorders; Obsessions and Compulsions; Hysteria; Depression; Suicide; Inadequacy/Immaturity; Personality Problems; Socialized Aggressive Reaction; Unsocialized Aggressive Reaction.
Services Provided Individual Therapy; Group Therapy; Parent Involvement; Behavior Therapy; Cognitive Developmental Therapy; Family Therapy; Drug Therapy; Art Therapy; Music Therapy; Reality Therapy; Work Adjustment Therapy; Recreation Therapy; Occupational Therapy. *Professionals on Staff* Psychiatrists 2; Psychologists 1; Social Workers 1; Child Care Staff 15; Nurses 4. *Service Facilities Available (with number of rooms)* Self-Contained Rooms 2; On Unit Academics. *Educational Professionals* Special Education Teachers 2. *Curricula* Career/Vocational Education; Individualized; Basic Skills; Prevocational. *Educational Intervention Approaches* Behavior Modification; Self-Control; Behavior Modification. *Degrees Awarded* Graduate Equivalency Diploma.

The Brown Schools

PO Box 4008, Austin, TX 78765 (800) 531-5305
Year Established 1940
Contact Bob Bennett, Admissions Dir
Facility Information *Placement* Special School; Private Residential Care; Residential Treatment Center. *Number of Beds* 506. *Children/Adolescents Served* 506 (3 hospitals). *Sexes Served* Both. *Room and Board Fees (Approx)* $175-295. *Sources of Funding* State Funds; Health Insurance; Medicaid; P.L. 94-142; CHAMPUS; Agency Contracts; Private; Other Insurance. Summer school available. *Teacher Certification Level* Elementary School; Junior High/Middle School; High School. *Special Certification Level* ED; LD; MR; Career/Vocational Education; Reading; Math.
Student/Patient Characteristics *Age Levels* 0-4; 5-8; 9-11; 12-14; 15-17; 18-21; Over 21. *IQ Ranges* 41-55; 56-70; 71-85; 85-130; Above 130. *Exceptionalities Served* Autistic; Emotionally Disturbed; Learning Disabled; Mentally Handicapped; Communication Disordered; Hearing Impaired/Deaf; Visually Impaired/Blind; Other Health Impaired; Physically Handicapped. *Learning Problems* Memory Disabilities; Perceptual Disabilities; Thinking Disabilities; Oral Language Disabilities; Reading Disabilities; Handwriting Disabilities; Spelling Disabilities; Arithmetic Disabilities; Written Expression. *Behavioral Problems* Attention Deficits; Hyperactivity; Hypoactivity; Impulsivity; Self-Aggression; Verbal Aggression; Physical Aggression; Indirect Aggression; Passive Aggression; Withdrawal. *Conditions Treated* Disintegrative Psychoses; Schizophrenia; Aphasia; Convulsive Disorders; Obsessions and Compulsions; Hysteria; Depression; Suicide; Asthma; Anorexia Nervosa; Inadequacy/Immaturity; Personality Problems; Socialized Aggressive Reaction; Unsocialized Aggressive Reaction.

Services Provided Individual Therapy; Group Therapy; Parent Involvement; Behavior Therapy; Cognitive Developmental Therapy; Biofeedback; Family Therapy; Drug Therapy; Art Therapy; Music Therapy; Reality Therapy; Play Therapy; Psychodrama. *Professionals on Staff* Psychiatrists 12; Psychologists 10; Counselors; Social Workers 29; Child Care Staff 491; Nurses 50; Physical Therapy 6; Occupational Therapy 6; Cognitive Retraining 5. *Service Facilities Available (with number of rooms)* Resource Rooms; Transition Rooms; Self-Contained Rooms. *Educational Professionals* Regular School Teachers; Special Education Teachers 24; Career/Vocational Teachers 21; Special Education Counselors 4; Paraprofessionals 4. *Curricula* Traditional Academic; Career/Vocational Education; Individualized; Basic Skills; Prevocational. *Educational Intervention Approaches* Progressive Discipline; Self-Control; Behavior Modification; Creative Conditioning. *Degrees Awarded* Certificate of Attendance; High School Diploma; Graduate Equivalency Diploma.

Comments The Brown Schools are 3 residential treatment centers that are also licensed and accredited as psychiatric hospitals. It provides psychiatric treatment programs. Services are available for children, adolescents, and young adults with emotional disturbances, behavior disorders, developmental delays, traumatic head injury, hearing impairment, or a combination of these conditions.

Child Study Center

1300 W Lancaster, Fort Worth, TX 76102 (817) 336-8611
Year Established 1966
Contact Larry Eason, Exec Dir
Facility Information *Placement* Special School; Special Program. *Sexes Served* Both. *Tuition Fees (Approx)* Sliding Scale. *Sources of Funding* Health Insurance; United Way; Contributions. *Special Certification Level* MR.
Student/Patient Characteristics *Age Levels* 0-4; 5-8; 9-11; 12-14. *IQ Ranges* 0-25; 26-40; 41-55; 56-70; 71-85; 85-130; Above 130. *Exceptionalities Served* Autistic; Emotionally Disturbed; Learning Disabled; Mentally Handicapped; Communication Disordered; Hearing Impaired/Deaf; Visually Impaired/Blind; Other Health Impaired; Physically Handicapped. *Learning Problems* Memory Disabilities; Perceptual Disabilities; Thinking Disabilities; Oral Language Disabilities; Reading Disabilities; Handwriting Disabilities; Spelling Disabilities; Arithmetic Disabilities; Written Expression. *Behavioral Problems* Attention Deficits; Hyperactivity; Hypoactivity; Impulsivity; Self-Aggression; Verbal Aggression; Physical Aggression; Indirect Aggression; Passive Aggression; Withdrawal. *Conditions Treated* Early Infantile Autism; Aphasia; Convulsive Disorders; Phobias; Obsessions and Compulsions; Hysteria; Depression; Suicide; Asthma; Anorexia Nervosa; Inadequacy/Immaturity; Personality Problems; Socialized Aggressive Reaction; Unsocialized Aggressive Reaction.
Services Provided Individual Therapy; Group Therapy; Parent Involvement; Behavior Therapy; Family Therapy; Drug Therapy; Play Therapy. *Professionals on Staff* Psychiatrists 5; Psychologists 5; Social Workers 4.5; Nurses 3; Speech Therapists; Occupational Therapists; Audiology; Pediatricians; Physical Therapist. *Service Facilities Available (with number of rooms)* Consultative (ERT) 6; Self-Contained Rooms 6. *Educational Professionals* Special Education Teachers 6; Paraprofessionals 6. *Curricula* Individualized; Basic Skills. *Educational Intervention Approaches* Engineered Classroom; Behavior Modification.

Comments The Child Study Center is a private nonprofit agency providing a variety of outpatient treatment and evaluation services: speech and language, psychology, social work, and educational diagnosticians. There are 6 classes of preschoolers and program and genetic services.

Children's Learning Center of San Antonio

5705 Blanco Rd, San Antonio, TX 78213 (512) 340-1121
Contact Terri Locke, Acting Dir
Facility Information *Placement* Private Day Care. *Children/Adolescents Served* 25. *Sexes Served* Both. *Sources of Funding* State Funds. Summer school available. *Teacher*

Certification Level Elementary School; Junior High/Middle School; High School. *Special Certification Level* ED; MR; Generic Special Education.
Student/Patient Characteristics *Age Levels* 0-4; 5-8; 9-11; 12-14; 15-17; 18-21. *IQ Ranges* 0-25; 26-40; 41-55; 56-70; 71-85; 85-130; Above 130. *Exceptionalities Served* Autistic; Emotionally Disturbed; Mentally Handicapped; Communication Disordered. *Learning Problems* Memory Disabilities; Perceptual Disabilities; Thinking Disabilities; Oral Language Disabilities; Reading Disabilities; Handwriting Disabilities; Spelling Disabilities; Arithmetic Disabilities; Written Expression. *Behavioral Problems* Attention Deficits; Hyperactivity; Hypoactivity; Impulsivity; Self-Aggression; Verbal Aggression; Physical Aggression; Indirect Aggression; Passive Aggression; Withdrawal; Self Stimulation. *Conditions Treated* Early Infantile Autism; Obsessions and Compulsions.
Services Provided Individual Therapy; Group Therapy; Parent Involvement; Behavior Therapy; Cognitive Developmental Therapy; Family Therapy. *Professionals on Staff* Speech Therapists. *Service Facilities Available (with number of rooms)* Special School 12; Vocational and Community Settings. *Educational Professionals* Special Education Teachers 4; Paraprofessionals 5. *Curricula* Career/Vocational Education; Individualized; Basic Skills; Functional Living. *Educational Intervention Approaches* Self-Control; Behavior Modification.

Comments This program is individualized and functional.

Children's Medical Center—Psychiatric Inpatient Unit

1935 Amelia, Dallas, TX 75235 (214) 920-2050
Year Established 1970
Contact Graham J Emslie, Dir Psychiatry Inpatient Unit
Facility Information *Placement* Private Hospital. *Number of Beds* 16. *Children/Adolescents Served* 16. *Sexes Served* Both. *Room and Board Fees (Approx)* $225. *Sources of Funding* Health Insurance; Medicaid. Summer school available. *Teacher Certification Level* Elementary School; Junior High/Middle School; High School. *Special Certification Level* ED; LD.
Student/Patient Characteristics *Age Levels* 0-4; 5-8; 9-11; 12-14; 15-17. *IQ Ranges* 71-85; 85-130; Above 130. *Exceptionalities Served* Emotionally Disturbed; Learning Disabled; Communication Disordered; Other Health Impaired; Physically Handicapped; Gifted. *Learning Problems* Memory Disabilities; Perceptual Disabilities; Thinking Disabilities; Oral Language Disabilities; Reading Disabilities; Handwriting Disabilities; Spelling Disabilities; Arithmetic Disabilities; Written Expression. *Behavioral Problems* Attention Deficits; Hyperactivity; Hypoactivity; Impulsivity; Self-Aggression; Verbal Aggression; Physical Aggression; Indirect Aggression; Passive Aggression; Withdrawal. *Conditions Treated* Disintegrative Psychoses; Schizophrenia; Convulsive Disorders; Phobias; Obsessions and Compulsions; Hysteria; Depression; Suicide; Asthma; Anorexia Nervosa; Ulcerative Colitis; Personality Problems; Socialized Aggressive Reaction; Unsocialized Aggressive Reaction.
Services Provided Individual Therapy; Group Therapy; Parent Involvement; Behavior Therapy; Cognitive Developmental Therapy; Family Therapy; Filial Therapy; Drug Therapy; Play Therapy; Psychodrama. *Professionals on Staff* Psychiatrists 5; Psychologists 3; Social Workers 2; Child Care Staff 20; Nurses 6. *Service Facilities Available (with number of rooms)* Self-Contained Rooms 3. *Educational Professionals* Special Education Teachers 2; Paraprofessionals 1. *Curricula* Traditional Academic; Individualized; Basic Skills.

Comments The unit is a 16 bed short to intermediate stay psychiatric unit for children 10-17 yrs. It is a children's hospital with an emphasis on children with combined medical and emotional problems.

Crockett State School Independent School District

PO Box 411, Loop 304, Crockett, TX 75835 (409) 544-5111
Year Established 1957
Contact Monroe D Werner, Personnel Dept

Facility Information *Placement* State School. *Number of Beds* 125. *Children/Adolescents Served* 125 (campus); 50 (wilderness camping program). *Sexes Served* Male. *Room and Board Fees (Approx)* $67 (campus); $52 (camp). *Sources of Funding* State Funds; Chapter I. *Teacher Certification Level* Elementary School; Junior High/Middle School; High School. *Special Certification Level* ED; LD; MR; Career/Vocational Education; Reading; Math.

Student/Patient Characteristics *Age Levels* 12-14; 15-17. *IQ Ranges* 71-85; 85-130. *Exceptionalities Served* Emotionally Disturbed; Learning Disabled; Juvenile Delinquent. *Learning Problems* Memory Disabilities; Perceptual Disabilities; Thinking Disabilities; Oral Language Disabilities; Reading Disabilities; Handwriting Disabilities; Spelling Disabilities; Arithmetic Disabilities; Written Expression. *Behavioral Problems* Attention Deficits; Hyperactivity; Impulsivity; Self-Aggression; Verbal Aggression; Physical Aggression; Indirect Aggression; Passive Aggression; Withdrawal. *Conditions Treated* Alcohol Abuse and/or Drug Abuse; Other Substance Abuse or Dependence; Depression; Inadequacy/Immaturity; Personality Problems; Socialized Aggressive Reaction; Unsocialized Aggressive Reaction.

Services Provided Individual Therapy; Group Therapy. *Professionals on Staff* Psychiatrists 1; Psychologists 1; Counselors 8; Social Workers 1; Child Care Staff 90; Nurses 8; Recreation Supervisor 1. *Service Facilities Available (with number of rooms)* Resource Rooms 1. *Educational Professionals* Regular School Teachers 7; Special Education Teachers 4; Career/Vocational Teachers 2. *Curricula* Traditional Academic; Career/Vocational Education; Individualized; Basic Skills. *Educational Intervention Approaches* Precision Teaching; Positive Peer Culture. *Degrees Awarded* High School Diploma; Graduate Equivalency Diploma.

Darden Hill Ranch School

PO Box 40, Rte 1, Box 23C, Driftwood, TX 78619
(512) 858-4258
Year Established 1973
Contact Charles Campise, Dir

Facility Information *Placement* Private Residential Care. *Number of Beds* 28. *Children/Adolescents Served* 25. *Sexes Served* Male. *Room and Board Fees (Approx)* $61. *Sources of Funding* State Funds; Private Donations. Summer school available.

Student/Patient Characteristics *Age Levels* 5-8; 9-11; 12-14; 15-17. *IQ Ranges* 71-85; 85-130. *Exceptionalities Served* Emotionally Disturbed; Learning Disabled. *Learning Problems* Memory Disabilities; Perceptual Disabilities; Thinking Disabilities; Oral Language Disabilities; Reading Disabilities; Handwriting Disabilities; Spelling Disabilities; Arithmetic Disabilities; Written Expression. *Behavioral Problems* Attention Deficits; Hyperactivity; Impulsivity; Self-Aggression; Verbal Aggression; Physical Aggression; Indirect Aggression; Passive Aggression; Withdrawal. *Conditions Treated* Obsessions and Compulsions; Hysteria; Depression; Inadequacy/Immaturity; Personality Problems; Socialized Aggressive Reaction; Unsocialized Aggressive Reaction; Borderline Personalities.

Services Provided Individual Therapy; Group Therapy; Parent Involvement; Behavior Therapy; Reality Therapy; Play Therapy; Psychodrama. *Professionals on Staff* Psychiatrists 1; Psychologists 1; Social Workers 1; Child Care Staff 15. *Service Facilities Available (with number of rooms)* Transition Rooms; Classroom at Ranch with Impact Unit at Public School; Special School. *Educational Professionals* Special Education Teachers 1. *Curricula* Career/Vocational Education; Individualized; Basic Skills. *Educational Intervention Approaches* Engineered Classroom; Self-Control; Behavior Modification; Creative Conditioning. *Degrees Awarded* Certificate of Attendance.

The Devereux Foundation—Texas Branch

PO BOX 2666, Goliad Hwy 59 S, Victoria, TX 77902
(512) 575-8271
Year Established 1959
Contact Betty H Templin, Admissions Dir

Facility Information *Placement* Private Residential Care; Psychiatric Hospital. *Number of Beds* 159. *Children/Adolescents Served* 159. *Sexes Served* Both. *Tuition Fees (Approx)* $39,200-$67,200. *Sources of Funding* State Funds; Health Insurance; P.L. 94-142. Summer school available. *Teacher Certification Level* Elementary School; Junior High/Middle School; High School. *Special Certification Level* ED; LD.

Student/Patient Characteristics *Age Levels* 5-8; 9-11; 12-14; 15-17; 18-21. *IQ Ranges* 71-85; 85-130; Above 130. *Exceptionalities Served* Emotionally Disturbed; Learning Disabled; Hearing Impaired/Deaf; Visually Impaired/Blind; Behaviorally Disordered. *Learning Problems* Memory Disabilities; Perceptual Disabilities; Thinking Disabilities; Oral Language Disabilities; Reading Disabilities; Handwriting Disabilities; Spelling Disabilities; Arithmetic Disabilities; Written Expression. *Behavioral Problems* Attention Deficits; Hyperactivity; Hypoactivity; Impulsivity; Self-Aggression; Verbal Aggression; Physical Aggression; Indirect Aggression; Passive Aggression; Withdrawal. *Conditions Treated* Alcohol Abuse and/or Drug Abuse; Other Substance Abuse or Dependence; Schizophrenia; Aphasia; Phobias; Obsessions and Compulsions; Hysteria; Depression; Suicide; Asthma; Inadequacy/Immaturity; Personality Problems; Socialized Aggressive Reaction; Unsocialized Aggressive Reaction.

Services Provided Individual Therapy; Group Therapy; Parent Involvement; Behavior Therapy; Family Therapy; Reality Therapy; Play Therapy; Milieu Therapy. *Professionals on Staff* Psychiatrists 3; Psychologists 9; Counselors 2; Social Workers 4; Child Care Staff 61; Nurses 22; Mental Health Technicians 41; Vocational Counselor 1. *Service Facilities Available (with number of rooms)* Resource Rooms 1; Self-Contained Rooms 6; Hospital School 4. *Educational Professionals* Regular School Teachers 5; Special Education Teachers 12; Career/Vocational Teachers 10; Paraprofessionals 4; Speech Pathologist 1; Therapeutic Recreational Therapists 2; Vocational Evaluator 1. *Curricula* Traditional Academic; Career/Vocational Education; Individualized; Basic Skills; Prevocational. *Educational Intervention Approaches* Self-Control; Behavior Modification; Level Systems. *Degrees Awarded* High School Diploma; Graduate Equivalency Diploma.

Comments The Devereux Texas Branch provides a continuum of treatment from the most restrictive to the least restrictive environment.

Education Service Center Region 10

400 E Spring Valley Rd, Richardson, TX 75080 (214) 231-6301
Year Established 1967
Contact Louis E Glover, Special Educ Dir

Facility Information *Placement* Information and Referral for Handicapped.

Comments The Region 10 Education Service Center is a public school support system providing information and referral for handicapped persons from birth through 22 years. Services are free and available to the public.

El Paso Guidance Center

1501 N Mesa, El Paso, TX 79902 (915) 542-1921
Year Established 1964
Contact Marian Given, Dir

Facility Information *Placement* Outpatient Guidance Center. *Children/Adolescents Served* 1,375. *Sexes Served* Both. *Sources of Funding* State Funds; P.L. 94-142; United Way; City; County; E.P.M.HMR; Dept of Human Resources.

Student/Patient Characteristics *Age Levels* 0-4; 5-8; 9-11; 12-14; 15-17. *IQ Ranges* 0-25; 26-40; 41-55; 56-70; 71-85; 85-130. *Exceptionalities Served* Autistic; Emotionally Disturbed; Learning Disabled; Mentally Handicapped; Gifted. *Learning Problems* Memory Disabilities; Perceptual Disabilities; Thinking Disabilities; Oral Language Disabilities; Reading Disabilities; Handwriting Disabilities; Spelling Disabilities; Arithmetic Disabilities. *Behavioral Problems* Attention Deficits; Hyperactivity; Hypoactivity; Impulsivity; Self-Aggression; Verbal Aggression; Physical Aggression; Indirect Aggression; Passive Aggression; Withdrawal. *Conditions Treated* Schizophrenia; Convulsive Disorders; Phobias; Obsessions and Compulsions; Hysteria; Depression; Suicide; Anorexia Nervosa; Inadequacy/Immaturity; Personality Problems; Socialized Aggressive Reaction; Unsocialized Aggressive Reaction.

Services Provided Individual Therapy; Group Therapy; Parent Involvement; Family Therapy. *Professionals on Staff* Psychiatrists 4; Psychologists 5; Counselors 2; Social Workers 6.

Comments This a public supported, nonprofit, outpatient, mental health agency for children and their families in El Paso County.

Eleanor Griffin Children's Development Center

710 Quincy, Plainview, TX 79072 (806) 293-4475
Contact Joyce Lacy, Coord
Facility Information *Placement* Special School.
Children/Adolescents Served 60. *Sexes Served* Both. *Sources of Funding* State Funds; P.L. 94-142. Summer school available. *Teacher Certification Level* Elementary School; Junior High/Middle School. *Special Certification Level* LD; MR; Reading; Early Childhood Handicapped.
Student/Patient Characteristics *Age Levels* 0-4; 5-8; 9-11; 12-14; 15-17; 18-21. *IQ Ranges* 0-25; 26-40; 41-55; 56-70; 71-85. *Exceptionalities Served* Autistic; Emotionally Disturbed; Learning Disabled; Mentally Handicapped; Communication Disordered; Hearing Impaired/Deaf; Visually Impaired/Blind; Other Health Impaired; Physically Handicapped. *Learning Problems* Memory Disabilities; Perceptual Disabilities; Thinking Disabilities; Oral Language Disabilities; Reading Disabilities; Handwriting Disabilities; Spelling Disabilities; Arithmetic Disabilities; Written Expression. *Behavioral Problems* Attention Deficits; Hyperactivity; Hypoactivity; Impulsivity; Self-Aggression; Physical Aggression; Withdrawal. *Conditions Treated* Early Infantile Autism; Aphasia; Convulsive Disorders.
Services Provided Individual Therapy; Group Therapy; Parent Involvement; Behavior Therapy; Cognitive Developmental Therapy. *Professionals on Staff* Psychologists 1; Social Workers 1. *Service Facilities Available (with number of rooms)* Self-Contained Rooms 4. *Educational Professionals* Special Education Teachers 5; Paraprofessionals 8; Program Coordinator; Speech Pathologist 2. *Curricula* Career/Vocational Education; Individualized; Basic Skills; Prevocational. *Educational Intervention Approaches* Self-Control; Behavior Modification; Applied Behavior Analysis; Creative Conditioning.

Comments The Eleanor Griffin Children's Development Center serves developmentally disabled children, ranging from birth to 3 years of age. Developmental disabilities include mental retardation, epilepsy, cerebral palsy, and autism; however, services are provided for the significantly delayed or impaired child, as in the blind, deaf, hyperactive, or emotionally disturbed child. The Children's Development Center contracts with the independent school system to provide special education services to eligible children. This unit also provides a free service to residents of the 9 county area through the Rural Infant Education Program (RIEP). It is a program of individual treatment for mentally and/or physically handicapped children and/or for developmentally delayed children provided by a Home Bound Teacher weekly at the child's home.

The Goldstaub Residence

5618 Rutherglenn Dr, Houston, TX 77096 (713) 729-9020
Year Established 1965
Contact Lorraine B Goldstaub, Assoc Dir
Facility Information *Placement* Private Residential Care. *Number of Beds* 6. *Children/Adolescents Served* 6. *Sexes Served* Both. *Room and Board Fees (Approx)* $65. *Sources of Funding* Fees.

Student/Patient Characteristics *Age Levels* 5-8; 9-11; 12-14. *IQ Ranges* 71-85; 85-130; Above 130. *Exceptionalities Served* Emotionally Disturbed. *Learning Problems* Memory Disabilities; Perceptual Disabilities; Thinking Disabilities; Oral Language Disabilities; Reading Disabilities; Handwriting Disabilities; Spelling Disabilities; Arithmetic Disabilities; Written Expression. *Behavioral Problems* Attention Deficits; Hyperactivity; Hypoactivity; Impulsivity; Self-Aggression; Verbal Aggression; Physical Aggression; Indirect Aggression; Passive Aggression; Withdrawal. *Conditions Treated* Alcohol Abuse and/or Drug Abuse; Other Substance Abuse or Dependence; Early Infantile Autism; Disintegrative Psychoses; Schizophrenia; Aphasia; Convulsive Disorders; Phobias; Obsessions and Compulsions; Hysteria; Depression; Suicide; Asthma; Anorexia Nervosa; Ulcerative Colitis; Inadequacy/Immaturity; Personality Problems; Socialized Aggressive Reaction; Unsocialized Aggressive Reaction.

Services Provided Individual Therapy; Group Therapy; Art Therapy; Music Therapy; Play Therapy. *Professionals on Staff* Social Workers 2.

Learning Inc

1118 Third St, Corpus Christi, TX 78414 (512) 883-6801
Year Established 1972
Contact Jacki Etheridge, Co-Dir
Facility Information *Placement* Private Individual Sessions.
Children/Adolescents Served 80. *Sexes Served* Both. Summer school available. *Teacher Certification Level* Elementary School; Junior High/Middle School; High School. *Special Certification Level* LD; MR.
Student/Patient Characteristics *Age Levels* 5-8; 9-11; 12-14; 15-17; 18-21; Over 21. *IQ Ranges* 85-130; Above 130. *Exceptionalities Served* Emotionally Disturbed; Learning Disabled. *Learning Problems* Memory Disabilities; Perceptual Disabilities; Reading Disabilities; Handwriting Disabilities; Spelling Disabilities; Arithmetic Disabilities; Written Expression. *Behavioral Problems* Attention Deficits; Hyperactivity; Hypoactivity; Impulsivity; Verbal Aggression.
Services Provided Individual Therapy. *Professionals on Staff* Counselors 2. *Educational Professionals* Special Education Teachers 2. *Curricula* Individualized; Basic Skills; Perceptual Training.

Meridell Achievement Center Inc

PO Box 9383, Austin, TX 78766 (512) 258-1691
Year Established 1961
Contact Bobbie Caviness, Admin
Facility Information *Placement* Private Residential Care. *Number of Beds* 35. *Children/Adolescents Served* 35. *Sexes Served* Both. *Room and Board Fees (Approx)* $195. *Sources of Funding* Health Insurance; P.L. 94-142; OCHAMPUS. Summer school available. *Teacher Certification Level* Elementary School; Junior High/Middle School; High School. *Special Certification Level* ED.
Student/Patient Characteristics *Age Levels* 5-8; 9-11; 12-14; 15-17; 18-21. *IQ Ranges* 85-130; Above 130. *Exceptionalities Served* Autistic; Emotionally Disturbed; Learning Disabled. *Learning Problems* Perceptual Disabilities; Thinking Disabilities; Reading Disabilities; Arithmetic Disabilities. *Behavioral Problems* Attention Deficits; Hyperactivity; Impulsivity; Verbal Aggression; Passive Aggression; Withdrawal. *Conditions Treated* Schizophrenia; Phobias; Obsessions and Compulsions; Hysteria; Depression; Inadequacy/Immaturity; Personality Problems; Socialized Aggressive Reaction; Unsocialized Aggressive Reaction.
Services Provided Individual Therapy; Group Therapy; Parent Involvement; Family Therapy; Reality Therapy; Play Therapy. *Professionals on Staff* Psychiatrists 2; Psychologists 1; Social Workers 6; Child Care Staff 15; Nurses 7. *Service Facilities Available (with number of rooms)* Self-Contained Rooms 4; On-Campus Residential School 4. *Educational Professionals* Special Education Teachers 4; Paraprofessionals 3. *Curricula* Traditional Academic; Individualized; Prevocational; Remedial. *Educational Intervention Approaches* Self-Control. *Degrees Awarded* High School Diploma.

MHMR of Southeast Texas—Daybreak Cottage

4303 N Tejas Pkwy, Orange, TX 77630 (409) 883-0962
Year Established 1978
Contact Sally Shearer, Admin

Facility Information *Placement* Public Residential Care. *Number of Beds* 16. *Children/Adolescents Served* 16 (residential); 8 (school). *Sexes Served* Both. *Room and Board Fees (Approx)* Sliding Scale. *Tuition Fees (Approx)* Sliding Scale. *Sources of Funding* State Funds; Health Insurance. *Teacher Certification Level* Elementary School; Junior High/Middle School; High School. *Special Certification Level* LD; Special Education.

Student/Patient Characteristics *Age Levels* 5-8; 9-11; 12-14; 15-17. *IQ Ranges* 71-85; 85-130; Above 130. *Exceptionalities Served* Emotionally Disturbed; Learning Disabled. *Learning Problems* Memory Disabilities; Perceptual Disabilities; Thinking Disabilities; Oral Language Disabilities; Reading Disabilities; Handwriting Disabilities; Spelling Disabilities; Arithmetic Disabilities; Written Expression. *Behavioral Problems* Attention Deficits; Hyperactivity; Hypoactivity; Impulsivity; Self-Aggression; Verbal Aggression; Physical Aggression; Indirect Aggression; Passive Aggression; Withdrawal. *Conditions Treated* Alcohol Abuse and/or Drug Abuse; Phobias; Obsessions and Compulsions; Hysteria; Depression; Inadequacy/Immaturity; Personality Problems; Socialized Aggressive Reaction; Unsocialized Aggressive Reaction.

Services Provided Individual Therapy; Group Therapy; Parent Involvement; Behavior Therapy; Cognitive Developmental Therapy; Biofeedback; Family Therapy; Filial Therapy; Drug Therapy; Art Therapy; Reality Therapy; Play Therapy. *Professionals on Staff* Psychiatrists 1; Psychologists 2; Social Workers 1; Child Care Staff 12; Nurses 1. *Service Facilities Available (with number of rooms)* Self-Contained Rooms 2; On-Campus Residential School 2. *Educational Professionals* Special Education Teachers 2; Paraprofessionals 3. *Curricula* Traditional Academic; Individualized. *Educational Intervention Approaches* Progressive Discipline; Self-Control; Behavior Modification.

Region VIII Education Service Center

100 N Riddle, Mount Pleasant, TX 75455 (214) 572-8553
Contact James R Riddle, Coord Spec Ed

Facility Information *Placement* Early Childhood Intervention Program. *Sexes Served* Both. *Sources of Funding* State Funds. *Teacher Certification Level* Elementary School. *Special Certification Level* Elementary; Speech Therapy; Counseling.

Student/Patient Characteristics *Age Levels* 0-4. *IQ Ranges* 0-25; 26-40; 41-55; 56-70; 71-85; 85-130; Above 130. *Exceptionalities Served* Autistic; Emotionally Disturbed; Learning Disabled; Mentally Handicapped; Communication Disordered; Hearing Impaired/Deaf; Visually Impaired/Blind; Other Health Impaired; Physically Handicapped. *Learning Problems* Memory Disabilities; Perceptual Disabilities; Thinking Disabilities. *Behavioral Problems* Attention Deficits; Hyperactivity; Hypoactivity; Impulsivity; Self-Aggression; Verbal Aggression; Physical Aggression; Indirect Aggression; Passive Aggression; Withdrawal. *Conditions Treated* Early Infantile Autism; Convulsive Disorders.

Services Provided Individual Therapy. *Professionals on Staff* Counselors 1; Early Childhood Intervention Teachers 3. *Service Facilities Available (with number of rooms)* Homebound Instruction. *Educational Professionals* Regular School Teachers 1; Special Education Teachers 1; Paraprofessionals 1; Counselor 1. *Curricula* Individualized. *Educational Intervention Approaches* Behavior Modification; Language Development, Motor Development, and other Educational Programming.

Region 16 Educational Service Center

PO Box 30600, Amarillo, TX 79120 (806) 376-5521
Contact Gene Norman, Special Ed Dir

Facility Information *Placement* Assists Public School in Residential Placement. *Sexes Served* Both. *Sources of Funding* State Funds; P.L. 94-142.

Student/Patient Characteristics *Age Levels* 0-4; 5-8; 9-11; 12-14; 15-17; 18-21. *IQ Ranges* 26-40; 41-55; 56-70; 71-85; 85-130. *Exceptionalities Served* Autistic; Emotionally Disturbed; Learning Disabled; Mentally Handicapped; Communication Disordered; Hearing Impaired/Deaf; Visually Impaired/Blind; Other Health Impaired; Physically Handicapped. *Learning Problems* Memory Disabilities; Perceptual Disabilities; Thinking Disabilities; Oral Language Disabilities; Reading Disabilities; Handwriting Disabilities; Spelling Disabilities; Arithmetic Disabilities; Written Expression. *Behavioral Problems* Attention Deficits; Hyperactivity; Hypoactivity; Impulsivity; Self-Aggression; Verbal Aggression; Physical Aggression; Indirect Aggression; Passive Aggression. *Conditions Treated* Early Infantile Autism; Schizophrenia; Aphasia; Convulsive Disorders; Phobias; Obsessions and Compulsions; Hysteria; Depression; Asthma; Anorexia Nervosa; Ulcerative Colitis; Socialized Aggressive Reaction.

Services Provided Diagnosis; Referral. *Professionals on Staff* Psychiatrists 3; Psychologists 2; Child Care Staff 2; Nurses 2.

Comments Services are provided to local school districts upon request.

Rusk State Hospital—Child and Adolescent Unit

PO Box 318, Hwy 69 N, Rusk, TX 75785 (214) 683-3441
Contact Kathleen Joslin, Unit Dir

Facility Information *Placement* State Hospital. *Number of Beds* 30. *Children/Adolescents Served* 30. *Sexes Served* Both. *Sources of Funding* State Funds. Summer school available. *Teacher Certification Level* Elementary School; Junior High/Middle School; High School. *Special Certification Level* ED; LD; Reading; Math.

Student/Patient Characteristics *Age Levels* 5-8; 9-11; 12-14; 15-17. *IQ Ranges* 71-85; 85-130. *Exceptionalities Served* Emotionally Disturbed. *Learning Problems* Reading Disabilities; Handwriting Disabilities; Arithmetic Disabilities. *Behavioral Problems* Attention Deficits; Hyperactivity; Impulsivity; Verbal Aggression; Physical Aggression. *Conditions Treated* Schizophrenia; Depression; Suicide; Anorexia Nervosa.

Services Provided Individual Therapy; Group Therapy; Parent Involvement; Behavior Therapy; Family Therapy. *Professionals on Staff* Psychiatrists 2.4; Psychologists 1; Social Workers 2; Child Care Staff 26; Nurses 4. *Service Facilities Available (with number of rooms)* Self-Contained Rooms 3; Homebound Instruction 2. *Educational Professionals* Special Education Teachers 3; Career/Vocational Teachers 3; Paraprofessionals 2. *Curricula* Traditional Academic; Individualized; Basic Skills. *Educational Intervention Approaches* Progressive Discipline; Self-Control; Behavior Modification; Applied Behavior Analysis. *Degrees Awarded* Certificate of Attendance; Graduate Equivalency Diploma.

Comments This program is designed to treat psychotic youngsters from within our 31 county catchment area. Referrals should be screened through the local MHMR centers.

San Marcos Treatment Center of The Brown Schools

PO Box 768, San Marcos, TX 78666 (512) 396-8500
Year Established 1940
Contact Peggy Hawthorne, Admissions Dir

Facility Information *Placement* Private Residential Care; Psychiatric Hospital. *Number of Beds* 225. *Children/Adolescents Served* 225. *Sexes Served* Both. *Room and Board Fees (Approx)* $175-$240. *Sources of Funding* State Funds; Health Insurance; P.L. 94-142. Summer school available. *Teacher Certification Level* Elementary School; Junior High/Middle School; High School. *Special Certification Level* ED; LD.

Student/Patient Characteristics *Age Levels* 5-8; 9-11; 12-14; 15-17; 18-21; Over 21. *IQ Ranges* 71-85; 85-130; Above 130. *Exceptionalities Served* Autistic; Emotionally Disturbed; Learning Disabled; Mentally Handicapped; Communication Disordered. *Learning Problems* Memory Disabilities; Perceptual Disabilities; Thinking Disabilities; Oral Language Disabilities; Reading Disabilities; Handwriting Disabilities; Spelling Disabilities; Arithmetic Disabilities; Written Expression. *Behavioral Problems* Attention Deficits; Hyperactivity; Impulsivity; Self-Aggression; Verbal Aggression; Physical Aggression; Indirect Aggression; Passive Aggression. *Conditions Treated* Alcohol Abuse and/or Drug Abuse; Other Substance Abuse or Dependence; Early Infantile Autism; Schizophrenia; Aphasia; Convulsive Disorders; Phobias; Obsessions and Compulsions; Hysteria; Depression; Suicide; Asthma; Anorexia Nervosa; Inadequacy/Immaturity; Personality Problems; Socialized Aggressive Reaction; Unsocialized Aggressive Reaction.

Services Provided Individual Therapy; Group Therapy; Parent Involvement; Family Therapy; Filial Therapy; Drug Therapy; Art Therapy; Play Therapy; Psychodrama. *Professionals on Staff* Psychiatrists 5; Psychologists 11; Social Workers 10; Child Care Staff; Nurses 21; Art Therapist 1; Speech Therapists 4; Physical Therapist 1. *Service Facilities Available (with number of rooms)* Self-Contained Rooms 27. *Educational Professionals* Special Education Teachers 25; Paraprofessionals 3. *Curricula* Traditional Academic; Career/Vocational Education; Individualized; Basic Skills; Prevocational. *Degrees Awarded* High School Diploma; Graduate Equivalency Diploma.

Timberlawn Psychiatric Hospital

Box 11288, Dallas, TX 75223 (214) 381-7181
Year Established 1917
Contact Mark J Blotcky, Dir Child and Adolescent Serv
Facility Information *Placement* Special School; Private Psychiatric Hospital. *Number of Beds* 75. *Children/Adolescents Served* 75. *Sexes Served* Both. *Room and Board Fees (Approx)* $300. *Sources of Funding* Health Insurance. *Teacher Certification Level* Elementary School; Junior High/Middle School; High School.
Student/Patient Characteristics *Age Levels* 5-8; 9-11; 12-14; 15-17; 18-21; Over 21. *IQ Ranges* 71-85; 85-130; Above 130. *Exceptionalities Served* Autistic; Emotionally Disturbed; Learning Disabled; Mentally Handicapped; Communication Disordered; Visually Impaired/Blind; Other Health Impaired. *Learning Problems* Perceptual Disabilities; Thinking Disabilities; Oral Language Disabilities; Reading Disabilities; Handwriting Disabilities; Spelling Disabilities; Arithmetic Disabilities; Written Expression. *Behavioral Problems* Attention Deficits; Hyperactivity; Hypoactivity; Impulsivity; Self-Aggression; Verbal Aggression; Physical Aggression; Indirect Aggression; Passive Aggression; Withdrawal. *Conditions Treated* Alcohol Abuse and/or Drug Abuse; Other Substance Abuse or Dependence; Early Infantile Autism; Disintegrative Psychoses; Schizophrenia; Aphasia; Convulsive Disorders; Phobias; Obsessions and Compulsions; Hysteria; Depression; Suicide; Asthma; Anorexia Nervosa; Ulcerative Colitis; Inadequacy/Immaturity; Personality Problems; Socialized Aggressive Reaction; Unsocialized Aggressive Reaction.
Services Provided Individual Therapy; Group Therapy; Parent Involvement; Behavior Therapy; Family Therapy; Filial Therapy; Drug Therapy; Music Therapy; Reality Therapy; Play Therapy; Psychodrama; Milieu Therapy. *Professionals on Staff* Psychiatrists 25; Psychologists 8; Social Workers 8; Child Care Staff 40; Nurses 12. *Service Facilities Available (with number of rooms)* Self-Contained Rooms 7; Hospital School. *Educational Professionals* Regular School Teachers; Special Education Teachers. *Curricula* Traditional Academic; Individualized; Basic Skills; Prevocational. *Educational Intervention Approaches* Self-Control; Behavior Modification. *Degrees Awarded* High School Diploma.

University of Texas Medical Branch—Division of Pediatric Psychology—Department of Pediatrics

Galveston, TX 77550 (409) 761-2355
Contact Mary C Cerreto, Chief Psychologist
Facility Information *Placement* University Medical School Outpatient Department. *Sexes Served* Both. *Sources of Funding* State Funds; Health Insurance; Medicaid; P.L. 94-142.
Student/Patient Characteristics *Age Levels* 0-4; 5-8; 9-11; 12-14. *IQ Ranges* 0-25; 26-40; 41-55; 56-70; 71-85; 85-130; Above 130. *Exceptionalities Served* Autistic; Emotionally Disturbed; Learning

Disabled; Mentally Handicapped; Other Health Impaired; Physically Handicapped. *Learning Problems* Memory Disabilities; Perceptual Disabilities; Thinking Disabilities. *Behavioral Problems* Attention Deficits; Hyperactivity; Impulsivity; Self-Aggression; Verbal Aggression; Physical Aggression; Withdrawal. *Conditions Treated* Early Infantile Autism; Convulsive Disorders; Phobias; Obsessions and Compulsions; Hysteria; Depression; Suicide; Asthma; Inadequacy/Immaturity; Personality Problems; Socialized Aggressive Reaction; Unsocialized Aggressive Reaction.
Services Provided Individual Therapy; Parent Involvement; Behavior Therapy; Biofeedback; Family Therapy; Play Therapy. *Professionals on Staff* Psychologists 4.
Comments Housed within a university medical school Department of Pediatrics, the Division of Pediatric Psychology addresses the emotional concomitants of chronic childhood illness.

University of Texas Medical Branch—Inpatient Service—Division of Child and Adolescent Psychiatry

1014 Texas Ave, Galveston, TX 77550 (409) 761-2418
Contact Kay G Holt, Med Dir
Facility Information *Placement* Inpatient Service. *Number of Beds* 32. *Children/Adolescents Served* 32. *Sexes Served* Both. *Sources of Funding* State Funds; Health Insurance; Medicaid. Summer school available. *Teacher Certification Level* Elementary School; Junior High/Middle School; High School. *Special Certification Level* ED; LD; MR; Career/Vocational Education; Reading; Math.
Student/Patient Characteristics *Age Levels* 5-8; 9-11; 12-14; 15-17. *IQ Ranges* 41-55; 56-70; 71-85; 85-130; Above 130. *Exceptionalities Served* Autistic; Emotionally Disturbed; Learning Disabled; Mentally Handicapped; Communication Disordered; Hearing Impaired/Deaf; Other Health Impaired; Gifted. *Learning Problems* Memory Disabilities; Perceptual Disabilities; Thinking Disabilities; Oral Language Disabilities; Reading Disabilities; Handwriting Disabilities; Spelling Disabilities; Arithmetic Disabilities; Written Expression. *Behavioral Problems* Attention Deficits; Hyperactivity; Hypoactivity; Impulsivity; Self-Aggression; Verbal Aggression; Physical Aggression; Indirect Aggression; Passive Aggression; Withdrawal. *Conditions Treated* Alcohol Abuse and/or Drug Abuse; Other Substance Abuse or Dependence; Early Infantile Autism; Disintegrative Psychoses; Schizophrenia; Aphasia; Convulsive Disorders; Phobias; Obsessions and Compulsions; Hysteria; Depression; Suicide; Asthma; Anorexia Nervosa; Ulcerative Colitis; Inadequacy/Immaturity; Personality Problems; Socialized Aggressive Reaction; Unsocialized Aggressive Reaction.
Services Provided Individual Therapy; Group Therapy; Parent Involvement; Behavior Therapy; Cognitive Developmental Therapy; Biofeedback; Family Therapy; Filial Therapy; Drug Therapy; Art Therapy; Music Therapy; Reality Therapy; Play Therapy; Psychodrama. *Professionals on Staff* Psychiatrists 10; Psychologists 6; Counselors 6; Social Workers 3; Child Care Staff; Nurses; Speech Therapists 2. *Service Facilities Available (with number of rooms)* Consultative (ERT) 4; Resource Rooms 3; Transition Rooms 2; Self-Contained Rooms 2; Hospital School. *Educational Professionals* Special Education Teachers 6; Special Education Counselors 1; Educational Diagnosticians 3. *Curricula* Traditional Academic; Career/Vocational Education; Individualized; Basic Skills; Prevocational. *Educational Intervention Approaches* Engineered Classroom; Self-Control; Behavior Modification; Applied Behavior Analysis. *Degrees Awarded* Certificate of Attendance; High School Diploma.

West Texas Boys' Ranch

PO Box 3568, San Angelo, TX 76902 (915) 949-1936
Year Established 1947
Contact Guy Roberts, Supt

Facility Information *Placement* Boys' Ranch. *Number of Beds* 56. *Children/Adolescents Served* 56. *Sexes Served* Male. *Sources of Funding* Private Donations. Summer school available. *Special Certification Level* Reading.

Student/Patient Characteristics *Age Levels* 5-8; 9-11; 12-14; 15-17. *IQ Ranges* 85-130. *Exceptionalities Served* Learning Disabled. *Learning Problems* Reading Disabilities; Handwriting Disabilities; Spelling Disabilities; Arithmetic Disabilities; Written Expression. *Behavioral Problems* Attention Deficits; Hyperactivity; Impulsivity; Self-Aggression; Verbal Aggression; Physical Aggression; Indirect Aggression; Passive Aggression; Withdrawal.

Conditions Treated Depression; Suicide; Asthma; Inadequacy/Immaturity; Personality Problems; Socialized Aggressive Reaction; Unsocialized Aggressive Reaction.

Services Provided Individual Therapy; Group Therapy; Parent Involvement; Behavior Therapy; Biofeedback; Family Therapy; Reality Therapy; Play Therapy. *Professionals on Staff* Psychologists 2; Counselors 1; Social Workers 1; Child Care Staff 14; Outside Services Purchased on an As Needed Basis. *Educational Professionals* Special Education Teachers 3; Career/Vocational Teachers 1. *Curricula* Traditional Academic; Career/Vocational Education; Basic Skills; Prevocational. *Educational Intervention Approaches* Progressive Discipline; Behavior Modification. *Degrees Awarded* High School Diploma.

Utah

Children's Behavior Therapy Unit

668 S 1300 E, Salt Lake City, UT 84102 (801) 581-0194
Year Established 1967
Contact George W Frangia, Dir
Facility Information *Placement* Day Treatment Unit.
Children/Adolescents Served 76. *Sexes Served* Both. *Room and Board Fees (Approx)* $70. *Sources of Funding* State Funds; Health Insurance; Medicaid; P.L. 94-142; Parent Fees. Summer school available. *Teacher Certification Level* Elementary School. *Special Certification Level* ED.
Student/Patient Characteristics *Age Levels* 0-4; 5-8; 9-11; 12-14; 15-17. *IQ Ranges* 56-70; 71-85; 85-130. *Exceptionalities Served* Autistic; Emotionally Disturbed; Learning Disabled; Mentally Handicapped; Communication Disordered; Hearing Impaired/Deaf; Visually Impaired/Blind. *Learning Problems* Memory Disabilities; Perceptual Disabilities; Thinking Disabilities; Oral Language Disabilities; Reading Disabilities; Handwriting Disabilities; Spelling Disabilities; Arithmetic Disabilities; Written Expression. *Behavioral Problems* Attention Deficits; Hyperactivity; Hypoactivity; Impulsivity; Self-Aggression; Verbal Aggression; Physical Aggression; Indirect Aggression; Passive Aggression; Withdrawal. *Conditions Treated* Early Infantile Autism; Schizophrenia; Phobias; Obsessions and Compulsions; Depression; Inadequacy/Immaturity; Personality Problems; Socialized Aggressive Reaction; Unsocialized Aggressive Reaction.
Services Provided Individual Therapy; Group Therapy; Parent Involvement; Behavior Therapy; Family Therapy; Drug Therapy. *Professionals on Staff* Psychiatrists 2; Psychologists 4; Social Workers 1; Child Care Staff; Behavior Therapists 10. *Service Facilities Available (with number of rooms)* Self-Contained Rooms 7; Special School 7. *Educational Professionals* Special Education Teachers 3; Paraprofessionals 15. *Curricula* Traditional Academic; Individualized; Basic Skills. *Educational Intervention Approaches* Engineered Classroom; Progressive Discipline; Self-Control; Behavior Modification; Applied Behavior Analysis. *Degrees Awarded* Certificate of Attendance.
Comments The Children's Behavior Therapy Unit is a psychoeducational program serving preschool through elementary school aged children and their families. CBTU is an intensive, data-based behavioral program which operates on an extended school year schedule.

The Children's Center

1855 Medical Circle, Salt Lake City, UT 84112 (801) 582-5534
Year Established 1962
Contact Agnes M Plenk, Exec Dir
Facility Information *Placement* Private Residential Care; Private Day Care. *Number of Beds* 9. *Children/Adolescents Served* 9. *Sexes Served* Both. *Sources of Funding* State Funds; Medicaid. Summer school available.

Student/Patient Characteristics *Age Levels* 5-8. *IQ Ranges* Above 130. *Exceptionalities Served* Emotionally Disturbed; Learning Disabled. *Behavioral Problems* Hyperactivity; Impulsivity; Self-Aggression; Verbal Aggression; Physical Aggression; Passive Aggression; Withdrawal. *Conditions Treated* Depression; Socialized Aggressive Reaction; Unsocialized Aggressive Reaction.
Services Provided Individual Therapy; Group Therapy; Parent Involvement; Behavior Therapy; Cognitive Developmental Therapy; Play Therapy. *Professionals on Staff* Psychiatrists 1; Psychologists 1; Social Workers 1; Child Care Staff 6.

Hillside School Inc

683 E 4th N, Logan, UT 84321 (801) 752-8901
Year Established 1970
Contact Phyllis R Publicover, Corp Treasurer
Facility Information *Placement* Private Residential Care. *Number of Beds* 15. *Children/Adolescents Served* 15. *Sexes Served* Both. *Room and Board Fees (Approx)* $60. *Tuition Fees (Approx)* $21,600. *Sources of Funding* P.L. 94-142; CHAMPUS; Private Funds. Summer school available. *Teacher Certification Level* High School. *Special Certification Level* ED; LD; Secondary Education.
Student/Patient Characteristics *Age Levels* 15-17; 18-21. *IQ Ranges* 85-130. *Exceptionalities Served* Emotionally Disturbed; Learning Disabled. *Learning Problems* Memory Disabilities; Perceptual Disabilities; Thinking Disabilities; Reading Disabilities; Spelling Disabilities; Arithmetic Disabilities; Written Expression. *Behavioral Problems* Attention Deficits; Hyperactivity; Impulsivity; Verbal Aggression; Indirect Aggression; Passive Aggression; Withdrawal. *Conditions Treated* Schizophrenia; Phobias; Obsessions and Compulsions; Depression; Inadequacy/Immaturity; Personality Problems; Socialized Aggressive Reaction; Unsocialized Aggressive Reaction.
Services Provided Individual Therapy; Group Therapy; Parent Involvement; Behavior Therapy; Cognitive Developmental Therapy; Biofeedback; Family Therapy; Filial Therapy; Drug Therapy; Art Therapy; Music Therapy; Reality Therapy. *Professionals on Staff* Psychiatrists 1; Psychologists 2; Counselors 1; Child Care Staff 15; Nurses 1; Dietician 1. *Educational Professionals* Special Education Teachers 2. *Curricula* Traditional Academic; Career/Vocational Education; Individualized; Basic Skills; Prevocational; College. *Educational Intervention Approaches* Engineered Classroom; Self-Control; Behavior Modification; Applied Behavior Analysis. *Degrees Awarded* Certificate of Attendance; High School Diploma; Graduate Equivalency Diploma.

Primary Children's Medical Center—Department of Child Psychiatry

320 12th Ave, Salt Lake City, UT 84103 (801) 521-1447
Year Established 1965
Contact Thomas A Halversen, Acting Chair

Facility Information *Placement* Private Residential Care; Children's Medical Center. *Number of Beds* 49. *Children/Adolescents Served* 49 (inpatient and residential); 200 (outpatient). *Sexes Served* Both. *Room and Board Fees (Approx)* $279 (inpatient); $85 (residential). *Sources of Funding* State Funds; Health Insurance; Medicaid; P.L. 94-142; Hospital Charity. Summer school available. *Teacher Certification Level* Elementary School; Junior High/Middle School. *Special Certification Level* ED; LD; Reading; Math.

Student/Patient Characteristics *Age Levels* 0-4; 5-8; 9-11; 12-14; 15-17. *IQ Ranges* 71-85; 85-130; Above 130. *Exceptionalities Served* Emotionally Disturbed; Learning Disabled; Mentally Handicapped; Communication Disordered. *Learning Problems* Memory Disabilities; Perceptual Disabilities; Thinking Disabilities; Reading Disabilities; Spelling Disabilities; Arithmetic Disabilities. *Behavioral Problems* Attention Deficits; Hyperactivity; Hypoactivity; Impulsivity; Self-Aggression; Verbal Aggression; Physical Aggression; Indirect Aggression; Passive Aggression; Withdrawal. *Conditions Treated* Disintegrative Psychoses; Schizophrenia; Phobias; Obsessions and Compulsions; Hysteria; Depression; Suicide; Anorexia Nervosa; Ulcerative Colitis; Inadequacy/Immaturity; Personality Problems; Socialized Aggressive Reaction; Unsocialized Aggressive Reaction.

Services Provided Individual Therapy; Group Therapy; Parent Involvement; Behavior Therapy; Family Therapy; Drug Therapy; Reality Therapy; Play Therapy. *Professionals on Staff* Psychiatrists 5; Psychologists 7; Social Workers 21; Child Care Staff 31; Nurses 23. *Service Facilities Available (with number of rooms)* Self-Contained Rooms 3; Hospital School 4; On-Campus Residential School 1. *Educational Professionals* Special Education Teachers 4; Paraprofessionals 4. *Curricula* Traditional Academic; Individualized; Basic Skills; Prevocational. *Educational Intervention Approaches* Behavior Modification; Applied Behavior Analysis.

Comments The department provides comprehensive treatment services for emotionally disturbed, behaviorally disordered, and learning disabled children and adolescents. Inpatient, outpatient, residential, and consultation services are offered by a large multidisciplinary staff. The program is approved by the Joint Commission on Accreditation of Hospitals.

Provo Canyon School

PO Box 1441, 4501 N University Ave, Provo, UT 84603
(801) 227-2000
Year Established 1971
Contact Eugene Thorne, Exec Dir

Facility Information *Placement* Private Residential Care. *Number of Beds* 220. *Children/Adolescents Served* 220. *Sexes Served* Male. *Tuition Fees (Approx)* $28,000. *Sources of Funding* State Funds; Health Insurance; P.L. 94-142. Summer school available. *Teacher Certification Level* Junior High/Middle School; High School. *Special Certification Level* ED; LD; Reading; Math.

Student/Patient Characteristics *Age Levels* 12-14; 15-17. *IQ Ranges* 85-130; Above 130. *Exceptionalities Served* Emotionally Disturbed; Learning Disabled; Behaviorally Disturbed. *Learning Problems* Perceptual Disabilities; Reading Disabilities; Handwriting Disabilities; Spelling Disabilities; Arithmetic Disabilities; Written Expression. *Behavioral Problems* Attention Deficits; Hyperactivity; Impulsivity; Verbal Aggression; Indirect Aggression; Passive Aggression; Withdrawal. *Conditions Treated* Phobias;

Obsessions and Compulsions; Depression; Inadequacy/Immaturity; Personality Problems; Socialized Aggressive Reaction; Unsocialized Aggressive Reaction.

Services Provided Individual Therapy; Parent Involvement; Behavior Therapy; Cognitive Developmental Therapy; Family Therapy; Reality Therapy. *Professionals on Staff* Psychiatrists 1; Psychologists 4; Counselors 1; Social Workers 5; Child Care Staff 35; Nurses 1; Marriage and Family Therapists 2. *Service Facilities Available (with number of rooms)* Resource Rooms; Self-Contained Rooms; On-Campus Residential School. *Educational Professionals* Regular School Teachers 25; Special Education Teachers 2; Paraprofessionals 3. *Curricula* Traditional Academic; Career/Vocational Education; Individualized; Basic Skills. *Educational Intervention Approaches* Precision Teaching; Progressive Discipline; Self-Control; Behavior Modification. *Degrees Awarded* High School Diploma; Special Education.

Comments Provo Canyon School is a residential school for boys ages 11-17, whose education is enhanced by a therapeutic environment.

Utah Boys' Ranch—Children and Youth Services Inc

PO Box 15888, 3685 W 6200 S, Salt Lake City, UT 84115
(801) 969-3252
Year Established 1964
Contact Richard C Forsyth, Exec Dir

Facility Information *Placement* Private Residential Care. *Number of Beds* 50. *Children/Adolescents Served* 50. *Sexes Served* Male. *Room and Board Fees (Approx)* $42. *Tuition Fees (Approx)* $15,330. *Sources of Funding* State Funds; Contributions. Summer school available. *Teacher Certification Level* Junior High/Middle School; High School. *Special Certification Level* ED; LD; Reading; Math.

Student/Patient Characteristics *Age Levels* 12-14; 15-17. *IQ Ranges* 71-85; 85-130; Above 130. *Exceptionalities Served* Emotionally Disturbed; Learning Disabled; Gifted. *Learning Problems* Thinking Disabilities; Reading Disabilities; Handwriting Disabilities; Spelling Disabilities; Arithmetic Disabilities; Written Expression. *Behavioral Problems* Attention Deficits; Hyperactivity; Impulsivity; Self-Aggression; Verbal Aggression; Physical Aggression; Passive Aggression. *Conditions Treated* Alcohol Abuse and/or Drug Abuse; Other Substance Abuse or Dependence; Obsessions and Compulsions; Depression; Suicide; Personality Problems; Socialized Aggressive Reaction; Unsocialized Aggressive Reaction.

Services Provided Individual Therapy; Group Therapy; Parent Involvement; Behavior Therapy; Cognitive Developmental Therapy; Family Therapy; Drug Therapy; Reality Therapy; Play Therapy. *Professionals on Staff* Psychiatrists 1; Psychologists 1; Counselors 1; Social Workers 2; Nurses. *Service Facilities Available (with number of rooms)* Itinerants 1; Resource Rooms; Self-Contained Rooms 2; On-Campus Residential School 1. *Educational Professionals* Special Education Teachers 3; Paraprofessionals 2. *Curricula* Individualized; Basic Skills. *Educational Intervention Approaches* Self-Control; Behavior Modification; Creative Conditioning. *Degrees Awarded* High School Diploma.

Utah State Division of Youth Corrections—Region 1 Observation and Assessment Center

645 AVC Ln, Ogden, UT 84404 (801) 621-0132
Year Established 1980
Contact Seranor T deJesus, Prog Dir

Facility Information *Placement* 90 Day Lock Up Facility for Juvenile Delinquents.

Vermont

The Baird Center for Children and Families Inc

1110 Pine St, Burlington, VT 05401 (802) 863-1326
Year Established 1865
Contact Carol Ann Haigis, Business Mgr
Facility Information *Placement* Special School; Private Residential Care. *Number of Beds* 10. *Children/Adolescents Served* 52.
Sexes Served Both. *Sources of Funding* State Funds; Medicaid;
P.L. 94-142; Private Endowment Funds; United Way. Summer
school available. *Teacher Certification Level* Elementary School.
Special Certification Level ED; LD; MR.
Student/Patient Characteristics *Age Levels* 5-8; 9-11; 12-14. *IQ
Ranges* 56-70; 71-85; 85-130. *Exceptionalities Served* Emotionally
Disturbed. *Behavioral Problems* Attention Deficits; Hyperactivity; Impulsivity; Self-Aggression; Verbal Aggression; Physical
Aggression; Indirect Aggression; Passive Aggression; Withdrawal.
Conditions Treated Disintegrative Psychoses; Schizophrenia;
Phobias; Obsessions and Compulsions; Depression; Suicide;
Inadequacy/Immaturity; Personality Problems; Socialized Aggressive Reaction; Unsocialized Aggressive Reaction.
Services Provided Individual Therapy; Group Therapy; Parent
Involvement; Behavior Therapy; Family Therapy; Filial Therapy;
Drug Therapy; Play Therapy. *Professionals on Staff* Psychiatrists
1; Psychologists 1; Social Workers 4.5; Child Care Staff 8;
Nurses 1; Nurse's Aide 1; Speech Therapist 1; Pediatrician 1.
Service Facilities Available (with number of rooms) Special School
2. *Educational Professionals* Special Education Teachers 4; Consulting Teachers 2. *Curricula* Traditional Academic; Individualized; Basic Skills. *Educational Intervention Approaches* Behavior
Modification; Applied Behavior Analysis; Direct Instruction.

Brattleboro Retreat

75 Linden St, Brattleboro, VT 05301 (802) 257-7785
Year Established 1834
Contact Glenna Annis, Admissions Dir
Facility Information *Placement* Special School; Private Residential Care; Special Program; Inpatient Psychiatric Retreat.
Number of Beds 54. *Children/Adolescents Served* 54. *Sexes Served*
Both. *Room and Board Fees (Approx)* $357 (inpatient); $160
(residential). *Tuition Fees (Approx)* $9,065. *Sources of Funding*
Health Insurance; P.L. 94-142. Summer school available. *Teacher
Certification Level* Junior High/Middle School; High School.
Special Certification Level ED; LD; Career/Vocational Education;
Reading; Math Science; Social Studies.
Student/Patient Characteristics *Age Levels* 12-14; 15-17; 18-21.
IQ Ranges 71-85; 85-130; Above 130. *Exceptionalities Served*
Autistic; Emotionally Disturbed; Learning Disabled; Communication Disordered; Visually Impaired/Blind; Other Health Impaired; Physically Handicapped; Gifted. *Learning Problems*
Memory Disabilities; Perceptual Disabilities; Thinking Disabilities; Reading Disabilities; Handwriting Disabilities; Spelling
Disabilities; Arithmetic Disabilities; Written Expression.
Behavioral Problems Attention Deficits; Hyperactivity; Hypoactivity; Impulsivity; Self-Aggression; Verbal Aggression; Physical
Aggression; Indirect Aggression; Passive Aggression; Withdrawal.
Conditions Treated Alcohol Abuse and/or Drug Abuse; Other
Substance Abuse or Dependence; Disintegrative Psychoses;
Schizophrenia; Aphasia; Convulsive Disorders; Phobias; Obsessions and Compulsions; Hysteria; Depression; Suicide; Asthma;
Anorexia Nervosa; Ulcerative Colitis; Inadequacy/Immaturity;
Personality Problems; Socialized Aggressive Reaction; Unsocialized Aggressive Reaction.
Services Provided Individual Therapy; Group Therapy; Parent
Involvement; Behavior Therapy; Cognitive Developmental Therapy; Biofeedback; Family Therapy; Filial Therapy; Drug Therapy; Art Therapy; Music Therapy; Reality Therapy; Play Therapy; Psychodrama; Dance and Movement Therapy. *Professionals
on Staff* Psychiatrists 4; Psychologists 2; Counselors 4; Social
Workers 4; Child Care Staff 40; Nurses 18; Activities and Support Personnel 10. *Service Facilities Available (with number of
rooms)* Self-Contained Rooms 8; Hospital School 12. *Educational
Professionals* Regular School Teachers 4; Special Education
Teachers 5; Career/Vocational Teachers 2; Paraprofessionals 1.
Curricula Traditional Academic; Career/Vocational Education;
Individualized; Basic Skills; Prevocational; Remedial.
Educational Intervention Approaches Progressive Discipline; Behavior Modification; Applied Behavior Analysis; Diagnostic Prescriptive Teaching; Interdisciplinary. *Degrees Awarded* Certificate
of Attendance; Graduate Equivalency Diploma.
Comments There are 3 separate programs for adolescents aged
12-19. It is an inpatient psychiatric program, an inpatient alcohol and drug treatment program, and a residential transitional
program.

The Clearing

Box 1600, RD 1, Marshfield, VT 05658 (802) 426-3810
Year Established 1978
Contact Robert Belenky, Clinical Dir
Facility Information *Placement* Short Term Residential Private
Counseling Center and Retreat. *Number of Beds* 5.
Children/Adolescents Served 150 (per annum). *Sexes Served* Both.
Room and Board Fees (Approx) $50. *Sources of Funding* HEW;
Health Insurance; Medicaid; P.L. 94-142; Out of Pocket. Summer school available.
Student/Patient Characteristics *Age Levels* 12-14; 15-17. *IQ
Ranges* 71-85; 85-130; Above 130. *Exceptionalities Served* Emotionally Disturbed; Learning Disabled; Mentally Handicapped;
Communication Disordered; Hearing Impaired/Deaf; Visually
Impaired/Blind; Other Health Impaired; Physically Handicapped;
Gifted. *Behavioral Problems* Attention Deficits; Hyperactivity;
Hypoactivity; Impulsivity; Self-Aggression; Verbal Aggression;
Physical Aggression; Indirect Aggression; Passive Aggression;
Withdrawal. *Conditions Treated* Phobias; Obsessions and Com-

pulsions; Hysteria; Depression; Suicide; Inadequacy/Immaturity; Personality Problems; Socialized Aggressive Reaction; Unsocialized Aggressive Reaction.

Services Provided Individual Therapy; Group Therapy; Parent Involvement; Cognitive Developmental Therapy; Family Therapy; Filial Therapy; Art Therapy; Play Therapy. *Professionals on Staff* Psychologists 1; Counselors 2. *Educational Intervention Approaches* Progressive Discipline; Self-Control.

Comments This is a counseling center for young people who have been expelled or suspended from school. The aim is to provide a moratorium in a natural setting as well as peer and professional help.

Franklin Grand Isle Mental Health Services Inc

8 Ferris St, Saint Albans, VT 05478 (802) 524-6554
Year Established 1958
Contact Frank MacNeil, Exec Dir

Facility Information *Placement* Community Mental Health Agency. *Children/Adolescents Served* 40 (per month). *Sexes Served* Both. *Sources of Funding* State Funds; HEW; Health Insurance; Medicaid; First Party Payor; Local Funds. *Special Certification Level* ED; MR.

Student/Patient Characteristics *Age Levels* 0-4; 5-8; 9-11; 12-14; 15-17; 18-21; Over 21. *IQ Ranges* 0-25; 26-40; 41-55; 56-70; 71-85; 85-130; Above 130. *Exceptionalities Served* Autistic; Emotionally Disturbed; Learning Disabled; Mentally Handicapped; Communication Disordered. *Learning Problems* Memory Disabilities; Perceptual Disabilities; Thinking Disabilities; Oral Language Disabilities; Reading Disabilities; Handwriting Disabilities; Spelling Disabilities; Arithmetic Disabilities; Written Expression. *Behavioral Problems* Attention Deficits; Hyperactivity; Impulsivity; Self-Aggression; Verbal Aggression; Physical Aggression; Indirect Aggression; Passive Aggression; Withdrawal. *Conditions Treated* Alcohol Abuse and/or Drug Abuse; Other Substance Abuse or Dependence; Early Infantile Autism; Disintegrative Psychoses; Schizophrenia; Aphasia; Convulsive Disorders; Phobias; Obsessions and Compulsions; Hysteria; Depression; Suicide; Anorexia Nervosa; Inadequacy/Immaturity; Personality Problems; Socialized Aggressive Reaction; Unsocialized Aggressive Reaction.

Services Provided Individual Therapy; Group Therapy; Parent Involvement; Behavior Therapy; Family Therapy; Drug Therapy; Reality Therapy; Play Therapy. *Professionals on Staff* Psychiatrists 3; Psychologists 5; Counselors 6; Social Workers 10; Nurses 4. *Educational Professionals* Special Education Teachers 5; Career/Vocational Teachers 2; Paraprofessionals 20; Social Workers 5. *Curricula* Career/Vocational Education; Basic Skills; Prevocational. *Educational Intervention Approaches* Engineered Classroom; Precision Teaching; Progressive Discipline; Self-Control; Behavior Modification; Applied Behavior Analysis; Creative Conditioning.

Comments This is a comprehensive mental health/mental retardation program.

Green Meadows School

PO Box 109, Stowe Hill Rd, Wilmington, VT 05363
(802) 464-8646
Year Established 1976
Contact Steven M Cohen, Dir

Facility Information *Placement* Private Residential Care. *Number of Beds* 34. *Children/Adolescents Served* 34. *Sexes Served* Both. *Room and Board Fees (Approx)* $28. *Tuition Fees (Approx)* $26,017. *Sources of Funding* State Funds. Summer school available. *Special Certification Level* MR.

Student/Patient Characteristics *Age Levels* 15-17; 18-21; Over 21. *IQ Ranges* 41-55; 56-70; 71-85. *Exceptionalities Served* Autistic; Mentally Handicapped. *Learning Problems* Memory Disabilities;

Perceptual Disabilities; Thinking Disabilities; Oral Language Disabilities; Reading Disabilities; Handwriting Disabilities; Spelling Disabilities; Arithmetic Disabilities; Written Expression. *Behavioral Problems* Hyperactivity; Impulsivity; Self-Aggression; Verbal Aggression; Physical Aggression; Indirect Aggression; Passive Aggression; Withdrawal. *Conditions Treated* Early Infantile Autism; Unsocialized Aggressive Reaction.

Services Provided Behavior Therapy; Cognitive Developmental Therapy; Reality Therapy. *Professionals on Staff* Psychiatrists 1; Social Workers 1; Child Care Staff 25; Nurses 1. *Service Facilities Available (with number of rooms)* Consultative (ERT) 1; Resource Rooms 3; On-Campus Residential School 7. *Educational Professionals* Special Education Teachers 4; Paraprofessionals 8. *Curricula* Individualized; Basic Skills; Work Activity Center. *Educational Intervention Approaches* Progressive Discipline; Behavior Modification; Creative Conditioning.

Spring Lake Ranch

Cuttingsville, VT 05738 (802) 492-3322
Year Established 1933
Contact Michael Wells, Dir

Facility Information *Placement* Private Residential Care. *Number of Beds* 10. *Children/Adolescents Served* 10. *Sexes Served* Both. *Room and Board Fees (Approx)* $65. *Tuition Fees (Approx)* $24,000.

Student/Patient Characteristics *Age Levels* 18-21; Over 21. *IQ Ranges* 85-130; Above 130. *Exceptionalities Served* Emotionally Disturbed; Learning Disabled. *Learning Problems* Thinking Disabilities; Reading Disabilities. *Behavioral Problems* Attention Deficits; Hyperactivity; Hypoactivity; Impulsivity. *Conditions Treated* Alcohol Abuse and/or Drug Abuse; Other Substance Abuse or Dependence; Disintegrative Psychoses; Schizophrenia; Phobias; Obsessions and Compulsions; Hysteria; Depression; Anorexia Nervosa; Inadequacy/Immaturity; Personality Problems.

Services Provided Drug Therapy; Reality Therapy; Milieu Therapy. *Professionals on Staff* Psychiatrists 1; Counselors 15.

Winston L Prouty Center

2 Oak St, Brattleboro, VT 05301 (802) 257-7852
Year Established 15
Contact Arthur Schubert, Exec Dir

Facility Information *Placement* Preschool Respite Care Treatment Center. *Number of Beds* 10. *Children/Adolescents Served* 70. *Sexes Served* Both. *Room and Board Fees (Approx)* $84. *Sources of Funding* State Funds; P.L. 94-142; Foundations; Fund Drives. *Special Certification Level* Physical Therapy; Speech Therapy; Occupational Therapy; Special Education.

Student/Patient Characteristics *Age Levels* 0-4. *IQ Ranges* 0-25; 26-40; 41-55; 56-70; 71-85; 85-130. *Exceptionalities Served* Autistic; Emotionally Disturbed; Mentally Handicapped; Communication Disordered; Hearing Impaired/Deaf; Visually Impaired/Blind; Other Health Impaired; Physically Handicapped. *Learning Problems* Memory Disabilities; Perceptual Disabilities; Thinking Disabilities; Oral Language Disabilities. *Behavioral Problems* Attention Deficits; Hyperactivity; Hypoactivity; Impulsivity; Self-Aggression; Verbal Aggression; Physical Aggression. *Conditions Treated* Early Infantile Autism; Schizophrenia; Aphasia; Convulsive Disorders; Obsessions and Compulsions.

Services Provided Individual Therapy; Group Therapy; Parent Involvement; Behavior Therapy; Cognitive Developmental Therapy; Family Therapy. *Service Facilities Available (with number of rooms)* Resource Rooms; Self-Contained Rooms. *Educational Professionals* Special Education Teachers 4; Physical Therapists; Occupational Therapists; Speech Therapists. *Curricula* Individualized. *Educational Intervention Approaches* Engineered Classroom; Precision Teaching; Self-Control; Behavior Modification.

Virginia

Alexandria Head Start

1501 Cameron St, Alexandria, VA 22314 (703) 836-5774
Year Established 1965
Contact Mary Peterson, Dir
Facility Information *Placement* Public Day Care.
Children/Adolescents Served 100. *Sexes Served* Both. *Sources of Funding* HEW.
Student/Patient Characteristics *Age Levels* 0-4; 5-8. *IQ Ranges* 71-85; 85-130. *Exceptionalities Served* Emotionally Disturbed; Learning Disabled; Communication Disordered; Other Health Impaired. *Learning Problems* Perceptual Disabilities; Oral Language Disabilities. *Behavioral Problems* Attention Deficits; Hyperactivity; Self-Aggression; Verbal Aggression; Withdrawal.
Services Provided Parent Involvement; Behavior Therapy.
Professionals on Staff Psychologists 2; Social Workers 1; Nurses 1.

Charter Westbrook Hospital

1500 Westbrook Ave, Richmond, VA 23227 (804) 266-9671
Year Established 1908
Contact Joanne Michael, Community Relations Coord
Facility Information *Placement* Private Residential Care. *Number of Beds* 96. *Children/Adolescents Served* 96. *Sexes Served* Both. *Sources of Funding* Health Insurance; Medicare; P.L. 94-142. Summer school available. *Teacher Certification Level* Elementary School; Junior High/Middle School; High School. *Special Certification Level* ED; LD.
Student/Patient Characteristics *Age Levels* 9-11; 12-14; 15-17; 18-21; Over 21. *IQ Ranges* 85-130. *Exceptionalities Served* Emotionally Disturbed; Learning Disabled; Gifted. *Behavioral Problems* Attention Deficits; Hyperactivity; Hypoactivity; Impulsivity; Self-Aggression; Verbal Aggression; Physical Aggression; Indirect Aggression; Passive Aggression; Withdrawal. *Conditions Treated* Alcohol Abuse and/or Drug Abuse; Other Substance Abuse or Dependence; Disintegrative Psychoses; Schizophrenia; Convulsive Disorders; Phobias; Obsessions and Compulsions; Hysteria; Depression; Suicide; Anorexia Nervosa; Inadequacy/Immaturity; Personality Problems; Socialized Aggressive Reaction; Unsocialized Aggressive Reaction.
Services Provided Individual Therapy; Group Therapy; Parent Involvement; Behavior Therapy; Cognitive Developmental Therapy; Biofeedback; Family Therapy; Drug Therapy; Art Therapy; Music Therapy; Reality Therapy; Play Therapy; Psychodrama; Occupational Therapy; Activities Therapy. *Professionals on Staff* Psychiatrists 16; Psychologists 6; Social Workers 6; Nurses 100. *Service Facilities Available (with number of rooms)* Self-Contained Rooms 3; Hospital School 8. *Educational Professionals* Regular School Teachers 3; Special Education Teachers 3; Educational Services Director 1. *Curricula* Tradi-

tional Academic; Individualized; Basic Skills. *Educational Intervention Approaches* Precision Teaching; Behavior Modification. *Degrees Awarded* High School Diploma.

DeJarnette Center

PO Box 2309, Staunton, VA 24401 (703) 885-9068
Year Established 1974
Contact Robert Garber, Admissions Coord
Facility Information *Placement* Public Residential Care; Psychiatric Hospital. *Number of Beds* 60. *Children/Adolescents Served* 60. *Sexes Served* Both. *Room and Board Fees (Approx)* Sliding Scale. *Sources of Funding* State Funds; Health Insurance; P.L. 94-142; CHAMPUS. Summer school available. *Teacher Certification Level* Elementary School; High School. *Special Certification Level* ED; LD; MR.
Student/Patient Characteristics *Age Levels* 0-4; 5-8; 9-11; 12-14; 15-17. *IQ Ranges* 41-55; 56-70; 71-85; 85-130; Above 130. *Exceptionalities Served* Autistic; Emotionally Disturbed; Learning Disabled; Communication Disordered. *Learning Problems* Memory Disabilities; Perceptual Disabilities; Thinking Disabilities; Oral Language Disabilities; Reading Disabilities; Handwriting Disabilities; Spelling Disabilities; Arithmetic Disabilities; Written Expression. *Behavioral Problems* Attention Deficits; Hyperactivity; Hypoactivity; Impulsivity; Self-Aggression; Verbal Aggression; Physical Aggression; Indirect Aggression; Passive Aggression; Withdrawal. *Conditions Treated* Early Infantile Autism; Disintegrative Psychoses; Schizophrenia; Phobias; Obsessions and Compulsions; Hysteria; Depression; Suicide; Anorexia Nervosa; Personality Problems; Socialized Aggressive Reaction; Unsocialized Aggressive Reaction.
Services Provided Individual Therapy; Group Therapy; Parent Involvement; Behavior Therapy; Cognitive Developmental Therapy; Family Therapy; Drug Therapy; Art Therapy; Reality Therapy; Play Therapy. *Professionals on Staff* Psychiatrists 2; Psychologists 3; Counselors 1; Social Workers 5; Child Care Staff 63; Nurses 9; Recreational Therapist 1. *Service Facilities Available (with number of rooms)* Resource Rooms 8; Self-Contained Rooms 3. *Educational Professionals* Regular School Teachers 3; Special Education Teachers 8; Speech Pathologists 2; Director of Education 1; Assistant Director of Education 1. *Curricula* Traditional Academic; Career/Vocational Education; Individualized; Basic Skills; Prevocational; Computer Literacy. *Educational Intervention Approaches* Behavior Modification; Applied Behavior Analysis; Creative Conditioning; Level System.
Comments DeJarnette Center is a 60-bed comprehensive child and adolescent psychiatric facility, licensed and operated by the Commonwealth of Virginia, Department of Mental Health and Mental Retardation. The mission of the center is to provide specialized, intensive, diagnostic, evaluation, and treatment services to children who live in Virginia between the ages of 2 and 18 years.

Department of Corrections—Hanover Learning Center

Hanover, VA 23069 (804) 798-9278
Year Established 1898
Contact James H Ball Jr, Supt
Facility Information *Placement* Correctional Facility. *Number of Beds* 110. *Sexes Served* Male. *Sources of Funding* State Funds. *Teacher Certification Level* High School. *Special Certification Level* ED; LD; MR.
Student/Patient Characteristics *Age Levels* 15-17. *IQ Ranges* 56-70; 71-85; 85-130. *Exceptionalities Served* Emotionally Disturbed; Learning Disabled; Mentally Handicapped. *Learning Problems* Memory Disabilities; Perceptual Disabilities; Thinking Disabilities; Oral Language Disabilities; Reading Disabilities; Handwriting Disabilities; Spelling Disabilities; Arithmetic Disabilities; Written Expression. *Behavioral Problems* Attention Deficits; Hyperactivity; Hypoactivity; Impulsivity; Self-Aggression; Verbal Aggression; Physical Aggression; Indirect Aggression; Passive Aggression; Withdrawal.
Services Provided Behavior Therapy. *Professionals on Staff* Psychiatrists 1; Psychologists 2; Counselors 9; Child Care Staff 70; Nurses 5.

Dominion Hospital—The Dominion School

2960 Sleepy Hollow Rd, Falls Church, VA 22044 (703) 536-2000
Year Established 1971
Contact Donald E Annis, Exec Dir; Debra Pell, Act Dir
Facility Information *Placement* Inpatient Psychiatric Hospitalization. *Number of Beds* 50. *Children/Adolescents Served* 50. *Sexes Served* Both. *Room and Board Fees (Approx)* $375. *Sources of Funding* Health Insurance; P.L. 94-142. Summer school available. *Teacher Certification Level* Junior High/Middle School; High School. *Special Certification Level* ED; LD.
Student/Patient Characteristics *Age Levels* 12-14; 15-17. *IQ Ranges* 85-130; Above 130. *Exceptionalities Served* Emotionally Disturbed; Learning Disabled. *Learning Problems* Memory Disabilities; Perceptual Disabilities; Thinking Disabilities; Oral Language Disabilities; Reading Disabilities; Handwriting Disabilities; Spelling Disabilities; Arithmetic Disabilities; Written Expression. *Behavioral Problems* Attention Deficits; Hyperactivity; Hypoactivity; Impulsivity; Self-Aggression; Verbal Aggression; Physical Aggression; Indirect Aggression; Passive Aggression; Withdrawal. *Conditions Treated* Alcohol Abuse and/or Drug Abuse; Other Substance Abuse or Dependence; Disintegrative Psychoses; Schizophrenia; Convulsive Disorders; Phobias; Obsessions and Compulsions; Hysteria; Depression; Suicide; Anorexia Nervosa; Inadequacy/Immaturity; Personality Problems; Socialized Aggressive Reaction; Unsocialized Aggressive Reaction.
Services Provided Individual Therapy; Group Therapy; Parent Involvement; Behavior Therapy; Cognitive Developmental Therapy; Family Therapy; Filial Therapy; Drug Therapy; Art Therapy; Reality Therapy. *Professionals on Staff* Psychiatrists 25; Psychologists 6; Social Workers 6; Nurses 29.5. *Service Facilities Available (with number of rooms)* Resource Rooms 2; Self-Contained Rooms 1. *Educational Professionals* Special Education Teachers 3; Diagnostic Prescriptive Specialists 2; Education Program Director 1. *Curricula* Traditional Academic; Individualized; Basic Skills. *Educational Intervention Approaches* Precision Teaching; Progressive Discipline; Self-Control.

Comments The Dominion School offers intensive, psychoeducational services for emotionally disturbed adolescents, within a comprehensive disciplinary inpatient treatment program.

Eastern Shore Mental Health Center

PO Box 434, Nassawadox, VA 23413 (804) 442-7707
Year Established 1960
Contact Michael D Johnson, Dir
Facility Information *Placement* Mental Health Center. *Sexes Served* Both. *Sources of Funding* Health Insurance; Medicaid; Medicare; Private Pay; Sliding Scale.

Student/Patient Characteristics *Age Levels* 5-8; 9-11; 12-14; 15-17; 18-21; Over 21. *IQ Ranges* 71-85; 85-130; Above 130. *Exceptionalities Served* Learning Disabled. *Behavioral Problems* Attention Deficits; Hyperactivity; Hypoactivity; Impulsivity; Self-Aggression; Verbal Aggression; Physical Aggression; Indirect Aggression; Passive Aggression; Withdrawal. *Conditions Treated* Disintegrative Psychoses; Schizophrenia; Phobias; Obsessions and Compulsions; Hysteria; Depression; Suicide; Asthma; Anorexia Nervosa; Ulcerative Colitis; Inadequacy/Immaturity; Personality Problems; Socialized Aggressive Reaction; Unsocialized Aggressive Reaction.
Services Provided Individual Therapy; Parent Involvement; Behavior Therapy; Cognitive Developmental Therapy; Family Therapy; Filial Therapy; Drug Therapy; Reality Therapy; Play Therapy. *Professionals on Staff* Psychiatrists 1.5; Psychologists 3; Social Workers 4; Nurses 1.

Grafton School

PO Box 112, Berryville, VA 22611 (703) 955-2400
Year Established 1958
Contact Tammy Miller Tucker, Admissions
Facility Information *Placement* Special School; Private Residential Care. *Number of Beds* 110. *Children/Adolescents Served* 135. *Sexes Served* Both. *Sources of Funding* State Funds. *Special Certification Level* ED; LD; MR.
Student/Patient Characteristics *Age Levels* 5-8; 9-11; 12-14; 15-17. *IQ Ranges* 41-55; 56-70; 71-85; 85-130. *Exceptionalities Served* Autistic; Emotionally Disturbed; Learning Disabled; Mentally Handicapped; Communication Disordered; Hearing Impaired/Deaf. *Learning Problems* Memory Disabilities; Thinking Disabilities; Oral Language Disabilities; Reading Disabilities; Handwriting Disabilities; Spelling Disabilities; Arithmetic Disabilities; Written Expression. *Behavioral Problems* Attention Deficits; Hyperactivity; Impulsivity; Self-Aggression; Verbal Aggression; Physical Aggression. *Conditions Treated* Early Infantile Autism.
Services Provided Individual Therapy; Group Therapy; Parent Involvement. *Professionals on Staff* Psychologists 2; Counselors 3; Social Workers 2; Child Care Staff 45; Nurses 2. *Service Facilities Available (with number of rooms)* Resource Rooms; On-Campus Residential School. *Educational Professionals* Special Education Teachers. *Curricula* Career/Vocational Education; Individualized; Basic Skills; Prevocational. *Educational Intervention Approaches* Precision Teaching; Behavior Modification.

Grafton School—Autism Program

Box 112, Berryville, VA 22611 (703) 955-2400
Year Established 1958
Contact Charles Perso, Prog Serv Dir
Facility Information *Placement* Special School; Private Residential Care. *Number of Beds* 30. *Children/Adolescents Served* 35. *Sexes Served* Both. *Sources of Funding* P.L. 94-142. Summer school available. *Teacher Certification Level* Elementary School; Junior High/Middle School. *Special Certification Level* ED; LD; MR.
Student/Patient Characteristics *Age Levels* 0-4; 5-8; 9-11; 12-14; 15-17. *IQ Ranges* 26-40; 41-55; 56-70; 71-85. *Exceptionalities Served* Autistic; Emotionally Disturbed; Mentally Handicapped; Communication Disordered; Hearing Impaired/Deaf. *Learning Problems* Memory Disabilities; Perceptual Disabilities; Thinking Disabilities; Oral Language Disabilities; Reading Disabilities; Handwriting Disabilities; Arithmetic Disabilities; Written Expression. *Behavioral Problems* Attention Deficits; Hyperactivity; Impulsivity; Self-Aggression; Physical Aggression; Withdrawal. *Conditions Treated* Early Infantile Autism; Aphasia; Convulsive Disorders.
Services Provided Parent Involvement; Behavior Therapy; Cognitive Developmental Therapy; Drug Therapy; Music Therapy; Speech Therapy; Occupational Therapy. *Professionals on Staff* Psychologists 1; Social Workers 3; Child Care Staff 36. *Service Facilities Available (with number of rooms)* Self-Contained

Rooms 7. *Educational Professionals* Special Education Teachers 8; Academic Specialists 10. *Curricula* Traditional Academic; Individualized; Basic Skills; Prevocational. *Educational Intervention Approaches* Engineered Classroom; Precision Teaching; Behavior Modification; Applied Behavior Analysis.

Comments The Grafton Autism Program provides intensive educational and residential instruction for children with autism and other communication disorders.

Graydon Manor

301 Children's Center Rd, Leesburg, VA 22075 (703) 777-3485
Year Established 1957
Contact William J Kropp, Dir of Admissions and Development
Facility Information *Placement* Private Residential Care. *Number of Beds* 61. *Children/Adolescents Served* 61. *Sexes Served* Both. *Room and Board Fees (Approx)* $212. *Sources of Funding* State Funds; Health Insurance; OCHAMPUS. Summer school available. *Teacher Certification Level* Elementary School; Junior High/Middle School; High School. *Special Certification Level* ED; LD; Career/Vocational Education; Reading; Math.
Student/Patient Characteristics *Age Levels* 5-8; 9-11; 12-14; 15-17. *IQ Ranges* 85-130. *Exceptionalities Served* Emotionally Disturbed; Learning Disabled. *Learning Problems* Memory Disabilities; Perceptual Disabilities; Thinking Disabilities; Oral Language Disabilities; Reading Disabilities; Handwriting Disabilities; Spelling Disabilities; Arithmetic Disabilities; Written Expression. *Behavioral Problems* Attention Deficits; Hyperactivity; Hypoactivity; Impulsivity; Self-Aggression; Verbal Aggression; Physical Aggression; Indirect Aggression; Passive Aggression; Withdrawal. *Conditions Treated* Disintegrative Psychoses; Schizophrenia; Convulsive Disorders; Phobias; Obsessions and Compulsions; Hysteria; Depression; Anorexia Nervosa; Inadequacy/Immaturity; Personality Problems; Socialized Aggressive Reaction; Unsocialized Aggressive Reaction.
Services Provided Individual Therapy; Group Therapy; Parent Involvement; Behavior Therapy; Cognitive Developmental Therapy; Family Therapy; Drug Therapy; Art Therapy; Music Therapy; Reality Therapy; Play Therapy; Psychodrama. *Professionals on Staff* Psychiatrists 4; Psychologists 5; Counselors 3; Social Workers 3; Child Care Staff 30; Nurses 6. *Service Facilities Available (with number of rooms)* On-Campus Residential School 9. *Educational Professionals* Special Education Teachers 9; Career/Vocational Teachers 1; Paraprofessionals 9. *Curricula* Traditional Academic; Individualized; Basic Skills; Prevocational. *Educational Intervention Approaches* Engineered Classroom; Precision Teaching; Progressive Discipline; Self-Control; Behavior Modification; Applied Behavior Analysis.

Comments Graydon Manor is JCAH accredited and provides a multidisciplinary approach to treatment of emotional illness within the context of a therapeutic milieu, for boys and girls ages 7 to 17.

Harbor House

6435 Columbia Pike, Annandale, VA 22003 (703) 354-0311
Year Established 1980
Contact Tim Harmon, Dir
Facility Information *Placement* Public Residential Care. *Number of Beds* 8. *Children/Adolescents Served* 8. *Sexes Served* Both. *Room and Board Fees (Approx)* $88. *Sources of Funding* State Funds; Title XX. Summer school available. *Teacher Certification Level* Junior High/Middle School; High School.
Student/Patient Characteristics *Age Levels* 12-14; 15-17. *IQ Ranges* 85-130; Above 130. *Exceptionalities Served* Emotionally Disturbed; Learning Disabled. *Learning Problems* Memory Disabilities; Perceptual Disabilities; Thinking Disabilities; Oral Language Disabilities; Reading Disabilities; Handwriting Disabilities; Spelling Disabilities; Arithmetic Disabilities; Written Expression. *Behavioral Problems* Attention Deficits; Hyperactivity; Hypoactivity; Impulsivity; Self-Aggression; Verbal Aggression; Physical Aggression; Indirect Aggression; Passive Aggression; Withdrawal.

Services Provided Individual Therapy; Group Therapy; Parent Involvement; Behavior Therapy; Family Therapy; Reality Therapy. *Professionals on Staff* Counselors 6; Social Workers 1. *Educational Professionals* Regular School Teachers; Special Education Teachers. *Curricula* Traditional Academic.

Comments Harbor House is a 90-day diagnostic group home for 8 ED adolescent boys and girls. It provides crisis and stabilization services through individual and group therapy.

Leary Educational Foundation—Timber Ridge

PO Box 3160, Winchester, VA 22601 (703) 888-3456
Year Established 1969
Contact Phil Arlotta, Social Serv Dir
Facility Information *Placement* Private Residential Care. *Number of Beds* 60. *Children/Adolescents Served* 60. *Sexes Served* Male. *Tuition Fees (Approx)* $30,545. *Sources of Funding* State Funds; P.L. 94-142. Summer school available. *Teacher Certification Level* Junior High/Middle School; High School. *Special Certification Level* ED; LD; Career/Vocational Education; Reading.
Student/Patient Characteristics *Age Levels* 12-14; 15-17; 18-21. *IQ Ranges* 85-130. *Exceptionalities Served* Emotionally Disturbed; Learning Disabled; Socially Maladjusted. *Learning Problems* Thinking Disabilities; Reading Disabilities; Handwriting Disabilities; Spelling Disabilities; Arithmetic Disabilities; Written Expression. *Behavioral Problems* Attention Deficits; Hyperactivity; Hypoactivity; Impulsivity; Verbal Aggression; Physical Aggression; Indirect Aggression; Passive Aggression; Withdrawal. *Conditions Treated* Inadequacy/Immaturity; Personality Problems; Socialized Aggressive Reaction.
Services Provided Individual Therapy; Group Therapy; Behavior Therapy; Art Therapy. *Professionals on Staff* Psychologists 1; Counselors 10; Social Workers 4; Child Care Staff 12; Nurses 1; Recreational Staff 10. *Service Facilities Available (with number of rooms)* Resource Rooms 1; Departmental Teacher 4. *Educational Professionals* Regular School Teachers 5; Special Education Teachers 3; Career/Vocational Teachers 2. *Curricula* Traditional Academic; Career/Vocational Education; Individualized; Basic Skills; Prevocational. *Educational Intervention Approaches* Behavior Modification. *Degrees Awarded* Certificate of Attendance; Graduate Equivalency Diploma.

Leary School Inc

6349 Lincolnia Rd, Alexandria, VA 22312 (703) 941-8150
Year Established 1964
Contact Gene Meale, Dir
Facility Information *Placement* Special Program. *Children/Adolescents Served* 65. *Sexes Served* Both. *Sources of Funding* P.L. 94-142. Summer school available. *Teacher Certification Level* Elementary School; Junior High/Middle School; High School. *Special Certification Level* ED; LD; MR; Career/Vocational Education; Physical Education.
Student/Patient Characteristics *Age Levels* 5-8; 9-11; 12-14; 15-17; 18-21. *IQ Ranges* 71-85; 85-130. *Exceptionalities Served* Emotionally Disturbed; Learning Disabled; Mentally Handicapped. *Learning Problems* Memory Disabilities; Perceptual Disabilities; Thinking Disabilities; Oral Language Disabilities; Reading Disabilities; Handwriting Disabilities; Spelling Disabilities; Arithmetic Disabilities; Written Expression. *Behavioral Problems* Attention Deficits; Hyperactivity; Impulsivity; Self-Aggression; Verbal Aggression; Physical Aggression; Indirect Aggression; Passive Aggression; Withdrawal. *Conditions Treated* Inadequacy/Immaturity; Personality Problems; Socialized Aggressive Reaction; Unsocialized Aggressive Reaction.
Services Provided Individual Therapy; Group Therapy; Parent Involvement; Behavior Therapy; Cognitive Developmental Therapy; Family Therapy; Art Therapy; Reality Therapy. *Professionals on Staff* Psychiatrists 1; Counselors 2; Social Workers 1. *Service Facilities Available (with number of rooms)* Consultative (ERT) 1; Resource Rooms 1; Self-Contained Rooms 6. *Educational Professionals* Special Education Teachers 6; Career/Vocational Teachers 2; Crisis Teachers 2; Special Education

Counselors 3; Paraprofessionals 6. *Curricula* Traditional Academic; Career/Vocational Education; Individualized; Basic Skills; Prevocational. *Educational Intervention Approaches* Precision Teaching; Self-Control; Behavior Modification; Positive Peer Culture. *Degrees Awarded* Certificate of Completion.

Massanutten Mental Health Center

1241 N Main St, Harrisonburg, VA 22801 (703) 434-1766
Contact Betty Kline, Children's Serv Coord
Facility Information *Placement* Mental Health Center. *Children/Adolescents Served* $100. *Sexes Served* Both. *Tuition Fees (Approx)* Sliding Scale. *Sources of Funding* State Funds; Local Matching Funds.

Student/Patient Characteristics *Age Levels* 0-4; 5-8; 9-11; 12-14; 15-17; 18-21; Over 21. *Exceptionalities Served* Emotionally Disturbed. *Behavioral Problems* Attention Deficits; Hyperactivity; Hypoactivity; Impulsivity; Self-Aggression; Verbal Aggression; Physical Aggression; Indirect Aggression; Passive Aggression; Withdrawal. *Conditions Treated* Early Infantile Autism; Disintegrative Psychoses; Schizophrenia; Aphasia; Phobias; Obsessions and Compulsions; Hysteria; Depression; Suicide; Anorexia Nervosa; Inadequacy/Immaturity; Personality Problems; Socialized Aggressive Reaction; Unsocialized Aggressive Reaction.

Services Provided Individual Therapy; Group Therapy; Parent Involvement; Behavior Therapy; Family Therapy; Art Therapy; Play Therapy. *Professionals on Staff* Psychiatrists 1; Psychologists 1; Counselors 1; Social Workers 1; Nurses 1. *Service Facilities Available (with number of rooms)* Consultative (ERT).

Psychiatric Institute of Richmond—Educational Development Center

3001 5th Ave, Richmond, VA 23222 (804) 329-4392
Year Established 1980
Contact Nancy Walker, Admissions Coord
Facility Information *Placement* Special School; Private Residential Care; Acute Care Hospital. *Number of Beds* 84. *Children/Adolescents Served* 84 (residential); 50 (day school). *Sexes Served* Both. *Sources of Funding* P.L. 94-142; Self-Pay. Summer school available. *Special Certification Level* ED; LD; MR; Reading; Math.

Student/Patient Characteristics *Age Levels* 0-4; 5-8; 9-11; 12-14; 15-17; 18-21. *IQ Ranges* 85-130. *Exceptionalities Served* Autistic; Emotionally Disturbed; Learning Disabled; Gifted. *Learning Problems* Memory Disabilities; Perceptual Disabilities; Thinking Disabilities; Oral Language Disabilities; Reading Disabilities; Handwriting Disabilities; Spelling Disabilities; Arithmetic Disabilities; Written Expression. *Behavioral Problems* Attention Deficits; Hyperactivity; Hypoactivity; Impulsivity; Self-Aggression; Verbal Aggression; Physical Aggression; Indirect Aggression; Passive Aggression; Withdrawal. *Conditions Treated* Alcohol Abuse and/or Drug Abuse; Schizophrenia; Depression; Suicide; Anorexia Nervosa.

Services Provided Individual Therapy; Group Therapy; Parent Involvement; Family Therapy; Individual and Group Counseling. *Professionals on Staff* Psychiatrists 6; Psychologists 4; Social Workers 2; Child Care Staff; Nurses. *Service Facilities Available (with number of rooms)* Self-Contained Rooms 6. *Educational Professionals* Regular School Teachers 1; Special Education Teachers 10; Career/Vocational Teachers 1; Special Education Counselors 2; Paraprofessionals 6. *Curricula* Traditional Academic; Career/Vocational Education; Individualized; Basic Skills; Prevocational. *Educational Intervention Approaches* Behavior Modification.

Comments The Educational Development Center is a therapeutic day school, providing educational services to emotionally disturbed and/or learning disabled students. Support services include group and individual counseling, career counseling, and basic computer literacy.

School for Contemporary Education

7203 Wimsatt Rd, Springfield, VA 22151 (703) 941-8810
Year Established 1967
Contact Marie Fort Withrow, Prog Coord
Facility Information *Placement* Special School; Private, Specialized Foster Care Program. *Children/Adolescents Served* 114. *Sexes Served* Both. *Sources of Funding* State Funds; P.L. 94-142; Corrections; Mental Health; Welfare. *Special Certification Level* ED; LD; MR; Career/Vocational Education; Math.

Student/Patient Characteristics *Age Levels* 5-8; 9-11; 12-14; 15-17; 18-21. *IQ Ranges* 26-40; 41-55; 56-70; 71-85; 85-130. *Exceptionalities Served* Autistic; Emotionally Disturbed; Learning Disabled; Mentally Handicapped; Communication Disordered; Hearing Impaired/Deaf; Other Health Impaired. *Learning Problems* Memory Disabilities; Perceptual Disabilities; Thinking Disabilities; Oral Language Disabilities; Reading Disabilities; Handwriting Disabilities; Spelling Disabilities; Arithmetic Disabilities; Written Expression. *Behavioral Problems* Attention Deficits; Hyperactivity; Impulsivity; Self-Aggression; Verbal Aggression; Physical Aggression; Indirect Aggression; Passive Aggression; Withdrawal. *Conditions Treated* Other Substance Abuse or Dependence; Early Infantile Autism; Schizophrenia; Aphasia; Convulsive Disorders; Obsessions and Compulsions; Depression; Asthma; Inadequacy/Immaturity; Personality Problems; Socialized Aggressive Reaction; Unsocialized Aggressive Reaction.

Services Provided Individual Therapy; Parent Involvement; Behavior Therapy; Family Therapy; Drug Therapy; Reality Therapy; Play Therapy; Psychodrama; Speech/Language Therapy; Occupational Therapy; Physical Therapy. *Professionals on Staff* Psychologists 5; Counselors 2; Social Workers 3; Speech Therapists 4; Occupational Therapists 4; Physical Therapist 1; Recreation Therapist 1; Behavior Coordinator 1; Assessment Specialist 1. *Service Facilities Available (with number of rooms)* Self-Contained Rooms 13. *Educational Professionals* Special Education Teachers 13; Career/Vocational Teachers 2; Crisis Teachers 1; Special Education Counselors 5; Paraprofessionals 17. *Curricula* Traditional Academic; Career/Vocational Education; Individualized; Basic Skills; Prevocational. *Educational Intervention Approaches* Progressive Discipline; Self-Control; Behavior Modification; Applied Behavior Analysis.

Comments In addition to providing special education to handicapped children, the school operates a specialized foster care program for emotionally disturbed children ages 6-18. Additionally, the Family Services Department extends its training and counseling to families whose children are not enrolled in the school, and a Tutoring Service provides additional service to the Metropolitan D.C. area.

Virginia Center for Psychiatry

301 Fort Ln, Portsmouth, VA 23704 (804) 393-0061
Year Established 1971
Contact T Jack Baker, Dir of Educ Therapy
Facility Information *Placement* Private Psychiatric Hospital. *Number of Beds* 90. *Children/Adolescents Served* 100. *Sexes Served* Both. *Sources of Funding* Health Insurance; Medicaid; P.L. 94-142. *Teacher Certification Level* Elementary School; Junior High/Middle School; High School. *Special Certification Level* ED; LD.

Student/Patient Characteristics *Age Levels* 5-8; 9-11; 12-14; 15-17; 18-21. *Exceptionalities Served* Emotionally Disturbed; Learning Disabled. *Learning Problems* Perceptual Disabilities; Spelling Disabilities; Arithmetic Disabilities; Written Expression. *Behavioral Problems* Attention Deficits; Hyperactivity; Hypoactivity; Impulsivity; Self-Aggression; Verbal Aggression; Physical Aggression; Indirect Aggression; Passive Aggression; Withdrawal. *Conditions Treated* Alcohol Abuse and/or Drug Abuse; Other Substance Abuse or Dependence; Schizophrenia; Phobias; Obsessions and Compulsions; Hysteria; Depression; Suicide; Anorexia Nervosa; Inadequacy/Immaturity; Personality Problems; Socialized Aggressive Reaction; Unsocialized Aggressive Reaction.

Services Provided Individual Therapy; Group Therapy; Parent Involvement; Behavior Therapy; Family Therapy; Drug Therapy; Art Therapy; Music Therapy; Play Therapy. *Professionals on Staff* Psychiatrists; Psychologists; Counselors; Social Workers; Child Care Staff; Nurses. *Service Facilities Available (with number of rooms)* Self-Contained Rooms 15. *Educational Professionals* Special Education Teachers; Crisis Teachers. *Curricula* Traditional Academic; Individualized; Basic Skills. *Degrees Awarded* Certificate of Attendance.

Virginia Center for Psychiatry

100 Kingsley Ln, Norfolk, VA 23505 (804) 489-1072
Year Established 1981
Contact T Jack Baker, Dir of Ed Therapy
Facility Information *Placement* Private Psychiatric Hospital. *Number of Beds* 40. *Children/Adolescents Served* 40. *Sexes Served* Both. *Sources of Funding* Health Insurance; Medicaid; P.L. 94-142. *Teacher Certification Level* Junior High/Middle School; High School. *Special Certification Level* ED; LD.

Student/Patient Characteristics *Age Levels* 15-17; 18-21. *IQ Ranges* 56-70; 71-85; 85-130; Above 130. *Exceptionalities Served* Emotionally Disturbed; Learning Disabled. *Learning Problems* Perceptual Disabilities; Spelling Disabilities; Arithmetic Disabilities; Written Expression. *Behavioral Problems* Attention Deficits; Hyperactivity; Hypoactivity; Impulsivity; Self-Aggression; Verbal Aggression; Physical Aggression; Indirect Aggression; Passive Aggression; Withdrawal. *Conditions Treated* Alcohol Abuse and/or Drug Abuse; Other Substance Abuse or Dependence; Schizophrenia; Phobias; Obsessions and Compulsions; Hysteria; Depression; Suicide; Anorexia Nervosa; Inadequacy/Immaturity; Personality Problems; Socialized Aggressive Reaction; Unsocialized Aggressive Reaction.

Services Provided Individual Therapy; Group Therapy; Parent Involvement; Family Therapy; Drug Therapy; Art Therapy; Music Therapy; Play Therapy. *Professionals on Staff* Psychiatrists; Psychologists; Counselors; Social Workers; Child Care Staff; Nurses. *Service Facilities Available (with number of rooms)* Self-Contained Rooms 5. *Educational Professionals* Special Education Teachers; Crisis Teachers. *Curricula* Traditional Academic; Individualized; Basic Skills. *Degrees Awarded* Certificate of Attendance.

Washington

Child Study and Treatment Center

8919 Steilacoom Blvd SW, Tacoma, WA 98498 (206) 756-2504
Year Established 1962
Contact Donna J Douglass, Chief Psychiatric Social Worker
Facility Information *Placement* Public Residential Care; Public
Day Hospital. *Number of Beds* 40. *Children/Adolescents Served*
60. *Sexes Served* Both. *Room and Board Fees (Approx)* $175
(inpatient); $44 (day hospital). *Sources of Funding* State Funds;
Medicaid. Summer school available. *Teacher Certification Level*
Elementary School; Junior High/Middle School; High School.
Special Certification Level Reading; Math; Special Education.
Student/Patient Characteristics *Age Levels* 5-8; 9-11; 12-14;
15-17. *IQ Ranges* 71-85; 85-130; Above 130. *Exceptionalities
Served* Emotionally Disturbed; Learning Disabled. *Learning
Problems* Memory Disabilities; Perceptual Disabilities; Thinking
Disabilities; Oral Language Disabilities; Reading Disabilities;
Handwriting Disabilities; Spelling Disabilities; Arithmetic Dis-
abilities; Written Expression. *Behavioral Problems* Attention
Deficits; Hyperactivity; Hypoactivity; Impulsivity; Self-
Aggression; Verbal Aggression; Physical Aggression; Indirect Ag-
gression; Passive Aggression; Withdrawal. *Conditions Treated* Al-
cohol Abuse and/or Drug Abuse; Disintegrative Psychoses;
Schizophrenia; Convulsive Disorders; Phobias; Obsessions and
Compulsions; Hysteria; Depression; Suicide; Asthma; Anorexia
Nervosa; Ulcerative Colitis; Inadequacy/Immaturity; Personality
Problems; Socialized Aggressive Reaction; Unsocialized Aggres-
sive Reaction.
Services Provided Individual Therapy; Group Therapy; Parent
Involvement; Behavior Therapy; Family Therapy; Drug Therapy;
Reality Therapy. *Professionals on Staff* Psychiatrists 2; Psycholo-
gists 2; Social Workers 5; Child Care Staff 35; Nurses 8. *Service
Facilities Available (with number of rooms)* Itinerants 1; Self-
Contained Rooms 4; On-Campus Residential School 12.
Educational Professionals Special Education Teachers 11; Para-
professionals 5; Administrator 1. *Curricula* Traditional Academic; Individualized; Basic Skills; Prevocational. *Educational
Intervention Approaches* Progressive Discipline; Behavior Modification; Creative Conditioning. *Degrees Awarded* High School
Diploma; Graduate Equivalency Diploma.
Comments The Child Study and Treatment Center is designed
and staffed for the treatment of the moderately to severely
emotionally disturbed child and family. The emphasis at the
center is on the establishment and maintenance of treatment
programs.

Luther Child Center—Children's Hospitalization Alternative Program

PO Box 2097, 4526 Federal, Everett, WA 98203 (206) 258-2371
Contact Mary Kay Brennan, Prog Supv
Facility Information *Placement* Public School; Therapeutic Foster
Care. *Number of Beds* 10. *Children/Adolescents Served* 10. *Sexes
Served* Both. *Sources of Funding* State Funds.
Student/Patient Characteristics *Age Levels* 5-8; 9-11; 12-14;
15-17. *IQ Ranges* 56-70; 71-85. *Exceptionalities Served* Emotion-
ally Disturbed; Learning Disabled; Communication Disordered.
Learning Problems Perceptual Disabilities; Thinking Disabilities.
Behavioral Problems Attention Deficits; Hyperactivity; Hypoac-
tivity; Impulsivity; Self-Aggression; Verbal Aggression; Physical
Aggression; Indirect Aggression; Passive Aggression; Withdrawal.
Conditions Treated Alcohol Abuse and/or Drug Abuse; Schizo-
phrenia; Phobias; Hysteria; Depression; Inadequacy/Immaturity;
Personality Problems; Socialized Aggressive Reaction; Un-
socialized Aggressive Reaction.
Services Provided Individual Therapy; Group Therapy; Parent
Involvement; Behavior Therapy; Family Therapy. *Professionals
on Staff* Psychiatrists 1; Psychologists 4; Counselors 4; Social
Workers 9. *Service Facilities Available (with number of rooms)*
Day Treatment School Program. *Educational Professionals* Regular School Teachers; Special Education Teachers; Special Education Counselors. *Educational Intervention Approaches* Self-
Control; Behavior Modification.
Comments The center's students attend public school. There are
some who attend a Day Treatment School for 1/2 day at Luther
Child Center. Children's Hospitalization Alternative Program is
a long-term intensive foster-care program for children who are
seriously emotionally disturbed. Intensive foster care is provided
by foster parents who have received specialized training.

Mid-Columbia Mental Health Center—Adolescent Psychiatric Department

1175 Gribble Ave, Richland, WA 99352 (509) 943-9104
Contact Doug Southard, Public Relations Dept
Facility Information *Placement* Public Residential Care. *Number
of Beds* 10. *Children/Adolescents Served* 18. *Sexes Served* Both.
Room and Board Fees (Approx) $379. *Sources of Funding* State
Funds. Summer school available. *Teacher Certification Level* Ele-
mentary School; Junior High/Middle School; High School.
Special Certification Level ED.
Student/Patient Characteristics *Age Levels* 9-11; 12-14; 15-17. *IQ
Ranges* 71-85; 85-130. *Exceptionalities Served* Autistic; Emotionally Disturbed; Learning Disabled; Mentally Handicapped; Hearing Impaired/Deaf; Visually Impaired/Blind; Other Health Im-
paired; Physically Handicapped; Gifted. *Learning Problems*
Memory Disabilities; Perceptual Disabilities; Thinking Disabil-
ities; Oral Language Disabilities; Reading Disabilities; Handwriting Disabilities; Spelling Disabilities; Arithmetic Disabilities;
Written Expression. *Behavioral Problems* Attention Deficits; Hyperactivity; Hypoactivity; Impulsivity; Self-Aggression; Verbal
Aggression; Physical Aggression; Indirect Aggression; Passive Ag-

gression; Withdrawal. *Conditions Treated* Disintegrative Psychoses; Schizophrenia; Obsessions and Compulsions; Hysteria; Depression; Suicide; Anorexia Nervosa; Personality Problems; Socialized Aggressive Reaction; Unsocialized Aggressive Reaction.

Services Provided Individual Therapy; Group Therapy; Parent Involvement; Behavior Therapy; Cognitive Developmental Therapy; Family Therapy; Reality Therapy; Play Therapy; Psychodrama. *Professionals on Staff* Psychiatrists 1; Psychologists 1; Counselors; Social Workers 3; Child Care Staff 20; Nurses 2. *Service Facilities Available (with number of rooms)* Consultative (ERT) 1; Itinerants 3; Resource Rooms 1; Transition Rooms 2; Self-Contained Rooms 2; Special School 1; Hospital School 1; On-Campus Residential School 1. *Educational Professionals* Regular School Teachers 1; Special Education Teachers 1; Career/Vocational Teachers; Crisis Teachers 1; Special Education Counselors 1; Paraprofessionals 1. *Curricula* Traditional Academic; Individualized; Basic Skills; Prevocational. *Educational Intervention Approaches* Precision Teaching; Behavior Modification. *Degrees Awarded* High School Diploma; Graduate Equivalency Diploma.

Secret Harbor School

PO Box 440, 1009 8th St, Anacortes, WA 98221 (206) 293-5151
Year Established 1949
Contact John D MacDonald, Exec Dir

Facility Information *Placement* Private Residential Care; Special Education Classes. *Number of Beds* 30. *Children/Adolescents Served* 30. *Sexes Served* Male. *Sources of Funding* Health Insurance; Medicaid; P.L. 94-142; Families. Summer school available. *Teacher Certification Level* Elementary School; Junior High/Middle School; High School.

Student/Patient Characteristics *Age Levels* 12-14; 15-17. *IQ Ranges* 85-130; Above 130. *Exceptionalities Served* Emotionally Disturbed; Learning Disabled; Mentally Handicapped; Communication Disordered; Gifted; Behaviorally Disordered. *Learning Problems* Perceptual Disabilities; Reading Disabilities; Handwriting Disabilities; Spelling Disabilities; Arithmetic Disabilities; Written Expression. *Behavioral Problems* Attention Deficits; Hyperactivity; Hypoactivity; Impulsivity; Verbal Aggression; Physical Aggression; Indirect Aggression; Passive Aggression; Withdrawal. *Conditions Treated* Alcohol Abuse and/or Drug Abuse; Other Substance Abuse or Dependence; Schizophrenia; Phobias; Obsessions and Compulsions; Hysteria; Depression; Asthma; Anorexia Nervosa; Inadequacy/Immaturity; Personality Problems; Socialized Aggressive Reaction; Unsocialized Aggressive Reaction; Affective Disorders; Attention Deficit Disorder; Identity Disorder.

Services Provided Individual Therapy; Group Therapy; Parent Involvement; Behavior Therapy; Family Therapy; Drug Therapy; Art Therapy; Reality Therapy; Play Therapy; Milieu Therapy. *Professionals on Staff* Psychiatrists 1; Psychologists 1; Social Workers 3; Child Care Staff 12; Nurses 1. *Service Facilities Available (with number of rooms)* Resource Rooms 1; On-Campus Residential School 30. *Educational Professionals* Regular School Teachers 3; Special Education Teachers 1; Special Education Certified Tutor 1. *Curricula* Traditional Academic; Career/Vocational Education; Individualized; Basic Skills; Prevocational; Tutoring. *Educational Intervention Approaches* Progressive Discipline; Self-Control; Behavior Modification; Applied Behavior Analysis. *Degrees Awarded* Certificate of Attendance; High School Diploma; Graduate Equivalency Diploma.

Comments Secret Harbor School is a self-contained island campus of 345 acres that permits concentration on remediation of emotional and educational handicaps free from the distractions of toxic peer pressure and family conflicts. Emotional maturity and productivity are the goals of the therapeutic milieu which includes psychotherapy, special education, and dedication to the work ethic.

West Virginia

Concord

Yellow Spring, WV 26865 (304) 856-3404
Year Established 1975
Contact Rolf H Mielzarek, Co Dir
Facility Information *Placement* Private Residential Care.
Children/Adolescents Served 52. *Sexes Served* Both. *Tuition Fees
(Approx)* $24,000. *Sources of Funding* State Funds; P.L. 94-142;
Private. *Special Certification Level* ED; MR.
Student/Patient Characteristics *Age Levels* 15-17; 18-21; Over 21.
IQ Ranges 0-25; 26-40; 41-55; 56-70; 71-85. *Exceptionalities
Served* Autistic; Emotionally Disturbed; Mentally Handicapped;
Hearing Impaired/Deaf; Visually Impaired/Blind. *Learning
Problems* Memory Disabilities; Perceptual Disabilities; Thinking
Disabilities; Oral Language Disabilities; Reading Disabilities;
Handwriting Disabilities; Spelling Disabilities; Arithmetic Dis-
abilities; Written Expression. *Behavioral Problems* Attention
Deficits; Hyperactivity; Hypoactivity; Impulsivity; Self-
Aggression; Verbal Aggression; Physical Aggression; Indirect Ag-
gression; Passive Aggression; Withdrawal. *Conditions Treated*
Inadequacy/Immaturity; Personality Problems; Socialized Aggressive Reaction; Unsocialized Aggressive Reaction.
Services Provided Behavior Therapy. *Professionals on Staff* Psychologists 1; Counselors 1. *Service Facilities Available (with
number of rooms)* Resource Rooms 1; Transition Rooms 2;
Self-Contained Rooms 5. *Educational Professionals* Special Education Teachers 4. *Curricula* Career/Vocational Education; Individualized; Basic Skills; Prevocational. *Educational
Intervention Approaches* Precision Teaching; Progressive Discipline; Behavior Modification; Applied Behavior Analysis.

Comments Concord provides training and residential living for
mentally retarded adults with emphasis on normal living, independent living skills, pre-vocational and vocational development, and the quality of life.

Lakin Hospital—Adolescent Services

Lakin, WV 25250 (304) 675-3230
Contact Charlie M Wamsley, Asst Dir and Prog Coord
Facility Information *Placement* Public School; Special School;
Public Residential Care; Group Home. *Number of Beds* 28.
Children/Adolescents Served 28. *Sexes Served* Both. *Room and
Board Fees (Approx)* $96. *Sources of Funding* State Funds; HEW;
Health Insurance; Medicaid; Medicare; P.L. 94-142. Summer
school available. *Teacher Certification Level* Junior High/Middle
School; High School. *Special Certification Level* ED; LD; Career/
Vocational Education; Reading; Math; Behavior Disorders.
Student/Patient Characteristics *Age Levels* 12-14; 15-17. *IQ
Ranges* 56-70; 71-85; 85-130; Above 130. *Exceptionalities Served*
Emotionally Disturbed; Learning Disabled; Mentally Handi-
capped; Behavior Disordered. *Learning Problems* Memory Dis-
abilities; Perceptual Disabilities; Thinking Disabilities; Oral Lan-

guage Disabilities; Reading Disabilities; Handwriting Disabilities;
Spelling Disabilities; Arithmetic Disabilities; Written Expression;
Motor Disabilities. *Behavioral Problems* Attention Deficits; Hy-
peractivity; Hypoactivity; Impulsivity; Self-Aggression; Verbal
Aggression; Physical Aggression; Indirect Aggression; Passive Ag-
gression; Withdrawal. *Conditions Treated* Alcohol Abuse and/or
Drug Abuse; Other Substance Abuse or Dependence; Schizophre-
nia; Convulsive Disorders; Phobias; Obsessions and Compul-
sions; Hysteria; Depression; Suicide; Inadequacy/Immaturity;
Personality Problems; Socialized Aggressive Reaction; Un-
socialized Aggressive Reaction.
Services Provided Individual Therapy; Group Therapy; Behavior
Therapy; Drug Therapy; Art Therapy; Music Therapy; Psycho-
drama. *Professionals on Staff* Psychiatrists 1; Psychologists 1;
Counselors 3; Social Workers 2; Child Care Staff 27; Nurses 6;
Behavioral Pediatrician 1. *Service Facilities Available (with
number of rooms)* Resource Rooms 1; Transition Rooms 3;
Self-Contained Rooms 2; Special School; On-Campus Residential
School 8; Homebound Instruction. *Educational Professionals*
Regular School Teachers 4; Special Education Teachers 11;
Career/Vocational Teachers 1; Crisis Teachers 1; Special Educa-
tion Counselors 1; Paraprofessionals 4; Art Therapist 1.
Curricula Individualized; Basic Skills; Prevocational. *Educational
Intervention Approaches* Precision Teaching; Progressive Disci-
pline; Self-Control; Behavior Modification; Applied Behavior
Analysis. *Degrees Awarded* Certificate of Attendance; High
School Diploma; Graduate Equivalency Diploma.

Comments Lakin Hospital/Adolescent Services is a public residential care facility serving emotionally disturbed, behavior disordered youth. Housing and treatment is provided by WV Dept.
of Health; the on-grounds school is operated by WV Dept. of
Education. While both evaluation/diagnostic workups and long-
term treatment are offered, emphasis is placed on the latter.
Length of stay varies from one to 24 months.

North Central Regional Education Service Agency

1000 Virginia Ave, Fairmont, WV 26554 (304) 367-1431
Year Established 1972
Contact Sandra McQuain, Special Ed Coord
Facility Information *Placement* Technical Assistance. *Sources of
Funding* State Funds; P.L. 94-142.
Services Provided *Professionals on Staff* Psychologists 1; Audiologist 1; Special Education Coordinator 1.
Comments North Central RESA assists member county school
systems in improving educational services and in coordinating
activities at a regional level both in special education and regular
education. Special education activities include regional inservice
workshops for teachers and administrators, coordination of advi-
sory committees for improvement in adolescent and vocational

programs, a project to assist teachers in upgrading teacher certification, a resource center that loans instructional material, and technical assistance in special education upon request.

Pressley Ridge School—Laurel Park

Box 697, Rte 5, Clarksburg, WV 26302 (304) 624-9879
Year Established 1983
Contact Mark Freado, Dir
Facility Information *Placement* Private Residential Care. *Number of Beds* 20. *Children/Adolescents Served* 20. *Sexes Served* Both. *Tuition Fees (Approx)* 25,000. *Sources of Funding* State Funds. Summer school available. *Teacher Certification Level* Elementary School; Junior High/Middle School; High School. *Special Certification Level* ED.
Student/Patient Characteristics *Age Levels* 12-14; 15-17. *IQ Ranges* 71-85; 85-130. *Exceptionalities Served* Emotionally Disturbed; Status Offenders. *Learning Problems* Memory Disabilities; Perceptual Disabilities; Thinking Disabilities; Oral Language Disabilities; Reading Disabilities; Handwriting Disabilities; Spelling Disabilities; Arithmetic Disabilities; Written Expression. *Behavioral Problems* Attention Deficits; Hyperactivity; Hypoactivity; Impulsivity; Self-Aggression; Verbal Aggression; Physical Aggression; Indirect Aggression; Passive Aggression; Withdrawal. *Conditions Treated* Alcohol Abuse and/or Drug Abuse; Other Substance Abuse or Dependence; Phobias; Obsessions and Compulsions; Hysteria; Depression; Suicide; Inadequacy/Immaturity; Personality Problems; Socialized Aggressive Reaction; Unsocialized Aggressive Reaction.
Services Provided Individual Therapy; Group Therapy; Parent Involvement; Behavior Therapy; Family Therapy. *Professionals on Staff* Psychiatrists 2; Psychologists 6; Counselors 6; Social Workers 2; Child Care Staff 2. *Service Facilities Available (with number of rooms)* Consultative (ERT); Resource Rooms; Self-Contained Rooms; On-Campus Residential School. *Educational Professionals* Special Education Teachers 2; Paraprofessionals 2. *Curricula* Traditional Academic; Career/Vocational Education; Individualized; Basic Skills; Prevocational. *Educational Intervention Approaches* Engineered Classroom; Self-Control; Behavior Modification; Applied Behavior Analysis. *Degrees Awarded* Certificate of Attendance; High School Diploma; Graduate Equivalency Diploma.

Western District Guidance Center

2121 7th St, Parkersburg, WV 26101 (304) 485-1721
Contact Marilyn P Aspuarelli, Therapist
Facility Information *Placement* Outpatient Facility. *Sexes Served* Both. *Sources of Funding* Health Insurance; Medicaid.
Student/Patient Characteristics *Age Levels* 0-4; 5-8; 9-11; 12-14; 15-17; 18-21; Over 21. *IQ Ranges* 56-70; 71-85; 85-130; Above 130. *Exceptionalities Served* Emotionally Disturbed; Learning Disabled; Mentally Handicapped; Gifted. *Learning Problems* Memory Disabilities; Perceptual Disabilities. *Behavioral Problems* Attention Deficits; Hyperactivity; Impulsivity; Self-Aggression; Verbal Aggression; Physical Aggression; Indirect Aggression; Passive Aggression; Withdrawal. *Conditions Treated* Alcohol Abuse and/or Drug Abuse; Other Substance Abuse or Dependence; Early Infantile Autism; Disintegrative Psychoses; Schizophrenia; Aphasia; Convulsive Disorders; Phobias; Obsessions and Compulsions; Hysteria; Depression; Suicide; Asthma; Anorexia Nervosa; Ulcerative Colitis; Inadequacy/Immaturity; Personality Problems; Socialized Aggressive Reaction; Unsocialized Aggressive Reaction.
Services Provided Individual Therapy; Group Therapy; Parent Involvement; Behavior Therapy; Family Therapy; Play Therapy. *Professionals on Staff* Psychiatrists 3; Psychologists 2; Counselors 4; Social Workers 2; Nurses 1.

Wisconsin

Brown County Mental Health Center—Children Services

2900 St Anthony Dr, Green Bay, WI 54301 (414) 468-1136
Year Established 1967
Contact Gene Gilbert, Chief of Children Serv
Facility Information *Placement* Public Residential Care. *Number of Beds* 25. *Children/Adolescents Served* 25. *Sexes Served* Both. *Room and Board Fees (Approx)* $195. *Sources of Funding* State Funds; Health Insurance; Medical Assistance. Summer school available. *Teacher Certification Level* Elementary School; Junior High/Middle School; High School. *Special Certification Level* ED; LD; MR.

Student/Patient Characteristics *Age Levels* 0-4; 5-8; 9-11; 12-14; 15-17; 18-21. *IQ Ranges* 56-70; 71-85; 85-130; Above 130. *Exceptionalities Served* Autistic; Emotionally Disturbed; Learning Disabled; Mentally Handicapped; Communication Disordered; Hearing Impaired/Deaf; Visually Impaired/Blind; Other Health Impaired; Physically Handicapped; Gifted. *Learning Problems* Memory Disabilities; Perceptual Disabilities; Thinking Disabilities; Oral Language Disabilities; Reading Disabilities; Arithmetic Disabilities. *Behavioral Problems* Attention Deficits; Hyperactivity; Hypoactivity; Impulsivity; Self-Aggression; Verbal Aggression; Physical Aggression; Indirect Aggression; Passive Aggression; Withdrawal. *Conditions Treated* Alcohol Abuse and/or Drug Abuse; Other Substance Abuse or Dependence; Disintegrative Psychoses; Schizophrenia; Aphasia; Convulsive Disorders; Phobias; Obsessions and Compulsions; Hysteria; Depression; Suicide; Asthma; Anorexia Nervosa; Ulcerative Colitis; Inadequacy/Immaturity; Personality Problems; Socialized Aggressive Reaction; Unsocialized Aggressive Reaction.

Services Provided Individual Therapy; Group Therapy; Parent Involvement; Behavior Therapy; Cognitive Developmental Therapy; Family Therapy; Drug Therapy; Reality Therapy; Play Therapy. *Professionals on Staff* Psychiatrists 1; Psychologists 3; Counselors 2; Social Workers 3; Child Care Staff 20; Nurses 6; Licensed Practical Nurse 6. *Service Facilities Available (with number of rooms)* Consultative (ERT) 2; Hospital School 3. *Educational Professionals* Special Education Teachers 2; Special Education Counselors 2. *Curricula* Traditional Academic; Basic Skills. *Educational Intervention Approaches* Behavior Modification. *Degrees Awarded* High School Diploma.

Comments The facility is an inpatient unit within a mental health center with an on campus school through the local school district.

Eau Claire Academy

PO Box 1168, 550 N Dewey, Eau Claire, WI 54702
(715) 834-6681
Year Established 1967
Contact Thomas P McMullin, Dir

Facility Information *Placement* Private Residential Care. *Number of Beds* 110. *Children/Adolescents Served* 110. *Sexes Served* Both. *Tuition Fees (Approx)* $35,952. *Sources of Funding* State Funds; Health Insurance; P.L. 94-142; County Social Service. Summer school available. *Teacher Certification Level* Junior High/Middle School; High School. *Special Certification Level* ED; Reading; Math.

Student/Patient Characteristics *Age Levels* 9-11; 12-14; 15-17; 18-21. *IQ Ranges* 85-130. *Exceptionalities Served* Emotionally Disturbed; Learning Disabled; Mentally Handicapped; Communication Disordered; Gifted. *Learning Problems* Memory Disabilities; Perceptual Disabilities; Thinking Disabilities; Reading Disabilities; Handwriting Disabilities; Spelling Disabilities; Arithmetic Disabilities; Written Expression. *Behavioral Problems* Attention Deficits; Hyperactivity; Hypoactivity; Impulsivity; Self-Aggression; Verbal Aggression; Physical Aggression; Indirect Aggression; Passive Aggression; Withdrawal. *Conditions Treated* Alcohol Abuse and/or Drug Abuse; Other Substance Abuse or Dependence; Convulsive Disorders; Phobias; Obsessions and Compulsions; Hysteria; Depression; Suicide; Inadequacy/Immaturity; Personality Problems; Socialized Aggressive Reaction; Unsocialized Aggressive Reaction.

Services Provided Individual Therapy; Group Therapy; Parent Involvement; Behavior Therapy; Cognitive Developmental Therapy; Family Therapy; Drug Therapy; Art Therapy; Music Therapy; Reality Therapy; Play Therapy. *Professionals on Staff* Psychiatrists .5; Psychologists .5; Social Workers 8; Child Care Staff 90; Nurses 6. *Service Facilities Available (with number of rooms)* Resource Rooms 1; Transition Rooms 4; Self-Contained Rooms 8. *Educational Professionals* Regular School Teachers 7; Special Education Teachers 14; Crisis Teachers 4; Paraprofessionals 4; School Psychologist; Speech Therapist; Recreational Therapist; Occupational Therapist. *Curricula* Traditional Academic; Career/Vocational Education; Individualized; Basic Skills; GED Preparation. *Educational Intervention Approaches* Progressive Discipline; Behavior Modification. *Degrees Awarded* High School Diploma; Graduate Equivalency Diploma.

Family and Children's Center

2507 Weston, LaCrosse, WI 54601 (608) 788-6333
Year Established 1888
Contact Robert D O'Connell, Exec Dir

Facility Information *Placement* Private Residential Care. *Number of Beds* 20. *Children/Adolescents Served* 20. *Sexes Served* Both. *Room and Board Fees (Approx)* $90. *Tuition Fees (Approx)* $32,844. *Sources of Funding* State Funds; Health Insurance. Summer school available. *Teacher Certification Level* Elementary School; Junior High/Middle School; High School. *Special Certification Level* ED; Reading.

Student/Patient Characteristics *Age Levels* 5-8; 9-11; 12-14; 15-17. *IQ Ranges* 85-130. *Exceptionalities Served* Emotionally Disturbed. *Learning Problems* Memory Disabilities; Reading Disabilities; Spelling Disabilities; Arithmetic Disabilities; Written Expression. *Behavioral Problems* Attention Deficits; Impulsivity; Verbal Aggression; Physical Aggression; Passive Aggression. *Conditions Treated* Depression; Inadequacy/Immaturity; Personality Problems; Socialized Aggressive Reaction; Unsocialized Aggressive Reaction.

Services Provided Individual Therapy; Group Therapy; Parent Involvement; Behavior Therapy; Family Therapy; Drug Therapy; Reality Therapy. *Professionals on Staff* Psychiatrists 1; Psychologists 1; Social Workers 3; Child Care Staff 14; Nurses .5. *Service Facilities Available (with number of rooms)* Self-Contained Rooms 1. *Educational Professionals* Special Education Teachers 2. *Curricula* Traditional Academic; Individualized; Basic Skills; Prevocational. *Educational Intervention Approaches* Progressive Discipline; Self-Control; Behavior Modification. *Degrees Awarded* Certificate of Attendance; High School Diploma.

Lad Lake Inc

Box 158, Dousman, WI 53118 (414) 965-2131
Year Established 1905
Contact Dennis J Neuenfeldt, Dir of Treatment Serv

Facility Information *Placement* Special School; Private Residential Care. *Number of Beds* 65. *Children/Adolescents Served* 65. *Sexes Served* Male. *Room and Board Fees (Approx)* $92. *Sources of Funding* State Funds; Health Insurance. Summer school available. *Teacher Certification Level* Elementary School; Junior High/Middle School; High School. *Special Certification Level* ED; LD; MR; Career/Vocational Education; Reading; Math. **Student/Patient Characteristics** *Age Levels* 9-11; 12-14; 15-17. *IQ Ranges* 56-70; 71-85; 85-130; Above 130. *Exceptionalities Served* Emotionally Disturbed; Learning Disabled; Communication Disordered; Gifted; Delinquent. *Learning Problems* Memory Disabilities; Perceptual Disabilities; Thinking Disabilities; Oral Language Disabilities; Reading Disabilities; Handwriting Disabilities; Spelling Disabilities; Arithmetic Disabilities; Written Expression. *Behavioral Problems* Attention Deficits; Hyperactivity; Hypoactivity; Impulsivity; Self-Aggression; Verbal Aggression; Physical Aggression; Indirect Aggression; Passive Aggression; Withdrawal. *Conditions Treated* Alcohol Abuse and/or Drug Abuse; Other Substance Abuse or Dependence; Phobias; Obsessions and Compulsions; Hysteria; Depression; Suicide; Inadequacy/Immaturity; Personality Problems; Socialized Aggressive Reaction; Unsocialized Aggressive Reaction.

Services Provided Individual Therapy; Group Therapy; Parent Involvement; Behavior Therapy; Cognitive Developmental Therapy; Family Therapy; Filial Therapy; Drug Therapy; Art Therapy; Reality Therapy; Art Therapy. *Professionals on Staff* Psychiatrists 1; Psychologists 1; Social Workers 7; Child Care Staff 25; Recreation Therapists 2. *Service Facilities Available (with number of rooms)* Resource Rooms 1; Transition Rooms 1; Self-Contained Rooms 1; On-Campus Residential School 5; Homebound Instruction 5. *Educational Professionals* Regular School Teachers 4; Special Education Teachers 3; Career/Vocational Teachers 2; Paraprofessionals 1. *Curricula* Traditional Academic; Career/Vocational Education; Individualized; Basic Skills; Prevocational. *Educational Intervention Approaches* Engineered Classroom; Precision Teaching; Progressive Discipline; Self-Control; Behavior Modification. *Degrees Awarded* Certificate of Attendance; High School Diploma; Graduate Equivalency Diploma.

Comments Lad Lake emphasizes the family or client and develops treatment, education, and supportive services around the family. Foster care treatment has been recently added.

Lakeside Child and Family Center Inc

2220 E North Ave, Milwaukee, WI 53202 (414) 271-9494
Year Established 1843
Contact Jean Johnson, Dir of Support Serv

Facility Information *Placement* Private Residential Care. *Number of Beds* 40. *Children/Adolescents Served* 40. *Sexes Served* Both. *Room and Board Fees (Approx)* $55. *Tuition Fees (Approx)* $17,274. *Sources of Funding* P.L. 94-142; Private. Summer school available. *Teacher Certification Level* Elementary School; Junior High/Middle School; High School. *Special Certification Level* ED; LD; Career/Vocational Education; Reading; Math. **Student/Patient Characteristics** *Age Levels* 5-8; 9-11; 12-14; 15-17. *IQ Ranges* 56-70; 71-85; 85-130. *Exceptionalities Served* Emotionally Disturbed; Learning Disabled. *Learning Problems* Thinking Disabilities; Oral Language Disabilities; Reading Disabilities; Written Expression. *Behavioral Problems* Attention Deficits; Hyperactivity; Impulsivity; Self-Aggression; Verbal Aggression; Physical Aggression; Passive Aggression; Withdrawal. *Conditions Treated* Disintegrative Psychoses; Schizophrenia; Phobias; Obsessions and Compulsions; Hysteria; Depression; Inadequacy/Immaturity; Personality Problems.

Services Provided Individual Therapy; Group Therapy; Parent Involvement; Behavior Therapy; Family Therapy; Art Therapy; Music Therapy; Play Therapy. *Professionals on Staff* Psychiatrists 1; Psychologists 1; Social Workers 6; Child Care Staff 25. *Service Facilities Available (with number of rooms)* Resource Rooms 2; Self-Contained Rooms 5; On-Campus Residential School 8. *Educational Professionals* Special Education Teachers 5; Career/Vocational Teachers 1; Crisis Teachers 1; Special Education Counselors 6. *Curricula* Traditional Academic; Career/Vocational Education; Individualized. *Educational Intervention Approaches* Precision Teaching; Behavior Modification; Creative Conditioning. *Degrees Awarded* Certificate of Attendance.

Manitowoc County Counseling Center

339 Reed Ave, Manitowoc, WI 54220 (414) 683-4300
Year Established 1962
Contact Judith M Doersch, Admin

Facility Information *Placement* Outpatient Community; Mental Health Program. *Sexes Served* Both. *Sources of Funding* State Funds; Health Insurance; Medicaid; Medicare; Sliding Scale. *Teacher Certification Level* Elementary School. *Special Certification Level* Reading. **Student/Patient Characteristics** *Age Levels* 0-4; 5-8; 9-11; 12-14; 15-17; 18-21; Over 21. *IQ Ranges* 0-25; 26-40; 41-55; 56-70; 71-85; 85-130; Above 130. *Exceptionalities Served* Autistic; Emotionally Disturbed; Learning Disabled; Mentally Handicapped; Communication Disordered; Hearing Impaired/Deaf; Visually Impaired/Blind; Other Health Impaired; Physically Handicapped; Gifted. *Learning Problems* Memory Disabilities; Perceptual Disabilities; Thinking Disabilities; Oral Language Disabilities; Reading Disabilities; Handwriting Disabilities; Spelling Disabilities; Arithmetic Disabilities; Written Expression. *Behavioral Problems* Attention Deficits; Hyperactivity; Hypoactivity; Impulsivity; Self-Aggression; Verbal Aggression; Physical Aggression; Indirect Aggression; Passive Aggression; Withdrawal. *Conditions Treated* Early Infantile Autism; Disintegrative Psychoses; Schizophrenia; Aphasia; Phobias; Obsessions and Compulsions; Hysteria; Depression; Suicide; Anorexia Nervosa; Inadequacy/Immaturity; Personality Problems; Socialized Aggressive Reaction; Unsocialized Aggressive Reaction.

Services Provided Individual Therapy; Parent Involvement; Behavior Therapy; Family Therapy; Filial Therapy; Drug Therapy. *Professionals on Staff* Psychiatrists 1; Psychologists 2; Social Workers 3. *Educational Professionals* Special Education Teachers 1.

Comments MCCC is a publicly funded and operated outpatient community mental health service.

Martin Luther Centers

2001 W Broadway, Madison, WI 53713 (608) 221-8786
Year Established 1898
Contact Frank Chase, Residential Dir

Facility Information *Placement* Public School; Special School; Private Residential Care. *Number of Beds* 46. *Children/Adolescents Served* 55. *Sexes Served* Both. *Room and*

Board Fees (Approx) $90. *Tuition Fees (Approx)* $32,722. *Sources of Funding* State Funds; Health Insurance; County Social Services. Summer school available. *Teacher Certification Level* Junior High/Middle School; High School. *Special Certification Level* ED; LD; Career/Vocational Education; Reading; Math.

Student/Patient Characteristics *Age Levels* 12-14; 15-17. *IQ Ranges* 71-85; 85-130. *Exceptionalities Served* Emotionally Disturbed; Learning Disabled; Physically Handicapped. *Learning Problems* Memory Disabilities; Perceptual Disabilities; Thinking Disabilities; Oral Language Disabilities; Reading Disabilities; Handwriting Disabilities; Spelling Disabilities; Arithmetic Disabilities; Written Expression. *Behavioral Problems* Attention Deficits; Hyperactivity; Impulsivity; Self-Aggression; Verbal Aggression; Physical Aggression; Indirect Aggression; Passive Aggression; Withdrawal. *Conditions Treated* Alcohol Abuse and/or Drug Abuse; Other Substance Abuse or Dependence; Schizophrenia; Phobias; Obsessions and Compulsions; Hysteria; Depression; Suicide; Asthma; Anorexia Nervosa; Personality Problems; Socialized Aggressive Reaction; Unsocialized Aggressive Reaction.

Services Provided Individual Therapy; Group Therapy; Parent Involvement; Behavior Therapy; Cognitive Developmental Therapy; Family Therapy; Drug Therapy; Art Therapy; Reality Therapy; Play Therapy. *Professionals on Staff* Psychiatrists 3; Psychologists 1; Social Workers 3; Child Care Staff 28; Nurses. *Service Facilities Available (with number of rooms)* Resource Rooms 3; Transition Rooms 6; Self-Contained Rooms 8; On-Campus Residential School 3. *Educational Professionals* Regular School Teachers 1; Special Education Teachers 2; Career/Vocational Teachers 1; Paraprofessionals 3. *Curricula* Traditional Academic; Career/Vocational Education; Individualized; Basic Skills; Prevocational. *Educational Intervention Approaches* Progressive Discipline; Self-Control; Behavior Modification; Creative Conditioning Positive Peer Group. *Degrees Awarded* High School Diploma; Graduate Equivalency Diploma.

Comments The center is a community based residential program serving boys and girls in 4 residential units. It provides in-home treatment and foster care treatment following a residential stay.

Mendota Mental Health Institute—Child and Adolescent Program

301 Troy Dr, Madison, WI 53704 (608) 244-2411
Contact William M Buzogany, Dir of the Child and Adolescent Prog

Facility Information *Placement* Special School; Public Residential Care; Special Program; Mental Health Institute. *Number of Beds* 65. *Children/Adolescents Served* 70. *Sexes Served* Both. *Room and Board Fees (Approx)* $236. *Sources of Funding* State Funds; Health Insurance; Medicaid. Summer school available. *Teacher Certification Level* Elementary School; Junior High/Middle School; High School. *Special Certification Level* ED; LD; MR; Career/Vocational Education; Reading; Math.

Student/Patient Characteristics *Age Levels* 5-8; 9-11; 12-14; 15-17. *IQ Ranges* 71-85; 85-130; Above 130. *Exceptionalities Served* Autistic; Emotionally Disturbed; Learning Disabled; Mentally Handicapped; Communication Disordered; Hearing Impaired/Deaf; Visually Impaired/Blind; Other Health Impaired; Physically Handicapped; Gifted. *Learning Problems* Memory Disabilities; Perceptual Disabilities; Thinking Disabilities; Oral Language Disabilities; Reading Disabilities; Handwriting Disabilities; Spelling Disabilities; Arithmetic Disabilities; Written Expression. *Behavioral Problems* Attention Deficits; Hyperactivity; Hypoactivity; Impulsivity; Self-Aggression; Verbal Aggression; Physical Aggression; Indirect Aggression; Passive Aggression; Withdrawal. *Conditions Treated* Alcohol Abuse and/or Drug Abuse; Other Substance Abuse or Dependence; Early Infantile Autism; Disintegrative Psychoses; Schizophrenia; Aphasia; Convulsive Disorders; Phobias; Obsessions and Compulsions; Hysteria; Depression; Suicide; Asthma; Anorexia Nervosa; Ulcerative Colitis; Inadequacy/Immaturity; Personality Problems; Socialized Aggressive Reaction; Unsocialized Aggressive Reaction.

Services Provided Individual Therapy; Group Therapy; Parent Involvement; Behavior Therapy; Cognitive Developmental Therapy; Family Therapy; Filial Therapy; Drug Therapy; Art Ther-

apy; Music Therapy; Reality Therapy; Play Therapy; Psychodrama. *Professionals on Staff* Psychiatrists 6; Psychologists 6; Counselors 2; Social Workers 6; Child Care Staff 40; Nurses 24; Occupational Therapist 1; Recreational Therapists 2. *Service Facilities Available (with number of rooms)* Consultative (ERT) 4; Resource Rooms 2; Self-Contained Rooms 8. *Educational Professionals* Special Education Teachers 14; Career/Vocational Teachers 1; Paraprofessionals 2. *Curricula* Traditional Academic; Career/Vocational Education; Individualized; Basic Skills; Prevocational. *Educational Intervention Approaches* Engineered Classroom; Precision Teaching; Progressive Discipline; Self-Control; Behavior Modification; Applied Behavior Analysis; Creative Conditioning. *Degrees Awarded* High School Diploma; Graduate Equivalency Diploma.

Comments Mendota Mental Health Institute is a public mental health facility serving the state of Wisconsin. Mendota has a specialized unit for youth transferred from the 2 state juvenile correctional facilities.

North Central Health Care Facilities

1100 Lake View Dr, Wausau, WI 54401 (715) 842-1636
Year Established 1894
Contact Peter DeSantis, Exec Dir

Facility Information *Placement* Public Day Care; Health Care Facility. *Sexes Served* Both. *Sources of Funding* State Funds; Health Insurance; Medicaid; Medicare. *Special Certification Level* LD; MR.

Student/Patient Characteristics *Age Levels* 0-4; 5-8; 9-11; 12-14; 15-17. *Exceptionalities Served* Autistic; Emotionally Disturbed; Learning Disabled; Mentally Handicapped; Communication Disordered; Hearing Impaired/Deaf; Visually Impaired/Blind; Other Health Impaired; Physically Handicapped. *Learning Problems* Memory Disabilities; Perceptual Disabilities; Thinking Disabilities; Oral Language Disabilities; Reading Disabilities; Handwriting Disabilities; Spelling Disabilities; Arithmetic Disabilities; Written Expression. *Behavioral Problems* Hyperactivity; Hypoactivity; Impulsivity; Self-Aggression; Verbal Aggression; Physical Aggression; Indirect Aggression; Passive Aggression; Withdrawal. *Conditions Treated* Alcohol Abuse and/or Drug Abuse; Other Substance Abuse or Dependence; Early Infantile Autism; Disintegrative Psychoses; Schizophrenia; Aphasia; Convulsive Disorders; Phobias; Obsessions and Compulsions; Hysteria; Depression; Suicide; Inadequacy/Immaturity; Personality Problems; Socialized Aggressive Reaction; Unsocialized Aggressive Reaction.

Services Provided Individual Therapy; Group Therapy; Parent Involvement; Behavior Therapy; Cognitive Developmental Therapy; Family Therapy; Filial Therapy; Drug Therapy; Art Therapy; Music Therapy; Reality Therapy. *Professionals on Staff* Psychiatrists 3; Psychologists 7; Counselors 12; Social Workers 13; Child Care Staff 7; Nurses 25; Speech Therapist; Physical Therapist; Occupational Therapist; Neuro Psychological Evaluator. *Educational Professionals* Special Education Teachers 7; Paraprofessionals 15. *Curricula* Individualized; Basic Skills.

Comments This is a comprehensive community mental health center serving mental health, alcohol-drug abuse, developmental disabilities, and geriatric patients.

Oconomowoc Developmental Training Center Inc

36100 Genesee Lake Rd, Oconomowoc, WI 53066
(414) 567-5515
Year Established 1975
Contact Debbie Frisk, Dir

Facility Information *Placement* Private Residential Care. *Number of Beds* 60. *Children/Adolescents Served* 60. *Sexes Served* Both. *Room and Board Fees (Approx)* $94. *Tuition Fees (Approx)* $6,600. *Sources of Funding* Department of Social Services; Developmental Disabilities Board. Summer school available. *Teacher Certification Level* Elementary School. *Special Certification Level* ED; LD; MR; Career/Vocational Education.

Student/Patient Characteristics *Age Levels* 0-4; 5-8; 9-11; 12-14; 15-17; 18-21. *IQ Ranges* 26-40; 41-55; 56-70. *Exceptionalities Served* Autistic; Emotionally Disturbed; Learning Disabled; Mentally Handicapped; Communication Disordered; Hearing Impaired/Deaf; Visually Impaired/Blind; Other Health Impaired; Physically Handicapped. *Learning Problems* Memory Disabilities; Perceptual Disabilities; Thinking Disabilities; Oral Language Disabilities; Reading Disabilities; Handwriting Disabilities; Spelling Disabilities; Arithmetic Disabilities; Written Expression. *Behavioral Problems* Attention Deficits; Hyperactivity; Hypoactivity; Impulsivity; Self-Aggression; Verbal Aggression; Physical Aggression; Indirect Aggression; Passive Aggression; Withdrawal. *Conditions Treated* Early Infantile Autism; Disintegrative Psychoses; Schizophrenia; Aphasia; Convulsive Disorders; Phobias; Obsessions and Compulsions; Hysteria; Depression; Suicide; Asthma; Anorexia Nervosa; Ulcerative Colitis; Inadequacy/Immaturity; Personality Problems; Socialized Aggressive Reaction; Unsocialized Aggressive Reaction.

Services Provided Individual Therapy; Group Therapy; Parent Involvement; Behavior Therapy; Cognitive Developmental Therapy; Family Therapy; Drug Therapy; Reality Therapy; Play Therapy. *Professionals on Staff* Psychiatrists 1; Psychologists 2; Counselors 1; Social Workers 5; Child Care Staff; Nurses 6; Crisis Supervisors. *Service Facilities Available (with number of rooms)* Self-Contained Rooms 4; Workshop Program. *Educational Professionals* Special Education Teachers 6; Paraprofessionals 15. *Curricula* Individualized; Basic Skills; Prevocational. *Educational Intervention Approaches* Precision Teaching; Self-Control; Behavior Modification; Applied Behavior Analysis.

Project for Psychotic and Neurologically Impaired Children

301 Troy Dr, Madison, WI 53704 (608) 244-2411
Year Established 1972
Contact Glen Sallans, Unit Chief
Facility Information *Placement* Public Residential Care. *Number of Beds* 10. *Children/Adolescents Served* 10. *Sexes Served* Both. *Room and Board Fees (Approx)* $235. *Tuition Fees (Approx)* $85,775. *Sources of Funding* State Funds; Health Insurance; Medicaid; Parent Fee; Sliding Scale. Summer school available. *Teacher Certification Level* Elementary School; Junior High/Middle School; High School. *Special Certification Level* ED; LD; MR.
Student/Patient Characteristics *Age Levels* 0-4; 5-8; 9-11; 12-14; 15-17. *IQ Ranges* 0-25; 26-40; 41-55; 56-70; 71-85; 85-130. *Exceptionalities Served* Autistic; Emotionally Disturbed; Learning Disabled; Mentally Handicapped; Communication Disordered; Hearing Impaired/Deaf; Visually Impaired/Blind; Other Health Impaired. *Learning Problems* Memory Disabilities; Perceptual Disabilities; Thinking Disabilities; Oral Language Disabilities; Reading Disabilities; Handwriting Disabilities; Spelling Disabilities; Arithmetic Disabilities; Written Expression. *Behavioral Problems* Attention Deficits; Hyperactivity; Hypoactivity; Impulsivity; Self-Aggression; Verbal Aggression; Physical Aggression; Indirect Aggression; Passive Aggression; Withdrawal. *Conditions Treated* Early Infantile Autism; Schizophrenia; Convulsive Disorders; Phobias; Depression; Inadequacy/Immaturity; Unsocialized Aggressive Reaction.
Services Provided Individual Therapy; Parent Involvement; Behavior Therapy; Family Therapy; Drug Therapy; Play Therapy. *Professionals on Staff* Psychologists 2; Social Workers 1; Child Care Staff 7; Nurses 4.5; Occupational Therapist 1; Speech Therapist .5; Pediatrician .5. *Service Facilities Available (with number of rooms)* On-Campus Residential School 2. *Educational Professionals* Special Education Teachers 2. *Curricula* Individualized; Basic Skills; Prevocational. *Educational Intervention Approaches* Precision Teaching; Self-Control; Behavior Modification; Applied Behavior Analysis.
Comments This is an inpatient setting for MR, autistic, and other ED children who cannot be maintained in the community. Treatment is behavioral. Training is provided for parents, teachers, and mental health personnel.

Sunburst Youth Homes

1210 W 5th, Neillsville, WI 54456 (715) 743-3154
Contact Donald W Clemens, Prog Dir
Facility Information *Placement* Special School; Private Residential Care; Private Day Care. *Number of Beds* 67. *Children/Adolescents Served* 67. *Sexes Served* Both. *Room and Board Fees (Approx)* $97. *Sources of Funding* State Funds; Health Insurance; P.L. 94-142; Contributions. Summer school available. *Teacher Certification Level* Elementary School; Junior High/Middle School; High School. *Special Certification Level* ED; LD; MR; Reading; Math.
Student/Patient Characteristics *Age Levels* 5-8; 9-11; 12-14; 15-17; 18-21. *IQ Ranges* 85-130. *Exceptionalities Served* Autistic; Emotionally Disturbed; Learning Disabled; Neurologically Impaired. *Learning Problems* Perceptual Disabilities; Thinking Disabilities; Reading Disabilities; Handwriting Disabilities; Spelling Disabilities; Arithmetic Disabilities; Written Expression. *Behavioral Problems* Attention Deficits; Hyperactivity; Impulsivity; Self-Aggression; Verbal Aggression; Physical Aggression; Indirect Aggression; Passive Aggression; Withdrawal. *Conditions Treated* Alcohol Abuse and/or Drug Abuse; Other Substance Abuse or Dependence; Convulsive Disorders; Phobias; Obsessions and Compulsions; Hysteria; Depression; Anorexia Nervosa; Inadequacy/Immaturity; Personality Problems; Socialized Aggressive Reaction; Unsocialized Aggressive Reaction.
Services Provided Individual Therapy; Group Therapy; Parent Involvement; Behavior Therapy; Family Therapy; Drug Therapy; Art Therapy; Music Therapy; Reality Therapy; Recreation Therapy. *Professionals on Staff* Psychiatrists .25; Psychologists .25; Counselors .25; Social Workers 6; Child Care Staff 30; Recreation Therapists 5. *Service Facilities Available (with number of rooms)* Consultative (ERT) 1; Resource Rooms 2; Self-Contained Rooms 11; On-Campus Residential School; Homebound Instruction 7. *Educational Professionals* Regular School Teachers 5; Special Education Teachers 7; Career/Vocational Teachers 1; Crisis Teachers 2; Special Education Counselors 1; Media Specialist 1. *Curricula* Traditional Academic; Career/Vocational Education; Individualized; Basic Skills; Prevocational; GED Preparation. *Educational Intervention Approaches* Engineered Classroom; Precision Teaching; Behavior Modification; Applied Behavior Analysis. *Degrees Awarded* High School Diploma; Graduate Equivalency Diploma.

Tomorrow's Children

Box 192, Waupaca, WI 54981 (715) 258-8351
Year Established 1973
Contact Greg Heindel, Social Worker
Facility Information *Placement* Private Residential Care. *Number of Beds* 22. *Children/Adolescents Served* 22. *Sexes Served* Both. *Room and Board Fees (Approx)* $92. *Tuition Fees (Approx)* $33,840. *Sources of Funding* State Funds; County. Summer school available. *Special Certification Level* ED; MR.
Student/Patient Characteristics *Age Levels* 5-8; 9-11; 12-14; 15-17. *IQ Ranges* 26-40; 41-55; 56-70; 71-85; 85-130. *Exceptionalities Served* Autistic; Emotionally Disturbed; Learning Disabled; Mentally Handicapped. *Learning Problems* Memory Disabilities; Perceptual Disabilities; Thinking Disabilities; Oral Language Disabilities; Reading Disabilities; Handwriting Disabilities; Spelling Disabilities; Arithmetic Disabilities; Written Expression. *Behavioral Problems* Attention Deficits; Hyperactivity; Hypoactivity; Impulsivity; Self-Aggression; Verbal Aggression; Physical Aggression; Indirect Aggression; Passive Aggression; Withdrawal. *Conditions Treated* Early Infantile Autism; Disintegrative Psychoses; Schizophrenia; Aphasia; Convulsive Disorders; Phobias; Obsessions and Compulsions; Hysteria; Depression; Suicide; Inadequacy/Immaturity; Personality Problems; Socialized Aggressive Reaction; Unsocialized Aggressive Reaction.
Services Provided Individual Therapy; Group Therapy; Parent Involvement; Behavior Therapy; Family Therapy; Drug Therapy. *Professionals on Staff* Psychiatrists 1; Psychologists 1; Social Workers 1; Child Care Staff 21. *Service Facilities Available (with number of rooms)* Home Setting; On-Campus Residential School 3. *Educational Professionals* Special Education Teachers 2;

Career/Vocational Teachers 1; Special Education Counselors 1. *Curricula* Traditional Academic; Individualized; Basic Skills; Prevocational. *Educational Intervention Approaches* Behavior Modification; Applied Behavior Analysis.

University of Wisconsin—Child Psychiatry Clinic

600 Highland Ave, Madison, WI 53792 (608) 263-6099
Year Established 1955
Contact William Smith, Clinic Dir
Facility Information *Placement* Outpatient Child Psychiatry Clinic.

Willowglen Academy Inc

3030 W Highland Blvd, Milwaukee, WI 53208 (414) 342-7040
Year Established 1972
Contact David S Perhach, Dir
Facility Information *Placement* Private Residential Care. *Number of Beds* 102. *Children/Adolescents Served* 102. *Sexes Served* Both. *Room and Board Fees (Approx)* $55-$80. *Sources of Funding* State Funds; Health Insurance; P.L. 94-142; County Funds. Summer school available. *Teacher Certification Level* Elementary School; Junior High/Middle School; High School. *Special Certification Level* ED; LD; MR; Career/Vocational Education; Reading; Speech Therapy; Occupational Therapy.
Student/Patient Characteristics *Age Levels* 5-8; 9-11; 12-14; 15-17; 18-21. *IQ Ranges* 0-25; 26-40; 41-55; 56-70; 71-85; 85-130; Above 130. *Exceptionalities Served* Autistic; Emotionally Disturbed; Learning Disabled; Mentally Handicapped; Communication Disordered; Hearing Impaired/Deaf. *Learning Problems* Memory Disabilities; Perceptual Disabilities; Thinking Disabilities; Oral Language Disabilities; Reading Disabilities; Handwriting Disabilities; Spelling Disabilities; Arithmetic Disabilities; Written Expression. *Behavioral Problems* Attention Deficits; Hyperactivity; Impulsivity; Self-Aggression; Verbal Aggression; Physical Aggression; Indirect Aggression; Passive Aggression; Withdrawal. *Conditions Treated* Early Infantile Autism; Disintegrative Psychoses; Schizophrenia; Convulsive Disorders; Phobias; Obsessions and Compulsions; Depression; Suicide; Anorexia Nervosa; Inadequacy/Immaturity; Personality Problems; Socialized Aggressive Reaction; Unsocialized Aggressive Reaction.
Services Provided Individual Therapy; Group Therapy; Parent Involvement; Behavior Therapy; Family Therapy; Art Therapy; Music Therapy; Reality Therapy; Play Therapy. *Professionals on Staff* Psychiatrists 6; Psychologists 2; Counselors 60; Social Workers 6; Nurses 3; Speech; Occupational Therapy; Activity Therapy. *Educational Professionals* Special Education Teachers 12; Career/Vocational Teachers 2; Crisis Teachers 5; Paraprofessionals. *Curricula* Career/Vocational Education; Individualized; Basic Skills; Prevocational. *Educational Intervention Approaches* Self-Control; Behavior Modification. *Degrees Awarded* Certificate of Attendance; High School Diploma; Graduate Equivalency Diploma.

Winnebago Mental Health Institute—Autistic Unit

Box 9, Winnebago, WI 54985 (414) 235-4910
Year Established 1962
Contact Dennis Meszaron, Prog Dir
Facility Information *Placement* Public Residential Care. *Number of Beds* 15. *Children/Adolescents Served* 15. *Sexes Served* Both. *Sources of Funding* State Funds; Health Insurance; Title 18; Title 19. Summer school available. *Teacher Certification Level* Elementary School; Junior High/Middle School; High School. *Special Certification Level* ED; LD; MR; Reading; Math.
Student/Patient Characteristics *Age Levels* 0-4; 5-8; 9-11; 12-14; 15-17; 18-21. *IQ Ranges* 0-25; 26-40. *Exceptionalities Served* Autistic; Mentally Handicapped; Behavioral Disorders. *Behavioral Problems* Attention Deficits; Hyperactivity; Hypoactivity; Impulsivity; Self-Aggression; Physical Aggression; Withdrawal. *Conditions Treated* Early Infantile Autism; Behavioral Disorders.

Services Provided Parent Involvement; Behavior Therapy. *Professionals on Staff* Psychiatrists .5; Psychologists .5; Social Workers .5; Child Care Staff 7; Nurses 2; Occupational Therapist 1. *Service Facilities Available (with number of rooms)* Self-Contained Rooms 3. *Educational Professionals* Special Education Teachers 4; Paraprofessionals 2. *Curricula* Individualized; Basic Skills; Prevocational. *Educational Intervention Approaches* Engineered Classroom; Precision Teaching; Self-Control; Behavior Modification; Applied Behavior Analysis.

Winnebago Mental Health Institute—Children's Unit

Box 9, Winnebago, WI 54985 (414) 235-4910
Year Established 1962
Contact Dennis Meszaros, Prog Dir
Facility Information *Placement* Public Residential Care. *Number of Beds* 60. *Children/Adolescents Served* 60. *Sexes Served* Both. *Sources of Funding* State Funds; Health Insurance; Title 18; Title 19. Summer school available. *Teacher Certification Level* Elementary School; Junior High/Middle School; High School. *Special Certification Level* ED; LD; MR; Reading; Math.
Student/Patient Characteristics *Age Levels* 0-4; 5-8; 9-11; 12-14; 15-17; 18-21. *IQ Ranges* 41-55; 56-70; 71-85; 85-130; Above 130. *Exceptionalities Served* Emotionally Disturbed. *Behavioral Problems* Attention Deficits; Hyperactivity; Hypoactivity; Impulsivity; Self-Aggression; Verbal Aggression; Physical Aggression; Indirect Aggression; Passive Aggression; Withdrawal. *Conditions Treated* Alcohol Abuse and/or Drug Abuse; Other Substance Abuse or Dependence; Early Infantile Autism; Disintegrative Psychoses; Schizophrenia; Aphasia; Convulsive Disorders; Phobias; Obsessions and Compulsions; Hysteria; Depression; Suicide; Anorexia Nervosa; Inadequacy/Immaturity; Personality Problems; Socialized Aggressive Reaction; Unsocialized Aggressive Reaction.
Services Provided Individual Therapy; Group Therapy; Parent Involvement; Behavior Therapy; Family Therapy; Drug Therapy. *Professionals on Staff* Psychiatrists 2; Psychologists 2; Social Workers 4; Child Care Staff 30; Nurses 10; Occupational Therapist 4. *Service Facilities Available (with number of rooms)* Self-Contained Rooms 8. *Educational Professionals* Special Education Teachers 12.5. *Curricula* Traditional Academic; Career/Vocational Education; Individualized; Basic Skills; Prevocational. *Educational Intervention Approaches* Engineered Classroom; Precision Teaching; Self-Control; Behavior Modification; Applied Behavior Analysis. *Degrees Awarded* High School Diploma; Graduate Equivalency Diploma.

Wyalusing Academy

601 S Beaumont Rd, Prairie du Chien, WI 53821
(608) 326-6481
Year Established 1969
Contact Robert Pickett, Ed Dir
Facility Information *Placement* Special School; Private Residential Care. *Number of Beds* 70. *Children/Adolescents Served* 70. *Sexes Served* Both. *Sources of Funding* State Funds; P.L. 94-142. Summer school available. *Teacher Certification Level* Junior High/Middle School; High School. *Special Certification Level* ED; LD; MR; Career/Vocational Education; Vocational Certification.
Student/Patient Characteristics *Age Levels* 12-14; 15-17. *IQ Ranges* 56-70; 71-85; 85-130. *Exceptionalities Served* Emotionally Disturbed; Learning Disabled; Mentally Handicapped; Communication Disordered; Physically Handicapped; Delinquent. *Learning Problems* Memory Disabilities; Perceptual Disabilities; Thinking Disabilities; Oral Language Disabilities; Reading Disabilities; Handwriting Disabilities; Spelling Disabilities; Arithmetic Disabilities; Written Expression; Gross and Fine Motor Disabilities. *Behavioral Problems* Attention Deficits; Hyperactivity; Hypoactivity; Impulsivity; Self-Aggression; Verbal Aggression; Physical Aggression; Indirect Aggression; Passive Aggression; Withdrawal. *Conditions Treated* Phobias; Obsessions

and Compulsions; Hysteria; Depression; Suicide; Inadequacy/
Immaturity; Personality Problems; Socialized Aggressive Reaction; Unsocialized Aggressive Reaction.

Services Provided Individual Therapy; Group Therapy; Parent Involvement; Behavior Therapy; Drug Therapy. *Professionals on Staff* Psychiatrists 5; Psychologists 1; Social Workers 5; Child Care Staff 30; Nurses 3; Speech Therapists 2; Occupational Therapist 1; Crisis Intervention Aids 3; Recreation Therapist 1. *Service Facilities Available (with number of rooms)* Consultative (ERT) 3; Resource Rooms 1; Self-Contained Rooms 3; Individual Academic Instruction 4; On-Campus Residential School. *Educational Professionals* Special Education Teachers 6; Career/ Vocational Teachers 9; Crisis Teachers 3. *Curricula* Traditional Academic; Career/Vocational Education; Individualized; Basic Skills; Prevocational. *Educational Intervention Approaches* Engineered Classroom; Precision Teaching; Self-Control; Behavior Modification. *Degrees Awarded* Certificate of Attendance; Graduate Equivalency Diploma.

Comments Wyalusing Academy emphasizes developing students' ability to get jobs through vocational training and actual community work experience. Students are in school from 9-4 all year long; most hours are spent learning job skills and behavior in welding, mechanics, metals, business education, home economics, building trades, food service, and work adjustment.

Wyoming

Cathedral Home for Children

PO Box E, Laramie, WY 82070 (307) 745-8997
Year Established 1910
Contact Richard Munchel, Prog Dir
Facility Information *Placement* Private Residential Care. *Number of Beds* 30. *Children/Adolescents Served* 30. *Sexes Served* Both. *Room and Board Fees (Approx)* $44. *Tuition Fees (Approx)* $9,000. *Sources of Funding* P.L. 94-142; Contract Service. Summer school available. *Teacher Certification Level* Junior High/Middle School; High School. *Special Certification Level* Reading; General Science; Phychology; Biology; Special Education.
Student/Patient Characteristics *Age Levels* 12-14; 15-17; 18-21. *IQ Ranges* 71-85; 85-130; Above 130. *Exceptionalities Served* Emotionally Disturbed; Learning Disabled. *Learning Problems* Memory Disabilities; Perceptual Disabilities; Thinking Disabilities; Oral Language Disabilities; Reading Disabilities; Handwriting Disabilities; Spelling Disabilities; Arithmetic Disabilities; Written Expression. *Behavioral Problems* Attention Deficits; Hyperactivity; Hypoactivity; Impulsivity; Self-Aggression; Verbal Aggression; Indirect Aggression; Passive Aggression; Withdrawal. *Conditions Treated* Alcohol Abuse and/or Drug Abuse; Other Substance Abuse or Dependence; Phobias; Obsessions and Compulsions; Depression; Anorexia Nervosa; Inadequacy/Immaturity; Personality Problems.
Services Provided Individual Therapy; Group Therapy; Behavior Therapy; Drug Therapy; Reality Therapy. *Professionals on Staff* Counselors 2; Social Workers 2; Child Care Staff 10. *Service Facilities Available (with number of rooms)* Self-Contained Rooms 2; On-Campus Residential School 2. *Educational Professionals* Special Education Teachers 1. *Curricula* Career/Vocational Education; Individualized; Basic Skills; Prevocational. *Educational Intervention Approaches* Progressive Discipline; Self-Control; Behavior Modification. *Degrees Awarded* Certificate of Attendance.

Comments This is a structured learning environment based on a sequential program approach. The program is based on individualized curriculum and is self-paced. Behavior modification is the method of discipline.

St Joseph's Children's Home

Box 1117, Torrington, WY 82240 (307) 532-4197
Contact Steven E Bogus, Prog Dir
Facility Information *Placement* Private Residential Care. *Number of Beds* 30. *Children/Adolescents Served* 30. *Sexes Served* Both. *Room and Board Fees (Approx)* $32. *Sources of Funding* State Funds; P.L. 94-142; Private Contributions. Summer school available. *Teacher Certification Level* Elementary School; Junior High/Middle School; High School. *Special Certification Level* ED; LD; MR; Career/Vocational Education; Elementary Education; Psychology; English; Physical Education; Health.

Student/Patient Characteristics *Age Levels* 9-11; 12-14; 15-17. *IQ Ranges* 71-85; 85-130. *Exceptionalities Served* Emotionally Disturbed; Learning Disabled. *Learning Problems* Memory Disabilities; Perceptual Disabilities; Reading Disabilities; Handwriting Disabilities; Spelling Disabilities; Arithmetic Disabilities; Written Expression. *Behavioral Problems* Attention Deficits; Hyperactivity; Hypoactivity; Impulsivity; Self-Aggression; Verbal Aggression; Physical Aggression; Indirect Aggression; Passive Aggression; Withdrawal. *Conditions Treated* Depression; Suicide; Asthma; Anorexia Nervosa; Ulcerative Colitis; Inadequacy/Immaturity; Personality Problems; Socialized Aggressive Reaction.
Services Provided Individual Therapy; Group Therapy; Parent Involvement; Family Therapy; Play Therapy. *Professionals on Staff* Counselors 2; Social Workers 3; Child Care Staff 16. *Service Facilities Available (with number of rooms)* Self-Contained Rooms 2; Vocational Education 1; Physical Education 1. *Educational Professionals* Special Education Teachers 2; Career/Vocational Teachers 1; Paraprofessionals 2; Psychological Diagnostician 1; Physical Education 1. *Curricula* Individualized; Basic Skills; Prevocational; Accelerated Curriculum. *Educational Intervention Approaches* Engineered Classroom; Precision Teaching; Behavior Modification; Applied Behavior Analysis; Adlerian Psychology.

Wyoming State Hospital

Box 177, Evanston, WY 82930 (307) 789-3464
Year Established 1886
Contact Gary R Parker, Dir Dept of Social Work Serv
Facility Information *Placement* Psychiatric Hospital. *Number of Beds* 30. *Children/Adolescents Served* 30. *Sexes Served* Both. *Room and Board Fees (Approx)* $180. *Sources of Funding* State Funds. Summer school available. *Teacher Certification Level* Elementary School; Junior High/Middle School; High School. *Special Certification Level* ED; LD; MR; Career/Vocational Education; Reading; Math.
Student/Patient Characteristics *Age Levels* 9-11; 12-14; 15-17; 18-21; Over 21. *Exceptionalities Served* Autistic; Mentally Handicapped. *Learning Problems* Memory Disabilities; Perceptual Disabilities; Thinking Disabilities; Oral Language Disabilities; Reading Disabilities; Handwriting Disabilities; Spelling Disabilities; Arithmetic Disabilities; Written Expression. *Behavioral Problems* Attention Deficits; Hyperactivity; Hypoactivity; Impulsivity; Self-Aggression; Verbal Aggression; Physical Aggression; Indirect Aggression; Passive Aggression; Withdrawal. *Conditions Treated* Alcohol Abuse and/or Drug Abuse; Other Substance Abuse or Dependence; Early Infantile Autism; Disintegrative Psychoses; Schizophrenia; Aphasia; Convulsive Disorders; Phobias; Obsessions and Compulsions; Depression; Suicide; Anorexia Nervosa.
Services Provided Individual Therapy; Group Therapy; Parent Involvement; Behavior Therapy; Cognitive Developmental Therapy; Family Therapy; Drug Therapy; Music Therapy; Reality

Therapy. *Professionals on Staff* Psychiatrists 1; Psychologists 1; Counselors 5; Social Workers 5; Child Care Staff 25; Nurses 10. *Service Facilities Available (with number of rooms)* Consultative (ERT) 1; Resource Rooms 4. *Educational Professionals* Regular School Teachers 2; Special Education Teachers 3; Career/Vocational Teachers 1; Crisis Teachers 4; Special Education Counselors 1. *Curricula* Traditional Academic; Career/Vocational Education; Individualized; Basic Skills; Sewing and Cooking. *Educational Intervention Approaches* Engineered Classroom; Precision Teaching; Progressive Discipline; Self-Control; Behavior Modification; Applied Behavior Analysis; Creative Conditioning. *Degrees Awarded* Graduate Equivalency Diploma.

Wyoming Youth Treatment Center

1514 E 12th St, Casper, WY 82601 (307) 261-2200
Year Established 1912
Contact George Brown, Supt

Facility Information *Placement* Public Residential Care. *Number of Beds* 50. *Children/Adolescents Served* 50. *Sexes Served* Both. *Room and Board Fees (Approx)* $107. *Sources of Funding* State Funds. Summer school available. *Teacher Certification Level* Elementary School; Junior High/Middle School; High School. *Special Certification Level* ED; LD; Regular Education; General Special Education.

Student/Patient Characteristics *Age Levels* 12-14; 15-17; 18-21. *IQ Ranges* 85-130. *Exceptionalities Served* Emotionally Disturbed; Learning Disabled. *Learning Problems* Reading Disabilities; Spelling Disabilities; Arithmetic Disabilities; Written Expression. *Behavioral Problems* Hyperactivity; Impulsivity; Self-Aggression; Verbal Aggression; Physical Aggression; Indirect Aggression; Passive Aggression; Withdrawal. *Conditions Treated* Alcohol Abuse and/or Drug Abuse; Depression; Suicide; Inadequacy/Immaturity; Personality Problems; Socialized Aggressive Reaction; Unsocialized Aggressive Reaction.

Services Provided Individual Therapy; Group Therapy; Parent Involvement; Reality Therapy. *Professionals on Staff* Psychiatrists 1; Psychologists 2; Counselors 5; Child Care Staff; Nurses 1. *Service Facilities Available (with number of rooms)* On-Campus Residential School. *Educational Professionals* Regular School Teachers 1; Special Education Teachers 2. *Curricula* Individualized; Basic Skills. *Educational Intervention Approaches* Progressive Discipline; Self-Control.

Exceptionalities Index

Autistic

ALA Costa Center for the Developmentally Disabled—After School, Berkeley, CA
Albuquerque Special Preschool, Albuquerque, NM
All Children's Hospital, St Petersburg, FL
Allendale School, Lake Villa, IL
American Institute—The Training School at Vineland, Vineland, NJ
Anne Arundel County Health Department Mental Health Clinic, Annapolis, MD
Archdiocese of Louisville—Guidance Clinic, Louisville, KY
Area Education Agency—Education Center, Waterloo, IA
Arizona State Hospital, Phoenix, AZ
Arrise Inc—Arrise Group Home for Autistic Children, Forest Park, IL
Arthur Brisbane Child Treatment Center, Farmingdale, NJ
Atlanta Public Schools, Atlanta, GA
Austin State Hospital, Austin, TX
Autistic Treatment Center—Richardson, Richardson, TX
Autistic Treatment Center—San Antonio, San Antonio, TX
Avalon Center—Avalon Schools, Lenox, MA
Avalon School at High Point, Lenox, MA
Avon Lenox Special Education, Memphis, TN
Avondale House, Houston, TX
The Bancroft School, Haddonfield, NJ
Bar-None Residential Treatment Services for Children, Anoka, MN
Battle Creek Child Guidance Center, Battle Creek, MI
Behavior Research Institute, Providence, RI
Behavioral Development Center Inc, Providence, RI
Benhaven, East Haven, CT
Berea Children's Home, Berea, OH
Bergen Center for Child Development, Haworth, NJ
Bergen County Special Services School District—Washington School Autistic Program, Paramus, NJ
Bergen Pines Hospital—Children's Psychiatric Unit, Paramus, NJ
Berks County Intermediate Unit, Reading, PA
Berrien County Intermediate School District, Berrien Springs, MI
Big Lakes Developmental Center Inc, Manhattan, KS
Birmingham Autistic Program, Birmingham, MI
Birmingham City Board of Education, Birmingham, AL
Bittersweet Farms, Whitehouse, OH
Blick Clinic for Developmental Disabilities, Akron, OH
Board of Cooperative Educational Services II—Special Education Division Instructional Support Center, Centereach, NY
BOCES Nassau, Westbury, NY
BOCES Southern Westchester—Rye Lake Campus, White Plains, NY

Bowman Gray School of Medicine Developmental Evaluation Clinic—Amos Cottage Rehabilitation Hospital, Winston-Salem, NC
Bradley Hospital, East Providence, RI
Brant Services Corporation—Brant Ryan House, Inkster, MI
Brattleboro Retreat, Brattleboro, VT
Brentwood Center, Los Angeles, CA
Bronx Developmental Center—Respite Service, Bronx, NY
Brown County Mental Health Center—Children Services, Green Bay, WI
The Brown Schools, Austin, TX
Bunche Park Elementary School, Opa Locka, FL
Burt Children's Center, San Francisco, CA
Burwell Psychoeducational Program, Carrollton, GA
Camphill Special Schools Inc, Glenmoore, PA
Cantalician Center for Learning, Buffalo, NY
Capitol Region Education Council's Day Treatment Service, West Hartford, CT
Cass County Social Services—Children's Social Service Center, Fargo, ND
Center for Autistic Children, Philadelphia, PA
Central Massachusetts Special Education Collaborative—Quimby School, Worcester, MA
Central New Hampshire Community Mental Health Services Inc—Early Intervention Services, Concord, NH
Charles Lea Center—Program for Children, Adolescents, and Young Adults with Autism, Spartanburg, SC
Charleston County School District—Charleston Program for the Behaviorally Handicapped, North Charleston, SC
Cheboygan-Otsego-Presque Isle Intermediate School District—Alpine Educational Facility, Gaylord, MI
Cheboygan-Otsego-Presque Isle Intermediate School District—Hawks Programs, Hawks, MI
Cheboygen-Otsego-Presque Isle Intermediate School District—Inverness Elementary, Cheboygen, MI
Chestnut Lodge Hospital—Adolescent and Child Division, Rockville, MD
Child Adolescent Service Center, Canton, OH
Child and Adolescent Psychoeducational Center, Dalton, GA
Child Development Service—Lakeview Center Inc, Pensacola, FL
Child Disability Clinic—Carle Clinic, Urbana, IL
Child Guidance Center of Southern Connecticut, Stanford, CT
Child Guidance Clinic of Southeastern Connecticut Inc, New London, CT
Child Mental Health Services Inc—Allan Cott School McDonough House, Birmingham, AL
Child Study Center, Fort Worth, TX
Childhaven, Saint Louis, MO
Children's and Adolescent Unit of Mental Health Institute of Cherokee Iowa, Cherokee, IA
Children's Behavior Therapy Unit, Salt Lake City, UT

Children's Day Hospital—New York Hospital—Cornell Medical Center—Westchester Division, White Plains, NY

The Children's Day School, Trenton, NJ

Children's Health Council, Palo Alto, CA

Children's Home Society of South Dakota, Sioux Falls, SD

Children's Hospital at Washington University Medical Center—Psychiatric Unit, Saint Louis, MO

The Children's Institute, South Orange, NJ

Children's Learning Center of San Antonio, San Antonio, TX

Children's Medical Center, Tulsa, OK

The Children's Mercy Hospital—Section of Psychiatry, Kansas City, MO

Children's Psychiatric Center of the Jewish Hospital, Cincinnati, OH

The Children's School of the Institute of Living, Hartford, CT

Christ Church Child Center, Bethesda, MD

Clear View School, Scarborough, NY

Cleveland County Area Mental Health Program—Division of Child and Youth Services, Shelby, NC

The Clinical Center of Southern Illinois University, Carbondale, IL

Cobb County—Cobb Douglas Psychoeducation Children's Program, Marietta, GA

Colorado Springs School District No. 11, Colorado Springs, CO

Community Child Guidance Clinic Preschool, Manchester, CT

The Community School of the Family Service and Child Guidance Center of the Oranges Maplewood and Millburn, Orange, NJ

Concord, Yellow Spring, WV

Connecticut College Program for Children with Special Needs, New London, CT

Convalescent Hospital for Children, Rochester, NY

Cooperative Educational Services Developmental Learning Center, Wilton, CT

Cousins Respite Care Program of the Parent Resource Center Inc, Orlando, FL

Craig House—Technoma, Pittsburgh, PA

Creative Arts Rehabilitation Center Inc, New York, NY

DeJarnette Center, Staunton, VA

The Delacato and Doman Autistic Unit, Morton, PA

The Delacato and Doman Autistic Unit, Plymouth Meeting, PA

Department of Public Instruction, Dover, DE

Development Evaluation Center, Fayetteville, NC

Developmental Living Center, Sacramento, CA

The Devereux Center in Arizona, Scottsdale, AZ

The Devereux Foundation, Devon, PA

The Devereux Foundation, Santa Barbara, CA

The Devereux Schools at Rutland, Rutland, MA

Douglass College—Gibbons Campus—Douglass Developmental Disabilities Center, New Brunswick, NJ

Durham County Group Home for Autistic Adults Inc, Durham, NC

Dysfunctioning Child Center—Respite Care Unit, Chicago, IL

Early Childhood Developmental Center Inc, Hays, KS

Early Education Center, Jackson, MS

East Alabama Mental Health Retardation Center, Opelika, AL

Eastern Area Residential Treatment Home (EARTH), Greenville, NC

Eastern Los Angeles Regional Center for the Developmentally Disabled, Alhambra, CA

Eden Family of Programs, Princeton, NJ

Educational Alliance—Camp Cummings, New York, NY

Educational Service Unit 3—Department of Special Education—Exceptional Children Resource Center, Omaha, NE

Efficacy Research Institute of Framingham, Framingham, MA

Efficacy Research Institute of Taunton Inc, Taunton, MA

El Paso Guidance Center, El Paso, TX

Eleanor Griffin Children's Development Center, Plainview, TX

Elizabeth Ives School, Hamden, CT

Elwyn Institutes, Elwyn, PA

Emma Pendleton Bradley Hospital Developmental Disabilities Program, East Providence, RI

Encor—Family and Medical Support Services—Home Based Services, Omaha, NE

Encor—Family and Medical Support Services—Respite Services, Omaha, NE

Escalon Inc, Altadena, CA

Escambia District Schools, Pensacola, FL

Evansville Vanderburgh School Corporation, Evansville, IN

Family Guidance Center, Reading, PA

Flint Community Schools, Flint, MI

Florence Program for Autistic Children and Adolescents—Lester Elementary School, Florence, SC

Forest Heights Lodge, Evergreen, CO

The Forum School, Waldwick, NJ

Franklin Grand Isle Mental Health Services Inc, Saint Albans, VT

Fremont Unified School District, Fremont, CA

Garden Sullivan Learning and Development Program, San Francisco, CA

Genesee Intermediate School District Center for Autism, Flint, MI

Grady Memorial Hospital—Division of Child and Adolescent Psychiatry, Atlanta, GA

Grafton School, Berryville, VA

Grafton School—Autism Program, Berryville, VA

Green Meadows School, Wilmington, VT

Greenshire School, Cheshire, CT

The Group Home for the Autistic Inc, Albemarle, NC

The Grove School, Lake Forest, IL

Hall-Mercer Children's Center of the McLean Hospital, Belmont, MA

Harbor View Mercy Hospital, Fort Smith, AR

Harford County Community Mental Health Center, Bel Air, MD

Harrison County Training Center for Exceptional Children, Gulfport, MS

Hartgrove Hospital—Hartgrove Academy, Chicago, IL

Hawaii State Department of Education—Special Needs Branch, Honolulu, HI

Hawthorn Center, Northville, MI

Henry Horner Children and Adolescent Center, Chicago, IL

High Plains Mental Health Center—Colby Office, Colby, KS

Homes Unlimited Inc, Bangor, ME

Honolulu District—Special Education Center of Oahu (SECO), Honolulu, HI

Humana Hospital Huntington Beach—Children's Behavioral Center, Huntington Beach, CA

Huntsville City School System, Hunstville, AL

Illinois Center for Autism, Fairview Heights, IL

Independence House of Avalon Inc, Sheffield, MA

Indiana University Developmental Training Center, Bloomington, IN

Indianapolis Public Schools—Special Education Department, Indianapolis, IN

Indianapolis Public Schools—James E Roberts School No. 97, Indianapolis, IN

Ingham Developmental Center, Mason, MI

ISIS Programs Inc—Individual Support Through Innovative Services for Autistic Persons, Orlando, FL

Jackson County Intermediate School District, Jackson, MI

Jackson Municipal Separate School District, Jackson, MS

Jane Wayland Center, Phoenix, AZ

Jeanine Schultz Memorial School, Park Ridge, IL

Jefferson County Public Schools, Lakewood, CO

Jefferson Parish School System—Department of Special Education, Gretna, LA

Jersey Shore Medical Center—Child Evaluation Center, Neptune, NJ

The John F Kennedy Institute, Baltimore, MD

Jowonio School, Syracuse, NY

Judevine Center for Autistic Children, Saint Louis, MO

Judge Baker Guidance Center, Boston, MA

Kalamazoo Child Guidance Clinic, Kalamazoo, MI

Kaplan Foundation, Orangevale, CA

Kenai Peninsula Borough School District, Soldotna, AK

Kimwood—Home for Autistic Opportunities Inc, Springfield, OH

Kings County Hospital—Downstate Medical Center—Division of Child and Adolescent Psychiatry, Brooklyn, NY

SEARCH Day Program Inc, Ocean, NJ
Seminole County Board of Public Instruction—Programs for
    Emotionally Handicapped, Sanford, FL
Shawnee Mission Public Schools, Shawnee Mission, KS
Sherwood Center for The Exceptional Child, Kansas City, MO
Solomon Mental Health Center, Lowell, MA
Sonia Shankman Orthogenic School of the University of Chi-
    cago, Chicago, IL
South Carolina State College—Autistic Nursery, Speech, Lan-
    guage, and Hearing Clinic, Orangeburg, SC
Southbury Training School, Southbury, CT
Southeast Mental Health Center—Child Development Institute,
    Memphis, TN
Southeastern Children's Center, Sioux Falls, SD
Southgate Regional Center for Developmental Disabilities,
    Southgate, MI
Southwest Georgia Psychoeducational Services—Thomas County
    Schools, Ochlocknee, GA
Spaulding Youth Center—Autistic Program, Tilton, NH
Special Care Program, Orofino, ID
Special Service School District of Bergen County, Paramus, NJ
Spectrum Center for Educational and Behavioral Development
    Inc, Berkeley, CA
Spence Chapin Services to Families and Children—The Chil-
    dren's House, New York, NY
The Spofford Home, Kansas City, MO
State University of New York at Albany—SUNY Pre-
    Kindergarten, Albany, NY
Stevencroft Inc, Saint Paul, MN
Suffolk Child Development Center, Smithtown, NY
Sunburst Youth Homes, Neillsville, WI
Sunny Hill Children's Center Inc, Greenwich, CT
Sunny Hills Children's Services, San Anselmo, CA
Therapeutic School and Preschool Community Mental Health
    Services, Belleville, NJ
Threshold Inc, Goldenrod, FL
Timberlawn Psychiatric Hospital, Dallas, TX
Timberridge Institute for Children and Adolescents Inc, Okla-
    homa City, OK
The Timothy School, Bryn Mawr, PA
Tomorrow's Children, Waupaca, WI
Total Living Continuum, Camarillo, CA
Trumbull County Board of Education, Warren, OH
Tupelo Municipal Public Schools, Tupelo, MS
United Affiliated Facilities Program at Winthrop College, Rock
    Hill, SC
University Hospitals of Cleveland—Hanna Pavilion Child Psy-
    chiatric Unit, Cleveland, OH
University of Arkansas Medical Sciences Division Child
    Psychiatry—Child Study Center, Little Rock, AR
The University of Chicago—Departments of Psychiatry and
    Pediatrics—Child Psychiatry, Chicago, IL
University of Colorado Health Sciences Center—Day Care Cen-
    ter, Denver, CO
University of Illinois Medical Center—Child Psychiatry Clinic,
    Chicago, IL
University of Minnesota Hospitals—Child and Adolescent Psy-
    chiatry, Minneapolis, MN
University of New Mexico Children's Psychiatric
    Hospital—Mimbres School, Albuquerque, NM
University of New Mexico—Children's Psychiatric Hospital, Al-
    buquerque, NM
University of North Carolina School of Medicine—Department
    of Psychiatry—Division TEACCH, Chapel Hill, NC
University of South Florida—Florida Mental Health
    Institute—Department of Child and Family Services,
    Tampa, FL
University of Texas Medical Branch—Division of Pediatric
    Psychology—Department of Pediatrics, Galveston, TX
University of Texas Medical Branch—Inpatient
    Service—Division of Child and Adolescent Psychiatry, Gal-
    veston, TX
Vanderbilt Medical Center—Division of Child and Adolescent
    Psychiatry, Nashville, TN
Variety Preschooler's Workshop, Syosset, NY

Villa Esperanza, Pasadena, CA
Walter Reed Army Medical Center Child and Adolescent Psychi-
    atry Service, Washington, DC
War Bonnet—Wilderness Pathways, Canaan, NH
Washington School District, Phoenix, AZ
Waterford Country School, Quaker Hill, CT
Wellerwood Autism Program, Grand Rapids, MI
West River Children's Center of the Children's Home Society of
    South Dakota, Rapid City, SD
Wheeler Clinic Inc—Northwest Village School, Plainville, CT
Wilder Children's Placement, Saint Paul, MN
Willowglen Academy Inc, Milwaukee, WI
Winnebago Mental Health Institute—Autistic Unit, Winnebago,
    WI
Winston L Prouty Center, Brattleboro, VT
Work Training Program Inc, Woodland Hills, CA
Work Training Program Inc, Santa Barbara, CA
Wyandotte Special Education Cooperative, Kansas City, KS
Wyoming State Hospital, Evanston, WY
Yuma School District One, Yuma, AZ
Yuma Union High School District, Yuma, AZ
Zonta Children's Center, San Jose, CA

Communication Disordered

Ahwahnee Hills School, Ahwahnee, CA
ALA Costa Center for the Developmentally Disabled—After
    School, Berkeley, CA
Albuquerque Special Preschool, Albuquerque, NM
Alexandria Head Start, Alexandria, VA
All Children's Hospital, St Petersburg, FL
Almansor Education Center, Alhambra, CA
American Institute—The Training School at Vineland, Vineland,
    NJ
Area Education Agency—Education Center, Waterloo, IA
Arizona Boys' Ranch, Boys Ranch, AZ
Arizona State Hospital, Phoenix, AZ
Arizona State Hospital—Nueva Vista School, Phoenix, AZ
Arthur Brisbane Child Treatment Center, Farmingdale, NJ
The Astor Home for Children—Residential Treatment
    Center—Residential Treatment Facility—Learning Center,
    Rhinebeck, NY
Atlanta Public Schools, Atlanta, GA
Austin State Hospital, Austin, TX
Avalon Center—Avalon Schools, Lenox, MA
Avalon School at High Point, Lenox, MA
Avon Lenox Special Education, Memphis, TN
Avondale House, Houston, TX
The Bancroft School, Haddonfield, NJ
Bar-None Residential Treatment Services for Children, Anoka,
    MN
The Battin Clinic, Houston, TX
Behavior Research Institute, Providence, RI
Behavioral Development Center Inc, Providence, RI
Bergen Center for Child Development, Haworth, NJ
Bergen Pines Hospital—Children's Psychiatric Unit, Paramus,
    NJ
Berks County Intermediate Unit, Reading, PA
Big Lakes Developmental Center Inc, Manhattan, KS
Birmingham City Board of Education, Birmingham, AL
Blick Clinic for Developmental Disabilities, Akron, OH
Board of Cooperative Educational Services II—Special Education
    Division Instructional Support Center, Centereach, NY
BOCES Nassau, Westbury, NY
BOCES Onondaga Madison, East Syracuse, NY
Bowman Gray School of Medicine Developmental Evaluation
    Clinic—Amos Cottage Rehabilitation Hospital, Winston-
    Salem, NC
Boys' and Girls' Aid Society of San Diego—Cottonwood Center
    and Community Based Psychiatric Program, El Cajon, CA
Brattleboro Retreat, Brattleboro, VT
Brea Neuropsychiatric Center, Brea, CA
Bridgeport Tutoring Center—Counseling Center of Connecticut,
    Bridgeport, CT
Brooklyn Community Counseling Center, Brooklyn, NY

Homes Unlimited Inc, Bangor, ME

Honolulu District—Special Education Center of Oahu (SECO), Honolulu, HI

Humana Hospital Huntington Beach—Children's Behavioral Center, Huntington Beach, CA

Huntsville City School System, Hunstville, AL

Idaho Youth Ranch Inc, Rupert, ID

Independence House of Avalon Inc, Sheffield, MA

Indianapolis Public Schools—Special Education Department, Indianapolis, IN

Ingham Developmental Center, Mason, MI

Institute for Developmental Disabilities—Crystal Springs School, Assonet, MA

Institute of Logopedics, Wichita, KS

Ittleson Center for Child Research, New York, NY

Jackson Municipal Separate School District, Jackson, MS

Jane Wayland Center, Phoenix, AZ

Jasper County Mental Health Center, Newton, IA

Jefferson County Public Schools, Lakewood, CO

Jefferson Parish School System—Department of Special Education, Gretna, LA

Jersey Shore Medical Center—Child Evaluation Center, Neptune, NJ

John C Corrigan Mental Health Center, Fall River, MA

The John F Kennedy Institute, Baltimore, MD

John G McGrath School, Napa, CA

John Umstead Hospital—Children's Psychiatric Institute, Butner, NC

Josephine County Mental Health Program—Children's Resource Team, Grants Pass, OR

Jowonio School, Syracuse, NY

Judevine Center for Autistic Children, Saint Louis, MO

Kenai Peninsula Borough School District, Soldotna, AK

Klamath County Mental Health Center—Mentally Retarded/Developmentally Disabled Program, Klamath Falls, OR

La Mel, San Francisco, CA

La Puente Valley Community Mental Health Center, La Puente, CA

Lad Lake Inc, Dousman, WI

Lafayette Clinic, Detroit, MI

Lakeshore Mental Health Institute—Riverbend School—Children and Youth Services, Knoxville, TN

Lakeside Center for Boys, Saint Louis, MO

The League School, Brooklyn, NY

League School of Boston Inc, Newtonville, MA

The Learning Center, State College, PA

Lighthouse School, Chelmsford, MA

Little Friends Inc—Little Friends Parent Infant Program, Naperville, IL

Little Friends Inc—Little Friends School, Naperville, IL

Little Rock School District, Little Rock, AR

The Little Village School, Garden City, NY

The Los Angeles Child Guidance Clinic, Los Angeles, CA

Los Angeles County Office of Education—Division of Special Education, Downey, CA

Los Angeles County Office of Education—Mark Twain School, Lawndale, CA

Los Ninos Education Center, San Diego, CA

Louisiana State University Medical Center—School of Allied Health Professions—Human Development Center, New Orleans, LA

Lovellton Academy, Elgin, IL

Luther Child Center—Children's Hospitalization Alternative Program, Everett, WA

Madeline Burg Counseling Services—Jewish Board of Family and Children Services, Bronx, NY

Main Street Human Resources, Great Barington, MA

Manhattan Children's Psychiatric Center, New York, NY

Manitowoc County Counseling Center, Manitowoc, WI

The Mary and Alexander Laughlin Children's Center, Sewickley, PA

Marymount Hospital Mental Health Center, Garfield Heights, OH

Medical Care Rehabilitation Hospital's Child Evaluation and Treatment Program, Grand Forks, ND

Medical University of South Carolina—Department of Psychiatry—Youth Division, Charleston, SC

Mendota Mental Health Institute—Child and Adolescent Program, Madison, WI

Menorah Medical Center—Hearing and Speech Department, Kansas City, MO

Mercy Hospital and Medical Center—Community Guidance Center, Chicago, IL

Michael Reese Hospital and Medical Center—Dysfunctioning Child Center, Chicago, IL

The Mid Fairfield Child Guidance Center Inc, Norwalk, CT

The Midland School, North Branch, NJ

Millcreek Schools Inc, Magee, MS

Minneapolis Children's Medical Center—Program for Autistic and Other Exceptional Children, Minneapolis, MN

Montrose School, Reisterstown, MD

Mt Airy Psychiatric Center—Children's Treatment Program—Adolescent Treatment Program, Denver, CO

Multidisciplinary Institute for Neuropsychological Development Inc—MIND, Cambridge, MA

Napa State Hospital—Children's Program, Imola, CA

The Nassau Center for the Developmentally Disabled Inc, Woodbury, NY

New England Home for Little Wanderers—Orchard Home, Watertown, MA

New England Salem Children's Trust, Rumney, NH

New Hope of Indiana Inc, Indianapolis, IN

North Central Health Care Facilities, Wausau, WI

North Dakota State Mental Hospital—Child and Adolescent Unit, Jamestown, ND

North Mississippi Retardation Center, Oxford, MS

Northwood Children's Home, Duluth, MN

Oconomowoc Developmental Training Center Inc, Oconomowoc, WI

Ohel Children's Home and Family Services, Brooklyn, NY

Orange County Public School System—Gateway School, Orlando, FL

Overlook Mental Health Center—Blount County Adolescent Partial Hospitalization Program, Maryville, TN

Pace School, Braintree, MA

Pacific Children's Center, Oakland, CA

Parkview Counseling Center Inc, Youngstown, OH

Parkwood Hospital, Atlanta, GA

Parry Center for Children, Portland, OR

Parsons Child and Family Center—Neil Hellman School, Albany, NY

Pawnee Mental Health Services, Concordia, KS

Peanut Butter and Jelly Therapeutic Pre-School, Albuquerque, NM

Penninsula Children's Center—Children and Youth Services, Palo Alto, CA

Philadelphia Child Guidance Clinic, Philadelphia, PA

Philadelphia Child Guidance Clinic—Child and Family Inpatient Service, Philadelphia, PA

Phoenix Union High School District No. 210, Phoenix, AZ

Prescott Child Development Center, Prescott, AZ

Primary Children's Medical Center—Department of Child Psychiatry, Salt Lake City, UT

Project for Psychotic and Neurologically Impaired Children, Madison, WI

Project Second Start's Alternative High School Program, Concord, NH

Protestant Youth Center, Baldwinville, MA

Psychiatric Services Inc, Haverhill, MA

Pulaski County Special School District, Little Rock, AR

Quincy School for the Handicapped, Quincy, IL

Raineswood Residential Center, Memphis, TN

Range Mental Health Center, Virginia, MN

The Re-Ed West Center for Children Inc, Sacramento, CA

Region VIII Education Service Center, Mount Pleasant, TX

Region 16 Educational Service Center, Amarillo, TX

Regional Intervention Program, Nashville, TN

The Rehabilitation Institute of Pittsburgh, Pittsburgh, PA

Rensselaer County Mental Health Department—Unified Services for Children and Adolescents, Troy, NY

The Rimland School for Autistic Children, Chicago, IL
Rise East School, Pomona, NY
Rochester Mental Health Center Inc—Day Treatment Unit Services—Children and Youth Division, Rochester, NY
Rockford School District No. 205, Rockford, IL
Rockland Psychological and Educational Center, Spring Valley, NY
Rusty's Morningstar Ranch, Cornville, AZ
St Cloud Children's Home, Saint Cloud, MN
St George Homes Inc, Berkeley, CA
St Mary's Home for Boys, Beaverton, OR
St Vincent Children's Center, Columbus, OH
St Vincent's Hospital and Medical Center of New York—Child and Adolescent Psychiatry Service, New York, NY
Samarkand Manor, Eagle Springs, NC
Samuel Gompers Memorial Rehabilitation Center Inc, Phoenix, AZ
San Diego County Mental Health Services—Loma Portal Facility, San Diego, CA
San Diego Unified School District, San Diego, CA
San Joaquin County Office of Education—Special Education Programs, Stockton, CA
San Marcos Treatment Center of The Brown Schools, San Marcos, TX
San Mateo County Office of Education, Redwood City, CA
School District of Philadelphia—Special Education—Stevens Administrative Center, Philadelphia, PA
School for Contemporary Education, Springfield, VA
Scottsdale Public School District, Phoenix, AZ
SEARCH Day Program Inc, Ocean, NJ
Secret Harbor School, Anacortes, WA
Shawnee Mission Public Schools, Shawnee Mission, KS
Sheldon Community Guidance Clinic Inc, New Britain, CT
Sherwood Center for The Exceptional Child, Kansas City, MO
South Carolina State College—Autistic Nursery, Speech, Language, and Hearing Clinic, Orangeburg, SC
South Dakota Human Services Center, Yankton, SD
South Oaks Hospital, Amityville, NY
Southbury Training School, Southbury, CT
Southeastern Children's Center, Sioux Falls, SD
Southgate Regional Center for Developmental Disabilities, Southgate, MI
Spaulding Youth Center—Autistic Program, Tilton, NH
Spaulding Youth Center—Emotional Handicap Program, Tilton, NH
Special Education Association of Adams County, Quincy, IL
Special Service School District of Bergen County, Paramus, NJ
Spectrum Center for Educational and Behavioral Development Inc, Berkeley, CA
Spence Chapin Services to Families and Children—The Children's House, New York, NY
State Training School, Eldora, IA
State University of New York at Albany—SUNY Pre-Kindergarten, Albany, NY
Suffolk Child Development Center, Smithtown, NY
Sunny Hill Children's Center Inc, Greenwich, CT
Switzer Center, Torrance, CA
Terry Children's Psychiatric Center, New Castle, DE
Therapeutic School and Preschool Community Mental Health Services, Belleville, NJ
Timberlawn Psychiatric Hospital, Dallas, TX
Timberridge Institute for Children and Adolescents Inc, Oklahoma City, OK
Towering Pines Center, Slidell, LA
Training Center for Youth, Columbus, OH
Trumbull County Board of Education, Warren, OH
Tupelo Municipal Public Schools, Tupelo, MS
University Hospitals of Cleveland—Hanna Pavilion Child Psychiatric Unit, Cleveland, OH
University of Colorado Health Sciences Center—Day Care Center, Denver, CO
University of Minnesota Hospitals—Child and Adolescent Psychiatry, Minneapolis, MN
University of New Mexico—Children's Psychiatric Hospital, Albuquerque, NM

University of North Carolina School of Medicine—Department of Psychiatry—Division TEACCH, Chapel Hill, NC
University of South Florida—Florida Mental Health Institute—Department of Child and Family Services, Tampa, FL
University of Texas Medical Branch—Inpatient Service—Division of Child and Adolescent Psychiatry, Galveston, TX
University Park Psychological Center, Denver, CO
Valleyhead Inc, Lenox, MA
Vanderbilt Medical Center—Division of Child and Adolescent Psychiatry, Nashville, TN
Variety Preschooler's Workshop, Syosset, NY
Villa Esperanza, Pasadena, CA
Walker Home and School, Needham, MA
Walter Reed Army Medical Center Child and Adolescent Psychiatry Service, Washington, DC
War Bonnet—Wilderness Pathways, Canaan, NH
Waterford Country School, Quaker Hill, CT
Westbridge, Phoenix, AZ
Western New York Children's Psychiatric Center, West Seneca, NY
West-Ros-Park Mental Health Center, Roslindale, MA
Wheeler Clinic Inc—Northwest Village School, Plainville, CT
Willowglen Academy Inc, Milwaukee, WI
Winston L Prouty Center, Brattleboro, VT
Work Training Program Inc, Woodland Hills, CA
Wyalusing Academy, Prairie du Chien, WI
Wyandotte Special Education Cooperative, Kansas City, KS
Yellowstone Boys' and Girls' Ranch, Billings, MT
Youth Center of Beloit—North Beloit High, Beloit, KS
Yuma School District One, Yuma, AZ
Yuma Union High School District, Yuma, AZ

Emotionally Disturbed

Adams County Adolescent Day Treatment Program, Denver, CO
Ahwahnee Hills School, Ahwahnee, CA
Alabama Youth Services—Chalkville Campus, Birmingham, AL
Albany Area Mental Health and Mental Retardation Center, Albany, GA
Alexander Children's Center, Charlotte, NC
Alexandria Head Start, Alexandria, VA
All Children's Hospital, St Petersburg, FL
Allendale School, Lake Villa, IL
Almansor Education Center, Alhambra, CA
American Institute—The Training School at Vineland, Vineland, NJ
Andrus Children's Home, Yonkers, NY
Anne Arundel County Health Department Mental Health Clinic, Annapolis, MD
Anneewakee Hospital, Douglasville, GA
Archdiocese of Louisville—Guidance Clinic, Louisville, KY
Area Education Agency—Education Center, Waterloo, IA
Arizona Baptist Children's Services—Little Canyon Campus, Phoenix, AZ
Arizona Boys' Ranch, Boys Ranch, AZ
Arizona Children's Home, Tucson, AZ
Arizona State Hospital, Phoenix, AZ
Arizona State Hospital—Nueva Vista School, Phoenix, AZ
Arlington School, Belmont, MA
Arnell Engstrom Children's Center, Traverse City, MI
Arthur Brisbane Child Treatment Center, Farmingdale, NJ
Aseltine School, San Diego, CA
The Astor Home for Children—Day Treatment Program, Poughkeepsie, NY
The Astor Home for Children—Day Treatment Program, Bronx, NY
The Astor Home for Children—Group Home Program, Bronx, NY
The Astor Home for Children—Residential Treatment Center—Residential Treatment Facility—Learning Center, Rhinebeck, NY
Atlanta Public Schools, Atlanta, GA
Atlantic Mental Health Center Inc, McKee City, NJ

Augusta School Department, Augusta, ME
Aurora Adolescent Day Resource Center, Aurora, CO
Austin State Hospital, Austin, TX
Autistic Treatment Center—San Antonio, San Antonio, TX
Avalon Center—Avalon Schools, Lenox, MA
Avalon School at High Point, Lenox, MA
Avondale House, Houston, TX
The Baird Center for Children and Families Inc, Burlington, VT
Baker Hall Inc, Lackawanna, NY
The Bancroft School, Haddonfield, NJ
Barat Human Services—Barat House, Detroit, MI
Bar-None Residential Treatment Services for Children, Anoka, MN
The Battin Clinic, Houston, TX
Battle Creek Child Guidance Center, Battle Creek, MI
Beacon Day Treatment Program, Romulus, MI
Behavioral Development Center Inc, Providence, RI
Benhaven, East Haven, CT
Berea Children's Home, Berea, OH
Bergen Center for Child Development, Haworth, NJ
Bergen Pines Hospital—Children's Psychiatric Unit, Paramus, NJ
Berks County Intermediate Unit, Reading, PA
Berkshire Farm Center and Services for Youth, Canaan, NY
Berrien County Intermediate School District, Berrien Springs, MI
Big Lakes Developmental Center Inc, Manhattan, KS
Big Spring State Hospital, Big Spring, TX
Birmingham City Board of Education, Birmingham, AL
Blick Clinic for Developmental Disabilities, Akron, OH
Board of Cooperative Educational Services II—Special Education Division Instructional Support Center, Centereach, NY
BOCES Nassau, Westbury, NY
BOCES Onondaga Madison, East Syracuse, NY
BOCES Southern Westchester—Rye Lake Campus, White Plains, NY
Boston Public Schools—The McKinley Schools, Mattapau, MA
Bowman Gray School of Medicine Developmental Evaluation Clinic—Amos Cottage Rehabilitation Hospital, Winston-Salem, NC
Boys' and Girls' Aid Society of San Diego—Cottonwood Center and Community Based Psychiatric Program, El Cajon, CA
Boys' Town of Missouri Inc, Saint James, MO
Boys' Village Inc—Boys' Village School, Smithville, OH
Boysville of Michigan, Clinton, MI
Bradley Hospital, East Providence, RI
Brant Services Corporation—Brant Ryan House, Inkster, MI
Brattleboro Retreat, Brattleboro, VT
Brea Neuropsychiatric Center, Brea, CA
Brentwood Center, Los Angeles, CA
Brewer-Porch Children's Center, University, AL
Bridgeport Tutoring Center—Counseling Center of Connecticut, Bridgeport, CT
Bridgeway Hospital Youthcare Program, North Little Rock, AR
Brighton School and Diagnostic Center, Phoenix, AZ
Brooklyn Community Counseling Center, Brooklyn, NY
Broom-Tioga Board of Cooperative Educational Services, Binghamton, NY
Brown County Mental Health Center—Children Services, Green Bay, WI
The Brown Schools, Austin, TX
Buckeye Boys' Ranch Inc, Grove City, OH
Bucks County Intermediate Unit—Looking Glass School, Doylestown, PA
Bunche Park Elementary School, Opa Locka, FL
Burt Children's Center, San Francisco, CA
Burwell Psychoeducational Program, Carrollton, GA
Butler County Mental Health Center Inc, Hamilton, OH
California Mental Health Center, Los Angeles, CA
Cantwell Academy Inc, Miami, FL
Capital City Schools, Topeka, KS
Capitol Region Education Council's Day Treatment Service, West Hartford, CT
Cass County Social Services—Children's Social Service Center, Fargo, ND

Cathedral Home for Children, Laramie, WY
Cayuga Home for Children, Auburn, NY
Cedu School, Running Springs, CA
Center for Autistic Children, Philadelphia, PA
Center for Life Management, Salem, NH
Center for Urban Living, Saint Louis, MO
Centerville Clinics Inc—Partial Hospital Program, Fredericktown, PA
Central Massachusetts Special Education Collaborative—Quimby School, Worcester, MA
Chaddock, Quincy, IL
Chancellor Academy, Pompton Plains, NJ
The Charlton School, Burnt Hills, NY
Charter Westbrook Hospital, Richmond, VA
Chestnut Lodge Hospital—Adolescent and Child Division, Rockville, MD
Child Adolescent Service Center, Canton, OH
Child and Adolescent Psychiatric Clinic Inc, Buffalo, NY
Child and Adolescent Psychoeducational Center, Dalton, GA
Child and Family Services, Knoxville, TN
Child Development Center, New York, NY
Child Development Service—Lakeview Center Inc, Pensacola, FL
Child Disability Clinic—Carle Clinic, Urbana, IL
Child Guidance Center of Southern Connecticut, Stanford, CT
Child Guidance Clinic—Day Treatment Program, Winston-Salem, NC
Child Guidance Clinic of Southeastern Connecticut Inc, New London, CT
Child Psychiatry Service—Department of Psychiatry—University Hospitals, Ann Arbor, MI
Child Study and Treatment Center, Tacoma, WA
Child Study Center, Fort Worth, TX
Childhaven, Saint Louis, MO
Children's Aid Society, Cleveland, OH
Children's and Adolescent Unit of Mental Health Institute of Cherokee Iowa, Cherokee, IA
Children's Behavior Therapy Unit, Salt Lake City, UT
Children's Bureau of Indianapolis Inc, Indianapolis, IN
Children's Center, Hamden, CT
The Children's Center, Salt Lake City, UT
Children's Center for Behavioral Development, East Saint Louis, IL
Children's Day Hospital—New York Hospital—Cornell Medical Center—Westchester Division, White Plains, NY
The Children's Day School, Trenton, NJ
Children's Day Treatment Center, Honolulu, HI
The Children's Guild Inc, Baltimore, MD
Children's Health Council, Palo Alto, CA
Children's Home of Cedar Rapids—Cedarwood Group Home, Cedar Rapids, IA
Children's Home of Cedar Rapids—Heartwood Diagnostic Evaluation Unit, Cedar Rapids, IA
Children's Home of Cedar Rapids—Heartwood Residential Treatment Center, Cedar Rapids, IA
Children's Home of Cedar Rapids—Maplewood Group Home, Cedar Rapids, IA
The Children's Home of Cincinnati, Cincinnati, OH
Children's Home of Kingston, Kingston, NY
Children's Home Society of South Dakota, Sioux Falls, SD
Children's Hospital at Washington University Medical Center—Psychiatric Unit, Saint Louis, MO
The Children's Institute, South Orange, NJ
Children's Learning Center of San Antonio, San Antonio, TX
Children's Medical Center, Tulsa, OK
Children's Medical Center—Psychiatric Inpatient Unit, Dallas, TX
Children's Mental Health Center Inc, Columbus, OH
The Children's Mercy Hospital—Section of Psychiatry, Kansas City, MO
Children's Psychiatric Center of the Jewish Hospital, Cincinnati, OH
The Children's School of the Institute of Living, Hartford, CT
The Children's Study Home, Springfield, MA

The Frost School, Rockville, MD
Garden Sullivan Learning and Development Program, San Francisco, CA
Garfield Girls' School, Phoenix, AZ
Gateway United Methodist Youth Center and Family Services, Williamsville, NY
The George Junior Republic Association Inc, Freeville, NY
Gerard of Minnesota Inc, Austin, MN
Gibault School For Boys, Terre Haute, IN
Gilfillan Center, Bemidji, MN
Gladman Memorial Hospital Adolescent Program, Oakland, CA
Glenholme School, Washington, CT
Glens Falls Hospital—Child and Family Services—Community Mental Health Center, Glens Falls, NY
The Goldstaub Residence, Houston, TX
Gould Farm, Monterey, MA
Grady Memorial Hospital—Division of Child and Adolescent Psychiatry, Atlanta, GA
Grafton School, Berryville, VA
Grafton School—Autism Program, Berryville, VA
The Gramon School, Livingston, NJ
Grant Center Hospital, Miami, FL
Graydon Manor, Leesburg, VA
Green Chimneys Children's Services Inc, Brewster, NY
Green Tree School, Philadelphia, PA
Greenshire School, Cheshire, CT
Grove School, Madison, CT
Hall-Mercer Children's Center of the McLean Hospital, Belmont, MA
Hall-Brooke Foundation—Hall-Brooke Hospital—Hall-Brooke School, Westport, CT
Hamilton Children's Center, Hyattsville, MD
The Hannah More Center, Reisterstown, MD
Harbor House, Annandale, VA
Harbor Schools Inc, Newburyport, MA
Harbor View Mercy Hospital, Fort Smith, AR
Harford County Community Mental Health Center, Bel Air, MD
The Harmony Center Inc, Baton Rouge, LA
Harmony Hill School Inc, Chedachet, RI
Harrison County Training Center for Exceptional Children, Gulfport, MS
Hartgrove Hospital—Hartgrove Academy, Chicago, IL
Hathaway School of Hathaway Home for Children, Pacoima, CA
Hawaii State Department of Education—Special Needs Branch, Honolulu, HI
Hawaii State Hospital—Adolescent Unit, Kaneohe, HI
Hawthorn Center, Northville, MI
Hawthorne Cedar Knolls School, Hawthorne, NY
Hawthorne Children's Psychiatric Hospital, Saint Louis, MO
Henderson Mental Health Center, Fort Lauderdale, FL
Henrietta Weill Memorial Child Guidance Clinic, Bakersfield, CA
Henry Horner Children and Adolescent Center, Chicago, IL
High Plains Mental Health Center—Colby Office, Colby, KS
High Point Adolescent School—Children's Psychiatric Center, Morganville, NJ
Highland Heights—St Francis Home for Children Inc, New Haven, CT
Highland Youth Services—The Highland School, Pittsburgh, PA
Hillside Children's Center, Rochester, NY
Hillside Inc, Atlanta, GA
Hillside School Inc, Logan, UT
Homes Unlimited Inc, Bangor, ME
Homewood School—Highland Hospital, Asheville, NC
Honolulu District—Special Education Center of Oahu (SECO), Honolulu, HI
Humana Hospital Huntington Beach—Children's Behavioral Center, Huntington Beach, CA
Hunterdon Learning Center, Califon, NJ
Huntsville City School System, Hunstville, AL
Idaho Youth Ranch Inc, Rupert, ID
Independence House of Avalon Inc, Sheffield, MA
Indianapolis Public Schools—Special Education Department, Indianapolis, IN
Ingham Intermediate School District, Mason, MI

Ingleside Hospital, Rosemead, CA
The Institute Day School, Lowell, MA
Institute for Developmental Disabilities—Crystal Springs School, Assonet, MA
Institute for Family and Life Learning Residential School, Danvers, MA
Institute for Learning, Philadelphia, PA
The Institute of Living School, Hartford, CT
Institute of Psychiatry and Human Behavior—Department of Psychiatry—Child and Adolescent Inpatient Service, Baltimore, MD
Italian Home for Children, Jamaica Plain, MA
Ittleson Center for Child Research, New York, NY
Jackson County Intermediate School District, Jackson, MI
Jackson Municipal Separate School District, Jackson, MS
Jane Wayland Center, Phoenix, AZ
Jasper County Mental Health Center, Newton, IA
Jeanine Schultz Memorial School, Park Ridge, IL
Jefferson County Public Schools, Lakewood, CO
Jefferson Parish School System—Department of Special Education, Gretna, LA
Jennie Clarkson Child Care Services Inc—St Christopher's, Dobbs Ferry, NY
Jersey Shore Medical Center—Child Evaluation Center, Neptune, NJ
Jewish Board of Family and Children Services—Linden Hill School, Hawthorne, NY
Jewish Child Care Association—Pleasantville Cottage School, Pleasantville, NY
Jewish Child Care Association—Youth Residence Center, New York, NY
Jewish Children's Bureau of Chicago, Chicago, IL
John C Corrigan Mental Health Center, Fall River, MA
The John F Kennedy Institute, Baltimore, MD
John G McGrath School, Napa, CA
John Umstead Hospital—Children's Psychiatric Institute, Butner, NC
Josephine County Mental Health Program—Children's Resource Team, Grants Pass, OR
Jowonio School, Syracuse, NY
Judge Baker Guidance Center, Boston, MA
Kalamazoo Child Guidance Clinic, Kalamazoo, MI
K-Bar-B Youth Ranch—Richard M Wise School, Lacombe, LA
Kenai Peninsula Borough School District, Soldotna, AK
Kings County Hospital—Downstate Medical Center—Division of Child and Adolescent Psychiatry, Brooklyn, NY
Kinsman School—Wittenmeyer Youth Center, Davenport, IA
Klamath County Mental Health Center—Natural Family Preservation Project, Klamath Falls, OR
La Amistad Foundation, Winter Park, FL
La Mel, San Francisco, CA
La Puente Valley Community Mental Health Center, La Puente, CA
Lad Lake Inc, Dousman, WI
Lafayette Clinic, Detroit, MI
Lake County Mental Health Center—Department of Children's Services, Mentor, OH
Lake Grove School, Lake Grove, NY
Lakeshore Mental Health Institute—Riverbend School—Children and Youth Services, Knoxville, TN
Lakeside Center for Boys, Saint Louis, MO
Lakeside Child and Family Center Inc, Milwaukee, WI
Lakin Hospital—Adolescent Services, Lakin, WV
Lane School Programs—Lane Education Service District, Eugene, OR
Lansing School District, Lansing, MI
Larned State Hospital—Child Psychiatric Unit—Adolescent Psychiatric Unit/Westside School, Larned, KS
LaSalle School, Albany, NY
LaVoy Exceptional Center, Tampa, FL
The League School, Brooklyn, NY
League School of Boston Inc, Newtonville, MA
Learning Center, Lafayette, IN
The Learning Center, State College, PA
Learning Inc, Corpus Christi, TX

Ohel Children's Home and Family Services, Brooklyn, NY

Orange County Public School System—Gateway School, Orlando, FL

Orlando Regional Medical Center—Mental Health Department—Children's Services, Orlando, FL

Osterlen Services for Youth, Springfield, OH

Otis R Bowen Center, Warsaw, IN

Our Lady of Providence Children's Center, West Springfield, MA

Overlook Mental Health Center—Blount County Adolescent Partial Hospitalization Program, Maryville, TN

Pace School, Braintree, MA

Pace School, Pittsburgh, PA

Pacific Children's Center, Oakland, CA

Paradise Valley School District No. 69—Therapeutic Educational Activities Milieu, Phoenix, AZ

Parkview Counseling Center Inc, Youngstown, OH

Parkwood Hospital, Atlanta, GA

Parmadale—The Youth Services Village, Parma, OH

Parry Center for Children, Portland, OR

Parsons Child and Family Center, Albany, NY

Parsons Child and Family Center—Neil Hellman School, Albany, NY

Partial Hospitalization Program Children's Service Center, Wilkes Barre, PA

Pawnee Mental Health Services, Concordia, KS

Peace River Center for Personal Development Inc, Bartow, FL

Peanut Butter and Jelly Therapeutic Pre-School, Albuquerque, NM

Penn Foundation for Mental Health, Sellersville, PA

Penninsula Children's Center—Children and Youth Services, Palo Alto, CA

Phil Smalley Children's Center, Norman, OK

Philadelphia Child Guidance Clinic, Philadelphia, PA

Philadelphia Child Guidance Clinic—Child and Family Inpatient Service, Philadelphia, PA

Philbrook Center—Special Education Program, Concord, NH

Phoenix Union High School District No. 210, Phoenix, AZ

Pikes Peak Board of Cooperative Services, Colorado Springs, CO

Pine Grove School, Elgin, SC

Pine Haven Boys' Center, Suncook, NH

Pomona Mental Health Center—Child Development Center, Pomona, NY

Porter Starke Services Inc—Vale Park Psychiatric Hospital, Valparaiso, IN

Post Script Consulting Service, Corning, NY

Prehab of Arizona Inc—Dorothy Mitchell Residence—Homestead Residence—Helaman House, Mesa, AZ

Prescott Child Development Center, Prescott, AZ

Pressley Ridge School—Day School, Pittsburgh, PA

Pressley Ridge School—Laurel Park, Clarksburg, WV

Pressley Ridge School—Pryde—Family Based Treatment, Pittsburgh, PA

Pressley Ridge School—Wilderness School, Ohiopyle, PA

Primary Children's Medical Center—Department of Child Psychiatry, Salt Lake City, UT

Project for Psychotic and Neurologically Impaired Children, Madison, WI

Project Second Start's Alternative High School Program, Concord, NH

Protestant Youth Center, Baldwinville, MA

Provo Canyon School, Provo, UT

Psychiatric Clinic of the Charlotte Hungerford Hospital, Torrington, CT

Psychiatric Institute of Richmond—Educational Development Center, Richmond, VA

Psychiatric Services Inc, Haverhill, MA

Pulaski County Special School District, Little Rock, AR

Queen of Angels School—Villa Maria Treatment Center, Timonium, MD

Queens Hospital Center Department of Psychiatry Child and Adolescent Clinic, Jamaica, NY

Ranch Hope Strang School, Alleway, NJ

Range Mental Health Center, Virginia, MN

Raritan Bay Mental Health Center, Perth Amboy, NJ

The Re-Ed West Center for Children Inc, Sacramento, CA

Red Rock Comprehensive Mental Health Center, Oklahoma City, OK

Region VIII Education Service Center, Mount Pleasant, TX

Region 16 Educational Service Center, Amarillo, TX

Regional Intervention Program, Nashville, TN

The Rehabilitation Institute of Pittsburgh, Pittsburgh, PA

Rensselaer County Mental Health Department—Unified Services for Children and Adolescents, Troy, NY

Richmond County Board of Education—Sand Hills Psychoeducational Program, Augusta, GA

Ridgeview Institute, Smyrna, GA

Ridgeview Psychiatric Hospital and Center, Oak Ridge, TN

The Rimland School for Autistic Children, Chicago, IL

Rise East School, Pomona, NY

River Street School, Hyde Park, MA

Rochester Mental Health Center Inc—Day Treatment Unit Services—Children and Youth Division, Rochester, NY

Rockford School District No. 205, Rockford, IL

Rockland Children's Psychiatric Center, Orangeburg, NY

Rockland Psychological and Educational Center, Spring Valley, NY

Rusk State Hospital—Child and Adolescent Unit, Rusk, TX

Rutland Psychoeducational Services, Athens, GA

Sacramento Children's Home—Helen E Cowell Children's Center, Sacramento, CA

Sagamore Hills Children's Psychiatric Hospital, Northfield, OH

St Ann's Home Inc—Day Treatment and Special Education Program, Methuen, MA

St Ann's Home Inc—Residential Treatment and Special Education Program, Methuen, MA

St Cabrini Home Inc, West Park, NY

St Clare's Hospital—Adult, Child and Family Services, Denville, NJ

St Cloud Children's Home, Saint Cloud, MN

St Elizabeth's Hospital—Division of Child and Adolescent Services, Washington, DC

The St Francis Boys' Homes Inc, Salina, KS

St Francis Boys' Home—Camelot, Lake Placid, NY

St Gabriel's Hall, Phoenixville, PA

St George Homes Inc, Berkeley, CA

St Joseph Center for Mental Health, Omaha, NE

St Joseph Residential Treatment and Child Care Center, Dayton, OH

St Joseph's Carondelet Child Center, Chicago, IL

St Joseph's Children's Home, Torrington, WY

St Louis County Child Mental Health Services, Saint Louis, MO

St Mary's Home for Boys, Beaverton, OR

St Vincent Children's Center, Columbus, OH

St Vincent's Hospital and Medical Center of New York—Child and Adolescent Psychiatry Service, New York, NY

The Salvation Army Residential Treatment Facilities for Children and Youth, Honolulu, HI

Samarkand Manor, Eagle Springs, NC

Samuel Gompers Memorial Rehabilitation Center Inc, Phoenix, AZ

San Diego County Mental Health Services—Loma Portal Facility, San Diego, CA

San Diego Unified School District, San Diego, CA

San Joaquin County Office of Education—Special Education Programs, Stockton, CA

San Marcos Treatment Center of The Brown Schools, San Marcos, TX

San Mateo County Office of Education, Redwood City, CA

School District of Philadelphia—Special Education—Stevens Administrative Center, Philadelphia, PA

School for Contemporary Education, Baltimore, MD

School for Contemporary Education, Springfield, VA

Scottsdale Public School District, Phoenix, AZ

Scranton Counseling Center—The Louis J Vitale Children and Youth Service, Scranton, PA

SEARCH Day Program Inc, Ocean, NJ

Secret Harbor School, Anacortes, WA

Wilder Children's Placement, Saint Paul, MN
Willowglen Academy Inc, Milwaukee, WI
Winnebago Mental Health Institute—Children's Unit, Winnebago, WI
Winston L Prouty Center, Brattleboro, VT
Woodbourne Center, Baltimore, MD
Woodward Mental Health Center, Freeport, NY
Work Training Program Inc, Santa Barbara, CA
Wyalusing Academy, Prairie du Chien, WI
Wyandotte Mental Health Center, Kansas City, KS
Wyandotte Special Education Cooperative, Kansas City, KS
Wyoming Youth Treatment Center, Casper, WY
Yellowstone Boys' and Girls' Ranch, Billings, MT
York Woods Center, Ypsilanti, MI
Youth and Family Services, Omaha, NE
Youth Center at Larned—Westside School, Larned, KS
Youth Center of Beloit—North Beloit High, Beloit, KS
Youth Evaluation and Treatment Centers (YETC), Phoenix, AZ
Yuma School District One, Yuma, AZ
Yuma Union High School District, Yuma, AZ
Zonta Children's Center, San Jose, CA

Gifted

All Children's Hospital, St Petersburg, FL
Almansor Education Center, Alhambra, CA
Andrus Children's Home, Yonkers, NY
Anne Arundel County Health Department Mental Health Clinic, Annapolis, MD
Anneewakee Hospital, Douglasville, GA
Archdiocese of Louisville—Guidance Clinic, Louisville, KY
Arizona Boys' Ranch, Boys Ranch, AZ
Arizona Children's Home, Tucson, AZ
Arthur Brisbane Child Treatment Center, Farmingdale, NJ
Aseltine School, San Diego, CA
Atlanta Public Schools, Atlanta, GA
Atlantic Mental Health Center Inc, McKee City, NJ
Austin State Hospital, Austin, TX
Bar-None Residential Treatment Services for Children, Anoka, MN
The Battin Clinic, Houston, TX
Battle Creek Child Guidance Center, Battle Creek, MI
Berks County Intermediate Unit, Reading, PA
Birmingham City Board of Education, Birmingham, AL
Board of Cooperative Educational Services II—Special Education Division Instructional Support Center, Centereach, NY
BOCES Onondaga Madison, East Syracuse, NY
Boys' Town of Missouri Inc, Saint James, MO
Brattleboro Retreat, Brattleboro, VT
Bridgeport Tutoring Center—Counseling Center of Connecticut, Bridgeport, CT
Bridgeway Hospital Youthcare Program, North Little Rock, AR
Brooklyn Community Counseling Center, Brooklyn, NY
Brown County Mental Health Center—Children Services, Green Bay, WI
California Mental Health Center, Los Angeles, CA
Cass County Social Services—Children's Social Service Center, Fargo, ND
Centerville Clinics Inc—Partial Hospital Program, Fredericktown, PA
Charter Westbrook Hospital, Richmond, VA
Child Disability Clinic—Carle Clinic, Urbana, IL
Children's and Adolescent Unit of Mental Health Institute of Cherokee Iowa, Cherokee, IA
Children's Day Hospital—New York Hospital—Cornell Medical Center—Westchester Division, White Plains, NY
Children's Hospital at Washington University Medical Center—Psychiatric Unit, Saint Louis, MO
Children's Medical Center—Psychiatric Inpatient Unit, Dallas, TX
The Children's Mercy Hospital—Section of Psychiatry, Kansas City, MO
The Clearing, Marshfield, VT
Cleveland County Area Mental Health Program—Division of Child and Youth Services, Shelby, NC

The Clinical Center of Southern Illinois University, Carbondale, IL
Cobb County—Cobb Douglas Psychoeducation Children's Program, Marietta, GA
College Hospital—College Park School, Cerritos, CA
Colorado Springs School District No. 11, Colorado Springs, CO
Connecticut College Program for Children with Special Needs, New London, CT
Creative Arts Rehabilitation Center Inc, New York, NY
De Neuville Heights School for Girls, Memphis, TN
Department of Education—Windward Oahu District, Kaneohe, HI
Department of Public Instruction, Dover, DE
DeSisto Schools Inc, West Stockbridge, MA
Development Evaluation Center, Fayetteville, NC
Donaldsonville Mental Health Center, Donaldsonville, LA
Early Childhood Developmental Center Inc, Hays, KS
East Alabama Mental Health Retardation Center, Opelika, AL
East St Louis Area Joint Agreement—Department of Special Education, East Saint Louis, IL
Eau Claire Academy, Eau Claire, WI
Edgefield Children's Center, Troutdale, OR
The Educational Clinic Inc, Columbus, OH
El Paso Guidance Center, El Paso, TX
Elmcrest Psychiatric Institute, Portland, CT
Escalon Inc, Altadena, CA
Escambia District Schools, Pensacola, FL
Excelsior Youth Center, Aurora, CO
Forest Hospital, Des Plaines, IL
The George Junior Republic Association Inc, Freeville, NY
Gladman Memorial Hospital Adolescent Program, Oakland, CA
The Gramon School, Livingston, NJ
Harbor View Mercy Hospital, Fort Smith, AR
Harford County Community Mental Health Center, Bel Air, MD
Hartgrove Hospital—Hartgrove Academy, Chicago, IL
Hawaii State Department of Education—Special Needs Branch, Honolulu, HI
High Plains Mental Health Center—Colby Office, Colby, KS
Highland Youth Services—The Highland School, Pittsburgh, PA
Homewood School—Highland Hospital, Asheville, NC
Jackson Municipal Separate School District, Jackson, MS
Jasper County Mental Health Center, Newton, IA
Jefferson Parish School System—Department of Special Education, Gretna, LA
Jersey Shore Medical Center—Child Evaluation Center, Neptune, NJ
Jewish Children's Bureau of Chicago, Chicago, IL
The John F Kennedy Institute, Baltimore, MD
John G McGrath School, Napa, CA
John Umstead Hospital—Children's Psychiatric Institute, Butner, NC
Josephine County Mental Health Program—Children's Resource Team, Grants Pass, OR
Kenai Peninsula Borough School District, Soldotna, AK
La Mel, San Francisco, CA
La Puente Valley Community Mental Health Center, La Puente, CA
Lad Lake Inc, Dousman, WI
Lake County Mental Health Center—Department of Children's Services, Mentor, OH
The Learning Center, State College, PA
Lovellton Academy, Elgin, IL
Lutheran Special Classes, Saint Louis, MO
Madeline Burg Counseling Services—Jewish Board of Family and Children Services, Bronx, NY
Manitowoc County Counseling Center, Manitowoc, WI
Mardan Center of Educational Therapy, Costa Mesa, CA
The Mary and Alexander Laughlin Children's Center, Sewickley, PA
Marymount Hospital Mental Health Center, Garfield Heights, OH
Medical University of South Carolina—Department of Psychiatry—Youth Division, Charleston, SC
Mendota Mental Health Institute—Child and Adolescent Program, Madison, WI

Mental Health Center of Boulder County—Adolescent Treatment Program, Boulder, CO

Mid-Columbia Mental Health Center—Adolescent Psychiatric Department, Richland, WA

Millcreek Schools Inc, Magee, MS

Multidisciplinary Institute for Neuropsychological Development Inc—MIND, Cambridge, MA

North Dakota State Mental Hospital—Child and Adolescent Unit, Jamestown, ND

Northeast Colorado Board of Cooperative Educational Services, Haxton, CO

Northwood Children's Home, Duluth, MN

Our Lady of Providence Children's Center, West Springfield, MA

Pawnee Mental Health Services, Concordia, KS

Peanut Butter and Jelly Therapeutic Pre-School, Albuquerque, NM

Philadelphia Child Guidance Clinic—Child and Family Inpatient Service, Philadelphia, PA

Phoenix Union High School District No. 210, Phoenix, AZ

Post Script Consulting Service, Corning, NY

Psychiatric Institute of Richmond—Educational Development Center, Richmond, VA

Psychiatric Services Inc, Haverhill, MA

Pulaski County Special School District, Little Rock, AR

Queens Hospital Center Department of Psychiatry Child and Adolescent Clinic, Jamaica, NY

Range Mental Health Center, Virginia, MN

The Re-Ed West Center for Children Inc, Sacramento, CA

Rensselaer County Mental Health Department—Unified Services for Children and Adolescents, Troy, NY

Ridgeview Psychiatric Hospital and Center, Oak Ridge, TN

Rockford School District No. 205, Rockford, IL

Rockland Psychological and Educational Center, Spring Valley, NY

St Joseph Center for Mental Health, Omaha, NE

St Louis County Child Mental Health Services, Saint Louis, MO

St Vincent's Hospital and Medical Center of New York—Child and Adolescent Psychiatry Service, New York, NY

Samarkand Manor, Eagle Springs, NC

San Diego Unified School District, San Diego, CA

School District of Philadelphia—Special Education—Stevens Administrative Center, Philadelphia, PA

Scottsdale Public School District, Phoenix, AZ

Secret Harbor School, Anacortes, WA

Shadow Mountain Institute, Tulsa, OK

Shawnee Mission Public Schools, Shawnee Mission, KS

South Dakota Human Services Center, Yankton, SD

Southeast Mental Health Center—Child Development Institute, Memphis, TN

Southwood Psychiatric Residential Treatment Center—Hillcrest, San Diego, CA

Springfield Park Central Hospital—Park Central School, Springfield, MO

Timberridge Institute for Children and Adolescents Inc, Oklahoma City, OK

Training Center for Youth, Columbus, OH

Trumbull County Board of Education, Warren, OH

University of Arkansas Medical Sciences Division Child Psychiatry—Child Study Center, Little Rock, AR

The University of Chicago—Departments of Psychiatry and Pediatrics—Child Psychiatry, Chicago, IL

University of Colorado Health Sciences Center—Day Care Center, Denver, CO

University of Minnesota Hospitals—Child and Adolescent Psychiatry, Minneapolis, MN

University of New Mexico—Children's Psychiatric Hospital, Albuquerque, NM

University of Texas Medical Branch—Inpatient Service—Division of Child and Adolescent Psychiatry, Galveston, TX

University Park Psychological Center, Denver, CO

Utah Boys' Ranch—Children and Youth Services Inc, Salt Lake City, UT

Valley View School, North Brookfield, MA

Vanderbilt Medical Center—Division of Child and Adolescent Psychiatry, Nashville, TN

Vista Del Mar Child Care Service, Los Angeles, CA

Vitam Center Inc—Vitam School, Norwalk, CT

Walter Reed Army Medical Center Child and Adolescent Psychiatry Service, Washington, DC

War Bonnet—Wilderness Pathways, Canaan, NH

West Hartford Public Schools Off-Campus Program, West Hartford, CT

Westbridge, Phoenix, AZ

Western District Guidance Center, Parkersburg, WV

Wyandotte Special Education Cooperative, Kansas City, KS

Yuma School District One, Yuma, AZ

Hearing Impaired/Deaf

All Children's Hospital, St Petersburg, FL

American Institute—The Training School at Vineland, Vineland, NJ

Area Education Agency—Education Center, Waterloo, IA

Arizona State Hospital, Phoenix, AZ

Arthur Brisbane Child Treatment Center, Farmingdale, NJ

Atlanta Public Schools, Atlanta, GA

Augusta School Department, Augusta, ME

Austin State Hospital, Austin, TX

Autistic Treatment Center—Richardson, Richardson, TX

Avalon School at High Point, Lenox, MA

The Bancroft School, Haddonfield, NJ

Bar-None Residential Treatment Services for Children, Anoka, MN

The Battin Clinic, Houston, TX

Behavior Research Institute, Providence, RI

Benhaven, East Haven, CT

Berea Children's Home, Berea, OH

Bergen Center for Child Development, Haworth, NJ

Berks County Intermediate Unit, Reading, PA

Big Lakes Developmental Center Inc, Manhattan, KS

Blick Clinic for Developmental Disabilities, Akron, OH

Board of Cooperative Educational Services II—Special Education Division Instructional Support Center, Centereach, NY

BOCES Nassau, Westbury, NY

Bowman Gray School of Medicine Developmental Evaluation Clinic—Amos Cottage Rehabilitation Hospital, Winston-Salem, NC

Brown County Mental Health Center—Children Services, Green Bay, WI

The Brown Schools, Austin, TX

Cass County Social Services—Children's Social Service Center, Fargo, ND

Centerville Clinics Inc—Partial Hospital Program, Fredericktown, PA

Central New Hampshire Community Mental Health Services Inc—Early Intervention Services, Concord, NH

Cheboygan-Otsego-Presque Isle Intermediate School District—Alpine Educational Facility, Gaylord, MI

Cheboygan-Otsego-Presque Isle Intermediate School District—Hawks Programs, Hawks, MI

Cheboygen-Otsego-Presque Isle Intermediate School District—Inverness Elementary, Cheboygen, MI

Child Disability Clinic—Carle Clinic, Urbana, IL

Child Study Center, Fort Worth, TX

Children's Behavior Therapy Unit, Salt Lake City, UT

Children's Bureau of Indianapolis Inc, Indianapolis, IN

Children's Health Council, Palo Alto, CA

Children's Medical Center, Tulsa, OK

The Children's Mercy Hospital—Section of Psychiatry, Kansas City, MO

The Children's School of the Institute of Living, Hartford, CT

The Children's Study Home, Springfield, MA

Christ Church Child Center, Bethesda, MD

The Clearing, Marshfield, VT

Clearwater Ranch Children's House Inc, Philo, CA

Cleveland Clinic Foundation, Cleveland, OH

Cleveland County Area Mental Health Program—Division of Child and Youth Services, Shelby, NC

The Clinical Center of Southern Illinois University, Carbondale, IL

Colorado Springs School District No. 11, Colorado Springs, CO

Concord, Yellow Spring, WV

Connecticut College Program for Children with Special Needs, New London, CT

Cooperative Educational Services Developmental Learning Center, Wilton, CT

Cousins Respite Care Program of the Parent Resource Center Inc, Orlando, FL

Covenant Children's Home and Family Services, Princeton, IL

CRATER of Broward Inc—Retreat Ranch Facility—24 Hour Residential Treatment Center, Fort Lauderdale, FL

De Neuville Heights School for Girls, Memphis, TN

The Delacato and Doman Autistic Unit, Morton, PA

Delaware Guidance Services for Children and Youth Inc, Wilmington, DE

The Delacato and Doman Autistic Unit, Plymouth Meeting, PA

Department of Education—Windward Oahu District, Kaneohe, HI

Department of Public Instruction, Dover, DE

Development Evaluation Center, Fayetteville, NC

The Devereux Foundation, Devon, PA

The Devereux Foundation, Santa Barbara, CA

The Devereux Foundation—Texas Branch, Victoria, TX

Dysfunctioning Child Center—Respite Care Unit, Chicago, IL

Early Childhood Developmental Center Inc, Hays, KS

Early Education Center, Jackson, MS

East Alabama Mental Health Retardation Center, Opelika, AL

East St Louis Area Joint Agreement—Department of Special Education, East Saint Louis, IL

The Educational Clinic Inc, Columbus, OH

Educational Service Unit 3—Department of Special Education—Exceptional Children Resource Center, Omaha, NE

Eleanor Griffin Children's Development Center, Plainview, TX

Elwyn Institutes, Elwyn, PA

Emma Pendleton Bradley Hospital Developmental Disabilities Program, East Providence, RI

Encor—Family and Medical Support Services—Home Based Services, Omaha, NE

Encor—Family and Medical Support Services—Respite Services, Omaha, NE

Escambia District Schools, Pensacola, FL

Evansville Vanderburgh School Corporation, Evansville, IN

Excelsior Youth Center, Aurora, CO

Forest Hospital, Des Plaines, IL

Fort Logan Mental Health Center, Denver, CO

Fremont Unified School District, Fremont, CA

Grafton School, Berryville, VA

Grafton School—Autism Program, Berryville, VA

Greenshire School, Cheshire, CT

Harbor View Mercy Hospital, Fort Smith, AR

Harrison County Training Center for Exceptional Children, Gulfport, MS

Hartgrove Hospital—Hartgrove Academy, Chicago, IL

Hawaii State Department of Education—Special Needs Branch, Honolulu, HI

Hawaii State Hospital—Adolescent Unit, Kaneohe, HI

Hawthorn Center, Northville, MI

High Plains Mental Health Center—Colby Office, Colby, KS

Hillside Children's Center, Rochester, NY

Homes Unlimited Inc, Bangor, ME

Honolulu District—Special Education Center of Oahu (SECO), Honolulu, HI

Huntsville City School System, Hunstville, AL

Illinois Center for Autism, Fairview Heights, IL

Independence House of Avalon Inc, Sheffield, MA

Indianapolis Public Schools—Special Education Department, Indianapolis, IN

Ingham Developmental Center, Mason, MI

Institute for Developmental Disabilities—Crystal Springs School, Assonet, MA

Institute of Logopedics, Wichita, KS

ISIS Programs Inc—Individual Support Through Innovative Services for Autistic Persons, Orlando, FL

Jackson Municipal Separate School District, Jackson, MS

Jasper County Mental Health Center, Newton, IA

Jefferson County Public Schools, Lakewood, CO

Jefferson Parish School System—Department of Special Education, Gretna, LA

Jersey Shore Medical Center—Child Evaluation Center, Neptune, NJ

The John F Kennedy Institute, Baltimore, MD

John G McGrath School, Napa, CA

John Umstead Hospital—Children's Psychiatric Institute, Butner, NC

Josephine County Mental Health Program—Children's Resource Team, Grants Pass, OR

Kenai Peninsula Borough School District, Soldotna, AK

Klamath County Mental Health Center—Mentally Retarded/Developmentally Disabled Program, Klamath Falls, OR

Lake Grove School, Lake Grove, NY

Lighthouse School, Chelmsford, MA

Little Rock School District, Little Rock, AR

The Little Village School, Garden City, NY

Los Angeles County Office of Education—Division of Special Education, Downey, CA

Los Ninos Education Center, San Diego, CA

Louisiana State University Medical Center—School of Allied Health Professions—Human Development Center, New Orleans, LA

Manhattan Children's Psychiatric Center, New York, NY

Manitowoc County Counseling Center, Manitowoc, WI

The Mary and Alexander Laughlin Children's Center, Sewickley, PA

Marymount Hospital Mental Health Center, Garfield Heights, OH

Medical Care Rehabilitation Hospital's Child Evaluation and Treatment Program, Grand Forks, ND

Mendota Mental Health Institute—Child and Adolescent Program, Madison, WI

Menorah Medical Center—Hearing and Speech Department, Kansas City, MO

Mercy Hospital and Medical Center—Community Guidance Center, Chicago, IL

Mid-Columbia Mental Health Center—Adolescent Psychiatric Department, Richland, WA

Mt Airy Psychiatric Center—Children's Treatment Program—Adolescent Treatment Program, Denver, CO

Multidisciplinary Institute for Neuropsychological Development Inc—MIND, Cambridge, MA

Napa State Hospital—Children's Program, Imola, CA

The Nassau Center for the Developmentally Disabled Inc, Woodbury, NY

New England Medical Center—Division of Child Psychiatry, Boston, MA

New Hope of Indiana Inc, Indianapolis, IN

North Central Health Care Facilities, Wausau, WI

North Mississippi Retardation Center, Oxford, MS

Northern Indiana State Hospital and Developmental Disabilities Center, South Bend, IN

Oconomowoc Developmental Training Center Inc, Oconomowoc, WI

Parsons Child and Family Center—Neil Hellman School, Albany, NY

Penninsula Children's Center—Children and Youth Services, Palo Alto, CA

Philadelphia Child Guidance Clinic, Philadelphia, PA

Philadelphia Child Guidance Clinic—Child and Family Inpatient Service, Philadelphia, PA

Phoenix Union High School District No. 210, Phoenix, AZ

Prescott Child Development Center, Prescott, AZ

Project for Psychotic and Neurologically Impaired Children, Madison, WI

Psychiatric Services Inc, Haverhill, MA

Pulaski County Special School District, Little Rock, AR

Quincy School for the Handicapped, Quincy, IL

Raineswood Residential Center, Memphis, TN

Range Mental Health Center, Virginia, MN
Region VIII Education Service Center, Mount Pleasant, TX
Region 16 Educational Service Center, Amarillo, TX
Regional Intervention Program, Nashville, TN
The Rehabilitation Institute of Pittsburgh, Pittsburgh, PA
Rensselaer County Mental Health Department—Unified Services
    for Children and Adolescents, Troy, NY
Rise East School, Pomona, NY
Rockford School District No. 205, Rockford, IL
St Vincent Children's Center, Columbus, OH
Samarkand Manor, Eagle Springs, NC
Samuel Gompers Memorial Rehabilitation Center Inc, Phoenix,
    AZ
San Diego Unified School District, San Diego, CA
San Joaquin County Office of Education—Special Education
    Programs, Stockton, CA
San Mateo County Office of Education, Redwood City, CA
School District of Philadelphia—Special Education—Stevens Ad-
    ministrative Center, Philadelphia, PA
School for Contemporary Education, Springfield, VA
Scottsdale Public School District, Phoenix, AZ
Scranton Counseling Center—The Louis J Vitale Children and
    Youth Service, Scranton, PA
SEARCH Day Program Inc, Ocean, NJ
Shawnee Mission Public Schools, Shawnee Mission, KS
Sherwood Center for The Exceptional Child, Kansas City, MO
Southbury Training School, Southbury, CT
Southeastern Children's Center, Sioux Falls, SD
Southgate Regional Center for Developmental Disabilities,
    Southgate, MI
Spaulding Youth Center—Autistic Program, Tilton, NH
Spaulding Youth Center—Emotional Handicap Program, Tilton,
    NH
Special Education Association of Adams County, Quincy, IL
Special Service School District of Bergen County, Paramus, NJ
Spectrum Center for Educational and Behavioral Development
    Inc, Berkeley, CA
Spence Chapin Services to Families and Children—The Chil-
    dren's House, New York, NY
State Agriculture and Industrial School, Industry, NY
State Training School, Eldora, IA
State University of New York at Albany—SUNY Pre-
    Kindergarten, Albany, NY
Sunny Hills Children's Services, San Anselmo, CA
Total Living Continuum, Camarillo, CA
Training Center for Youth, Columbus, OH
Trumbull County Board of Education, Warren, OH
University Hospitals of Cleveland—Hanna Pavilion Child Psy-
    chiatric Unit, Cleveland, OH
University of Minnesota Hospitals—Child and Adolescent Psy-
    chiatry, Minneapolis, MN
University of South Florida—Florida Mental Health
    Institute—Department of Child and Family Services,
    Tampa, FL
University of Tennessee—Child Development Center School,
    Memphis, TN
University of Texas Medical Branch—Inpatient
    Service—Division of Child and Adolescent Psychiatry, Gal-
    veston, TX
University Park Psychological Center, Denver, CO
Valleyhead Inc, Lenox, MA
Vanderbilt Medical Center—Division of Child and Adolescent
    Psychiatry, Nashville, TN
Walter Reed Army Medical Center Child and Adolescent Psychi-
    atry Service, Washington, DC
West Central Community Services Center Inc, Willmar, MN
Westbridge, Phoenix, AZ
Western New York Children's Psychiatric Center, West Seneca,
    NY
Wilder Children's Placement, Saint Paul, MN
Willowglen Academy Inc, Milwaukee, WI
Winston L Prouty Center, Brattleboro, VT
Wyandotte Special Education Cooperative, Kansas City, KS
Yuma Union High School District, Yuma, AZ

Learning Disabled

Adams County Adolescent Day Treatment Program, Denver, CO
Ahwahnee Hills School, Ahwahnee, CA
ALA Costa Center for the Developmentally Disabled—After
    School, Berkeley, CA
Alabama Youth Services—Chalkville Campus, Birmingham, AL
Albuquerque Special Preschool, Albuquerque, NM
Alexander Children's Center, Charlotte, NC
Alexandria Head Start, Alexandria, VA
All Children's Hospital, St Petersburg, FL
Allendale School, Lake Villa, IL
Almansor Education Center, Alhambra, CA
American Institute—The Training School at Vineland, Vineland,
    NJ
Andrus Children's Home, Yonkers, NY
Anneewakee Hospital, Douglasville, GA
Archdiocese of Louisville—Guidance Clinic, Louisville, KY
Area Education Agency—Education Center, Waterloo, IA
Arizona Baptist Children's Services—Little Canyon Campus,
    Phoenix, AZ
Arizona Boys' Ranch, Boys Ranch, AZ
Arizona Children's Home, Tucson, AZ
Arizona State Hospital, Phoenix, AZ
Arlington School, Belmont, MA
Arthur Brisbane Child Treatment Center, Farmingdale, NJ
Aseltine School, San Diego, CA
The Astor Home for Children—Day Treatment Program, Bronx,
    NY
The Astor Home for Children—Group Home Program, Bronx,
    NY
The Astor Home for Children—Residential Treatment
    Center—Residential Treatment Facility—Learning Center,
    Rhinebeck, NY
Atlanta Public Schools, Atlanta, GA
Atlantic Mental Health Center Inc, McKee City, NJ
Augusta School Department, Augusta, ME
Aurora Adolescent Day Resource Center, Aurora, CO
Austin State Hospital, Austin, TX
Avalon School at High Point, Lenox, MA
Baker Hall Inc, Lackawanna, NY
The Bancroft School, Haddonfield, NJ
Barat Human Services—Barat House, Detroit, MI
Bar-None Residential Treatment Services for Children, Anoka,
    MN
The Battin Clinic, Houston, TX
Battle Creek Child Guidance Center, Battle Creek, MI
Behavior Research Institute, Providence, RI
Berea Children's Home, Berea, OH
Bergen Center for Child Development, Haworth, NJ
Bergen Pines Hospital—Children's Psychiatric Unit, Paramus,
    NJ
Berks County Intermediate Unit, Reading, PA
Berkshire Farm Center and Services for Youth, Canaan, NY
Big Lakes Developmental Center Inc, Manhattan, KS
Birmingham City Board of Education, Birmingham, AL
Blick Clinic for Developmental Disabilities, Akron, OH
Board of Cooperative Educational Services II—Special Education
    Division Instructional Support Center, Centereach, NY
BOCES Nassau, Westbury, NY
BOCES Onondaga Madison, East Syracuse, NY
Boston Public Schools—The McKinley Schools, Mattapau, MA
Bowman Gray School of Medicine Developmental Evaluation
    Clinic—Amos Cottage Rehabilitation Hospital, Winston-
    Salem, NC
Boys' and Girls' Aid Society of San Diego—Cottonwood Center
    and Community Based Psychiatric Program, El Cajon, CA
Boys' Town of Missouri Inc, Saint James, MO
Boys' Village Inc—Boys' Village School, Smithville, OH
Boysville of Michigan, Clinton, MI
Brattleboro Retreat, Brattleboro, VT
Brea Neuropsychiatric Center, Brea, CA
Brewer-Porch Children's Center, University, AL
Bridgeport Tutoring Center—Counseling Center of Connecticut,
    Bridgeport, CT

Bridgeway Hospital Youthcare Program, North Little Rock, AR
Bronx Developmental Center—Respite Service, Bronx, NY
Brooklyn Community Counseling Center, Brooklyn, NY
Brown County Mental Health Center—Children Services, Green Bay, WI
The Brown Schools, Austin, TX
Buckeye Boys' Ranch Inc, Grove City, OH
Bunche Park Elementary School, Opa Locka, FL
Camphill Special Schools Inc, Glenmoore, PA
Cantwell Academy Inc, Miami, FL
Capitol Region Education Council's Day Treatment Service, West Hartford, CT
Cass County Social Services—Children's Social Service Center, Fargo, ND
Cathedral Home for Children, Laramie, WY
Cayuga Home for Children, Auburn, NY
Center for Life Management, Salem, NH
Center for Urban Living, Saint Louis, MO
Centerville Clinics Inc—Partial Hospital Program, Fredericktown, PA
Central Massachusetts Special Education Collaborative—Quimby School, Worcester, MA
Central New Hampshire Community Mental Health Services Inc—Early Intervention Services, Concord, NH
Chaddock, Quincy, IL
The Charlton School, Burnt Hills, NY
Charter Westbrook Hospital, Richmond, VA
Child Adolescent Service Center, Canton, OH
Child Development Center, New York, NY
Child Disability Clinic—Carle Clinic, Urbana, IL
Child Guidance Center of Southern Connecticut, Stanford, CT
Child Guidance Clinic of Southeastern Connecticut Inc, New London, CT
Child Psychiatry Service—Department of Psychiatry—University Hospitals, Ann Arbor, MI
Child Study and Treatment Center, Tacoma, WA
Child Study Center, Fort Worth, TX
Childhaven, Saint Louis, MO
Children's Aid Society, Cleveland, OH
Children's and Adolescent Unit of Mental Health Institute of Cherokee Iowa, Cherokee, IA
Children's Behavior Therapy Unit, Salt Lake City, UT
Children's Bureau of Indianapolis Inc, Indianapolis, IN
Children's Center, Hamden, CT
The Children's Center, Salt Lake City, UT
Children's Center for Behavioral Development, East Saint Louis, IL
Children's Day Hospital—New York Hospital—Cornell Medical Center—Westchester Division, White Plains, NY
The Children's Day School, Trenton, NJ
The Children's Guild Inc, Baltimore, MD
Children's Health Council, Palo Alto, CA
Children's Home of Cedar Rapids—Cedarwood Group Home, Cedar Rapids, IA
Children's Home of Cedar Rapids—Heartwood Diagnostic Evaluation Unit, Cedar Rapids, IA
Children's Home of Cedar Rapids—Heartwood Residential Treatment Center, Cedar Rapids, IA
Children's Home of Cedar Rapids—Maplewood Group Home, Cedar Rapids, IA
The Children's Home of Cincinnati, Cincinnati, OH
Children's Home of Kingston, Kingston, NY
Children's Home Society of South Dakota, Sioux Falls, SD
Children's Hospital at Washington University Medical Center—Psychiatric Unit, Saint Louis, MO
The Children's Institute, South Orange, NJ
Children's Medical Center, Tulsa, OK
Children's Medical Center—Psychiatric Inpatient Unit, Dallas, TX
The Children's Mercy Hospital—Section of Psychiatry, Kansas City, MO
The Children's School of the Institute of Living, Hartford, CT
The Children's Study Home, Springfield, MA
The Children's Village, Dobbs Ferry, NY
Christ Church Child Center, Bethesda, MD

Christian Church—Children's Campus, Danville, KY
Christian Haven Homes—Central Indiana Campus, Wheatfield, IN
Christie School, Marylhurst, OR
The Clearing, Marshfield, VT
Clearwater Ranch Children's House Inc, Philo, CA
Cleveland Christian Home for Children Inc, Cleveland, OH
Cleveland Clinic Foundation, Cleveland, OH
Cleveland County Area Mental Health Program—Division of Child and Youth Services, Shelby, NC
The Cleveland Home, Versailles, KY
The Clinical Center of Southern Illinois University, Carbondale, IL
Cobb County—Cobb Douglas Psychoeducation Children's Program, Marietta, GA
College Hospital—College Park School, Cerritos, CA
Colorado Springs School District No. 11, Colorado Springs, CO
Colorado West Regional Mental Health Center, Glenwood Springs, CO
Community Child Guidance Clinic Preschool, Manchester, CT
Community Counseling Center—Rural Clinics, Ely, NV
Community Mental Health Center South, Lee's Summit, MO
Community Psychiatric Clinic Inc, Wheaton; Bethesda; Gaithersburg, MD
Comprehensive Mental Health Center of St Clair County Inc, East Saint Louis, IL
Connecticut College Program for Children with Special Needs, New London, CT
Connecticut Junior Republic—Litchfield District, Litchfield, CT
Convalescent Hospital for Children, Rochester, NY
Covenant Children's Home and Family Services, Princeton, IL
CPC Belmont Hills Hospital, Belmont, CA
Craig House—Technoma, Pittsburgh, PA
CRATER of Broward Inc—Retreat Ranch Facility—24 Hour Residential Treatment Center, Fort Lauderdale, FL
Creative Learning Systems Inc, Tucson, AZ
Crockett State School Independent School District, Crockett, TX
Dakota Boys' Ranch, Minot, ND
Darden Hill Ranch School, Driftwood, TX
De Neuville Heights School for Girls, Memphis, TN
DeJarnette Center, Staunton, VA
The Delacato and Doman Autistic Unit, Morton, PA
Delaware Guidance Services for Children and Youth Inc, Wilmington, DE
The Delacato and Doman Autistic Unit, Plymouth Meeting, PA
Delta School, Philadelphia, PA
Department of Corrections—Hanover Learning Center, Hanover, VA
Department of Education—Windward Oahu District, Kaneohe, HI
Department of Public Instruction, Dover, DE
DePaul Hospital and Residential Treatment Center, New Orleans, LA
Des Moines Children's Home—Orchard Place, Des Moines, IA
Desert Hills, Tucson, AZ
DeSisto Schools Inc, West Stockbridge, MA
Development Evaluation Center, Fayetteville, NC
The Devereux Center in Arizona, Scottsdale, AZ
The Devereux Foundation, Devon, PA
The Devereux Foundation, Santa Barbara, CA
The Devereux Foundation—Deerhaven, Chester, NJ
The Devereux Foundation—Texas Branch, Victoria, TX
Devereux in Georgia, Kennesaw, GA
The Devereux Schools at Rutland, Rutland, MA
District of Columbia Public Schools—Division of Special Education and Pupil Personnel Services, Washington, DC
Dominion Hospital—The Dominion School, Falls Church, VA
Donaldsonville Mental Health Center, Donaldsonville, LA
Douglas A Thom Clinic Inc, Boston, MA
Early Childhood Developmental Center Inc, Hays, KS
Early Education Center, Jackson, MS
East Alabama Mental Health Retardation Center, Opelika, AL
East Bay Activity Center, Oakland, CA
East St Louis Area Joint Agreement—Department of Special Education, East Saint Louis, IL

K-Bar-B Youth Ranch—Richard M Wise School, Lacombe, LA
Kenai Peninsula Borough School District, Soldotna, AK
Kings County Hospital—Downstate Medical Center—Division of Child and Adolescent Psychiatry, Brooklyn, NY
La Mel, San Francisco, CA
La Puente Valley Community Mental Health Center, La Puente, CA
Lad Lake Inc, Dousman, WI
Lafayette Clinic, Detroit, MI
Lake County Mental Health Center—Department of Children's Services, Mentor, OH
Lake Grove School, Lake Grove, NY
Lakeshore Mental Health Institute—Riverbend School—Children and Youth Services, Knoxville, TN
Lakeside Center for Boys, Saint Louis, MO
Lakeside Child and Family Center Inc, Milwaukee, WI
Lakin Hospital—Adolescent Services, Lakin, WV
Lane School Programs—Lane Education Service District, Eugene, OR
Lansing School District, Lansing, MI
Larned State Hospital—Child Psychiatric Unit—Adolescent Psychiatric Unit/Westside School, Larned, KS
League School of Boston Inc, Newtonville, MA
The Learning Center, State College, PA
Learning Inc, Corpus Christi, TX
Leary Educational Foundation—Timber Ridge, Winchester, VA
Leary School Inc, Alexandria, VA
Lighthouse School, Chelmsford, MA
Little Friends Inc—Little Friends Parent Infant Program, Naperville, IL
Little Friends Inc—Little Friends School, Naperville, IL
Little Friends Inc—The Therapeutic Workshop, Downers Grove, IL
Little Rock School District, Little Rock, AR
The Little Village School, Garden City, NY
Lookout Mountain School, Golden, CO
Lord Stirling School, Basking Ridge, NJ
The Los Angeles Child Guidance Clinic, Los Angeles, CA
Los Angeles County Office of Education—Division of Special Education, Downey, CA
Los Angeles County Office of Education—Mark Twain School, Lawndale, CA
Los Ninos Education Center, San Diego, CA
Lovellton Academy, Elgin, IL
Luther Child Center—Children's Hospitalization Alternative Program, Everett, WA
Lutheran Special Classes, Saint Louis, MO
Madden Mental Health Center Campus—Institute for Juvenile Research—Inpatient Services, Hines, IL
Madeline Burg Counseling Services—Jewish Board of Family and Children Services, Bronx, NY
Manhattan Children's Psychiatric Center, New York, NY
Manitowoc County Counseling Center, Manitowoc, WI
The Mansion, Naperville, IL
Mardan Center of Educational Therapy, Costa Mesa, CA
Martin Luther Centers, Madison, WI
The Mary and Alexander Laughlin Children's Center, Sewickley, PA
Maryhurst School, Louisville, KY
Marymount Hospital Mental Health Center, Garfield Heights, OH
Marymount Hospital Mental Health Center, Garfield Heights, OH
Maryvale, Rosemead, CA
McKinley Home for Boys, San Dimas, CA
McKinley Therapeutic Center, Chicago, IL
Medical Care Rehabilitation Hospital's Child Evaluation and Treatment Program, Grand Forks, ND
Medical University of South Carolina—Department of Psychiatry—Youth Division, Charleston, SC
Meharry Community Mental Health Center, Nashville, TN
Mendota Mental Health Institute—Child and Adolescent Program, Madison, WI
The Menninger Foundation—Pre-School Day Treatment Center, Topeka, KS

The Menninger Foundation—The Children's Division, Topeka, KS
Menorah Medical Center—Hearing and Speech Department, Kansas City, MO
Mental Health Care Center of the Lower Keys, Key West, FL
Mental Health Center of Boulder County—Adolescent Treatment Program, Boulder, CO
Meridell Achievement Center Inc, Austin, TX
MHMR of Southeast Texas—Daybreak Cottage, Orange, TX
Michael Reese Hospital and Medical Center—Dysfunctioning Child Center, Chicago, IL
The Mid Fairfield Child Guidance Center Inc, Norwalk, CT
Mid-Columbia Mental Health Center—Adolescent Psychiatric Department, Richland, WA
The Midland School, North Branch, NJ
Milford Assistance Program Day School, Milford, MA
Millcreek Schools Inc, Magee, MS
Minneapolis Children's Medical Center—Program for Autistic and Other Exceptional Children, Minneapolis, MN
Minnesota Learning Center, Brainerd, MN
Monroe County Intermediate School District—Programs for Emotionally Impaired, Monroe, MI
Montrose School, Reisterstown, MD
Mt Airy Psychiatric Center—Children's Treatment Program—Adolescent Treatment Program, Denver, CO
Mt Scott Institute, Washington, NJ
Mountain Board of Cooperative Services—Adolescent Day Treatment Program, Leadville, CO
Multidisciplinary Institute for Neuropsychological Development Inc—MIND, Cambridge, MA
Mystic Valley Mental Health Center, Lexington, MA
Nannahagur School Day Treatment Program—(JCCA), Pleasantville, NY
Napa State Hospital—Children's Program, Imola, CA
National Foundation for the Treatment of the Emotionally Handicapped, Sepulveda, CA
New England Home for Little Wanderers—Longview Farm, Walpole, MA
New England Home for Little Wanderers—Orchard Home, Watertown, MA
New England Home for Little Wanderers—Knight Children's Center, Boston, MA
New England Medical Center—Bay Cove Day Center for Children Day Hospital, Boston, MA
New England Medical Center—Division of Child Psychiatry, Boston, MA
New England Salem Children's Trust, Rumney, NH
New Hope Guild, Brooklyn, NY
New Hope of Indiana Inc, Indianapolis, IN
North Central Health Care Facilities, Wausau, WI
North Dakota State Mental Hospital—Child and Adolescent Unit, Jamestown, ND
Northeast Colorado Board of Cooperative Educational Services, Haxton, CO
Northwood Children's Home, Duluth, MN
Ocean Institute—Adolescent Day School—Mental Health Clinic of Ocean County, Toms River, NJ
Oconomowoc Developmental Training Center Inc, Oconomowoc, WI
Ohel Children's Home and Family Services, Brooklyn, NY
Orange County Public School System—Gateway School, Orlando, FL
Orlando Regional Medical Center—Mental Health Department—Children's Services, Orlando, FL
Osterlen Services for Youth, Springfield, OH
Our Lady of Providence Children's Center, West Springfield, MA
Overlook Mental Health Center—Blount County Adolescent Partial Hospitalization Program, Maryville, TN
Pace School, Pittsburgh, PA
Pacific Children's Center, Oakland, CA
Paradise Valley School District No. 69—Therapeutic Educational Activities Milieu, Phoenix, AZ
Parkview Counseling Center Inc, Youngstown, OH
Parkwood Hospital, Atlanta, GA

University of Arkansas Medical Sciences Division Child Psychiatry—Child Study Center, Little Rock, AR
University of California at Los Angeles—Fernald, Los Angeles, CA
The University of Chicago—Departments of Psychiatry and Pediatrics—Child Psychiatry, Chicago, IL
University of Colorado Health Sciences Center—Day Care Center, Denver, CO
University of Illinois Medical Center—Child Psychiatry Clinic, Chicago, IL
University of Minnesota Hospitals—Child and Adolescent Psychiatry, Minneapolis, MN
University of New Mexico Children's Psychiatric Hospital—Mimbres School, Albuquerque, NM
University of New Mexico—Children's Psychiatric Hospital, Albuquerque, NM
University of North Carolina School of Medicine—Department of Psychiatry—Division TEACCH, Chapel Hill, NC
University of Rochester Medical School—Child and Adolescent Psychiatry Clinic, Rochester, NY
University of South Florida—Florida Mental Health Institute—Department of Child and Family Services, Tampa, FL
University of Tennessee—Child Development Center School, Memphis, TN
University of Texas Medical Branch—Division of Pediatric Psychology—Department of Pediatrics, Galveston, TX
University of Texas Medical Branch—Inpatient Service—Division of Child and Adolescent Psychiatry, Galveston, TX
University Park Psychological Center, Denver, CO
Utah Boys' Ranch—Children and Youth Services Inc, Salt Lake City, UT
Valley View School, North Brookfield, MA
Valleyhead Inc, Lenox, MA
Vanderbilt Medical Center—Division of Child and Adolescent Psychiatry, Nashville, TN
Variety Preschooler's Workshop, Syosset, NY
Villa Esperanza, Pasadena, CA
Village of St Joseph, Atlanta, GA
Virginia Center for Psychiatry, Portsmouth, VA
Virginia Center for Psychiatry, Norfolk, VA
Vista Del Mar Child Care Service, Los Angeles, CA
Vista Maria, Dearborn Heights, MI
Vitam Center Inc—Vitam School, Norwalk, CT
Walker Home and School, Needham, MA
Walter Reed Army Medical Center Child and Adolescent Psychiatry Service, Washington, DC
War Bonnet—Wilderness Pathways, Canaan, NH
Warm Springs Center, Boise, ID
Washington School District, Phoenix, AZ
Waterford Country School, Quaker Hill, CT
Waterloo Community Schools, Waterloo, IA
Waverly Children's Home, Portland, OR
West Hartford Public Schools Off-Campus Program, West Hartford, CT
West River Children's Center of the Children's Home Society of South Dakota, Rapid City, SD
West Texas Boys' Ranch, San Angelo, TX
Westbridge, Phoenix, AZ
Westchester Day Treatment Program, Hawthorne, NY
Western District Guidance Center, Parkersburg, WV
Western New York Children's Psychiatric Center, West Seneca, NY
West-Ros-Park Mental Health Center, Roslindale, MA
Wheeler Clinic Inc—Northwest Village School, Plainville, CT
Wichita Guidance Center, Wichita, KS
Wilder Children's Placement, Saint Paul, MN
Willowglen Academy Inc, Milwaukee, WI
Woodbourne Center, Baltimore, MD
Work Training Program Inc, Woodland Hills, CA
Work Training Program Inc, Santa Barbara, CA
Wyalusing Academy, Prairie du Chien, WI
Wyandotte Mental Health Center, Kansas City, KS
Wyandotte Special Education Cooperative, Kansas City, KS

Wyoming Youth Treatment Center, Casper, WY
Yellowstone Boys' and Girls' Ranch, Billings, MT
York Woods Center, Ypsilanti, MI
Youth and Family Services, Omaha, NE
Youth Center at Larned—Westside School, Larned, KS
Youth Center of Beloit—North Beloit High, Beloit, KS
Yuma School District One, Yuma, AZ
Yuma Union High School District, Yuma, AZ

Mentally Handicapped

Ahwahnee Hills School, Ahwahnee, CA
ALA Costa Center for the Developmentally Disabled—After School, Berkeley, CA
Alabama Youth Services—Chalkville Campus, Birmingham, AL
Albany Area Mental Health and Mental Retardation Center, Albany, GA
Albuquerque Special Preschool, Albuquerque, NM
All Children's Hospital, St Petersburg, FL
Almansor Education Center, Alhambra, CA
American Institute—The Training School at Vineland, Vineland, NJ
Archdiocese of Louisville—Guidance Clinic, Louisville, KY
Area Education Agency—Education Center, Waterloo, IA
Area Education Agency 4—River Valley School, Rock Valley, IA
Arizona State Hospital, Phoenix, AZ
Arizona State Hospital—Nueva Vista School, Phoenix, AZ
Arthur Brisbane Child Treatment Center, Farmingdale, NJ
The Astor Home for Children—Day Treatment Program, Bronx, NY
The Astor Home for Children—Residential Treatment Center—Residential Treatment Facility—Learning Center, Rhinebeck, NY
Atlanta Public Schools, Atlanta, GA
Atlantic Mental Health Center Inc, McKee City, NJ
Augusta School Department, Augusta, ME
Aurora Adolescent Day Resource Center, Aurora, CO
Austin State Hospital, Austin, TX
Autistic Treatment Center—San Antonio, San Antonio, TX
Avalon Center—Avalon Schools, Lenox, MA
Avalon School at High Point, Lenox, MA
Avon Lenox Special Education, Memphis, TN
Avondale House, Houston, TX
Baker Hall Inc, Lackawanna, NY
The Bancroft School, Haddonfield, NJ
Barat Human Services—Barat House, Detroit, MI
Bar-None Residential Treatment Services for Children, Anoka, MN
Battle Creek Child Guidance Center, Battle Creek, MI
Behavior Research Institute, Providence, RI
Benhaven, East Haven, CT
Berks County Intermediate Unit, Reading, PA
Big Lakes Developmental Center Inc, Manhattan, KS
Big Spring State Hospital, Big Spring, TX
Birmingham City Board of Education, Birmingham, AL
Blick Clinic for Developmental Disabilities, Akron, OH
Board of Cooperative Educational Services II—Special Education Division Instructional Support Center, Centereach, NY
BOCES Nassau, Westbury, NY
BOCES Southern Westchester—Rye Lake Campus, White Plains, NY
Bowman Gray School of Medicine Developmental Evaluation Clinic—Amos Cottage Rehabilitation Hospital, Winston-Salem, NC
Brentwood Center, Los Angeles, CA
Bridgeway Hospital Youthcare Program, North Little Rock, AR
Bronx Developmental Center—Respite Service, Bronx, NY
Brooklyn Community Counseling Center, Brooklyn, NY
Brown County Mental Health Center—Children Services, Green Bay, WI
The Brown Schools, Austin, TX
Bunche Park Elementary School, Opa Locka, FL
Butler County Mental Health Center Inc, Hamilton, OH
Camphill Special Schools Inc, Glenmoore, PA
Cantalician Center for Learning, Buffalo, NY

Capitol Region Education Council's Day Treatment Service, West Hartford, CT

Cass County Social Services—Children's Social Service Center, Fargo, ND

Center for Autistic Children, Philadelphia, PA

Center for Life Management, Salem, NH

Center for Urban Living, Saint Louis, MO

Centerville Clinics Inc—Partial Hospital Program, Fredericktown, PA

Central Massachusetts Special Education Collaborative—Quimby School, Worcester, MA

Central New Hampshire Community Mental Health Services Inc—Early Intervention Services, Concord, NH

Cheboygan-Otsego-Presque Isle Intermediate School District—Alpine Educational Facility, Gaylord, MI

Cheboygan-Otsego-Presque Isle Intermediate School District—Hawks Programs, Hawks, MI

Cheboygen-Otsego-Presque Isle Intermediate School District—Inverness Elementary, Cheboygen, MI

Child Adolescent Service Center, Canton, OH

Child and Family Services, Knoxville, TN

Child Development Service—Lakeview Center Inc, Pensacola, FL

Child Disability Clinic—Carle Clinic, Urbana, IL

Child Psychiatry Service—Department of Psychiatry—University Hospitals, Ann Arbor, MI

Child Study Center, Fort Worth, TX

Childhaven, Saint Louis, MO

Children's Behavior Therapy Unit, Salt Lake City, UT

Children's Center for Behavioral Development, East Saint Louis, IL

Children's Day Hospital—New York Hospital—Cornell Medical Center—Westchester Division, White Plains, NY

Children's Health Council, Palo Alto, CA

Children's Home of Cedar Rapids—Heartwood Diagnostic Evaluation Unit, Cedar Rapids, IA

Children's Home of Cedar Rapids—Heartwood Residential Treatment Center, Cedar Rapids, IA

Children's Hospital at Washington University Medical Center—Psychiatric Unit, Saint Louis, MO

Children's Learning Center of San Antonio, San Antonio, TX

Children's Medical Center, Tulsa, OK

The Children's Mercy Hospital—Section of Psychiatry, Kansas City, MO

The Children's School of the Institute of Living, Hartford, CT

The Children's Village, Dobbs Ferry, NY

Christ Church Child Center, Bethesda, MD

Christian Haven Homes—Central Indiana Campus, Wheatfield, IN

Clear View School, Scarborough, NY

The Clearing, Marshfield, VT

Clearwater Ranch Children's House Inc, Philo, CA

Cleveland Clinic Foundation, Cleveland, OH

Cleveland County Area Mental Health Program—Division of Child and Youth Services, Shelby, NC

The Clinical Center of Southern Illinois University, Carbondale, IL

Cobb County—Cobb Douglas Psychoeducation Children's Program, Marietta, GA

Colorado Springs School District No. 11, Colorado Springs, CO

Colorado West Regional Mental Health Center, Glenwood Springs, CO

Community Counseling Center—Rural Clinics, Ely, NV

Community Psychiatric Clinic Inc, Wheaton; Bethesda; Gaithersburg, MD

Concord, Yellow Spring, WV

Connecticut College Program for Children with Special Needs, New London, CT

Cooperative Educational Services Developmental Learning Center, Wilton, CT

Cousins Respite Care Program of the Parent Resource Center Inc, Orlando, FL

Covenant Children's Home and Family Services, Princeton, IL

CPC Belmont Hills Hospital, Belmont, CA

CRATER of Broward Inc—Retreat Ranch Facility—24 Hour Residential Treatment Center, Fort Lauderdale, FL

Creative Arts Rehabilitation Center Inc, New York, NY

The Delacato and Doman Autistic Unit, Morton, PA

Delaware Guidance Services for Children and Youth Inc, Wilmington, DE

Delta School, Philadelphia, PA

Department of Corrections—Hanover Learning Center, Hanover, VA

Department of Education—Windward Oahu District, Kaneohe, HI

Department of Public Instruction, Dover, DE

DePaul Hospital and Residential Treatment Center, New Orleans, LA

Development Evaluation Center, Fayetteville, NC

The Devereux Foundation, Devon, PA

The Devereux Foundation, Santa Barbara, CA

The Devereux Schools at Rutland, Rutland, MA

Doctor Franklin Perkins School, Lancaster, MA

Donaldsonville Mental Health Center, Donaldsonville, LA

Dysfunctioning Child Center—Respite Care Unit, Chicago, IL

Early Childhood Developmental Center Inc, Hays, KS

Early Education Center, Jackson, MS

East Alabama Mental Health Retardation Center, Opelika, AL

East St Louis Area Joint Agreement—Department of Special Education, East Saint Louis, IL

Eastern Los Angeles Regional Center for the Developmentally Disabled, Alhambra, CA

Eau Claire Academy, Eau Claire, WI

Edgefield Children's Center, Troutdale, OR

Edgemeade of Maryland, Upper Marlboro, MD

Edgewood Children's Center, Saint Louis, MO

Edgewood Day Treatment—The Lucinda Weeks Center, San Francisco, CA

Educational Alliance—Camp Cummings, New York, NY

The Educational Clinic Inc, Columbus, OH

Educational Service Unit 3—Department of Special Education—Exceptional Children Resource Center, Omaha, NE

Efficacy Research Institute of Framingham, Framingham, MA

Efficacy Research Institute of Taunton Inc, Taunton, MA

El Paso Guidance Center, El Paso, TX

Eleanor Griffin Children's Development Center, Plainview, TX

Elizabeth Ives School, Hamden, CT

Elwyn Institutes, Elwyn, PA

Emma Pendleton Bradley Hospital Developmental Disabilities Program, East Providence, RI

Encor—Family and Medical Support Services—Home Based Services, Omaha, NE

Encor—Family and Medical Support Services—Respite Services, Omaha, NE

Escalon Inc, Altadena, CA

Escambia District Schools, Pensacola, FL

Evansville Vanderburgh School Corporation, Evansville, IN

Family Guidance Center, Reading, PA

Five Acres Boys' and Girls' Aide Society, Altadena, CA

Fort Logan Mental Health Center, Denver, CO

Franklin Grand Isle Mental Health Services Inc, Saint Albans, VT

Fred Finch Youth Center, Oakland, CA

Fremont Unified School District, Fremont, CA

Garden Sullivan Learning and Development Program, San Francisco, CA

Gilfillan Center, Bemidji, MN

Gladman Memorial Hospital Adolescent Program, Oakland, CA

Grady Memorial Hospital—Division of Child and Adolescent Psychiatry, Atlanta, GA

Grafton School, Berryville, VA

Grafton School—Autism Program, Berryville, VA

The Gramon School, Livingston, NJ

Green Chimneys Children's Services Inc, Brewster, NY

Green Meadows School, Wilmington, VT

Greenshire School, Cheshire, CT

The Grove School, Lake Forest, IL

Hall-Mercer Children's Center of the McLean Hospital, Belmont, MA

Harbor View Mercy Hospital, Fort Smith, AR

Harford County Community Mental Health Center, Bel Air, MD

The Harmony Center Inc, Baton Rouge, LA

Harrison County Training Center for Exceptional Children, Gulfport, MS

Hartgrove Hospital—Hartgrove Academy, Chicago, IL

Hawaii State Department of Education—Special Needs Branch, Honolulu, HI

Hawaii State Hospital—Adolescent Unit, Kaneohe, HI

Hawthorne Cedar Knolls School, Hawthorne, NY

Henderson Mental Health Center, Fort Lauderdale, FL

High Plains Mental Health Center—Colby Office, Colby, KS

Hillside Children's Center, Rochester, NY

Hillside Inc, Atlanta, GA

Homes Unlimited Inc, Bangor, ME

Homewood School—Highland Hospital, Asheville, NC

Honolulu District—Special Education Center of Oahu (SECO), Honolulu, HI

Huntsville City School System, Hunstville, AL

Idaho Youth Ranch Inc, Rupert, ID

Independence House of Avalon Inc, Sheffield, MA

Indianapolis Public Schools—Special Education Department, Indianapolis, IN

Ingham Developmental Center, Mason, MI

Ingleside Hospital, Rosemead, CA

Institute for Developmental Disabilities—Crystal Springs School, Assonet, MA

Institute of Logopedics, Wichita, KS

Institute of Psychiatry and Human Behavior—Department of Psychiatry—Child and Adolescent Inpatient Service, Baltimore, MD

ISIS Programs Inc—Individual Support Through Innovative Services for Autistic Persons, Orlando, FL

Jackson Municipal Separate School District, Jackson, MS

Jasper County Mental Health Center, Newton, IA

Jefferson County Public Schools, Lakewood, CO

Jefferson Parish School System—Department of Special Education, Gretna, LA

Jennie Clarkson Child Care Services Inc—St Christopher's, Dobbs Ferry, NY

Jersey Shore Medical Center—Child Evaluation Center, Neptune, NJ

John C Corrigan Mental Health Center, Fall River, MA

The John F Kennedy Institute, Baltimore, MD

John G McGrath School, Napa, CA

Josephine County Mental Health Program—Children's Resource Team, Grants Pass, OR

Jowonio School, Syracuse, NY

Judevine Center for Autistic Children, Saint Louis, MO

Judge Baker Guidance Center, Boston, MA

Kenai Peninsula Borough School District, Soldotna, AK

Kings County Hospital—Downstate Medical Center—Division of Child and Adolescent Psychiatry, Brooklyn, NY

Klamath County Mental Health Center—Mentally Retarded/Developmentally Disabled Program, Klamath Falls, OR

La Puente Valley Community Mental Health Center, La Puente, CA

Lake County Mental Health Center—Department of Children's Services, Mentor, OH

Lakin Hospital—Adolescent Services, Lakin, WV

Lansing School District, Lansing, MI

LaVoy Exceptional Center, Tampa, FL

The League School, Brooklyn, NY

League School of Boston Inc, Newtonville, MA

Leary School Inc, Alexandria, VA

Lighthouse School, Chelmsford, MA

Little Friends Inc—Little Friends Parent Infant Program, Naperville, IL

Little Friends Inc—Little Friends School, Naperville, IL

Little Friends Inc—The Therapeutic Workshop, Downers Grove, IL

Little Rock School District, Little Rock, AR

The Little Village School, Garden City, NY

Los Angeles County Office of Education—Division of Special Education, Downey, CA

Los Angeles County Office of Education—Mark Twain School, Lawndale, CA

Los Lunas Hospital and Training School—Behavioral Services Unit, Los Lunas, NM

Los Ninos Education Center, San Diego, CA

Louisiana State University Medical Center—School of Allied Health Professions—Human Development Center, New Orleans, LA

Lutheran Special Classes, Saint Louis, MO

Madeline Burg Counseling Services—Jewish Board of Family and Children Services, Bronx, NY

Main Street Human Resources, Great Barington, MA

Manitowoc County Counseling Center, Manitowoc, WI

Mardan Center of Educational Therapy, Costa Mesa, CA

Marymount Hospital Mental Health Center, Garfield Heights, OH

McKinley Therapeutic Center, Chicago, IL

Medical Care Rehabilitation Hospital's Child Evaluation and Treatment Program, Grand Forks, ND

Medical University of South Carolina—Department of Psychiatry—Youth Division, Charleston, SC

Meharry Community Mental Health Center, Nashville, TN

Mendota Mental Health Institute—Child and Adolescent Program, Madison, WI

Menorah Medical Center—Hearing and Speech Department, Kansas City, MO

Mental Health Centers of Central Illinois—Child and Adolescent Day Treatment Program, Springfield, IL

Mercy Hospital and Medical Center—Community Guidance Center, Chicago, IL

Michael Reese Hospital and Medical Center—Dysfunctioning Child Center, Chicago, IL

Mid-Columbia Mental Health Center—Adolescent Psychiatric Department, Richland, WA

Millcreek Schools Inc, Magee, MS

Minneapolis Children's Medical Center—Program for Autistic and Other Exceptional Children, Minneapolis, MN

Minnesota Learning Center, Brainerd, MN

Montrose School, Reisterstown, MD

Mt Airy Psychiatric Center—Children's Treatment Program—Adolescent Treatment Program, Denver, CO

Multidisciplinary Institute for Neuropsychological Development Inc—MIND, Cambridge, MA

Mystic Valley Mental Health Center, Lexington, MA

Nannahagur School Day Treatment Program—(JCCA), Pleasantville, NY

Napa State Hospital—Children's Program, Imola, CA

The Nassau Center for the Developmentally Disabled Inc, Woodbury, NY

National Foundation for the Treatment of the Emotionally Handicapped, Sepulveda, CA

New Hope of Indiana Inc, Indianapolis, IN

North Central Health Care Facilities, Wausau, WI

North Dakota State Mental Hospital—Child and Adolescent Unit, Jamestown, ND

North Mississippi Retardation Center, Oxford, MS

Northeast Colorado Board of Cooperative Educational Services, Haxton, CO

Northern Indiana State Hospital and Developmental Disabilities Center, South Bend, IN

Northwood Children's Home, Duluth, MN

Oconomowoc Developmental Training Center Inc, Oconomowoc, WI

Ohel Children's Home and Family Services, Brooklyn, NY

Osterlen Services for Youth, Springfield, OH

Our Lady of Providence Children's Center, West Springfield, MA

Pace School, Braintree, MA

Parkview Counseling Center Inc, Youngstown, OH

Parmadale—The Youth Services Village, Parma, OH

Parsons Child and Family Center—Neil Hellman School, Albany, NY

Pawnee Mental Health Services, Concordia, KS

Youth Center of Beloit—North Beloit High, Beloit, KS
Yuma School District One, Yuma, AZ
Yuma Union High School District, Yuma, AZ

Other Health Impaired

ALA Costa Center for the Developmentally Disabled—After School, Berkeley, CA
Albuquerque Special Preschool, Albuquerque, NM
Alexandria Head Start, Alexandria, VA
All Children's Hospital, St Petersburg, FL
American Institute—The Training School at Vineland, Vineland, NJ
Area Education Agency 4—River Valley School, Rock Valley, IA
Arizona State Hospital, Phoenix, AZ
Arthur Brisbane Child Treatment Center, Farmingdale, NJ
Atlanta Public Schools, Atlanta, GA
Atlantic Mental Health Center Inc, McKee City, NJ
Austin State Hospital, Austin, TX
Avalon Center—Avalon Schools, Lenox, MA
Avon Lenox Special Education, Memphis, TN
The Bancroft School, Haddonfield, NJ
Berks County Intermediate Unit, Reading, PA
Big Lakes Developmental Center Inc, Manhattan, KS
Blick Clinic for Developmental Disabilities, Akron, OH
Board of Cooperative Educational Services II—Special Education Division Instructional Support Center, Centereach, NY
BOCES Nassau, Westbury, NY
Bowman Gray School of Medicine Developmental Evaluation Clinic—Amos Cottage Rehabilitation Hospital, Winston-Salem, NC
Brattleboro Retreat, Brattleboro, VT
Brown County Mental Health Center—Children Services, Green Bay, WI
The Brown Schools, Austin, TX
Bunche Park Elementary School, Opa Locka, FL
Cass County Social Services—Children's Social Service Center, Fargo, ND
Centerville Clinics Inc—Partial Hospital Program, Fredericktown, PA
Central New Hampshire Community Mental Health Services Inc—Early Intervention Services, Concord, NH
Cheboygan-Otsego-Presque Isle Intermediate School District—Alpine Educational Facility, Gaylord, MI
Cheboygan-Otsego-Presque Isle Intermediate School District—Hawks Programs, Hawks, MI
Cheboygan-Otsego-Presque Isle Intermediate School District—Inverness Elementary, Cheboygen, MI
Child Adolescent Service Center, Canton, OH
Child Disability Clinic—Carle Clinic, Urbana, IL
Child Study Center, Fort Worth, TX
Children's Aid Society, Cleveland, OH
Children's Hospital at Washington University Medical Center—Psychiatric Unit, Saint Louis, MO
Children's Medical Center, Tulsa, OK
Children's Medical Center—Psychiatric Inpatient Unit, Dallas, TX
The Children's Mercy Hospital—Section of Psychiatry, Kansas City, MO
The Children's School of the Institute of Living, Hartford, CT
The Clearing, Marshfield, VT
Cleveland Clinic Foundation, Cleveland, OH
Cleveland County Area Mental Health Program—Division of Child and Youth Services, Shelby, NC
The Cleveland Home, Versailles, KY
The Clinical Center of Southern Illinois University, Carbondale, IL
Cobb County—Cobb Douglas Psychoeducation Children's Program, Marietta, GA
Colorado Springs School District No. 11, Colorado Springs, CO
Colorado West Regional Mental Health Center, Glenwood Springs, CO
Connecticut College Program for Children with Special Needs, New London, CT

Cousins Respite Care Program of the Parent Resource Center Inc, Orlando, FL
Covenant Children's Home and Family Services, Princeton, IL
CRATER of Broward Inc—Retreat Ranch Facility—24 Hour Residential Treatment Center, Fort Lauderdale, FL
Delaware Guidance Services for Children and Youth Inc, Wilmington, DE
Department of Education—Windward Oahu District, Kaneohe, HI
Department of Public Instruction, Dover, DE
Development Evaluation Center, Fayetteville, NC
The Devereux Foundation, Santa Barbara, CA
Early Childhood Developmental Center Inc, Hays, KS
Early Education Center, Jackson, MS
East Alabama Mental Health Retardation Center, Opelika, AL
East St Louis Area Joint Agreement—Department of Special Education, East Saint Louis, IL
The Educational Clinic Inc, Columbus, OH
Educational Service Unit 3—Department of Special Education—Exceptional Children Resource Center, Omaha, NE
Eleanor Griffin Children's Development Center, Plainview, TX
Elwyn Institutes, Elwyn, PA
Encor—Family and Medical Support Services—Home Based Services, Omaha, NE
Encor—Family and Medical Support Services—Respite Services, Omaha, NE
Escambia District Schools, Pensacola, FL
Evansville Vanderburgh School Corporation, Evansville, IN
Excelsior Youth Center, Aurora, CO
Fremont Unified School District, Fremont, CA
Garden Sullivan Learning and Development Program, San Francisco, CA
Gilfillan Center, Bemidji, MN
Grady Memorial Hospital—Division of Child and Adolescent Psychiatry, Atlanta, GA
The Gramon School, Livingston, NJ
Greenshire School, Cheshire, CT
The Grove School, Lake Forest, IL
Harbor View Mercy Hospital, Fort Smith, AR
The Harmony Center Inc, Baton Rouge, LA
Harrison County Training Center for Exceptional Children, Gulfport, MS
Harry S Truman Children's Neurological Center, Kansas City, MO
Hawaii State Department of Education—Special Needs Branch, Honolulu, HI
Hawaii State Hospital—Adolescent Unit, Kaneohe, HI
High Plains Mental Health Center—Colby Office, Colby, KS
Homes Unlimited Inc, Bangor, ME
Honolulu District—Special Education Center of Oahu (SECO), Honolulu, HI
Huntsville City School System, Hunstville, AL
Independence House of Avalon Inc, Sheffield, MA
Indianapolis Public Schools—Special Education Department, Indianapolis, IN
Indianapolis Public Schools—James E Roberts School No. 97, Indianapolis, IN
Ingham Developmental Center, Mason, MI
Institute for Developmental Disabilities—Crystal Springs School, Assonet, MA
Institute of Logopedics, Wichita, KS
Jackson Municipal Separate School District, Jackson, MS
Jasper County Mental Health Center, Newton, IA
Jefferson County Public Schools, Lakewood, CO
Jefferson Parish School System—Department of Special Education, Gretna, LA
Jersey Shore Medical Center—Child Evaluation Center, Neptune, NJ
The John F Kennedy Institute, Baltimore, MD
John Umstead Hospital—Children's Psychiatric Institute, Butner, NC
Josephine County Mental Health Program—Children's Resource Team, Grants Pass, OR
Jowonio School, Syracuse, NY

Physically Handicapped

Austin State Hospital, Austin, TX
The Bancroft School, Haddonfield, NJ
Bar-None Residential Treatment Services for Children, Anoka, MN
Bergen Pines Hospital—Children's Psychiatric Unit, Paramus, NJ
Berks County Intermediate Unit, Reading, PA
Big Lakes Developmental Center Inc, Manhattan, KS
Birmingham City Board of Education, Birmingham, AL
Blick Clinic for Developmental Disabilities, Akron, OH
Board of Cooperative Educational Services II—Special Education Division Instructional Support Center, Centereach, NY
BOCES Nassau, Westbury, NY
Brattleboro Retreat, Brattleboro, VT
Brewer-Porch Children's Center, University, AL
Brown County Mental Health Center—Children Services, Green Bay, WI
The Brown Schools, Austin, TX
Cass County Social Services—Children's Social Service Center, Fargo, ND
Centerville Clinics Inc—Partial Hospital Program, Fredericktown, PA
Central New Hampshire Community Mental Health Services Inc—Early Intervention Services, Concord, NH
Cheboygan-Otsego-Presque Isle Intermediate School District—Alpine Educational Facility, Gaylord, MI
Cheboygan-Otsego-Presque Isle Intermediate School District—Hawks Programs, Hawks, MI
Cheboygen-Otsego-Presque Isle Intermediate School District—Inverness Elementary, Cheboygen, MI
Child Adolescent Service Center, Canton, OH
Child Disability Clinic—Carle Clinic, Urbana, IL
Child Study Center, Fort Worth, TX
Childhaven, Saint Louis, MO
Children's Health Council, Palo Alto, CA
Children's Hospital at Washington University Medical Center—Psychiatric Unit, Saint Louis, MO
Children's Medical Center, Tulsa, OK
Children's Medical Center—Psychiatric Inpatient Unit, Dallas, TX
The Children's Mercy Hospital—Section of Psychiatry, Kansas City, MO
The Clearing, Marshfield, VT
Cleveland County Area Mental Health Program—Division of Child and Youth Services, Shelby, NC
The Clinical Center of Southern Illinois University, Carbondale, IL
Cobb County—Cobb Douglas Psychoeducation Children's Program, Marietta, GA
College Hospital—College Park School, Cerritos, CA
Colorado Springs School District No. 11, Colorado Springs, CO
Colorado West Regional Mental Health Center, Glenwood Springs, CO
Connecticut College Program for Children with Special Needs, New London, CT
Cousins Respite Care Program of the Parent Resource Center Inc, Orlando, FL
Covenant Children's Home and Family Services, Princeton, IL
CRATER of Broward Inc—Retreat Ranch Facility—24 Hour Residential Treatment Center, Fort Lauderdale, FL
De Neuville Heights School for Girls, Memphis, TN
Delaware Guidance Services for Children and Youth Inc, Wilmington, DE
Department of Education—Windward Oahu District, Kaneohe, HI
Department of Public Instruction, Dover, DE
Development Evaluation Center, Fayetteville, NC
Early Childhood Developmental Center Inc, Hays, KS
Early Education Center, Jackson, MS
East Alabama Mental Health Retardation Center, Opelika, AL
East St Louis Area Joint Agreement—Department of Special Education, East Saint Louis, IL
Eastern Los Angeles Regional Center for the Developmentally Disabled, Alhambra, CA

Edgewood Day Treatment—The Lucinda Weeks Center, San Francisco, CA
Educational Service Unit 3—Department of Special Education—Exceptional Children Resource Center, Omaha, NE
Eleanor Griffin Children's Development Center, Plainview, TX
Elwyn Institutes, Elwyn, PA
Encor—Family and Medical Support Services—Home Based Services, Omaha, NE
Escalon Inc, Altadena, CA
Escambia District Schools, Pensacola, FL
Evansville Vanderburgh School Corporation, Evansville, IN
Excelsior Youth Center, Aurora, CO
Forest Hospital, Des Plaines, IL
Fremont Unified School District, Fremont, CA
Gerard of Minnesota Inc, Austin, MN
Grady Memorial Hospital—Division of Child and Adolescent Psychiatry, Atlanta, GA
Green Tree School, Philadelphia, PA
The Grove School, Lake Forest, IL
Harbor View Mercy Hospital, Fort Smith, AR
Harford County Community Mental Health Center, Bel Air, MD
Harry S Truman Children's Neurological Center, Kansas City, MO
Hartgrove Hospital—Hartgrove Academy, Chicago, IL
Hawaii State Department of Education—Special Needs Branch, Honolulu, HI
High Plains Mental Health Center—Colby Office, Colby, KS
Homewood School—Highland Hospital, Asheville, NC
Honolulu District—Special Education Center of Oahu (SECO), Honolulu, HI
Huntsville City School System, Hunstville, AL
Independence House of Avalon Inc, Sheffield, MA
Indianapolis Public Schools—Special Education Department, Indianapolis, IN
Indianapolis Public Schools—James E Roberts School No. 97, Indianapolis, IN
Institute for Developmental Disabilities—Crystal Springs School, Assonet, MA
Institute of Logopedics, Wichita, KS
Jackson Municipal Separate School District, Jackson, MS
Jasper County Mental Health Center, Newton, IA
Jefferson County Public Schools, Lakewood, CO
Jefferson Parish School System—Department of Special Education, Gretna, LA
Jersey Shore Medical Center—Child Evaluation Center, Neptune, NJ
Jewish Children's Bureau of Chicago, Chicago, IL
The John F Kennedy Institute, Baltimore, MD
John Umstead Hospital—Children's Psychiatric Institute, Butner, NC
Josephine County Mental Health Program—Children's Resource Team, Grants Pass, OR
Judge Baker Guidance Center, Boston, MA
Kenai Peninsula Borough School District, Soldotna, AK
La Mel, San Francisco, CA
Lake County Mental Health Center—Department of Children's Services, Mentor, OH
Lighthouse School, Chelmsford, MA
Little Friends Inc—Little Friends Parent Infant Program, Naperville, IL
Little Rock School District, Little Rock, AR
The Little Village School, Garden City, NY
Los Angeles County Office of Education—Division of Special Education, Downey, CA
Louisiana State University Medical Center—School of Allied Health Professions—Human Development Center, New Orleans, LA
Lovellton Academy, Elgin, IL
Manitowoc County Counseling Center, Manitowoc, WI
Martin Luther Centers, Madison, WI
Marymount Hospital Mental Health Center, Garfield Heights, OH
Medical Care Rehabilitation Hospital's Child Evaluation and Treatment Program, Grand Forks, ND

Visually Impaired/Blind

Cleveland County Area Mental Health Program—Division of Child and Youth Services, Shelby, NC

Cobb County—Cobb Douglas Psychoeducation Children's Program, Marietta, GA

Colorado Springs School District No. 11, Colorado Springs, CO

Concord, Yellow Spring, WV

Connecticut College Program for Children with Special Needs, New London, CT

Cousins Respite Care Program of the Parent Resource Center Inc, Orlando, FL

Covenant Children's Home and Family Services, Princeton, IL

CRATER of Broward Inc—Retreat Ranch Facility—24 Hour Residential Treatment Center, Fort Lauderdale, FL

The Delacato and Doman Autistic Unit, Morton, PA

Department of Education—Windward Oahu District, Kaneohe, HI

Department of Public Instruction, Dover, DE

Development Evaluation Center, Fayetteville, NC

The Devereux Foundation—Texas Branch, Victoria, TX

Dysfunctioning Child Center—Respite Care Unit, Chicago, IL

Early Childhood Developmental Center Inc, Hays, KS

Early Education Center, Jackson, MS

East Alabama Mental Health Retardation Center, Opelika, AL

East St Louis Area Joint Agreement—Department of Special Education, East Saint Louis, IL

The Educational Clinic Inc, Columbus, OH

Educational Service Unit 3—Department of Special Education—Exceptional Children Resource Center, Omaha, NE

Eleanor Griffin Children's Development Center, Plainview, TX

Elwyn Institutes, Elwyn, PA

Emma Pendleton Bradley Hospital Developmental Disabilities Program, East Providence, RI

Encor—Family and Medical Support Services—Home Based Services, Omaha, NE

Encor—Family and Medical Support Services—Respite Services, Omaha, NE

Escambia District Schools, Pensacola, FL

Evansville Vanderburgh School Corporation, Evansville, IN

Forest Hospital, Des Plaines, IL

Fremont Unified School District, Fremont, CA

Greenshire School, Cheshire, CT

Harbor View Mercy Hospital, Fort Smith, AR

Harrison County Training Center for Exceptional Children, Gulfport, MS

Harry S Truman Children's Neurological Center, Kansas City, MO

Hawaii State Department of Education—Special Needs Branch, Honolulu, HI

Hawaii State Hospital—Adolescent Unit, Kaneohe, HI

High Plains Mental Health Center—Colby Office, Colby, KS

Honolulu District—Special Education Center of Oahu (SECO), Honolulu, HI

Huntsville City School System, Hunstville, AL

Indianapolis Public Schools—Special Education Department, Indianapolis, IN

Ingham Developmental Center, Mason, MI

Institute for Developmental Disabilities—Crystal Springs School, Assonet, MA

Institute of Logopedics, Wichita, KS

Jackson Municipal Separate School District, Jackson, MS

Jasper County Mental Health Center, Newton, IA

Jefferson County Public Schools, Lakewood, CO

Jefferson Parish School System—Department of Special Education, Gretna, LA

Jersey Shore Medical Center—Child Evaluation Center, Neptune, NJ

The John F Kennedy Institute, Baltimore, MD

John Umstead Hospital—Children's Psychiatric Institute, Butner, NC

Josephine County Mental Health Program—Children's Resource Team, Grants Pass, OR

Kenai Peninsula Borough School District, Soldotna, AK

Klamath County Mental Health Center—Mentally Retarded/Developmentally Disabled Program, Klamath Falls, OR

Lighthouse School, Chelmsford, MA

Little Friends Inc—Little Friends Parent Infant Program, Naperville, IL

Little Rock School District, Little Rock, AR

The Little Village School, Garden City, NY

Los Angeles County Office of Education—Division of Special Education, Downey, CA

Los Lunas Hospital and Training School—Behavioral Services Unit, Los Lunas, NM

Los Ninos Education Center, San Diego, CA

Louisiana State University Medical Center—School of Allied Health Professions—Human Development Center, New Orleans, LA

Manhattan Children's Psychiatric Center, New York, NY

Manitowoc County Counseling Center, Manitowoc, WI

Marymount Hospital Mental Health Center, Garfield Heights, OH

Medical Care Rehabilitation Hospital's Child Evaluation and Treatment Program, Grand Forks, ND

Mendota Mental Health Institute—Child and Adolescent Program, Madison, WI

Michael Reese Hospital and Medical Center—Dysfunctioning Child Center, Chicago, IL

Mid-Columbia Mental Health Center—Adolescent Psychiatric Department, Richland, WA

Millcreek Schools Inc, Magee, MS

Mt Airy Psychiatric Center—Children's Treatment Program—Adolescent Treatment Program, Denver, CO

Multidisciplinary Institute for Neuropsychological Development Inc—MIND, Cambridge, MA

New Hope of Indiana Inc, Indianapolis, IN

North Central Health Care Facilities, Wausau, WI

North Dakota State Mental Hospital—Child and Adolescent Unit, Jamestown, ND

North Mississippi Retardation Center, Oxford, MS

Northern Indiana State Hospital and Developmental Disabilities Center, South Bend, IN

Oconomowoc Developmental Training Center Inc, Oconomowoc, WI

Penninsula Children's Center—Children and Youth Services, Palo Alto, CA

Philadelphia Child Guidance Clinic—Child and Family Inpatient Service, Philadelphia, PA

Phoenix Union High School District No. 210, Phoenix, AZ

Project for Psychotic and Neurologically Impaired Children, Madison, WI

Psychiatric Services Inc, Haverhill, MA

Pulaski County Special School District, Little Rock, AR

Quincy School for the Handicapped, Quincy, IL

Range Mental Health Center, Virginia, MN

Region VIII Education Service Center, Mount Pleasant, TX

Region 16 Educational Service Center, Amarillo, TX

Regional Intervention Program, Nashville, TN

The Rehabilitation Institute of Pittsburgh, Pittsburgh, PA

Rensselaer County Mental Health Department—Unified Services for Children and Adolescents, Troy, NY

Rise East School, Pomona, NY

Rockford School District No. 205, Rockford, IL

Samuel Gompers Memorial Rehabilitation Center Inc, Phoenix, AZ

San Diego Unified School District, San Diego, CA

San Joaquin County Office of Education—Special Education Programs, Stockton, CA

San Mateo County Office of Education, Redwood City, CA

School District of Philadelphia—Special Education—Stevens Administrative Center, Philadelphia, PA

Scottsdale Public School District, Phoenix, AZ

Shawnee Mission Public Schools, Shawnee Mission, KS

Southbury Training School, Southbury, CT

Southeastern Children's Center, Sioux Falls, SD

Southgate Regional Center for Developmental Disabilities, Southgate, MI

Spaulding Youth Center—Autistic Program, Tilton, NH

Spaulding Youth Center—Emotional Handicap Program, Tilton, NH

Psychopathological Conditions Treated Index

Alcohol Abuse and/or Drug Abuse

Adams County Adolescent Day Treatment Program, Denver, CO
Ahwahnee Hills School, Ahwahnee, CA
Alabama Youth Services—Chalkville Campus, Birmingham, AL
Albany Area Mental Health and Mental Retardation Center, Albany, GA
Anneewakee Hospital, Douglasville, GA
Archdiocese of Louisville—Guidance Clinic, Louisville, KY
Arizona Boys' Ranch, Boys Ranch, AZ
Arizona State Hospital—Nueva Vista School, Phoenix, AZ
Arlington School, Belmont, MA
Aseltine School, San Diego, CA
The Astor Home for Children—Group Home Program, Bronx, NY
Atlantic Mental Health Center Inc, McKee City, NJ
Augusta School Department, Augusta, ME
Aurora Adolescent Day Resource Center, Aurora, CO
Baker Hall Inc, Lackawanna, NY
The Battin Clinic, Houston, TX
Battle Creek Child Guidance Center, Battle Creek, MI
Beacon Day Treatment Program, Romulus, MI
Bergen Pines Hospital—Children's Psychiatric Unit, Paramus, NJ
Berks County Intermediate Unit, Reading, PA
Berkshire Farm Center and Services for Youth, Canaan, NY
Birmingham City Board of Education, Birmingham, AL
Blick Clinic for Developmental Disabilities, Akron, OH
Boston Public Schools—The McKinley Schools, Mattapau, MA
Boys' and Girls' Aid Society of San Diego—Cottonwood Center and Community Based Psychiatric Program, El Cajon, CA
Bradley Hospital, East Providence, RI
Brattleboro Retreat, Brattleboro, VT
Brea Neuropsychiatric Center, Brea, CA
Bridgeway Hospital Youthcare Program, North Little Rock, AR
Brighton School and Diagnostic Center, Phoenix, AZ
Brown County Mental Health Center—Children Services, Green Bay, WI
Butler County Mental Health Center Inc, Hamilton, OH
Capital City Schools, Topeka, KS
Cathedral Home for Children, Laramie, WY
Cedu School, Running Springs, CA
Center for Life Management, Salem, NH
Chancellor Academy, Pompton Plains, NJ
Charter Westbrook Hospital, Richmond, VA
Child and Adolescent Psychiatric Clinic Inc, Buffalo, NY
Child Disability Clinic—Carle Clinic, Urbana, IL
Child Guidance Clinic of Southeastern Connecticut Inc, New London, CT
Child Study and Treatment Center, Tacoma, WA
Children's Center, Hamden, CT
Children's Center for Behavioral Development, East Saint Louis, IL

Children's Home of Kingston, Kingston, NY
Children's Mental Health Center Inc, Columbus, OH
The Children's Mercy Hospital—Section of Psychiatry, Kansas City, MO
The Children's School of the Institute of Living, Hartford, CT
Christian Haven Homes—Central Indiana Campus, Wheatfield, IN
Christie School, Marylhurst, OR
Clear View School, Scarborough, NY
Cleveland Clinic Foundation, Cleveland, OH
Cleveland County Area Mental Health Program—Division of Child and Youth Services, Shelby, NC
The Clinical Center of Southern Illinois University, Carbondale, IL
College Hospital—College Park School, Cerritos, CA
Colorado Springs School District No. 11, Colorado Springs, CO
Colorado West Regional Mental Health Center, Glenwood Springs, CO
Community Counseling Center—Rural Clinics, Ely, NV
Community Mental Health Center South, Lee's Summit, MO
Community Psychiatric Clinic Inc, Wheaton; Bethesda; Gaithersburg, MD
Connecticut Junior Republic—Litchfield District, Litchfield, CT
Covenant Children's Home and Family Services, Princeton, IL
CPC Belmont Hills Hospital, Belmont, CA
Craig House—Technoma, Pittsburgh, PA
Creative Learning Systems Inc, Tucson, AZ
Crockett State School Independent School District, Crockett, TX
De Neuville Heights School for Girls, Memphis, TN
DePaul Hospital and Residential Treatment Center, New Orleans, LA
DeSisto Schools Inc, West Stockbridge, MA
The Devereux Foundation, Devon, PA
The Devereux Foundation—Texas Branch, Victoria, TX
Dominion Hospital—The Dominion School, Falls Church, VA
East Alabama Mental Health Retardation Center, Opelika, AL
Eau Claire Academy, Eau Claire, WI
The Eckerd Wilderness Educational System Camping System, Clearwater, FL
Edgefield Children's Center, Troutdale, OR
Edgemeade of Maryland, Upper Marlboro, MD
Edgemont Hospital, Los Angeles, CA
The Educational Clinic Inc, Columbus, OH
Educational Department of Institute of Pennsylvania Hospital—Mill Creek School, Philadelphia, PA
Elm Acres Youth Home Inc, Pittsburg, KS
Elmcrest Children's Center, Syracuse, NY
Elmcrest Psychiatric Institute, Portland, CT
Emerson North, Cincinati, OH
Epworth Village Inc, York, NE
Escambia District Schools, Pensacola, FL
Ettie Lee Homes Inc, Baldwin Park, CA
Excelsior Youth Center, Aurora, CO

Forest Hospital, Des Plaines, IL

Fort Logan Mental Health Center, Denver, CO

Four Winds Hospital—Adolescent Services, Katonah, NY

Franklin Grand Isle Mental Health Services Inc, Saint Albans, VT

The Frost School, Rockville, MD

Garfield Girls' School, Phoenix, AZ

Gibault School For Boys, Terre Haute, IN

Gladman Memorial Hospital Adolescent Program, Oakland, CA

The Goldstaub Residence, Houston, TX

Grady Memorial Hospital—Division of Child and Adolescent Psychiatry, Atlanta, GA

Hall-Brooke Foundation—Hall-Brooke Hospital—Hall-Brooke School, Westport, CT

Hamilton Children's Center, Hyattsville, MD

The Hannah More Center, Reisterstown, MD

Harbor View Mercy Hospital, Fort Smith, AR

Hartgrove Hospital—Hartgrove Academy, Chicago, IL

Hawaii State Department of Education—Special Needs Branch, Honolulu, HI

Hawaii State Hospital—Adolescent Unit, Kaneohe, HI

Hawthorn Center, Northville, MI

High Plains Mental Health Center—Colby Office, Colby, KS

Hillside Children's Center, Rochester, NY

Homewood School—Highland Hospital, Asheville, NC

Idaho Youth Ranch Inc, Rupert, ID

Indiana Girls' School, Indianapolis, IN

Ingleside Hospital, Rosemead, CA

Institute for Family and Life Learning Residential School, Danvers, MA

The Institute of Living School, Hartford, CT

Institute of Psychiatry and Human Behavior—Department of Psychiatry—Child and Adolescent Inpatient Service, Baltimore, MD

Jackson County Intermediate School District, Jackson, MI

Jasper County Mental Health Center, Newton, IA

Jefferson Parish School System—Department of Special Education, Gretna, LA

Jewish Children's Bureau of Chicago, Chicago, IL

Kalamazoo Child Guidance Clinic, Kalamazoo, MI

K-Bar-B Youth Ranch—Richard M Wise School, Lacombe, LA

Klamath County Mental Health Center—Natural Family Preservation Project, Klamath Falls, OR

Lad Lake Inc, Dousman, WI

Lake County Mental Health Center—Department of Children's Services, Mentor, OH

Lakeshore Mental Health Institute—Riverbend School—Children and Youth Services, Knoxville, TN

Lakin Hospital—Adolescent Services, Lakin, WV

Lane School Programs—Lane Education Service District, Eugene, OR

LaSalle School, Albany, NY

Lookout Mountain School, Golden, CO

The Los Angeles Child Guidance Clinic, Los Angeles, CA

Lovellton Academy, Elgin, IL

Luther Child Center—Children's Hospitalization Alternative Program, Everett, WA

Main Street Human Resources, Great Barington, MA

The Mansion, Naperville, IL

Martin Luther Centers, Madison, WI

Maryhurst School, Louisville, KY

Marymount Hospital Mental Health Center, Garfield Heights, OH

Maryvale, Rosemead, CA

Medical University of South Carolina—Department of Psychiatry—Youth Division, Charleston, SC

Meharry Community Mental Health Center, Nashville, TN

Mendota Mental Health Institute—Child and Adolescent Program, Madison, WI

The Menninger Foundation—The Children's Division, Topeka, KS

Menorah Medical Center—Hearing and Speech Department, Kansas City, MO

Mental Health Care Center of the Lower Keys, Key West, FL

Mental Health Center of Boulder County—Adolescent Treatment Program, Boulder, CO

The Mental Health Institute for Children at Allentown State Hospital, Allentown, PA

MHMR of Southeast Texas—Daybreak Cottage, Orange, TX

Milford Assistance Program Day School, Milford, MA

Monroe County Intermediate School District—Programs for Emotionally Impaired, Monroe, MI

Montrose School, Reisterstown, MD

Mt Airy Psychiatric Center—Children's Treatment Program—Adolescent Treatment Program, Denver, CO

Mountain Board of Cooperative Services—Adolescent Day Treatment Program, Leadville, CO

Napa State Hospital—Children's Program, Imola, CA

New Hope Guild, Brooklyn, NY

New Mexico Boys' School, Springer, NM

Normon Westlund Child Guidance Clinic, Saginaw, MI

North Central Health Care Facilities, Wausau, WI

North Dakota State Mental Hospital—Child and Adolescent Unit, Jamestown, ND

Northeast Colorado Board of Cooperative Educational Services, Haxton, CO

Norton Psychiatric Clinic—Norton Adolescent Treatment Program and Norton Academy, Louisville, KY

Oconee Area Psycho Educational Program, Milledgeville, GA

Orlando Regional Medical Center—Mental Health Department—Children's Services, Orlando, FL

Overlook Mental Health Center—Blount County Adolescent Partial Hospitalization Program, Maryville, TN

Parkwood Hospital, Atlanta, GA

Parmadale—The Youth Services Village, Parma, OH

Pawnee Mental Health Services, Concordia, KS

Penn Foundation for Mental Health, Sellersville, PA

Porter Starke Services Inc—Vale Park Psychiatric Hospital, Valparaiso, IN

Prehab of Arizona Inc—Dorothy Mitchell Residence—Homestead Residence—Helaman House, Mesa, AZ

Prescott Child Development Center, Prescott, AZ

Pressley Ridge School—Day School, Pittsburgh, PA

Pressley Ridge School—Laurel Park, Clarksburg, WV

Pressley Ridge School—Pryde—Family Based Treatment, Pittsburgh, PA

Pressley Ridge School—Wilderness School, Ohiopyle, PA

Project Second Start's Alternative High School Program, Concord, NH

Psychiatric Clinic of the Charlotte Hungerford Hospital, Torrington, CT

Psychiatric Institute of Richmond—Educational Development Center, Richmond, VA

Psychiatric Services Inc, Haverhill, MA

Range Mental Health Center, Virginia, MN

Raritan Bay Mental Health Center, Perth Amboy, NJ

The Re-Ed West Center for Children Inc, Sacramento, CA

Red Rock Comprehensive Mental Health Center, Oklahoma City, OK

Rensselaer County Mental Health Department—Unified Services for Children and Adolescents, Troy, NY

Ridgeview Institute, Smyrna, GA

River Street School, Hyde Park, MA

Rockland Psychological and Educational Center, Spring Valley, NY

St Elizabeth's Hospital—Division of Child and Adolescent Services, Washington, DC

St Gabriel's Hall, Phoenixville, PA

St Joseph Center for Mental Health, Omaha, NE

St Louis County Child Mental Health Services, Saint Louis, MO

Samarkand Manor, Eagle Springs, NC

San Diego County Mental Health Services—Loma Portal Facility, San Diego, CA

San Marcos Treatment Center of The Brown Schools, San Marcos, TX

Secret Harbor School, Anacortes, WA

Shadow Mountain Institute, Tulsa, OK

Shawnee County Youth Center Services, Topeka, KS

Sheldon Community Guidance Clinic Inc, New Britain, CT
Sibley Hospital—Groome Center—Hayes Hall, Washington, DC
South Bend Community School Corporation—Adolescent Day Treatment Center, South Bend, IN
South Dakota Human Services Center, Yankton, SD
South Oaks Hospital, Amityville, NY
South Shore Child Guidance Center, Freeport, NY
Southeast Kansas Mental Health Center, Humboldt, KS
Southwood Psychiatric Residential Treatment Center—Hillcrest, San Diego, CA
Spaulding Youth Center—Emotional Handicap Program, Tilton, NH
Special Education Association of Adams County, Quincy, IL
Special Service School District of Bergen County, Paramus, NJ
Spring Lake Ranch, Cuttingsville, VT
Springfield Park Central Hospital—Park Central School, Springfield, MO
State Training School, Eldora, IA
Stuyvesant Residence Club, New York City, NY
Sunburst Youth Homes, Neillsville, WI
Sunset Learning Center, Fort Lauderdale, FL
Taylor Manor Hospital, Ellicott City, MD
Timberlawn Psychiatric Hospital, Dallas, TX
Training Center for Youth, Columbus, OH
Tri-County Community Mental Health Center, Kansas City, MO
University Hospitals of Cleveland—Hanna Pavilion Child Psychiatric Unit, Cleveland, OH
University of Arkansas Medical Sciences Division Child Psychiatry—Child Study Center, Little Rock, AR
The University of Chicago—Departments of Psychiatry and Pediatrics—Child Psychiatry, Chicago, IL
University of Minnesota Hospitals—Child and Adolescent Psychiatry, Minneapolis, MN
University of Rochester Medical School—Child and Adolescent Psychiatry Clinic, Rochester, NY
University of South Florida—Florida Mental Health Institute—Department of Child and Family Services, Tampa, FL
University of Texas Medical Branch—Inpatient Service—Division of Child and Adolescent Psychiatry, Galveston, TX
University Park Psychological Center, Denver, CO
Utah Boys' Ranch—Children and Youth Services Inc, Salt Lake City, UT
Valleyhead Inc, Lenox, MA
Virginia Center for Psychiatry, Portsmouth, VA
Virginia Center for Psychiatry, Norfolk, VA
Vista Maria, Dearborn Heights, MI
Vitam Center Inc—Vitam School, Norwalk, CT
Walter Reed Army Medical Center Child and Adolescent Psychiatry Service, Washington, DC
West Central Community Services Center Inc, Willmar, MN
West Hartford Public Schools Off-Campus Program, West Hartford, CT
Westbridge, Phoenix, AZ
Western District Guidance Center, Parkersburg, WV
West-Ros-Park Mental Health Center, Roslindale, MA
Wheeler Clinic Inc—Northwest Village School, Plainville, CT
Winnebago Mental Health Institute—Children's Unit, Winnebago, WI
Woodward Mental Health Center, Freeport, NY
Wyandotte Mental Health Center, Kansas City, KS
Wyoming State Hospital, Evanston, WY
Wyoming Youth Treatment Center, Casper, WY
Yellowstone Boys' and Girls' Ranch, Billings, MT
York Woods Center, Ypsilanti, MI
Youth and Family Services, Omaha, NE
Youth Center of Beloit—North Beloit High, Beloit, KS
Yuma Union High School District, Yuma, AZ

Anorexia Nervosa

Adams County Adolescent Day Treatment Program, Denver, CO
Albuquerque Child Guidance Center, Albuquerque, NM
All Children's Hospital, St Petersburg, FL
Almansor Education Center, Alhambra, CA
Anne Arundel County Health Department Mental Health Clinic, Annapolis, MD
Arizona Children's Home, Tucson, AZ
Arizona State Hospital, Phoenix, AZ
Arizona State Hospital—Nueva Vista School, Phoenix, AZ
Arlington School, Belmont, MA
Arnell Engstrom Children's Center, Traverse City, MI
Atlantic Mental Health Center Inc, McKee City, NJ
Augusta School Department, Augusta, ME
Aurora Adolescent Day Resource Center, Aurora, CO
Austin State Hospital, Austin, TX
Battle Creek Child Guidance Center, Battle Creek, MI
Beacon Day Treatment Program, Romulus, MI
Bergen Pines Hospital—Children's Psychiatric Unit, Paramus, NJ
Berks County Intermediate Unit, Reading, PA
Bradley Hospital, East Providence, RI
Brattleboro Retreat, Brattleboro, VT
Brea Neuropsychiatric Center, Brea, CA
Bridgeway Hospital Youthcare Program, North Little Rock, AR
Brighton School and Diagnostic Center, Phoenix, AZ
Brooklyn Community Counseling Center, Brooklyn, NY
Brown County Mental Health Center—Children Services, Green Bay, WI
The Brown Schools, Austin, TX
Butler County Mental Health Center Inc, Hamilton, OH
California Mental Health Center, Los Angeles, CA
Cantwell Academy Inc, Miami, FL
Capital City Schools, Topeka, KS
Cass County Social Services—Children's Social Service Center, Fargo, ND
Cathedral Home for Children, Laramie, WY
Center for Life Management, Salem, NH
Chancellor Academy, Pompton Plains, NJ
The Charlton School, Burnt Hills, NY
Charter Westbrook Hospital, Richmond, VA
Chestnut Lodge Hospital—Adolescent and Child Division, Rockville, MD
Child and Adolescent Psychiatric Clinic Inc, Buffalo, NY
Child Disability Clinic—Carle Clinic, Urbana, IL
Child Guidance Center of Southern Connecticut, Stanford, CT
Child Guidance Clinic of Southeastern Connecticut Inc, New London, CT
Child Psychiatry Service—Department of Psychiatry—University Hospitals, Ann Arbor, MI
Child Study and Treatment Center, Tacoma, WA
Child Study Center, Fort Worth, TX
Children's and Adolescent Unit of Mental Health Institute of Cherokee Iowa, Cherokee, IA
Children's Bureau of Indianapolis Inc, Indianapolis, IN
Children's Health Council, Palo Alto, CA
The Children's Home of Cincinnati, Cincinnati, OH
Children's Home Society of South Dakota, Sioux Falls, SD
Children's Hospital at Washington University Medical Center—Psychiatric Unit, Saint Louis, MO
Children's Medical Center, Tulsa, OK
Children's Medical Center—Psychiatric Inpatient Unit, Dallas, TX
Children's Mental Health Center Inc, Columbus, OH
The Children's Mercy Hospital—Section of Psychiatry, Kansas City, MO
The Children's School of the Institute of Living, Hartford, CT
The Children's Study Home, Springfield, MA
Cabinet for Human Resources—Children's Treatment Service, Louisville, KY
Cleveland Clinic Foundation, Cleveland, OH
Cleveland County Area Mental Health Program—Division of Child and Youth Services, Shelby, NC

The Clinical Center of Southern Illinois University, Carbondale, IL

College Hospital—College Park School, Cerritos, CA

Colorado Springs School District No. 11, Colorado Springs, CO

Colorado West Regional Mental Health Center, Glenwood Springs, CO

Community Counseling Center—Rural Clinics, Ely, NV

Community Mental Health Center South, Lee's Summit, MO

Comprehensive Mental Health Center of St Clair County Inc, East Saint Louis, IL

Covenant Children's Home and Family Services, Princeton, IL

CPC Belmont Hills Hospital, Belmont, CA

Craig House—Technoma, Pittsburgh, PA

Creative Arts Rehabilitation Center Inc, New York, NY

Dakota House, Aberdeen, SD

De Neuville Heights School for Girls, Memphis, TN

DeJarnette Center, Staunton, VA

Delaware Guidance Services for Children and Youth Inc, Wilmington, DE

DePaul Hospital and Residential Treatment Center, New Orleans, LA

Des Moines Children's Home—Orchard Place, Des Moines, IA

DeSisto Schools Inc, West Stockbridge, MA

The Devereux Foundation, Devon, PA

The Devereux Foundation, Santa Barbara, CA

Devereux in Georgia, Kennesaw, GA

Dominion Hospital—The Dominion School, Falls Church, VA

Donaldsonville Mental Health Center, Donaldsonville, LA

East Alabama Mental Health Retardation Center, Opelika, AL

Eastern Shore Mental Health Center, Nassawadox, VA

Edgemont Hospital, Los Angeles, CA

The Educational Clinic Inc, Columbus, OH

Educational Department of Institute of Pennsylvania Hospital—Mill Creek School, Philadelphia, PA

El Paso Guidance Center, El Paso, TX

Elmcrest Psychiatric Institute, Portland, CT

Emerson North, Cincinati, OH

Escalon Inc, Altadena, CA

Escambia District Schools, Pensacola, FL

Evansville Vanderburgh School Corporation, Evansville, IN

Excelsior Youth Center, Aurora, CO

Family Guidance Center, Reading, PA

Family Guidance Service—Ingham Community Mental Health Center, Lansing, MI

Forest Hospital, Des Plaines, IL

Ft Wayne Children's Home—Crossroad, Fort Wayne, IN

Four Winds Hospital—Adolescent Services, Katonah, NY

Franklin Grand Isle Mental Health Services Inc, Saint Albans, VT

The Frost School, Rockville, MD

Gerard of Minnesota Inc, Austin, MN

Gladman Memorial Hospital Adolescent Program, Oakland, CA

Glens Falls Hospital—Child and Family Services—Community Mental Health Center, Glens Falls, NY

The Goldstaub Residence, Houston, TX

Grady Memorial Hospital—Division of Child and Adolescent Psychiatry, Atlanta, GA

The Gramon School, Livingston, NJ

Grant Center Hospital, Miami, FL

Graydon Manor, Leesburg, VA

Hall-Mercer Children's Center of the McLean Hospital, Belmont, MA

Hall-Brooke Foundation—Hall-Brooke Hospital—Hall-Brooke School, Westport, CT

Hamilton Children's Center, Hyattsville, MD

Harbor View Mercy Hospital, Fort Smith, AR

Harford County Community Mental Health Center, Bel Air, MD

Hartgrove Hospital—Hartgrove Academy, Chicago, IL

Hawaii State Department of Education—Special Needs Branch, Honolulu, HI

Hawthorn Center, Northville, MI

Henderson Mental Health Center, Fort Lauderdale, FL

Henrietta Weill Memorial Child Guidance Clinic, Bakersfield, CA

Henry Horner Children and Adolescent Center, Chicago, IL

High Plains Mental Health Center—Colby Office, Colby, KS

Hillside Children's Center, Rochester, NY

Homewood School—Highland Hospital, Asheville, NC

Humana Hospital Huntington Beach—Children's Behavioral Center, Huntington Beach, CA

Ingleside Hospital, Rosemead, CA

The Institute of Living School, Hartford, CT

ISIS Programs Inc—Individual Support Through Innovative Services for Autistic Persons, Orlando, FL

Jasper County Mental Health Center, Newton, IA

Jeanine Schultz Memorial School, Park Ridge, IL

Jefferson Parish School System—Department of Special Education, Gretna, LA

Jewish Child Care Association—Pleasantville Cottage School, Pleasantville, NY

Jewish Child Care Association—Youth Residence Center, New York, NY

Jewish Children's Bureau of Chicago, Chicago, IL

John C Corrigan Mental Health Center, Fall River, MA

John G McGrath School, Napa, CA

John Umstead Hospital—Children's Psychiatric Institute, Butner, NC

Kalamazoo Child Guidance Clinic, Kalamazoo, MI

Kings County Hospital—Downstate Medical Center—Division of Child and Adolescent Psychiatry, Brooklyn, NY

La Mel, San Francisco, CA

La Puente Valley Community Mental Health Center, La Puente, CA

Lafayette Clinic, Detroit, MI

Lake County Mental Health Center—Department of Children's Services, Mentor, OH

Lakeshore Mental Health Institute—Riverbend School—Children and Youth Services, Knoxville, TN

Lane School Programs—Lane Education Service District, Eugene, OR

Los Ninos Education Center, San Diego, CA

Lovellton Academy, Elgin, IL

Lutheran Medical Center—Psychiatric Division, Saint Louis, MO

Madden Mental Health Center Campus—Institute for Juvenile Research—Inpatient Services, Hines, IL

Madeline Burg Counseling Services—Jewish Board of Family and Children Services, Bronx, NY

Main Street Human Resources, Great Barington, MA

Manitowoc County Counseling Center, Manitowoc, WI

Martin Luther Centers, Madison, WI

Marymount Hospital Mental Health Center, Garfield Heights, OH

Marymount Hospital Mental Health Center, Garfield Heights, OH

Massanutten Mental Health Center, Harrisonburg, VA

Medical University of South Carolina—Department of Psychiatry—Youth Division, Charleston, SC

Mendota Mental Health Institute—Child and Adolescent Program, Madison, WI

The Menninger Foundation—The Children's Division, Topeka, KS

Mental Health Care Center of the Lower Keys, Key West, FL

Mental Health Center of Boulder County—Adolescent Treatment Program, Boulder, CO

Mental Health Center of Mid-Iowa, Marshalltown, IA

Mental Health Services of North Central Hamilton Co Inc, Cincinnati, OH

Mid-Columbia Mental Health Center—Adolescent Psychiatric Department, Richland, WA

Milford Assistance Program Day School, Milford, MA

The Millcreek Psychiatric Center for Children, Cincinnati, OH

Miramonte Mental Health Services Inc, Palo Alto, CA

Mt Airy Psychiatric Center—Children's Treatment Program—Adolescent Treatment Program, Denver, CO

Mystic Valley Mental Health Center, Lexington, MA

Napa State Hospital—Children's Program, Imola, CA

New England Home for Little Wanderers—Orchard Home, Watertown, MA

New Hope Guild, Brooklyn, NY

Normon Westlund Child Guidance Clinic, Saginaw, MI
North Dakota State Mental Hospital—Child and Adolescent Unit, Jamestown, ND
Northeast Colorado Board of Cooperative Educational Services, Haxton, CO
Northwest Florida Mental Health Center, Panama City, FL
Norton Psychiatric Clinic—Norton Adolescent Treatment Program and Norton Academy, Louisville, KY
Oconee Area Psycho Educational Program, Milledgeville, GA
Oconomowoc Developmental Training Center Inc, Oconomowoc, WI
Ohel Children's Home and Family Services, Brooklyn, NY
Orlando Regional Medical Center—Mental Health Department—Children's Services, Orlando, FL
Otis R Bowen Center, Warsaw, IN
Parkview Counseling Center Inc, Youngstown, OH
Parkwood Hospital, Atlanta, GA
Partial Hospitalization Program Children's Service Center, Wilkes Barre, PA
Pawnee Mental Health Services, Concordia, KS
Penn Foundation for Mental Health, Sellersville, PA
Philadelphia Child Guidance Clinic, Philadelphia, PA
Philadelphia Child Guidance Clinic—Child and Family Inpatient Service, Philadelphia, PA
Prescott Child Development Center, Prescott, AZ
Primary Children's Medical Center—Department of Child Psychiatry, Salt Lake City, UT
Psychiatric Clinic of the Charlotte Hungerford Hospital, Torrington, CT
Psychiatric Institute of Richmond—Educational Development Center, Richmond, VA
Psychiatric Services Inc, Haverhill, MA
Queens Hospital Center Department of Psychiatry Child and Adolescent Clinic, Jamaica, NY
Range Mental Health Center, Virginia, MN
Raritan Bay Mental Health Center, Perth Amboy, NJ
Red Rock Comprehensive Mental Health Center, Oklahoma City, OK
Region 16 Educational Service Center, Amarillo, TX
The Rehabilitation Institute of Pittsburgh, Pittsburgh, PA
Rensselaer County Mental Health Department—Unified Services for Children and Adolescents, Troy, NY
Ridgeview Institute, Smyrna, GA
Ridgeview Psychiatric Hospital and Center, Oak Ridge, TN
River Street School, Hyde Park, MA
Rockland Children's Psychiatric Center, Orangeburg, NY
Rockland Psychological and Educational Center, Spring Valley, NY
Rusk State Hospital—Child and Adolescent Unit, Rusk, TX
Sagamore Hills Children's Psychiatric Hospital, Northfield, OH
St Clare's Hospital—Adult, Child and Family Services, Denville, NJ
St Joseph Center for Mental Health, Omaha, NE
St Joseph's Children's Home, Torrington, WY
St Louis County Child Mental Health Services, Saint Louis, MO
St Vincent's Hospital and Medical Center of New York—Child and Adolescent Psychiatry Service, New York, NY
San Marcos Treatment Center of The Brown Schools, San Marcos, TX
Secret Harbor School, Anacortes, WA
Serendipity Diagnostic and Treatment Center, Citrus Heights, CA
Shadow Mountain Institute, Tulsa, OK
Sheldon Community Guidance Clinic Inc, New Britain, CT
Sibley Hospital—Groome Center—Hayes Hall, Washington, DC
Sonia Shankman Orthogenic School of the University of Chicago, Chicago, IL
South Carolina State Hospital—Child and Adolescent Unit—Blanding House, Columbia, SC
South Dakota Human Services Center, Yankton, SD
South Oaks Hospital, Amityville, NY
South Shore Child Guidance Center, Freeport, NY
Southeast Kansas Mental Health Center, Humboldt, KS
Southeast Mental Health Center—Child Development Institute, Memphis, TN

Special Care Program, Orofino, ID
Special Education Association of Adams County, Quincy, IL
Special Service School District of Bergen County, Paramus, NJ
Spring Lake Ranch, Cuttingsville, VT
Strafford Guidance Center Inc, Dover, NH
Summit Children's Residence Center, Upper Nyack, NY
Sunburst Youth Homes, Neillsville, WI
Taylor Manor Hospital, Ellicott City, MD
Terry Children's Psychiatric Center, New Castle, DE
Timberlawn Psychiatric Hospital, Dallas, TX
Tri City Community Mental Health and Retardation Center, Malden, MA
Tri-County Community Mental Health Center, Kansas City, MO
University Hospitals of Cleveland—Hanna Pavilion Child Psychiatric Unit, Cleveland, OH
University of Arkansas Medical Sciences Division Child Psychiatry—Child Study Center, Little Rock, AR
The University of Chicago—Departments of Psychiatry and Pediatrics—Child Psychiatry, Chicago, IL
University of Illinois Medical Center—Child Psychiatry Clinic, Chicago, IL
University of Minnesota Hospitals—Child and Adolescent Psychiatry, Minneapolis, MN
University of New Mexico Children's Psychiatric Hospital—Mimbres School, Albuquerque, NM
University of New Mexico—Children's Psychiatric Hospital, Albuquerque, NM
University of Rochester Medical School—Child and Adolescent Psychiatry Clinic, Rochester, NY
University of Texas Medical Branch—Inpatient Service—Division of Child and Adolescent Psychiatry, Galveston, TX
University Park Psychological Center, Denver, CO
Valleyhead Inc, Lenox, MA
Vanderbilt Medical Center—Division of Child and Adolescent Psychiatry, Nashville, TN
Virginia Center for Psychiatry, Portsmouth, VA
Virginia Center for Psychiatry, Norfolk, VA
Vista Del Mar Child Care Service, Los Angeles, CA
Vista Maria, Dearborn Heights, MI
Vitam Center Inc—Vitam School, Norwalk, CT
Walter Reed Army Medical Center Child and Adolescent Psychiatry Service, Washington, DC
Warm Springs Center, Boise, ID
West Central Community Services Center Inc, Willmar, MN
West Hartford Public Schools Off-Campus Program, West Hartford, CT
West Nassau Mental Health Center, Franklin Square, NY
West River Children's Center of the Children's Home Society of South Dakota, Rapid City, SD
Westbridge, Phoenix, AZ
Westchester Day Treatment Program, Hawthorne, NY
Western District Guidance Center, Parkersburg, WV
Western New York Children's Psychiatric Center, West Seneca, NY
West-Ros-Park Mental Health Center, Roslindale, MA
Wheeler Clinic Inc—Northwest Village School, Plainville, CT
Wichita Guidance Center, Wichita, KS
Wilder Children's Placement, Saint Paul, MN
Willowglen Academy Inc, Milwaukee, WI
Winnebago Mental Health Institute—Children's Unit, Winnebago, WI
Woodward Mental Health Center, Freeport, NY
Wyandotte Mental Health Center, Kansas City, KS
Wyandotte Special Education Cooperative, Kansas City, KS
Wyoming State Hospital, Evanston, WY
Yellowstone Boys' and Girls' Ranch, Billings, MT
York Woods Center, Ypsilanti, MI

Aphasia

Albuquerque Special Preschool, Albuquerque, NM
All Children's Hospital, St Petersburg, FL
Almansor Education Center, Alhambra, CA
Area Education Agency—Education Center, Waterloo, IA

Little Friends Inc—Little Friends School, Naperville, IL
Los Angeles County Office of Education—Mark Twain School, Lawndale, CA
Los Ninos Education Center, San Diego, CA
Lovellton Academy, Elgin, IL
Manitowoc County Counseling Center, Manitowoc, WI
The Mary and Alexander Laughlin Children's Center, Sewickley, PA
Marymount Hospital Mental Health Center, Garfield Heights, OH
Massanutten Mental Health Center, Harrisonburg, VA
Medical Care Rehabilitation Hospital's Child Evaluation and Treatment Program, Grand Forks, ND
Medical University of South Carolina—Department of Psychiatry—Youth Division, Charleston, SC
Mendota Mental Health Institute—Child and Adolescent Program, Madison, WI
Menorah Medical Center—Hearing and Speech Department, Kansas City, MO
Mental Health Center of Boulder County—Adolescent Treatment Program, Boulder, CO
Michael Reese Hospital and Medical Center—Dysfunctioning Child Center, Chicago, IL
Mt Airy Psychiatric Center—Children's Treatment Program—Adolescent Treatment Program, Denver, CO
Multidisciplinary Institute for Neuropsychological Development Inc—MIND, Cambridge, MA
Mystic Valley Mental Health Center, Lexington, MA
Napa State Hospital—Children's Program, Imola, CA
New Hope of Indiana Inc, Indianapolis, IN
Normon Westlund Child Guidance Clinic, Saginaw, MI
North Central Health Care Facilities, Wausau, WI
North Dakota State Mental Hospital—Child and Adolescent Unit, Jamestown, ND
Northeast Colorado Board of Cooperative Educational Services, Haxton, CO
Northwest Psychoeducational Program, Rome, GA
Oconomowoc Developmental Training Center Inc, Oconomowoc, WI
Ohel Children's Home and Family Services, Brooklyn, NY
Otis R Bowen Center, Warsaw, IN
Parkview Counseling Center Inc, Youngstown, OH
Parry Center for Children, Portland, OR
Parsons Child and Family Center—Neil Hellman School, Albany, NY
Peninsula Children's Center—Children and Youth Services, Palo Alto, CA
Philadelphia Child Guidance Clinic—Child and Family Inpatient Service, Philadelphia, PA
Phoenix Union High School District No. 210, Phoenix, AZ
Prescott Child Development Center, Prescott, AZ
Psychiatric Clinic of the Charlotte Hungerford Hospital, Torrington, CT
Psychiatric Services Inc, Haverhill, MA
Quincy School for the Handicapped, Quincy, IL
Range Mental Health Center, Virginia, MN
Region 16 Educational Service Center, Amarillo, TX
Regional Intervention Program, Nashville, TN
Rensselaer County Mental Health Department—Unified Services for Children and Adolescents, Troy, NY
Rise East School, Pomona, NY
Rockland Psychological and Educational Center, Spring Valley, NY
St Joseph Center for Mental Health, Omaha, NE
St Joseph's Carondelet Child Center, Chicago, IL
St Vincent Children's Center, Columbus, OH
St Vincent's Hospital and Medical Center of New York—Child and Adolescent Psychiatry Service, New York, NY
San Diego Unified School District, San Diego, CA
San Joaquin County Office of Education—Special Education Programs, Stockton, CA
San Marcos Treatment Center of The Brown Schools, San Marcos, TX
San Mateo County Office of Education, Redwood City, CA
School for Contemporary Education, Springfield, VA

SEARCH Day Program Inc, Ocean, NJ
South Metropolitan Association—Interventions Residential School, Matteson, IL
South Oaks Hospital, Amityville, NY
Southbury Training School, Southbury, CT
Spaulding Youth Center—Emotional Handicap Program, Tilton, NH
Special Education Association of Adams County, Quincy, IL
Special Service School District of Bergen County, Paramus, NJ
Spectrum Center for Educational and Behavioral Development Inc, Berkeley, CA
The Spofford Home, Kansas City, MO
State University of New York at Albany—SUNY Pre-Kindergarten, Albany, NY
Strafford Guidance Center Inc, Dover, NH
Suffolk Child Development Center, Smithtown, NY
Switzer Center, Torrance, CA
Therapeutic School and Preschool Community Mental Health Services, Belleville, NJ
Timberlawn Psychiatric Hospital, Dallas, TX
The Timothy School, Bryn Mawr, PA
Tomorrow's Children, Waupaca, WI
Tri-County Community Mental Health Center, Kansas City, MO
Trumbull County Board of Education, Warren, OH
University Hospitals of Cleveland—Hanna Pavilion Child Psychiatric Unit, Cleveland, OH
University of Arkansas Medical Sciences Division Child Psychiatry—Child Study Center, Little Rock, AR
The University of Chicago—Departments of Psychiatry and Pediatrics—Child Psychiatry, Chicago, IL
University of Colorado Health Sciences Center—Day Care Center, Denver, CO
University of Minnesota Hospitals—Child and Adolescent Psychiatry, Minneapolis, MN
University of South Florida—Florida Mental Health Institute—Department of Child and Family Services, Tampa, FL
University of Tennessee—Child Development Center School, Memphis, TN
University of Texas Medical Branch—Inpatient Service—Division of Child and Adolescent Psychiatry, Galveston, TX
University Park Psychological Center, Denver, CO
Vanderbilt Medical Center—Division of Child and Adolescent Psychiatry, Nashville, TN
Variety Preschooler's Workshop, Syosset, NY
Walter Reed Army Medical Center Child and Adolescent Psychiatry Service, Washington, DC
Wellerwood Autism Program, Grand Rapids, MI
West Nassau Mental Health Center, Franklin Square, NY
West River Children's Center of the Children's Home Society of South Dakota, Rapid City, SD
Western District Guidance Center, Parkersburg, WV
Wheeler Clinic Inc—Northwest Village School, Plainville, CT
Winnebago Mental Health Institute—Children's Unit, Winnebago, WI
Winston L Prouty Center, Brattleboro, VT
Work Training Program Inc, Woodland Hills, CA
Wyandotte Special Education Cooperative, Kansas City, KS
Wyoming State Hospital, Evanston, WY
Youth Evaluation and Treatment Centers (YETC), Phoenix, AZ
Yuma Union High School District, Yuma, AZ

Asthma

Adams County Adolescent Day Treatment Program, Denver, CO
Albuquerque Special Preschool, Albuquerque, NM
All Children's Hospital, St Petersburg, FL
Almansor Education Center, Alhambra, CA
Andrus Children's Home, Yonkers, NY
Anne Arundel County Health Department Mental Health Clinic, Annapolis, MD
Archdiocese of Louisville—Guidance Clinic, Louisville, KY
Arizona Boys' Ranch, Boys Ranch, AZ
Arizona Children's Home, Tucson, AZ

The Astor Home for Children—Day Treatment Program, Bronx, NY

Aurora Adolescent Day Resource Center, Aurora, CO

Austin State Hospital, Austin, TX

Avon Lenox Special Education, Memphis, TN

Barat Human Services—Barat House, Detroit, MI

Bar-None Residential Treatment Services for Children, Anoka, MN

Battle Creek Child Guidance Center, Battle Creek, MI

Bergen Center for Child Development, Haworth, NJ

Bergen Pines Hospital—Children's Psychiatric Unit, Paramus, NJ

Berks County Intermediate Unit, Reading, PA

Berkshire Farm Center and Services for Youth, Canaan, NY

Board of Cooperative Educational Services II—Special Education Division Instructional Support Center, Centereach, NY

Bradley Hospital, East Providence, RI

Brattleboro Retreat, Brattleboro, VT

Brooklyn Community Counseling Center, Brooklyn, NY

Brown County Mental Health Center—Children Services, Green Bay, WI

The Brown Schools, Austin, TX

California Mental Health Center, Los Angeles, CA

Cantwell Academy Inc, Miami, FL

Center for Life Management, Salem, NH

Chancellor Academy, Pompton Plains, NJ

Child Development Center, New York, NY

Child Disability Clinic—Carle Clinic, Urbana, IL

Child Psychiatry Service—Department of Psychiatry—University Hospitals, Ann Arbor, MI

Child Study and Treatment Center, Tacoma, WA

Child Study Center, Fort Worth, TX

Children's and Adolescent Unit of Mental Health Institute of Cherokee Iowa, Cherokee, IA

Children's Day Hospital—New York Hospital—Cornell Medical Center—Westchester Division, White Plains, NY

Children's Home of Kingston, Kingston, NY

Children's Home Society of South Dakota, Sioux Falls, SD

Children's Hospital at Washington University Medical Center—Psychiatric Unit, Saint Louis, MO

Children's Medical Center, Tulsa, OK

Children's Medical Center—Psychiatric Inpatient Unit, Dallas, TX

The Children's Mercy Hospital—Section of Psychiatry, Kansas City, MO

The Children's School of the Institute of Living, Hartford, CT

The Children's Study Home, Springfield, MA

The Children's Village, Dobbs Ferry, NY

Christian Church—Children's Campus, Danville, KY

Clearwater Ranch Children's House Inc, Philo, CA

Cleveland Clinic Foundation, Cleveland, OH

Community Counseling Center—Rural Clinics, Ely, NV

Connecticut College Program for Children with Special Needs, New London, CT

Cooperative Educational Services Developmental Learning Center, Wilton, CT

Covenant Children's Home and Family Services, Princeton, IL

Craig House—Technoma, Pittsburgh, PA

Creative Arts Rehabilitation Center Inc, New York, NY

Creative Learning Systems Inc, Tucson, AZ

De Neuville Heights School for Girls, Memphis, TN

Delaware Guidance Services for Children and Youth Inc, Wilmington, DE

Desert Hills, Tucson, AZ

DeSisto Schools Inc, West Stockbridge, MA

The Devereux Foundation, Devon, PA

The Devereux Foundation, Santa Barbara, CA

The Devereux Foundation—Texas Branch, Victoria, TX

Devereux in Georgia, Kennesaw, GA

East Alabama Mental Health Retardation Center, Opelika, AL

Eastern Shore Mental Health Center, Nassawadox, VA

Edgemont Hospital, Los Angeles, CA

Elmcrest Psychiatric Institute, Portland, CT

The Episcopal Church Home for Children—York Place, York, SC

Escambia District Schools, Pensacola, FL

Evansville Vanderburgh School Corporation, Evansville, IN

Excelsior Youth Center, Aurora, CO

Family Guidance Center, Reading, PA

Forest Hospital, Des Plaines, IL

Gladman Memorial Hospital Adolescent Program, Oakland, CA

Glenholme School, Washington, CT

Glens Falls Hospital—Child and Family Services—Community Mental Health Center, Glens Falls, NY

The Goldstaub Residence, Houston, TX

Grady Memorial Hospital—Division of Child and Adolescent Psychiatry, Atlanta, GA

Greenshire School, Cheshire, CT

Hall-Mercer Children's Center of the McLean Hospital, Belmont, MA

Hamilton Children's Center, Hyattsville, MD

Harbor View Mercy Hospital, Fort Smith, AR

Hartgrove Hospital—Hartgrove Academy, Chicago, IL

Hawaii State Department of Education—Special Needs Branch, Honolulu, HI

Hawthorn Center, Northville, MI

Hawthorne Cedar Knolls School, Hawthorne, NY

Henderson Mental Health Center, Fort Lauderdale, FL

High Plains Mental Health Center—Colby Office, Colby, KS

Hillside Children's Center, Rochester, NY

Homewood School—Highland Hospital, Asheville, NC

Humana Hospital Huntington Beach—Children's Behavioral Center, Huntington Beach, CA

Indianapolis Public Schools—James E Roberts School No. 97, Indianapolis, IN

Ingleside Hospital, Rosemead, CA

The Institute of Living School, Hartford, CT

Institute of Psychiatry and Human Behavior—Department of Psychiatry—Child and Adolescent Inpatient Service, Baltimore, MD

ISIS Programs Inc—Individual Support Through Innovative Services for Autistic Persons, Orlando, FL

Italian Home for Children, Jamaica Plain, MA

Jasper County Mental Health Center, Newton, IA

Jefferson Parish School System—Department of Special Education, Gretna, LA

Jewish Children's Bureau of Chicago, Chicago, IL

John Umstead Hospital—Children's Psychiatric Institute, Butner, NC

Kalamazoo Child Guidance Clinic, Kalamazoo, MI

K-Bar-B Youth Ranch—Richard M Wise School, Lacombe, LA

Kings County Hospital—Downstate Medical Center—Division of Child and Adolescent Psychiatry, Brooklyn, NY

La Mel, San Francisco, CA

La Puente Valley Community Mental Health Center, La Puente, CA

Lake County Mental Health Center—Department of Children's Services, Mentor, OH

Lake Grove School, Lake Grove, NY

Lakeside Center for Boys, Saint Louis, MO

Lane School Programs—Lane Education Service District, Eugene, OR

LaSalle School, Albany, NY

Lookout Mountain School, Golden, CO

Lovellton Academy, Elgin, IL

Manhattan Children's Psychiatric Center, New York, NY

Martin Luther Centers, Madison, WI

Maryvale, Rosemead, CA

McAuley Nazareth Home for Boys, Leicester, MA

Medical University of South Carolina—Department of Psychiatry—Youth Division, Charleston, SC

Mendota Mental Health Institute—Child and Adolescent Program, Madison, WI

The Menninger Foundation—The Children's Division, Topeka, KS

Mercy Hospital and Medical Center—Community Guidance Center, Chicago, IL

Michael Reese Hospital and Medical Center—Dysfunctioning Child Center, Chicago, IL

Montrose School, Reisterstown, MD

Mt Airy Psychiatric Center—Children's Treatment Program—Adolescent Treatment Program, Denver, CO

Mt Scott Institute, Washington, NJ

Napa State Hospital—Children's Program, Imola, CA

New England Home for Little Wanderers—Orchard Home, Watertown, MA

New England Medical Center—Bay Cove Day Center for Children Day Hospital, Boston, MA

New England Medical Center—Division of Child Psychiatry, Boston, MA

North Dakota State Mental Hospital—Child and Adolescent Unit, Jamestown, ND

Oconomowoc Developmental Training Center Inc, Oconomowoc, WI

Ohel Children's Home and Family Services, Brooklyn, NY

Orlando Regional Medical Center—Mental Health Department—Children's Services, Orlando, FL

Osterlen Services for Youth, Springfield, OH

Paradise Valley School District No. 69—Therapeutic Educational Activities Milieu, Phoenix, AZ

Parkwood Hospital, Atlanta, GA

Partial Hospitalization Program Children's Service Center, Wilkes Barre, PA

Philadelphia Child Guidance Clinic—Child and Family Inpatient Service, Philadelphia, PA

Prescott Child Development Center, Prescott, AZ

Psychiatric Clinic of the Charlotte Hungerford Hospital, Torrington, CT

Psychiatric Services Inc, Haverhill, MA

Ranch Hope Strang School, Alleway, NJ

Range Mental Health Center, Virginia, MN

Region 16 Educational Service Center, Amarillo, TX

The Rehabilitation Institute of Pittsburgh, Pittsburgh, PA

Rensselaer County Mental Health Department—Unified Services for Children and Adolescents, Troy, NY

River Street School, Hyde Park, MA

Rockland Psychological and Educational Center, Spring Valley, NY

St Elizabeth's Hospital—Division of Child and Adolescent Services, Washington, DC

St George Homes Inc, Berkeley, CA

St Joseph Center for Mental Health, Omaha, NE

St Joseph's Carondelet Child Center, Chicago, IL

St Joseph's Children's Home, Torrington, WY

St Mary's Home for Boys, Beaverton, OR

St Vincent's Hospital and Medical Center of New York—Child and Adolescent Psychiatry Service, New York, NY

San Diego Unified School District, San Diego, CA

San Marcos Treatment Center of The Brown Schools, San Marcos, TX

San Mateo County Office of Education, Redwood City, CA

School for Contemporary Education, Springfield, VA

Secret Harbor School, Anacortes, WA

Southbury Training School, Southbury, CT

Southeast Mental Health Center—Child Development Institute, Memphis, TN

Special Care Program, Orofino, ID

Special Education Association of Adams County, Quincy, IL

Special Service School District of Bergen County, Paramus, NJ

Summit Children's Residence Center, Upper Nyack, NY

Taylor Manor Hospital, Ellicott City, MD

Timberlawn Psychiatric Hospital, Dallas, TX

Training Center for Youth, Columbus, OH

Tri-County Community Mental Health Center, Kansas City, MO

Trumbull County Board of Education, Warren, OH

University Hospitals of Cleveland—Hanna Pavilion Child Psychiatric Unit, Cleveland, OH

University of Arkansas Medical Sciences Division Child Psychiatry—Child Study Center, Little Rock, AR

The University of Chicago—Departments of Psychiatry and Pediatrics—Child Psychiatry, Chicago, IL

University of Colorado Health Sciences Center—Day Care Center, Denver, CO

University of Minnesota Hospitals—Child and Adolescent Psychiatry, Minneapolis, MN

University of Rochester Medical School—Child and Adolescent Psychiatry Clinic, Rochester, NY

University of Texas Medical Branch—Division of Pediatric Psychology—Department of Pediatrics, Galveston, TX

University of Texas Medical Branch—Inpatient Service—Division of Child and Adolescent Psychiatry, Galveston, TX

University Park Psychological Center, Denver, CO

Vanderbilt Medical Center—Division of Child and Adolescent Psychiatry, Nashville, TN

Village of St Joseph, Atlanta, GA

Vista Del Mar Child Care Service, Los Angeles, CA

Vitam Center Inc—Vitam School, Norwalk, CT

Walter Reed Army Medical Center Child and Adolescent Psychiatry Service, Washington, DC

Waterford Country School, Quaker Hill, CT

West Hartford Public Schools Off-Campus Program, West Hartford, CT

West Texas Boys' Ranch, San Angelo, TX

Western District Guidance Center, Parkersburg, WV

West-Ros-Park Mental Health Center, Roslindale, MA

Wheeler Clinic Inc—Northwest Village School, Plainville, CT

Wilder Children's Placement, Saint Paul, MN

Wyandotte Special Education Cooperative, Kansas City, KS

York Woods Center, Ypsilanti, MI

Yuma Union High School District, Yuma, AZ

Convulsive Disorders

Adams County Adolescent Day Treatment Program, Denver, CO

Albuquerque Special Preschool, Albuquerque, NM

All Children's Hospital, St Petersburg, FL

Almansor Education Center, Alhambra, CA

Arizona Baptist Children's Services—Little Canyon Campus, Phoenix, AZ

Arizona Boys' Ranch, Boys Ranch, AZ

Arizona Children's Home, Tucson, AZ

Arizona State Hospital, Phoenix, AZ

Arlington School, Belmont, MA

Arnell Engstrom Children's Center, Traverse City, MI

The Astor Home for Children—Day Treatment Program, Bronx, NY

Austin State Hospital, Austin, TX

Avalon School at High Point, Lenox, MA

Avon Lenox Special Education, Memphis, TN

Avondale House, Houston, TX

Baker Hall Inc, Lackawanna, NY

The Bancroft School, Haddonfield, NJ

Bar-None Residential Treatment Services for Children, Anoka, MN

Battle Creek Child Guidance Center, Battle Creek, MI

Benhaven, East Haven, CT

Bergen Center for Child Development, Haworth, NJ

Bergen Pines Hospital—Children's Psychiatric Unit, Paramus, NJ

Berks County Intermediate Unit, Reading, PA

Big Lakes Developmental Center Inc, Manhattan, KS

Big Spring State Hospital, Big Spring, TX

Birmingham City Board of Education, Birmingham, AL

Blick Clinic for Developmental Disabilities, Akron, OH

Board of Cooperative Educational Services II—Special Education Division Instructional Support Center, Centereach, NY

BOCES Nassau, Westbury, NY

Bowman Gray School of Medicine Developmental Evaluation Clinic—Amos Cottage Rehabilitation Hospital, Winston-Salem, NC

Boys' Town of Missouri Inc, Saint James, MO

Bradley Hospital, East Providence, RI

Brattleboro Retreat, Brattleboro, VT

Brentwood Center, Los Angeles, CA

Brewer-Porch Children's Center, University, AL

Brighton School and Diagnostic Center, Phoenix, AZ

Brown County Mental Health Center—Children Services, Green Bay, WI

The Brown Schools, Austin, TX

Cantalician Center for Learning, Buffalo, NY
Cantwell Academy Inc, Miami, FL
Cass County Social Services—Children's Social Service Center, Fargo, ND
Central New Hampshire Community Mental Health Services Inc—Early Intervention Services, Concord, NH
Charter Westbrook Hospital, Richmond, VA
Child Adolescent Service Center, Canton, OH
Child Development Center, New York, NY
Child Development Service—Lakeview Center Inc, Pensacola, FL
Child Disability Clinic—Carle Clinic, Urbana, IL
Child Study and Treatment Center, Tacoma, WA
Child Study Center, Fort Worth, TX
Childhaven, Saint Louis, MO
Children's Aid Society, Cleveland, OH
Children's and Adolescent Unit of Mental Health Institute of Cherokee Iowa, Cherokee, IA
Children's Bureau of Indianapolis Inc, Indianapolis, IN
Children's Day Hospital—New York Hospital—Cornell Medical Center—Westchester Division, White Plains, NY
Children's Home of Cedar Rapids—Heartwood Residential Treatment Center, Cedar Rapids, IA
Children's Home of Kingston, Kingston, NY
Children's Home Society of South Dakota, Sioux Falls, SD
Children's Hospital at Washington University Medical Center—Psychiatric Unit, Saint Louis, MO
Children's Medical Center, Tulsa, OK
Children's Medical Center—Psychiatric Inpatient Unit, Dallas, TX
The Children's Mercy Hospital—Section of Psychiatry, Kansas City, MO
The Children's School of the Institute of Living, Hartford, CT
The Children's Study Home, Springfield, MA
The Children's Village, Dobbs Ferry, NY
Christ Church Child Center, Bethesda, MD
Christian Church—Children's Campus, Danville, KY
Cleveland Clinic Foundation, Cleveland, OH
Cleveland County Area Mental Health Program—Division of Child and Youth Services, Shelby, NC
The Clinical Center of Southern Illinois University, Carbondale, IL
Colorado West Regional Mental Health Center, Glenwood Springs, CO
Community Counseling Center—Rural Clinics, Ely, NV
Cooperative Educational Services Developmental Learning Center, Wilton, CT
Covenant Children's Home and Family Services, Princeton, IL
Craig House—Technoma, Pittsburgh, PA
Dakota House, Aberdeen, SD
De Neuville Heights School for Girls, Memphis, TN
The Delacato and Doman Autistic Unit, Morton, PA
Delaware Guidance Services for Children and Youth Inc, Wilmington, DE
Department of Education—Windward Oahu District, Kaneohe, HI
Department of Public Instruction, Dover, DE
DePaul Hospital and Residential Treatment Center, New Orleans, LA
The Devereux Foundation, Devon, PA
The Devereux Foundation, Santa Barbara, CA
Devereux in Georgia, Kennesaw, GA
The Devereux Schools at Rutland, Rutland, MA
Dominion Hospital—The Dominion School, Falls Church, VA
Early Childhood Developmental Center Inc, Hays, KS
East Alabama Mental Health Retardation Center, Opelika, AL
Eau Claire Academy, Eau Claire, WI
Edgewood Day Treatment—The Lucinda Weeks Center, San Francisco, CA
The Educational Clinic Inc, Columbus, OH
Educational Service Unit 3—Department of Special Education—Exceptional Children Resource Center, Omaha, NE
El Paso Guidance Center, El Paso, TX
Eleanor Griffin Children's Development Center, Plainview, TX

Elmcrest Psychiatric Institute, Portland, CT
Elwyn Institutes, Elwyn, PA
Emma Pendleton Bradley Hospital Developmental Disabilities Program, East Providence, RI
Encor—Family and Medical Support Services—Respite Services, Omaha, NE
The Episcopal Church Home for Children—York Place, York, SC
Escalon Inc, Altadena, CA
Escambia District Schools, Pensacola, FL
Evansville Vanderburgh School Corporation, Evansville, IN
Excelsior Youth Center, Aurora, CO
Fairmount Children's Center, Syracuse, NY
Forest Hospital, Des Plaines, IL
The Forum School, Waldwick, NJ
Franklin Grand Isle Mental Health Services Inc, Saint Albans, VT
Garden Sullivan Learning and Development Program, San Francisco, CA
Genesee Intermediate School District Center for Autism, Flint, MI
The George Junior Republic Association Inc, Freeville, NY
Gerard of Minnesota Inc, Austin, MN
Gladman Memorial Hospital Adolescent Program, Oakland, CA
The Goldstaub Residence, Houston, TX
Grafton School—Autism Program, Berryville, VA
The Gramon School, Livingston, NJ
Graydon Manor, Leesburg, VA
Green Chimneys Children's Services Inc, Brewster, NY
Greenshire School, Cheshire, CT
Hall-Mercer Children's Center of the McLean Hospital, Belmont, MA
Hamilton Children's Center, Hyattsville, MD
Harbor View Mercy Hospital, Fort Smith, AR
Hartgrove Hospital—Hartgrove Academy, Chicago, IL
Hawaii State Department of Education—Special Needs Branch, Honolulu, HI
Hawthorn Center, Northville, MI
Hawthorne Children's Psychiatric Hospital, Saint Louis, MO
High Plains Mental Health Center—Colby Office, Colby, KS
Hillside Children's Center, Rochester, NY
Homes Unlimited Inc, Bangor, ME
Honolulu District—Special Education Center of Oahu (SECO), Honolulu, HI
Humana Hospital Huntington Beach—Children's Behavioral Center, Huntington Beach, CA
Independence House of Avalon Inc, Sheffield, MA
Indianapolis Public Schools—Special Education Department, Indianapolis, IN
Indianapolis Public Schools—James E Roberts School No. 97, Indianapolis, IN
Ingleside Hospital, Rosemead, CA
Institute for Developmental Disabilities—Crystal Springs School, Assonet, MA
The Institute of Living School, Hartford, CT
ISIS Programs Inc—Individual Support Through Innovative Services for Autistic Persons, Orlando, FL
Jane Wayland Center, Phoenix, AZ
Jeanine Schultz Memorial School, Park Ridge, IL
Jefferson County Public Schools, Lakewood, CO
Jefferson Parish School System—Department of Special Education, Gretna, LA
Jersey Shore Medical Center—Child Evaluation Center, Neptune, NJ
John C Corrigan Mental Health Center, Fall River, MA
The John F Kennedy Institute, Baltimore, MD
John G McGrath School, Napa, CA
John Umstead Hospital—Children's Psychiatric Institute, Butner, NC
Jowonio School, Syracuse, NY
Kaplan Foundation, Orangevale, CA
K-Bar-B Youth Ranch—Richard M Wise School, Lacombe, LA
Kenai Peninsula Borough School District, Soldotna, AK
Kimwood—Home for Autistic Opportunities Inc, Springfield, OH

Kings County Hospital—Downstate Medical Center—Division of Child and Adolescent Psychiatry, Brooklyn, NY

Klamath County Mental Health Center—Mentally Retarded/Developmentally Disabled Program, Klamath Falls, OR

La Mel, San Francisco, CA

Lafayette Clinic, Detroit, MI

Lake County Mental Health Center—Department of Children's Services, Mentor, OH

Lake Grove School, Lake Grove, NY

Lakeshore Mental Health Institute—Riverbend School—Children and Youth Services, Knoxville, TN

Lakeside Center for Boys, Saint Louis, MO

Lakin Hospital—Adolescent Services, Lakin, WV

Lane School Programs—Lane Education Service District, Eugene, OR

League School of Boston Inc, Newtonville, MA

Little Friends Inc—Little Friends Parent Infant Program, Naperville, IL

Los Lunas Hospital and Training School—Behavioral Services Unit, Los Lunas, NM

Los Ninos Education Center, San Diego, CA

Louisiana State University Medical Center—School of Allied Health Professions—Human Development Center, New Orleans, LA

Lovellton Academy, Elgin, IL

Lutheran Medical Center—Psychiatric Division, Saint Louis, MO

Madden Mental Health Center Campus—Institute for Juvenile Research—Inpatient Services, Hines, IL

Manhattan Children's Psychiatric Center, New York, NY

Marymount Hospital Mental Health Center, Garfield Heights, OH

Medical Care Rehabilitation Hospital's Child Evaluation and Treatment Program, Grand Forks, ND

Medical University of South Carolina—Department of Psychiatry—Youth Division, Charleston, SC

Mendota Mental Health Institute—Child and Adolescent Program, Madison, WI

The Menninger Foundation—The Children's Division, Topeka, KS

Menorah Medical Center—Hearing and Speech Department, Kansas City, MO

Mental Health Care Center of the Lower Keys, Key West, FL

The Mental Health Institute for Children at Allentown State Hospital, Allentown, PA

Mercy Hospital and Medical Center—Community Guidance Center, Chicago, IL

Michael Reese Hospital and Medical Center—Dysfunctioning Child Center, Chicago, IL

The Millcreek Psychiatric Center for Children, Cincinnati, OH

Millcreek Schools Inc, Magee, MS

Minneapolis Children's Medical Center—Program for Autistic and Other Exceptional Children, Minneapolis, MN

Minnesota Learning Center, Brainerd, MN

Mt Airy Psychiatric Center—Children's Treatment Program—Adolescent Treatment Program, Denver, CO

Mt Scott Institute, Washington, NJ

Multidisciplinary Institute for Neuropsychological Development Inc—MIND, Cambridge, MA

Nannahagur School Day Treatment Program—(JCCA), Pleasantville, NY

Napa State Hospital—Children's Program, Imola, CA

New Hope of Indiana Inc, Indianapolis, IN

North Central Health Care Facilities, Wausau, WI

North Dakota State Mental Hospital—Child and Adolescent Unit, Jamestown, ND

North Mississippi Retardation Center, Oxford, MS

Northeast Colorado Board of Cooperative Educational Services, Haxton, CO

Northern Indiana State Hospital and Developmental Disabilities Center, South Bend, IN

Northwood Children's Home, Duluth, MN

Norton Psychiatric Clinic—Norton Adolescent Treatment Program and Norton Academy, Louisville, KY

Oconomowoc Developmental Training Center Inc, Oconomowoc, WI

Orlando Regional Medical Center—Mental Health Department—Children's Services, Orlando, FL

Our Lady of Providence Children's Center, West Springfield, MA

Pace School, Braintree, MA

Parkwood Hospital, Atlanta, GA

Parsons Child and Family Center, Albany, NY

Peanut Butter and Jelly Therapeutic Pre-School, Albuquerque, NM

Philadelphia Child Guidance Clinic—Child and Family Inpatient Service, Philadelphia, PA

Prescott Child Development Center, Prescott, AZ

Pressley Ridge School—Pryde—Family Based Treatment, Pittsburgh, PA

Project for Psychotic and Neurologically Impaired Children, Madison, WI

Project Second Start's Alternative High School Program, Concord, NH

Protestant Youth Center, Baldwinville, MA

Psychiatric Clinic of the Charlotte Hungerford Hospital, Torrington, CT

Psychiatric Services Inc, Haverhill, MA

Public School No. 176, Bronx, NY

Queen of Angels School—Villa Maria Treatment Center, Timonium, MD

Quincy School for the Handicapped, Quincy, IL

Raineswood Residential Center, Memphis, TN

Range Mental Health Center, Virginia, MN

Region VIII Education Service Center, Mount Pleasant, TX

Region 16 Educational Service Center, Amarillo, TX

The Rehabilitation Institute of Pittsburgh, Pittsburgh, PA

Rensselaer County Mental Health Department—Unified Services for Children and Adolescents, Troy, NY

Ridgeview Institute, Smyrna, GA

Rise East School, Pomona, NY

Sagamore Hills Children's Psychiatric Hospital, Northfield, OH

St Clare's Hospital—Adult, Child and Family Services, Denville, NJ

St Cloud Children's Home, Saint Cloud, MN

St John's Child Development Center, Washington, DC

St Joseph Center for Mental Health, Omaha, NE

St Mary's Home for Boys, Beaverton, OR

St Vincent Children's Center, Columbus, OH

St Vincent's Hospital and Medical Center of New York—Child and Adolescent Psychiatry Service, New York, NY

Samuel Gompers Memorial Rehabilitation Center Inc, Phoenix, AZ

San Diego Unified School District, San Diego, CA

San Marcos Treatment Center of The Brown Schools, San Marcos, TX

San Mateo County Office of Education, Redwood City, CA

School for Contemporary Education, Springfield, VA

Seminole County Board of Public Instruction—Programs for Emotionally Handicapped, Sanford, FL

Serendipity Diagnostic and Treatment Center, Citrus Heights, CA

Shawnee Mission Public Schools, Shawnee Mission, KS

South Carolina State Hospital—Child and Adolescent Unit—Blanding House, Columbia, SC

South Dakota Human Services Center, Yankton, SD

South Metropolitan Association—Interventions Residential School, Matteson, IL

South Oaks Hospital, Amityville, NY

Southbury Training School, Southbury, CT

Southeastern Children's Center, Sioux Falls, SD

Southgate Regional Center for Developmental Disabilities, Southgate, MI

Spaulding Youth Center—Autistic Program, Tilton, NH

Spaulding Youth Center—Emotional Handicap Program, Tilton, NH

Special Care Program, Orofino, ID

Special Education Association of Adams County, Quincy, IL

Special Service School District of Bergen County, Paramus, NJ

Depression

Brighton School and Diagnostic Center, Phoenix, AZ

Brooklyn Community Counseling Center, Brooklyn, NY

Brown County Mental Health Center—Children Services, Green Bay, WI

The Brown Schools, Austin, TX

Buckeye Boys' Ranch Inc, Grove City, OH

Bucks County Intermediate Unit—Looking Glass School, Doylestown, PA

Butler County Mental Health Center Inc, Hamilton, OH

California Mental Health Center, Los Angeles, CA

Cantwell Academy Inc, Miami, FL

Capital City Schools, Topeka, KS

Capitol Region Education Council's Day Treatment Service, West Hartford, CT

Cass County Social Services—Children's Social Service Center, Fargo, ND

Cathedral Home for Children, Laramie, WY

Cayuga Home for Children, Auburn, NY

Cedu School, Running Springs, CA

Center for Life Management, Salem, NH

Chaddock, Quincy, IL

Chancellor Academy, Pompton Plains, NJ

The Charlton School, Burnt Hills, NY

Charter Westbrook Hospital, Richmond, VA

Chestnut Lodge Hospital—Adolescent and Child Division, Rockville, MD

Child Adolescent Service Center, Canton, OH

Child and Adolescent Psychiatric Clinic Inc, Buffalo, NY

Child and Adolescent Psychoeducational Center, Dalton, GA

Child and Family Services, Knoxville, TN

Child Development Center, New York, NY

Child Development Service—Lakeview Center Inc, Pensacola, FL

Child Disability Clinic—Carle Clinic, Urbana, IL

Child Guidance Center of Southern Connecticut, Stanford, CT

Child Guidance Clinic—Day Treatment Program, Winston-Salem, NC

Child Guidance Clinic of Southeastern Connecticut Inc, New London, CT

Child Psychiatry Service—Department of Psychiatry—University Hospitals, Ann Arbor, MI

Child Study and Treatment Center, Tacoma, WA

Child Study Center, Fort Worth, TX

Children's Aid Society, Cleveland, OH

Children's and Adolescent Unit of Mental Health Institute of Cherokee Iowa, Cherokee, IA

Children's Behavior Therapy Unit, Salt Lake City, UT

Children's Bureau of Indianapolis Inc, Indianapolis, IN

Children's Center, Hamden, CT

The Children's Center, Salt Lake City, UT

Children's Center for Behavioral Development, East Saint Louis, IL

Children's Day Hospital—New York Hospital—Cornell Medical Center—Westchester Division, White Plains, NY

The Children's Day School, Trenton, NJ

Children's Day Treatment Center, Honolulu, HI

The Children's Guild Inc, Baltimore, MD

Children's Health Council, Palo Alto, CA

Children's Home of Cedar Rapids—Cedarwood Group Home, Cedar Rapids, IA

Children's Home of Cedar Rapids—Heartwood Residential Treatment Center, Cedar Rapids, IA

Children's Home of Cedar Rapids—Maplewood Group Home, Cedar Rapids, IA

The Children's Home of Cincinnati, Cincinnati, OH

Children's Home of Kingston, Kingston, NY

Children's Home Society of South Dakota, Sioux Falls, SD

Children's Hospital at Washington University Medical Center—Psychiatric Unit, Saint Louis, MO

The Children's Institute, South Orange, NJ

Children's Medical Center, Tulsa, OK

Children's Medical Center—Psychiatric Inpatient Unit, Dallas, TX

Children's Mental Health Center Inc, Columbus, OH

The Children's Mercy Hospital—Section of Psychiatry, Kansas City, MO

Children's Psychiatric Center of the Jewish Hospital, Cincinnati, OH

The Children's School of the Institute of Living, Hartford, CT

The Children's Study Home, Springfield, MA

Cabinet for Human Resources—Children's Treatment Service, Louisville, KY

The Children's Village, Dobbs Ferry, NY

Christian Church—Children's Campus, Danville, KY

Christian Haven Homes—Central Indiana Campus, Wheatfield, IN

Christie School, Marylhurst, OR

Clear View School, Scarborough, NY

The Clearing, Marshfield, VT

Clearwater Ranch Children's House Inc, Philo, CA

Cleveland Christian Home for Children Inc, Cleveland, OH

Cleveland Clinic Foundation, Cleveland, OH

Cleveland County Area Mental Health Program—Division of Child and Youth Services, Shelby, NC

The Clinical Center of Southern Illinois University, Carbondale, IL

Cobb County—Cobb Douglas Psychoeducation Children's Program, Marietta, GA

College Hospital—College Park School, Cerritos, CA

Colorado Springs School District No. 11, Colorado Springs, CO

Colorado West Regional Mental Health Center, Glenwood Springs, CO

Community Counseling Center—Rural Clinics, Ely, NV

Community Mental Health Center South, Lee's Summit, MO

Community Psychiatric Clinic Inc, Wheaton; Bethesda; Gaithersburg, MD

The Community School of the Family Service and Child Guidance Center of the Oranges Maplewood and Millburn, Orange, NJ

Comprehensive Mental Health Center of St Clair County Inc, East Saint Louis, IL

Connecticut Junior Republic—Litchfield District, Litchfield, CT

Convalescent Hospital for Children, Rochester, NY

Covenant Children's Home and Family Services, Princeton, IL

CPC Belmont Hills Hospital, Belmont, CA

Craig House—Technoma, Pittsburgh, PA

CRATER of Broward Inc—Retreat Ranch Facility—24 Hour Residential Treatment Center, Fort Lauderdale, FL

Creative Arts Rehabilitation Center Inc, New York, NY

Creative Learning Systems Inc, Tucson, AZ

Crockett State School Independent School District, Crockett, TX

Cumberland County Guidance Center Inc, Millville, NJ

Dakota House, Aberdeen, SD

Daniel Memorial Inc, Jacksonville, FL

Darden Hill Ranch School, Driftwood, TX

De Neuville Heights School for Girls, Memphis, TN

DeJarnette Center, Staunton, VA

Delaware Guidance Services for Children and Youth Inc, Wilmington, DE

DePaul Hospital and Residential Treatment Center, New Orleans, LA

Des Moines Children's Home—Orchard Place, Des Moines, IA

Desert Hills, Tucson, AZ

DeSisto Schools Inc, West Stockbridge, MA

The Devereux Center in Arizona, Scottsdale, AZ

The Devereux Foundation, Devon, PA

The Devereux Foundation, Santa Barbara, CA

The Devereux Foundation—Deerhaven, Chester, NJ

The Devereux Foundation—Texas Branch, Victoria, TX

Devereux in Georgia, Kennesaw, GA

The Devereux Schools at Rutland, Rutland, MA

Dominion Hospital—The Dominion School, Falls Church, VA

Donaldsonville Mental Health Center, Donaldsonville, LA

Douglas A Thom Clinic Inc, Boston, MA

Early Childhood Developmental Center Inc, Hays, KS

East Alabama Mental Health Retardation Center, Opelika, AL

East Bay Activity Center, Oakland, CA

East St Louis Area Joint Agreement—Department of Special Education, East Saint Louis, IL

Eastern Shore Mental Health Center, Nassawadox, VA

Eau Claire Academy, Eau Claire, WI

The Eckerd Wilderness Educational System Camping System, Clearwater, FL

Edgefield Children's Center, Troutdale, OR

Edgemeade of Maryland, Upper Marlboro, MD

Edgemont Hospital, Los Angeles, CA

Edgewood Children's Center, Saint Louis, MO

Edgewood Children's Center, San Francisco, CA

Edgewood Day Treatment—The Lucinda Weeks Center, San Francisco, CA

The Educational Clinic Inc, Columbus, OH

Educational Department of Institute of Pennsylvania Hospital—Mill Creek School, Philadelphia, PA

El Paso Guidance Center, El Paso, TX

Elm Acres Youth Home Inc, Pittsburg, KS

Elmcrest Children's Center, Syracuse, NY

Elmcrest Psychiatric Institute, Portland, CT

Emerson North, Cincinati, OH

Emma Pendleton Bradley Hospital Developmental Disabilities Program, East Providence, RI

The Episcopal Center for Children, Washington, DC

The Episcopal Church Home for Children—York Place, York, SC

Epworth Village Inc, York, NE

Escalon Inc, Altadena, CA

Escambia District Schools, Pensacola, FL

Ettie Lee Homes Inc, Baldwin Park, CA

Evansville Vanderburgh School Corporation, Evansville, IN

Excelsior Youth Center, Aurora, CO

Fairmount Children's Center, Syracuse, NY

Family and Children's Center, LaCrosse, WI

Family Guidance Center, Reading, PA

Family Guidance Service—Ingham Community Mental Health Center, Lansing, MI

Five Acres Boys' and Girls' Aide Society, Altadena, CA

Flint Community Schools, Flint, MI

Forest Heights Lodge, Evergreen, CO

Forest Hospital, Des Plaines, IL

Fort Logan Mental Health Center, Denver, CO

Ft Wayne Children's Home—Crossroad, Fort Wayne, IN

Four Winds Hospital—Adolescent Services, Katonah, NY

Franklin Grand Isle Mental Health Services Inc, Saint Albans, VT

Fred Finch Youth Center, Oakland, CA

The Frost School, Rockville, MD

Garfield Girls' School, Phoenix, AZ

Gateway United Methodist Youth Center and Family Services, Williamsville, NY

Genesee Intermediate School District Center for Autism, Flint, MI

The George Junior Republic Association Inc, Freeville, NY

Gerard of Minnesota Inc, Austin, MN

Gilfillan Center, Bemidji, MN

Gladman Memorial Hospital Adolescent Program, Oakland, CA

Glenholme School, Washington, CT

Glens Falls Hospital—Child and Family Services—Community Mental Health Center, Glens Falls, NY

The Goldstaub Residence, Houston, TX

Gould Farm, Monterey, MA

Grady Memorial Hospital—Division of Child and Adolescent Psychiatry, Atlanta, GA

The Gramon School, Livingston, NJ

Grant Center Hospital, Miami, FL

Graydon Manor, Leesburg, VA

Green Chimneys Children's Services Inc, Brewster, NY

Greenshire School, Cheshire, CT

Grove School, Madison, CT

Hall-Mercer Children's Center of the McLean Hospital, Belmont, MA

Hall-Brooke Foundation—Hall-Brooke Hospital—Hall-Brooke School, Westport, CT

Hamilton Children's Center, Hyattsville, MD

The Hannah More Center, Reisterstown, MD

Harbor Schools Inc, Newburyport, MA

Harbor View Mercy Hospital, Fort Smith, AR

Harford County Community Mental Health Center, Bel Air, MD

Hartgrove Hospital—Hartgrove Academy, Chicago, IL

Hathaway School of Hathaway Home for Children, Pacoima, CA

Hawaii State Department of Education—Special Needs Branch, Honolulu, HI

Hawaii State Hospital—Adolescent Unit, Kaneohe, HI

Hawthorn Center, Northville, MI

Hawthorne Cedar Knolls School, Hawthorne, NY

Hawthorne Children's Psychiatric Hospital, Saint Louis, MO

Henderson Mental Health Center, Fort Lauderdale, FL

Henrietta Weill Memorial Child Guidance Clinic, Bakersfield, CA

Henry Horner Children and Adolescent Center, Chicago, IL

High Plains Mental Health Center—Colby Office, Colby, KS

High Point Adolescent School—Children's Psychiatric Center, Morganville, NJ

Highland Youth Services—The Highland School, Pittsburgh, PA

Hillside Children's Center, Rochester, NY

Hillside Inc, Atlanta, GA

Hillside School Inc, Logan, UT

Homes Unlimited Inc, Bangor, ME

Homewood School—Highland Hospital, Asheville, NC

Humana Hospital Huntington Beach—Children's Behavioral Center, Huntington Beach, CA

Hunterdon Learning Center, Califon, NJ

Idaho Youth Ranch Inc, Rupert, ID

Independence House of Avalon Inc, Sheffield, MA

Indiana Girls' School, Indianapolis, IN

Ingleside Hospital, Rosemead, CA

The Institute Day School, Lowell, MA

Institute for Family and Life Learning Residential School, Danvers, MA

Institute for Learning, Philadelphia, PA

The Institute of Living School, Hartford, CT

Institute of Psychiatry and Human Behavior—Department of Psychiatry—Child and Adolescent Inpatient Service, Baltimore, MD

Italian Home for Children, Jamaica Plain, MA

Ittleson Center for Child Research, New York, NY

Jane Wayland Center, Phoenix, AZ

Jasper County Mental Health Center, Newton, IA

Jeanine Schultz Memorial School, Park Ridge, IL

Jefferson County Public Schools, Lakewood, CO

Jefferson Parish School System—Department of Special Education, Gretna, LA

Jennie Clarkson Child Care Services Inc—St Christopher's, Dobbs Ferry, NY

Jersey Shore Medical Center—Child Evaluation Center, Neptune, NJ

Jewish Board of Family and Children Services—Linden Hill School, Hawthorne, NY

Jewish Child Care Association—Pleasantville Cottage School, Pleasantville, NY

Jewish Child Care Association—Youth Residence Center, New York, NY

Jewish Children's Bureau of Chicago, Chicago, IL

John C Corrigan Mental Health Center, Fall River, MA

John G McGrath School, Napa, CA

John Umstead Hospital—Children's Psychiatric Institute, Butner, NC

Josephine County Mental Health Program—Children's Resource Team, Grants Pass, OR

Kalamazoo Child Guidance Clinic, Kalamazoo, MI

K-Bar-B Youth Ranch—Richard M Wise School, Lacombe, LA

Kenai Peninsula Borough School District, Soldotna, AK

Kings County Hospital—Downstate Medical Center—Division of Child and Adolescent Psychiatry, Brooklyn, NY

La Amistad Foundation, Winter Park, FL

La Mel, San Francisco, CA

La Puente Valley Community Mental Health Center, La Puente, CA

Lad Lake Inc, Dousman, WI

Lafayette Clinic, Detroit, MI

Lake County Mental Health Center—Department of Children's Services, Mentor, OH

Lake Grove School, Lake Grove, NY

Lakeshore Mental Health Institute—Riverbend School—Children and Youth Services, Knoxville, TN

Lakeside Center for Boys, Saint Louis, MO

Lakeside Child and Family Center Inc, Milwaukee, WI

Lakin Hospital—Adolescent Services, Lakin, WV

Lane School Programs—Lane Education Service District, Eugene, OR

Lansing School District, Lansing, MI

LaSalle School, Albany, NY

Lighthouse School, Chelmsford, MA

Little Friends Inc—Little Friends Parent Infant Program, Naperville, IL

Little Friends Inc—Little Friends School, Naperville, IL

Little Friends Inc—The Therapeutic Workshop, Downers Grove, IL

Lookout Mountain School, Golden, CO

The Los Angeles Child Guidance Clinic, Los Angeles, CA

Los Lunas Hospital and Training School—Behavioral Services Unit, Los Lunas, NM

Lovellton Academy, Elgin, IL

Luther Child Center—Children's Hospitalization Alternative Program, Everett, WA

Lutheran Medical Center—Psychiatric Division, Saint Louis, MO

Lutherbrook Children's Center, Addison, IL

Madden Mental Health Center Campus—Institute for Juvenile Research—Inpatient Services, Hines, IL

Madeline Burg Counseling Services—Jewish Board of Family and Children Services, Bronx, NY

Main Street Human Resources, Great Barington, MA

Manhattan Children's Psychiatric Center, New York, NY

Manitowoc County Counseling Center, Manitowoc, WI

The Mansion, Naperville, IL

Martin Luther Centers, Madison, WI

The Mary and Alexander Laughlin Children's Center, Sewickley, PA

Marymount Hospital Mental Health Center, Garfield Heights, OH

Marymount Hospital Mental Health Center, Garfield Heights, OH

Maryvale, Rosemead, CA

Massanutten Mental Health Center, Harrisonburg, VA

McAuley Nazareth Home for Boys, Leicester, MA

McKinley Home for Boys, San Dimas, CA

Mears House, Highland, IN

Medical Care Rehabilitation Hospital's Child Evaluation and Treatment Program, Grand Forks, ND

Medical University of South Carolina—Department of Psychiatry—Youth Division, Charleston, SC

Meharry Community Mental Health Center, Nashville, TN

Mendota Mental Health Institute—Child and Adolescent Program, Madison, WI

The Menninger Foundation—Pre-School Day Treatment Center, Topeka, KS

The Menninger Foundation—The Children's Division, Topeka, KS

Menorah Medical Center—Hearing and Speech Department, Kansas City, MO

Mental Health Care Center of the Lower Keys, Key West, FL

Mental Health Center of Boulder County—Adolescent Treatment Program, Boulder, CO

Mental Health Center of Mid-Iowa, Marshalltown, IA

Mental Health Centers of Central Illinois—Child and Adolescent Day Treatment Program, Springfield, IL

The Mental Health Institute for Children at Allentown State Hospital, Allentown, PA

Mental Health Services of North Central Hamilton Co Inc, Cincinnati, OH

Mercy Hospital and Medical Center—Community Guidance Center, Chicago, IL

Meridell Achievement Center Inc, Austin, TX

MHMR of Southeast Texas—Daybreak Cottage, Orange, TX

Michael Reese Hospital and Medical Center—Dysfunctioning Child Center, Chicago, IL

The Mid Fairfield Child Guidance Center Inc, Norwalk, CT

Mid-Columbia Mental Health Center—Adolescent Psychiatric Department, Richland, WA

Milford Assistance Program Day School, Milford, MA

The Millcreek Psychiatric Center for Children, Cincinnati, OH

Millcreek Schools Inc, Magee, MS

Minnesota Learning Center, Brainerd, MN

Miramonte Mental Health Services Inc, Palo Alto, CA

Monroe County Intermediate School District—Programs for Emotionally Impaired, Monroe, MI

Montrose School, Reisterstown, MD

Mt Airy Psychiatric Center—Children's Treatment Program—Adolescent Treatment Program, Denver, CO

Mt Scott Institute, Washington, NJ

Mountain Board of Cooperative Services—Adolescent Day Treatment Program, Leadville, CO

Multidisciplinary Institute for Neuropsychological Development Inc—MIND, Cambridge, MA

Mystic Valley Mental Health Center, Lexington, MA

Nannahagur School Day Treatment Program—(JCCA), Pleasantville, NY

Napa State Hospital—Children's Program, Imola, CA

National Foundation for the Treatment of the Emotionally Handicapped, Sepulveda, CA

New England Home for Little Wanderers—Orchard Home, Watertown, MA

New England Home for Little Wanderers—Knight Children's Center, Boston, MA

New England Medical Center—Bay Cove Day Center for Children Day Hospital, Boston, MA

New England Medical Center—Division of Child Psychiatry, Boston, MA

New England Salem Children's Trust, Rumney, NH

New Hope Guild, Brooklyn, NY

New Hope of Indiana Inc, Indianapolis, IN

New Mexico Boys' School, Springer, NM

Normon Westlund Child Guidance Clinic, Saginaw, MI

North Central Health Care Facilities, Wausau, WI

North Dakota State Mental Hospital—Child and Adolescent Unit, Jamestown, ND

North Metro Psychoeducational Program, Atlanta, GA

Northeast Colorado Board of Cooperative Educational Services, Haxton, CO

Northwest Florida Mental Health Center, Panama City, FL

Northwest Psychoeducational Program, Rome, GA

Northwood Children's Home, Duluth, MN

Norton Psychiatric Clinic—Norton Adolescent Treatment Program and Norton Academy, Louisville, KY

Ocean Institute—Adolescent Day School—Mental Health Clinic of Ocean County, Toms River, NJ

Oconee Area Psycho Educational Program, Milledgeville, GA

Oconomowoc Developmental Training Center Inc, Oconomowoc, WI

Office of Riverside County Superintendent of Schools, Riverside, CA

Ohel Children's Home and Family Services, Brooklyn, NY

Orange County Public School System—Gateway School, Orlando, FL

Orlando Regional Medical Center—Mental Health Department—Children's Services, Orlando, FL

Osterlen Services for Youth, Springfield, OH

Otis R Bowen Center, Warsaw, IN

Our Lady of Providence Children's Center, West Springfield, MA

Overlook Mental Health Center—Blount County Adolescent Partial Hospitalization Program, Maryville, TN

Pacific Children's Center, Oakland, CA

Paradise Valley School District No. 69—Therapeutic Educational Activities Milieu, Phoenix, AZ

Parkview Counseling Center Inc, Youngstown, OH

Parkwood Hospital, Atlanta, GA

Parmadale—The Youth Services Village, Parma, OH

Parry Center for Children, Portland, OR

Strafford Guidance Center Inc, Dover, NH
Stuyvesant Residence Club, New York City, NY
Summit Children's Residence Center, Upper Nyack, NY
Sunburst Youth Homes, Neillsville, WI
Sunset Learning Center, Fort Lauderdale, FL
Switzer Center, Torrance, CA
The Sycamores, Altadena, CA
Taylor Manor Hospital, Ellicott City, MD
Terry Children's Psychiatric Center, New Castle, DE
Timberlawn Psychiatric Hospital, Dallas, TX
Timberridge Institute for Children and Adolescents Inc, Oklahoma City, OK
Tomorrow's Children, Waupaca, WI
Towering Pines Center, Slidell, LA
Training Center for Youth, Columbus, OH
Tri City Community Mental Health and Retardation Center, Malden, MA
Tri-County Community Mental Health Center, Kansas City, MO
United Methodist Youthville, Newton, KS
University Hospitals of Cleveland—Hanna Pavilion Child Psychiatric Unit, Cleveland, OH
University of Arkansas Medical Sciences Division Child Psychiatry—Child Study Center, Little Rock, AR
The University of Chicago—Departments of Psychiatry and Pediatrics—Child Psychiatry, Chicago, IL
University of Colorado Health Sciences Center—Day Care Center, Denver, CO
University of Illinois Medical Center—Child Psychiatry Clinic, Chicago, IL
University of Minnesota Hospitals—Child and Adolescent Psychiatry, Minneapolis, MN
University of New Mexico Children's Psychiatric Hospital—Mimbres School, Albuquerque, NM
University of New Mexico—Children's Psychiatric Hospital, Albuquerque, NM
University of Rochester Medical School—Child and Adolescent Psychiatry Clinic, Rochester, NY
University of South Florida—Florida Mental Health Institute—Department of Child and Family Services, Tampa, FL
University of Texas Medical Branch—Division of Pediatric Psychology—Department of Pediatrics, Galveston, TX
University of Texas Medical Branch—Inpatient Service—Division of Child and Adolescent Psychiatry, Galveston, TX
University Park Psychological Center, Denver, CO
Utah Boys' Ranch—Children and Youth Services Inc, Salt Lake City, UT
Valleyhead Inc, Lenox, MA
Vanderbilt Medical Center—Division of Child and Adolescent Psychiatry, Nashville, TN
Variety Preschooler's Workshop, Syosset, NY
Ventura County Superintendent of Schools, Ventura, CA
Village of St Joseph, Atlanta, GA
Virginia Center for Psychiatry, Portsmouth, VA
Virginia Center for Psychiatry, Norfolk, VA
Vista Del Mar Child Care Service, Los Angeles, CA
Vista Maria, Dearborn Heights, MI
Vitam Center Inc—Vitam School, Norwalk, CT
Walker Home and School, Needham, MA
Wallace Village for Children, Broomfield, CO
Walter Reed Army Medical Center Child and Adolescent Psychiatry Service, Washington, DC
War Bonnet—Wilderness Pathways, Canaan, NH
Warm Springs Center, Boise, ID
Waterford Country School, Quaker Hill, CT
Waterloo Community Schools, Waterloo, IA
West Central Community Services Center Inc, Willmar, MN
West Hartford Public Schools Off-Campus Program, West Hartford, CT
West Nassau Mental Health Center, Franklin Square, NY
West River Children's Center of the Children's Home Society of South Dakota, Rapid City, SD
West Texas Boys' Ranch, San Angelo, TX
Westbridge, Phoenix, AZ

Westchester Day Treatment Program, Hawthorne, NY
Western District Guidance Center, Parkersburg, WV
Western New York Children's Psychiatric Center, West Seneca, NY
West-Ros-Park Mental Health Center, Roslindale, MA
Wheeler Clinic Inc—Northwest Village School, Plainville, CT
Wichita Guidance Center, Wichita, KS
Wilder Children's Placement, Saint Paul, MN
Willowglen Academy Inc, Milwaukee, WI
Winnebago Mental Health Institute—Children's Unit, Winnebago, WI
Woodbourne Center, Baltimore, MD
Woodward Mental Health Center, Freeport, NY
Work Training Program Inc, Santa Barbara, CA
Wyalusing Academy, Prairie du Chien, WI
Wyandotte Mental Health Center, Kansas City, KS
Wyandotte Special Education Cooperative, Kansas City, KS
Wyoming State Hospital, Evanston, WY
Wyoming Youth Treatment Center, Casper, WY
Yellowstone Boys' and Girls' Ranch, Billings, MT
York Woods Center, Ypsilanti, MI
Youth and Family Services, Omaha, NE
Youth Center of Beloit—North Beloit High, Beloit, KS
Youth Evaluation and Treatment Centers (YETC), Phoenix, AZ
Yuma Union High School District, Yuma, AZ
Zonta Children's Center, San Jose, CA

Disintegrative Psychoses

All Children's Hospital, St Petersburg, FL
Anne Arundel County Health Department Mental Health Clinic, Annapolis, MD
Area Education Agency—Education Center, Waterloo, IA
Arizona State Hospital, Phoenix, AZ
Arizona State Hospital—Nueva Vista School, Phoenix, AZ
Arlington School, Belmont, MA
Arnell Engstrom Children's Center, Traverse City, MI
The Astor Home for Children—Day Treatment Program, Poughkeepsie, NY
The Astor Home for Children—Day Treatment Program, Bronx, NY
Atlantic Mental Health Center Inc, McKee City, NJ
Augusta School Department, Augusta, ME
Austin State Hospital, Austin, TX
Avalon Center—Avalon Schools, Lenox, MA
The Baird Center for Children and Families Inc, Burlington, VT
Baker Hall Inc, Lackawanna, NY
Bar-None Residential Treatment Services for Children, Anoka, MN
Battle Creek Child Guidance Center, Battle Creek, MI
Bergen Center for Child Development, Haworth, NJ
Bergen Pines Hospital—Children's Psychiatric Unit, Paramus, NJ
Big Spring State Hospital, Big Spring, TX
Birmingham City Board of Education, Birmingham, AL
Board of Cooperative Educational Services II—Special Education Division Instructional Support Center, Centereach, NY
BOCES Nassau, Westbury, NY
Bradley Hospital, East Providence, RI
Brattleboro Retreat, Brattleboro, VT
Brea Neuropsychiatric Center, Brea, CA
Brentwood Center, Los Angeles, CA
Bridgeway Hospital Youthcare Program, North Little Rock, AR
Brighton School and Diagnostic Center, Phoenix, AZ
Brown County Mental Health Center—Children Services, Green Bay, WI
The Brown Schools, Austin, TX
Burt Children's Center, San Francisco, CA
Capital City Schools, Topeka, KS
Capitol Region Education Council's Day Treatment Service, West Hartford, CT
Center for Autistic Children, Philadelphia, PA
Charter Westbrook Hospital, Richmond, VA
Child Disability Clinic—Carle Clinic, Urbana, IL
Child Guidance Center of Southern Connecticut, Stamford, CT

Monroe County Intermediate School District—Programs for Emotionally Impaired, Monroe, MI
Mystic Valley Mental Health Center, Lexington, MA
Napa State Hospital—Children's Program, Imola, CA
New Hope Guild, Brooklyn, NY
New Mexico Boys' School, Springer, NM
Normon Westlund Child Guidance Clinic, Saginaw, MI
North Central Health Care Facilities, Wausau, WI
North Dakota State Mental Hospital—Child and Adolescent Unit, Jamestown, ND
Northeast Colorado Board of Cooperative Educational Services, Haxton, CO
Northwest Florida Mental Health Center, Panama City, FL
Norton Psychiatric Clinic—Norton Adolescent Treatment Program and Norton Academy, Louisville, KY
Ocean Institute—Adolescent Day School—Mental Health Clinic of Ocean County, Toms River, NJ
Oconee Area Psycho Educational Program, Milledgeville, GA
Oconomowoc Developmental Training Center Inc, Oconomowoc, WI
Orlando Regional Medical Center—Mental Health Department—Children's Services, Orlando, FL
Otis R Bowen Center, Warsaw, IN
Our Lady of Providence Children's Center, West Springfield, MA
Paradise Valley School District No. 69—Therapeutic Educational Activities Milieu, Phoenix, AZ
Parkwood Hospital, Atlanta, GA
Parsons Child and Family Center, Albany, NY
Peace River Center for Personal Development Inc, Bartow, FL
Philadelphia Child Guidance Clinic—Child and Family Inpatient Service, Philadelphia, PA
Prescott Child Development Center, Prescott, AZ
Primary Children's Medical Center—Department of Child Psychiatry, Salt Lake City, UT
Psychiatric Clinic of the Charlotte Hungerford Hospital, Torrington, CT
Psychiatric Services Inc, Haverhill, MA
Range Mental Health Center, Virginia, MN
Raritan Bay Mental Health Center, Perth Amboy, NJ
Red Rock Comprehensive Mental Health Center, Oklahoma City, OK
Rensselaer County Mental Health Department—Unified Services for Children and Adolescents, Troy, NY
Richmond County Board of Education—Sand Hills Psychoeducational Program, Augusta, GA
Ridgeview Institute, Smyrna, GA
Ridgeview Psychiatric Hospital and Center, Oak Ridge, TN
River Street School, Hyde Park, MA
Rockland Children's Psychiatric Center, Orangeburg, NY
Sagamore Hills Children's Psychiatric Hospital, Northfield, OH
St Clare's Hospital—Adult, Child and Family Services, Denville, NJ
St Elizabeth's Hospital—Division of Child and Adolescent Services, Washington, DC
St George Homes Inc, Berkeley, CA
St Joseph Center for Mental Health, Omaha, NE
St Joseph's Carondelet Child Center, Chicago, IL
St Vincent's Hospital and Medical Center of New York—Child and Adolescent Psychiatry Service, New York, NY
San Diego County Mental Health Services—Loma Portal Facility, San Diego, CA
San Diego Unified School District, San Diego, CA
Shadow Mountain Institute, Tulsa, OK
Shawnee Mission Public Schools, Shawnee Mission, KS
Solomon Mental Health Center, Lowell, MA
South Metropolitan Association—Interventions Residential School, Matteson, IL
Southbury Training School, Southbury, CT
Southeast Kansas Mental Health Center, Humboldt, KS
Special Care Program, Orofino, ID
Special Education Association of Adams County, Quincy, IL
Special Service School District of Bergen County, Paramus, NJ
Spectrum Center for Educational and Behavioral Development Inc, Berkeley, CA

Spring Lake Ranch, Cuttingsville, VT
Strafford Guidance Center Inc, Dover, NH
Summit Children's Residence Center, Upper Nyack, NY
Sunny Hill Children's Center Inc, Greenwich, CT
Taylor Manor Hospital, Ellicott City, MD
Timberlawn Psychiatric Hospital, Dallas, TX
Tomorrow's Children, Waupaca, WI
Tri-County Community Mental Health Center, Kansas City, MO
University Hospitals of Cleveland—Hanna Pavilion Child Psychiatric Unit, Cleveland, OH
University of Arkansas Medical Sciences Division Child Psychiatry—Child Study Center, Little Rock, AR
The University of Chicago—Departments of Psychiatry and Pediatrics—Child Psychiatry, Chicago, IL
University of Minnesota Hospitals—Child and Adolescent Psychiatry, Minneapolis, MN
University of New Mexico—Children's Psychiatric Hospital, Albuquerque, NM
University of Rochester Medical School—Child and Adolescent Psychiatry Clinic, Rochester, NY
University of South Florida—Florida Mental Health Institute—Department of Child and Family Services, Tampa, FL
University of Texas Medical Branch—Inpatient Service—Division of Child and Adolescent Psychiatry, Galveston, TX
Vanderbilt Medical Center—Division of Child and Adolescent Psychiatry, Nashville, TN
Variety Preschooler's Workshop, Syosset, NY
Ventura County Superintendent of Schools, Ventura, CA
Walter Reed Army Medical Center Child and Adolescent Psychiatry Service, Washington, DC
Warm Springs Center, Boise, ID
Waterloo Community Schools, Waterloo, IA
West Hartford Public Schools Off-Campus Program, West Hartford, CT
West Nassau Mental Health Center, Franklin Square, NY
West River Children's Center of the Children's Home Society of South Dakota, Rapid City, SD
Westchester Day Treatment Program, Hawthorne, NY
Western District Guidance Center, Parkersburg, WV
Western New York Children's Psychiatric Center, West Seneca, NY
West-Ros-Park Mental Health Center, Roslindale, MA
Wheeler Clinic Inc—Northwest Village School, Plainville, CT
Wilder Children's Placement, Saint Paul, MN
Willowglen Academy Inc, Milwaukee, WI
Winnebago Mental Health Institute—Children's Unit, Winnebago, WI
Work Training Program Inc, Santa Barbara, CA
Wyandotte Special Education Cooperative, Kansas City, KS
Wyoming State Hospital, Evanston, WY
Youth and Family Services, Omaha, NE

Early Infantile Autism

ALA Costa Center for the Developmentally Disabled—After School, Berkeley, CA
Albuquerque Special Preschool, Albuquerque, NM
All Children's Hospital, St Petersburg, FL
Area Education Agency—Education Center, Waterloo, IA
Arrise Inc—Arrise Group Home for Autistic Children, Forest Park, IL
The Astor Home for Children—Day Treatment Program, Poughkeepsie, NY
Austin State Hospital, Austin, TX
Autistic Treatment Center—Richardson, Richardson, TX
Autistic Treatment Center—San Antonio, San Antonio, TX
Avalon Center—Avalon Schools, Lenox, MA
Avalon School at High Point, Lenox, MA
Avondale House, Houston, TX
Bar-None Residential Treatment Services for Children, Anoka, MN
Battle Creek Child Guidance Center, Battle Creek, MI
Behavior Research Institute, Providence, RI

Independence House of Avalon Inc, Sheffield, MA
Indiana University Developmental Training Center, Bloomington, IN
Indianapolis Public Schools—James E Roberts School No. 97, Indianapolis, IN
Ingham Developmental Center, Mason, MI
The Institute of Living School, Hartford, CT
ISIS Programs Inc—Individual Support Through Innovative Services for Autistic Persons, Orlando, FL
Ittleson Center for Child Research, New York, NY
Jackson Municipal Separate School District, Jackson, MS
Jeanine Schultz Memorial School, Park Ridge, IL
Jefferson County Public Schools, Lakewood, CO
Jefferson Parish School System—Department of Special Education, Gretna, LA
Jersey Shore Medical Center—Child Evaluation Center, Neptune, NJ
The John F Kennedy Institute, Baltimore, MD
Jowonio School, Syracuse, NY
Judevine Center for Autistic Children, Saint Louis, MO
Kalamazoo Child Guidance Clinic, Kalamazoo, MI
Kaplan Foundation, Orangevale, CA
Kenai Peninsula Borough School District, Soldotna, AK
Kimwood—Home for Autistic Opportunities Inc, Springfield, OH
Klamath County Mental Health Center—Mentally Retarded/Developmentally Disabled Program, Klamath Falls, OR
Lafayette Clinic, Detroit, MI
Lake Grove School, Lake Grove, NY
Lakeshore Mental Health Institute—Riverbend School—Children and Youth Services, Knoxville, TN
LaVoy Exceptional Center, Tampa, FL
League School of Boston Inc, Newtonville, MA
Lighthouse School, Chelmsford, MA
Linwood Children's Center, Elliott City, MD
Little Friends Inc—Group Home for Autistic Children, Wheaton, IL
Little Friends Inc—Little Friends Parent Infant Program, Naperville, IL
Little Friends Inc—Little Friends School, Naperville, IL
The Little Village School, Garden City, NY
Los Angeles County Office of Education—Mark Twain School, Lawndale, CA
Los Lunas Hospital and Training School—Behavioral Services Unit, Los Lunas, NM
Los Ninos Education Center, San Diego, CA
Louisiana State University Medical Center—School of Allied Health Professions—Human Development Center, New Orleans, LA
Manitowoc County Counseling Center, Manitowoc, WI
Massanutten Mental Health Center, Harrisonburg, VA
Medical Care Rehabilitation Hospital's Child Evaluation and Treatment Program, Grand Forks, ND
Medical University of South Carolina—Department of Psychiatry—Youth Division, Charleston, SC
Mendota Mental Health Institute—Child and Adolescent Program, Madison, WI
The Menninger Foundation—Pre-School Day Treatment Center, Topeka, KS
Menorah Medical Center—Hearing and Speech Department, Kansas City, MO
Michael Reese Hospital and Medical Center—Dysfunctioning Child Center, Chicago, IL
Millcreek Schools Inc, Magee, MS
Minneapolis Children's Medical Center—Program for Autistic and Other Exceptional Children, Minneapolis, MN
Monroe County Intermediate School District—Programs for Emotionally Impaired, Monroe, MI
Multidisciplinary Institute for Neuropsychological Development Inc—MIND, Cambridge, MA
Mystic Valley Mental Health Center, Lexington, MA
The Nassau Center for the Developmentally Disabled Inc, Woodbury, NY
New England Medical Center—Bay Cove Day Center for Children Day Hospital, Boston, MA

New England Medical Center—Division of Child Psychiatry, Boston, MA
New Hope of Indiana Inc, Indianapolis, IN
North Central Health Care Facilities, Wausau, WI
North Dakota State Mental Hospital—Child and Adolescent Unit, Jamestown, ND
North Metro Psychoeducational Program, Atlanta, GA
North Mississippi Retardation Center, Oxford, MS
Northeast Colorado Board of Cooperative Educational Services, Haxton, CO
Northern Indiana State Hospital and Developmental Disabilities Center, South Bend, IN
Northwest Florida Mental Health Center, Panama City, FL
Northwest Psychoeducational Program, Rome, GA
Northwood Children's Home, Duluth, MN
O D Heck Developmental Center Autism Program, Schenectady, NY
Oconee Area Psycho Educational Program, Milledgeville, GA
Oconomowoc Developmental Training Center Inc, Oconomowoc, WI
Ohel Children's Home and Family Services, Brooklyn, NY
Orlando Regional Medical Center—Mental Health Department—Children's Services, Orlando, FL
Our Lady of Providence Children's Center, West Springfield, MA
Pace School, Braintree, MA
Pacific Children's Center, Oakland, CA
Parkview Counseling Center Inc, Youngstown, OH
Parkwood Hospital, Atlanta, GA
Parry Center for Children, Portland, OR
Parsons Child and Family Center, Albany, NY
Parsons Child and Family Center—Neil Hellman School, Albany, NY
Partial Hospitalization Program Children's Service Center, Wilkes Barre, PA
Peanut Butter and Jelly Therapeutic Pre-School, Albuquerque, NM
Penninsula Children's Center—Children and Youth Services, Palo Alto, CA
Pine Grove School, Elgin, SC
Pomona Mental Health Center—Child Development Center, Pomona, NY
Prescott Child Development Center, Prescott, AZ
Princeton Child Development Institute, Princeton, NJ
Project for Psychotic and Neurologically Impaired Children, Madison, WI
Psychiatric Clinic of the Charlotte Hungerford Hospital, Torrington, CT
Psychiatric Services Inc, Haverhill, MA
Public School No. 176, Bronx, NY
Quad Cities Center for Autistic Children Inc, Davenport, IA
Raineswood Residential Center, Memphis, TN
Range Mental Health Center, Virginia, MN
Red Rock Comprehensive Mental Health Center, Oklahoma City, OK
Region VIII Education Service Center, Mount Pleasant, TX
Region 16 Educational Service Center, Amarillo, TX
Regional Intervention Program, Nashville, TN
Rensselaer County Mental Health Department—Unified Services for Children and Adolescents, Troy, NY
Richmond County Board of Education—Sand Hills Psychoeducational Program, Augusta, GA
The Rimland School for Autistic Children, Chicago, IL
Rise East School, Pomona, NY
Rochester Mental Health Center Inc—Day Treatment Unit Services—Children and Youth Division, Rochester, NY
Rockford School District No. 205, Rockford, IL
Rutland Psychoeducational Services, Athens, GA
St John's Child Development Center, Washington, DC
St Joseph Center for Mental Health, Omaha, NE
St Joseph's Carondelet Child Center, Chicago, IL
Samuel Gompers Memorial Rehabilitation Center Inc, Phoenix, AZ
San Diego County Mental Health Services—Loma Portal Facility, San Diego, CA

San Diego Unified School District, San Diego, CA
San Joaquin County Office of Education—Special Education Programs, Stockton, CA
San Marcos Treatment Center of The Brown Schools, San Marcos, TX
San Mateo County Office of Education, Redwood City, CA
School for Contemporary Education, Springfield, VA
SEARCH Day Program Inc, Ocean, NJ
Seminole County Board of Public Instruction—Programs for Emotionally Handicapped, Sanford, FL
Shawnee Mission Public Schools, Shawnee Mission, KS
Sherwood Center for The Exceptional Child, Kansas City, MO
Sonia Shankman Orthogenic School of the University of Chicago, Chicago, IL
South Carolina State College—Autistic Nursery, Speech, Language, and Hearing Clinic, Orangeburg, SC
Southbury Training School, Southbury, CT
Southeast Kansas Mental Health Center, Humboldt, KS
Southeastern Children's Center, Sioux Falls, SD
Southgate Regional Center for Developmental Disabilities, Southgate, MI
Southwest Georgia Psychoeducational Services—Thomas County Schools, Ochlocknee, GA
Spaulding Youth Center—Autistic Program, Tilton, NH
Special Care Program, Orofino, ID
Special Education Association of Adams County, Quincy, IL
Special Service School District of Bergen County, Paramus, NJ
Spectrum Center for Educational and Behavioral Development Inc, Berkeley, CA
Spence Chapin Services to Families and Children—The Children's House, New York, NY
State University of New York at Albany—SUNY Pre-Kindergarten, Albany, NY
Stevencroft Inc, Saint Paul, MN
Suffolk Child Development Center, Smithtown, NY
Sunny Hill Children's Center Inc, Greenwich, CT
Therapeutic School and Preschool Community Mental Health Services, Belleville, NJ
Threshold Inc, Goldenrod, FL
Timberlawn Psychiatric Hospital, Dallas, TX
Timberridge Institute for Children and Adolescents Inc, Oklahoma City, OK
The Timothy School, Bryn Mawr, PA
Tomorrow's Children, Waupaca, WI
Total Living Continuum, Camarillo, CA
Tri-County Community Mental Health Center, Kansas City, MO
Tupelo Municipal Public Schools, Tupelo, MS
United Affiliated Facilities Program at Winthrop College, Rock Hill, SC
University Hospitals of Cleveland—Hanna Pavilion Child Psychiatric Unit, Cleveland, OH
University of Arkansas Medical Sciences Division Child Psychiatry—Child Study Center, Little Rock, AR
The University of Chicago—Departments of Psychiatry and Pediatrics—Child Psychiatry, Chicago, IL
University of Colorado Health Sciences Center—Day Care Center, Denver, CO
University of Minnesota Hospitals—Child and Adolescent Psychiatry, Minneapolis, MN
University of New Mexico Children's Psychiatric Hospital—Mimbres School, Albuquerque, NM
University of New Mexico—Children's Psychiatric Hospital, Albuquerque, NM
University of North Carolina School of Medicine—Department of Psychiatry—Division TEACCH, Chapel Hill, NC
University of Rochester Medical School—Child and Adolescent Psychiatry Clinic, Rochester, NY
University of South Florida—Florida Mental Health Institute—Department of Child and Family Services, Tampa, FL
University of Texas Medical Branch—Division of Pediatric Psychology—Department of Pediatrics, Galveston, TX
University of Texas Medical Branch—Inpatient Service—Division of Child and Adolescent Psychiatry, Galveston, TX

Vanderbilt Medical Center—Division of Child and Adolescent Psychiatry, Nashville, TN
Variety Preschooler's Workshop, Syosset, NY
Villa Esperanza, Pasadena, CA
Walter Reed Army Medical Center Child and Adolescent Psychiatry Service, Washington, DC
Washington School District, Phoenix, AZ
Waterloo Community Schools, Waterloo, IA
Wellerwood Autism Program, Grand Rapids, MI
West River Children's Center of the Children's Home Society of South Dakota, Rapid City, SD
Western District Guidance Center, Parkersburg, WV
West-Ros-Park Mental Health Center, Roslindale, MA
Wheeler Clinic Inc—Northwest Village School, Plainville, CT
Willowglen Academy Inc, Milwaukee, WI
Winnebago Mental Health Institute—Autistic Unit, Winnebago, WI
Winnebago Mental Health Institute—Children's Unit, Winnebago, WI
Winston L Prouty Center, Brattleboro, VT
Wyandotte Special Education Cooperative, Kansas City, KS
Wyoming State Hospital, Evanston, WY
York Woods Center, Ypsilanti, MI
Zonta Children's Center, San Jose, CA

Hysteria

Alexander Children's Center, Charlotte, NC
All Children's Hospital, St Petersburg, FL
Almansor Education Center, Alhambra, CA
Anne Arundel County Health Department Mental Health Clinic, Annapolis, MD
Archdiocese of Louisville—Guidance Clinic, Louisville, KY
Arizona Baptist Children's Services—Little Canyon Campus, Phoenix, AZ
Arizona Children's Home, Tucson, AZ
Arizona State Hospital, Phoenix, AZ
Arizona State Hospital—Nueva Vista School, Phoenix, AZ
Arlington School, Belmont, MA
Arnell Engstrom Children's Center, Traverse City, MI
The Astor Home for Children—Day Treatment Program, Bronx, NY
Atlantic Mental Health Center Inc, McKee City, NJ
Aurora Adolescent Day Resource Center, Aurora, CO
Austin State Hospital, Austin, TX
Bar-None Residential Treatment Services for Children, Anoka, MN
Battle Creek Child Guidance Center, Battle Creek, MI
Beacon Day Treatment Program, Romulus, MI
Bergen Pines Hospital—Children's Psychiatric Unit, Paramus, NJ
Berks County Intermediate Unit, Reading, PA
Big Spring State Hospital, Big Spring, TX
Birmingham City Board of Education, Birmingham, AL
Blick Clinic for Developmental Disabilities, Akron, OH
Boston Public Schools—The McKinley Schools, Mattapau, MA
Bowman Gray School of Medicine Developmental Evaluation Clinic—Amos Cottage Rehabilitation Hospital, Winston-Salem, NC
Boys' Village Inc—Boys' Village School, Smithville, OH
Bradley Hospital, East Providence, RI
Brattleboro Retreat, Brattleboro, VT
Brea Neuropsychiatric Center, Brea, CA
Brentwood Center, Los Angeles, CA
Brewer-Porch Children's Center, University, AL
Bridgeway Hospital Youthcare Program, North Little Rock, AR
Brighton School and Diagnostic Center, Phoenix, AZ
Brooklyn Community Counseling Center, Brooklyn, NY
Brown County Mental Health Center—Children Services, Green Bay, WI
The Brown Schools, Austin, TX
Buckeye Boys' Ranch Inc, Grove City, OH
Butler County Mental Health Center Inc, Hamilton, OH
California Mental Health Center, Los Angeles, CA
Cantwell Academy Inc, Miami, FL

Cass County Social Services—Children's Social Service Center, Fargo, ND

Chancellor Academy, Pompton Plains, NJ

Charter Westbrook Hospital, Richmond, VA

Chestnut Lodge Hospital—Adolescent and Child Division, Rockville, MD

Child and Adolescent Psychiatric Clinic Inc, Buffalo, NY

Child and Family Services, Knoxville, TN

Child Development Service—Lakeview Center Inc, Pensacola, FL

Child Disability Clinic—Carle Clinic, Urbana, IL

Child Guidance Center of Southern Connecticut, Stanford, CT

Child Guidance Clinic of Southeastern Connecticut Inc, New London, CT

Child Psychiatry Service—Department of Psychiatry—University Hospitals, Ann Arbor, MI

Child Study and Treatment Center, Tacoma, WA

Child Study Center, Fort Worth, TX

Children's and Adolescent Unit of Mental Health Institute of Cherokee Iowa, Cherokee, IA

Children's Day Hospital—New York Hospital—Cornell Medical Center—Westchester Division, White Plains, NY

The Children's Day School, Trenton, NJ

Children's Day Treatment Center, Honolulu, HI

The Children's Guild Inc, Baltimore, MD

Children's Health Council, Palo Alto, CA

Children's Home of Cedar Rapids—Heartwood Residential Treatment Center, Cedar Rapids, IA

Children's Home of Kingston, Kingston, NY

Children's Home Society of South Dakota, Sioux Falls, SD

Children's Hospital at Washington University Medical Center—Psychiatric Unit, Saint Louis, MO

The Children's Institute, South Orange, NJ

Children's Medical Center, Tulsa, OK

Children's Medical Center—Psychiatric Inpatient Unit, Dallas, TX

The Children's Mercy Hospital—Section of Psychiatry, Kansas City, MO

The Children's School of the Institute of Living, Hartford, CT

The Children's Study Home, Springfield, MA

Cabinet for Human Resources—Children's Treatment Service, Louisville, KY

The Clearing, Marshfield, VT

Clearwater Ranch Children's House Inc, Philo, CA

Cleveland Clinic Foundation, Cleveland, OH

Cleveland County Area Mental Health Program—Division of Child and Youth Services, Shelby, NC

The Clinical Center of Southern Illinois University, Carbondale, IL

College Hospital—College Park School, Cerritos, CA

Colorado Springs School District No. 11, Colorado Springs, CO

Colorado West Regional Mental Health Center, Glenwood Springs, CO

Community Counseling Center—Rural Clinics, Ely, NV

Community Psychiatric Clinic Inc, Wheaton; Bethesda; Gaithersburg, MD

The Community School of the Family Service and Child Guidance Center of the Oranges Maplewood and Millburn, Orange, NJ

Comprehensive Mental Health Center of St Clair County Inc, East Saint Louis, IL

Connecticut Junior Republic—Litchfield District, Litchfield, CT

Convalescent Hospital for Children, Rochester, NY

Covenant Children's Home and Family Services, Princeton, IL

CPC Belmont Hills Hospital, Belmont, CA

Craig House—Technoma, Pittsburgh, PA

Creative Arts Rehabilitation Center Inc, New York, NY

Cumberland County Guidance Center Inc, Millville, NJ

Dakota House, Aberdeen, SD

Darden Hill Ranch School, Driftwood, TX

De Neuville Heights School for Girls, Memphis, TN

DeJarnette Center, Staunton, VA

Delaware Guidance Services for Children and Youth Inc, Wilmington, DE

DePaul Hospital and Residential Treatment Center, New Orleans, LA

Des Moines Children's Home—Orchard Place, Des Moines, IA

Desert Hills, Tucson, AZ

DeSisto Schools Inc, West Stockbridge, MA

The Devereux Foundation, Devon, PA

The Devereux Foundation, Santa Barbara, CA

The Devereux Foundation—Deerhaven, Chester, NJ

The Devereux Foundation—Texas Branch, Victoria, TX

Devereux in Georgia, Kennesaw, GA

The Devereux Schools at Rutland, Rutland, MA

Dominion Hospital—The Dominion School, Falls Church, VA

Donaldsonville Mental Health Center, Donaldsonville, LA

Douglas A Thom Clinic Inc, Boston, MA

East Alabama Mental Health Retardation Center, Opelika, AL

Eastern Shore Mental Health Center, Nassawadox, VA

Eau Claire Academy, Eau Claire, WI

Edgemont Hospital, Los Angeles, CA

Edgewood Children's Center, Saint Louis, MO

Edgewood Day Treatment—The Lucinda Weeks Center, San Francisco, CA

The Educational Clinic Inc, Columbus, OH

El Paso Guidance Center, El Paso, TX

Elm Acres Youth Home Inc, Pittsburg, KS

Elmcrest Psychiatric Institute, Portland, CT

Emerson North, Cincinati, OH

Evansville Vanderburgh School Corporation, Evansville, IN

Fairmount Children's Center, Syracuse, NY

Family Guidance Center, Reading, PA

Family Guidance Service—Ingham Community Mental Health Center, Lansing, MI

Five Acres Boys' and Girls' Aide Society, Altadena, CA

Forest Heights Lodge, Evergreen, CO

Forest Hospital, Des Plaines, IL

Fort Logan Mental Health Center, Denver, CO

Ft Wayne Children's Home—Crossroad, Fort Wayne, IN

Franklin Grand Isle Mental Health Services Inc, Saint Albans, VT

The Frost School, Rockville, MD

Gerard of Minnesota Inc, Austin, MN

Gilfillan Center, Bemidji, MN

Gladman Memorial Hospital Adolescent Program, Oakland, CA

Glens Falls Hospital—Child and Family Services—Community Mental Health Center, Glens Falls, NY

The Goldstaub Residence, Houston, TX

Gould Farm, Monterey, MA

Grady Memorial Hospital—Division of Child and Adolescent Psychiatry, Atlanta, GA

Graydon Manor, Leesburg, VA

Green Chimneys Children's Services Inc, Brewster, NY

Hall-Mercer Children's Center of the McLean Hospital, Belmont, MA

Hall-Brooke Foundation—Hall-Brooke Hospital—Hall-Brooke School, Westport, CT

Hamilton Children's Center, Hyattsville, MD

The Hannah More Center, Reisterstown, MD

Harbor Schools Inc, Newburyport, MA

Harbor View Mercy Hospital, Fort Smith, AR

Harford County Community Mental Health Center, Bel Air, MD

Hartgrove Hospital—Hartgrove Academy, Chicago, IL

Hathaway School of Hathaway Home for Children, Pacoima, CA

Hawaii State Department of Education—Special Needs Branch, Honolulu, HI

Hawthorn Center, Northville, MI

Hawthorne Children's Psychiatric Hospital, Saint Louis, MO

Henderson Mental Health Center, Fort Lauderdale, FL

Henrietta Weill Memorial Child Guidance Clinic, Bakersfield, CA

Henry Horner Children and Adolescent Center, Chicago, IL

High Plains Mental Health Center—Colby Office, Colby, KS

Hillside Children's Center, Rochester, NY

Homewood School—Highland Hospital, Asheville, NC

Humana Hospital Huntington Beach—Children's Behavioral Center, Huntington Beach, CA

Indiana Girls' School, Indianapolis, IN

Region 16 Educational Service Center, Amarillo, TX
Rensselaer County Mental Health Department—Unified Services for Children and Adolescents, Troy, NY
Richmond County Board of Education—Sand Hills Psychoeducational Program, Augusta, GA
Ridgeview Institute, Smyrna, GA
Rockland Children's Psychiatric Center, Orangeburg, NY
Rockland Psychological and Educational Center, Spring Valley, NY
Sagamore Hills Children's Psychiatric Hospital, Northfield, OH
St Ann's Home Inc—Day Treatment and Special Education Program, Methuen, MA
St Ann's Home Inc—Residential Treatment and Special Education Program, Methuen, MA
St Cabrini Home Inc, West Park, NY
St Clare's Hospital—Adult, Child and Family Services, Denville, NJ
St Cloud Children's Home, Saint Cloud, MN
St Elizabeth's Hospital—Division of Child and Adolescent Services, Washington, DC
St George Homes Inc, Berkeley, CA
St Joseph Center for Mental Health, Omaha, NE
St Joseph Residential Treatment and Child Care Center, Dayton, OH
St Joseph's Carondelet Child Center, Chicago, IL
St Louis County Child Mental Health Services, Saint Louis, MO
St Vincent Children's Center, Columbus, OH
St Vincent's Hospital and Medical Center of New York—Child and Adolescent Psychiatry Service, New York, NY
San Diego County Mental Health Services—Loma Portal Facility, San Diego, CA
San Diego Unified School District, San Diego, CA
San Marcos Treatment Center of The Brown Schools, San Marcos, TX
San Mateo County Office of Education, Redwood City, CA
Secret Harbor School, Anacortes, WA
Seminole County Board of Public Instruction—Programs for Emotionally Handicapped, Sanford, FL
Serendipity Diagnostic and Treatment Center, Citrus Heights, CA
Shadow Mountain Institute, Tulsa, OK
Shawnee Mission Public Schools, Shawnee Mission, KS
Solomon Mental Health Center, Lowell, MA
Sonia Shankman Orthogenic School of the University of Chicago, Chicago, IL
South Bend Community School Corporation—Adolescent Day Treatment Center, South Bend, IN
South Carolina State Hospital—Child and Adolescent Unit—Blanding House, Columbia, SC
South Metropolitan Association—Interventions Residential School, Matteson, IL
South Oaks Hospital, Amityville, NY
South Shore Child Guidance Center, Freeport, NY
Southeast Kansas Mental Health Center, Humboldt, KS
Southeast Mental Health Center—Child Development Institute, Memphis, TN
Southlake Center for Mental Health, Merriville, IN
Southwest Georgia Psychoeducational Services—Thomas County Schools, Ochlocknee, GA
Southwood Psychiatric Residential Treatment Center—Hillcrest, San Diego, CA
Special Education Association of Adams County, Quincy, IL
Special Service School District of Bergen County, Paramus, NJ
The Spofford Home, Kansas City, MO
Spring Lake Ranch, Cuttingsville, VT
Springfield Park Central Hospital—Park Central School, Springfield, MO
Stetson School Inc, Barre, MA
Strafford Guidance Center Inc, Dover, NH
Summit Children's Residence Center, Upper Nyack, NY
Sunburst Youth Homes, Neillsville, WI
Taylor Manor Hospital, Ellicott City, MD
Terry Children's Psychiatric Center, New Castle, DE
Timberlawn Psychiatric Hospital, Dallas, TX
Tomorrow's Children, Waupaca, WI

Training Center for Youth, Columbus, OH
Tri City Community Mental Health and Retardation Center, Malden, MA
Tri-County Community Mental Health Center, Kansas City, MO
University Hospitals of Cleveland—Hanna Pavilion Child Psychiatric Unit, Cleveland, OH
University of Arkansas Medical Sciences Division Child Psychiatry—Child Study Center, Little Rock, AR
The University of Chicago—Departments of Psychiatry and Pediatrics—Child Psychiatry, Chicago, IL
University of Colorado Health Sciences Center—Day Care Center, Denver, CO
University of Illinois Medical Center—Child Psychiatry Clinic, Chicago, IL
University of Minnesota Hospitals—Child and Adolescent Psychiatry, Minneapolis, MN
University of New Mexico—Children's Psychiatric Hospital, Albuquerque, NM
University of Rochester Medical School—Child and Adolescent Psychiatry Clinic, Rochester, NY
University of Texas Medical Branch—Division of Pediatric Psychology—Department of Pediatrics, Galveston, TX
University of Texas Medical Branch—Inpatient Service—Division of Child and Adolescent Psychiatry, Galveston, TX
University Park Psychological Center, Denver, CO
Vanderbilt Medical Center—Division of Child and Adolescent Psychiatry, Nashville, TN
Variety Preschooler's Workshop, Syosset, NY
Ventura County Superintendent of Schools, Ventura, CA
Virginia Center for Psychiatry, Portsmouth, VA
Virginia Center for Psychiatry, Norfolk, VA
Walker Home and School, Needham, MA
Walter Reed Army Medical Center Child and Adolescent Psychiatry Service, Washington, DC
Warm Springs Center, Boise, ID
Waterford Country School, Quaker Hill, CT
West Central Community Services Center Inc, Willmar, MN
West Hartford Public Schools Off-Campus Program, West Hartford, CT
West Nassau Mental Health Center, Franklin Square, NY
West River Children's Center of the Children's Home Society of South Dakota, Rapid City, SD
Westbridge, Phoenix, AZ
Westchester Day Treatment Program, Hawthorne, NY
Western District Guidance Center, Parkersburg, WV
Western New York Children's Psychiatric Center, West Seneca, NY
West-Ros-Park Mental Health Center, Roslindale, MA
Wheeler Clinic Inc—Northwest Village School, Plainville, CT
Wichita Guidance Center, Wichita, KS
Wilder Children's Placement, Saint Paul, MN
Winnebago Mental Health Institute—Children's Unit, Winnebago, WI
Woodward Mental Health Center, Freeport, NY
Work Training Program Inc, Santa Barbara, CA
Wyalusing Academy, Prairie du Chien, WI
Wyandotte Special Education Cooperative, Kansas City, KS
York Woods Center, Ypsilanti, MI
Youth Evaluation and Treatment Centers (YETC), Phoenix, AZ

Inadequacy/Immaturity

Adams County Adolescent Day Treatment Program, Denver, CO
Ahwahnee Hills School, Ahwahnee, CA
Alabama Youth Services—Chalkville Campus, Birmingham, AL
Alexander Children's Center, Charlotte, NC
All Children's Hospital, St Petersburg, FL
Allendale School, Lake Villa, IL
Almansor Education Center, Alhambra, CA
Andrus Children's Home, Yonkers, NY
Anne Arundel County Health Department Mental Health Clinic, Annapolis, MD
Anneewakee Hospital, Douglasville, GA
Archdiocese of Louisville—Guidance Clinic, Louisville, KY

Area Education Agency—Education Center, Waterloo, IA

Arizona Baptist Children's Services—Little Canyon Campus, Phoenix, AZ

Arizona Boys' Ranch, Boys Ranch, AZ

Arizona Children's Home, Tucson, AZ

Arizona State Hospital, Phoenix, AZ

Arlington School, Belmont, MA

Arnell Engstrom Children's Center, Traverse City, MI

The Astor Home for Children—Day Treatment Program, Bronx, NY

The Astor Home for Children—Residential Treatment Center—Residential Treatment Facility—Learning Center, Rhinebeck, NY

Atlantic Mental Health Center Inc, McKee City, NJ

Aurora Adolescent Day Resource Center, Aurora, CO

Austin State Hospital, Austin, TX

The Baird Center for Children and Families Inc, Burlington, VT

Baker Hall Inc, Lackawanna, NY

The Bancroft School, Haddonfield, NJ

Barat Human Services—Barat House, Detroit, MI

Bar-None Residential Treatment Services for Children, Anoka, MN

The Battin Clinic, Houston, TX

Battle Creek Child Guidance Center, Battle Creek, MI

Beacon Day Treatment Program, Romulus, MI

Bergen Center for Child Development, Haworth, NJ

Bergen Pines Hospital—Children's Psychiatric Unit, Paramus, NJ

Berks County Intermediate Unit, Reading, PA

Berkshire Farm Center and Services for Youth, Canaan, NY

Big Lakes Developmental Center Inc, Manhattan, KS

Big Spring State Hospital, Big Spring, TX

Birmingham City Board of Education, Birmingham, AL

Bittersweet Farms, Whitehouse, OH

Blick Clinic for Developmental Disabilities, Akron, OH

Board of Cooperative Educational Services II—Special Education Division Instructional Support Center, Centereach, NY

BOCES Nassau, Westbury, NY

BOCES Onondaga Madison, East Syracuse, NY

Boston Public Schools—The McKinley Schools, Mattapau, MA

Bowman Gray School of Medicine Developmental Evaluation Clinic—Amos Cottage Rehabilitation Hospital, Winston-Salem, NC

Boys' and Girls' Aid Society of San Diego—Cottonwood Center and Community Based Psychiatric Program, El Cajon, CA

Boys' Town of Missouri Inc, Saint James, MO

Boys' Village Inc—Boys' Village School, Smithville, OH

Bradley Hospital, East Providence, RI

Brant Services Corporation—Brant Ryan House, Inkster, MI

Brattleboro Retreat, Brattleboro, VT

Brea Neuropsychiatric Center, Brea, CA

Brentwood Center, Los Angeles, CA

Brewer-Porch Children's Center, University, AL

Bridgeway Hospital Youthcare Program, North Little Rock, AR

Brooklyn Community Counseling Center, Brooklyn, NY

Broom-Tioga Board of Cooperative Educational Services, Binghamton, NY

Brown County Mental Health Center—Children Services, Green Bay, WI

The Brown Schools, Austin, TX

Buckeye Boys' Ranch Inc, Grove City, OH

Bucks County Intermediate Unit—Looking Glass School, Doylestown, PA

Butler County Mental Health Center Inc, Hamilton, OH

Cantwell Academy Inc, Miami, FL

Capital City Schools, Topeka, KS

Capitol Region Education Council's Day Treatment Service, West Hartford, CT

Cass County Social Services—Children's Social Service Center, Fargo, ND

Cathedral Home for Children, Laramie, WY

Cedu School, Running Springs, CA

Center for Life Management, Salem, NH

Center for Urban Living, Saint Louis, MO

Chaddock, Quincy, IL

Chancellor Academy, Pompton Plains, NJ

The Charlton School, Burnt Hills, NY

Charter Westbrook Hospital, Richmond, VA

Chestnut Lodge Hospital—Adolescent and Child Division, Rockville, MD

Child Adolescent Service Center, Canton, OH

Child and Adolescent Psychiatric Clinic Inc, Buffalo, NY

Child and Adolescent Psychoeducational Center, Dalton, GA

Child and Family Services, Knoxville, TN

Child Development Center, New York, NY

Child Development Service—Lakeview Center Inc, Pensacola, FL

Child Disability Clinic—Carle Clinic, Urbana, IL

Child Guidance Center of Southern Connecticut, Stanford, CT

Child Guidance Clinic of Southeastern Connecticut Inc, New London, CT

Child Psychiatry Service—Department of Psychiatry—University Hospitals, Ann Arbor, MI

Child Study and Treatment Center, Tacoma, WA

Child Study Center, Fort Worth, TX

Children's and Adolescent Unit of Mental Health Institute of Cherokee Iowa, Cherokee, IA

Children's Behavior Therapy Unit, Salt Lake City, UT

Children's Bureau of Indianapolis Inc, Indianapolis, IN

Children's Center, Hamden, CT

Children's Center for Behavioral Development, East Saint Louis, IL

Children's Day Hospital—New York Hospital—Cornell Medical Center—Westchester Division, White Plains, NY

The Children's Day School, Trenton, NJ

Children's Day Treatment Center, Honolulu, HI

The Children's Guild Inc, Baltimore, MD

Children's Health Council, Palo Alto, CA

Children's Home of Cedar Rapids—Cedarwood Group Home, Cedar Rapids, IA

Children's Home of Cedar Rapids—Heartwood Residential Treatment Center, Cedar Rapids, IA

Children's Home of Cedar Rapids—Maplewood Group Home, Cedar Rapids, IA

The Children's Home of Cincinnati, Cincinnati, OH

Children's Home of Kingston, Kingston, NY

Children's Home Society of South Dakota, Sioux Falls, SD

Children's Hospital at Washington University Medical Center—Psychiatric Unit, Saint Louis, MO

Children's Medical Center, Tulsa, OK

Children's Mental Health Center Inc, Columbus, OH

The Children's Mercy Hospital—Section of Psychiatry, Kansas City, MO

Children's Psychiatric Center of the Jewish Hospital, Cincinnati, OH

The Children's School of the Institute of Living, Hartford, CT

The Children's Study Home, Springfield, MA

Christ Church Child Center, Bethesda, MD

Christian Church—Children's Campus, Danville, KY

Christie School, Marylhurst, OR

The Clearing, Marshfield, VT

Clearwater Ranch Children's House Inc, Philo, CA

Cleveland Christian Home for Children Inc, Cleveland, OH

Cleveland Clinic Foundation, Cleveland, OH

Cleveland County Area Mental Health Program—Division of Child and Youth Services, Shelby, NC

The Clinical Center of Southern Illinois University, Carbondale, IL

Colorado Springs School District No. 11, Colorado Springs, CO

Colorado West Regional Mental Health Center, Glenwood Springs, CO

Community Child Guidance Clinic Preschool, Manchester, CT

Community Counseling Center—Rural Clinics, Ely, NV

The Community School of the Family Service and Child Guidance Center of the Oranges Maplewood and Millburn, Orange, NJ

Comprehensive Mental Health Center of St Clair County Inc, East Saint Louis, IL

Concord, Yellow Spring, WV

Convalescent Hospital for Children, Rochester, NY

Cooperative Educational Services Developmental Learning Center, Wilton, CT

Covenant Children's Home and Family Services, Princeton, IL

CPC Belmont Hills Hospital, Belmont, CA

Craig House—Technoma, Pittsburgh, PA

CRATER of Broward Inc—Retreat Ranch Facility—24 Hour Residential Treatment Center, Fort Lauderdale, FL

Creative Arts Rehabilitation Center Inc, New York, NY

Creative Learning Systems Inc, Tucson, AZ

Crockett State School Independent School District, Crockett, TX

Cumberland County Guidance Center Inc, Millville, NJ

Dakota Boys' Ranch, Minot, ND

Darden Hill Ranch School, Driftwood, TX

De Neuville Heights School for Girls, Memphis, TN

The Delacato and Doman Autistic Unit, Morton, PA

Delaware Guidance Services for Children and Youth Inc, Wilmington, DE

Department of Education—Windward Oahu District, Kaneohe, HI

DePaul Hospital and Residential Treatment Center, New Orleans, LA

Desert Hills, Tucson, AZ

DeSisto Schools Inc, West Stockbridge, MA

The Devereux Center in Arizona, Scottsdale, AZ

The Devereux Foundation, Santa Barbara, CA

The Devereux Foundation—Deerhaven, Chester, NJ

The Devereux Foundation—Texas Branch, Victoria, TX

Devereux in Georgia, Kennesaw, GA

Dominion Hospital—The Dominion School, Falls Church, VA

Donaldsonville Mental Health Center, Donaldsonville, LA

Douglas A Thom Clinic Inc, Boston, MA

East Alabama Mental Health Retardation Center, Opelika, AL

East St Louis Area Joint Agreement—Department of Special Education, East Saint Louis, IL

Eastern Shore Mental Health Center, Nassawadox, VA

Eau Claire Academy, Eau Claire, WI

The Eckerd Wilderness Educational System Camping System, Clearwater, FL

Edgefield Children's Center, Troutdale, OR

Edgemont Hospital, Los Angeles, CA

Edgewood Children's Center, Saint Louis, MO

Edgewood Children's Center, San Francisco, CA

Edgewood Day Treatment—The Lucinda Weeks Center, San Francisco, CA

The Educational Clinic Inc, Columbus, OH

Educational Department of Institute of Pennsylvania Hospital—Mill Creek School, Philadelphia, PA

Educational Service Unit 3—Department of Special Education—Exceptional Children Resource Center, Omaha, NE

El Paso Guidance Center, El Paso, TX

Elizabeth Ives School, Hamden, CT

Elmcrest Children's Center, Syracuse, NY

Elmcrest Psychiatric Institute, Portland, CT

Elwyn Institutes, Elwyn, PA

The Episcopal Church Home for Children—York Place, York, SC

Epworth Village Inc, York, NE

Escalon Inc, Altadena, CA

Ettie Lee Homes Inc, Baldwin Park, CA

Evansville Vanderburgh School Corporation, Evansville, IN

Excelsior Youth Center, Aurora, CO

Fairmount Children's Center, Syracuse, NY

Family and Children's Center, LaCrosse, WI

Family Guidance Center, Reading, PA

Family Guidance Service—Ingham Community Mental Health Center, Lansing, MI

Five Acres Boys' and Girls' Aide Society, Altadena, CA

Florence Program for Autistic Children and Adolescents—Lester Elementary School, Florence, SC

Forest Heights Lodge, Evergreen, CO

Forest Hospital, Des Plaines, IL

Ft Wayne Children's Home—Crossroad, Fort Wayne, IN

Franklin Grand Isle Mental Health Services Inc, Saint Albans, VT

Fred Finch Youth Center, Oakland, CA

The Frost School, Rockville, MD

Garden Sullivan Learning and Development Program, San Francisco, CA

Garfield Girls' School, Phoenix, AZ

Gateway United Methodist Youth Center and Family Services, Williamsville, NY

The George Junior Republic Association Inc, Freeville, NY

Gerard of Minnesota Inc, Austin, MN

Gilfillan Center, Bemidji, MN

Gladman Memorial Hospital Adolescent Program, Oakland, CA

Glenholme School, Washington, CT

Glens Falls Hospital—Child and Family Services—Community Mental Health Center, Glens Falls, NY

The Goldstaub Residence, Houston, TX

Gould Farm, Monterey, MA

Grady Memorial Hospital—Division of Child and Adolescent Psychiatry, Atlanta, GA

The Gramon School, Livingston, NJ

Grant Center Hospital, Miami, FL

Graydon Manor, Leesburg, VA

Green Chimneys Children's Services Inc, Brewster, NY

Green Tree School, Philadelphia, PA

Greenshire School, Cheshire, CT

Grove School, Madison, CT

Hall-Mercer Children's Center of the McLean Hospital, Belmont, MA

Hall-Brooke Foundation—Hall-Brooke Hospital—Hall-Brooke School, Westport, CT

Hamilton Children's Center, Hyattsville, MD

The Hannah More Center, Reisterstown, MD

Harbor Schools Inc, Newburyport, MA

Harbor View Mercy Hospital, Fort Smith, AR

Harford County Community Mental Health Center, Bel Air, MD

Harmony Hill School Inc, Chedachet, RI

Hartgrove Hospital—Hartgrove Academy, Chicago, IL

Hathaway School of Hathaway Home for Children, Pacoima, CA

Hawaii State Department of Education—Special Needs Branch, Honolulu, HI

Hawthorn Center, Northville, MI

Hawthorne Cedar Knolls School, Hawthorne, NY

Hawthorne Children's Psychiatric Hospital, Saint Louis, MO

Henderson Mental Health Center, Fort Lauderdale, FL

Henrietta Weill Memorial Child Guidance Clinic, Bakersfield, CA

Henry Horner Children and Adolescent Center, Chicago, IL

High Plains Mental Health Center—Colby Office, Colby, KS

High Point Adolescent School—Children's Psychiatric Center, Morganville, NJ

Highland Heights—St Francis Home for Children Inc, New Haven, CT

Highland Youth Services—The Highland School, Pittsburgh, PA

Hillside Inc, Atlanta, GA

Hillside School Inc, Logan, UT

Homes Unlimited Inc, Bangor, ME

Homewood School—Highland Hospital, Asheville, NC

Humana Hospital Huntington Beach—Children's Behavioral Center, Huntington Beach, CA

Hunterdon Learning Center, Califon, NJ

Idaho Youth Ranch Inc, Rupert, ID

Independence House of Avalon Inc, Sheffield, MA

Indiana Girls' School, Indianapolis, IN

Ingleside Hospital, Rosemead, CA

The Institute Day School, Lowell, MA

Institute for Family and Life Learning Residential School, Danvers, MA

The Institute of Living School, Hartford, CT

ISIS Programs Inc—Individual Support Through Innovative Services for Autistic Persons, Orlando, FL

Italian Home for Children, Jamaica Plain, MA

Jackson County Intermediate School District, Jackson, MI

Jackson Municipal Separate School District, Jackson, MS

Jane Wayland Center, Phoenix, AZ

Jasper County Mental Health Center, Newton, IA

Jeanine Schultz Memorial School, Park Ridge, IL

Orlando Regional Medical Center—Mental Health Department—Children's Services, Orlando, FL

Otis R Bowen Center, Warsaw, IN

Our Lady of Providence Children's Center, West Springfield, MA

Pace School, Pittsburgh, PA

Pacific Children's Center, Oakland, CA

Parkview Counseling Center Inc, Youngstown, OH

Parkwood Hospital, Atlanta, GA

Parsons Child and Family Center—Neil Hellman School, Albany, NY

Partial Hospitalization Program Children's Service Center, Wilkes Barre, PA

Pawnee Mental Health Services, Concordia, KS

Peace River Center for Personal Development Inc, Bartow, FL

Penn Foundation for Mental Health, Sellersville, PA

Penninsula Children's Center—Children and Youth Services, Palo Alto, CA

Philadelphia Child Guidance Clinic, Philadelphia, PA

Philadelphia Child Guidance Clinic—Child and Family Inpatient Service, Philadelphia, PA

Phoenix Union High School District No. 210, Phoenix, AZ

Pikes Peak Board of Cooperative Services, Colorado Springs, CO

Pine Haven Boys' Center, Suncook, NH

Porter Starke Services Inc—Vale Park Psychiatric Hospital, Valparaiso, IN

Prescott Child Development Center, Prescott, AZ

Pressley Ridge School—Day School, Pittsburgh, PA

Pressley Ridge School—Laurel Park, Clarksburg, WV

Pressley Ridge School—Pryde—Family Based Treatment, Pittsburgh, PA

Pressley Ridge School—Wilderness School, Ohiopyle, PA

Primary Children's Medical Center—Department of Child Psychiatry, Salt Lake City, UT

Project for Psychotic and Neurologically Impaired Children, Madison, WI

Protestant Youth Center, Baldwinville, MA

Provo Canyon School, Provo, UT

Psychiatric Clinic of the Charlotte Hungerford Hospital, Torrington, CT

Psychiatric Services Inc, Haverhill, MA

Queen of Angels School—Villa Maria Treatment Center, Timonium, MD

Queens Hospital Center Department of Psychiatry Child and Adolescent Clinic, Jamaica, NY

Ranch Hope Strang School, Alleway, NJ

Range Mental Health Center, Virginia, MN

Raritan Bay Mental Health Center, Perth Amboy, NJ

The Re-Ed West Center for Children Inc, Sacramento, CA

Red Rock Comprehensive Mental Health Center, Oklahoma City, OK

The Rehabilitation Institute of Pittsburgh, Pittsburgh, PA

Rensselaer County Mental Health Department—Unified Services for Children and Adolescents, Troy, NY

Richmond County Board of Education—Sand Hills Psychoeducational Program, Augusta, GA

Ridgeview Institute, Smyrna, GA

Ridgeview Psychiatric Hospital and Center, Oak Ridge, TN

River Street School, Hyde Park, MA

Rochester Mental Health Center Inc—Day Treatment Unit Services—Children and Youth Division, Rochester, NY

Rockford School District No. 205, Rockford, IL

Rockland Children's Psychiatric Center, Orangeburg, NY

Rockland Psychological and Educational Center, Spring Valley, NY

Rutland Psychoeducational Services, Athens, GA

Sacramento Children's Home—Helen E Cowell Children's Center, Sacramento, CA

Sagamore Hills Children's Psychiatric Hospital, Northfield, OH

St Ann's Home Inc—Day Treatment and Special Education Program, Methuen, MA

St Ann's Home Inc—Residential Treatment and Special Education Program, Methuen, MA

St Clare's Hospital—Adult, Child and Family Services, Denville, NJ

St Cloud Children's Home, Saint Cloud, MN

St Elizabeth's Hospital—Division of Child and Adolescent Services, Washington, DC

St Francis Boys' Home—Camelot, Lake Placid, NY

St Gabriel's Hall, Phoenixville, PA

St George Homes Inc, Berkeley, CA

St Joseph Center for Mental Health, Omaha, NE

St Joseph Residential Treatment and Child Care Center, Dayton, OH

St Joseph's Carondelet Child Center, Chicago, IL

St Joseph's Children's Home, Torrington, WY

St Louis County Child Mental Health Services, Saint Louis, MO

St Mary's Home for Boys, Beaverton, OR

St Vincent Children's Center, Columbus, OH

St Vincent's Hospital and Medical Center of New York—Child and Adolescent Psychiatry Service, New York, NY

The Salvation Army Residential Treatment Facilities for Children and Youth, Honolulu, HI

Samarkand Manor, Eagle Springs, NC

San Diego County Mental Health Services—Loma Portal Facility, San Diego, CA

San Diego Unified School District, San Diego, CA

San Marcos Treatment Center of The Brown Schools, San Marcos, TX

San Mateo County Office of Education, Redwood City, CA

School for Contemporary Education, Baltimore, MD

School for Contemporary Education, Springfield, VA

Secret Harbor School, Anacortes, WA

Seminole County Board of Public Instruction—Programs for Emotionally Handicapped, Sanford, FL

Serendipity Diagnostic and Treatment Center, Citrus Heights, CA

Shadow Mountain Institute, Tulsa, OK

Shawnee County Youth Center Services, Topeka, KS

Shawnee Mission Public Schools, Shawnee Mission, KS

Sheldon Community Guidance Clinic Inc, New Britain, CT

Solomon Mental Health Center, Lowell, MA

Sonia Shankman Orthogenic School of the University of Chicago, Chicago, IL

South Bend Community School Corporation—Adolescent Day Treatment Center, South Bend, IN

South Dakota Human Services Center, Yankton, SD

South Metropolitan Association—Interventions Residential School, Matteson, IL

South Oaks Hospital, Amityville, NY

South Shore Child Guidance Center, Freeport, NY

Southbury Training School, Southbury, CT

Southeast Kansas Mental Health Center, Humboldt, KS

Southeast Mental Health Center—Child Development Institute, Memphis, TN

Southlake Center for Mental Health, Merriville, IN

Southwood Psychiatric Residential Treatment Center—Hillcrest, San Diego, CA

Spaulding Youth Center—Emotional Handicap Program, Tilton, NH

Special Care Program, Orofino, ID

Special Education Association of Adams County, Quincy, IL

Special Service School District of Bergen County, Paramus, NJ

Spectrum Center for Educational and Behavioral Development Inc, Berkeley, CA

Spence Chapin Services to Families and Children—The Children's House, New York, NY

The Spofford Home, Kansas City, MO

Spring Lake Ranch, Cuttingsville, VT

Springfield Park Central Hospital—Park Central School, Springfield, MO

Springfield Public School District No. 186, Springfield, IL

The Starr Commonwealth Schools, Albion, MI

Starr Commonwealth Schools—Hannah Neil Center for Children, Columbus, OH

State Agriculture and Industrial School, Industry, NY

State Training School, Eldora, IA

Stetson School Inc, Barre, MA

Strafford Guidance Center Inc, Dover, NH

Stuyvesant Residence Club, New York City, NY

Summit Children's Residence Center, Upper Nyack, NY
Sunburst Youth Homes, Neillsville, WI
Switzer Center, Torrance, CA
Taylor Manor Hospital, Ellicott City, MD
Terry Children's Psychiatric Center, New Castle, DE
Timberlawn Psychiatric Hospital, Dallas, TX
Tomorrow's Children, Waupaca, WI
Towering Pines Center, Slidell, LA
Training Center for Youth, Columbus, OH
Tri City Community Mental Health and Retardation Center,
    Malden, MA
Tri-County Community Mental Health Center, Kansas City, MO
United Methodist Youthville, Newton, KS
University Hospitals of Cleveland—Hanna Pavilion Child Psy-
    chiatric Unit, Cleveland, OH
University of Arkansas Medical Sciences Division Child
    Psychiatry—Child Study Center, Little Rock, AR
The University of Chicago—Departments of Psychiatry and
    Pediatrics—Child Psychiatry, Chicago, IL
University of Illinois Medical Center—Child Psychiatry Clinic,
    Chicago, IL
University of Minnesota Hospitals—Child and Adolescent Psy-
    chiatry, Minneapolis, MN
University of New Mexico—Children's Psychiatric Hospital, Al-
    buquerque, NM
University of Rochester Medical School—Child and Adolescent
    Psychiatry Clinic, Rochester, NY
University of South Florida—Florida Mental Health
    Institute—Department of Child and Family Services,
    Tampa, FL
University of Texas Medical Branch—Division of Pediatric
    Psychology—Department of Pediatrics, Galveston, TX
University of Texas Medical Branch—Inpatient
    Service—Division of Child and Adolescent Psychiatry, Gal-
    veston, TX
University Park Psychological Center, Denver, CO
Valley View School, North Brookfield, MA
Valleyhead Inc, Lenox, MA
Vanderbilt Medical Center—Division of Child and Adolescent
    Psychiatry, Nashville, TN
Variety Preschooler's Workshop, Syosset, NY
Ventura County Superintendent of Schools, Ventura, CA
Villa Esperanza, Pasadena, CA
Village of St Joseph, Atlanta, GA
Virginia Center for Psychiatry, Portsmouth, VA
Virginia Center for Psychiatry, Norfolk, VA
Vista Del Mar Child Care Service, Los Angeles, CA
Vista Maria, Dearborn Heights, MI
Vitam Center Inc—Vitam School, Norwalk, CT
Walker Home and School, Needham, MA
Wallace Village for Children, Broomfield, CO
Walter Reed Army Medical Center Child and Adolescent Psychi-
    atry Service, Washington, DC
War Bonnet—Wilderness Pathways, Canaan, NH
Warm Springs Center, Boise, ID
Washington School District, Phoenix, AZ
Waterford Country School, Quaker Hill, CT
Waterloo Community Schools, Waterloo, IA
Waverly Children's Home, Portland, OR
West Central Community Services Center Inc, Willmar, MN
West Hartford Public Schools Off-Campus Program, West Hart-
    ford, CT
West Nassau Mental Health Center, Franklin Square, NY
West River Children's Center of the Children's Home Society of
    South Dakota, Rapid City, SD
West Texas Boys' Ranch, San Angelo, TX
Westbridge, Phoenix, AZ
Westchester Day Treatment Program, Hawthorne, NY
Western District Guidance Center, Parkersburg, WV
Western New York Children's Psychiatric Center, West Seneca,
    NY
West-Ros-Park Mental Health Center, Roslindale, MA
Wheeler Clinic Inc—Northwest Village School, Plainville, CT
Wichita Guidance Center, Wichita, KS
Wilder Children's Placement, Saint Paul, MN

Willowglen Academy Inc, Milwaukee, WI
Winnebago Mental Health Institute—Children's Unit, Win-
    nebago, WI
Woodbourne Center, Baltimore, MD
Woodward Mental Health Center, Freeport, NY
Work Training Program Inc, Santa Barbara, CA
Wyalusing Academy, Prairie du Chien, WI
Wyandotte Mental Health Center, Kansas City, KS
Wyandotte Special Education Cooperative, Kansas City, KS
Wyoming Youth Treatment Center, Casper, WY
Yellowstone Boys' and Girls' Ranch, Billings, MT
York Woods Center, Ypsilanti, MI
Youth Evaluation and Treatment Centers (YETC), Phoenix, AZ
Yuma School District One, Yuma, AZ
Yuma Union High School District, Yuma, AZ

Obsessions and Compulsions

Adams County Adolescent Day Treatment Program, Denver, CO
Albany Area Mental Health and Mental Retardation Center,
    Albany, GA
Albuquerque Child Guidance Center, Albuquerque, NM
Alexander Children's Center, Charlotte, NC
All Children's Hospital, St Petersburg, FL
Almansor Education Center, Alhambra, CA
Anne Arundel County Health Department Mental Health Clinic,
    Annapolis, MD
Archdiocese of Louisville—Guidance Clinic, Louisville, KY
Area Education Agency—Education Center, Waterloo, IA
Arizona Children's Home, Tucson, AZ
Arizona State Hospital, Phoenix, AZ
Arizona State Hospital—Nueva Vista School, Phoenix, AZ
Arlington School, Belmont, MA
Arnell Engstrom Children's Center, Traverse City, MI
Aseltine School, San Diego, CA
The Astor Home for Children—Day Treatment Program, Bronx,
    NY
Atlantic Mental Health Center Inc, McKee City, NJ
Augusta School Department, Augusta, ME
Aurora Adolescent Day Resource Center, Aurora, CO
Austin State Hospital, Austin, TX
Avalon School at High Point, Lenox, MA
Avon Lenox Special Education, Memphis, TN
Avondale House, Houston, TX
The Baird Center for Children and Families Inc, Burlington, VT
The Bancroft School, Haddonfield, NJ
Bar-None Residential Treatment Services for Children, Anoka,
    MN
The Battin Clinic, Houston, TX
Battle Creek Child Guidance Center, Battle Creek, MI
Beacon Day Treatment Program, Romulus, MI
Berea Children's Home, Berea, OH
Bergen Center for Child Development, Haworth, NJ
Bergen Pines Hospital—Children's Psychiatric Unit, Paramus,
    NJ
Berks County Intermediate Unit, Reading, PA
Berkshire Farm Center and Services for Youth, Canaan, NY
Big Lakes Developmental Center Inc, Manhattan, KS
Big Spring State Hospital, Big Spring, TX
Birmingham City Board of Education, Birmingham, AL
Blick Clinic for Developmental Disabilities, Akron, OH
BOCES Nassau, Westbury, NY
Bowman Gray School of Medicine Developmental Evaluation
    Clinic—Amos Cottage Rehabilitation Hospital, Winston-
    Salem, NC
Boys' Village Inc—Boys' Village School, Smithville, OH
Bradley Hospital, East Providence, RI
Brant Services Corporation—Brant Ryan House, Inkster, MI
Brattleboro Retreat, Brattleboro, VT
Brea Neuropsychiatric Center, Brea, CA
Brentwood Center, Los Angeles, CA
Brewer-Porch Children's Center, University, AL
Bridgeway Hospital Youthcare Program, North Little Rock, AR
Brighton School and Diagnostic Center, Phoenix, AZ
Brooklyn Community Counseling Center, Brooklyn, NY

Broom-Tioga Board of Cooperative Educational Services, Binghamton, NY
Brown County Mental Health Center—Children Services, Green Bay, WI
The Brown Schools, Austin, TX
Buckeye Boys' Ranch Inc, Grove City, OH
Butler County Mental Health Center Inc, Hamilton, OH
California Mental Health Center, Los Angeles, CA
Cantwell Academy Inc, Miami, FL
Capitol Region Education Council's Day Treatment Service, West Hartford, CT
Cass County Social Services—Children's Social Service Center, Fargo, ND
Cathedral Home for Children, Laramie, WY
Center for Autistic Children, Philadelphia, PA
Center for Life Management, Salem, NH
Central Massachusetts Special Education Collaborative—Quimby School, Worcester, MA
Chancellor Academy, Pompton Plains, NJ
Charter Westbrook Hospital, Richmond, VA
Chestnut Lodge Hospital—Adolescent and Child Division, Rockville, MD
Child Adolescent Service Center, Canton, OH
Child and Adolescent Psychiatric Clinic Inc, Buffalo, NY
Child and Family Services, Knoxville, TN
Child Development Service—Lakeview Center Inc, Pensacola, FL
Child Disability Clinic—Carle Clinic, Urbana, IL
Child Guidance Center of Southern Connecticut, Stanford, CT
Child Guidance Clinic—Day Treatment Program, Winston-Salem, NC
Child Guidance Clinic of Southeastern Connecticut Inc, New London, CT
Child Psychiatry Service—Department of Psychiatry—University Hospitals, Ann Arbor, MI
Child Study and Treatment Center, Tacoma, WA
Child Study Center, Fort Worth, TX
Children's Aid Society, Cleveland, OH
Children's and Adolescent Unit of Mental Health Institute of Cherokee Iowa, Cherokee, IA
Children's Behavior Therapy Unit, Salt Lake City, UT
Children's Bureau of Indianapolis Inc, Indianapolis, IN
Children's Center, Hamden, CT
Children's Day Hospital—New York Hospital—Cornell Medical Center—Westchester Division, White Plains, NY
The Children's Day School, Trenton, NJ
Children's Day Treatment Center, Honolulu, HI
The Children's Guild Inc, Baltimore, MD
Children's Health Council, Palo Alto, CA
Children's Home of Cedar Rapids—Heartwood Residential Treatment Center, Cedar Rapids, IA
The Children's Home of Cincinnati, Cincinnati, OH
Children's Home of Kingston, Kingston, NY
Children's Home Society of South Dakota, Sioux Falls, SD
Children's Hospital at Washington University Medical Center—Psychiatric Unit, Saint Louis, MO
The Children's Institute, South Orange, NJ
Children's Learning Center of San Antonio, San Antonio, TX
Children's Medical Center, Tulsa, OK
Children's Medical Center—Psychiatric Inpatient Unit, Dallas, TX
Children's Mental Health Center Inc, Columbus, OH
The Children's Mercy Hospital—Section of Psychiatry, Kansas City, MO
Children's Psychiatric Center of the Jewish Hospital, Cincinnati, OH
The Children's School of the Institute of Living, Hartford, CT
The Children's Study Home, Springfield, MA
Cabinet for Human Resources—Children's Treatment Service, Louisville, KY
Christian Church—Children's Campus, Danville, KY
The Clearing, Marshfield, VT
Clearwater Ranch Children's House Inc, Philo, CA
Cleveland Christian Home for Children Inc, Cleveland, OH
Cleveland Clinic Foundation, Cleveland, OH

Cleveland County Area Mental Health Program—Division of Child and Youth Services, Shelby, NC
The Clinical Center of Southern Illinois University, Carbondale, IL
College Hospital—College Park School, Cerritos, CA
Colorado Springs School District No. 11, Colorado Springs, CO
Colorado West Regional Mental Health Center, Glenwood Springs, CO
Community Counseling Center—Rural Clinics, Ely, NV
Community Psychiatric Clinic Inc, Wheaton; Bethesda; Gaithersburg, MD
The Community School of the Family Service and Child Guidance Center of the Oranges Maplewood and Millburn, Orange, NJ
Comprehensive Mental Health Center of St Clair County Inc, East Saint Louis, IL
Connecticut College Program for Children with Special Needs, New London, CT
Convalescent Hospital for Children, Rochester, NY
Covenant Children's Home and Family Services, Princeton, IL
CPC Belmont Hills Hospital, Belmont, CA
Craig House—Technoma, Pittsburgh, PA
CRATER of Broward Inc—Retreat Ranch Facility—24 Hour Residential Treatment Center, Fort Lauderdale, FL
Creative Arts Rehabilitation Center Inc, New York, NY
Creative Learning Systems Inc, Tucson, AZ
Cumberland County Guidance Center Inc, Millville, NJ
Dakota House, Aberdeen, SD
Daniel Memorial Inc, Jacksonville, FL
Darden Hill Ranch School, Driftwood, TX
De Neuville Heights School for Girls, Memphis, TN
DeJarnette Center, Staunton, VA
The Delacato and Doman Autistic Unit, Morton, PA
Delaware Guidance Services for Children and Youth Inc, Wilmington, DE
Department of Public Instruction, Dover, DE
DePaul Hospital and Residential Treatment Center, New Orleans, LA
Des Moines Children's Home—Orchard Place, Des Moines, IA
Desert Hills, Tucson, AZ
DeSisto Schools Inc, West Stockbridge, MA
The Devereux Foundation, Devon, PA
The Devereux Foundation, Santa Barbara, CA
The Devereux Foundation—Deerhaven, Chester, NJ
The Devereux Foundation—Texas Branch, Victoria, TX
Devereux in Georgia, Kennesaw, GA
The Devereux Schools at Rutland, Rutland, MA
Dominion Hospital—The Dominion School, Falls Church, VA
Donaldsonville Mental Health Center, Donaldsonville, LA
Douglas A Thom Clinic Inc, Boston, MA
Durham County Group Home for Autistic Adults Inc, Durham, NC
Early Childhood Developmental Center Inc, Hays, KS
East Alabama Mental Health Retardation Center, Opelika, AL
Eastern Shore Mental Health Center, Nassawadox, VA
Eau Claire Academy, Eau Claire, WI
The Eckerd Wilderness Educational System Camping System, Clearwater, FL
Edgefield Children's Center, Troutdale, OR
Edgemont Hospital, Los Angeles, CA
Edgewood Children's Center, Saint Louis, MO
Edgewood Day Treatment—The Lucinda Weeks Center, San Francisco, CA
The Educational Clinic Inc, Columbus, OH
Educational Department of Institute of Pennsylvania Hospital—Mill Creek School, Philadelphia, PA
El Paso Guidance Center, El Paso, TX
Elizabeth Ives School, Hamden, CT
Elm Acres Youth Home Inc, Pittsburg, KS
Elmcrest Psychiatric Institute, Portland, CT
Elwyn Institutes, Elwyn, PA
Emerson North, Cincinnati, OH
The Episcopal Church Home for Children—York Place, York, SC
Escalon Inc, Altadena, CA

Escambia District Schools, Pensacola, FL
Evansville Vanderburgh School Corporation, Evansville, IN
Excelsior Youth Center, Aurora, CO
Fairmount Children's Center, Syracuse, NY
Family Guidance Center, Reading, PA
Family Guidance Service—Ingham Community Mental Health
Center, Lansing, MI
Five Acres Boys' and Girls' Aide Society, Altadena, CA
Florence Program for Autistic Children and Adolescents—Lester
Elementary School, Florence, SC
Forest Heights Lodge, Evergreen, CO
Forest Hospital, Des Plaines, IL
Fort Logan Mental Health Center, Denver, CO
Ft Wayne Children's Home—Crossroad, Fort Wayne, IN
Franklin Grand Isle Mental Health Services Inc, Saint Albans,
VT
Fremont Unified School District, Fremont, CA
The Frost School, Rockville, MD
The George Junior Republic Association Inc, Freeville, NY
Gerard of Minnesota Inc, Austin, MN
Gilfillan Center, Bemidji, MN
Gladman Memorial Hospital Adolescent Program, Oakland, CA
Glenholme School, Washington, CT
Glens Falls Hospital—Child and Family Services—Community
Mental Health Center, Glens Falls, NY
The Goldstaub Residence, Houston, TX
Gould Farm, Monterey, MA
Grady Memorial Hospital—Division of Child and Adolescent
Psychiatry, Atlanta, GA
The Gramon School, Livingston, NJ
Grant Center Hospital, Miami, FL
Graydon Manor, Leesburg, VA
Green Chimneys Children's Services Inc, Brewster, NY
Greenshire School, Cheshire, CT
Grove School, Madison, CT
Hall-Mercer Children's Center of the McLean Hospital, Belmont,
MA
Hall-Brooke Foundation—Hall-Brooke Hospital—Hall-Brooke
School, Westport, CT
Hamilton Children's Center, Hyattsville, MD
The Hannah More Center, Reisterstown, MD
Harbor Schools Inc, Newburyport, MA
Harbor View Mercy Hospital, Fort Smith, AR
Harford County Community Mental Health Center, Bel Air, MD
Hartgrove Hospital—Hartgrove Academy, Chicago, IL
Hathaway School of Hathaway Home for Children, Pacoima, CA
Hawaii State Department of Education—Special Needs Branch,
Honolulu, HI
Hawthorn Center, Northville, MI
Hawthorne Children's Psychiatric Hospital, Saint Louis, MO
Henderson Mental Health Center, Fort Lauderdale, FL
Henrietta Weill Memorial Child Guidance Clinic, Bakersfield,
CA
Henry Horner Children and Adolescent Center, Chicago, IL
High Plains Mental Health Center—Colby Office, Colby, KS
Highland Youth Services—The Highland School, Pittsburgh, PA
Hillside Children's Center, Rochester, NY
Hillside School Inc, Logan, UT
Homewood School—Highland Hospital, Asheville, NC
Honolulu District—Special Education Center of Oahu (SECO),
Honolulu, HI
Humana Hospital Huntington Beach—Children's Behavioral
Center, Huntington Beach, CA
Independence House of Avalon Inc, Sheffield, MA
Indiana University Developmental Training Center, Blooming-
ton, IN
Indianapolis Public Schools—Special Education Department, In-
dianapolis, IN
Ingleside Hospital, Rosemead, CA
Institute for Learning, Philadelphia, PA
The Institute of Living School, Hartford, CT
Institute of Psychiatry and Human Behavior—Department of
Psychiatry—Child and Adolescent Inpatient Service, Bal-
timore, MD

ISIS Programs Inc—Individual Support Through Innovative Ser-
vices for Autistic Persons, Orlando, FL
Italian Home for Children, Jamaica Plain, MA
Ittleson Center for Child Research, New York, NY
Jane Wayland Center, Phoenix, AZ
Jasper County Mental Health Center, Newton, IA
Jeanine Schultz Memorial School, Park Ridge, IL
Jefferson County Public Schools, Lakewood, CO
Jefferson Parish School System—Department of Special Educa-
tion, Gretna, LA
Jewish Child Care Association—Pleasantville Cottage School,
Pleasantville, NY
Jewish Child Care Association—Youth Residence Center, New
York, NY
Jewish Children's Bureau of Chicago, Chicago, IL
John C Corrigan Mental Health Center, Fall River, MA
John Umstead Hospital—Children's Psychiatric Institute, Butner,
NC
Kalamazoo Child Guidance Clinic, Kalamazoo, MI
K-Bar-B Youth Ranch—Richard M Wise School, Lacombe, LA
Kenai Peninsula Borough School District, Soldotna, AK
Kings County Hospital—Downstate Medical Center—Division of
Child and Adolescent Psychiatry, Brooklyn, NY
La Mel, San Francisco, CA
La Puente Valley Community Mental Health Center, La Puente,
CA
Lad Lake Inc, Dousman, WI
Lafayette Clinic, Detroit, MI
Lake County Mental Health Center—Department of Children's
Services, Mentor, OH
Lake Grove School, Lake Grove, NY
Lakeshore Mental Health Institute—Riverbend School—Children
and Youth Services, Knoxville, TN
Lakeside Child and Family Center Inc, Milwaukee, WI
Lakin Hospital—Adolescent Services, Lakin, WV
Lane School Programs—Lane Education Service District, Eu-
gene, OR
Lansing School District, Lansing, MI
Lighthouse School, Chelmsford, MA
Little Friends Inc—Group Home for Autistic Children, Wheaton,
IL
Little Friends Inc—Little Friends School, Naperville, IL
Little Friends Inc—The Therapeutic Workshop, Downers Grove,
IL
Lookout Mountain School, Golden, CO
The Los Angeles Child Guidance Clinic, Los Angeles, CA
Los Angeles County Office of Education—Mark Twain School,
Lawndale, CA
Los Lunas Hospital and Training School—Behavioral Services
Unit, Los Lunas, NM
Los Ninos Education Center, San Diego, CA
Lourdesmont—Good Shepherd Youth and Family Services,
Clarks Summit, PA
Lovellton Academy, Elgin, IL
Lutheran Medical Center—Psychiatric Division, Saint Louis,
MO
Madden Mental Health Center Campus—Institute for Juvenile
Research—Inpatient Services, Hines, IL
Madeline Burg Counseling Services—Jewish Board of Family
and Children Services, Bronx, NY
Main Street Human Resources, Great Barington, MA
Manhattan Children's Psychiatric Center, New York, NY
Manitowoc County Counseling Center, Manitowoc, WI
The Mansion, Naperville, IL
Martin Luther Centers, Madison, WI
Marymount Hospital Mental Health Center, Garfield Heights,
OH
Maryvale, Rosemead, CA
Massanutten Mental Health Center, Harrisonburg, VA
Medical Care Rehabilitation Hospital's Child Evaluation and
Treatment Program, Grand Forks, ND
Medical University of South Carolina—Department of
Psychiatry—Youth Division, Charleston, SC
Mendota Mental Health Institute—Child and Adolescent Pro-
gram, Madison, WI

The Menninger Foundation—Pre-School Day Treatment Center, Topeka, KS

The Menninger Foundation—The Children's Division, Topeka, KS

Mental Health Center of Boulder County—Adolescent Treatment Program, Boulder, CO

Mental Health Center of Mid-Iowa, Marshalltown, IA

Mental Health Centers of Central Illinois—Child and Adolescent Day Treatment Program, Springfield, IL

Mental Health Services of North Central Hamilton Co Inc, Cincinnati, OH

Mercy Hospital and Medical Center—Community Guidance Center, Chicago, IL

Meridell Achievement Center Inc, Austin, TX

MHMR of Southeast Texas—Daybreak Cottage, Orange, TX

The Mid Fairfield Child Guidance Center Inc, Norwalk, CT

Mid-Columbia Mental Health Center—Adolescent Psychiatric Department, Richland, WA

The Millcreek Psychiatric Center for Children, Cincinnati, OH

Millcreek Schools Inc, Magee, MS

Minnesota Learning Center, Brainerd, MN

Miramonte Mental Health Services Inc, Palo Alto, CA

Monroe County Intermediate School District—Programs for Emotionally Impaired, Monroe, MI

Mt Airy Psychiatric Center—Children's Treatment Program—Adolescent Treatment Program, Denver, CO

Mt Scott Institute, Washington, NJ

Mountain Board of Cooperative Services—Adolescent Day Treatment Program, Leadville, CO

Multidisciplinary Institute for Neuropsychological Development Inc—MIND, Cambridge, MA

Mystic Valley Mental Health Center, Lexington, MA

Napa State Hospital—Children's Program, Imola, CA

National Foundation for the Treatment of the Emotionally Handicapped, Sepulveda, CA

New England Home for Little Wanderers—Orchard Home, Watertown, MA

New England Home for Little Wanderers—Knight Children's Center, Boston, MA

New England Medical Center—Bay Cove Day Center for Children Day Hospital, Boston, MA

New England Medical Center—Division of Child Psychiatry, Boston, MA

New England Salem Children's Trust, Rumney, NH

New Hope Guild, Brooklyn, NY

New Mexico Boys' School, Springer, NM

Normon Westlund Child Guidance Clinic, Saginaw, MI

North Central Health Care Facilities, Wausau, WI

North Dakota State Mental Hospital—Child and Adolescent Unit, Jamestown, ND

North Metro Psychoeducational Program, Atlanta, GA

Northeast Colorado Board of Cooperative Educational Services, Haxton, CO

Northwest Florida Mental Health Center, Panama City, FL

Northwest Psychoeducational Program, Rome, GA

Northwood Children's Home, Duluth, MN

Norton Psychiatric Clinic—Norton Adolescent Treatment Program and Norton Academy, Louisville, KY

Ocean Institute—Adolescent Day School—Mental Health Clinic of Ocean County, Toms River, NJ

Oconomowoc Developmental Training Center Inc, Oconomowoc, WI

Office of Riverside County Superintendent of Schools, Riverside, CA

Ohel Children's Home and Family Services, Brooklyn, NY

Orlando Regional Medical Center—Mental Health Department—Children's Services, Orlando, FL

Otis R Bowen Center, Warsaw, IN

Our Lady of Providence Children's Center, West Springfield, MA

Pacific Children's Center, Oakland, CA

Paradise Valley School District No. 69—Therapeutic Educational Activities Milieu, Phoenix, AZ

Parkview Counseling Center Inc, Youngstown, OH

Parkwood Hospital, Atlanta, GA

Parry Center for Children, Portland, OR

Parsons Child and Family Center, Albany, NY

Parsons Child and Family Center—Neil Hellman School, Albany, NY

Partial Hospitalization Program Children's Service Center, Wilkes Barre, PA

Pawnee Mental Health Services, Concordia, KS

Peace River Center for Personal Development Inc, Bartow, FL

Penninsula Children's Center—Children and Youth Services, Palo Alto, CA

Philadelphia Child Guidance Clinic, Philadelphia, PA

Philadelphia Child Guidance Clinic—Child and Family Inpatient Service, Philadelphia, PA

Phoenix Union High School District No. 210, Phoenix, AZ

Pikes Peak Board of Cooperative Services, Colorado Springs, CO

Porter Starke Services Inc—Vale Park Psychiatric Hospital, Valparaiso, IN

Prescott Child Development Center, Prescott, AZ

Pressley Ridge School—Day School, Pittsburgh, PA

Pressley Ridge School—Laurel Park, Clarksburg, WV

Pressley Ridge School—Pryde—Family Based Treatment, Pittsburgh, PA

Pressley Ridge School—Wilderness School, Ohiopyle, PA

Primary Children's Medical Center—Department of Child Psychiatry, Salt Lake City, UT

Project Second Start's Alternative High School Program, Concord, NH

Protestant Youth Center, Baldwinville, MA

Provo Canyon School, Provo, UT

Psychiatric Clinic of the Charlotte Hungerford Hospital, Torrington, CT

Psychiatric Services Inc, Haverhill, MA

Queen of Angels School—Villa Maria Treatment Center, Timonium, MD

Queens Hospital Center Department of Psychiatry Child and Adolescent Clinic, Jamaica, NY

Ranch Hope Strang School, Alloway, NJ

Range Mental Health Center, Virginia, MN

Raritan Bay Mental Health Center, Perth Amboy, NJ

The Re-Ed West Center for Children Inc, Sacramento, CA

Red Rock Comprehensive Mental Health Center, Oklahoma City, OK

Region 16 Educational Service Center, Amarillo, TX

Rensselaer County Mental Health Department—Unified Services for Children and Adolescents, Troy, NY

Richmond County Board of Education—Sand Hills Psychoeducational Program, Augusta, GA

Ridgeview Institute, Smyrna, GA

River Street School, Hyde Park, MA

Rockford School District No. 205, Rockford, IL

Rockland Children's Psychiatric Center, Orangeburg, NY

Rockland Psychological and Educational Center, Spring Valley, NY

Rutland Psychoeducational Services, Athens, GA

Sagamore Hills Children's Psychiatric Hospital, Northfield, OH

St Ann's Home Inc—Day Treatment and Special Education Program, Methuen, MA

St Ann's Home Inc—Residential Treatment and Special Education Program, Methuen, MA

St Clare's Hospital—Adult, Child and Family Services, Denville, NJ

St Cloud Children's Home, Saint Cloud, MN

St Elizabeth's Hospital—Division of Child and Adolescent Services, Washington, DC

St George Homes Inc, Berkeley, CA

St John's Child Development Center, Washington, DC

St Joseph Center for Mental Health, Omaha, NE

St Joseph's Carondelet Child Center, Chicago, IL

St Louis County Child Mental Health Services, Saint Louis, MO

St Mary's Home for Boys, Beaverton, OR

St Vincent Children's Center, Columbus, OH

St Vincent's Hospital and Medical Center of New York—Child and Adolescent Psychiatry Service, New York, NY

Samarkand Manor, Eagle Springs, NC

San Diego County Mental Health Services—Loma Portal Facility, San Diego, CA

San Diego Unified School District, San Diego, CA

San Marcos Treatment Center of The Brown Schools, San Marcos, TX

San Mateo County Office of Education, Redwood City, CA

School for Contemporary Education, Baltimore, MD

School for Contemporary Education, Springfield, VA

Secret Harbor School, Anacortes, WA

Seminole County Board of Public Instruction—Programs for Emotionally Handicapped, Sanford, FL

Serendipity Diagnostic and Treatment Center, Citrus Heights, CA

Shadow Mountain Institute, Tulsa, OK

Shawnee Mission Public Schools, Shawnee Mission, KS

Sherwood Center for The Exceptional Child, Kansas City, MO

Sibley Hospital—Groome Center—Hayes Hall, Washington, DC

Solomon Mental Health Center, Lowell, MA

Sonia Shankman Orthogenic School of the University of Chicago, Chicago, IL

South Bend Community School Corporation—Adolescent Day Treatment Center, South Bend, IN

South Carolina State Hospital—Child and Adolescent Unit—Blanding House, Columbia, SC

South Dakota Human Services Center, Yankton, SD

South Metropolitan Association—Interventions Residential School, Matteson, IL

South Oaks Hospital, Amityville, NY

South Shore Child Guidance Center, Freeport, NY

Southbury Training School, Southbury, CT

Southeast Kansas Mental Health Center, Humboldt, KS

Southeast Mental Health Center—Child Development Institute, Memphis, TN

Southlake Center for Mental Health, Merriville, IN

Southwest Georgia Psychoeducational Services—Thomas County Schools, Ochlocknee, GA

Southwood Psychiatric Residential Treatment Center—Hillcrest, San Diego, CA

Spaulding Youth Center—Autistic Program, Tilton, NH

Spaulding Youth Center—Emotional Handicap Program, Tilton, NH

Special Care Program, Orofino, ID

Special Education Association of Adams County, Quincy, IL

Special Service School District of Bergen County, Paramus, NJ

Spence Chapin Services to Families and Children—The Children's House, New York, NY

The Spofford Home, Kansas City, MO

Spring Lake Ranch, Cuttingsville, VT

Springfield Park Central Hospital—Park Central School, Springfield, MO

State University of New York at Albany—SUNY Pre-Kindergarten, Albany, NY

Stetson School Inc, Barre, MA

Strafford Guidance Center Inc, Dover, NH

Stuyvesant Residence Club, New York City, NY

Summit Children's Residence Center, Upper Nyack, NY

Sunburst Youth Homes, Neillsville, WI

Switzer Center, Torrance, CA

Taylor Manor Hospital, Ellicott City, MD

Terry Children's Psychiatric Center, New Castle, DE

Threshold Inc, Goldenrod, FL

Timberlawn Psychiatric Hospital, Dallas, TX

Timberridge Institute for Children and Adolescents Inc, Oklahoma City, OK

Tomorrow's Children, Waupaca, WI

Total Living Continuum, Camarillo, CA

Towering Pines Center, Slidell, LA

Training Center for Youth, Columbus, OH

Tri City Community Mental Health and Retardation Center, Malden, MA

Tri-County Cooperative Center No. 946, Grand Rapids, MN

Tri-County Community Mental Health Center, Kansas City, MO

University Hospitals of Cleveland—Hanna Pavilion Child Psychiatric Unit, Cleveland, OH

University of Arkansas Medical Sciences Division Child Psychiatry—Child Study Center, Little Rock, AR

The University of Chicago—Departments of Psychiatry and Pediatrics—Child Psychiatry, Chicago, IL

University of Colorado Health Sciences Center—Day Care Center, Denver, CO

University of Illinois Medical Center—Child Psychiatry Clinic, Chicago, IL

University of Minnesota Hospitals—Child and Adolescent Psychiatry, Minneapolis, MN

University of New Mexico—Children's Psychiatric Hospital, Albuquerque, NM

University of Rochester Medical School—Child and Adolescent Psychiatry Clinic, Rochester, NY

University of South Florida—Florida Mental Health Institute—Department of Child and Family Services, Tampa, FL

University of Texas Medical Branch—Division of Pediatric Psychology—Department of Pediatrics, Galveston, TX

University of Texas Medical Branch—Inpatient Service—Division of Child and Adolescent Psychiatry, Galveston, TX

University Park Psychological Center, Denver, CO

Utah Boys' Ranch—Children and Youth Services Inc, Salt Lake City, UT

Vanderbilt Medical Center—Division of Child and Adolescent Psychiatry, Nashville, TN

Variety Preschooler's Workshop, Syosset, NY

Ventura County Superintendent of Schools, Ventura, CA

Villa Esperanza, Pasadena, CA

Village of St Joseph, Atlanta, GA

Virginia Center for Psychiatry, Portsmouth, VA

Virginia Center for Psychiatry, Norfolk, VA

Vista Del Mar Child Care Service, Los Angeles, CA

Vista Maria, Dearborn Heights, MI

Vitam Center Inc—Vitam School, Norwalk, CT

Walker Home and School, Needham, MA

Walter Reed Army Medical Center Child and Adolescent Psychiatry Service, Washington, DC

War Bonnet—Wilderness Pathways, Canaan, NH

Warm Springs Center, Boise, ID

Waterford Country School, Quaker Hill, CT

Waterloo Community Schools, Waterloo, IA

West Central Community Services Center Inc, Willmar, MN

West Hartford Public Schools Off-Campus Program, West Hartford, CT

West Nassau Mental Health Center, Franklin Square, NY

West River Children's Center of the Children's Home Society of South Dakota, Rapid City, SD

Westbridge, Phoenix, AZ

Westchester Day Treatment Program, Hawthorne, NY

Western District Guidance Center, Parkersburg, WV

Western New York Children's Psychiatric Center, West Seneca, NY

West-Ros-Park Mental Health Center, Roslindale, MA

Wheeler Clinic Inc—Northwest Village School, Plainville, CT

Wichita Guidance Center, Wichita, KS

Wilder Children's Placement, Saint Paul, MN

Willowglen Academy Inc, Milwaukee, WI

Winnebago Mental Health Institute—Children's Unit, Winnebago, WI

Winston L Prouty Center, Brattleboro, VT

Woodbourne Center, Baltimore, MD

Woodward Mental Health Center, Freeport, NY

Work Training Program Inc, Santa Barbara, CA

Wyalusing Academy, Prairie du Chien, WI

Wyandotte Special Education Cooperative, Kansas City, KS

Wyoming State Hospital, Evanston, WY

Yellowstone Boys' and Girls' Ranch, Billings, MT

York Woods Center, Ypsilanti, MI

Youth and Family Services, Omaha, NE

Youth Center of Beloit—North Beloit High, Beloit, KS

Youth Evaluation and Treatment Centers (YETC), Phoenix, AZ

Zonta Children's Center, San Jose, CA

Other Substance Abuse or Dependence

Albany Area Mental Health and Mental Retardation Center, Albany, GA

Anne Arundel County Health Department Mental Health Clinic, Annapolis, MD

Anneewakee Hospital, Douglasville, GA

Arizona Boys' Ranch, Boys Ranch, AZ

Arizona State Hospital—Nueva Vista School, Phoenix, AZ

Arlington School, Belmont, MA

Aseltine School, San Diego, CA

The Astor Home for Children—Group Home Program, Bronx, NY

Atlantic Mental Health Center Inc, McKee City, NJ

Aurora Adolescent Day Resource Center, Aurora, CO

Baker Hall Inc, Lackawanna, NY

The Battin Clinic, Houston, TX

Battle Creek Child Guidance Center, Battle Creek, MI

Bergen Pines Hospital—Children's Psychiatric Unit, Paramus, NJ

Berks County Intermediate Unit, Reading, PA

Berkshire Farm Center and Services for Youth, Canaan, NY

Blick Clinic for Developmental Disabilities, Akron, OH

Boston Public Schools—The McKinley Schools, Mattapau, MA

Boys' Town of Missouri Inc, Saint James, MO

Boys' Village Inc—Boys' Village School, Smithville, OH

Bradley Hospital, East Providence, RI

Brattleboro Retreat, Brattleboro, VT

Bridgeway Hospital Youthcare Program, North Little Rock, AR

Brighton School and Diagnostic Center, Phoenix, AZ

Brown County Mental Health Center—Children Services, Green Bay, WI

Butler County Mental Health Center Inc, Hamilton, OH

Cathedral Home for Children, Laramie, WY

Cedu School, Running Springs, CA

Center for Life Management, Salem, NH

Charter Westbrook Hospital, Richmond, VA

Child and Adolescent Psychiatric Clinic Inc, Buffalo, NY

Child Disability Clinic—Carle Clinic, Urbana, IL

Child Guidance Clinic of Southeastern Connecticut Inc, New London, CT

Children's Home Society of South Dakota, Sioux Falls, SD

The Children's Mercy Hospital—Section of Psychiatry, Kansas City, MO

The Children's School of the Institute of Living, Hartford, CT

Clear View School, Scarborough, NY

Cleveland Clinic Foundation, Cleveland, OH

Cleveland County Area Mental Health Program—Division of Child and Youth Services, Shelby, NC

The Clinical Center of Southern Illinois University, Carbondale, IL

College Hospital—College Park School, Cerritos, CA

Colorado Springs School District No. 11, Colorado Springs, CO

Colorado West Regional Mental Health Center, Glenwood Springs, CO

Community Counseling Center—Rural Clinics, Ely, NV

Covenant Children's Home and Family Services, Princeton, IL

CPC Belmont Hills Hospital, Belmont, CA

Craig House—Technoma, Pittsburgh, PA

Creative Learning Systems Inc, Tucson, AZ

Crockett State School Independent School District, Crockett, TX

De Neuville Heights School for Girls, Memphis, TN

DePaul Hospital and Residential Treatment Center, New Orleans, LA

DeSisto Schools Inc, West Stockbridge, MA

The Devereux Foundation, Devon, PA

The Devereux Foundation—Texas Branch, Victoria, TX

Dominion Hospital—The Dominion School, Falls Church, VA

East Alabama Mental Health Retardation Center, Opelika, AL

Eau Claire Academy, Eau Claire, WI

Edgemont Hospital, Los Angeles, CA

The Educational Clinic Inc, Columbus, OH

Educational Department of Institute of Pennsylvania Hospital—Mill Creek School, Philadelphia, PA

Elmcrest Psychiatric Institute, Portland, CT

Emerson North, Cincinati, OH

Escambia District Schools, Pensacola, FL

Ettie Lee Homes Inc, Baldwin Park, CA

Excelsior Youth Center, Aurora, CO

Forest Hospital, Des Plaines, IL

Fort Logan Mental Health Center, Denver, CO

Four Winds Hospital—Adolescent Services, Katonah, NY

Franklin Grand Isle Mental Health Services Inc, Saint Albans, VT

Garfield Girls' School, Phoenix, AZ

Gilfillan Center, Bemidji, MN

Gladman Memorial Hospital Adolescent Program, Oakland, CA

The Goldstaub Residence, Houston, TX

Gould Farm, Monterey, MA

Grady Memorial Hospital—Division of Child and Adolescent Psychiatry, Atlanta, GA

Hall-Brooke Foundation—Hall-Brooke Hospital—Hall-Brooke School, Westport, CT

Hamilton Children's Center, Hyattsville, MD

Harbor View Mercy Hospital, Fort Smith, AR

Hartgrove Hospital—Hartgrove Academy, Chicago, IL

Hawaii State Department of Education—Special Needs Branch, Honolulu, HI

Hawaii State Hospital—Adolescent Unit, Kaneohe, HI

Hawthorn Center, Northville, MI

Hawthorne Children's Psychiatric Hospital, Saint Louis, MO

High Plains Mental Health Center—Colby Office, Colby, KS

Highland Heights—St Francis Home for Children Inc, New Haven, CT

Homewood School—Highland Hospital, Asheville, NC

Ingleside Hospital, Rosemead, CA

Institute for Family and Life Learning Residential School, Danvers, MA

The Institute of Living School, Hartford, CT

Institute of Psychiatry and Human Behavior—Department of Psychiatry—Child and Adolescent Inpatient Service, Baltimore, MD

Jasper County Mental Health Center, Newton, IA

Jefferson Parish School System—Department of Special Education, Gretna, LA

John G McGrath School, Napa, CA

Kalamazoo Child Guidance Clinic, Kalamazoo, MI

K-Bar-B Youth Ranch—Richard M Wise School, Lacombe, LA

Klamath County Mental Health Center—Natural Family Preservation Project, Klamath Falls, OR

La Puente Valley Community Mental Health Center, La Puente, CA

Lad Lake Inc, Dousman, WI

Lake County Mental Health Center—Department of Children's Services, Mentor, OH

Lakeshore Mental Health Institute—Riverbend School—Children and Youth Services, Knoxville, TN

Lakin Hospital—Adolescent Services, Lakin, WV

LaSalle School, Albany, NY

Lookout Mountain School, Golden, CO

The Los Angeles Child Guidance Clinic, Los Angeles, CA

Lovellton Academy, Elgin, IL

Main Street Human Resources, Great Barington, MA

Martin Luther Centers, Madison, WI

Maryhurst School, Louisville, KY

Marymount Hospital Mental Health Center, Garfield Heights, OH

Mendota Mental Health Institute—Child and Adolescent Program, Madison, WI

The Mental Health Institute for Children at Allentown State Hospital, Allentown, PA

Milford Assistance Program Day School, Milford, MA

Monroe County Intermediate School District—Programs for Emotionally Impaired, Monroe, MI

Montrose School, Reisterstown, MD

Mt Airy Psychiatric Center—Children's Treatment Program—Adolescent Treatment Program, Denver, CO

Napa State Hospital—Children's Program, Imola, CA

New Hope Guild, Brooklyn, NY

New Jersey Training School for Boys, Jamesburg, NJ

New Mexico Boys' School, Springer, NM
North Central Health Care Facilities, Wausau, WI
North Dakota State Mental Hospital—Child and Adolescent Unit, Jamestown, ND
Northeast Colorado Board of Cooperative Educational Services, Haxton, CO
Norton Psychiatric Clinic—Norton Adolescent Treatment Program and Norton Academy, Louisville, KY
Orlando Regional Medical Center—Mental Health Department—Children's Services, Orlando, FL
Overlook Mental Health Center—Blount County Adolescent Partial Hospitalization Program, Maryville, TN
Parkwood Hospital, Atlanta, GA
Parmadale—The Youth Services Village, Parma, OH
Pawnee Mental Health Services, Concordia, KS
Penn Foundation for Mental Health, Sellersville, PA
Porter Starke Services Inc—Vale Park Psychiatric Hospital, Valparaiso, IN
Prescott Child Development Center, Prescott, AZ
Pressley Ridge School—Day School, Pittsburgh, PA
Pressley Ridge School—Laurel Park, Clarksburg, WV
Pressley Ridge School—Pryde—Family Based Treatment, Pittsburgh, PA
Pressley Ridge School—Wilderness School, Ohiopyle, PA
Project Second Start's Alternative High School Program, Concord, NH
Psychiatric Clinic of the Charlotte Hungerford Hospital, Torrington, CT
Psychiatric Services Inc, Haverhill, MA
Range Mental Health Center, Virginia, MN
The Re-Ed West Center for Children Inc, Sacramento, CA
Red Rock Comprehensive Mental Health Center, Oklahoma City, OK
Rensselaer County Mental Health Department—Unified Services for Children and Adolescents, Troy, NY
Ridgeview Institute, Smyrna, GA
Rockland Psychological and Educational Center, Spring Valley, NY
Rusty's Morningstar Ranch, Cornville, AZ
St Cabrini Home Inc, West Park, NY
St Elizabeth's Hospital—Division of Child and Adolescent Services, Washington, DC
St Gabriel's Hall, Phoenixville, PA
St Joseph Center for Mental Health, Omaha, NE
St Louis County Child Mental Health Services, Saint Louis, MO
Samarkand Manor, Eagle Springs, NC
San Diego County Mental Health Services—Loma Portal Facility, San Diego, CA
San Marcos Treatment Center of The Brown Schools, San Marcos, TX
School for Contemporary Education, Springfield, VA
Secret Harbor School, Anacortes, WA
Shadow Mountain Institute, Tulsa, OK
Shawnee County Youth Center Services, Topeka, KS
South Bend Community School Corporation—Adolescent Day Treatment Center, South Bend, IN
South Dakota Human Services Center, Yankton, SD
South Oaks Hospital, Amityville, NY
South Shore Child Guidance Center, Freeport, NY
Southwood Psychiatric Residential Treatment Center—Hillcrest, San Diego, CA
Spaulding Youth Center—Emotional Handicap Program, Tilton, NH
Special Education Association of Adams County, Quincy, IL
Special Service School District of Bergen County, Paramus, NJ
Spring Lake Ranch, Cuttingsville, VT
Springfield Park Central Hospital—Park Central School, Springfield, MO
State Agriculture and Industrial School, Industry, NY
State Training School, Eldora, IA
Sunburst Youth Homes, Neillsville, WI
Taylor Manor Hospital, Ellicott City, MD
Timberlawn Psychiatric Hospital, Dallas, TX
Training Center for Youth, Columbus, OH
Tri-County Community Mental Health Center, Kansas City, MO

University Hospitals of Cleveland—Hanna Pavilion Child Psychiatric Unit, Cleveland, OH
University of Arkansas Medical Sciences Division Child Psychiatry—Child Study Center, Little Rock, AR
The University of Chicago—Departments of Psychiatry and Pediatrics—Child Psychiatry, Chicago, IL
University of Minnesota Hospitals—Child and Adolescent Psychiatry, Minneapolis, MN
University of Rochester Medical School—Child and Adolescent Psychiatry Clinic, Rochester, NY
University of Texas Medical Branch—Inpatient Service—Division of Child and Adolescent Psychiatry, Galveston, TX
University Park Psychological Center, Denver, CO
Utah Boys' Ranch—Children and Youth Services Inc, Salt Lake City, UT
Valleyhead Inc, Lenox, MA
Virginia Center for Psychiatry, Portsmouth, VA
Virginia Center for Psychiatry, Norfolk, VA
Vista Maria, Dearborn Heights, MI
Walter Reed Army Medical Center Child and Adolescent Psychiatry Service, Washington, DC
War Bonnet—Wilderness Pathways, Canaan, NH
West Hartford Public Schools Off-Campus Program, West Hartford, CT
Westbridge, Phoenix, AZ
Western District Guidance Center, Parkersburg, WV
West-Ros-Park Mental Health Center, Roslindale, MA
Wheeler Clinic Inc—Northwest Village School, Plainville, CT
Winnebago Mental Health Institute—Children's Unit, Winnebago, WI
Woodward Mental Health Center, Freeport, NY
Wyandotte Mental Health Center, Kansas City, KS
Wyoming State Hospital, Evanston, WY
Yellowstone Boys' and Girls' Ranch, Billings, MT
York Woods Center, Ypsilanti, MI
Youth Center of Beloit—North Beloit High, Beloit, KS

Personality Problems

Adams County Adolescent Day Treatment Program, Denver, CO
Ahwahnee Hills School, Ahwahnee, CA
Albuquerque Child Guidance Center, Albuquerque, NM
Alexander Children's Center, Charlotte, NC
All Children's Hospital, St Petersburg, FL
Allendale School, Lake Villa, IL
Almansor Education Center, Alhambra, CA
Andrus Children's Home, Yonkers, NY
Anne Arundel County Health Department Mental Health Clinic, Annapolis, MD
Anneewakee Hospital, Douglasville, GA
Archdiocese of Louisville—Guidance Clinic, Louisville, KY
Area Education Agency—Education Center, Waterloo, IA
Arizona Baptist Children's Services—Little Canyon Campus, Phoenix, AZ
Arizona Children's Home, Tucson, AZ
Arizona State Hospital, Phoenix, AZ
Arizona State Hospital—Nueva Vista School, Phoenix, AZ
Arlington School, Belmont, MA
Arnell Engstrom Children's Center, Traverse City, MI
Aseltine School, San Diego, CA
The Astor Home for Children—Day Treatment Program, Poughkeepsie, NY
The Astor Home for Children—Day Treatment Program, Bronx, NY
The Astor Home for Children—Group Home Program, Bronx, NY
The Astor Home for Children—Residential Treatment Center—Residential Treatment Facility—Learning Center, Rhinebeck, NY
Atlantic Mental Health Center Inc, McKee City, NJ
Augusta School Department, Augusta, ME
Aurora Adolescent Day Resource Center, Aurora, CO
Austin State Hospital, Austin, TX
Avalon Center—Avalon Schools, Lenox, MA

The Baird Center for Children and Families Inc, Burlington, VT
Baker Hall Inc, Lackawanna, NY
The Bancroft School, Haddonfield, NJ
Barat Human Services—Barat House, Detroit, MI
Bar-None Residential Treatment Services for Children, Anoka, MN
Battle Creek Child Guidance Center, Battle Creek, MI
Beacon Day Treatment Program, Romulus, MI
Berea Children's Home, Berea, OH
Bergen Center for Child Development, Haworth, NJ
Bergen Pines Hospital—Children's Psychiatric Unit, Paramus, NJ
Berks County Intermediate Unit, Reading, PA
Berkshire Farm Center and Services for Youth, Canaan, NY
Big Lakes Developmental Center Inc, Manhattan, KS
Big Spring State Hospital, Big Spring, TX
Birmingham City Board of Education, Birmingham, AL
Blick Clinic for Developmental Disabilities, Akron, OH
Board of Cooperative Educational Services II—Special Education Division Instructional Support Center, Centereach, NY
BOCES Nassau, Westbury, NY
BOCES Onondaga Madison, East Syracuse, NY
BOCES Southern Westchester—Rye Lake Campus, White Plains, NY
Boston Public Schools—The McKinley Schools, Mattapau, MA
Bowman Gray School of Medicine Developmental Evaluation Clinic—Amos Cottage Rehabilitation Hospital, Winston-Salem, NC
Boys' and Girls' Aid Society of San Diego—Cottonwood Center and Community Based Psychiatric Program, El Cajon, CA
Boys' Town of Missouri Inc, Saint James, MO
Boys' Village Inc—Boys' Village School, Smithville, OH
Bradley Hospital, East Providence, RI
Brant Services Corporation—Brant Ryan House, Inkster, MI
Brattleboro Retreat, Brattleboro, VT
Brea Neuropsychiatric Center, Brea, CA
Brentwood Center, Los Angeles, CA
Brewer-Porch Children's Center, University, AL
Bridgeport Tutoring Center—Counseling Center of Connecticut, Bridgeport, CT
Bridgeway Hospital Youthcare Program, North Little Rock, AR
Brighton School and Diagnostic Center, Phoenix, AZ
Brooklyn Community Counseling Center, Brooklyn, NY
Brown County Mental Health Center—Children Services, Green Bay, WI
The Brown Schools, Austin, TX
Buckeye Boys' Ranch Inc, Grove City, OH
Bucks County Intermediate Unit—Looking Glass School, Doylestown, PA
Butler County Mental Health Center Inc, Hamilton, OH
California Mental Health Center, Los Angeles, CA
Cantwell Academy Inc, Miami, FL
Capital City Schools, Topeka, KS
Capitol Region Education Council's Day Treatment Service, West Hartford, CT
Cass County Social Services—Children's Social Service Center, Fargo, ND
Cathedral Home for Children, Laramie, WY
Cayuga Home for Children, Auburn, NY
Cedu School, Running Springs, CA
Center for Life Management, Salem, NH
Chaddock, Quincy, IL
Chancellor Academy, Pompton Plains, NJ
The Charlton School, Burnt Hills, NY
Charter Westbrook Hospital, Richmond, VA
Chestnut Lodge Hospital—Adolescent and Child Division, Rockville, MD
Child Adolescent Service Center, Canton, OH
Child and Adolescent Psychiatric Clinic Inc, Buffalo, NY
Child and Adolescent Psychoeducational Center, Dalton, GA
Child and Family Services, Knoxville, TN
Child Development Center, New York, NY
Child Development Service—Lakeview Center Inc, Pensacola, FL
Child Disability Clinic—Carle Clinic, Urbana, IL

Child Guidance Center of Southern Connecticut, Stanford, CT
Child Guidance Clinic—Day Treatment Program, Winston-Salem, NC
Child Guidance Clinic of Southeastern Connecticut Inc, New London, CT
Child Psychiatry Service—Department of Psychiatry—University Hospitals, Ann Arbor, MI
Child Study and Treatment Center, Tacoma, WA
Child Study Center, Fort Worth, TX
Children's and Adolescent Unit of Mental Health Institute of Cherokee Iowa, Cherokee, IA
Children's Behavior Therapy Unit, Salt Lake City, UT
Children's Bureau of Indianapolis Inc, Indianapolis, IN
Children's Center, Hamden, CT
Children's Center for Behavioral Development, East Saint Louis, IL
Children's Day Hospital—New York Hospital—Cornell Medical Center—Westchester Division, White Plains, NY
The Children's Day School, Trenton, NJ
Children's Day Treatment Center, Honolulu, HI
The Children's Guild Inc, Baltimore, MD
Children's Health Council, Palo Alto, CA
Children's Home of Cedar Rapids—Cedarwood Group Home, Cedar Rapids, IA
Children's Home of Cedar Rapids—Heartwood Residential Treatment Center, Cedar Rapids, IA
Children's Home of Cedar Rapids—Maplewood Group Home, Cedar Rapids, IA
The Children's Home of Cincinnati, Cincinnati, OH
Children's Home of Kingston, Kingston, NY
Children's Home Society of South Dakota, Sioux Falls, SD
Children's Hospital at Washington University Medical Center—Psychiatric Unit, Saint Louis, MO
The Children's Institute, South Orange, NJ
Children's Medical Center, Tulsa, OK
Children's Medical Center—Psychiatric Inpatient Unit, Dallas, TX
Children's Mental Health Center Inc, Columbus, OH
The Children's Mercy Hospital—Section of Psychiatry, Kansas City, MO
Children's Psychiatric Center of the Jewish Hospital, Cincinnati, OH
The Children's School of the Institute of Living, Hartford, CT
The Children's Study Home, Springfield, MA
The Children's Village, Dobbs Ferry, NY
Christ Church Child Center, Bethesda, MD
Christian Church—Children's Campus, Danville, KY
Christian Haven Homes—Central Indiana Campus, Wheatfield, IN
Christie School, Marylhurst, OR
Clear View School, Scarborough, NY
The Clearing, Marshfield, VT
Clearwater Ranch Children's House Inc, Philo, CA
Cleveland Christian Home for Children Inc, Cleveland, OH
Cleveland Clinic Foundation, Cleveland, OH
Cleveland County Area Mental Health Program—Division of Child and Youth Services, Shelby, NC
The Clinical Center of Southern Illinois University, Carbondale, IL
Cobb County—Cobb Douglas Psychoeducation Children's Program, Marietta, GA
College Hospital—College Park School, Cerritos, CA
Colorado Springs School District No. 11, Colorado Springs, CO
Colorado West Regional Mental Health Center, Glenwood Springs, CO
Community Child Guidance Clinic Preschool, Manchester, CT
Community Counseling Center—Rural Clinics, Ely, NV
Community Mental Health Center South, Lee's Summit, MO
Community Psychiatric Clinic Inc, Wheaton; Bethesda; Gaithersburg, MD
The Community School of the Family Service and Child Guidance Center of the Oranges Maplewood and Millburn, Orange, NJ
Comprehensive Mental Health Center of St Clair County Inc, East Saint Louis, IL

Hunterdon Learning Center, Califon, NJ
Idaho Youth Ranch Inc, Rupert, ID
Indiana Girls' School, Indianapolis, IN
Indianapolis Public Schools—Special Education Department, Indianapolis, IN
Indianapolis Public Schools—James E Roberts School No. 97, Indianapolis, IN
Ingleside Hospital, Rosemead, CA
The Institute Day School, Lowell, MA
Institute for Family and Life Learning Residential School, Danvers, MA
Institute for Learning, Philadelphia, PA
The Institute of Living School, Hartford, CT
Institute of Psychiatry and Human Behavior—Department of Psychiatry—Child and Adolescent Inpatient Service, Baltimore, MD
Italian Home for Children, Jamaica Plain, MA
Ittleson Center for Child Research, New York, NY
Jackson County Intermediate School District, Jackson, MI
Jackson Municipal Separate School District, Jackson, MS
Jane Wayland Center, Phoenix, AZ
Jasper County Mental Health Center, Newton, IA
Jeanine Schultz Memorial School, Park Ridge, IL
Jefferson County Public Schools, Lakewood, CO
Jefferson Parish School System—Department of Special Education, Gretna, LA
Jennie Clarkson Child Care Services Inc—St Christopher's, Dobbs Ferry, NY
Jewish Board of Family and Children Services—Linden Hill School, Hawthorne, NY
Jewish Child Care Association—Pleasantville Cottage School, Pleasantville, NY
Jewish Child Care Association—Youth Residence Center, New York, NY
Jewish Children's Bureau of Chicago, Chicago, IL
John C Corrigan Mental Health Center, Fall River, MA
John G McGrath School, Napa, CA
John Umstead Hospital—Children's Psychiatric Institute, Butner, NC
Josephine County Mental Health Program—Children's Resource Team, Grants Pass, OR
Kalamazoo Child Guidance Clinic, Kalamazoo, MI
K-Bar-B Youth Ranch—Richard M Wise School, Lacombe, LA
Kenai Peninsula Borough School District, Soldotna, AK
Kimwood—Home for Autistic Opportunities Inc, Springfield, OH
Kings County Hospital—Downstate Medical Center—Division of Child and Adolescent Psychiatry, Brooklyn, NY
Klamath County Mental Health Center—Natural Family Preservation Project, Klamath Falls, OR
La Amistad Foundation, Winter Park, FL
La Mel, San Francisco, CA
La Puente Valley Community Mental Health Center, La Puente, CA
Lad Lake Inc, Dousman, WI
Lafayette Clinic, Detroit, MI
Lake County Mental Health Center—Department of Children's Services, Mentor, OH
Lake Grove School, Lake Grove, NY
Lakeshore Mental Health Institute—Riverbend School—Children and Youth Services, Knoxville, TN
Lakeside Center for Boys, Saint Louis, MO
Lakeside Child and Family Center Inc, Milwaukee, WI
Lakin Hospital—Adolescent Services, Lakin, WV
Lane School Programs—Lane Education Service District, Eugene, OR
LaSalle School, Albany, NY
Leary Educational Foundation—Timber Ridge, Winchester, VA
Leary School Inc, Alexandria, VA
Lighthouse School, Chelmsford, MA
Little Friends Inc—Little Friends Parent Infant Program, Naperville, IL
Little Friends Inc—Little Friends School, Naperville, IL
Little Friends Inc—The Therapeutic Workshop, Downers Grove, IL

Lookout Mountain School, Golden, CO
Lord Stirling School, Basking Ridge, NJ
The Los Angeles Child Guidance Clinic, Los Angeles, CA
Los Lunas Hospital and Training School—Behavioral Services Unit, Los Lunas, NM
Lourdesmont—Good Shepherd Youth and Family Services, Clarks Summit, PA
Lovellton Academy, Elgin, IL
Luther Child Center—Children's Hospitalization Alternative Program, Everett, WA
Lutheran Medical Center—Psychiatric Division, Saint Louis, MO
Lutherbrook Children's Center, Addison, IL
Madden Mental Health Center Campus—Institute for Juvenile Research—Inpatient Services, Hines, IL
Madeline Burg Counseling Services—Jewish Board of Family and Children Services, Bronx, NY
Main Street Human Resources, Great Barington, MA
Manhattan Children's Psychiatric Center, New York, NY
Manitowoc County Counseling Center, Manitowoc, WI
The Mansion, Naperville, IL
Martin Luther Centers, Madison, WI
The Mary and Alexander Laughlin Children's Center, Sewickley, PA
Marymount Hospital Mental Health Center, Garfield Heights, OH
Marymount Hospital Mental Health Center, Garfield Heights, OH
Maryvale, Rosemead, CA
Massanutten Mental Health Center, Harrisonburg, VA
McAuley Nazareth Home for Boys, Leicester, MA
McKinley Home for Boys, San Dimas, CA
McKinley Therapeutic Center, Chicago, IL
Mears House, Highland, IN
Medical University of South Carolina—Department of Psychiatry—Youth Division, Charleston, SC
Meharry Community Mental Health Center, Nashville, TN
Mendota Mental Health Institute—Child and Adolescent Program, Madison, WI
The Menninger Foundation—Pre-School Day Treatment Center, Topeka, KS
The Menninger Foundation—The Children's Division, Topeka, KS
Menorah Medical Center—Hearing and Speech Department, Kansas City, MO
Mental Health Care Center of the Lower Keys, Key West, FL
Mental Health Center of Boulder County—Adolescent Treatment Program, Boulder, CO
Mental Health Center of Mid-Iowa, Marshalltown, IA
Mental Health Centers of Central Illinois—Child and Adolescent Day Treatment Program, Springfield, IL
The Mental Health Institute for Children at Allentown State Hospital, Allentown, PA
Mental Health Services of North Central Hamilton Co Inc, Cincinnati, OH
Mercy Hospital and Medical Center—Community Guidance Center, Chicago, IL
Meridell Achievement Center Inc, Austin, TX
MHMR of Southeast Texas—Daybreak Cottage, Orange, TX
Michael Reese Hospital and Medical Center—Dysfunctioning Child Center, Chicago, IL
The Mid Fairfield Child Guidance Center Inc, Norwalk, CT
Mid-Columbia Mental Health Center—Adolescent Psychiatric Department, Richland, WA
Milford Assistance Program Day School, Milford, MA
The Millcreek Psychiatric Center for Children, Cincinnati, OH
Millcreek Schools Inc, Magee, MS
Monroe County Intermediate School District—Programs for Emotionally Impaired, Monroe, MI
Montrose School, Reisterstown, MD
Mt Airy Psychiatric Center—Children's Treatment Program—Adolescent Treatment Program, Denver, CO
Mt Scott Institute, Washington, NJ
Mountain Board of Cooperative Services—Adolescent Day Treatment Program, Leadville, CO

San Diego County Mental Health Services—Loma Portal Facility, San Diego, CA

San Diego Unified School District, San Diego, CA

San Marcos Treatment Center of The Brown Schools, San Marcos, TX

San Mateo County Office of Education, Redwood City, CA

School for Contemporary Education, Baltimore, MD

School for Contemporary Education, Springfield, VA

Secret Harbor School, Anacortes, WA

Seminole County Board of Public Instruction—Programs for Emotionally Handicapped, Sanford, FL

Serendipity Diagnostic and Treatment Center, Citrus Heights, CA

Shadow Mountain Institute, Tulsa, OK

Shawnee County Youth Center Services, Topeka, KS

Shawnee Mission Public Schools, Shawnee Mission, KS

Sheldon Community Guidance Clinic Inc, New Britain, CT

Sherwood Center for The Exceptional Child, Kansas City, MO

Sibley Hospital—Groome Center—Hayes Hall, Washington, DC

Solomon Mental Health Center, Lowell, MA

Sonia Shankman Orthogenic School of the University of Chicago, Chicago, IL

South Bend Community School Corporation—Adolescent Day Treatment Center, South Bend, IN

South Carolina State Hospital—Child and Adolescent Unit—Blanding House, Columbia, SC

South Dakota Human Services Center, Yankton, SD

South Metropolitan Association—Interventions Residential School, Matteson, IL

South Oaks Hospital, Amityville, NY

South Shore Child Guidance Center, Freeport, NY

Southbury Training School, Southbury, CT

Southeast Kansas Mental Health Center, Humboldt, KS

Southeast Mental Health Center—Child Development Institute, Memphis, TN

Southlake Center for Mental Health, Merriville, IN

Southwest Georgia Psychoeducational Services—Thomas County Schools, Ochlocknee, GA

Southwood Psychiatric Residential Treatment Center—Hillcrest, San Diego, CA

Spaulding Youth Center—Emotional Handicap Program, Tilton, NH

Special Care Program, Orofino, ID

Special Education Association of Adams County, Quincy, IL

Special Service School District of Bergen County, Paramus, NJ

Spectrum Center for Educational and Behavioral Development Inc, Berkeley, CA

Spence Chapin Services to Families and Children—The Children's House, New York, NY

The Spofford Home, Kansas City, MO

Spring Lake Ranch, Cuttingsville, VT

Springfield Park Central Hospital—Park Central School, Springfield, MO

Springfield Public School District No. 186, Springfield, IL

The Starr Commonwealth Schools, Albion, MI

Starr Commonwealth Schools—Hannah Neil Center for Children, Columbus, OH

State Agriculture and Industrial School, Industry, NY

State Training School, Eldora, IA

State University of New York at Albany—SUNY Pre-Kindergarten, Albany, NY

Stetson School Inc, Barre, MA

Strafford Guidance Center Inc, Dover, NH

Stuyvesant Residence Club, New York City, NY

Summit Children's Residence Center, Upper Nyack, NY

Sunburst Youth Homes, Neillsville, WI

Sunny Hill Children's Center Inc, Greenwich, CT

Sunset Learning Center, Fort Lauderdale, FL

Switzer Center, Torrance, CA

The Sycamores, Altadena, CA

Taylor Manor Hospital, Ellicott City, MD

Terry Children's Psychiatric Center, New Castle, DE

Timberlawn Psychiatric Hospital, Dallas, TX

Timberridge Institute for Children and Adolescents Inc, Oklahoma City, OK

Tomorrow's Children, Waupaca, WI

Towering Pines Center, Slidell, LA

Training Center for Youth, Columbus, OH

Tri City Community Mental Health and Retardation Center, Malden, MA

Tri-County Cooperative Center No. 946, Grand Rapids, MN

Tri-County Community Mental Health Center, Kansas City, MO

United Methodist Youthville, Newton, KS

University Hospitals of Cleveland—Hanna Pavilion Child Psychiatric Unit, Cleveland, OH

University of Arkansas Medical Sciences Division Child Psychiatry—Child Study Center, Little Rock, AR

The University of Chicago—Departments of Psychiatry and Pediatrics—Child Psychiatry, Chicago, IL

University of Colorado Health Sciences Center—Day Care Center, Denver, CO

University of Illinois Medical Center—Child Psychiatry Clinic, Chicago, IL

University of Minnesota Hospitals—Child and Adolescent Psychiatry, Minneapolis, MN

University of New Mexico Children's Psychiatric Hospital—Mimbres School, Albuquerque, NM

University of New Mexico—Children's Psychiatric Hospital, Albuquerque, NM

University of Rochester Medical School—Child and Adolescent Psychiatry Clinic, Rochester, NY

University of South Florida—Florida Mental Health Institute—Department of Child and Family Services, Tampa, FL

University of Tennessee—Child Development Center School, Memphis, TN

University of Texas Medical Branch—Division of Pediatric Psychology—Department of Pediatrics, Galveston, TX

University of Texas Medical Branch—Inpatient Service—Division of Child and Adolescent Psychiatry, Galveston, TX

University Park Psychological Center, Denver, CO

Utah Boys' Ranch—Children and Youth Services Inc, Salt Lake City, UT

Valley View School, North Brookfield, MA

Valleyhead Inc, Lenox, MA

Vanderbilt Medical Center—Division of Child and Adolescent Psychiatry, Nashville, TN

Variety Preschooler's Workshop, Syosset, NY

Ventura County Superintendent of Schools, Ventura, CA

Villa Esperanza, Pasadena, CA

Village of St Joseph, Atlanta, GA

Virginia Center for Psychiatry, Portsmouth, VA

Virginia Center for Psychiatry, Norfolk, VA

Vista Del Mar Child Care Service, Los Angeles, CA

Vista Maria, Dearborn Heights, MI

Vitam Center Inc—Vitam School, Norwalk, CT

Walker Home and School, Needham, MA

Wallace Village for Children, Broomfield, CO

Walter Reed Army Medical Center Child and Adolescent Psychiatry Service, Washington, DC

War Bonnet—Wilderness Pathways, Canaan, NH

Warm Springs Center, Boise, ID

Washington School District, Phoenix, AZ

Waterford Country School, Quaker Hill, CT

Waterloo Community Schools, Waterloo, IA

Waverly Children's Home, Portland, OR

West Central Community Services Center Inc, Willmar, MN

West Hartford Public Schools Off-Campus Program, West Hartford, CT

West Nassau Mental Health Center, Franklin Square, NY

West River Children's Center of the Children's Home Society of South Dakota, Rapid City, SD

West Texas Boys' Ranch, San Angelo, TX

Westbridge, Phoenix, AZ

Westchester Day Treatment Program, Hawthorne, NY

Western District Guidance Center, Parkersburg, WV

Western New York Children's Psychiatric Center, West Seneca, NY

West-Ros-Park Mental Health Center, Roslindale, MA

Wheeler Clinic Inc—Northwest Village School, Plainville, CT
Wichita Guidance Center, Wichita, KS
Wilder Children's Placement, Saint Paul, MN
Willowglen Academy Inc, Milwaukee, WI
Winnebago Mental Health Institute—Children's Unit, Winnebago, WI
Woodbourne Center, Baltimore, MD
Woodward Mental Health Center, Freeport, NY
Work Training Program Inc, Santa Barbara, CA
Wyalusing Academy, Prairie du Chien, WI
Wyandotte Mental Health Center, Kansas City, KS
Wyandotte Special Education Cooperative, Kansas City, KS
Wyoming Youth Treatment Center, Casper, WY
Yellowstone Boys' and Girls' Ranch, Billings, MT
York Woods Center, Ypsilanti, MI
Youth and Family Services, Omaha, NE
Youth Center of Beloit—North Beloit High, Beloit, KS
Youth Evaluation and Treatment Centers (YETC), Phoenix, AZ
Yuma School District One, Yuma, AZ
Yuma Union High School District, Yuma, AZ
Zonta Children's Center, San Jose, CA

Phobias

Adams County Adolescent Day Treatment Program, Denver, CO
Albany Area Mental Health and Mental Retardation Center, Albany, GA
Albuquerque Child Guidance Center, Albuquerque, NM
All Children's Hospital, St Petersburg, FL
Allendale School, Lake Villa, IL
Almansor Education Center, Alhambra, CA
Anne Arundel County Health Department Mental Health Clinic, Annapolis, MD
Archdiocese of Louisville—Guidance Clinic, Louisville, KY
Area Education Agency—Education Center, Waterloo, IA
Arizona Children's Home, Tucson, AZ
Arizona State Hospital, Phoenix, AZ
Arizona State Hospital—Nueva Vista School, Phoenix, AZ
Arlington School, Belmont, MA
Arnell Engstrom Children's Center, Traverse City, MI
Aseltine School, San Diego, CA
The Astor Home for Children—Day Treatment Program, Poughkeepsie, NY
The Astor Home for Children—Day Treatment Program, Bronx, NY
Atlantic Mental Health Center Inc, McKee City, NJ
Augusta School Department, Augusta, ME
Aurora Adolescent Day Resource Center, Aurora, CO
Austin State Hospital, Austin, TX
Avondale House, Houston, TX
The Baird Center for Children and Families Inc, Burlington, VT
Bar-None Residential Treatment Services for Children, Anoka, MN
The Battin Clinic, Houston, TX
Battle Creek Child Guidance Center, Battle Creek, MI
Beacon Day Treatment Program, Romulus, MI
Bergen Center for Child Development, Haworth, NJ
Bergen Pines Hospital—Children's Psychiatric Unit, Paramus, NJ
Berks County Intermediate Unit, Reading, PA
Berkshire Farm Center and Services for Youth, Canaan, NY
Birmingham City Board of Education, Birmingham, AL
Blick Clinic for Developmental Disabilities, Akron, OH
Board of Cooperative Educational Services II—Special Education Division Instructional Support Center, Centereach, NY
BOCES Nassau, Westbury, NY
Bowman Gray School of Medicine Developmental Evaluation Clinic—Amos Cottage Rehabilitation Hospital, Winston-Salem, NC
Boys' Village Inc—Boys' Village School, Smithville, OH
Bradley Hospital, East Providence, RI
Brattleboro Retreat, Brattleboro, VT
Brea Neuropsychiatric Center, Brea, CA
Brentwood Center, Los Angeles, CA
Brewer-Porch Children's Center, University, AL

Bridgeway Hospital Youthcare Program, North Little Rock, AR
Brighton School and Diagnostic Center, Phoenix, AZ
Brooklyn Community Counseling Center, Brooklyn, NY
Brown County Mental Health Center—Children Services, Green Bay, WI
Buckeye Boys' Ranch Inc, Grove City, OH
Butler County Mental Health Center Inc, Hamilton, OH
California Mental Health Center, Los Angeles, CA
Capital City Schools, Topeka, KS
Capitol Region Education Council's Day Treatment Service, West Hartford, CT
Cass County Social Services—Children's Social Service Center, Fargo, ND
Cathedral Home for Children, Laramie, WY
Center for Autistic Children, Philadelphia, PA
Center for Life Management, Salem, NH
Center for Urban Living, Saint Louis, MO
Central Massachusetts Special Education Collaborative—Quimby School, Worcester, MA
The Charlton School, Burnt Hills, NY
Charter Westbrook Hospital, Richmond, VA
Child and Adolescent Psychiatric Clinic Inc, Buffalo, NY
Child and Adolescent Psychoeducational Center, Dalton, GA
Child and Family Services, Knoxville, TN
Child Development Service—Lakeview Center Inc, Pensacola, FL
Child Disability Clinic—Carle Clinic, Urbana, IL
Child Guidance Center of Southern Connecticut, Stanford, CT
Child Guidance Clinic—Day Treatment Program, Winston-Salem, NC
Child Guidance Clinic of Southeastern Connecticut Inc, New London, CT
Child Psychiatry Service—Department of Psychiatry—University Hospitals, Ann Arbor, MI
Child Study and Treatment Center, Tacoma, WA
Child Study Center, Fort Worth, TX
Children's Aid Society, Cleveland, OH
Children's and Adolescent Unit of Mental Health Institute of Cherokee Iowa, Cherokee, IA
Children's Behavior Therapy Unit, Salt Lake City, UT
Children's Bureau of Indianapolis Inc, Indianapolis, IN
Children's Day Hospital—New York Hospital—Cornell Medical Center—Westchester Division, White Plains, NY
The Children's Day School, Trenton, NJ
Children's Day Treatment Center, Honolulu, HI
The Children's Guild Inc, Baltimore, MD
Children's Health Council, Palo Alto, CA
Children's Home of Cedar Rapids—Heartwood Residential Treatment Center, Cedar Rapids, IA
The Children's Home of Cincinnati, Cincinnati, OH
Children's Home of Kingston, Kingston, NY
Children's Home Society of South Dakota, Sioux Falls, SD
Children's Hospital at Washington University Medical Center—Psychiatric Unit, Saint Louis, MO
The Children's Institute, South Orange, NJ
Children's Medical Center, Tulsa, OK
Children's Medical Center—Psychiatric Inpatient Unit, Dallas, TX
Children's Mental Health Center Inc, Columbus, OH
The Children's Mercy Hospital—Section of Psychiatry, Kansas City, MO
Children's Psychiatric Center of the Jewish Hospital, Cincinnati, OH
The Children's School of the Institute of Living, Hartford, CT
The Children's Study Home, Springfield, MA
Cabinet for Human Resources—Children's Treatment Service, Louisville, KY
Christian Church—Children's Campus, Danville, KY
Christie School, Marylhurst, OR
The Clearing, Marshfield, VT
Clearwater Ranch Children's House Inc, Philo, CA
Cleveland Clinic Foundation, Cleveland, OH
Cleveland County Area Mental Health Program—Division of Child and Youth Services, Shelby, NC

The Clinical Center of Southern Illinois University, Carbondale, IL

Cobb County—Cobb Douglas Psychoeducation Children's Program, Marietta, GA

College Hospital—College Park School, Cerritos, CA

Colorado Springs School District No. 11, Colorado Springs, CO

Colorado West Regional Mental Health Center, Glenwood Springs, CO

Community Counseling Center—Rural Clinics, Ely, NV

Community Psychiatric Clinic Inc, Wheaton; Bethesda; Gaithersburg, MD

The Community School of the Family Service and Child Guidance Center of the Oranges Maplewood and Millburn, Orange, NJ

Comprehensive Mental Health Center of St Clair County Inc, East Saint Louis, IL

Connecticut College Program for Children with Special Needs, New London, CT

Connecticut Junior Republic—Litchfield District, Litchfield, CT

Convalescent Hospital for Children, Rochester, NY

Covenant Children's Home and Family Services, Princeton, IL

CPC Belmont Hills Hospital, Belmont, CA

Craig House—Technoma, Pittsburgh, PA

CRATER of Broward Inc—Retreat Ranch Facility—24 Hour Residential Treatment Center, Fort Lauderdale, FL

Creative Arts Rehabilitation Center Inc, New York, NY

Cumberland County Guidance Center Inc, Millville, NJ

Dakota House, Aberdeen, SD

De Neuville Heights School for Girls, Memphis, TN

DeJarnette Center, Staunton, VA

Delaware Guidance Services for Children and Youth Inc, Wilmington, DE

DePaul Hospital and Residential Treatment Center, New Orleans, LA

Des Moines Children's Home—Orchard Place, Des Moines, IA

Desert Hills, Tucson, AZ

DeSisto Schools Inc, West Stockbridge, MA

The Devereux Center in Arizona, Scottsdale, AZ

The Devereux Foundation, Devon, PA

The Devereux Foundation, Santa Barbara, CA

The Devereux Foundation—Texas Branch, Victoria, TX

Devereux in Georgia, Kennesaw, GA

The Devereux Schools at Rutland, Rutland, MA

Dominion Hospital—The Dominion School, Falls Church, VA

Donaldsonville Mental Health Center, Donaldsonville, LA

Douglas A Thom Clinic Inc, Boston, MA

East Alabama Mental Health Retardation Center, Opelika, AL

Eastern Shore Mental Health Center, Nassawadox, VA

Eau Claire Academy, Eau Claire, WI

Edgemont Hospital, Los Angeles, CA

Edgewood Children's Center, Saint Louis, MO

Edgewood Day Treatment—The Lucinda Weeks Center, San Francisco, CA

The Educational Clinic Inc, Columbus, OH

Educational Department of Institute of Pennsylvania Hospital—Mill Creek School, Philadelphia, PA

El Paso Guidance Center, El Paso, TX

Elizabeth Ives School, Hamden, CT

Elm Acres Youth Home Inc, Pittsburg, KS

Elmcrest Psychiatric Institute, Portland, CT

Emerson North, Cincinati, OH

Escalon Inc, Altadena, CA

Escambia District Schools, Pensacola, FL

Ettie Lee Homes Inc, Baldwin Park, CA

Excelsior Youth Center, Aurora, CO

Fairmount Children's Center, Syracuse, NY

Family Guidance Center, Reading, PA

Family Guidance Service—Ingham Community Mental Health Center, Lansing, MI

Five Acres Boys' and Girls' Aide Society, Altadena, CA

Flint Community Schools, Flint, MI

Forest Heights Lodge, Evergreen, CO

Forest Hospital, Des Plaines, IL

Fort Logan Mental Health Center, Denver, CO

Ft Wayne Children's Home—Crossroad, Fort Wayne, IN

Franklin Grand Isle Mental Health Services Inc, Saint Albans, VT

The Frost School, Rockville, MD

Gateway United Methodist Youth Center and Family Services, Williamsville, NY

Gerard of Minnesota Inc, Austin, MN

Gilfillan Center, Bemidji, MN

Gladman Memorial Hospital Adolescent Program, Oakland, CA

Glenholme School, Washington, CT

Glens Falls Hospital—Child and Family Services—Community Mental Health Center, Glens Falls, NY

The Goldstaub Residence, Houston, TX

Gould Farm, Monterey, MA

Grady Memorial Hospital—Division of Child and Adolescent Psychiatry, Atlanta, GA

The Gramon School, Livingston, NJ

Grant Center Hospital, Miami, FL

Graydon Manor, Leesburg, VA

Green Chimneys Children's Services Inc, Brewster, NY

Greenshire School, Cheshire, CT

Grove School, Madison, CT

Hall-Mercer Children's Center of the McLean Hospital, Belmont, MA

Hall-Brooke Foundation—Hall-Brooke Hospital—Hall-Brooke School, Westport, CT

Hamilton Children's Center, Hyattsville, MD

The Hannah More Center, Reisterstown, MD

Harbor Schools Inc, Newburyport, MA

Harbor View Mercy Hospital, Fort Smith, AR

Harford County Community Mental Health Center, Bel Air, MD

Hartgrove Hospital—Hartgrove Academy, Chicago, IL

Hathaway School of Hathaway Home for Children, Pacoima, CA

Hawaii State Department of Education—Special Needs Branch, Honolulu, HI

Hawaii State Hospital—Adolescent Unit, Kaneohe, HI

Hawthorn Center, Northville, MI

Hawthorne Children's Psychiatric Hospital, Saint Louis, MO

Henderson Mental Health Center, Fort Lauderdale, FL

Henrietta Weill Memorial Child Guidance Clinic, Bakersfield, CA

Henry Horner Children and Adolescent Center, Chicago, IL

High Plains Mental Health Center—Colby Office, Colby, KS

Highland Heights—St Francis Home for Children Inc, New Haven, CT

Highland Youth Services—The Highland School, Pittsburgh, PA

Hillside Children's Center, Rochester, NY

Hillside School Inc, Logan, UT

Homes Unlimited Inc, Bangor, ME

Homewood School—Highland Hospital, Asheville, NC

Humana Hospital Huntington Beach—Children's Behavioral Center, Huntington Beach, CA

Independence House of Avalon Inc, Sheffield, MA

Indianapolis Public Schools—Special Education Department, Indianapolis, IN

Ingleside Hospital, Rosemead, CA

Institute for Learning, Philadelphia, PA

The Institute of Living School, Hartford, CT

Institute of Psychiatry and Human Behavior—Department of Psychiatry—Child and Adolescent Inpatient Service, Baltimore, MD

Italian Home for Children, Jamaica Plain, MA

Ittleson Center for Child Research, New York, NY

Jane Wayland Center, Phoenix, AZ

Jasper County Mental Health Center, Newton, IA

Jeanine Schultz Memorial School, Park Ridge, IL

Jefferson County Public Schools, Lakewood, CO

Jefferson Parish School System—Department of Special Education, Gretna, LA

Jewish Child Care Association—Pleasantville Cottage School, Pleasantville, NY

Jewish Children's Bureau of Chicago, Chicago, IL

John C Corrigan Mental Health Center, Fall River, MA

The John F Kennedy Institute, Baltimore, MD

John Umstead Hospital—Children's Psychiatric Institute, Butner, NC

Queens Hospital Center Department of Psychiatry Child and Adolescent Clinic, Jamaica, NY

Ranch Hope Strang School, Alleway, NJ

Range Mental Health Center, Virginia, MN

Raritan Bay Mental Health Center, Perth Amboy, NJ

The Re-Ed West Center for Children Inc, Sacramento, CA

Red Rock Comprehensive Mental Health Center, Oklahoma City, OK

Region 16 Educational Service Center, Amarillo, TX

Rensselaer County Mental Health Department—Unified Services for Children and Adolescents, Troy, NY

Richmond County Board of Education—Sand Hills Psychoeducational Program, Augusta, GA

Ridgeview Institute, Smyrna, GA

Rochester Mental Health Center Inc—Day Treatment Unit Services—Children and Youth Division, Rochester, NY

Rockford School District No. 205, Rockford, IL

Rockland Children's Psychiatric Center, Orangeburg, NY

Rockland Psychological and Educational Center, Spring Valley, NY

Rutland Psychoeducational Services, Athens, GA

Sagamore Hills Children's Psychiatric Hospital, Northfield, OH

St Ann's Home Inc—Day Treatment and Special Education Program, Methuen, MA

St Ann's Home Inc—Residential Treatment and Special Education Program, Methuen, MA

St Clare's Hospital—Adult, Child and Family Services, Denville, NJ

St Cloud Children's Home, Saint Cloud, MN

St Elizabeth's Hospital—Division of Child and Adolescent Services, Washington, DC

St Francis Boys' Home—Camelot, Lake Placid, NY

St George Homes Inc, Berkeley, CA

St Joseph Center for Mental Health, Omaha, NE

St Joseph's Carondelet Child Center, Chicago, IL

St Louis County Child Mental Health Services, Saint Louis, MO

St Mary's Home for Boys, Beaverton, OR

St Vincent's Hospital and Medical Center of New York—Child and Adolescent Psychiatry Service, New York, NY

San Diego County Mental Health Services—Loma Portal Facility, San Diego, CA

San Diego Unified School District, San Diego, CA

San Joaquin County Office of Education—Special Education Programs, Stockton, CA

San Marcos Treatment Center of The Brown Schools, San Marcos, TX

San Mateo County Office of Education, Redwood City, CA

School for Contemporary Education, Baltimore, MD

Scottsdale Public School District, Phoenix, AZ

Secret Harbor School, Anacortes, WA

Seminole County Board of Public Instruction—Programs for Emotionally Handicapped, Sanford, FL

Serendipity Diagnostic and Treatment Center, Citrus Heights, CA

Shadow Mountain Institute, Tulsa, OK

Shawnee Mission Public Schools, Shawnee Mission, KS

Sheldon Community Guidance Clinic Inc, New Britain, CT

Sibley Hospital—Groome Center—Hayes Hall, Washington, DC

Solomon Mental Health Center, Lowell, MA

Sonia Shankman Orthogenic School of the University of Chicago, Chicago, IL

South Bend Community School Corporation—Adolescent Day Treatment Center, South Bend, IN

South Carolina State Hospital—Child and Adolescent Unit—Blanding House, Columbia, SC

South Metropolitan Association—Interventions Residential School, Matteson, IL

South Oaks Hospital, Amityville, NY

South Shore Child Guidance Center, Freeport, NY

Southbury Training School, Southbury, CT

Southeast Kansas Mental Health Center, Humboldt, KS

Southeast Mental Health Center—Child Development Institute, Memphis, TN

Southlake Center for Mental Health, Merriville, IN

Southwest Georgia Psychoeducational Services—Thomas County Schools, Ochlocknee, GA

Southwood Psychiatric Residential Treatment Center—Hillcrest, San Diego, CA

Spaulding Youth Center—Autistic Program, Tilton, NH

Spaulding Youth Center—Emotional Handicap Program, Tilton, NH

Special Education Association of Adams County, Quincy, IL

Special Service School District of Bergen County, Paramus, NJ

Spence Chapin Services to Families and Children—The Children's House, New York, NY

The Spofford Home, Kansas City, MO

Spring Lake Ranch, Cuttingsville, VT

Springfield Park Central Hospital—Park Central School, Springfield, MO

State University of New York at Albany—SUNY Pre-Kindergarten, Albany, NY

Stetson School Inc, Barre, MA

Strafford Guidance Center Inc, Dover, NH

Stuyvesant Residence Club, New York City, NY

Summit Children's Residence Center, Upper Nyack, NY

Sunburst Youth Homes, Neillsville, WI

Sunset Learning Center, Fort Lauderdale, FL

Switzer Center, Torrance, CA

The Sycamores, Altadena, CA

Taylor Manor Hospital, Ellicott City, MD

Terry Children's Psychiatric Center, New Castle, DE

Timberlawn Psychiatric Hospital, Dallas, TX

Timberridge Institute for Children and Adolescents Inc, Oklahoma City, OK

Tomorrow's Children, Waupaca, WI

Towering Pines Center, Slidell, LA

Training Center for Youth, Columbus, OH

Tri City Community Mental Health and Retardation Center, Malden, MA

Tri-County Community Mental Health Center, Kansas City, MO

University Hospitals of Cleveland—Hanna Pavilion Child Psychiatric Unit, Cleveland, OH

University of Arkansas Medical Sciences Division Child Psychiatry—Child Study Center, Little Rock, AR

The University of Chicago—Departments of Psychiatry and Pediatrics—Child Psychiatry, Chicago, IL

University of Colorado Health Sciences Center—Day Care Center, Denver, CO

University of Illinois Medical Center—Child Psychiatry Clinic, Chicago, IL

University of Minnesota Hospitals—Child and Adolescent Psychiatry, Minneapolis, MN

University of New Mexico Children's Psychiatric Hospital—Mimbres School, Albuquerque, NM

University of New Mexico—Children's Psychiatric Hospital, Albuquerque, NM

University of Rochester Medical School—Child and Adolescent Psychiatry Clinic, Rochester, NY

University of South Florida—Florida Mental Health Institute—Department of Child and Family Services, Tampa, FL

University of Texas Medical Branch—Division of Pediatric Psychology—Department of Pediatrics, Galveston, TX

University of Texas Medical Branch—Inpatient Service—Division of Child and Adolescent Psychiatry, Galveston, TX

University Park Psychological Center, Denver, CO

Vanderbilt Medical Center—Division of Child and Adolescent Psychiatry, Nashville, TN

Variety Preschooler's Workshop, Syosset, NY

Ventura County Superintendent of Schools, Ventura, CA

Virginia Center for Psychiatry, Portsmouth, VA

Virginia Center for Psychiatry, Norfolk, VA

Vista Del Mar Child Care Service, Los Angeles, CA

Vista Maria, Dearborn Heights, MI

Vitam Center Inc—Vitam School, Norwalk, CT

Walker Home and School, Needham, MA

Walter Reed Army Medical Center Child and Adolescent Psychiatry Service, Washington, DC

War Bonnet—Wilderness Pathways, Canaan, NH
Warm Springs Center, Boise, ID
Waterford Country School, Quaker Hill, CT
Waterloo Community Schools, Waterloo, IA
West Central Community Services Center Inc, Willmar, MN
West Hartford Public Schools Off-Campus Program, West Hartford, CT
West Nassau Mental Health Center, Franklin Square, NY
West River Children's Center of the Children's Home Society of South Dakota, Rapid City, SD
Westbridge, Phoenix, AZ
Westchester Day Treatment Program, Hawthorne, NY
Western District Guidance Center, Parkersburg, WV
Western New York Children's Psychiatric Center, West Seneca, NY
West-Ros-Park Mental Health Center, Roslindale, MA
Wheeler Clinic Inc—Northwest Village School, Plainville, CT
Wichita Guidance Center, Wichita, KS
Wilder Children's Placement, Saint Paul, MN
Willowglen Academy Inc, Milwaukee, WI
Winnebago Mental Health Institute—Children's Unit, Winnebago, WI
Woodbourne Center, Baltimore, MD
Woodward Mental Health Center, Freeport, NY
Work Training Program Inc, Santa Barbara, CA
Wyalusing Academy, Prairie du Chien, WI
Wyandotte Mental Health Center, Kansas City, KS
Wyandotte Special Education Cooperative, Kansas City, KS
Wyoming State Hospital, Evanston, WY
York Woods Center, Ypsilanti, MI
Youth and Family Services, Omaha, NE
Youth Center of Beloit—North Beloit High, Beloit, KS
Youth Evaluation and Treatment Centers (YETC), Phoenix, AZ

Schizophrenia

Albany Area Mental Health and Mental Retardation Center, Albany, GA
Alexander Children's Center, Charlotte, NC
All Children's Hospital, St Petersburg, FL
Allendale School, Lake Villa, IL
Almansor Education Center, Alhambra, CA
Anne Arundel County Health Department Mental Health Clinic, Annapolis, MD
Anneewakee Hospital, Douglasville, GA
Area Education Agency—Education Center, Waterloo, IA
Arizona State Hospital, Phoenix, AZ
Arizona State Hospital—Nueva Vista School, Phoenix, AZ
Arlington School, Belmont, MA
Arnell Engstrom Children's Center, Traverse City, MI
The Astor Home for Children—Day Treatment Program, Poughkeepsie, NY
The Astor Home for Children—Day Treatment Program, Bronx, NY
The Astor Home for Children—Residential Treatment Center—Residential Treatment Facility—Learning Center, Rhinebeck, NY
Atlantic Mental Health Center Inc, McKee City, NJ
Augusta School Department, Augusta, ME
Aurora Adolescent Day Resource Center, Aurora, CO
Austin State Hospital, Austin, TX
Avalon Center—Avalon Schools, Lenox, MA
Avalon School at High Point, Lenox, MA
The Baird Center for Children and Families Inc, Burlington, VT
Baker Hall Inc, Lackawanna, NY
The Bancroft School, Haddonfield, NJ
Bar-None Residential Treatment Services for Children, Anoka, MN
Battle Creek Child Guidance Center, Battle Creek, MI
Behavior Research Institute, Providence, RI
Benhaven, East Haven, CT
Berea Children's Home, Berea, OH
Bergen Center for Child Development, Haworth, NJ
Bergen County Special Services School District—Washington School Autistic Program, Paramus, NJ

Bergen Pines Hospital—Children's Psychiatric Unit, Paramus, NJ
Berks County Intermediate Unit, Reading, PA
Big Lakes Developmental Center Inc, Manhattan, KS
Big Spring State Hospital, Big Spring, TX
Birmingham City Board of Education, Birmingham, AL
Blick Clinic for Developmental Disabilities, Akron, OH
Board of Cooperative Educational Services II—Special Education Division Instructional Support Center, Centereach, NY
BOCES Nassau, Westbury, NY
Boston Public Schools—The McKinley Schools, Mattapau, MA
Boys' and Girls' Aid Society of San Diego—Cottonwood Center and Community Based Psychiatric Program, El Cajon, CA
Boys' Town of Missouri Inc, Saint James, MO
Bradley Hospital, East Providence, RI
Brattleboro Retreat, Brattleboro, VT
Brea Neuropsychiatric Center, Brea, CA
Brentwood Center, Los Angeles, CA
Brewer-Porch Children's Center, University, AL
Bridgeway Hospital Youthcare Program, North Little Rock, AR
Brighton School and Diagnostic Center, Phoenix, AZ
Brooklyn Community Counseling Center, Brooklyn, NY
Brown County Mental Health Center—Children Services, Green Bay, WI
The Brown Schools, Austin, TX
Butler County Mental Health Center Inc, Hamilton, OH
Capital City Schools, Topeka, KS
Capitol Region Education Council's Day Treatment Service, West Hartford, CT
Cass County Social Services—Children's Social Service Center, Fargo, ND
Center for Autistic Children, Philadelphia, PA
Central Massachusetts Special Education Collaborative—Quimby School, Worcester, MA
Charles Lea Center—Program for Children, Adolescents, and Young Adults with Autism, Spartanburg, SC
Charter Westbrook Hospital, Richmond, VA
Chestnut Lodge Hospital—Adolescent and Child Division, Rockville, MD
Child Adolescent Service Center, Canton, OH
Child and Adolescent Psychoeducational Center, Dalton, GA
Child Development Service—Lakeview Center Inc, Pensacola, FL
Child Disability Clinic—Carle Clinic, Urbana, IL
Child Guidance Center of Southern Connecticut, Stanford, CT
Child Guidance Clinic of Southeastern Connecticut Inc, New London, CT
Child Psychiatry Service—Department of Psychiatry—University Hospitals, Ann Arbor, MI
Child Study and Treatment Center, Tacoma, WA
Childhaven, Saint Louis, MO
Children's and Adolescent Unit of Mental Health Institute of Cherokee Iowa, Cherokee, IA
Children's Behavior Therapy Unit, Salt Lake City, UT
Children's Center for Behavioral Development, East Saint Louis, IL
Children's Day Hospital—New York Hospital—Cornell Medical Center—Westchester Division, White Plains, NY
The Children's Day School, Trenton, NJ
The Children's Guild Inc, Baltimore, MD
Children's Health Council, Palo Alto, CA
Children's Home Society of South Dakota, Sioux Falls, SD
Children's Hospital at Washington University Medical Center—Psychiatric Unit, Saint Louis, MO
The Children's Institute, South Orange, NJ
Children's Medical Center, Tulsa, OK
Children's Medical Center—Psychiatric Inpatient Unit, Dallas, TX
The Children's Mercy Hospital—Section of Psychiatry, Kansas City, MO
The Children's School of the Institute of Living, Hartford, CT
The Children's Study Home, Springfield, MA
Cabinet for Human Resources—Children's Treatment Service, Louisville, KY
The Children's Village, Dobbs Ferry, NY

Clear View School, Scarborough, NY
Clearwater Ranch Children's House Inc, Philo, CA
Cleveland Clinic Foundation, Cleveland, OH
Cleveland County Area Mental Health Program—Division of Child and Youth Services, Shelby, NC
The Clinical Center of Southern Illinois University, Carbondale, IL
Cobb County—Cobb Douglas Psychoeducation Children's Program, Marietta, GA
Colorado West Regional Mental Health Center, Glenwood Springs, CO
Community Child Guidance Clinic Preschool, Manchester, CT
Community Counseling Center—Rural Clinics, Ely, NV
Community Psychiatric Clinic Inc, Wheaton; Bethesda; Gaithersburg, MD
The Community School of the Family Service and Child Guidance Center of the Oranges Maplewood and Millburn, Orange, NJ
Comprehensive Mental Health Center of St Clair County Inc, East Saint Louis, IL
Connecticut College Program for Children with Special Needs, New London, CT
Convalescent Hospital for Children, Rochester, NY
Cooperative Educational Services Developmental Learning Center, Wilton, CT
Covenant Children's Home and Family Services, Princeton, IL
CPC Belmont Hills Hospital, Belmont, CA
Craig House—Technoma, Pittsburgh, PA
Creative Arts Rehabilitation Center Inc, New York, NY
Cumberland County Guidance Center Inc, Millville, NJ
Dakota House, Aberdeen, SD
Daniel Memorial Inc, Jacksonville, FL
DeJarnette Center, Staunton, VA
Delaware Guidance Services for Children and Youth Inc, Wilmington, DE
Department of Public Instruction, Dover, DE
DePaul Hospital and Residential Treatment Center, New Orleans, LA
Des Moines Children's Home—Orchard Place, Des Moines, IA
Desert Hills, Tucson, AZ
DeSisto Schools Inc, West Stockbridge, MA
The Devereux Center in Arizona, Scottsdale, AZ
The Devereux Foundation, Devon, PA
The Devereux Foundation, Santa Barbara, CA
The Devereux Foundation—Texas Branch, Victoria, TX
Devereux in Georgia, Kennesaw, GA
The Devereux Schools at Rutland, Rutland, MA
Dominion Hospital—The Dominion School, Falls Church, VA
Donaldsonville Mental Health Center, Donaldsonville, LA
East Alabama Mental Health Retardation Center, Opelika, AL
East Bay Activity Center, Oakland, CA
Eastern Area Residential Treatment Home (EARTH), Greenville, NC
Eastern Shore Mental Health Center, Nassawadox, VA
Edgemeade of Maryland, Upper Marlboro, MD
Edgewood Day Treatment—The Lucinda Weeks Center, San Francisco, CA
The Educational Clinic Inc, Columbus, OH
Educational Department of Institute of Pennsylvania Hospital—Mill Creek School, Philadelphia, PA
El Paso Guidance Center, El Paso, TX
Elmcrest Psychiatric Institute, Portland, CT
Emerson North, Cincinati, OH
Emma Pendleton Bradley Hospital Developmental Disabilities Program, East Providence, RI
The Episcopal Center for Children, Washington, DC
The Episcopal Church Home for Children—York Place, York, SC
Escalon Inc, Altadena, CA
Evansville Vanderburgh School Corporation, Evansville, IN
Fairmount Children's Center, Syracuse, NY
Family Guidance Center, Reading, PA
Family Guidance Service—Ingham Community Mental Health Center, Lansing, MI
Flint Community Schools, Flint, MI

Forest Heights Lodge, Evergreen, CO
Forest Hospital, Des Plaines, IL
Fort Logan Mental Health Center, Denver, CO
The Forum School, Waldwick, NJ
Franklin Grand Isle Mental Health Services Inc, Saint Albans, VT
Fred Finch Youth Center, Oakland, CA
Fremont Unified School District, Fremont, CA
The Frost School, Rockville, MD
Genesee Intermediate School District Center for Autism, Flint, MI
Gerard of Minnesota Inc, Austin, MN
Gladman Memorial Hospital Adolescent Program, Oakland, CA
Glens Falls Hospital—Child and Family Services—Community Mental Health Center, Glens Falls, NY
The Goldstaub Residence, Houston, TX
Gould Farm, Monterey, MA
Grady Memorial Hospital—Division of Child and Adolescent Psychiatry, Atlanta, GA
The Gramon School, Livingston, NJ
Grant Center Hospital, Miami, FL
Graydon Manor, Leesburg, VA
Green Chimneys Children's Services Inc, Brewster, NY
Greenshire School, Cheshire, CT
The Grove School, Lake Forest, IL
Hall-Mercer Children's Center of the McLean Hospital, Belmont, MA
Hall-Brooke Foundation—Hall-Brooke Hospital—Hall-Brooke School, Westport, CT
Hamilton Children's Center, Hyattsville, MD
The Hannah More Center, Reisterstown, MD
Harbor Schools Inc, Newburyport, MA
Harbor View Mercy Hospital, Fort Smith, AR
Harford County Community Mental Health Center, Bel Air, MD
Hartgrove Hospital—Hartgrove Academy, Chicago, IL
Hathaway School of Hathaway Home for Children, Pacoima, CA
Hawaii State Department of Education—Special Needs Branch, Honolulu, HI
Hawaii State Hospital—Adolescent Unit, Kaneohe, HI
Hawthorn Center, Northville, MI
Hawthorne Children's Psychiatric Hospital, Saint Louis, MO
Henderson Mental Health Center, Fort Lauderdale, FL
Henrietta Weill Memorial Child Guidance Clinic, Bakersfield, CA
Henry Horner Children and Adolescent Center, Chicago, IL
High Plains Mental Health Center—Colby Office, Colby, KS
High Point Adolescent School—Children's Psychiatric Center, Morganville, NJ
Highland Youth Services—The Highland School, Pittsburgh, PA
Hillside Children's Center, Rochester, NY
Hillside Inc, Atlanta, GA
Hillside School Inc, Logan, UT
Homes Unlimited Inc, Bangor, ME
Homewood School—Highland Hospital, Asheville, NC
Honolulu District—Special Education Center of Oahu (SECO), Honolulu, HI
Humana Hospital Huntington Beach—Children's Behavioral Center, Huntington Beach, CA
Illinois Center for Autism, Fairview Heights, IL
Independence House of Avalon Inc, Sheffield, MA
Ingleside Hospital, Rosemead, CA
The Institute of Living School, Hartford, CT
Ittleson Center for Child Research, New York, NY
Jane Wayland Center, Phoenix, AZ
Jasper County Mental Health Center, Newton, IA
Jeanine Schultz Memorial School, Park Ridge, IL
Jefferson County Public Schools, Lakewood, CO
Jefferson Parish School System—Department of Special Education, Gretna, LA
Jersey Shore Medical Center—Child Evaluation Center, Neptune, NJ
Jewish Board of Family and Children Services—Linden Hill School, Hawthorne, NY
Jewish Child Care Association—Pleasantville Cottage School, Pleasantville, NY

Jewish Child Care Association—Youth Residence Center, New York, NY

Jewish Children's Bureau of Chicago, Chicago, IL

John C Corrigan Mental Health Center, Fall River, MA

John G McGrath School, Napa, CA

John Umstead Hospital—Children's Psychiatric Institute, Butner, NC

Kalamazoo Child Guidance Clinic, Kalamazoo, MI

Kaplan Foundation, Orangevale, CA

Kenai Peninsula Borough School District, Soldotna, AK

Kings County Hospital—Downstate Medical Center—Division of Child and Adolescent Psychiatry, Brooklyn, NY

La Amistad Foundation, Winter Park, FL

La Mel, San Francisco, CA

La Puente Valley Community Mental Health Center, La Puente, CA

Lafayette Clinic, Detroit, MI

Lake County Mental Health Center—Department of Children's Services, Mentor, OH

Lake Grove School, Lake Grove, NY

Lakeshore Mental Health Institute—Riverbend School—Children and Youth Services, Knoxville, TN

Lakeside Child and Family Center Inc, Milwaukee, WI

Lakin Hospital—Adolescent Services, Lakin, WV

Lane School Programs—Lane Education Service District, Eugene, OR

League School of Boston Inc, Newtonville, MA

Lighthouse School, Chelmsford, MA

Little Friends Inc—Little Friends Parent Infant Program, Naperville, IL

Little Friends Inc—Little Friends School, Naperville, IL

Little Friends Inc—The Therapeutic Workshop, Downers Grove, IL

The Los Angeles Child Guidance Clinic, Los Angeles, CA

Los Angeles County Office of Education—Mark Twain School, Lawndale, CA

Los Lunas Hospital and Training School—Behavioral Services Unit, Los Lunas, NM

Los Ninos Education Center, San Diego, CA

Lovellton Academy, Elgin, IL

Luther Child Center—Children's Hospitalization Alternative Program, Everett, WA

Lutheran Medical Center—Psychiatric Division, Saint Louis, MO

Madden Mental Health Center Campus—Institute for Juvenile Research—Inpatient Services, Hines, IL

Madeline Burg Counseling Services—Jewish Board of Family and Children Services, Bronx, NY

Main Street Human Resources, Great Barington, MA

Manhattan Children's Psychiatric Center, New York, NY

Manitowoc County Counseling Center, Manitowoc, WI

Martin Luther Centers, Madison, WI

Maryhurst School, Louisville, KY

Marymount Hospital Mental Health Center, Garfield Heights, OH

Massanutten Mental Health Center, Harrisonburg, VA

Medical University of South Carolina—Department of Psychiatry—Youth Division, Charleston, SC

Meharry Community Mental Health Center, Nashville, TN

Mendota Mental Health Institute—Child and Adolescent Program, Madison, WI

The Menninger Foundation—Pre-School Day Treatment Center, Topeka, KS

The Menninger Foundation—The Children's Division, Topeka, KS

Menorah Medical Center—Hearing and Speech Department, Kansas City, MO

Mental Health Care Center of the Lower Keys, Key West, FL

Mental Health Center of Boulder County—Adolescent Treatment Program, Boulder, CO

Mental Health Center of Mid-Iowa, Marshalltown, IA

Mental Health Centers of Central Illinois—Child and Adolescent Day Treatment Program, Springfield, IL

The Mental Health Institute for Children at Allentown State Hospital, Allentown, PA

Mental Health Services of North Central Hamilton Co Inc, Cincinnati, OH

Mercy Hospital and Medical Center—Community Guidance Center, Chicago, IL

Meridell Achievement Center Inc, Austin, TX

Mid-Columbia Mental Health Center—Adolescent Psychiatric Department, Richland, WA

Milford Assistance Program Day School, Milford, MA

The Millcreek Psychiatric Center for Children, Cincinnati, OH

Millcreek Schools Inc, Magee, MS

Minnesota Learning Center, Brainerd, MN

Miramonte Mental Health Services Inc, Palo Alto, CA

Monroe County Intermediate School District—Programs for Emotionally Impaired, Monroe, MI

Montrose School, Reisterstown, MD

Mt Airy Psychiatric Center—Children's Treatment Program—Adolescent Treatment Program, Denver, CO

Mt Scott Institute, Washington, NJ

Mountain Board of Cooperative Services—Adolescent Day Treatment Program, Leadville, CO

Mystic Valley Mental Health Center, Lexington, MA

Nannahagur School Day Treatment Program—(JCCA), Pleasantville, NY

Napa State Hospital—Children's Program, Imola, CA

New England Home for Little Wanderers—Orchard Home, Watertown, MA

New England Medical Center—Bay Cove Day Center for Children Day Hospital, Boston, MA

New England Medical Center—Division of Child Psychiatry, Boston, MA

New Hope Guild, Brooklyn, NY

New Mexico Boys' School, Springer, NM

North Central Health Care Facilities, Wausau, WI

North Dakota State Mental Hospital—Child and Adolescent Unit, Jamestown, ND

North Metro Psychoeducational Program, Atlanta, GA

Northeast Colorado Board of Cooperative Educational Services, Haxton, CO

Northwest Florida Mental Health Center, Panama City, FL

Northwest Psychoeducational Program, Rome, GA

Northwood Children's Home, Duluth, MN

Norton Psychiatric Clinic—Norton Adolescent Treatment Program and Norton Academy, Louisville, KY

Ocean Institute—Adolescent Day School—Mental Health Clinic of Ocean County, Toms River, NJ

Oconee Area Psycho Educational Program, Milledgeville, GA

Oconomowoc Developmental Training Center Inc, Oconomowoc, WI

Office of Riverside County Superintendent of Schools, Riverside, CA

Ohel Children's Home and Family Services, Brooklyn, NY

Orlando Regional Medical Center—Mental Health Department—Children's Services, Orlando, FL

Otis R Bowen Center, Warsaw, IN

Our Lady of Providence Children's Center, West Springfield, MA

Pacific Children's Center, Oakland, CA

Paradise Valley School District No. 69—Therapeutic Educational Activities Milieu, Phoenix, AZ

Parkview Counseling Center Inc, Youngstown, OH

Parkwood Hospital, Atlanta, GA

Parry Center for Children, Portland, OR

Parsons Child and Family Center, Albany, NY

Parsons Child and Family Center—Neil Hellman School, Albany, NY

Partial Hospitalization Program Children's Service Center, Wilkes Barre, PA

Peace River Center for Personal Development Inc, Bartow, FL

Penn Foundation for Mental Health, Sellersville, PA

Penninsula Children's Center—Children and Youth Services, Palo Alto, CA

Philadelphia Child Guidance Clinic, Philadelphia, PA

Philadelphia Child Guidance Clinic—Child and Family Inpatient Service, Philadelphia, PA

Pikes Peak Board of Cooperative Services, Colorado Springs, CO

Pomona Mental Health Center—Child Development Center, Pomona, NY

Porter Starke Services Inc—Vale Park Psychiatric Hospital, Valparaiso, IN

Prescott Child Development Center, Prescott, AZ

Pressley Ridge School—Day School, Pittsburgh, PA

Pressley Ridge School—Pryde—Family Based Treatment, Pittsburgh, PA

Primary Children's Medical Center—Department of Child Psychiatry, Salt Lake City, UT

Project for Psychotic and Neurologically Impaired Children, Madison, WI

Psychiatric Clinic of the Charlotte Hungerford Hospital, Torrington, CT

Psychiatric Institute of Richmond—Educational Development Center, Richmond, VA

Psychiatric Services Inc, Haverhill, MA

Queen of Angels School—Villa Maria Treatment Center, Timonium, MD

Queens Hospital Center Department of Psychiatry Child and Adolescent Clinic, Jamaica, NY

Ranch Hope Strang School, Alleway, NJ

Range Mental Health Center, Virginia, MN

Raritan Bay Mental Health Center, Perth Amboy, NJ

The Re-Ed West Center for Children Inc, Sacramento, CA

Red Rock Comprehensive Mental Health Center, Oklahoma City, OK

Region 16 Educational Service Center, Amarillo, TX

The Rehabilitation Institute of Pittsburgh, Pittsburgh, PA

Rensselaer County Mental Health Department—Unified Services for Children and Adolescents, Troy, NY

Richmond County Board of Education—Sand Hills Psychoeducational Program, Augusta, GA

Ridgeview Institute, Smyrna, GA

Ridgeview Psychiatric Hospital and Center, Oak Ridge, TN

Rise East School, Pomona, NY

Rockford School District No. 205, Rockford, IL

Rockland Children's Psychiatric Center, Orangeburg, NY

Rusk State Hospital—Child and Adolescent Unit, Rusk, TX

Rutland Psychoeducational Services, Athens, GA

Sagamore Hills Children's Psychiatric Hospital, Northfield, OH

St Clare's Hospital—Adult, Child and Family Services, Denville, NJ

St Cloud Children's Home, Saint Cloud, MN

St Elizabeth's Hospital—Division of Child and Adolescent Services, Washington, DC

St George Homes Inc, Berkeley, CA

St Joseph Center for Mental Health, Omaha, NE

St Joseph's Carondelet Child Center, Chicago, IL

St Louis County Child Mental Health Services, Saint Louis, MO

St Vincent Children's Center, Columbus, OH

St Vincent's Hospital and Medical Center of New York—Child and Adolescent Psychiatry Service, New York, NY

Samarkand Manor, Eagle Springs, NC

San Diego County Mental Health Services—Loma Portal Facility, San Diego, CA

San Diego Unified School District, San Diego, CA

San Marcos Treatment Center of The Brown Schools, San Marcos, TX

School for Contemporary Education, Springfield, VA

SEARCH Day Program Inc, Ocean, NJ

Secret Harbor School, Anacortes, WA

Seminole County Board of Public Instruction—Programs for Emotionally Handicapped, Sanford, FL

Serendipity Diagnostic and Treatment Center, Citrus Heights, CA

Shadow Mountain Institute, Tulsa, OK

Shawnee Mission Public Schools, Shawnee Mission, KS

Sherwood Center for The Exceptional Child, Kansas City, MO

Sibley Hospital—Groome Center—Hayes Hall, Washington, DC

Solomon Mental Health Center, Lowell, MA

Sonia Shankman Orthogenic School of the University of Chicago, Chicago, IL

South Carolina State Hospital—Child and Adolescent Unit—Blanding House, Columbia, SC

South Dakota Human Services Center, Yankton, SD

South Metropolitan Association—Interventions Residential School, Matteson, IL

South Oaks Hospital, Amityville, NY

South Shore Child Guidance Center, Freeport, NY

Southbury Training School, Southbury, CT

Southeast Kansas Mental Health Center, Humboldt, KS

Southwest Georgia Psychoeducational Services—Thomas County Schools, Ochlocknee, GA

Southwood Psychiatric Residential Treatment Center—Hillcrest, San Diego, CA

Special Care Program, Orofino, ID

Special Education Association of Adams County, Quincy, IL

Special Service School District of Bergen County, Paramus, NJ

Spectrum Center for Educational and Behavioral Development Inc, Berkeley, CA

Spence Chapin Services to Families and Children—The Children's House, New York, NY

The Spofford Home, Kansas City, MO

Spring Lake Ranch, Cuttingsville, VT

Springfield Park Central Hospital—Park Central School, Springfield, MO

Strafford Guidance Center Inc, Dover, NH

Stuyvesant Residence Club, New York City, NY

Summit Children's Residence Center, Upper Nyack, NY

Sunny Hill Children's Center Inc, Greenwich, CT

Sunset Learning Center, Fort Lauderdale, FL

Switzer Center, Torrance, CA

Taylor Manor Hospital, Ellicott City, MD

Terry Children's Psychiatric Center, New Castle, DE

Therapeutic School and Preschool Community Mental Health Services, Belleville, NJ

Threshold Inc, Goldenrod, FL

Timberlawn Psychiatric Hospital, Dallas, TX

Tomorrow's Children, Waupaca, WI

Total Living Continuum, Camarillo, CA

Towering Pines Center, Slidell, LA

Tri City Community Mental Health and Retardation Center, Malden, MA

Tri-County Community Mental Health Center, Kansas City, MO

Tupelo Municipal Public Schools, Tupelo, MS

University Hospitals of Cleveland—Hanna Pavilion Child Psychiatric Unit, Cleveland, OH

University of Arkansas Medical Sciences Division Child Psychiatry—Child Study Center, Little Rock, AR

The University of Chicago—Departments of Psychiatry and Pediatrics—Child Psychiatry, Chicago, IL

University of Colorado Health Sciences Center—Day Care Center, Denver, CO

University of Illinois Medical Center—Child Psychiatry Clinic, Chicago, IL

University of Minnesota Hospitals—Child and Adolescent Psychiatry, Minneapolis, MN

University of New Mexico Children's Psychiatric Hospital—Mimbres School, Albuquerque, NM

University of New Mexico—Children's Psychiatric Hospital, Albuquerque, NM

University of Rochester Medical School—Child and Adolescent Psychiatry Clinic, Rochester, NY

University of South Florida—Florida Mental Health Institute—Department of Child and Family Services, Tampa, FL

University of Texas Medical Branch—Inpatient Service—Division of Child and Adolescent Psychiatry, Galveston, TX

Valleyhead Inc, Lenox, MA

Vanderbilt Medical Center—Division of Child and Adolescent Psychiatry, Nashville, TN

Variety Preschooler's Workshop, Syosset, NY

Ventura County Superintendent of Schools, Ventura, CA

Virginia Center for Psychiatry, Portsmouth, VA

Virginia Center for Psychiatry, Norfolk, VA

Wallace Village for Children, Broomfield, CO

Walter Reed Army Medical Center Child and Adolescent Psychiatry Service, Washington, DC

War Bonnet—Wilderness Pathways, Canaan, NH
Warm Springs Center, Boise, ID
Waterloo Community Schools, Waterloo, IA
West Central Community Services Center Inc, Willmar, MN
West Hartford Public Schools Off-Campus Program, West Hartford, CT
West Nassau Mental Health Center, Franklin Square, NY
West River Children's Center of the Children's Home Society of South Dakota, Rapid City, SD
Westbridge, Phoenix, AZ
Westchester Day Treatment Program, Hawthorne, NY
Western District Guidance Center, Parkersburg, WV
Western New York Children's Psychiatric Center, West Seneca, NY
West-Ros-Park Mental Health Center, Roslindale, MA
Wheeler Clinic Inc—Northwest Village School, Plainville, CT
Wichita Guidance Center, Wichita, KS
Wilder Children's Placement, Saint Paul, MN
Willowglen Academy Inc, Milwaukee, WI
Winnebago Mental Health Institute—Children's Unit, Winnebago, WI
Winston L Prouty Center, Brattleboro, VT
Woodward Mental Health Center, Freeport, NY
Work Training Program Inc, Santa Barbara, CA
Wyandotte Mental Health Center, Kansas City, KS
Wyandotte Special Education Cooperative, Kansas City, KS
Wyoming State Hospital, Evanston, WY
Yellowstone Boys' and Girls' Ranch, Billings, MT
York Woods Center, Ypsilanti, MI
Youth and Family Services, Omaha, NE
Youth Evaluation and Treatment Centers (YETC), Phoenix, AZ
Yuma Union High School District, Yuma, AZ
Zonta Children's Center, San Jose, CA

Socialized Aggressive Reaction

Adams County Adolescent Day Treatment Program, Denver, CO
Ahwahnee Hills School, Ahwahnee, CA
Alabama Youth Services—Chalkville Campus, Birmingham, AL
Albuquerque Child Guidance Center, Albuquerque, NM
Alexander Children's Center, Charlotte, NC
All Children's Hospital, St Petersburg, FL
Allendale School, Lake Villa, IL
Almansor Education Center, Alhambra, CA
Andrus Children's Home, Yonkers, NY
Anne Arundel County Health Department Mental Health Clinic, Annapolis, MD
Anneewakee Hospital, Douglasville, GA
Area Education Agency—Education Center, Waterloo, IA
Arizona Baptist Children's Services—Little Canyon Campus, Phoenix, AZ
Arizona Boys' Ranch, Boys Ranch, AZ
Arizona Children's Home, Tucson, AZ
Arizona State Hospital, Phoenix, AZ
Arizona State Hospital—Nueva Vista School, Phoenix, AZ
Arlington School, Belmont, MA
Arnell Engstrom Children's Center, Traverse City, MI
Aseltine School, San Diego, CA
The Astor Home for Children—Day Treatment Program, Poughkeepsie, NY
The Astor Home for Children—Day Treatment Program, Bronx, NY
The Astor Home for Children—Group Home Program, Bronx, NY
The Astor Home for Children—Residential Treatment Center—Residential Treatment Facility—Learning Center, Rhinebeck, NY
Atlantic Mental Health Center Inc, McKee City, NJ
Augusta School Department, Augusta, ME
Aurora Adolescent Day Resource Center, Aurora, CO
Austin State Hospital, Austin, TX
Avalon Center—Avalon Schools, Lenox, MA
Avondale House, Houston, TX
The Baird Center for Children and Families Inc, Burlington, VT
Baker Hall Inc, Lackawanna, NY

The Bancroft School, Haddonfield, NJ
Barat Human Services—Barat House, Detroit, MI
Bar-None Residential Treatment Services for Children, Anoka, MN
The Battin Clinic, Houston, TX
Battle Creek Child Guidance Center, Battle Creek, MI
Beacon Day Treatment Program, Romulus, MI
Behavior Research Institute, Providence, RI
Berea Children's Home, Berea, OH
Bergen Center for Child Development, Haworth, NJ
Bergen Pines Hospital—Children's Psychiatric Unit, Paramus, NJ
Berks County Intermediate Unit, Reading, PA
Berkshire Farm Center and Services for Youth, Canaan, NY
Big Lakes Developmental Center Inc, Manhattan, KS
Big Spring State Hospital, Big Spring, TX
Birmingham City Board of Education, Birmingham, AL
Blick Clinic for Developmental Disabilities, Akron, OH
Board of Cooperative Educational Services II—Special Education Division Instructional Support Center, Centereach, NY
BOCES Nassau, Westbury, NY
BOCES Onondaga Madison, East Syracuse, NY
Boston Public Schools—The McKinley Schools, Mattapau, MA
Bowman Gray School of Medicine Developmental Evaluation Clinic—Amos Cottage Rehabilitation Hospital, Winston-Salem, NC
Boys' and Girls' Aid Society of San Diego—Cottonwood Center and Community Based Psychiatric Program, El Cajon, CA
Boys' Town of Missouri Inc, Saint James, MO
Boys' Village Inc—Boys' Village School, Smithville, OH
Bradley Hospital, East Providence, RI
Brant Services Corporation—Brant Ryan House, Inkster, MI
Brattleboro Retreat, Brattleboro, VT
Brea Neuropsychiatric Center, Brea, CA
Brewer-Porch Children's Center, University, AL
Bridgeway Hospital Youthcare Program, North Little Rock, AR
Brighton School and Diagnostic Center, Phoenix, AZ
Brooklyn Community Counseling Center, Brooklyn, NY
Brown County Mental Health Center—Children Services, Green Bay, WI
The Brown Schools, Austin, TX
Buckeye Boys' Ranch Inc, Grove City, OH
Bucks County Intermediate Unit—Looking Glass School, Doylestown, PA
Burt Children's Center, San Francisco, CA
Butler County Mental Health Center Inc, Hamilton, OH
California Mental Health Center, Los Angeles, CA
Capital City Schools, Topeka, KS
Capitol Region Education Council's Day Treatment Service, West Hartford, CT
Cass County Social Services—Children's Social Service Center, Fargo, ND
Cayuga Home for Children, Auburn, NY
Cedu School, Running Springs, CA
Center for Life Management, Salem, NH
Center for Urban Living, Saint Louis, MO
Chancellor Academy, Pompton Plains, NJ
The Charlton School, Burnt Hills, NY
Charter Westbrook Hospital, Richmond, VA
Chestnut Lodge Hospital—Adolescent and Child Division, Rockville, MD
Child Adolescent Service Center, Canton, OH
Child and Adolescent Psychiatric Clinic Inc, Buffalo, NY
Child and Adolescent Psychoeducational Center, Dalton, GA
Child and Family Services, Knoxville, TN
Child Development Service—Lakeview Center Inc, Pensacola, FL
Child Disability Clinic—Carle Clinic, Urbana, IL
Child Guidance Center of Southern Connecticut, Stanford, CT
Child Guidance Clinic—Day Treatment Program, Winston-Salem, NC
Child Guidance Clinic of Southeastern Connecticut Inc, New London, CT
Child Psychiatry Service—Department of Psychiatry—University Hospitals, Ann Arbor, MI

Child Study and Treatment Center, Tacoma, WA
Child Study Center, Fort Worth, TX
Childhaven, Saint Louis, MO
Children's Aid Society, Cleveland, OH
Children's and Adolescent Unit of Mental Health Institute of Cherokee Iowa, Cherokee, IA
Children's Behavior Therapy Unit, Salt Lake City, UT
Children's Bureau of Indianapolis Inc, Indianapolis, IN
Children's Center, Hamden, CT
The Children's Center, Salt Lake City, UT
Children's Center for Behavioral Development, East Saint Louis, IL
Children's Day Hospital—New York Hospital—Cornell Medical Center—Westchester Division, White Plains, NY
The Children's Day School, Trenton, NJ
Children's Day Treatment Center, Honolulu, HI
The Children's Guild Inc, Baltimore, MD
Children's Health Council, Palo Alto, CA
Children's Home of Cedar Rapids—Cedarwood Group Home, Cedar Rapids, IA
Children's Home of Cedar Rapids—Heartwood Residential Treatment Center, Cedar Rapids, IA
Children's Home of Cedar Rapids—Maplewood Group Home, Cedar Rapids, IA
The Children's Home of Cincinnati, Cincinnati, OH
Children's Home of Kingston, Kingston, NY
Children's Home Society of South Dakota, Sioux Falls, SD
Children's Hospital at Washington University Medical Center—Psychiatric Unit, Saint Louis, MO
The Children's Institute, South Orange, NJ
Children's Medical Center, Tulsa, OK
Children's Medical Center—Psychiatric Inpatient Unit, Dallas, TX
Children's Mental Health Center Inc, Columbus, OH
The Children's Mercy Hospital—Section of Psychiatry, Kansas City, MO
Children's Psychiatric Center of the Jewish Hospital, Cincinnati, OH
The Children's School of the Institute of Living, Hartford, CT
The Children's Study Home, Springfield, MA
The Children's Village, Dobbs Ferry, NY
Christ Church Child Center, Bethesda, MD
Christian Church—Children's Campus, Danville, KY
Christian Haven Homes—Central Indiana Campus, Wheatfield, IN
Christie School, Marylhurst, OR
Clear View School, Scarborough, NY
The Clearing, Marshfield, VT
Clearwater Ranch Children's House Inc, Philo, CA
Cleveland Christian Home for Children Inc, Cleveland, OH
Cleveland Clinic Foundation, Cleveland, OH
Cleveland County Area Mental Health Program—Division of Child and Youth Services, Shelby, NC
The Clinical Center of Southern Illinois University, Carbondale, IL
Cobb County—Cobb Douglas Psychoeducation Children's Program, Marietta, GA
College Hospital—College Park School, Cerritos, CA
Colorado Springs School District No. 11, Colorado Springs, CO
Colorado West Regional Mental Health Center, Glenwood Springs, CO
Community Counseling Center—Rural Clinics, Ely, NV
Community Mental Health Center South, Lee's Summit, MO
Community Psychiatric Clinic Inc, Wheaton; Bethesda; Gaithersburg, MD
The Community School of the Family Service and Child Guidance Center of the Oranges Maplewood and Millburn, Orange, NJ
Comprehensive Mental Health Center of St Clair County Inc, East Saint Louis, IL
Concord, Yellow Spring, WV
Connecticut Junior Republic—Litchfield District, Litchfield, CT
Convalescent Hospital for Children, Rochester, NY
Cooperative Educational Services Developmental Learning Center, Wilton, CT

Covenant Children's Home and Family Services, Princeton, IL
CPC Belmont Hills Hospital, Belmont, CA
Craig House—Technoma, Pittsburgh, PA
CRATER of Broward Inc—Retreat Ranch Facility—24 Hour Residential Treatment Center, Fort Lauderdale, FL
Creative Arts Rehabilitation Center Inc, New York, NY
Creative Learning Systems Inc, Tucson, AZ
Crockett State School Independent School District, Crockett, TX
Cumberland County Guidance Center Inc, Millville, NJ
Dakota House, Aberdeen, SD
Daniel Memorial Inc, Jacksonville, FL
Darden Hill Ranch School, Driftwood, TX
De Neuville Heights School for Girls, Memphis, TN
DeJarnette Center, Staunton, VA
The Delacato and Doman Autistic Unit, Morton, PA
Delaware Guidance Services for Children and Youth Inc, Wilmington, DE
Department of Education—Windward Oahu District, Kaneohe, HI
DePaul Hospital and Residential Treatment Center, New Orleans, LA
Des Moines Children's Home—Orchard Place, Des Moines, IA
Desert Hills, Tucson, AZ
DeSisto Schools Inc, West Stockbridge, MA
The Devereux Center in Arizona, Scottsdale, AZ
The Devereux Foundation, Devon, PA
The Devereux Foundation, Santa Barbara, CA
The Devereux Foundation—Deerhaven, Chester, NJ
The Devereux Foundation—Texas Branch, Victoria, TX
Devereux in Georgia, Kennesaw, GA
The Devereux Schools at Rutland, Rutland, MA
Dominion Hospital—The Dominion School, Falls Church, VA
Donaldsonville Mental Health Center, Donaldsonville, LA
Douglas A Thom Clinic Inc, Boston, MA
Early Childhood Developmental Center Inc, Hays, KS
East Alabama Mental Health Retardation Center, Opelika, AL
East St Louis Area Joint Agreement—Department of Special Education, East Saint Louis, IL
Eastern Area Residential Treatment Home (EARTH), Greenville, NC
Eastern Shore Mental Health Center, Nassawadox, VA
Eau Claire Academy, Eau Claire, WI
The Eckerd Wilderness Educational System Camping System, Clearwater, FL
Edgefield Children's Center, Troutdale, OR
Edgemont Hospital, Los Angeles, CA
Edgewood Children's Center, Saint Louis, MO
Edgewood Children's Center, San Francisco, CA
Edgewood Day Treatment—The Lucinda Weeks Center, San Francisco, CA
Educational Alliance—Camp Cummings, New York, NY
The Educational Clinic Inc, Columbus, OH
Educational Department of Institute of Pennsylvania Hospital—Mill Creek School, Philadelphia, PA
El Paso Guidance Center, El Paso, TX
Elm Acres Youth Home Inc, Pittsburg, KS
Elmcrest Children's Center, Syracuse, NY
Elmcrest Psychiatric Institute, Portland, CT
Elwyn Institutes, Elwyn, PA
Emerson North, Cincinati, OH
The Episcopal Center for Children, Washington, DC
The Episcopal Church Home for Children—York Place, York, SC
Epworth Village Inc, York, NE
Escalon Inc, Altadena, CA
Escambia District Schools, Pensacola, FL
Ettie Lee Homes Inc, Baldwin Park, CA
Evansville Vanderburgh School Corporation, Evansville, IN
Excelsior Youth Center, Aurora, CO
Fairmount Children's Center, Syracuse, NY
Family and Children's Center, LaCrosse, WI
Family Guidance Center, Reading, PA
Family Guidance Service—Ingham Community Mental Health Center, Lansing, MI
Five Acres Boys' and Girls' Aide Society, Altadena, CA

Flint Community Schools, Flint, MI
Forest Heights Lodge, Evergreen, CO
Forest Hospital, Des Plaines, IL
Fort Logan Mental Health Center, Denver, CO
Ft Wayne Children's Home—Crossroad, Fort Wayne, IN
The Forum School, Waldwick, NJ
Four Winds Hospital—Adolescent Services, Katonah, NY
Franklin Grand Isle Mental Health Services Inc, Saint Albans, VT
Fred Finch Youth Center, Oakland, CA
The Frost School, Rockville, MD
Garfield Girls' School, Phoenix, AZ
Gerard of Minnesota Inc, Austin, MN
Gilfillan Center, Bemidji, MN
Gladman Memorial Hospital Adolescent Program, Oakland, CA
Glenholme School, Washington, CT
Glens Falls Hospital—Child and Family Services—Community Mental Health Center, Glens Falls, NY
The Goldstaub Residence, Houston, TX
Gould Farm, Monterey, MA
Grady Memorial Hospital—Division of Child and Adolescent Psychiatry, Atlanta, GA
The Gramon School, Livingston, NJ
Grant Center Hospital, Miami, FL
Graydon Manor, Leesburg, VA
Green Chimneys Children's Services Inc, Brewster, NY
Green Tree School, Philadelphia, PA
Greenshire School, Cheshire, CT
Grove School, Madison, CT
Hall-Mercer Children's Center of the McLean Hospital, Belmont, MA
Hall-Brooke Foundation—Hall-Brooke Hospital—Hall-Brooke School, Westport, CT
Hamilton Children's Center, Hyattsville, MD
The Hannah More Center, Reisterstown, MD
Harbor Schools Inc, Newburyport, MA
Harbor View Mercy Hospital, Fort Smith, AR
Harford County Community Mental Health Center, Bel Air, MD
Hartgrove Hospital—Hartgrove Academy, Chicago, IL
Hathaway School of Hathaway Home for Children, Pacoima, CA
Hawaii State Department of Education—Special Needs Branch, Honolulu, HI
Hawaii State Hospital—Adolescent Unit, Kaneohe, HI
Hawthorn Center, Northville, MI
Hawthorne Cedar Knolls School, Hawthorne, NY
Hawthorne Children's Psychiatric Hospital, Saint Louis, MO
Henderson Mental Health Center, Fort Lauderdale, FL
Henrietta Weill Memorial Child Guidance Clinic, Bakersfield, CA
Henry Horner Children and Adolescent Center, Chicago, IL
High Plains Mental Health Center—Colby Office, Colby, KS
High Point Adolescent School—Children's Psychiatric Center, Morganville, NJ
Highland Heights—St Francis Home for Children Inc, New Haven, CT
Highland Youth Services—The Highland School, Pittsburgh, PA
Hillside Children's Center, Rochester, NY
Hillside Inc, Atlanta, GA
Hillside School Inc, Logan, UT
Homewood School—Highland Hospital, Asheville, NC
Honolulu District—Special Education Center of Oahu (SECO), Honolulu, HI
Humana Hospital Huntington Beach—Children's Behavioral Center, Huntington Beach, CA
Hunterdon Learning Center, Califon, NJ
Idaho Youth Ranch Inc, Rupert, ID
Indiana Girls' School, Indianapolis, IN
Ingleside Hospital, Rosemead, CA
The Institute Day School, Lowell, MA
Institute for Family and Life Learning Residential School, Danvers, MA
Institute for Learning, Philadelphia, PA
The Institute of Living School, Hartford, CT

Institute of Psychiatry and Human Behavior—Department of Psychiatry—Child and Adolescent Inpatient Service, Baltimore, MD
ISIS Programs Inc—Individual Support Through Innovative Services for Autistic Persons, Orlando, FL
Jackson Municipal Separate School District, Jackson, MS
Jane Wayland Center, Phoenix, AZ
Jasper County Mental Health Center, Newton, IA
Jeanine Schultz Memorial School, Park Ridge, IL
Jefferson County Public Schools, Lakewood, CO
Jefferson Parish School System—Department of Special Education, Gretna, LA
Jennie Clarkson Child Care Services Inc—St Christopher's, Dobbs Ferry, NY
Jewish Child Care Association—Pleasantville Cottage School, Pleasantville, NY
Jewish Child Care Association—Youth Residence Center, New York, NY
Jewish Children's Bureau of Chicago, Chicago, IL
John C Corrigan Mental Health Center, Fall River, MA
The John F Kennedy Institute, Baltimore, MD
John G McGrath School, Napa, CA
John Umstead Hospital—Children's Psychiatric Institute, Butner, NC
Josephine County Mental Health Program—Children's Resource Team, Grants Pass, OR
Kalamazoo Child Guidance Clinic, Kalamazoo, MI
K-Bar-B Youth Ranch—Richard M Wise School, Lacombe, LA
Kenai Peninsula Borough School District, Soldotna, AK
Kings County Hospital—Downstate Medical Center—Division of Child and Adolescent Psychiatry, Brooklyn, NY
Klamath County Mental Health Center—Natural Family Preservation Project, Klamath Falls, OR
La Mel, San Francisco, CA
La Puente Valley Community Mental Health Center, La Puente, CA
Lad Lake Inc, Dousman, WI
Lafayette Clinic, Detroit, MI
Lake County Mental Health Center—Department of Children's Services, Mentor, OH
Lake Grove School, Lake Grove, NY
Lakeshore Mental Health Institute—Riverbend School—Children and Youth Services, Knoxville, TN
Lakeside Center for Boys, Saint Louis, MO
Lakin Hospital—Adolescent Services, Lakin, WV
Lane School Programs—Lane Education Service District, Eugene, OR
Lansing School District, Lansing, MI
Larned State Hospital—Child Psychiatric Unit—Adolescent Psychiatric Unit/Westside School, Larned, KS
LaSalle School, Albany, NY
Leary Educational Foundation—Timber Ridge, Winchester, VA
Leary School Inc, Alexandria, VA
Lighthouse School, Chelmsford, MA
Little Friends Inc—Little Friends School, Naperville, IL
Lord Stirling School, Basking Ridge, NJ
The Los Angeles Child Guidance Clinic, Los Angeles, CA
Los Lunas Hospital and Training School—Behavioral Services Unit, Los Lunas, NM
Lourdesmont—Good Shepherd Youth and Family Services, Clarks Summit, PA
Lovellton Academy, Elgin, IL
Luther Child Center—Children's Hospitalization Alternative Program, Everett, WA
Lutheran Medical Center—Psychiatric Division, Saint Louis, MO
Madden Mental Health Center Campus—Institute for Juvenile Research—Inpatient Services, Hines, IL
Madeline Burg Counseling Services—Jewish Board of Family and Children Services, Bronx, NY
Main Street Human Resources, Great Barington, MA
Manhattan Children's Psychiatric Center, New York, NY
Manitowoc County Counseling Center, Manitowoc, WI
The Mansion, Naperville, IL
Martin Luther Centers, Madison, WI

The Mary and Alexander Laughlin Children's Center, Sewickley, PA

Marymount Hospital Mental Health Center, Garfield Heights, OH

Marymount Hospital Mental Health Center, Garfield Heights, OH

Maryvale, Rosemead, CA

Massanutten Mental Health Center, Harrisonburg, VA

McAuley Nazareth Home for Boys, Leicester, MA

McKinley Therapeutic Center, Chicago, IL

Mears House, Highland, IN

Medical Care Rehabilitation Hospital's Child Evaluation and Treatment Program, Grand Forks, ND

Medical University of South Carolina—Department of Psychiatry—Youth Division, Charleston, SC

Meharry Community Mental Health Center, Nashville, TN

Mendota Mental Health Institute—Child and Adolescent Program, Madison, WI

The Menninger Foundation—Pre-School Day Treatment Center, Topeka, KS

The Menninger Foundation—The Children's Division, Topeka, KS

Menorah Medical Center—Hearing and Speech Department, Kansas City, MO

Mental Health Care Center of the Lower Keys, Key West, FL

Mental Health Center of Boulder County—Adolescent Treatment Program, Boulder, CO

Mental Health Center of Mid-Iowa, Marshalltown, IA

Mental Health Centers of Central Illinois—Child and Adolescent Day Treatment Program, Springfield, IL

The Mental Health Institute for Children at Allentown State Hospital, Allentown, PA

Mental Health Services of North Central Hamilton Co Inc, Cincinnati, OH

Mercy Hospital and Medical Center—Community Guidance Center, Chicago, IL

Meridell Achievement Center Inc, Austin, TX

MHMR of Southeast Texas—Daybreak Cottage, Orange, TX

Michael Reese Hospital and Medical Center—Dysfunctioning Child Center, Chicago, IL

The Mid Fairfield Child Guidance Center Inc, Norwalk, CT

Mid-Columbia Mental Health Center—Adolescent Psychiatric Department, Richland, WA

Milford Assistance Program Day School, Milford, MA

The Millcreek Psychiatric Center for Children, Cincinnati, OH

Millcreek Schools Inc, Magee, MS

Minnesota Learning Center, Brainerd, MN

Monroe County Intermediate School District—Programs for Emotionally Impaired, Monroe, MI

Montrose School, Reisterstown, MD

Mt Airy Psychiatric Center—Children's Treatment Program—Adolescent Treatment Program, Denver, CO

Mt Scott Institute, Washington, NJ

Mountain Board of Cooperative Services—Adolescent Day Treatment Program, Leadville, CO

Multidisciplinary Institute for Neuropsychological Development Inc—MIND, Cambridge, MA

Mystic Valley Mental Health Center, Lexington, MA

Nannahagur School Day Treatment Program—(JCCA), Pleasantville, NY

Napa State Hospital—Children's Program, Imola, CA

National Foundation for the Treatment of the Emotionally Handicapped, Sepulveda, CA

New England Home for Little Wanderers—Orchard Home, Watertown, MA

New England Home for Little Wanderers—Knight Children's Center, Boston, MA

New England Medical Center—Bay Cove Day Center for Children Day Hospital, Boston, MA

New England Medical Center—Division of Child Psychiatry, Boston, MA

New England Salem Children's Trust, Rumney, NH

New Hope Guild, Brooklyn, NY

New Jersey Training School for Boys, Jamesburg, NJ

New Mexico Boys' School, Springer, NM

North Central Health Care Facilities, Wausau, WI

North Dakota State Mental Hospital—Child and Adolescent Unit, Jamestown, ND

North Metro Psychoeducational Program, Atlanta, GA

Northeast Colorado Board of Cooperative Educational Services, Haxton, CO

Northwest Florida Mental Health Center, Panama City, FL

Northwest Psychoeducational Program, Rome, GA

Northwood Children's Home, Duluth, MN

Norton Psychiatric Clinic—Norton Adolescent Treatment Program and Norton Academy, Louisville, KY

Oconee Area Psycho Educational Program, Milledgeville, GA

Oconomowoc Developmental Training Center Inc, Oconomowoc, WI

Office of Riverside County Superintendent of Schools, Riverside, CA

Ohel Children's Home and Family Services, Brooklyn, NY

Orlando Regional Medical Center—Mental Health Department—Children's Services, Orlando, FL

Osterlen Services for Youth, Springfield, OH

Otis R Bowen Center, Warsaw, IN

Our Lady of Providence Children's Center, West Springfield, MA

Overlook Mental Health Center—Blount County Adolescent Partial Hospitalization Program, Maryville, TN

Pace School, Braintree, MA

Pace School, Pittsburgh, PA

Pacific Children's Center, Oakland, CA

Paradise Valley School District No. 69—Therapeutic Educational Activities Milieu, Phoenix, AZ

Parkview Counseling Center Inc, Youngstown, OH

Parkwood Hospital, Atlanta, GA

Parmadale—The Youth Services Village, Parma, OH

Parry Center for Children, Portland, OR

Parsons Child and Family Center, Albany, NY

Parsons Child and Family Center—Neil Hellman School, Albany, NY

Partial Hospitalization Program Children's Service Center, Wilkes Barre, PA

Pawnee Mental Health Services, Concordia, KS

Peace River Center for Personal Development Inc, Bartow, FL

Peanut Butter and Jelly Therapeutic Pre-School, Albuquerque, NM

Penn Foundation for Mental Health, Sellersville, PA

Penninsula Children's Center—Children and Youth Services, Palo Alto, CA

Philadelphia Child Guidance Clinic, Philadelphia, PA

Philadelphia Child Guidance Clinic—Child and Family Inpatient Service, Philadelphia, PA

Philbrook Center—Special Education Program, Concord, NH

Phoenix Union High School District No. 210, Phoenix, AZ

Pikes Peak Board of Cooperative Services, Colorado Springs, CO

Pine Haven Boys' Center, Suncook, NH

Pomona Mental Health Center—Child Development Center, Pomona, NY

Porter Starke Services Inc—Vale Park Psychiatric Hospital, Valparaiso, IN

Prehab of Arizona Inc—Dorothy Mitchell Residence—Homestead Residence—Helaman House, Mesa, AZ

Prescott Child Development Center, Prescott, AZ

Pressley Ridge School—Day School, Pittsburgh, PA

Pressley Ridge School—Laurel Park, Clarksburg, WV

Pressley Ridge School—Pryde—Family Based Treatment, Pittsburgh, PA

Pressley Ridge School—Wilderness School, Ohiopyle, PA

Primary Children's Medical Center—Department of Child Psychiatry, Salt Lake City, UT

Protestant Youth Center, Baldwinville, MA

Provo Canyon School, Provo, UT

Psychiatric Clinic of the Charlotte Hungerford Hospital, Torrington, CT

Psychiatric Services Inc, Haverhill, MA

Queen of Angels School—Villa Maria Treatment Center, Timonium, MD

Queens Hospital Center Department of Psychiatry Child and Adolescent Clinic, Jamaica, NY
Raineswood Residential Center, Memphis, TN
Ranch Hope Strang School, Alleway, NJ
Range Mental Health Center, Virginia, MN
Raritan Bay Mental Health Center, Perth Amboy, NJ
The Re-Ed West Center for Children Inc, Sacramento, CA
Red Rock Comprehensive Mental Health Center, Oklahoma City, OK
Region 16 Educational Service Center, Amarillo, TX
The Rehabilitation Institute of Pittsburgh, Pittsburgh, PA
Rensselaer County Mental Health Department—Unified Services for Children and Adolescents, Troy, NY
Ridgeview Institute, Smyrna, GA
Ridgeview Psychiatric Hospital and Center, Oak Ridge, TN
River Street School, Hyde Park, MA
Rochester Mental Health Center Inc—Day Treatment Unit Services—Children and Youth Division, Rochester, NY
Rockford School District No. 205, Rockford, IL
Rockland Children's Psychiatric Center, Orangeburg, NY
Rockland Psychological and Educational Center, Spring Valley, NY
Rutland Psychoeducational Services, Athens, GA
Sacramento Children's Home—Helen E Cowell Children's Center, Sacramento, CA
Sagamore Hills Children's Psychiatric Hospital, Northfield, OH
St Ann's Home Inc—Day Treatment and Special Education Program, Methuen, MA
St Ann's Home Inc—Residential Treatment and Special Education Program, Methuen, MA
St Cabrini Home Inc, West Park, NY
St Clare's Hospital—Adult, Child and Family Services, Denville, NJ
St Cloud Children's Home, Saint Cloud, MN
St Elizabeth's Hospital—Division of Child and Adolescent Services, Washington, DC
The St Francis Boys' Homes Inc, Salina, KS
St Francis Boys' Home—Camelot, Lake Placid, NY
St Gabriel's Hall, Phoenixville, PA
St John's Child Development Center, Washington, DC
St Joseph Center for Mental Health, Omaha, NE
St Joseph Residential Treatment and Child Care Center, Dayton, OH
St Joseph's Carondelet Child Center, Chicago, IL
St Joseph's Children's Home, Torrington, WY
St Louis County Child Mental Health Services, Saint Louis, MO
St Mary's Home for Boys, Beaverton, OR
St Vincent Children's Center, Columbus, OH
St Vincent's Hospital and Medical Center of New York—Child and Adolescent Psychiatry Service, New York, NY
The Salvation Army Residential Treatment Facilities for Children and Youth, Honolulu, HI
Samarkand Manor, Eagle Springs, NC
San Diego County Mental Health Services—Loma Portal Facility, San Diego, CA
San Diego Unified School District, San Diego, CA
San Joaquin County Office of Education—Special Education Programs, Stockton, CA
San Marcos Treatment Center of The Brown Schools, San Marcos, TX
San Mateo County Office of Education, Redwood City, CA
School for Contemporary Education, Baltimore, MD
School for Contemporary Education, Springfield, VA
Secret Harbor School, Anacortes, WA
Seminole County Board of Public Instruction—Programs for Emotionally Handicapped, Sanford, FL
Serendipity Diagnostic and Treatment Center, Citrus Heights, CA
Shadow Mountain Institute, Tulsa, OK
Shawnee County Youth Center Services, Topeka, KS
Shawnee Mission Public Schools, Shawnee Mission, KS
Solomon Mental Health Center, Lowell, MA
Sonia Shankman Orthogenic School of the University of Chicago, Chicago, IL

South Bend Community School Corporation—Adolescent Day Treatment Center, South Bend, IN
South Carolina State Hospital—Child and Adolescent Unit—Blanding House, Columbia, SC
South Dakota Human Services Center, Yankton, SD
South Metropolitan Association—Interventions Residential School, Matteson, IL
South Oaks Hospital, Amityville, NY
South Shore Child Guidance Center, Freeport, NY
Southbury Training School, Southbury, CT
Southeast Kansas Mental Health Center, Humboldt, KS
Southeast Mental Health Center—Child Development Institute, Memphis, TN
Southlake Center for Mental Health, Merriville, IN
Southwest Georgia Psychoeducational Services—Thomas County Schools, Ochlocknee, GA
Southwood Psychiatric Residential Treatment Center—Hillcrest, San Diego, CA
Spaulding Youth Center—Emotional Handicap Program, Tilton, NH
Special Care Program, Orofino, ID
Special Education Association of Adams County, Quincy, IL
Special Service School District of Bergen County, Paramus, NJ
Spectrum Center for Educational and Behavioral Development Inc, Berkeley, CA
The Spofford Home, Kansas City, MO
Springfield Park Central Hospital—Park Central School, Springfield, MO
Starr Commonwealth Schools—Hannah Neil Center for Children, Columbus, OH
State Agriculture and Industrial School, Industry, NY
State Training School, Eldora, IA
State University of New York at Albany—SUNY Pre-Kindergarten, Albany, NY
Stetson School Inc, Barre, MA
Strafford Guidance Center Inc, Dover, NH
Stuyvesant Residence Club, New York City, NY
Summit Children's Residence Center, Upper Nyack, NY
Sunburst Youth Homes, Neillsville, WI
Sunny Hill Children's Center Inc, Greenwich, CT
Sunset Learning Center, Fort Lauderdale, FL
Switzer Center, Torrance, CA
The Sycamores, Altadena, CA
Taylor Manor Hospital, Ellicott City, MD
Terry Children's Psychiatric Center, New Castle, DE
Therapeutic School and Preschool Community Mental Health Services, Belleville, NJ
Timberlawn Psychiatric Hospital, Dallas, TX
Timberridge Institute for Children and Adolescents Inc, Oklahoma City, OK
Tomorrow's Children, Waupaca, WI
Towering Pines Center, Slidell, LA
Training Center for Youth, Columbus, OH
Tri City Community Mental Health and Retardation Center, Malden, MA
Tri-County Community Mental Health Center, Kansas City, MO
Trumbull County Board of Education, Warren, OH
United Methodist Youthville, Newton, KS
University Hospitals of Cleveland—Hanna Pavilion Child Psychiatric Unit, Cleveland, OH
University of Arkansas Medical Sciences Division Child Psychiatry—Child Study Center, Little Rock, AR
The University of Chicago—Departments of Psychiatry and Pediatrics—Child Psychiatry, Chicago, IL
University of Colorado Health Sciences Center—Day Care Center, Denver, CO
University of Illinois Medical Center—Child Psychiatry Clinic, Chicago, IL
University of Minnesota Hospitals—Child and Adolescent Psychiatry, Minneapolis, MN
University of New Mexico Children's Psychiatric Hospital—Mimbres School, Albuquerque, NM
University of New Mexico—Children's Psychiatric Hospital, Albuquerque, NM

University of Rochester Medical School—Child and Adolescent Psychiatry Clinic, Rochester, NY
University of South Florida—Florida Mental Health Institute—Department of Child and Family Services, Tampa, FL
University of Tennessee—Child Development Center School, Memphis, TN
University of Texas Medical Branch—Division of Pediatric Psychology—Department of Pediatrics, Galveston, TX
University of Texas Medical Branch—Inpatient Service—Division of Child and Adolescent Psychiatry, Galveston, TX
University Park Psychological Center, Denver, CO
Utah Boys' Ranch—Children and Youth Services Inc, Salt Lake City, UT
Valley View School, North Brookfield, MA
Valleyhead Inc, Lenox, MA
Vanderbilt Medical Center—Division of Child and Adolescent Psychiatry, Nashville, TN
Variety Preschooler's Workshop, Syosset, NY
Ventura County Superintendent of Schools, Ventura, CA
Village of St Joseph, Atlanta, GA
Virginia Center for Psychiatry, Portsmouth, VA
Virginia Center for Psychiatry, Norfolk, VA
Vista Del Mar Child Care Service, Los Angeles, CA
Vista Maria, Dearborn Heights, MI
Vitam Center Inc—Vitam School, Norwalk, CT
Walker Home and School, Needham, MA
Wallace Village for Children, Broomfield, CO
Walter Reed Army Medical Center Child and Adolescent Psychiatry Service, Washington, DC
War Bonnet—Wilderness Pathways, Canaan, NH
Warm Springs Center, Boise, ID
Washington School District, Phoenix, AZ
Waterford Country School, Quaker Hill, CT
Waterloo Community Schools, Waterloo, IA
West Hartford Public Schools Off-Campus Program, West Hartford, CT
West Nassau Mental Health Center, Franklin Square, NY
West River Children's Center of the Children's Home Society of South Dakota, Rapid City, SD
West Texas Boys' Ranch, San Angelo, TX
Westbridge, Phoenix, AZ
Westchester Day Treatment Program, Hawthorne, NY
Western District Guidance Center, Parkersburg, WV
Western New York Children's Psychiatric Center, West Seneca, NY
West-Ros-Park Mental Health Center, Roslindale, MA
Wheeler Clinic Inc—Northwest Village School, Plainville, CT
Wichita Guidance Center, Wichita, KS
Wilder Children's Placement, Saint Paul, MN
Willowglen Academy Inc, Milwaukee, WI
Winnebago Mental Health Institute—Children's Unit, Winnebago, WI
Woodbourne Center, Baltimore, MD
Woodward Mental Health Center, Freeport, NY
Wyalusing Academy, Prairie du Chien, WI
Wyandotte Mental Health Center, Kansas City, KS
Wyandotte Special Education Cooperative, Kansas City, KS
Wyoming Youth Treatment Center, Casper, WY
Yellowstone Boys' and Girls' Ranch, Billings, MT
York Woods Center, Ypsilanti, MI
Youth and Family Services, Omaha, NE
Youth Evaluation and Treatment Centers (YETC), Phoenix, AZ
Yuma Union High School District, Yuma, AZ
Zonta Children's Center, San Jose, CA

Suicide

Adams County Adolescent Day Treatment Program, Denver, CO
Alabama Youth Services—Chalkville Campus, Birmingham, AL
Albany Area Mental Health and Mental Retardation Center, Albany, GA
Albuquerque Child Guidance Center, Albuquerque, NM
All Children's Hospital, St Petersburg, FL

Almansor Education Center, Alhambra, CA
Anne Arundel County Health Department Mental Health Clinic, Annapolis, MD
Anneewakee Hospital, Douglasville, GA
Archdiocese of Louisville—Guidance Clinic, Louisville, KY
Arizona Baptist Children's Services—Little Canyon Campus, Phoenix, AZ
Arizona State Hospital, Phoenix, AZ
Arizona State Hospital—Nueva Vista School, Phoenix, AZ
Arlington School, Belmont, MA
Arnell Engstrom Children's Center, Traverse City, MI
The Astor Home for Children—Day Treatment Program, Bronx, NY
The Astor Home for Children—Group Home Program, Bronx, NY
Atlantic Mental Health Center Inc, McKee City, NJ
Augusta School Department, Augusta, ME
Aurora Adolescent Day Resource Center, Aurora, CO
Austin State Hospital, Austin, TX
The Baird Center for Children and Families Inc, Burlington, VT
Baker Hall Inc, Lackawanna, NY
Barat Human Services—Barat House, Detroit, MI
Bar-None Residential Treatment Services for Children, Anoka, MN
The Battin Clinic, Houston, TX
Battle Creek Child Guidance Center, Battle Creek, MI
Beacon Day Treatment Program, Romulus, MI
Bergen Pines Hospital—Children's Psychiatric Unit, Paramus, NJ
Berks County Intermediate Unit, Reading, PA
Berkshire Farm Center and Services for Youth, Canaan, NY
Big Spring State Hospital, Big Spring, TX
Birmingham City Board of Education, Birmingham, AL
Boston Public Schools—The McKinley Schools, Mattapau, MA
Boys' and Girls' Aid Society of San Diego—Cottonwood Center and Community Based Psychiatric Program, El Cajon, CA
Boys' Town of Missouri Inc, Saint James, MO
Bradley Hospital, East Providence, RI
Brattleboro Retreat, Brattleboro, VT
Brea Neuropsychiatric Center, Brea, CA
Bridgeway Hospital Youthcare Program, North Little Rock, AR
Brighton School and Diagnostic Center, Phoenix, AZ
Brooklyn Community Counseling Center, Brooklyn, NY
Brown County Mental Health Center—Children Services, Green Bay, WI
The Brown Schools, Austin, TX
Buckeye Boys' Ranch Inc, Grove City, OH
Butler County Mental Health Center Inc, Hamilton, OH
Capital City Schools, Topeka, KS
Cass County Social Services—Children's Social Service Center, Fargo, ND
Center for Life Management, Salem, NH
Chancellor Academy, Pompton Plains, NJ
The Charlton School, Burnt Hills, NY
Charter Westbrook Hospital, Richmond, VA
Chestnut Lodge Hospital—Adolescent and Child Division, Rockville, MD
Child and Adolescent Psychiatric Clinic Inc, Buffalo, NY
Child and Family Services, Knoxville, TN
Child Development Service—Lakeview Center Inc, Pensacola, FL
Child Disability Clinic—Carle Clinic, Urbana, IL
Child Guidance Center of Southern Connecticut, Stanford, CT
Child Guidance Clinic of Southeastern Connecticut Inc, New London, CT
Child Psychiatry Service—Department of Psychiatry—University Hospitals, Ann Arbor, MI
Child Study and Treatment Center, Tacoma, WA
Child Study Center, Fort Worth, TX
Children's and Adolescent Unit of Mental Health Institute of Cherokee Iowa, Cherokee, IA
The Children's Day School, Trenton, NJ
Children's Day Treatment Center, Honolulu, HI
The Children's Home of Cincinnati, Cincinnati, OH
Children's Home Society of South Dakota, Sioux Falls, SD

Children's Hospital at Washington University Medical Center—Psychiatric Unit, Saint Louis, MO
The Children's Institute, South Orange, NJ
Children's Medical Center, Tulsa, OK
Children's Medical Center—Psychiatric Inpatient Unit, Dallas, TX
Children's Mental Health Center Inc, Columbus, OH
The Children's Mercy Hospital—Section of Psychiatry, Kansas City, MO
Children's Psychiatric Center of the Jewish Hospital, Cincinnati, OH
The Children's School of the Institute of Living, Hartford, CT
The Children's Study Home, Springfield, MA
Cabinet for Human Resources—Children's Treatment Service, Louisville, KY
The Children's Village, Dobbs Ferry, NY
Christie School, Marylhurst, OR
Clear View School, Scarborough, NY
The Clearing, Marshfield, VT
Clearwater Ranch Children's House Inc, Philo, CA
Cleveland Clinic Foundation, Cleveland, OH
Cleveland County Area Mental Health Program—Division of Child and Youth Services, Shelby, NC
The Clinical Center of Southern Illinois University, Carbondale, IL
Cobb County—Cobb Douglas Psychoeducation Children's Program, Marietta, GA
College Hospital—College Park School, Cerritos, CA
Colorado Springs School District No. 11, Colorado Springs, CO
Colorado West Regional Mental Health Center, Glenwood Springs, CO
Community Counseling Center—Rural Clinics, Ely, NV
Community Mental Health Center South, Lee's Summit, MO
Community Psychiatric Clinic Inc, Wheaton; Bethesda; Gaithersburg, MD
The Community School of the Family Service and Child Guidance Center of the Oranges Maplewood and Millburn, Orange, NJ
Comprehensive Mental Health Center of St Clair County Inc, East Saint Louis, IL
Covenant Children's Home and Family Services, Princeton, IL
CPC Belmont Hills Hospital, Belmont, CA
Craig House—Technoma, Pittsburgh, PA
Creative Arts Rehabilitation Center Inc, New York, NY
Creative Learning Systems Inc, Tucson, AZ
Cumberland County Guidance Center Inc, Millville, NJ
Dakota House, Aberdeen, SD
Daniel Memorial Inc, Jacksonville, FL
De Neuville Heights School for Girls, Memphis, TN
DeJarnette Center, Staunton, VA
Delaware Guidance Services for Children and Youth Inc, Wilmington, DE
DePaul Hospital and Residential Treatment Center, New Orleans, LA
Des Moines Children's Home—Orchard Place, Des Moines, IA
Desert Hills, Tucson, AZ
DeSisto Schools Inc, West Stockbridge, MA
The Devereux Foundation, Devon, PA
The Devereux Foundation, Santa Barbara, CA
The Devereux Foundation—Deerhaven, Chester, NJ
The Devereux Foundation—Texas Branch, Victoria, TX
Devereux in Georgia, Kennesaw, GA
Dominion Hospital—The Dominion School, Falls Church, VA
Donaldsonville Mental Health Center, Donaldsonville, LA
East Alabama Mental Health Retardation Center, Opelika, AL
East Bay Activity Center, Oakland, CA
Eastern Shore Mental Health Center, Nassawadox, VA
Eau Claire Academy, Eau Claire, WI
Edgemont Hospital, Los Angeles, CA
Edgewood Children's Center, Saint Louis, MO
Edgewood Children's Center, San Francisco, CA
The Educational Clinic Inc, Columbus, OH
Educational Department of Institute of Pennsylvania Hospital—Mill Creek School, Philadelphia, PA
El Paso Guidance Center, El Paso, TX

Elmcrest Psychiatric Institute, Portland, CT
Emerson North, Cincinati, OH
Epworth Village Inc, York, NE
Escalon Inc, Altadena, CA
Ettie Lee Homes Inc, Baldwin Park, CA
Evansville Vanderburgh School Corporation, Evansville, IN
Excelsior Youth Center, Aurora, CO
Fairmount Children's Center, Syracuse, NY
Family Guidance Center, Reading, PA
Family Guidance Service—Ingham Community Mental Health Center, Lansing, MI
Five Acres Boys' and Girls' Aide Society, Altadena, CA
Forest Heights Lodge, Evergreen, CO
Forest Hospital, Des Plaines, IL
Fort Logan Mental Health Center, Denver, CO
Ft Wayne Children's Home—Crossroad, Fort Wayne, IN
Four Winds Hospital—Adolescent Services, Katonah, NY
Franklin Grand Isle Mental Health Services Inc, Saint Albans, VT
Fred Finch Youth Center, Oakland, CA
The Frost School, Rockville, MD
Genesee Intermediate School District Center for Autism, Flint, MI
Gerard of Minnesota Inc, Austin, MN
Gilfillan Center, Bemidji, MN
Gladman Memorial Hospital Adolescent Program, Oakland, CA
Glens Falls Hospital—Child and Family Services—Community Mental Health Center, Glens Falls, NY
The Goldstaub Residence, Houston, TX
Gould Farm, Monterey, MA
Grady Memorial Hospital—Division of Child and Adolescent Psychiatry, Atlanta, GA
Grant Center Hospital, Miami, FL
Green Chimneys Children's Services Inc, Brewster, NY
Hall-Mercer Children's Center of the McLean Hospital, Belmont, MA
Hall-Brooke Foundation—Hall-Brooke Hospital—Hall-Brooke School, Westport, CT
Hamilton Children's Center, Hyattsville, MD
Harbor Schools Inc, Newburyport, MA
Harbor View Mercy Hospital, Fort Smith, AR
Harford County Community Mental Health Center, Bel Air, MD
Hartgrove Hospital—Hartgrove Academy, Chicago, IL
Hathaway School of Hathaway Home for Children, Pacoima, CA
Hawaii State Department of Education—Special Needs Branch, Honolulu, HI
Hawaii State Hospital—Adolescent Unit, Kaneohe, HI
Hawthorn Center, Northville, MI
Hawthorne Children's Psychiatric Hospital, Saint Louis, MO
Henderson Mental Health Center, Fort Lauderdale, FL
Henrietta Weill Memorial Child Guidance Clinic, Bakersfield, CA
Henry Horner Children and Adolescent Center, Chicago, IL
High Plains Mental Health Center—Colby Office, Colby, KS
High Point Adolescent School—Children's Psychiatric Center, Morganville, NJ
Hillside Children's Center, Rochester, NY
Hillside Inc, Atlanta, GA
Homes Unlimited Inc, Bangor, ME
Homewood School—Highland Hospital, Asheville, NC
Humana Hospital Huntington Beach—Children's Behavioral Center, Huntington Beach, CA
Indiana Girls' School, Indianapolis, IN
Ingleside Hospital, Rosemead, CA
The Institute Day School, Lowell, MA
Institute for Family and Life Learning Residential School, Danvers, MA
The Institute of Living School, Hartford, CT
Institute of Psychiatry and Human Behavior—Department of Psychiatry—Child and Adolescent Inpatient Service, Baltimore, MD
Jane Wayland Center, Phoenix, AZ
Jasper County Mental Health Center, Newton, IA
Jeanine Schultz Memorial School, Park Ridge, IL

Jefferson Parish School System—Department of Special Education, Gretna, LA

Jewish Board of Family and Children Services—Linden Hill School, Hawthorne, NY

Jewish Child Care Association—Pleasantville Cottage School, Pleasantville, NY

Jewish Children's Bureau of Chicago, Chicago, IL

John C Corrigan Mental Health Center, Fall River, MA

John G McGrath School, Napa, CA

John Umstead Hospital—Children's Psychiatric Institute, Butner, NC

Josephine County Mental Health Program—Children's Resource Team, Grants Pass, OR

Kalamazoo Child Guidance Clinic, Kalamazoo, MI

K-Bar-B Youth Ranch—Richard M Wise School, Lacombe, LA

Kenai Peninsula Borough School District, Soldotna, AK

Kings County Hospital—Downstate Medical Center—Division of Child and Adolescent Psychiatry, Brooklyn, NY

La Mel, San Francisco, CA

La Puente Valley Community Mental Health Center, La Puente, CA

Lad Lake Inc, Dousman, WI

Lafayette Clinic, Detroit, MI

Lake County Mental Health Center—Department of Children's Services, Mentor, OH

Lake Grove School, Lake Grove, NY

Lakeshore Mental Health Institute—Riverbend School—Children and Youth Services, Knoxville, TN

Lakeside Center for Boys, Saint Louis, MO

Lakin Hospital—Adolescent Services, Lakin, WV

Lane School Programs—Lane Education Service District, Eugene, OR

LaSalle School, Albany, NY

Little Friends Inc—Little Friends School, Naperville, IL

Little Friends Inc—The Therapeutic Workshop, Downers Grove, IL

Lookout Mountain School, Golden, CO

The Los Angeles Child Guidance Clinic, Los Angeles, CA

Lovellton Academy, Elgin, IL

Lutheran Medical Center—Psychiatric Division, Saint Louis, MO

Madden Mental Health Center Campus—Institute for Juvenile Research—Inpatient Services, Hines, IL

Main Street Human Resources, Great Barington, MA

Manhattan Children's Psychiatric Center, New York, NY

Manitowoc County Counseling Center, Manitowoc, WI

The Mansion, Naperville, IL

Martin Luther Centers, Madison, WI

Marymount Hospital Mental Health Center, Garfield Heights, OH

Massanutten Mental Health Center, Harrisonburg, VA

McAuley Nazareth Home for Boys, Leicester, MA

Medical University of South Carolina—Department of Psychiatry—Youth Division, Charleston, SC

Meharry Community Mental Health Center, Nashville, TN

Mendota Mental Health Institute—Child and Adolescent Program, Madison, WI

The Menninger Foundation—Pre-School Day Treatment Center, Topeka, KS

The Menninger Foundation—The Children's Division, Topeka, KS

Menorah Medical Center—Hearing and Speech Department, Kansas City, MO

Mental Health Care Center of the Lower Keys, Key West, FL

Mental Health Center of Boulder County—Adolescent Treatment Program, Boulder, CO

Mental Health Center of Mid-Iowa, Marshalltown, IA

Mental Health Centers of Central Illinois—Child and Adolescent Day Treatment Program, Springfield, IL

The Mental Health Institute for Children at Allentown State Hospital, Allentown, PA

Mental Health Services of North Central Hamilton Co Inc, Cincinnati, OH

Mercy Hospital and Medical Center—Community Guidance Center, Chicago, IL

The Mid Fairfield Child Guidance Center Inc, Norwalk, CT

Mid-Columbia Mental Health Center—Adolescent Psychiatric Department, Richland, WA

Milford Assistance Program Day School, Milford, MA

The Millcreek Psychiatric Center for Children, Cincinnati, OH

Minnesota Learning Center, Brainerd, MN

Montrose School, Reisterstown, MD

Mt Airy Psychiatric Center—Children's Treatment Program—Adolescent Treatment Program, Denver, CO

Multidisciplinary Institute for Neuropsychological Development Inc—MIND, Cambridge, MA

Mystic Valley Mental Health Center, Lexington, MA

Napa State Hospital—Children's Program, Imola, CA

National Foundation for the Treatment of the Emotionally Handicapped, Sepulveda, CA

New England Home for Little Wanderers—Orchard Home, Watertown, MA

New England Medical Center—Bay Cove Day Center for Children Day Hospital, Boston, MA

New England Medical Center—Division of Child Psychiatry, Boston, MA

New England Salem Children's Trust, Rumney, NH

New Hope Guild, Brooklyn, NY

New Mexico Boys' School, Springer, NM

Normon Westlund Child Guidance Clinic, Saginaw, MI

North Central Health Care Facilities, Wausau, WI

North Dakota State Mental Hospital—Child and Adolescent Unit, Jamestown, ND

Northeast Colorado Board of Cooperative Educational Services, Haxton, CO

Northwest Florida Mental Health Center, Panama City, FL

Northwood Children's Home, Duluth, MN

Norton Psychiatric Clinic—Norton Adolescent Treatment Program and Norton Academy, Louisville, KY

Ocean Institute—Adolescent Day School—Mental Health Clinic of Ocean County, Toms River, NJ

Oconee Area Psycho Educational Program, Milledgeville, GA

Oconomowoc Developmental Training Center Inc, Oconomowoc, WI

Office of Riverside County Superintendent of Schools, Riverside, CA

Ohel Children's Home and Family Services, Brooklyn, NY

Orlando Regional Medical Center—Mental Health Department—Children's Services, Orlando, FL

Osterlen Services for Youth, Springfield, OH

Otis R Bowen Center, Warsaw, IN

Our Lady of Providence Children's Center, West Springfield, MA

Paradise Valley School District No. 69—Therapeutic Educational Activities Milieu, Phoenix, AZ

Parkview Counseling Center Inc, Youngstown, OH

Parkwood Hospital, Atlanta, GA

Parsons Child and Family Center, Albany, NY

Partial Hospitalization Program Children's Service Center, Wilkes Barre, PA

Pawnee Mental Health Services, Concordia, KS

Peace River Center for Personal Development Inc, Bartow, FL

Penn Foundation for Mental Health, Sellersville, PA

Penninsula Children's Center—Children and Youth Services, Palo Alto, CA

Philadelphia Child Guidance Clinic—Child and Family Inpatient Service, Philadelphia, PA

Phoenix Union High School District No. 210, Phoenix, AZ

Porter Starke Services Inc—Vale Park Psychiatric Hospital, Valparaiso, IN

Prescott Child Development Center, Prescott, AZ

Pressley Ridge School—Day School, Pittsburgh, PA

Pressley Ridge School—Laurel Park, Clarksburg, WV

Pressley Ridge School—Pryde—Family Based Treatment, Pittsburgh, PA

Pressley Ridge School—Wilderness School, Ohiopyle, PA

Primary Children's Medical Center—Department of Child Psychiatry, Salt Lake City, UT

Psychiatric Clinic of the Charlotte Hungerford Hospital, Torrington, CT

Psychiatric Institute of Richmond—Educational Development
  Center, Richmond, VA
Psychiatric Services Inc, Haverhill, MA
Queens Hospital Center Department of Psychiatry Child and
  Adolescent Clinic, Jamaica, NY
Range Mental Health Center, Virginia, MN
Raritan Bay Mental Health Center, Perth Amboy, NJ
Red Rock Comprehensive Mental Health Center, Oklahoma
  City, OK
Rensselaer County Mental Health Department—Unified Services
  for Children and Adolescents, Troy, NY
Richmond County Board of Education—Sand Hills
  Psychoeducational Program, Augusta, GA
Ridgeview Institute, Smyrna, GA
Ridgeview Psychiatric Hospital and Center, Oak Ridge, TN
River Street School, Hyde Park, MA
Rockland Children's Psychiatric Center, Orangeburg, NY
Rockland Psychological and Educational Center, Spring Valley,
  NY
Rusk State Hospital—Child and Adolescent Unit, Rusk, TX
Rutland Psychoeducational Services, Athens, GA
Sagamore Hills Children's Psychiatric Hospital, Northfield, OH
St Clare's Hospital—Adult, Child and Family Services, Denville,
  NJ
St Cloud Children's Home, Saint Cloud, MN
St Elizabeth's Hospital—Division of Child and Adolescent Ser-
  vices, Washington, DC
St Gabriel's Hall, Phoenixville, PA
St George Homes Inc, Berkeley, CA
St Joseph Center for Mental Health, Omaha, NE
St Joseph's Carondelet Child Center, Chicago, IL
St Joseph's Children's Home, Torrington, WY
St Louis County Child Mental Health Services, Saint Louis, MO
St Vincent's Hospital and Medical Center of New York—Child
  and Adolescent Psychiatry Service, New York, NY
Samarkand Manor, Eagle Springs, NC
San Diego County Mental Health Services—Loma Portal Fa-
  cility, San Diego, CA
San Marcos Treatment Center of The Brown Schools, San Mar-
  cos, TX
Serendipity Diagnostic and Treatment Center, Citrus Heights,
  CA
Shadow Mountain Institute, Tulsa, OK
Shawnee Mission Public Schools, Shawnee Mission, KS
Sibley Hospital—Groome Center—Hayes Hall, Washington, DC
Solomon Mental Health Center, Lowell, MA
South Bend Community School Corporation—Adolescent Day
  Treatment Center, South Bend, IN
South Carolina State Hospital—Child and Adolescent
  Unit—Blanding House, Columbia, SC
South Dakota Human Services Center, Yankton, SD
South Oaks Hospital, Amityville, NY
Southbury Training School, Southbury, CT
Southeast Kansas Mental Health Center, Humboldt, KS
Southeast Mental Health Center—Child Development Institute,
  Memphis, TN
Southwood Psychiatric Residential Treatment Center—Hillcrest,
  San Diego, CA
Spaulding Youth Center—Emotional Handicap Program, Tilton,
  NH
Special Care Program, Orofino, ID
Special Education Association of Adams County, Quincy, IL
Special Service School District of Bergen County, Paramus, NJ
The Spofford Home, Kansas City, MO
Springfield Park Central Hospital—Park Central School, Spring-
  field, MO
Starr Commonwealth Schools—Hannah Neil Center for Chil-
  dren, Columbus, OH
Strafford Guidance Center Inc, Dover, NH
Summit Children's Residence Center, Upper Nyack, NY
Sunset Learning Center, Fort Lauderdale, FL
Switzer Center, Torrance, CA
Taylor Manor Hospital, Ellicott City, MD
Terry Children's Psychiatric Center, New Castle, DE
Timberlawn Psychiatric Hospital, Dallas, TX

Tomorrow's Children, Waupaca, WI
Training Center for Youth, Columbus, OH
Tri City Community Mental Health and Retardation Center,
  Malden, MA
Tri-County Community Mental Health Center, Kansas City, MO
University Hospitals of Cleveland—Hanna Pavilion Child Psy-
  chiatric Unit, Cleveland, OH
University of Arkansas Medical Sciences Division Child
  Psychiatry—Child Study Center, Little Rock, AR
The University of Chicago—Departments of Psychiatry and
  Pediatrics—Child Psychiatry, Chicago, IL
University of Colorado Health Sciences Center—Day Care Cen-
  ter, Denver, CO
University of Illinois Medical Center—Child Psychiatry Clinic,
  Chicago, IL
University of Minnesota Hospitals—Child and Adolescent Psy-
  chiatry, Minneapolis, MN
University of New Mexico Children's Psychiatric
  Hospital—Mimbres School, Albuquerque, NM
University of New Mexico—Children's Psychiatric Hospital, Al-
  buquerque, NM
University of Rochester Medical School—Child and Adolescent
  Psychiatry Clinic, Rochester, NY
University of Texas Medical Branch—Division of Pediatric
  Psychology—Department of Pediatrics, Galveston, TX
University of Texas Medical Branch—Inpatient
  Service—Division of Child and Adolescent Psychiatry, Gal-
  veston, TX
University Park Psychological Center, Denver, CO
Utah Boys' Ranch—Children and Youth Services Inc, Salt Lake
  City, UT
Valleyhead Inc, Lenox, MA
Vanderbilt Medical Center—Division of Child and Adolescent
  Psychiatry, Nashville, TN
Ventura County Superintendent of Schools, Ventura, CA
Virginia Center for Psychiatry, Portsmouth, VA
Virginia Center for Psychiatry, Norfolk, VA
Vista Maria, Dearborn Heights, MI
Walker Home and School, Needham, MA
Walter Reed Army Medical Center Child and Adolescent Psychi-
  atry Service, Washington, DC
Warm Springs Center, Boise, ID
Waterford Country School, Quaker Hill, CT
West Central Community Services Center Inc, Willmar, MN
West Hartford Public Schools Off-Campus Program, West Hart-
  ford, CT
West Nassau Mental Health Center, Franklin Square, NY
West River Children's Center of the Children's Home Society of
  South Dakota, Rapid City, SD
West Texas Boys' Ranch, San Angelo, TX
Westbridge, Phoenix, AZ
Westchester Day Treatment Program, Hawthorne, NY
Western District Guidance Center, Parkersburg, WV
Western New York Children's Psychiatric Center, West Seneca,
  NY
West-Ros-Park Mental Health Center, Roslindale, MA
Wheeler Clinic Inc—Northwest Village School, Plainville, CT
Wichita Guidance Center, Wichita, KS
Wilder Children's Placement, Saint Paul, MN
Willowglen Academy Inc, Milwaukee, WI
Winnebago Mental Health Institute—Children's Unit, Win-
  nebago, WI
Woodbourne Center, Baltimore, MD
Woodward Mental Health Center, Freeport, NY
Wyalusing Academy, Prairie du Chien, WI
Wyandotte Special Education Cooperative, Kansas City, KS
Wyoming State Hospital, Evanston, WY
Wyoming Youth Treatment Center, Casper, WY
Yellowstone Boys' and Girls' Ranch, Billings, MT
York Woods Center, Ypsilanti, MI
Youth and Family Services, Omaha, NE
Youth Center of Beloit—North Beloit High, Beloit, KS
Youth Evaluation and Treatment Centers (YETC), Phoenix, AZ
Yuma Union High School District, Yuma, AZ

Ulcerative Colitis

All Children's Hospital, St Petersburg, FL
Anne Arundel County Health Department Mental Health Clinic, Annapolis, MD
Aurora Adolescent Day Resource Center, Aurora, CO
Austin State Hospital, Austin, TX
The Bancroft School, Haddonfield, NJ
Bergen Pines Hospital—Children's Psychiatric Unit, Paramus, NJ
Berks County Intermediate Unit, Reading, PA
Bradley Hospital, East Providence, RI
Brattleboro Retreat, Brattleboro, VT
Brooklyn Community Counseling Center, Brooklyn, NY
Brown County Mental Health Center—Children Services, Green Bay, WI
Cantwell Academy Inc, Miami, FL
Child Disability Clinic—Carle Clinic, Urbana, IL
Child Psychiatry Service—Department of Psychiatry—University Hospitals, Ann Arbor, MI
Child Study and Treatment Center, Tacoma, WA
Children's and Adolescent Unit of Mental Health Institute of Cherokee Iowa, Cherokee, IA
Children's Home of Cedar Rapids—Heartwood Residential Treatment Center, Cedar Rapids, IA
Children's Home Society of South Dakota, Sioux Falls, SD
Children's Hospital at Washington University Medical Center—Psychiatric Unit, Saint Louis, MO
Children's Medical Center, Tulsa, OK
Children's Medical Center—Psychiatric Inpatient Unit, Dallas, TX
The Children's Mercy Hospital—Section of Psychiatry, Kansas City, MO
Cleveland Clinic Foundation, Cleveland, OH
The Clinical Center of Southern Illinois University, Carbondale, IL
Colorado West Regional Mental Health Center, Glenwood Springs, CO
Community Counseling Center—Rural Clinics, Ely, NV
The Community School of the Family Service and Child Guidance Center of the Oranges Maplewood and Millburn, Orange, NJ
Covenant Children's Home and Family Services, Princeton, IL
Craig House—Technoma, Pittsburgh, PA
De Neuville Heights School for Girls, Memphis, TN
Delaware Guidance Services for Children and Youth Inc, Wilmington, DE
DeSisto Schools Inc, West Stockbridge, MA
The Devereux Foundation, Santa Barbara, CA
Devereux in Georgia, Kennesaw, GA
East Alabama Mental Health Retardation Center, Opelika, AL
Eastern Shore Mental Health Center, Nassawadox, VA
Edgemont Hospital, Los Angeles, CA
The Educational Clinic Inc, Columbus, OH
Elmcrest Psychiatric Institute, Portland, CT
Evansville Vanderburgh School Corporation, Evansville, IN
Excelsior Youth Center, Aurora, CO
Family Guidance Center, Reading, PA
Forest Hospital, Des Plaines, IL
Gladman Memorial Hospital Adolescent Program, Oakland, CA
The Goldstaub Residence, Houston, TX
Grady Memorial Hospital—Division of Child and Adolescent Psychiatry, Atlanta, GA
Hamilton Children's Center, Hyattsville, MD
Hartgrove Hospital—Hartgrove Academy, Chicago, IL
Hawaii State Department of Education—Special Needs Branch, Honolulu, HI
Hawthorn Center, Northville, MI
High Plains Mental Health Center—Colby Office, Colby, KS
The Institute of Living School, Hartford, CT
Jasper County Mental Health Center, Newton, IA
Jeanine Schultz Memorial School, Park Ridge, IL
Jewish Child Care Association—Youth Residence Center, New York, NY
Jewish Children's Bureau of Chicago, Chicago, IL

John Umstead Hospital—Children's Psychiatric Institute, Butner, NC
Kings County Hospital—Downstate Medical Center—Division of Child and Adolescent Psychiatry, Brooklyn, NY
La Mel, San Francisco, CA
La Puente Valley Community Mental Health Center, La Puente, CA
Lake County Mental Health Center—Department of Children's Services, Mentor, OH
Lovellton Academy, Elgin, IL
Main Street Human Resources, Great Barington, MA
Marymount Hospital Mental Health Center, Garfield Heights, OH
Medical University of South Carolina—Department of Psychiatry—Youth Division, Charleston, SC
Mendota Mental Health Institute—Child and Adolescent Program, Madison, WI
The Menninger Foundation—The Children's Division, Topeka, KS
Menorah Medical Center—Hearing and Speech Department, Kansas City, MO
Mercy Hospital and Medical Center—Community Guidance Center, Chicago, IL
The Millcreek Psychiatric Center for Children, Cincinnati, OH
Napa State Hospital—Children's Program, Imola, CA
New England Home for Little Wanderers—Orchard Home, Watertown, MA
Normon Westlund Child Guidance Clinic, Saginaw, MI
Northeast Colorado Board of Cooperative Educational Services, Haxton, CO
Norton Psychiatric Clinic—Norton Adolescent Treatment Program and Norton Academy, Louisville, KY
Oconomowoc Developmental Training Center Inc, Oconomowoc, WI
Ohel Children's Home and Family Services, Brooklyn, NY
Orlando Regional Medical Center—Mental Health Department—Children's Services, Orlando, FL
Parkview Counseling Center Inc, Youngstown, OH
Philadelphia Child Guidance Clinic—Child and Family Inpatient Service, Philadelphia, PA
Prescott Child Development Center, Prescott, AZ
Primary Children's Medical Center—Department of Child Psychiatry, Salt Lake City, UT
Psychiatric Services Inc, Haverhill, MA
Range Mental Health Center, Virginia, MN
Region 16 Educational Service Center, Amarillo, TX
Rensselaer County Mental Health Department—Unified Services for Children and Adolescents, Troy, NY
Rockland Psychological and Educational Center, Spring Valley, NY
St Joseph Center for Mental Health, Omaha, NE
St Joseph's Children's Home, Torrington, WY
St Mary's Home for Boys, Beaverton, OR
St Vincent's Hospital and Medical Center of New York—Child and Adolescent Psychiatry Service, New York, NY
Sibley Hospital—Groome Center—Hayes Hall, Washington, DC
South Shore Child Guidance Center, Freeport, NY
Special Education Association of Adams County, Quincy, IL
Special Service School District of Bergen County, Paramus, NJ
Strafford Guidance Center Inc, Dover, NH
Summit Children's Residence Center, Upper Nyack, NY
Timberlawn Psychiatric Hospital, Dallas, TX
Tri-County Community Mental Health Center, Kansas City, MO
University Hospitals of Cleveland—Hanna Pavilion Child Psychiatric Unit, Cleveland, OH
The University of Chicago—Departments of Psychiatry and Pediatrics—Child Psychiatry, Chicago, IL
University of Minnesota Hospitals—Child and Adolescent Psychiatry, Minneapolis, MN
University of New Mexico—Children's Psychiatric Hospital, Albuquerque, NM
University of Rochester Medical School—Child and Adolescent Psychiatry Clinic, Rochester, NY

University of Texas Medical Branch—Inpatient Service—Division of Child and Adolescent Psychiatry, Galveston, TX
University Park Psychological Center, Denver, CO
Vanderbilt Medical Center—Division of Child and Adolescent Psychiatry, Nashville, TN
Walter Reed Army Medical Center Child and Adolescent Psychiatry Service, Washington, DC
Western District Guidance Center, Parkersburg, WV
West-Ros-Park Mental Health Center, Roslindale, MA
Wilder Children's Placement, Saint Paul, MN
Wyandotte Special Education Cooperative, Kansas City, KS

Unsocialized Aggressive Reaction

Adams County Adolescent Day Treatment Program, Denver, CO
Ahwahnee Hills School, Ahwahnee, CA
Alabama Youth Services—Chalkville Campus, Birmingham, AL
Albuquerque Child Guidance Center, Albuquerque, NM
Alexander Children's Center, Charlotte, NC
All Children's Hospital, St Petersburg, FL
Allendale School, Lake Villa, IL
Almansor Education Center, Alhambra, CA
Andrus Children's Home, Yonkers, NY
Anneewakee Hospital, Douglasville, GA
Area Education Agency—Education Center, Waterloo, IA
Arizona Baptist Children's Services—Little Canyon Campus, Phoenix, AZ
Arizona Boys' Ranch, Boys Ranch, AZ
Arizona Children's Home, Tucson, AZ
Arizona State Hospital, Phoenix, AZ
Arizona State Hospital—Nueva Vista School, Phoenix, AZ
Arlington School, Belmont, MA
Arnell Engstrom Children's Center, Traverse City, MI
Aseltine School, San Diego, CA
The Astor Home for Children—Day Treatment Program, Poughkeepsie, NY
The Astor Home for Children—Day Treatment Program, Bronx, NY
The Astor Home for Children—Group Home Program, Bronx, NY
The Astor Home for Children—Residential Treatment Center—Residential Treatment Facility—Learning Center, Rhinebeck, NY
Atlantic Mental Health Center Inc, McKee City, NJ
Augusta School Department, Augusta, ME
Aurora Adolescent Day Resource Center, Aurora, CO
Austin State Hospital, Austin, TX
Avalon Center—Avalon Schools, Lenox, MA
Avondale House, Houston, TX
The Baird Center for Children and Families Inc, Burlington, VT
Baker Hall Inc, Lackawanna, NY
Barat Human Services—Barat House, Detroit, MI
Bar-None Residential Treatment Services for Children, Anoka, MN
The Battin Clinic, Houston, TX
Battle Creek Child Guidance Center, Battle Creek, MI
Beacon Day Treatment Program, Romulus, MI
Behavior Research Institute, Providence, RI
Behavioral Development Center Inc, Providence, RI
Berea Children's Home, Berea, OH
Bergen Center for Child Development, Haworth, NJ
Bergen Pines Hospital—Children's Psychiatric Unit, Paramus, NJ
Berks County Intermediate Unit, Reading, PA
Berkshire Farm Center and Services for Youth, Canaan, NY
Big Lakes Developmental Center Inc, Manhattan, KS
Big Spring State Hospital, Big Spring, TX
Birmingham City Board of Education, Birmingham, AL
Blick Clinic for Developmental Disabilities, Akron, OH
Board of Cooperative Educational Services II—Special Education Division Instructional Support Center, Centereach, NY
BOCES Nassau, Westbury, NY
BOCES Onondaga Madison, East Syracuse, NY

BOCES Southern Westchester—Rye Lake Campus, White Plains, NY
Boston Public Schools—The McKinley Schools, Mattapau, MA
Bowman Gray School of Medicine Developmental Evaluation Clinic—Amos Cottage Rehabilitation Hospital, Winston-Salem, NC
Boys' and Girls' Aid Society of San Diego—Cottonwood Center and Community Based Psychiatric Program, El Cajon, CA
Boys' Town of Missouri Inc, Saint James, MO
Boys' Village Inc—Boys' Village School, Smithville, OH
Bradley Hospital, East Providence, RI
Brant Services Corporation—Brant Ryan House, Inkster, MI
Brattleboro Retreat, Brattleboro, VT
Brea Neuropsychiatric Center, Brea, CA
Brentwood Center, Los Angeles, CA
Brewer-Porch Children's Center, University, AL
Bridgeway Hospital Youthcare Program, North Little Rock, AR
Brighton School and Diagnostic Center, Phoenix, AZ
Brooklyn Community Counseling Center, Brooklyn, NY
Broom-Tioga Board of Cooperative Educational Services, Binghamton, NY
Brown County Mental Health Center—Children Services, Green Bay, WI
The Brown Schools, Austin, TX
Buckeye Boys' Ranch Inc, Grove City, OH
Burt Children's Center, San Francisco, CA
Butler County Mental Health Center Inc, Hamilton, OH
Capital City Schools, Topeka, KS
Cass County Social Services—Children's Social Service Center, Fargo, ND
Cayuga Home for Children, Auburn, NY
Center for Life Management, Salem, NH
Center for Urban Living, Saint Louis, MO
Chancellor Academy, Pompton Plains, NJ
The Charlton School, Burnt Hills, NY
Charter Westbrook Hospital, Richmond, VA
Chestnut Lodge Hospital—Adolescent and Child Division, Rockville, MD
Child Adolescent Service Center, Canton, OH
Child and Adolescent Psychiatric Clinic Inc, Buffalo, NY
Child and Adolescent Psychoeducational Center, Dalton, GA
Child and Family Services, Knoxville, TN
Child Development Service—Lakeview Center Inc, Pensacola, FL
Child Disability Clinic—Carle Clinic, Urbana, IL
Child Guidance Center of Southern Connecticut, Stanford, CT
Child Guidance Clinic—Day Treatment Program, Winston-Salem, NC
Child Guidance Clinic of Southeastern Connecticut Inc, New London, CT
Child Psychiatry Service—Department of Psychiatry—University Hospitals, Ann Arbor, MI
Child Study and Treatment Center, Tacoma, WA
Child Study Center, Fort Worth, TX
Childhaven, Saint Louis, MO
Children's Aid Society, Cleveland, OH
Children's and Adolescent Unit of Mental Health Institute of Cherokee Iowa, Cherokee, IA
Children's Behavior Therapy Unit, Salt Lake City, UT
Children's Bureau of Indianapolis Inc, Indianapolis, IN
Children's Center, Hamden, CT
The Children's Center, Salt Lake City, UT
Children's Center for Behavioral Development, East Saint Louis, IL
Children's Day Hospital—New York Hospital—Cornell Medical Center—Westchester Division, White Plains, NY
The Children's Day School, Trenton, NJ
Children's Day Treatment Center, Honolulu, HI
Children's Health Council, Palo Alto, CA
Children's Home of Cedar Rapids—Cedarwood Group Home, Cedar Rapids, IA
Children's Home of Cedar Rapids—Heartwood Residential Treatment Center, Cedar Rapids, IA
Children's Home of Cedar Rapids—Maplewood Group Home, Cedar Rapids, IA

The Children's Home of Cincinnati, Cincinnati, OH
Children's Home of Kingston, Kingston, NY
Children's Home Society of South Dakota, Sioux Falls, SD
Children's Hospital at Washington University Medical Center—Psychiatric Unit, Saint Louis, MO
The Children's Institute, South Orange, NJ
Children's Medical Center, Tulsa, OK
Children's Medical Center—Psychiatric Inpatient Unit, Dallas, TX
Children's Mental Health Center Inc, Columbus, OH
The Children's Mercy Hospital—Section of Psychiatry, Kansas City, MO
Children's Psychiatric Center of the Jewish Hospital, Cincinnati, OH
The Children's School of the Institute of Living, Hartford, CT
The Children's Study Home, Springfield, MA
The Children's Village, Dobbs Ferry, NY
Christ Church Child Center, Bethesda, MD
Christian Church—Children's Campus, Danville, KY
Christian Haven Homes—Central Indiana Campus, Wheatfield, IN
Christie School, Marylhurst, OR
Clear View School, Scarborough, NY
The Clearing, Marshfield, VT
Clearwater Ranch Children's House Inc, Philo, CA
Cleveland Christian Home for Children Inc, Cleveland, OH
Cleveland Clinic Foundation, Cleveland, OH
Cleveland County Area Mental Health Program—Division of Child and Youth Services, Shelby, NC
The Clinical Center of Southern Illinois University, Carbondale, IL
Cobb County—Cobb Douglas Psychoeducation Children's Program, Marietta, GA
College Hospital—College Park School, Cerritos, CA
Colorado Springs School District No. 11, Colorado Springs, CO
Colorado West Regional Mental Health Center, Glenwood Springs, CO
Community Counseling Center—Rural Clinics, Ely, NV
Community Mental Health Center South, Lee's Summit, MO
The Community School of the Family Service and Child Guidance Center of the Oranges Maplewood and Millburn, Orange, NJ
Comprehensive Mental Health Center of St Clair County Inc, East Saint Louis, IL
Concord, Yellow Spring, WV
Connecticut Junior Republic—Litchfield District, Litchfield, CT
Convalescent Hospital for Children, Rochester, NY
Cooperative Educational Services Developmental Learning Center, Wilton, CT
Covenant Children's Home and Family Services, Princeton, IL
CPC Belmont Hills Hospital, Belmont, CA
Craig House—Technoma, Pittsburgh, PA
CRATER of Broward Inc—Retreat Ranch Facility—24 Hour Residential Treatment Center, Fort Lauderdale, FL
Creative Learning Systems Inc, Tucson, AZ
Crockett State School Independent School District, Crockett, TX
Cumberland County Guidance Center Inc, Millville, NJ
Dakota Boys' Ranch, Minot, ND
Dakota House, Aberdeen, SD
Daniel Memorial Inc, Jacksonville, FL
Darden Hill Ranch School, Driftwood, TX
De Neuville Heights School for Girls, Memphis, TN
DeJarnette Center, Staunton, VA
The Delacato and Doman Autistic Unit, Morton, PA
Delaware Guidance Services for Children and Youth Inc, Wilmington, DE
Department of Education—Windward Oahu District, Kaneohe, HI
DePaul Hospital and Residential Treatment Center, New Orleans, LA
Des Moines Children's Home—Orchard Place, Des Moines, IA
Desert Hills, Tucson, AZ
DeSisto Schools Inc, West Stockbridge, MA
The Devereux Center in Arizona, Scottsdale, AZ
The Devereux Foundation, Devon, PA

The Devereux Foundation, Santa Barbara, CA
The Devereux Foundation—Deerhaven, Chester, NJ
The Devereux Foundation—Texas Branch, Victoria, TX
Devereux in Georgia, Kennesaw, GA
The Devereux Schools at Rutland, Rutland, MA
Dominion Hospital—The Dominion School, Falls Church, VA
Donaldsonville Mental Health Center, Donaldsonville, LA
Douglas A Thom Clinic Inc, Boston, MA
Early Childhood Developmental Center Inc, Hays, KS
East Alabama Mental Health Retardation Center, Opelika, AL
East St Louis Area Joint Agreement—Department of Special Education, East Saint Louis, IL
Eastern Area Residential Treatment Home (EARTH), Greenville, NC
Eastern Shore Mental Health Center, Nassawadox, VA
Eau Claire Academy, Eau Claire, WI
The Eckerd Wilderness Educational System Camping System, Clearwater, FL
Edgefield Children's Center, Troutdale, OR
Edgemont Hospital, Los Angeles, CA
Edgewood Children's Center, Saint Louis, MO
Edgewood Children's Center, San Francisco, CA
Edgewood Day Treatment—The Lucinda Weeks Center, San Francisco, CA
The Educational Clinic Inc, Columbus, OH
Educational Department of Institute of Pennsylvania Hospital—Mill Creek School, Philadelphia, PA
El Paso Guidance Center, El Paso, TX
Elm Acres Youth Home Inc, Pittsburg, KS
Elmcrest Children's Center, Syracuse, NY
Elmcrest Psychiatric Institute, Portland, CT
Emerson North, Cincinnati, OH
Emma Pendleton Bradley Hospital Developmental Disabilities Program, East Providence, RI
The Episcopal Center for Children, Washington, DC
The Episcopal Church Home for Children—York Place, York, SC
Epworth Village Inc, York, NE
Escalon Inc, Altadena, CA
Escambia District Schools, Pensacola, FL
Ettie Lee Homes Inc, Baldwin Park, CA
Evansville Vanderburgh School Corporation, Evansville, IN
Excelsior Youth Center, Aurora, CO
Fairmount Children's Center, Syracuse, NY
Family and Children's Center, LaCrosse, WI
Family Guidance Center, Reading, PA
Family Guidance Service—Ingham Community Mental Health Center, Lansing, MI
Five Acres Boys' and Girls' Aide Society, Altadena, CA
Flint Community Schools, Flint, MI
Forest Heights Lodge, Evergreen, CO
Forest Hospital, Des Plaines, IL
Fort Logan Mental Health Center, Denver, CO
The Forum School, Waldwick, NJ
Franklin Grand Isle Mental Health Services Inc, Saint Albans, VT
Fred Finch Youth Center, Oakland, CA
The Frost School, Rockville, MD
Garfield Girls' School, Phoenix, AZ
Gateway United Methodist Youth Center and Family Services, Williamsville, NY
The George Junior Republic Association Inc, Freeville, NY
Gerard of Minnesota Inc, Austin, MN
Gibault School For Boys, Terre Haute, IN
Gilfillan Center, Bemidji, MN
Gladman Memorial Hospital Adolescent Program, Oakland, CA
Glens Falls Hospital—Child and Family Services—Community Mental Health Center, Glens Falls, NY
The Goldstaub Residence, Houston, TX
Grady Memorial Hospital—Division of Child and Adolescent Psychiatry, Atlanta, GA
Grant Center Hospital, Miami, FL
Graydon Manor, Leesburg, VA
Green Chimneys Children's Services Inc, Brewster, NY
Green Meadows School, Wilmington, VT

Green Tree School, Philadelphia, PA

Greenshire School, Cheshire, CT

Grove School, Madison, CT

Hall-Mercer Children's Center of the McLean Hospital, Belmont, MA

Hall-Brooke Foundation—Hall-Brooke Hospital—Hall-Brooke School, Westport, CT

Hamilton Children's Center, Hyattsville, MD

The Hannah More Center, Reisterstown, MD

Harbor Schools Inc, Newburyport, MA

Harbor View Mercy Hospital, Fort Smith, AR

Harford County Community Mental Health Center, Bel Air, MD

Hartgrove Hospital—Hartgrove Academy, Chicago, IL

Hathaway School of Hathaway Home for Children, Pacoima, CA

Hawaii State Department of Education—Special Needs Branch, Honolulu, HI

Hawaii State Hospital—Adolescent Unit, Kaneohe, HI

Hawthorn Center, Northville, MI

Hawthorne Cedar Knolls School, Hawthorne, NY

Hawthorne Children's Psychiatric Hospital, Saint Louis, MO

Henderson Mental Health Center, Fort Lauderdale, FL

Henrietta Weill Memorial Child Guidance Clinic, Bakersfield, CA

Henry Horner Children and Adolescent Center, Chicago, IL

High Plains Mental Health Center—Colby Office, Colby, KS

High Point Adolescent School—Children's Psychiatric Center, Morganville, NJ

Highland Youth Services—The Highland School, Pittsburgh, PA

Hillside Children's Center, Rochester, NY

Hillside Inc, Atlanta, GA

Hillside School Inc, Logan, UT

Homewood School—Highland Hospital, Asheville, NC

Honolulu District—Special Education Center of Oahu (SECO), Honolulu, HI

Humana Hospital Huntington Beach—Children's Behavioral Center, Huntington Beach, CA

Hunterdon Learning Center, Califon, NJ

Idaho Youth Ranch Inc, Rupert, ID

Independence House of Avalon Inc, Sheffield, MA

Indiana Girls' School, Indianapolis, IN

Ingleside Hospital, Rosemead, CA

The Institute Day School, Lowell, MA

Institute for Developmental Disabilities—Crystal Springs School, Assonet, MA

Institute for Family and Life Learning Residential School, Danvers, MA

The Institute of Living School, Hartford, CT

Institute of Psychiatry and Human Behavior—Department of Psychiatry—Child and Adolescent Inpatient Service, Baltimore, MD

ISIS Programs Inc—Individual Support Through Innovative Services for Autistic Persons, Orlando, FL

Italian Home for Children, Jamaica Plain, MA

Ittleson Center for Child Research, New York, NY

Jackson Municipal Separate School District, Jackson, MS

Jane Wayland Center, Phoenix, AZ

Jasper County Mental Health Center, Newton, IA

Jeanine Schultz Memorial School, Park Ridge, IL

Jefferson County Public Schools, Lakewood, CO

Jefferson Parish School System—Department of Special Education, Gretna, LA

Jennie Clarkson Child Care Services Inc—St Christopher's, Dobbs Ferry, NY

Jersey Shore Medical Center—Child Evaluation Center, Neptune, NJ

Jewish Child Care Association—Pleasantville Cottage School, Pleasantville, NY

Jewish Children's Bureau of Chicago, Chicago, IL

The John F Kennedy Institute, Baltimore, MD

John G McGrath School, Napa, CA

John Umstead Hospital—Children's Psychiatric Institute, Butner, NC

Josephine County Mental Health Program—Children's Resource Team, Grants Pass, OR

Kalamazoo Child Guidance Clinic, Kalamazoo, MI

K-Bar-B Youth Ranch—Richard M Wise School, Lacombe, LA

Kenai Peninsula Borough School District, Soldotna, AK

Kings County Hospital—Downstate Medical Center—Division of Child and Adolescent Psychiatry, Brooklyn, NY

Klamath County Mental Health Center—Natural Family Preservation Project, Klamath Falls, OR

La Mel, San Francisco, CA

La Puente Valley Community Mental Health Center, La Puente, CA

Lad Lake Inc, Dousman, WI

Lafayette Clinic, Detroit, MI

Lake County Mental Health Center—Department of Children's Services, Mentor, OH

Lake Grove School, Lake Grove, NY

Lakeshore Mental Health Institute—Riverbend School—Children and Youth Services, Knoxville, TN

Lakeside Center for Boys, Saint Louis, MO

Lakin Hospital—Adolescent Services, Lakin, WV

Lane School Programs—Lane Education Service District, Eugene, OR

Lansing School District, Lansing, MI

Larned State Hospital—Child Psychiatric Unit—Adolescent Psychiatric Unit/Westside School, Larned, KS

LaSalle School, Albany, NY

Leary School Inc, Alexandria, VA

Lighthouse School, Chelmsford, MA

Little Friends Inc—Little Friends School, Naperville, IL

The Los Angeles Child Guidance Clinic, Los Angeles, CA

Los Angeles County Office of Education—Mark Twain School, Lawndale, CA

Lourdesmont—Good Shepherd Youth and Family Services, Clarks Summit, PA

Lovellton Academy, Elgin, IL

Luther Child Center—Children's Hospitalization Alternative Program, Everett, WA

Lutheran Medical Center—Psychiatric Division, Saint Louis, MO

Lutherbrook Children's Center, Addison, IL

Madden Mental Health Center Campus—Institute for Juvenile Research—Inpatient Services, Hines, IL

Madeline Burg Counseling Services—Jewish Board of Family and Children Services, Bronx, NY

Main Street Human Resources, Great Barington, MA

Manhattan Children's Psychiatric Center, New York, NY

Manitowoc County Counseling Center, Manitowoc, WI

Martin Luther Centers, Madison, WI

Marymount Hospital Mental Health Center, Garfield Heights, OH

Maryvale, Rosemead, CA

Massanutten Mental Health Center, Harrisonburg, VA

McAuley Nazareth Home for Boys, Leicester, MA

McKinley Therapeutic Center, Chicago, IL

Mears House, Highland, IN

Medical Care Rehabilitation Hospital's Child Evaluation and Treatment Program, Grand Forks, ND

Meharry Community Mental Health Center, Nashville, TN

Mendota Mental Health Institute—Child and Adolescent Program, Madison, WI

The Menninger Foundation—Pre-School Day Treatment Center, Topeka, KS

The Menninger Foundation—The Children's Division, Topeka, KS

Menorah Medical Center—Hearing and Speech Department, Kansas City, MO

Mental Health Care Center of the Lower Keys, Key West, FL

Mental Health Center of Mid-Iowa, Marshalltown, IA

The Mental Health Institute for Children at Allentown State Hospital, Allentown, PA

Mental Health Services of North Central Hamilton Co Inc, Cincinnati, OH

Mercy Hospital and Medical Center—Community Guidance Center, Chicago, IL

Meridell Achievement Center Inc, Austin, TX

MHMR of Southeast Texas—Daybreak Cottage, Orange, TX

Michael Reese Hospital and Medical Center—Dysfunctioning Child Center, Chicago, IL

The Mid Fairfield Child Guidance Center Inc, Norwalk, CT

Mid-Columbia Mental Health Center—Adolescent Psychiatric Department, Richland, WA

Milford Assistance Program Day School, Milford, MA

Millcreek Schools Inc, Magee, MS

Minnesota Learning Center, Brainerd, MN

Monroe County Intermediate School District—Programs for Emotionally Impaired, Monroe, MI

Mt Airy Psychiatric Center—Children's Treatment Program—Adolescent Treatment Program, Denver, CO

Mt Scott Institute, Washington, NJ

Mountain Board of Cooperative Services—Adolescent Day Treatment Program, Leadville, CO

Nannahagur School Day Treatment Program—(JCCA), Pleasantville, NY

Napa State Hospital—Children's Program, Imola, CA

National Foundation for the Treatment of the Emotionally Handicapped, Sepulveda, CA

New England Home for Little Wanderers—Knight Children's Center, Boston, MA

New England Medical Center—Bay Cove Day Center for Children Day Hospital, Boston, MA

New England Medical Center—Division of Child Psychiatry, Boston, MA

New England Salem Children's Trust, Rumney, NH

New Hope Guild, Brooklyn, NY

New Jersey Training School for Boys, Jamesburg, NJ

New Mexico Boys' School, Springer, NM

North Central Health Care Facilities, Wausau, WI

North Dakota State Mental Hospital—Child and Adolescent Unit, Jamestown, ND

North Metro Psychoeducational Program, Atlanta, GA

Northeast Colorado Board of Cooperative Educational Services, Haxton, CO

Northwest Florida Mental Health Center, Panama City, FL

Northwest Psychoeducational Program, Rome, GA

Northwood Children's Home, Duluth, MN

Norton Psychiatric Clinic—Norton Adolescent Treatment Program and Norton Academy, Louisville, KY

Oconee Area Psycho Educational Program, Milledgeville, GA

Oconomowoc Developmental Training Center Inc, Oconomowoc, WI

Office of Riverside County Superintendent of Schools, Riverside, CA

Orlando Regional Medical Center—Mental Health Department—Children's Services, Orlando, FL

Osterlen Services for Youth, Springfield, OH

Otis R Bowen Center, Warsaw, IN

Our Lady of Providence Children's Center, West Springfield, MA

Overlook Mental Health Center—Blount County Adolescent Partial Hospitalization Program, Maryville, TN

Pace School, Braintree, MA

Pace School, Pittsburgh, PA

Pacific Children's Center, Oakland, CA

Paradise Valley School District No. 69—Therapeutic Educational Activities Milieu, Phoenix, AZ

Parkview Counseling Center Inc, Youngstown, OH

Parkwood Hospital, Atlanta, GA

Parmadale—The Youth Services Village, Parma, OH

Parry Center for Children, Portland, OR

Parsons Child and Family Center, Albany, NY

Parsons Child and Family Center—Neil Hellman School, Albany, NY

Partial Hospitalization Program Children's Service Center, Wilkes Barre, PA

Pawnee Mental Health Services, Concordia, KS

Peace River Center for Personal Development Inc, Bartow, FL

Peanut Butter and Jelly Therapeutic Pre-School, Albuquerque, NM

Peninsula Children's Center—Children and Youth Services, Palo Alto, CA

Philadelphia Child Guidance Clinic, Philadelphia, PA

Philadelphia Child Guidance Clinic—Child and Family Inpatient Service, Philadelphia, PA

Philbrook Center—Special Education Program, Concord, NH

Phoenix Union High School District No. 210, Phoenix, AZ

Pikes Peak Board of Cooperative Services, Colorado Springs, CO

Pine Haven Boys' Center, Suncook, NH

Pomona Mental Health Center—Child Development Center, Pomona, NY

Porter Starke Services Inc—Vale Park Psychiatric Hospital, Valparaiso, IN

Prehab of Arizona Inc—Dorothy Mitchell Residence—Homestead Residence—Helaman House, Mesa, AZ

Prescott Child Development Center, Prescott, AZ

Pressley Ridge School—Day School, Pittsburgh, PA

Pressley Ridge School—Laurel Park, Clarksburg, WV

Pressley Ridge School—Pryde—Family Based Treatment, Pittsburgh, PA

Pressley Ridge School—Wilderness School, Ohiopyle, PA

Primary Children's Medical Center—Department of Child Psychiatry, Salt Lake City, UT

Project for Psychotic and Neurologically Impaired Children, Madison, WI

Protestant Youth Center, Baldwinville, MA

Provo Canyon School, Provo, UT

Psychiatric Clinic of the Charlotte Hungerford Hospital, Torrington, CT

Psychiatric Services Inc, Haverhill, MA

Queen of Angels School—Villa Maria Treatment Center, Timonium, MD

Queens Hospital Center Department of Psychiatry Child and Adolescent Clinic, Jamaica, NY

Raineswood Residential Center, Memphis, TN

Ranch Hope Strang School, Alleway, NJ

Range Mental Health Center, Virginia, MN

Raritan Bay Mental Health Center, Perth Amboy, NJ

The Re-Ed West Center for Children Inc, Sacramento, CA

Red Rock Comprehensive Mental Health Center, Oklahoma City, OK

The Rehabilitation Institute of Pittsburgh, Pittsburgh, PA

Rensselaer County Mental Health Department—Unified Services for Children and Adolescents, Troy, NY

Ridgeview Institute, Smyrna, GA

Ridgeview Psychiatric Hospital and Center, Oak Ridge, TN

Rochester Mental Health Center Inc—Day Treatment Unit Services—Children and Youth Division, Rochester, NY

Rockford School District No. 205, Rockford, IL

Rockland Children's Psychiatric Center, Orangeburg, NY

Rockland Psychological and Educational Center, Spring Valley, NY

Rutland Psychoeducational Services, Athens, GA

Sagamore Hills Children's Psychiatric Hospital, Northfield, OH

St Ann's Home Inc—Day Treatment and Special Education Program, Methuen, MA

St Ann's Home Inc—Residential Treatment and Special Education Program, Methuen, MA

St Cabrini Home Inc, West Park, NY

St Clare's Hospital—Adult, Child and Family Services, Denville, NJ

St Cloud Children's Home, Saint Cloud, MN

St Elizabeth's Hospital—Division of Child and Adolescent Services, Washington, DC

The St Francis Boys' Homes Inc, Salina, KS

St Francis Boys' Home—Camelot, Lake Placid, NY

St Gabriel's Hall, Phoenixville, PA

St George Homes Inc, Berkeley, CA

St John's Child Development Center, Washington, DC

St Joseph Center for Mental Health, Omaha, NE

St Joseph Residential Treatment and Child Care Center, Dayton, OH

St Joseph's Carondelet Child Center, Chicago, IL

St Louis County Child Mental Health Services, Saint Louis, MO

St Mary's Home for Boys, Beaverton, OR

St Vincent Children's Center, Columbus, OH

St Vincent's Hospital and Medical Center of New York—Child and Adolescent Psychiatry Service, New York, NY

The Salvation Army Residential Treatment Facilities for Children and Youth, Honolulu, HI

Samarkand Manor, Eagle Springs, NC

San Diego County Mental Health Services—Loma Portal Facility, San Diego, CA

San Diego Unified School District, San Diego, CA

San Joaquin County Office of Education—Special Education Programs, Stockton, CA

San Marcos Treatment Center of The Brown Schools, San Marcos, TX

San Mateo County Office of Education, Redwood City, CA

School for Contemporary Education, Baltimore, MD

School for Contemporary Education, Springfield, VA

Secret Harbor School, Anacortes, WA

Seminole County Board of Public Instruction—Programs for Emotionally Handicapped, Sanford, FL

Serendipity Diagnostic and Treatment Center, Citrus Heights, CA

Shadow Mountain Institute, Tulsa, OK

Shawnee Mission Public Schools, Shawnee Mission, KS

Solomon Mental Health Center, Lowell, MA

Sonia Shankman Orthogenic School of the University of Chicago, Chicago, IL

South Bend Community School Corporation—Adolescent Day Treatment Center, South Bend, IN

South Carolina State Hospital—Child and Adolescent Unit—Blanding House, Columbia, SC

South Dakota Human Services Center, Yankton, SD

South Oaks Hospital, Amityville, NY

South Shore Child Guidance Center, Freeport, NY

Southbury Training School, Southbury, CT

Southeast Kansas Mental Health Center, Humboldt, KS

Southeast Mental Health Center—Child Development Institute, Memphis, TN

Southgate Regional Center for Developmental Disabilities, Southgate, MI

Southlake Center for Mental Health, Merriville, IN

Southwest Georgia Psychoeducational Services—Thomas County Schools, Ochlocknee, GA

Southwood Psychiatric Residential Treatment Center—Hillcrest, San Diego, CA

Spaulding Youth Center—Autistic Program, Tilton, NH

Spaulding Youth Center—Emotional Handicap Program, Tilton, NH

Special Care Program, Orofino, ID

Special Education Association of Adams County, Quincy, IL

Special Service School District of Bergen County, Paramus, NJ

Spectrum Center for Educational and Behavioral Development Inc, Berkeley, CA

Spence Chapin Services to Families and Children—The Children's House, New York, NY

The Spofford Home, Kansas City, MO

Springfield Park Central Hospital—Park Central School, Springfield, MO

The Starr Commonwealth Schools, Albion, MI

Starr Commonwealth Schools—Hannah Neil Center for Children, Columbus, OH

State Agriculture and Industrial School, Industry, NY

State Training School, Eldora, IA

Stetson School Inc, Barre, MA

Strafford Guidance Center Inc, Dover, NH

Stuyvesant Residence Club, New York City, NY

Summit Children's Residence Center, Upper Nyack, NY

Sunburst Youth Homes, Neillsville, WI

Sunny Hill Children's Center Inc, Greenwich, CT

Sunset Learning Center, Fort Lauderdale, FL

Switzer Center, Torrance, CA

The Sycamores, Altadena, CA

Taylor Manor Hospital, Ellicott City, MD

Terry Children's Psychiatric Center, New Castle, DE

Timberlawn Psychiatric Hospital, Dallas, TX

Timberridge Institute for Children and Adolescents Inc, Oklahoma City, OK

Tomorrow's Children, Waupaca, WI

Towering Pines Center, Slidell, LA

Training Center for Youth, Columbus, OH

Tri-County Community Mental Health Center, Kansas City, MO

Trumbull County Board of Education, Warren, OH

United Methodist Youthville, Newton, KS

University Hospitals of Cleveland—Hanna Pavilion Child Psychiatric Unit, Cleveland, OH

The University of Chicago—Departments of Psychiatry and Pediatrics—Child Psychiatry, Chicago, IL

University of Colorado Health Sciences Center—Day Care Center, Denver, CO

University of Illinois Medical Center—Child Psychiatry Clinic, Chicago, IL

University of Minnesota Hospitals—Child and Adolescent Psychiatry, Minneapolis, MN

University of New Mexico Children's Psychiatric Hospital—Mimbres School, Albuquerque, NM

University of New Mexico—Children's Psychiatric Hospital, Albuquerque, NM

University of Rochester Medical School—Child and Adolescent Psychiatry Clinic, Rochester, NY

University of South Florida—Florida Mental Health Institute—Department of Child and Family Services, Tampa, FL

University of Texas Medical Branch—Division of Pediatric Psychology—Department of Pediatrics, Galveston, TX

University of Texas Medical Branch—Inpatient Service—Division of Child and Adolescent Psychiatry, Galveston, TX

University Park Psychological Center, Denver, CO

Utah Boys' Ranch—Children and Youth Services Inc, Salt Lake City, UT

Valleyhead Inc, Lenox, MA

Vanderbilt Medical Center—Division of Child and Adolescent Psychiatry, Nashville, TN

Variety Preschooler's Workshop, Syosset, NY

Ventura County Superintendent of Schools, Ventura, CA

Village of St Joseph, Atlanta, GA

Virginia Center for Psychiatry, Portsmouth, VA

Virginia Center for Psychiatry, Norfolk, VA

Vista Del Mar Child Care Service, Los Angeles, CA

Vista Maria, Dearborn Heights, MI

Vitam Center Inc—Vitam School, Norwalk, CT

Walker Home and School, Needham, MA

Wallace Village for Children, Broomfield, CO

Walter Reed Army Medical Center Child and Adolescent Psychiatry Service, Washington, DC

War Bonnet—Wilderness Pathways, Canaan, NH

Warm Springs Center, Boise, ID

Waterford Country School, Quaker Hill, CT

Waterloo Community Schools, Waterloo, IA

West Nassau Mental Health Center, Franklin Square, NY

West River Children's Center of the Children's Home Society of South Dakota, Rapid City, SD

West Texas Boys' Ranch, San Angelo, TX

Westbridge, Phoenix, AZ

Western District Guidance Center, Parkersburg, WV

Western New York Children's Psychiatric Center, West Seneca, NY

West-Ros-Park Mental Health Center, Roslindale, MA

Wheeler Clinic Inc—Northwest Village School, Plainville, CT

Wichita Guidance Center, Wichita, KS

Wilder Children's Placement, Saint Paul, MN

Willowglen Academy Inc, Milwaukee, WI

Winnebago Mental Health Institute—Children's Unit, Winnebago, WI

Woodbourne Center, Baltimore, MD

Woodward Mental Health Center, Freeport, NY

Wyalusing Academy, Prairie du Chien, WI

Wyandotte Special Education Cooperative, Kansas City, KS

Wyoming Youth Treatment Center, Casper, WY

Yellowstone Boys' and Girls' Ranch, Billings, MT

York Woods Center, Ypsilanti, MI

Youth and Family Services, Omaha, NE

Youth Evaluation and Treatment Centers (YETC), Phoenix, AZ
Yuma Union High School District, Yuma, AZ
Zonta Children's Center, San Jose, CA

Cakes & Pastries

ROBERT CARRIER'S KITCHEN

Cakes & Pastries

Marshall Cavendish   London Sydney & New York

Editor	Roz Fishel
Editorial Staff	Caroline Macy
	Penny Smith
	Kate Toner
	Anne Wiltsher
Designer	Alan White
Series Editor	Pepita Aris
Production Executive	Robert Paulley
Production Controller	Steve Roberts

Photography
Bryce Attwell: 28
Paul Bussell: 8, 9, 10, 11, 42, 55, 63, 65, 78, 86, 91, 93, 94, 98, 106
Alan Duns: 32, 68, 102
Laurie Evans: 29, 31, 36, 58, 75, 97, 100
Melvin Grey: 70, 72, 104
James Jackson: 2, 15, 35, 37, 60, 61, 62, 73, 74, 92, 96
Anthony Kay: 67
Chris Knaggs: 20, 22, 24, 25, 26, 27, 77, 88, 89, 107
David Levin: 99
Peter Myers: 17, 18, 39, 40, 44, 57, 59
Roger Phillips: 14, 71
Paul Webster: 54, 101
Paul Williams: 13, 38, 56, 76
Cover picture: **Alan Duns**

Weights and measures
Both metric and imperial measurements are given. As these are not exact equivalents, please work from one set of figures or the other. Use graded measuring spoons levelled across.

Time symbols
The time needed to prepare the dish is given on each recipe. The symbols are as follows:

 simple to prepare and cook

 straightforward but requires more skill or attention

 time-consuming to prepare or requires extra skill

 must be started 1 day or more ahead

On the cover: Chocolate cake, page 32

This edition published 1985
© Marshall Cavendish Limited 1985

Printed in Italy by
L.E.G.O. S.p.a. Vicenza

Typeset by Quadraset Limited, Midsomer Norton, Bath, Avon

Published by Marshall Cavendish House
58 Old Compton Street London W1V 5PA
ISBN 0 86307 264 X (series)
ISBN 0 86307 410 3 (this volume)

Contents

In this superb volume, *Cakes & Pastries*, I cover a wonderful range of recipes from the simple to the sublime. If your taste is for rich, creamy gateaux, my opening chapter includes such sumptuous creations as chilled Italian tipsy gateau, a chocolate sponge soaked in brandy and orange liqueur, filled with thick cream, cherries, hazelnuts and chocolate, and then finished with Crème chantilly.

Chocolate-lovers are catered for in a section designed to show the versatility of chocolate. Try my recipes for rich Chocolate roulade and irresistible Chocolate éclairs, with my tempting variations on fillings and icings.

Do you have a special occasion approaching, such as a birthday or engagement party? If so, you'll enjoy my chapter on Celebration cakes. Using a simple genoise sponge base, I show you how to create three spectacular-looking cakes with creamy fillings, beautiful icings and pretty decorations. For more suggestions on these aspects of cake-making, see my chapters on Simple toppings and fillings, and Piping and icing techniques.

For the busy cook, my chapter on Batch baking for the freezer will prove extremely useful. I give you a recipe for a basic sponge mix from which you can make four delicious cakes — a Chocolate cake, a Lemon cake, a spicy Dutch apple cake and a walnut-topped Streussel cake.

Improve your pastry-making skills by following my invaluable tips. Open-plate tarts with fancy pastry edges or lattice tops that allow the filling to show, are not expensive to make and look both pretty and colourful. Or be adventurous and produce something really special like Strawberry mille-feuilles — layers of the lightest puff pastry oozing with Crème pâtissière and jam, then topped with glazed fresh strawberries.

In my chapter on Tea-time treats I give recipes for traditional favourites like crumpets, scones and Bakewell slices, as well as some ideas for biscuits and a lovely pineapple fruit cake. In the section on Family fare you'll find recipes to suit all age groups and tastes, from fruity Chelsea buns to scrumptious Walnut ice cream roll.

Happy cooking and bon appétit!

Robert Carrier

Cakes

GATEAUX

Gorgeous, gooey, grand and a gourmet's delight, these gateaux are pleasing to the eye and the palate. They are magnificent whether made for a special celebration or just as a treat for the family.

The word *gâteau* in French actually covers all kinds of pastries and cakes, but to many people it usually means a rich, layered sponge cake filled with cream or flavoured butter cream which is then beautifully decorated or iced. Most of the gateaux in this chapter are of this type, although Gâteau Paris-Brest is a good example of how choux pastry can be used as the base for a special cake. It was created 100 years ago to celebrate a famous bicycle race from Paris to Brest and back.

In this chapter, too, I have included my version of the popular Black Forest gateau. This confection does take time to prepare, but the results are mouth-watering. It is best made in two stages — first the cake should be baked and the filling prepared, then the gateau can be completed the next day. Using egg whites without yolks makes a rather dry and therefore perfect base for absorbing the juice from the cherries.

An interesting and unusual cake is Italian tipsy gateau which is a rich chocolate sponge, cut up to line a mould and spread with a cream and cherry mixture. The centre of the sponge circle is filled with Crème chantilly.

Orange gateau

 1 hour 50 minutes

Serves 8–10
butter and flour, for the tin
50 g /2 oz butter, in small pieces
4 eggs
100 g /4 oz caster sugar
100 g /4 oz flour, sifted twice
5 ml /1 tsp orange oil or 10 ml /2 tsp orange essence
50 g /2 oz flaked almonds, toasted
For the crème au beurre
75 g /3 oz caster sugar
2 egg yolks
100 g /4 oz unsalted butter
15 ml /1 tbls orange-flower water
orange oil or orange essence
orange food colouring (optional)
For the glacé icing
175 g /6 oz icing sugar, sifted
15 ml /1 tbls orange-flower water
orange oil or orange essence
orange food colouring (optional)

1 Heat the oven to 180C /350F /gas 4. Butter a 20 cm /8 in cake tin which has a loose base and dust it lightly with flour.
2 Place the butter in a bowl and stand this over a saucepan containing 5 cm /2 in of simmering water. When the butter has melted, remove the bowl from the pan and set it aside to allow the butter to cool until it is needed.
3 Place the eggs and sugar in a bowl of more than 1.5 L /2½ pt capacity and place this over the saucepan. Whisk with a hand-held electric beater, if you wish, until the volume is doubled and the mixture is white in colour. (Alternatively if you have a table-top mixer, whisk the eggs and sugar at high speed for 5 minutes until the volume is doubled and the mixture is pale and firm enough to leave a thick trail from the beaters when they are lifted.)
4 Sift a third of the flour into the bowl and gently fold it in with a metal spoon. Repeat with a second third of the flour.
5 Add the orange oil or essence to the butter and fold this, a tablespoon at a time, into the whisked mixture. When well blended, fold in the remaining flour.
6 Transfer to the prepared tin and bake for about 30 minutes, or until the cake is golden brown and firm to the touch. Turn it out onto a wire rack to cool.
7 To make the crème au beurre, place 45 ml /3 tbls water and the caster sugar in a heavy pan. Heat gently until the sugar has completely dissolved, then bring it to boiling point and continue boiling steadily until it reaches 115C /240F on a sugar thermometer; at this temperature a sample of the syrup dropped into a bowl of cold water will make a soft ball.
8 Place the egg yolks in a bowl and whisk well. Gradually add the syrup, whisking well all the time, until the mixture is both thick and cold.
9 In a separate bowl, beat the butter until it is creamy, then gradually beat in the egg mixture until the filling is smooth. Blend in the orange-flower water and add 1–2 drops of orange essence to flavour the filling to your taste. If wished, add a few drops of orange food colouring, a drop at a time, to tint it pale orange.
10 Split the cake in half horizontally, and use half the crème au beurre to sandwich the cake together. Use half the remaining crème to cover the sides of the cake.
11 Arrange the almonds on a sheet of greaseproof paper. Holding the cake between the palms of your hands, roll the creamy sides in the almonds to coat them all over.
12 Make the glacé icing by mixing the icing sugar with the orange-flower water and sufficient hot water (about 5 ml /1 tsp) to give a fairly thick consistency. Add 1–2 drops orange oil or 2–3 drops orange essence to flavour to your taste and tint with a few drops of orange food colouring, if wished. Use this icing to cover the top of the cake. Leave it to set.
13 Fill a piping bag fitted with a shell nozzle with the remaining crème au beurre and pipe a decoration around the top edge of the cake before serving.

Orange gateau

Black Forest cherry gateau

⏰ ||| 2 hours, overnight cooling, then 2½ hours

Makes 12 generous slices
butter and flour, for the tin
180 g /6½ oz plain chocolate, broken up
210 g /7½ oz butter
7 medium-sized egg whites, at room
  temperature
180 g /6½ oz icing sugar, sifted
180 g /6½ oz flour
For the filling
700 g /1½ lb cherries
90 ml /6 tbls icing sugar
30 ml /2 tbls vanilla caster sugar (see note
  following method)
225 ml /8 fl oz kirsch
500 ml /18 fl oz thick cream
50 g /2 oz chocolate shavings

1 Heat the oven to 180C /350F /gas 4. Grease and lightly dust with flour a 22–25 cm /9–10 in round cake tin. Melt the chocolate pieces in a bowl over hot water; remove the bowl as soon as the chocolate has melted.
2 Beat the butter until fluffy, then beat in the barely warm, melted chocolate.

3 Whisk the egg whites until very stiff, then whisk in the sifted icing sugar. Fold the chocolate mixture into the egg whites a quarter at a time, adding the sifted flour a quarter at a time, too. As soon as the chocolate is dispersed, stop mixing or you will break up the egg white bubbles. Continue folding in the flour and chocolate mixture until they have all been used. Pour the mixture into the prepared cake tin and bake in the centre of the oven for 1 hour. Test the cake before removing it from the oven — it should be well risen and springy to the touch. Allow the cake to cool for 5 minutes, then turn it out of the tin onto a rack and leave it overnight to become completely cold.
4 For the filling, reserve 13 whole cherries for decoration (stone them if you wish) and stone and halve the rest. Put all the cherries in a bowl, dust them with 60 ml /4 tbls icing sugar and 15 ml /1 tbls vanilla caster sugar; pour 100 ml /4 fl oz kirsch over them. Cover the bowl and leave for 3–4 hours.
5 Pour the liquid from the cherries into a small saucepan; heat it gently, but do not let the liquid boil, then pour it over the cherries again. Cover them and leave them overnight.
6 The next day, slice the cake horizontally into 3 layers and place them on 3 separate large plates.
7 Pour off the liquid from the cherries and measure it. If there is more than 200 ml /

7 fl oz, reduce it in a saucepan over a low heat. Add 50 ml /2 fl oz of kirsch and spoon the liquid over the cake layers; leave them to soak for 30 minutes.
8 Whip the cream until fairly stiff, whisk in the rest of the icing sugar, vanilla sugar to taste and the rest of the kirsch. (If any more liquid has leaked from the cherries, you can whip this into the cream as well, although it may tinge the cream pink.)
9 Reserve the flat bottom of the cake, upside down, for the top layer. Spread one layer of the cake with a third of the whipped cream, cover with half the halved cherries, put the second layer of cake on top of the first layer of cake, cream and cherries and repeat the procedure.
10 Put the top layer on the cake and mask the gateau with the remaining whipped cream. Decorate the top with the reserved cherries and cover the sides of the cake with chocolate shavings. Chill the cake for at least 1 hour before serving.

● A vanilla pod buried in a jar of icing or caster sugar for at least two weeks will impregnate the sugar with a delicate flavour.
● If you are using leftover egg whites and cannot remember how many there are, weigh them: 1 medium-to-large egg white weighs 35 g /1½ oz.

Black Forest cherry gateau

Italian tipsy gateau

🔪🔪 1 hour for the cake, plus cooling, then ½ hour, plus chilling

Serves 8
melted butter and flour, for the tins
75 g /3 oz flour
25 g /1 oz cocoa powder
5 eggs
75 g /3 oz caster sugar
25 g /1 oz butter, melted and cooled
60 ml /4 tbls brandy
60 ml /4 tbls orange liqueur
For the cream filling
575 ml /1 pt thick cream
25 g /1 oz icing sugar, sifted
50 g /2 oz hazelnuts, coarsely chopped
225 g /8 oz black cherries, halved
100 g /4 oz plain chocolate, grated
To decorate
Crème chantilly (see page 41)
icing sugar

1 First make the chocolate sponge. Heat the oven to 180C /350F /gas 4. Brush 2 × 19–20 cm/7½–8 in sandwich tins with melted butter. Line the bases with grease-proof paper and brush them again with butter. Lightly dust the tins with flour.
2 Sift the flour and cocoa powder together 3 times. Mix the eggs and caster sugar in a large bowl. Set the bowl over a pan of barely simmering water and whisk until thick, light and lukewarm.
3 Remove the bowl from the heat and continue whisking until the mixture has cooled and is thick so that the whisk leaves a trail.
4 Gradually resift the flour and cocoa over the surface of the egg mixture, folding it in lightly with a metal spoon. Fold in the cooled, melted butter quickly and lightly. Divide the mixture between the tins.
5 Bake for 15–20 minutes, or until the cakes are well risen and springy to the touch.

Italian tipsy gateau

Turn out onto a wire rack. Peel off the lining papers and leave the cakes until cold.
6 Slice the cold sponge cakes in 3 horizontally, to make 6 layers. Cut the edges off 3 layers leaving 3 squares. Cut each square in half. Place them in a 1.4 L /2½ pt ring mould. Reserve the trimmings for the top. Cut the remaining 3 layers into triangles and use them to fill the gaps, reserving the excess for the top. Trim the sponge lining, then sprinkle the lining with 45 ml /3 tbls brandy and 45 ml /3 tbls orange liqueur. Chill.
7 To make the filling, whisk the cream until it is stiff and combine it with the sifted icing sugar. Fold in the chopped hazelnuts, cherries and chocolate. Chill.
8 Spoon the cream mixture into the mould onto the sponge, leaving the outer edge clear. Top the mould with the remaining bits of sponge, sealing the outer edge, and sprinkle the remaining brandy and orange liqueur over it. Chill the mould for 2 hours.
9 Run a knife around the edge of the cake to loosen it. Invert a serving plate over the mould and, holding the two firmly together, reverse them. The cake should slide out of the mould easily.
10 Fill the centre of the ring with Crème chantilly. Immediately before serving, sprinkle with icing sugar.

Gâteau Paris-Brest

🔪🔪 45 minutes preparation, then 30 minutes cooking

Serves 6
65 g /2½ oz flour
50 g /2 oz unsalted butter, plus extra for greasing
3 medium-sized eggs
15 g /½ oz flaked almonds
icing sugar, to dredge and decorate

For the praline filling
50 g /2 oz caster sugar
50 g /2 oz unblanched almonds
250 ml /9 fl oz thick cream

1 Heat the oven to 200C /400F /gas 6. Sift the flour. Put 150 ml /5 fl oz water and the butter in a saucepan and bring to the boil. Add the flour all at once and beat with a wooden spoon over a low heat until the paste is smooth and leaves the sides of the pan cleanly. Remove from the heat and beat in 2 eggs, one at a time, until the paste is smooth and very shiny.
2 Mark a 20 cm /8 in circle on a greased baking sheet. Place the paste in a piping bag fitted with a plain 25 mm /1 in nozzle and pipe a ring following the marked shape on the baking sheet.
3 Beat the remaining egg and use it to brush the ring. Sprinkle the ring with the flaked almonds and dredge it evenly with icing sugar. Bake the ring in the oven for about 30 minutes or until the choux pastry is well risen and browned. Remove from the oven and split the ring horizontally. Cool both halves, with their rounded sides downwards, on a wire rack.
4 Meanwhile, make the praline. Place the sugar and almonds in a heavy-based saucepan over a medium heat and cook until the sugar melts. Stir with a metal spoon and remove from the heat when the sugar is brown. Turn the mixture onto a greased baking sheet and allow it to cool and harden.
5 Turn the hard praline out of the tin and crush it with a rolling pin or reduce it to a powder in a food processor or a blender.
6 Whip the cream until it is thick and then fold in the praline powder.
7 Just before serving, fill the choux pastry ring with the praline cream. Replace the top of the ring lightly — the cream filling should be visible between the halves of the ring. Sift icing sugar over the top.

Dobostorte

This layered sponge cake has an attractive caramelized top.

🔪🔪🔪 2 hours

Serves 6
butter and flour, for the baking trays
4 eggs
150 g /6 oz caster sugar
125 g /5 oz flour
a pinch of salt
125 g /5 oz sugar
2 × Crème au beurre (page 39), plus either 100 g /4 oz plain chocolate, melted and cooled, or 60 ml /4 tbls cocoa, sifted

1 Heat the oven to 190C /375F /gas 5. Cut six 20 cm /8 in diameter greaseproof paper circles. Lightly butter and flour each one and lay them flat on baking trays.
2 Choose a large bowl for whisking up the ingredients and select a large saucepan over which it will fit firmly. Pour 5 cm /2 in water into the pan and bring it to the boil. Reduce the heat. Place the eggs and the caster sugar

in the bowl and set it over the barely simmering water. Whisk until the mixture is light and thick enough to hold a trail on the surface when the beaters are lifted. Remove it from the heat and then continue whisking until it is cool.

3 Sift the flour with the salt and fold it into the egg and sugar mixture with a large metal spoon. Divide the sponge mixture evenly among the prepared paper circles, smoothing it with a palette knife to cover the circles in an even layer. Bake the sponges in batches for 10–12 minutes, or until they are golden and springy when touched. Transfer them to wire racks. Leave them to cool completely,

then peel off the greaseproof paper circles.

4 In a small saucepan dissolve the sugar in 150 ml /5 fl oz water; bring to the boil and boil for 15 minutes, or until the sugar caramelizes to a deep golden brown.

5 Select the best looking sponge layer and place it on a baking tray. Pour the caramel all over the sponge layer and leave it for 45 seconds to harden slightly. With an oiled knife and pressing deeply, mark the caramel into 6 sections. Allow it to become completely cold.

6 Make up the chocolate Crème au beurre and use half of it to sandwich the remaining sponge layers. Spread a little extra on the top

Dobostorte

of the fifth layer and carefully put the caramel-coated layer in position on top. Spread the sides of the cake with a quarter of the remaining crème au beurre. Transfer the Dobostorte to a large serving platter using 2 fish slices or palette knives.

7 Fill a piping bag which has been fitted with a star nozzle with the remaining chocolate crème au beurre and pipe a rosette on each marked-out section. Pipe a line in between each rosette and double back on it to form an arched effect. Do not refrigerate the Dobostorte or the caramel will spoil.

CHOCOLATE CAKES

Some of the most luxurious, rich cakes contain chocolate. Use it as a creamy filling, add it to the ingredients or smooth it on as a dark, tempting covering. Here are some irresistible chocolate cake recipes.

You can't go far wrong using chocolate as a cake flavouring. Few people dislike it and it complements a great number of different ingredients — particularly mint, nuts, orange and other citrus fruit and ginger. You can use grated or melted chocolate or cocoa for the flavouring but cocoa is more economical. Melted chocolate gives an attractive, hard glossy finish to biscuits and cakes.

You may have some difficulty in finding cooking chocolate (sometimes called baking chocolate) in shops but you can use plain dessert chocolate instead, adding sugar to taste if necessary.

My delicious Chocolate Swiss roll is easier to make than you may at first think, although care and patience are required when you are unrolling it. Don't let this put you off, the cake is too scrumptious to miss.

If, in the past, you have been a little reticent about making choux pastry for chocolate éclairs, do try it now. I think you'll find that the recipe is not too difficult to follow. One tip for success is to assemble everything you need before you start to bake. If the choux paste is left halfway through, the end results will be disappointing. Choux pastry is at its best on the day it is made, but it can be stored, after cooking, in an airtight tin for up to three days. On the other hand it also freezes successfully and can then be kept for six months.

I have included several suggestions for filling and icing the éclairs, so you can have different fillings for different occasions!

Chocolate éclairs

Everyone loves chocolate éclairs, whether they are filled with a chocolate crème pâtissière, as in the recipe, with sweetened whipped cream (see picture), or one of the variations listed below. Add the filling shortly before serving to prevent the éclairs from becoming soggy.

┃┃ 1 hour,
┃┃ plus cooling

Makes 10–12
75 g /3 oz butter
a pinch of salt
25 g /1 oz sugar
150 g /5 oz flour, sifted
3 medium-sized eggs
For the filling
3 medium-sized egg yolks
175 g /6 oz caster sugar
65 g /2½ oz flour, sifted
275 ml /10 fl oz milk
75 g /3 oz plain chocolate, grated
2.5 ml /½ tsp vanilla essence
For the icing
50 g /2 oz plain chocolate
200 g /7 oz icing sugar, sifted

1　First make the choux pastry. Heat the oven to 200C /400F /gas 6. Line a baking sheet with foil or non-stick baking paper.
2　Bring 275 ml /10 fl oz water to the boil in a pan with the butter, salt and sugar. Remove from the heat and add the flour, all at once. Beat with a wooden spoon until smooth. Return the pan to a low heat and continue to beat vigorously until the mixture leaves the sides of the pan. Remove from the heat and leave it to cool for 10 minutes.
3　Add the eggs one at a time, beating each one in thoroughly. Continue to beat until the mixture is smooth and glossy.
4　Fit a piping bag with a large plain nozzle and fill it with the mixture. Pipe 7.5 cm /3 in lengths onto the prepared baking sheet.
5　Bake for 15 minutes, or until the pastry cases are lightly coloured. Remove them from the oven and turn the oven off. Carefully slit the pastry cases along each side. Return the cases, on the baking sheet, to the oven, leaving the door propped open, for 10 minutes. Next, cool the cases on a wire rack while you make the filling.
6　To make the filling, beat the egg yolks and sugar in a bowl until light and creamy. Add the flour and continue beating until the mixture is smooth.
7　Heat the milk to just below boiling point and very slowly add it to the yolk mixture, stirring constantly. Add the grated chocolate and vanilla essence and stir the mixture over a very low heat until it is thick and smooth. On no account allow it to boil. Remove it from the heat and leave it to cool.
8　To make the icing, put 60 ml /4 tbls water and the chocolate, broken into pieces, in a saucepan and set it over a low heat. Stir until the chocolate has melted. Remove the pan from the heat and mix until it is smooth. Add the icing sugar, a little at a time, stirring continuously with a wooden spoon until smooth and thick. Leave to cool.
9　Fill the choux pastry cases with the chocolate cream, using a piping bag if you like, or a teaspoon.
10　Spread the icing on top of each filled pastry case. When the icing has set, use a metal spatula dipped in hot water to make a smooth finish.
11　Carefully lift the éclairs onto a serving dish and serve.

● Try some of these variations for filling and icing your éclairs:
● Flavour the filling with 15–30 ml /1–2 tbls rum, or rum essence, and substitute milk chocolate for plain chocolate to make the icing.
● For a coffee-flavoured filling, use 30 ml /1–2 tbls coffee essence or very strong black coffee.
● For orange or lemon flavouring, use the grated zest of either one small orange or one small lemon.

● Mix equal quantities of fruit purée with Crème pâtissière (page 66) to fill the éclairs.
● Try using Crème au beurre (see page 39), flavoured with vanilla essence, or sweetened whipped cream as fillings.
● Use both plain and milk chocolate for a decorative effect when icing the éclairs.
● Sprinkle chopped nuts or flaked nuts, or chopped glacé cherries or chopped crystallized fruit on top of the icing before it sets.
● Caramel topping made with 175 g /6 oz granulated sugar boiled for 4 minutes with 75 ml /5 tbls water gives a crisp, golden surface to the éclairs.
● The chocolate cream filling for the éclairs also makes an excellent filling for a chocolate meringue pie.

Chocolate roulade

🕐 ┃┃ 1 hour,
　　 plus overnight resting

Serves 6
butter, for greasing (optional)
100 g /4 oz plain chocolate
4 medium-sized eggs, separated
100 g /4 oz caster sugar
icing sugar, sifted, for dredging
200 ml /7 fl oz thick cream
75 ml /3 fl oz thin cream
15 ml /1 tbls chocolate liqueur
sugar, to taste (optional)

1　First prepare a 38×25 cm /15×10 in Swiss roll tin. Line the tin with non-stick silicone paper or with greased greaseproof paper. Heat the oven to 180C /350F /gas 4.
2　Break the chocolate into pieces and put it in a bowl with 45 ml /3 tbls water. Set the bowl over simmering water. Stir from time to time until it is melted.
3　In a bowl, beat the egg yolks until they are light and fluffy. Slowly add the sugar, continuing to beat. In a separate bowl whisk the egg whites until they are stiff.
4　Add the melted chocolate mixture to the beaten egg yolks, stirring it in thoroughly. Take a spoonful of the beaten whites and fold it into the yolk mixture to lighten it a little. Now very gently fold in the rest of the whites. Put the mixture into the prepared tin; spread it evenly. Bake for 15 minutes.
5　Remove from the oven and cover the crisp top of the sponge with a clean damp cloth — this will make it easier to roll. Leave it until it is cold — overnight if possible.
6　Shake some sifted icing sugar over a clean tea-towel and turn the baked sponge onto the tea-towel. Carefully peel off the paper, which will now be on top. The sponge is very fragile, so ease the paper off gently.
7　Whip the creams together with the liqueur. (You can add a little sugar if you like.) Very carefully spread the whipped cream over the surface of the sponge.
8　Using the tea-towel to help you, gently lift the longer edge of the sponge up until it rolls over. Continue until the roll is completed. Dredge with icing sugar and serve.

Chocolate roulade (in the foreground) and a plate of Chocolate éclairs with a sweetened, whipped cream filling

12

Chocolate orange sandwich cake

🍴 55 minutes,
plus cooling

Makes one 18 cm /7 in cake
175 g /6 oz soft margarine
100 g /4 oz caster sugar
100 g /4 oz self-raising flour
5 ml /1 tsp baking powder
2 medium-sized eggs
juice and grated zest of 1 small orange
65 g /2½ oz plain chocolate, grated
butter, for greasing
100 g /4 oz icing sugar

1 Heat the oven to 180C /350F /gas 4. Beat 125 g /4 oz margarine, the caster sugar, flour, baking powder, eggs, half the juice and half the zest of the orange and 50 g /2 oz of the chocolate until smooth.
2 Grease two 18 cm /7 in sandwich tins. Divide the mixture between them and bake for 25–30 minutes until golden brown and springy to the touch. Cool on a wire rack.
3 For the filling, beat together 50 g /2 oz margarine and the remaining orange zest until creamy and light. Gradually beat in the icing sugar, and stir in the remaining juice.
4 Spread two-thirds of the filling over one layer. Sandwich the layers together and

Chocolate nut torte

spread the top with the rest of the filling. Sprinkle with the remaining grated chocolate.

Chocolate nut torte

🍴🍴 1¾–2 hours,
plus chilling

Serves 6–8
7 medium-sized eggs, separated
butter and flour, for the tins (optional)
2.5 ml /½ tsp salt
225 g /8 oz granulated sugar
5 ml /1 tsp vanilla essence
175 g /6 oz ground pecans
150 g /5 oz ground hazelnuts
60 ml /4 tbls dry breadcrumbs
5 ml /1 tsp baking powder
For the filling
275 ml /10 fl oz thick cream, chilled
50 g /2 oz icing sugar, sifted
5 ml /1 tsp vanilla essence
For the chocolate coffee icing
100 g /4 oz plain dark dessert chocolate, broken into pieces
50 g /2 oz butter
225 g /8 oz icing sugar, sifted
60 ml /4 tbls instant coffee
7.5 ml /1½ tsp vanilla essence
To decorate
whole hazelnuts or pecans

1 Place the egg whites in a large electric mixer bowl; leave to stand at room temperature for 1 hour. Line the bases of three 20 cm /

8 in diameter sandwich tins with non-stick silicone paper or greaseproof paper which has been greased with butter and dusted lightly with flour.
2 Heat the oven to 190C /375F /gas 5. Add 1.5 ml /¼ tsp salt to the egg whites; with the mixer at high speed, beat the whites until soft peaks form when the beaters are slowly raised. Beat in half the granulated sugar, 30 ml /2 tbls at a time, and continue beating until stiff peaks form. Now turn the stiffly whisked whites into a clean bowl and reserve them.
3 Beat the egg yolks in a mixing bowl until they become thick and light; gradually beat in the remaining granulated sugar. Beat for 3 minutes more until thick; beat in vanilla essence. Combine the ground pecans and hazelnuts, breadcrumbs, baking powder and remaining salt and blend into the egg yolk mixture with a plastic spatula. Next, fold in the whisked egg whites.
4 Divide the mixture equally among the lined tins and then smooth the tops. Bake for 25 minutes or until the tops spring back when gently pressed. Turn the 3 cakes upside down in their tins onto a wire rack covered with non-stick paper. Allow them to cool completely.
5 To make the filling, whisk the cream to the soft peak stage. Next, gradually whisk in the icing sugar, beat in the vanilla essence and then chill the filling.
6 To make the icing, melt the chocolate and butter in a bowl over hot water. Remove this from the heat and whisk in the icing sugar. Dissolve the coffee in 60 ml /4 tbls hot water and whisk it into the melted chocolate with the vanilla essence.
7 Run a spatula around the edges of the cold cakes to loosen them, then turn them out and peel off the lining paper. Trim the sides of each layer with a sharp knife. Place 1 cake on a serving plate and spread it with half the filling. Place a second layer on top and spread it with the remaining filling. Top with the last layer. Use most of the icing to cover the top and sides of the cake. Place the remaining icing in a piping bag fitted with a star nozzle and pipe rosettes around the top of the cake. Decorate each rosette with a nut. Refrigerate the cake for at least 1 hour before serving. This will make it much easier to cut.

Chocolate Swiss roll

🕐🍴 overnight marinating,
then 1¼ hours

Serves 4
3 eggs
75 g /3 oz caster sugar
5 ml /1 tsp vanilla essence
50 g /2 oz flour
a pinch of salt
25 g /1 oz cocoa powder
For the filling
125 g /4 oz glacé cherries
45 ml /3 tbls kirsch
150 ml /5 oz thick cream, whipped
For the decoration
1 large orange
30 ml /2 tbls icing sugar

1 For the filling, marinate the glacé cherries in the kirsch overnight.

2 The next day, for the decoration, pare the zest from the orange with a potato peeler, cut it into 25 mm /1 in lengths and then into very fine julienne strips. Blanch these for 5 minutes in simmering water. Drain them, refresh them under cold running water and drain again.

3 Heat the oven to 200C /400F /gas 6. Line a Swiss roll tin with silicone or other non-stick baking paper.

4 Choose a bowl that fits over a saucepan of simmering water and put in the eggs, caster sugar and vanilla essence. Whisk, pre-ferably with a hand-held electric whisk, until the mixture increases in bulk and becomes very thick and light. When the beaters are lifted, they should leave a trail (this takes at least 10 minutes).

5 Remove the bowl from the saucepan and whisk the mixture until it is cold.

6 Sift the flour, salt and cocoa powder over the egg and sugar mixture and fold it in with a large metal spoon. Pour this into the tin and level the surface. Bake for 12–15 minutes or until the sponge shrinks slightly from the sides of the tin and the surface springs back when touched.

7 Lay a large piece of greaseproof paper on

Chocolate Swiss roll

a flat surface. Turn the sponge out onto the paper and peel away the lining paper.

8 Trim the edges with a sharp knife. Lay another piece of greaseproof paper on top of the cake and carefully roll up the Swiss roll with the paper inside it. Leave it to become cold on a wire rack.

9 To fill the cake, unroll it carefully, dis-carding the paper. Spread the cake with the whipped cream. Drain the cherries and spread them evenly over the cream. Re-roll the Swiss roll and sift icing sugar over the top of the cake. Sprinkle with the orange julienne.

CELEBRATION CAKES

Celebrate engagements, important birthdays and other special occasions with spectacular shaped and decorated cakes. You can make cakes in ordinary tins and then follow my recipes to turn them into elaborate designs.

There are occasions which call for a special celebration, and what better centrepiece to a table than a beautifully decorated home-made cake. Eighteenth and twenty-first birthdays only happen once, and I have chosen a cake suitable for each of these important events. Engagement parties are incomplete without an engagement cake, and Valentine's day can be made into an extra-special event with a beautifully decorated cake, as well as the usual cards. Christmas being another time of general celebration, I have included a traditional iced fruit cake for this particular day. (See the chapter on Piping & icing techniques for more decorating ideas.)

A simple, moist genoise sponge makes an excellent base for many celebration cakes. It can be kept for several days while you complete the shaping and the icing. Store it in an airtight container or securely wrapped in silver foil, until it is needed.

It is best to cut the cake the day after baking. Assemble it 24 hours later if possible — this gives the cut surfaces time to settle, so that they are not too crumbly when you come to ice the cake.

The coming-of-age and the Twenty-first birthday cakes can be finished a day or even two ahead of the celebrations. Keep them in the refrigerator or else in a cool dry place. Do not, however, fill the Heart-shaped engagement cake, which uses fresh cream, more than 24 hours before cutting it.

Crème au beurre and butter cream, made with egg yolks, are useful coverings for shaped and decorated cakes. They can be used to stick cakes together and for making up any deficiencies in shape, for icing the cakes and for piping the decorations. When icing with butter cream, put on a very thin layer and chill it. When the icing is firm, put on a second thin layer. In this way any loose crumbs will be well covered and not spoil the final effect.

Remember though, that whichever cake you choose to make for your special celebration, the main thing is to leave yourself plenty of time to ice the cake carefully so as to give it a really professional finish.

Key-shaped coming-of-age cake

🕐❙❙❙ 1 hour, plus cooling, then 40 minutes, plus setting

Makes about 24 slices
For the genoise cake
50 g /2 oz butter, plus extra for greasing
3 eggs
2 egg yolks
100 g /4 oz sugar
100 g /4 oz flour, sifted several times
5 ml /1 tsp vanilla essence

For the filling and decoration
175 g /6 oz butter, softened
350 g /12 oz icing sugar, sifted
3 egg yolks
5 ml /1 tsp vanilla essence
3 × Chocolate rum icing (see page 40)
silver cake balls (optional)

1 To make the genoise cake, heat the oven to 180C /350F /gas 4. Grease, line and grease again an 18 cm /7 in sandwich tin and a 28×18 cm /11×7 in oblong tin.
2 Clarify the butter by melting it over a low heat. When the butter foams, allow the foam to fall to the bottom of the pan, then carefully pour off the oil-like clarified butter from the surface ready for use.
3 In a large bowl set over a pan of gently simmering water, whisk together the eggs and egg yolks, the sugar and the vanilla essence until the mixture is very thick and lukewarm — this usually takes about 10 minutes when using an electric hand whisk.
4 Remove the bowl from the heat and continue whisking for a further 5 minutes or until the mixture has cooled and leaves a trail when the whisk is lifted.
5 Sift the sifted flour into the mixture and fold it in, using a metal spoon. Add the cooled clarified butter, a little at a time, and fold it in carefully.
6 Divide the mixture between the prepared cake tins. Bake in the oven for 20–25 minutes until the cakes are springy to the touch. Cool for 1–2 minutes in the tin, then turn out. Turn the cakes the right way up and leave until cold.
7 Using a 7 cm /2½ in plain round cutter, remove the centre from the round cake. Carefully mark a third lengthways on the oblong cake. Allowing for the extensions of the key from the main stem, cut along the marking, as shown in the diagram below. Square off the round edge of the ring of the cake, so that it fits onto the stem of the key. Leave it overnight in an airtight container.
8 Make the butter cream filling: beat the butter until soft. Gradually beat in the icing sugar, followed by the egg yolks and the vanilla essence.
9 Cut the two pieces of cake horizontally and then sandwich them together with a little of the butter cream. Put the two pieces of cake on a wire rack over a large tray and join them in a key-shape with the butter cream, reserving some for decoration.
10 Coat the top and sides of the key with Chocolate rum icing and leave to set.
11 Transfer the key to a cake board. Fit a piping bag with a large writing nozzle, and spoon in the remaining butter cream. Pipe a line around the top edges of the key. Pipe large dots around the bottom edge and decorate with silver balls, if wished.

● Try 25 g /1 oz cocoa powder instead of 25 g /1 oz flour in the basic cake mixture.

Twenty-first birthday cake

🕐❙❙❙ 1 hour, plus cooling, then 1¼ hours

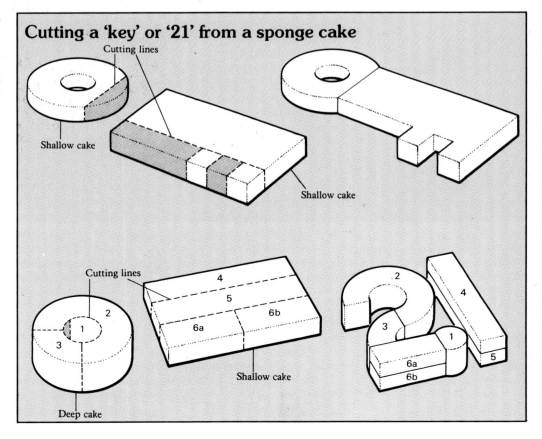

Cutting a 'key' or '21' from a sponge cake

Cutting lines

Shallow cake

Shallow cake

Cutting lines

4
5
6a
6b

Shallow cake

Deep cake

2
1
3

2
4
3
1
6a
6b
5

Makes about 20 slices
butter, for greasing
1 × genoise cake mixture (see previous page)
For the butter cream
350 g /12 oz unsalted butter, softened
700 g /1½ lb icing sugar, sifted
2 eggs
30 ml /2 tbls Cointreau or Grand Marnier
a few drops of orange food colouring
To decorate
21 candle-holders
21 candles

1 Heat the oven to 180C /350F /gas 4. Grease, line and grease again a deep 18 cm / 7 in round cake tin and a shallow 28 × 18 cm /11 × 7 in tin. Prepare the genoise cake, following the instructions in the previous recipe, and divide the mixture between the tins, so that it comes about halfway up each tin.

2 Bake the cakes until they are springy to the touch — about 20 minutes for the oblong cake, about 30 minutes for the round one. Leave them in the tins for 1–2 minutes to settle, then turn them out onto a rack. Turn them the right way up and then leave them

on the wire cooling rack to get completely cold.

3 Using a 7 cm /2½ in plain cutter, remove the centre of the round cake. The small round piece is 1 in the diagram (see previous page). Thinking of the large ring as a clock, cut through it along the small hands of 6 o'clock and 9 o'clock to give piece 2 and piece 3 (see diagram).

4 Cut the oblong cake into three equal pieces along its length to give pieces 4, 5, 6. Cut across piece 6 so that it forms two short oblongs, 6a and 6b in the diagram. Leave all the cake pieces overnight in an airtight container to settle.

5 To make the butter cream, beat the butter until it is light and fluffy. Beat in the icing sugar, a little at a time. Add the egg and beat it in. Now add the Cointreau or Grand Marnier and the orange food colouring and beat thoroughly.

6 Split pieces 1, 2 and 3 horizontally and sandwich them together with a small amount of butter cream. Sandwich together pieces 4 and 5, and pieces 6a and 6b, with butter cream.

7 For the numeral 2, arrange pieces 2, 3, 6a, 6b and 1 together as shown in the

diagram, trimming piece 1 to fit, then sticking them together with butter cream. Now arrange the cake numerals 2 and 1 in the appropriate position on the cake board.

8 Spread numerals 2 and 1 with a thin layer of butter cream to cover. Chill for 30 minutes, then spread the numerals with a second layer.

9 Fit a piping bag with a 10 mm /¾ in star nozzle and spoon in the remaining butter cream. Pipe shells around the top and bottom edge of the cakes to give a neat finish. To complete the cake, arrange the candles in their holders on the top.

● Vary the colour and flavour of the butter cream for this cake depending on your taste and on the colour theme you have chosen for the party. You can add 30 ml /2 tbls kirsch or maraschino in place of the Cointreau or Grand Marnier and tint the butter cream a pale pink, or flavour it with Tia Maria and tint it a pale coffee colour. You can also try a delicate yellow-coloured and apricot brandy-flavoured butter cream, if you prefer.

Heart-shaped engagement cake (page 18)

Eighteenth birthday cake

You do not need to have specially shaped tins for the numerals '1' and '8', you can use two ordinary baking tins: the '1' needs a tin of 1.1 L /2 pt capacity, 23 cm /9 in long and 6 cm /2½ in deep, the '8' needs a tin of 1.4 L /2½ pt capacity, 23 cm /9 in long and 6 cm /2½ in deep. Cut templates of the numbers, and use these to shape the cakes.

2¼ hours, plus cooling, making and using the paste and icing

Makes 2 cakes (about 50 slices)
275 g /10 oz unsalted butter, plus extra for greasing
275 g /10 oz soft brown sugar
5 eggs
grated zest of half a lemon
350 g /12 oz flour
5 ml /1 tsp cinnamon
5 ml /1 tsp mace
450 g /1 lb currants
200 g /7 oz raisins
200 g /7 oz sultanas
150 g /5 oz glacé cherries, chopped
60 g /2½ oz mixed peel
60 g /2½ oz blanched almonds, chopped
30 ml /2 tbls brandy
For the decoration
1½ × Almond paste (see page 21)
1½ × Royal icing (see page 21)
a few drops of yellow food colouring

1 Heat the oven to 150C /300F /gas 2 and grease the cake tins.
2 Cream the butter and sugar until light and fluffy. Beat the eggs lightly and then beat them into the butter mixture, a little at a time. Add lemon zest and beat thoroughly.
3 Sift the flour, cinnamon and mace into the butter mixture and fold in, using a metal spoon. Add the dried fruit, cherries, peel, almonds and the brandy; fold in carefully.
4 Divide the mixture between the two tins and level the surfaces. Bake in the centre of the oven — the '1' will take about 1½ hours, the '8' will take about 1¾ hours. Cut out templates for the numbers.
5 When cooked, allow the cakes to cool in their tins before turning them out onto a wire rack. Using the templates, cut out the numerals when the cakes are cold.
6 Follow the rules for covering a cake in Almond paste (see White Christmas cake recipe, page 21). Allow to dry for 24 hours.
7 Colour three-quarters of the Royal icing pale yellow. Flat ice the cakes (see page 21).
8 Pipe a border along the edges. Allow the cake to dry for 24 hours before serving.

Heart-shaped engagement cake

making the icing, then 1¼ hours, plus cooling and finishing

Makes 24 slices
1½ × Genoise cake mixture (see page 16)

For the icing and decoration
300 ml /10 fl oz thick cream
50 g /2 oz sugar
90 ml /6 tbls apricot jam
1½ × Fondant icing (see page 40)
a little sifted icing sugar
a few drops of pink food colouring
2.5 ml /½ tsp rose-water
small fresh flowers, to decorate
ribbons and lace, to decorate

1 Heat the oven to 180C /350F /gas 4. Grease, line and grease again a deep 25 cm / 10 in square cake tin.
2 Make the sponge cake, following the instructions on page 16, and bake it for 40 minutes, or until it is springy to the touch.
3 Take the cake from the oven and cool it in the tin for 5 minutes, then turn it out onto a rack. Turn it the right way up and leave it, preferably overnight, until cold.
4 Arrange the cold cake with one corner towards you. Mark a line from the corner furthest from you to the nearest one as a guide. Using a saucer as a further guide, cut out the two rounded tops of the heart (see the photograph on the previous page). Leave the cake in an airtight container to settle before filling and icing it.
5 Whip the thick cream until stiff peaks form. Cut the cake in half horizontally and sandwich it together again with half the whipped cream. Make a sugar syrup: put the sugar in a small saucepan with 100 ml /4 fl oz cold water. Stir over a low heat until the sugar has dissolved, then bring it to the boil and boil it until the temperature reaches 105C /220F — about 10 minutes.
6 Sieve the apricot jam into a small pan, add 30 ml /2 tbls water and heat gently, stirring until melted. Cool slightly, then brush it over the top and sides of the cake.
7 In a pan, warm the fondant with 45 ml / 3 tbls sugar syrup. Then reserve 50 g /2 oz. Add a few drops of pink colouring to the rest of the fondant and reserve 50 g /2 oz. Roll out the two reserved quantities on a surface lightly dusted with icing sugar then cut out one pink and one white heart. Leave to harden in a cool place.
8 Put the rest of the fondant in the pan and thin it to a pouring consistency with extra sugar syrup. Add the rose-water and mix.
9 Stand the cake on a wire rack over a tray. Pour the pink fondant over it, spreading it with a palette knife dipped in warm water to cover the top and sides. Leave it to set.
10 Scoop up any icing from the tray. Thin it down, if necessary, with warm water and coat the cake again. Leave the icing to set.
11 Transfer the cake carefully to a silver board or cake plate. Place the two fondant hearts on top of the cake with a tiny bunch of flowers tied with ribbon. Put lace and ribbon around the side.
12 Fit a piping bag with a small star nozzle and spoon in the remaining whipped cream. Pipe stars or shells around the bottom edge of the cake. Refrigerate until needed.

Valentine cake

2 hours, plus cooling and overnight settling, then 1 hour

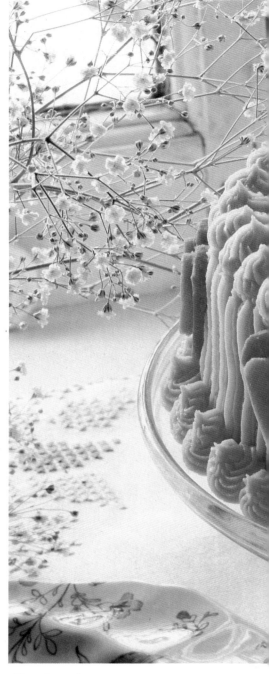

For the cake
225 g /8 oz butter, plus extra for greasing
4 medium-sized eggs, separated and at room temperature
225 g /8 oz caster sugar
225 g /8 oz flour
5 ml /1 tsp baking powder
30 ml /2 tbls rose-water
150 g /5 oz blanched almonds, ground
For the decoration
icing sugar, for dusting
½ × Almond paste (see page 21)
a few drops of red food colouring
silver cake balls
butter cream made with 225 g /8 oz unsalted butter, 500 g /1 lb icing sugar, 2 egg yolks, made following step 8 on page 16
45 ml /3 tbls rose-water

1 Heat the oven to 180C /350F /gas 4. Grease a 20 cm /8 in round cake tin.
2 In a bowl set over a pan of simmering

water, beat together the egg yolks and the sugar until the mixture holds a trail when the beaters are lifted. Remove from the heat and continue beating until the mixture returns to room temperature. Melt the butter and allow it to become tepid.

3 Whisk the egg whites until they are stiff, then gradually whisk in the remaining sugar until soft peaks form.

4 Sift the flour and baking powder into the egg yolk mixture, about a quarter at a time, folding it in after each addition. Now fold in the melted butter, rose-water and almonds, followed by the whisked egg whites.

5 Put the cake mixture into the prepared tin, then bake for 1¼–1½ hours until a warmed skewer inserted into the centre comes out clean. Cool on a wire rack, then wrap in foil and leave overnight to settle.

6 While the cake is baking, make the almond paste hearts. Cut 3 different sized heart-shaped templates from thick cardboard.

On a board dusted with icing sugar, knead the almond paste to soften it. Tint it pale pink and continue kneading, adding sifted icing sugar if necessary. Cut off enough almond paste to make 4 large and 8 medium-sized hearts and set it aside. Add colouring to the remaining paste to darken it.

7 Dust a sheet of greaseproof paper with icing sugar and roll out the darker almond paste to a 3 mm /⅛ in thickness. Cut out 12 large hearts and 4 small hearts from this. Roll out the reserved lighter almond paste and cut out 4 large and 8 medium-sized hearts. Brush all the hearts very lightly with water to remove surplus sugar. Press silver balls into the points of the small hearts and dry overnight.

8 The next day, slice a thin piece from the top of the cake to level it, if necessary, then cut it into 3 layers. Flavour the butter cream with rose-water (instead of vanilla essence as on page 16) and tint it very pale pink. Spread

Valentine cake

a thin coat of the butter cream on the 2 bottom layers and sandwich the 3 layers together. Transfer the cake to a stand. Spread the top layer with butter cream and smooth it, using a palette knife.

9 Fit a large piping bag with a small star piping nozzle and spoon in the remaining butter cream. Pipe vertical lines, touching each other, all around the cake and rosettes on the cake at the top of the lines.

10 Arrange hearts on the top of the cake as shown in the picture. Press them into the butter cream and stick the small dark pink hearts to them with the butter cream.

11 Pipe rosettes around the base of the cake. Decorate the sides with the remaining hearts: place a medium light pink heart in each of 8 large dark pink hearts, first pressing them together, then pressing them gently but firmly onto the cake.

White Christmas cake

⏱ ⦀ 5 hours, plus
3 days standing

Makes a 20 cm /8 in cake
butter and flour, for the tin
275 g /10 oz flour
2.5 ml /½ tsp salt
5 ml /1 tsp baking powder
2.5 ml /½ tsp ground allspice
225 g /8 oz butter
225 g /8 oz caster sugar
5 eggs
grated zest of 1 orange
grated zest of 1 lemon
2.5 ml /½ tsp almond essence
2.5 ml /½ tsp vanilla essence
30 ml /2 tbls brandy
225 g /8 oz chopped walnuts
225 g /8 oz glacé pineapple, chopped
225 g /8 oz glacé cherries, chopped
225 g /8 oz mixed peel, chopped
100 g /4 oz candied angelica, chopped
For the almond paste
350 g /12 oz ground almonds
175 g /6 oz caster sugar
*175 g /6 oz icing sugar, sifted, plus extra
 for dusting*
2.5 ml /½ tsp vanilla essence
a few drops of almond essence
5 ml /1 tsp lemon juice
2 small eggs, lightly beaten
For the apricot glaze
45 ml /3 tbls apricot jam
15 ml /1 tbls kirsch
For the Royal icing
4 egg whites
900 g /2 lb icing sugar
10 ml /2 tsp lemon juice
a few drops of glycerine
For the decoration
silver cake balls
red ribbon

1 Heat the oven to 150C /300F /gas 2. Butter and lightly flour a deep 20cm /8 in round cake tin. Sift the flour, salt, baking powder and allspice into a medium-sized bowl and set it aside.
2 In a large mixing bowl, beat the butter, using an electric whisk, until it is light and fluffy. Add the caster sugar and cream the mixture until it is smooth. Beat in the eggs, 1 at a time, adding 15 ml /1 tbls of the flour mixture with each egg. Beat in the grated orange and lemon zest, the almond and the vanilla essences and the brandy.
3 Using a metal spoon, fold in the remaining flour mixture, the chopped nuts, chopped glacé pineapple and cherries, mixed peel and angelica. Combine the mixture thoroughly and spoon it into the prepared cake tin. Smooth the surface, making a slight well in the centre so that when the cake rises during cooking it will produce a flat top.
4 Place the cake in the centre of the oven and bake for 2½ hours or until a warm skewer inserted in the centre comes out clean. When cooked, remove the cake from the oven and

White Christmas cake

leave it in the tin until it is completely cold.
5 To make the almond paste, thoroughly mix together the ground almonds and the two sugars. Add the vanilla and almond essences, the lemon juice and the lightly beaten egg. Using your hand, knead the mixture until it forms a completely smooth and pliable paste.
6 To make the apricot glaze, sieve the jam into a small pan, add the kirsch and heat gently. When the jam is melted, allow the glaze to cool slightly. If necessary cut a thin slice from the top of the cake to make it completely flat and then brush the cake with the glaze.
7 On a surface lightly dusted with icing sugar, roll out one third of the almond paste to a thickness of 5–8 mm /¼–⅓ in. Cut this into a circle which is slightly larger than the top of the cake. Roll the remaining paste into a long, thin strip and cut a band to fit around the sides of the cake. Press first the band and then the circle onto the cake and smooth the edges using either a rolling pin or a jam jar. Leave the cake in a cool dry place for 24 hours. This is long enough to allow the almond paste to dry before icing.
8 For the Royal icing, whisk the egg whites until they are slightly foamy. Gradually sift in the icing sugar, whisking thoroughly between each addition. Add the lemon juice and a few drops of glycerine and whisk again until light peaks form.
9 Cover the bowl with a damp tea-towel and leave the icing to stand for 24 hours — this helps to smooth out any air bubbles and makes the mixture easier to use.
10 To ice the cake, first stick it to a cake-board with a dab of icing. Spread some of the icing over the top of the cake, levelling the surface with an icing ruler or a long palette knife. Put aside enough icing to use for piping and decoration and then spread the remainder around the sides of the cake, smoothing carefully. Leave the cake to stand for 24 hours before piping so that the surface icing is hard.
11 Trace a star design onto a piece of greaseproof paper cut the same size as the top of the cake. Place this on top of the cake and, using a clean pin, prick the design onto the icing.
12 Fill a small piping bag (see below) with the last of the icing and carefully pipe out the star shape onto the cake. Pipe icing inside the star, (see picture). Pipe a border at the base of the cake, using a shell nozzle, and also on the top outer edge where the flat icing on the top and sides of the cake meet. Place silver cake balls on the points of the star.
13 Leave for 24 hours for the icing to dry and then tie a red ribbon around the cake to finish the decoration.

● When piping the decoration onto the cake, you may prefer to use a paper piping bag which can be thrown away after use and so save sticky washing-up. To make this, use a strong triangle of greaseproof paper: roll the paper into a cone shape so that the corners meet. Fold the top of the bag over to secure. You can either cut a very small hole in the point of the bag and pipe from this, or alternatively fit the bag with a piping nozzle of your choice.

FRUIT CAKES

Whether it is used fresh, dried, canned or as jam, fruit is an invaluable ingredient in cake-making. Cherries, apples, plums and pineapple are just some of the fruits used imaginatively in this lovely selection of cakes.

The great attractions of using fruit in cake-making are that it is delicious and extremely versatile. When fruit is in season, use it to make scrumptious cakes like Yeast cake with fresh plums and Apple strudel (see recipes).

Apple strudel, although a pastry, is actually the national cake of Bavaria, so I have included it in this section. It is superb served warm or cold with chilled, thick whipped cream. Add a little brandy to the filling for a special occasion, and vary the spice flavourings according to your taste.

When preparing the apples, use a stainless steel knife and apple-corer to prevent the flesh discolouring. Once cut, apples quickly begin to turn brown. When you are going to cook them and wish to preserve their natural colour, drop the fruit, as you prepare it, into a bowl of cold water into which you have squeezed a few drops of lemon juice; drain the apples thoroughly before using.

For something a little different, try my Currant leaf cake (see recipe). Filled with a cream cheese mixture and apricot jam, it is a light sponge with the unusual and delicate flavour of aromatic blackcurrant leaves.

If fresh fruit is not available, you can often use the canned variety instead. Either fresh or canned fruit is perfectly suitable for cakes such as spicy Pumpkin cake and delicious Cherry sponge (see recipes). Pineapple cheesecake is a lovely rich mixture which includes canned pineapple and grated lemon zest for a really tangy flavour (see recipe).

Keep a variety of dried fruits in your store-cupboard for making cakes like the famous Dundee cake, which is dark, moist and full of plump sultanas and currants; and for Light fruit cake, which incorporates glacé pineapple, ginger and cherries (see recipes). Apricot Griestorte (see recipe) is very light and has a filling made from dried apricots.

If you're looking for a cake for a children's party, my Banana party cake (see recipe) is ideal. It is made with banana purée and is decorated with thick vanilla butter cream and slices of banana. Children will love it!

Cherry and almond sherry cake

🍴 2½ hours

Makes an 18 cm /7 in cake
175 g /6 oz butter, plus extra for greasing
100 g /4 oz flour
100 g /4 oz self-raising flour
a pinch of salt
250 g /9 oz glacé cherries
175 g /6 oz caster sugar
3 medium-sized eggs, lightly beaten
75 g /3 oz ground almonds
90 ml /6 tbls sweet sherry

1 Heat the oven to 180C /350F /gas 4, then grease an 18 cm /7 in diameter deep cake tin.
2 Sift the flours and salt together in a bowl. Halve, wash and dry the glacé cherries and then toss them with 45 ml /3 tbls of the mixed flour.
3 In a large mixing bowl, beat the butter to a cream. Add the sugar and beat until the mixture is light and fluffy.
4 Gradually add the eggs, beating well after each addition. Fold in the flour and the almonds with a metal spoon until they are completely mixed with the butter and eggs. Stir in the sherry and then fold the cherries into the mixture.
5 Put the mixture into the prepared cake tin and bake for 1¾ hours, or until the cake has shrunk slightly from the sides of the tin and a warmed skewer inserted into the centre comes out clean.
8 Remove the cake from the oven and leave it in the tin for 15 minutes. Turn it onto a wire rack and leave until cold.

Apple and ginger cake

🍴 1¼ hours

Serves 6
65 g /2½ oz softened butter
60 ml /4 tbls soft brown sugar
1–2 tart dessert apples, peeled, cored and sliced
For the cake
100 g /4 oz self-raising flour
2.5 ml /½ tsp salt
7.5 ml /1½ tsp ground ginger
2.5 ml /½ tsp grated nutmeg
100 g /4 oz butter
100 g /4 oz soft brown sugar
grated zest and juice of 1 lemon
2 eggs

1 Heat the oven to 180C /350F /gas 4. Grease the sides of a 20 cm /8 in diameter sandwich tin with 15 g /½ oz of the softened butter.
2 To make the topping, cream together 50 g /2 oz butter and the soft brown sugar. Spread the mixture over the base of the buttered cake tin. Arrange the apple slices evenly over the mixture.
3 To make the cake, in a medium-sized bowl sift together the flour, salt and spices. In another bowl, cream the butter and the sugar with the lemon zest and juice until the mixture is light and fluffy. (You may find the mixture looks curdled owing to the combination of butter and lemon juice, but don't worry about it.) Beat in the eggs one at a time and fold in the sieved flour and spices. Spread the mixture carefully and evenly over the top of the apples.

4 Bake the cake in the oven for 45 minutes. Turn it out onto a serving dish so that the apples are on top.

● The cake may be served either hot or cold and with custard or cream.

Pineapple cheesecake

🍴 25 minutes preparation, 1 hour baking, then cooling

Serves 10–12

75 g /3 oz butter, melted
175 g /6 oz digestive biscuits, crushed
15 ml /1 tbls grated lemon zest
300 g /11 oz sugar
250 g /9 oz canned crushed pineapple in syrup,
    well drained
750 g /1 lb 11 oz curd cheese
5 ml /1 tsp salt
25 g /1 oz flour
45 ml /3 tbls lemon juice
100 ml /3½ fl oz thick cream
4 medium-sized eggs
extra crushed pineapple, to garnish

1 Heat the oven to 170C /325F /gas 3. To make the cheesecake crust, stir the melted butter into the biscuit crumbs, then thoroughly mix in 5 ml /1 tsp grated lemon zest and 50 g /2 oz sugar. Use all but 60 ml / 4 tbls of the mixture to line a 23 cm /9 in tin, pressing the mixture well into the base, using the back of a spoon. Cover the crust with the well drained crushed pineapple.

2 Sieve the curd cheese into a bowl. Add the salt, flour, remaining lemon zest, lemon juice and thick cream and beat well.

3 In another bowl, beat the eggs with the remaining sugar until the mixture is light and fluffy. Fold it into the cheese mixture.

4 Pour the filling into the tin and sprinkle the top with the reserved crumb mixture.

5 Bake the cheesecake for 1 hour, then turn off the heat and let the cake stand in the oven for 1 hour. Transfer it to a wire rack to cool completely before removing from the tin. Decorate with extra pineapple before serving.

● It is advisable to use a spring-release tin with a removable rim and bottom when making this cheesecake classic.

Cherry and almond sherry cake

23

Orange foam cake

1 hour (1½ hours with a hand whisk), plus cooling and finishing

Makes 6 slices
melted butter and flour, for the sandwich tins
75 g /3 oz flour
45 ml /3 tbls cornflour
4 ml /¾ tsp baking powder
a pinch of salt
4 eggs, separated
2.5 ml /½ tsp cream of tartar
100 g /4 oz caster sugar
finely grated zest of 2 small oranges
45 ml /3 tbls orange juice
15 ml /1 tbls lemon juice
jam and whipped cream, for the filling
icing sugar, to decorate

1 Heat the oven to 170C /325F /gas 3.
2 Brush the bases and sides of two 19 cm / 7½ in sandwich tins with melted butter. Line the base of each tin with a neat circle of greaseproof paper and brush that with melted butter as well. Lightly dust the bases and sides of the tins with flour, knocking the tins to shake off the surplus.
3 Sift the flour, cornflour, baking powder and salt into a bowl and set aside.
4 Whisk the egg whites and cream of tartar in a large bowl until foamy. Now gradually

Banana party cake

whisk in 50 g /2 oz caster sugar. Continue whisking until the mixture is glossy and soft peaks form, then reserve.
5 Choose a bowl of not less than 1.5 L / 2½ pt capacity and select a large saucepan over which it will fit firmly. Pour 5 cm /2 in water into the pan and bring it to the boil. Reduce the heat until the water is barely simmering.
6 Put the egg yolks and remaining sugar in the selected bowl. Set it over the simmering water and whisk until the mixture is thick and lightly coloured. This will take about 10 minutes if you use a hand-held electric mixer at high speed.
7 Remove the bowl from the heat. Stand it on a cool surface and continue to whisk until the mixture leaves a distinct trail on the surface when the beaters are lifted and the mixture has cooled (5 minutes if beating with an electric mixer at high speed).
8 Combine the grated orange zest, orange juice and lemon juice in a bowl. Using a large metal spoon, fold them alternately with the sifted flour into the yolk mixture.
9 Fold the whisked egg whites gently into the batter until completely blended, again using a large metal spoon.
10 Divide the batter evenly between the prepared sandwich tins. If necessary, level the tops lightly with a spatula. Place the tins in the hot oven and bake for 30–35 minutes. The cakes are cooked when they shrink away slightly from the sides of the tins and spring back into shape when pressed lightly.
11 Remove the cakes from the oven and

leave them for 1–2 minutes to settle. Next, turn them out onto a clean tea-towel. Peel off the greaseproof paper and invert the cakes onto a wire rack to cool, resting right side up.
12 When the cakes are cold, sandwich the layers with jam and whipped cream and dust the top with icing sugar.

Banana party cake

1 hour 25 minutes, plus cooling and finishing

Makes 8 slices
butter, for greasing
3 bananas
about 30 ml /2 tbls milk
2 eggs
100 g /4 oz softened butter, in small pieces
100 g /4 oz sugar
225 g /8 oz flour
20 ml /4 tsp cocoa powder
2.5 ml /½ tsp bicarbonate of soda
2.5 ml /½ tsp baking powder
5 ml /1 tsp ground ginger
1.5 ml /¼ tsp salt
100 g /4 oz sultanas
For the vanilla butter cream
100 g /4 oz unsalted butter
175 g /6 oz icing sugar, sifted
2.5 ml /½ tsp vanilla essence
For the topping
1 medium-sized banana
15 ml /1 tbls lemon juice

off the paper and leave it until it is cold. Store in an air-tight tin and let the cake mature for 2 days before eating.

● To use as a wedding or Christening cake, store the cake for 2–3 months. Wrap it in tin foil when completely cold, leaving the lining paper attached. Prick the surface every week and brush with brandy, rum or sherry.

Apricot Griestorte

This cake is very light, with a slightly crunchy texture

🔪🔪 soaking the apricots,
then 2 hours, plus cooling

Serves 4–5
75 g /3 oz dried apricots, quartered and soaked
   for 1 hour in cold water to cover
25 g /1 oz soft light brown sugar
15 ml /1 tbls lemon juice
butter, for greasing
3 medium-sized eggs, separated
100 g /4 oz caster sugar
juice and grated zest of ½ lemon
30 ml /2 tbls ground almonds
50 g /2 oz semolina
icing sugar, for dusting
For the filling
125 ml /4 fl oz whipping cream
25 g /1 oz amaratti (Italian macaroons) or
   ratafias, crushed

1 First make the apricot purée: simmer the apricots in their soaking water with the brown sugar and lemon juice for 30–45 minutes, until the apricots are soft and the mixture is very thick. Purée them in a blender, cool and then chill.
2 Heat the oven to 180C /350F /gas 4. Grease two 18 cm /7 in round shallow cake tins, line the bottoms with greaseproof paper and grease that as well.
3 Beat the egg yolks and caster sugar in a large bowl until the mixture is thick and light, using an electric or hand whisk. Add the lemon juice and continue beating until the mixture is very thick. Stir in the lemon zest, ground almonds and semolina.
4 Clean and dry the whisk thoroughly and whisk the egg whites until they are stiff. Gently stir one-quarter of them into the semolina mixture to lighten it, then lightly fold in the rest, using a metal spoon.
5 Divide the mixture between the prepared tins, place immediately in the oven and bake for about 40 minutes, until the cakes are firm in the centre and beginning to shrink away from the sides of the tins.
6 Cool the cakes in the tins for 10 minutes, then turn them out onto a wire rack until they are cold.
7 Not more than 2 hours before serving, make the filling. Whip the cream until it is stiff and then fold in the crushed amaretti or ratafias.
8 Spread one cake with the apricot purée, then top it with the cream. Place the second cake on the cream and chill in the refrigerator until ready to serve.
9 Just before serving, dust the top of the cake with sifted icing sugar.

Dundee cake

1 Heat the oven to 180C /350F / gas 4. Grease a 20 cm /8 in cake tin and line it with greased greaseproof paper.
2 Chop the bananas roughly and purée them in a blender with the milk, adding more milk if necessary to make the quantity up to 275 ml /10 fl oz.
3 Add the eggs, butter and sugar. Blend until smooth.
4 Sift the flour, cocoa, bicarbonate of soda, baking powder, ginger and salt into a large mixing bowl and stir in the sultanas.
5 Gradually add the banana mixture from the blender to the dry ingredients. Stir well.
6 Pour the mixture into the prepared tin and bake for about 1 hour 10 minutes, or until a warmed skewer inserted into the centre comes out clean. Remove the cake from the oven, cool it slightly and turn it out onto a wire rack to cool completely.
7 To make the butter cream, beat together the butter, icing sugar and vanilla essence until smooth and fluffy. Spread the butter cream over the top of the cold cake.
8 To decorate, just before serving, slice the banana and dip each piece in lemon juice. Arrange on top of the cake.

Dundee cake

🕐🔪🔪 3¾–4 hours,
then 2 days maturing

Serves 8
175g /6 oz butter, plus extra for greasing
175 g /6 oz soft light brown sugar
3 medium-sized eggs, beaten
50 g /2 oz ground almonds
150 g /5 oz currants
150 g /5 oz sultanas
25 g /1 oz mixed candied peel, chopped
175 g /6 oz flour
5 ml /1 tsp baking powder
15 ml /1 tbls milk
50 g /2 oz blanched almonds

1 Grease an 18 cm /7 in deep cake tin, line the base and sides with two thicknesses of greaseproof paper and grease the paper. Heat the oven to 150C /300F /gas 2.
2 Cream together the butter and sugar until light and fluffy. Gradually beat in the eggs. Next, stir in the ground almonds, currants, sultanas and peel.
3 Sift together the flour and baking powder and gradually fold this into the mixture alternately with the milk.
4 Turn the mixture into the prepared tin and level the top, making a slight depression in the centre. Arrange the almonds in rings over the top of the cake.
5 Bake the cake for 3¼–3½ hours or until it is cooked. Test by piercing the middle of the cake with a warmed skewer: it should come out clean.
6 When the cake is cooked, remove the tin from the oven and stand it on a wire rack to cool for 30 minutes. Turn out the cake, peel

Apple strudel

2 hours,
then 35–40 minutes baking

Makes 6–8 slices

225 g /8 oz flour, plus extra for dusting
2.5 ml /½ tsp salt
1 small egg, lightly beaten
30 ml /2 tbls vegetable oil
50 g /2 oz butter, melted, for brushing
sifted icing sugar, to dredge
chilled whipped thick cream, to serve
  (optional)

For the filling

50 g /2 oz butter
75 g /3 oz dry white breadcrumbs
100 g /4 oz sugar
2.5 ml /½ tsp ground cinnamon
2.5 ml /½ tsp ground cloves
grated zest of ½ lemon
75 g /3 oz blanched almonds, coarsely chopped
50 g /2 oz sultanas
900 g /2 lb cooking apples
lemon juice

1 Sift the flour and salt into a large bowl and make a well in the centre. Beat the egg together with the vegetable oil and 60 ml /4 tbls warm water; pour this into the well and mix to a soft dough.

2 Turn the dough out onto a lightly floured surface and knead it vigorously for about 15 minutes until it is smooth and elastic. Shape the dough into a ball, invert a clean, warmed bowl over it and leave it to relax for 1 hour.
3 Meanwhile, prepare the filling. Melt the butter in a small pan, add the breadcrumbs and fry gently until crisp and browned; set aside. In a small bowl, mix together the sugar, ground spices, lemon zest, almonds and sultanas. Quarter, core and peel the apples; cut them into medium-thick slices, brush with lemon juice or leave them in a bowl of acidulated water so that they do not discolour. Put to one side.
4 Heat the oven to 190C /375F /gas 5. Use some of the melted butter to grease 2 large baking sheets. Warm and lightly flour a rolling pin. Cover a very large surface with a clean, patterned cotton cloth about 75 × 63 cm /30 × 25 in; lightly flour the cloth.
5 Place the dough on the cloth and roll it out as thinly as possible. Flour your hands and ease them, palms down, under the dough. Working from the centre outwards and moving your hands repeatedly apart, gently stretch the dough until transparent. (You should be able to see the pattern of the cloth clearly through the dough.) Don't worry if small holes appear, but do not tear the dough. If the dough begins to dry out, brush it quickly and lightly with melted butter.

6 With a sharp knife, trim away the edges of the dough to leave a rectangle about 63 × 50 cm /25 × 20 in. Arrange the dough so that one of the long edges is facing you. Now quickly brush the surface with melted butter.
7 Scatter the browned breadcrumbs over the dough. Spread the sliced apples horizontally over half the dough, leaving a clear border of 5 cm /2 in from the long edge nearest you and 25 mm /1 in from the sides. Sprinkle the sugar and sultana mixture over the apples. Fold the side edges, and then the long edge nearest you, over the apple filling.
8 With the aid of the cloth, roll up the strudel, starting with the edge nearest you. Stop after each turn and pat the roll into shape.
9 Cut the strudel in half and transfer each piece to a greased baking sheet. Brush the surface of the strudel with melted butter.
10 Bake the strudel for 35–40 minutes until crisp and golden. Cool slightly, then dredge with icing sugar. Serve sliced, warm or cold, with whipped cream if liked.

Pumpkin cake

1 hour 15 minutes,
plus cooling

Apple strudel

Serves 8

100 g /4 oz self-raising flour
5 ml /1 tsp ground cinnamon
1.5 ml /¼ tsp freshly grated nutmeg
2.5 ml /½ tsp salt
1 medium-sized egg
40 g /1½ oz soft margarine, plus extra for
greasing
50 g /2 oz caster sugar
50 g /2 oz soft light brown sugar
225 ml /8 fl oz pumpkin purée (fresh or
canned)
50 g /2 oz chopped walnuts
50 g /2 oz raisins
For the frosting
15 g /½ oz soft margarine
grated zest of 1 lemon
100 g /4 oz icing sugar, sifted
5 ml /1 tsp lemon juice
15 ml /1 tbls thick cream

1 Heat the oven to 180C /350F /gas 4. Grease an 18 cm /7 in square cake tin.
2 Sift together the flour, cinnamon, nutmeg and salt and beat in the egg. In another bowl, cream together the margarine and sugars and beat until light and fluffy. Beat the dry ingredients and the pumpkin purée alternately into the margarine mixture, then stir in the walnuts and the raisins.
3 Turn the mixture into the prepared tin and bake in the centre of the oven for 45–50 minutes, or until the cake is done. Leave it to cool in the tin, then turn it out.
4 To make the cake frosting, cream together the margarine and the lemon zest. Add the sugar, the lemon juice and the cream

Cherry sponge

and beat until the mixture becomes smooth.
5 Spread the frosting on top of the cold cake. Draw a fork from side to side, making parallel lines in one direction. Now draw it across 3 or 4 times in the opposite direction to make a wavy pattern. Cut the pumpkin cake into 8 fingers to serve.

Light fruit cake

⏱ 🍴 35 minutes, plus 2½ hours baking, then 2 days maturing

Makes 1×18 cm /7 in square or 20 cm / 8in round cake

225 g /8 oz butter, plus extra for greasing
225 g /8 oz flour
a pinch of salt
50 g /2 oz ground hazelnuts, toasted
125 g /4 oz glacé pineapple
50 g /2 oz glacé ginger
225 g /8 oz chopped mixed peel
50 g /2 oz walnuts, chopped
50 g /2 oz almonds, chopped
175 g /6 oz caster sugar
4 eggs
grated zest and juice of 1 lemon
grated zest and juice of 1 orange
about 30 ml /2 tbls sweet sherry
For the decoration
45–60 ml /3–4 tbls clear honey
large piece of candied peel
12–15 glacé cherries
12–15 blanched almonds, split

1 Completely line an 18 cm /7 in square or a 20 cm /8 in round cake tin with a double thickness of greased greaseproof paper. Tie a double thickness of brown paper around the outside to prevent burning. Heat the oven to 170C /325F /gas 3.
2 Sieve the flour, salt and ground hazelnuts together. Wash and thoroughly dry the glacé fruits, then chop them roughly. Mix them with the mixed peel, the walnuts and the almonds.
3 Cream the butter and sugar together until light and fluffy. Gradually beat in the eggs. Add a little flour mixture with the last few additions of the egg mixture. With a metal spoon, fold in the remaining flour, the mixed fruits, nuts and peel and the fruit zests and juices. Lastly, fold in the sherry to make the mixture a soft consistency.
4 Spoon the cake mixture into the prepared tin, smooth the surface and form a small hollow in the centre. Place on a pad of brown paper on the lowest shelf in the oven and bake for 2½ hours, covering the top if it becomes too brown in colour.
5 Remove from the oven, take off the outer paper and leave the cake to cool for 15 minutes. Remove it from the tin, leave it for about 15 minutes on a wire rack, then gently ease away the lining paper. Leave until cold.
6 To decorate, brush the top of the cold cake with half the honey. Wash the peel and cut it into strips. Dry well. Wash and dry the cherries and cut them into quarters.
7 Arrange the fruits and nuts in a pattern on top of the cake. Warm the remaining honey and brush it over the decoration.
8 Cover with an inverted cake tin and leave for at least 2 days before cutting.

Cherry sponge

🍴🍴 50 minutes, plus cooling

Serves 6–8

150 g /5 oz butter, softened, plus extra for
greasing
150 g /5 oz caster sugar
3 eggs, separated
150 g /5 oz flour, sifted
450 g /1 lb fresh black cherries or canned
black cherries, drained
icing sugar, to dust

1 Heat the oven to 180C /350F /gas 4. Line a 30×23 cm /12×9 in roasting tin with buttered greaseproof paper.
2 Beat the butter and sugar together until they are light and creamy. Add the egg yolks and beat thoroughly.
3 Whisk the egg whites until they form stiff peaks and add them alternately with spoonfuls of the flour, to the egg, butter and sugar mixture. Spread the sponge mixture evenly over the prepared tin.
4 Lay the cherries thickly over the sponge mixture. Bake for 30–35 minutes or until a warmed skewer pushed into the sponge comes out clean. Cool, dust with icing sugar, then cut the cake into slices and serve cold.

● This particular sponge is a traditional Czechoslovakian cake.

Yeast cake with fresh plums

This plum cake can be found all over Germany, but its real home is Bavaria. Although the base for the cake is often made with shortcrust pastry, yeast pastry is used here, because it soaks up the juice from the plums without becoming soggy.

 1 hour 40 minutes, plus 1–2 hours rising

Makes about 16 slices
250 g /9 oz strong plain flour
50 g /2 oz icing or caster sugar
15 g /½ oz fresh yeast
125 ml /4 fl oz milk, lukewarm
60 g /2¼ oz butter
1 medium-sized egg
1 medium-sized egg yolk
2.5 ml /½ tsp lemon zest, grated
butter and flour, for the baking dish
700 g /1½ lb plums, washed, dried and
  stoned
icing sugar, sifted
vanilla caster sugar, sifted (see page 9)
ground cinnamon

1 Sift the flour and the icing or caster sugar into a warmed bowl. In a cup, blend the yeast with half the lukewarm milk, sprinkle it with a little of the flour and set it aside until bubbles form on the surface — this should take about 10 minutes.
2 Meanwhile, melt the butter in a cup over hot water. When the yeast is ready, make a well in the flour and pour in the yeast.
3 Whisk together the rest of the lukewarm milk and the melted butter and whisk in the egg and the egg yolk: the temperature should be no more than lukewarm. Whisk the egg mixture into the flour and yeast, then beat until the mixture is very smooth and blisters begin to form on the surface. Mix in the grated lemon zest.
4 Butter and flour a deep baking dish or roasting tin, about 28 cm /11 in square, tipping out the loose flour. Put the dough in the centre of the dish and press it out with your fingers until it covers the bottom of the tin completely. Halve or quarter the plums according to their size and cover the dough closely with the plums, cut side down and slightly overlapping. Cover the tin with a clean kitchen cloth and leave the dough to rise in a warm place away from draughts for about 1 hour.
5 Heat the oven to 200C /400F /gas 6. When the dough has risen to about twice its original height put the tin in the oven and immediately lower the heat to 190C /375F / gas 5. Bake for 45 minutes, then lower the temperature to 180C /350F /gas 4 and bake for another 15 minutes or until golden.
6 Dust the cake with icing sugar, vanilla sugar and cinnamon while still hot. When warm, mark the cake into slices.

● The two sugars, icing and vanilla caster, add different textures to the top of this cake.

Currant leaf cake

Aromatic blackcurrant leaves give a delicate flavour to this light sponge cake.

1½ hours

Makes a 18cm /7 in cake
8 blackcurrant leaves, washed thoroughly
125 g /4 oz cream cheese
200 g /7 oz butter, softened
grated zest of ½ lemon
200 g /7 oz caster sugar
200 g /7 oz self-raising flour
a pinch of salt
3 eggs, beaten
75 ml /3 fl oz milk
butter, for greasing
For finishing
30 ml /2 tbls caster sugar
45 ml /3 tbls apricot jam

1 Heat the oven to 180C /350F /gas 4. Bruise 2 of the blackcurrant leaves by folding them and crushing them on a board using a rolling pin. Make sure the leaves remain whole. Put the cream cheese in a bowl and carefully mix in the leaves. Set aside.

2 Cream the butter with the lemon zest in a large mixing bowl. Beat in the sugar until the mixture is light and fluffy. Sift the flour with the salt and beat it into the butter and sugar mixture alternately with the beaten eggs. Mix in enough milk to make a soft dropping consistency.
3 Butter 2×18 cm /7 in sandwich tins and line the base of each with a circle of buttered greaseproof paper. On top of each circle place 3 blackcurrant leaves, evenly spaced.
4 Divide the cake mixture evenly between the tins, smooth the top and bake for 30 minutes in the centre of the oven until the cake halves are golden brown and firm and have shrunk slightly from the sides of the tins. Cool them for 5 minutes in the tins, then turn them onto wire cooling racks. Remove the greaseproof paper and black-currant leaves from the base of each.
5 Remove the blackcurrant leaves from the cream cheese in the bowl and beat 15 ml / 1 tbls caster sugar into the cheese. When the cakes are cold, spread one of them first with the cheese, then with the apricot jam. Place the other cake on top and dredge with the remaining sugar.

● Geranium leaves may be substituted for the blackcurrant leaves.

IDEAS FOR SMALL CAKES

Tiny iced cakes are deliciously rich, pretty to look at and fun to prepare. Make them from a basic sponge recipe and use a variety of coatings and decorations to make them temptingly colourful and tasty.

The concentration of icing and decoration on little cakes is much higher than on big cakes, therefore they taste richer. People enjoy eating more than one of these treats, so provide lots of little cakes with contrasting colours and flavours.

A sponge baked in a Swiss roll tin will give you from 20–36 small fancies for icing and decorating.

Bake a sponge cake which contains butter, or the sponge will go stale too quickly. Choose between a Genoise sponge (page 16) or an All-in-one sponge cake (page 106), baked in a shallow tin, 28 × 18 cm / 11 × 7 in.

Cutting the shapes

Allow the cake to cool, then leave it for 24 hours in an airtight container to settle. Cut it into a selection of shapes, not longer than about 5 cm / 2 in or narrower than 25 mm / 1 in. If the shapes are to have straight or uniform sides, cut off the crusty edges of the sponge first. Use a sharp, long-bladed knife to cut squares, triangles, fingers and diamonds from the basic rectangle. Cut rounds using a biscuit cutter.

For more ambitious shapes, such as ovals, leaves or hearts, use paper templates. Glaze the cakes on all sides (except the bottom) with Apricot glaze (page 21) to make a really smooth base before icing.

Icing and decorating

Decorate the shapes differently and use a variety of flavours and textured icings following the ideas in this chapter. Butter cream (page 17) and water icing (below) are both easy to make. Glacé icing (page 39), which is made over hot water, sets more quickly than water icing. Fondant icing (page 40) gives a finer finish.

Water icing is the easiest soft icing to make and it is ideal for icing small cakes as it flows easily down the sides of the cakes to cover them. It sets to a crisp, glossy crust, remaining soft underneath. Add hard decorations to it before it sets.

● To make water icing to cover 12 small cakes, put 30 ml / 2 tbls hot water in a bowl. Gradually stir in 225 g / 8 oz sifted icing sugar, until the mixture is smooth. If it is runny, add a little more sugar. Add the flavouring and colouring of your choice.

Icing cakes: put the glazed cakes on a wire rack over a tray. Pour 10 ml / 2 tsp water icing over each cake. As it runs slowly down the sides, guide it with a small, round-bladed knife into any corners and crevices. Spoon on

more icing if it is needed to cover any gaps. Scoop up any crumb-free icing from the tray and use it again. Before the icing sets put decorations such as nuts or cherries in place. Add other decorations, such as piped butter cream, when the icing surface is completely dry.

Water icing can be piped in decorative lines using a fine plain small nozzle (see Piping & icing techniques, page 42). Or make a greaseproof paper bag and snip off the point of the bag. When several icings for a number of cakes are needed, mix each batch as required.

Coatings add a different texture; pile them on kitchen paper and dip or roll the cakes in them immediately after glazing. Pat them with your fingers if necessary and shake off any excess. Use chopped nuts, vermicelli or coloured sugar strands, or dip the cakes in some crisped sponge cake crumbs or baked, desiccated coconut.

Chocolate squares are popular to surround the cake on all sides for a 'box' effect. Smaller shapes can be used to 'spike' decorations on top.

● For 40 squares, melt 350 g / 12 oz plain chocolate in a bowl set over a saucepan of gently simmering water. Leave the chocolate until it is cool and just beginning to solidify. Now spread it evenly over non-stick paper to make three 18 cm / 7 in squares. When set, but not hard, cut the chocolate with a sharp, long-bladed knife into 40 pieces.

Icing shaped cakes

For 6 hearts

6 × 5 cm / 2 in long sponge hearts
60 ml / 4 tbls Apricot glaze (page 21)
5 ml / 1 tsp lemon juice
150 g / 5 oz icing sugar, sifted
a few drop of yellow food colouring
40 g / 1½ oz Butter cream (page 17)
18 silver balls

Coat the sponge sides with the glaze. Stir 2.5 ml / ½ tsp lemon juice and 20 ml / 1¼ tbls hot water into the icing sugar and ice the cakes. Stir the remaining lemon juice and colouring into the butter cream. Using a small rose nozzle, pipe a line around the top of each cake, and a rosette in the centre. Decorate with silver balls.

For 6 triangles

6 × sponge triangles (5 cm / 2 in on matching sides)
45 ml / 3 tbls Apricot glaze (page 21)
2.5 ml / ½ tsp coffee and chicory essence
100 g / 4 oz icing sugar, sifted
40 g / 1½ oz Butter cream (page 17)
6 walnut pieces

Coat the sponge sides with glaze. Stir 1.5 ml / ¼ tsp coffee and chicory essence and 15 ml / 1 tbls hot water into the icing sugar and ice all the cakes. Stir a few drops of coffee essence into the butter cream. Using a small star nozzle, pipe scrolls on the tops of the cakes from each of three corners to the centre. Place a walnut piece in the centre of each cake.

Little iced fancy cakes

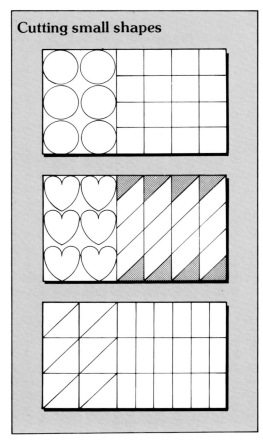

Cutting small shapes

Icing squares

For 8 vanilla squares

8×4 cm /1½ in sponge squares
90 ml /6 tbls Raspberry glaze (page 38)
90 ml /6 tbls sponge crumbs, browned
100 g /4 oz Butter cream (page 17)
4–6 drops vanilla essence

Coat the sponge sides with some of the glaze and with the crumbs. Mix the butter cream with the vanilla essence and pipe it in lines on top of the squares. Drizzle the remaining jam glaze in lines across the cream.

For 8 cherry and marzipan boxes

275 g /10 oz marzipan
8×4 cm /1½ in sponge squares
100 g /4 oz Butter cream (page 17)
4–8 drops vanilla essence
60 ml /4 tbls icing sugar, sifted
a few drops of red food colouring
4 glacé cherries, halved
16 almond flakes

Roll out the marzipan and cut it into 32 squares which are slightly taller than the sides of the sponge squares. Mix the butter cream with the essence and coat the sponge sides. Attach the marzipan. Mix the icing sugar with 5 ml /1 tsp warm water and the colouring. Fill the tops with icing and decorate with cherries and almonds.

For 8 chocolate boxes

8×4 cm /1½ in sponge squares
60 ml /4 tbls Apricot glaze (page 21)
40 Chocolate squares (page 29)
200 g /7 oz Butter cream (page 17)
2.5 ml /½ tsp vanilla essence or brandy
8 pieces crystallized violet

Coat the sponge sides with the glaze and fix the chocolate squares to them. Mix the butter cream with vanilla essence or brandy. Pipe rosettes on top so that they rise in the middle. Rest a chocolate square on top as a lid and put the crystallized violets under the lids.

For 8 almond squares

175 g /6 oz Butter cream (page 17)
4–6 drops almond essence
a few drops of green food colouring
8×4 cm /1½ in sponge squares
25 g /1 oz flaked almonds, toasted

Mix the butter cream with the almond essence and the colouring. To make the lids, cut a slice across each sponge square, leaving it attached on one side. Coat the sponge sides and tops with butter cream and almonds. Carefully lift the lids and pipe a swirl of butter cream underneath them.

Icing rectangles or diamonds

For 8 cherry tops

8×5 cm /2 in sponge fingers
60 ml /4 tbls Raspberry or Strawberry
  glaze (page 38)
40 g /1½ oz walnuts, finely chopped
a few drops of red food colouring
25 g /1 oz Butter cream (page 17)
4 glacé cherries, halved

Coat the sponge sides with the glaze and then the walnuts. Add the colouring to the butter cream and mix until pink. Pipe a small swirl in the centre of each cake. Put cherry halves on top and brush with the remaining glaze.

For 6 iced diamonds

6×5 cm /2 in sponge diamonds
45 ml /3 tbls Raspberry glaze (page 38)
150 g /5 oz icing sugar, sifted
a few drops red food colouring
a few drops green food colouring
3 pieces glacé cherry
6 almond pieces

Coat the sponge sides with the glaze. Mix all but 5 ml /1 tsp icing sugar with 15 ml /1 tbls hot water. Halve the icing sugar mixture and colour one half pink and the other half green. Ice 3 cakes pink and 3 cakes green. Decorate the pink cakes with the cherry and almond pieces. Mix the reserved icing sugar with a little water. Drizzle this in fine lines over the green cakes.

For 6 chocolate marzipan fingers

25 g /1 oz marzipan
30 ml /2 tbls Apricot glaze (page 21)
6×5 cm /2 in sponge fingers
100 g /4 oz icing sugar, sifted
15 ml /1 tbls cocoa powder, sifted
3 crystallized violets or rose petals

Shape the marzipan into 2 × 15 cm /6 in rolls. Dip one side in glaze, then secure along the centres of 2 rows of 3 sponge fingers placed end to end. Cut the marzipan at the edge of each sponge finger. Coat the sponge sides with the glaze. Mix the icing sugar and cocoa powder with 15 ml /1 tbls hot water. Ice the cakes and decorate with flower petals.

Shapes and decorations for small cakes

For 8 pineapple or orange tops
8 × 5 cm /2 in sponge fingers
75 ml /5 tbls Apricot glaze (page 21)
75 ml /5 tbls coconut, coloured yellow
8 chunks pineapple or mandarin orange
   segments, drained

Coat the cakes with glaze and then coconut. Dip the fruit segments in the glaze and place 1 on top of each cake, then glaze.

For 8 sweetie tops
100 g /4 oz Butter cream (page 17)
10 ml /2 tsp cocoa powder, sifted
8 × 5 cm /2 in sponge fingers
75 ml /5 tbls coloured sugar strands
24 coloured chocolate buttons

Mix the butter cream, cocoa and 7.5 ml /1½ tsp water. Coat the sponge sides with butter cream and sugar strands, swirl butter cream on top. Dot with chocolate buttons.

Icing round cakes

For 6 lemon tops
75 g /3 oz Butter cream (page 17)
2.5 ml /½ tsp lemon juice
a little finely grated lemon zest
6 × 4.5 cm /1¾ in sponge rounds
30 ml /2 tbls coconut, browned
30 ml /2 tbls lemon curd

Mix the butter cream with the lemon juice and zest. Coat the sponge sides with butter cream and then coconut. Pipe butter cream around the top edge and then fill the centres with the lemon curd.

For 6 Mocha tops
6 × 4.5 cm /1¾ in sponge rounds
45 ml /3 tbls Apricot glaze (page 21)
45 ml /3 tbls chocolate sugar strands
50 g /2 oz Butter cream (page 17)
2.5 ml /½ tsp coffee essence
30 ml /2 tbls icing sugar, sifted
6 chocolate dots

Coat the sponge sides with the glaze and the chocolate strands. Mix the butter cream with half the coffee essence and pipe it around the top edge of the sponges. Mix the icing sugar with the remaining essence and 5 ml / 1 tsp warm water. Spread inside the cream border and place a chocolate dot in the centre.

For 6 chocolate rounds
100 g /4 oz Butter cream (page 17)
3–4 drops peppermint essence
a few drops of green food colouring
6 × 4.5 cm /1¾ in sponge rounds
40 g /1½ oz plain chocolate
angelica leaves, to decorate

Mix together the butter cream, peppermint essence and green colouring and use it to coat the sponge cake sides. Melt the chocolate, let it cool and spread it over the top, then pipe rosettes of butter cream on top. Dot with angelica leaves.

For 6 tulip rounds
175 g /6 oz marzipan
175 g /6 oz Butter cream (page 17)
10 ml /2 tsp lemon juice
a few drops green or yellow food colouring
6 × 4.5 cm /1¾ in sponge rounds
16 tiny angelica leaves

Roll out the marzipan and cut it into 24 × 4 cm /1½ in circles. Mix the butter cream with the lemon juice and colouring. Coat the sponge sides with it and secure 4 marzipan circles to the sides of each cake, overlapping them. Pipe rosettes of butter cream on top and decorate with angelica leaves.

BATCH BAKING FOR THE FREEZER

One of the best ways of using your freezer is to bake and freeze in large quantities. Here I give a recipe for a basic mixture and then suggest four ways in which it can be divided to give you a selection of cakes.

Batch-baking planner

2½ hours, 4 hours chilling, plus ½ hour decorating then freezing

1 Collect together all the ingredients and prepare the baking tins.
2 Dutch apple cake: make the apple purée.
3 Lemon cake: grate the zest of the lemon and squeeze the juice.
4 Make basic mixture and heat the oven.
5 Prepare the Chocolate cake, Lemon cake and Dutch apple cake in that order.
6 Bake the Chocolate cake on the top shelf of the oven and the Lemon cake and Dutch apple cake on the lower shelf.
7 Meanwhile, prepare the Struessel cake.
8 After 20 minutes baking, remove the Chocolate cake and put the Struessel cake tin in the oven. Cool the Chocolate cake.
9 After a further 35 minutes baking, remove the Streussel cake and the Lemon cake from the oven. Allow both cakes to cool.
10 After a further 15 minutes baking, remove the Dutch apple cake. Cool.
11 Decorate the cold Chocolate cake and Lemon cake and freeze.
12 Freeze the cold Struessel cake and Dutch apple cake.

Freezer sponge mix

350 g /12 oz flour
350 g /12 oz self-raising flour
10 ml /2 tsp salt
175 g /6 oz butter, softened
350 g /12 oz margarine, softened
500 g /18 oz caster sugar
9 medium-sized eggs, beaten
15 ml /1 tbls vanilla essence

1 Sift the flours and salt together. In a large mixing bowl cream the butter and margarine together until they are pale. Beat in the sugar until the mixture is smooth, fluffy and light.
2 Gradually beat in the eggs, taking care to beat well after each addition to prevent the mixture curdling. Next, thoroughly beat in the vanilla essence.
3 Fold in the sifted flour and salt mixture, a little at a time, until it is evenly incorporated. Alternatively, combine the ingredients in a food mixer or processor.
4 Heat the oven to 180C /350F /gas 4. Place one shelf just above the centre and another just below the centre, making sure that there is enough room for all the tins.
5 Now refer to the following recipes for cake variations.

Chocolate cake

Makes 8 slices
butter, for greasing
¼ of the freezer sponge mix, weighing 525–550 g / 19–20 oz
30 ml /2 tbls evaporated milk
50 g /2 oz cocoa powder

For the filling and icing
425 ml /15 fl oz whipping cream
50 g /2 oz plain chocolate, grated

1   Grease two 15 cm /6 in sandwich tins.
2   Weigh out the sponge mixture and pour on the evaporated milk, then sift the cocoa powder over it. Gently fold this in with a metal spoon until it is evenly blended.
3   Divide the mixture between the two prepared tins and smooth the surfaces. Position the tins on the top shelf of the oven and bake for 20 minutes. The cakes should feel springy to the touch — if they are still moist, return them to the oven for a few minutes more.
4   Leave the cakes in the tins to cool for a few minutes, then turn them onto a wire rack and leave them to cool completely.
5   To assemble, place one of the sponges on a plate. Whip the cream until it stands in peaks and put about 90 ml /6 tbls in a piping bag fitted with a star nozzle.
6   Spoon a third of the remaining cream on the sponge base and smooth it over. Place the other sponge on top and use the rest of the cream to cover the top and sides.

Left to right: Streussel cake squares, Lemon cake decorated with walnuts, Chocolate cake and Dutch apple cake, partly sliced

7   Using the cream in the piping bag, pipe a border around the top outer edge of the cake then sprinkle the top of the cake with the grated chocolate.
8   To serve, decorate the lower part of the cake with more whipped cream and grated chocolate, if wished.

● To freeze: place the cake, unwrapped, in the freezer until the cream is firm. Wrap it in heavy-duty foil or freezer film and cover it with a rigid container to protect the decoration. Label and freeze.
● Freezer life: 3 months.
● Thawing: unwrap the cake and leave it in a cool room for 3–4 hours or slice whilst semi-frozen and thaw for 1–2 hours. Alternatively, unwrap it and then thaw it overnight in the refrigerator.

Lemon cake

Makes 8 slices
butter, for greasing
¼ of the freezer sponge mix, weighing 525–550 g / 19–20 oz
10 ml /2 tsp grated lemon zest
15 ml /1 tbls lemon juice
For the icing
150 g /5 oz butter, softened
400 g /14 oz icing sugar, sifted
20 ml /4 tsp lemon juice
100 g /4 oz honey
75 g /3 oz walnut halves

1   Grease a deep round 15 cm /6 in cake tin and line the base with greaseproof paper.
2   Weigh out the sponge mixture into a large mixing bowl. Fold in the lemon zest and juice. Put the mixture into the prepared cake tin and smooth the surface.
3   Place the tin on the lower shelf of the oven for 55 minutes. When cooked, remove from the oven and leave the cake in the tin for a few minutes before turning it out onto a wire rack to cool completely. Peel off the greaseproof paper.
4   Meanwhile, prepare the icing. In a medium-sized bowl, cream the butter, icing sugar, lemon juice and honey together. Finely chop 50 g /2 oz of the nuts and fold them in with a metal spoon.
5   Using a serrated knife, cut the cold cake in half horizontally. Put the bottom half on a plate and spread it with a third of the lemon icing mixture.
6   Place the other half of the cake on top and cover the top and sides with the remaining butter icing. Use a round-bladed knife to swirl the icing into peaks. Decorate with the reserved walnut halves.

● To freeze: leave the cake uncovered in the freezer until the icing is completely hard. Next, cover the cake in freezer foil or cling film and put it in a rigid container to prevent the decoration being damaged during storage. Label and freeze.
● Freezer life: 3 months.
● Thawing: uncover the cake and leave it for 3–4 hours in a cool, but not cold, place. Alternatively, uncover the cake and then leave it to thaw in the refrigerator for about 12 hours.

Dutch apple cake

Makes 10 slices
butter, for greasing
500 g /1 lb sharp eating apples
finely grated zest and juice of 1 lemon
25 g /1 oz caster sugar
¼ of the freezer sponge mix, weighing 525–550 g / 19–20 oz
1.5 ml /¼ tsp cinnamon
1.5 ml /¼ tsp fresh nutmeg, grated
1.5 ml /¼ tsp mixed ground spice
25 g /1 oz self-raising flour
2.5 ml /½ tsp baking powder

1   Grease a 2 L /3 pt loaf tin and line the base with greaseproof paper.
2   Peel, core and chop the apples. Place them in a pan with 45 ml /3 tbls water, the lemon zest and juice and the sugar. Simmer over a low heat until the apples are reduced to a purée. Leave them to cool completely. Weigh out ¼ of the sponge mix.
3   Fold the apple purée into the sponge mixture and then sift the spices, flour and baking powder over the surface. Gently fold in with a metal spoon until incorporated.
4   Spoon the mixture into the loaf tin and smooth over the surface. Place the tin on the lower shelf in the oven and bake for 1 hour 10 minutes. When cooked, turn onto a cooling rack, peel off the greaseproof paper and leave to cool.

● To freeze: Wrap the cold cake in heavy-duty foil or freezer film. Label and freeze.
● Freezer life: 6 months.
● Thawing: unwrap and leave to thaw at room temperature for 2–3 hours. Serve sliced either plain, or with butter or cream.

Streussel cake

Makes 15 slices
butter, for greasing
¼ of the freezer sponge mix, weighing 525–550 g / 19–20 oz
75 g /3 oz soft brown sugar
5 ml /1 tsp ground cinnamon
25 g /1 oz self-raising flour
50 g /2 oz walnuts, finely chopped
25 g /1 oz butter, melted

1   Grease a shallow 25 × 15 cm /10 × 6 in cake tin. Scrape the remaining sponge mixture into the tin. Smooth the surface.
2   Put the sugar, cinnamon, flour, walnuts and melted butter in a bowl. Mix well, then sprinkle over the cake mixture.
3   Place the tin on the top shelf of the oven and bake for 35 minutes. Test that the cake is cooked by inserting a skewer into the centre: it should come out clean. Leave it in the tin for a few minutes before turning out onto a wire rack to cool completely.

● To freeze: with a sharp knife, cut the cold cake into 5 cm /2 in squares. Wrap in heavy-duty foil or freezer film, expelling all the air. Label and freeze.
● Freezer life: 6 months.
● Thawing: unwrap and thaw at room temperature for 1–2 hours.

DOUGHNUTS & YEAST CAKES

Sweet foods made with yeast are often sadly neglected, although they are not difficult to make. Deep fried or baked in the oven, doughnuts and yeast cakes make an excellent tea-time treat or mid-morning snack.

Some doughnuts are made from a traditional sweet yeast dough (see recipes for English doughnuts and Dutch doughnuts), while others (see recipes for American chocolate doughnut rings and Crisp-coated plaited doughnuts) use different raising agents. The yeast cakes all need time allowed for the dough to rise, but actually are not very complicated to make.

Doughnuts

Doughnuts are famous the world over and are often eaten on special holidays: Mardi Gras in France and Fasching in Germany. In England most bakers cook fresh, jam-filled doughnuts every day, and in America doughnut rings are sold in shops specially created for the purpose. The Americans also like to dress up their doughnuts with icings and chocolate coatings.

Traditional doughnuts are made with a yeast dough, shaped into rings. I like my doughnuts served warm if possible — this means that they should not be cooked ahead of time, but as they cook very quickly, you can afford to leave them to the last moment. However, if the doughnuts are filled or coated, they usually need to be left to cool a little first.

Equipment and oil

The main equipment you will need to deep fry doughnuts is a large heavy-based pan, a thermometer and a draining spoon or frying-basket. You will find that most doughnuts float as they cook, so they will need plenty of room in the pan to roll and turn.

To deep-fry doughnuts it is best to use a light, flavourless oil so the taste of the oil does not overpower the dough. Providing you strain it well, the oil can be stored and used again.

Heat the oil to the required temperature and carefully lower the doughnuts into the oil. If you overcrowd the pan the doughnuts will stick together and cook unevenly. Cook the doughnuts on one side until they are golden brown and then turn them over to allow the other side to cook. You may have to hold the doughnuts under the surface of the oil with a long-handled spoon — if not you could find a white, uncooked circle in the middle.

When both sides are golden brown lift the doughnuts out of the hot oil with a slotted spoon. Drain them well on absorbent paper. If you have to keep them warm, put them in the oven in an uncovered dish. Doughnuts can be served sprinkled with sifted icing sugar or with caster sugar flavoured with vanilla, cinnamon or grated citrus zest.

Cinnamon-topped cakes

East Germany has produced many excellent yeast cakes and I have chosen two for this chapter. The first one, Crumb-topped cake, is called *Streuselkuchen* in Germany, and is a wonderfully light cake which is covered in a topping flavoured with cinnamon. The second cake I have included, *Butterkuchen*, or Buttery yeast cake, has a slightly breadlike texture. While it is still hot, it is brushed with a generous amount of melted butter and then sprinkled with sugar and cinnamon.

Swedish nut ring

This version of a sweet yeast cake is filled with nuts, glazed with icing and decorated with chopped nuts and glacé cherries, making it perfect for morning coffee parties. Shaped into a ring and cut at intervals so that the rich filling peeps through, it is both sweet and crunchy at the same time.

Rum babas

Among the many culinary creations credited to King Stanislas Leczinski of Poland is that of the *baba au rhum*, one of the world's most delicious confections. The traditional explanation is that he dunked his favourite yeast cake in a rum-flavoured syrup. Declaring the result a triumph, he named it after the hero of his favourite story, *Ali Baba and the 40 thieves*. The original recipe was baked in a tall mould and had dried fruit in it, (see recipe for my version).

The rum baba is a feather-light concoction of flour, sugar and eggs, made airy with yeast and moistened with a rum-flavoured syrup. If you succeed in getting the consistency of your raw dough right, my recipe will provide one of the lightest babas. Remember though, that as with all yeast doughs, it is far better to thicken the consistency with extra flour than to have to thin down a stiff dough with extra liquid.

English doughnuts

1 hour 40 minutes, plus cooling

Makes about 12
225 g /8 oz flour
2.5 ml /½ tsp salt
150 ml /5 fl oz milk
15 g /½ oz fresh yeast
45 ml /3 tbls sugar
2 egg yolks
oil for deep frying, plus extra for brushing
caster sugar, for coating
125 g /4 oz strawberry jam
lemon juice

1 Sift the flour and salt into a large mixing bowl and make a well in the centre. Warm the milk to blood temperature (37C /98F). Combine the yeast and sugar and mix well with 60 ml /4 tbls warmed milk.
2 Put the egg yolks and the yeast mixture in the centre of the flour and mix with your hand to gradually incorporate all the flour. Gradually add the remaining milk until the mixture forms a dough. You may find that you do not need the full 150 ml /5 fl oz.
3 Knead the dough until it is smooth, brush it lightly with oil and put it in a warm place to rise to double its original size (approximately 30 minutes at 24C /75F).
4 Knock back the dough with your knuckles to break any air bubbles, then cut the dough into 25 g /1 oz pieces. Roll the pieces into evenly shaped, smooth balls and place them on a baking sheet. Leave to prove in a warm place until they are at least twice their original size.
5 Heat the oil in a deep-fat frier to 180C /350F.
6 Fry the doughnuts, 3 or 4 at a time, in the hot oil for 5 minutes, turning them over during cooking. You may find it necessary to push them down into the fat with a spoon to prevent a white uncooked circle remaining around the middle. Remove them from the oil with a slotted spoon and drain them on absorbent paper. Coat them immediately with caster sugar. Set them aside to cool and cook the remaining doughnuts.
7 Heat the strawberry jam with a little lemon juice to heighten the flavour and make the jam a little more liquid. Strain the jam through a sieve and allow it to cool.
8 When the jam and doughnuts have cooled, place the jam in a piping bag with a small pointed nozzle. Make a hole in each doughnut with a skewer and fill each one with jam. Serve at once.

Dutch doughnuts

30 minutes, then 2 hours rising, plus 45 minutes

Makes about 24 doughnuts
25 g /1 oz fresh yeast or 15 ml /1 tbls dried yeast
300 ml /11 fl oz tepid milk
30 ml /2 tbls sugar
300 g /11 oz strong white flour
7.5 ml /1½ tsp salt
2 medium-sized eggs, lightly beaten
50 g /2 oz raisins
15 ml /1 tbls candied peel, finely chopped
grated zest of 1 lemon
about 500 ml /18 fl oz fresh vegetable oil, for deep frying
about 100 g /4 oz icing sugar, sieved, or caster sugar

1 In a small bowl or cup, add the yeast to 75 ml /3 fl oz of the milk and the sugar. Stir to dissolve, then cover with a cloth and leave in a warm place away from drafts for 20 minutes or until the yeast foams.
2 Sift the flour and salt into a warmed bowl. Beat the eggs into the flour until they are well incorporated. Slowly beat in the rest of the milk until the mixture is smooth. Continue beating while adding the yeast mixture, the raisins, candied peel and lemon zest.
3 Cover the mixture with a light, damp

American chocolate doughnut rings

cloth and leave it in a warm place to rise for 2 hours or until it has doubled in bulk.
4 Heat the oil in a deep-fat frier with a basket, to about 190C /375F. At this temperature a bread cube will brown in 50 seconds. Put the batter, 15 ml /1 tbls at a time, in batches of 3, into the frying basket and fry until they are puffy and golden-brown. Cook for 5 minutes on each side.
5 Remove the doughnuts from the fat with a slotted spoon and drain them on absorbent paper. Then you can either roll the doughnuts in caster sugar immediately, or keep them warm, and just before serving sprinkle them with icing sugar.

American chocolate doughnut rings

🍴 35 minutes, plus cooling

Makes 12
225 g /8 oz flour, plus extra for dusting
a pinch of salt
2.5 ml /½ tsp baking powder
150 ml /5 fl oz milk
50 g /2 oz butter, melted
2 eggs, beaten
60 ml /4 tbls sugar
oil, for deep frying
For the coating
caster sugar, for dusting
175 g /6 oz plain chocolate

1 Make the dough: sift the flour, the salt and the baking powder into a mixing bowl. Heat the milk to blood temperature (37C /98F). In another bowl, mix together the melted butter, half the beaten egg and the sugar.
2 Make a well in the centre of the flour and pour in the egg and butter mixture, stirring to gradually incorporate the flour. Add the warmed milk, stirring constantly, until all the flour is absorbed and the mixture is smooth. The mixture should be soft but firm enough to handle without being sticky.
3 Cut the dough into 12 pieces and, with floured hands, roll each piece into a sausage shape, about 7.5–10 cm /3–4 in long. Form it into a ring using the remaining beaten egg to stick the ends together.
4 Heat the oil in a deep-fat frier to 180C /350F.
5 Cook 4 doughnut rings at a time in the hot oil until they are a light golden colour. Remove and drain them on absorbent paper. Dip one side of each doughnut in the caster sugar while the doughnut is still hot. Cook the remaining doughnuts in 2 batches. Coat them with sugar and allow them to cool.
6 Break the chocolate into the top pan of a double boiler. Place over simmering water until the chocolate has melted, then dip the unsugared side of each cold doughnut into the chocolate. Allow the chocolate to set, then serve the doughnuts.

● Another popular American idea for these doughnuts is to dip the chocolate side, while it is still warm, in chopped nuts, to give a lovely crunchy finish.

Crisp-coated plaited doughnuts

The secret of the crisp syrupy outside of these doughnuts is that they are taken straight from the hot oil and are immediately dipped into ice-cold sugar syrup. This seals the syrup on the outside and leaves the inside dry in contrast.

🍴 15 minutes, plus chilling for the syrup, then 2 hours

Makes about 18 doughnuts
225 g /8 oz flour
a good pinch of salt
15 ml /1 tbls baking powder
15 ml /1 tbls butter
225 ml /8 fl oz milk, soured with 30 ml /2 tbls distilled or white wine vinegar
vegetable oil, for deep frying
For the syrup
450 g /1 lb sugar
2.5 ml /½ tsp cream of tartar
7.5 ml /1½ tsp golden syrup
2.5 ml /½ tsp ground ginger

1 For the syrup, stir the sugar into 225 ml /8 fl oz boiling water in a heavy-based saucepan. Continue stirring until the sugar dissolves. Add the cream of tartar, then raise the heat and boil fast for 5 minutes. Remove the pan from the heat and stir in the golden syrup and the ground ginger.
2 Divide the syrup equally between 2 bowls and cool thoroughly. Put them in the refrigerator to chill well.
3 To make the doughnuts, sift the flour, the salt and the baking powder into a bowl. Rub in the butter. Add the soured milk and mix to a smooth dough. Leave the dough to stand for 1 hour.
4 Roll out the dough 5 mm /¼ in thick. Cut it into strips about 5 × 10 cm /2 × 4 in. Cut each strip lengthways into 3 equal-sized strips leaving one end joined. Plait the strips by weaving the outside strips alternately over the centre strip. Press them together at the free ends to join them.
5 Take one of the bowls of syrup out of the refrigerator. Heat the oil in a deep frying-pan over medium-high heat. Put a few doughnuts at a time into the oil, and fry them until they are lightly browned and puffed.
6 Lift them out of the pan using a slotted spoon, shake them over the pan to remove any excess oil, and dip them at once in the chilled syrup. Turn them over to make sure that they are covered in syrup, then drain them in a sieve standing on absorbent paper.
7 Repeat the process until all the doughnuts have been fried, dipped and drained. When the syrup starts to get warm, change the bowl for the one still in the refrigerator. Serve the doughnuts cold, and store them in an airtight tin if necessary.

● These doughnuts can also be served while they are still warm, accompanied either with thick cream, or with an ice cream of your choice.
● If you have any syrup left, you can add it to a fresh fruit salad or another dessert.

Crumb-topped cake

🍴 about 2¼ hours,
including rising

Makes 12 slices
*65 g /2½ oz butter, melted, plus extra
for greasing*
20 g /¾ oz fresh yeast
40 ml /2½ tbls caster sugar
125 ml /4 fl oz tepid milk
250 g /9 oz flour, plus extra for dusting
4 medium-sized egg yolks
icing sugar, for dusting (optional)
For the topping
150 g /5 oz flour
75 g /3 oz caster sugar
15 ml /1 tbls vanilla sugar (see page 9)
125 g /4½ oz butter
finely grated zest of ½ lemon
5 ml /1 tsp ground cinnamon
65 g /2½ oz ground almonds

1 Grease a large mixing bowl and set it
aside. Cream the yeast in a small bowl with 5
ml /1 tsp of the sugar, stir in the milk and set
aside. Sift the flour into a warmed bowl and
make a little well in the centre.
2 As soon as the yeast begins to bubble,
about 5 minutes, stir the mixture into the
centre of the flour. Add the remaining sugar,
the egg yolks and the butter. Mix the ingredients with a wooden spoon, then knead until
the dough is smooth, shiny and begins to
blister.
3 Pat the dough into a neat ball, then place

it in the greased bowl, cover the top with a
tea-towel and set it in a warm place until it
is doubled in bulk. This usually takes about
1 hour.
4 Meanwhile, thoroughly butter and flour a
baking tin measuring about 33×28 cm /
13×11 in.
5 Make the topping in a large bowl,
rubbing together the flour, the caster sugar,
the vanilla sugar, the butter, the lemon zest,
the cinnamon and the ground almonds, until
they are the consistency of coarse breadcrumbs, then reserve.
6 Knead the dough briefly, then put in the
centre of the prepared tin. Press the dough
out with your knuckles until it completely
covers the bottom of the tin and fills the
corners. Sprinkle the topping over, cover the
tin with a clean tea-towel and set it in a warm
place to rise a second time, 45–60 minutes or
until the dough has doubled in size. While
the dough is rising, heat the oven to 190C
/375F /gas 5.
7 Bake the cake for about 40 minutes or
until the centre is firm when pressed with the
fingertips. Cool it in the tin. Dust the top of
the cake with a little more icing sugar if
wished, but traditionally the cake should not
be very sweet. Slice it to serve.

Swedish nut ring

🍴 2½ hours, plus cooling,
then decorating

Rum babas

Serves 6
oil, for greasing
15 g /½ oz fresh yeast
175 ml /6 fl oz milk
75 g /3 oz butter, softened
25 g /1 oz caster sugar
2.5 ml /½ tsp salt
*500 g /1 lb strong flour, plus extra for
dusting*
50 g /2 oz walnuts, chopped
50 g /2 oz soft dark brown sugar
1 egg, beaten
175 g /6 oz icing sugar, sifted
15 ml /1 tbls walnuts, chopped, to decorate
*maraschino cherries, drained and sliced, to
decorate*

1 Lightly oil a large mixing bowl and set it
to one side. In a small bowl, crumble the
yeast over 50 ml /2 fl oz lukewarm water and
stir until the yeast is dissolved. In a
saucepan, scald the milk and add 50 g /2 oz
of the butter, the caster sugar and the salt.
Allow to cool to blood temperature (37C /
98F).
2 Sift three-quarters of the flour into a bowl
and pour in the milk mixture and the
dissolved yeast. Draw in the flour and mix it
well with one hand. Knead the dough until it
comes away from the sides of the bowl. Now
turn it onto a lightly floured board and knead
for 5 minutes, adding more flour if necessary,
until the dough is smooth and elastic. Place
the dough in the oiled bowl, cover it with
cling film and allow it to stand until it
doubles in bulk.
3 Turn the dough out, punch it down to its

Swedish nut ring

original size and roll it into a rectangle 45×18 cm /18×7 in and about 15 mm /½ in thick. Spread it with the remaining softened butter, 50 g /2 oz chopped walnuts and the brown sugar. Roll it up as for Swiss roll, starting from the long edge. There should be about three turns.

4   Place the roll on a baking sheet and, with the seal on the bottom, shape it into a circle. Tuck the ends inside each other. Make 6 slashes in the top of the ring and flatten the roll slightly. Cover it loosely with cling film and put it in a warm place to rise and double in bulk again.

5   While the dough is rising, heat the oven to 180C /350F /gas 4.

6   Brush the loaf with the beaten egg. Bake the nut ring in the oven for 20–25 minutes or until it is a golden brown colour. Transfer to a wire rack and allow it to cool. Remove it from the tin.

7   Mix the icing sugar with 75–90 ml /5–6 tbls cold water, stirring well, until the icing is thick and smooth. Spread the icing over each section of the ring between the slashes, allowing the icing to run down the sides of the ring. Next, sprinkle the remaining chopped nuts and sliced maraschino cherries over the top of the ring.

Rum babas

2½ hours, plus cooling,
2–3 hours soaking, then 15 minutes

Serves 6
40 ml /1½ fl oz milk
15 g /½ oz fresh yeast
25 g /1 oz sugar
15 g /½ oz butter, softened, plus extra
  for greasing
1 egg, beaten
125 g /4 oz strong flour
2 small egg yolks
75 g /3 oz raisins
300 ml /10 fl oz thick cream, whipped, to serve
For the syrup
125 g /4 oz sugar
45 ml /3 tbls dark rum
For the glaze
45–60 ml /3–4 tbls apricot jam
7.5 ml /½ tbls lemon juice

1   In a saucepan, heat the milk to lukewarm, crumble the yeast over the milk and stir until it is dissolved.

2   Put the milk mixture in a large bowl and add the sugar, the softened butter and the beaten egg. Now sift the flour into the bowl. Mix well with one hand and then add the egg yolks and the raisins. Mix well again until the raisins are evenly distributed and you have a soft, smooth dough. Cover the bowl with cling film and leave in a warm place until the dough has risen and doubled in bulk.

3   In the bowl, knead the dough until it has returned to its original size.

4   Brush six 150 ml /5 fl oz dariole moulds with melted butter and divide the dough between them, to fill each mould one-third full. Place the moulds on a baking sheet and

cover loosely with cling film. Leave the moulds in a warm place until the dough rises and fills them.

5   While the dough is rising, heat the oven to 180C /350F /gas 4.

6   Bake the babas in the oven for 15 minutes or until they are golden brown.

7   Remove the babas from the oven, allow them to cool for 5 minutes in the moulds, then turn them out onto a wire rack.

8   To make the syrup, put the sugar in a saucepan with 150 ml /5 fl oz water. Stir over a gentle heat until the sugar has dissolved, then bring the syrup to the boil and boil it for 5 minutes. Remove it from the heat and add the rum.

9   Place each baba on an individual serving dish and prick each one all over with a fork. Spoon the hot rum syrup over them and leave them to soak for 2–3 hours.

10   To make the glaze, combine the apricot jam with 15 ml /1 tbls water and the lemon juice in a saucepan, and heat until the jam has melted. Bring it to the boil and then sieve it to remove any lumps. Brush the glaze over the babas. Serve them with whipped cream.

Buttery yeast cake

This recipe makes a popular, tasty cake which can either be served with coffee during the morning, or with afternoon tea.

2 hours,
including rising

Makes 12 slices
500 g /18 oz flour, plus extra for dusting
25 g /1 oz fresh yeast
75 g /3 oz caster sugar
250 ml /9 fl oz tepid milk
75 g /3 oz butter, softened, plus extra for
  greasing
150 g /5 oz butter, melted
150 g /5 oz icing sugar
7.5 ml /1½ tsp ground cinnamon

1   Sift the flour into a warmed bowl. Make a well in the centre using a spoon. Now cream the yeast with 10 ml /2 tsp of the sugar, add 150 ml /5 fl oz of the milk and pour the mixture into the centre of the flour. Cover the bowl with a clean cloth and set it aside until the yeast starts to bubble — this usually takes about 5 minutes.

2   Work the flour into the yeast mixture using a wooden spoon, adding the rest of the milk and the sugar and 75 g /3 oz softened butter to form a dough. Knead the dough with your hands until it is smooth, shiny and blisters.

3   Butter and flour a deep roasting tin, about 33×28 cm /13×11 in. Put the dough into the centre of the tin and press it out with your knuckles, towards the sides of the tin, until it covers the bottom of the tin. Cover the top lightly with a cloth and leave the tin in a warm place until the dough almost doubles in bulk, this should take 1 hour.

4   While the dough is rising, heat the oven to 190C /275F /gas 5. Bake the cake for about 30 minutes. Brush the cake with the melted butter and sprinkle with the sugar and the cinnamon while it is still hot. Serve warm.

SIMPLE TOPPINGS & FILLINGS

Turning an ordinary cake into something special can be enormous fun and a simple icing is often the most effective kind to use. This chapter gives you some suggestions for easy icings, toppings and fillings.

Let me introduce you to icings and cake decorations which require a minimum of skill and only a few basic tools — with the possible exception of a sugar thermometer. Whether you want a simple glacé or a rich fudge icing, the next few pages give you ideas about how best to make and use them.

Glacé icing

Glacé icing is the simplest of all the icings. To make it, warm the icing sugar gently with a little water or liquid flavouring, until it melts. Poured warm over the cake, it gives a smooth, shiny coating when set.

Glacé icing is perfect left unadorned — in particular, chocolate glacé icing has a richness, smoothness and density that white glacé icing lacks. But you can also use it for piping fine designs and writing, and for simple designs such as those shown below.

Simple glacé icing decorations

There are two basic glacé icing techniques. **Feather icing,** shown on the left below, is usually seen as dark-coloured feathering on white icing but it can also be done the other way, for instance using a chocolate icing with white feathering.

Ice the cake with most of the glacé icing. While the coating is still soft, thin the remaining icing by adding water and colouring.

Fill a small piping bag with the coloured icing. Carefully pipe it in parallel lines 15–20 mm /1/2–3/4 in apart, across the cake.

Quickly draw a skewer at right angles to the piping, again at 15–20 mm /1/2–3/4 in intervals, drawing the skewer alternately in opposite directions to give a feathered effect. Wipe the skewer clean each time you draw

it through the icing, to ensure a smooth, even finish.

Cobweb icing: shown on the right, below. Pipe the coloured icing in a spiral on a round cake and draw the skewer into and out from the centre alternately.

Butter creams

Butter creams are soft creamy icings, which are used as fillings as well as toppings. They are easy to spread and swirl and are frequently used around the sides of a cake to hold chopped nuts or chocolate vermicelli.

One is made by creaming butter and sugar together until the mixture is light and fluffy. Flavouring and colouring are then added, as are egg yolks for extra richness.

French butter cream, known as *crème au beurre,* is made of the same ingredients but they are combined in a more elaborate way. The sugar is boiled with water to make a syrup. This is then poured onto the yolks and whisked to make a fluffy sauce. Butter is then creamed in, a little at a time, for extra smoothness and richness.

Both these butter creams are used in the same way. Smooth them onto the cake fairly thickly and then use a fork or palette knife to make the decorations. Butter cream icings are also good for piping.

Fudge icings and frosting

Icings made from melted ingredients are ideal fillings for cakes as well as toppings. The simplest are made from melted chocolate with butter or cream stirred in. Or, you can make a fudge by boiling together the sugar and cream and then beating in the butter.

Orange cream icing (see recipe) is made

like a custard. Sugar and egg are cooked together in the top of a double boiler until they become thickened, and whipped cream is folded in when they are cold. The result is a soft icing which is less sugary than the fudge icings.

Fondant icing

Fondant icing is probably the most difficult icing to make in this section. It is very white and soft to the bite, even when set.

It is made by boiling sugar to a very precise temperature and so a sugar thermometer is essential for success. At 115C /240F the boiled sugar changes its form. When cool enough to handle, it is kneaded by hand. Unlike other icings, the major part of the work can be done ahead of time and the fondant base can be kept for up to a year in an airtight container, in a cool, dry place.

To coat the cake, the fondant base is melted with a little sugar syrup and poured over the cake. It is worth the extra trouble involved for the fine finish it gives. This kind of icing can also be modelled into flowers and other shapes.

Royal icing

The traditional icing for a celebration fruit cake is Royal icing. It is very hard when set, and therefore is excellent when used on the lower sections of a wedding cake. It is simple to make and the addition of a few drops of glycerine soften it just enough to make it easy to cut — such as in my White Christmas cake (see page 21).

Royal icing can be made, piped onto the cake, and then kept for several weeks before it is eaten. For wedding and anniversary cakes the icing is usually piped in a formal design. It can also be used to rough-ice a cake (see illustration on next page) which can then be decorated to resemble a snow scene.

A completely smooth base is essential for Royal icing. To achieve this you must cover the cake with almond paste. Though this can be bought, it is always nicer if you make it at home by kneading together ground almonds, sugar and flavourings (see page 21).

A glaze made with a melted jam of your choice (traditionally apricot jam is used), and a liquid such as water or alcohol, is spread under many icings to prevent crumbs spoiling the finish. If you use it under almond paste, it also helps the paste stick firmly to the cake.

Roll out the almond paste and cover the cake. Now roll the rolling pin over the cake to smooth away any awkward seams. If you have any almond paste left over, work some drops of food colouring into the paste and make edible decorations.

Fillings

As well as using an icing to cover a cake, it can also be used to stick two halves of a sandwich cake together. Most icings are suitable for use in this way, but glacé, fondant and Royal icings are best used only on the top and sides of cakes. To fill cakes covered in these icings you can use Creme au beurre,

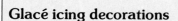

Glacé icing decorations

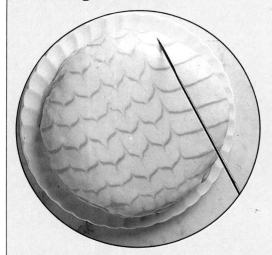

Pipe icing in parallel lines across the cake, then draw a skewer across the wet lines in alternate directions for a feathered effect.

Pipe in a spiral around the cake, then draw a skewer alternately into and out from the centre to make a cobweb design.

Simple American frosting, Orange cream icing, Crème chantilly (see recipes), Kirsch cream (page 50), a praline filling (page 10), or any jam of your choice.

Finishing the cake
To keep the cake plate clean and free from messy icing trails while you are decorating the cake, cut 4 strips of waxed paper or foil. Lay the strips in a square pattern around the rim of the plate and place the cake carefully on the strips, making sure the cake rests on the paper all round. After you have finished icing the cake, carefully remove these strips from under the cake, leaving the cake to sit on an unmarked plate.

Glacé icing

This is probably the most useful of all the icings. Use glacé icing on sponge cakes, light pastries and iced buns to give a crisp, smooth, shiny glaze without too much added sweetness.

 10 minutes

Covers a 22 cm /8½ in cake
225 g /8 oz icing sugar
flavouring (see notes below)
colouring (optional)
For the apricot glaze
45 ml /3 tbls apricot jam

1   Sift the icing sugar into the top half of a double boiler.
2   Add 50 ml /3 tbls plus 1 tsp water, or a liquid flavouring (see notes below) and a few drops of colouring, if you wish, made up with water to give the same quantity. Stir with a wooden spoon over a low heat. Do not let the water in the bottom of the double boiler get too warm, otherwise the icing will become lumpy.
3   The icing is the right consistency when it coats the back of a spoon. If the icing becomes too soft, stiffen it by adding a little extra sifted icing sugar.
4   Place the cake to be iced on a wire rack over a baking sheet or a sheet of greaseproof paper. For the apricot glaze, sieve the jam into a small saucepan, add 15 ml /1 tbls water and heat it gently. When the jam has completely melted, let it stand a moment or two and then brush the warm glaze smoothly all over the cake.
5   While the glacé icing is still soft, pour it over the cake and guide it down the sides with a palette knife to completely cover them. Any icing that runs over may be spooned up and used again.

● Liquid flavourings must only be used instead of the water and not in addition to the water.
Vanilla: use 5 ml /1 tsp vanilla essence to replace 5 ml /1 tsp water.
Chocolate: replace 30 ml /2 tbls icing sugar with 30 ml /2 tbls cocoa, sifted.
Coffee: use 15 ml /1 tbls instant coffee dissolved in 5 ml /1 tsp boiling water to replace 5 ml /1 tsp water. Allow this to cool before adding it to the icing.

Decorations for thicker icings

To rough ice a cake, smooth the icing over the cake with a palette knife, then pull it up into peaks with the knife tip.

For swirled icing, use the tip of a palette knife and work from the centre outwards to make a Catherine wheel pattern.

Another alternative is to fork the smoothed icing in wavy or straight lines, spacing them evenly across the top of the cake.

To decorate the sides of a cake, ice the sides first and then roll the cake in chopped nuts or vermicelli.

Liqueur: use 15 ml /1 tbls liqueur to replace 15 ml /1 tbls water.
● Add a few drops of food colouring to the icing, if wished.

Crème au beurre

This rich butter cream has a soft, mousse-like texture, but it is still suitable for using in a piping bag. If you wish to pipe a decoration around the rim and base of the cake as well as filling and covering it, make double the quantity of crème au beurre.

25 minutes

Fills and covers a 22 cm /8½ in sandwich cake
3 egg yolks
60 g /2½ oz sugar
175 g /6 oz unsalted butter, softened
flavouring, to taste
colouring (optional)

1   Lightly whisk the egg yolks in a bowl.
2   In a small pan, heat the sugar with 50 ml /2 fl oz water until it has dissolved. Bring it to the boil until the temperature on a sugar thermometer reaches 115C /240F. At this temperature a sample dropped into cold water will form a soft ball between your fingers. The syrup must not be allowed to heat above this temperature, so start testing it early.
3   As soon as the syrup is ready, remove it from the heat and immediately pour it onto the egg yolks, all at once, as you whisk them — this is easiest with an electric whisk. Continue whisking until the mixture is pale, cool, very thick and mousse-like.
4   In another bowl, cream the butter until it is really soft and the same consistency as the egg yolk mixture. Gradually beat the creamed butter into the egg yolk mixture, a little at a time to begin with, until the mixture thickens, then it can be added more quickly. When all the butter is beaten in, add a flavouring which complements your cake, and food colouring if you wish.

Fudge icing

 30 minutes

**Fills and covers the top of a 22 cm /
8½ in sandwich cake**
225 g /8 oz caster sugar
50 ml /2 fl oz evaporated milk
75 ml /3 fl oz thin cream
100 g /4 oz unsalted butter
flavouring (see notes below)

1 In a medium-sized, heavy saucepan, mix
together the sugar, the evaporated milk and
the cream. Place over a low heat and stir
constantly until the sugar has dissolved.
2 Increase the heat slightly and boil the
mixture, stirring constantly with a wooden
spoon, for about 9 minutes until it reaches
115C /240F on a sugar thermometer. At this
temperature a sample dropped into cold
water will form a soft ball. Allow the syrup
to cool for 5 minutes.
3 Cut the butter into small pieces and then
stir them into the fudge mixture, followed by
your chosen flavouring. Beat the fudge until
thick and smooth — about 3 minutes.
4 Fill and cover the cake immediately,
using a palette knife to spread the icing.
Allow the fudge icing to run down the sides
of the cake rather than spreading it with a
palette knife, because overworking it will
make it granular.

● **Vanilla:** use 10 ml /2 tsp vanilla essence.
● **Coffee:** use 30 ml /2 tbls coffee dissolved
in 15 ml /1 tbls boiling water, cooled.
● **Almond:** use 10 ml /2 tsp almond
essence.

Chocolate rum icing

**This chocolate icing has a rich, shiny finish
which makes a cake luxurious.**

 15 minutes

Covers the top of a 22 cm /8½ in cake
50 g /2 oz plain chocolate
25 g /1 oz unsalted butter
15 ml /1 tbls rum

1 Break the chocolate into pieces and melt
it in the top of a double boiler or in a bowl
over simmering water. Beat in the butter.
Add the rum and beat until the icing is
glossy. Leave it to cool and harden slightly.
2 Pour the icing over the top of the cake,
spread evenly with a palette knife and allow
it to set before serving.

Chocolate soured-
cream icing

**This icing is too soft for piping — it simply
drips over the sides of the cake.**

 10 minutes,
plus 30 minutes cooling

**Fills and covers a 22 cm /8½ in
sandwich cake**
225 g /8 oz plain chocolate
150 ml /5 fl oz soured cream
15 ml /1 tbls caster sugar (optional)

1 Break the chocolate into pieces and melt
it in the top of a double boiler or in a bowl
over simmering water. As soon as the chocolate has melted, remove it from the heat.
2 Stir in the soured cream and add the
sugar if you wish.
3 Leave the icing to cool and thicken for 30
minutes. When it becomes as thick as
whipped cream, use it to fill the cake and to
cover the top and sides.

Simple American frosting

**American frosting spreads easily and the
whisked egg whites in it give a marsh-
mallowy texture. To make it successfully,
you do need a sugar thermometer.**

 30 minutes

**Fills and covers a 20 cm /8 in ring
mould**
350 g /12 oz sugar
2 egg whites
flavourings (see notes below)

1 Put the sugar and 150 ml /5 fl oz water
together in a heavy-based saucepan and
gently dissolve the sugar over a low heat.
Bring the syrup to boiling point and then
boil it rapidly for 15–20 minutes, or until it
reaches 115C /240F.
2 Meanwhile, whisk the egg whites in a
large bowl until they are stiff. When the
syrup is ready, pour it onto the egg whites in
a thin stream, whisking continuously until
the frosting is cool and very thick. If you are
using a hand whisk and only have one hand
free, you may find it better to put the sugar
syrup into a jug so you can pour it in a
stream more easily.
3 Add your chosen flavouring — see
suggestions listed below. Whisk this in
thoroughly, then cover the cake with the
icing, making a swirling pattern all over the
surface.

● **Vanilla:** use 20 ml /4 tsp vanilla essence.
● **Chocolate:** use 60 ml /4 tbls cocoa,
sifted.
● **Coffee:** use 30 ml /2 tbls instant coffee
dissolved in 10 ml /2 tsp boiling water, and
then cooled.

Fondant icing

**For this all-sugar icing the sugar is heated to
the temperature which allows it to become
white when firm. A sugar thermometer is
essential when you are making fondant
icing, which can also be used for modelling
cake decorations — flowers or names.**

 30 minutes, plus 1 hour resting,
then 15 minutes

A ring mould cake decorated with Simple American frosting

dissolved in 5 ml /1 tsp boiling water.
Lemon or orange: use 10–15 ml /2–3 tsp lemon or orange juice and 2.5 ml /½ tsp grated zest. Add yellow, or yellow and red colouring if you wish.
Rose-water: use 2.5 ml /½ tsp triple distilled rose-water and add a few drops of red food colouring to make the icing a light pink colour.
● When adding food colouring to fondant icing, dip a skewer into the bottle of colouring and use this to drip the colouring into the fondant mixture and so prevent any over-colouring.

Orange cream icing

 30 minutes, plus cooling

Fills and covers a 22cm /8½ sandwich cake
1 egg
150 g /5 oz caster sugar
finely grated zest of 1 orange
30 ml /2 tbls flour, sifted
juice from 1 orange
275 ml /10 fl oz thick cream

1 In a bowl, whisk together the egg, sugar and finely grated orange zest until foamy. With a wooden spoon, beat in the flour. Add enough water to the orange juice to make it up to 150 ml /5 fl oz and then beat it into the egg mixture.
2 Pour the mixture into the top of a double boiler and then cook it over simmering water, stirring constantly, for 10–15 minutes, until the mixture becomes smooth and thick. Remove the pan from the heat and leave it to cool.
3 Whip the cream lightly, then fold the whipped cream into the cold mixture using a large metal spoon.
4 Sandwich the cake layers with a little of the orange cream and use the remainder to cover the top and sides, smoothing it on with a palette knife.

Crème chantilly

15 minutes

Fills and covers a 22 cm /8½ in sandwich cake
275–425 ml /10–15 fl oz thick cream
15–30 ml /1–2 tbls icing sugar
15–30 ml /1–2 tbls iced water

1 In a medium-sized bowl, whisk the cream until soft peaks form when the whisk is lifted from the cream.
2 Sieve the icing sugar and add it to the cream to taste. Beat until the mixture is stiff, then add the iced water. Fold this in until the cream is smooth. Chill.

● If liked, Crème chantilly can be flavoured with a few drops of vanilla essence.

Covers the top of a 22 cm /8½ in cake
450 g /1 lb sugar
25 ml /1 fl oz liquid glucose or 2.5 ml /½ tsp cream of tartar
icing sugar, for dusting
To finish the fondant
50 g /2 oz sugar
flavouring (see notes below)
sifted icing sugar, if necessary
colouring (optional)
Apricot glaze, (see under Glacé icing, page 39)

1 Put the sugar and 150 ml /5 fl oz water in a large, heavy-based saucepan and dissolve the sugar over a low heat. You may find that you get a rim of sugar around the pan above the level of the liquid. If so, dip a pastry brush in cold water and wipe any sugar crystals not dissolved back down into the syrup to keep the texture smooth.
2 Bring the syrup to the boil. Meanwhile, add either the glucose or the cream of tartar. If you are using cream of tartar, dissolve it in 5 ml /1 tsp water before adding it to the syrup. Boil the syrup steadily for 10–15 minutes until it reaches 115C /240F.
3 Remove the pan from the heat and allow the bubbles to subside. Next pour the syrup slowly into a heatproof bowl. Leave it to stand for about 1 minute until a skin forms on the surface.
4 Using a wooden spoon, work the icing in figure-of-eight movements until it becomes white and firm.
5 Dust your hands with icing sugar and knead the fondant icing until it is completely smooth and free from lumps.
6 Pack the fondant into a small bowl, cover with a damp cloth and leave it to stand for 1 hour. Then either use it immediately or wrap the fondant in waxed paper and keep it in an airtight container until it is needed. It will keep for up to a year.
7 To use the icing, you will need to add a little sugar syrup to make it soft and flowing. To make this, dissolve 50 g /2 oz sugar in 125 ml /4 fl oz water in a small pan over a low heat. Bring it to the boil and boil until the temperature reaches 105C /220F. This will take about 10 minutes.
8 Warm the fondant in a double boiler, adding 30–45 ml /2–3 tbls sugar syrup and a flavouring (see below). Heat it, stirring, until the icing is the consistency of thick cream. If the icing becomes too runny, add a little sifted icing sugar to correct it. Finally add colouring if you wish.
9 Place the cake on a wire rack over a baking sheet or greaseproof paper. Make the apricot glaze, let it stand for a moment or two, then brush the warm glaze over the cake and leave it to cool.
10 Pour the fondant icing over the top of the cake and smooth it to the edge with a palette knife.

● All liquid flavourings should be added to the icing at step 8, with a little of the sugar syrup, not after the syrup, otherwise the fondant will be too runny. However, when using chocolate flavouring the cocoa should be added after the sugar syrup.
Vanilla: use 5 ml /1 tsp vanilla essence.
Chocolate: use 30–45 ml /2–3 tbls cocoa, sifted, adding this after the sugar syrup.
Coffee: use 15 ml /1 tbls instant coffee

PIPING & ICING TECHNIQUES

Special occasions call for extra-special cakes. Whatever the reason, plan the design and decorations well in advance. The result — a beautifully iced cake — will impress and delight your guests.

Piping may appear to be an extremely complicated skill, and indeed the more elaborate designs are difficult to get right. However, if you start with simple designs using one, or perhaps two, nozzles, you can still produce professional-looking results. Of course, the more you are able to practise, the better the end results will be.

Equipment

The only special tools you need for piping are a piping bag and a small selection of nozzles. For piping intricate patterns with Royal icing (see page 21) and Glacé icing (see page 39), it is best to make your own bag from greaseproof paper. You can make several bags at a time to make life easier when you are using different coloured icings or nozzles. If you buy a piping bag it will be made from nylon, plastic or cotton — this type of bag is particularly good for piping butter icing and whipped cream.

Icing pump: instead of a piping bag you may prefer to use an icing pump. This resembles a syringe and, once you have acquired the knack, is much cleaner to use than a bag; follow the manufacturer's instructions for assembly and use. However, a pump is suitable only for thick icings.

Nozzles: a greaseproof paper piping bag can be used without a metal nozzle for simple designs, but for any other bag a nozzle is essential. There are numerous shapes of nozzle available but three basic shapes are adequate for most needs. Choose two plain (or writing) nozzles of different sizes, perhaps a fine and a medium, a star nozzle and a shell nozzle. With these three shapes you can produce a wide range of designs.

Other equipment you may need for piping icing includes small bowls for holding small quantities of differently coloured icing; a spatula for scraping all the icing out of a bowl; and a damp cloth to cover the bowl of icing to prevent it drying out.

Filling the bag

To fill a fabric piping bag with icing, slip the chosen nozzle into the bag so that it projects through the hole at the point of the bag. Place the assembled bag inside a tall jar, nozzle end first (see photograph on page 43). Fold the rim of the bag over the rim of the jar and half fill the bag with icing. Now fold over the top of the bag and twist, to force out any trapped air.

Piping

Piping requires a light, yet firm, hold and a very steady touch. Hold the bag so that one hand secures the twist at the top of the bag ready for squeezing. Leave the other free for guiding the bag as you work — start by practising simple designs and then gradually progress to more complicated patterns.

The same technique applies to all forms of piping, whether you are using icing or cream. The picture on the left shows examples of what the various types of nozzles are able to produce:

The plain nozzle is used for piping straight lines, a trellis, curved lines or loops, writing (names and numbers), dots and lacework. This nozzle comes in many sizes.

The star nozzle is used to create stars, rosettes, rope, zigzag and scrolls. The number of points to the star may vary but will not affect how you use it.

The shell nozzle is used to make a shell border around the edge of a cake.

Piping with a plain nozzle

These plain-nozzle patterns are very basic:
Straight lines: hold the bag firmly with one hand, keeping the top tightly closed. Use the other hand to guide the bag and apply a gentle pressure. Holding the bag at an angle of 45 degrees, squeeze out enough icing so that it just touches the surface of the cake. With an even pressure, continue to squeeze the bag gently, lift the nozzle a little above the surface and pull it gently towards you.

For the piping shown (left), use a plain nozzle for the trellis, lacework and loops in the four corners. Pipe the central design with a plain nozzle too. Use a shell nozzle for the vertical shell borders on the far left and right and a star nozzle for the rows of zigzags and stars next to the shell borders. Use a star nozzle for the scroll at the bottom and top

Anna

For easy filling, place the bag in a jar

The icing will come out in a slightly sagging line which can be manoeuvred to keep it straight. To finish the line, touch the surface gently with the nozzle.

Trellis: pipe a series of parallel lines using a medium nozzle. When dry, turn the cake 45 degrees and pipe another layer of parallel lines over the first layer, to give a diamond effect. For a more delicate result, use a finer plain nozzle to pipe a third and fourth layer, each time turning the cake 45 degrees, allowing each layer to dry first.

Loops: these are usually used for the sides of a cake, though they can be effective on the top. Practise by drawing a series of loops on a piece of paper first. For a loop on top of the cake, place the tip of the nozzle at the beginning of the loop and squeeze out a little icing. Lift the nozzle and allow the line to drape along the curve of the loop. Lower the nozzle as you reach the end.

To make a loop on the side of a cake, tilt the cake slightly and hold the nozzle away from the cake to allow the icing to fall in an even shape. Touch the cake with the nozzle to finish the loop, turn the cake slightly and pipe another loop. Repeat all round.

Dots: dots are a useful decoration — they make a simple border around the top of a cake, or look effective used on the sides, piped in graduated sizes.

To pipe a dot, place the tip of the nozzle on the surface of the cake and hold the bag upright. Squeeze the bag gently and at the same time lift the nozzle slightly. Use a quick down and up movement, so that the dot is not lifted into too much of a point.

Writing: any of the plain nozzles can be used for writing. Try piping capital letters first. Once this has been mastered, you can progress to script. Write the words on a piece of greaseproof paper, the same size as the top of the cake. Lay the paper on the cake and attach it with pins. Using a pin, prick through the paper into the icing so that you can see the design on the cake. With a medium nozzle, follow the pin-pricks.

Lacework: using a fine nozzle, pipe a continuous wiggly line.

Piping with a star nozzle

These patterns are more intricate:

Stars: hold the bag just above the surface of the cake in an upright position. Squeeze out the icing, using a quick down and up movement, so that you create a squat star.

Rosettes: hold the bag upright just above the surface of the cake. Squeeze out the icing in a circular movement, working from the outside and curling into the centre. Finish off sharply, leaving a point in the centre.

Rope: move the piping bag over and over in a circular movement, making a series of overlapping circles.

Scroll: hold the bag at a 45-degree angle just above the surface of the cake. Squeeze out the icing in the shape of a comma, beginning with a thick head and releasing the pressure on the bag while pulling into a long tail.

Zigzag: hold the bag at a slight angle, just above the surface of the cake. Squeeze out the icing in a continuous line, moving it from side to side to give a zigzag effect.

Piping with a shell nozzle

The shell border can in fact be piped with the star nozzle as well as the shell nozzle. The shell nozzle has more ridges than the star nozzles, producing a fatter shell.

Shell border: hold the nozzle just above the surface of the cake at a 45-degree angle. Squeeze out the icing to form a head, then pull the nozzle away, gently releasing the pressure, until the head tapers to a neat point. Pipe the next shell onto the pointed end of the previous shell, and then continue piping in this way to form a border.

Planning and design

Think carefully about the event and the shape of the cake. A simple design, subtle colour combinations and imaginative ideas will all add to the effectiveness of the end result.

Make sure the cake board is suitable; it needs to be 25 mm /1 in larger all round than the cake, and 5–7 cm /2–3 in larger if the piping design continues onto the board.

Remember that cakes must look attractive. If the occasion is a wedding, take a cutting of

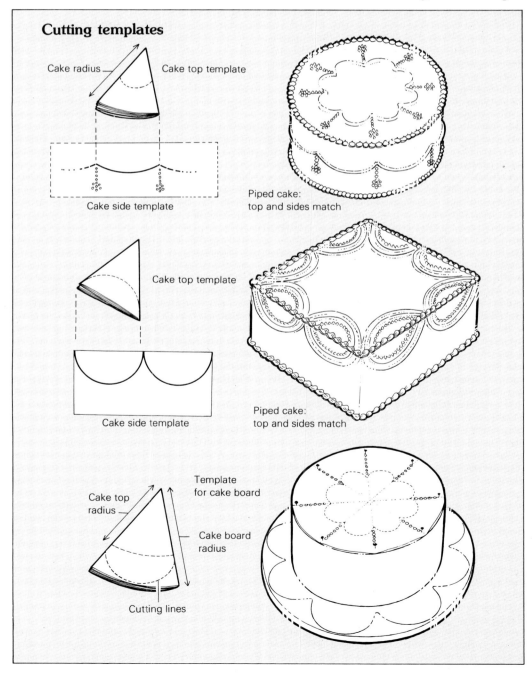

Cutting templates

Cake radius — Cake top template

Cake side template

Piped cake: top and sides match

Cake top template

Cake side template

Piped cake: top and sides match

Cake top radius —

Template for cake board

Cake board radius

Cutting lines

the dress fabric, so that you can match the cake's ribbon, flowers and icing to it.

Make a trial batch of icing; making a note of the number of drops of food colouring added, mix the colours in the daylight and leave the icing to stand. The colour tends to deepen several shades when dry. Experiment until you have a colour you want. If you have to make more than one batch, always keep some of the original icing in reserve to match each fresh batch as it is made.

When piping with coloured icing, first pipe fine designs in white icing, then overpipe with a colour. This protects the cake from becoming stained.

Designs

Plan your design carefully before you begin icing the cake, taking into consideration the overall look of the sides and the top of the cake.

Template: cake designing is like geometry — accuracy is essential. Cut a template out of greaseproof paper (see diagrams on page 43) to fit the top of the cake, and a strip of paper to fit the sides of the cake. Fold the template for the top of the cake in half, and then in

---

Ideas for decorations

● Choose icing colours to suit the occasion: pastel shades for engagement, weddings and anniversaries.
● For christenings, try a pastel pink, yellow or blue cake, white decorations and a run-out of a cradle, stork with a bundle, or a pram. To finish, tie a lace ribbon around the cake.
● For an anniversary or engagement party, choose a motif such as horseshoes or bells. Try pink hearts and bows, or a pair of facing blue birds. For a silver wedding try a silver and white theme.
● For Christmas, try a simple candle, lantern or angel. Alternatively try a scheme with more colour: a ring of holly leaves with red berries, a Father Christmas, or even a sleigh and reindeer.
● Make a template of the words 'Merry Christmas'. Cut the words out in coloured marzipan and stick them on the top of the cake with a dab of icing.
● Try a Poinsettia flower cake for Christmas. Cover the cake with almond paste, then ice with white icing. Colour equal quantities of reserved almond paste red and green. Make a template of the flowers and leaves and stick them on with a dab of icing.
● For Easter, yellow and blue are appropriate: make chicks, bunnies, eggs, flowers, lambs and ducks from marzipan.
● For children's parties, funny faces in primary colours are always popular. Try your children's favourite cartoon character or a clown, making up his hat and nose separately in differently coloured icings.
● For Hallowe'en, make an orange-iced cake with chocolate-coloured cats, and witches on broomsticks.
● For a birthday cake, cut out a template of the number, or name, and make a run-out on your design. Stick it to the cake with a dab of icing when it is dry.
● For further suggestions see the chapter on Celebration cakes.

---

half twice more to divide it into eight identical sections.

Work out a design for the top and sides using simple lines and curves, and mark them on the greaseproof template. When the design is ready, draw or trace it onto clean greaseproof paper and cut it out.

When the iced cake is completely dry, place the new template carefully on top of the cake, pencil lines upward. Hold it lightly in position and use a stainless steel pin or needle to prick around the shape on the template. This will transfer the shape of the design onto the top of the cake. Repeat this for the sides, resting the template on the cake board, to keep the design level.

Piping: use only two or three piping nozzles or the effect will be too complicated. Make sure the icing is the correct colour and consistency. Use greaseproof paper icing bags, with or without nozzles, and small quantities of icing. This way the bags are easy to handle and the nozzles, if you are using them, are easy to remove.

Pipe the design following the marked pattern on top of the cake. Repeat the piping on the sides to match the top. Tilt the cake so the surface is not vertical. Pipe retaining lines or scallops first, and then any infill or extra pattern. Finally pipe the borders around the top and bottom of the cake.

When the icing is dry, with a little reserved icing, secure the remaining decorations, such as run-outs (see below), ribbons and flowers. Leave the cake in a dry place lightly covered.

Icing run-outs

Icing run-outs are one of the most useful forms of decoration as they allow you to experiment, without spoiling the top of the cake. Try out your ideas on waxed paper, then, when you have achieved several neat examples of the design you have chosen, you can transfer them to the iced cake.

Choosing shapes: decide on a shape or a name in not more than three colours. Draw or trace it onto a piece of paper. Repeat the design several times, so you have a few spares to work with. Secure the design to a board with tape and cover the design with a piece of waxed paper; secure the paper with several beads of icing.

Piping the outline: use Royal icing (see page 21) made with egg whites only and omit additives like lemon juice and glycerine. The icing should be like a light glossy meringue. When the spoon is lifted, a soft peak should form which will bend at the top. If, when you are icing, the icing thread keeps breaking, it is because the consistency of the icing is too stiff or the icing has not been beaten enough.

Using a fine writing nozzle, pipe carefully around the outline with as few breaks as possible. Small run-outs can be piped with one thread of icing. Pipe internal lines to separate areas of different colours. The outline piping can be the same colour as the soft icing, or simply pipe a white outline and fill it in with a coloured icing.

Filling the run-out: complete the run-out in one go, otherwise it will crack when the area is filled with the soft icing. The icing used to fill in the run-out must be much softer than that used for piping. Add a little

---

more egg white, then let the icing stand so that the air bubbles disperse. The consistency needed for satisfactorily filling the run-out is not so liquid that it will flow, but sufficiently soft to spread smoothly with the aid of a fine paint brush or cocktail stick. Remember, icing shrinks when drying, so be generous, the run-out should look overfilled.

To fill the run-out, start from the edges and work into the centre. This keeps the outline soft and stops it setting too quickly. When you have completed the run-out with soft icing, use a paint brush or cocktail stick to ensure that the whole area is smoothly covered. Gently vibrate the run-out so that any air bubbles rise to the surface. Burst them with a pin. Carefully remove the waxed paper and the run-out and place it on a tray to dry. If using more than one run-out, make more the same way.

Drying: leave the icing run-outs to dry in a warm, dry place overnight or until completely hard and dry. The quicker they dry, the more glossy they will be. When they are completely dry, carefully peel them off the paper. When ready to use them, arrange the run-outs on the cake and secure them with beads of icing.

If you make the run-outs ahead, store them between layers of soft paper in an airtight container for up to three months.

Cake board run-outs

A design which matches the cake top is sometimes repeated around the cake on the cake board. This can be made in separate pieces (like other run-outs) and then fitted together around the cake base. However, a better fit is achieved by working directly onto the cake board. If you do this remember to choose a board large enough to leave a border around the cake.

Complete the design for the top of the cake, then make a greaseproof paper template the same size as the cake board. Draw around the cake tin to give you an idea of the size of the border around the cake.

Inside the circle representing the cake, trace the pattern for the cake top (this will give you some guidance for the border). Now work out the border design; for example, if you have scallops or arches on top of the cake, repeat the same shapes, rather larger, on the board template. Do not take the pattern too close to the edge of the template. When you are happy with the pattern, fold the template into eight and cut away the spare paper on the edge and in the centre. You will now have a template of the edge. Cut through the template in one place.

At this point put the cake on the board and ice it. Leave it to dry for 24 hours after the last coat of icing.

Put the template around the base of the cake. Pin it onto the cake board and prick around the edge of the design, then remove it. Place the top template on the cake, being careful that the shapes on the top are exactly above those on the board. Prick around the edge of the design, then remove the template. Make the run-out icing the same colour as the icing on the cake. Pipe around the outline on the board then flood it with soft icing. Pipe the design on the top of the cake, and then finally pipe a neat border around the bottom of the cake where it joins the run-out to neaten the join.

Left, a Christening cake and right, a Golden Wedding Anniversary cake

French meringue cake

Serves 6
butter and oil, for greasing
flour, for dusting
6 eggs, separated
175g /6 oz sugar
grated zest of 1 lemon
75 g /3 oz flour
30 ml /2 tbls cornflour
a pinch of salt

440 g /15½ oz canned halved
  apricots, drained
For the filling
440 g /15½ oz canned halved
  apricots, drained
60 ml /4 tbls marmalade
For the meringue
4 egg whites
120 ml /8 tbls caster sugar

1 Heat the oven to 180C /350F /gas 4. Grease two 23 cm /9 in sandwich cake tins with butter. Line the bases with buttered greaseproof paper and dust with flour, shaking out the excess.
2 Put the egg yolks and the sugar, 30 ml /2 tbls water and the lemon zest in a large bowl. Set the bowl over barely simmering water and whisk until the mixture is pale, light and fluffy. The mixture should leave a trail when the beaters are lifted.
3 Off the heat, sift the flour, cornflour and salt over the whisked mixture and fold in with a large metal spoon.
4 Whisk the egg whites until they are stiff but not dry and fold them gently into the cake mixture. Divide the mixture between the two tins and bake for 30–35 minutes or until golden. Turn the cakes out onto wire racks to cool. Cover and leave for 1 day.
5 Heat the oven to 220C /425F /gas 7. For the filling, blend the apricots until they are smooth, or purée them with a vegetable mill. Pour them into a bowl, add the marmalade and mix well.
6 Cut each cake horizontally into 2 thin layers. Sandwich 3 layers with the apricot mixture and put the plain layer on top. Cover a baking sheet with foil, oil it lightly and place the cake on it.
7 In a bowl, whisk the egg whites until they are stiff. Add the sugar gradually and continue to whisk until the meringue stands in stiff peaks. Mask the cake with the meringue, using a palette knife to spread it evenly. Bake in the oven for 10–15 minutes or until the meringue is lightly golden and set.
8 To garnish, slice the remaining apricots thinly. Arrange an overlapping circle of slices around the top edge of the cake. Serve immediately, while the meringue is still warm.

 45 minutes, overnight maturing,
then 30 minutes

Chocolate and orange cake with almonds

Serves 6
butter, for greasing
225 g /8 oz plain chocolate,
  broken up
45 ml /3 tbls strong black coffee
225 g /8 oz softened butter
225 g /8 oz caster sugar
grated zest of 1 orange
5 eggs, separated

100 g /4 oz fresh white breadcrumbs
100 g /4 oz ground almonds
2 large oranges, peeled and
  segmented, to garnish
For the icing
225 g /8 oz dark cooking chocolate,
  broken up
75 ml /5 tbls dark rum
50 /2 oz butter, diced

1 Heat the oven to 190C /375F /gas 5. Grease a round 20 cm /8 in, 7.5 cm /3 in deep cake tin. Cut out a circle of greaseproof paper, butter it generously and put it in the tin bottom, butter-side upwards.
2 In a small saucepan, combine the chocolate with the strong black coffee. Place over a low heat and stir frequently until melted. Leave to cool, but do not let the mixture harden again.
3 In a large mixing bowl, cream the butter until soft. Gradually add the sugar and grated orange zest and continue beating until the mixture is light and fluffy. Add the egg yolks one at a time, beating constantly. Stir in the cooled chocolate, then the breadcrumbs and the ground almonds and continue stirring until well blended.
4 In a medium-sized clean bowl, whisk the egg whites until stiff peaks form. Fold the whisked egg whites into the chocolate mixture.
5 Spoon the mixture into the prepared tin and bake in the centre of the oven for 50 minutes. Cover the top with foil to prevent the cake from browning too much and return to the oven for 25 minutes, or until a skewer inserted into the centre of the cake comes out clean.
6 Remove the tin from the oven. Leave the cake to cool in the tin for five minutes, then turn it out onto a wire rack to get cold.
7 When the cake is cold, make the icing. In a small saucepan, combine the dark cooking chocolate and rum. Place over a low heat, stirring frequently. When the chocolate has melted, and the mixture has the consistency of thick cream, remove it from the heat and whisk in the diced butter, piece by piece, whisking constantly.
8 Place the cold cake on a serving dish. Pour the icing over the cake and spread it all over, working quickly. Leave to set.
9 Just before serving, garnish with orange segments.

 2 hours,
plus cooling and setting

Angel food cake with orange rum sauce

Makes 10–12 slices
75 g /3 oz flour
25 g /1 oz cornflour
2.5 ml /½ tsp salt
225 g /8 oz caster sugar
10 medium-sized egg whites
15 ml /1 tbls lemon juice
5 ml /1 tsp cream of tartar
2.5 ml /½ tsp vanilla essence

For the orange and rum sauce
4 medium-sized oranges
juice of half a lemon
15 ml /1 tbls cornflour
45 ml /3 tbls caster sugar
25 g /1 oz butter
1 medium-sized egg yolk, beaten
10 ml /2 tsp rum

1 Heat the oven to 180C /350F /gas 4. Have ready a clean, dry and ungreased 22 cm /9 in Angel cake or Guglhupf tin. Sieve the flour with the cornflour and salt. Sieve the caster sugar separately. Add 75 g /3 oz of the sifted sugar to the flour; sieve together 3 times.
2 Lightly whisk together the egg whites and lemon juice. Continue whisking until foamy, then add the cream of tartar and whisk until stiff but not dry. Whisk in the remaining sugar, 15 ml /1 tbls at a time. Whisk in the vanilla.
3 Sieve the flour mixture, 30 ml /2 tbls at a time, over the whisked whites and fold in quickly and gently but thoroughly.
4 When all the flour has been incorporated, turn the mixture into the tin. Smooth the surface and draw a palette knife through the mixture to release any large air bubbles. Bake immediately for about 45 minutes or until the surface springs back when gently pressed.
5 Remove from the oven and stand the tin upside down on a wire rack. Leave for about 1½ hours or until the cake is quite cold and set.
6 Prepare the sauce. Finely grate the zest from 1 orange and reserve. Squeeze the juice from all the oranges and pour into a measuring jug. Add the orange zest and lemon juice and make up to 600 ml /1 pt with water. Pour into a small saucepan and bring it to the boil.
7 Blend the cornflour with 60 ml /4 tbls water and add to the sauce. Simmer, stirring, for 2–3 minutes until it is thick and translucent.
8 Remove from the heat, add the sugar and butter and stir until the sugar is dissolved. Now pour it in a thin stream onto the egg yolk, beating constantly. Return the mixture to a clean pan and stir over a very low heat for 1–2 minutes until the sauce has thickened slightly. Do not boil. Strain into a sauce-boat. Cool slightly; stir in the rum.
9 Transfer the cake to a serving plate. Serve with the cold sauce.

1½ hours, plus cooling

Chocolate Madeira cake

Serves 8–12
butter, for greasing
175 g /6 oz softened butter
175 g /6 oz caster sugar
3 eggs, beaten
150 g /5 oz self-raising flour
100 g /4 oz plain flour
a pinch of salt
grated zest and juice of 1 lemon
For the filling
450 g /1 lb cottage cheese
60 ml /4 tbls thick cream

50 g /2 oz caster sugar
45 ml /3 tbls Cointreau
45 ml /3 tbls mixed chopped candied fruit
50 g /2 oz plain chocolate, grated
For the icing
350 g /12 oz plain chocolate
175 ml /6 fl oz strong black coffee
30 ml /2 tbls dark rum
200 g /8 oz unsalted butter, diced candied angelica leaves, to decorate

1 Prepare the Madeira cake. Heat the oven to 160C /325F /gas 3. Cut a disc of greaseproof paper to fit the bottom of a deep 12.5 cm / 7 in cake tin. Grease the tin and paper disc with butter.
2 In a bowl, cream the butter, beating in the sugar gradually until light and fluffy. Beat in the eggs, a little at a time.
3 Sift the flours and salt into a clean bowl. Fold them into the mixture alternately with the lemon zest and juice.
4 Spoon the cake mixture into the prepared tin and level off with a palette knife. Bake for 1¼ hours.
5 Leave the cake to cool in the tin for 10 minutes. Turn it out onto a wire rack and leave it to get cold, then slice horizontally into 3 layers.
6 Meanwhile, prepare the filling. Press the cottage cheese through a sieve into a bowl, using the back of a wooden spoon. Beat in the thick cream, sugar, Cointreau, candied fruit and grated chocolate.
7 Place the bottom layer of the cake on a serving plate and spread smoothly with half the filling. Place the middle layer on top and spread with the remaining filling. Add the last layer. Wrap the cake in foil and chill for 2 hours, or until the filling is set.
8 When the filling is almost set, prepare the icing. Grate the chocolate. In a saucepan, combine the chocolate, coffee and rum. Melt over a low heat, stirring constantly with a wooden spoon. Remove from the heat and beat in the diced butter, a piece at a time. Leave to set until the mixture has the consistency of thick cream.
9 With a palette knife, coat the cake evenly with ⅔ of the mixture. Fit a piping bag with a 15 mm /½ in star nozzle and spoon the remaining icing into it. Pipe rosettes around the top edge of the cake and a pattern around the base. Decorate the rosettes with angelica leaves.

2½ hours, then chilling

Honey and date fingers

Serves 6–8
butter, for greasing
30 ml /2 tbls flour
a pinch of salt
2.5 ml /½ tsp baking powder
75 g /3 oz fresh white breadcrumbs
2 eggs, separated
325 g /11 oz clear honey
grated zest of 1 orange
225 g /8 oz chopped dates
100 g /4 oz chopped walnuts
5 ml /1 tsp vanilla essence
275 ml /10 fl oz whipped cream, chilled, to serve (optional)

1 Heat the oven to 190C /375F /gas 5.
2 Grease the base of a 19 cm /7½ in square cake tin and line it with greaseproof paper. Grease the paper and sides of the tin lightly.
3 Sift the flour, a pinch of salt and baking powder into a bowl. Mix in the breadcrumbs and set aside.
4 In a mixing bowl, lightly beat the egg yolks. Add the clear honey and the grated orange zest, mixing thoroughly. Stir in the chopped dates, walnuts and vanilla essence.
5 Gently fold in the dry ingredients.
6 In a separate clean bowl, whisk the egg whites until stiff but not dry, then fold them into the date and honey mixture, working thoroughly but lightly.
7 Pour the mixture into the prepared tin, then bake in the oven for 30–35 minutes, or until golden brown and nearly firm to the touch.
8 Remove the cake from the oven and then leave it to cool in the tin for 30 minutes.
9 Run a knife around between the cake and the sides of the tin and turn out the cake onto a wire rack. Leave to become cold, then cut it into 6–8 rectangles. Serve with chilled whipped cream, if wished.

 1 hour,
plus cooling

Caribbean cake

Serves 6–8
butter, for greasing
250 g /9 oz flour
a pinch of salt
17.5 ml /3½ tsp baking powder
225 g /8 oz caster sugar
100 g /4 oz softened butter
225 ml /8 fl oz milk

5 ml /1 tsp vanilla essence
4 egg whites
275 g /10 oz Brazil nuts, finely
  chopped
For the icing
75 g /3 oz soft dark brown sugar
100 g /5 oz golden syrup
2 egg whites

1 Heat the oven to 190C /375F /gas 5. Cut out 2 circles of greaseproof paper and use them to line 2 × 20 cm /8 in sandwich tins. Butter the tins and paper circles.
2 Into a large bowl, sift the flour, salt and baking powder. Stir in the caster sugar. Add the softened butter, milk and vanilla essence and beat the mixture until smooth.
3 Add the egg whites and beat the mixture for 2 minutes, then stir in half the finely chopped nuts.
4 Divide the cake mixture evenly between the prepared tins and then level the tops with a palette knife. Bake for 35–40 minutes, or until the cake is golden and springs back when touched.
5 Leave to cool in the tins for 5 minutes, then turn out onto a wire rack and peel off the circles of paper. Leave the cake to get cold.
6 When cold, make the icing. In a medium-sized heavy-based saucepan, combine the soft dark brown sugar and golden syrup with 45 ml /3 tbls water. Heat slowly, stirring frequently, until the sugar has dissolved, then bring to the boil and boil until it reaches 116C /242F.
7 While the syrup is heating, in a clean bowl whisk the egg whites to stiff peaks. Pour the hot syrup in a thin stream onto the whisked egg whites. Beat until the icing is stiff and glossy and holds firm peaks.
8 Assemble the cake. Place one layer on a serving dish and spread it with enough icing to coat. Place the second layer on top. Coat with the remaining icing, using a palette knife to smooth the surface. Use the tip of the knife to draw parallel lines across the top for an attractive finish. Using a clean palette knife, press the remaining Brazil nuts into the sides of the cake. Brush away any nuts that have fallen and use again.

● Do not make the icing until the cake is completely cold because the icing must be used immediately. A sugar thermometer is essential for successful results.

1½ hours

Apple and chocolate squares

Serves 4–6
butter and flour, for the tin
60 ml /4 tbls flour
5 ml /1 tsp baking powder
a pinch of salt
225 g /8 oz butter
75 g /3 oz cocoa powder
400 g /14 oz caster sugar
4 eggs, beaten

7.5 ml /1½ tsp vanilla essence
100 g /4 oz chopped walnuts
2 apples, peeled, cored and sliced
For the icing
40 g /1½ oz butter
45 ml /3 tbls cocoa powder
125 ml /4 fl oz milk
2.5 ml /½ tsp vanilla essence
275 g /10 oz icing sugar

1 Heat the oven to 180C /350F /gas 4. Cut a square of greaseproof paper to fit a cake tin 22.5 cm /9 in square and 5 cm /2 in deep. Butter the tin, line it with the greaseproof paper and butter and flour the greaseproof paper.
2 Sift the flour, baking powder and salt onto another piece of greaseproof paper.
3 Melt the butter in a saucepan. Stir in the cocoa powder with a wooden spoon and beat to a smooth paste. Stir in the sugar and gradually add the beaten eggs, vanilla essence, sifted flour mixture, chopped walnuts and apple slices.
4 Pour the mixture into the prepared tin and bake for about 55 minutes, or until set. When a skewer is inserted, it should come out clean. Turn out onto a wire rack and leave to cool completely.
5 Make the icing. In a saucepan, melt the butter, stir in the cocoa powder and beat until smooth. Pour in the milk and heat, whisking until smooth. Remove from the heat, stir in the vanilla essence and leave to cool.
6 Sift the icing sugar and beat it into the cooled chocolate mixture. Keep beating until the mixture is smooth and glossy, then chill the chocolate icing until thick.
7 Peel the greaseproof paper from the bottom of the cold apple and chocolate square. Using a palette knife, spread the chocolate icing evenly over the top and cut into 16 pieces.

1 hour 20 minutes,
plus cooling and chilling

Strawberry cream cake

Serves 4–6
butter, for greasing
4 eggs
225 g /8 oz caster sugar
a few drops of almond essence
125 g /4 oz ground almonds
300 ml /10 fl oz thick cream
225 g /8 oz flour, sifted
salt
5 ml /1 tsp baking powder
60 ml /4 tbls melted butter

For the filling
425 ml /15 fl oz thick cream
30–45 ml /2–3 tbls caster sugar
30–45 ml /2–3 tbls curaçao
  or Cointreau
225 g /8 oz strawberries, hulled
  and sliced
For the decoration
large strawberries, hulled
candied angelica, cut into small
  strips

1 Heat the oven to 180C /350F /gas 4.
2 Grease two 23 cm /9 in sandwich tins, line them with discs of buttered greaseproof paper and set them aside.
3 Choose a medium-sized bowl which fits over a saucepan. Add the eggs and sugar and whisk together until they are well blended. Set the bowl over simmering water and whisk the egg and sugar mixture until it is thick, greatly increased in volume and the whisk leaves a ribbon trail when it is lifted.
4 Remove the bowl from the pan and whisk the mixture until cool. Using a large metal spoon, fold in the almond essence, ground almonds and thick cream.
5 Sift the flour, salt and baking powder together, then sift one third over the egg mixture and fold in. Repeat twice more. Lastly, gently fold in the butter.
6 Pour equal amounts of the almond mixture into each prepared sandwich tin. Bake in the centre of the oven for 25–30 minutes, or until the cakes are golden.
7 Remove the cakes from the oven and allow to cool in tins for 1 minute before turning them out onto a wire rack to cool completely.
8 For the filling, whisk together the cream, caster sugar and liqueur until stiff peaks form. Spread one-quarter of the cream over one cake. Arrange the strawberries over the cream and spread another quarter of the cream over the strawberries. Place the other cake on top. Spread a thin layer of cream over the top and around the cake, then use a fork to make a pattern around the sides.
9 Spoon the remaining cream into a piping bag fitted with a 10 mm /½ in star nozzle, and pipe rosettes and a lattice on top of the cake. Decorate with the strawberries, and angelica arranged to look like stems of the fruit. Chill for at least 30 minutes before serving.

1¼ hours, cooling,
then decorating and chilling

Iced chocolate brownies

Makes 12
100 g /4 oz butter, plus extra for greasing
50 g /2 oz bitter chocolate
100 g /4 oz flour, sifted
2.5 ml /½ tsp baking powder
a pinch of salt
225 g /8 oz sugar
2 eggs
2.5 ml /½ tsp vanilla essence
50 g /2 oz chopped walnuts
For the icing
40 g /1½ oz butter
100 g /4 oz icing sugar, sifted
25 g /1 oz cocoa powder

1 Heat the oven to 180C /350F /gas 4.
2 Lightly butter a baking tin 25 × 15 cm /10 × 6 in and 25 mm /1 in deep. Line with greaseproof paper.
3 Melt the bitter chocolate in the top of a double saucepan over simmering water.
4 Sift the flour with the baking powder and the salt into a bowl. In another bowl, beat the butter and the sugar together with a wooden spoon until light and creamy. Beat in the eggs one at a time, followed by the vanilla essence and the melted chocolate.
5 With a large metal spoon, fold the flour mixture and the chopped walnuts into the chocolate mixture. Spoon the mixture into the prepared baking tin and bake in the oven for 20–30 minutes, or until the surface is firm to the touch. Cool for a few minutes in the tin before turning the cake out onto a wire rack.
6 To make the icing, melt the butter in a saucepan and stir in the sifted icing sugar and cocoa powder. Gradually add 30 ml /2 tbls water, beating with a wooden spoon until smooth.
7 With a palette knife, spread the icing over the top of the cake and leave it to set. When it is set, cut into 12 portions and serve.

 1 hour,
plus setting

Danish kirsch cake

Serves 6–8
6 medium-sized eggs, 2 separated
225 g /8 oz sugar
grated zest of 1 orange
5 ml /1 tsp vanilla essence
150 g /5 oz self-raising flour
softened butter, for greasing
For the kirsch cream
700 ml /1½ pt thick cream

45 ml /3 tbls caster sugar
4 ml /¾ tsp vanilla essence
30 ml /2 tbls kirsch
For the decoration
425 g /15 oz canned black
    stoneless cherries, drained
60 ml /4 tbls redcurrant jelly,
    dissolved in 30 ml /2 tbls
    water or kirsch

1 Heat the oven to 180C /350F /gas 4. Butter a loose-bottomed round 22 cm /8½ in cake tin and line the bottom with greaseproof paper; grease again.
2 Combine 4 whole eggs and 2 egg yolks in a large mixing bowl. Add the sugar, grated orange zest and vanilla essence. Using a wire whisk or rotary beater, beat for about 15 minutes, until the mixture is thick and pale yellow.
3 With a metal spoon, fold the self-raising flour into the egg and sugar mixture.
4 Whisk the 2 egg whites until they form stiff peaks, then gradually fold them into the egg and flour mixture.
5 Turn the sponge mixture into the prepared cake tin and bake in the centre of the oven. After 10 minutes, lower the heat to 160C /325F /gas 3 and bake for a further 50 minutes, or until the cake is golden brown. Let the cake stand for 10 minutes before removing it from the tin to cool on a wire rack.
6 To make the kirsch cream, whisk the cream and sugar until it forms stiff peaks. Stir in the vanilla essence and kirsch to taste.
7 Not more than 1 hour before serving, trim the top and sides of the cold cake. Carefully cut it horizontally into three layers of equal thickness with a long, sharp knife. Put the bottom layer on a serving dish and spread 10 mm /1½ in thick layer of kirsch cream over the top. Place the second layer of cake on top, and spread with cream. Place the third layer onto the cream and spread about half the remaining kirsch cream around the sides of the cake.
8 Cover the top of the cake decoratively with canned black cherries, leaving a border around the edge. Coat the fruit with the redcurrant glaze, using the glaze to cover any spaces between the fruit.
9 Pipe the remaining cream around the top and cake base.

● Use 500 g /1 lb fresh, hulled strawberries instead of black cherries as an alternative decoration.

 1½ hours, plus cooling,
then 20 minutes decorating

Orange ginger cake

Serves 8
butter and flour, for tins
275 g /10 oz flour
a pinch of salt
10 ml /2 tsp baking powder
1.5 ml /¼ tsp bicarbonate
* of soda*
10 ml /2 tsp ground ginger
10 ml /2 tsp ground cinnamon
225 g /8 oz caster sugar
100 g /4 oz butter
90 ml /6 tbls molasses
200 ml /7 fl oz milk
2 eggs, beaten
For the orange icing
25 g /1 oz butter
150 g /5 oz icing sugar, sifted
1 egg yolk
orange food colouring
* (optional)*
7.5 ml /1½ tsp lemon juice
finely grated zest of ½ orange
15 ml /1 tbls orange liqueur
15 ml /1 tbls thick cream

1 Heat the oven to 180C /350F /gas 4. Butter two 20 cm /8 in square cake tins, line the bases with buttered greaseproof paper and dust with flour.
2 Sift the flour, salt, baking powder, bicarbonate of soda, ground ginger and cinnamon into a large mixing bowl.
3 Place the caster sugar in a saucepan with the butter and molasses. Melt over a low heat, stirring with a wooden spoon. Do not allow the mixture to simmer.
4 Make a well in the centre of the flour mixture and pour in the molasses mixture. Beat with a wooden spoon, gradually incorporating the flour, and continue to beat until smooth. Beat in the milk, a little at a time, and finally add the beaten eggs.
5 Divide the cake batter between the prepared tins and smooth over the mixture with a palette knife or a spatula. Bake in the oven for 25–30 minutes, or until the cake is dark golden brown and springy to the touch.
6 Meanwhile, make the orange icing: cream the butter in a bowl, gradually beat in the sifted icing sugar and continue to beat until smooth. Add the egg yolk, orange food colouring (if wished), lemon juice, finely grated orange zest and orange liqueur and mix well. Finally, beat in the thick cream and then chill the icing, covered, until it is needed.
7 When the cakes are cooked, turn them onto a wire rack to cool.
8 Sandwich the cold cakes with half of the orange icing. Use the rest of the icing to cover the top of the cake, smoothing and then swirling it in an attractive pattern with a palette knife.

1–1¼ hours,
plus cooling

Maple syrup gateau

Serves 8
butter, for greasing
100 g /4 oz butter
100 g /4 oz soft brown sugar
2 eggs, lightly beaten
225 g /8 oz maple syrup
225 g /8 oz self-raising flour
1.5 ml /¼ tsp salt
15 ml /1 tbls ground ginger
5 ml /1 tsp ground mixed spice, or allspice
2.5 ml /½ tsp grated nutmeg
275 ml /10 fl oz thick cream
22.5 ml /1½ tbls icing sugar, sifted
50 g /2 oz walnuts
25 g /1 oz sultanas

1 Heat the oven to 180C /350F /gas 4. Lightly grease two 20 cm /8 in sandwich tins and set aside.
2 In a large mixing bowl, cream the butter until soft. Gradually add the soft brown sugar, beating until the mixture becomes fluffy and soft. Beat in the eggs, then gradually add the maple syrup, beating constantly.
3 Place the flour, salt, ground ginger, mixed spice (or allspice) and grated nutmeg in a sieve and sift a little at a time into the creamed mixture, beating until the mixture forms a smooth batter.
4 Divide the batter equally between the prepared sandwich tins. Place the tins in the oven and bake for 30 minutes, or until a warmed skewer inserted in the centre of each cake comes out clean.
5 Remove the cakes from the oven and allow them to cool in their tins for 1 hour. Turn the cakes out onto a wire rack and leave them to cool completely.
6 In a bowl, whip the thick cream until it forms stiff peaks. Fold in 15 ml /1 tbls of the icing sugar, the walnuts and the sultanas. Spread the cream over one layer and sandwich the two layers together.
7 To serve, place four 25 mm /1 in wide paper bands across the cake, equally spaced. Sift the remaining icing sugar over the top of the cake and then carefully remove the paper bands, so the sugar gives a striped effect.

1 hour, plus cooling,
then 15 minutes

Tropical fruit roll

Serves 6

melted butter, for greasing
75 g /3 oz flour, plus extra for
   dusting
3 eggs
caster sugar, see method
icing sugar, to decorate

For the filling
150 ml /5 fl oz thick cream
30 ml /2 tbls kirsch
1 small banana, peeled and diced
2 kiwi fruit, peeled and diced
½ mango, peeled, stoned and diced

1 Heat the oven to 180C /350F /gas 4.
2 Brush the base and sides of a 30×20 cm /12×8 in Swiss roll tin with melted butter. Line with a sheet of greaseproof paper and brush with melted butter. Lightly dust the base and sides with flour, knocking the tin against a hard surface to shake off any excess flour.
3 Choose a bowl in which to whisk up the mixture and a large saucepan over which it fits firmly. Pour 5 cm /2 in water into the pan and bring to the boil, then reduce the heat until the water simmers.
4 In the bowl, over barely simmering water, combine the eggs and 75 g /3 oz caster sugar. Whisk the mixture until it is increased in volume, very thick and lukewarm, preferably using a hand-held electric whisk (10 minutes at high speed).
5 Remove the bowl from the pan and stand it on a cool surface. Continue to whisk until the mixture has cooled and there is a distinct trail on the surface when the beaters are lifted (5 minutes if using a hand-held electric whisk at high speed).
6 Sift the flour over the egg mixture and fold it in lightly but thoroughly with a large metal spoon.
7 Pour the batter into the prepared tin and level it off. Bake for 25–30 minutes, or until the cake shrinks slightly away from the sides of the tin and springs back into shape when touched.
8 While the cake is in the oven, lay a sheet of greaseproof paper on a table and sprinkle it with 5 ml /1 tsp caster sugar. Turn the cake out onto the sugared paper and carefully peel off the lining. Trim the crusty edges with a sharp knife. Lay a fresh sheet of greaseproof paper on top of the cake and carefully roll it up with the paper inside, starting at one of the longer sides. Leave the cake on a rack to cool.
9 Meanwhile, prepare the filling. In a bowl, whisk the cream and kirsch to soft peaks, then fold in the prepared fruits.
10 Carefully unroll the cold Swiss roll and remove the top paper. Spread it evenly with the filling and then roll the cake up again, leaving the paper out. Sprinkle it with sifted icing sugar and then transfer it to a serving platter.

 1½ hours

Devil's food cake

Serves 8

75 ml /5 tbls cocoa powder
1 medium-sized egg yolk
300 ml /10 fl oz milk
100 g /4 oz butter, softened
350 g /12 oz caster sugar
5 ml /1 tsp vanilla essence
2 medium-sized eggs
250 g /9 oz flour, sifted

10 ml /2 tsp baking powder
1.5 ml /¼ tsp bicarbonate of soda
2.5 ml /½ tsp salt
butter and flour, for the tins
For the lemon butter icing
225 g /8 oz butter
225 g /8 oz icing sugar, sifted
juice of 1½ lemons
icing sugar, to decorate

1 Heat the oven to 180C /350F /gas 4. In a saucepan, mix the cocoa powder, egg yolk and 150 ml /5 fl oz of the milk. Cook over a very low heat for about 5 minutes, stirring, until smooth and thickened. Cool the mixture.
2 In a mixing bowl and using a wooden spoon, cream the butter until light and fluffy. Gradually add the sugar, beating until light and fluffy. Add the vanilla essence, then the eggs one at a time, beating well after each addition. Mix in the cocoa mixture.
3 Sift together the dry ingredients into a bowl and add these to the creamed mixture alternately with the remaining milk, beginning and ending with dry ingredients. Beat the cake mixture until smooth.
4 Line the bottoms of 2×23 cm /9 in sandwich tins with circles of greaseproof paper; grease them, then divide the cake mixture between the two. Bake in the oven for about 30 minutes. If the tins do not fit on the same level, be sure to swap their positions during the cooking time. Cool for 5 minutes, then turn the cakes out onto a wire tray and carefully peel off the paper. Leave to cool completely.
5 Make up the lemon butter icing. Place the butter in a bowl with the sifted icing sugar and beat with a wooden spoon or spatula until light and fluffy. Add the lemon juice and mix well. With a palette knife, spread half the icing on the bottom layer of the cold cake. Sandwich the cakes together and use the remaining icing to decorate the top with a rough, swirled finish. Before serving, sprinkle icing sugar on top.

 1 hour

Pastries

PASTRY-CASE SKILLS

Pretty flans and tarts with colourful sweet or savoury fillings can be made in a variety of shaped rings and moulds. The techniques vary, but in this chapter I show you how to accomplish them.

Pastry cases can be made in a variety of tins or dishes. Metal containers are the best heat conductors and produce a crisper pastry case. If you are using ceramic dishes, you may have to make an adjustment to the times allowed for baking blind and the final baking to counteract this.

Shortcrust is the best lining pastry. For the basic ingredients, method and different quantities of pastry, see Little chocolate boats (page 56).

Flan rings and tins

These can be divided into two categories:
English flan rings are approximately 25 mm /1 in deep and do not have a bottom. They must be placed on a flat baking sheet before lining them with the pastry. There are two types: plain rings are usually used for savoury dishes. Fluted rings are more versatile, although they are traditionally used for sweet dishes. These rings are made with an inner fluted ring and a plain outer band for added strength.

After baking a flan in a flan ring, let it stand for 5 minutes, then transfer it to a wire rack and remove the ring. This allows the steam to escape and air to circulate so that the pastry becomes dry and crisp as it cools.
French flan tins are shallower than flan rings and so require less pastry and less filling — the difference becoming greater as the diameter increases. These flan tins are always fluted and have loose bottoms; the edges are usually unturned. As the flan remains on the metal base after baking, moving and serving it are much easier. To remove the ring, stand the flan on a bowl and pull the outside ring gently downwards.

Flan dishes

There is a large selection of attractive flan dishes available.
Glazed ceramic flan dishes are often white and always fluted. They are thicker and heavier than the metal flan rings or tins and, because the heat penetration is slow and the conduction poor, the pastry tends to be softer and paler than when baked in metal. To help correct this, choose a dish with an unglazed base. Heat a baking sheet while you heat the oven, then place the flan dish on it. Allow extra time (2–4 minutes) for the dish to heat when baking the pastry.

As the steam is trapped by the dish and the dish cools slowly, it is best to eat the flan while it is hot or warm because the pastry can become soggy if it is allowed to cool.

Flans always look good served in these dishes but it is almost impossible to remove a presentable first slice. The best way is to cut a very thin slice and take it out with a flexible spatula, then use a fish or pastry slice to remove the next portion. Be careful, as a sharp knife can mark the surface of the dish.
Heatproof glass dishes have similar disadvantages to ceramic ware, although they have better heat conducting properties, so the pastry will be crisper. Allow the pastry a few extra minutes cooking time.

Small pastry cases

Try using some of these attractive shapes:
Barquettes are small, metal, boat-shaped moulds, 7.5–10 cm /3–4 in long. They may be fluted or plain; plain ones have rims. Bake the pastry blind in the moulds, turn them out and cool. Fill with sweet mixtures.
French tartlet tins are like miniature loose-bottomed French flan tins. They may be fluted or plain and small ones are between 5–7.5 cm /2–3 in in diameter and about 1.5 cm /½ in deep. There are also tins available which are 10 cm /4 in in diameter and 25 mm /1 in deep.
Fancy shapes: there are many other small metal shapes, such as miniature brioche tins, used for baking small pastry shells.
Patty or bun tins are arranged in groups of 6, 9 or 12 and have quite deep straight sides and a diameter of 6.5 cm /2½ in.
Tart tins are similar to patty tins but are shallow with sloping sides and flat bases.
Yorkshire pudding tins are grouped in fours and are similar in shape to bun tins but are larger in diameter.
Horn-shaped metal moulds are ideal for use with Puff pastry (see page 72) to make containers for cold food and creams.

Lining flan tins and dishes

Follow these tips to help line your tins satisfactorily.
For a large flan, roll out the pastry on a lightly floured surface with a lightly floured

Making pastry cases

To move a large piece of pastry, roll it around the rolling pin. Lift it over the centre of the tin, then unroll it loosely.

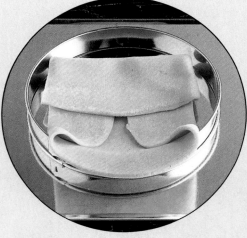

Alternatively, for a deep ring, fold the rolled-out pastry into a square. Lift it into the ring and then unfold it.

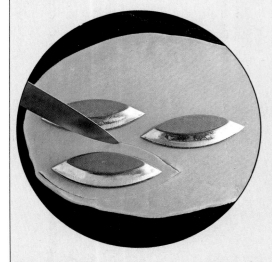

For small moulds, invert them over the pastry and cut out a similar shape but 15 mm /½ in larger all round than the mould.

To fit pastry into a mould, work from the base centre outwards. With a small ball of pastry, work up each flute from the bottom.

rolling pin to a circle 3 mm /⅛ in thick and 4–5 cm /1½–2 in larger than the diameter of the ring or dish. Now transfer the pastry to the ring or dish (see pictures, left).

Working from the centre with lightly floured fingers, gently but firmly press the pastry down, taking care not to stretch or tear it or to trap air under it. Make sure the sides are loose until the base has been fitted right to the edges.

Next, see that the pastry fits very snugly up the sides of the tin. If the tin is fluted, use a small ball of floured pastry or a floured finger to work the pastry well up the flutes.

To remove excess pastry, roll the rolling pin firmly across the top of the tin and with floured fingers press up the sides again. If fluted, press into the flutes again. Prick the base all over with a fork, cover and chill for 30 minutes. Cover the pastry with tin foil and beans and bake blind (see Little chocolate boats, both the method and the notes following the recipe).

To remove a flan from a loose-bottomed tin or ring, lower the cooked flan centrally onto an upturned pudding bowl or wide jar and let the outer ring fall away.

To line small individual moulds, roll the pastry out until it is approximately 3 mm / ⅛ in thick. Moulds of about 25 mm /1 in

Make use of colourful seasonal fruits to fill pastry cases of varying shapes and sizes. Savoury fillings can look just as effective — perfect for a buffet spread

diameter can be lined by laying a sheet of pastry over them and then pressing the pastry into each indentation. Roll the pin over the top to cut them clear. Other moulds are best lined individually.

With lightly floured fingers, gently ease the pastry into the shape of the mould, then use a ball of floured dough to make sure it fits snugly. Prick well with a fork, line with foil and beans and chill before baking.

Little chocolate boats

🔪🔪🔪 making and baking the pastry,
then 1 hour, plus chilling

Serves 6
**For the shortcrust pastry (225 g /8 oz
made-weight)**
100 g /4 oz flour
15 ml /1 tbls icing sugar
a pinch of salt
50 g /2 oz butter
1 medium-sized egg yolk
5 ml /1 tsp lemon juice
iced water
For the filling
150 ml /5 fl oz chocolate ice cream
100 g /4 oz plain chocolate

1 To make the pastry, sift the flour, the
icing sugar and the salt into a large bowl. Cut
the butter into 5 mm /¼ in dice and add it to
the bowl. Then, using a pastry blender or
2 knives, cut the butter into the flour until
the mixture has the consistency of coarse
breadcrumbs.
2 Scoop up some of the mixture with your
fingers, holding them high above the bowl,
lightly rub the mixture between your thumbs
and fingertips, letting it fall back into the
bowl. Repeat 6 or 7 times until the mixture
resembles fine breadcrumbs.

3 In a small jug, beat together the egg yolk,
lemon juice and 15 ml /1 tbls iced water.
Sprinkle this over the flour mixture, mixing
with a fork until the pastry begins to hold
together.
4 When three-quarters of the pastry is
holding together, use one cupped hand to
press the pastry lightly and quickly into one
piece, gathering up all the crumbs. Gently
press the moist dough into a ball.
5 Wrap the pastry in greaseproof paper,
followed by a dampened cloth or a sheet of
foil, or in cling film. Leave in the refrigerator
for at least one hour to rest, or up to 24 hours
to give it time to really relax.
6 Heat the oven to 200C /400F /gas 6.
7 Roll out the pastry and use it to line 12
barquette moulds, 9.5 cm /3½ in long. Bake
blind until fully cooked, by covering the
pastry with tin foil and beans and baking for
10 minutes. Turn down the oven to 180C /
350F /gas 4 and bake without the foil for a
further 10–15 minutes. Leave to cool.
8 Meanwhile, put the ice cream in the
main part of the refrigerator to soften it just
enough for spooning. Now spoon it into the
barquette cases, forming a dome shape.
Smooth the ice cream on each barquette with
a palette knife and place the whole batch in
the freezer until the ice cream has set hard.
9 Break the chocolate into the top pan of a
double boiler and melt it over simmering
water. Coat the top of the barquettes with the

Grape tart

chocolate, using either a spoon or dipping
them in the chocolate. Return them to the
freezer to harden.
10 Remove the chocolate barquettes from
their moulds and serve.

● For 350 g /12 oz shortcrust pastry use:
175 g /6 oz flour, 22.5 ml /1½ tbls icing
sugar, 1.5 ml /¼ tsp salt, 75 g /3 oz butter,
1 medium egg yolk and 5 ml /1 tsp lemon
juice, iced water.
● For 450 g /1 lb pastry use: 225 g /8 oz
flour, 30 ml /2 tbls icing sugar, 2.5 ml /½ tsp
salt, 150 g /5 oz butter, 1 medium egg yolk,
5 ml /1 tsp lemon juice, iced water.
● For 900 g /2 lb pastry use: 450 g /1 lb
flour, 275 g /10 oz butter, 60 ml /4 tbls icing
sugar, 5 ml /1 tsp salt, 2 small egg yolks,
10 ml /2 tsp lemon juice, iced water.
● For a half-baked pastry case, cook at
200C /400F /gas 6 for 10 minutes, then bake
for a further 8–10 minutes at 180C /350F /
gas 4 without the foil and beans.

Grape tart

***Pâte brisée* is French for 'shortcrust pastry'.**

🔪🔪🔪 making and resting the pastry,
then 1¼ hours

Serves 4–5
For the pâte brisée
175 g /6 oz flour
1.5 g /¼ tsp salt
25 g /1 oz caster sugar
100 g /4 oz unsalted butter, diced small
45 ml /3 tbls iced water
For the filling
350 g /12 oz large green grapes
a little egg white, for brushing
50 g /2 oz caster sugar
45 ml /3 tbls greengage or crab-apple jelly

1 To make the pâte brisée, sift the flour with the salt and sugar. Rub the butter into the flour mixture with your fingertips, sprinkle in the cold water and pull the pastry together with a fork. Use your hands to make the pastry into a ball. Knead it briefly by pressing it with the heel of your hand and then forming it into a ball again. Wrap the pastry in cling film and refrigerate for at least 1 hour.
2 Heat the oven to 190C /375F /gas 5.
3 Remove the seeds from the grapes by slicing them in half and easing out the seeds with the point of a knife. Reserve the grapes.
4 Roll out the pastry and line a 20 cm /8 in flan tin. Prick it with a fork, brush with egg white and fill the tart with the grapes, cut side down. Sprinkle with sugar and bake for 35–45 minutes.
5 As soon as the tart is baked, heat the jelly until it becomes liquid and brush it all over the tart.

French pear tart

making the pastry, baking blind then 1¾ hours

Serves 4
350 g /12 oz made-weight shortcrust pastry (see note following Little chocolate boats)
100 g /4 oz sugar
3 small, ripe dessert pears
30 ml /2 tbls brandy
200 ml /7 fl oz thick cream
50 g /2 oz caster sugar
15 ml /1 tbls cornflour
15 ml /1 tbls lemon juice
1 egg, separated
45 ml /3 tbls apricot jam (optional)

1 Make the pastry (see recipe for Little chocolate boats for method, steps 1–5) and leave it in the refrigerator for at least 1 hour to relax. Roll it out and use it to line an 18 cm /7 in tart tin. Half bake the pastry case and leave to cool.
2 Put the sugar and 850 ml /1½ pt water in a saucepan and heat gently, stirring, until the sugar is dissolved. Now bring it to the boil and let it simmer gently.
3 Peel the pears and cut them in half lengthways. With a teaspoon, scoop out the central core and seeds.
4 As soon as the pears are ready, lower them into the simmering syrup and poach them until soft but not disintegrating. This will take 5–10 minutes.
5 Lift the pears out of the syrup with a slotted spoon, draining them thoroughly, and put them in a bowl. Pour the brandy over

and leave them to steep in it as they cool.
6 Heat the oven to 150C /300F /gas 2.
7 In a saucepan, gently heat the thick cream and 25 g /1 oz of the caster sugar. In a small bowl, blend the cornflour with the lemon juice to a smooth paste. Pour a few tablespoons of the warmed cream into the cornflour and then add it to the remaining cream. Bring to the boil and simmer gently for 3 minutes, or until thickened, stirring constantly. Remove from the heat.
8 In a small bowl, lightly beat the egg yolk. Stir it into the warm cream. Pour off the brandy syrup from the pears and add it to the

custard cream. Drain the pears on absorbent paper and slice them thinly.
9 Brush the pastry case with the lightly beaten egg white and pour in the custard. Arrange the pears in an overlapping circle to cover the entire surface. Sprinkle with the remaining caster sugar and cook until the custard is set. Remove the tart from the tin.
10 Serve lukewarm or cold. If serving cold, the pears can be coated with a very thin apricot glaze (see page 21). Brush the glaze over the pears and pour into any gaps.

Little chocolate boats

Apple mince tarts

making the pastry,
then about 1¼ hours, plus cooling

Makes 12

900 g /2 lb made-weight shortcrust pastry (see the notes following Little chocolate boats, page 56)
175 g /6 oz soft brown sugar
45 ml /3 tbls flour
8 medium-sized, tart dessert apples
30 ml /2 tbls brandy
450 g /1 lb bought mincemeat
2 large dessert apples
15 g /½ oz butter

1 Make the shortcrust pastry (for method see Little chocolate boats recipe steps 1–5). Roll it out and use it to line 12 × 7.5 cm /3 in individual tart tins. Heat the oven to 200C /400F /gas 6.
2 In a bowl, combine the soft brown sugar and flour and mix well. Sprinkle 10 ml /2 tsp of the mixture in the bottom of each tart shell. Reserve 60 ml /4 tbls of the mixture for the topping.
3 Peel, core and slice the medium-sized dessert apples. Layer them in the pastry shells, sprinkling each layer of apples with some of the rest of the sugar and flour mixture.
4 In a bowl mix the brandy with the mincemeat. Reserve 100 g /4 oz of the mincemeat

Apple mince tarts

and spread the rest in an even layer in each tart case.
5 Peel and core the 2 large dessert apples and cut them into 12 rings, 5 mm /¼ in thick. Place an apple ring on top of the mincemeat in each tart case.
6 Divide the reserved mincemeat between the tart cases, spooning it into the hole in each apple ring. Sprinkle the top with the reserved sugar-flour mixture and dot the tarts with butter.
7 Place the tarts on baking sheets and bake for 20–25 minutes, or until the apples are tender. Let the tarts cool a little before removing them from the tins.

OPEN-PLATE TARTS

If individual jam tarts are popular favourites for tea, open-plate tarts with fancy pastry edges or lattice tops, are even more appealing. They are one of the easiest pies to make and colourful to look at too.

Open-plate tarts are made in pie dishes — round, shallow, ovenproof dishes with a slightly raised and very wide rim. You can also use a gratin or flan dish for making a lattice tart.

Lining a pie plate

When you have made your shortcrust pastry (see page 56), chill it for 30 minutes, then allow it to soften a little before rolling out. Roll it out on a lightly floured surface to 3 mm /⅛ in thick and 25 mm /1 in larger than the plate. Check the size by placing the plate upside down on the pastry. Roll the pastry over the rolling pin, gently lift it, then unroll it onto the pie plate.

With your fingers, press it gently but firmly into the shape of the plate, working from the centre outwards, without stretching or pulling the pastry. Prick it with a fork and trim the excess pastry to 5 mm /¼ in beyond the plate.

Fold the pastry under to lie flush with the pie plate. This extra thickness will stop the edge cooking more quickly than the rest and becoming too brown.

Decorating the edge

An open-plate tart or pie is easy, quick and inexpensive to decorate using the pastry itself. Unlike a pie with a solid pastry topping, an open-plate tart does not need glazing. Try the following ideas for finishing the edges:

Forked: lightly flour the prongs of a fork and gently press all around the edge, with the prongs pointing inwards.

Daisy: flour the handle of a teaspoon and press all around the edge, leaving a very slight gap between each indentation. Keep the 'petals' straight and of equal length.

Sunflower (see diagram overleaf): with the point of a floured sharp knife, cut the pastry at 25 mm /1 in intervals. Now lift the corner of each strip and fold diagonally in half to form a triangle.

Overlapping (see diagram overleaf): with the point of a floured sharp knife, cut the pastry edge at 20 mm /¾ in intervals. Gently lift the strips and bend them over so that they overlap slightly. Make sure they overlap to the same degree all the way around the edge of the tart.

Castellated: with the point of a floured sharp knife, cut the pastry at 25 mm /1 in intervals around the edge. Fold every second strip inwards.

Goffered (see diagram overleaf): slip the floured tip of a knife under the pastry edge, put your thumb and index finger on either side of the knife and pinch together to slightly raise the pastry in a ridge around the edge of the tart.

Crimping: press your thumb on the edge and push the thumb and forefinger of your other hand against the pastry on either side of your first thumb.

Scallops: snip the edges with floured scissors at regular intervals, 6 mm /¼ in apart for most tarts. Another method is to place your thumb on the edge of the pastry and, holding a floured knife downwards in a slanting direction, draw it towards you with a very quick, short stroke, making a slanting kink in the pastry.

Pastry wheel: flour a pastry wheel and roll it around the edge. Do this one, two or even three times, depending on the depth of the

An open-plate tart with a decorated edge and interwoven lattice topping

Decorative edges

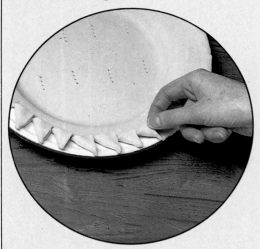

Sunflower: cut the pastry edge at 25 mm / 1 in intervals. Lift the corner of each strip and fold it in half to form a triangle.

Overlapping: cut the pastry edge at 20 mm / ¾ in intervals. Lift and bend the strips so that they overlap slightly.

Goffered: slip a floured knife tip under the edge, put your thumb and index finger on either side and slightly raise the pastry.

border you have around your tart or pie.
Twisted edge: with a floured thumb and index finger, pinch the edge of the pastry and slightly twist and turn it towards the centre. Repeat at 10 mm /½ in intervals.
Cut-out decorations: surplus pastry can be shaped in many ways and used to decorate the edge of the tart. Roll it into a neat shape, with an even thickness of 3 mm /⅛ in. Cut out the decorations, using a small floured biscuit or pastry cutters. Dampen them to stick to the pastry edge.
Scalloped strips: flour a pastry wheel and cut the trimmings into strips. Use them flat or twisted. For a single strand, lift slightly and twist over and over along the length of the strip. For a double strand, cut two strips, dampen one end of each strip and press lightly on top of each other. Lift the two strands slightly and twist around each other.
Plait: with a lightly floured knife, cut the

rolled out pastry trimmings into three strips of the same width. Dampen one end of each and press on top of each other. Lift the strips gently and plait them together. At the finish, dampen the ends of the strips and again press them on top of each other to make a neat edge.
Leaves: with a floured sharp knife, cut the rolled out trimmings into strips 25 mm /1 in wide. Now cut across at an angle to make diamond shapes. Mark veins with the back of a knife, and pinch one end in.
Necklace: roll the pastry trimmings into small even-sized balls. Place them around the edge of the tart touching each other. Press them lightly to seal.

Decorating the filling
Decorating the filling helps to prevent the filling from drying out. Do not forget that you will need to allow extra pastry, at least

25–50 g /1–2 oz, for a simple lattice and twice that amount if you are going to make an interwoven one.
To make a simple lattice, roll out the trimmings to 3 mm /⅛ in thick and 10 mm / ½ in longer than the diameter of the pie plate. Cut it into strips 10 mm /½ in wide using a sharp knife or preferably with a pastry wheel for a scalloped effect. Dampen the edge of the filled tart and lay half the strips over the filling in parallel lines. Lay the remaining strips across the first layer, at right angles. Next, trim the ends so that they are flush with the plate, and then press the ends gently to seal them.
To make an interwoven lattice, if the filling is very moist, place the empty plate upside-down on a sheet of greaseproof paper and draw its outline. Line the pie plate, fill and set aside. Roll out the trimmings and cut into strips. Place half the strips in parallel lines on the outline on the paper. Working at right angles, interweave the remaining strips in parallel lines. Dampen the edge of the tart pastry. Carefully lift the greaseproof paper and gently shake it to ease the lattice onto the filling. Trim the edges; then press to seal them.

Alternatively, if the filling is quite firm, place half the strips in parallel lines on the filling. Turn the pie plate round and work at right angles, to interweave the remaining strips in parallel lines.
To make a wheel, cut strips as for a simple lattice tart decoration, using a sharp knife. Now lift each strip carefully and gently twist it over and over along the whole length of the strip. Cut each strip in half. Lay them across the top of the tart, making them meet in the centre to form a pattern like the spokes of a wheel. Trim the ends of the twisted strips of pastry so they are flush with the edge of the tart, and press the ends gently in order to seal them.

Lattices

To make an interwoven lattice, place half the strips on the tart, then interweave each remaining strip at right angles.

Once a simple or interwoven lattice is in place, trim the ends of the strips to meet the rim of the plate and press to seal.

A selection of decorated open-plate tarts, showing the attractive edgings that can be easily created

Red cherry lattice pie

A lattice topping is a very attractive and professional-looking way to decorate your pies and ring the changes. Made from strips of pastry laid diagonally across each other, it allows you to see the filling of the pie. This recipe has a cherry filling but you can try it with almost any fruit.

🔪 making the pastry, 40 minutes, plus cooling, then 1 hour

Serves 6–8
900 g /2 lb made-weight shortcrust pastry (see note following and method for Little chocolate boats, page 56)
60–90 ml /4–6 tbls sugar
1.4 kg /3 lb red cherries, stoned
30 ml /2 tbls lemon juice
60 ml /4 tbls redcurrant jelly
1 egg, beaten
thick cream, whipped, to serve

1 Make the pastry following steps 1–5 for Little chocolate boats (page 56). Reserve one-fifth of the pastry, and roll out the rest on a lightly floured board or between sheets of cling film. Use it to line a 750 ml / 1¼ pt pie plate. Do not stretch the pastry. Make sure that you leave a 12 mm /½ in border of pastry around the edge of the plate. Leave it to relax in the refrigerator for at least 30 minutes.
2 In a heavy based saucepan, combine the sugar and 600 ml /1 pt water; heat gently, stirring constantly, until the sugar is dissolved. Bring to the boil and simmer for 20 minutes. Add the stoned cherries and poach for 3–4 minutes or until *al dente*.
3 Remove the cherries from the syrup with a slotted spoon and allow them to cool. Boil the remaining syrup for about 10 minutes or until it becomes thick.
4 Remove the pan from the heat and stir in the lemon juice and the redcurrant jelly; stir constantly until the jelly has completely melted. Allow the liquid to cool, then stir in the cherries.
5 Heat the oven to 200C /400F /gas 6.
6 Spoon the cold cherries and syrup into the prepared pie case. Roll out the remaining pastry thinly and cut into long 12 mm /½ in wide strips. Twist each strip several times and place about 20 mm /¾ in apart across the pie; then place the remaining strips across the pie in the opposite direction to form a lattice. Attach the strips loosely to the edge of the pie to allow for shrinkage, fixing the end of each strip with a little beaten egg. Cut off the loose ends of pastry around the edge of the pie and then brush the pastry with the beaten egg.
6 Bake the pie in the oven for 10 minutes and then reduce the temperature to 190C / 375F /gas 5 for 25–30 minutes or until the pastry is golden, covering the top loosely with foil if the pastry starts to brown too quickly.
7 Serve the hot pie immediately, accompanied by whipped cream.

● Keep the lattice pastry strips untwisted if preferred and decorate with a pastry wheel.

Multi-coloured tart

🔪 making the pastry, then 1 hour

Serves 6
350 g /12 oz made-weight shortcrust pastry (see note following and method for Little chocolate boats, page 56)
15–30 ml /1–2 tbls lemon curd
15–30 ml /1–2 tbls black cherry jam
15–30 ml /1–2 tbls apricot jam
15–30 ml /1–2 tbls strawberry jam

1 Make the pastry following steps 1–5 for Little chocolate boats (page 56). Roll it out and line a 20 cm /8 in pie plate with it. Reserve the trimmings and set the dish aside.
2 Heat the oven to 200C /400F /gas 6.
3 Gather up the pastry trimmings, make them into a ball and roll it out to a rectangle about 2.5×25.5 cm /1×10 in and 6 mm /¼ in thick.
4 Cut two strips from the rectangle, each 12 mm /½ in wide.
5 Brush one side of each strip of pastry with cold water. Now place one strip, damp side down, on the pastry lining. Cut a 12 mm /½ in piece from the centre of the second strip and discard. Position the two short strips on the lined dish to make a neat cross with the first pastry strip.
6 Gently press the strips against the pastry lining to seal and trim the ends to align with the rim of the dish.
7 Spoon a different jam into each of the four sections and spread it out.
8 Bake the tart in the centre of the oven for 25–30 minutes. Serve hot or cold.

● You can vary the fillings in the tart using raspberry jam, or tinned or fresh fruit, for

Multi-coloured tart

example, but it looks at its very best with different fillings of contrasting colours.

Bakewell tart

🔪 making the pastry, then 1 hour

Serves 6
225 g /8 oz made-weight shortcrust pastry (see recipe and method for Little chocolate boats, page 56)
30 ml /2 tbls raspberry jam
50 g /2 oz self-raising flour
2.5 ml /½ tsp baking powder
2 medium-sized eggs
50 g /2 oz soft margarine
50 g /2 oz caster sugar
50 g /2 oz ground almonds
icing sugar, for dusting

1 Make the pastry following steps 1–5 for Little chocolate boats (page 56). Roll it out and line a 20 cm /8 in pie plate with it.
2 Heat the oven to 190C /375F /gas 5.
3 Spoon the jam into the bottom of the pastry-lined dish and spread it evenly over the base.
4 Sift the flour together with the baking powder into a warmed mixing bowl.
5 Add the eggs, the soft margarine, the caster sugar and the almonds and mix them together for 2–3 minutes until the mixture is light and glossy.
6 Spoon the cake mixture over the jam and smooth the top with a knife.
7 Bake in the centre of the oven for 35–40 minutes, or until a warmed skewer inserted into the cake filling comes out clean.
8 Serve dusted with icing sugar.

Duke of Cambridge tart

🍴 making the pastry,
then 1¼ hours

Serves 6
225 g /8 oz made-weight shortcrust pastry (see recipe and method for Little chocolate boats, page 56)
50 g /2 oz glacé cherries, coarsely chopped
25 g /1 oz angelica, coarsely chopped
50 g /2 oz chopped mixed peel
75 g /3 oz unsalted butter
75 g /3 oz caster sugar
2 medium-sized egg yolks

1 Make the shortcrust pastry following steps 1–5 for Little chocolate boats (page 56).
2 Heat the oven to 190C /375F /gas 5.
3 Roll out the pastry and line a 20 cm /8 in pie plate with it but do not make a folded edge.
4 Snip the pastry edge into 2.5 cm /1 in wide strips and fold diagonally over itself, making a sunflower pattern (see page 60).
5 Scatter the glacé cherries and angelica over the inside of the tart together with the chopped mixed peel.
6 Melt the butter over a very low heat in a heavy-based saucepan, stirring constantly — make sure it does not burn.
7 Add the egg yolks and caster sugar to the melted butter and stir over a medium heat.
8 Take care not to let the mixture boil or the egg yolks will overcook and the tart will be spoilt. When the sauce is thick and smooth and about to boil, remove it from the heat.
9 Immediately pour the butter mixture over the glacé fruit and bake the tart in the centre of the oven for 30 minutes or until the filling has risen and is well browned.

● Surface decoration is not possible with this tart as it must be baked as soon as it has been filled with the butter mixture.

Linzertorte

🍴 2 hours,
including chilling

Makes 8 slices
150 g /5 oz icing or caster sugar
150 g /5 oz unblanched almonds, ground
150 g /5 oz flour, plus extra for dusting
a pinch of ground cloves
a pinch of ground cinnamon
a pinch of grated nutmeg
a pinch of ground allspice
150 g /5 oz chilled butter, cut into small pieces, plus extra for greasing
3 medium-sized egg yolks
juice of ½ lemon
1.5 ml /¼ tsp grated lemon zest
225–275 g /8–10 oz raspberry jam
15 ml /1 tbls vanilla icing sugar (see page 9)

1 In a large bowl, mix together the first 7 ingredients. Cut in the butter with a palette

knife, then rub it in briefly with your fingers. Add the egg yolks, the lemon juice, and the lemon zest to the centre of the bowl and quickly pull the dry ingredients into the liquid with your fingertips. When a ball is formed, knead briefly, then chill, wrapped, for 30 minutes.
2 Heat the oven to 180C /350F /gas 4. Grease and flour a 23 cm /9 in flan case. The pastry is so malleable that there is no need to roll it out. Reserve one-third for the top, then flatten the rest into the tin and line the bottom and sides of the case, pressing it in place with your fingers. Prick the pastry lightly with a fork. Spread the jam over the bottom.
3 Roll out the remaining pastry 3 mm /⅛ in thick and cut it into strips 12 mm /½ in wide. Arrange the strips in a lattice pattern over the jam. Arrange one strip in a circle around the top to cover all the ends.
4 Bake the tart in the oven for 40 minutes or until the pastry is dark golden. Dust the tart with icing sugar while still warm but allow it to cool completely before serving.

Treacle tart

🍴 making the pastry,
then 1 hour

Serves 6
225 g /8 oz made-weight shortcrust pastry (see recipe and method for Little chocolate boats, page 56)
175 g /6 oz golden syrup
50 g /2 oz fresh white breadcrumbs

1 Make the shortcrust pastry following steps 1–5 for Little chocolate boats (page 56).
2 Heat the oven to 200C /400F /gas 6.
3 Measure the syrup into a saucepan and heat gently until very runny. Stir in the breadcrumbs and remove from the heat.
4 Roll out the pastry and line a 23 cm /9 in pie plate with it. Do not make a folded edge.
5 Cut about 24 pastry strips 2 cm /1 in wide around the rim (there must be an even number).
6 Spoon the syrup mixture into the centre of the pastry and spread it over the base.
7 Fold alternate pastry strips over the filling leaving the others on the rim of the pie plate to make a castellated edge (see page 60).
8 Fold under the edges of the strips left lying on the rim of the pie plate to neaten them.
9 Bake the treacle tart on the centre shelf of the oven for 25 minutes or until golden.

Linzertorte

FLAKY PASTRIES

They take a little extra time to make, but the end result is well worth it. Use your puff, rough puff or flaky pastry for recipes which range from old favourites like Eccles cakes to wonderful Strawberry mille-feuilles.

These three pastries are delicate and sophisticated — and though time-consuming to make they are not difficult if you follow each step of the preparation carefully. Choose the right pastry for the recipe you are going to make: mille-feuilles and palmiers are best with puff pastry; mince pies and Eccles cakes suit rough puff pastry and cream horns are at their very best with flaky pastry.

Flaky pastry is the easiest to make and is generally used for topping pies and making tarts. Rough puff, quicker and easier to make than puff pastry, is similar to flaky, but tends to be lighter. Puff pastry is the finest of the flaked pastries, and as the name mille-feuilles suggests, it is lots of very thin layers of light pastry leaves.

General tips

All these three pastries have some steps in common. Firstly, the best results are obtained if all the ingredients are chilled — for at least an hour before you use them. This includes the mixing bowl and any water that you need to use. If you are lucky enough to have a marble slab then this will help to keep the ingredients cool as you work with them. Do try and work in a cool room and as soon as the butter and pastry start to soften, return them to the refrigerator to chill and firm up again.

Always roll your pastry from the centre, one roll away from you and one roll towards you. Make sure your rolling pin overlaps the piece of pastry and doesn't leave ridges when you roll it. Don't push hard or you may tear the layers you have worked so hard to produce. Keep your corners and sides straight so that your layers build up evenly all over the pastry.

Do make sure that there is time to rest the pastry thoroughly in the refrigerator before shaping it, and then again after it has been shaped. It is advisable, though, to remove the prepared pastry from the refrigerator while the oven is heating up just to take the extreme chill off it, especially if it has been chilling overnight.

All these pastries take time, so it is worth making a big batch at one go and then freezing the surplus for future use. Pack the dough in 500 g /1 lb or 250 g /8 oz packs as convenient quantities to be thawed and used at a later date.

Pastry shapes

Flaky, Rough puff and Puff pastry can all be used for making pastry shapes — either sprinkled with sugar or filled with jam, fruit or cream.

Palmiers (see recipe) look like two curls side by side, and these can be eaten singly or alternatively sandwiched together with thick cream.

Arcs are made by rolling the pastry into a roll and cutting off slices which look like pinwheels. Then a cut is made with a sharp knife from the centre of the pin wheel to the outside edge and the cut edges are slightly separated to allow for expansion when they cook. Bake at 200C /400F /gas 6 for 15 minutes or so.

Papillons are made by placing four layers of pastry one on top of another, then cutting them into strips, laying them on their sides, cut side down on the baking sheet and squeezing the centre to make a butterfly shape. Bake as for Arcs.

Sacristans and bow-ties are thin strips cut from pastry that has been brushed with lightly beaten egg white and sprinkled with flaked almonds and granulated sugar. To make a sacristan, hold both ends and twist in opposite directions; for a bow-tie, hold both ends of a strip and make a loop in the middle. Bake at 200C /400F /gas 6 for 15 minutes.

Puff pastry

This can be used for many different items.
Vol au vents can be from 5 cm /2 in to 10 cm /4 in for several servings. Make them by cutting out a circle of pastry, then cutting a smaller circle inside it, cutting almost but not quite through the dough. When cooked, the soft centre is scooped out and the top is reserved to form the lid.

Bouchées are tiny vol au vents, no bigger than 4 cm /1½ in, which is enough for a single mouthful.

Mille-feuilles can be large or small. My recipe for Strawberry mille-feuilles serves four.

Tranche is a long puff pastry container made by sticking a border on a rectangle of pastry. After baking, it is filled with fruit (see recipe).

The fillings for all of these items can be chosen from fresh, whipped cream, crème pâtissière (see recipe page 66), crème chantilly (see page 41) or fresh fruit of your choice, depending on the season. Puff pastry trimmings can be used to make petits fours — cut the pastry into little fingers and sprinkle them with caster sugar, chopped almonds, pistachio nuts or coffee sugar crystals. Bake at 200C /400F /gas 6 for 15 minutes.

Rough puff pastry

Most of what has been said about puff pastry can be applied to rough puff pastry, but it is accepted by most cooks that rough puff pastry will hold its shape better if used as decorations.

Fleurons (the name is derived from *fleur*, the French word for flower), which are half-moon shapes, are attractive when used as a garnish. They can be brushed with beaten egg and sprinkled with poppy seeds, sesame seeds or finely chopped walnuts.

If cooked rough puff pastry is stored for too long it will loose its freshness. Three days in an airtight tin, or wrapped in foil or cling film is the maximum advised.

Flaky pastry

This does not have to be kept as icy cold as the other two pastries, although it always produces better results if it is. When glazing flaky pastry, generally eggs are used in one form or another — as whole beaten egg, beaten egg and milk, or beaten egg white which can have a little sugar included.

If the pastry looks as if it is browning too quickly while it is cooking, then a piece of greaseproof paper placed on the top of the pastry will solve that problem.

Do make sure not to bake your flaky pastry in the oven with something that gives off steam as it is cooking, otherwise the flaky pastry will go soggy. It will also go soggy if you put pastry on top of hot fillings, always allow the fillings to cool first.

Do not leave pies to keep warm for any length of time since the pastry will toughen. If you want to eat a pie cold, then let it cool evenly in a draught-free place.

Uncooked flaky pastry will keep in the freezer for 6 months, and cooked pastry for 3.

Filling pastry

There are three classic cream fillings for puff, rough puff and flaky pastry: *crème au beurre ménagère*, *crème au beurre en sucre cuit* and *crème au beurre à l'anglaise*.

Crème au beurre ménagère is best used for filling rather than decorating since it has a 'grainy' appearance due to the fact that the crème is not cooked and therefore the sugar does not melt. Unsalted butter is beaten until it is smooth and then the sugar, egg yolks and flavouring are beaten in. The crème should be chilled before it is used.

Crème au beurre en sucre cuit is made by beating unsalted butter until smooth in one bowl, and eggs in another. Sugar is then heated with a little water until it reaches 110C /230F. The resulting syrup is then added to the eggs and beaten. This mixture is heated on a double boiler and beaten until it doubles in volume. This is cooled, while still beating, and added a spoonful at a time to the creamed butter — then any flavouring is included.

Crème au beurre à l'anglaise has a custard base and a lighter texture than either of the other crèmes. Unsalted butter is beaten into the custard, and then any flavouring.

All these crèmes store well, if covered, for up to three days in a refrigerator, but do remove them 30 minutes before use.

Toppings

Pastry is often glazed with an egg or milk glaze, but if you want a slightly different topping, then try glacé icing instead. It gives a crisp, smooth glaze without adding too much sweetness to the pastry (see page 39).

A caramel topping is another suggestion for your pastries. Put sugar and water in a saucepan, heat them until the sugar is dissolved, then bring the syrup to the boil and boil it for 10 minutes when it should be a golden colour. Brush this over the pastry.

Strawberry mille-feuilles (page 66)

Basic puff pastry

🔪🔪🔪 chilling the ingredients,
🔪🔪🔪 then 3 hours, plus chilling

Made-weight of pastry is 1.2 kg /2¾ lb
500 g /1 lb unsalted butter, in 2 blocks
500 g /1 lb strong flour, plus extra for rolling
2.5 ml /½ tsp salt
30 ml /2 tbls lemon juice

1 Chill all the ingredients, a mixing bowl and 250 ml /9 fl oz water in the refrigerator.
2 Remove the ingredients from the refrigerator. Finely dice 40 g /1½ oz butter. Set the remaining butter aside.
3 Sift 500 g /1 lb flour and the salt into the mixing bowl; add the diced butter and work it with your fingers until it is completely coated with the flour. Make a well in the centre of the bowl.
4 Add the water and lemon juice to the well, and work the ingredients with your hand to a moist, but not sticky, dough. Add more water if necessary.
5 Turn the dough out onto a floured board and knead it into a ball.
6 Flatten the dough to 25 mm /1 in thick, wrap it closely in cling film and refrigerate for 15 minutes.
7 Meanwhile, place the remaining butter on a floured board and shape it into a rectangle 15 × 12.5 cm /6 × 5 in. Chill.
8 Remove the dough from the refrigerator, then pat the pastry down with your hands and roll the dough into a rectangle. Push the sides and corners as straight as possible.
9 Place the 'brick' of butter in the centre of the rectangle and fold over the 4 edges to make a parcel. Seal the pastry joins by pressing gently with your fingertips.
10 To make the first turn, roll the pastry to a rectangle 38 × 30 cm /15 × 12 in. Fold the bottom ⅓ over the centre; now fold the top ⅓ down on top of it. Seal the joins. Turn the pastry 90 degrees.
11 To make the second turn, roll the pastry out to a rectangle 38 × 30 cm /15 × 12 in. Fold both the short edges of the dough to meet in the centre. Next, fold one half on top of the other. Seal the pastry joins. Turn the pastry through 90 degrees.
12 To rest the pastry for the first time, wrap it in cling film and leave it to relax in the refrigerator for at least 15 minutes.
13 Repeat both the 'turns' as described in steps 10, 11, 12 another 3 times.
14 Rest the pastry for the second time for at least 15 minutes, then use it.

Strawberry mille-feuilles

This is a mouthwatering confection of light, crisp pastry; the French name means 'one-thousand leaves'.

🔪🔪 making the crème pâtissière,
🔪🔪 then 1¼ hours, plus cooling

Serves 4
215 g /7½ oz made-weight Basic puff pastry
  (see recipe)
60 ml /4 tbls strawberry jam, warmed and sieved
100–150 g /4–6 strawberries, hulled
For the crème pâtissière
15 ml /1 tbls caster sugar
7.5 ml /1½ tsps flour
5 ml /1 tsp cornflour
125 ml /4 fl oz milk
1 egg yolk
7.5 g /¼ oz butter
1.5 ml /¼ tsp vanilla essence (optional)
7.5 ml /1½ tsp kirsch (optional)
whipped cream, for decoration (optional)

1 Heat the oven to 230C /450F /gas 8. Roll out the pastry to a 25 cm /10 in square. Using a sharp knife, trim the edges and cut the pastry into 3 equal strips. Place the strips on 1 or 2 large dampened baking sheet(s) and prick well with the prongs of a fork. Chill in the refrigerator for 5 minutes.
2 Bake the pastry for 10–12 minutes until well browned. Turn over the strips and return to the oven for 3–4 minutes to dry the undersides. Leave on wire racks until cold.
3 Make the crème pâtissière. In a saucepan, mix together the sugar, flour and cornflour. Gradually stir in the milk. Bring to the boil, stirring constantly. Boil for 1 minute.
4 Beat the egg yolk lightly in the top of a double boiler, then beat in the butter and a little of the hot milk mixture and mix well. Pour in the remaining hot milk mixture and cook over hot water, stirring, until the mixture is smooth and thick. This will take about 20 minutes. Strain into a bowl and leave to cool. Flavour with vanilla essence and kirsch, if you wish. Cover the surface closely with cling film to prevent a skin forming. Chill until quite firm.
5 Not more than 1 hour before serving, trim the edges of each pastry strip with a sharp knife. Brush the surface of 1 strip very thinly with jam and spread with half the crème pâtissière, to within 5 mm /¼ in of the edges. Place the strip on a flat dish. Lightly brush a second strip with jam and spread with the remaining crème pâtissière. Place it on top of the first strip.
6 Brush the surface of the last strip with half the remaining jam. Cut the strawberries in half and arrange them, cut side down, on top of the strip. Glaze the fruit with the remaining jam. Place the strawberry-covered pastry on top of the other two strips and pipe a cream border if you wish. Leave the mille-feuilles in a cool place for 15 minutes before serving.

Gâteau Pithiviers

🔪🔪🔪 making the pastry,
🔪🔪🔪 then 2 hours

Serves 6–8
500 g /1 lb made-weight Basic puff pastry
  (see recipe)
flour, for rolling
1 egg yolk, beaten with 15 ml /1 tbls water, for the egg glaze
For the filling
125 g /4 oz butter, softened
125 g /4 oz sugar
1 egg
1 egg yolk
125 g /4 oz ground almonds
15 ml /1 tbls flour
30 ml /2 tbls rum

1 To make the filling, beat the butter and sugar together in a bowl until they are light and fluffy. Beat in the egg and the egg yolk and then stir in the ground almonds, flour and rum.
2 On a lightly floured board, roll out the pastry and cut out a 23 cm /9 in circle and a 25 cm /10 in circle. Place the 23 cm /9 in circle upside down on a baking sheet.
3 Pile the almond filling in the centre, leaving a 25 mm /1 in border around the edge. Brush the border with egg glaze and place the remaining circle on top, upside down, sealing the edges well. Brush off the excess flour. Knock up and scallop the edges. Make a hole in the centre to allow the steam to escape and score the pastry like a wheel with a knife. Chill in the refrigerator for 30 minutes.
4 Meanwhile, heat the oven to 230C /450F /gas 8.
5 Brush the pastry with egg glaze, making sure that the glaze does not drip over the edges. Sprinkle the baking sheet with cold water. Bake in the oven for 20–25 minutes or until the pastry is crisp and golden brown. Remove it from the oven and transfer it to a wire rack. Allow it to cool completely before serving.

Palmiers

This recipe is an ideal way to use up the pastry trimmings from another dish. A classic French recipe, made with puff pastry, rolled and folded with sugar, Palmiers are recognizable by their familiar 'v' shape.

🔪🔪🔪 making the pastry,
🔪🔪🔪 then 1½ hours, plus cooling

Makes 36
500 g /1 lb made-weight Basic puff pastry
  (see recipe)
125 g /4 oz icing sugar, plus extra for sifting

1 Roll the puff pastry into a rectangle 45 × 15 cm /18 × 6 in. Sprinkle with icing sugar, fold in three, turn at right angles and roll again. Sprinkle with sugar and again fold in three. Chill for 15 minutes.
2 Sprinkle the board with icing sugar and roll the pastry into a rectangle 38 × 25 cm / 15 × 10 in. With the long side towards you, fold each short edge over twice to reach the centre. Now fold one half on top of the other, as if you were closing a book. Press down lightly and, with a sharp knife, cut across into slices, 15 mm /½ in wide.
3 Place them on baking sheets cut side

down, leaving them space to expand. Open the slices slightly and flatten the pastry with the heel of your hand. Chill in the refrigerator for 30 minutes.

4   Meanwhile, heat the oven to 230C /425F /gas 8.

5   Carefully sprinkle the baking sheet with cold water between the pastries. Sprinkle the palmiers with more icing sugar. Bake in the oven for 8–12 minutes or until they are puffed and golden brown. Transfer them to a rack to cool before decorating (see notes below) and serving.

● Sandwich two palmiers together with crème chantilly (see page 41) or fresh whipped cream and strawberries or raspberries. You can use any soft fresh fruit to decorate.

● Add Cointreau, to taste, to your crème chantilly cream and then decorate the palmiers with well-drained, canned mandarin orange segments.

● Sprinkle Demerara sugar and chopped, mixed nuts over the top of the palmiers before baking.

Tranche aux fruits

making the pastry, then 45 minutes, plus cooling and decorating

Serves 6–8
500 g /1 lb made-weight Basic puff pastry
(see recipe)
1 small egg, beaten
275 ml /10 fl oz thick cream
1 banana
100 g /4 oz grapes
100 g /4 oz strawberries
1 large ripe peach
30 ml /2 tbls apricot jam

1   Heat the oven to 230C /450F /gas 8. Dampen a baking tray.

2   Roll the pastry out to a rectangle 33×20 cm /13×8 in. Trim the edges to neaten them, then fold it in half lengthwise. Using a sharp knife, cut away a border of pastry 4 cm /1½ in wide. Set this border aside.

3   Roll out a centre piece to the same size as the border. Brush the edges with beaten egg. Lift the centre piece onto the baking tray. Prick the base well with a fork. Lift the border on top. Press the edges lightly. Brush them with beaten egg. Mark a pattern (see picture) on the top. Bake for 30–35 minutes until the pastry is golden and puffy.

4   Allow it to cool on a wire tray. Whip the cream until it will just hold its shape. Fill the tranche with the cream, smoothing it to make an even layer.

5   Peel and slice the banana. Skin and de-seed the grapes. Wash, hull and halve the strawberries. Peel and slice the peach.

6   Arrange the fruit decoratively over the cream so that the cream is covered.

7   Push the apricot jam through a sieve into a small heavy-based pan. Set over a low heat until it is liquid.

8   Spoon the jam over the fruit. Allow it to set before serving.

Tranche aux fruits

Basic rough puff pastry

🔪🔪 chilling the ingredients, then 40 minutes, plus chilling

Made-weight of pastry is 500 g /1 lb
250 g /8 oz strong flour, plus extra for rolling
a pinch of salt
175 g /6 oz unsalted butter
5 ml /1 tsp lemon juice

1 Put flour, the salt, the unsalted butter and the lemon juice, plus about 150 ml /5 fl oz water, and the mixing bowl in the refrigerator to chill.
2 Remove the ingredients from the refrigerator. Sift the flour and the salt into the chilled bowl.
3 Dice the chilled butter into 15 mm /½ in cubes and drop them into the flour. Add the lemon juice and 125 ml /4 fl oz water and mix it all very quickly to a light dough. Add 15–30 ml /1–2 tbls more water, if necessary.
4 Turn the dough onto a lightly floured board and, with a lightly floured rolling pin, roll it out to a rectangle 30 × 15 cm /12 × 6 in, pushing the sides as straight and the corners as square as possible with a ruler.
5 Fold one-third of the pastry up towards the centre, then fold the top third of the pastry down over the centre. Seal the edges with your hand or a rolling pin. Turn the pastry through 90 degrees.
6 Roll and fold and turn the pastry, following the instructions in steps 4 and 5, once more, then wrap and rest the pastry in the refrigerator for 20 minutes.
7 Repeat the rolling, folding and resting four more times.
8 Wrap the pastry in cling film, or in greaseproof paper and a damp cloth and chill it in the refrigerator for at least 1 hour.

Mince pies

🔪🔪 making the pastry, then 1 hour

Makes 12 pies
500 g /1 lb made-weight Basic rough puff pastry (see recipe)
350 g /12 oz mincemeat
beaten egg, to glaze
caster sugar, to sprinkle

1 Position the shelf just above the centre and heat the oven to 230C /450F /gas 8. Roll out the pastry to 3 mm /⅛ in thick.
2 Using a fluted cutter the same diameter as the hollows of the tartlet tins, cut out the lids for the tarts. Using a small fancy star-shaped cutter, cut star shapes out of the centre of each pastry lid. Using a cutter 2.5 cm /1 in larger than the first, cut out as many bases as you can from the remaining pastry.
3 Combine the pastry trimmings and re-roll them. Stamp out the remaining number of rounds that are needed. Line the tartlet tin hollows with the larger rounds of pastry,

moulding them to fit. Place a heaped teaspoonful of mincemeat in each.
4 Brush the edges of each lid with cold water and place them, damp side down, over the mincemeat. Press the edges to seal them.
5 Place the pies in the refrigerator for 20 minutes to relax. Brush the top of the pies with beaten egg to glaze and sprinkle lightly with sugar.
6 Bake the pies in the oven for 20–25 minutes. Remove the pies from the oven and leave them in the tin for a few minutes.
7 Now remove the pies from the tin. If you are serving the pies cold, put them on a wire rack to cool.

● Sprinkle the pastry bases with ground almonds and a little rum or brandy before filling them with mincemeat.
● Instead of using all mincemeat to fill the tarts, use half mincemeat, a quarter chopped walnuts and a quarter of stewed apple.
● Serve the mince pies with a cube of Stilton or even a blob of cream cheese on top of each one.

Peach and banana puffs

🔪🔪🔪 2 hours, plus cooling

Makes 8 small pastries
4 small fresh peaches or 8 small canned peach halves, well drained
250 ml /½ pt dry white wine, or syrup from canned peaches
45 ml /3 tbls lemon juice
5 ml /1 tsp ground allspice
40 g /1½ oz soft brown sugar
500 g /1 lb made-weight Basic rough puff pastry (see recipe)
1 medium-sized banana
1 egg white, beaten
caster sugar, to sprinkle

1 If using fresh peaches, pour the wine, or the same quantity of water, into a large saucepan. Add 30 ml /2 tsp lemon juice, the allspice and the brown sugar. Stir it once, then bring to the boil. Simmer it for 2 minutes until the sugar has dissolved.
2 Skin, halve and remove the stones from the fresh peaches. Remove the pan from the heat and add the fresh peach halves. Reduce the heat, cover and simmer the peaches gently for 10–15 minutes, until they are tender. Uncover the pan and set it aside until the fruit is completely cold.
3 Carefully lift the peaches out of the cold liquid and pat them dry. Reserve the poaching liquid.
4 If using canned peaches, drain them well, reserving the syrup.
5 Position the shelf just above the centre of the oven and heat the oven to 230C /450F /gas 8.
6 Roll out the pastry to 3 mm /⅛ in thick. Using a 7.5 cm /3 in fluted cutter, cut out eight circles from the pastry. Then, using a 10 cm /4 in fluted cutter, cut out another eight circles.
7 Put the trimmings on top of each other

Peach and banana puffs

and roll this out to 3 mm /⅛ in thick. Using a very small fancy cutter, cut out 24 fancy shapes from the trimmings and put them to one side for later.
8 Peel the banana and cut it into 24 thin

decorations with egg white. Sprinkle the lids with a little caster sugar.

11 Bake the puffs in the oven for 25–30 minutes, until the pastry is puffed and golden brown.

● Serve these hot with the poaching liquid (or canned peach syrup) thickened with arrowroot and served as a sauce; or cold with ice cream.
● Use apricots instead of peaches and add a little Amaretti (almond liqueur) to the poaching liquid or syrup.
● Place a small ball of marzipan in each peach cavity before baking.

Eccles cakes

making the pastry,
then 1¼ hours

Makes 16 cakes
500 g /1 lb made-weight Basic rough puff pastry (see recipe)
For the filling
25 g /1 oz butter or margarine
15 ml /1 tbls light, soft brown sugar
100 g /4 oz currants
50 g /2 oz mixed peel
2.5 ml /½ tsp mixed spice
For the glaze:
milk
caster sugar

1 Position the shelf just above the centre and heat oven to 230C /450F /gas 8.
2 Place the butter or margarine in a small saucepan and add the remaining filling ingredients. Heat over a low heat until the butter has melted, then stir to mix together and allow to cool.
3 Roll out the pastry to 3 mm /⅛ in thick. Using a 8.5 cm /3½ in plain cutter, cut out 16 circles. If necessary, put the pastry trimmings on top of each other and re-roll. Stamp the remaining number of rounds needed. Very lightly roll the pastry circles with a rolling pin to make them slightly larger.
4 Dampen the pastry edges with a little milk and place a heaped teaspoon of the filling in the centre of each circle. Using your fingertips, gather the pastry edges up over the filling and pinch them together to seal.
5 Turn the cakes over so that the joins are underneath and gently flatten each cake with the palm of your hand. Place the cakes on a baking sheet and put them in the refrigerator for 20 minutes to relax.
6 Using a sharp knife, make three diagonal slits across the top of each cake. Brush the tops with milk and sprinkle them with a little caster sugar.
7 Bake the cakes for 20–25 minutes until they are puffed and golden.

● Substitute mincemeat for the filling.
● Make cherry Eccles cakes by omitting the mixed peel and substituting 50 g /2 oz chopped glacé cherries. Soak the currants in 30 ml /2 tbls cherry brandy before using.
● Omit 25 g /1 oz currants and replace them with 25 g /1 oz chopped walnuts. Use ground cinnamon instead of mixed spice.

slices. Place the slices in a bowl and add the remaining lemon juice. Toss the slices to coat them with lemon juice.
9 Place the eight smaller pastry circles on a baking sheet or tray and brush the edges with a little beaten egg white. Place 3 slices of banana, overlapping, in the centre of each

pastry circle. Place a peach half, cavity side downwards, on top of the banana.
10 Cover each peach with a larger circle of pastry. Press the edges together to seal. Brush the top surface of each pie with a little beaten egg white. Arrange three fancy pastry shapes on top of each pie and also brush the

Basic flaky pastry

⚔ 2 hours making the pastry,
then resting

Made-weight of pastry is 900 g /2 lb
500 g /1 lb strong flour, plus extra for rolling
5 ml /1 tsp salt
225 g /8 oz butter
15 ml /1 tbls lemon juice
125 g /4 oz lard

1 Chill the ingredients, 250 ml /9 fl oz water and the mixing bowl.
2 Sift the flour and the salt into the bowl. Dice half the butter and then rub it into the flour until it resembles fine breadcrumbs.

Make a well in the centre of the flour.
3 Measure 150 ml /5 fl oz iced water into the well; add the lemon juice. Stir vigorously, adding more iced water if necessary. The dough should not be too sticky, nor too dry.
4 Turn the dough out and work it lightly with just a few turns.
5 Roll the dough out into a rectangle 40×20 cm /16×8 in, pushing the sides straight and the corners square.
6 Use the tip of a knife to dot the upper two-thirds of the pastry with half the lard. Leave a border, 15mm /½ in wide, clear on the 3 outer sides.
7 Fold the rectangle in 3 as follows: fold the free-of-fat third of the dough up towards the centre. Now fold the remaining third down over the top of it. Seal the edges.

8 Wrap the pastry in cling film and chill it for 15 minutes. Make a note that the pastry has had one 'turn'.
9 Unwrap the pastry and lay it on a lightly floured surface so that the fold is on your left-hand side and the longest sealed edge on your right. Roll it out again.
10 Repeat steps 6 and 7 with half the remaining butter. Seal the edges, wrap and chill it for 15 minutes. Make a note of the second 'turn'.
11 Give the pastry its third and fourth 'turns' using the remaining lard, then the remaining butter. Chill the pastry for 15 minutes each time.
12 After the final folding, seal the edges. Wrap it in cling film and leave it to rest in the refrigerator for at least 1 hour.

Coffee cream squares

⚔⚔ making the pastry,
then 2¼ hours

Makes 8 squares
450 g /1 lb made-weight Basic flaky pastry
(see recipe)
50 g /2 oz granulated sugar
For the crème au beurre au sucre cuit
225 g /8 oz unsalted butter, softened
1 medium-sized egg
3 medium-sized egg yolks
125 g /4 oz granulated sugar
30 ml /2 tbls strong black coffee
50 g /2 oz sugar-coated coffee beans, to decorate

1 Position the oven shelf in the middle of the oven, then heat to 230C /450F /gas 8.
2 Sprinkle the pastry board with the granulated sugar. Roll out the pastry and trim it to a rectangle 23×18 cm /9×7 in.
3 Rinse a baking sheet with water. Trim the pastry edges to neaten, then cut the pastry into two strips down the length, then cut each strip equally into four squares. Place pastry squares on the baking sheet and prick them well with a fork. Place the pastry in the refrigerator for 30 minutes to relax.
4 Bake the pastry for 15–20 minutes until it is risen and golden brown. Transfer the squares to a cooling rack and leave until cold.
5 Meanwhile, prepare the crème au beurre sucre cuit. Place the butter in a warmed mixing bowl and beat it with a wooden spoon, or hand-held electric whisk, until it is very light and fluffy.

A Coffee cream square

6 Place the egg and yolks in a mixing bowl. Briskly beat them together.
7 Place the sugar in a small, heavy-based saucepan. Add 45 ml /3 tbls water and bring to the boil. Boil, shaking the saucepan from time to time until a sugar thermometer registers 110–116C /230–240F or the sugar reaches the soft ball stage. As soon as this stage has been reached, pour the sugar syrup into the yolk mixture in a steady stream. Beat continually.
8 When all the syrup has been incorporated into the egg mixture, place the bowl over a saucepan of hot, but not boiling, water. Continue to beat the sugar and egg mixture for 4–5 minutes until it has doubled in volume and is foamy.
9 Place the bowl in a larger bowl half filled with cold water and continue beating until the mixture is tepid.
10 Beat the egg mixture, a spoonful at a time, into the creamed butter, until it has all been incorporated. Finally, beat in the black coffee, a little at a time.
11 Using a small sharp knife, carefully split each square of pastry into two, through the flakes, lengthwise.
12 Using half the crème au beurre sucre cuit, generously sandwich the pastry squares back together in pairs. Spread the remaining butter cream evenly onto the tops of the pastry squares. Decorate either end of each square with the sugar-coated coffee beans.

Chantilly fruit tartlets

⚔ making the pastry,
then 1¼ hours

Makes 12
350 g /12 oz made-weight Basic flaky pastry
(see recipe)
For the filling
25 g /1 oz ratafia biscuits
30 ml /2 tbls redcurrant jelly
225 g /8 oz soft fruit, strawberries,
cherries, raspberries etc
150 ml /5 fl oz thick cream
a few drops vanilla essence

1 Place a shelf just above centre of the oven and heat it to 230C /450F /gas 8.
2 Roll out the pastry to 6 mm /¼ in thick.

Using a 7.5 cm /3 in round cutter, cut out 12 circles to fit a 12-hole tartlet tin. If necessary, re-roll the pastry by placing the trimmings one on top of the other. Roll and cut out the desired number of pastry circles. Carefully line the tartlet tin with pastry circles and place the tin in the refrigerator to rest for at least 15 minutes.

3 Cut out circles of greaseproof paper or foil slightly larger than the tins. Place these linings on the pastry and cover them with baking beans.

4 Bake the pastry blind for 10 minutes. Remove the linings and beans and return the pastry to the oven for a further 10 minutes.
5 Remove the pastry from the oven and leave it in the tin to cool for 3 minutes. Carefully remove the pastry cases from the tins, place them on a wire rack and leave to cool.
6 Put the ratafia biscuits in a polythene bag and crush them finely with a rolling pin.
7 Place the redcurrant jelly in a bowl and beat it with a wooden spoon. Sieve the jelly into a small saucepan and heat it gently

(without boiling) until the jelly melts. Remove it from the heat. Prepare your fruit.
8 Put the cream and a few drops of vanilla essence in a bowl. Whip it until the cream just holds its shape, then fold in the biscuit crumbs.
9 Pipe or spoon the cream mixture into the tartlet cases. Arrange the fruit on top of the cream. Brush the melted jelly over the fruit and serve immediately.

Chantilly fruit tartlets

Strawberry cream horns

♦♦♦ making the pastry,
then 1½ hours, plus cooling

Makes 8 pastries
500 g /1 lb made-weight Basic flaky pastry
(see recipe)
50 g /2 oz granulated sugar
milk, to glaze
caster sugar, to sprinkle
175 g /6 oz unsalted butter
50 g /2 oz icing sugar, plus extra for sifting
2 medium-sized egg yolks
a few drops of vanilla essence
125 g /4 oz strawberries, hulled and quartered
8 whole strawberries, to decorate
angelica, to decorate

1 Sprinkle the pastry board with the granulated sugar and roll out the pastry 3 mm / ⅛ in thick into a rectangle approximately 25 × 32.5 cm /10 × 13 in. Trim the pastry. Cut it into strips 2.5 cm /1 in wide, each measuring approximately 30 cm /12 in long.

2 Dampen the pastry strips along one long edge of the strip with water. Rinse a baking sheet and have ready the ungreased horn moulds. Starting at the pointed end, wind the pastry strips around the moulds. Remember that the pastry should overlap on the dampened strip.

3 Gently press the pastry together with the fingertips to make sure that it securely and evenly covers the moulds. Fix the end of the pastry strips by pressing down gently. Place the horns on a rinsed baking sheet. Put the pastry horns in the refrigerator to relax for 30 minutes.

4 Position the oven shelf in the centre of the oven and heat to 230C /450F /gas 8.

5 Brush the pastry horns with milk and sprinkle each one lightly with caster sugar. Bake them for 15–20 minutes, until the pastry is puffed and golden brown. Allow them to cool for 5 minutes before carefully removing the moulds. Transfer the horns to a rack and leave until they are cold.

6 Meanwhile, make the filling. Place the softened butter in a warmed mixing bowl and then beat it until it is smooth and creamy. Sift the icing sugar into the bowl and then add the egg yolks.

One of the many variations of fillings that can be used in pastry horns

7 Beat the mixture until it is creamy and add a few drops of vanilla essence to taste. Fold in the quartered strawberries.

8 Fill the horns with the cream and strawberry mixture, top each horn with a whole fresh strawberry and a couple of 'leaves' of angelica. Sift a little icing sugar over the top of the pastry.

● For apricot and almond horns, omit the strawberries and, at step 6, beat in 30 ml /2 tbls apricot brandy. Drop a small spoonful of apricot preserve into the bottom of each horn and sprinkle each with a few chopped almonds. Fill the horns with the butter cream and sift a little icing sugar over the top for a decoration.

● Fill the horns with crème chantilly (see page 41) and top with a generous teaspoon of thick fruit preserve, such as blackcurrant or strawberry or apricot.

● Omit the flavouring from the butter cream and use 50 g /2 oz melted chocolate, stir in rum to taste and a scant 25 g /1 oz seedless raisins. Use this to fill the horns.

CROISSANTS

What better way to start the day than with a delicious buttery croissant and a large cup of fresh coffee? Making croissants is a combination of techniques, those for dough and puff pastry — here I show you how to make them.

Most of us think of croissants as being a typically French pastry seen on breakfast tables in hotels and restaurants all over France but, in fact, they originated in Budapest. In 1686 the city was besieged by Turks and it was bakers, working at night, who heard the enemy tunnelling under the city and raised the alarm. The bakers were rewarded with the privilege of making pastries in a crescent, the symbol of the Ottoman empire, so 'cocking a snook' at their attackers.

These days there are various styles of croissant, some have a consistency more like bread dough whilst others are closer to flaky pastry. The lightest are made of puff pastry, but this is very rich to eat and the yeast dough type is more popular.

Variations on the basic croissant are popular as mid-morning snacks with coffee or afternoon snacks with tea. They are sweet and very similar in style to Danish pastries (see following chapter).

Croissant dough

My croissant dough is rich with butter and eggs (all good croissants are made with butter — that's what gives them their special flavour), but it is also light and airy. It has a very high proportion of yeast, and the basic dough is soft and sticky.

After mixing the basic dough, cover the bowl with cling film and leave the dough to rise until it is doubled in bulk. I find it is best if allowed to rise for about 1 hour in the refrigerator — if kept at a warm temperature, as you would normally for a yeast dough, it is difficult to handle. Butter is then rolled into the risen dough as if for puff pastry; a block of chilled butter is folded up in the dough which is then rolled out and turned four times in all. In between each rolling and turning of the dough it is chilled in the refrigerator to relax it. You do have to work quickly as you roll and fold because the dough actually rises while you are working it. If it gets too difficult to handle, pop the dough back in the refrigerator to chill again.

For the final shaping of the croissants, roll the dough out quite thinly — 5 mm /¼ in thick is about right. Cut it into triangles using a sharp, floured knife. Roll up the triangles, starting at the wide base (see step-by-step instructions overleaf). Place each roll on a dampened baking sheet and pull the two ends inwards to form a crescent shape, with the points almost touching. Make sure the tip of the triangle is on top of the roll.

After shaping, leave the rolls to prove for about 20 minutes — this time in a warm place as for conventional yeast doughs. Now bake the croissants in a hot oven; the steam from the damp baking sheet will help to make the croissants puffier and lighter.

Croissants

Making croissants

First roll the dough to a rectangle. Now put the butter in the centre of the rectangle and fold over the 4 edges.

Roll the dough to a rectangle. Fold the bottom third up over the middle third and then the top down over this.

After chilling and rolling 4 times, roll to a rectangle 75×30 cm /30×12 in. Cut in half lengthways, cut 9 triangles from each half.

Brush the edges with egg glaze. Roll up the triangles, beginning at the wide base, and arrange them with the triangle points on top.

Croissants

🍴🍴🍴 3½ hours, then
🍴🍴🍴 1¼ hours, plus cooling

Makes 18

225 ml /8 fl oz milk
25 g /1 oz fresh yeast
550 g /1¼ lb strong flour, plus extra
   for rolling
30 ml /2 tbls caster sugar
5 ml /1 tsp salt
275 g /10 oz butter, chilled
2 eggs, lightly beaten
1 egg, lightly beaten, to glaze

1 In a saucepan, heat the milk to 37C /98F. Put 30–45 ml /2–3 tbls of the milk in a small bowl, crumble the yeast over it and stir until dissolved.

2 In a large mixing bowl, sift 450 g /1 lb flour, the sugar and the salt. Cut 50 g /2 oz of the chilled butter into small dice and add it to the flour mixture. Rub in the fat with your fingertips until the mixture resembles fine breadcrumbs.

3 Make a well in the centre. of the flour mixture and pour in the yeast mixture, the remaining milk and the eggs. Using your fingers, gradually draw the flour into the liquid. Continue mixing until all the flour is incorporated and a soft sticky dough is formed.

4 Cover the bowl with cling film and transfer to the refrigerator for 1 hour or until the dough has risen to twice its original size.

5 Meanwhile, place the remaining 225 g / 8 oz butter between 2 pieces of cling film. With a rolling pin, roll out the butter into a rectangle 23×12.5 cm /9×5 in. Leave the butter wrapped in the cling film and put it in the refrigerator.

6 Sift the remaining 100 g /4 oz of flour onto a board or marble slab and turn out the dough onto the flour. Knead the dough for about 10 minutes or until all the flour on the board or slab has been worked in. The dough should be elastic and smooth.

7 With the rolling pin, roll out the dough to a rectangle 45×25 cm /18×10 in. Unwrap the butter and place it in the centre of the dough. Fold over all 4 edges of the dough to enclose the butter (see picture).

8 Roll the dough lengthways into a rectangle about 38 cm /15 in long. Mark the dough lightly across into 3. Fold the bottom third up over the centre third and then fold the top third down to cover this. Wrap the dough in cling film and place in the refrigerator to chill for about 10 minutes. Repeat the rolling out and the folding of the dough 3 more times. Place it in the refrigerator to chill for 10 minutes between each rolling.

9 After the final rolling, leave the dough to chill in the refrigerator for 1 hour. Sprinkle 3 baking sheets with cold water.

10 Place the dough on a floured board or marble slab and roll it out into a rectangle 75×30 cm /30×12 in and about 5 mm /¼ in thick. Cut in half lengthways and cut 9×15 cm /6 in triangles from each strip.

11 To shape the croissants, roll up the triangles beginning at the wide base. Brush the edges with egg glaze to seal them. Place the croissants on the dampened baking sheets with the triangle point on the top and pull the ends together to form a crescent shape. Leave them in a warm place for 20 minutes, or until they have doubled in bulk.

12 Meanwhile, heat the oven to 200C / 400F /gas 6.

13 Brush the croissants with egg glaze. Bake for 15 minutes or until golden. Allow to cool a little and serve while still warm.

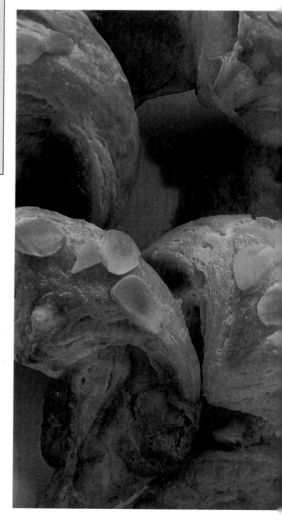

Croissants d'amandes

For the following three variations on my basic Croissant recipe, make the dough as directed in the original recipe and cut it into triangles. Flavour the croissants as directed in the individual recipes below and then shape them according to the main recipe.

making the croissant dough, then 1¼ hours, plus cooling

Makes 18

1 × Croissant dough (see recipe)
250 g /9 oz marzipan
1 egg, beaten, to glaze
125 g /4 oz flaked almonds
icing sugar, to serve

1 Prepare the croissant dough and cut it into 18 triangles as before.
2 Cut the marzipan into 15 g /½ oz pieces and roll each piece into a cigar-shape. Place a marzipan cigar on the wide edge of each dough triangle and roll up, beginning at the wide base. Brush the edges with egg glaze to seal them. Place the croissants on dampened baking sheets and pull the ends together to form a crescent shape. Leave the croissants to rise in a warm place for 20 minutes until they have doubled in bulk.
3 Heat the oven to 200C /400F /gas 6.
4 Brush the croissants with egg glaze and sprinkle them with flaked almonds. Cook in the oven for 15 minutes.
5 Remove the croissants from the oven and allow them to cool a little on a wire rack. Sprinkle with icing sugar and serve warm.

Spiced croissants

making the croissant dough, then 1¼ hours, plus cooling

Makes 18

1 × Croissant dough (see recipe)
90 ml /6 tbls caster sugar
15 ml /1 tbls ground cinnamon
1 egg, beaten, to glaze

1 Prepare the croissant dough and cut 18 triangles as before. Roll up the triangles beginning at the wide base. Brush the edges with egg glaze to seal them. Place on dampened baking sheets with the triangle points at the top. Pull the ends together to form a crescent shape and leave the croissants to rise in a warm place for 20 minutes or until they have doubled in bulk.
2 In a small bowl, mix together the caster sugar and the ground cinnamon.
3 Heat the oven to 200C /400F /gas 6.
4 Brush the croissants with egg glaze and sprinkle them with the cinnamon sugar. Cook in the oven for 15 minutes. Cool a little on a wire rack and serve warm.

Cheese croissants

These croissants are equally good served in the morning with a cup of steaming coffee or later in the day as a delicious savoury afternoon snack.

making the croissant dough, then 1¼ hours, plus cooling

Serves 18

1 × Croissant dough (see recipe)
90 ml /6 tbls grated Cheddar cheese
1 egg, beaten, to glaze

1 Prepare the croissant dough and cut it into 18 triangles as before.
2 Sprinkle 5 ml /1 tsp grated cheese over each triangle. Roll the triangles up, beginning at the wide base. Brush the edges with egg glaze to seal them. Place on dampened baking sheets with the pointed tip of each triangle on top. Pull the ends of each rolled triangle together to form a crescent shape. Leave to rise in a warm place for 20 minutes, or until doubled in bulk.
3 Heat the oven to 200C /400F /gas 6.
4 Brush the croissants with egg glaze and cook them in the oven for 15 minutes.
5 Remove them from the oven and allow them to cool a little on a wire rack. Serve the croissants while they are still warm.

Croissants d'amandes

DANISH PASTRIES

Home-baked Danish pastries are not difficult to make if you keep your ingredients cool. They are delicious and you can choose your favourite shapes and fillings from my large selection here.

If you can make croissants (see page 74) you should be able to make Danish pastries. Using the same combination of yeast dough with puff pastry techniques, you can make a light puffy dough to use for all sorts and shapes of Danish pastry. Fillings can range from a custard, apple purée, almond paste to vanilla butter.

A Danish pastry is always a surprise — the shape may be round or starred, curled like a snail or folded into a square. The centre may be filled with one of the classics already mentioned, or with jam or currants or another fruit. The outside may be crunchy with spiced sugar or smooth with glacé icing.

They should be eaten fresh; preferably when they are cold, but certainly on the day they are made.

Fancy pastries

Use fine, soft flour — not strong bread flour — to make these delectable pastries.

🔪🔪🔪 1½-1¾ hours, including resting, then 1 hour shaping and baking

Makes 24 small pastries
225 g /8 oz flour, plus extra for kneading
a large pinch of salt
15 ml /1 tbls caster sugar
25 g /1 oz lard or white cooking fat
15 g /½ oz fresh yeast
1 medium-sized egg, beaten
150 g /5 oz unsalted butter, beaten until soft
oil, for greasing
For the egg wash
1 small egg
2.5 ml /½ tsp caster sugar

For the pineapple turnovers
50 g /2 oz cottage cheese with pineapple
30 ml /2 tbls flaked almonds, coarsely chopped
30 ml /2 tbls apricot jam, sieved and dissolved in 10 ml /2 tsp boiling water
For the almond envelopes and stars
50 g /2 oz almond paste
icing sugar, for dredging
redcurrant jelly
For the spice pinwheels
15 g /½ oz butter, softened
15 g /½ oz caster sugar
2.5 ml /½ tsp ground mixed spice
25 g /1 oz currants
45 ml /3 tbls icing sugar, sifted
2 glacé cherries, quartered

1 Sift the flour and salt into a large, cool mixing bowl; stir in the sugar and rub in the fat. Blend the yeast with 75 ml /5 tbls cold water, combine with the beaten egg and pour onto the flour mixture.
2 Mix the ingredients thoroughly. Gather the dough together with your fingers, turn it out onto a lightly floured surface and knead it briefly until smooth. Place the dough in an oiled polythene bag and chill it in the refrigerator for 10 minutes.
3 Place the soft butter on a sheet of greaseproof paper. With a palette knife, spread the butter into a 23×7.5 cm /9×3 in rectangle. Chill until firm.
4 Roll out the chilled dough to a 25 cm /10 in square. Place the butter down the centre of the dough and peel off the greaseproof paper. Fold the sides of the dough over the butter so that they overlap. With the rolling pin, press the top and bottom edges to seal.
5 Roll out the dough to a 45×15 cm / 18×6 in rectangle. Fold the dough evenly in 3 to make a 15 cm /6 in square. Seal the open edges of the dough with the rolling pin. Place the dough in an oiled polythene bag and rest it in the refrigerator for 10 minutes.
6 Repeat the rolling out, folding and resting 3 times, rolling the dough in a different direction each time. Rest the dough for 10 minutes after the final rolling.
7 Make the egg wash by beating the egg together with the sugar and a few drops of water. Heat the oven to 220C /425F /gas 7.
8 Shape the pineapple turnovers. Roll a third of the dough out to a 30×15 cm /12×6 in rectangle. (Return the remaining two-thirds to the refrigerator.) Trim the edges with a sharp knife and cut the dough into 8×7.5 cm /3 in squares. Brush each square lightly with egg wash. Place 5 ml /1 tsp cottage cheese with pineapple in the centre of each square. Fold each square diagonally in half to make triangular-shaped turnovers; gently press the edges to seal. Brush the turnovers with egg wash and sprinkle them with chopped almonds.
9 Place the pastries on a large, lightly oiled baking sheet, cover loosely with a clean cloth and leave to prove at room temperature for about 10 minutes until they are puffy. Bake the pastries for 10 minutes. Transfer them to a wire rack and brush them with the warm apricot jam glaze. Leave them to cool.
10 While the pineapple turnovers prove, shape the almond envelopes and stars. Roll out another third of the dough to a rectangle as before and cut it into 8×7.5 cm / 3 in squares. Cut the almond paste into 8 equal sized pieces and flatten each. Brush each dough square with egg wash and place a circle of almond paste in the centre.
11 Shape 4 of the squares into envelopes: fold the corner of each square to the centre and press them gently together (see picture). Shape the remaining 4 squares into stars: make a diagonal cut from the tip of each corner to within 5 mm /¼ in of the almond paste; fold alternate points to centre (see picture). Press to seal.
12 Brush the envelopes and stars with egg wash and place them on an oiled baking sheet. Prove for 10 minutes and bake for 10 minutes. Transfer the baked pastries to a wire rack and dredge with sifted icing sugar. Place a dab of redcurrant jelly in the centre of each. Leave to cool.
13 While the almond envelopes and stars are proving, shape the spice pinwheels. Roll out the remaining dough to a 20×15 cm /8×6 in rectangle; trim the edges with a sharp knife. Beat together the butter, sugar and mixed spice and spread it evenly over the dough. Sprinkle with the currants.
14 Roll up the dough from one short end. Cut into 8 equal sized slices. Place the slices, cut side down, on an oiled baking sheet; flatten slightly and brush with egg wash. Prove for 10 minutes and bake for 10 minutes.
15 Transfer the baked pinwheels to a wire rack and leave to cool. Blend the icing sugar with a little cold water and drizzle the icing over the cold pinwheels. Place a piece of cherry in the centre of each. Leave to set.

Top left, Almond stars; top right, Pineapple turnovers; foreground, Spice pinwheels (topped with icing) and Almond squares

Making almond envelopes and stars

For envelopes: place almond paste on the dough squares; fold the corners to the centre.

For stars: cut from the corners of the square almost to the centre; fold alternately.

Cream buns, snails and spandauers

In this recipe I have given three different shapes for forming Danish pastries; cream buns, snails and spandauers. It is much more fun to make and eat the pastries if they vary in shape.

3¾ hours

Makes 32 pastries
300 ml /10 fl oz milk
500 g /1 lb butter, plus extra for greasing
40 g /1½ oz sugar
1 egg, beaten
1 egg yolk, beaten
a pinch of ground cardamom
40 g /1½ oz fresh yeast
500 g /1 lb strong flour, plus extra for
   rolling and kneading
a pinch of salt
For the vanilla butter
½ vanilla pod
85 g /3½ oz caster sugar
85 g /3½ oz butter
For the almond filling
225 g /8 oz ground almonds
225 g /8 oz caster sugar
1 egg
For the custard
150 ml /5 fl oz milk
30 ml /2 tbls sugar
1 egg yolk
20 ml /4 tsp cornflour
1 drop of vanilla essence
For the decorations
1 egg, beaten with 15 ml /1 tbls milk,
   to glaze
25 g /1 oz raisins
45 ml /3 tbls flaked almonds
75 ml /5 tbls chopped almonds
45 ml /3 tbls melted butter
135 ml /9 tbls vanilla-flavoured caster
   sugar (see page 9)
225 g /8 oz icing sugar
40 ml /8 tsp milk

1 Put the milk and 65 g /2½ oz butter in a saucepan and heat gently, stirring, until the butter has melted. Add the sugar and stir until it has dissolved. Remove from the heat and allow to cool to lukewarm.
2 Add the egg, egg yolk and ground cardamom. Crumble the fresh yeast over the egg mixture and stir it until the yeast is dissolved.
3 Sift the flour and salt into a large bowl and make a well in the centre. Add the milk and yeast mixture and mix together with your hand to make a dough.
4 Turn the dough onto a well floured surface and knead until smooth. Shape the dough into a cube, wrap it in cling film and allow it to rest in the refrigerator for 30 minutes. Pat the remaining butter into a slightly smaller cube.
5 Meanwhile, make the fillings. For the vanilla butter, scrape the seeds from the vanilla pod into a bowl and beat them with the sugar and butter until the mixture is smooth. Set aside.

6 For the almond filling, put the ground almonds, sugar and egg in a bowl, mix with a wooden spoon until smooth; set aside.
7 For the custard, put the milk and half the sugar in a saucepan and gently bring it to the boil. In a bowl, mix the remaining sugar with the egg yolk and cornflour to a smooth paste; gradually add the hot milk to this mixture and mix well. Strain it through a fine sieve into the top part of a double boiler. Place over simmering water and bring it back to the boil, stirring, and simmer for a few minutes until it has thickened. Stir in the vanilla essence and remove it from the heat. Set aside enough custard to decorate the spandauers when they are cooked and leave

this and the rest of the custard to cool.
8 Remove the dough from the refrigerator and, on a lightly floured board, roll and pull the dough into the shape of a four-leaf clover, just large enough so that when wrapped over it will completely contain the cube of butter.
9 Put the butter in the middle of the dough and bring the 'leaves' up to meet each other over the butter.
10 Roll out the dough to a rectangle about 20 mm /¾ in thick. Mark it lightly across into three. Fold the bottom third up and over the middle third and the top third down and over this. Wrap the dough in cling film and leave it to rest in the refrigerator for at least 10 minutes.

11 Roll out the dough again, as before, fold it in three and allow it to rest. Repeat the rolling and folding for the third time, leave it to rest for 10 minutes, then roll it out and fold it in three again. Cut it across into three with a floured knife.

12 Butter and flour 3 baking sheets.

13 Make the cream bun shapes; on a lightly floured board, roll out one portion of the dough to a 23 cm /9 in square. With a floured knife, cut this into nine 7.5 cm /3 in squares. Place 5 ml /1 tsp custard in the centre of each square. Bring the four corners into the centre of the square, overlapping the edges and sealing in the custard. Turn it over, seams underneath, and shape it into a round. Brush off the excess flour and place each pastry on a baking sheet.

14 Make the spandauer shapes; roll out a second portion of the dough to a 26 cm /10½ in square. Using a floured knife, cut it into nine 9 cm /3½ in squares. Take 125 g /4 oz of the vanilla butter and divide it into 9 portions. Roll each portion into a small ball and place it in the centre of a pastry square. Bring the four corners of the pastry into the centre, so that they just touch the vanilla butter, and press lightly with your finger to make a small indentation in the centre. Brush off the excess flour and place the spandauer on the second baking sheet.

15 Leave the cream buns and spandauer shapes to rise in a warm place while you make the snail shapes. Meanwhile, heat the oven to 200C /400F /gas 6.

16 Make the snail shapes; roll out the remaining portion of dough to a rectangle 35×23 cm /14×9 in. Roll out the almond filling to a rectangle just slightly smaller than the rectangle of dough and place it on top of the pastry. Spread the remaining vanilla butter over the almond filling and sprinkle the raisins on top.

17 Roll up the pastry from the long side, brushing off the excess flour as you go and, with a floured knife, cut it into slices 25 mm / 1 in thick, to make 14 pastries. Place them, cut side down, on the third baking sheet. Leave them to rise in a warm place.

18 Brush the tops of the risen spandauers with egg glaze and spoon 5 ml /1 tsp of the custard into the centre of each pastry, on top of the vanilla butter. Sprinkle the pastry with the flaked almonds.

19 Place the spandauers and cream buns in the oven and bake for 12 minutes, or until they are golden in colour and cooked through. Transfer them to a wire rack.

20 Brush the risen snails with the egg glaze and sprinkle them with the chopped almonds. Bake them in the oven for 10 minutes, then reduce the temperature to 180C /350F /gas 4 and cook for a further 5 minutes, or until the snails are golden. Transfer them to a wire rack.

21 While the cream buns are still hot, brush each one with melted butter and sprinkle the tops with vanilla sugar.

22 Make a glacé icing by blending together the icing sugar and milk; place the bowl over simmering water to heat gently.

23 When the snail shapes are cooked, transfer them to a wire rack. Spoon the rest of the icing into a greaseproof paper piping bag and pipe a spiral on the top of each snail, following the line of the pastry.

24 When the spandauers are cool, place a dab of the reserved custard in the centre of each one.

25 Leave all the pastries to cool before eating, but serve them fresh, the day that they are made.

● Currants, finely chopped mixed peel or sultanas can be used instead of raisins.

● For a ginger filling, cream together butter, caster sugar, and a little ground ginger. Add some finely chopped crystallized ginger, if wished.

● For a vanilla filling, cream together butter and sugar with a few drops of vanilla essence. Now add either sultanas or finely chopped, blanched almonds.

● Do not use too much filling in the pastries or it will run out during the baking and spoil them — usually 5 ml /1 tsp of filling per pastry is sufficient.

● Use 10 ml /2 tsp dried active baking yeast instead of each 15 g /½ oz fresh yeast.

● The uncooked dough can be stored in a freezer for up to six weeks.

● Though best eaten on the day they are made, most pastries will keep for 1–2 days in an airtight tin.

Danish pastries: (from left to right), Snails, Cream buns and Spandauers

Chocolate almond pie

Serves 6

20 cm /8 in half-baked pastry case, using 450 g /1 lb made-weight pastry,
(see note following Little chocolate boats, page 56, for ingredients, and
method steps 1–7)
50 g /2 oz blanched, toasted almonds, coarsely chopped
275 ml /10 fl oz milk
75 g /3 oz plain chocolate
2 eggs, separated
40 g /1½ oz caster sugar
grated zest of 1 orange
30 ml /2 tbls rum
15 g /½ oz gelatine
275 ml /10 fl oz thick cream
25 g /1 oz plain chocolate, grated

1   Cover the base of the pastry case with coarsely chopped almonds.
2   Pour the milk into a saucepan. Break in the chocolate and melt it over a low heat, whisking continuously.
3   Whisk the egg yolks with the sugar in the top pan of double boiler, off the heat, until they are pale and fluffy. Pour the chocolate milk onto the egg yolk mixture, stirring vigorously.
4   Put the pan onto the top of the double boiler over gently simmering water. Cook, stirring continuously, until the custard thickens enough to coat the back of a wooden spoon — about 10 minutes. Do not allow the mixture to come to the boil or the eggs will curdle. Remove from the heat.
5   Stir in the grated orange zest and the rum and stand the pan in a large bowl containing crushed ice to cool.
6   In a small bowl, sprinkle the gelatine over 45 ml /3 tbls water. Place the bowl in a saucepan of simmering water and stir until the gelatine has completely dissolved. Add the dissolved gelatine to the custard and stir constantly until it is on the point of setting. Remove from the ice.
7   Whisk the egg whites in a bowl until they are stiff but not dry. Now lightly whisk the thick cream.
8   With a metal spoon, fold half the lightly whipped cream gently into the custard. Next, fold in all the egg whites, taking care not to stir or let them lose their fluffiness. Pour the mixture into the pastry case and chill it for 30 minutes or until set.
9   Fill a piping bag, fitted with a 10 mm /½ in star nozzle, with the remaining whipped cream and pipe rosettes around the border. Sprinkle each rosette with a little grated chocolate.

 making pastry case,
then 40 minutes, plus setting

Banana tart

Serves 4–6

23 cm /9 in fluted pastry case,
fully baked blind, using 450 g /
1 lb made-weight pastry (see note
following Little chocolate boats,
page 56, for ingredients, and
method steps 1–7)

For the banana crème
pâtissière
2 egg yolks, beaten
60 ml /4 tbls icing sugar
5 ml /1 tsp cornflour

275 ml /10 fl oz milk
2 bananas
10 ml /2 tsp lemon juice
2.5 ml /½ tsp vanilla essence
grated zest of 1 orange
10 ml /2 tsp gelatine
150 ml /5 fl oz thick cream

For the syrup glaze
juice of 2 oranges
15 ml /1 tbls lemon juice
60 ml /4 tbls sugar
2 bananas, to decorate

1   To make the banana crème pâtissière, mix together the egg yolks, icing sugar and cornflour in the top pan of a double boiler. Gradually stir in the milk and cook over simmering water, stirring constantly with a wooden spoon, until the crème pâtissière is smooth and thick. Do not let it come to the boil or it will curdle. Remove it from the heat and leave it to cool slightly.
2   Peel and slice the bananas and purée them in a blender with a little of the crème pâtissière until smooth, or press them through a sieve into a bowl and beat in a little of the crème pâtissière until smooth. Pour the blended banana into the remainder of the crème, add the lemon juice, vanilla essence and grated orange zest, stirring with a wooden spoon.
3   In a small bowl, sprinkle the gelatine over 30 ml /2 tbls water. Stand the bowl in a saucepan of simmering water and stir until the gelatine is completely dissolved. Pour the gelatine into the banana crème pâtissière and stir to blend.
4   Set the bowl of banana crème pâtissière in a bowl of cracked ice and stir until it is on the point of setting. Whip the cream until soft peaks form, then fold it into the banana mixture. Pour the filling into the tart case and chill.
5   For the syrup glaze, combine the orange juice, lemon juice and sugar in a small saucepan. Stir over a gentle heat until the sugar has dissolved, then increase the heat and bring to the boil. Boil for 10 minutes until the mixture is thick and syrupy. Remove from the heat and leave it to cool slightly.
6   Peel and slice the bananas and arrange them in overlapping circles on top of the banana crème pâtissière filling. Quickly brush the syrup glaze over the top of the tart and transfer it to a flat plate.

 making the pastry case,
then 1½ hours including chilling

Raspberry mille-feuilles

Serves 6–8

*225 g /8 oz made-weight puff
  pastry*
For the crème pâtissière
*425 ml /15 fl oz milk
5 cm /2 in piece vanilla pod, split
5 egg yolks
100 g /4 oz caster sugar*

*30 ml /2 tbls flour, sifted
15 ml /1 tbls cornflour
15 g /½ oz butter*
For the garnish
*350 g /12 oz raspberries
120 ml /8 tbls raspberry jam
15 ml /1 tbls lemon juice*

1 Heat the oven to 220C /425F /gas 7. Roll out the pastry as thinly as possible to cover a 30×40 cm /12×16 in dampened baking sheet. With a fork, prick the pastry thoroughly. Chill for 10 minutes.
2 Cook the pastry in the oven for 7–10 minutes, until it is golden brown and risen. Trim the edges of the pastry and cut it into 3 equal strips lengthways. Turn each strip over carefully and return them to the oven for 2–3 minutes to allow the undersides to cook. Remove the pastry from the oven and transfer it to a wire rack to cool.
3 Scald the milk in a heavy-based saucepan with the split vanilla pod. Remove it from the heat, cover and leave to infuse until needed.
4 In a bowl, whisk the egg yolks with the sugar until light and thick. Gradually whisk in the flour and cornflour.
5 Remove the vanilla pod from the milk and pour the milk in a thin stream onto the egg yolk mixture, whisking until well blended.
6 Return the mixture to the pan and bring it to the boil over a moderate heat, stirring constantly. Simmer for 3 minutes, beating vigorously with the spoon to disperse any lumps in the mixture. Remove it from the heat and beat in the butter. Continue to beat for 1–2 minutes, then leave to cool.
7 To assemble the mille-feuilles, spread one strip of pastry evenly with half the crème pâtissière. Lay a second strip of pastry on top, pressing down very lightly. Spread it evenly with the remaining crème and carefully place the third strip of top. With a palette knife, scrape away any mixture which overhangs the edge.
8 To decorate, arrange the raspberries, hulled side down, over the top strip of pastry. Put the raspberry jam, lemon juice and 15 ml / 1 tbls water in a small saucepan and bring it to the boil. Sieve it and brush it over the raspberries to glaze and cover any gaps on the pastry. Serve on a long flat platter.

● For extra flavour, add 350 g /12 oz raspberries to the crème pâtissière before assembling the mille-feuilles

 1½ hours

American-style pumpkin pie

Serves 8

*400 g /14 oz canned pumpkin purée
3 eggs, beaten
30 ml /2 tbls melted butter
2.5 ml /½ tsp salt
75 g /3 oz soft brown sugar
2.5 ml /½ tsp ground cinnamon
2.5 ml /½ tsp ground ginger
2.5 ml /½ tsp ground nutmeg
1.5 ml /¼ ground cloves
1.5 ml /¼ powdered mace
600 ml /1 pt thick cream
23 cm /9 in pastry case, baked blind, using 450 g /1 lb made-weight
  pastry (see note following Little chocolate boats, page 56, for
  ingredients, and method steps 1–7)*

1 Heat the oven to 230C /450F /gas 8. Put the pumpkin purée in a mixing bowl and beat in the eggs, the melted butter, the salt, the soft brown sugar, the cinnamon, the ginger, the nutmeg, the cloves and the mace.
2 In a bowl, whisk 300 ml /10 fl oz of the thick cream until it forms soft peaks. Gently fold it into the pumpkin mixture with a large metal spoon. Pour the mixture into the baked pastry case and bake in the oven for 10 minutes.
3 Reduce the heat to 180C /350F /gas 4 and continue baking for about 30 minutes, or until the filling is firm. Take the pie from the oven and allow it to cool, then whisk the remaining cream and pipe it around the edge of the pie.

● If using fresh pumpkin, stew 1 kg /2 lb over a low heat until nearly all the liquid has evaporated.

 making the pastry case,
then 1 hour, plus cooling

Coffee chiffon flan

Serves 6

11.5 ml /2¼ tsp gelatine
300 ml /11 fl oz milk
3 eggs, separated
75 g /3 oz sugar
30 ml /2 tbls instant coffee
30 ml /2 tbls brandy
125 ml /4 fl oz thick cream, lightly whipped
23 cm /9 in pastry case, fully baked blind, using 450 g /1 lb made-weight pastry (see note following Little chocolate boats, page 56, for ingredients, and method steps 1–7)

For the chocolate caraque
125 g /4 oz plain chocolate

1   In a small bowl, sprinkle the gelatine over 45 ml /3 tbls cold water and leave it to soften. Meanwhile, bring the milk to simmering point.
2   In the top pan of a double boiler, whisk together the egg yolks, half the sugar and the instant coffee, until they are light and fluffy. Pour in the hot milk, whisking vigorously.
3   Place the pan over simmering water and stir with a wooden spoon for 10 minutes or until the custard coats the back of the spoon. Do not let the water boil or the eggs will curdle. Leave the custard to cool, stirring occasionally to prevent a skin forming.
4   Place the bowl of gelatine in a saucepan of simmering water until the gelatine is dissolved, then leave it to cool slightly.
5   Pour the dissolved gelatine in a thin stream into the coffee custard, stirring constantly. Set the bowl of coffee custard in a bowl of cracked ice and stir until the custard starts to thicken and set.
6   Stir in the brandy and, with a large metal spoon, fold in the whipped cream.
7   In a clean bowl, whisk the egg whites until stiff peaks form, then gradually whisk in the remaining sugar, until the mixture is stiff and glossy. Fold this into the gelatine mixture with a large metal spoon and pour it all into the prepared pastry case. Leave the flan in the refrigerator for about 1 hour or until it is set.
8   To make the chocolate caraque, melt the chocolate in a bowl set over a pan of gently simmering water. Pour it onto a cold, hard surface and allow it to set. Using a sharp knife, scrape the chocolate into curls and place them on top of the flan, then serve.

making the pastry case and chocolate caraque,
then about 2 hours

Almond tarts

Serves 6

6 × 10 cm /4 in fluted shortcrust pastry cases, half-baked, using 450 g /1 lb made-weight pastry (see note following Little chocolate boats, page 56, for ingredients, and method steps 1–7), pastry trimmings reserved
1 egg white
60 ml /4 tbls raspberry jam
flour, for dusting

For the almond filling
2 eggs
75 ml /5 tbls caster sugar
90 ml /6 tbls thick cream
100 g /4 oz ground almonds
juice and grated zest of 1 large lemon
1–2 drops almond essence

1   Heat the oven to 170C /325F /gas 3.
2   Place the half-baked tart cases on a baking tray. Brush the bases and sides with egg white, which will stop the pastry becoming soggy when you put in your filling, and spread 10 ml /2 tsp raspberry jam over the base of each case.
3   On a lightly floured board, roll out the reserved scraps of pastry very thinly and cut it into 5 mm /¼ in lengths.
4   Prepare the almond filling. In a bowl, whisk together the eggs and caster sugar until they are thick and creamy. Add the thick cream, ground almonds, lemon juice and zest and the almond essence. Beat them all vigorously with a wooden spoon until smoothly blended.
5   Pour the mixture into the prepared pastry cases. Arrange strips of pastry on top of each almond-filled tart case to make a cross. Trim the ends neatly.
6   Cook the tarts in the oven for 30 minutes, or until golden and firm to the touch. Remove them from the oven and leave them to get cold on a wire rack.
7   To serve, arrange the almond tarts on a doily-covered plate.

preparing the pastry cases,
then 45 minutes, plus cooling

French raisin flan

For the pastry
175 g /6 oz flour
5 ml /1 tsp icing sugar
1.5 ml /¼ tsp salt
75 g /3 oz butter, chilled
1 medium-sized egg yolk
5 ml /1 tsp lemon juice
about 20 ml /4 tsp iced water

For the filling
30 ml /2 tbls flour
30 ml /2 tbls cornflour
45 ml /3 tbls caster sugar
2 medium-sized eggs, separated
225 ml /8 fl oz milk
45 ml /3 tbls rum
50 g /2 oz raisins

1 Soak the raisins in the rum for at least 2 hours. Drain and reserve the rum.
2 To make the pastry, sift the flour, icing sugar and salt into a large bowl. Cut the cold butter into 5 mm /¼ in dice and add to the bowl. Using a pastry blender or 2 knives, one in each hand, cut the diced butter into the flour mixture until it resembles coarse breadcrumbs. Now rub the crumbs of fat between your fingertips until the mixture is reduced to fine breadcrumbs.
3 Beat the egg yolk in a small bowl. Add the lemon juice and 10 ml / 2 tsp iced water, and beat lightly until well mixed. Sprinkle this over the flour mixture, tossing and mixing with a fork. Rinse out the bowl with another 10 ml /2 tsp iced water and mix this into the pastry in the same way. Continue tossing and mixing with the fork until about three-quarters of the pastry is holding together. Now use your hand, cupped, to press the pastry into one piece. Shape the pastry into a round. Wrap it in a sheet of greaseproof paper, then a dampened tea-towel, and chill for 1 hour.
4 Heat the oven to 190C /375F /gas 5. Roll out the pastry and use it to line 20 cm /8 in greased flan tin with a removable base. Bake blind, filled with foil and beans, for 10 minutes. Remove the foil and beans and bake for a further 5 minutes. Leave the pastry in the tin to cool.
5 To make the filling, mix together the flour, cornflour and sugar in the top pan of a double boiler. Beat the egg yolks and stir them in. Heat the milk to just below boiling point and pour it onto the egg yolk mixture, stirring constantly.
6 Put the pan onto the bottom half of the double boiler filled with simmering water and cook, stirring frequently, for about 10 minutes until thickened. The water in the double boiler must not touch the top pan. Add the rum.
7 Whisk the egg whites until they form soft peaks and fold them into the egg mixture. Pour the mixture into the pastry case and distribute the raisins on top. Bake in the oven for 20 minutes.

 2 hours 20 minutes

Pear and ginger galette

Serves 6
225 g /8 oz flour, plus extra for dusting
a pinch of salt
175 g /6 oz butter, softened
100 g /4 oz icing sugar
2 egg yolks
2–3 drops vanilla essence
1.1 kg /2½ lb firm pears

the juice of ½ a lemon
2 pieces of preserved stem ginger, drained and thinly sliced
15 ml /1 tbls preserved ginger syrup
For the icing
100 g /4 oz icing sugar
1–2 drops vanilla essence
30 ml /2 tbls redcurrant jelly, sieved

1 Make the pastry: sift the flour and salt onto a clean working surface. Make a well in the centre and add the softened butter. Sift the icing sugar over the butter and place the egg yolks on top, with a few drops of vanilla essence. Work it to a smooth paste with your fingertips, gradually incorporating the flour, then work it to a smooth dough. Wrap in cling film and chill for 1 hour.
2 Meanwhile, make the filling. Peel, quarter, core and thickly slice the pears. Put them into a heavy-based saucepan. Add the lemon juice and 15 ml /1 tbls water. Cover and cook them gently for 10 minutes, or until the pears are tender but not mushy, shaking the pan constantly. Remove from the heat and leave to cool completely.
3 Heat the oven to 190C /375F /gas 5.
4 Divide the chilled pastry into 3. On a floured board, roll out each piece to a 20 cm /8 in circle. Lift the circles onto 2 baking sheets. Prick the pastry with a fork and bake for 10–12 minutes, or until it is a pale golden colour, then remove from the oven and leave to cool.
5 Slide 1 cold circle of pastry onto a serving platter. Cover with half the cooked pears. Scatter with half the ginger slices and syrup. Carefully place the second pastry circle on top and cover with the remaining pears, ginger and syrup. Place the third circle on top.
6 For the icing, sift the icing sugar into the top pan of a double boiler and gradually stir in 15–30 ml /1–2 tbls water until the icing is thick enough to coat the back of a wooden spoon. Flavour with vanilla essence. Heat the icing gently over simmering water. Pour the icing over the top pastry circle and smooth the surface with a palette knife.
8 Put the sieved redcurrant jelly into a greaseproof paper piping bag and pipe five straight lines of redcurrant jelly over the icing. Draw a skewer across the lines to make a feathered effect. Serve within 1 hour.

 2 hours, plus cooling

Old English treacle tart

Serves 6
425 ml /15 fl oz golden syrup
50 g /2 oz fresh breadcrumbs
2.5 ml /½ tsp powdered ginger
the grated zest and juice of ½ a lemon
the grated zest and juice of ½ an orange
30 ml /2 tbls soft brown sugar
30 ml /2 tbls thick cream
1 apple, peeled, cored and grated
5 ml /1 tsp butter
20 cm /8 in pastry case, half-baked (for ingredients and method see
*   French raisin flan, page 83), excess pastry reserved for lattice*
1 egg yolk, beaten

1 Heat the oven to 180C /350F /gas 4.
2 In a saucepan, melt the syrup and stir in the breadcrumbs, the powdered ginger, the grated zest and juice of the lemon and orange, the soft brown sugar, the thick cream, the grated apple and the butter. Blend them well and pour the mixture into the half-baked pastry case.
3 Roll out the remaining pastry to an oval 20 cm /8 in long and cut it into strips about 10 mm /½ in wide. Arrange these on top of the tart, weaving them under and over each other to make a lattice over the filling (see Pastry case skills, page 54). Brush this lattice with the beaten egg yolk. Bake the tart in the oven for 20–25 minutes or until the pastry is golden brown. Allow the tart to cool before serving.

Apple jalousie

Serves 6
400 g /14 oz made-weight puff pastry
flour, for dusting
225 g /8 oz sweet mincemeat
1 large cooking apple
1 egg, beaten
15 ml /1 tbls icing sugar, sifted

1 Heat the oven to 230C /450F /gas 8. Place a baking tray on a shelf in the oven to heat it through. The jalousie is placed on this so that the bottom cooks as well as the top.
2 Cut the puff pastry in half. Roll it out into 2 oblong strips about 30 × 15 cm /12 × 6 in and 5–10 mm /¼–½ in thick. Lightly dust another baking sheet with flour and place one oblong of pastry on it. Spread this pastry with mincemeat, leaving a good 25 mm /1 in of pastry visible around the edge.
3 Peel, core and thinly slice the apple and arrange this on top of the mincemeat in overlapping rows. Trim any uneven edges of the pastry to give a neat rectangle and brush with the beaten egg.
4 Fold the second piece of pastry in half lengthways and with a sharp knife cut slits into the fold, about 5 mm /¼ in apart and to 25 mm /1 in from the edges, making sure that the cuts go right through to the second side. Open out the pastry and place it carefully on top of the filling.
5 Seal the edges of the jalousie. To flute the edges, place a thumb on the rim of the pastry and, holding a floured knife downwards, draw the knife back against the pastry edge, towards the centre of the jalousie. Use a quick short stroke to make a slanting kink. Repeat at intervals of 5 mm /¼ in around the edge of the pastry.
6 Brush the pastry with the rest of the beaten egg, place the jalousie on the heated baking tray and bake in the oven for 10 minutes. Reduce the heat to 190C /375F /gas 5 and cook for a further 10 minutes. Remove the jalousie from the oven, sprinkle it with a little of the sifted icing sugar and cook it for a further 5–10 minutes, or until the glaze is golden and the pastry crisp. Just before serving, sprinkle it with the remainder of the icing sugar.

● This tea-time treat can also be served hot, with whipped cream.

 making the pastry case,
then 45 minutes

 1 hour

Everyday Baking

A COFFEE MORNING SPREAD

From gorgeous creamy cakes, which are light and enticing, to crisp, golden, cream-filled brandy snaps, you can offer your coffee morning guests some of these delicious treats when they come to visit.

A coffee morning is a relaxed way either of entertaining your friends or raising money for your favourite charity. Why not try it.

Many of the items in this section can be conveniently made in advance and just finished on the morning. Choose a selection from the recipes I have included — remember that most people will sample everything that you have provided, and most guests will manage without lunch on that day. Apart from these cakes and biscuits you could include gateaux (see page 8), croissants (see page 73) or even Danish pastries (see page 76).

Coffee hedgehogs (see recipe) are novelty cakes which will amuse your guests, and the Brandy snaps are a delicious biscuit which can be filled with a mixture of cream and fruit — or just cream, depending on what you prefer.

Coffee is traditionally served on these occasions, although there is no reason why you should not serve tea if you prefer, or even a glass of wine.

Potize

🍴🍴 2¾ hours,
plus cooling

Makes 14–16 slices
150 ml /5 fl oz milk, warmed to 25C /80F
25 g /1 oz caster sugar
15 g /½ oz fresh yeast
250 g /9 oz strong flour
5 ml /1 tsp salt
50 g /2 oz butter
2 medium-sized eggs
1 medium-sized egg yolk
oil, for greasing
butter and flour, for the tin
icing sugar, for dredging
For the filling
125 g /4 oz sugar
50 g /2 oz sultanas
50 g /2 oz pine nuts
5 ml /1 tsp ground cinnamon

1   To make the filling, combine the sugar, sultanas, pine nuts and cinnamon in a bowl and set aside.
2   For the cake, place the warmed milk in a bowl, add 5 ml /1 tsp of the sugar and crumble in the yeast. Stir until the yeast has dissolved. Sift in 50 g /2 oz flour and mix to a paste.
3   Cover the paste and set it aside in a warm place to rise and double in size — it will take about 10 minutes.
4   Meanwhile, sift the rest of the flour and the salt together 2 or 3 times.
5   Beat the butter and remaining sugar until

pale and fluffy. Or, if you have one, use an electric mixer and beat with the dough hook. Add 1 egg and egg yolk and continue beating until they are combined.
6   Add the flour and the yeast mixture together, a little at a time, and mix well until combined.
7   Knead the dough by hand until it comes away from the sides of the bowl and is very soft and smooth.
8   Put the dough in a large, oiled polythene

bag, tie lightly and leave in a warm place (a maximum temperature of 25C /80F) to rise until it has doubled in bulk — this should take about 1 hour.
9   Heat the oven to 200C /400F /gas 6 and then grease and flour a deep 24–26 cm /9½–10½ in cake tin.
10   You will need a surface about 1.2 m /4 ft long for the rolling out. Lay a clean tea-towel along it. Dust it, and the surface at either end, with flour.
11   Untie the bag and shape the dough into a long sausage. Turn it out of the bag and lay it down the centre of the cloth.
12   Using a rolling pin, working very lightly and starting in the middle, roll the

At the back, German apple cake (page 90); in front, Hazelnut tartlets and Iced biscuits

dough towards one end of the cloth. Return to the centre and roll towards the other end. Keep the surface well-floured to prevent sticking and try to prevent the dough spreading sidewards. Roll it to a rectangle which is about 1 m /3 ft 6 in long about 10 cm /4 in wide and 5 mm /¼ in thick.

13 Spread the filling over the pastry, working to within 15 mm /½ in of the edges.

14 Using the cloth to support and roll the dough, roll up the pastry into a long thin roll from the longest edge.

15 Still using the towel as support, lift up the pastry and coil it gently round inside the prepared tin, starting in the middle and working towards the sides. Take care not to crush the dough as it needs room to rise.

16 Cover and leave it to rise in a warm place for a further 20 minutes or until puffy.

17 Lightly beat the remaining egg and

brush the risen dough with it. Now bake it in the oven for 20 minutes. Remove it from the tin and cool it on a wire rack.

18 Place it on a serving plate and dredge with icing sugar. To serve cut into slices.

Iced biscuits

Make these vanilla-flavoured biscuits well ahead. They will keep fresh for several weeks in an airtight container.

 1¼ hours

Makes 40 biscuits
125 g /4½ oz flour
a pinch of salt
100 g /4 oz butter, diced
40 g /1½ oz icing sugar
1 drop of vanilla essence
1 medium-sized egg yolk
butter, for greasing
flour, for dusting
For the icing
200 g /7 oz icing sugar, plus more if necessary
4 drops of vanilla essence

1 Sift the flour and salt together two or three times into a large mixing bowl. Cut in the diced butter, then rub it in with your fingertips until the mixture resembles fine breadcrumbs.

2 Sift the icing sugar into the mixture and add the vanilla essence and the egg yolk. Work the mixture with your hand to a dough. Knead until the dough is smooth. Wrap it in cling film and refrigerate it for 30 minutes.

3 Heat the oven to 200C /400F /gas 6 and lightly grease 2 baking sheets.

4 On a lightly floured surface roll out the pastry until it is 3 mm /⅛ in thick and cut out 40 circles using a 5 cm /2 in crimped cutter lightly dusted with flour.

5 With a smaller cutter 10 mm /⅓ in across, cut a hole from the middle of each circle. Space the biscuits well apart on the prepared baking sheets. Set them on one side until you have made the icing.

6 Make the icing. Sift the icing sugar into a small heatproof bowl, which fits over a pan of simmering water, or into the top pan of a double boiler. Add 30–45 ml /2–3 tbls of very hot water, a little at a time, stirring with a wooden spoon, until the icing coats the back of the spoon and is smooth, thick and creamy in texture. If it is too thin, add more icing sugar; if it is too thick, add more water. Add the vanilla essence and mix well. Put the bowl over the simmering water, but do not let it touch the surface of the water. Warm the icing until it runs. Remove the pan from the heat but leave the bowl in place over it.

7 Bake the biscuits for 10–12 minutes until they are golden and slightly soft to the touch. Immediately transfer the biscuits with a palette knife to a wire rack. While they are still warm, dip each biscuit face down in the glacé icing, then arrange them on the rack to cool completely.

8 When the icing has set, pack the biscuits in airtight containers. They will keep for several weeks.

Hazelnut tartlets

These tartlets are shaped on the back of your tartlet moulds; this is quicker than baking blind, but serves the same purpose.

 35 minutes, plus cooling

Makes 24 tartlets
100 g /4 oz butter, diced, plus extra for greasing
150 g /5 oz flour, plus extra for flouring
75 g /3 oz caster sugar
75 g /3 oz ground hazelnuts
100 g /4 oz apricot jam
700 g /1½ lb fresh soft fruit (raspberries, strawberries or redcurrants), hulled
whipped cream, for serving

1 Heat the oven to 170C /325F /gas 3 and lightly grease the undersides of 24 tartlet moulds with a little butter.

2 Sift the flour into a mixing bowl. Rub in the butter with your fingertips, until the mixture resembles fine breadcrumbs. Add the sugar and hazelnuts and work them into the mixture. Press the pastry into a ball shape.

3 Roll it out on a lightly floured surface until it is about 3 mm /⅛ in thick. Flour an 8 cm /3½ in cutter and cut out 24 circles. Lay each one over the back of a tartlet mould and press gently to the shape.

4 Bake like this for 10–15 minutes, until lightly coloured but still soft: they crisp as they cool. Remove them from the oven. After a few minutes, lift the pastry shapes off the moulds onto a wire rack, to finish cooling. At this stage they can be stored for 2–3 weeks in an airtight tin.

5 Just before serving, heat the apricot jam in a small saucepan and sieve it. Brush the base of each tart with the apricot jam and then fill with the prepared fruit. Pipe rosettes of cream onto the filled tarts.

Coffee hedgehogs

30 minutes

Serves 8
8 small sponge cakes
125 ml /4 fl oz brandy or rum
100 g /4 oz unsalted butter
30 ml /2 tbls icing sugar
2 medium-sized egg yolks
30 ml /2 tbls strong black coffee
50 g /2 oz toasted almond slivers

1 Place the sponge cakes on a serving dish, sprinkle them with the brandy or rum and put them in the refrigerator.

2 Meanwhile, beat the butter in a mixing bowl until it is soft and light. Add the icing sugar and continue beating until the mixture is light and fluffy, then beat in the egg yolks, one by one. Gradually beat in the black coffee, drop by drop.

3 Put a little of the mixture on top of each sponge cake and coat the sides with the rest. Stick in the toasted almond slivers like hedgehog's prickles.

Brandy snaps

Rose cakes

These fried pastry cakes need to be cooked individually and served warm, so you may need an extra pair of hands in the kitchen if you are greeting guests.

 50 minutes

Makes about 12
150 g /5 oz flour
a pinch of salt
45 g /1½ oz vanilla icing sugar (see page 9)
2 medium-sized egg yolks
10 ml /2 tsp thick cream
10 ml /2 tsp rum or brandy
40 g /1½ oz butter, diced small
a little egg white, beaten
vegetable oil, for frying
red jam (redcurrant, strawberry or raspberry)

1 Sift together the flour, salt and 25 g /1 oz icing sugar, then sift them again onto a pastry board. Make a well in the centre, drop in the egg yolks, add the cream, the rum or brandy and the butter. Pull the flour into the centre, gradually working it with your fingertips until a stiff paste is formed. Cover the dough with a cloth and leave for at least 20 minutes.
2 Have ready 3 round pastry cutters graduated in size. Roll out the pastry 1.5 mm /¹⁄₁₆ in thick and cut out equal numbers of rounds in each size.
3 Select one round of each size and moisten the centre of each one with egg white. Pile

them up, largest at the bottom, smallest at the top. Push firmly in the centre of each 'rose' with a fingertip to make a small hollow. Make a few incisions with a knife around each circle of dough to mark the 'petals'.
4 Put oil in a small pan to a depth of 4 cm /1½ in and heat to 180C /350F, or until a small cube of bread turns golden in 60 seconds. Carefully put in the roses one at a time, petal sides downwards. Turn them over carefully when one side has browned and fry them on the other side. Drain the roses on absorbent paper and keep them warm, while you cook the rest of the batch.
5 Dust the roses with the rest of the vanilla sugar. Place a small dot of jam in the centre of each rose and serve them warm.

Brandy snaps

Brandy snaps can be made ahead and stored in an airtight tin.

 45 minutes

Makes 14–18 large brandy snaps
100 g /4 oz butter, plus extra for greasing
100 g /4 oz caster sugar
100 g /4 oz flour
60 ml /4 tbls golden syrup
10 ml /2 tsp brandy
2.5 ml /½ tsp ground ginger
250 ml /9 fl oz thick cream

1 Heat the oven to 180C /350F /gas 4 and grease two baking sheets. Put all the ingredients except the cream into a mixing bowl

and mix them together to a smooth paste.
2 Divide the mixture into 25 g /1 oz pieces and lightly roll them into balls. Place 3 balls on each baking sheet, well spaced apart. Flatten them a little.
3 Bake one sheet for about 5 minutes, until the mixture is golden brown. Remove the baking sheet from the oven and put in the second sheet.
4 Let the biscuits on the first sheet cool slightly until you can touch them. With a metal spatula, very carefully ease up the edge of one biscuit and gently wrap it around the handle of a wooden spoon. Although it is quite delicate, the biscuit is pliable at this stage and you should be able to roll it to make a secure cylinder. It will set and become crisp quite quickly. Gently ease the roll off the handle and continue with the remaining biscuits. Cool on a wire tray.
5 Remove the second sheet from the oven and repeat the rolling process. Continue to bake 3 balls at a time, rolling the cooked biscuits while the next batch is cooking. If they go hard before you have rolled them, put the baking sheet back in the oven for a few seconds to soften the biscuits.
6 Store the rolled brandy snaps in an airtight tin until they are required.
7 Whip the cream and put it into a piping bag with a small nozzle. Just before serving, pipe a small whirl of whipped cream into one end of each brandy snap. Arrange the brandy snaps carefully on a serving dish. To keep the texture of the snaps crisp, they should only be filled at the last minute before serving. The cream softens the biscuits if it is put into them too long beforehand.

Kirsch cream cake

Kirsch cream cake

🍴 1½ hours, plus chilling
and cooling

Serves 8
butter and flour, for the cake tins
150 ml /5 fl oz milk
25 g /1 oz butter
2 eggs
225 g /8 oz caster sugar
1.5 ml /¼ tsp vanilla essence
150 g /5 oz flour
5 ml /1 tsp baking powder
1.5 ml /¼ tsp salt
For the kirsch cream
425 ml /15 fl oz milk
4 egg yolks
90 ml /6 tbls caster sugar
45 ml /3 tbls cornflour
30 ml /2 tbls kirsch
For the chocolate topping
75 g /3 oz plain chocolate, broken
25 g /1 oz butter
10 ml /2 tsp instant coffee granules

1 Heat the oven to 180C /350F /gas 4. Grease two 20 cm /8 in deep, round cake tins and line the bottoms with discs of buttered greaseproof paper. Lightly flour the tins.
2 In a saucepan, bring milk to simmer; then whisk in the butter. Cover and keep warm.
3 In a large bowl, whisk the eggs. Gradually add the sugar and whisk until light and lemon coloured. Add the vanilla essence. Sift the flour, baking powder and salt over the egg mixture and, with a large metal spoon, fold them in until well blended. Add the milk to the cake batter and continue to fold in until smooth. Pour the batter into the prepared tins and bake for 25–30 minutes, or until they are well risen and golden. Remove them from the oven and allow them to cool for a few minutes before turning out onto wire racks. Remove the greaseproof discs.
4 To make the kirsch cream, bring the milk to the boil in a saucepan. In a bowl, whisk the egg yolks and the sugar until they are thick and light. Whisk in the cornflour. Gradually pour the boiling milk into the egg yolk mixture, beating with a whisk until it is all well blended. Pour the liquid back into the pan and bring to the boil over a moderate heat, stirring constantly. Simmer for 3 minutes, beating vigorously with a wooden spoon to disperse any lumps. Remove the pan from the heat and allow the mixture to cool a little before stirring in the kirsch. Cover the surface with greaseproof paper, cool and chill.
5 To make the topping, put the chocolate in a bowl over simmering water and add the butter. Dissolve the coffee in 10 ml /2 tsp water, then add it to the chocolate. Stir the chocolate frequently until it has melted and is smooth and glossy. Allow to cool slightly.
6 Assemble the cake by placing one layer on a serving platter. Stir the kirsch cream until it is smooth, and pile it onto the layer using a palette knife. Place the remaining cake layer on top. Pour the chocolate topping over the top of the cake and, using a palette knife, smooth the chocolate out to the sides.

● In the United States this recipe is known as Boston cream pie — although not a pie at all! It is usually eaten as a dessert rather than a cake, by the Bostonians.

Walnut gateau

The Viennese, it was said, argued as to which was the better cake — *Nusscremetorte* or *Alpenbuttertorte* (nut-cream gateau or butter gateau) — until an inspiration led to the best of both worlds, the basic walnut cake with an *Alpenbuttertorte* filling.

2½ hours, plus overnight cooling

Makes 12 slices
butter and ground walnuts, for the cake tin
40 g /1½ oz fine breadcrumbs
30 ml /2 tbls dark rum
6 eggs, separated
150 g /5 oz icing sugar, sifted
150 g /5 oz ground walnuts
For the butter filling
3 egg yolks
5 ml /1 tsp flour
150 ml /5 fl oz thick cream
150 g /5 oz unsalted butter
100 g /4 oz icing sugar
15 g /½ oz vanilla icing sugar (see page 9)
For the icing and garnish
75 g /3 oz redcurrant jelly
200 g /7 oz icing sugar
lemon juice or white rum
12 walnut halves

1 Heat the oven to 180C /350F /gas 4. Butter a 23 cm /9 in round cake tin and dust it with ground walnuts. Mix the fine breadcrumbs with the dark rum and leave them to soften. Whisk the egg yolks with the icing sugar until they are thick and creamy, then beat in the breadcrumbs and the ground walnuts.
2 Whisk the egg whites in a large bowl until they are stiff but not dry, then fold in the egg yolk mixture. Turn the mixture into the cake tin and bake in the oven for 45–50 minutes, until the cake shrinks away from the side of the tin.
3 Allow the walnut cake to cool in the tin for 5 minutes before turning it out onto a wire rack. Leave it overnight to cool completely.
4 For the filling, whisk the egg yolks, flour and cream in the top of a double boiler over just simmering water (make sure that the water does not touch the top pan) until the mixture is thick. Remove the top pan from the heat and continue whisking until the mixture is cool. Beat the butter with the icing sugar and the vanilla icing sugar until it is very fluffy, then beat in the egg mixture by teaspoonfuls so that the consistency is like thick mayonnaise.
5 Slice the cake horizontally into 2 or 3 layers. Spread the filling between the layers.
6 Gently warm the redcurrant jelly until it is liquid, then spread it over the top and sides of the cake. Allow the jelly an hour to dry before icing.
7 For the icing, beat the icing sugar with enough lemon juice or white rum to make a stiff paste and spread this over the sides and top of the cake with a palette knife. When the icing is beginning to harden, decorate the cake with walnut halves by pressing them lightly around the top outer edge.

Guglhupf

There are many different spellings for this cake — Gougelhof, Gougelhopf, Kugelhupf or Suglhupf. Guglhupf is the Austrian spelling for what is acknowledged to be their creation. It is said that the original recipe was given to the master chef Carême by the chef to Prince Schwartzenberg, the Austrian Ambassador to France, in the early nineteenth century.

about 2 hours, including rising

Makes 12 slices
100 g /4 oz butter, plus extra for greasing
15 g /½ oz fresh yeast
30 ml /2 tbls sugar
100 ml /3½ fl oz milk
250 g /9 oz flour, sifted, plus extra for dusting
65 g /2½ oz almonds, blanched and slivered
3 eggs, lightly beaten
65 g /2½ oz raisins
zest of 1 lemon, grated
5 ml /1 tsp vanilla icing sugar (see page 9)

1 Heat the oven to 220C /425F /gas 7. Melt the butter in a bowl, which should be standing in a little hot water. Cream the fresh yeast with 5 ml /1 tsp of the sugar in a small bowl. Heat the milk in a small saucepan over a low heat until it is just tepid, then pour it onto the yeast and mix well.
2 Sift the flour into a warmed bowl, make a well in the centre and pour in the yeast mixture. Sprinkle a little of the flour on top of the yeast, cover the bowl with a cloth and leave it in a warm place.
3 Brush a 900 ml /1 pt 12 fl oz Guglhupf mould with a little melted butter, dust with flour and sprinkle it evenly with the almond slivers. When the yeast begins to bubble, start mixing in the flour from the sides of the bowl. Add the rest of the sugar and the eggs. Beat the mixture well to make a smooth batter, gradually adding the melted butter. Stir in the raisins and lemon zest.
4 Pour the mixture into the Guglhupf tin (it should be about two-thirds full), cover it with a cloth and stand it in a warm place away from draughts to rise.
5 When the mixture has risen to within 15 mm /½ in of the top of the mould, place it in the oven and turn down the heat to 180C /350F /gas 4.
6 Continue baking for up to 40 minutes. Test the cake by pressing the top with your fingertips (it should feel firm) before removing it from the oven. If the top browns too quickly, cover it with buttered greaseproof paper or open the door of the oven slightly during the last few minutes of the baking time.
7 Allow the cake to cool for 5 minutes before carefully removing it from the mould. Dust it with the vanilla sugar while it is still warm and serve.

● Guglhupf moulds have a narrow funnel which is very similar to an Angel cake tin but the sides may be fluted in a traditional design. Buy them in any good hardware or department store.

German apple cake

It may be more convenient for your guests to have this delicious deep apple tart already decorated with cream, rather than to pass around a bowl of cream separately.

1 hour 20 minutes, plus cooling

Makes 10–20 slices
1 kg /2¼ lb apples
a few drops lemon juice
150 g /5 oz self-raising flour
150 g /5 oz butter, cut into 5 mm /¼ in dice, plus extra for greasing
75 g /2½ oz sugar
1 small egg, lightly beaten
caster sugar, for dredging
ground cinnamon, for dredging
whipped, sweetened cream, to decorate or serve

1 Peel, core and evenly slice the apples. Place them in a bowl of cold water acidulated with the lemon juice to prevent them from discolouring.
2 Sift the self-raising flour into a large bowl. Cut the diced butter into the flour with a knife; now lightly rub the mixture between your finger tips until it resembles fine breadcrumbs.
3 Mix in the sugar; then with a spatula, blend in the egg. Pull the pastry together by hand and work to make it a smooth, soft dough. Press it gently into a ball. Use it immediately or wrap it in cling film and chill in the refrigerator.
4 Heat the oven to 190C /375F /gas 5.
5 Lightly grease a 24 cm /9½ in loose-bottomed deep flan tin. Roll out the pastry. Press it lightly and evenly into the flan tin with your fingertips, from the centre outwards and up the sides.
6 Drain the apple slices and pat them dry with absorbent paper. Arrange a layer of slightly overlapping slices on top of the pastry in a regular pattern. Dredge it with caster sugar and cinnamon. Next, arrange further layers, dredging each layer with the sugar and cinnamon.
7 Place the cake in the centre of the oven and bake for about 50 minutes or until the pastry begins to shrink away from the sides of the tin, and the fruit starts to colour. Lift the tin out of the oven and put it on a wire rack to cool. Do not remove the cake from the tin until it is cold. If you wish to store the tart, cover it with cling film while still in the tin and it will keep for 3–4 days in a cool place.
8 When ready to serve the apple cake, remove it from the tin to a serving plate. Dredge generously with caster sugar. Decorate the top with whipped, sweetened cream or pass a bowl of cream separately to serve.

● Other orchard fruit can be used instead of apples. Stone and quarter them, then pack them, skin side down, so close together that they overlap.

Clockwise from left: Coffee hedgehogs (page 87), Walnut gateau, Rose cakes (page 88) and Guglhupf

TEA-TIME TREATS

For an enthusiastic cook, tea time provides a chance to display skill and imagination, and to offer a wide variety of mouthwatering temptations to family and guests alike.

Even after a big Sunday lunch, people start to feel peckish as the afternoon draws on. A good cup of tea and a bite or two to accompany it, are always welcomed. How much you provide depends on how hungry you think your guests — or family — are going to be.

In this section I have included a variety of recipes ranging from muffins and crumpets, to scones, biscuits and a beautiful American pineapple fruit cake, which has glacé pineapple, dates, raisins, Brazil nuts and walnuts in the ingredients.

For summer teas, try small sandwiches with fillings ranging from cheese and pickle, cheese and tomato, cheese and pineapple, egg mayonnaise, tuna and cucumber, meat or fish pastes, ham and lettuce or, as a really luxury filling, smoked salmon. Sweet fillings can include jam, sliced, fresh eating apple and syrup or banana. For winter teas try your hand at making a batch of Crumpets, Pikelets or Muffins. Served with lashings of butter these are a warming and filling start to any afternoon tea.

Another suggestion for tea, which is traditional, is cinnamon toast; toast slices of white bread, cut off the crusts and butter them while they are warm, then sprinkle the slices with a mixture of equal quantities of caster sugar and ground cinnamon. Place the slices in a warm oven for a few minutes, cut them into fingers and serve at once.

Scones are a real favourite whether served with cream, clotted or whipped, or jam, home-made for preference, or just with butter. The savoury Caerphilly scones (see recipe) make a change for those who do not have such a sweet tooth, and these can be served with a variety of cheeses and sticks of crisp celery.

Try some of my unusual recipes for biscuits — Allspice biscuits and Muesli fingers. These have the added advantage that they can be kept in an airtight tin for sometime, thus easing the pressure on the cook at the last minute. Cheesecake biscuits are another unusual but delicious recipe well worth trying. Bakewell slices, with their almond and jam flavour, are always a popular treat.

Most people seem to find room for a slice of cake too. I have given you recipes for an Orange and hazelnut cake, a Ginger fruit cake and a Dried apple cake. You can, of course, make an All-in-one sponge in different flavours (see page 106) or a fruit cake, or even a Lardy cake (see page 104).

In fact, you don't have to offer all these goodies at one time. If the children in the family are going to be into tea, then a selection of substantial 'fillers' will be the order of the day. If, however, the appetites are likely to be less voracious, then you can choose a mixture of recipes to fill a small gap and just tide you over until it is time for the next meal.

Many of these tea-time treats are a bonus to the cook since they can be prepared ahead, then kept in the refrigerator, an airtight container or even the freezer until they are needed. In fact the American pineapple fruit cake needs to be kept for a couple of weeks after it has been made — and it is 'fed' a couple of times with brandy to help the maturing process.

Gateaux (see page 8) can always be included on the bill of fare as a luxurious touch and if it is a birthday tea then the birthday cake will be a central part of the occasion (see page 16). These type of cakes, of necessity, take much longer to prepare, make and decorate so you should choose to make other items which are not too time consuming to prepare and so keep your workload to manageable proportions.

Finally, remember that the cup of tea itself is very important. It does not matter whether your preference is for China or Indian tea as long as it is made correctly, with the right amount of tea, a kettle of freshly drawn boiling water, a heated teapot — and time to allow the tea to draw. The argument as to milk in the cup first or last is unimportant — do what ever you wish.

Crumpets

1¼ hours,
then toasting or grilling

Makes 16
15 g /½ oz fresh yeast or 10 ml /2 tsp dried yeast
5 ml /1 tsp caster sugar
600 ml /1 pt milk, lukewarm
450 g /1 lb strong flour, plus extra for flouring
5 ml /1 tsp salt
1 medium-sized egg, beaten
50 g /2 oz butter, melted, plus extra for greasing
butter and honey, to serve

1 Place the fresh yeast in a small bowl, stir in the sugar and 45 ml /3 tbls of the milk. Add half of the remaining milk and mix well. (For dried yeast, stir the sugar into half the milk, sprinkle the yeast over the top and mix well.) Now set the mixture aside in a warm place for 15–20 minutes until it becomes frothy.
2 In a bowl, sift together the flour and salt. Pour in the yeast mixture, the remaining milk, egg and melted butter and mix well. Beat until a light and frothy batter is formed.
3 Cover the bowl and leave it in a warm place for about 45 minutes, until the batter has doubled in size.
4 Gently heat the griddle or a heavy frying-pan. Check that is is hot enough by

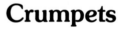

Muffins

92

sprinkling flour over it — the flour should turn brown in 2–3 minutes. Brush it off and grease the griddle lightly. Grease 7.5 cm /3 in crumpet rings or metal biscuit cutters and place them on the heated griddle.

5 Pour about 20 mm /¾ in of batter into each ring. The batter should come about halfway up the sides of the rings. Cook the crumpets until bubbles appear on the surface — in about 5 minutes.

6 Transfer to a wire rack to cool, then cook the remaining batter in the same way.

7 To serve, toast (or grill) the crumpets on both sides and spread them generously with butter and honey.

Muffins

1½ hours,
45 minutes, then toasting

Makes 16
15 g /½ oz fresh yeast, or 10 ml /2 tsp dried
* yeast*
5 ml /1 tsp caster sugar
300 ml /10 fl oz milk, lukewarm
450 g /1 lb strong flour
5 ml /1 tsp salt
1 medium-sized egg, beaten
25 g /1 oz melted butter, plus extra for greasing
butter, to serve

1 Place the fresh yeast in a small bowl, stir in the sugar and 45 ml /3 tbls of the milk. Add half of the remaining milk and mix well. (For dried yeast, stir the sugar into half the milk, sprinkle the yeast over the top and mix well.) Set the mixture aside in a warm place for 15–20 minutes until it becomes frothy.

2 In a bowl, sift together the flour and salt, then stir in the yeast mixture, the remaining milk, egg and melted butter. Beat until the mixture is frothy. Cover the bowl and set it aside in a warm place for 45 minutes, until the batter has doubled in size.

3 Gently heat the griddle or heavy frying-pan. Check to see if it is hot enough by sprinkling flour over it — the flour should turn brown in 2–3 minutes. Dust the flour off and grease the griddle lightly. Grease crumpet rings or 7.5 cm /3 in biscuit cutters.

4 Lightly flour your hands and divide the mixture into 16 pieces. Shape the pieces into 7.5 cm /3 in rounds. Next, press the dough into the metal rings and cook, in batches, on one side for 5–6 minutes. Remove the rings, turn the muffins over with a spatula and cook on the other side for 3–4 minutes until evenly brown. Transfer to a wire rack and leave to cool.

5 Split and toast (or grill) the muffins and serve them hot with butter.

● Fill the split and toasted muffins with a hot thick apple purée, in which raisins, dates or sultanas have been stirred.

● Make delicious fruit muffins by adding up to 100 g /4 oz cooked, well-drained black-currants or blueberries to the batter.

● Make savoury muffins by adding 75 g /3 oz grated Cheddar cheese and 10 ml /2 tsp chopped herbs to the batter. Split the muffins and top them with more cheese before toasting them under the grill.

Pikelets

These delicately textured drop scones are usually served for tea. Many different recipes exist, some of which include eggs and yeast in their ingredients.

25 minutes

Makes about 18
250 g /9 oz flour
40 g /1½ oz caster sugar
2.5 ml /½ tsp salt
2.5 ml /½ tsp bicarbonate of soda
about 400 ml /14 fl oz buttermilk

1 Mix together the flour, sugar and salt and make a well in the centre. Dissolve the bicarbonate of soda in a little of the buttermilk and pour it into the flour mixture. Beat well, adding enough buttermilk to make a thick, smooth batter.

2 Grease a hot griddle or heavy frying-pan and 7.5 cm /3 in crumpet rings or you can use a series of plain metal biscuit cutters. Place the rings on the griddle or in the pan and spoon in about 30 ml /2 tbls batter for each pikelet. Cook gently until the bubbles burst and the pikelets are brown. Turn the pikelets over and brown the other sides.

3 Transfer the cooked pikelets to a warm plate and cover them with a clean tea towel while you cook more pikelets, re-greasing the rings before using them again. Serve hot.

Buttermilk scones

30 minutes

Makes 8 scones
butter and flour, for the baking sheet
225 g /8 oz flour
2.5 ml /½ tsp cream of tartar
2.5 ml /½ tsp bicarbonate of soda
2.5 ml /½ tsp salt
50 g /2 oz butter
150 ml /5 fl oz buttermilk
beaten egg or buttermilk, for glazing
butter, to serve
jam, to serve
whipped cream, to serve

1 Heat the oven to 230C /450F /gas 8. Grease and lightly flour a baking sheet.

2 Sift the flour 3 times with the cream of tartar, bicarbonate of soda and salt into a large mixing bowl. Cut the butter into the flour with a knife, then rub in the pieces with your fingertips until the mixture resembles fine breadcrumbs.

3 Make a well in the centre and pour in most of the buttermilk. Mix with a fork to a soft but not sticky dough, adding the remaining buttermilk if necessary. Gather the dough into a ball with your fingers, turn it onto a lightly floured surface and knead briefly and lightly until smooth.

4 Pat out the dough to a round about 10–20 mm /½–¾ in thick. With a 6.5 cm / 2½ in pastry cutter, stamp out 8 scones.

5 Transfer the scones to the prepared baking sheet and brush with beaten egg or buttermilk. Bake for about 15 minutes, until the scones are well risen and browned. Cool them wrapped in a soft, clean cloth. Serve them halved and thickly buttered, or with jam and cream. Serve on the day of baking as scones stale quickly. Any left-over scones can be toasted next day.

Buttermilk scones

Caerphilly scones

⏲ 30 minutes

Makes about 12
350 g /12 oz flour, plus extra for flouring
15 ml /1 tbls baking powder
1.5 ml /¼ tsp salt
50 g /2 oz butter, plus extra for greasing
100 g /4 oz Caerphilly cheese, finely grated
about 200 ml /7 fl oz milk
butter, for serving

1 Heat the oven to 220C /425F /gas 7. Sift flour with baking powder and salt into a bowl and rub in the butter. Stir in the cheese. Add enough milk to make a soft dough.
2 Pat the dough on a floured surface to a thickness of about 20 mm /¾ in. Stamp it out into 6 cm /2½ in rounds with a fluted cutter.
3 Arrange on a greased baking sheet and bake for about 15 minutes, or until the scones are well risen and golden brown. Serve warm, split and spread with butter.

● Try using other cheeses such as Cheddar with chopped herbs such as thyme.

Oat wedges

⏲ 30 minutes,
then cooling

Makes 8
50 g /2 oz butter, plus extra for greasing
50 g /2 oz soft brown sugar (dark or light)
100 g /4 oz rolled oats
yeast extract, to serve

1 Heat the oven to 180C /350F /gas 4. In a small saucepan, melt the butter and sugar, stirring. Add the oats and stir them in.
2 Grease a 20 cm /8 in loose-bottomed cake tin on a greased baking sheet. Press the oat mixture into this to form a round. Bake the oat cake for 20 minutes.
3 Cut it into wedges while still hot, then remove them to a wire rack to cool. Serve them with a little yeast extract spread on top.

Allspice biscuits

⏲⏲ 20 minutes, plus chilling,
then 30 minutes, plus cooling

Makes 50–60
225 g /8 oz white flour, sifted
7.5 ml /1½ tsp baking powder
5 ml /1 tsp allspice
2.5 ml /½ tsp finely ground black pepper
a pinch of cayenne pepper
2.5 ml /½ tsp cinnamon
75 g /3 oz unsweetened cocoa powder
175 g /6 oz butter
7.5 ml /1½ tsp vanilla extract
225 g /8 oz sugar
1 egg

1 Sift together the flour, baking powder, allspice, black pepper, cayenne pepper, cinnamon and cocoa powder.

2 In a large bowl, cream the butter until it is light. Add the vanilla extract and sugar and beat well. Beat in the egg and gradually add the dry ingredients, scraping the bowl with a rubber spatula. Beat the mixture until it is thoroughly mixed.
3 Have ready a strip of greaseproof paper about 40 cm /16 in long. Spoon the dough in heaped tablespoonfuls down the length of the paper, forming a sausage-like strip about 30 cm /12 in long. Now roll the dough in the paper in order to cover it, pressing with your hands to shape the dough evenly into a sausage shape.
4 Slide a baking sheet under the wrapped dough to prevent breakage, then transfer it to the refrigerator or freezer for several hours until firm (or several days, if wished).
5 Heat the oven to 190C /375F /gas 5. Line 2 baking sheets with baking parchment or non-stick baking paper.
6 Unwrap the dough and, with a sharp knife, cut it into 5 mm /¼ in slices. Place the slices, a little apart, on the sheets. Bake for 10–12 minutes, changing the sheets over on the shelves halfway through, until the tops of the biscuits spring back when pressed. Do not overbake.
7 Transfer the biscuits to a wire rack to cool while you bake the remaining biscuits.

Cheesecake biscuits

⏲ 1 hour,
plus cooling

Makes 16
150 g /5 oz soft light brown sugar
175 g /6 oz flour
75 g /3 oz walnuts, chopped
75 g /3 oz butter, melted
225 g /8 oz cream cheese
100 g /4 oz sugar
1 medium-sized egg, beaten
15 ml /1 tbls lemon juice
30 ml /2 tbls milk
5 ml /1 tsp vanilla extract

1 Heat the oven to 180C /350F /gas 4. Combine the brown sugar, flour and nuts in a large bowl. Stir in the butter and mix with your hands until it is light and crumbly.
2 Reserve one-third of the mixture. Place the remainder in a 20 cm /8 in square tin and press down firmly. Bake for 15 minutes.
3 Meanwhile, beat the cream cheese and sugar together in a large bowl until smooth. Beat in the egg, lemon juice, milk and vanilla extract.
4 Pour the filling over the baked crust, top

with the reserved nut mixture, return to the oven and bake for 25 minutes.

5 Leave it to cool in the tin, then cut it into 16 squares and remove them from the tin. Store them in an airtight container in the refrigerator for up to 2 days.

Muesli fingers

Make a batch of these crunchy, spicy and nutritious biscuits which can be eaten at any time to fill a gap — not just at tea time.

20 minutes,
plus cooling

Makes about 16 fingers
350 g /12 oz packet of muesli
60 ml /4 tbls thick honey
60 ml /4 tbls golden syrup
60 ml /4 tbls vegetable oil
5 ml /1 tsp ground cinnamon

1 Heat the oven to 180C /350F /gas 4. Put all the ingredients in a bowl and stir until thoroughly combined. Press the muesli biscuit mixture into a buttered 28 × 18 cm /

Cheesecake biscuits and Ginger fruit cake

11 × 7 in shallow tin and bake for 15 minutes.
2 Leave to cool in the tin for 5 minutes, then mark into fingers cutting right through the mixture. Leave it until cold, then remove it from the tin. The fingers will keep for several weeks in an airtight container.

Bakewell slices

1½ hours,
plus cooking and decorating

Makes 20 slices
butter, for greasing
100 g /4 oz flour
a pinch of salt
40 g /1½ oz butter
15 g /½ oz lard
For the filling
45 ml /3 tbls raspberry or apricot jam
100 g /4 oz butter, softened
100 g /4 oz caster sugar
2 medium-sized eggs, beaten
5 ml /1 tsp almond essence
75 g /3 oz self-raising flour
25 g /1 oz ground rice
For the topping
150 g /5 oz icing sugar
15 g /½ oz flaked almonds, browned

1 Grease the sides of a 20 × 15 cm /10 × 6 in tin, 4 cm /1½ in deep, with butter.
2 To make the pastry, mix the flour and salt in a bowl. Add the butter and lard; rub in to make fine crumbs. Mix with 10–15 ml /2–3 tsp cold water to make a firm dough.
3 Roll out to the size of the tin base and press it evenly in the tin. Heat oven to 180C /350F /gas 4.
4 For the filling, spread jam all over the pastry. Put the butter, sugar, eggs, almond essence, flour and ground rice into a bowl. Beat with a wooden spoon or an electric mixer for 2–3 minutes until it is evenly mixed. Spread the mixture carefully over the top of the jam.
5 Bake in the centre of the oven for 40–45 minutes until it is firm when pressed lightly in the middle.
6 Remove it from the oven, leave to cool for 15 minutes, then turn it out onto a wire rack. Leave until it is cold, then turn the tart the right way up.
7 To make the icing, sift the icing sugar into a bowl, add 15 ml /1 tbls warm water and mix it in, adding up to 7 ml /½ tbls more water as needed to make an icing that just coats the back of the spoon. Spread the icing over the tart and scatter the almonds on top. Leave until it is set.
8 Cut in half lengthwise, then into 20 slices. Store in an airtight container for up to 2 days.

● Seal the fingers in a rigid container and freeze them. They keep for up to 6 weeks.

Ginger fruit cake

1½–2 hours, plus cooling
and 2–3 days maturing

Makes 18 cm /7 in cake
225 g /8 oz butter, plus extra for greasing
225 g /8 oz white or soft light brown sugar
450 g /1 lb dried pears, chopped
225 g /8 oz dried apricots, chopped
50 g /2 oz ground almonds
50 g /2 oz blanched almonds, flaked
100 g /4 oz crystallized ginger, finely chopped
grated zest of ½ lemon
3 eggs, lightly beaten
225 g /8 oz flour
2.5 ml /½ tsp baking powder
45 ml /3 tbls whisky

1 Heat the oven to 180C /350F /gas 4. Grease a deep 18 cm /7 in round cake tin; line with greaseproof paper. Grease again.
2 In a large bowl, cream the butter. Add the sugar and beat well. Beat in the chopped dried fruit, ground and flaked almonds, ginger, lemon zest and eggs, plus a little of the flour to prevent the mixture from curdling.
3 Sift the baking powder with the rest of the flour and stir it into the fruit mixture with the whisky. Turn this into the prepared tin and bake for 1–1½ hours, or until the cake is done.
4 Cool it in the tin for 10 minutes, then turn it out and leave it on a wire rack until cold.
5 Wrap the cake in foil and store it in an airtight tin for 2–3 days before serving.

Dried apple cake

overnight soaking, 2½ hours, plus cooling

Makes 8
175 g /6 oz dried apple rings
175 ml /6 fl oz molasses
100 g /4 oz butter
2 medium-sized eggs
225 ml /8 fl oz milk
175 g /6 oz soft brown sugar
5 ml /1 tsp bicarbonate of soda
225 g /8 oz flour
butter, for greasing
Glacé icing (see page 39), to decorate

1 Soak the apple rings in plenty of warm water overnight. Drain, reserving 175 ml /6 fl oz of the soaking liquid. Chop the apple rings roughly.
2 Put the chopped apple, 175 ml /6 fl oz of

Dried apple cake

the soaking liquid and the molasses in a heavy saucepan. Mix well and simmer uncovered over a low heat for 1 hour or until the liquid is reduced to a thin layer of syrupy glaze on the bottom of the pan.
3 Off the heat, beat in the butter with an electric beater until well blended. Heat the oven to 180C /350F /gas 4.
4 Beat the eggs into the milk and reserve. Mix the sugar, bicarbonate of soda and flour together in a bowl. One third at a time, beat the dry ingredients into the molasses-butter mixture, adding them alternately with the egg-milk mixture.
5 Grease a 22 cm /8½ in round cake tin and stand a greased 450 g /1 lb jam jar in the middle. Half-fill the jar with water to make it heavier.
6 Carefully pour the mixture into the prepared tin without moving the jar. Level the top and bake for 1–1¼ hours or until the cake begins to shrink from the sides of the pan.
7 Let the cake cool in the tin for 10 minutes. Twist the jar and remove it. Leave

the cake for another 10 minutes, then remove it from the tin. Finish by cooling it on a wire rack, if possible for 24 hours.
8 Make the glacé icing. Put the icing on the top of the cake, allowing some of it to dribble down the sides.

● If wished, fill the hole in the centre of the cake with stewed apples and serve with whipped cream.

Orange and hazelnut cake

toasting the nuts, then 1½ hours, plus cooling and maturing

Makes 1 × 30 cm /12 in cake
150 g /5 oz butter, plus extra for greasing
275 g /10 oz soft light brown sugar
225 ml /8 fl oz milk
5 ml /1 tsp vanilla extract
3 medium-sized eggs, separated
225 g /8 oz wholemeal flour
10 ml /2 tsp baking powder
2.5 ml /½ tsp salt
100 g /4 oz whole hazelnuts, lightly toasted
100 g /4 oz raisins
grated zest of 2 oranges

For the syrup

75 g /3 oz honey
the juice of 1 orange

1 Heat the oven to 180C /350F /gas 4. Grease a round cake tin 30 cm /12 in in diameter and 5 cm /2 in deep.
2 Cream together the butter and sugar. Add the milk, vanilla and yolks and beat them together.
3 Sift together the flour, baking powder and salt and gradually beat this into the butter mixture. Stir in the nuts, raisins and orange zest.
4 Whisk the egg whites in a large, clean bowl until stiff peaks form, then gently fold it into the cake mixture with a large metal spoon. Pour it into the tin and bake for 50–55 minutes, or until a skewer inserted in the centre comes out clean.
5 While the cake is baking, place the honey and orange juice in a small saucepan and heat gently until the honey is dissolved. As soon as you take the cake from the oven, spoon the syrup over it. Let the cake cool in the tin for 10 minutes, then remove it from the tin and leave it on a wire rack until cold.
6 Wrap the cake in foil and store it in an airtight tin for 1–2 days before serving.

American pineapple fruit cake

American pineapple fruit cake

⏱🍴 4 hours, plus cooling, then 2½ weeks or more maturing

Makes one 2.5 kg /5½ lb cake

350 g /12 oz glacé pineapple, chopped
350 g /12 oz pressed stoned dates, chopped
200 g /7 oz glacé cherries, rinsed, dried and chopped
200 g /7 oz sultanas
275 g /10 oz seedless raisins
200 g /7 oz mixed candied peel, finely chopped
225 g /8 oz walnuts, finely chopped
225 g /8 oz Brazil nuts, finely chopped
75 g /3 oz desiccated coconut
50 ml /2 fl oz brandy, plus extra for sprinkling
125 g /4½ oz butter or margarine, softened, plus extra for greasing
175 g /6 oz clear honey
6 medium-sized eggs
5 ml /1 tsp vanilla essence
350 g /12 oz flour
1.5 ml /¼ tsp bicarbonate of soda
1.5 ml /¼ tsp salt
1.5 ml /¼ tsp ground mixed spice
1.5 ml /¼ tsp ground cinnamon
a large pinch of ground mace

1 Heat the oven to 140C /275F /gas 1. Put the pineapple in a small bowl and cover with boiling water. Leave for 10 minutes, then drain. Mix it together thoroughly with the other fruits, peel and nuts, then mix in the coconut. Pour in 2 fl oz of the brandy.
2 Grease a 25 cm /10 in loose-bottomed ring cake tin with a little of the butter or margarine. In a large bowl, beat the remaining butter or margarine, gradually adding the honey until it is completely blended into the butter or margarine.
3 Beat in the eggs, 2 at a time, blending each addition in thoroughly before adding the next. Add the vanilla essence.
4 Sift together the flour, bicarbonate of soda, salt and spices. Add this to the butter mixture in 3 or 4 batches, stirring each in thoroughly before adding the next. Lastly, stir in the fruit mixture. Press the mixture into the prepared tin and bake it for 3 hours.
5 Cool the cake in the tin on a wire rack for 15 minutes, then remove the ring and base and finish cooling it on the rack.
6 When the cake is cold, sprinkle it with brandy, wrap it closely in a cloth or foil and place in an airtight tin. Leave for 2–3 days.
7 Sprinkle again with brandy, wrap and store in the tin for at least 2 weeks before cutting. You can sprinkle again with brandy after the first week, if wished.

TEABREADS

Teabreads are cakes which usually include nuts or fruit and are served in the same way as yeast bread — sliced with butter. More economical than fancy cakes, they make a delicious addition to any tea-table.

Teabreads are halfway between a cake and a bread, and help to fill the table at tea time. They are best when eaten on the same day as they were made, either warm or cold, but most of them do freeze satisfactorily and so can be made in advance, if necessary.

Nearly all of the teabreads in this chapter are cooked in the oven, but one, the Northumberland Singin' Hinny, is made on a griddle or girdle. The griddle is a thick, round, cast-iron plate with a half-hoop handle. It is heated on the top of the cooker and is usually used for cooking scones.

Most of the recipes for teabreads come from Scotland, Ireland and the North of England where they were an important part of the high tea ritual. There really is very little to beat a slice of warm, fruity and spicy bread spread with butter and eaten in front of the fire on a cold, wet winter's day. The fact that these recipes can equally be made and eaten with pleasure in the summer, shows the versatility of tea breads.

One slightly more unusual teabread which I have included is the Light-weight banana bread. This uses ripe bananas, yoghurt and whole wheat flour. To give the bread its

Fruity teabread

lightness, the butter is creamed with the sugar, rather than rubbed in with the flour, as with a traditional tea bread. This is a truly healthy, filling recipe for all the family.

Fruity teabread

overnight soaking the dried fruit, then 2 hours, plus cooling

Makes 3 small loaves (or 1 large, 1 small)
450 g /1 lb sultanas
450 g /1 lb raisins
450 g /1 lb soft brown sugar
425 ml /15 fl oz brewed tea
butter and flour, for the tins
450 g /1 lb flour
3 eggs, beaten
15 ml /1 tbls baking powder
15 ml /1 tbls mixed spice
45 ml /3 tbls honey, warmed, to glaze

1 Put the fruit, the sugar and tea in a large mixing bowl and soak overnight.
2 Heat the oven to 170C /325F /gas 3. Butter 3 × 1 L /1½ pt loaf tins (or one small tin and one twice the size) and dust them

with flour. Add the flour and beaten eggs alternately to the tea mixture. Add the baking powder and the spice and mix together.
3 Divide the batter equally among the prepared tins, level it off with a palette knife and place the tins in the oven for 1½ hours (add an extra ½ hour for the large loaf). Test each loaf with a skewer inserted in the centre, if it comes out clean it is cooked.
4 Allow the loaves to cool for 5 minutes and turn them out of their tins onto a wire rack. When cold, gently warm the honey, brush it over the tops of the loaves and allow it to set. Serve sliced with plenty of butter.

● In Ireland, on Hallowe'en, a ring is baked inside this cake; it is said whoever gets the slice with the ring will be the first to marry.

Cherry teabread

This simple teabread is best eaten on the same day it is baked. Serve it thickly sliced with lots of butter.

1 hour

Makes about 8 slices
75 g /3 oz butter, plus extra for greasing
100 g /4 oz glacé cherries
225 g /8 oz flour, plus extra for dusting
10 ml /2 tsp baking powder
a pinch of salt
75 g /3 oz caster sugar
2 medium-sized eggs, beaten
75–150 ml /3–5 fl oz milk

1 Grease, line with greaseproof paper and re-grease a deep 18 cm /7 in square cake tin. Heat the oven to 180C /350F /gas 4.
2 Wash the cherries and dry them on absorbent paper. Cut the glacé cherries into quarters and dust them lightly with a little flour to prevent them sinking to the bottom of the bread when it is cooked.
3 Sift the flour, baking powder and salt into a large warmed mixing bowl. Cut in the butter and rub it in until the mixture resembles fine breadcrumbs.
4 Stir in the sugar and cherry quarters, then mix in the beaten eggs. Add the milk, a spoonful at a time, stirring and checking the consistency. Stop adding the milk when you find that the mixture will easily drop from the spoon.
5 Pat the mixture into the prepared cake tin and smooth over the top. Bake for 45 minutes, or until a fine, warmed skewer inserted into the centre of the cake comes out clean.
6 Remove the cherry teabread from the oven and leave it to cool in the tin for 5 minutes. Now turn it out onto a wire rack. Remove the lining paper and leave the teabread to cool before serving.

Date and walnut loaf

Dates and walnuts give this teabread a **wonderful texture and flavour. The inclusion of black treacle also improves the loaf's storing qualities.**

 2¼ hours

Makes 12–15 slices
175 g /6 oz butter, plus extra for greasing
450 g /1 lb flour
20 ml /4 tsp baking powder
5 ml / 1 tsp salt
2.5 ml /½ tsp mixed ground spice
175 g /6 oz stoned dates, finely chopped
50 g /2 oz walnuts, finely chopped
175 g /6 oz caster sugar
2 medium-sized eggs, beaten
150 ml /5 fl oz milk
125 ml /4 fl oz black treacle, warmed

1 Heat the oven to 180C /350F /gas 4. Grease a 1.5 L /3 pt loaf tin, then line it with greaseproof paper and re-grease the base.
2 Sift the flour, baking powder, salt and spice into a large, warmed mixing bowl. Cut in the butter and rub it in until the mixture resembles breadcrumbs.
3 Stir in the dates, walnuts and sugar. Now stir in the beaten eggs. Mix the milk with the warmed black treacle and stir this into the other ingredients, a little at a time. If the mixture is too dry, gradually add extra milk, a spoonful at a time, until a soft dropping consistency is reached.
4 Using a spatula, scrape the mixture into the prepared tin and smooth over the top. Bake for 2 hours, or until a fine, warmed skewer inserted into the centre of the loaf comes out quite clean.
5 Remove the loaf from the oven and allow

it to stand in the tin for 5 minutes. Then turn it out onto a wire rack, peel off the lining paper, and leave it to cool.

Light-weight banana bread

Deliciously light but with a cake-like **consistency, banana bread is an excellent way of using up over-ripe bananas.**

 1½ hours

Makes 8–10 slices
65 g /2½ oz margarine
100 g /4 oz soft brown sugar
1 medium-sized egg, beaten
2 small ripe bananas, weighing 150 g /5 oz, mashed
15 ml /1 tbls yoghurt
25 g /1 oz whole wheat flour
75 g /3 oz flour
2.5 ml /½ tsp bicarbonate of soda
a pinch of salt

1 Heat the oven to 170C /325F /gas 3. Cream the fat with the sugar until light and fluffy. Beat in the egg until well incorporated. In another bowl, combine the mashed bananas with the yoghurt.
2 Sift the flours, bicarbonate of soda and salt into a large bowl. Fold the sifted flour into the butter and egg mixture alternately with the mashed bananas.
3 Transfer the mixture to a greased 850 ml / 1½ pt loaf tin and bake in the oven for 1¼ hours. Remove from the oven and leave it to stand in the tin for 10 minutes or so before turning out onto a wire rack to cool.

Date and walnut loaf

Singin' Hinny

 20 minutes

Serves 6
225 g /8 oz self-raising flour
1.5 ml /¼ tsp cream of tartar
a pinch of salt
50 g /2 oz lard
75 g /3 oz currants
about 150 ml /5 fl oz milk
flour, for sprinkling
butter, to serve

1 Heat a griddle or heavy-based frying-pan over a medium heat.
2 Sift the flour into a bowl with the cream of tartar and salt. Rub in the lard until the mixture resembles breadcrumbs, then stir in the currants and add enough milk to make a soft dough. Pat it out on a floured surface to a round about 20 cm /8 in in diameter.
3 Sprinkle a little flour on the hot griddle or pan to keep the dough from sticking. Cook it over a medium heat for 5 minutes, then turn it over. The cooked side should be a deep golden brown. Cook the dough for a further 5 minutes or until the second side is brown.
4 Divide the hinny into 6 wedges, then split each one in half horizontally. Spread the inside with butter, put the halves back together and serve the teabread warm.

● This recipe gets its name from the noise the dough makes cooking on the griddle.
● Children enjoy the buttered surface sprinkled with soft dark brown sugar.

Bishop's bread

Apricot nut bread

🍴 3–4 hours soaking, then 1½ hours, plus cooling

Makes about 30 slices
175 g /6 oz dried apricots
300 g /11 oz flour, plus extra for dusting
butter, for greasing
5 ml /1 tsp baking powder
5 ml /1 tsp salt
225 g /8 oz caster sugar
150 g /5 oz flaked almonds
grated zest and juice of 1 large orange
2 medium-sized eggs
50 g /2 oz butter, melted and cooled
150 ml /5 fl oz soured cream

1 Soak the apricots in water for 3–4 hours. Drain them and dry them carefully with absorbent paper. Chop them into small pieces and dust them with a little flour to absorb any excess moisture.
2 Heat the oven to 180C /350F /gas 4. Grease with butter and then flour an 850 ml /1½ pt loaf tin.

3 Sift the flour with the baking powder and the salt into a mixing bowl. Add the apricots, sugar, almonds and orange zest and mix well. In another bowl, beat the eggs with the melted and cooled butter and the orange juice. Blend in the soured cream, then add this to the flour mixture beating until well combined.
4 Pour the batter into the prepared tin and bake for 1½ hours. To test that it is cooked, insert a skewer into the middle — it should come out dry. Remove the bread from the oven and cool it in the tin for 10 minutes before turning it out onto a wire rack. Leave it until cold. Then serve it sliced, plain or spread with butter.

Orange bread

This teabread, served either with tea or coffee, or as a dessert, is a speciality of Barbados and is also popular in other parts of the West Indies. The Trinidad-Tobago version of this recipe adds grated coconut to the batter.

🍴 50 minutes

Makes 1 small loaf
225 g /8 oz flour
15 ml /1 tbls baking powder
2.5 ml /½ tsp salt
50 g /2 oz butter, diced small
100 g /4 oz sugar
15 ml /1 tbls grated orange zest
1 egg, well beaten
225 ml /8 fl oz orange juice
melted butter, for the loaf tin

1 Heat the oven to 180C /350F /gas 4. Sift together the flour, baking powder and salt in a mixing bowl. Rub the butter into the flour with your fingertips. Mix in the sugar and orange zest.
2 Stir the egg into the orange juice and fold these into the flour mixture.
3 Pour the mixture into a buttered 1.5 L / 3 pt loaf tin and bake in the oven for 30 minutes, or until a skewer inserted in the centre comes out clean. Cool the cake in the tin for 5 minutes, then turn it out onto a wire rack to finish cooling. Wait until it is completely cold before cutting into slices.

Bishop's bread

The fruit and nut mixture in this cake may be varied, but it must include the small lumps of plain chocolate. These retain their shape during baking.

🕐🍴 about 1½ hours, plus overnight maturing

Serves 4–6
butter and flour, for the tin
25 g /1 oz good quality, plain chocolate
40 g /1½ oz walnuts, hazelnuts or unblanched almonds
25 g /1 oz sultanas or glacé cherries
25 g /1 oz raisins
25 g /1 oz candied peel
a little grated lemon zest
3 medium-sized eggs, separated
125 g /4½ oz icing sugar
5 ml /1 tsp vanilla sugar, plus extra for dusting (see page 9)
125 g /4½ oz flour

1 Butter and flour a 1.7 L /3 pt loaf tin.
2 Chop the chocolate into small uneven lumps and do the same with the nuts. Chop the glacé cherries, if using, or pick over the sultanas and the raisins. Mix the fruit, nuts, candied peel, lemon zest and chocolate together and reserve.
3 Whisk the egg yolks with 100 g /4 oz icing sugar until they are very thick and creamy.
4 Heat the oven to 180C /350F /gas 4.
5 Whisk the egg whites until they are stiff, then whisk in the remaining icing sugar and vanilla sugar. Fold the egg whites into the egg yolks alternately with the flour and fruit mixture. Now put the mixture in the prepared tin.
6 Bake for about 45 minutes or until it is firm in the centre when tested and the cake shrinks away from the sides of the tin. Dust the cake with vanilla sugar, leaving it in the tin to cool, but wait to cut it until the next day, so the flavours can mature.

Fruit bread

As filling as Christmas cake, but moister, this confection can be eaten all year round. It is best kept for a week after baking to allow it to mature properly.

🕐 🍴 20 minutes, plus soaking, then 2 hours plus maturing

Makes 2 loaves
225 g /8 oz dried mixed fruit (apples, apricots, pears, plums, etc.)
225 g /8 oz seedless raisins
175 g /6 oz mixed chopped candied orange and lemon peel
75 ml /3 fl oz kirsch
175 g /6 oz caster sugar
15 g /½ oz ground cinnamon
50 g /2 oz almonds, flaked
100 g /4 oz walnuts, chopped
about 100 g /4 oz flour
butter, for greasing
milk, for brushing
icing sugar, for sprinkling
For the bread dough
2.5 ml /½ tsp caster sugar
150 ml /5 fl oz warm milk and water mixed
7.5 ml /1½ tsp dried yeast
225 g /8 oz strong white flour
a pinch of salt
15 g /½ oz butter
flour, for kneading

Fruit bread

1 Place the dried mixed fruit in a saucepan, add water to cover it, bring to the boil and cook for 4 minutes. Drain and cut the fruit into large pieces, removing any stones. Put the fruit in a bowl with the raisins and candied peel and pour the kirsch over it. Stir well, cover and leave to soak overnight.
2 Next day, make the bread dough. Dissolve the sugar in the milk mixture, sprinkle the yeast on top of it and leave it in a warm place for 10 minutes until it is frothy.
3 Sift the flour and salt into a bowl and rub in the butter. Add the yeast mixture and mix it into a dough. Turn it out onto a floured surface and knead for 10 minutes.
4 Return the dough to the mixing bowl, cover it with greased cling film and leave it in a warm place for about 40 minutes, or until it doubles in bulk.
5 Add the soaked fruit mixture to the bread dough with the sugar, cinnamon and nuts and mix well with your hands, gradually adding the flour.
6 Heat the oven to 190C /375F /gas 5. Divide the dough into 2 equal portions and shape each into a ball. Place them on greased baking sheets, brush them with milk and bake in the oven for 40 minutes, or until they are golden brown. Cool on a wire rack.
7 Seal the loaves in foil and store them for 1 week before cutting. Sprinkle with icing sugar and serve very thinly sliced.

Prune and walnut teabread

🕐 🍴 overnight soaking, then 2 hours

Serves 6
grated zest and juice of 1 large orange
175 g /6 oz stoned prunes, roughly chopped
sunflower oil, for greasing
400 g /14 oz flour
7.5 ml /1½ tsp baking powder
2.5 ml /½ tsp bicarbonate of soda
a pinch of salt
175 g /6 oz dark brown sugar
75 g /3 oz shelled walnuts, roughly chopped
1 medium-sized egg, beaten
50 g /2 oz margarine, melted

1 Make up the orange juice to 225 ml /8 fl oz with water. Add the prunes and orange zest and soak overnight.
2 Heat the oven to 180C /350F /gas 4. Grease with sunflower oil and then line a 1.7 L /3 pt loaf tin.
3 Sift the flour, baking powder, bicarbonate of soda and salt in a mixing bowl. Add the sugar, walnuts, beaten egg, margarine and drained prunes. Mix thoroughly.
4 Place the mixture in the prepared tin. Bake for 1–1½ hours until well risen and a knife inserted into the loaf comes out clean.

FAMILY FARE

Special treats for tea to thrill the children and please quite a few adults, too! Make a batch of buns to see you through the week, or try one of my more unusual recipes for a change.

North, south, London — I've included cake recipes from all around England in this section. Traditional recipes which have been favourites for centuries are bound to be just as successful with your own family. Johnny cakes and Chelsea buns are ideal for filling hungry children at tea time; Sponge drops and Cornish splits are richer (messier!) as they are served with jam and cream. Almond cheesecake tarts are for those with a less sweet tooth.

Why not try a fruity traditional Lardy cake from Yorkshire? It is especially delicious eaten warm. Or serve a home-made Battenburg? This sweet, pretty pink and yellow cake, covered in marzipan, is always popular.

My recipe for a basic All-in-one-sponge cake has almost limitless variations and I've included just a few ideas. The Walnut layer cake is a cinch — easy to make, lovely to look at — a moist cake combining cream cheese, honey and walnuts. Your family won't be able to resist it!

Almond cheesecake tarts

These tasty tarts used to be sold by pie vendors in the streets of London during the seventeenth century.

 40 minutes

Makes 20
400 g /14 oz made-weight puff pastry, defrosted if frozen
flour, for dusting
2 medium-sized egg yolks
30 ml /2 tbls caster sugar
100 g /4 oz ground almonds
25 g /1 oz butter, softened
zest of ½ lemon, finely grated
15 ml /1 tbls rose-water
75 ml /5 tbls thin cream

1 Heat the oven to 190C /375F /gas 5. Lightly flour a flat surface, then roll out the pastry thinly and cut circles, each 10 cm /4 in in diameter. Re-roll the trimmings to make more circles. Line 20 holes in two bun tins with the pastry circles. Chill the pastry while making the filling.
2 Beat together the egg yolks, sugar, almonds, butter, lemon zest and rose-water. Finally, stir in the cream.
3 Divide the filling among the pastry cases and bake them in the oven for about 15 minutes or until well risen and golden. Serve warm at tea time or as a dessert.

● Buy rose-water at most chemists.
● The filling can be made even richer by substituting brandy for the rose-water.

Johnny cakes and Chelsea buns

Enriched yeast mixtures have always been used for sweet buns by London bakers who excelled in making them. Customers who could not afford rich fruit or fancy cream cakes often had a few coppers to spare for buns crusted with sugar and fruit or embellished with thick icing.

🍴🍴 1 hour, plus rising, then 45 minutes baking, plus cooling

Makes 12 cakes and 9 buns
For the yeast mixture
175 g /6 oz strong white flour
25 ml /5 tsp dried yeast
7.5 ml /1½ tsp caster sugar
200 ml /7 fl oz milk
75 ml /3 fl oz boiling water
For the dough
500 g /18 oz strong white flour
5 ml /1 tsp ground nutmeg
75 g /3 oz butter
50 g /2 oz caster sugar
2 medium-sized eggs
flour, for dusting
butter, for greasing
For the Johnny cakes
100 g /4 oz currants
2.5 ml /½ tsp caraway seeds
butter, for greasing
For the Chelsea buns
25 g /1 oz butter, melted
75 g /3 oz sultanas and seedless raisins, mixed
25 g /1 oz chopped mixed peel
25 g /1 oz soft brown sugar
butter, for greasing
For the icing
200 g /7 oz icing sugar, sifted
about 15 ml /1 tbls hot water

1 Beat together all the ingredients for the yeast mixture and allow them to stand in a warm place until they are foamy — about 10 minutes.
2 Sift the flour and nutmeg for the basic dough into a bowl and rub in the butter. Stir in the sugar, then add the yeast mixture and eggs and mix to a soft dough. Turn the dough out onto a floured surface and knead for 10 minutes, then form it into a ball.
3 Grease the mixing bowl, return the ball of dough to it. Turn the dough once in the bowl to coat the ball evenly with the grease. Cover the bowl and allow the dough to rise in a warm place until it doubles in bulk — about 1 hour.
4 When it has risen, turn the dough out onto a floured surface and knead it for 2 minutes, until it is firm.
5 To make the Johnny cakes, take two-thirds of the dough and work in the currants

and caraway seeds. Divide the dough mixture into 12 equal portions. Form each piece into a finger shape, about 12.5 cm /5 in long and arrange them well apart on a greased baking sheet.
6 Cover the dough fingers with greased cling film and allow them to rise until double in size — about 15 minutes. Meanwhile, heat the oven to 190C /375F /gas 5. Bake the buns for about 15 minutes, or until golden brown. Cool on a wire rack.
7 To make the Chelsea buns, take the remaining dough and roll it out to a rectangle about 23 × 30 cm /9 × 12 in. Brush the rectangle with the melted butter and sprinkle it with the fruit, peel and the soft brown sugar.
8 Roll up carefully, starting from one long side. Cut into 9 equal slices and stand them, cut sides downwards, in 3 rows of 3 on a greased tin 18 cm /7 in square.
9 Cover the buns with greased cling film and allow them to rise in a warm place until they double in size — about 25 minutes. Bake at 190C /375F /gas 5 for about 25 minutes, or until the buns are evenly brown. Cool them in the tin while you make the icing.
10 To make the icing, mix the icing sugar with just enough of the water to make a thick consistency. Use almost all of this icing to coat the tops of the Johnny cakes. Add a little extra water to the left-over icing until it is the consistency of thin cream. Brush this over the tops of the Chelsea buns and separate the buns to serve them.

Sponge drops

Also known as Devonshire creams, these are crisp rounds of sponge sandwiched together with cream and jam. The proportion of flour and sugar is high as a thick mix is required to ensure that the drops hold their shape during cooking.

🍴 1¼ hours,
plus cooling

Makes 12–14
oil, for greasing
125 g /4 oz plain flour
a pinch of salt
5 ml /1 tsp baking powder
2 eggs
150 g /5 oz caster sugar
For the filling
125–175 g /4–6 oz red jam
225 ml /8 fl oz thick cream

1 Position the oven shelf in the centre, then heat the oven to 190C /375F /gas 5. Brush two baking trays with oil.
2 Half fill a saucepan with water, bring it to the boil, then remove it from the heat. Meanwhile, sift the flour twice with the salt and baking powder.
3 Place the eggs in a large mixing bowl and whisk them lightly together using a balloon, rotary or electric hand-held whisk. Gradually beat in 125 g /4 oz of the caster sugar.
4 Place the bowl over the saucepan — it should sit comfortably without touching the water. Whisk the eggs and sugar together until the mixture is pale and thick and holds the trail of the whisk for 3 seconds.
5 Remove from the heat and continue whisking for about 5 minutes or until cool.
6 Sift the flour gradually and evenly over the surface of the mixture and lightly fold in.
7 Using a teaspoon, place spoonfuls of the mix onto the greased baking sheets. Space them about 2.5 cm /1 in apart to allow for spreading during baking.
8 Dredge the drops with the remaining caster sugar, then bake for 10 minutes.
9 Remove from the oven and stand the baking sheets on a damp tea towel for 30 seconds. Ease the sponge drops off the sheets with a palette knife and then allow them to cool completely on a wire rack.
10 To serve, place the drops upside down so that the flat base is uppermost. Spread half the drops with jam. Whip the cream until it is thick, then pipe a swirl of cream on each of the remaining drops. Sandwich them together.

● There are a number of easy variations to this recipe, which are listed below. Try all of them.
● For sponge fingers, put the mixture into a forcing bag fitted with a 1.2 cm /½ in nozzle

Sponge drops

and pipe it out onto prepared baking sheets in 7.5 cm /3 in lengths or 5 cm /2 in rounds. Baking time will be about 6 minutes.
● For chocolate sponge drops, replace 15 ml /1 tbls flour with 15 ml /1 tbls cocoa powder. Sieve the cocoa with the flour.
● For fruit-filled sponge drops, use crushed raspberries, strawberries or mashed banana in place of the jam.
● For iced drops, omit the filling, and ice the top of each drop with 2.5 ml /½ tsp coffee or chocolate flavoured glacé icing. Decorate each with a piece of glacé cherry, chocolate vermicelli or half a walnut.

Cornish splits

In Devonshire these are called cut rounds or chudleighs. In Dorset the same recipe is used to make tuff cakes — pieces of dough are placed closely together on a baking sheet like cobblestones. After baking they are pulled apart.

🍴 1¾ hours,
including rising

Makes 16 buns
5 ml /1 tsp caster sugar
250 ml /9 fl oz milk and water, mixed in equal
proportions, lukewarm
15 g /½ oz dried yeast
400 g /14 oz strong or bread flour, plus extra
for dusting
2.5 ml /½ tsp salt
50 g /2 oz butter, melted, plus extra for
greasing
whipped or clotted cream and jam, to serve

1 Dissolve the sugar in the lukewarm liquid, sprinkle on the yeast and allow it to stand in a warm place for about 10 minutes, until frothy.
2 Sift the flour and salt into a bowl, make a well in the centre and add the yeast liquid and butter and mix to a dough. Turn out the dough on a floured surface and knead for about 5 minutes.
3 Return to the bowl, cover with greased polythene and leave in a warm place for about 45 minutes, until it doubles in bulk.
4 Heat the oven to 220C /425F /gas 7. Turn the dough out again and knead lightly. Divide it into 16 equal portions and shape each one into a ball. Arrange on a greased baking sheet, allowing space for spreading. Cover again with greased polythene and leave to rise for 30 minutes or until double the size.
5 Place the buns in the oven for 15 minutes or until golden brown. They will sound hollow when tapped with the knuckles if fully cooked. Cover them immediately with a clean cloth to give a soft crust.
6 Fill the buns with whipped or clotted cream and jam, then serve.

● Fresh yeast can be used instead of dried yeast in this recipe but the quantity should be doubled. Blend the yeast into the lukewarm milk, water and sugar mixture. Make a well in the dry ingredients, pour in the yeast liquid and sprinkle a little flour over the surface. Leave until frothy, then add the butter and proceed as above.

Oatmeal gingerbread

This recipe comes from Scotland and is sometimes called a 'holding bannock' because it can be stored.

 1¼ hours

Makes one large cake
butter, for greasing
flour, for sprinkling
175 g /6 oz flour
2.5 ml /½ tsp bicarbonate of soda
75 g /3 oz butter
175 g /6 oz medium oatmeal
7.5 ml /1½ tsp ground ginger
75 g /3 oz dark soft brown sugar
1 medium-sized egg
50 g /2 oz black treacle
275 ml /10 fl oz buttermilk or soured milk

1 Heat the oven to 180C /350F /gas 4. Grease and lightly flour a 1.7 L /3 pt loaf tin. Sift the flour and the bicarbonate of soda into a large mixing bowl and rub in the butter until the mixture resembles fine breadcrumbs. Stir in the oatmeal, the ground ginger and the dark soft brown sugar.
2 Make a well in the centre of the mixture and add the egg, the black treacle and half the buttermilk or soured milk. Gradually draw in the dry ingredients, with a wooden spoon, until blended. Now mix in the remaining buttermilk or soured milk.
3 Transfer the mixture to the prepared loaf tin. Bake in the centre of the oven for about 55 minutes, or until the gingerbread is just firm in the centre.
4 Leave the cake to cool in the tin for 15 minutes, then turn it out and when cold store it in an airtight container. It is delicious warm, but improves if left to mature for 3 days before cutting.

Orange gingerbread

This delicious orange-flavoured gingerbread is at its nicest when served thickly sliced and generously buttered.

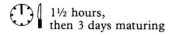 1½ hours, then 3 days maturing

Makes an 18 cm /7 in cake
butter, for greasing
225 g /8 oz flour
a pinch of salt
7.5 ml /1½ tsp baking powder
2.5 ml /½ tsp bicarbonate of soda
5 ml /1 tsp ground ginger
2.5 ml /½ tsp ground mixed spice
100 g /4 oz soft light brown sugar
75 g /3 oz margarine
75 g /3 oz black treacle
75 g /3 oz golden syrup
1 medium-sized egg
125 ml /4 fl oz milk
grated zest of 1 orange

Battenburg cake

1 Heat the oven to 170C /325F /gas 3. Grease and line a deep, 18 cm /7 in square cake tin with greased greaseproof paper.
2 Sift the flour with the salt, baking powder, bicarbonate of soda, ginger and mixed spice.
3 Put the sugar, margarine, black treacle and golden syrup in a heavy-based saucepan and stir, with a wooden spoon, over a low heat until the ingredients are melted and thoroughly blended. Remove from the heat and allow to cool slightly.
4 Beat the egg with the milk and pour on to the sifted flour mixture. Add the cooled melted treacle mixture and grated orange zest. Using a metal spoon, stir until thoroughly blended.
5 Pour the cake mixture into the prepared tin. Bake for about 1 hour, until the top of the gingerbread is firm to the touch. Let the cake cool in the tin for 10 minutes before turning it out onto a wire rack. Remove the lining paper and leave the cake to become quite cold. Wrap the cake in foil and store for 3 days before cutting.

Lardy cake

This traditional fruit bread is made in both Yorkshire and Wiltshire. The fat gives it extra richness. Eat it at tea time while it is still warm.

 2½ hours

Makes one 18 cm /7 in square cake
butter, for greasing
225 g /8 oz strong plain flour
a pinch of salt
6 g /¼ oz fresh yeast
5 ml /1 tsp sugar
15 ml /1 tbls sugar, to glaze
For the filling
50 g /2 oz lard
50 g /2 oz sugar
50 g /2 oz sultanas

1 Grease an 18 cm /7 in square cake tin. Sieve the flour and salt into a warm bowl. In another bowl, cream the yeast with the sugar, stir in 150 ml /5 fl oz warm water and

Saffron cake

The crumbly, bread-like texture of this rich yeast cake does not in any way resemble that of a cake raised with baking powder. It is an eighteenth century cake from Britain's West country and is traditionally baked in a round tin, sliced across and served with clotted cream.

soaking the saffron, then about 2½ hours, plus cooling

Makes a deep 20 cm /8 in cake
175 g /6 oz butter, diced small, plus extra for greasing
300 ml /10 fl oz milk
a pinch of saffron strands
15 g /½ oz fresh yeast
75 g /3 oz caster sugar
500 g /18 oz flour
100 g /4 oz currants
100 g /4 oz chopped mixed orange and lemon peel
a few drops yellow food colouring (optional)

1 Grease a 20 cm /8 in cake tin. In a saucepan, heat the milk, stir in the saffron strands and leave to stand for at least 2 hours, to infuse.
2 Strain the flavoured milk and then heat it until it is lukewarm.
3 Cream the yeast with 5 ml /1 tsp of the sugar and gradually blend in the flavoured milk. Sprinkle the surface with 5 ml /1 tsp of the flour and leave the yeast liquid to stand for about 10 minutes, or until frothy.
4 Sift the remaining flour into a warm bowl and rub in the butter with your fingertips until the mixture resembles fine bread-crumbs. Stir in the rest of the sugar, the currants and the mixed peel.
5 Make a well in the centre, add the yeast liquid and mix to a soft dough. Add a few drops of yellow food colouring to the dough, if wished.
6 Turn the dough into the prepared cake tin, cover loosely with greased cling film and leave in a warm place until doubled in size — about 1 hour. Meanwhile, heat the oven to 180C /350F /gas 4.
7 Bake in the oven for about 1 hour, or until golden brown and firm to the touch. Leave the cake to cool in the tin for 10 minutes, then turn it out onto a wire rack and leave until cold.

Battenburg cake

2 hours, plus cooling

Serves 10
butter, for greasing
225 g /8 oz self-raising flour
4 eggs
225 g /8 oz butter or margarine
225 g /8 oz caster sugar
a few drops of vanilla essence
a few drops or red food colouring
30 ml /2 tbls apricot jam
caster sugar, for sprinkling
225 g /8 oz marzipan

1 Heat the oven to 190C /375F /gas 5. Grease and line a 28 × 18 cm /11 × 7 in Swiss roll tin, drawing the greaseproof paper into a pleat lengthways. Grease the paper again.
2 Sift the flour into a bowl and set it aside. In another bowl, lightly whisk the eggs.
3 In a third, larger bowl, beat the butter or margarine until light and creamy. Add the sugar and cream it with the fat until fluffy.
4 Beat in a few drops of vanilla essence, then the whisked eggs, a little at a time.
5 Fold in the reserved flour, then place half of the mixture in a separate bowl. Add a few drops of red food colouring and beat well.
6 Place the pink mixture down one side of the divided Swiss roll tin and place the uncoloured mixture down the other side. Smooth the top of both mixtures. Bake just above centre of oven for 45–50 minutes or until cooked.
7 Turn out the cakes onto a wire rack to cool. Cut each cake in half lengthways and trim them to exactly the same size.
8 Spread the sides of the cakes with the jam and stick them together, alternating the colours (see picture). Press together.
9 Spread the outside of the cake with jam.
10 Sprinkle the board liberally with caster sugar and roll out the marzipan to an oblong 30 × 25 cm /12 × 10 in. Spread the marzipan evenly with jam.
11 Place the cake on the marzipan and wrap the marzipan around it. Seal the join with jam and trim the edges. Pinch the top edges together to form a pattern and criss-cross the top with a sharp knife.

Cornish heavy cake

This recipe resembles Wiltshire lardy cake except that butter is used instead of lard.

50 minutes

Serves 8
500 g /1 lb butter, chilled, plus extra for greasing
500 g /1 lb flour, plus extra for dusting
a pinch of salt
200 g /7 oz currants
15 ml /1 tbls milk

1 Heat the oven to 220C /425F /gas 7. Grease a large baking sheet. Sift the flour and salt into a bowl and rub in one quarter of the butter until the mixture resembles fine breadcrumbs. Stir in the currants and just enough water to make a firm dough.
2 Roll the dough out on a floured surface to a rectangle, 60 × 25 cm /24 × 10 in. Using a further quarter of the butter, dot this over the top two-thirds of the rectangle.
3 Fold the bottom third up, the top third down and seal the edges by pressing with the pin. Give the dough one quarter turn and repeat the rolling, dotting and folding process twice more until all the butter is used.
4 Roll out the dough to a square about 25 mm /1 in thick and place it on the greased baking sheet. Score the surface with a sharp knife to make a diamond pattern and brush it with milk. Place it in the oven for about 30 minutes, or until golden brown on top.

then mix it with the flour to a soft dough.
2 Knead for about 5 minutes, until smooth. Shape into a ball, put into the bowl, cover and leave in a warm place for about 45 minutes, or until doubled in size.
3 Roll out to an oblong about 5 mm /¼ in thick. Dot half the lard over the top two-thirds of the oblong and sprinkle the lard with half the sugar and half the sultanas. Fold the bottom third up and the top third down.
4 Give the dough a quarter turn and repeat the rolling, dotting and folding process using the remaining lard, sugar and sultanas.
5 Roll out and fold to fit the prepared cake tin. Leave in a warm place to rise for about 30 minutes. Meanwhile, heat the oven to 220C /425F /gas 7.
6 For the glaze, dissolve the sugar in 15 ml / 1 tbls water and brush over the cake. Score the surface into squares and bake in the centre of the oven for about 30 minutes, or until golden brown. Turn the cake out of the tin and pour any juice over it.

● Lardy cake is best eaten warm. Serve it sliced, plain or buttered.

Carrot cake

 2 hours,
plus standing

Makes a 22 cm /9 in cake
5 eggs, separated
250 g /8 oz sugar
250 g /8 oz carrots, finely grated
350 g /12 oz almonds, blanched and ground
grated zest of ½ lemon
50 g /2 oz flour
5 ml /1 tsp baking powder
a pinch of salt
5 ml /1 tsp ground cinnamon
butter and flour, for the tin

For the frosting
125 g /4 oz cream cheese
30 ml /2 tbls thin cream
100 g /4 oz icing sugar, sifted
grated zest of ½ lemon
2.5 ml /½ tsp ground cinnamon
50 g /2 oz almonds, blanched and ground

Cornish heavy cake (page 105) and
Cornish splits (page 103)

1 Heat the oven to 180C /350F /gas 4. In a large mixing bowl, whisk the egg yolks until they begin to thicken. Whisk in the sugar and continue whisking until the mixture is thick and frothy.
2 Mix in the grated carrots, the ground almonds and lemon zest. Sift the flour with the baking powder, salt and cinnamon and fold into the carrot and almond mixture. Whisk the egg whites until stiff and fold them in.
3 Put the mixture in a buttered and floured 23 cm /9 in cake tin and bake the cake for 1 hour 10 minutes or until a fine skewer inserted in the centre of the cake comes out clean. Turn the cake onto a wire rack to cool completely.
4 To make the frosting, put the cream cheese in a bowl and beat in the cream until thoroughly blended. Gradually beat in the icing sugar and then add the lemon zest and cinnamon. Beat well.
5 Cut the cake horizontally in half, and sandwich it together with one-third of the frosting. Spread the rest of the frosting over the top and sides.
6 For the decoration, put the ground

almonds into a heavy ungreased frying-pan and stir them over a medium heat until they become light brown. Tip them onto a plate and leave them to cool completely. Sprinkle the almonds evenly over the top and sides of the cake.
7 Let the cake stand for 2 hours before serving, to allow the frosting to set.

● It is always better to use home-prepared ground almonds since they will be fresher.

All-in-one sponge cake

This is a basic recipe for a plain jam sandwich sponge cake. Ring the changes with different flavourings: add lemon zest for a fresh-tasting lemon cake; concentrated orange cordial for an orange cake; cocoa for a chocolate cake; coffee and chichory essence for a coffee cake.

1 hour,
plus cooling

Makes 6–8 slices
melted fat or oil, for the tin
100 g /4 oz self-raising flour
5 ml /1 tsp baking powder
100 g /4 oz soft margarine
100 g /4 oz caster sugar or soft brown sugar
2 medium-sized eggs
45 ml /3 tbls jam, for filling
icing sugar, for decorating

1 Position shelf in the centre of the oven and heat to 170C /325F /gas 3.
2 Grease and line two 18 cm /7 in sandwich tins and grease again.
3 Sift the flour and baking powder into a warm mixing bowl. Add the soft margarine, caster sugar or brown sugar and eggs and beat them together for 2–3 minutes until glossy and light.
4 Scrape the mixture into the prepared cake tins and smooth the tops with a palette knife.
5 Bake for 25–35 minutes.
6 Remove from the oven, cool in the tin for 3 minutes and then turn out onto a wire rack. Leave until cold.
7 Spread jam on one cake and top with the other. Sprinkle on icing sugar and serve.

● Try different fillings for this sponge cake: cream cheese mixed with thick cream; mashed bananas mixed with unsweetened chestnut purée.

Walnut layer cake

20 minutes, 1¼ hours baking, plus cooling

Makes 8 slices
melted fat or oil, for the tin
175 g /6 oz self-raising flour
7.5 ml /1½ tsp baking powder
175 g /6 oz soft margarine
175 g /6 oz soft light brown sugar
3 eggs
50 g /2 oz walnut pieces, chopped
2–3 drops of vanilla essence
For the filling and topping
350 g /12 oz full fat cream cheese
30 ml /2 tbls thin honey
walnut halves, to decorate

1 Heat the oven to 170C /325F /gas 3. Grease and line a deep 19 cm /7½ in round

Walnut layer cake

cake tin, and then grease the lining paper.
2 Sift the flour with the baking powder into a large bowl. Add the soft margarine, light brown sugar, eggs, chopped walnut pieces and vanilla essence and beat with a wooden spoon for 2–3 minutes until evenly blended.
3 Turn the mixture into the prepared tin and make a shallow hollow in the centre. Bake the cake for about 1¼ hours, until a fine, warm skewer inserted in the centre comes out clean.
4 Let the cake stand in the tin for 5 minutes before turning it out onto a wire rack. Remove the lining paper and leave the cake to cool.
5 Make the filling and topping. Beat the cream cheese with a wooden spoon until smooth and creamy, then gradually beat in the honey. Chill until required.
6 Slice the cold cake across into 3 equal layers. Use some of the cream cheese mixture to sandwich the layers together and spread the rest over the top, using a palette knife to make an attractive wheel pattern on the surface. Decorate with walnut halves.

German cheesecake

Serves 6–8
100 g /4 oz butter, softened
50 g /2 oz caster sugar
1 egg yolk
1.5 ml /¼ tsp finely grated lemon zest
175 g /6 oz flour
a pinch of salt
For the cheese filling
50 g /2 oz sultanas
15–30 ml /1–2 tbls dark rum
350 g /12 oz cottage cheese
4 eggs, separated
5 ml /1 tsp finely grated lemon zest
100 g /4 oz caster sugar
15 ml /1 tbls flour, sifted

1 Heat the oven to 170C /325F /gas 3.
2 Make the pastry base: in a bowl, cream the butter and the sugar together until they are light and fluffy. Gradually beat in the egg yolk and the finely grated lemon zest. Sift the flour and salt into the butter mixture and mix to form a softish dough.
3 Press the dough evenly over the base of a 20 cm /8 in deep, loose-bottomed cake tin.
4 Bake for 20 minutes until firm but not coloured. Remove the pastry from the oven, allow it to cool for 10 minutes. Reduce the oven temperature to 160C /300F /gas 2.
5 To make the cheese filling, toss the sultanas with the rum in a small bowl and leave to macerate until needed.
6 Rub the cottage cheese through a fine sieve into a large bowl. Beat in the egg yolks and finely grated lemon zest until smoothly blended.
7 In another bowl that is perfectly clean and dry, whisk the egg whites until they are stiff but not dry. Now gradually whisk in the caster sugar and sifted flour, and continue to whisk until the mixture is stiff, glossy and meringue-like.
8 With a large metal spoon or spatula, carefully fold the whites into the cheese mixture. Spoon the mixture over the pastry case. Sprinkle the surface with rum-soaked sultanas.
9 Bake the cheesecake for 40–50 minutes or until firm to the touch. Cool, then remove from the tin and chill lightly before serving.

2 hours,
then chilling

Sponge whirls

Serves 4
softened butter, for greasing
1 egg
75 ml /5 tbls caster sugar
grated zest of ½ orange
50 g /2 oz flour
a pinch of salt
2.5 ml /½ tsp baking powder
For the filling
45 ml /3 tbls raspberry jam
5 ml /1 tsp lemon juice
150 ml /5 fl oz thick cream, whipped

1 Heat the oven to 190C /375F /gas 5. Brush 2 baking trays or sheets with the softened butter.
2 Select a bowl in which to whisk up the cake and a large saucepan over which it will fit firmly. Pour 5 cm /2 in water into the pan and bring to the boil. Reduce the heat.
3 Place the egg, 60 ml /4 tbls caster sugar and the grated orange zest in the bowl. Set it over the barely simmering water and whisk until the mixture is thick and mousse-like.
4 Remove the bowl from the heat and continue whisking until cool.
5 Sift the flour, the pinch of salt and the baking powder into the cooled mixture and fold it in with a large metal spoon.
6 Place heaped teaspoons of the mixture on the prepared baking trays or sheets, spacing them about 25 mm /1 in from each other, to allow for spreading during baking. Sprinkle the tops with the remaining sugar and bake for about 10 minutes, or until golden.
7 Remove the sponge whirls from the oven and allow them to cool for 30 seconds. Ease the sponge whirls from the baking trays or sheets with a spatula and allow them to cool completely on a wire rack.
8 Meanwhile, combine the jam and lemon juice in a small saucepan. Stir over a gentle heat until blended. Remove from the heat and spread the melted jam and lemon mixture over half the sponge whirls.
9 Fit a piping bag with a 10 mm /½ in plain nozzle and spoon the whipped cream into it. Pipe spirals of cream onto the remaining sponge whirls and sandwich together the jam and cream sponge halves in pairs. Serve as soon as possible.

45 minutes,
plus cooling

Little cherry cakes

Makes 10 cakes
100 g /4 oz flour
a pinch of salt
5 ml /1 tsp baking powder
100 g /4 oz softened butter, plus extra for greasing
100 g /4 oz caster sugar
2 eggs, lightly beaten
grated zest of 1 orange
For the decoration
60 ml /4 tbls cherry jam
50 g /2 oz desiccated coconut
10 glacé cherries
10 angelica leaves

1   Heat the oven to 220C /425F /gas 7.
2   Sift the flour, salt and baking powder together 3 times. Grease 10 small dariole moulds thoroughly with softened butter.
3   Cream 100 g /4 oz softened butter and the sugar together until light and fluffy. Gradually beat in the eggs and finely grated orange zest. With a metal spoon, fold in the sifted dry ingredients.
4   Divide the mixture equally among the dariole moulds to half fill them, levelling the top of the mixture with the back of a teaspoon. Bake for 12–15 minutes or until the cakes are golden brown and spring back when touched.
5   Run a knife around the edge of each dariole mould and turn each cake out onto a wire rack to cool.
6   Heat the cherry jam in a small saucepan and brush each cold cake with cherry glaze. Sprinkle desiccated coconut onto a plate and roll each cake in the coconut to completely cover the sides and top, pressing the coconut on firmly with a palette knife.
7   Decorate each cake with a glacé cherry and an angelica leaf.

30 minutes,
plus cooling

American pound cake

Makes about 25 slices
9 medium-sized eggs, separated
450 g /1 lb softened butter
450 g /1 lb sugar
finely grated zest of 1 orange
10 ml /2 tsp vanilla or almond essence
450 g /1 lb flour
5 ml /1 tsp baking powder
2.5 ml /½ tsp salt
icing sugar, for sifting
butter, to serve

1   Let the egg whites warm to room temperature in a large mixing bowl for about 1 hour. Heat the oven to 190C /375F /gas 5.
2   Thoroughly grease a 24–25 cm /9½–10 in diameter, 12 cm /4¾ in deep, loose-bottomed decorative ring cake mould with a little of the softened butter.
3   Whisk the egg whites until stiff. Now gradually whisk in half the sugar. Continue whisking until soft peaks form.
4   Beat the egg yolks and place them, with the remaining sugar, grated orange zest and vanilla or almond essence, in a bowl. Set the bowl over a pan of simmering water. Whisk until the mixture will hold a trail when the beaters are lifted.
5   Remove the bowl from the heat and whisk until the mixture cools to room temperature. Melt the remaining butter and allow it to cool.
6   Sift the flour, baking powder and salt gradually into the beaten egg yolk mixture, about one quarter at a time, and fold it in after each addition. Now fold in the melted butter. Fold the beaten egg white and sugar mixture into the flour and egg yolk mixture.
7   Transfer the mixture to the prepared ring mould and bake for about 1½ hours. If the cake looks as if it is becoming too brown towards the end of the cooking time, cover it with a piece of greaseproof paper, with a hole in the centre, to allow the steam to escape. To test that the cake is done, insert a warmed skewer 10 mm /½ in from the centre wall of the pan; if the skewer comes out clean, the cake is done.
8   Invert the mould onto a wire rack, and let it cool for 15 minutes. Now remove the mould and allow the cake to cool completely.
9   Just before serving, sift icing sugar over the cake. Serve cut into thin slices and spread with butter.

● This cake owes its name to the even balance of ingredients — eggs, sugar, butter and flour are all equal weights.

2 hours,
plus cooling time

Scotch shortbread

Makes 24 biscuits
275 g /10 oz butter, diced, plus extra for greasing
225 g /8 oz flour, plus extra for rolling
225 g /8 oz rice flour
100 g /4 oz caster sugar, plus extra for dusting
2.5 ml /½ tsp vanilla essence
1 medium-sized egg
45–60 ml /3–4 tbls thick cream

1 Heat the oven to 190C /375F /gas 5. Lightly grease a baking sheet.
2 Sift the flour and rice flour into a mixing bowl. Rub in the butter lightly with your fingertips, then add the sugar and vanilla essence.
3 Whisk the egg with the cream in a small bowl. Pour this over the dry ingredients, mixing them to a smooth paste with your hands, using more cream if necessary.
4 Turn the dough out on a floured board and knead lightly until the dough is free from cracks. Flour a rolling pin and roll the dough out to about 15 mm /½ thick. Stamp out rounds with a 5 cm /2 in biscuit cutter and place them on the baking sheet, re-rolling as necessary until all the dough is used.
5 Bake the biscuits for 10–15 minutes or until they are lightly coloured. Dust them with caster sugar while they are still hot and transfer them to a wire rack to cool. Serve when cold.

 45 minutes,
plus cooling

Walnut ice cream roll

Serves 4
oil, for greasing
30 ml /2 tbls flour
a pinch of salt
2.5 ml /½ tsp baking powder
6 eggs, separated
150 g / 5 oz caster sugar
100 g /4 oz walnuts, coarsely ground
425 ml /15 fl oz vanilla ice cream, softened
icing sugar, for dusting

1 Grease a 35 × 23 cm /14 × 9 in Swiss roll tin. Line with greaseproof paper, then grease the paper. Heat the oven to 180C /350F /gas 4.
2 Sift the flour, salt and baking powder into a bowl and reserve.
3 Place the egg yolks and 100 g /4 oz caster sugar in a large heatproof mixing bowl and whisk lightly. Set the bowl over a pan of hot water, making sure it does not touch the water. Continue whisking until the mixture is increased in volume, very thick and lukewarm.
4 Remove from the heat and whisk until the mixture holds the trail of the whisk and is cool. Gently fold in the walnuts.
5 In a clean bowl and using a dry whisk, whisk the egg whites until they are stiff but not dry. Fold the whites into the walnut mixture. Now fold in the flour mixture, working lightly with the metal spoon.
6 Pour the mixture into the prepared tin, smoothing the surface with a spatula. Bake for 20–30 minutes, or until the cake is well risen and springs back when lightly pressed.
7 While the cake is baking, cut 2 pieces of greaseproof paper slightly larger than the size of the tin. Lay 1 piece on a flat surface and sprinkle with 15–30 ml /1–2 tbls caster sugar.
8 Turn out the baked cake onto the sugared paper and peel off the lining paper. Trim away the crusty edges, then lay the remaining piece of greaseproof paper over the cake. Roll up the cake carefully from one of the long ends, with the top piece of paper inside.
9 Place the cake seam side down on a wire rack, cover with a clean damp tea-towel and leave until completely cold.
10 Just before serving, carefully unroll the cake and remove the paper. Spread the softened ice cream over the surface, then roll the cake up again without the paper. Dust with icing sugar and serve.

1¼ hours,
plus cooling and filling

Index

111